DESCRIPTIONARY

FOURTH EDITION

MARC MCCUTCHEON

Checkmark Books
An imprint of Infobase Publishing

DESCRIPTIONARY, Fourth Edition

Checkmark Books
An imprint of Infobase Publishing
132 West 31st Street
New York NY 10001

Library of Congress Cataloging-in-Publication Data

McCutcheon, Marc.
Descriptionary / Marc McCutcheon. — 4th ed.
p. cm.
Includes bibliographical references and index.
ISBN 978-0-8160-7946-9 (alk. paper)
ISBN 978-0-8160-7947-6 (pbk.: alk. paper)
1. English language—Synonyms and antonyms—Dictionaries. 2. Description (Rhetoric)—Dictionaries. 3. English language—Terms and phrases. 4. Figures of speech—Dictionaries. I. Title.
PE1591.M415 2010
423'.12—dc22 2009020462

Checkmark Books are available at special discounts when purchased in bulk quantities for businesses, associations, institutions, or sales promotions. Please call our Special Sales Department in New York at (212) 967-8800 or (800) 322-8755.

You can find Facts On File on the World Wide Web at http://www.factsonfile.com

Text design by Kerry Casey
Composition by Hermitage Publishing Services
Cover printed by Sheridan Books, Inc., Ann Arbor, Mich.
Book printed and bound by Sheridan Books, Inc., Ann Arbor, Mich.
Date printed: May 2010
Printed in the United States of America

10 9 8 7 6 5 4 3 2 1

This book is printed on acid-free paper.

Contents

Introduction

Welcome to the expanded and updated *Descriptionary.* This fourth edition includes some extremely interesting and useful new categories, such as Anthropology and Archaeology, Brain, Chemistry, Dinosaurs, Evolution, Fishing, Gems, Jewelry, Prison Slang, Rocks and Gems, Sleep, Surfing, and Torture and Punishment, to name a few. It has also greatly broadened its lists of terms related to farming, finance, geology, Internet, meteorology, occult, psychology, and politics, among others.

As in the last edition, the end of the book features the vocabulary builder, Words You Should Know, which contains more than 1,050 words and expressions every articulate person should know.

Why use *Descriptionary*?

Descriptionary provides indispensable glossaries of terms to help you define and describe a subject you are writing about, be it cathedrals or castles, the stock market or stock cars. Consult *Descriptionary* whenever you are tempted to use words such as *watchamacallit, thingamajig,* or *doohickey* or whenever you are at a loss for a precise term.

Let's say, for example, you need the word for a sharp, steely descending peak, but you just cannot seem to bring the word to mind. Consult the standard dictionary and you will confront the age-old question of how to look up a word when you do not know what the word is. The answer is, you cannot—not with a standard dictionary, anyway. Nor will a thesaurus offer much help. A thesaurus lists the synonyms of mountains, not the components of mountains.

Enter *Descriptionary* to find the word you are looking for: *matterhorn.* This book lists not only definitions and synonyms, but also all the technically accurate words used in *describing* a mountain—words like *cairn, cordillera, couloir, Krummholz zone, ridgeback, saddle, scree,* and *sierra,* to name just a few.

Through a *Descriptionary* listing you will discover that there *is* a phrase for the leeward side of a mountain (*rain shadow*), and there *is* a name for the beautiful light that bathes a peak at sunset (*alpenglow*), and there *is* a word for the lateral ridge that projects from the side of a mountain (*spur*). And unlike when you are using a dictionary, you need only look under Mountains to find them all.

The value of having related words all in one place will become obvious the more you use *Descriptionary.* For example, you may discover words that you never dreamed existed (do you know where the *murder holes* are in a castle?) but that you might find useful in giving your work added authority or pizzazz.

Unlike most dictionaries, *Descriptionary* can be picked up and read for sheer entertainment alone, or for inspiration or ideas.

Place *Descriptionary* between your standard dictionary and thesaurus. We think you will find it equally as useful as either of these standard references, with one difference: It is twice as much fun.

ANIMALS AND INSECTS

ANIMAL GROUPS

Animal	Group	Male	Female	Young
ant	colony			
antelope	herd	buck	doe	kid
ass	herd/drove	jack	jenny	colt/foal
badger	cete	boar	sow	cub
bear	sloth	boar	sow	cub
bee	swarm/hive	drone	queen	
buffalo	herd	bull	cow	calf
camel	herd/flock	bull	cow	foal/calf
cattle	herd/drove	bull	cow	calf/heifer
deer	herd	buck/stag	doe	fawn
dog	pack	hound	bitch	puppy/whelp
elephant	herd	bull	cow	calf
elk	gang	bull	cow	calf
ferret	business	dog	bitch	
fish	shoal/school			
fox	skulk	vix	vixen	cub
frog	army		tadpole	
goat	herd/tribe	billy	nanny	kid
horse	herd/stable	stallion	mare	colt/foal/filly
kangaroo	troop	buck/jack	doe/jill	joey
leopard	leap	leopard	leopardess	cub
lion	pride/troop	lion	lioness	cub
monkey	troop/tribe			
moose		bull	cow	calf
mouse	nest			
mule	barren/rake			
otter		dog	bitch	
ox	herd/drove/yoke			
pig	litter/herd	boar	sow	piglet/farrow/shoat
polecat		hob	jill	
rabbit	nest	buck	doe	bunny
rhino	crash			
seal	herd/pod	bull	cow	pup
sheep	drove/flock	ram	ewe	lamb
squirrel	dray/scurry	buck	doe	pup/kit/kitten

ANIMAL GROUPS (continued)

Animal	Group	Male	Female	Young
tiger	streak/ambush	tiger	tigress	cub
toad	knot			
turtle	bale			
whale	gam/pod	bull	cow	calf
wolf	pack/rout	dog	bitch	cub/pup/whelp

BIRDS

aerie the lofty nest of a predatory bird, such as an eagle.

altricial of chicks, born blind and helpless.

alula the group of feathers on the leading edge of a wing, used to keep airflow smooth as the wing is tilted; also known as a false wing.

Anseriformes the order of ducks, geese, and swans.

anting the practice of some birds of placing live ants within their feathers, thought to help rid them of parasites.

apterous without wings, wingless.

aquiline of a beak, curved or hooked, as an eagle's.

Archaeopteryx the earliest known bird, semireptilian in nature, and living about 150 million years ago.

avian referring to birds.

aviary an enclosure or large cage for birds.

barbs the filaments emanating from the shaft of a feather.

bevy a group or flock of quail.

brood to sit on eggs; also, a group or flock of chickens.

brood spots bare patches on a bird's underbody that are rich in blood vessels and used for warming or incubating eggs.

Charadriiformes birds that live in ravines or cliffs, such as gulls, terns, and plovers.

charm a group or flock of finches.

chattering a group or flock of starlings.

clutch a group of eggs.

cob a male swan.

colony a group or flock of gulls.

Columbiformes the order of doves and pigeons.

comb the fleshy crest on the head of a fowl.

contour feathers the feathers involved in flying and regulating body temperature.

convocation a group of eagles.

covey a group of grouse.

craw the crop or enlargement of the gullet, aiding in digestion.

cygnet a young swan or swan chick.

dancing grounds a mating area where ritualistic displays are performed, especially of grouse and prairie chickens.

down the soft, fluffy plumage beneath the feathers and on the breasts of many birds.

drake male adult duck.

egg tooth a small tooth or nubbin in the upper jaw, used by newborn chicks to chip their way out of an egg; it disappears soon after birth.

exaltation a group or flock of larks.

falconer one who trains hawks or falcons to hunt for oneself.

Falconiformes the order of vultures, falcons, hawks, and eagles.

falconry the sport of hunting game with trained falcons or other birds of prey.

fall a group of woodcock.

fledgling a young bird with new feathers.

flight a group of doves or swallows.

flyway a migratory route.

gaggle a group or flock of geese.

Galliformes the order of grouse, quail, and turkeys.

gander a male adult goose.

gizzard the second stomach in which food is finely ground, thought to compensate for a bird's lack of teeth.

herd a group or flock of swans.

host a group or flock of sparrows.

keel the breastbone ridge in which most of the flight muscles are attached.

molt to shed the feathers.

murder a group or flock of crows.

murmuration a group or flock of starlings.

muster a group or flock of peacocks.

nye a group or flock of pheasants.

ocellus one of the eyelike spots in the tail of a peacock.

ornithologist one who studies birds.

ornithology the study of birds.

parliament a group of owls.

Passeriformes the order of birds that perch, such as larks, swallows, wrens, sparrows, and warblers, the largest order of birds.

pecking order the order of dominance and submission among a bird group, where a dominant bird may peck a weaker or lower status bird, but not vice versa; once established there is little fighting among the group.

pen a female adult swan.

phoenix the bird of legend that rises from the ashes.

pigeon milk a thick, cheesy secretion of pigeons and some parrots, fed to the young.

pinnate like a feather or having the shape of a feather.

precocial of chicks, born mature and becoming active almost immediately.

Procellariiformes the order of albatrosses, fulmars, and petrels.

Psittaciformes the order of parrots, parakeets, cockatoos, macaws, and lovebirds.

quill one of the large, strong flight feathers in the wings or tail.

raptor a bird of prey, such as a falcon, hawk, or eagle.

roc the giant elephant-carrying bird of Arabian legend.

rookery a nesting or breeding colony of sea birds.

ruff a projecting collar of hair or feathers around the neck.

siege a group or flock of herons.

skein a group of flying geese.

static soaring floating on a warm thermal of air.

Strigiformes the order of owls.

syrinx the throat component producing a bird's voice, located at the lower end of the trachea.

talon a claw of a bird.

team a group or flock of ducks.

thermal a rising current of warm air, used by birds to carry them aloft.

wattle the naked, fleshy component hanging from the neck, as in a turkey.

CATS

Abyssinian a long, lean breed of cat known for its athleticism and playful personality.

ailurophile one who loves and admires cats.

ailurophobe one who fears cats.

allogrooming the grooming of one cat by another.

Angora Turkish breed of cat with long, silky hair.

blaze a white marking running from a cat's forehead to its nose.

blue coloring from blue gray to slate gray.

brush a bushy or plumelike tail.

Burmese breed related to the Siamese, having short, usually sable-colored hair.

calico coloring combination of tortoiseshell and white.

calling the cries of a sexually receptive female.

caterwaul the cry of cats at mating time.

catnip plant, member of the mint family, known for its intoxicating effect on cats.

catus a tabbylike wildcat from North Africa, thought to be the primary ancestor of all domestic cats.

chinchilla coloring in which the tips of the hairs are black or another color, with the under hairs being white or pale.

cobby having a low-lying body on short legs.

dam mother.

FAIDS Feline Acquired Immune Deficiency Syndrome, a weakened immune system often brought on by feline leukemia.

feline relating to or resembling a cat.

feral domesticated but living in the wild.

flehmen response the trancelike sneer often seen on the face of a male as it smells the urine of a sexually receptive female.

frill the hairs framing the head in long-haired breeds, also known as the ruff.

furball hair swallowed by a cat and forming a mass or "ball" in the stomach.

ghost markings faint markings on solid-colored cats, revealing a slight trait of another breed.

gloves white patches on the feet, also known as mittens.

haw the third eyelid, or nictitating membrane.

heat the sexually receptive period of a female.

laces white markings on the back of the rear legs of some cats.

lilac coloring of pale pinkish gray, also known as lavender.

litter a group of newborn kittens.

locket a white or other-colored patch under the neck.

lordosis the crouched position of a sexually receptive female inviting entry by the male.

Manx breed of cat without a tail, thought to have originated in the Orient.

milk-treading the "kneading" motion of a kitten's paws in an attempt to stimulate the flow of its mother's milk, the same behavior often seen in adult cats kneading the bellies of their human owners.

moggie a mongrel cat.

muzzle the jaws and nose of a cat.

pads the soles of the paws.

Persian breed originating from Asia, known for its flattened or pushed-in face and thick, luxuriant fur.

pheromones chemical substance released in urine and from certain areas of the skin to mark territories or attract the opposite sex.

piebald having black-and-white coloring.

pricked having ears that point high and erect.

purebred a cat descended from a long line of its own kind.

queen female cat used for breeding.

rangy long-limbed and long-bodied.

Rex breed of cat known for its curly hair and higher body temperature than other cats.

sheath the protective covering over retracted claws.

Siamese angular, elongated breed known for its noisy personality.

sire father.

spaying the neutering of a female cat.

spraying the male's act of marking with urine.

tabby a striped cat.

tapetum the light-reflecting layer at the back of a cat's eyes, aiding nocturnal vision and causing the "glowing" effect at night.

tom a male cat.

Tonkinese a crossbreed of the Burmese and Siamese.

vibrissae the highly sensitive whiskers and hairs found on the cheeks, on the chin, over the eyes, and at the back of the front legs, thought capable of detecting subtle air currents and the movement of prey in the dark.

whip long, thin, tapering tail, typically found on a Siamese.

DINOSAURS

acrocanthosaurus in the Cretaceous period, a very large meat eater with spikes down its back, which may have been part of a sail.

allosaur a large bipedal meat eater with a long, narrow, and often crested head and three-fingered hands that lived in the Jurassic period.

Alvarez extinction theory a proposal by the physicist Luis Alvarez and his son, the geologist Walter Alvarez, that an asteroid striking Earth 65 million years ago caused massive fires, dust clouds, geological upheavals, atmospheric disturbances, and tsunamis, all of which contributed to the death of vegetation, which in turn caused the starvation and death of the dinosaurs. See CHICXULUB, MULTIPLE IMPACT THEORY, SHIVA.

ankylosaur a short-legged plant eater characterized by its bony armor and clublike tail. It first appeared in the early Jurassic and survived to the end of the Cretaceous.

apatosaurus formerly known as a brontosaurus, a sauropod that grew to be 70 to 90 feet (21 to 27 m) long during the Jurassic period.

archaeopteryx a Jurassic bird with teeth, feathers, clawed wings and a long, bony tail.

archosaur "ruling lizard," one of a group of common land reptiles from which dinosaurs evolved, sometime during the Triassic period.

argentinosaurus a massive sauropod, one of the largest dinosaurs, measuring 130 to 140 feet (40–43 m) and characterized by a very long tail and equally long neck. It lived in what is now South America during the Cretaceous period.

articulated skeleton a skeleton that is found with many of its bones still attached.

baryonyx a fish-eating theropod with crocodile-like jaws that lived during the Cretaceous period.

bipedal walking on two legs instead of four, as a predatory dinosaur.

bone bed a large mass of dinosaur bones in one location.

boneheaded dinosaur another name for pachycephalosaurid.

brachiosaurus a giant, long-necked sauropod from the Jurassic period.

browser any herbivore that ate portions of trees, shrubs, and other tall plants.

carnivore any meat-eating dinosaur.

carnotaurus a 25-foot (7.5-m) long, meat-eating theropod with horns on its head that lived during the Cretaceous.

caudipteryx zoui a 3-foot-tall (1-m) theropod adorned with insulating (but not flightworthy) feathers that lived from the Jurassic to the Cretaceous.

ceratopsian one of a group of four-legged plant-eaters with beaks and bony head frills. Protoceratops and triceratops were ceratopsians.

Chicxulub a 120-mile (180-km) impact crater in the Yucatán Peninsula believed to be from the asteroid, meteor, or comet that played a large role in wiping out the dinosaurs 65 million years ago. See ALVAREZ EXTINCTION THEORY, MULTIPLE IMPACT THEORY, SHIVA.

chimera paleontologists' term for a fossil mixture composed of more than one species, named after the mythical monster with a lion's head, goat's body, and snake's tail.

compsognathus during the Jurassic, a theropod that ranged in size from a chicken to a small dog.

Cope's rule a scientific observation that, given adequate food sources, a species will tend to evolve into larger forms over time, which explains the massive growth of the dinosaurs. Although there are a few exceptions, a larger animal tends to be better at winning mates, killing competitors, and fighting off predators.

coprolite literally, "dung stone," fossilized dinosaur feces.

crest a growth or bony plate on top of the head, through which some dinosaurs may have made sounds.

Cretaceous period the time period that encompasses from 146 to 65 million years ago, at the end of which came the extinction of the dinosaurs.

cycad an evergreen, palmlike tree that served as one of the primary sources of food for herbivores in the Jurassic.

deinocheirus a giant birdlike meat eater with a toothless beak and arms that stretched 8 feet (2.4 m) and is believed to have been able to run as fast as 50 miles per hour (80 km/hr). It lived during the Cretaceous period.

digitigrade walking on the toes. Predator dinosaurs walked and ran on their toes or the front of their feet for better speed, similar to cats and dogs.

diplodocid a huge, four-legged sauropod with a small head, long neck and tail, and peg teeth. Apatosaurus, diplodocus, seismosaurus, and supersaurus were all diplodocids.

disarticulated skeleton paleontologists' term for a fossil skeleton that is found with its bones detached and in various positions and locations.

dromaeosaurid a family of small but fast theropods with retractable, sicklelike claws for slashing prey. The best known were the velociraptors.

duck-billed dinosaur see HADROSAUR.

ectothermic cold-blooded, or requiring the Sun or outside warmth to heat one's body to function normally, as with many dinosaurs.

endothermic warm-blooded, or not requiring the Sun's heat to warm one's body to function normally, as a mammal.

extinction the complete dying out of a species, as with the dinosaurs 65 million years ago.

fossil the remains of any living organism from a past geological period. Mineralized bone, teeth, claws, skulls, eggshells, coprolites, and rock-hardened footprints are all fossils.

frill a bony shield protecting the neck and head of a ceratopsian, such as triceratops and protoceratops.

gastrolith a rock purposely swallowed by sauropod dinosaurs to help grind food and aid in digestion, also believed to be used as ballast by plesiosaurs. Such rocks, rounded and polished from being knocked about, are often found among dinosaur bones.

gigantosaurus a massive meat eater, slightly larger than *Tyrannosaurus rex*, that lived during the Cretaceous.

gingko also known as the maidenhair tree, which in the Cretaceous and Jurassic periods served as a primary food source for plant-eating dinosaurs.

grazer any dinosaur that ate grasses and other low-lying plants, such as an ankylosaur or triceratops.

Great Dying, the also known as the Permian-Triassic extinction event, the most massive die-off of marine and land organisms in the history of Earth, occurring in spurts around 251.4 million years ago, which may have played a role in the eventual development of the dinosaurs. Like the demise of the dinosaurs, the complete wiping out of 70 percent of all land vertebrates and more than 90 percent of marine species may have been due to an asteroid impact.

hadrosaur any one of various types of duck-billed dinosaur, a plant eater that lived during the Cretaceous period. Unlike the sauropods' dependence on gastroliths to help digest food, the hadrosaurs developed a prodigious number of teeth, possibly the main reason they became so successful.

hallux in predatory dinosaurs, a superfluous claw, also known as a dewclaw, above the side of the foot.

herbivore any dinosaur that ate vegetation instead of meat.

hypacrosaurus a 30-foot (9-m) hadrosaur known for the small fin rising out of its back.

ichnite a non-bone fossil, such as footprints, coprolites, gastroliths, nests, etc. Also known as ichnofossil.

ichthyosaur Greek term for "fish lizard," a dolphinlike reptile that lived during the Mesozoic.

iguanodontid from the late Jurassic to the Cretaceous, very large plant eaters with beaks and thumb spikes, including iguanodon and camptosaurus, that eventually evolved into the hadrosaurs.

iridium layer a heavy element seen in meteorites and found in an unusually high concentration in a widespread geological deposit known as the K-T layer, dated from 65 million years ago. It is believed to have been dispersed around the earth by the asteroid impact that killed the dinosaurs.

Jurassic period the time period from 208 to 146 million years ago, when many dinosaurs thrived.

K-T extinction short for the Cretaceous-Tertiary extinction that killed off the dinosaurs 65 million years ago.

marginocephalian any Cretaceous plant eater with horns, beak, or thick and bony skull.

megaraptor a 26-foot (8-m) bipedal meat eater characterized by a very long, sicklelike claw on the side of each foot.

Mesozoic era a broad expanse of geological time that encompasses the Cretaceous, Jurassic, and Triassic, from 251 million to 65 million years ago, when the dinosaurs lived.

microraptor among the smallest of the dinosaurs, a dromaeosaurid that grew from 1.5 to 2.5 feet (0.5–0.8 m) long and sported feathered wings on its arms, tail, and legs and probably glided from tree to tree. Thought to be a possible forerunner of birds, it lived during the early Cretaceous.

mosasaur a marine reptile, growing up to 57 feet (17.5 m) long; living during the Cretaceous, it was the deadliest marine predator of the period.

multiple impact theory the theory held by some scientists that more than one asteroid or chunk of asteroid struck the earth 65 million years ago and killed off the dinosaurs. See ALVAREZ EXTINCTION THEORY, CHICXULUB, SHIVA.

omnivore a dinosaur that ate both plants and meat.

ornithischian a family of plant-eating dinosaurs with hip structures similar to birds, including triceratops, stegosaurus, ankylosaurs, and others. They are not, however, the ancestors of birds.

ornithopod from the Jurassic to the Cretaceous, any two- or four-legged plant eater without body armor.

oviraptor a theropod with a beaked, birdlike head and long fingers.

pachycephalosaurid a bipedal plant eater with an extraordinarily thick or bony head that lived in the Cretaceous period. Some, like pachycephalosaurus, had skulls 10 inches (25 cm) thick. Also known as a bonehead.

paleontologist a scientist who gathers fossils in the field and studies them to learn more about living organisms, such as dinosaurs, from past geological periods.

paleontology the study of living organisms and fossils from past geological periods.

parasaurolophus a beaked or duck-billed plant eater with a long crest that lived during the Cretaceous.

pterodactyl see PTEROSAUR.

pterosaur closely related to the dinosaurs, a group of flying, fish-eating reptiles that lived from the Triassic to the end of the Jurassic period. Hollow-boned, with membranelike wings, they ranged in size from a few inches to as large as 40 feet (12 m). Pterodactyls are probably the best-known pterosaurs.

quetzalcoatlus a reptile closely related to the dinosaurs; a massive pterosaur with a 40-foot (12-m) wingspan that lived during the Cretaceous.

saurischian an order of dinosaurs that were the ancestors of birds, but with hip structures similar to lizards. Sauropods and theropods were both saurischians.

sauropod any large, four-legged plant eater with a long neck and tail, ranging in size from 7 feet (2 m) to more than 100 feet (30 m) long.

scute a bony or horny plate or scale, as found on the skin of crocodiles, which many dinosaurs may have had.

seismosaurus "quake lizard," a massive diplodocid dinosaur that grew as long as 170 feet (52 m) and lived during the late Jurassic. It had an extremely long neck, which it used to peer into and forage along the edges of thick woods, especially useful when the rest of its body was simply too big to pass through.

shantungosaurus the largest of all the duck-billed dinosaurs, or hadrosaurs, growing up to 48 feet (15 m) in length. It lived during the late Cretaceous.

Shiva located under the Arabian Sea off India, a massive crater, stretching 370 miles (600 km) across, 280 miles (450 km) wide, and 7.5 miles (12 km) deep, possibly created by an asteroid or meteoroid 65 million years ago, which may have, along with the impact at Chicxulub in the Yucatán, brought on the extinction of the dinosaurs. See ALVAREZ EXTINCTION THEORY, CHICXULUB, MULTIPLE IMPACT THEORY.

spinosaurid during the Cretaceous, a large meat eater characterized by a 6-foot (1.8-m) high sail on its back, thought to have been a heat regulator or possibly used for mating displays.

stegosauria during the Jurassic and into the Cretaceous, a group of ornithischian plant eaters characterized by a double row of armor plates running down their backs and ending in spikes at the end of the tails. Stegosaurus is the best-known example, also famous for its tiny head and walnut-sized brain.

strata layers of sediment or rock, often marking distinct geological periods (sing., *stratum*).

Tertiary period the geological period from 1.8 to 65 million years ago, following the extinction of the dinosaurs, within which mammals took center stage.

theropod any bipedal carnivore with hands and claws, ranging from the size of a chicken to 50 feet (15 m) tall, that lived from the Triassic to the end of the Cretaceous. Birds are believed to have evolved from theropods.

thyreophoran living from the Jurassic to the Cretaceous, any four-legged plant eaters with armored plates, including stegosaurs and ankylosaurs.

titanosaurid a group of very large, four-legged sauropods, characterized by long necks and tails, small heads, and armored backs that lived during the Cretaceous.

T. rex see *TYRANNOSAURUS REX*.

Triassic period the geological time period from 251 million to 199.6 million years ago, it marked the beginning of the reign of dinosaurs.

triceratops during the late Cretaceous, a four-legged plant eater that grew to be up to 29.5 feet (9 m) long, characterized by its three horns and neck frill.

Tyrannosaurus rex "tyrant lizard," a very large bipedal predator that grew as tall as 43 feet (13 m), had a 5-foot (1.5-m) long skull, and lived in North America during the Cretaceous.

velociraptor a small, swift-footed meat eater that had a slashing, sicklelike claw on each foot and lived during the Cretaceous period. According to the size of its brain case to body size ratio, it was likely among the most intelligent of the dinosaurs.

DOGS

alpha the dominant dog in a pack.

apple head a rounded or domed skull, as in the English toy spaniel.

apron the longer hairs found on the chest of many breeds.

badger-marked having a coat consisting of gray or black markings on white.

bat ear an erect ear that is rounded at the top, as in a bat.

bay a deep bark.

beard the tuft or long hairs under the chin.

belton a coat consisting of blue or orange and white hair.

bitch female dog.

blaze a white or light-colored streak running along the center of the head.

blond having a coat of light yellow or yellowish tan.

bloom the glossiness of the coat.

bobtail a tail cut short; also known as a docked tail.

brindle having a streaked or spotted coat.

brisket part of the chest between and slightly behind the forelegs.

brush a bushy tail.

bullbaiting the long-banned English sport of dogs tormenting bulls.

butterfly nose a nose with two or more different colors.

buttocks the rump.

button ear an ear that folds forward toward the eye, as in a fox terrier.

canine of the dog family, or like a dog.

chops the lower cheeks, especially in a bulldog.

cloddy thickset and low to the ground, as a Scottish terrier.

cobby short-bodied.

crest the ridge of the neck.

crop trimming the ears to make them pointed.

cynology the study of dogs and their history.

cynophobia fear of dogs.

dam mother.

dewclaw one of the short vestigial claws or digits, the remnant of a first toe, now useless.

dewlap the loose fold of skin hanging from the neck of many breeds, such as the bulldog and the bloodhound.

dingo wild dog of the Australian outback.

distemper an infectious disease of puppies and young dogs, caused by a virus.

docking the surgical removal or shortening of the tail.

eyeteeth the two projecting canine teeth in the upper jaw.

fawn having a pale, yellowish brown coat.

feather the fringe of hair along the tail and back of the legs.

feral domesticated but living in the wild.

fiddle front forelegs that are bowlegged.

frill a fringe of hair around the neck.

grizzle having a coat that is gray or streaked with gray.

gun dog any of the sport hunting dogs, such as a setter, pointer, spaniel or retriever.

hackles neck and back hairs that bristle when a dog is angry or fearful.

harlequin having a white coat with black spots of various sizes.

haw the red membrane inside the lower eyelid.

heartworm a worm parasite living in the bloodstream of infected dogs.

heat the female's mating period.

hock the backward-bending joint in the hindleg, corresponding to the ankle in humans.

leather the external part of the ear.

litter the puppies brought forth at one birth.

liver having a reddish brown or purplish brown coat.

lop-eared having loose, dangling ears.

lupine of the wolf family, or like a wolf.

mane the long hair growing from the top or sides of the neck, as in a collie.

mange skin disease caused by parasitic mites, causing hair loss.

mask the dark shading found on the muzzle of several breeds.

mongrel a mixed breed.

muzzle the mouth, nose, and jaws. Or a leather device harnessed around the jaws to prevent biting.

overshot a jaw in which the top extends over the bottom.

pack a group of dogs.

pads the cushioned padding of the feet.

parti-colored having a multicolored coat.

pastern the foreleg part between the knee joint and the foot.

pedigree a record of lineage. Also, lineage that can be traced to the same breed for at least three generations.

philocynic one who loves dogs.

pied having a coat covered with patches or spots of two or more colors.

pit fighting the outlawed gambling sport of dog-fighting in a small pit or arena.

plume a feathery tail.

pompon the sculpted tufts of hair left on a dog's tail or body when artistically clipped, especially in poodles.

prick ear an ear carried stiffly erect, as in a German shepherd.

quarter to range over a field in search of game, especially of pointers, setters, and spaniels.

rabies an infectious viral disease affecting the central nervous system, characterized by convulsions, choking, and an inability to swallow.

racy long-legged and slight of build, as a greyhound.

ringtail a tail that is carried in a tight curl or ring.

ruff a collar of thick hair around the neck.

sable having a black or dark brown coat.

screwtail a short, kinky, twisted tail, as in a Boston terrier.

sire father.

snipy a sharply pointed muzzle.

spay to remove the ovaries of the female.

swayback a sagging back.

tie a male and female locked together in intercourse for up to 30 minutes, allowing for adequate ejaculation of sperm.

tulip ears erect ears with a slight forward curve.

undershot of a jaw, having the bottom further out than the top.

walleye a blue eye.

whelp to give birth to pups; also, one of the young of a dog.

whip a stiff, straight tail, as in a pointer.

withers part of the back between the shoulder blades.

HORSES

appointments equipment and clothing used in a specific riding event.

bag the udder of a mare.

barrel between the fore- and hindquarters, the trunk of a horse.

bloom the condition of a healthy-looking coat.

breastplate leather section strapped across a horse's chest that attaches to the saddle to prevent the saddle from sliding back.

bridle head harness used to control a horse, which includes a bit, cheek straps, crownpiece, throatlatch, headband, and reins. Also, a quick or violent upjerk of the horse's head.

bridlewise trained to change direction by laying the bridle reins on the side of the horse's neck the rider wishes to turn.

broodmare a mare used for breeding.

broomtail a long, bushy tail.

cannon the leg portion between the hock and the fetlock.

canter a three-beat gait or slow gallop.

cantle the rear of an English saddle.

capriole an upward leap with no forward motion, as made by a trained horse.

caracole a half-turn.

cast the condition in which a horse lying down in its stall is unable to get up again without assistance.

cavesson the noseband and headpiece of an English bridle.

cayuse an American Indian pony.

cheek straps bridle straps that run down the side of the cheeks to hold the bit or noseband.

cinch the girth of a Western saddle.

cob a stocky, thickset, short-legged horse.

cold back a horse who bolts or bucks when a saddle is placed on its back, due to inexperience or improper training or treatment.

colt a male under age four.

conformation a horse's overall physique or build.

conformation fault any one of several faults found in a horse's build.

coronet the upper portion of a horse's hoof.

cow-hocked a conformation fault in which the hocks are too close together.

crest the top of a horse's neck.

crop a short, looped whip used in horseback riding.

croup the rump of a horse.

crownpiece the bridle leather fitted over a horse's head and attached to the cheekpieces.

currycomb a horse comb.

cutting horse a horse trained to cut cattle out of a herd.

dam the mother of a horse.

dishing a movement in which the horse's feet swing sideways at a trot, usually a fault of pigeon-toed animals.

dobbin a gentle farm horse.

draft horse a powerful horse bred for farm work, such as plowing.

dressage a refined riding style in which the horse's gait is smooth, flat, and graceful.

driving horse a horse trained or bred to pull wagons or sulkies.

equerry one who acts as a stableman or supervisor of horses in a royal or other household.

equestrian pertaining to horses or horse riding; one who rides horses.

equine pertaining to or resembling a horse.

fetlock the projection and accompanying tuft of hair growing above and behind the hoof, or the joint marked by this projection.

filly a female under the age of four.

foal a newborn horse of either sex.

forehand the front portion of a horse, including the head, neck, shoulders, and front legs.

forelock bangs or hair of the horse's mane that hangs down over its forehead between its ears.

forging the striking of the rear hoof and the toe of the front hoof during a trot, caused by overextending.

fox trot walking with the front legs and trotting with the rear.

gait the speed and sequence of a horse's walk or run; gaits include walk, trot, canter, gallop, and rack.

gallop a full run.

gambado a low, four-legged leap, as when frolicking.

gaskin part of the hind leg between the stifle and the hock.

gee a traditional horse command meaning to "turn right." Opposite of haw.

gelding a castrated or gelded male.

girth the band of leather that goes around the trunk of a horse for fastening the saddle to its back.

grade a horse of unknown ancestry.

green horse an untrained horse.

green jumper a horse that has been taught to jump.

gymkhana a riding meet or competition.

hack a horse used for pleasure riding.

hackney a horse of English origin, characterized by its flexed knee gait.

halter a rope used for leading or tying a horse.

hand a unit of measurement in which 1 hand equals 4 inches, used to estimate the size of a horse.

haw traditional horse command meaning "turn left."

headband part of the bridle placed over the horse's forehead to prevent the bridle from slipping back.

heat the breeding period of a mare, occurring at three-week intervals and lasting about five days.

hock the joint located in the lower leg, corresponding to the ankle in humans.

hogback a horse having a rounded back, opposite of a swayback.

hunter a horse bred or trained for hunting, usually a fast runner and strong jumper.

jib a nervous or fidgety movement sideways or backwards.

jodhpurs horse-riding pants made of heavy cloth, fitting tightly at the knees and ankles, and typically worn with ankle-height leather boots also known as jodhpurs.

jog a slow trot.

lather sweat.

lope canter.

lunge a long rope or rein used for breaking or training a horse by leading it around in a circle.

manger a horse's wooden feeding trough, attached to a stall wall.

mare an adult female.

mudder a horse that runs well on muddy ground, as on a wet racetrack.

muzzle collective term for the nose, nostrils, lips, and chin of a horse.

neigh the cry of a horse.

noseband a strap fitted over the nose as part of the Western bridle.

offside the right side of a horse when viewed from behind; also known as the far side.

paddock a fenced-in area adjoining a barn where horses may play.

palfrey a post-horse, or historically a small horse used by ladies.

passade a backward movement.

pastern part of the foot between the fetlock and the hoof.

Pegasus the great steed of Greek mythology, known for its wings.

piaffe a test of horsemanship, in which the horse trots slowly in place.

pigeon-toed standing with toes pointed inward.

pillion a pad used for an extra rider behind the saddle.

poll the top of a horse's neck behind the ears.

pommel the front portion of the English saddle, fitting over the withers.

posting in English riding, the rising and falling of the rider with the rhythm of the trot.

rack a difficult four-beat gait or gallop used by a trained horse.

rear to stand up on the hind legs.

rip a wornout or useless horse.

sire father of a horse.

span horses in a matched pair.

splayfoot standing with toes pointed outward.

staggers a cerebrospinal disease characterized by loss of coordination, staggering, and falling down.

stallion adult male used for breeding.

steed a spirited horse, or a horse ridden in combat.

stifle the joint corresponding to the knee in humans.

swayback an old horse with a swayed back.

volt a partially sideways gait or step.

whinny a low and gentle neigh.

withers highest part of the back, between the shoulder blades.

Horse Breeds

American albino a Nebraska-bred, snow-white horse having pinkish skin and blue, brown, or hazel eyes.

Andalusian an elegant, good-natured Spanish horse, usually gray or bay and standing about 15 hands high.

Appaloosa bred for endurance by the North American Plains Indians, a horse widely recognized by its spotted rump.

Arab greatly admired, highly prized desert horse, known for its distinctive forehead bump shaped like a shield. Since it has fewer ribs and lumbar bones than other breeds, it has a distinctively short back. The Arab is said to "float" when it runs.

Boulonnais French breed; heavy but elegant, bred today mostly for its meat.

Camargue the ancient breed of southern France; thought to be that depicted in prehistoric cave paintings at Niaux and Lascaux.

Cleveland bay a popular coach-pulling or harness horse in the 19th century. Noted for its stamina and strength, it is now used as a hunter or as a show jumper.

Clydesdale a strong, heavy draught horse of Scottish breed; the Budweiser beer mascot.

cob not a breed, but a stocky short-legged horse noted for its jumping ability.

Connemara intelligent Irish breed known for its sure-footedness and jumping ability.

Criollo Argentine, dun-colored horse having great endurance and toughness, ridden by the gauchos of the pampas.

Dale hardy, calm Yorkshire breed, usually black, and used for riding or as pack horses.

Dartmoor a small, European riding horse having a kind, quiet nature.

Dutch draught massive, strong horse with a docile temperament, originally bred for farm work.

Exmoor British pony breed, thought to have pulled Roman chariots, now used as fox hunter and children's riding pony.

Fell European breed similar to a Dale but smaller, used as a hunter and as a riding horse.

French trotter Normandy-bred harness-racing horse, known for its stamina.

Friesian Holland-bred work and harness horse.

hack a refined, well-mannered and elegant show horse having a trot that appears to "float." The term *hack* is also used to denote any type of riding horse.

Hackney a high-stepping, trotting horse of English breed. It was once a popular carriage horse.

Hanoverian German breed renowned for its show-jumping ability.

Highland Scottish pony breed used for hunting, jumping, and everyday riding.

Holstein a tall (16 to 17 hands high) German carriage horse noted for its intelligence, today used in show jumping.

hunter European breed ridden in England and Ireland for hunting purposes. It is noted for its agility, stamina, and jumping ability.

Icelandic a small, muscular horse known for its toughness and agility.

Irish draught a large horse bred for farm work and riding.

Knabstrup ancient Denmark breed having a distinctive spotted coat (like a dalmatian), widely used as a circus horse.

Lipizzaner world-famous leaping white horse breed of Vienna.

Lusitano courageous and agile Portuguese horse ridden by Portuguese bullfighters.

Missouri fox-trotting horse Missouri breed that is able to walk with its front legs while trotting with its rear legs, thus producing a smoother ride that can be maintained over long distances.

Morgan American breed, strong and muscular, and noted for its versatility.

Norwegian fjord Norwegian breed once ridden by the Vikings, noted for its surefootedness and straight-cut mane.

palomino a golden horse having a cream-colored mane and tail.

Percheron strong, massive draught horse of French breed; it usually has a dark, dappled coat.

pinto not a breed but a color type—brown and white or black and white. A popular horse with Native Americans. Also known as a paint.

quarter horse widely popular American racing breed, famous for its ability to gallop at high speed over short distances. Its speed, agility, and intelligence has also made it a favorite cutting horse among cowboys.

saddlebred Kentucky-bred, all purpose ranch and show horse, noted for its superior rack gait.

Selle Français French, all-purpose horse, often bred for its jumping ability.

Shetland thick-set, short-legged, small (40 inches high; Shetlands are not measured with hands) horse having great strength and a shaggy mane.

shire very strong, heavy draught horse of English breed.

standardbred an American harness-racing horse.

Suffolk a strong, heavy draught horse having especially powerful shoulders; an English breed usually chestnut in color.

tarpan ancient Russian breed thought to be nearly extinct.

Tennessee walking horse an American, all-purpose breed.

thoroughbred a long-distance racer, usually a cross of an Arabian stallion and an English mare.

Welsh mountain pony small breed (no bigger than 12 hands) resembling an Arab and noted for its hardiness and intelligence.

Welsh pony larger version (13 hands) of the Welsh mountain pony.

Horse Colors and Markings

albino white with pinkish skin and blue or hazel eyes.

Appaloosa a distinct breed noted for its spotted rump.

bald a white streak on a horse's face and covering one of its eyes. See BLAZE.

bars black stripes on the legs of some breeds; also known as zebra striping.

bay a reddish brown with a black mane and tail.

blaze a broad, white streak running from between the eyes to the muzzle.

blood bay a deep red bay.

buckskin beige with a black mane and tail; may or may not have an eel stripe.

buttermilk another name for a palomino.

calico a spotted or piebald color; a pinto.

California sorrel reddish gold.

chestnut chestnut, bronze, or coppery. Also known as sorrel.

claybank yellowish cross of a sorrel and a dun.

cremello cream albino with pink skin and blue eyes.

dappled spotted or mottled.

dun beige with a beige or brown mane and tail.

eel stripe a dark stripe extending from the withers to the tail.

flaxen chestnut-colored with a white or cream-colored mane and tail.

grulla bluish gray or mouse-colored. Also known as smokey.

medicine hat black speckles found on mustangs, considered good luck by American Indians.

moros bluish.

paint irregularly patterned white with colored areas. Same as pinto.

palomilla milk white with white mane and tail.

palomino light tan or golden with an ivory or cream-colored mane and tail.

piebald black and white.

pinto a piebald; a spotted or irregularly marked horse. Also known as paint or Indian pony.

race a crooked blaze on the forehead.

roan bay, chestnut, or sorrel sprinkled with gray and white.

sabino light red or roan with a white belly.

skewbald patches of white over any color except black. Sometimes humorously referred to as a stewball.

snip a white marking along the nostril.

sock white on leg below the fetlock.

sorrel chestnut or brown.

star small white marking between eyes.

stocking any white extending above the fetlock. See SOCK.

zebra dun dun-colored with a dorsal stripe and stripes on its legs.

INSECTS AND SPIDERS

abdomen the posterior segment of an insect's body.

antennae sensory appendages used for probing or smelling.

arachnid the class of insects with four pairs of legs, including spiders, scorpions, mites, and ticks.

arachnoid resembling a spider's web, or pertaining to arachnids.

bristle any stiff hair arising from the body.

carapace a hard covering of the body of some insects, for protection from predators.

caste system a social system in which each insect in a colony has a clearly defined role. Termites, for example, have four castes: workers, soldiers, kings, and queens.

cephalothorax the first segment of a spider's body, including the head and thorax.

cercus a sensory appendage on the abdomen.

chitin the main component in an insect's outer structure or exoskeleton.

claspers part of the male sex organs in some insects, two clasping appendages used to hold the female during mating.

colony a community of insects that work together for one another's benefit.

compound eye multifaceted eyes consisting of several individual lenses.

cryptic coloration coloration that provides camouflage to help an insect blend into its surroundings without detection by predators.

diapause a period of suspended growth or development during the life cycle.

dimorphism the existence of two different forms within the same species.

elytra the hard wing covers of beetles.

entomology the study of insects.

exoskeleton the exterior supporting structure of the insect body.

fang an appendage similar to a sharp tooth, also known as the chelicera.

formic acid the acid injected or sprayed by some ants as a defense.

fritiniency insect noises.

gallmaker an insect that causes plants or trees to grow warty protuberances, or "galls," around them.

herbivore an insect that feeds exclusively on plants.

histamine one of the main components of the poison injected by the sting of a wasp.

honeydew the sugary excretion of aphids and some other insects.

insectivore any animal or insect that eats insects.

instar any single stage of insect development in which the insect is transformed from one form to another; some insects have more than a half dozen such instars or stages.

larva the wormlike form of a newly hatched insect before metamorphosis.

leg segments from top to bottom these are the coxa, the trochanter, the femur, the tibia, and the footlike tarsus.

mandible the upper jaw of an insect, used in chewing.

mesothorax the middle segment of the thorax from which are attached the second pair of legs.

metamorphosis the transformation process that changes one form of an insect into another, such as a caterpillar becoming a butterfly.

metathorax the third or last segment of the thorax from which the third pair of legs are attached.

mimicry imitation of shape, colorization, or size of an insect (usually poisonous) by an insect of another species for the purpose of deceiving predators. (For example, a nonpoisonous insect with the exact appearance of a poisonous insect.)

mine a shaft dug by ants or caterpillars.

molt the shedding of skin to allow for metamorphosis or growth.

mouthparts a vast array of tiny mouth instruments, depending on the species, from a sucking proboscis to tools for boring, sawing, cutting, clamping, injecting, and piercing.

nymph the young of insects that undergo incomplete metamorphosis.

ocelli tiny simple eyes (usually three) between the compound eyes.

omnivore an animal or insect that eats plants and animals.

ovipositor a long, tubelike organ on the abdomen of females for depositing eggs.

palp an elongated sensory organ associated with the mouthparts.

parthenogenesis reproduction by unfertilized females with the unfertilized eggs usually developing into one-sex young.

pedipalp on the cephalothorax of a spider, a leglike appendage used for guiding food to the mouth, but also used by the male to transfer sperm.

pheromones scents discharged by some insects to attract members of the opposite sex.

prehensile adapted for grabbing and holding, as the legs of a praying mantis.

proboscis a slender, tubular feeding instrument.

prothorax the first of the three thoracic segments, from which the head and first set of legs are attached.

pulvillus the adhesive foot lobe moistened by secretion that allows insects to cling to smooth surfaces.

pupa the inactive stage of metamorphosis following the larval stage and preceding the adult stage.

pupate to become a pupa.

spinneret one of the two to four pairs of nozzlelike outgrowths in the rear of a spider through which silk is extruded for the construction of webs.

spiracles respiratory holes in the sides of the abdomen and thorax. Also known as stigmata.

stridulation insect chirping sounds, especially that of crickets and grasshoppers.

thorax the segment of the body between the head and abdomen, which in itself consists of three subdivisions (prothorax, mesothorax, metathorax).

ultrasounds whistles, tones, and other insect noises pitched too high for humans to hear.

venation the arrangement of veins in the wings that help distinguish orders, families, and genera of insects.

warning coloration conspicuous colors of some insects that warn predators of the presence of poison or other hazard.

LIVESTOCK

abomasum the fourth or true stomach of a ruminant, where most digestion takes place.

anthrax a frequently fatal blood poisoning disease of cattle, sheep, and goats (pigs to a lesser degree) that is highly contagious and characterized by dark, bloody discharges from mouth, nose, and rectum.

barn itch see MANGE.

boar a male hog or pig.

buck a male goat.

bummer an orphaned lamb.

cloven-footed having feet that are divided by clefts.

crossbreed a cross between two different breeds; a hybrid.

crutching trimming the wool around a ewe's udder and flanks.

cud regurgitated food chewed a second time and then reswallowed, part of the natural digestive process of ruminants.

cull to remove an undesirable animal from a herd.

dam the mother of a pig, cow, sheep, or goat.

dewlap a loose fold of skin hanging from the neck of some breeds of cattle.

disbud to dehorn. Also known as to poll.

dock to bob or cut off the end of a tail, usually of lambs for health reasons.

double-muscled of some breeds of cattle, having bulging muscles and a rounded rump, supplying greater meat than other breeds.

elastration livestock castration method in which a rubber band is wound tightly around the scrotum to cut off blood supply, ultimately resulting in the death, drying up, and falling off of the testicles.

estrus the period when the female is sexually receptive to the male, or in heat.

ewe a female sheep.

facing trimming the wool around a ewe's face.

farrow a litter of pigs; to give birth to such a litter.

flock book a register of purebred sheep.

flushing a method of increasing fertility in animals by increasing their feed a few weeks prior to breeding.

fodder various coarse foods for livestock, including cornstalks, hay, and straw.

foot-and-mouth disease a long-lasting, highly contagious disease of cloven-footed animals characterized by fever and blisters in the mouth and around the hooves and teats.

gilt a young sow who has not yet produced a litter.

grade an animal with one purebred parent and one grade or scrub.

heat the period of sexual arousal in animals, especially the estrus of females.

heifer a young cow yet to produce young.

herdbook a register of cattle or hog breeds.

hircine like a goat; pertaining to goats.

kid a young goat.

listeriosis a brain inflammation disease in cattle, sheep, and goats associated with corn silage feeding and characterized by facial paralysis, a "depressed" look, and aimless wandering or walking in tight circles. Also known as circling disease.

mad cow disease a disease of cattle, caused by proteins called prions, which clog brain cells. The prions are spread through the ingestion of infected tissue from a cow's nervous system and are not destroyed by cooking the meat after slaughter.

mange dermatitis caused by mite infestation, characterized by itching and wrinkling of the skin. Also known as barn itch.

mastitis a common disease of sows, dairy goats, and dairy cattle, characterized by reduced milk flow, fever, lack of appetite, and a hot, swollen udder.

omasum the third stomach of a ruminant.

ovine like a sheep; pertaining to sheep.

pedigree a written record or registry of the ancestry of an animal. Also, the registration certificate itself.

poll to cut off or cut short the horns.

pollard an animal with its horns removed.

porcine like a pig; pertaining to a pig or hog.

purebred an animal from two registered parents or from unmixed descent.

ram a male sheep.

reticulum the second stomach of a ruminant.

rumen the first stomach of a ruminant.

ruminant any of the cud-chewing animals, including cattle, sheep, and goats.

ruminate to chew the cud.

rutting sexual excitement of the male.

scours severe diarrhea suffered by livestock animals.

scrub an animal of unknown or unimproved ancestry.

service to stud.

silage green fodder stored in a silo.

sire to father an animal; the father of an animal.

sow an adult female pig.

stud a male used for breeding.

swine collective term for pigs or hogs.

switch the hairy part of a tail.

taurine like a bull; pertaining to bulls.

tribe closely related families within a breed.

ungulate any animal with hooves.

yearling a newly born sheep or goat.

Beef Cattle Breeds

Angus originated in Scotland, black, polled head.

Barzona originated in Arizona, red, specially adapted to arid ranges.

beefalo a crossbreed of a buffalo, a Charolais, and a Hereford, cold-tolerant, lean, flavorful meat, originating in the United States.

beef Friesian bred in the United States, black and white, broad-muzzled, and strong-jawed.

beefmaster Texas breed, red or varied colors, horned or polled, good milk producer.

belted Galloway originally bred in Galloway, Scotland, black with brown tinge or dun-colored with white belt encircling the body, polled head.

Brahman originating in India, gray, red, or spotted, long face with drooping ears, hump over shoulders, pendulous dewlap, heat- and insect-tolerant.

Brangus Oklahoma breed, cross between Brahman and Angus, black, polled, sleek coat, crest on neck.

Charbray Texas breed, creamy white, horned, slight vestigial dewlap.

Charolais French breed, creamy white, horned, large size.

Chianina Italian origin, white, horned, black tongue, the largest cattle in the world, with some bulls weighing in at 4,000 pounds.

Devon English breed, red, horns with black tips.

Dexter Irish breed, black or red, horned, small with short legs.

Fleckvieh German breed, red and white-spotted, horned.

Galloway Scottish breed, black or black with brown or red tint, or dun; polled, long, curly hair, cold-tolerant.

Gelbvieh German breed, golden red or rust, horned, large, long, and muscular.

Hays converter Canadian breed, black with white face, white feet and white tail, good milk producer.

Hereford English breed, red with white markings and white face, horned, thick hair.

Indu Brazil Brazilian breed, light gray silver, dun or red; long, drooping ears, horns pointing up to the rear, hump on shoulders, pendulous dewlap.

Limousin French breed, wheat or rust, horned, long and large, abundant meat.

Lincoln red English breed, cherry red, horned or polled, long, fast-growing, good milk producer.

Maine-Anjou French breed, dark red with white, long, large, fast-growing.

Marchigiana Italian breed, grayish white, small horns, large-bodied.

Normande French breed, dark red and white, spectaclelike patches over eyes, large-bodied.

Norwegian red Norwegian breed, red or red and white, horned, good milk producer.

Piedmont Italian breed, white or pale gray, double-muscled, excellent meat producer.

polled Hereford Iowa breed, red with white markings, white face, polled, thick coat of hair.

polled Shorthorn U.S. breed, red or white, or red and white, polled.

ranger U.S. breed of the western range, all colors, hardy, medium-sized.

red Angus Scottish breed, red, polled, similar to black Angus.

red Brangus U.S. breed, cross of a Brahman and Angus, broad head, sleek coat.

Salers French breed, deep cherry red, horned or polled, hardy, fast-growing, and large.

Scotch Highland Scottish breed, red, yellow, silver, white, dun, black, or brindle; long, shaggy hair, cold-tolerant.

Shorthorn English breed, red, white, or red and white; short horns curving inward.

Simmental Swiss breed, red and white-spotted, white face, horned, fast-growing, excellent meat and milk producer.

Sussex English breed, mahogany red, mostly polled, high yield of lean meat.

Tarentaise French breed, wheat-colored or light cherry or dark blond, small-bodied.

Texas longhorn Texas breed, all colors; long, spreading horns, long head, long legs.

Welsh black Welsh breed, black, mostly horned, good milk producer.

DAIRY CATTLE BREEDS

Ayrshire Scottish breed, cherry red, mahogany, brown, or a mixture of these colors; mostly horned.

brown Swiss alpine breed, solid brown, black nose and tongue, horned, strong and muscular, placid.

Dutch belted Dutch breed, black and white with white belt extending around the body, horned.

Guernsey originating on the Isle of Guernsey, fawn with white marks, horned; yellow milk.

Holstein-Friesian Netherlands breed, black and white or red and white, broad-muzzled, strong-jawed.

Illawarra Australian breed, red or red and white, horned.

Jersey originating on the Island of Jersey, usually fawn-colored with or without white marks; large, bright eyes.

milking Shorthorn English breed, red, white, or red and white, horned.

GOAT BREEDS

American La Mancha U.S. breed, all colors, short or no ears, hornless, milk producer.

Angora Turkish breed, white face, legs and mohair, horned or polled, long locks of mohair.

French Alpine French Alps breed, multicolored, horned or polled, large and deerlike, milk producer.

Nubian a cross of Indian and Egyptian breeds, multicolors, horned or polled, long and droopy ears, Roman nose, milk producer.

Rock Alpine U.S. breed, multicolored, horned or polled, milk producer.

Saanen Swiss breed, white or creamy, horned or polled, large, milk producer.

Swiss Alpine Swiss breed, ocher or brown, polled, erect ears, milk producer.

Toggenburg Swiss breed, fawn to dark brown with white stripes on face and white on legs, polled, milk producer.

PIG BREEDS

American Landrace Danish breed, white with small black spots.

Berkshire English breed, black with white feet.

Chester white U.S. breed, white with or without small bluish spots.

Conner prairie U.S. breed, all colors, large litters.

Duroc U.S. breed, red, medium size.

Hampshire Kentucky breed, black with white belt encircling body; white face.

Hereford U.S. breed, red with white face, similar coloring to that of Hereford cattle.

Lacombe Canadian breed, white, floppy ears.

Managra Canadian breed, white, lop-eared, large litters.

Poland China U.S. breed, black with or without white spots; droopy ears.

spotted U.S. U.S. breed, spotted black and white.

Tamworth English breed, red with or without black spots.

Wessex saddleback English breed, black with white belt encircling body.

Yorkshire English breed, white with or without black freckles; long-bodied.

Sheep Breeds

American merino Spanish breed, white, strong flocking instinct, produces fine wool.

black-faced Highland Scottish breed, black or mottled, horned, produces carpet wool.

Cheviot Scottish breed, white with black nose, polled, no wool on head or legs.

Columbia Wyoming and Idaho breed, white, polled, face free of wool.

Corriedale New Zealand breed, white with or without black marks, polled.

Cotswold English breed, white or white with gray specks, polled, wavy ringlets and curls, long wool.

Debouillet New Mexico breed, white, horned or polled, produces fine wool.

Delaine merino Spanish breed, white, rams with horns, strong flocking instinct, produces fine wool.

Dorset English breed, white, horned or polled.

Finnsheep Finnish breed, white, head free of wool, usually polled; medium wool.

Hampshire English breed, deep brown, polled, large, produces medium wool.

Leicester English, white with or without bluish tinge, polled.

Lincoln English breed, white with or without black spots, polled, the largest of all sheep breeds with rams weighing as much as 375 pounds; produces heavy fleece.

montadale U.S. breed, white, polled, head free of wool, produces medium wool.

Oxford English breed, gray to brown, polled, large.

Panama U.S. breed, white, polled, long wool.

Shropshire English breed, dark-faced, polled, dense wool on head.

Southdown English breed, light or dark brown, polled, produces medium wool.

Suffolk English breed, black head and legs, polled, no wool around head or ears, produces medium wool.

Targhee U.S. breed, white, polled, open-faced.

Tunis North African breed, reddish brown to light tan, polled, long drooping ears, no wool on head, produces medium wool.

MOTHS AND BUTTERFLIES

abdomen the hind body portion, consisting of 10 segments.

androconia special scales on the abdomen, legs, or wings of males that release sex pheromones.

antennae the sensory appendages on the head.

birdwing the largest of all butterflies, with wingspans as long as 12 inches in some species.

chorion the shell of an insect egg.

chrysalis the pupa of a butterfly, the form reached between the larval or caterpillar stage and the winged butterfly stage.

cocoon the silky protective casing made by a moth caterpillar, in which it passes the pupa stage.

cocoon cutter a ridgelike growth on the head of some species that enables them to cut their way out of a cocoon when they're ready to emerge.

compound eye similar to other insects, each eye consisting of several individual units or facets.

cremaster at the tip of the abdomen of a pupa, an extension used to attach the pupa to the place of pupation.

crepuscular active or flying during the twilight, as some species of moths and butterflies.

dagger moth a family of moths recognized by black daggers or dashes on their gray brown forewings.

dash a sharp, short black line on the forewing of many species; also known as a dagger.

diapause a period of suspended growth or development during the life cycle.

diurnal flying or active during the day, as most butterflies.

epiphysis the leaflike appendage on the foreleg, thought to be used for cleaning mouthparts and antennae.

eyespot an eyelike spot found on the wings of some species, thought to frighten birds away. Also known as ocellus (pl., *ocelli*).

forewing the front wing, attached to the mesothorax.

frass the excrement pellets of caterpillars.

frons the front of the head, between the eyes and above the mouthparts.

geometer the second largest family of moths, recognized by their slender bodies and small to medium overall size. The larvae are inchworms.

gossamer wing a family of butterflies recognized for their small size and bright wings with metallic or iridescent hues.

hawk moth a family of medium to very large moths with robust bodies, narrow wings without ocelli, long probosci, and a hovering flight similar to a bird. Also known as sphinx moths or hummingbird moths.

Hesperiidae the butterfly family of skippers.

hind wing the back wing, attached to the metathorax.

instar in the larval stage, the period between molts.

larva the caterpillar stage.

Lepidoptera the order of moths and butterflies.

lepidopterist an entomologist specializing in moths and butterflies.

Lycaenidae the butterfly family of gossamer wings.

mandible the chewing mouthpart of a caterpillar.

Megathymidae the butterfly family of giant skippers.

mesothorax the midportion of a thorax on which the forewings and middle legs are attached.

metamorphosis a transformation of the structure or nature of an organism resulting in a radically different organism; the transformation of a caterpillar to a butterfly, for example; the transformation of Lepidoptera from an egg to a larva to a pupa to a butterfly.

Microlepidoptera a family of medium to small moths recognized by long, slender legs and T-shaped appearance when at rest (its rolled wings are kept folded at right angles to the body).

nectaring the act of gathering nectar by butterflies.

nocturnal active or flying at night, as most moths.

Nymphalidae the large family of brushfooted butterflies, with forelegs reduced to useless brushes.

ocelli collective term for all eyelike spots found on a wing.

orbicular spot a round or elliptical spot resembling an eye in the middle of a forewing in some species.

owlet (noctuid) moth the largest family (Noctuidae) of moths, with some 20,000 species worldwide, recognized by gray brown coloring with a complex pattern of lines and spots and obscured orbicular spots.

Papilionidae the butterfly family of swallowtails, recognized by their spectacular colors, and with wings shaped like a swallow's.

pheromone a sex attractant released by male and female.

Pieridae the butterfly family of whites, sulfurs, and marbles, each resembling its namesake.

proboscis the double-coiled tongue, which is extended to suck up nectar or water.

prothorax the first or frontmost of the three thoracic segments to which the forelegs are attached.

pupa the quiet, metamorphic stage that grows into a butterfly or moth.

reniform spot a kidney-shaped spot on the forewing, similar to an orbicular spot.

skipper once thought to be a link between butterflies and moths, actually a small, quick-flying, short-winged butterfly.

sphragis a device deposited by a male moth on the abdomen of a female to prevent her from mating with another male.

spinneret the silk-spinning organ near the mouth of a caterpillar.

thorax the middle of the three body sections consisting of the prothorax, the mesothorax, and the metathorax.

underwing a large family of moths, recognized by their hind wings, which are all black or brightly colored with black bands; the forewings resemble the bark of trees.

venation the pattern formed by branching veins in wings, helpful in identification.

WHALES

ambergris a waxy substance formed in the intestines of sperm whales and used in the manufacture of perfumes.

baleen in baleen whales, the comblike plates hanging from the palate that strain out small fish and crustaceans.

baleen whale a toothless whale that eats plankton.

blowhole the nostril(s) on top of the head.

breaching jumping out of the water.

calf a juvenile whale.

cetacean the order of fishlike aquatic mammals, including whales, dolphins, and porpoises.

cetology the study of whales, porpoises, and dolphins.

dorsal fin the stabilizing fin on the top of the back of many species.

finning of a whale on its side, slapping the water with its fin.

flukes the horizontal tail fins.

Jonah biblical character who survived three days in the belly of a whale.

lobtailing raising the flukes high out of the water then slapping them down hard on the water.

mysticeti "mustached whales"; the suborder of baleen whales, with 10 species known.

odontoceti the suborder of toothed whales, with more than 66 species known.

orca the species of killer whales.

pod a school of whales.

right whale once considered by whalers as the "right" whale to catch because it is slow and floats when dead.

scrimshaw the decorating and carving of whale bones and teeth.

sonar the use of sound by some whales to locate objects obscured in dark or murky water; echolocation.

sounding diving.

spermaceti a waxy, fatty substance taken from the heads of sperm whales and used for making candles, ointments, and cosmetics.

spy-hop to stick the head upright out of the water.

stranding stranding or beaching in shallow waters.

zeuglodon a prehistoric forerunner of the whale from the Eocene epoch, 50 million years ago.

ARCHITECTURE

ARCHITECTURE TERMS

abutment the mass of masonry that receives the thrust of an arch or vault.

acanthus Mediterranean plant whose leaves are represented as decoration on the capitals of Corinthian and composite columns.

allegory any symbolic sculpture.

amphiprostyle having columns only at the front and back of a temple or a templelike building.

amphistylar having columns along both sides of a temple or a templelike building.

anteroom a room next to a larger, more important room. Also known as an antechamber.

arabesques decorative acanthus scrolls, swags, candelabrum shafts, and animal and human figures appearing on the pilasters and panels of Roman and Renaissance architecture. Also, decorative geometric designs appearing on same.

arcade a series of arches on raised columns; also, a covered walk with such arches.

arcading a line of columned arches represented as decorative relief against a wall.

arcature arcading or miniature arcading.

arch the curved supporting structure of masonry spanning an opening.

arch brick a wedge-shaped brick used in an arch or any circular masonry construction. Also known as compass brick, radial brick, and voussoir brick.

architrave in classical orders, the lowest member of the entablature; the common beam that spans a series of columns.

arcuated having arches.

ashlar any type of squared building stone.

astylar without columns; a facade lacking columns or pilasters of any kind.

atlas a figure of a man used in place of a supporting column.

backing brick a lower-quality brick used behind face brick.

balconet a false balconet projecting out slightly from a window and intended only for decoration.

balloon framing in a wooden building, studwork that extends the full height of the frame from floor to roof.

baluster any one of the vertical posts supporting a stair handrail or other railing.

balustrade an entire railing system, including rail, balusters, and other components.

banister the handrail of a staircase.

bargeboard a decorative board hanging from the projecting end of a roof and covering the gables; the older versions are elaborately carved. Also known as gableboard and vergeboard.

barrel ceiling a semicylindrical ceiling.

barrel vault a masonry vault with a semicylindrical roof.

bar tracery within the arch of a gothic window, the interlocking stone forming a decorative pattern and filled with glass.

basket weave a checkerboard pattern of bricklaying.

bas-relief low relief or protrusion of a carving, embossing, or casting.

bay window a window set in a protruding bay.

bead molding a strip of metal or wood used around a pane of glass to keep it in place. Also, any convex, decorative molding.

belvedere a rooftop pavilion providing an excellent view.

blindstory a floor level without windows.

blindwall a wall unbroken by doors or windows. Also known as a dead wall.

boss a carved ornament placed at the intersection of beams, ribs, or groins.

bowstring beam a girder or truss having a curved or bowed member and a straight member to tie it together.

bow window a window in a rounded or semicylindrical bay. Also known as a compass window.

brick nogging the laying of bricks in the spaces of a timber frame.

brownstone a brown or reddish brown sandstone used in the facades of many eastern U.S. apartment houses in the 19th century.

buttress an exterior mass of masonry bonded into or angled against a wall to add strength and support.

cable molding decorative molding with the appearance of stranded cable or rope.

camberbeam a beam that curves upward slightly.

camber window an arched window.

campanile a freestanding bell tower.

cantilever a beam or truss that projects beyond its supporting foundation, wall, or column. Also, a bracket supporting a balcony.

capital the uppermost member, often ornately carved, of a column or pilaster.

caryatid the figure of a woman used in place of a supporting column, pilaster, or pier.

casement window a hinged window that swings open along its length.

catslide a long, sloping roof, as on a saltbox-style house.

checkerwork in a wall or pavement, masonry laid in a checkerboard pattern.

Christian door a colonial door in which the exterior paneling forms a cross.

cilery the decorative carving around a column's capital.

clapboard overlapping horizontal wood siding used on home and building exteriors. Also known as bevel siding or lap siding.

classicism style inspired by ancient Roman, ancient Greek, and Italian Renaissance architecture.

clerestory the windowed upper story of the nave and choir in a church.

cloister a covered or sheltered walkway surrounding an open courtyard.

cloister garth the courtyard surrounded by a cloister.

clustered column several columns massed together to form one large supporting member.

coffer any one of the decorative sunken panels in a coffered ceiling.

coffered ceiling a highly decorative ceiling characterized by sunken panels.

collar beam a beam or plank that ties together two opposing rafters in a roof.

colonnade a series of columns supporting an entablature.

column a long, vertical, and cylindrical support member that includes a base, a shaft, and a capital.

Composite order in classical architecture, one of the five orders, specifically a composite of Corinthian and Ionic orders.

concourse any open space in a building for accommodating large crowds.

console a decorative bracket, often of wood or stone, projecting from a wall and supporting a cornice, a door head, a bust, or a shelf.

console table a table or large shelf attached to a wall and supported by consoles.

coping the top portion, usually slanting to shed water, of a wall or roof. Also known as copestone or capstone.

corbel a masonry or wood bracket, often decorative, projecting from a wall and supporting a cornice, arch, or other overhanging member.

corbeling a layering of masonry in which each course or row of bricks or stones projects further from the wall than the last row.

corbie steps step or stairlike projections running up the gables of a pitched roof, found on many houses of the 17th century. Also known as catsteps or crowsteps.

Corinthian order the most ornate of the five classical orders, characterized by a voluted, bell-shaped capital with acanthus leaf carvings, and an intricately decorated entablature.

cornerstone an inscribed stone situated near the base of any corner in a building, sometimes ceremoniously laid and hollowed out to store historical documents or objects.

cornice a molded projection that crowns a building or wall. Also, any ornamental molding around the walls just below a ceiling.

cosmati cut-stone mosaic inlay forming geometric patterns.

course one row of bricks or stones in a wall.

cove ceiling a ceiling that curves down to meet the walls.

crocket an ornament, usually in the form of a leaf, found along the sloping or vertical edges of gothically styled spires, pinnacles, and gables.

cupola a small dome or domelike structure on a roof.

curtail the spiraling or scroll-like termination at the end of a stair railing.

dais a raised platform for speakers.

day one division in a window.

deadlight any window not designed to open.

decastyle of a portico, having 10 columns or rows of 10 columns.

dentil any of the small, square blocks projecting like teeth beneath an entablature.

diamond work masonry laid out to form the shape of diamonds in a wall or pavement.

distyle having two columns.

Doric order in classical architecture, the least adorned of the orders, characterized by a heavy, fluted column and a simple capital.

dormer a structure or gable projecting out from a sloping roof and containing a window.

drip the protective molding over the top of a window or door to discharge rainwater.

Dutch door a split door consisting of separate bottom-opening and top-opening segments.

eaves the portion of a lower roof projecting beyond the wall.

embedded column a column that is partially within the face of a wall. Also known as an engaged column.

English bond a bricklaying method characterized by alternating courses of headers (heads of the bricks facing out) and stretchers (laid out horizontally in the direction of the wall).

entablature in a classical order, the upper section resting on the capital, consisting of the architrave, the frieze, and the cornice.

facade the exterior face of a building.

fanlight a semicircular window with radiating sash bars, usually placed over a door.

fascia a flat trim board around the eaves or gables of roofs.

fenestra a small window.

fenestration the design and arrangement of windows in a building.

finial an ornament at the top of a spire or pinnacle.

Flemish bond brickwork in which every other brick laid is a header.

floriated decorated with floral carvings or patterns.

florid highly ornate, heavily embellished.

fluting grooves or channels, as in the shaft of a column.

flying buttress a bar of masonry rising from a pier or arch and abutting against a roof or vault to receive thrust.

French door a door with glass panes running nearly its full length and usually hung in pairs. Also known as a casement door.

French roof a mansard roof.

fresco a painting on plaster.

fret a banded ornament consisting of geometrical patterns.

frieze the middle horizontal member of an entablature, often decorated with carvings of leaves or human and animal figures.

gable the triangular wall portion at either end of a pitched roof.

gableboard see BARGEBOARD.

gable roof a roof having gables.

gambrel roof a roof pitched twice on each side, with the lowest pitch being the steepest.

gargoyle a grotesque sculpture projecting from a roof gutter and acting as a spout for wastewater or rainwater.

gingerbread highly decorative woodwork of gingerbread-style houses of the 19th century.

grotesque sculptured ornamentation representing animal or human forms in bizarre and fanciful ways.

header a brick or stone laid so that its head or short side faces out.

hecatonstylon a building with 100 columns.

herringbone pattern masonry work laid in a zigzagging fashion.

hexastyle having six columns.

hip the angle formed at the junction of two sloping roofs.

hip roof a roof having four sloping sides instead of two.

historiated ornamented with a representation of a narrative of some historic event, usually in the form of human or animal figures.

horseshoe arch a rounded arch in the distinct shape of a horseshoe. Also known as a Moorish arch.

intercolumniation the system of spacing between a colonnade for varying effects. Roman styles of intercolumniation include pycnostyle—1½ diameters; systyle—2 diameters; eustyle—2¼ diameters; diastyle—3 diameters; araeostyle—4 diameters.

Ionic order the classical order of intercolumniation characterized by elegant detailing, although less ornate than Corinthian and less massive than Doric.

jib door a door with no visible hardware on the room side and that stands flush with the wall so as to blend in neatly.

joist one of any of the parallel beams used to support the load from a floor and ceiling.

keystone the central block, sometimes embellished, of an arch.

lancet window a narrow window with a pointed arch, commonly found in churches.

lantern a decorative, lighted structure crowning a dome, turret, or roof.

lintel a horizontal member forming the upper portion of a door or window frame and that supports the load above it.

lozenge a small window.

mansard roof a roof having two slopes on all four sides, the upper portion being almost flat and the lower portion being almost nearly vertical. Similar to a gambrel roof.

marigold window a round window with radiating mullions. Also known as a rose window.

marquetry wood inlay work.

mezzanine a partial floor level between two main levels in a building; an extended balcony or gallery.

minaret a tall tower associated with a mosque.

molding trim, usually of wood, providing decorative outline and contouring.

monopteron a Greek circular building surrounded by a single row of columns.

motif any repeated decorative design or pattern.

mullion any one of the vertical members supporting or dividing a window or door.

newel the central supporting column or post around which a winding staircase climbs.

obelisk a four-sided stone tower or monument, tapering to a pyramidal tip.

octastyle having eight columns.

onion dome a Russian bulbous dome ending in a point and resembling an onion.

order in classical architecture, the style of intercolumniation and entablature. The Greek orders are Ionic, Doric, and Corinthian. The Roman orders are Tuscan and Composite.

ornament any carved, sculpted, engraved, or painted architectural decoration.

oversailing course a row of bricks that project beyond the face of a wall.

palmette an ornament representing palm leaves.

parapet a low, safeguarding wall along the edges of a rooftop.

parquet inlaid wood flooring, usually forming a geometric pattern.

pavilion roof a pyramidal roof.

pediment in classical architecture, the triangular gable end of a roof. Also, an ornamental feature, such as found over doors and windows, having this shape.

pentastyle having five columns.

pepperbox turret a turret with a conical or domed roof.

peripteral surrounded by a single colonnade.

peristyle a colonnade surrounding a building or courtyard.

pier a vertical masonry support.

pilaster a flat, rectangular column having a base and capital and set or engaged into a wall.

pilastrade a line of pilasters.

pinnacle a tower or turret.

plinth the square base for a column or pilaster. Also, a block serving as a base for a statue.

portcullis a large iron or timber grated door that can be raised or lowered, as in the entrance to a castle.

portico a porch consisting of a roof supported by columns.

pyramidion a small pyramid, as a cap on an obelisk.

quadrangle a rectangular courtyard surrounded by buildings.

quarry-faced rough, unfinished.

quoin the stones used to reinforce an external wall corner, sometimes decoratively distinguished from surrounding masonry. Also known as coin.

random course a row of masonry of unequal sizes.

random work masonry laid in irregular courses, with random sizes of stone.

reinforced concrete concrete reinforced with iron or steel mesh or bars embedded within it.

relief a carving or embossing raised against its background.

rib a slender supporting arch.

rose window a large round window, frequently with stained glass and stone tracery. Also known as a marigold window.

rubblework masonry consisting of rubble.

rusticated stone rough-faced stone that has been beveled, popular during the Renaissance and in modern banks and courthouses because of the impregnable appearance they provide to a facade.

sash any window framework.

scroll an ornament resembling a scroll or spiral.

scrollwork ornately carved wood, cut with a scroll saw.

sill a horizontal timber at the bottom of a door or window frame. Also, the horizontal timber resting on a foundation in a wood house.

skirt roof a small false roof between levels of a building, forming a decorative skirt.

sleeper any horizontal beam laid near the ground or foundation of a building.

soffit the exposed surface underneath an architectural member, such as an arch, beam, or lintel.

splay a large bevel.

stretcher a brick or stone laid lengthwise; opposite of a header.

stringer in a stairway, the cut, inclined board on which the steps rest.

stucco textured plaster or cement used on walls for a decorative effect.

swag a relief ornament resembling garlands and gathered drapery.

terra-cotta hard, fired clay, unglazed, glazed, or painted, used for ornamental designs and roof and floor tiles.

tessellated having small squares of stone, marble, or glass set in a mosaic pattern, in a floor or wall.

tetrastyle having four columns or rows of four columns.

tholos in Greek architecture, a round building.

trabeated constructed with horizontal beams and lintels instead of arches and vaults.

tracery ornamental stonework supporting glass in a gothically styled window.

travertine a creamy, banded limestone, used for facing a floor.

turret a miniature tower, corbeled out from a corner of a wall, as in a castle.

vault a masonry roof or ceiling over an arched area.

vaulting vaulted ceilings, roofs, hallways, or other structures.

volute a spiral scroll, as found on Ionic, Corinthian, and Composite capitals.

wagon vault a semicylindrical vault, or barrel vault.

wainscot decorative paneling or facing placed on a wall near the floor.

widow's walk a platformed walkway on the roofs of early New England houses.

BRIDGES

abutment the support at either end of a bridge.

aqueduct bridge structure designed to convey water over a river or hollow and over long distances to supply communities.

arcade collective term for the series of arches and columns that support some types of bridges.

arch structural member supporting and displacing stress under a span.

balustrade a row of balusters topped by a rail serving as a barrier along the edges of a bridge.

bascule type of drawbridge with span arms that pivot and swing upward to let boat traffic pass.

bridle-chord bridge type of bridge in which the girders are supported by steel cables passing over the tops of towers on the main piers.

caisson a watertight chamber filled with compressed air for use in underwater construction by bridge builders.

cantilever type of bridge in which two beams or trusses project from shore toward each other and are connected.

cofferdam enclosure built in the water and continuously pumped dry to allow construction or repair of bridge piers.

gantry bridge structure supporting the rails of a moving construction crane.

gephyrophobia fear of bridges.

parapet any low wall or barrier that protects—as a railing—the edges of a bridge.

pier support at either end of a span.

pile long timber driven in the earth, used to support piers or abutments, or as a direct support for the bridge itself.

pontoon a flat-bottomed boat, or any float, used in the construction of bridges.

saddles blocks over which the cables of a suspension bridge pass.

suspension bridge similar to a bridle-chord bridge but using more cables to support and relieve stress on the girders.

swing bridge bridge with a span that opens by swinging around horizontally to let boat traffic pass.

trestle open-braced framework for supporting a railroad bridge.

truss assembly of beams, bars, or rods forming a rigid framework.

vertical lift bridge bridge with a span section that is lifted at both ends from towers to allow boat traffic to pass.

viaduct an arched masonry bridge that carries a roadway over a valley or ravine.

CASTLES AND MEDIEVAL BUILDINGS

(includes castle weaponry, castle staffing, and related subjects)

alcazar a Spanish fortress or castle.

alure a gallery or passage along the parapets of a castle.

arbalest a medieval crossbow used to shoot arrows. Also, a large bow mounted on a stand to launch darts, lances, or metal bolts.

archeria apertures through which archers could shoot arrows. Also known as arrow loops, loopholes, balistraria, and arrow slits.

assommoir a gallery built over a doorway from which heavy objects could be dropped down on the heads of intruding enemies.

bailey an open ground or courtyard encircled by walls. Also known as a ward.

balistraria a room in which crossbows were kept. Also, small holes in walls to allow the shooting of arrows.

barbican a walled outwork or tower protecting a drawbridge or a gateway.

bartizan a projecting or overhanging turret.

bastille a castle or castle tower used as a prison.

bastion a mass of earth faced with stones or sods projecting out from a rampart.

battlement an indented or notched parapet for observing or shooting.

belfry a tall, mobile tower erected at a siege site and pushed up against an outer wall to allow archers or other military men to advance against or shoot at castle defenders. Also known as a bear.

brattice any one of the wooden planks or timbers in a stockade or palisade. Also, any castle tower made of timbers.

butler a castle staff member in charge of drinks and the buttery (bottlery).

buttery a bottlery, or a room used for stocking or preparing drinks.

castellated like a castle in structure.

castellum a fort surrounded by a village or a fortified town.

catapult one of several types of siege engines used to launch such projectiles as rocks and firebombs onto or over castle walls.

cesspit a pit that receives waste from a garderobe.

chamberlain serving under a monarch or lord, an official in charge of the domestic affairs of a castle, especially in supplying the great hall or chamber, where most of the daily living activities took place.

chandlery a storeroom for candles and lighting supplies.

chaplain in medieval times, the religious head who conducted services in a castle chapel but who also kept castle accounts and conducted correspondence because of his ability to read and write.

château a French castle.

chatelaine the lady or mistress of a castle.

chatelet a small castle.

citadel any fortress near a city and keeping its inhabitants in subjugation.

corbel a projection of stones from the face of a wall to support a roof or parapet.

crenel any one of the gaps at the top of a battlement wall for shooting and observation.

crossbowmen archers.

curtain wall any one of the inner or outer protective walls ringing a castle.

dais a raised platform in a great hall or chamber where a lord and lady sat.

donjon (dungeon) the main tower or keep, usually the central and strongest location where fighters withdrew when the enemy had penetrated, often containing a well, apartments, offices, service rooms, and supplies. In early castles, the living quarters of a lord; in later castles, the dungeon or prison, especially the lower or underground portion.

drawbridge spanning a moat or ditch, a bridge that could be raised or drawn back to prevent an enemy from entering.

dungeon see DONJON.

embrasure an opening in a wall, sloped to enlarge its interior portion, for shooting and observation; the low portion of a battlement.

falcon one of the predatory birds (also hawks) often kept as pets in a castle for sport hunting purposes.

falconer one who trained a predatory bird to sport hunt.

farrier a castle staff member in charge of shoeing or caring for horses.

feudal system a political and economic system in medieval Europe in which a servant, peasant, or tenant was granted land in exchange for service, often involving the guarding or defending of castles.

finial a slender, ornamental stone sometimes fixed on the tops of merlons.

garderobe a latrine or privy, usually located in an outer wall over a ditch, moat, or cesspit.

gargoyle a grotesque sculpture adorning the upper walls of some castles and often used to discharge dirty water.

gatehouse a tower protecting the drawbridge.

Greek fire a mixture of naphtha, sulfur, and quicklime, which ignited by moistening and burned fiercely, hurled as a firebomb over castle walls.

half timber in many medieval castles, a construction method in which wood frame walls are filled with wattle (a mat of woven sticks) and daub (mud or clay).

hedgehog the equivalent of modern barbed wire, thorn bushes and stakes erected to protect an outer wall from the enemy. Also known as a herrison or zareba.

hoarding a makeshift balconylike structure hung from the tops of walls to provide a platform for archers and other warriors during a battle; hoardings were made of wood and were usually only temporary.

inner ward in the center of a castle, an open yard.

jester a court fool or comic.

jousting sport in which a knight on horseback tries to knock off another knight on horseback with the use of lance and shield.

keep the donjon or strongest building in a castle.

list the open area immediately in front of a castle's defenses, kept clear to avoid giving cover to the enemy.

lord in feudal law, the owner of a manor or castle.

machicolation a slit or opening between corbels, allowing projectiles or boiling liquids to be dropped down on an enemy.

maiden tower the keep or main tower.

mangon a catapult with a spoon-shaped end in which large stones, timbers, and firebombs were launched; because of its violent kicking after each throw, the Romans called these siege engines "wild asses;" the 12th-century Normans called them "nags."

merlons the solid sections between a wall's crenels or notches.

mining tunneling under a castle during a siege to bring about the collapse of its walls or foundation.

moat a deep, wide trench, usually filled with water around a castle to keep an enemy from penetrating.

motte a mound of hard-packed earth used as a base for early castles.

motte-and-bailey castle an early type of castle perched on a mound of hard-packed earth and surrounded by an open courtyard or bailey and a palisade.

mouse an iron gouge or bore used to pry away bits of stone on a castle wall during a siege.

murder holes arrow loops and other holes or openings in an upper floor, through which defenders could fire down upon an intruding enemy.

oubliette a secret pit with a trapdoor within the floor of a dungeon through which prisoners could be dropped and left to rot.

outer ward an open yard outside of an inner curtain wall.

palisade a barrier or stockade made of strong timbers, often surrounding early castles.

pantler a castle staff member in charge of the pantry.

parapet a low wall along the edge of a roof to protect soldiers from falling off or from being attacked by enemies.

pas-de-souris steps leading from a moat to the entrance.

pepperbox turret a circular turret with a conical roof. Same as a pinnacle.

pikeman a warrior adept at killing with a pike.

portcullis a large, grated door made of oak and iron that could be wound up or down by a windlass and sometimes acted as a counterweight to a drawbridge.

porter a castle official who made sure no one entered or left a castle without the proper authority.

postern a minor gateway set inside a wall, usually at the rear of a castle.

privy latrine.

quintain a wooden dummy that spun on a post, used for lancing practice in a castle's courtyards by knights.

ram a battering ram, usually a large tree trunk fitted with an iron snout.

rampart a surrounding mound or embankment on which a parapet was frequently raised.

rushlights twisted strands of rush dipped in grease or tallow, ignited, and held in wall brackets for lighting.

sapper during a siege, a warrior specifically assigned to batter down the stonework of a castle wall.

scaling ladder a ladder used in scaling castle walls.

scarp a steep slope to slow the advance of an enemy in front of a castle. Also known as an escarpment.

screw stair a winding staircase.

seneschal a steward or majordomo in charge of such domestic affairs as buying provisions, managing servants, planning feasts, or keeping accounts.

shell keep an early castle consisting of a stone-walled motte.

siege the surrounding and attacking of a fortification to gain possession.

siege engine any one of several catapult or battering devises used in a siege against a castle.

solar a sunny room adjacent to the upper end of a hall, used by a lord, his family, and honored guests.

stable marshal an officer in charge of a castle's stables and horses.

stair turret any turret completely filled by a winding staircase.

tiltyard a list or open courtyard where knights practiced their riding and lancing skills.

tortoise a portable shelter made of hides or metal in which attackers could be protected from the arrows and bombs of castle defenders; sometimes used to get safely across a moat.

trebuchet a large siege engine employing counterweights to thrust rocks, firebombs, and the decayed carcasses of dead horses as far as a quarter mile; also known as a tripgate.

turret a small tower set above a larger structure.

usher a castle doorman.

ward the open ground or bailey between encircling walls.

wattle and daub woven sticks and grass sealed with mud or clay (daub), common construction material of medieval times.

Medieval Villages

(*Also see* CASTLES AND MEDIEVAL BUILDINGS)

assize of bread and ale laws that fix the prices and standards of goods.

bailiff an official who manages business (looking after crops, stocking supplies, etc.) and enforces the laws of a lord's manor.

beadle a manorial assistant to a reeve; in charge of preserving and sowing seeds from the previous year's crops.

cellarer a monastery official responsible for food stores.

censuarius a tenant who pays rent in lieu of labor.

charter an official document, such as a deed.

cotter a tenant of a cottage.

croft the garden area of a village house.

curia a courtyard.

demesne the portion of a manor cultivated for the lord's personal use.

distraint an arrest or summons.

eyre royal circuit court.

farm lease.

feudalism the political and social system of medieval days.

fief a grant of land made by a lord in exchange for services. Also known as a fee.

frankpledge the responsibility of each division of a community to carry out police duties and to see to it that the law is upheld.

glebe land cultivated to help support a parish church.

hue and cry a law requiring that all citizens within earshot give chase to a fleeing criminal.

infangenethef the right to confiscate the belongings of a convicted thief.

leirwite a fine given a single woman for sexual indiscretions.

manor a lord's estate, including those portions cultivated by tenants.

merchet a serf's payment for a daughter's marriage.

messuage a house and yard in a village.

mortuary a duty, usually one's second-best beast, paid to the church upon death.

pannage a fee paid to a lord to allow one's pigs to forage for acorns, nuts, and apples on a forest floor.

reeve a manor official who made sure that tenants who owed the lord of the manor labor repaid him promptly.

serf a peasant; a villein.

tallage an annual tax paid by villeins to a lord.

tithe traditional donation of 10 percent of all crops to the church.

tithing a group of 10 to 12 men, each responsible for the other's behavior in a village.

toft a yard of a house in a village.

villein a serf.

virgate a unit of land from 18 to 32 acres, thought to be sufficient to support a peasant and his family.

woodward a manor official responsible for a lord's woodland.

HOUSE CONSTRUCTION

aggregate sand, stone, or gravel used to make concrete.

anchor bolts bolts set in the top of a concrete foundation to hold structural members in place.

backfill earth mounded up around a foundation's walls to create a slope for water runoff.

balloon framing a form of house construction in which the upright studs extend all the way from the sill to the roof, a technique that has largely grown out of favor.

balusters the spindles or poles that support a stair railing.

balustrade a row of balusters topped with a rail.

baseboard the interior trim that runs around the walls next to the floor.

batten a strip of wood used to cover a joint, especially between siding boards.

bay window any curved, rectangular, or polygonal window that projects out from a wall.

beam a large, supportive structural member, usually running from one foundation wall to another and held up by pillars or poles.

bearing wall any wall that bears the weight of a ceiling, floor, or roof above it. Also known as a load-bearing wall or a bearing partition.

belvedere a small, glass-enclosed room used as a lookout on the roof of a house.

berm a mound or bank of earth formed to shunt drainage away from a house.

bevel to cut at an angle, as in beveled siding; thicker on one end than the other.

bibcock or bib nozzle a faucet on the outside of the house around or above the foundation. Also known as a sill cock.

board-and-batten siding siding of broad boards lined together with narrow boards or battens nailed over their joints.

breezeway a sheltered passageway between a garage and a house.

bricklaying The following are common terms.

common bond a bricklaying style characterized by several courses of overlapping stretchers interspersed with an occasional course of headers.

course one row of bricks.

English bond a bricklaying style characterized by alternating courses of headers and stretchers.

Flemish bond a bricklaying style characterized by courses consisting of alternating headers and stretchers forming an overall diamond pattern.

garden wall a bricklaying style characterized by courses in which every fourth brick is a header.

header a brick laid with its short end facing out.

rowlock a header laid on its narrow side.

running bond a bricklaying style characterized by overlapping courses of stretchers and no headers.

shiner a stretcher with its broad side facing out.

soldier a brick laid standing on end.

stacked bond a bricklaying style characterized by nonoverlapping courses of stretchers.

stretcher a brick laid lengthwise.

bridging small pieces of wood crossed between studs to add rigidity and to distribute load.

casement window a hinged window that swings open along one vertical edge.

casing the trim around a door or a window.

caulking sealing material used to waterproof cracks and joints, especially around doors and windows.

clapboard a long, beveled board used for siding.

collar beam a beam that connects rafters. Also known as a rafter tie.

conduit, electrical a pipe or tube through which wiring is run.

corbel a projection of wood or masonry to add structural support to a wall.

counterflashing extra flashing used around a chimney to help prevent rain from entering a house.

cripple stud a stud placed over a wall opening, above a header.

curtain wall a non-load-bearing wall.

doorsill a door framing member that serves as a threshold.

dormer a projecting structure, usually containing one or more windows, on a sloping roof.

double-hung window a window that has two sashes that can be moved up or down independently of one another.

drip cap exterior molding above a window or door to direct rainwater away from woodwork.

drop siding tongue-and-groove board siding.

drywall any wallboard or other wall covering not needing a plaster finish; gypsum wallboard.

eaves the lowest or overhanging portion of a roof.

English basement a house or apartment building with its first floor halfway underground.

fascia the horizontal trim board running along the roof line; it is attached to the ends of the rafters.

firestop a block placed between framing studs to slow the spread of fire.

flashing sheet metal, weather stripping, or other material used to prevent the entry of rainwater through the joints in a roof.

floating foundation a foundation without footings, used in swampy or other unstable areas.

footings concrete supports under a foundation.

foundation the large supporting structure below ground, forming a basement or a slab.

gable the portion of a wall between the two slopes of a roof.

gambrel roof a double-sloped roof, with the lower portion being the steepest.

gingerbread any elaborate or excessive ornamentation on a house. Also known as gingerbread work.

glazing installing glass into sashes and doors.

grout a thin mortar used in tile work.

gusset a bracket or board applied to intersections of a frame to add rigidity.

gypsum wallboard wall panels made of gypsum and faced with paper.

header the topmost frame member over a door, window, or other wall opening. Also known as a lintel.

hip roof a roof that rises on all four sides of a house; a roof with no gable ends.

jack rafter a short rafter frame between the wall plate and a hip rafter.

jalousie a window or door composed of adjustable glass louvers.

joist a large timber laid horizontally to support a floor or ceiling.

lintel see HEADER.

live load the variable load a structural member must bear, such as snow on a roof or people walking across a floor, as distinguished from dead load or permanent, nonvariable load.

load the weight a structural member bears or supports.

lookout a structural member running between the lower end of rafters; the underside of a roof overhang.

mansard roof a roof having two slopes on all four sides of a house.

masonry stone, brick, tile, concrete block, and such like.

molding any narrow, usually rounded, trim used decoratively to cover joints.

mullion a vertical bar or strip dividing the panes of a window.

newel the principal post supporting the handrail at the bottom of a staircase.

nogging bricks placed between the timbers of a wall, for a decorative effect or as a firestop.

on center builder's term referring to a measurement taken from the center of one structural member to the center of another.

plaster a mixture of lime, cement, and sand, used on walls.

plate a structural member laid horizontally over the top of studs in a wall. It serves as a support for the attic joists and roof rafters.

platform framing a framing method in which the subfloor extends out into a platform for stud walls; walls are usually prefabricated and tilted into place.

plumb a weight hung from a line to determine if a structural member is perfectly vertical; used to test vertical alignments.

post-and-beam construction a framing method characterized by the use of heavy timbers set further apart than standard framing.

purlins the horizontal members that support rafters.

rabbet joint a recess or groove on the end of a board.

rafter a sloping roof framing member extending from the ridge to the eaves.

rake the slope of a roof or roof rafter.

ridgeboard the uppermost horizontal roof member, to which the top of the rafters are attached.

riser the vertical board rising under a stair tread.

roughing-in the installation of drainage and water pipes for hookup with fixtures and appliances. Also, partial completion of electrical wiring.

R-value a number that signifies the efficiency of an insulating material, such as R-19.

sash the framework that holds the glass in a window.

scuttle a small opening giving access to the attic.

shake a handsplit wood shingle.

sheathing collective term for any covering boards, panels, or other materials.

sheathing paper a building paper used in the roof and walls to block the passing of air.

sheetrock commonly used commercial name for gypsum wallboard.

shim a thin wedge of wood used to help level framing members, especially window and door frames.

shiplap siding siding comprised of boards that connect with one another with rabbeted joints.

shoe the lowest framing member laid horizontally on a subfloor and used as a base for a stud wall.

sill the lowest of all horizontal structural members; it lies directly on the foundation.

skylight a roof window.

slab a solid concrete foundation without a basement.

sleeper a sill; any large structural member laid horizontally.

soffit the underside of a structural member, such as a beam, a staircase, or a roof overhang.

soil stack the large, vertical pipe that receives wastewater from all plumbing fixtures and appliances.

soleplate the lowest horizontal member in a wall frame.

stringer the inclined, precut framing member that serves as one of two supports for stair risers and treads.

stucco a wall covering made of cement or plaster.

stud a vertical framing member, usually made of wood.

subfloor the rough flooring laid directly over the floor joists.

sump in the basement, a hole or depression that collects leaking water.

termite shield sheet metal placed in and around a foundation and its openings to prevent entry by termites.

tie beam a collar beam or rafter tie.

toenail to pound a nail in at an angle in order to make it penetrate a second structural member. Also, to drive a nail so that its head will not be visible on the surface.

transom bar a horizontal bar dividing a window.

truss a large, triangular framing unit, often prefabricated, constructed of beams, bars, and ties, and used to span a large space.

valley rafter a rafter rising where two roof slopes of different angles meet; an inside corner rafter. Similar to a hip rafter.

vapor barrier any material applied to a wall to block the passage of moisture.

wainscot a decorative wall covering skirting the lower portion of a wall.

wallboard Sheetrock, gypsum, waferboard, and similar items.

weephole a small hole cut in masonry to drain moisture.

widow's walk an open, railed walkway around a peaked roof, particularly in some New England seacoast homes.

HOUSE STYLES

adobe a Spanish clay-and-straw brick home.

bothy a small cottage of northern England, Scotland, and Ireland.

brownstone a house or apartment building faced with a brown or reddish brown sandstone.

bungalow a one-story, cottagelike house characterized by overhanging gables forming the front porch. Also, a one-story tiled or thatched house surrounded by a wide veranda in India.

Cajun cottage a tin-roofed shack of Louisiana.

Cape Cod a rectangular, 1½-story house with a pitched roof, originating in colonial Cape Cod, Massachusetts.

carpenter Gothic a 19th-century American homebuilding technique characterized by the application of elaborate gothic motifs with wood.

catslide house slang for a saltbox house, named for its long, sloping roof in the rear and short roof in front.

château a French country estate.

colonial any one of several house styles imported from a motherland. For example, a clapboard colonial saltbox with a massive central chimney; a German colonial with heavy stone walls; a fieldstone Dutch colonial with a broad gambrel roof; a stuccoed adobe Spanish colonial with arcaded veranda and red-tiled roof.

Creole townhouse a New Orleans townhouse characterized by iron balconies, slate or tiled roofs, arched and shuttered windows, and plastered or stuccoed facades with colors that include pink, ocher, and yellow.

Dutch colonial originating in Dutch-settled areas of New York and the Hudson River valley in the 17th century, a house characterized by a gambrel roof (two pitches on each side) and overhanging eaves.

Elizabethan an English country house originating in the late 1500s and characterized by large, mullioned windows and decorative strapwork.

English magpie a style of house popular in medieval England.

Federal style classic revival style popular from 1790 to 1830 in the United States. Notable features include two or four chimneys flanking either end of the house, elaborate fan doorways (some with porticos), paired or twin front stairways, and brass and iron hardware. Rooms in Federal houses are often round or oval.

Georgian popular in 18th-century Britain and its American colonies, and characterized by a columned or pilaster-flanked front entry, heavy stone sills, brass hardward, and ornate roof balustrades.

gambrel see DUTCH COLONIAL.

gingerbread an ornately decorated American house of the 19th century, reminiscent of the fairytale namesake.

Greek revival a revival of Greek and Roman forms early in 19th-century America and England; characterized by Corinthian, Doric, or Ionic wood-columned porticos creating the famous "temple" look. Door surrounds and eaves are carefully carved in Greek foliate or geometric motifs as well.

Gothic revival popular in 18th- and early 19th-century Europe and America, a house characterized by the revival of Gothic forms of architecture.

hacienda a large Spanish estate.

half-timbered 16th- and 17th-century American and European houses built with large timber foundations, supports, and studs, with walls filled in with bricks or plaster.

Italianate (Italian villa-style) popular in United States and England in the mid-1800s, characterized by slightly pitched roofs, square towers, and round-arched windows.

octagon an eight-sided Victorian house.

pueblo a stone or adobe community dwelling as high as five stories, built by the Native Americans of the southwestern United States.

Queen Anne a house style popular in the 1870s and 1880s in England and America, actually based on a combination of Elizabethan, Tudor, Gothic, and English Renaissance forms. Features include polygonal or cylindrical towers, bay windows, balconies, and richly decorative woodwork.

Romanesque style popular from 1840 to 1860, characterized by tall towers, arched windows, and decorative arcading beneath the eaves.

row house any one of an unbroken line or series of houses.

saltbox a New England house characterized by a long, sloping roof in the back and a short, pitched roof in front.

Second Empire popular Victorian style characterized by mansard roofs, tall arched windows and doors, and iron roof pinnacles.

shingle style later 19th-century Victorian style, characterized by the dominant use of unpainted wood shingles on roofs and walls.

stick style a wood exposed-frame style popular in the later 19th century.

Tudor a house style characterized by its exposed beams.

vernacular Victorian an understated Victorian, less ornate than earlier styles and usually adopting local forms.

INTERNATIONAL AND NATIVE AMERICAN ARCHITECTURE

Ancient Greek and Roman Architecture

acaina in ancient Greece, a measure of length equal to 1,215 inches.

acroaterion in ancient Greece, a hall or place where lectures were given.

acrobaticon the scaffolding used in ancient Greek construction.

acropolis the elevated stronghold or plateau-plaza of a Greek city.

additus maximus a main entrance in an ancient Roman amphitheater.

aerarium the public treasury of ancient Rome.

aethousa a sunny portico of a Greek dwelling.

agalma any ancient Greek work of art dedicated to a god.

agger an ancient Roman rampart or earthwork.

agora in ancient Greece, an outdoor public assembly place or marketplace.

agyieus an altar or statue of Apollo traditionally placed at a street-facing door of a Greek house.

ahenum a boiler system consisting of three copper vessels and a furnace for providing water to ancient Roman baths.

ala a small room or alcove off the atrium of an ancient Roman house.

albani stone the stone commonly used in the construction of ancient Roman buildings before the introduction of marble.

album in ancient Rome, a section of white plaster on a wall in a public place on which public announcements were written.

aleatorium in ancient Rome, a room where dice games were played.

alipterium a room in which ancient Roman bathers anointed themselves.

alveus a Roman sunken bath.

ambivium an ancient Roman road that circumnavigated a site but did not go through it.

amphitheater an elliptical, circular, or semicircular auditorium.

anatarium a house and yard for raising ducks in ancient Rome.

andron a room used exclusively by men in ancient Greece.

angiportus a narrow road between rows of houses in ancient Rome.

anserarium an ancient Roman porticolike structure used for raising geese.

anthemion a common ornamentation based on the honeysuckle or palmette plants, frequently seen in Greek architecture.

apodyterium a room where Greek or Roman bathers undressed.

apotheca a Greek or Roman storeroom that frequently held wines.

aqueduct a water channel placed on high arches when crossing valleys or low ground.

arabesque in Roman architecture, a decorative pattern of acanthus scrolls, swags, candelabrum shafts, and animal and human forms appearing on panels and pilasters. (Differs from the arabesque pattern of Muslim countries.)

area custodiae an ancient Roman prison cell.

archivium a building in which archives were kept in ancient Rome and Greece.

arena the sanded central area in a Roman circus or amphitheater.

arenarium an ancient Roman cemetery, crypt, or grave.

argurokopeion in ancient Greece, a place where money was coined; a mint.

athenaeum a Roman temple or place of scientific or literary studies, named after Athena.

atrium in a Roman house, a large inner hall with an opening in the roof for rainwater and a basin on the floor to catch it.

auditorium a place where orators, poets, and critics spoke.

baccha a Roman lighthouse.

baphium a Roman establishment for dyeing cloth.

bestiarium where wild animals were kept before their appearance in an ancient Roman amphitheater.

bronteum in Greek and Roman theaters, a heavy vase filled with stones and shaken to simulate the sound of thunder.

caldarium one of the three components of an ancient Roman bath, consisting of the hot water bath itself. See FRIGIDARIUM, TEPIDARIUM.

capeleion a place where wine and provisions were sold in ancient Greece.

caprile a Roman structure used to house goats.

carnificina a Roman underground dungeon in which criminals were tortured or killed.

cartibulum a supported marble slab serving as a table in a Roman atrium.

catadrome a Roman racecourse used by chariots, horses, or men.

caupona a place where wine and provisions were sold in ancient Rome.

cavaedium an atrium or inner courtroom in a Roman house.

cavea cage for wild animals under the seats of an ancient Roman amphitheater.

cenatio a formal dining room in a Roman house.

choragic monument a Greek commemorative structure.

choragium in Greek and Roman theaters, a storage and rehearsal space behind the stage.

cinerarium a Roman depository for urns holding the ashes of the dead.

circus a Roman stadium for races and gladiator shows.

clavus in ancient Roman construction, a nail.

cloaca in ancient Rome, a sewer.

coenaculum any of the upper eating rooms in Roman houses.

colosseum any large Roman amphitheater.

Columna Maenia a column erected in the Roman Forum to which criminals and slaves were tied and publicly punished.

compitum any crossroads in ancient Rome where altars and shrines were erected.

compluvium in the atrium of a Roman house, an opening in the roof through which rain fell.

conclavium any rectangular room in a Roman house.

conditorium a Roman underground vault in which a corpse was deposited.

Corinthian a highly elaborate and ornate style of Greek architecture.

crepido on a Roman street, a raised sidewalk for pedestrians.

crypta associated with a Roman farmhouse or villa, a long, narrow vault, usually underground, for storing grains and fruits.

cubiculum a Roman bed chamber.

culina a Roman kitchen.

cyzicene an apartment in a Greek house.

delubrum an ancient Roman temple or sanctuary.

deversorium a Roman inn for travelers.

Doric the oldest and simplest order of Greek architecture, characterized by plain capitals and heavily fluted columns.

ekklesiasterion in a Greek town, a public hall.

elaeothesium where oil was kept in a Roman bath.

emblemata in Roman construction, a decorative, inlaid flooring.

emporium in Roman towns, a building housing imported merchandise for sale to local retailers.

ergastulum on a Roman farm, a prison where slaves worked.

farrarium a Roman grain barn.

favissa a Roman crypt or cellar.

ferriterion a Roman prison keeping chained slaves.

forica public toilets located throughout ancient Rome.

forum any Roman public square surrounded by important buildings.

frigidarium the third of the three chambers in a Roman bath, consisting of the final cold bath and sometimes a swimming pool. See CALDARIUM, TEPIDARIUM.

gymnasium same as a modern gymnasium.

gynaeceum the portion of a Greek church or house set apart for women.

hastarium a Roman public auction room.

hemicyclium a semicircular alcovelike structure providing seating for several persons in Roman pleasure gardens or other public spots.

hippodrome a Greek racecourse for horses and chariots and considerably wider to accommodate more racers than a Roman circus.

hippodromus a Roman promenade or garden area used for equestrian exercises.

horreum a Roman barn or granary.

hortus a Roman garden.

hospitalium a guest room in a Roman house.

hypocaustum a Roman central heating system in which warm air was blown from a furnace through flues within walls and floors.

hypodromus a Roman covered walkway.

ianua the outer door of a Roman house.

imagine a memorial busts of deceased family member placed in a wooden shrine within the wall of an atrium in a Roman house. The busts were accompanied by descriptive inscriptions.

impluvium the cistern or basin within the floor of an atrium, used to collect the rainwater that fell through the compluvium.

Ionic the Greek style of architecture characterized by ornamental scrolls and elegant detailing, but less elaborate than the Corinthian style.

laconicum a sweat room in a Roman bath.

lararium a shrine to the household gods in a Roman house.

latifundium a large Roman estate.

latrina a Roman bathroom or washroom.

lesche a Greek public clubhouse where people gathered to talk and receive news.

lithostrotum opus a Greek or Roman ornamental pavement such as mosaic.

logeum the stage in Greek and Roman theaters.

lucullite a type of black marble used in Roman construction.

macellum a Roman meat and produce market.

maenianum a balcony or gallery in a Roman theater.

mesaulos in a Greek house, the passage connecting the men's section (andron) with the women's section (gynaeceum).

milliarium on the side of Roman roads, a column erected at intervals of 1 Roman mile (0.92 mile) to indicate distance traveled.

moneta a Roman mint.

monopteron any circular Greek building surrounded by a single row of columns.

necropolis any large cemetery of ancient Greece.

nosocomium a Greek or Roman hospital for the poor.

opaion in Greek or Roman architecture, any aperture in a roof for smoke to escape.

oppidum a Roman town. Also, a collective term for the towers, gates, and horse stalls at the end of a Roman circus, said to resemble a town.

opus tectorium a type of stucco used in Roman construction.

orchestra in Greek theater, the place occupied by the dancers and chorus. In later Roman theater, a space between the stage and first row of seats reserved for senators and other important people.

order an architectural style, particular of columns and entablatures. The Greek orders are Doric, Ionic, and Corinthian. The Romans later added Tuscan and Composite.

ornithon an ancient Roman poultry house; an aviary.

palaestra an athletic training room, smaller than a gymnasium, used by Greek and Roman athletes.

pandokeion a Greek travelers' inn.

pantheon a Roman temple dedicated to the gods.

parastatica a pilaster of a Greek temple.

parathura the back door of a Greek house.

paries in Roman construction, a wall.

paries e lapide quadrato a Roman wall made of cut stone or ashlar.

paries lateritius a Roman brick wall.

passus a Roman measure of length, equal to 58.2 inches.

pastas a Greek vestibule.

pavimentum a Roman pavement formed of crushed stone, flint, and tile rammed and composited in a bed of cement.

pavonazzo in Roman construction, a type of marble characterized by dark red veins.

pes (pl. pedes) a Roman measure of length equal to 11.65 inches.

pharos a Greek or Roman lighthouse.

phyrctorion a Greek watchtower used for military purposes.

pinaculum in Greek or Roman construction, any roof that forms a ridge. Most houses of the day had flat roofs.

piscina in Roman construction, a reservoir. Also a pool or basin of water in a Roman bathroom.

platea any wide Roman street.

plethron an ancient Greek measure of length equal to 101¼ feet.

podium the plateau or platform on which Roman temples were built. Also, in a circus, the first or closest row of seats to the racecourse that was protected from the wild animal acts by a 10-foot trench.

polyandrion an ancient Greek monument or burial place dedicated to men killed in battle.

popina a Roman restaurant or tavern patronized by the lower classes.

porta the gateway to a Roman city.

posticum the back door of a Roman house.

postscenium the dressing rooms and storage rooms of the actors in Greek and Roman theaters.

pretorium the Roman residence of a governor.

propnigeum the sweat room furnace in a Greek gymnasium.

prothyron an entrance vestibule in a Greek house.

puteus in Roman construction, a manhole in an aqueduct. Also, a fountain in a Roman house.

robur a chamber below an underground dungeon where criminals were put to death.

ruderatio in Roman construction a common floor made of pieces of brick, stone, and tile.

sacrarium an in-house family shrine or chapel in Roman residences.

scabellum a Roman, freestanding pedestal.

scaena ductilis in Roman and Greek theater, a mobile screen that served as a scenic backdrop.

scalpturatum an ancient Roman pavement inlaid with patterned, colored marble.

scandula a Roman roof shingle.

scansorium Roman scaffolding.

senaculum a Roman council chamber.

specula a Roman watchtower and signal tower.

sphaeristerium part of a Roman gymnasium, a place for ball playing.

spica testacea an ancient Roman flooring, oblong tiles laid in a herringbone pattern.

spicatum opus Roman masonry set in a herringbone pattern.

spina the lengthwise barrier that divided a circus and around which athletes and charioteers raced.

spoliarium a room where the dead were dragged after being defeated in combat in a Roman amphitheater show.

spoliatorium in a Roman bath, a place for keeping the bathers' clothing.

stadium a sports arena, or a Roman measure of length equal to 607 feet.

sudatorium in ancient Rome, a sweat room used by athletes.

synoecia in ancient Greece, a dwelling shared by several families.

taberna a Roman booth, stall, or shop.

telonium a Roman customhouse.

tepidarium in Roman baths, a warm room. See CALDARIUM, FRIGIDARIUM.

thesaurus a Greek treasury house.

tholos any round building in Greek architecture.

thymele in the central orchestra section of a Greek theater, an altar dedicated to Bacchus.

tribunal in a Roman theater, a place of high status to the immediate right or left of a stage, reserved for magistrates, emperors, empresses, and the vestal virgins.

triclinium a Roman dining room with a low table surrounded by couches.

ustrinum where corpses were cremated in ancient Rome.

valetudinarium a Roman infirmary or hospital.

velarium an awning that protected the audience from the elements in a Roman theatre or amphitheater.

via any paved Roman road.

Via Appia the first Roman highway, built in 312 B.C., and joining Rome with Capua.

via munita a Roman road paved with polygonal blocks of stone or lava.

villa an elaborate Roman residence with gardens and outbuildings.

villa rustica an agricultural villa with apartments for a steward, bookkeeper, and slaves.

vitrum in Roman construction, glass.

vomitory an entrance or exit in a bank of seats in a Roman theater or amphitheater.

water leaf in Greek or Roman ornamentation, a lotus leaf or ivy motif.

FAR EASTERN ARCHITECTURE

amado in traditional Japanese architecture, a sliding storm shutter, usually set at night.

byo a Japanese mausoleum.

ch'an t'ang in Chinese architecture, a room set apart for meditation.

chashitsu a small rustic house equipped for the Japanese tea ceremony; also, a room so equipped.

chen ch'uan a Chinese triangular arch.

ch'iao a Chinese bridge.

chigai-dana in a Japanese house, steplike shelving placed in an alcove.

chu in Chinese construction, a column.

ch'uan in Chinese construction, an arch.

chuang in Chinese construction, a window of any kind.

daikoku-bashira in the center of a traditional Japanese house, a large post associated with the god of fortune.

fang in traditional Chinese architecture, a building with the appearance of a barge, used as a tavern or restaurant, on the shore of a lake or pond.

feng huo t'ai one of the regularly spaced (1½ miles) rectangular towers along the Great Wall of China.

fusuma in a Japanese house, a decoratively painted, sliding interior partition made of wood lattice covered with heavy paper or cloth.

genkan in traditional Japanese architecture, a vestibule where shoes are set before entering a building.

goju-no-tu a five-story pagoda.

haiden a Japanese hall of worship.

hashira in Japanese construction, a column.

hogyo-yane in traditional Japanese architecture, a pyramidal roof.

kaidan Japanese steps.

mado in Japanese architecture, a window.

men in Chinese architecture, a door.

minka a traditional Japanese farmhouse.

mu a Chinese tomb.

nagare-zukuri a popular style of Japanese shrine, characterized by a gabled roof that extends over and beyond the front stairs.

nagaya in traditional Japanese architecture, an elongated apartment house.

nijiriguchi a tiny guest entrance to a Japanese tea-ceremony house, through which one must pass on one's knees.

ping feng in a traditional Chinese house, a wood or bamboo partition moved when needed for privacy.

she li t'a a Chinese pagoda made of masonry and used as a shrine.

shikkui a traditional Japanese architecture, plaster, mortar, stucco, or whitewash made from lime and clay.

sorin the uppermost or crowning spire of a Japanese pagoda.

sukiya a Japanese tearoom or teahouse.

tatami one of several thick, 6-foot-long straw floor-mats used in a Japanese house.

tea garden a Japanese garden next to a teahouse or tearoom.

to a Japanese pagoda of two to seven stories, a shrine for Buddhist relics.

yagura in Japanese architecture, a tower.

zashiki in a Japanese house, a room for entertaining guests.

Indian Architecture

alinda a veranda.

aryaka an alignment of five columns symbolizing the five Dhiyana Buddhas.

basadi a Jain temple or monastery.

bhumi a floor or story of a building.

bodhika the capital of a column.

chavada a pavilion.

choultry a public assembly place or hall.

dhvajastambham a high pillar in front of a temple.

ghat a stairway leading to a body of water.

gumpha a monastery.

manastambha a freestanding pillar in front of a temple.

mandapa a hall in a temple.

matha a convent or monastery.

sikhara a tower or spire, tapering on both ends, of an Indian temple.

siras the capital of a column.

sringa in southern India, the dome of a Hindu temple.

stupa a Buddhist memorial mound, shaped like a beehive or a bell.

vihara a Buddhist monastery.

Middle Eastern Architecture

apadana a columned audience hall in an Iranian palace.

ataurique a Moorish plasterwork design featuring leaves and flowers.

bagnio a Turkish prison.

bazaar an outdoor marketplace of shops and stalls.

chahr bagh an Islamic garden divided into four parts of water channels symbolizing the four rivers of paradise.

cubit an ancient Egyptian and biblical measure of length equal to 20.62 inches.

horseshoe arch an Arabic or Moorish arch shaped distinctly like a horseshoe.

hosh an inner court of an Egyptian house.

kasr an Arabian castle or palace.

kiosk a Turkish pavilion or feasting pavilion.

kubba a domed tomb, a common Islamic burial structure. Also known as a turbe.

mihrab a niche in the wall of a mosque indicating the direction of Mecca.

minaret a tower within or alongside a mosque from which the faithful are called to prayer.

muristan Iranian term for hospital.

musall Iranian term for burial ground.

qa'a a reception hall in an Egyptian house.

qibla the wall of a mosque oriented toward Mecca.

serai a Turkish palace.

serefe the balcony of a minaret from which the faithful are called to prayer.

Native American Architecture

adobe a blend of clay and straw formed into sun-dried bricks.

banco a shelf around the interior of a kiva or pit house.

burial mound an elevated earthen grave.

cache a hole or chamber for storing dried food or other items.

chinking grass, mud, or clay sealing material applied between the cracks of a log home.

corbeled roof a roof frame composed of horizontal tiers that graduate in size from peak to base.

cordage hide or plant fiber used to tie structural members together.

cosmic tree the center pole in some Indian structures, noted for its religious symbolism. Also known as the earth navel.

cribbed logs notched horizontal logs that overlap at the corner of a building.

dew cloth a cloth used by Plains Indians to line and insulate the inside of a tipi.

foot drums hollow log ceremonial drums played with the feet.

hogan an earth-covered dwelling built by the Navajo.

horno a pueblo baking oven shaped like a beehive.

italwa Creek Indian word for "town."

kashim a large Eskimo building used for social and religious gatherings.

kiva a chamber, frequently underground, where Pueblo Indians meet, conduct rituals, and weave cloth.

latillas in a pueblo roof, the small, round poles spanning between the vigas.

longhouse an Indian meeting house. Also, a long, multifamily dwelling of the Iroquois.

palisade a fence or wall composed of upright logs, frequently pointed, protecting a village.

pit house a partially underground, one-room house with an earthen roof.

plaza a public center for large gatherings outside.

puddled adobe a wet clay mixture used to finish a floor or wall.

pueblo a stone or adobe community building up to five stories high, built by southwestern Indians.

puncheon a slablike plank.

ramada a log sunshade or overhead trellis.

smoke flaps the adjustable portion of a tipi cover; it opens and closes to keep out wind and rain and to let out smoke.

tipi ring a circle of stones used to hold down tipi coverings.

totem pole a large post carved into faces and fantastic figures by northwestern Indians.

travois the V-shaped frame of tipi poles, used as a conveyance, pulled by dogs or horses.

tupik a summer tent used by Eskimos.

viga a log beam used as a frame member on a pueblo roof.

wattle and daub a framing technique employing upright or interwoven saplings to hold mud fill, used by southeastern and southwestern tribes.

wickiup a domed hut covered with bark or brush, used by the Kickapoo and Apache tribes.

wigwam an arched or conical dwelling covered with bark, hide, or mats, used by Indians from the Northeast and Great Lakes region.

Russian Architecture

dacha a country home.

dvoine a twin-pyramid-towered church.

izba a log cabin or small wooden cottage.

kokoshniki decorative gables or arches not needed for support and usually found in multiple tiers around the drums supporting onion domes.

kremlin a citadel of a city.

krest a cross.

lukovitsa an onion dome.

nalichniki in older wooden cottages, the carved decorations at the ends of gables and around window frames.

onion dome capping a cupola or tower, a bulbous dome ending in a point and resembling an onion.

shatrovy pyramid-shaped towers, commonly found on older Russian churches.

troine a triple-pyramid-towered church.

Spanish Architecture

adobe sun-dried, unburned clay and straw, a common building material.

alcazar a Spanish castle.

azothea on the roof of a house, a terrace or platform.

capilla mayor the main chapel in a Spanish church.

hacienda a large estate, plantation, or ranch.

mirador a window or roof pavilion with a commanding or spectacular view.

mission architecture Spanish colonial church and monastery architecture, often characterized by twin bell towers.

mission tile semicylindrical clay roofing tile. Also known as Spanish tile.

posada an inn.

ramada a rustic arbor or an open porch.

LIGHTHOUSES

ANTS short for Aid to Navigation Teams; Coast Guard personnel who inspect and maintain automated lighthouses quarterly or annually.

caisson a lighthouse mounted on a large foundation.

cupola the domed top of a lighthouse.

diaphone fog signal a two-tone fog signal, making a sound similar to breeeeeooooooo.

gallery a railed walkway around a lantern.

keeper a person who maintains and/or lives in a lighthouse, all but abolished by 1990.

lamp the light inside the lens.

lamp changer a device that automatically changes a worn-out lightbulb.

lantern collective term for the lamp, the lens, and their containment.

lens a Fresnel lens used to magnify and concentrate light.

lightship a ship fitted with lanterns and anchored permanently at sea to serve as a floating lighthouse.

range lights paired towers consisting of a short lighthouse at the entrance to a harbor or a channel, and a distant, taller lighthouse; a safe course is followed by keeping the lights one atop the other.

screwpile a lighthouse with legs of huge screws that are twisted into the ground as anchors.

skeleton light a lighthouse with an open framework tower.

walkway on a large lighthouse, a railed walkway above the gallery that gives access for cleaning the outside of the lantern glass.

RELIGIOUS BUILDINGS

abat-voix a sound reflector above the pulpit.

abbey a monastery or convent.

agnus dei any artwork representing a lamb that is emblematic of Christ.

aguilla the obelisk or spire of a church tower.

almariol a storage room or niche for ecclesiastical vestments. Also known as an ambry.

almehrabh a niche in an Arabian mosque that marks the direction of Mecca.

almemar in a synagogue, a desk on which the Torah rests while being read from to the congregation.

altar the elevated table or structure used for religious offerings or rites.

altar frontal an ornamental hanging or panel fronting the altar.

altar of repose a repository or niche where the Host is kept from Maundy Thursday to Good Friday in a Roman Catholic church.

altarpiece above and behind the altar, an ornamental painting or screen or sculpture.

altar screen a decorative partition separating the altar from the space behind.

altar slab a stone or slab forming the top of an altar.

ambry a repository or niche for sacraments.

ambulatory an aisle or walkway around the apse of a church.

ambulatory church a church with a dome surrounded on three sides by aisles.

antechapel an entrance, porch, or vestibule in front of a chapel.

antenave a porch leading into the nave of a church.

antepodium behind the dais in a choir, seating for the clergy.

apostolaeum any church dedicated to or named after an apostle.

apse the semicylindrical or semidomed space or room housing the altar.

archiepiscopal cross a cross with two transverse arms, the shorter one on top, the longer one near the center.

ark in a synagogue, an ornamental repository for the scrolls of the Torah.

armariolum in a cathedral or monastic church, a wardrobe for keeping vestments.

aspersorium a font for holy water.

aureole the glory or radiance surrounding the head of a sacred figure.

baptistery a building or portion of a building where baptisms are held.

basilica an elongated church with a central high nave with clerestory, side aisles, and a semicircular apse.

bell canopy a gable roof that shelters a bell.

bell cot a small belfry astride the ridge of a roof.

bell gable a roof-ridge turret holding one or more bells.

bellhouse a tower holding a bell.

belltower any tall structure containing a bell.

bénitier a basin for holy water.

bestiary in a medieval church, a group of painted or sculpted creatures.

bethel a chapel for seamen.

box pew a pew enclosed by a high back and sides.

calvary sculptures, often life-size, depicting the Crucifixion.

Calvary cross a Latin cross set on three steps.

cantoria a choir gallery.

carrel a pew in a monastery.

catacumba the atrium or courtyard of a basilican church.

cathedral the home church of a bishop.

Catherine wheel window a large circular, ornamental window at the front of many cathedrals. Also known as a rose window.

Celtic cross a tall cross with short horizontal arms partially enclosed by a circle.

chatya a Buddhist sanctuary.

chancel the sanctuary of a church, or the space near the altar reserved for the clergy and choir.

chancel arch in some churches, an arch that divides the chancel from the nave.

chancel screen a screen separating the chancel from the nave.

chapel a small church or parish or a room or building set apart for worship within a school, college, hospital, or other institution. Also, an area within a church set aside for private prayer.

chapel royal the chapel of a royal palace or castle.

chevet an apse surrounded by an ambulatory.

choir between the nave and the sanctuary, the area occupied by the clergy and choir.

choir loft a balcony occupied by the choir.

choir stall seating for choir and clergy.

choraula a rehearsal room for the choir.

chrismatory a niche holding the consecrated oil for baptism near the font.

church stile an old term for pulpit.

cimeliarch a treasury where holy objects and other valuables are stored in a church.

clausura the part of a monastery or convent occupied by the monks or nuns and closed to the public.

clerestory the windowed, upper portion of the nave, transepts, and choir; any upper wall windowed for light and ventilation.

cloister a place devoted to religious seclusion, as a monastery or convent. Also, a covered walk surrounding an open courtyard, used as a link between buildings in a monastery.

cloister garth the courtyard surrounded by a cloister.

confessional the private booth where a priest sits and listens to confessions from the penitent.

convent a community of nuns; a nunnery.

credence near the altar, a shelf or stand for holding holy objects, service books, and other objects.

crowde a cellar or crypt of a church.

cruciform in the shape of a cross, as many Gothic churches whose nave, chancel, and apse intersect with the transepts.

crypt an underground or partially underground level containing separate chapels or, sometimes, tombs.

double monastery a monastery and a convent sharing the same church and authority.

duomo an Italian cathedral.

east end where the main altar is located, a tradition of medieval churches.

ecclesiology the study of the decoration and architecture of churches.

epistle side the south side of a church when the main altar is at the east end, the side the epistle is read from.

esonarthex when present, the second narthex from the entrance.

expiatory chapel a chapel erected to atone for a great crime, such as a murder.

fauwara in the court of a mosque, a fountain.

feretory a space where church relics are kept.

font the stone basin that holds water for baptism.

frater house a common eating hall in a monastery.

galilee a chapel for worship at the west side of a church.

galilee porch a galilee acting as a vestibule to the main church.

garbha-griha the darkened sanctuary where the statue of a deity is placed in a Hindu temple.

glory the halo and radiance surrounding the head of a religious figure in a painting.

Gospel side the north side of the church when the main altar is in the east, where the Gospel is read.

hall church a church without clerestories, having an interior of more or less uniform height, as a hall.

high altar the main altar.

inner sanctum the most sacred of places.

interstitium the crossing of a cruciform church.

jami a mosque specially designed for large congregations.

kubba a dome in a mosque.

Lady chapel at the east end of a church, a chapel dedicated to the Virgin Mary.

lancet window a narrow window with a pointed arch, commonly found in many churches.

lectern a stand with a slanting top for convenient reading from the Scriptures.

li pai tien a Christian church in China.

lozenge a small window just above a double lancet window.

manse a clergyman's dwelling.

mensa the top slab or surface of an altar.

mihrab a niche in any religious Muslim building indicating the direction of Mecca.

minaret a tower in or flanking a mosque from which the faithful are called to prayer.

minbar in a mosque, the pulpit.

minster a monastic church.

minstrel gallery a small balcony over the entrance of a church interior.

mission a church supported by a larger church.

mission architecture Spanish colonial church and monastery architecture.

mosque a Muslim house of worship.

musalla a Muslim prayer hall.

narthex a vestibule or portico of early Christian or Byzantine churches; any entrance hall leading to the nave.

nave the central portion of a church flanked by aisles, and intended for the congregation.

nimbus in any artwork, the halo of light around the head of a holy figure.

nunnery a convent.

oratory a small, private chapel.

organ loft the loft or gallery where the organ is placed.

parlatory in a monastery or convent, a place where visitors are received.

parsonage the parson's house; a rectory.

pede window next to a large window, a smaller window symbolizing one of the feet of Christ.

pew a bench for seating of the congregation.

presbytery the place or sanctuary reserved for clergy beyond the choir.

pulpit an elevated platform or lectern where most of the preaching is done. In some churches, an elevated, enclosed stand.

rectory the residence of a minister, priest, or pastor.

refectory a dining room for monks or nuns.

riddle one of a pair of curtains enclosing an altar on either side.

rood a large cross, sometimes supported on a beam (the rood beam) across the entrance of a chancel.

rood screen an ornamental wood or stone screen surmounted by a cross and separating the nave and the chancel.

rood spire a roof spire rising up over the crossing of the transepts and nave.

rose window a large, circular, stained glass window of Gothic or medieval design set in the front entrance of a cathedral. Also known as a Catherine wheel window, a marigold window, or a wheel window.

sacristy near the chancel, a room for storing the altar vessels and vestments.

sanctuary same as presbytery; the immediate area around an altar.

sanctus bell a bell hung in a turret over the chancel to call people to service.

seminary a school for preparing men to be Roman Catholic or Episcopal priests, Protestant ministers, or Jewish rabbis.

sepulcher in an altar, a receptacle for sacred relics.

shrine a receptacle or building housing sacred relics, or the tomb of a saint or other revered person.

sounding board a canopy above the pulpit used to reflect the preacher's voice into the congregation.

squint a small opening or window in the wall of a church allowing a view from the transept to the main altar.

steeple the tower and spire of a church.

stupa a Buddhist shrine consisting of a built mound, sometimes in the shape of a beehive or bell.

tabernacle a box on an altar for holding the consecrated host and wine of the Eucharist. Also, an ornamental niche in a wall housing a statue.

transept the crossing or transverse portion of a church, forming the arms of a cruciform layout.

transept chapel a chapel entered from the transept.

triapsidal having three apses, sometimes forming a cloverleaf at the altar end of the church.

triforium a gallery or arches above the nave and below the clerestory, sometimes serving as attic space or as a gallery for spectators.

vestry a room near the altar for storing robes of the clergy and choir.

Cemeteries, Tombs, and Monuments

Bateson's belfry a coffin device consisting of a bell and cord that the interred could ring in case he miraculously revived, popular in Victorian times when people were occasionally pronounced dead prematurely.

bier a stand in which a coffin containing a corpse rests to lie in state.

Boot Hill in the American West, a cemetery for gunfighters.

Calvary a sculptured representation, often life-size, of the Crucifixion.

catacomb an underground passage with niches or recesses for graves or urns.

catafalque a draped scaffold on which is placed a coffin or effigy of the deceased during a state funeral.

cemetery beacon a graveyard lighthouse and altar used in Europe in the 12th and 13th centuries.

cenotaph a monument erected in memory of one not buried under it or interred within it.

centry-garth a burial ground.

cinerarium a vault for storing urns containing the ashes of the dead.

crematory a building for incinerating the bodies of the deceased.

crypt an underground vault, usually under a church, used for burials.

cubiculum an underground chamber with wall compartments for the reception of the dead.

effigy a painted or sculpted representation of the deceased on a monument.

ghoul a grave robber.

golgotha any burial place, named after the hill of Calvary, where Jesus was crucified.

lanterne des morts in medieval France, a graveyard towerlike structure and turret serving as a lantern.

mausoleum a large tomb or building housing one or more tombs.

monument any stone, pillar, sculpture, structure, or building erected in memory of the deceased.

mortuary where bodies are prepared for burial or cremation.

necropolis a large cemetery or city of the dead associated with an ancient city.

ossuary an urn or vault for holding the bones of the dead.

potter's field a cemetery for paupers.

sarcophagus a stone coffin.

septum a low wall surrounding a tomb.

sepulcher a burial vault.

shaft tomb a vertical shaft leading to underground burial chambers.

solium an elaborately sculpted sarcophagus made of marble, used for kings and other important people.

weepers mourning statues placed within or around some tombs.

STYLES OF ARCHITECTURE

Anglo-Saxon architecture prominent in England before the Norman conquest in 1066, characterized by round arches and huge walls.

art deco a decorative "futuristic" style popular in the 1930s, characterized by zigzags, chevrons, and similar geometrical ornamentation typically found on the skyscrapers of the period.

art nouveau decorative style of later 19th-century France and Belgium, characterized by curvilinear design and whiplash lines. Known as Jugendstil in Germany and modernismo in Spain.

Aztec from the Indian people of central Mexico, an architecture characterized by pyramids and temples dedicated to the gods.

baroque European style prominent between 1550 and the early 1700s characterized by oval spaces, curved surfaces, elaborate decoration, sculpture, and color.

Byzantine architecture of the eastern Roman Empire from the fourth century to the Middle Ages, largely in Greece, and characterized by large domes, round arches, and elaborate columns.

classical architecture of Hellenic Greece and imperial Rome, the five orders of which are Corinthian, Doric, Ionic, Tuscan, and Composite.

colonial any architectural style borrowed by an overseas colony from the motherland, such as the transplantation of English Georgian to North America in the 18th century.

Dutch colonial Dutch style of architecture transplanted to America and particularly New York State in the 17th century, characterized by gambrel roofs and overhanging eaves.

Egyptian from the third millennium B.C. to the Roman period, a style characterized by temples, pyramids, and funeral monuments.

flamboyant style in the 15th century, a phase of French Gothic architecture characterized by tracery with the appearance of dancing flames.

Georgian prominent in 18th-century Britain and North America, a style derivative of classical, Renaissance, and baroque forms.

Gothic prominent in western Europe from the 12th to the 15th centuries, characterized by pointed arches, rib vaulting, and flying buttresses.

Islamic (also known as **Muslim**) an architectural style originating around the Mediterranean and spreading as far as India and China, characterized by round and horseshoe arches, domes, tunnel vaults, and geometric ornamentation.

Japanese from the 5th century A.D. and borrowing from Chinese style, a largely wood timber architecture characterized by pavilion-like and pagoda-like buildings.

Maya dating from approximately A.D. 600 to 900, the architecture of the Indian people of Mexico, Guatemala, and Honduras, characterized by temples, pyramids, plazas, and similar structures, with most buildings raised high on platforms.

Renaissance from the 14th through the 16th centuries and developed in Italy, derivative of the classical orders.

revival any style reviving or deriving from another earlier style.

rococo developed largely in 18th-century France, the final phase of baroque, characterized by florid or elaborate ornamentation intended to produce a delicate effect.

Romanesque begun in early 11th-century western Europe and borrowing from Roman and Byzantine forms, a style characterized by massive walls, round arches, and powerful vaults.

WINDMILLS

air brakes at the leading edge of a sail, boards that spring open in heavy gusts to slow rotation.

axle the windshaft.

backwind a wind hitting the mill from the opposite direction the sails are facing.

beard a decorative board behind the canister.

beehive cap a domed cap.

brake wheel a large cogged wheel that drives the millstone; it is mounted on the windshaft.

bran the husks of grain.

buck the body of a mill that revolves above the trestle to keep the sails facing into the wind.

canister at the end of a windshaft, the socket that receives the stocks of the sails.

cap a movable top on some windmills; it is turned by a fantail so the sails face into the wind at all times.

cloth sail wood-frame sail covered with cloth. Also, the cloth itself.

common sails cloth sails.

concentrator a device used with a modern wind turbine to concentrate the windstream.

cross trees the heavy horizontal beams that rest on piers and carry the weight of the main structure.

crown wheel the horizontal gear that meshes with the vertical gear.

cut-in speed the speed of wind at which the sails of a windmill begin to turn.

fantail a small, helper windmill that turns the cap to face the wind. Also known as a fly tackle.

furling speed speed at which a windmill or wind turbine should be stopped to prevent structural damage from strong wind gusts.

grain hopper a holding bin for grain to be milled.

heel the inner edge of a sail.

jib sails cloth sails that could be furled by a miller to slow the sails in high winds.

leader boards the boards on the leading edge of a sail.

main post the post on which a post-mill is turned.

millstones the two stones that grind grain.

patent sails wood-shuttered sails attached to an opening and closing apparatus.

pepper pot a high, domed cap with a flat top.

post-mill a mill in which the entire body or buck revolves around on a trestle to face the wind.

quarter a mill to turn a mill slightly away from the wind to slow the sails.

reef to furl or take in a cloth sail to slow it down.

roundhouse the enclosed trestle portion of a post-mill, used for a storage space for grain and sometimes used as the miller's quarters.

runner stone the top millstone; the one turned by the mill.

sails the long blades or sweeps blown by the wind that drive the mill.

scoop wheel a cast iron wheel fitted with scoops to convey water to another level.

shroud a structure employed to concentrate or deflect wind.

shutter bar a bar linking shutters together.

shutters movable, spring-loaded boards that open and close according to the wind's power.

smock mill a multisided, wooden mill with a movable cap.

spring sail a sail having wind-activated, spring shutters.

sweeps another name for sails.

tower mill a brick or stone mill having a movable cap.

trestle the supporting members on which a postmill rests and revolves.

vanes the shutters of patent sails. Also, the sails of a fantail.

wallower the first wheel turned by the windshaft; it meshes with the brake wheel.

winded turned to face the wind.

windshaft the axle that is turned by the rotating sails; it turns the gears that run the mill's machinery.

ART

ART TERMS

(*Also see* ART TOOLS AND MATERIALS, SCULPTURE)

abozzo Italian for "sketch." In painting, the initial outline or drawing.

abstract art art composed of distorted, abstruse, stylized, or unrecognizable forms that may or may not represent a person, place, or object.

abstract expressionism a nonrepesentational painting style characterized by the use of abstract and stylized forms to express inner experience or emotion.

academic any style of art based on traditional standards.

acanthus a popular motif featuring the thistlelike acanthus plant of the Mediterranean, most notably found on Corinthian columns.

achromatic colors the noncolors white, black, and gray.

action painting a style of abstract expressionism in which paint is splattered, hurled, or brushed on the canvas impulsively as a reflection of the artist's moods.

advancing and retreating colors the perceived tendency of warm colors to appear at the forefront of a painting while cool colors (blues, violets) recede into the background, an optical illusion.

alla prima an oil painting executed in one application rather than layer by layer. A painting done in one sitting.

alligatoring a network of cracks resembling an alligator's hide on old or damaged paintings.

amphora a type of large Greek vase with two handles.

anamorphosis a method of distorted painting or drawing in which the subject is unrecognizable unless viewed from a particular angle or distance. Also refers to a subject that appears to transform into a different subject when viewed from various angles.

anthemion a traditional flower and leaf motif featuring palm leaf and/or honeysuckle.

appliqué a style of decoration characterized by the application of materials over other materials to form a design.

aquarelle a painting composed of transparent watercolors.

arabesque an ornate motif featuring intertwined floral, foliate, and geometric figures.

art nouveau originating in the 1880s, an art form characterized by cursive, flowing lines, interlaced patterns, and whiplash curves.

art rupestre French term for prehistoric cave art.

assemblage a three-dimensional art form characterized by the integration of various objects into a meaningful or decorative whole.

asymmetry the use of nonsymmetry in art to more accurately depict reality, as in a portrait of the human face.

à trois crayons a three-colored chalk drawing.

aureole the radiance surrounding a depiction of a holy or religious figure. Also known as a glory.

automatism spontaneous painting or creation without conscious thought or plan.

avant-garde of any art, experimental, original, nontraditional, new, or untried.

bas-relief low relief. Any sculpture or carving that is raised only slightly (such as coins) from its background.

biomorphic form any nongeometric form, such as that of a plant or animal.

bird's-eye view a painting of a scene as it might be viewed from overhead.

bisque firing the first firing of a ceramic.

bleed the migration of some oil paints into adjoining areas on a canvas.

blending in a painting, the imperceptible fusing or merging of two hues.

blister in a painting, a damaged area characterized by a raised spot, caused by moisture or foreign matter.

bloom on a varnished oil painting, an undesirable cloudy or misty surface effect, caused by moisture.

blush a bloom, but on clear lacquer.

bottega an Italian art studio or shop where a master painter and assistants work.

brown coat in a fresco, the second coat of plaster, made of sand and lime putty or marble dust and lime putty.

buckeye a poor quality, mass market landscape painting.

cabinet picture a small painting, usually 30 inches wide or less.

cachet a distinctive mark, monogram, or cipher used to authenticate an art work in lieu of a signature.

calendering the process of giving paper a smooth finish by running it under heavy pressure between rollers.

calligraphy artistic, stylized, or elegant handwriting.

en camaïeu painting in several shades of the same color.

caricature a drawing of a person that exaggerates the physical characteristics of that person.

ceramics art objects made of clay that have been fired in a kiln.

chalking disintegration of surface paint that turns to powder and eventually falls off.

chasing in sculpture, the ornamenting of a metal surface with indentations.

checking a series of square cracks on a painting.

chiaroscuro Italian for "light-dark," designating an art technique employing the use of several different shades of the same color, or a high contrast between light and dark elements to create depth, most often seen in baroque art. Also, any painting using this style.

chromatic colors all colors other than white, black, or gray.

chromaticity the properties of color.

chrysography lettering in gold or silver ink, a practice originating with the ancient Greeks.

cinquefoil decoration in the form of five joined leaves or lobes.

cissing an uneven coat of paint that streaks.

classical any ancient Greek or Roman art form. Also, any historic period that produced exceptional art works in a particular style.

classicism the adherence to or borrowing from ancient Greek and Roman styles in art works.

cleavage the separating of paint layers on a painting, due to poor materials or improper application.

collage a composition of paper, fabric, or other materials glued on a panel or canvas.

colorist an artist particularly masterful with the use of color.

commercial artist an artist who works in advertising, publishing, industry, design, and related fields.

concours in art school, a student exhibition of selected works at the end of a semester.

cool colors blues, green, violets; the opposite of warm colors.

crackle a network of cracks in a damaged painting.

crawl see CISSING.

cribbled decorative dots or punctures on wood or metal surfaces.

cubism style of art originating in Paris in the early 20th century and characterized by the reduction of natural forms into geometric patterns.

Dada art movement of World War I era; it rejected tradition and advocated unusual or outlandish art forms. Its credo was "everything the artist spits is art."

découpage a decoration consisting of cut-out paper figures or designs covering a surface.

deep relief a sculpted or carved design that projects high off its background. Also known as high relief.

diorama an illuminated, three-dimensional scene with or without a painted background, a popular museum display.

double image a painting that is cleverly designed to represent two different objects, such as a tree that is also a hand, a cloud that is also a face.

dragging stroke a light stroke that covers only the high areas of rough paper with paint.

drollery a humorous picture, often featuring animals who dress and act as humans.

drypoint a picture printed from an engraving made by a hard needle.

ébauche in oil painting, the first paint layer.

eclecticism borrowing from other art styles to create a new style.

écorché a drawing or status of a figure with its skin peeled and its inner musculature revealed; it is used as a study aid.

electroplate to coat with a thin layer of metal through an electrochemical process.

emboss to mold or carve in relief.

encaustic a painting painted with heated, colored beeswax. Also, the method of executing this type of painting.

epigone a second-rate imitator.

etching the process of the partial eating away of a surface to create designs or a relief printing surface.

exploded view in technical drawing, the illustration of separate components and their relationship to one another in a complex object, such as a motor.

expressionism an early 20th-century art movement that emphasized the expression of emotion through distorted forms.

fauvism art movement characterized by the use of colorful expressionist forms.

fecit Latin for "he made it," sometimes inscribed after the artist's name on a painting.

festoon a painting of a garland of leaves, flowers, and ribbons. Also known as a swag.

figurine a statue 10 inches or less in height.

filigree delicate ornamental work made from gold, silver, or silver-gilt wire.

film a continuous layer or coating of paint.

fine art any art created for its own sake as opposed to art created for purely commercial reasons.

flat without luster, as in flat paint.

flesh color human flesh tone, a color achieved by mixing white and yellow ocher.

floating signature a signature inscribed after a painting has been varnished, a sign of possible fraud.

foliated ornamented with depictions of foliage.

foreground the part of a painting that appears closest to the viewer.

foreshortening the reduction or diminishing of a subject in order to present an accurate picture of perspective as the subject grows into the distance.

foxing on paintings executed on paper, spotting and splotching caused by molds.

fresco Italian for "fresh." The art of painting on fresh plaster. Also, a mural painted by this method.

frilling the formation of waves in thin paint.

frottage the process of making an impression of the texture of stone, wood, fabric, string, and other materials by placing a piece of paper over the material and rubbing the paper with a pencil or crayon. Similar to a rubbing. Also, the impression made by this method.

fugitive colors pigments that gradually fade when exposed to sunlight.

gallery tone on an old painting, the darkening of varnish and the accumulation of grime creating a brownish haze or tone.

garzone Italian term for studio assistant or apprentice.

geometric abstraction an abstract painting featuring geometric shapes.

gilded covered with gold.

gilding the application of thin metal leaf to a surface.

glost fire the second firing of ceramics.

glyptic art the art of carving designs on gems and semiprecious stones.

goffer to decorate by embossing.

gouache the technique of painting on paper with opaque watercolors. Also, the picture rendered in this manner.

graphic arts any linear visual art, such as drawings, paintings, engravings, etchings, woodcuts, and lithographs.

grisaille a monochrome painting done in shades of gray to simulate sculpture.

grotesque ornamental painting or sculpture featuring a motif of leaves and flowers with imaginary or bizarre animal or human figures.

ground on a painting, the prime coat on which the painting is executed.

guilloche a decorative work consisting of interlaced curved lines.

hatching in drawing or painting, shading created with a series of close-set lines.

hue a color or gradation of a color.

icon a picture, image, or sculpture of a holy person.

idiom the predominant art style of a particular period or person.

illumination any drawings and calligraphy used to decorate a manuscript.

impasto a style of painting in which paint is applied in thick layers or strokes, as in many Rembrandts.

impressionism a French art style originating in the 1870s and characterized by discontinuous brush strokes, vague outlines, and the use of bright colors and light effects, as in the works of Claude Monet.

inherent vice an art conservation term referring to anything present within the materials of an art work that may eventually bring about its deterioration.

inlay to insert decorative pieces of wood, metal, stone, or other material in a depression on a surface.

inpainting an art conservation term referring to the painting over of a damaged area so that it blends in with the rest of the painting.

intaglio an incised design, as used in dies for coins. Also, an etching process in which the printing areas are recessed.

intarsia inlay work of small pieces of wood veneer and sometimes marble or mother-of-pearl.

intonaco in a fresco, the last coat of plaster; the coat that is painted on.

journeyman a craftsman or artist who has served an apprenticeship and is qualified to work under a master.

kickwheel a pedal-operated potter's wheel.

kiln a furnace in which ceramics are fired.

kinetic art any art that moves or which has movable components.

kitsch any cheap, pretentious, or sentimental art work that appeals to the masses.

lacuna Latin for "gap." A portion of an art work that is missing due to damage.

landscape a drawing or painting of natural scenery.

limited edition a replica of an art work produced in a predetermined quantity, after which the plate, mold, or die is destroyed so no further copies can be made.

line drawing a drawing executed by lines only.

lithochromy the art of painting on stone.

lithograph a print made by lithography.

lithography a printmaking process employing a metal plate or stone on which a drawing is made with a crayon or greasy ink from which an impression is pressed onto paper.

local color in painting, the real or actual color of an object as distinguished from that subjected to unusual lighting.

magic realism in painting, a highly realistic rendering of a subject accompanied by an air of surrealism due to the subject being placed in a strange or unexpected place or time. Also, a form of realism rendered with flat paint and an absence of shadows.

marbling a form of decoration imitating the swirling patterns of marble.

marouflage the technique of cementing a painted canvas on a wall with strong adhesives.

marquetry inlay work of small pieces of wood, mother-of-pearl, marble, and such-like, set in a floral or decorative pattern.

master an artist recognized as having great skill.

masterpiece one of an artist's best works.

mat a kind of inner painting frame or border made of cardboard or other still material.

matte of a finish, dull, flat.

mechanical drawing drafting.

medium the type of art form in which an artist works.

mezzo fresco a painting executed on partially dry plaster, Also, the method itself.

mobile a three-dimensional art work hung from a stand or from the ceiling and moved by slight air currents.

moiré effect an optical illusion of a nonexistent pattern created by superimposing a repetitive design over another repetitive design.

monochrome a painting painted in shades of one color. Also, the part of painting in this manner.

montage a picture made up of parts of other pictures or prints that are overlapped.

mosaic an assemblage of small pieces of tile, marble, wood, glass, or stone that form a picture or decorative pattern in a wall or floor.

motif in an art work, an element with a recurrent theme.

mural a painting executed directly on a wall or ceiling or on a canvas that is cemented directly to a wall.

neoclassical art any art influenced by the art of ancient Greece or Rome.

neutral color any color between warm and cool colors. Brown is a neutral color.

nonobjective art art that does not represent anything recognizable.

nouveau French term for a beginning artist or student.

objective art art that represents a person, place, or thing.

objet d'art a small, valuable artistic article.

op art a style of art popular in the 1960s and characterized by repeating abstract patterns that create optical illusions.

opening a private showing the day before an art exhibition opens to the public.

optical mixing painting small dots or strokes of different colors close together so they create the illusion of a mixed color when viewed from a distance. (For example, blue and red dots painted close together will appear as violet from a distance.)

overpainting in oil and tempera painting, the final coat applied after the underpainting.

painterly highly artistic. Also, like a painting.

palmette a palm leaf ornament or design.

pastel a colored crayon made of pigment and chalk. Also known as a pastille. A work of art executed with pastels.

pastel shades soft, delicate hues.

pastiche an art work imitating the style of previous works, or executed in different styles; a hodgepodge.

pâte-sur-pâte low-relief decoration on ceramics.

perspective the technique of accurately rendering a three-dimensional object or scene on a two-dimensional surface.

petite nature a painting in which the figures are smaller than life-size but larger than half-size.

pochade a quick color sketch on which details are added at a later time.

pointillism a style of painting characterized by the creation of an image through the use of painted dots and short strokes, as developed by Georges Seurat in the late 19th century.

polychrome executed in several colors, especially referring to a wood or stone carving.

pop art an art style made famous by Andy Warhol and characterized by larger-than-life replicas of commercial or widely recognized objects, such as food labels, packages, comic strip panels, etc.

portrait any work of art representing someone's face. It can also be used to describe a rendering of a full-body shot.

postiche a fake; an imitation.

pouncing a technique of transferring a drawing on one surface to another by perforating the lines of the original drawing and then passing pounce powder through the holes to the transfer surface.

pricking a test to determine a painting's relative age and possible authenticity, characterized by sticking a pin into a thick area of paint; if the pin can be pushed through easily, it means the paint is soft and relatively new and therefore a possible forgery.

primary colors the colors red, yellow, and blue, from which most other hues can be obtained by mixing with one another or with black or white.

primer a white base layer of paint on which a painting is executed. A ground.

primitive an art style uninfluenced by historical or contemporary forms. Also known as naive art.

profil perdu a profile or sideview showing more of the back of the head (or object) than the front.

psychedelic art U.S. abstract art of the 1960s, characterized by wild, swirling curves inspired by the use of hallucinogenic drugs.

realism an art style characterized by the realistic depictions of people, places, or things without abstraction or distortion.

relief a projection from a flat surface; a raised area.

Renaissance French for "rebirth." A period of western European history (roughly 1300s to 1500s) known for its many advances and innovations in the arts.

repoussé a method of forming a relief design by hammering a metal plate from the back.

retouching adding to or changing a finished painting.

rococo a French art style of the 1700s, characterized by elaborate, florid, and delicate ornamentation, especially in architecture.

rubbing a method of making a rough copy of a relief work by placing paper over the design and rubbing it with crayon, charcoal, pencil, or other writing instrument, as in a tombstone rubbing.

scale drawing a drawing whose dimensions are of the same ratio as those of the object drawn.

scrambled colors superficially blended colors that create swirls of different hues, a deliberate effect.

scrimshaw the art of carving on whalebone. Also, the art work itself.

scroll any spiral-like decoration.

scumble a thin layer of semitransparent paint applied over a painting to create a hazy effect.

secco a method of painting on dry lime plaster. Also, a mural painted in this manner.

secondary colors the colors green, orange, and purple, formed by mixing primary colors.

serigraph a print made from the silk screen process.

sfumato the soft blending of outlines in a painting, especially in the works of Leonardo da Vinci.

sgraffito creating a design by cutting lines into pottery, plaster, or stucco to reveal a layer of different color beneath.

shading the subtle blending of one color into another.

silhouette a portrait profile executed in a single color.

silk screen a method of color stenciling in which a squeegee is used to force color through a fine screen on which the designless areas are blocked out.

sketch a quick, rough drawing.

smooch a deliberate smudge made with the fingers on a drawing to produce shading.

sotto in su severe foreshortening of figures in a ceiling painting, an effect that makes them appear suspended in air. Italian for "from below upwards."

squaring a technique in which a drawing is transferred from one surface to another on a different scale by ruling the drawing and transfer surface into small squares.

stenciling a method of making copies of a design by cutting out a template and painting or spraying over its openings.

still life any drawing or painting of inanimate objects, such as a bowl of fruit.

stipple to apply color in dots.

study a rough, preliminary drawing (but more detailed than a sketch), painting, or sculpture.

surrealism an art style characterized by subjects of a dreamy, fantastic, or irrational nature.

tempera pigment dispersed in an emulsion of egg yolk and water. Also, the method of painting with these colors.

tenebrism painting in dark, shadowy hues.

tertiary colors any hues made from the mixing of secondary colors.

tessellated in the form of a checkered mosaic.

thumbnail sketch a tiny, rough sketch.

tondo a circular painting.

tone the prevailing color in a painting.

topographic landscape an accurate rendering of a landscape.

tormented color in an oil painting, a color that has been overworked and rendered drab or ineffective.

traction fissure in an old painting, a wide crack that reveals the ground layer beneath.

trompe l'oeil a style of painting in which the subject is rendered as realistically as possible; the highest form of realism, as in a photograph.

underpainting on a canvas or panel, a preliminary layer of color over which the overpainting is made.

vanishing point in parallel lines showing perspective, the point of convergence at the horizon line.

veduta a painting or drawing showing all or a large part of a town or city.

vignette a photograph or painting in which the subject gradually fades away and disappears toward the borders.

warm colors red, yellow, and any hues between them.

wash in a watercolor, a broad brushstroke or an area painted with broad brushstrokes.

wash brush a large camel hair brush used to paint washes with watercolors.

watercolors pigments dispersed in water instead of oils, characterized by a transparent quality.

wedging kneading clay to make it more pliable.

woodcut a technique of printing from relief carved on a block of wood. Also, the print made by this method.

worm's-eye view in a painting, a scene or subject depicted from a ground-level perspective.

ART TOOLS AND MATERIALS

acetone a flammable fluid used as a paint solvent.

acrylic brush any brush made with nylon bristles as opposed to hair.

acrylic colors fast-drying, easily removed plastic paints.

airbrush a small, spray-painting apparatus held like a pen and operated by compressed air or carbonic gas; it is used to delicately smooth out tones and create subtle shading effects in commercial art or in retouching of photographs.

alabaster a white, translucent variety of gypsum that is soft and easily carved.

angular liner a paint brush with a slanted end, used for lining. Also known as a fresco liner.

architect's rendering brush a large brush used by watercolor painters.

armature the skeletonlike frame upon which plaster, clay, or other substances is applied to construct a sculpture.

badger blender a round brush with a square end, made of badger hair, and used to create soft effects.

bamboo pen a Japanese pen made from bamboo and used for drawing and calligraphy.

banding wheel a turntable or wheel on which pottery is turned in order to easily apply decorative stripes or bands.

bisque ceramic ware that has been fired once but is unglazed, as in bisque figurines. Also known as biscuit.

blender brush a badger-haired brush that flares out instead of coming to a point; it is used for blending colors.

bright a flat, thin, square-ended brush used in creating effects similar to that provided by a painting knife.

bristle brush the standard oil painting brush, made from hog bristles.

bulletin cutter a large, flag-tipped brush used by sign painters to outline large letters.

burnisher any tool used to smooth, polish, or remove imperfections, especially in etching or gilding.

camel hair brush a brush made not from camel hair but from squirrel hair, commonly used with watercolors.

camera lucida an optical device comprising a stand, an adjustable arm, and a prism; it projects an image of an object or scene into a plane surface for tracing.

canvas the heavy fabric or linen on which oil paintings are painted after it is primed.

charcoal a black marker made of charred wood and used for drawing and creating special effects by smudging.

charcoal paper a paper with a grain that holds charcoal well.

chassis the framework that holds an artist's canvas.

chisel brush a straight-edged brush with a beveled tip, like a chisel, used for sign writing.

compass an adjustable instrument with two hinged legs, used for describing perfect circles or arcs.

crayon any drawing material in stick form.

dagger striper a brush having long hairs that taper to a sharp point, used for striping.

earth colors paint pigments derived from colored clays and rocks. Also known as mineral pigments.

easel a freestanding framework or support that holds an artist's canvas during painting.

ellipse guide a template that aids in the drawing of ovals or ellipses.

enamel a vitreous protective and/or decorative coating baked on metal, glass, or ceramics.

fan brush a flat, fan-shaped brush used for blending and creating wispy effects.

filbert brush an oval-ended bristle brush used in oil painting.

fitch brush a brush made from the hair of a polecat. Also, a chisel brush made of bristle and used in sign painting.

fixative a fluid sprayed over pastels and drawings to help prevent smudging.

flag the free end of a brush; opposite of the base.

fluorescent paint paints with a particularly luminous quality, especially after being exposed to ultraviolet light; Day-Glo.

French curve a scroll-like, plastic template used as a guide for ruling curves.

highliner a long-bristled, square-ended brush used for lettering and striping.

lay figure a jointed mannequin that substitutes for a human model in art study.

lettering brush a wide, square-ended brush made of red sable, camel hair, or ox hair and used for lettering or making clean lines.

mahlstick a short rod used by a painter to steady his hand or brush while executing delicate detail work.

mop a large camel hair brush used with watercolors.

mordant an acid mixture used in producing etchings.

oil colors pigments that have been ground with oil.

painting knives a family of thin, flexible knives used in painting and preferred by some artists over brushes.

palette an oval board or tablet with a hand grip and thumb hole, on which a painter lays out and mixes paints.

palette knife a spatulalike knife used to mix oil paints.

panel a wood or wallboard panel sometimes used instead of a canvas for painting on.

pantograph an adjustable hinged-arm device used to trace, reduce or enlarge a drawing.

papier-mâché a mixture of paper pulp and glue that can be molded into various shapes and painted when dried.

pastel a colored crayon made of pigment and chalk. Also known as pastille.

pâte the clay from which ceramic pottery is formed.

potter's wheel a turntable on which pottery is formed.

pounce a powder made from charcoal or chalk used to transfer a drawing from one surface to another.

rigger a narrow, lettering brush.

single-stroke brush a broad brush used for creating broad washes with watercolors.

spatula a large painting knife used for mixing and stirring.

spotting brush a fine, red sable brush with a small point, used to retouch photos and lithographs.

stenciling brush a short, stiff, flat-ended brush used in stenciling.

striper a brush used for making delicate lines and stripes.

stump a cigar-shaped drawing tool made of rolled chamois or paper, used for making smudges and smoothing out tones.

taboret an artist's cabinet table for tools and materials.

tempera pigment dispersed in an emulsion of egg yolk and water.

tessera a small piece of tile, glass, or stone used in creating a mosaic.

turning tools a family of spatulalike tools used to shape clay on a potter's wheel.

wash brush any broad brush used to paint washes with watercolors.

watercolors pigments dispersed in water instead of oils, characterized by a transparent quality.

PHOTOGRAPHY

airbush a lab technique of creating or eliminating tone effects in a photo.

anaglyph a three-dimensional photo effect composed of a slightly contrasting dual image.

aperture the amount of opening in a lens; it controls the amount of light entering the camera.

artifact in digital images, an image distortion.

backlight to illuminate a subject from behind.

barrel distortion an aberration in a camera lens that causes abnormal curvature of square images in a photo.

beam combiner a two-way mirror that reflects light, allowing photos to be taken of the real and reflected image simultaneously.

blowback the reenlargement to the original size of a reduced photo.

blowup an enlargement of a photo.

bounce light a flash pointed at the ceiling or wall to reflect light onto the subject.

bugeye see FISHEYE.

burn to expose a negative to light to retouch an area or to remove areas.

card in a digital camera, an electronic memory chip for storing images.

CCD charged-coupled device. A light-sensitive device that converts light images into electronic signals to form digital pictures, used in cameras, scanners, copiers, and camcorders.

changing bag a black bag in which 35 mm film magazines can be loaded or unloaded in daylight; used when a camera jams.

close down to reduce the opening of the camera lens by increasing the depth of field.

color transparencies another name for color slides.

computer enhancement the use of a computer to bring out fine or hazy details in a photograph.

contre jour to take photos with a light source directly facing the camera.

courtesy line the name of the photographer or other source that appears under a photo published in a newspaper, magazine, or book.

crop to trim a portion of a photo.

depth of field the in-focus portion of an image from the closest object to the furthest; the range of sharp focus through a camera lens.

double exposure a dual-image photo of two subjects.

duotone a photo printed in two colors.

84 Charlie military slang for a combat photographer.

enlarger an apparatus that projects an enlarged image of a negative on light-sensitive paper to produce a larger photo.

enlarging paper paper used for printing enlarged images.

expose to admit light.

f short for focal length. See F-STOP.

fast of a film, more sensitive to light than other (slow) film. Also, of a lens, allowing more light to enter the camera than others.

film speed film sensitivity to light. Fast film is more sensitive to light and is used in low-light situations; slow film is less sensitive to light and is used in bright, clear weather.

filter one of a variety of special lenses placed over the main lens to produce a number of color, light, or special effects.

fisheye a wide-angle (providing 180-degree view) lens, noted for the distorted circular image it produces. Also known as a bugeye.

fixer the chemical solution used to complete the development of a photo.

flat a photo having dull contrast.

focal length the distance between a point in the lens and the film when the lens is focused at infinity.

focal plane at the back of the camera, the area where the image is focused on the film.

fog filter a special-effects filter used to produce a foggy or hazy effect in a photograph.

f-stop a lens aperture setting; the higher the f-stop number the more the aperture is reduced.

glossy a photo having a glossy or smooth finish.

halftone a photo having varying tones of gray.

high hat a short tripod used for making low-angle shots.

hot shoe the receptacle or holder for a camera flash unit.

infinity through a camera lens, any distance at which the subject is a few hundred feet away or more.

iris diaphragm the opening and closing device that regulates the amount of light entering the lens aperture.

light meter a device that measures light to determine proper camera settings. Also known as an exposure meter.

macro lens a lens used to photograph very small objects closeup.

magic hour the hour at dawn and again at dusk, when the sun produces the most flattering light.

mask a cardboard cutout placed over a lens to create a variety of effects, such as making a picture appear as if it was taken through binoculars or through a keyhole.

mat a decorative cardboard border around a photo. Also spelled matte.

monochrome a photo in several shades of one color.

paparazzi freelance photographers who follow celebrities around and take their photographs for sale to publications. The singular form is paparazzo.

photoflood a studio light of 275 to 1,000 watts.

photogenic photographically attractive.

photomacography photography of small objects.

photometer a light-exposure meter.

photomicrography photography through a microscope.

pixel an individual electronic image point.

red eye in a photograph, the reddish glint that sometimes appears in the eye of a subject when a flashbulb has been used.

reflector a studio light reflector used to bounce light in the desired direction.

retouch to touch up or alter a photograph, as with an airbrush.

scrim a mesh fabric used to produce diffuse lighting.

shutter speed the speed at which the camera shutter opens and closes. A fast speed is needed to capture moving objects without blur.

sky filter a colored filter used in landscape photography.

slow of a film, less sensitive to light than other (fast) film. Also, of a lens, allowing less light to enter the camera than others.

SLR single-lens reflex camera, noted for its viewfinder that shows the image exactly as it will be recorded on film.

solarize to overexpose a photograph, sometimes done intentionally for effect.

stop bath a chemical solution used in stopping film from developing further, before the fixing process.

stop down to reduce the size of the camera aperture and amount of light entering it.

telephoto a lens used to focus on distant objects.

thumbnail in a digital camera, a reduced image of a stored photograph.

time exposure a photograph made with the camera shutter left open for several seconds or minutes to show movement of, for example, clouds and stars, or to gather more light from very dim objects.

tripod a three-legged camera stand.

unretouched photo an unaltered photo.

Vaseline petroleum jelly sometimes applied on glass to shoot pictures through; it produces a hazy effect.

vignette a photo whose edges blend into the surrounding background.

wide-angle lens a lens that allows a wide field of view.

zoom lens a telephoto lens with a range of different focal lengths.

SCULPTURE

acrolith a Greek marble statue.

armature the skeletonlike frame upon which plaster, clay, or other substance is applied to construct a sculpture.

bas-relief low relief. Any sculpture or carving (such as a coin) that is raised only slightly from its background.

bushhammer a brick-shaped hammer with teeth on either end, used in stone carving to pulverize rock.

bust a sculpture consisting of the subject's head, neck, and part of the shoulders.

bust peg a post on which a bust is sculpted.

butterfly in a large sculpture, a crosslike piece of wood hung inside the framework or armature to help hold up heavy masses of material; a cross-shaped support.

calipers a tool with two movable arms, used by sculptors to measure diameters.

colossal any sculpture that is more than twice as large as life-size.

contrapposto a sculpture of a figure poised with most of its weight resting on one leg.

damascene the inlaying of a precious metal into a plain metal surface.

deep relief a sculpted or carved design that projects high off its background. Also known as high relief.

direct carving creating a sculpture directly without a clay or wax model.

draperie mouillée wet drapery; in figure sculpture, a thin, clingy, form-revealing drapery.

dress to finish or smooth out stone.

fettle to trim a sculpture of rough edges and any other extraneous matter.

firing the subjecting of a clay body to high heat in order to harden it.

grotesque any sculpture featuring a motif of leaves and flowers with imaginary or bizarre animal or human figures.

heroic a figure sculpture that is larger than life-size but smaller than a colossal.

icon a sculpture or picture of a holy person.

isocephaly the arrangement of figures so that the heads are at the same level.

mallet a wooden sculptor's mallet having a barrel-shaped head.

maquette a small wax or clay model of a potential sculpture and presented to a client for approval.

modeling clay reusable, nonhardening clay used for modeling.

rasp an abrasive tool used in rough-shaping, striating, and wearing down surfaces.

relief any projection from a flat surface, a raised area.

repoussé a method of forming a relief design by hammering a metal plate from the back.

sculpture in the round freestanding figures carved in three dimensions, as distinguished from relief work.

statuary marble any white marble suitable for sculpture.

statuette a statue that is half life-size or less.

stun to split, chip, or splinter stone deliberately or by accident.

terra-cotta a fired, brownish red clay, commonly used by sculptors and potters.

Sculpting Marbles

bardiglio capella an Italian marble, gray with gray and black streaks.

benou jaune French marble, mottled gold, yellow, and violet.

brèche rose Italian marble, mottled brown, white, and lavender.

campan griotte French marble, mottled brown.

Carrara popular Italian marble, white with few gray streaks.

compage mélange vert French marble, green.

escalette French marble, yellowish green and pink.

French grand antique French marble, mottled black and white.

giallo antico popular with ancient Greeks and Romans, an antique yellow marble.

Languedoc French marble, red or scarlet with occasional white splash.

loredo chiaro Italian marble, mottled brown and yellow.

lumachelle French marble, mottled green.

Napoleon gray New England marble, gray.

pavonazzo Italian marble, multicolored with peacocklike markings.

Petworth English marble, multicolored and fossil-bearing.

porto marble Italian marble, black with gold veins.

rance Belgian marble, dull red with blue and white streaks.

Roman brèche French marble, mottled pink and blue.

rosso magnaboschi Italian marble, reddish orange.

royal Jersey green eastern U.S. marble, green, serpentine.

saccharoidal marble statuary marble.

Saint-Béat French marble, pure white.

Sainte-Anne marble Belgian marble, blue black with white veins.

Sainte-Baume marble French marble, yellow with brown and red veins.

sienna French marble, deep yellow with white and purple veins.

sienna travertine German marble, mottled brown.

CLOTHING AND FASHION

CLOTHING OF ANCIENT GREECE

ampyx a metal diadem or women's headband, often worn with a hairnet.

cestus an elaborate outer girdle.

chiton a short or long tunic. The short version was sometimes attached to only one shoulder. The long version tended to be worn by older men or men of prestige.

chitoniscus a knitted vest worn over a chiton.

chlamys a man's oblong wrap or cape made of wool; it fastened with a clasp in front or at the right shoulder.

diplax a woman's outdoor wrap, similar to a chlamys.

Greek fillet a braid of hair wound about the head several times, worn by women and by male athletes.

himation a long, loose outer garment wrapped about the body and arranged in folds and sometimes pulled up over the head. It was worn by men and women, and its elaborate wrapping was difficult to master.

petasos a flat felt hat with flaps over the front and back and over the ears.

pilos a conical felt or leather hat worn by sailors, fishermen, and artisans.

sakkos a slinglike headdress made of goat's hair, worn by women.

splendone a slinglike headress made of decorated cloth or leather and ending in a tie or band, worn by women.

stephane a metal circlet hair bow.

tribon a small, oblong shawl worn by men.

CLOTHING OF ANCIENT ROME

abolla a man's woolen cloak folded double and fastened with a brooch.

baltaeus a belt formed from the twisted folds of a toga.

birrus a hooded cape worn in inclement weather.

calceus an untanned leather boot having slits at the ankle, drawn together by leather thongs.

clavus a stripe.

crepida a low half-boot exposing the toes.

cucullus a hood.

cuirass a protective tunic, hinged front to back and molded to fit the figure, worn by the military.

laena a man's thick, woolen cloak worn in very cold weather.

loincloth worn under the toga before tunics came into vogue.

paenula a poncholike, wool cape, sometimes having a hood, worn by both sexes.

palla long, loose outer garment worn by women; similar to the Greek himation.

paludamentum a purple cloak clasping at the right shoulder, worn by military officers.

pilleus a felt, conical hat, worn by men.

sagum a thick, woolen cloak, usually red, worn by those who were not officers in the military. Similar to the abolla.

sandals the popular footwear of the period.

stola a long tunic reaching to the feet. When it had sleeves, they were attached separately by means of brooches.

toga a circular segment of fabric about 18 feet long and 7 feet wide; it was elaborately wrapped and draped about the body (and sometimes over the head in religious ceremonies) and was made of natural-colored wool.

toga candida a plain, white toga worn by campaigning politicians.

toga cinctus Gabinus a toga worn with the balteus passed twice around the waist instead of over the left shoulder.

toga picta a purple toga with gold embroidery, worn by emperors, consuls, and generals.

toga praetexta a white toga having a purple or scarlet band along its straight edge, worn by children under age 16 and by magistrates.

toga pulla a black or dark-colored toga for mourning.

toga pura the natural-colored wool toga for everyday wear.

tunica a wool or linen tunic.

tunica palmata a purple tunic richly embroidered in gold, worn by emperors and consuls.

CLOTHING OF MEDIEVAL ENGLAND AND FRANCE

(13th, 14th, and 15th centuries)

aglets metal tips at the ends of laces to facilitate lacing of garments.

agrafe a large metal brooch used to fasten cloaks and robes.

alb a long white tunic made of linen, a vestment of the clergy.

almuce a large, fur-lined cape, often edged with fur tails and having a hood, worn by doctors of divinity and canons.

amice a white linen napkin adjusted about the neck, a vestment of the clergy.

anelace a long dagger worn from the belt by civilians.

baguette a lappet of mail.

bainbergs lower leg armor. Also known as bamberges.

balandrana a wide cloak, popularly used in the 13th and 14th centuries when traveling.

balays pink rubies.

baldric a wide, decorative belt, sometimes worn over the shoulder and hung with bells.

barmecloth an apron.

bascinet a domed, pointed helmet of the 14th and 15th centuries.

beaver facial armor.

bliant a garment resembling the surcoat, sometimes fur-lined; worn by both sexes.

bouchette a breastplate fastener.

bourdon a decorative walking staff.

brassards steel arm plates or armor.

brayette a steel petticoat, similar to a baguette.

buskins high boots popularly worn by rural people and travelers.

bycocket a hat turned down in the front and turned up in the back.

camail the mail encircling the bottom of a bascinet and protecting the wearer's neck and upper chest.

capa a hooded robe.

cappa clausa a closed cape having only a small slit in the center to extend the hands out in an attitude of prayer; worn by the clergy.

cappa nigra a black choir cape, sometimes hooded.

capuchon a hood or cowl. Also known as a chaperon.

caputium a combination hood and cape. In the 15th century the color and lining of the hood denoted academic rank.

casque a helmet.

cassock a very long coat, fur-lined, and having tight sleeves; it fastened down the front and was worn by men.

cendal a material made of woven silk.

chain mail wrought iron rings riveted together and sewn onto a leather foundation for use as protective armor.

chapel de fer an iron hat of war.

chasuble a large, round garment with a center hole, slipped over the head and covering the body in voluminous folds, a clergyman's vestment.

chausses tight hose worn over the legs.

cingulum a waist belt.

cockers high-laced boots worn by rural men.

coif a close-fitting skullcap held on with a chin strap, worn by men.

coif-de-mailles a protective hat of mail.

colobium a plain tunic.

cope a large, full-bodied, decorative cape, frequently hooded and worn by the clergy.

cote an ordinary dress or gownlike garment worn by both sexes.

cote-hardie a tight-fitting tunic worn by men. Also, a long, tight-fitting gown worn by women.

coudières elbow guards, a form of armor.

cowl see CAPUCHON.

cracowes long-toed boots or shoes.

crespine a woman's headdress of the 14th century, characterized by two jeweled cauls or nets of wires holding hair in on either side of the head.

cuirass breast and back armor.

cuir-bouilli leather that has been boiled to harden it for use as protective armor.

cuissards armor pieces covering the thighs. Also known as cuisses.

dagges ornamental edgings on garments of the 14th century.

dalmatic a vestment similar to but shorter than an alb and having wider sleeves and a slit at the sides.

damask a rich, patterned fabric.

diaper ornamental embroidery.

dorelet a jewel-embroidered hairnet.

doublet a short, padded tunic.

dunster a broadcloth of the 14th century.

enbraude embroidery.

epaulières armor pieces protecting the shoulders.

ermine the most highly desired fur, worn by kings.

fitchets slits in outer garments used to provide access to inner garments or to purses, keys, and so forth.

fret a decorative hair net.

frontlet a cloth, silk, or velvet band worn on the forehead by 15th-century women.

frounce a flounce.

fustian cotton or wool cloth.

gambeson an early form of gipon.

gardcorp an outdoor garment worn by both sexes.

gauntlet a glove with protective metal plates to protect the hand, worn by knights.

gazzatum a fine silk of the 13th century.

genuilliers armor pieces protecting the knees.

gipon a close-fitting, waisted, quilted garment worn over a shirt; it evolved from the tunic. Also known as a doublet.

gipser a purse.

girdle a belt, usually decorative.

gite a gown.

gorget an armor piece protecting the throat. Also, the lower portion of a hood, covering the neck and upper chest.

greaves armor pieces protecting the shins. Also known as jambs, or jambarts.

grise a gray fur from the Russian squirrel, popular with the upper middle classes.

hatere attire.

hauberk a coat or shirt of mail.

helm a helmet.

heuke a cloak worn by men or women.

hure a cap.

jambarts see GREAVES.

kennel a form of hood forming a gable or pyramid shape over the forehead, popular with women in the 15th century. Also known as a gable or pedimental headdress.

kersche a kerchief.

kirtle a long, loose gown with flowing draperies and trains. Also, a waistcoat.

latchet a shoe or clog fastener.

lettice a pale, gray fur.

liripipe a short or long hanging tail extending from the point of some hoods and hats, sometimes twisting around the head like a turban.

mahoôtres padded shoulders, popular in the late 15th century.

mantle a loose, sleeveless coat.

mentonières armor pieces protecting the throat and chin.

misericord a dagger worn by knights on the right hip.

miter a pointed or horned cap worn by bishops and cardinals during services.

nifles a 15th-century veil.

nouch a jeweled clasp.

pauldrons shoulder guards.

pelicon a long, loose outer garment.

petticoat a small coat worn under a larger one in the late 15th century.

pilch a coat make of skins of fur.

pilion a round hat of the 14th and 15th centuries.

plate steel armor pieces that eventually replaced chain mail.

points laces or ties with metal tips, used most frequently for attaching hose.

ponge a purse.

poulaines long-pointed shoes.

ray striped cloth.

rerebrace an armor piece protecting the upper arm.

roskyn squirrel fur.

sabbatons very broad, square-toed shoes. Also known as duck-billed shoes.

sable highly prized (but less so than ermine) fur worn by princes.

samite a rich silk interwoven with gold thread.

slops in the 14th century, a jacket. In the 15th century, a shoe or cassock. In the 16th century, wide breeches.

standard of mail a collar of mail for protecting the neck.

sequanie a loose outer frock, worn by rural women.

surcoat a tunic worn over armor.

taces a skirt of protective plate, extending from the waist to the thighs.

tilting helm a large helmet.

tippet a long hanging end of cloth or cape.

tunic a long or short, sleeved or sleeveless garment, sometimes having slits at the front or sides; eventually replaced by the gipon.

vair black and white squirrel skins arranged in decorative patterns.

vambraces armor pieces protecting the lower arms.

visor a slitted face shield that pivoted on a knight's helmet.

volupere a nightcap of the 14th century.

wimple a veil worn over the neck and chin in the 13th century.

CLOTHING OF THE 16TH CENTURY

apron an apron made of wool or linen, worn with a bib by working-class or rural women and without a bib by higher classes.

band a linen collar.

bases a knee-length skirt worn by men over their armor.

beaver a hat. Also, the fur used to make this hat.

biggin a close-fitting cap worn by infants and children.

billiment a decorative and frequently jeweled border on a French hood.

blackwork black embroidery on white linen.

bodyes a bodice.

bonnet a soft hat worn by both men and women.

boothose stockings with decorative tops turned down over boots.

breastplate an armor piece protecting the chest.

breeches pants extending from the waist to the knees and worn with stockings.

carcenet a heavy, bejeweled necklace made of gold and worn like a collar.

caul a decorative hairnet made of gold thread or silk.

chemise a woman's smock or undergarment.

chin-clout a type of light scarf worn over the chin and mouth of rural women.

chopines clogs; shoes with raised platforms made of wood or cork.

cod-piece a projecting pouch or appendage allowing room for the groin area in men's tight-fitting breeches or hose.

coif a linen skullcap, tied under the chin by straps.

copotain a very high domed hat with a brim turned up on one side, made from block felt. Also known as a sugarloaf hat.

damask rich silk having floral or geometric decoration.

doublet a short, tuniclike garment worn over the shirt.

English hood a woman's hood that drapes over the sides of the face and forms an arch or gable over the forehead. Also known as a gable or pediment headdress.

ermine the most highly prized fur of the time, worn only by the nobility and royalty.

falling band a turned-down collar.

farthingale a hooped understructure employed to widen a woman's skirt from the waist down. Also, the skirt worn over this understructure.

French cloak a long cloak, usually worn draped over one shoulder.

French hood a small hood having a horseshoe-shaped crown, worn far back on the head.

galligaskins baggy breeches.

garters decorative bands used to hold up stockings.

girdle a decorative belt, band, or chain.

gorget a steel collar, an armor piece.

guards bands of material employed to cover seams, usually of contrasting color.

head-rail a linen square arranged about the head. In the later portion of the century it was wired into elaborate shapes and trimmed with lace.

hose a man's body stockings, from waist to feet.

jacket same as today's jacket.

jerkin a sleeved or sleeveless waistcoat, worn over the doublet.

kerchief a large square of material worn as a shawl over the shoulders.

kirtle before 1545, a bodice and skirt; after 1545, the skirt alone.

lappet a decorative border on an English hood; it hung down on either side of the face or was turned up and pinned to the crown.

loose gown a garment that hung loosely in folds from the shoulders.

mandilion a loose, hip-length jacket with a standing collar.

mantle a large, diaphanous piece of material worn as a shawl.

Mary Stuart hood a hood wired into a heart shape.

Milan bonnet a cornered hat with a turned-up, slit brim and a soft, pleated crown.

muckminder slang for handkerchief or napkin.

mules flat shoes without backs.

nightcap a men's indoor, linen cap.

nightgown a fur-lined gown worn by men and women either indoors or outdoors.

panes a decorative technique of slashing material vertically, as in a doublet or other outer garment.

pantofles short leather boots with thick cork soles.

pauldrons armor pieces that covered the shoulders.

peascod a form of doublet having a swollen belly, reminiscent of the shape of a pea pod.

petticoat an underskirt.

pinking a decorative pattern of small holes or slits.

points ribbon, linen, or silk laces tipped with aglets, used most frequently to tie hose to a doublet.

puffs material pulled through slashes in an outer garment. See PANES.

rail a square of material worn around the head or on the shoulders like a shawl.

rebato a wired collar that stands up around the back of the head and fans out in a series of pleats, worn by women.

rerebrace an armor piece that protects the upper arm.

ruching folded gathers used as a form of trim.

ruff a radiating, pleated, and layered neckband made of lace or linen. A ruff of lace folded in a figure-8 pattern was popular.

shag a thick cloth and fur lining.

shoe rose a ribbon or lace rosette used to decorate shoes.

smock a woman's T-shaped undergarment.

spangles decorative metal pieces.

Spanish breeches long breeches ending below the knee.

Steinkerk a loosely tied scarf or cravat worn with its ends drawn through a buttonhole or pinned to a coat.

stomacher an inverted triangle of stiffened material on a bodice.

sugarloaf hat a very high domed hat with a brim turned up on one side, made from block felt and worn by women. Formerly known as a copotain.

tippet a waist-length cape.

tricorne a triangular or three-cornered hat with turned-up brim, worn by men.

trunk hose padded or billowing round breeches.

wings decorative epaulettes on doublets and jerkins.

CLOTHING OF THE 17TH CENTURY

aigrette a tuft of feathers held together by gemstones.

basque a wide band that attached below a bodice or doublet. Also, a close-fitting bodice.

beaver a hat made from beaver fur.

blackwork black embroidery on white linen.

bombast cotton padding used to fill out garments.

boot hose an everyday hose worn over fine hose to protect it from boot wear.

breeches knee-length pants.

canions short, pantlike extensions worn with trunk hose.

cloak a coat, sometimes sleeved, and sometimes having a cape.

clocks embroidery on the sides of stockings.

cornet a woman's cap, having ribbons and streamers, and worn on the back of the head.

doublet a man's sleeved jacket, buttoned down the front.

Dutch breeches breeches ending above the knee.

echelles bows of graduating length in a row running down the front of a stomacher.

falling band a turned-down collar.

farthingale the hooped understructure of a hoop skirt. Also, the skirt itself.

fontange a high, tiered, frilled woman's headdress worn on the back of the head.

frogging ornamental braids, buttons, and loops running down the front of a garment, most often associated with military uniforms.

gaberdine a long, loose coat having wide sleeves.

gauntlets gloves reminiscent of the armored gloves worn by knights but having decorative embroidery and fringes; worn by both sexes.

gorget a steel collar that protected the throat.

jerkin a sleeveless jacket worn over the doublet by men.

kerchief a folded square of material worn around the neck and shoulders.

lappets lace or linen streamers running down from the back of a woman's hat.

mantua a loose gown sashed or belted at the waist.

mules flat shoes with toe caps and no backs.

nightcap an embroidered, informal hat worn by men, not necessarily at night.

panes strips or ribbons of material produced by slashing a garment; fashionable in sleeves, doublets, and bodices. Also known as slashing.

peascod a padded doublet making the belly appear similar to a pea pod.

periwig a man's wig.

Persian vest a loose coat closed by a sash or a belt, worn by men.

petticoat breeches voluminously wide, pleated pants, reminiscent of a skirt, worn by men.

pickadil a framework used to support a ruff or a standing collar.

pinking a decorative pattern of small holes and slits.

plumpers cork balls placed in each cheek to plump them out, a fashion of women toward the end of the century.

points ribbon, linen, or silk laces tipped with aglets, used most frequently to tie hose to a doublet.

ruching decorative gathers and pleats.

ruff the elaborate frill that radiated around standing collars of men and women.

russet a coarse wool worn by rural people.

sable a highly desired fur.

shag thick cloth used in linings.

slashing see PANES.

slops wide breeches.

snoskyn a woman's muff.

Spanish cloak a short, hooded cloak.

Spanish farthingale a bell- or funnel-shaped skirt, formed by an understructure of this shape. See FARTHINGALE.

startups loose leather shoes.

stomacher on the front of the bodice, an inverted triangle of stiffened material.

tippet a short cape.

trunk hose hose that swelled out from the waist to the thighs.

trunk sleeve a sleeve swelled out from the upper arm and closing at the wrist.

underpropper a collar wire that supported the ruff.

vambrace an armor piece that protected the forearm.

velvet popular material of the upper classes.

Venetians breeches that stopped at the knee. These were either baggy, close-fitting, or pear-shaped.

waistcoat a type of jacket worn by men or women.

CLOTHING OF THE 18TH CENTURY

Artois buckles large, square shoe buckles worn by both sexes in the second half of the century.

bag an ornamental purse of silk tied to men's hair. See BAGWIG.

bagwig a dress wig with the pigtail tucked into a black silk bag in the back of the neck. Also known as a bag.

banyan men's calf-length dressing gown.

beaver a hat made from beaver fur.

bedgown a full-length muslin or silk gown tied with a sash, worn by women.

bob wig a curly or frizzy wig in various lengths, worn by the middle class from the 1720s on.

breeches knee-length pants, buckled below the knee.

Brunswick a type of sack having a false bodice front and long, tight sleeves.

buffon a large handkerchief covering the open area left by a low-neck bodice.

buffskin buff-colored leather, fashionable in breeches and waistcoats.

bustle a gathering of material on the back of a woman's skirt forming a false rump.

cadogan a thick tail of hair, formed into a loop on the back of men's heads, fashionable in the 1770s to 1780s.

caraco a woman's thigh-length jacket.

cardinal a woman's knee-length, scarlet coat.

chatelaine a clasp or chain worn from the waist for holding perfume bottles, stay hooks, and other cosmetic accessories.

chemise a woman's full-length shift with ruffled neck and sleeves.

commode a woman's lace and linen headdress with lappets.

corset a sleeveless bodice laced from the back.

cravat a light linen scarf tied around the neck.

fantail hat a hat with a broad, turned-up front rim, worn by men.

fly cap a lace and wire cap shaped like a butterfly and sometimes decorated with jewels.

frock a long, loose, informal coat with a turned-down collar, worn by men for sport, riding, or other activities.

frogging looped braid fastenings, derived from military uniforms.

great coat a large, loose, calf-length overcoat with capelike collars for shedding rain, favored by coachmen. Also known as a surtout or a wrap-rascal.

Hessians short riding boots decorated with tassels.

hoop a hooped petticoat used for puffing out skirts.

indispensable a handbag introduced at the end of the century. Also known as a reticule.

lappet a woman's hat streamer.

lawn a fine linen.

major wig a wig with two short pigtails.

milkmaid hat a round, low-crowned hat having a wide brim, worn at various angles by women. Also known as a bergère.

mob cap a bonnetlike cap with a puffed-out crown and frill and ribbon trim, worn by women.

modesty piece a strip of lace that covered the open area left by a low-necked bodice.

morning gown a gown worn by either sex before formally dressing in the morning.

nightgown a loose, indoor coat, not worn to bed.

night rail a long, indoor cape worn by women.

open robe a bodice and skirt, open in the front to reveal an elegant underskirt.

pantaloons introduced in the 1790s, long pants that extended to the ankles; worn by men.

paste glass cut and polished to look like gems.

petenlair a lady's thigh-length jacket with a sack back.

petticoat the name used for a woman's skirt.

physical wig a bushy, long wig worn by doctors and surgeons.

pinner a cap surrounded by a linen frill, worn by women.

polonaise an open gown bunched up in the back of the waist to form three separate bunches or swags.

pompon jeweled feathers or ribbons worn on the hair or on a cap.

riding habit a lady's dress with riding coat and waistcoat.

rollups stockings pulled up over the breeches at the knee.

rump a crescent-shaped bustle.

sack a voluminous gown with a back having box pleats stitched down each side.

shift a woman's linen and lace undergarment.

spencer a waist-length jacket having a roll collar and cuffs, worn by both sexes.

stomacher on the front of a bodice, an inverted triangle of stiffened material, usually elaborately embroidered.

tie wig a wig having a pigtail tied with a bow at the nape of the neck.

tippet a short shoulder cape, often white in color, worn by women over the bosom or tucked into the bodice.

tricorne a three-cornered hat with the brim turned up on all sides.

tucker white edging around the top of a low-necked bodice.

waistcoat a sleeved or sleeveless jacket having slit sleeves and worn under a coat.

witch's hat a hat with a pointed crown, worn most often by rural women.

CLOTHING OF THE 19TH CENTURY

adelaide boots women's boots with fur around the tops.

albert a short chain connecting a watch to a buttonhole, popular from 1849 on.

albert overcoat a calf-length overcoat having breast and hip pockets and a half-circle cape resting on the shoulders.

alberts side-lacing half boots with cloth tops and false mother-of-pearl buttons on the front.

ankle jacks half-boots.

Apollo knot two or more wide loops of false hair wired to stand up on top of the head with decorative lace, flowers, or jeweled combs, popular with women from 1824 to the 1830s.

banyan a long informal coat with flared skirts, worn around the house in the morning.

batswing a variation of the bowtie having a very small knot, fashionable in the 1890s.

bavolet a frill attached to the back of a bonnet to protect the neck from sun.

Benjamin a loose topcoat worn when traveling.

Benoiton chains long beads of black wood or filigreed gold or silver that hung from each side of the head and draped across the bosom, popular from 1865 to 1870.

beret a crepe or silk evening hat, usually decorated with ribbons, flowers, or feathers. Also, a turban decorated with a plume.

bertha a frilled and ribboned border or collar covering the sleeves and falling over the top of a bodice.

bloomers frilled trousers gathered about the ankles and worn under a short skirt.

boa a scarf of feathers. Also, a scarf of fur made from skunk, opossum, beaver, sable, or fox.

bodice the corsetlike, fitted portion of a dress from the waist to the upper chest, fastened up the back with hooks and eyes and boned in front, often heavily padded at the bosom.

bolero a short jacket joined only at the breast or not at all.

bollinger a hat with a wide brim topped by a domed crown or "hemisphere." Also known as a hemisphere hat.

bosom, artificial any material used to plump out the bosom, most frequently cotton or wax.

bowler a stiff felt hat with a narrow brim and a round crown.

braces suspenders.

breeches tight, high-waisted pants extending nearly to mid-calf.

burnoose a small cape or shawl with a hood attached.

bustle a crescent-shaped, wool-stuffed pad, worn in the back of the dress to plump out the behind.

calash a hood that could be folded by means of cane hoops and carried in a bag to an evening function.

capote a puffy bonnet with a stiff brim projecting around the face.

cardigan a short, close-fitting jacket without a collar, made of wool or English worsted.

catagan a chignon brought down to the nape of the neck.

chemise robe a dress or frock buttoning down the front from the neck to the hem.

chemisette white edging around the top of a low-necked bodice. Also known as a tucker.

chesterfield a large overcoat or topcoat with a velvet collar and several pockets, widely popular from the 1840s on.

chignon a mass of coiled or plaited hair, sometimes supplemented with false hair, gathered at the back of the head and often covered with a net.

cloak a long and voluminous overcoat without sleeves and fastened around the body like a cape. In the second half of the century cloaks had sleeves, and many had detachable capes.

cornette a generic term for any bonnet tied under the chin.

cossacks loose, voluminous trousers having leg bottoms drawn closed by ribbons, popular from about 1817 to the 1830s.

cravat a light, linen scarf tied around the neck in a knot or bow.

crinoline a dome-, funnel-, or pyramidal-shaped understructure made of whalebone or spring hoops used to distend or widen skirts to as large as 18 feet in circumference. The skirt itself was often hitched up to show a scarlet petticoat beneath.

cummerbund a wide silk sash worn around the waist with a dress suit, popular with men from the 1890s on.

deerstalker cap a Harris tweed cap with ear flaps.

Dolly Varden dress a variation of the polonaise, having a short overskirt bunched up severely in the back.

duster a short summer overcoat.

follow-me-lads popular name for ribbon streamers trailing behind a woman's hat.

frock coat a knee-length, military-style overcoat.

gaiters leather or cloth leggings extended from the knee to the instep. Ankle-length gaiters were known as spats.

Garibaldi shirt a black-buttoned, red merino shirt worn with a belt and a black or other colored skirt.

gibus a top hat capable of being squashed flat and carried under the arm.

greatcoat a knee- or ankle-length overcoat, buttoning to just below the waist.

Grecian bend a fad in which a stooped posture was considered fashionable among women; a bustle was worn high on the back of the skirt to enhance this effect, popular from 1815 to 1819 and revived in 1868.

Hessians boots rising to just below the knee and decorated with tassels, worn most frequently with pantaloons.

highlows ankle boots buckled or strapped in front.

indispensable a circular or lozenge-shaped handbag favored by women. Also known as a reticule.

inexpressibles prudish name given to trousers to avoid being vulgar in speech. Also known as unmentionables and unwhisperables.

Inverness a greatcoat having a deep cape, popular from 1859 on.

jacket bodice a full-sleeved, form-fitting bodice spreading out over the waist.

knickerbockers a loose form of breeches, but longer and wider; they buckled at the knee and were worn from the 1870s on for shooting, boating, golf, and riding.

mackintosh an overcoat made of rubber bonded over cloth, a source of complaints due to its unpleasant odor.

mantle a long cloak, frequently having a cape.

mob cap a bonnetlike cap with a puffed-out crown and frill and ribbon trim, worn most frequently in the kitchen by women.

muff a handwarmer made of fur or feathers.

paletot a short overcoat for men. Also, a large jacket that spread over a crinoline dress.

pantaloons close-fitting pants, held to the feet by straps. Also known as tights.

pelerine a cape.

pelisse a long, short-waisted, ankle-length overcoat with a broad, turned-down collar.

piccadilly a man's stand-up collar.

poke bonnet a bonnet with a forward projecting brim.

polonaise a very popular dress having an overskirt attached at the bodice and draped up at the rump. It was sometimes left unbuttoned from the waist down. Also known as a princess polonaise.

porkpie hat a lady's hat having a low, flat crown, resembling a pie.

princess dress a dress having a bodice extending down to serve as an overskirt. Also known as an Isabeau dress.

pumps dress shoes open at the instep and just covering the toes, tied with ribbons.

rationals bicycle bloomers, popular in the 1890s.

reticule a small, drawstringed handbag made of silk, satin, or velvet.

riding habit skirt a very long skirt worn when riding to hide the legs from view.

sailor suit a popular boy's suit, consisting of a sailor's hat, knickerbockers, and a blouse with a square flat collar and V neck, worn from the 1860s on.

shawl a garment draped over the shoulders to warm the upper body.

skeleton suit a young boy's suit consisting of highwaisted trousers buttoned up over a fitted jacket having a broad, white collar, from 1800 to 1834.

spats see GAITERS.

spencer a short jacket pulled in at the waist, worn by women.

surtout a long overcoat.

tam-o'-shanter a close-fitting, Scottish cap having a pompon, feather, or tassel sticking up from the center.

tea gown a loose dress without a corset, frequently trimmed with flounces and ruffled sleeves.

three storeys and a basement a woman's high-crowned hat.

tippet a cape.

top coat a greatcoat or overcoat.

top hat a narrow-brimmed hat with a tall crown, most frequently shiny black in color. Also called a chimney pot hat.

trilby a soft felt hat having a dent along the crown from front to back.

ugly on a bonnet, an extra brim tied over the existing brim for extra shading against the sun.

ulster an overcoat worn with a belt and having a detachable hood, introduced in 1869.

unmentionables see inexpressibles.

unwhisperables see INEXPRESSIBLES.

waistcoat a sleeved or sleeveless jacket; a vest.

whangee a popular cane or walking stick.

wideawake a popular wide-brimmed straw or felt hat having a low crown, worn by men.

CLOTHING OF THE 20TH AND 21ST CENTURIES

Caps and Hats

Alpine a fur felt hat with a slightly peaked crown. Also known as a Tyrolean.

bearskin a soft, furry, high-domed hat having a chain or strap under the chin, worn by the guards at Buckingham Palace.

bellhop a small pillbox cap, sometimes having a chin-strap, worn by old-time bellhops.

beret a wool or cloth tam; a visorless, pancakelike hat.

boater a straw hat having a flat, oval crown, previously worn by men, now by women.

bobby a hat having a high, domed crown and a narrow brim, worn by English police (bobbies).

bowler English stiff-felt hat having a curving brim and a round crown. Same as the American derby.

bubble beret a brimless, puffed-out beret, worn tilted to one side, popular in the 1960s.

buff see DO-RAG.

busby a tall, fur or feather hat having an ornamental baglike drapery hanging from the crown to one side of the head, worn by some regiments of the British army.

bush an Australian, cowboylike hat with a large brim turned up on one side.

calotte a beanielike cap made of leather or suede with a stemmed top.

cartwheel a woman's hat having a very broad brim and a low, round crown.

cloche a soft, domelike hat pulled down low over the forehead, worn by women.

coolie a bamboo or straw parasol-like hat worn as protection against the sun by the Chinese.

cossack a high, brimless Russian fur hat worn by men.

crusher a soft felt hat that can be rolled up and stowed in the pocket for traveling, popular in the early 1900s and again in the 1980s.

Davy Crockett coonskin cap famous for its raccoon fur and tail hanging from the back, popular with boys in the 1950s and early 1960s.

deerstalker a tweed cap having ear flaps and a visor extending from the front and back, made famous by Sherlock Holmes.

derby American name for the English bowler.

do-rag also known as a buff, a kerchief that is worn around the head and ties at the back of the neck.

Dutch boy a visored wool cap having a soft, broad crown.

eight-point cap a cap having an octagon-shaped crown, worn by policemen.

engineer's cap a blue-and-white striped cap with a visor, worn by railroad workers.

envoy a man's fur-crowned hat, similar to a cossack, popular in the 1960s.

fatigue cap an army cap similar in cut to an engineer's cap.

fedora a man's soft felt hat having a medium brim usually worn turned up and a crown that is creased down the middle from front to back.

fez a red felt hat in the shape of a truncated cone; a black tassel hangs from the crown; worn by Turkish men.

French beret see PANCAKE BERET.

French sailor a large cotton tam, usually blue or white with a red pompon on the crown.

garrison cap an olive or khaki-colored cloth dress cap creased lengthwise to facilitate folding, worn by army and air force personnel in World War I and World War II. Also known as an overseas cap.

gaucho a black felt hat having a broad brim and a flat, cylindrical crown, held in place by a chin strap; a South American cowboy hat fashionable with women in the 1960s.

glengarry a creased cloth cap having a regiment badge on the front side and two black ribbons streaming from the back, worn by Scottish Highland Military.

Greek fisherman's a soft denim or wool cap with a braided visor, a popular boating hat worn by both sexes in the 1980s.

homburg a man's felt hat having a creased crown and a narrow, rolled brim.

hunt a riding cap worn with a riding habit, characterized by a round crown with a button on top along with a chin strap and small visor.

hunting a bright orange cap with a visor.

jockey cap a visored cap similar to a baseball cap but with a deeper crown, worn by jockeys.

Juliet a skullcap made of chain, jewels, pearls, or rich fabric, worn with wedding veils or with evening attire.

kepi the French Foreign Legion cap having a flat, cylindrical crown and a visor, sometimes worn with a cloth havelock to protect the back of the neck from sunburn.

leghorn a woman's broad-brimmed, yellow straw hat.

Legionnaire's see KEPI.

matador a hat reminiscent of the top of a bull's head, having two hornlike projections and a crown made of embroidered velvet.

mod a popular cap of the 1960s, actually an exaggerated form of the newsboy cap of the 1920s.

mortarboard square, cloth-covered cardboard with tassel and skullcap worn at graduations.

mountie's a broad-brimmed hat with a tall crown creased into four sections, worn by state police and by the Royal Canadian Mounted Police.

newsboy a visored cap with a puffed or bloused crown that could be snapped to the visor; worn by newsboys in the early 1900s and made famous by Jackie Coogan in the films of the 1920s.

opera hat a tall, silk hat having a crown that could be collapsed, similar to a top hat but having a duller finish.

overseas cap see GARRISON CAP.

painter's cap a visored cap having a rounded, flat-topped crown, worn by painters.

Panama a man's hand-plaited hat made from the straw of the jipijapa plant.

pancake beret a flat felt tam, sometimes worn tilted to one side by artists. Also called a French beret.

picture hat a large-brimmed hat made of straw, worn by women.

pillbox a small, round, brimless hat worn on the front, side, or back of the head, a popular woman's fashion since the 1920s.

planter's a broad-brimmed, banded straw hat with a dented crown.

porkpie a man's snap-brim hat with a low, flat crown.

profile a woman"s hat having a brim turned sharply down at one side, popular in the 1930s.

Puritan a man's tall black hat, adorned with a black band and silver buckle, worn by 17th-century Puritans and revived for women's fashion in the 1970s.

Rex Harrison a man's wool tweed, snap-brim hat, popularized by Rex Harrison in *My Fair Lady.*

safari hat a straw or fabric hat with a medium brim and a round, shallow crown.

Scottie a brimless hat having a creased crown ornamented with ribbons or feathers in the back, similar to a glengarry.

shako a tall, cylinderlike hat with a visor and a feather cockade in front, worn by members of a marching band.

skimmer a boater with a wider brim and a shallower crown.

skullcap any cap, such as a swimmer's cap, that fits snugly around the crown of the head.

snap-brim a hat having a brim that can be adjusted at different angles.

sombrero a straw or felt hat having a tall, tapering crown and a broad, upturned brim, worn in Mexico.

sou'wester a rain hat with a domelike crown and a broad brim that is longer in the back, originally a New England fisherman's hat.

Stetson the trademark name for a cowboy or 10-gallon hat.

stocking cap a knitted winter cap with a long tail frequently fitted with a pompon or tassel. Also known as a toboggan cap.

tam short for tam-o'-shanter. A flat, Scottish cap, having a pompon or tassel in the center, similar to a beret.

top hat a man's tall, stovepipelike hat with narrow brim and shiny, silk finish; not collapsible like an opera hat.

trooper a fur- or pile-lined leather or imitation leather cap having a flap at the sides and back that can be folded down to protect the ears or left up to show the lining, worn by mailmen, policemen, and, originally, by state troopers.

turban a head-wrapping; a linen scarf wound around the head.

Tyrolean see ALPINE.

watch cap a close-fitting, knitted cap having a turned-up cuff, originally navy blue and worn by sailors on watch, now a popular winter cap.

yarmulke an embroidered or crocheted fabric skullcap, worn by Orthodox Jewish men and, on religious occasions, by non-Orthodox Jewish men.

zucchetto a skullcap worn by a pope (white), a cardinal (red), or a bishop (purple).

COATS

admiral a double-breasted coat with gold buttons, modeled after those worn by U.S. Navy officers.

balmacaan a loose, full overcoat having raglan sleeves and small, turned-down collar, usually made of tweed.

car coat a short coat, originally designed to be worn while driving. Also known as a stadium coat, or mackinaw.

chesterfield a classic, single- or double-breasted overcoat with black velvet collar and concealed buttons.

clutch a woman's buttonless coat designed to be clutched together with the hand or worn open.

coachman's a double-breasted coat having large lapels and frequently, a cape collar and brass buttons; modeled after a 19th-century British coachman's coat.

cocoon a coat having large shoulders, batwing sleeves; it is cut to wrap about the body then taper to the hem like a cocoon.

coolie a short, square-shaped coat with kimono sleeves and frogs fasteners, modeled after those worn by Chinese workers.

duffel coat a short coat closed with toggles, designed after that worn by the British navy in World War II.

duster a woman's long, large-shouldered coat having large pockets.

greatcoat a large overcoat, worn by either sex.

Inverness a long coat with a detachable cape.

maxi an ankle-length coat, popular in the early 1970s.

midi any calf-length coat.

pink coat a crimson hunt coat with peaked lapels and black velvet collar, worn by both sexes. Also known as a hunt coat.

raccoon coat a long, large coat made of raccoon fur, popular in the 1920s and revived in the 1960s.

raglan a long, loose coat having extra-wide sleeves cut in one piece with the shoulders.

reefer a double-breasted car coat.

Regency a double-breasted coat with wide lapels and high rolled collar.

stadium a long, waterproof coat having two large pockets and a drawstring hood, worn at sporting events.

swallow-tailed a man's formal, open coat with long, scissorlike tails in the back.

tent woman's coat with a sharply flaring hem, like a tent, popular in the 1930s, 1940s, and 1960s.

toggle three-quarter length coat closed by toggles—barrel-shaped buttons passed through loops.

trench coat a long, loose-fitting overcoat or raincoat having several pockets and a belt.

yachting a double-breasted, navy blue wool coat with brass buttons.

Zhivago a long coat trimmed with fur at the neck, cuffs, and hem, modeled after that worn in the 1965 film *Dr. Zhivago*.

Collars

banded a stand-up collar that buttons.

Bermuda on a woman's blouse, a small, round collar forming right-angled corners and lying flat down the front.

bib any collar that extends over the top of a blouse or dress and drapes down like a child's bib.

bishop a large, rounded collar.

butterfly an oversized collar that hangs down in front in two points nearly to the waist, reminiscent of butterfly wings.

button-down a collar folded down and buttoned with tiny buttons to the front of the shirt.

choker a tight stand-up collar, often made of lace, that rises nearly to the chin and fastens in back. Also known as a Victorian collar.

clerical a stiff, white standing band collar worn by members of the clergy.

cowl a loose draperylike collar that rests around the shoulders.

cowl hood a cowl collar that can be pulled over the head and worn as a hood.

dog's ear a flat collar having rounded ends, reminiscent of a spaniel's ears.

jabot a standing collar with a ruffle hanging from the front.

Mandarin a standing band collar that does not quite meet in the front. Same as a Nehru.

Nehru a standing band collar that does not quite meet in the front, named after that worn by Prime Minister Nehru of India in the early 1960s.

Puritan a large, falling white band that drapes over the shoulders and is tied at the neck.

rolled any collar that extends up the neck and is then folded over.

sailor a large, square collar that drapes over the shoulders, forming a square in back and a V in front.

stand-up a banded collar.

swallow-tail a collar having long, narrow points, reminiscent of a swallow's tail.

turtleneck a soft or knitted, high-band collar extending nearly to the chin and often folded over.

Victorian see CHOKER.

Dresses

American Indian a suede or buckskin dress trimmed with beads and fringe.

Andean shift a Peruvian, straight-cut, embroidered dress.

baby doll a smocklike dress having a high neckline and a yoke, designed after doll clothes of the 1930s.

backless a dress having a low or no back.

ball gown a long, formal dress worn for high functions, characterized by a fitted bodice and full skirt.

bare-midriff a tropical, East Indian dress consisting of two pieces that leave the ribs bare.

bathrobe dress a wraparound dress held together by a sash.

blouson a bloused-top dress.

bouffant a dress having a snug-fitting bodice and a full, bell-shaped pleated or ruffled skirt.

bra-shift a sleeveless, figure-conforming shift.

bubble dress a dress having a fitted bodice and a full, bubblelike skirt, popular in the late 1950s.

bustle any dress having gathers of fabric protruding from the rump, popular in the 19th century.

caftan a full-length, robelike dress having embroidery around the neckline, a Moroccan design.

cardigan a dress reminiscent of a cardigan sweater, buttoned down the front and collarless, popular in the 1960s in various lengths, including minis.

chemise a straight-cut dress hanging straight from the shoulders with no waistline. Also known as a sack dress.

cheongsam a fitted, traditional Chinese dress, usually having a high collar and hanging to calf length, made of silk or satin.

coatdress a wool or wool blend dress with buttons or toggles, worn in professional or business settings.

cocktail dress a short evening dress with a décolleté neckline.

cutout a dress having holes or cutouts around the arms or midriff, popular in the 1960s.

dashiki an African-inspired, chemiselike dress having bell-shaped sleeves and decorated with an African panel or border print.

diamanté a glittery article of clothing, consisting of beads, sequins, or paillettes.

dinner a formal dress with covered shoulders, worn with a jacket.

dirndl a bell-shaped dress having a gathered waistline and attached to a snugfitting bodice.

Empire dress a dress with a very high waistline, raised right below the bust.

Ethiopian shirtdress a basic shift trimmed with embroidery of Ethiopian design.

evening gown any formal gown or ball gown.

fitted formfitting or clinging to one's body outline.

flamenco a dress having a long top and a flounced skirt, reminiscent of Spanish flamenco dancers.

flapper a dress having a long torso and a short skirt, popular in the 1920s and revived in the 1960s.

granny dress an old fashioned, ankle-length dress having a high, tight neckline and long sleeves trimmed with ruffles.

halter dress a sleeveless dress with either spaghetti straps or material that ties at the back of the neck.

Juliet a medieval-style dress having puffy sleeve tops and a high waistline, inspired by Shakespeare's Juliet.

kabuki a wraparound dress having kimono sleeves and no collar, held together by sash; inspired by Japanese actors in the kabuki theater.

kiltie dress designed after the Scottish kilt, with wrap skirt closed with a safety pin.

kimono a wraparound dress held together by a sash, inspired by the Japanese kimono robe.

maternity any dress designed with a full front for the comfort of pregnant women.

maxi an ankle-length dress, popular 1969 to 1970.

mermaid formfitting, curve-revealing dress that fits tightly around the torso and waist and flares at the calf.

micro a very short minidress, riding to the top of the thigh, popular in the 1960s.

midi any calf-length dress; first introduced in 1967.

minidress a short-skirted dress popular in the 1960s and reintroduced in the mid-1980s.

monk a cowl-necked dress having bell sleeves and a cord belt, designed after a monk's robe.

muumuu a loose-fitting, ankle-length, Hawaiian, floral-print dress.

patio a light, floral-print shift.

peasant European peasant-style dress having a tight bodice, puffed sleeves, drawstring neckline, and a gathered skirt.

peplum a narrow dress having a short overskirt or ruffle extending below the waistline, popular in the 1930s, 1960s, and again in the 1980s.

pinafore a child's sleeveless dress worn with a separate bib-top apron tied in the back, introduced in 1870.

Pocahontas dress see AMERICAN INDIAN.

prairie an old-fashioned dress having a stand-up neckline, gathered sleeves at the shoulders and bands at the wrist, accompanied by a gored skirt with ruffled hem.

rhumba a dress having a ruffled skirt split up the front, inspired by Carmen Miranda in the 1940s.

sack a chemise.

safari a dress reminiscent of a safari or bush jacket, having multiple pockets on the chest.

sailor a dress having a sailor-suit collar, popular from 1890 to 1930.

sari a gold-embroidered silk or cotton dress wrapped about the waist with one loose end draped over the shoulder or covering the head, a Hindu design.

sarong a brightly colored dress wrapped about the waist and draped to one side, an Indonesian design.

seloso a long, flowing African dress.

sheath a snug-fitting dress with a narrow skirt slashed in the back to make walking possible.

shift a chemise.

shirtdress a dress hanging straight from the shoulders and buttoned down the front, as a man's shirt.

shirtwaist dress a classic dress with a shirtlike top, buttoned down to the waist, accompanied by a full or straight skirt, popular in the 1930s, 1940s, and 1980s.

slip dress a dress hanging straight from shoulder straps.

spaghetti straps thin strips of material that hold a dress or shirt at the shoulders, leaving the arms bare.

square dancing a dress having puffed sleeves and a full, circular skirt, for square and folk dancing.

step-in a coat-like dress that buttons or zips three-fourths of the way down.

strapless a dress ending at the top of the bosom and held in place by shirring or boning.

sundress a strapless or halter-style dress.

sweater dress a knitted dress.

tent dress a triangular-shaped dress, introduced in the 1960s.

toga an elegant dress that leaves one shoulder uncovered; from the Roman design.

T-shirt dress a dress with the fabric and style of a T-shirt.

vintage any classic dress from another era.

wedge a tapering, V-shaped dress having large shoulders and dolman sleeves.

wrap a wraparound dress.

FABRICS AND FABRIC DESIGNS

abattre quilted or depressed effects in fabric.

abercrombie Scottish tartan with a blue and black ground and a green and white overcheck.

accordion pleat see PLEAT.

acrylic a synthetic fiber derived from coal, water, petroleum, and limestone.

alpaca cousin of the llama, from which fleece of variegated color is obtained.

angora the hair of the Angora rabbit or Angora goat.

antique lace see LACE.

appliqué fabric pieces cut out and attached to another fabric for decorative effect.

argyle knit a decorative design pattern in which diamonds are crossed by narrow stripes, found on socks and sweaters.

artificial silk an early name for rayon.

awning stripes see STRIPES, AWNING.

bagheera a crease-resistant, uncut pile velvet.

bargello decorative needlepoint characterized by geometric designs, diamonds, and flames.

batik Indonesian dyeing method using wax to cover areas to be left undyed. It often has a streaked or veined appearance where dye has worked through cracks in the wax.

batiste a light, sheer, combed muslin.

beetling a method of pounding linen to produce a surface with a sheen.

bird's-eye a woven fabric with a bird's-eye or dot in the center of the pattern.

blister any design, such as a flower, that bumps out from the fabric.

bolt a quantity of fabric, usually from 15 to 20 yards.

box pleat see PLEAT.

braid fabric made by interlacing three or more yarns or fabrics.

broadcloth a lustrous, tightly woven fabric having a fine rib.

brocade a heavy, jacquard-woven fabric having raised floral or other patterns, often made with metallic threads.

brushing a technique in which a fabric is combed by wire bristles to produce a nap, as in blankets or brushed denim.

buckskin deer or elk leather.

calico any fabric having small, bright, and colorful print designs.

canvas strong, plain-weave fabric, usually made of cotton. Also known as duck-cloth or sailcloth.

cashmere fabric or yarn made from the very soft wool that grows underneath the outer hair of the cashmere (Kashmir) goat.

cavalry twill a strong, twilled fabric used in uniforms and riding breeches.

chalk stripe see STRIPES, CHALK.

challis a soft, light fabric printed with bright floral patterns or paisley patterns.

chambray a fine, light gingham having a colored warp and a white filling.

chamois a soft, pliable leather from the chamois goat. Also, a cloth woven to imitate this leather.

chantilly see LACE, CHANTILLY.

check any small pattern of squares, woven or printed on a fabric.

check, houndstooth pointed checks.

check, pin very small checks.

chenille a soft, tufted cord used for fringes.

chiffon a sheer silk or rayon fabric, used in women's dresses.

chino a sturdy, twilled cotton fabric having a slight sheen, used in uniforms and men's work or casual pants.

chintz a glazed cotton fabric printed in bright designs, used mostly in drapes and upholstery.

cloque a blistered fabric.

corded a fabric having lengthwise ribs, as in corduroy.

corduroy corded, cut-pile fabric, usually made from cotton.

crepe a soft fabric having a crinkled surface.

damask a fabric having a heavy jacquard weave, used in tablecloths and in some clothing.

denim a coarse twill-weave fabric, used in jeans.

dobby a fabric with woven geometric figures.

duckcloth another name for canvas.

duffel cloth a thick, heavy fabric used in some coats.

dungaree heavy blue denim.

embroidery decorative stitches made with thread or yarn.

faille a finely ribbed, dressy fabric used in evening clothes and shoes.

fishnet a coarse fabric with holes, used for curtains and for hosiery.

flannel a soft wool or cotton fabric having a brushed surface.

fleece the wool of an animal.

flock waste fibers in near-powder form, applied in decorative patterns (flock printing) on other fabrics.

Fortrel trademark name for a polyester fiber.

foulard a plain or twill-weaved, lightweight, soft fabric used for neckties and scarves.

gabardine a strong, twill-weaved fabric, made from all types of fibers.

georgette a sheer, crepelike fabric, similar to chiffon.

gingham a yarn-dyed fabric woven with checks, plaids, or stripes.

glazed of a fabric, having a shiny surface. Also known as glace.

gossamer any very sheer, light fabric.

ground the background color on which other colors or designs are made.

harlequin a diamond design, from the original harlequin costume of the 16th century.

Harris tweed hand-woven tweed, derived from yarns spun on islands off the coast of Scotland, including Harris Island.

heather resembling heather, referring to a misty effect on fabric produced by cross-dyeing or by using contrasting warp and filling yarns.

herringbone a twill weave with a V pattern.

honeycomb a weave that resembles a honeycomb pattern.

houndstooth see CHECK, HOUNDSTOOTH.

Irish tweed a tweed made in Ireland, characterized by a white warp with colored filling threads.

jacquard any fabric with a woven or knitted design.

khaki a fabric having an earth or olive green color, as in military uniforms.

knit, double a fabric made in two layers.

knit, jacquard any design knit into a fabric.

lace, aloe a lace made from aloe plant fibers.

lace, antique a heavy, coarse, open form of darned lace, used in curtains. Also called spider work.

lace, binch a lace of handmade motifs attached to a net ground.

lace, bourdon scroll-patterned lace with heavy thread outline.

lace, Chantilly a popular bridal lace characterized by delicate scrolls, branches, and flowers.

lace, Irish crochet and needlepoint type laces made in Ireland.

lace, Venise needlepoint lace in a floral pattern edged with small, decorative loops.

lamé fabric made from metallic yarns, used in evening dresses.

lawn a sheer, lightweight, plain-weave fabric.

leather the cleaned hide of an animal.

linen one of the oldest fabrics, made from flax.

lisle two-ply cotton or wool yarn used for socks.

Lycra trademark name for spandex fiber.

mackinaw a thick, heavy, coarse fabric, named after blankets made by the Mackinaw Indians, now found in plaid or checked hunting jackets.

macramé a method of knotting and weaving to produce a coarse lacework.

madras a fine-textured cotton cloth from Madras, India, usually having a checked, striped, or plaid pattern whose dyes eventually bleed into one another after several washings.

marl a yarn made from different colored yarns.

matelassé fabric having a quilted or blistered appearance, produced with the use of puckered material.

matte having a dull, flat finish.

merino a fine, dense wool derived from the merino sheep.

metallic fibers human-made metal or metal-covered fibers.

middy twill a durable twill-weave fabric.

mohair the long, shiny hair of the Angora goat.

monk's cloth a heavy, coarse fabric that is loosely woven, used in draperies and in some clothing.

motif a design that is usually repeated in a pattern on a fabric.

muslin a plain weave fabric made of cotton and human-made fibers in various weights; used in sheets and in making prototypes of garments to save cutting expensive material.

naked wool sheer, lightweight woolen fabric.

nap a hairy, fuzzy, or soft surface, produced by brushing with wire bristles.

napping the brushing process that produces nap on a fabric.

needlepoint decorative needlework or embroidery on open fabric.

nun's veiling a plain-weave, light-weight, sheer fabric used by nuns for veils.

oilskin waterproof raincoat fabric.

organdy a sheer, lightweight fabric used in curtains, blouses, and evening wear.

Orlon trademark name for DuPont acrylic fiber.

ottoman wool, silk, or human-made fabric having wide, horizontal ribs, used in evening wear.

Oxford gray a very dark gray used in men's suits and slacks.

paisley swirling, conelike design woven or printed on fabric. A soft wool fabric having this design.

Panama a lightweight wool worsted used in summer suits.

patchwork combining bits or patches of different materials to create a large piece, as a quilt.

pebble refers to fabric having a bumpy or grainy surface.

percale a blend of combed and carded cotton and human-made fibers, used in sheets; softer and smoother than muslin.

picot an edging consisting of a series of small, decorative loops.

pile a nappy fabric surface composed of cut or uncut loops of yarn.

piqué a fabric having woven, raised geometrical patterns.

plaid, argyle a plaid pattern of diamonds.

pleat a permanently set fold of fabric.

pleats, accordion very narrow, straight pleats.

pleats, box a double pleat made by two facing folds.

pleats, knife narrow, straight pleats running in one direction.

pleats, sunburst pleats that radiate out to the edge of a skirt.

plissé a fabric that has been permanently puckered by a chemical or heat process.

plush thick deep pile.

pointillism printing dots on a fabric to give the illusion of a solid color from a distance.

polyester a strong, wrinkle-resistant, human-made fiber.

poodle cloth looped fabric used in coats.

poplin shiny, durable imitation silk with a fine, horizontal rib, used for dresses.

printing the application of a colored pattern or design onto a fabric.

rayon the first human-made fiber, originally known as artificial silk, used in some women's apparel.

rib a cord or ridge running vertically or horizontally.

sailcloth see CANVAS.

sateen a strong, shiny satin weave fabric made of cotton.

satin a glossy-faced fabric made of silk, cotton, rayon, or nylon.

satin, crepe-backed fabric having a satin face and a crepe back, used in jacket or coat linings.

satin, duchesse a rich, heavy satin used in formal wear.

scallops decorative edging composed of semicircular curves.

seersucker a lightweight, puckered fabric that is often striped but may also be plain, plaid, or printed.

sequin a decorative, metallic spangle.

serge a smooth, twill-weave fabric used in suits.

sheer transparent or nearly transparent.

Shetland yarn very soft, fluffy, two-ply yarn, spun from the wool of sheep on the Shetland Islands off the coast of Scotland.

shirring gathers of fabric used to create fullness, used in women's apparel.

silk material produced by the silk worm, now largely replaced by human-made fibers.

smocking rows of shirring given to a fabric to provide stretch and decoration.

spandex a synthetic elastic fiber used in stretch pants and other elastic clothing.

stripes, awning stripes at least 1½ inches wide.

stripes, chalk narrow white stripes on a dark fabric.

stripes, pin very narrow stripes of any color.

stripes, Roman narrow, colored stripes that cover the entire surface of a fabric.

studs small, decorative, rivetlike ornaments attached to fabrics (especially denim jackets) when in style.

suede leather having a soft, napped surface.

taffeta a crisp, plain-weave fabric with a shiny surface, used in women's apparel and noted for its "rustling" noise.

taffeta, antique a stiff taffeta reminiscent of that made in the 18th century.

taffeta paper a very light, crisp taffeta for evening wear.

tartan a pattern of intersecting, colored stripes, associated with a specific Scottish family or clan. A plaid.

tartan, Barclay a yellow background crossed with wide black stripes and narrower white stripes.

tartan, Black Watch a light blue background crossed with green stripes, worn by the 42nd Royal Highland Regiment.

tartan, Campbell a blue background crossed with green stripes and dark blue stripes.

tartan, Cumming dark and light green stripes combined with red and blue stripes.

tartan, Ogilvie a complex pattern of red, yellow, greenish blue, and dark blue stripes.

tartan, Rob Roy red and black check pattern, as that used on hunting jackets.

tartan, Stewart a red or white background spaced widely with narrow stripes of blue, white, and yellow.

terry cloth soft, absorbent cotton or cotton-blend fabric having uncut loops on one or both sides, used in robes and towels.

textured yarn yarn that has been crimped, coiled, or curled.

tweed a rough, strong, nubby wool or human-made fabric, used primarily in suits and coats.

twill a fabric woven with diagonal ribs.

velour a soft fabric having a thick, short pile.

velvet rich, soft-textured warp (made from warp threads) pile fabric.

velveteen a soft, cotton fabric with a cut pile thicker than corduroy. Pile is made of filling threads, as distinguished from the warp threads used in velvet.

vicuña expensive wool from the vicuña, a wild relative of the South American llama.

virgin fibers fibers that have never been processed (as remnant fibers) in a fabric before.

virgin wool see virgin fibers of wool.

voile a crisp, lightweight, sheer fabric used in blouses and curtains.

wale the lengthwise ribs on corduroy or other fabric.

wale, pin narrow ribbing.

wale, wide wide ribbing.

warp the yarns woven first on a loom when a fabric is made; it forms the length of a fabric, as distinguished from the filling threads that are woven under and over the warp in a crosswise fashion.

wash-and-wear needing little or no ironing.

weft another name for the filling threads woven over and under the warp.

wool fleece of a sheep or other animal.

worsted fabric made of yarns that have been combed and carded; it is smoother and cleaner (less fuzzy) than ordinary wool.

FASHION STYLES

Afro native African style characterized by Afro haircuts and such African garments as bubas, dashikis, and selosos, popular in the late 1960s and early 1970s.

American Indian style characterized by beads and fringed, deerskin dresses and pants.

androgynous a style combining male and female characteristics, for example, women wearing men's haircuts and suits and men wearing long hair and earrings.

Annie Hall a style characterized by baggy pants, challis skirts, and a general uncoordinated look, inspired by the movie of the same name in the 1970s.

baby doll a style characterized by childlike or doll-like attire, such as baby doll or Mary Jane shoes, gathered or pleated dresses.

Bonnie and Clyde inspired by the movie *Bonnie and Clyde,* an attire that includes pinstripe gangster suits, above-the-knee skirts from the 1930s, and a woman's beret worn to the side.

Brooks Brothers tailored businessperson's look characterized by button-down collars, tailored skirts, Ivy League suits, trenchcoats, balmacaan coats, and so on.

Carnaby the mod look of the 1960s, featuring miniskirts, polka-dot shirts with large white collars, bell-bottom pants, and newsboy caps, named after Carnaby Street in London where it originated.

cowpunk an amalgamation of punk and western looks, for example, fringed jackets, miniskirts, chains, western belts, punk or dyed hairstyles.

dandy a style characterized by ruffles at the neck and wrists, worn by both sexes in the 1960s and 1970s.

denim jeans and jeans jackets.

Edwardian an early 1900s fashion characterized by regency collars, capes, and neck ruffles.

ethnic any style that borrows from the fashions of other nations; may include gypsy, harem, and peasant clothes.

flapper look style borrowing from the flappers of the 1920s, featuring long-torso dresses ornamented with beads and ropes of pearls, short bob haircuts, and so on.

funky a 1960s or early 1970s look featuring platform shoes, newsboy hats, or faded dresses.

gaucho Argentine cowboy style featuring calf-length pants, long-sleeved blouses, boleros, and gaucho hats, popular with women in the 1960s and 1970s.

Gibson girl classic look of the late 1800s to early 1900s and revived many times; it features lace-trim blouses with leg-of-mutton sleeves and high, choker collars, long, gathered skirts, pompadour hairstyles, and so on.

goth originating in the 1980s, a style characterized by the use of black or dark-colored clothes and shoes, black lipstick, pale face makeup, and large silver jewelry.

granny look old-fashioned, ankle-length dresses with ruffled neckline and hem.

grunge look a dirty or unkempt look.

gypsy a look featuring hoop earrings, head scarves, shawls, boleros, and full skirts.

harem a look typified by ankle-length harem pants, bare midriff, chains, and sandals. Also known as the Arabian Nights look.

hip hop a style and cultural movement originating in the late 1970s, but not gaining mainstream acceptance until the 1980s, 1990s, and later. It was introduced to the mainstream by rap stars appearing on rap videos. It is largely characterized by loose, droopy clothing, such as baggy pants or oversized jerseys, expensive sneakers, sports or trucker's caps worn partially to the side, and large, clunky jewelry, or "bling bling." Do-rags, velour suits, and designer clothing are also widely worn.

hippie a slack, unkempt look featuring long hair, tie-dyed shirts, tank tops, old jeans, miniskirts, love beads, and peace symbols.

hunt look a riding apparel look featuring jodhpurs, stirrup pants, derby, stock tie, pleated trousers, full-length coat; mid-length, side-slitted skirt worn with boots, velvet jacket.

Japanese any bulky, oversized robelike fashions.

kiltie look Scottish look featuring kiltlike skirts in plaids, knee socks, tam-o'-shanter or glengarry caps.

maxi ankle-length skirts, dresses, coats.

midi calf-length skirts, dresses, coats.

military armed forces look featuring camouflage pants, fatigues, combat boots.

peasant old-world fashions featuring full skirts, puffed sleeves, drawstring necklines, aprons.

prairie a Midwest style characterized by long, calico dresses with long sleeves and high neckline.

preppy the upper-class student look featuring Ivy League shirts, cashmere sweaters, chinos and corduroys, oxfords, loafers, pumps.

punk rebellious teen look of the 1980s, featuring chains, safety pins, torn clothes, heavy lipstick, strange haircuts (mohawk, spikes, shaved, dyed), black leather jackets, slitted skirts.

retro any styles from the past.

Tyrolean an Austrian or Bavarian look featuring dirndl skirts and embroidered vests, Lederhosen, knee socks, and Alpine hats.

vintage classic fashions from the past.

western western cowboy look featuring tight jeans, cowboy shirts, string ties, Stetson hats, tooled-leather belts.

FOOTWEAR

BOOTS

Beatle ankle-high boots with pointed toes, made famous by the Beatles in the 1960s.

chukka ankle-high boot having a rubber sole, laced down the front.

combat a rugged leather, waterproof, laced boot worn by the military.

cowboy high boots having pointed or square toes and ornate, tooled leather.

galoshes waterproof boots worn over shoes and fastened with a buckle or a zipper.

go-go woman's calf-high, white boots, fashionable with miniskirts in the 1960s.

granny woman's old-fashioned high boot laced up the front.

hip thigh-high, rubber fishing boots.

jodhpur ankle-high boot buckled at the side, worn with horseback-riding attire.

mukluk calf-high Eskimo boots made from walrus, seal, or reindeer hide.

pac boot calf-high, insulated or noninsulated, leather or rubber boot having a heavy tread, a popular work and hunting boot.

police high, black leather boot, worn by motorcycle police.

squaw bootie ankle-high buckskin boot fringed around the top and trimmed with beads.

uggs Australian fleece-lined, sheepskin boots, in various colors and heights, made popular by celebrities in 2003 and after.

waders waterproof pant-boots extending to the waist or higher and held up by suspenders.

Wellington a boot covering the leg to the knee in front but cut lower in back.

PARTS OF A SHOE

aglet the metal tag at the end of a lace. Also known as a tag.

cuff the upper ridge around the back of the shoe.

eyelet a hole through which a lace is threaded.

eyelet tab a reinforced leather or fabric in which eyelets are punched.

heel a flat or platformed section corresponding with the heel of the foot.

insole the inner sole of a shoe.

instep the arching portion of the upper foot.

shank the narrow portion of the sole, under the instep. Also the material used to reinforce this area.

sole the bottom supporting member of the shoe.

tongue the flap under the laces or buckle of a shoe.

upper the part of the shoe above the sole.

vamp the part of the shoe covering the instep.

welt the material wedged between the sole and the upper.

SANDALS

alpargata rope-soled sandals with canvas uppers around the heels, worn in South America and Spain.

clog sandals having a thick wooden or cork sole and either a toe-covering material or straps.

flip-flops see ZORI.

Ganymede a Greek-style sandal with straps that lace up the calf.

geta a Japanese sandal raised on two wooden blocks at the toe and the heel.

gladiator Roman-style sandal with several straps running around the foot from the toes to the lower ankle.

huarache a sling-backed, leather thong with a flat heel, a Mexican design.

platform an open sandal noted for its high-heeled, platformed sole.

thongs flat sandals with leather straps running between the first and second toes.

zori a rubber sandal with straps running between the first and second toes. Also called flip-flops.

SHOES

baby doll shoes having wide, round toes and low heels, similar to Mary Janes.

boat a canvas shoe having a nonskid, rubber sole to prevent slipping on wet decks. Also called deck shoes.

brogan a heavy, ankle-high work shoe.

chain loafer a slip-on, moccasinlike shoe trimmed with metal links.

Chinese a fabric shoe having a crepe sole, a flat heel, and rounded toe, the most common shoe in China.

clog a sandal-like shoe having a thick cork or wood sole.

deck see BOAT.

espadrille a canvas shoe with a rope sole and laced up around the ankle. Most modern versions, however, have no laces.

golf oxford-style shoe with a rubber sole and rubber spikes.

Indian moccasin a heel-less, soft leather shoe, often trimmed with beads or fringe.

kiltie flat a low-heeled shoe with a fringed tongue.

loafer a moccasinlike shoe with a strap attached to the vamp. Popular types are the chain loafer and the penny loafer.

Mary Jane a low-heeled shoe with a blunt toe and a strap buttoned or buckled at the center or the side.

Miranda pump a pump with a high, flaring heel, named after Carmen Miranda.

mule a woman's backless shoe or slipper.

open-toed a woman's shoe with an open toe.

oxford a low, strong shoe that laces over the instep; it is made in a variety of styles.

penny loafer a loafer with a strap with a slot over the instep for the insertion of a penny or other coin.

platform a shoe with a raised wood or cork platform, popular with people who wished to appear taller in the 1960s and 1990s.

pump a woman's low-cut, strapless shoe with a medium to high heel and fitting snugly around the toe and heel.

Ruby Keeler a woman's low-heeled pump tied with a ribbon across the instep.

saddle shoe an oxford made of white buck calf with a brown leather "saddle" extending over the middle of the shoe.

safety shoe a work shoe having a reinforced or steel toe to help prevent injuries.

skimmer a very low cut woman's pump with a flat heel.

slingback any pump or other shoe with an open back and a heel strap.

stocking shoe a soft shoe permanently attached to a heavy stocking.

tuxedo pump a low-heeled pump with a round toe.

wedgies a woman's shoe having a thick wedge-shaped heel that joins with the sole.

white bucks white leather oxfords.

wing-tip an oxford decorated with perforations at the toe and extending along the sides.

GLASSES AND SUNGLASSES

aviator's sunglasses modeled after the goggles worn by early airplane pilots, characterized by oversized lenses.

Ben Franklins delicate glasses having small, elliptical, octagonal or oblong lenses, worn on the middle of the nose. Also known as granny glasses.

bifocals glasses having lenses divided to aid both closeup and distant vision.

butterfly glasses rimless sunglasses with lenses shaped like butterfly wings.

clip-ons frameless sunglasses that clip on over the lenses of prescription glasses.

Courrèges headband-like sunglasses consisting of a strip of opaque plastic wrapping around the face to the ears, with a narrow strip of glass or plastic in the center.

granny see BEN FRANKLINS.

half-glasses reading glasses having half-lenses to allow the eyes to peer over the rims to focus on a distant object.

harlequin glasses with diamond-shaped lenses.

horn-rimmed glasses having heavy, dark, or mottled brown frames.

Lennon specs sunglasses having circular, metal-rimmed lenses, named after those worn by Beatle John Lennon.

lorgnette glasses having a handle for holding instead of frames.

monocle a single lens attached to a ribbon worn around the neck.

owl oversized sunglasses with wide rims and broad lenses.

pince-nez frameless glasses having circular lenses that pinch in place over the bridge of the nose.

planos fake glasses having dark rims to provide a "studious look," worn only for fashion.

tortoiseshell glasses having frames made from authentic or imitation tortoiseshell, usually mottled brown.

wraparound wide sunglasses that wrap around the front of the head like a headband.

JACKETS

(*Also see* COATS)

bellhop a waist-length jacket with a standing collar and two rows of brass buttons, sometimes ornamented with gold braid.

blouson a bloused jacket with a knitted or gathered waistband.

bolero a sleeveless, collarless, buttonless, waist-length, vestlike jacket, worn by Spanish bullfighters and adopted for general fashion.

box a woman's straight, unfitted suit or dress jacket.

dinner jacket a man's white jacket worn at semiformal occasions.

gendarme a jacket having brass buttons down the front, on the sleeves and on the pockets, fashioned after those worn by French policemen.

Mandarin a Chinese-style jacket with a standing band collar.

Nehru an Indian-style jacket with a standing band collar.

smoking jacket a man's velvet jacket tied with a sash.

toreador a woman's waist-length jacket with epaulet shoulders, fashioned after that worn by bullfighters.

JEWELRY

(*Also see* ROCKS AND GEMS)

aigrette a bejeweled, featherlike ornament worn in the hair.

alloy a mix of two or more metals, for example, gold and copper.

alpaca a silver substitute, an alloy made of copper, nickel, zinc, and tin.

amber a yellowish, semi-clear stone, made of fossilized tree resin. It is not officially considered amber unless it is at least 1 million years old.

amulet a good luck charm or fetish worn around the neck.

ankh a cross with a loop at the top, often used as an Egyptian amulet.

anneal to heat metal so that it can be softened and worked for jewelry making.

arabesque ornamental metalwork, in the shape of scrolls, leaves, flowers, and lines.

Ascher cut an octagon-like cut consisting of 72 facets.

assaying the measuring of the precise percentage of pure gold or silver in a piece of gold or silver.

baguette resembling the French bread of the same name, a gemstone cut into a rectangular shape.

bail an attachment on a pendant that allows it to be hung on a chain or a necklace.

Bakelite a moldable plastic used in jewelry, popular during the Great Depression.

bananabell a curved or banana-shaped shaft worn as a piercing through the navel or brow.

band another name for a ring, especially a wedding band.

bangle any solid or nonflexible bracelet.

bar and ring clasp an attaching device, consisting of a toggle or bar and a ring clasp, used to fasten the two ends of a bracelet or necklace.

bar brooch a long, rectangular brooch.

baroque an irregular pearl or an irregular bead or stone.

baroque pearl any pearl with an irregular shape.

bar pin a long or rectangular pin.

barrel clasp a chain attachment that screws the ends of a chain together and resembles a barrel.

barrette a hair ornament.

basket a lacy setting.

baton a stone cut into a narrow, rectangular length, larger than a baguette.

bauble any showy but cheap or worthless piece of jewelry.

bayadere strands of pearls entwined to form a necklace.

bead made of plastic, glass, or wood, a small ball with a hole in its center and threaded together with other beads to make a necklace or bracelet.

belly ring any ring worn in the belly button.

beveled in a gem, cut off at the corners or sides at less than 90 degrees.

bezel setting a ring setting in which the stone is surrounded by a collar of gold or silver instead of prongs.

bib necklace any necklace with strands or components that hang down and cover the top of the chest, like a bib.

birthstone originating from astrology, a stone that represents the month in which one is born. The official Jewelers of America list is as follows:

January—garnet
February—amethyst
March—aquamarine
April—diamond
May—emerald
June—pearl or moonstone
July—ruby
August—peridot
September—sapphire
October—opal
November—citrine
December—turquoise or blue topaz

Biwa pearl a lustrous, irregularly shaped pearl from Lake Biwa in Japan.

black gold gold that has been electroplated with black rhodium or rutherium or which has been subjected to a lasering technique that turns the metal deep black.

blemish a chip, scratch, or any other imperfection in a stone.

bling modern slang for jewelry that tends to be oversized and often diamond-studded, for the purpose of showing off.

blister pearl see BOUTON PEARL.

bloomed gold any gold jewelry that has been treated with acid in order to give it a textured appearance.

blue gold an alloy of gold and iron, which creates a bluish tinge.

bodkin a long, decorative, and sometimes bejeweled hairpin.

body jewelry any jewelry, such as a ring or stud, attached to the belly button, nose, lip, eyebrow, toe, or nipple.

Bohemian diamond a fake diamond, actually rock crystal.

Bohemian ruby a fake ruby, actually pyrope garnet.

bolo a cord with an ornamental clasp worn like a necktie.

bombe a bulging setting.

bone any animal bone used to make jewelry.

book chain popular in Victorian times, a chain, usually gold or silver, with rectangular links resembling tiny books.

botanical gem any gem that originates with a plant, such as amber from tree resin or pearl opal from bamboo.

bouton pearl also known as a blister pearl, a naturally formed, hemispherical or half-pearl, most often used in earrings.

box chain a chain with square links.

box clasp on either end of a chain, a tiny, notched box and a knobbed spring, used to attach the ends together.

bracelet a loop of chain, beads, gems, or other decorative components worn around the wrist.

Brazilian chain a chain with cuplike links. Also known as a snake chain.

bridal set a matching engagement and wedding ring.

bridge piercing pierced studs, jewels or balls, worn on either side of the bridge of the nose.

brilliance another term for a stone's sparkle.

brilliant cut a round cut with 58 facets to produce the highest level of brilliance.

briolette a teardrop-shaped pendant cut with triangular facets.

brooch a decorative pin that attaches to clothing or may be used to clasp a garment together.

brushed finish tiny lines brushed or scratched onto a surface to add texture.

buttercup setting resembling a buttercup flower, a setting with six prongs.

button earring an earring that lies flush against the earlobe and does not dangle.

cable chain a chain with ringlike links.

cabochon a domed, nonfaceted gemstone, usually cut in an opal shape and having a flat bottom.

calibrated referring to a stone that has been cut to a standard size.

calibre cut oblong-shaped cuts made in small stones.

California ruby a fake ruby, actually pyrope garnet.

cameo originating in ancient Greece and popular again in the 18th and 19th centuries, an ornamental pin of a low-relief portrait of a woman, goddess, or a royal figure on a plain background and often carved from shell.

cameo habille a cameo in which a carved likeness of a woman or a goddess is herself wearing a tiny component of jewelry, such as a diamond necklace.

camphor glass a cloudy white glass from which jewelry was often made in the second half of the 19th century.

cannetille decorative scrolling made from gold wire.

captive bead ring in body piercing, a ring with a tiny opening, into which a tiny bead or gem is inserted to secure attachment to a nostril, ear lobe, nipple, or other body part.

carat a measure of weight used for gemstones, with one carat equaling one-fifth of a gram, or 200 milligrams.

carbon spot a flaw in a diamond.

carbuncle any deep red garnet cut into a cabochon.

celluloid an imitation ivory made of cellulose plastic.

Celtic jewelry originating in Ireland, Scotland, Wales, and Brittany, various pieces of jewelry made from bronze, silver, gold, cairngorm, and amethyst.

Celtic revival a style of jewelry fashioned after the original Celtic jewelry, popular in the 19th century.

center stone in a ring setting, the most valuable stone, often a diamond, situated in the center.

certification a certified grading of a gem's quality and characteristics, provided by a gem expert.

chain a metal strand with links in the shape of rings, squares, cable, etc., used for bracelets and necklaces.

chandelier earrings any showy, dangling earrings that resemble chandeliers.

channel inlay in a piece of jewelry, a recess or groove lined with mother of pearl, turquoise, or other gemstones.

chaplet a circlet, garland, or wreath, sometimes bejeweled, worn on the head.

charm any kind of small trinket or novelty hung from a bracelet, necklace, or earring. Charms may be simple ornaments or tiny figures of a book, bicycle, heart, animal, or virtually any object.

charm bracelet any chain bracelet decorated or hung with charms.

charm ring any ring decorated with a charm.

chasing decorative indentations made in metal.

chatelaine an ornamental clasp worn at the waist and hung with chains that held a purse or a case with various housekeeping items, from keys to pencils to scissors, popular in the 19th century.

chaton a rhinestone or crystal shaped like a cone.

choker a necklace worn snugly around the neck, like a collar.

Christina a piercing through which a bead or ball is attached, in the outer labia of the female genitals, just below the pubic mound.

cigar band on a ring, a broad band.

Claddagh ring a traditional Irish ring, originating in the 17th century in the town of Claddagh, and given as a gesture of friendship or to symbolize a formal engagement or marriage. It typically has two hands clasping a heart topped with a crown. When worn on the right hand, with the heart pointed out, the wearer can be assumed to be unattached or single. With the heart pointing in, the wearer is typically involved with someone. On the left hand, an outward pointing heart symbolizes that the wearer is engaged and an inward-pointing one, married.

clarity the clearness of a gem, with the highest clarity having no imperfections.

clasp a connector or attaching device for a bracelet, necklace, or watch.

class ring an engraved ring commemorating graduation from school.

claw any of the metal prongs that holds a gem in place in a setting.

claw setting a ring setting in which a stone is held in place by prongs.

clip-on designating any piece of jewelry, such as an earring, that can be attached with a simple clip or pinching device.

cloud any milky spot in a diamond.

cluster a grouping of stones in a setting.

cluster earring an earring having multiple stones or beads.

cluster ring any ring having a large central stone surrounded by several smaller ones.

cocktail ring popular in the 1950s and 1960s, a very large, showy ring set with various stones.

coiffe a silver or gold-threaded netting worn on the head, often decorated with various gems or pearls.

collar see CHOKER.

collarette see BIB NECKLACE.

color in a diamond, referring to the absolute absence of color.

composite suite any piece of jewelry having two or more components that can be disassembled and worn separately.

conch a white or pink shell with a pearl-like finish, used in making cameos, beads, or other jewelry.

conch piercing an earring piercing located in cartilage near the middle of the ear instead of in the lobe.

costume jewelry inexpensive and flashy jewelry, made with imitation gemstones and other cheap materials.

cowrie shell brightly colored tropical seashell used to make beads.

Crawford see MONROE.

crown in a setting, the topmost part of a diamond or any cut stone.

crystal any clear or partially clear natural stone, such as diamonds, emeralds, or quartz. Also, a manufactured glass containing at least 10 percent lead oxide, which produces exceptional clearness.

crystalline containing a crystal or crystals or resembling a crystal.

crystallize to form into a crystal or crystals.

Cuban link chain any metal chain with twisting, ropelike links.

cubic zirconia composed of zirconium oxide and yttrium oxide melted together, a clear, dense crystal that closely resembles and is often substituted for diamonds.

cuff bracelet a wide bangle or bracelet.

cuff link a fastener that serves as a fancy or decorative alternative to a button to close the cuff of a shirt.

cultured pearl a pearl naturally produced after a human artificially introduces an irritant, such as a sand grain or piece of shell into the opening of an oyster. The oyster secretes a lustrous substance called nacre to cover the irritant, and over time successive layers form into a pearl.

cut referring to the shaping and faceting of a finished gem.

cut beads beads that have been cut with facets.

cut glass any glass that has been cut with facets, for a decorative effect.

daith piercing a piercing for an earring that is not in the earlobe but above it, in the middle of the ear, in a portion of cartilage.

demilune any gemstone shaped like a half moon.

demiparure earrings, necklace, and pin that come in a matching set.

diadem a jeweled tiara.

diamanté a rhinestone.

diamond cut rope any chain made with diamond-shaped links.

dichoric glass specially made glass that reflects dual colors and is made into cabochons.

diffusion heating a stone along with iron oxide or chrome oxide to create additional surface color, sometimes used with sapphires and topaz.

dog collar a chokerlike necklace.

domed convex in shape, as with many earring and pendant styles.

doublet a thin or fragile piece of gemstone layered on top of a less expensive piece of stone, such as ironstone. Also a thin gemstone topped with a protective layer of quartz.

drop earring any earring that dangles beneath the earlobe.

dull referring to a low level of luster and reflectivity.

ebony a dark, dense wood sometimes used in jewelry.

electroplating the process of passing an electrical current through a base metal and coating it with a thin layer of gold.

electrum a natural, yellowish-white alloy of gold, silver, and platinum, originally used in ancient Greek coins and now used in jewelry.

emerald cut a square or rectangular cut, with additional faceting along edges and corners.

engrave to gouge a design, pattern, words, or a name into metal.

estate jewelry previously owned or used jewelry.

facet the smooth plane made by a strategic cut in a gemstone. Most stones are multifaceted.

fancy cut any gemstone cut other than a brilliant cut, such as emerald, heart, pear, or baguette.

fantasy cut a freeform cut with multiple facets.

faux French word for fake or imitation, as a faux pearl.

feather in a gemstone, a flaw.

fede ring a ring characterized by two hands clasped together, as a Claddagh ring.

fetish a charm or amulet, sometimes believed to have magical properties.

fibula a brooch that works like a safety pin to attach clothing.

figaro chain a chain having alternating round and oval links.

filigree any delicate, open metalwork, usually of fine wire.

findings all fasteners, hooks, clasps, posts, and attaching components used in jewelry.

finish the texture or lack thereof on the surface of a piece of jewelry.

fire any streaks of color seen within a gemstone.

flaw any imperfection, such as a crack, in a gemstone.

fob a short chain that attaches to a pocket watch.

freeform any cut or faceting other than a standard type.

French ivory imitation ivory made from plastic.

freshwater pearl an irregularly shaped pearl formed by a mussel taken from a lake or river.

full cut describing any gemstone having 58 facets.

gallery an open, decoratively pierced mounting, reminiscent of the woodwork on the sterns of old sailing ships.

gem any precious or semiprecious stone, usually cut and polished and used in jewelry.

gilding a thin layer of gold.

gilt gold plating.

girdle the middle portion of a faceted gem or diamond, between the crown and the pavilion.

glyptography the art of engraving and carving gemstones.

gold a soft and pliable precious metal widely used in jewelry. It is usually alloyed with other metals to add strength and durability.

gold filled a misleading term, actually made of base metal covered by gold.

gold plate a surfacing or coating of electroplated gold.

gold tone not necessarily made of gold but colored gold.

gold washed having an extremely thin layer of gold.

grain in diamonds or pearls, a unit of weight, with four grains equaling one carat.

greasy descriptive term for a kind of luster found most commonly on jades and soapstones.

green gold gold that has been alloyed with silver, copper, and zinc, giving it a greenish hue.

grey gold gold alloyed with 15 to 20 percent iron.

gypsy setting any setting in which the gemstone has been sunk into the surrounding metal, so that it is level with the surface.

hair jewelry popular in the 19th century, a style of jewelry that incorporated locks of hair, often braided, from loved ones or from strangers who sold their hair for cash. The hair would often be displayed in a small glass enclosure on a brooch, but it was also woven into bands for bracelets and watches and other jewelry items. Some hair jewelry was worn as a memorial to a deceased loved one and, often surrounded with gold or gems, could be expensive to make.

hallmark a mark or stamp placed on gold, silver, or platinum by an assay office to authenticate purity, as a protection against fraud.

hammered dimpled with hammer blows, for a textured effect.

heishi made originally by the Pueblo Indians, beaded necklaces made of ground shells, with modern versions also ornamented with turquoise, serpentine, or jet.

helix piercing an earring piercing in cartilage of the upper ear, instead of in the lobe.

hemp fibrous material taken from a plant in the cannabis family, used with beads to make bracelets and necklaces.

herringbone chain a chain consisting of slanting links, reminiscent of a herring spine.

high polish having a mirrorlike finish.

hoop earring any large, circular-shaped earring, with or without hanging ornaments.

inclusion in a gemstone, any natural flaw, such as a bubble, crack, carbon spot, feather, or cloud.

inlay an imbedding of gemstones, mother of pearl, or other jewel material in a groove or hollowed-out section.

intaglio carving or engraving in a gem.

iridescent having bright, rainbowlike colors, as a pearl.

Irish diamond a diamond in name only, actually a rock crystal.

irradiation subjecting gemstones to X-rays or gamma rays in order to create different colors.

ivory the yellowish-white material cut from the tusks of elephants and formerly used in jewelry, now illegal.

jabot pin a brooch or pin used to attach a jabot to a shirt.

jade glass an imitation jade made from green glass.

japanned having a finish of shiny, black lacquer.

jet a dense, black coal used in mourning jewelry. Also known as black amber.

Job's tears the dried, polished, and painted seeds from a tropical grass plant, used as beads in necklaces and bracelets.

karat a measure of the purity of gold: 24 karat is pure gold, 18 karat is 75 percent gold, 14 karat is 58.3 percent gold, and 10 karat is 41.7 percent.

labret a pierced ring, ball, gem, or other ornament worn anywhere in or around the lip. See MONROE.

lapidary the art of cutting and polishing stones for jewelry. Also, one who does this.

lavaliere a chain or necklace from which a pendant is hung.

loupe a special magnifying glass used by jewelers to check gems for color, cut, clarity, and flaws.

Madison piercing a piercing where a stud, gem, or ball is attached just at the bottom of the neck.

Madonna see MONROE.

marina chain a chain made up of flat, diamond-shaped links.

marquise cut a gemstone cut, characterized by an oval shape with pointy ends.

matte a flat or nonshiny finish.

maw sit sit stunning green gem discovered in Burma in the 1960s; it is never faceted but generally Cabochon cut or cut into beads.

Medusa pierced through the center of the philtrum above the upper lip, a labret stud, with the ball resting in the hollow part of the lip.

melange a mix of diamond sizes.

melee a class of small diamonds weighing less than a carat.

mesh a woven wire chain.

Mexican jade not actual jade but stalagmitic calcite dyed green.

mill grain edge an edge cut with ridges or beads.

Monroe designed to mimic the beauty spot made famous by Marilyn Monroe, a piercing that holds a stud, metal ball, or jewel just above the lip and off to one side. Also known as a Crawford, after Cindy Crawford, the model, and a Madonna, after the pop singer.

mother-of-pearl the iridescent shell layer from the inside of a pearl-bearing mollusk.

mount to seat or place a stone in a setting.

mounting the framework on which a gem is set.

mourning jewelry any jewelry appropriate to be worn when grieving the loss of a loved one. Traditionally, the components are black or dark and are made of jet, but hair jewelry may also be worn as a permanent memorial.

nacre the lustrous substance secreted by an oyster to cover over an irritant and which eventually forms a pearl.

night emerald not a real emerald, but another name for peridot.

nipple ring a captive bead ring pierced through a nipple.

nose stud a single stone or pearl attached to the nostril.

nugget any unshaped stone or a lump of precious metal, such as gold.

olive an olive-shaped bead.

opera necklace any very long necklace, up to 34 inches (86 cm), sometimes worn doubled over.

oxidation a darkening of metal, giving an antique appearance, that occurs over time due to exposure to air and humidity or to perspiration. Pure gold does not oxidize.

palladium a gray variety of platinum, useful in jewelry because of its resistance to corrosion.

parure a matching set of jewelry that includes bracelet, earrings, necklace, and brooch.

paste a glass that is faceted to look like gemstones.

patina a discoloration that appears most notably on silver and bronze, due to aging.

pave setting a setting in which stones are placed very close together, reminiscent of paving stones.

pear cut any cut shaped like a pear or a teardrop.

pearlescent having the rainbowlike sheen of a pearl.

pendalique in a gemstone, a lozenge-shaped cut.

pendant an ornament suspended from a chain or necklace.

pierced earring any earring that is inserted through a hole in the earlobe.

pink gold see ROSE GOLD.

posy ring a ring, most often a gold band, engraved with a verse or inscription, such as "love is enough" or "dear love of mine my heart is thine," usually on the outer surface, and popular in the 15th, 16th, and 17th centuries.

precious stones the most valuable of all gems, particularly diamonds, emeralds, rubies, and sapphires.

prong any one of the tiny claws used to secure a gemstone in a setting.

quadrillion cut in a gemstone, a square cut.

radiant cut a rectangular cut with clipped corners and 58 or more facets.

reconstituted stones ground-up stones bound with resin and then compressed and cut into beads and cabochons.

reticulation a textured surface of decorative ridges and ripples, created by heating metal to a near molten state with a blowtorch.

retro a style of jewelry popular in the United States in the 1940s, characterized by chunky, geometric forms and the frequent use of pink gold.

rhinestone an imitation gemstone made of glass.

rhodium flashing a highly reflective, silvery-white form of platinum, sometimes electroplated onto jewelry.

ring guard any ring worn in front of a more valuable one, to prevent the more valuable one from slipping off.

rivière any necklace with a single strand of uniformly sized and cut diamonds.

rolled gold a thin sheet of gold that is pressurized onto a cheaper base metal and used to make various jewelry pieces.

rope a string of pearls more than 40 inches (102 cm) long.

rope chain a metal chain of woven strands, resembling a rope.

rose cut in a diamond, a cut with a flat base and triangular facets, popular in the 17th and 18th centuries.

rose gold gold alloyed with copper and silver, creating a pinkish hue. Also known as pink gold.

satin finish a pearl-like finish.

scintillation the sparkle or flashes of light created by a faceted diamond.

semiprecious stones gemstones such as amethyst, garnets, opals, and others that are valued in jewelry but not at the level of precious stones.

signet a ring having a flat plane setting on which is inscribed an insignia, monogram, or coat of arms.

silver-plated coated with a thin surfacing of silver.

silver tone having a silver color but without being actual silver.

simulated imitation; manufactured to look like something valuable, as gold or silver.

slave beads ornamental glass beads used by the Europeans as currency with African nations in the 16th through 19th centuries, to purchase goods and slaves.

snake bite a dual piercing of studs or balls, attached under the bottom lip, and resembling fangs.

solitaire a piece of jewelry with one stone in one setting.

square cut cut into the shape of a square and angled with facets along the edges.

sterling silver silver that is 92.5 percent pure.

stud an earring made of a single gem or small ornament and attached directly to the earlobe.

table the top surface of a gem.

tongue barbell a shaft pierced through the tongue and held in place with tiny balls at each end.

tragus piercing an earring piercing made in cartilage in front of the ear canal, instead of in the lobe.

translucent allowing light to pass through in cloudy or scattered fashion, as in an opal or moonstone.

trillion shape a triangular diamond with 50 facets.

tumbling placing rough stones in a small rotating barrel with abrasive grit and lubricant, a process that smooths the stones over time.

white gold an alloy of gold and either nickel or palladium.

Pants

bell-bottoms jeans or other pants having broadly flaring hems, popular in the late 1960s, early 1970s, and late 1990s.

breaker pants having a side zipper that reveals a contrasting lining when opened.

camouflage brown and green military pants.

Capri tight, calf-length pants having short side slits at the hems.

cargo pants having two patch pockets in front and two bellows pockets in back.

chaps seatless leggings worn over pants, originally a cowboy accessory but adopted for women's fashions in the late 1960s.

chinos men's khaki-colored sport pants, made of chino cloth.

choori-dars pants fitting tightly around the thighs and rumpled below the knees, popular in the 1960s and revived in the 1980s.

Clamdiggers trade name for a pair of tight-fitting pants ending at the calf.

continental man's pants with fitted waistband and horizontal front pockets, popular in the 1960s.

crawlers bib-overall pants for infants.

culottes pants of various length cut with broad legs to give the appearance of a skirt.

deck pants boat pants ending below the knee, popular with both sexes in the 1950s and 1960s.

dhoti Indian pants having a gathered waistline and broad legs tapering to the ankles.

dirndl culottes or pants with a gathered waistline.

drawstring cotton pants cinched around the waist with a drawstring.

fatigues work pants worn by U.S. army personnel. Also known as field pants.

gaucho woman's leather, calf-length pants inspired by South American cowboy pants, popular in the 1960s.

harem pants puffy pants gathered at the waist and ankles, popular in the 1960s.

Harlow pants wide straight pants, inspired by those worn by actress Jean Harlow in the 1930s.

high-rise pants that ride high above the waistline.

hip-huggers 1960s pants that rode low on the hips.

hunt breeches riding pants cut wide at the thighs and hips and tight at the knees, usually tan or canary in color.

Ivy League men's narrow-legged pants, popular in the 1950s.

jockey pants breeches having jodhpurlike legs worn tucked into riding boots.

jodhpurs riding pants with flaring thighs and narrow legs below the knee.

luau pants Hawaiian print, calf-length pants, worn by men at Hawaiian luaus.

overalls denim pants and bib top held up by suspenders.

painter's pants having loops on legs to hold brushes, adopted for general fashions in the 1970s and 1980s.

parachute pants having three pockets at the side of the leg and 6-inch zippers at the hems to provide a snug fit around the ankles.

pedal pushers women's straight-cut, below-the-knee pants with cuffs, popular in the 1940s and 1950s for bike riding, revived in the 1980s.

pleated pants having pleats around the waistband to provide a fuller look in the hip area.

seven-eighths pants any pants ending just below the calf.

stirrup pants pants having straps or loops hanging from the hems.

stovepipe pants that are straight-cut and snug-fitting from the knee down, intermittently popular.

surfers knee-length pants popular in the 1960s.

toreador tight-fitting pants that end below the knee, made popular by Spanish bullfighters.

SHIRTS

(*Also see* TOPS)

body shirt a shirt that conforms to the curves of the body, popular in the 1960s.

calypso a shirt tied in a knot in front to bare the midriff.

clerical a black or gray shirt with a standing collar, worn by the clergy.

cowboy a western-style shirt, sometimes having pockets and sometimes worn with a string tie or a neckerchief.

C.P.O. a light wool, navy blue shirt with patch pockets, modeled after that worn by chief petty officers in the U.S. Navy.

dandy a shirt with lace or ruffles running down the front center and at the cuffs.

drawstring a shirt having a hem closed with a drawstring to create a bloused effect.

dress shirt traditional dress shirt worn with necktie.

dueling a slip-on shirt with large, full sleeves. Also known as a fencing shirt.

epaulet a long-sleeved, buttoned shirt with patch pockets and epaulet tabs on the shoulders.

fiesta man's white cotton shirt decorated with two bands of embroidery down the front, popular in the 1960s.

flannel a shirt made of flannel, for warmth.

formal a man's white, long-sleeved shirt with pleated front, wing collar, and French cuffs.

Hawaiian man's colorful, floral-print shirt.

hunting shirt a bright red wool shirt worn by hunters to increase their visibility in the woods.

jockey a colorful woman's shirt fashioned after a jockey's silks, popular in the late 1960s.

medic a white shirt-jacket with standing band collar, worn by some medical professionals. Also known as a Ben Casey shirt.

midriff a woman's shirt cut or tied just below the bustline.

safari a woman's button shirt with lapels and four large pockets in front.

western dress shirt an embroidered cowboy shirt trimmed with fringe, leather, or sequins.

SKIRTS

accordion-pleated a pleated skirt that flares out from the waistline to the hem.

A-line any flaring skirt, reminiscent of the letter A.

bell a large, full skirt gathered at the waist and flaring like a bell to the hem, sometimes worn with hoops underneath, popular intermittently since mid-1800s.

bias any skirt whose fabric is cut on the diagonal, popular in the 1920s, 1930s, and 1980s.

bouffant any full, gathered skirt.

box pleated a skirt having double pleats formed by two facing folds.

bubble a skirt gathered at the waist then puffing out and tapering—like a bubble; popular in the 1950s. Also known as a tulip skirt.

bustle any skirt with gathered material, ruffles, or a bow at the back.

crinoline an understructure or fabric worn to puff out skirts.

culottes a pair of pants cut with broad, short legs to give the appearance of a skirt. Also known as a pantskirt.

dance skirt a short skirt worn over a dancer's leotard and tights.

dirndl a Tyrolean peasant skirt; a full skirt gathered at the waistline.

Empire a straight skirt having a very high waistline, popular periodically since the early 1800s.

gathered a skirt made of straight panels shirred at the top.

gored a flaring skirt made from four to 24 tapering panels or sections. The separate panels are called gores.

granny ankle-length skirt with a ruffled hem.

handkerchief skirt a skirt with a hemline that hangs down in handkerchief-like points.

hip-hugger a 1960s, belted skirt that rode low on the hips.

hoop any skirt puffed out in a bell, cone, or pyramid shape by a crinoline or hoops.

kilt a wraparound skirt, usually plaid, and fastened with a pin.

knife-pleated a skirt composed of 1-inch pleats going all around.

layered a skirt made up of tiered sections.

maxi an ankle-length skirt.

midi a calf-length skirt.

miniskirt a very short, thigh-length skirt.

pantskirt see CULOTTES.

peasant a full, plain or embroidered skirt, sometimes worn with an apron.

prairie skirt a calico-patterned skirt gathered at the waist and having a ruffled hem.

sarong a floral-print wrap skirt.

sheath a narrow, nonflaring or straight skirt, often with a slit in the back to facilitate walking.

slit a skirt having a slit up both legs, originally worn by Vietnamese women.

square dance a full, puffed-out skirt with ruffled hem.

tiered a skirt layered with flounces.

trumpet skirt a skirt with a sharply flaring flounce at the hem.

tulip skirt see bubble.

wrap any skirt that wraps around the waist and is fastened with buttons, pins, or ties.

yoke a skirt with a fitted decorative piece attached at the waist.

Sport Jackets

Afghanistan a lambskin jacket with fur left on, worn leather side out with fringe showing around edges, popular in the 1960s.

anorak a short, hooded sealskin jacket worn by Greenland Eskimos.

battle jacket a waist-length army jacket worn in World War II. Also known as an Eisenhower jacket.

blazer a single-breasted suit jacket with patch pockets.

bomber see FLIGHT JACKET.

buckskin a fringed, deerskin jacket.

bulletproof trade name for a zippered safari-type or flight-type jacket lined with two bulletproof panels (Kevlar) in front and one in back.

bush see SAFARI JACKET.

deck a hooded, zippered, water-resistant jacket with knitted trim around cuffs and neck.

Eisenhower see BATTLE JACKET.

fishing parka a long, waterproof jacket having an attached hood and a large, kangaroo pocket across the chest.

flight jacket a zippered, waist-length jacket, made of nylon or leather, with standing collar, ribbed waistband, and patch or slot pockets.

golf a lightweight, waist-length, zippered jacket made of nylon.

hacking a single-breasted suit jacket with slanting flap pockets and a center vent in back, worn for horseback riding or for general fashion.

lumber jacket a waist-length, plaid wool jacket with ribbed waist and cuffs.

mackinaw a heavy wool, hip-length jacket with blanketlike patterns and designs.

motorcycle a waist-length black leather jacket, often fastened in front to one side.

Norfolk a hip-length jacket belted at the abdomen and having box pleats from the shoulders to the hem.

parka an insulated jacket with fur-trimmed hood.

pea jacket a straight, double-breasted, navy blue coat, modeled after those worn by U.S. sailors.

racing a lightweight, waterproof, zippered nylon jacket with drawstring hem.

safari jacket a khaki-colored jacket with peaked lapels and four large bellows pockets in front; may also have a belt. Also known as a bush jacket.

shearling a sheepskin jacket, worn leather side out with wool showing around collar, cuffs, and hem.

snorkel a hooded parka that zips up over the wearer's chin, giving the hood the appearance of a snorkel.

tweed a man's single-breasted, textured wool sport jacket.

windbreaker trade name for a lightweight, nylon-zippered jacket with fitted waistband.

SWEATERS

Aran Isle a round or V-necked pullover with raised cable knit and diamond-shaped patterns, originating in Ireland.

argyle a jacquard-knit sweater having diamond designs, often worn with matching socks.

bolero a waist-length or shorter sweater with rounded ends and worn open with no fasteners.

cardigan a coatlike sweater, usually with a crew neck and ribbed cuffs and hem.

cashmere any type of sweater made with the hair of a cashmere goat, noted for its softness.

coat sweater a long, cardiganlike sweater, usually having a long V neck and buttons.

cowl-neck a pullover with a draping, rolled collar.

crew-neck a pullover with a round neck.

dolman a pullover with batwing sleeves.

Fair Isle traditional knitted sweater named for Fair Isle, a tiny island in Scotland, consisting of patterns in multiple colors.

fanny sweater a long coat sweater pulled over the buttocks.

fisherman's an Irish-designed sweater made of water-repellant wool, known for its bulkiness and natural color.

Icelandic a hand-knit, natural-color sweater made of water-repellant wool, decorated with bands around the neck.

jacquard a sweater having elaborate geometric patterns or a deer on the front or back.

karaca a pullover turtleneck with Turkish embroidered panel down the front.

letter a coat sweater with a school letter on the chest, originally worn by members of a school's sports teams.

Norwegian thick sweater originating in Norway's freezing climate that has contrasting colors and intricate patterns and is finished with buttons and clasps made of metals like pewter or silver.

shell a sleeveless pullover.

tennis a white, long-sleeved, pullover, cable-knit sweater.

turtleneck a pullover with a soft, foldedover collar covering the neck.

TOPS

bib top a top having a bare back and a front similar to the top of overalls.

bustier a snug-fitting top sometimes laced in corset or camisole fashion.

camisole a top having either thin straps over the shoulders or no straps and held in place by elastic hem, formerly a lingerie piece.

cropped top a half top, frequently made from a cutoff T-shirt or sweatshirt, that bares the midriff, popular in the 1980s.

diamanté top a top covered with sequins, beads, or pailettes.

flashdance a sweatshirtlike top with large, low-cut neck that leaves one shoulder bare.

halter top a bare-backed top with front supported by a tie around the neck.

smock long-sleeved overgarment, worn to protect clothes.

tank top an undershirt or hot weather shirt with shoulder straps and a low neckline.

tube a snug-fitting, shirred, strapless top.

ELECTRONICS

COMPUTERS

acoustic coupler a modem that attaches to a telephone handset to transmit computer information over telephone lines.

address refers to the specific location of a piece of data in a computer's memory.

AI artificial intelligence.

ALGOL algorithmic language. Originating in 1963, a programming language characterized by blocks of statements, now nearly obsolete.

algorithm a set of specific, sequenced directions illustrating how to perform a task or solve a problem; a computer program.

ALU arithmetic/logic unit. In the central processing unit, the component that carries out arithmetic and logic functions.

analog computer a computer in which numerical data are represented by analogous quantities, such as variable voltage. See DIGITAL COMPUTER.

application a program designed for a specific purpose.

archival storage any medium, such as tape cartridges, disks, or diskettes (floppy disks) used to store computer information.

array a collection of related data stored under one name.

artificial intelligence creative computer intelligence, as in solving problems by thinking as the human brain does rather than by mindlessly spitting out numbers and data; the highest form of computer intelligence.

ASCII American Standard Code for Information Interchange. A universal code allowing files to be retrieved and read from an otherwise incompatible computer program or system.

audit a scan of a PC to determine if it is infected by parasites, viruses, or spyware.

audit trail a chronological record of users who have logged on to a particular computer and what they have done on it and when. It is useful in criminal investigations.

authenticate to identify a computer user or a device.

avatar an icon representing a real person.

back up to make an extra or duplicate file in memory in case the original is lost or accidentally erased.

BASIC a simple computer language in which line numbers precede each statement, popularly used by students and microcomputer owners.

baud a measurement, in bits per second, of the time it takes a computer to transfer data.

BBS bulletin board system. A central computer system that can be accessed over telephone lines to relay data to a remote computer or to exchange messages with other computer users.

bells and whistles sales jargon for any unnecessary gadgetry or features on a computer.

beta test a manufacturer's test of new programming software among selected computer users.

bidirectional printer a printer that can print with its head moving backward or forward over a page.

biometrics computer-driven devices capable of scanning and identifying fingerprints, faces, and retinas, for security purposes. Also, the science of this.

bit short for binary digit, the smallest unit of information, represented by either a 1 or a 0.

blue affectionate nickname for an IBM computer, named after Big Blue.

board a printed circuit board.

bomb any computer failure in which a program ends prematurely and must be restarted.

boot to start up a computer.

bootstrap a brief program that gets a computer started.

bps bits per second.

Bps bytes per second.

buffer an area of memory that temporarily holds incoming or outgoing data.

bug a mistake in a computer program.

bundled software any software supplied with a computer at no extra cost.

burn to write (record) data, images, or music on to a computer disk.

bus the connections or wires through which information is relayed to all of a computer's components.

byte 8 bits of memory space.

cache a data storage area that can be accessed quickly.

CAD computer-aided design; a computer system for creating blueprints and drafting layouts.

caddy a tray that slides out of the computer and holds a CD-ROM.

CAM acronym for computer-aided manufacturing.

card a printed circuit board.

carpal tunnel syndrome swelling around a main nerve in the wrist, causing pain and numbness that can extend from the wrist to the fingers. It is caused by repetitive keyboard work and sometimes results in permanent injury.

cartridge a medium for storing programs.

catalog a list of a disk's contents.

cathode-ray tube the picture tube in a monitor, consisting of a vacuum tube and fluorescent screen on which electrons are focused.

CD-ROM compact disk read-only memory. A compact disk (similar to the audio disk version) that stores huge volumes of computer information coded into it by the manufacturer.

chip see INTEGRATED CIRCUIT.

chiphead a computer enthusiast.

cipher text encrypted data.

clip art ready-made, non-copyrighted artwork or graphics that can be stored on a computer and incorporated into any document.

clipboard a temporary data storage area.

clone an imitation; it refers to a computer brand that imitates another computer brand or model.

COBOL an easy-to-read program for business data processing.

command an instruction to a computer.

compatibles any same-brand or competitive-brand computers or components that can work together.

compression the compaction of data to reduce the space needed to store it.

computerese computer jargon, slang, acronyms, etc.

computer forensics investigative techniques used to uncover illicit computer use.

CPU central processing unit. The part of a computer that executes directions and performs arithmetic and logic functions.

cracker one who breaks through security systems and infiltrates a computer system or network with criminal or mischievous intent.

cracking the illegal copying of commercial software by breaking down copy and registration protections.

crash any condition in which a computer malfunctions or stops operating.

Cray a family of state-of-the-art supercomputers manufactured by Cray Research, Inc.

CRT see CATHODE RAY TUBE.

crunch to process calculations or figures with the computer; to number crunch.

cursor on a computer screen or monitor, the symbol that points out where the next typed-in character will appear.

cyberphobe one who has an aversion to computers.

cyberpunk a subgenre of science fiction involving computer culture.

database a computer catalog of information.

data communication the passing of data from one computer to another.

DDT a debugging program.

debug to work the bugs out of or remove the mistakes from a computer program.

defrag to clean up a computer's hard drive; defragment.

desktop publishing a computer program that handles all publishing tasks, from printing to editing to graphics. Also, the design and production of publications by a small computer.

diagnostic any computer program used to track down programming errors.

digital computer a computer in which quantities are represented by digits electronically, as distinguished from an analog. Most modern computers are digital computers.

digital fingerprinting any digital identification marker used to legally protect original documents from unauthorized use.

digitize to convert signals, text, or imagery into digital code for use in a computer.

digitizer the device that converts signals, text, etc., into code for computer use.

disk a medium, either built-in or independent, that stores computer information.

disk drive the device that gives a computer the ability to read and write information on disks.

DOS disk operating system.

dot matrix printer a printer that prints characters as a pattern of dots.

down malfunctioning or inoperable.

download to transfer information from a main computer to a smaller computer or a remote computer.

DRAM dynamic random access memory.

editor a program that allows the user to add, delete, or change information in a file or program.

emulator software that enables a computer to download pirated video games over the Internet and "emulate" any video gaming platform.

ENIAC Electronic Numerical Integrator and Calculator, the first electronic computer, composed of some 18,000 vacuum tubes, and built in the 1940s.

EPROM a memory chip that can be erased by exposing it to ultraviolet light.

expert system a computer program using a form of artificial intelligence drawn from an extensive knowledge base and an inference engine.

fatal error any internal error causing a program to stop or abort, sometimes resulting in a loss of data.

file a document or collection of documents stored in the same place or under the same name.

file compression the electronic reduction of a file to make it fit into a smaller memory space.

flash drive an electronic device that stores digital data.

flat screen an alternative to cathode ray tubes, any video display employing liquid crystals or electroluminescence, as in laptop and notebook computers. Also known as flat-panel display.

floppy disk a small disk of magnetic film used for storing computer data.

flowchart a chart composed of characters and words to help guide a user through an algorithm.

font a group of type characters in one style, such as boldface or italics.

FORTRAN Formula Translation, a programming language developed in the 1950s.

fuzzy logic a form of computer intelligence that recognizes partial truths and variabilities, as a human brain does.

GIGO acronym for garbage in, garbage out, referring to the fact that poor information fed into the computer always results in poor information coming out.

GPF general protection fault; a crash of a Windows program caused by one application attempting to use another application's memory.

Graffiti software that recognizes handwriting.

graphene an electrically conductive, one-atom-thick sheet of carbon, which is currently being developed to replace copper and silicon in a vast array of electronics applications.

grid computing a network of large computers pooled together to supply power and storage capability to smaller computers.

hacker originally a computer programming wizard, but now more often one who breaks through security systems and infiltrates other systems or networks with criminal or mischievous intent.

Hal Arthur C. Clarke's mad computer in the novel and movie, *2001: A Space Odyssey.*

hang to crash so that the keyboard and mouse fail to respond to new inputs, requiring rebooting.

hard card a hard disk in the shape of a card.

hard copy a paper printout of computer data.

hard disk an information storage medium in the form of a built-in, nonremovable platter. Also known as a Winchester disk.

hardware the physical components of a computer system, such as the terminal, the monitor, and the integrated circuits, as distinguished from software.

hash useless information.

homeshoring in business, the growing practice of having contracted workers perform computer tasks at home on their home computers, saving on insurance and equipment costs.

host a master unit in a computer network.

icon a symbol or small graphic representation designating a specific function or file on a computer program, as a tiny typewriter representing a word processing program.

import to retrieve and display files or information from another application.

ink-jet printer a printer that forms type characters with dots of ink.

integrated circuit a conglomeration of tiny transistors and other components on a silicon wafer less than ¼-inch square. Also known as a chip.

intranet a company's in-house network of computers.

ISDN Integrated Services Digital Network, an all-digital telephone line that transmits digital data and voice without a modem.

IT information technology.

joystick a stick-like controller used with games, instead of a mouse.

K short for kilobyte, the equivalent of approximately 1,024 bytes. Each kilobyte memory unit is capable of storing 1,024 characters. Also KB.

kilobyte see K.

LAN local area network; a network confined to a single building, floor, or area.

laptop a portable, battery-operated computer that can be operated on one's lap while traveling.

laser printer a printer that uses a laser beam to produce characters and images that are transferred to paper electrostatically.

LCD liquid crystal display; a system of liquid crystal capsules that when electrified provide lighted displays for digital watches and some computer screens.

letter quality refers to the high-quality type print produced by some computer printers, as distinguished from poorer-quality dot matrix.

light pen an instrument used to manipulate or change pictures on a computer screen.

LISP list processing, a programming language characterized by its prolific use of lists and parentheses and used in handling complex data, such as that involved in artificial intelligence.

load to pass information on a disk to a computer.

Logo a simplified programming language used to familiarize children with computers.

log on to sign in with a computer and identify oneself as an authorized user.

mainframe computer a large computer that can be set up to serve as many as 500 users at one time.

MB megabyte, the equivalent of 1,024 kilobytes or 1,048,576 bytes. As a unit of memory, it can store over 1 million characters.

memory where data is stored in a computer; the core.

memory chips add-on memory in the form of RAM chips.

menu a list of options appearing on screen in a program.

micro- a prefix standing for one-millionth, as in microsecond, which stands for one-millionth of a second.

microcomputer a small computer intended for one user at a time, as a home computer, and characterized by a central processing unit (CPU) composed of only one integrated circuit called a microprocessor.

microprocessor a computer central processing unit composed of only one chip or integrated circuit.

MIDI Musical Instrument Digital Interface, used to transfer musical data between electronic instruments or between an electronic instrument and a computer.

minicomputer a computer that is smaller than a mainframe but larger than a microcomputer.

modem short for modulator-demodulator, a device that enables computers to communicate with other computers over telephone lines.

monitor the TV-like screen that shows the computer input and output.

Moore's law the observation held for many years that the power available in computers doubled every 18 months while their cost stayed the same.

morphing the transformation of images, such as that of a kitten turning into a pumpkin, by use of special effects software.

motherboard a computer's main circuit board.

mouse a small, external input device connected to a computer by a wire; moving and clicking a mouse moves the cursor on a computer screen, useful for selecting commands without having to type them in.

MS-DOS short for Microsoft disk operating system.

multitasking running more than one program in the same computer at the same time.

nano- a prefix for one-billionth, as in a nanosecond.

nanotechnology collective term for technological components on the scale of molecules, currently being developed for a wide range of applications, from medicine to computers.

network several computers linked together.

nibble half of a byte.

number cruncher slang for any computer used largely for carrying out highly complex numerical calculations. Also, the programmer involved in this work.

offshoring in business, the practice of having computer work performed overseas, which saves money because of lower pay and benefits.

OLEDs organic light emitting diodes; natural carbon-based molecules or synthetic polymers used in layers between electrodes to create an illuminated, superthin screen used in cell phones, computers, and TVs.

organizer see PDA.

PASCAL a popular, general-purpose programming language for use with microcomputers.

password a secret word that must be logged in to the computer in order to authorize use.

patch a small correction or modification loaded onto a defective program or software.

PC short for personal computer, a computer designed for a single user, as opposed to a mainframe computer.

PDA personal digital assistant; a handheld, battery-powered computer. Also known as an organizer.

peripheral any device that connects to a computer, such as a terminal, a disk drive, or a printer.

photoshopped named after the Adobe Photoshop program, referring to the touching up of photographs through digital alteration.

plotter a computer-controlled device that draws pictures on paper.

plug-in any software designed to boost the performance of an application.

port any connection through which information enters or leaves a computer.

program instructions to a computer.

programmer one who writes instructions for a computer.

PROLOG a programming language used for writing logic programs.

PROM short for programmable read-only memory; computer memory that cannot be erased or reprogrammed.

protocol a set of rules for data transfer between computers.

RAM short for random-access memory, a computer's main memory store, from which all information can be located roughly within the same amount of time.

reboot to restart a computer.

reverse engineering an engineering process of deciphering how something works by taking it apart. It is sometimes used to figure out alternative ways to perform certain tasks in order to sidestep established patents.

rip to digitize CDs to MP3 format.

robust of hardware or software, holding up well when another component or application fails.

ROM short for read-only memory, a chip containing manufacturer-installed information that cannot be erased or changed.

scanner a computer device that reads printed or handwritten pages.

screen saver a self-activating program that automatically displays a wide variety of moving imagery on a monitor that has been left idle for a set amount of time; the program prevents a static image from being permanently "burned in" to the screen.

scrolling the downward and/or upward movement of text on a computer screen.

semiconductor a material, such as silicon, that is both a poor conductor and a poor insulator. Semiconductor devices include diodes, transistors, and chips.

silicon the nonmetallic, silica-based element used in the manufacture of semiconductors.

Silicon Valley the area outside San Francisco where a large number of computer-related firms are located.

sim simulated; simulation.

simulation computer creation of a real-world environment or event, widely used in games, television reenactments, motion pictures, and in-flight training programs.

software the nonphysical components of a computer system, such as programming information.

speech synthesis a computer and program with the ability to read typed words and speak them aloud with a synthesized voice.

spike an abnormal surge of electricity, sometimes caused by a lightning strike, that can damage a computer.

spreadsheet a spreadsheet program, specifically any calculations based on rows and columns of numbers.

store to commit data to a computer's memory.

supercomputer a computer with more power or speed than a typical mainframe computer.

surge protector a device that protects a computer from a spike.

tape magnetic tape, similar to that used in a tape recorder, that can be used to store computer information.

tape drive a device that enables data on magnetic tape to be transmitted via signals to a computer.

telecommuting the process by which one may be employed at home and send one's work through a computer modem to a remote employer.

terminal collective term for the keyboard and CRT or TV screen portion of a computer.

timesharing a method of running multiple programs on a computer at the same time.

tractor feed on a printer, the moving, toothed gears that propel paper forward.

trap door a programming gap inserted intentionally as a means of bypassing security and gaining access to the program at a later date.

turtle in some computer graphics systems, an imaginary turtle that moves about the computer screen and draws patterns on command.

tutorial any file or menu that displays step-by-step instructions for various applications, for beginners.

unzip to decompress a file.

upload to transfer data from a small or remote computer to a large or central computer.

user-friendly easy to understand and use.

virtual reality realistic computer simulation of a world or environment, often featuring three-dimensional and audio effects.

voice recognition a process in which advanced computers can recognize human speech and type out words as the user speaks them into a microphone.

wallpaper slang for any long printout.

window on a computer screen, a superimposed square or rectangle containing commands or other information.

word processing a program that facilitates the typing, editing, and storing of documents.

zap slang term meaning to erase information.

zip to compress a file to facilitate storage.

CHATTING SHORTHAND

ACK acknowledge.

afk away from keyboard.

ASAP as soon as possible.

BAK back at keyboard.

BBN bye-bye now.

BBS bulletin board system.

BCNU be seeing you.

B4N bye for now.

BG big grin.

BRB be right back.

BTW by the way.

BWL bursting with laughter.

C&G chuckle and grin.

CNP continued in next post.

CUL see you later.

CYA see ya.

CYAL8R see ya later.

FUBAR fouled up beyond all repair/recognition.

FYEO for your eyes only.

FYI for your information.

GA go ahead.

GG gotta go.

G/S? gay or straight?

ILY I love you.

IM instant message.

IMHO in my humble opinion.

IMO in my opinion.

K kiss.

KIT keep in touch.

L8R later.

LOL laughed out loud.

M/F? male or female?

NTMY nice to meet you.

OIC oh I see.

OMG Oh, my God!

PM private message.

PMJI pardon my jumping in.

ROTF rolling on the floor.

ROFL rolling on the floor laughing.

SYS see you soon.

THX thanks.

WUF where are you from?

Zup? What's up?

The Internet

address a string of letters (often spelling out a name), characters, and/or numbers designating the electronic location of a Web site, computer user, organization, etc. Used for e-mail and to download a specific site on the Web.

adware a type of spyware consisting of a program that is secretly piggybacked onto another, albeit legitimate program, which a user downloads. The adware then infects the user's PC and causes annoying pop-up ads.

antispyware software that weeds out spyware from a user's PC and prevents other spyware from being downloaded.

archive a repository for the storage of data, software, etc. Also, a method for combining several files into one.

astroturfing the attempt to create a grassroots buzz about one's product or service by touting it anonymously in forums, chat rooms, and message boards.

attachment any file attached to and sent with an e-mail.

autobot see BOT.

backbone a large network serving to interconnect other networks.

back door program see TROJAN HORSE.

bait and switch a devious marketing ploy in which key words such as *sex* are used to draw search engines to a Web site.

bandwidth the amount of data, in bits per second, that can be sent over a network connection in a specific time period.

banner ad a Web page advertisement, usually appearing over the top of a page.

banner exchange the trading of advertisements between Web sites.

below the fold referring to the screen portion one must scroll down to see.

bitloss loss of data during a transmission.

BitTorrent a free program that allows simultaneous uploading and downloading of movie, video game, and other files, allowing users to share pieces of those with others and increase the speed of trading content.

blog short for Web log. A cybermagazine or online forum that may cover everything from politics to sports, with links to communicate with participants. Also, to participate in a Web log.

blogger one who contributes to a blog.

blogosphere slang for the medium of Web logs, and their contributors and readers.

bookmark an electronic bookmark, allowing the user to mark any site on the Web in order to return to it quickly, without searching again. Also known as a favorite.

bot short for robot. Any of several automated software programs, such as a crawler or spider, especially those involved in Web cataloging.

bounce return of an e-mail to its sender due to a delivery glitch or an incorrect address.

broadband a high-speed, high-capacity transmission channel using fiber-optic or coaxial cable.

browser Internet navigating software employed to find and display Web sites.

buffering temporarily holding data in computer storage that is being transmitted as an aid to compensate for different processing rates.

bulletin board an online medium through which users with a common interest may exchange messages or software.

cache a computer's storage repository for recently visited Web sites, used to expedite loading of Web files on future visits.

case sensitive referring to an e-mail address that must be typed in upper- or lower-case letters to be viable, largely a requirement of the past.

chain letter a spam or hoax letter directing the receiver to forward it to others, with negative consequences if unheeded, sometimes used in conjunction with fraudulent money-making schemes.

chat to converse online in real time.

chat room an online medium or Web site through which users can have real-time conversations.

click ad a Web page advertisement that, when clicked on, takes the viewer to a page with more information, often for ordering a product or service.

click fraud the dishonest and repeated clicking of an advertiser's ad with no intention of buying anything, in order to drive up that advertiser's fees, sometimes perpetrated by a rival advertiser.

codec technology that compresses or decompresses data, such as is necessary when viewing video on demand.

.com at the end of an e-mail or Web address, the designation for a commercial enterprise.

compression the electronic reduction of a file or data stream to speed transmission or take up less space in memory storage.

congestion a data path overload resulting in a slow or no response from a server.

contentjacking the copying or stealing of material in blogs or other sites to use in one's own site. Also known as pagejacking.

cookie a brief personal file created for a specific visitor and loaded on to his or her browser by a Web server to facilitate usage of its Web site. The file logs personal preferences and habits and often stores the user's ID and password.

cracker one who removes or defeats the security components in protected software to allow copying and pirating.

cracking the illegal removal or defeating of security components in software to allow copying and pirating.

crawler a program that searches new Internet resources.

cryptography mathematical coding used to secure Internet transactions.

cybercafe a coffee house with public computer access to the Internet.

cybercrime any crime committed online, such as credit card fraud or unauthorized access violations.

cyberfraud online fraud.

cybernaut one who frequently surfs the Internet; also known as an internaut.

cybersex simulated sex—actually, dirty talk—conveyed via a private chat room or e-mail.

cyberspace the electronic medium and culture of the World Wide Web.

cybersquatting the unethical practice of registering an Internet address or domain name consisting of the letters of a company name and selling that name to the company. A company is unable to use their own name in their Internet address unless it registers it before others do.

cyberstalking harassing someone through e-mails, instant messaging, etc.

cyberterrorism the criminal destruction or disruption of Internet communications through the use of mail bombs, viruses, or other means.

darknet an underground network of users who illegally trade copyrighted software and game files.

dead link a link that is either broken or connected to a Web page that is no longer available.

decryption the decoding of encrypted or secret messages.

dial-up online transmission service over telephone lines.

digirati collective term for people who are savvy with digital technology, particularly with computers and the Internet.

distance learning college or other classroom learning that takes place over the Internet.

DNS Domain Name System.

domain at the end of an e-mail or Internet address, an abbreviation designating the nature of the addressee, such as *.com* for "commercial enterprise," *.edu* for "educational institution," *.mil* for "military installation," and so on.

Domain Name System collective term for any one or all of several e-mail routing and Internet connection servers.

down inaccessible or inoperable due to technical difficulty.

download to transfer information or graphics of files from a Web location onto a computer.

DSL digital subscriber line. A transmission circuit that is superior to a regular phone circuit.

e-business commerce over the Internet; a company that sells goods or services via the Internet.

.edu at the end of an Internet or e-mail address, the domain designation for an educational institution.

e-mail electronic mail typed into a computer and sent through a modem over the Internet or online server to a receiver.

emoticon any fanciful "facial expression," such as a smiley face :), created on a keyboard, to help convey emotion in one's e-mail or post online.

encryption the coding of data into an unreadable form, to increase security.

ethernet a networking system used in a small or confined area.

evil twins a fraudulent technique through which an illegitimate, wireless network mimics a legitimate one and, by offering a public wi-fi connection to the Internet, such as those in coffeehouses and hotels, captures passwords, credit card numbers, etc.

extranet a partially closed network providing access to company employees and a select group of outsiders, such as vendors and contractors.

e-zine an online magazine.

FAQ frequently asked question.

favorite see BOOKMARK.

filter a sorting system used to block unwanted e-mail or spam.

finger a program or utility that can identify a person online from an e-mail address.

firewall a security system employed to protect access to a closed network by means of special software, passwords, and authentication checks.

flame war angry and insulting communications between two or more people via e-mail, chat forums, newsgroups, etc.

flaming angry and insulting communications or posts via e-mail, chat forums, newsgroups, etc.

flog a fake blog, used to promote a product or service.

flooding clogging one's mail server and blocking a recipient's mailbox by sending him or her a mass of spam.

frames separate windows on a Web page that can be scrolled down and accessed while keeping the main page and its menu in view.

fraudulent link a link that appears to be legitimate but in fact directs users to a phony site for criminal purposes.

freeware free software available for downloading from various Internet sites.

FTP file transfer protocol; a program used to send and receive files over the Internet.

geek slang for an Internet know-it-all.

ghost site an abandoned Web site that is no longer maintained. Also known as an Orphan Annie.

Google one of the Internet's most popular search engines.

Google bomb a method of increasing a search engine's ranking of a Web page by having several sites link to it with the same anchor text.

Gopher an information retrieval system or database searcher.

.gov at the end of an Internet or e-mail address, the domain designation for a government institution.

handle in a chat or other online forum, a participant's moniker or name.

hijacker any spyware designed to unethically monitor another's browsing, infect one's computer with pop-up ads, or change search or homepages.

history a list or log of Web sites recently visited.

hits the recorded number of times a Web site has been visited, useful for measuring popularity.

home page the opening Web page of an individual, organization, company, etc.

honeymonkey a computer set up to surf the Web on its own and survey for sites that may load malicious code.

honeypot a computer or operating system set up specifically to lure hackers and log all attempts at access in order to catch scammers or identity thieves.

host a network computer providing multiple services, such as e-mail, for other computers.

host name the first portion of an e-mail or Internet address, identifying a specific computer user.

hotlink see HYPERLINK.

hot spot any place, such as a coffee shop, with a wireless Internet connection.

HTML hypertext markup language; the language coding used to create Web pages.

http hypertext transfer protocol; the protocol that enables the linking of Web sites.

hyperlink a link made up of glowing text or graphics that when clicked leads directly to another related Web page or site. Also known as a hotlink.

hypermedia an integration of text, graphics, video, and sound.

hypertext a text system used to create links to related documents.

instant message an online medium through which one may communicate instantly a message on another's computer screen. Also, the message itself.

internaut see CYBERNAUT.

Internet a network of computer networks linking computer users worldwide.

Internet2 created by scientists in 1996, an independent, fee-based Internet employing faster, more advanced technology, used by universities, government agencies, and some organizations.

interactive of any communications medium, allowing direct, two-way contact.

intranet a communication network of computers restricted to a single company, organization, or building.

IP address an identification number assigned to every computer on the Internet.

IRC Internet relay chat. The protocol that enables computers users who are online to chat or "talk" to one another in real time.

ISP Internet Service Provider, which provides users with access to the Internet.

IT information technology.

JAVA a virus-safe programming language for use on the Internet.

JPEG Joint Photographic Experts Group; a common graphics format used to convey photographs, three-dimensional images, etc.

keylogger a form of spyware from which someone can remotely monitor keystrokes on another user's PC in order to read e-mails or determine which Web sites are visited.

kiosk mode a screen presentation without toolbars, menus, or borders. Also, presentation mode.

LAN a computer network used only on a single floor or in a single building.

leeching the downloading of game and movie files and subsequent refusal to share them with other online users.

link a connection to another Web page or site.

link rot the process over time by which a link may become irrelevant or unneeded, especially when connected to a Web site that is closed or outdated.

LINUX an open source operating system, derived from the Unix system by Linus Torvalds in 1991 and further developed and refined by many collaborators.

listserv an e-mail subscription service that relays all messages posted by the individuals in a common-interest group to each of its members. Also, the software that manages the member mailing list.

log a record of activity at a Web site.

log on to connect or sign on to a Web site.

lurk to read the posts or messages of a newsgroup discussion without participating in the dialogue oneself.

mail bomb an intentional mass e-mailing sent to a single recipient to wreak havoc on a server.

mailbox memory repository for storing e-mail or other transmissions.

mailing list all of the members of a common-interest group who subscribe to a listserv.

mashup a Web page composed of a combination of content shared by two or more Web sites, for example, that of Google Maps and Microsoft's Virtual Earth.

.mil at the end of an e-mail or Internet address, the domain designation for a military facility.

mirror site a Web site that is an exact copy of another, employed to broaden user access.

modem the electronic device that converts computer data into sound signals, which can be transmitted over telephone lines to other modems and computers.

.mov designation for a movie clip or still image, contained in a file.

MPEG Moving Pictures Expert Group; a compressed format for movies and sound files, which can be accessed or downloaded from the Internet.

MP3 a file used for storing high-fidelity, digitally transmitted, compressed audio.

nag screen a bulletin similar to a pop-up ad that urges users to upgrade outdated software.

Napster an application used for downloading and trading music files.

navigate to find one's way around the Internet.

Net short for Internet.

.net at the end of an e-mail or Internet address, the domain designation for a network.

netiquette online etiquette, manners, accepted procedures and behavior, etc.

network the interconnection of two or more computers.

newbie an online neophyte who does not know his or her way around yet and asks lots of questions.

newsgroup an online discussion group. A newsgroup usually focuses on any one of hundreds of specific subject areas.

node any individual computer connected to a network.

offline disconnected from a server or the Internet.

online logged on to an Internet or e-mail service.

open content any information in the public domain, allowing free use to those other than the original copyright holders.

open source software any software that is not protected under copyright or is in the public domain and that can be altered or improved by any member of the public and freely distributed to others.

.org at the end of an e-mail or Internet address, a domain designation for an organization.

Orphan Annie see GHOST SITE.

overpayment scam an online scam in which a product is purchased with a phony cashier's check that is written with a higher amount than the sale calls for, with the difference refunded to the buyer by the seller. By the time the seller learns the check is bad, the sale item is gone, along with the refunded money.

packet one portion of any data transmitted or received.

pagejacking the theft and unauthorized use of another's Web page.

password a word, name, or grouping of letters and numbers, often kept secret, and used to gain access to Web sites, account information, or other confidential data.

PDF Portable Document Format, a file format created by Adobe Systems.

permalink a permanent link, usually referring to one connected to a Web archive.

pharming a fraudulent practice in which scammers redirect Internet surfers to phony Web sites that mimic legitimate ones, in order to mine account and credit card information.

phishing a fraudulent practice in which scammers send phony e-mails that appear to come from banks or other businesses and request credit card numbers, passwords, etc., often under the pretense of updating an account.

ping to send a packet of data to a site and wait for an echo to verify accessibility to that site.

piracy the illegal copying of software, music, or movies, especially for resale or redistribution.

pirating the stealing of copyrighted content on the Internet, especially for redistribution or sale.

podcast an audio broadcast of music, interviews, news, etc., transmitted over the Internet.

pop-up an advertisement that pops up suddenly on a Web site, often an annoyance.

post a message posted on a bulletin board for an online discussion group. Also, to place a message in any online forum.

P2P peer-to-peer; a community of computers connected together through database software that facilitates the sharing of files. Also, the software itself.

pump and dump an unethical practice through which anonymous posters on message boards and forums claim to have insider information and persuade readers to buy shares in a risky stock. When the price is artificially driven up, the scammers sell for a quick profit.

refresh to reload a Web page for updated content.

router an electronic connector of networks.

scumware see SPYWARE.

search engine a program that searches Web sites, collects information and links, and then indexes all the data for easy user access.

search engine optimization the employment of various means to heighten placement of a Web site in a search engine's ranking, thus pulling in more visitors.

search engine optimizer one who is expert at getting Web sites placed high in a search engine's ranking, thus pulling in more visitors and more business.

server a network's host computer.

session one period of use of an Internet connection.

shareware free software that is shared among users.

shouting when posting a message, using all caps. ALL CAPS GIVES THE IMPRESSION OF SHOUTING and is perceived as such by the receiver.

site a Web site or Web page; an electronic location on the Internet that displays Web pages, links, etc.

snail mail "old-fashioned" mail, delivered the slow and traditional way, as opposed to almost-instantaneous e-mail.

snoopware see SPYWARE.

social networking site any Web site on which people can post personal details and network or communicate with others. A virtual community.

spam annoying advertisements and promotional messages distributed en masse throughout the Internet and via e-mail. Also, to distribute such advertisements.

spamdexing a method of increasing page viewings through the dishonest manipulation of search engine rankings with altered HTML pages.

spider a program that searches new Internet resources.

spim spam that is sent via instant messaging rather than e-mail.

splog combining *spam* and *blog*, a Web log specifically devised to promote an affiliated Web site and to boost search engine rankings to that site; a form of sneaky advertising.

spyware insidious software that is often unwittingly downloaded onto one's PC and can secretly steal and report e-mail dialogue, instant messages, and monitor Web sites visited to another party. Also known as scumware, snoopware.

streaming the transmission of compressed video and audio signals from a Web site to a remote receiver.

surf to explore various sites on the Internet, for fun or for research purposes.

swarming the sharing by multiple users of small pieces of movie or game files, which speeds up downloading and prevents leeching.

TCP/IP the standard communications protocol of the Internet.

telnet a communications protocol used to connect computers throughout the Internet.

thread in a newsgroup or other forum, a series of posts or messages on the same topic, actually a string of replies and counter-replies to an opening question or comment.

thumbnail a miniaturized picture clicked on to display a larger version.

Trojan horse a program embedded in an e-mail attachment used by hackers to infiltrate another's computer system. The program, also known as a back door program, can be employed to operate another's computer from remote control while its user is logged on to an Internet chat room or game site. Among other things, it can be used to erase hard drives.

troll one who posts controversial or irritating comments in order to produce heated responses from others. Also, the owner or employee of a company who anonymously posts negative comments about a competitor's products in forums and on message boards.

Twitter an online service that offers a social networking and blogging venue through the display of short texts known as tweets on users' profile pages.

upload to send a file from one's own computer to another via the Internet.

URL uniform resource locator; a Web address beginning with http://.

USENET a network of discussion groups called newsgroups.

video conferencing an Internet meeting with participants who appear on video.

viral advertising Internet advertising that is presented in a novel or entertaining way to encourage people to get their friends to look at it.

virtual simulated.

vlog a blog presented with video.

VOD video on demand; any service that offers immediate viewing of video or movies over the Internet.

VOIP voice-over-Internet protocol; a set of rules for voice transmission or telephone calls over the Internet. Also, the Internet telephone service itself.

VRML virtual reality modeling language; a graphics systems that can produce three-dimensional effects with changing perspectives and lighting as a user "moves" through an environment, as in a game program.

warez any software or game stripped of its copy-prevention components and illegally traded on file-sharing networks.

Web short for the World Wide Web.

webcam a camera used to send video or pictures over the Internet.

web designer a Web site architect or graphics designer.

Web log see BLOG.

webmaster a web site manager or administrator.

Web page an online file page.

Web ring a group of related Web sites joined together by links.

WebTV an online television service.

wi-fi a system capable of transmitting wireless signals from the Internet.

WiMax a wi-fi system capable of transmitting signals 30 miles.

wireless any wire-free Internet access.

World Wide Web the Internet; collective term for all of the Web pages, links, and sites accessible through cyberspace. Also, the protocols that allow a user to link to all the various sites.

WWW the World Wide Web.

Yahoo! a popular search engine.

Viruses, Parasites, and Other Computer Invaders

antidote any program designed to protect a computer from being infected with a virus.

antivirus any program that identifies, weeds out, or protects a computer from a virus.

back door an opening left intentionally by designers in a computer security system for practical reasons but often exploited by hackers with mischievous or criminal intent. Also known as a wormhole.

data-driven attack a stealthy virus or other form of attack encoded in harmless data in order to fool firewalls.

dictionary attack the attempt to uncover codes, passwords, or e-mail addresses by using exhaustive lists of words or word combinations.

hygiene collective term for measures taken to prevent a computer from being infected with a virus.

impersonating see SPOOFING.

logic bomb a secretly embedded code in an application or operating system that can be triggered when certain conditions are met to cause damage or breach security.

masquerading see SPOOFING.

parasite a type of insidious software or program that can be installed on a computer via the Internet without the owner's knowledge. It can be loaded simply by visiting certain Web sites, by clicking on a misleading pop-up ad, or by downloading shareware, music, games, or movie clips. The software, also known as spyware or scumware, can then transmit what one types, including passwords and credit card numbers, and record the sites one visits and any items purchased online. They can also serve up pop-up ads, alter browser settings, divert one's surfing to porn sites, and even steal from the Web sites visited.

polymorphic virus a virus designed to change its binary pattern as it replicates itself in order to elude detection by antivirus programs.

replicator a program that once installed makes copies of itself, as some worms and viruses.

sheepdip to run floppy disks and CD-ROM through antivirus programs on an auxiliary computer to clean them of viruses before they are loaded into a main computer, much like the farming practice of bathing sheep in chemical solutions to rid them of fleas and lice.

sniffing using a computer to monitor someone's network traffic in order to capture data, especially unencrypted passwords.

spoofing stealing identification and authentication data to gain access to a computer network. Also called impersonating, masquerading.

stealth virus a virus designed to hide itself from antivirus software by replacing itself with a copy in another location or file.

strain a virus type.

vaccine any program designed to protect a computer from being infected with a virus.

virus a prank program that disrupts computer operations by erasing, adding, or altering information and by making copies of itself and infecting other programs.

worm a rigged program that makes endless copies of itself and disrupts computer functioning. Similar to a virus.

wormhole see BACK DOOR.

ELECTRONIC TERMS

ampere a measure of electric current, specifically the number of electrons that flow by a given point each second. Also known as an amp.

brownout a drop in the amount of voltage running through a power line. Brownouts are known to cause damage to some electronic equipment.

capacitance the amount of electric charge a capacitor can store.

capacitor a device that stores an electric charge.

cathode-ray tube a type of vacuum tube in which an electron beam is focused electrostatically or electromagnetically onto a sensitized screen, forming a picture, as in a television set.

chip an integrated circuit.

circuit a closed pathway through which electricity can flow.

conductor any element through which electricity can freely flow.

current electricity; a flow of electrons through a conductive medium.

diode a device that permits electrons to pass in only one direction.

doping adding an impurity, such as phosphorus, to semiconducting silicon, to alter its conducting properties.

electrode any of the elements in a transistor that emits or controls the movement of electrons.

electron a subatomic particle with a negative charge.

farad a unit of capacitance.

germanium a semiconducting material used in making electronic components.

ground a large, conducting body, such as the earth, to which an electrical circuit is connected to prevent cables from picking up noise or emitting radio frequency interference.

henry the unit of inductance in which the variation of current at 1 ampere per second induces an electromotive force of 1 volt.

hole an area where no electron is present on the crystal of a P-type semiconductor; it acts as a positive charge.

impedance a measure of the opposition to the flow of current in an alternating-current circuit.

inductance the measure of a magnetic field generated by current passing through an inductor.

inductor a wire coil that stores energy in the form of a magnetic field.

insulator any material through which electricity cannot flow. Opposite of a conductor.

integrated circuit a conglomeration of transistors and other electronic components on a silicon wafer.

junction on a transistor or a diode, the area where opposite types of semiconductor elements meet.

LED an acronym for light-emitting diode, as used in lighted calculator displays.

MEMS microelectromechanical system; microscopic gears, springs, mirrors, sensors, or other devices mounted on chips only millimeters wide. MEMS are used to sense motion, light, temperature, chemicals, and so on in everything from toys to pacemakers.

N-type a region of a semiconductor that has been treated (doped) with an impurity to create free negative charges.

ohm a measurement of electrical resistance, equal to the resistance of a conductor carrying 1 ampere of current at a potential difference of 1 volt between the terminals.

P-type a region of a semiconductor that has been treated with an impurity to create holes (an absence of electrons), which act as positive charges.

resistance a measure of how difficult it is for electricity to flow through a component, measured in ohms.

resistor a device used to introduce resistance into an electrical circuit.

semiconductor any element that is both a poor conductor and a poor insulator, such as silicon.

series two or more components connected end to end so that the same current flows through each component.

silicon the most widely used semiconductor material; it goes into the manufacture of transistors, diodes, integrated circuits, and other components.

solid-state of electronic components, with no moving parts.

transistor a miniature electronic component that controls and amplifies electric current; it is composed of a layer of semiconducting material sandwiched between two opposing layers of semiconducting material.

vacuum tube a glass tube from which all air has been removed and containing electrodes between which current may be passed.

volt a unit of electromotive force.

watt a unit of power.

ROBOTICS

(*Also see* COMPUTERS)

actuator a servo mechanism.

AGV automated guided vehicle.

algorithm a series of programmable steps used to solve a mathematically based problem.

android a robot having a humanlike form, as distinguished from a boxlike robot or an industrial robot arm.

armed robotic vehicle an unmanned, robotically-controlled vehicle armed with missiles and a gun turret, currently under development with the military abbreviated as ARV.

automation a mechanical system that automatically controls its own tasks.

automaton robot.

bionics artificial organs or other human parts designed to replace real parts.

bugs errors in software.

Cartesian coordinates a system that defines an object's position; that is, an X coordinate (left to right) along one dimension, a Y coordinate (front to back) along another, and a Z coordinate indicating up and down. A robot arm may be capable of moving along these coordinates.

CIAM computerized, integrated, and automated manufacturing.

cybernetics the science of communication and control as they apply to complex machines and living organisms.

cyborg in science fiction, a human equipped with bionic parts.

degrees of freedom the distance or amount a robot arm is capable of moving along any dimension, for example, up, down, left, right, cylindrically.

drive system the power plant and components that enable a robot to move.

droid a robot programmed to cause no harm to humans, a popular device used in science fiction.

end effectors devices or tools, such as drills, saws, screwdrivers, and grippers, attached to the end of a robot arm to perform different tasks.

feedback a robot's ability to sense external stimuli and respond to it.

first-generation robot a deaf, dumb, and blind robot; an early model with no sensory ability.

fixed-stop robot a simple robot in which motion is controlled by a series of mechanical stops.

gripper a hand or manipulator used for grasping; an end effector.

hard automation a low-tech form of automation that can be altered only by shutting down the system and changing its physical components. See SOFT AUTOMATION.

humanoid any robot similar to a human in appearance or behavior.

interface a mechanical connection between two components, say a computer and a robot arm.

joystick control a stick moved by an operator to control a robot's motions.

manipulator the arm or hand of an industrial robot.

menu a list of possible motions of a robot, used by an operator in programming tasks.

micromotor a microscopic motor, powered by piezoelectricity, and currently being developed to navigate the human bloodstream to target diseased arteries.

MULE multifunction utility/logistics and equipment vehicle; currently under development for the military, a robotically-controlled vehicle designed to carry ammunition to troops on the battlefield, to carry out the wounded, and to fire machine guns or antitank weapons.

neuroengineering the emerging technology of connecting the human brain with machines or robots and controlling them through thought.

pick-and-place robot a simple form of robot consisting of an arm that transfers objects from one place to another.

point-to-point control programming a robot's arm movement along a series of points.

program a series of computer commands processed in binary language of 0's and 1's to control a robot's actions.

programmable robot a robot that can be programmed and reprogrammed to perform various tasks.

proximity sensor a device that senses position and distance of objects.

PUMA programmable universal machine for assembly; commercial name for a widely used manufacturing robot arm.

resolution a robot's accuracy at placing its end effectors within the desired parameters.

revolute coordinate robot a robot arm jointed at the shoulder, elbow, and wrist.

second-generation robot a robot equipped with sensory apparatus allowing it to react to visual, auditory, or tactile stimuli.

sensor any detection device used to sense temperature, moisture, radiation, light, distance, or motion.

servo mechanism an actuator or motor and a feedback device that conduct accurate movement and correct any deviation in intended movement. Also called a servo motor.

soft automation an automated system that can be altered or modified by software programming. See HARD AUTOMATION.

Soldier Unmanned Ground Vehicle currently under development for the military, a remote-controlled renaissance robot capable of climbing stairs, inspecting interiors, and serving sentry duty. Abbreviated as SUGV.

syntaxeur a machine used to teach a robot a series of movements by driving a control device through the same motions.

systems fusion the successful blending of various components, such as a global positing system (GPS) navigation system with radar and visual cameras.

telechiric device a robot hand or arm manipulated by an operator from a remote location.

teleoperated any machine or robot arm controlled from a remote location by an operator.

telepresence manipulating a mechanical arm or hand and receiving stimulus or feedback from it while in a remote location.

third-generation robot a robot having a high form of artificial intelligence, for example, the ability to make decisions on its own.

work envelope the collective area within which a robot arm can reach and work.

wrist articulation the ability of a robot wrist to bend up and down, turn side to side, and rotate.

yaw side to side movement of a robot arm.

ENVIRONMENT

ATMOSPHERE AND SKY

air the mixture of Earth's atmospheric gases, consisting of approximately 78 percent nitrogen, 21 percent oxygen, and small amounts of argon, carbon dioxide, neon, helium, methane, krypton, nitrous oxide, hydrogen, ozone, xenon, nitric oxide, and radon.

airglow the distinct glow or luminescence emanating from the ionosphere, caused by complex electrochemical reactions.

astronomical dawn the time when the Sun is 18 degrees below the horizon and lightening of the sky begins.

astronomical dusk the time when the Sun drops 18 degrees below the horizon and illumination of the sky fades out.

atmospheric layers the series of distinctive layers that make up the Earth's atmosphere; the lowest is the troposhere, followed by the stratosphere, the mesosphere, the ionosphere, the thermosphere, and the exosphere.

chlorofluorocarbon any of several compounds used as refrigerants and in aerosol cans that, when released into the atmosphere, rise to the stratosphere and deplete or destroy the Earth's protective ozone layer.

circumzenithal arc seen from the ground as an upside-down rainbow, usually in the far north and high in the sky—actually the bottom quarter or half of a circle of light, caused by sunlight passing through ice crystals several miles above Earth, and not associated with rain.

civil dawn the period when the Sun is six degrees below the horizon, when the Earth is partly illuminated.

civil dusk the period when the Sun drops six degrees below the horizon, when darkness begins to fall.

exosphere the uppermost stratum of the Earth's atmosphere, starting about 300 miles up and eventually giving way to the radiation belts and magnetic fields of space.

fata morgana complex multiple mirage seen along the Atlantic and Pacific coasts, where cliffs and rock formations may appear suspended in the sky or take on the appearance of castles and towers, caused by refraction of light in atmospheric zones of varying densities; named for the legendary castles of Morgan le Fay.

global warming see GREENHOUSE EFFECT.

glory a bull's-eye-light rainbow or aura caused by diffraction of sunlight through a thin cloud of water vapor, most frequently seen surrounding an airplane's shadow. Also known as a corona.

green flash a light-refracting phenomenon in which the last portion or bead of the setting Sun and surrounding sky flash out in a brilliant green, usually lasting only an instant and rarely seen.

greenhouse effect the trapping of heat and solar radiation in the atmosphere by excess carbon dioxide released by the increased burning of wood and fossil fuels, with the projected long-range effect of warming the Earth's overall climate and raising sea level by melting the polar ice caps.

hydrocarbon pollution pollution of the Earth's atmosphere by unburned or partially burned gasoline vapors.

hydrologic cycle the natural cycle in which water evaporates, forms clouds, and returns water back to Earth in the form of precipitation.

ionosphere the ion-rich layer of Earth's atmosphere found within the thermosphere between 50 and 180 miles up, used for reflecting radio beams in long-distance radio communication.

jet streams rivers of high-speed winds, usually travelling from west to east, from 30,000 to 45,000 feet up.

magnetosphere the huge magnetic envelope that protects the Earth from the Sun's constant blast of ions, found above the atmosphere as part of space.

mesosphere the strata of Earth's atmosphere from 30 to 50 miles up where extremely dry air drops to temperatures as low as –225°F.

mock sun a false image of the Sun, often watery in appearance, formed by the refraction or bending of light by hexagonal crystals of ice in the air. Also known as a sun dog.

ozone hole any one of various atmospheric "holes," which expand seasonally, such as has been measured over Antarctica, resulting from the chemical depletion of the protective layer of ozone from polluting chlorofluorocarbons.

ozone layer the layer of ozone gas (an explosive form of oxygen) that extends from 10 to 30 miles up in the stratosphere, and protects the Earth by absorbing hazardous ultraviolet radiation from the Sun.

Rayleigh scattering the scientific explanation for why the sky is blue. Blue wavelengths of sunlight are scattered by air molecules in all directions while yellow, red, and orange are not and pass to Earth unobstructed.

stratosphere the stratum of the Earth's atmosphere from 10 to 30 miles up that contains the ozone layer.

thermal a rising column of warm air.

thermosphere the stratum of Earth's atmosphere from 50 to 300 miles up that contains ionized bands, collectively known as the ionosphere.

troposphere the stratum of Earth's atmosphere from 0 to 10 miles up, where most weather systems occur.

ultraviolet radiation a form of radiation from the sun, most of which is absorbed or blocked by the Earth's ozone layer.

X-rays a form of the Sun's radiation, which is filtered or absorbed by the Earth's thermosphere.

BEACHES AND SHORES

barchan a crescent-shaped sand dune.

barrier beach a large, low-lying sand bar surrounded by the sea.

barrier reef a long, narrow ridge or rock or coral running parallel to the shore and separated from the beach by deep water.

bay a broad-mouthed inlet of the sea that is larger than a cove but smaller than a gulf.

berm a large terracelike ledge or shelf of sand deposited on a beach over time.

bluff a steep embarkment or headland cut or eroded by the sea.

bore a dangerous, often high wave caused by an incoming tide surging upstream in a narrowing estuary; can also be caused by the collision of tidal currents. Also known as an eagre.

cape any body of land projecting into the ocean.

cay a small island composed of sand or coral.

channel a waterway between two land masses. Also, a deep course navigable by large boats or ships.

cove a small bay, especially one that is sheltered by steep banks or promontories.

crest the top of a wave.

cusps curving mounds of sand several feet long set at regular intervals, caused by the sea breaking at right angles to the beach.

detritus eroded particles of plants, sea creatures, and rocks littering the beach.

eagre high, dangerous wave caused by an incoming tide surging upstream in a narrowing estuary.

ebb tide a receding tide.

eel grass a type of seaweed.

embayment a small bay or cove.

estuary an area where a river flows into the ocean.

feldspar common mineral particle found in beach sand.

fetch the distance wind travels from one point on the sea to another and its relation to the size of waves created; the longer the fetch or distance, the bigger the waves.

fjord a long inland arm of ocean surrounded on either side by cliffs or steep banks.

flotsam and jetsam debris, goods, or cargo cast or washed from an imperiled or wrecked ship.

foredune the dune or dunes immediately facing the sea; the closest dune to the shore.

foreshore the shore uncovered by a receding tide.

garnet a common mineral component found in beach sand.

graybeards any frothy or gray-crested waves.

groin a short jetty of stone or other material built at right angles to the shore to catch sand and help combat beach erosion.

gulf a broad expanse of ocean that extends inland and is considerably larger than a bay.

headland a high point of land extending out into the water; a promontory.

inlet an estuary or narrow bay.

isthmus a narrow strip of land extending into the water and joining two land masses, such as a mainland beach and an island.

jetty a structure of rocks or other material extending out into the water to protect a harbor.

key a low coral island, islet, or reef.

lagoon a small, shallow body of water sheltered from the sea by a reef or sandbar.

lee shore a shore protected from the wind, a haven for vessels because of its calmer sea.

littoral pertaining to the shore area.

longshore current a narrow current caused by diagonally breaking waves, known to move large quantities of sand and to build up new or existing beaches.

mermaid's purse a brown, pillowlike object with a tendril extending from each corner; the leathery egg case of a skate, commonly found on many beaches.

neap tide the minimal or low-moving tide occurring after the first and third quarters of the Moon, when the Sun's tidal force acts at right angles to that of the Moon.

parabolic dune a U-shaped beach dune with the open end toward the sea.

peninsula a large land mass bordered on three sides by the sea and connected to a mainland by an isthmus.

plunger a wave with a convex back and a crest that falls suddenly and violently, the most common type of beach wave.

pocket beach a small sand beach contained within an embayment between two cliffed headlands.

point a land mass that projects into the sea and ends in a narrow tip.

promontory headland.

quartz the most common component of beach sand.

red tide a bloom of phytoplankton that colors the water red and releases powerful toxins that kill large populations of fish and taint clams and mussels, making them hazardous for humans to eat.

rill a small water channel formed when a beach is saturated.

riptide a cross or conflicting current making for dangerous swimming conditions.

rockweed a rock-clinging seaweed.

sandbar a ridge of sand formed along beaches.

seaboard a coastline.

seashell The following are common types of seashells: abalone, angel wings, baby bonnet, cask, clam, cockle, conch, cone, cowrie, horn, horse conch, limpet, mottled Venus, mussel, nautilus, oyster, periwinkle, razor, scallop, sea pen, slipper, triton, wentletrap.

shingle beach a beach consisting of small, flat stones and a steep slope descending into deep water with little or no surf, commonly seen in England.

shoal a shallow area formed by a reef or sandbar, hazardous to boating.

skerry a small reef or rocky island.

spiller a wave with a concave back and a crest that breaks gradually and continuously, most often seen offshore.

spindrift sea spray.

spit a narrow point of land extending into the water.

spring tide the highest and lowest tide occurring at new and full Moon and reinforced by the alignment with the Sun.

stack a small island of rock isolated from land and set apart from the head of a promontory.

strait any narrow channel connecting two larger bodies of water.

strand a beach or shoreline.

swash a wave's shallow sweep up a beach; a receding swash is also known as backwash.

swashmarks long, interlacing ripples and strands of marine debris left by a receding swash.

tide the rise and fall of the sea due to the gravitational pull of the Sun and Moon.

tideland any land that is submerged at high tide.

tidemark any human-made or organic mark that indicates the sea's highest point during high tide.

tide pool a small body of seawater—varying from the size of a bathtub to that of a swimming pool—left behind by a withdrawing tide, and frequently teeming with marine life.

tidewater water that floods tideland at high tide.

tombolo a sand bar connecting an island to the mainland or two islands together.

train a series of waves of the same or nearly the same size.

trough the depression or hollow between waves.

wrack any marine vegetation washed to shore; also, the wreckage of a ship cast ashore.

CAVES

angel's hair the delicate needles of gypsum found growing in some caves.

breakdown a pile of rocks in a passage resulting from the collapse of a wall or ceiling.

breathing cave a cave passage in which airstreams can be felt moving in two different directions, as in respiration.

calcite calcium carbonate mineral, frequently white and mixing with water and other minerals to form stalactites, stalagmites, and other cave encrustations.

canyon any cave passage that is at least twice as high as it is wide.

cave pearl a flowerlike mineral formation made largely of calcite; also known as a pisolith.

caver a spelunker.

ceiling pocket a small dome formation on the ceiling of a cave.

chimney a narrow, vertical shaft. Also, the term used to describe the method of climbing a vertical shaft.

claustrophobia the fear of enclosed places.

column formation created by the joining of a stalactite with a stalagmite.

conduit a subterranean passage through which water flows or has flowed in the past.

crawl speleological term for any crawl space.

crouchway any passage that can be gotten through only by crouching or stooping.

dome a large, oval opening in the ceiling of a cave passage, closed at the top.

domepit a circular shaft in the floor of a cave, usually consisting of limestone or other soluble rock that has worn away.

dripstone collective term for any stalactite, stalagmite, or other formation created by dripping water and minerals.

flowstone calcium carbonate deposit forming sheets, drapery, and coatings over rocks.

fluting vertical striations in cave walls.

gallery a large chamber or hall.

glaciere a cave in a glacier.

glaciospeleology the study of glacier caves.

gour a small basin or pool of clear water edged with calcite encrustations.

grape a calcium carbonate deposit with the appearance of a grape or tea, encrusted on a cave wall.

gypsum a white or colorless mineral deposited in caves as calcium sulfate and forming flowers, needles, cotton balls, and other shapes.

karst an area of land characterized by numerous sinkholes and caves, formed by eroded limestone.

knee crawler knee pad used by spelunkers in crawl spaces.

lava tube cave a conduit or passage through which lava once flowed.

limestone sedimentary rock consisting largely of calcium carbonate. Most caves are limestone formations carved out by water.

master cave the main or largest cave in a group.

moon milk a white, puttylike form of flowstone.

pinched out a narrowing passage that becomes impenetrable. Also known as a pinch.

pitch a vertical shaft.

ponor the point where a stream disappears under a shelf of rock.

pothole any cave system where vertical shafts predominate.

sink a rounded depression often containing water.

sinkhole a hole, depression, or basin formed on the surface of karst land through which water drains underground.

sinkhole entrance access to a cave through a sinkhole.

soda straw a tiny stalactite in the shape of a soda straw.

speleology the study of caves.

spelunker one who studies or explores caves.

stalactite a long, tapering formation hanging from the roof of caves, formed by dripping water, calcium carbonate, and other minerals.

stalagmite conical calcium carbonate formation standing on the floor of caves; the counterpart of a stalactite.

sump an underwater passage in a cave; also known as a syphon.

troglobite any animal specially adapted to live in caves.

troglodyte a caveman.

troglophile any animal who inhabits a cave but may not be specially adapted to live there, such as a bat.

CLOUDS

altocumulus elliptical globular masses, forming individually, in groups, or in bands between 6,500 and 23,000 feet; also known as sheep or woolpack clouds.

altostratus bluish or grayish white sheets covering most or all of the sky between 6,500 and 23,000 feet.

anvil the flat top of a spreading cumulonimbus cloud, which resembles an anvil.

arcus any low, horizontal cloud seen at the leading edge of a thunderstorm, but particularly a roll or shelf cloud.

banner cloud a stationary, bannerlike plume seen frequently over the lee side of a mountain.

barber pole slang for any curving cloud striation, resembling the stripes on a barber pole, caused by updrafting in a thunderstorm.

ceiling the height of the lowest clouds.

cirriform thin, wispy clouds appearing at high altitude.

cirrocumulus rippled or banded clouds, often referred to as a "mackerel sky," forming between 16,000 and 45,000 feet.

cirrostratus high, thin, white veils covering all or most of the sky between 16,000 and 45,000 feet.

cirrus detached, feather or tufted clouds forming between 16,000 and 45,000 feet; also known as mares's tails.

clinometer device used to measure the height of clouds.

cloud seeding a technique in which various chemicals, especially silver iodide and dry ice, are dispersed into clouds via aircraft or rockets in an attempt to produce precipitation.

cloud tag cloud fragment. Also known as scud, fractus.

congestus a towering, cauliflower-like cumulus cloud.

contrails vapor trails left by aircraft.

cumuliform any mound or dome-shaped cloud or one that towers.

cumulonimbus towering clouds arising from cumulus 2 to 5 miles in height, yielding rain and sometimes thunderstorms. The thunderstorm cloud itself is called a thunderhead.

cumulus individual cloud masses vertically domed with a cauliflower-like appearance; associated with fair weather.

debris cloud at the base of a tornado, a rotating cloud of dust and debris.

eye wall the cloud band immediately surrounding a hurricane, the most intense area of the storm.

fractocumulus a ragged-looking cumulus cloud.

fractus any broken-off cloud fragment. Also known as scud.

funnel cloud a funnel-shaped cloud descending from a cumulus or cumulonimbus cloud, technically becoming a tornado only when debris and dust can be seen churning below it at ground level.

halo apparent circle around the sun or moon, caused by the refraction of sunlight by ice crystals in high, thin cirrus or cirrostratus clouds.

incus the anvil-shaped top of a thunderhead.

mammatocumulus cloud with extreme billowing or boiling appearance, accompanying severe thunderstorms and tornado conditions.

nephology the study of clouds.

nephoscope a device that measures the height and speed of clouds.

nimbostratus thick, dark gray, and shapeless cloud sheets associated with steady precipitation, forming between 6,500 and 23,000 feet.

noctilucent cloud a cloud that appears to "glow" at night, caused by reflected sunlight below the horizon.

roll cloud associated with a thunderstorm, a low, horizontal, tube-shaped cloud.

scud ragged patch broken off from main cloud by the wind.

shelf cloud associated with a thunderstorm, a low, horizontal, wedgelike cloud.

stratocumulus heavy rolls or globular masses arranged in bands covering most of the sky, forming between 0 and 6,500 feet.

stratus continuous, layerlike cloud deck, with no individual units, forming between 0 and 6,500 feet.

updraft rising moist, warm air that condenses into cumulus and cumulonimbus clouds.

virga wisps or trails suspended from clouds, often composed of rain that evaporates before reaching the ground.

DESERTS

alluvial fan the deposits of alluvial material, such as rocks and silt, that fan out at a mountain base or slope.

alluvium deposits of sand, silt, gravel, or rocks transported by water and laid down near stream or lake beds or around the base of mountains.

arroyo a dried-up stream or riverbed.

badlands a barren area where soft rocks or clays became eroded, creating ridges, mesas, channels, and gullies.

bajada the overlapping area of two or more alluvial fans, creating a wide expanse of deposited debris.

barchan a crescent-shaped sand dune, created by a one-directional wind.

Bedouin one of the groups of nomadic Arabs that roam the deserts of Syria and Arabia.

desert pavement a sand-free area of rocks and pebbles fitted together and highly polished by abrasion, forming a colorful mosaic bed. Known as gibber plain in Australia, serir in Libya, and reg in the Sahara.

erg the vast area where sand accumulates in the Sahara, opposed to the sand-free areas of desert known as reg.

gypsum the white mineral making up many of the sand dunes at White Sands National Monument in New Mexico.

inselberg a vestigial mountain reduced by erosion to a rocky nubbin or isolated "island," found in the most ancient desert areas.

mesa an eroded mountain with a flattened top and sheer rock walls; a smaller version of a mesa is known as a butte.

mirage an optical illusion caused by the refraction of light, sometimes causing the illusion of water in the desert, which in reality is only a mirror image of a shimmering blue sky.

oasis an isolated fertile area in the desert, fed by groundwater or irrigation and surrounded by lush vegetation.

phantom rain rain that passes through hot, dry desert air and evaporates before hitting the ground.

playa a level plain that can become a temporary lake after a rain.

pyramid a pyramid-shaped dune.

rain shadow the leeward side of a mountain, where little or no rain falls.

seif a sand dune elongated in the prevailing wind direction, known to grow up to 300 feet high and 1,500 feet long. Also known as a sword or longitudinal dune.

star sand dune formed by winds from several different directions, creating a stationary series of hummocks in the shape of a star.

steppe a semidesert plain devoid of trees.

transverse type of dunes characterized by ridges, giving the appearance of a series of ocean waves.

whaleback a giant sand dune that may stretch as far as 100 miles, sometimes seen in the Sahara.

DESERT VEGETATION

barrel cactus a succulent of the U.S. Southwest, known for its stout, branchless barrel shape.

century plant a succulent of the amaryllis family, flowering after about 25 years of growth but popularly thought to bloom after a century; tequila and mescal are derived from it.

cereus a night-blooming succulent that stores water in an underground container.

cholla a cactus with detachable joints that sticks to anything that brushes it, popularly known as a jumping cholla or teddybear cactus.

creosote bush shrub of the American Southwest whose name is derived from the acrid odor it gives off after a rain.

elephant tree tree found in Baja California, having a pulpy trunk serving as a water reservoir.

hedgehog cactus ground-hugging succulent producing brilliant blooms and red fruit.

ironwood a desert tree known for its unusually hard wood.

Joshua tree a member of the yucca family that grows up to 25 feet high and may live for hundreds of years, commonly found in the Mojave.

mesquite a spiny tree yielding pods and particularly dense wood.

ocotillo barbed shrub with small leaves.

paloverde desert plant with minute leaves, whose stems and branches contain chlorophyll, allowing photosynthesis even after the leaves have dropped.

prickly pear cactus a cactus growing in clumps of spiny paddles.

sagebrush an aromatic shrub commonly found throughout the U.S. Southwest.

saguaro a giant cactus known to grow as tall as 50 feet.

EARTHQUAKES

aftershock an earthquake that follows a larger earthquake.

dendrochronology the study of forest trees' growth rings to determine the location of past earthquakes; the rings reveal when a tree has been partially toppled over—evidence of an earthquake.

earthquake lights mysterious flickering glow seen over the ground during an earthquake, thought to be a natural reaction of rocks when stressed to the breaking point.

earthquake storm a cluster of earthquakes, with each quake triggered by the movement of the previous one.

epicenter the area directly above the center of an earthquake, where the largest vibrations are usually felt.

fault a fracture in rock strata or, on a larger scale, in the Earth's crust.

foreshock a small earthquake that precedes a larger one by several days or weeks.

liquefaction the shaking and churning of wet clay and sand into a dense liquid, as in severe earthquake activity.

Love waves earthquake waves causing side-to-side shaking, similar to the motion of a snake.

megathrust earthquake a massive earthquake generated by shifting tectonic plates at subduction zones.

megatsunami a towering tsunami, reaching heights far above normal, caused by landslides, volcanic collapse, or an asteroid impact in water close to shore. The largest megatsunami, at an estimated 1,720 feet (524 m) in height, was caused when an earthquake dislodged a massive block of rock and ice directly into Lituya Bay in 1958.

Mercalli intensity scale a scale of earthquake intensity based on observed structural damage and people's responses in questionnaires after a local quake, unrelated to the Richter scale, which measures magnitude.

microearthquake an earthquake with a magnitude of 2.0 or less as measured by the Richter scale, generally not felt by people.

moment magnitude scale introduced in 1979, a scale that more accurately measures the energy released by earthquakes stronger than 7 on the Richter scale, with the ability to measure more accurately from distances greater than 350 miles (600 km).

plate tectonics the interaction and subsequent effects of the Earth's continental plates colliding and scraping up against each other, as seen most notably in the San Andreas Fault in California.

precursor a geological event that immediately precedes an earthquake, including a change in seismic velocities, and groundwater levels and a tilting of ground surface.

primary wave the fastest traveling earthquake wave, also known as a P-wave or compressional wave. It is a pressure wave that compresses and decompresses the Earth as it travels out from an epicenter. P-waves are faster moving but less destructive than S-waves. The roar often heard at the start of an earthquake is actually a burst of P-waves reaching the Earth's surface and agitating air molecules.

P-wave see PRIMARY WAVE.

Richter scale a scale determining the magnitude of an earthquake as recorded by seismographs. Due to the logarithmic basis of the scale, each whole number increase in magnitude represents a 10-fold increase in magnitude. For example, an earthquake measuring 6.7 on the Richter scale would be considered 10 times worse than one measuring 5.7.

right-lateral fault faulted ground that moves or has moved to the right as you face it.

sand blow a small, volcano-like formation made by the explosion of liquefied soil during an earthquake, also known as sand volcano.

seaquake see SUBMARINE EARTHQUAKE.

secondary wave an earthquake wave, also known as an S-wave or shake wave, slower than a P-wave but more powerful. An S-wave causes the Earth to shake back and forth as it travels out from an epicenter; however, it cannot move through water.

seismic referring to earthquake activity.

seismic prospecting a technique of determining the nature of an underground rock structure by setting off explosive charges and measuring the time it takes the shock waves to travel varying paths; a seismic profile is attained this way.

seismic wave a wave of movement that travels through the Earth.

seismograph an instrument that records vibrations of the Earth.

seismology the study of earthquakes and other vibrations of the Earth.

seismometer an electronic instrument that measures and records ground motion. Also known as a seismograph.

subduction zone any area where one tectonic plate descends and forces its way beneath another tectonic plate, a source of earthquake and volcanic activity.

submarine earthquake an earthquake originating beneath the seafloor.

S-wave see SECONDARY WAVE.

temblor a tremor or earthquake.

tremor a small earthquake or vibration, often occurring before or after a major earthquake.

tsunami the Japanese term for *harbor wave,* formerly and erroneously known as a tidal wave. A tsunami is actually any one of what is usually a series of waves that may reach a height of 100 feet (30.5 m) and can cross an entire ocean at speeds up to 600 miles per hour (966 km/h), usually caused by an earthquake, underwater landslide, or collapse of an onshore landmass, such as a volcano, into a large body of water.

tsunami detection buoy a surface buoy connected to an underwater pressure sensor that can detect tsunamis and relay alerts via satellite.

tsunami warning network a series of tsunami detection buoys anchored throughout the ocean, capable of sending alerts via satellite.

FIELDS, MEADOWS, AND MARSHES

bracken any moist area with a heavy growth of a fern by the same name.

brake an area of thick brush.

everglade a marshland with tall stands of grass.

heath a large field or plain covered with small shrubs, such as heather.

moor a frequently elevated field covered with heather, bracken, and marshy areas.

pampas the grassy plains in South America lying from the Andes to the Atlantic Ocean. The equivalent of the North American prairie.

plain a large area of mostly treeless grassland.

prairie grassy plains of midwest North America.

rush any of various marsh plants or grasses having hollow stems.

savanna a tropical or subtropical grassland, sometimes having scattered trees.

sedge a grasslike marsh plant.

steppes grasslands of Eurasia.

tundra treeless plains with marshy areas, in Siberia and arctic North America.

tussock a thick tuft of grass.

veld elevated, treeless grassland of South Africa.

FLOWERS AND PLANTS

achene a small, hard, dry, one-seeded fruit that doesn't split open or yawn when ripe, typically found with buttercups and dandelions.

aerial rootlets small rootlike branches growing out of the stems of some climbing vines.

ananthous flowerless.

annual living and growing only one year or season.

anther at the top of a stamen, the tiny organ that secretes and discharges pollen.

armed bearing prickles, spines, or thorns.

aromatic spicy- or sweet-smelling.

axis the main stem or center around which plant parts or branches grow.

beard a group of bristles or hairs on a plant.

biennial a plant with the cycle of two years, producing leaves the first year, and fruit or flowers the second.

blade the flat, green expanse portion of a leaf, as opposed to the stalk.

bloom a white, powdery coating found on some fruits, such as plums, and the leaves and stems of various plants.

bract a small leaf beneath a flower or on the stalk of a flower cluster.

bud a leafy stem or flower unopened and undeveloped.

bulb an underground root or stem with fleshy scales and a food store for the undeveloped plant within.

calyx a collective term for the sepals of a flower; the leaflike green segments forming the outer circle in a flower.

catkin small flower cluster, drooping and resembling a kitten's tail; commonly found on willow and birch trees.

chaff husks of grain separated from the seed.

chlorophyll the green pigment found in plants.

claw the stalklike base of a petal.

corm a scaleless bulb or stem base.

corolla the collective term for the petals of a flower, separate or joined.

corymb a flat-topped flower cluster in which the outer flowers open first.

cyme a flat-topped flower cluster in which the middle or central flowers open first.

disk flower the tubular flowers that project from the center of the heads of daisies, sunflowers, and asters.

downy a coating of short, fine, soft hairs.

drupe any fruit, such as a peach, plum, or cherry, that has a hard pit or stone.

effloresce to blossom, bloom.

elliptic shaped like an ellipse, wide in the middle, tapered at both ends, as a leaf or petal.

evergreen a plant whose leaves remain green all year.

eye a mark or spot in the middle of the flower, prominent and of a different color from the rest of the flower.

filament the stalk of a stamen.

flora the native plants of a region.

floret any small flower, also known as a floweret.

gland any secreting organ of a plant.

head a dense cluster of stalkless flowers.

heliotropic of or any of the various plants that turn toward or follow the sun's path across the sky, relating to a condition also known as the phototropic response.

horticulture the art and science of cultivating plants, particularly ornamentals.

hortus siccus a collection of dried plants; a herbarium.

humus decomposed, dead vegetation.

hydroponics a soil-less growing method in which plant roots are bathed in dissolved nutrients.

lip an irregularly sized petal on an unequally divided corolla.

midrib the main or central vein of a leaf.

nosegay a small bouquet of flowers.

ornamental a plant growth for the purpose of decoration; a beautiful plant.

palmate a plant with lobes or leaves that spread out as the extended fingers of a hand.

perennial describing a plant with a life span or more than two years; a plant that lives on season after season.

photosynthesis the process through which plants convert sunlight to energy and synthesize organic compounds from inorganic ones.

phototropism the growth or movement of a plant in response to sunlight.

pistil the female organ of a flower, which develops into a fruit.

pollen tiny grains containing the male germ cells, released by the anthers of flowering plants.

pollen count the average number of ragweed pollen grains in a specific volume of air over a 24-hour period, used as a scale to estimate the severity of hayfever attacks.

pollen tube the thin tube emitted by a grain of pollen that infiltrates an ovule and fertilizes it.

pollinate to transfer pollen from an anther to a stigma for the purpose of fertilization.

pome any fruit with a papery, inner chamber containing the seeds, such as an apple.

pubescent having leaves or stems that are covered with fine hairs.

raceme a cluster of flowers in which each flower blooms on a short stalk arising at different points on a common stem.

ray flower any of the flat, strap-shaped flowers crowning the heads of composite flowers, such as daisies. Also known as a ray floret.

rosette a circle of leaves lying nearly flat on the ground.

saprophytic living on dead organic matter, as a plant.

scurfy covered with small scales.

sepal the leaflike green segments forming under the corolla.

slip a cutting from a plant used for grafting or planting; also known as a scion.

spadix a dense spike of flowers.

spathe a large bract surrounding or enclosing a flower cluster.

spatulate having leaves that are spoon-shaped with a rounded tip tapering to a stalk tip.

spike a spike-shaped cluster of flowers.

stamen the male element of a flower, consisting of a filament and pollen-bearing anther.

stigma the top of the pistil where pollen is received.

throat the opening into the tube of a corolla or calyx.

tropophyte a plant adapted to extreme weather changes.

umbel a flower cluster in which each flower stalk rises from the same or nearly the same point.

woolly covered with tangled hairs.

FOG

advection fog fog resulting from air being cooled by horizontal movement; the passing of cool air over warm water causes the advection fog known as steam fog or sea smoke to form. Most maritime fogs, however, are caused by warm, humid air passing over cooler water.

dew point the temperature at which air becomes saturated; further cooling beyond the dew point causes condensation and fog.

pogonip fog containing ice crystals.

rime freezing fog that deposits frost.

GARDENS AND LANDSCAPING

AAS see ALL AMERICA SELECTIONS.

accent plant usually a bold, colorful, or "interesting" plant that acts as a focal point for the rest of the garden.

aeration turning over soil or creating small holes in it in order to expose it to air.

alkaline soil soil with a pH level of 7 or more. Also known as sweet soil.

All America Selections new, award-winning cultivars of flowers and vegetables rigorously tested by a group of horticulturists.

allelopathy the chemical warfare launched by some plants to prevent the growth of competing plants nearby.

allée in a French garden, a tree-lined walk or avenue.

amend to correct or improve poor soils, by adding nutrients, drainage materials, etc.

annual a plant that grows only for one season then dies.

arbor a latticework structure on which vines or climbing roses are trained to grow.

arboretum a type of museum where plants and trees, especially rare ones, are grown, studied, and displayed.

balled and burlap of a plant, sold with its roots wrapped in burlap.

bedding the planting of established (already grown) plants together in a group.

berceau an arched trellis over a walkway.

berm a mound of earth, created to control runoff, improve privacy, or raise a plant bed.

biennial a plant that grows only leaves in its first season and then blooms and seeds in its second, after which it dies. Foxglove and hollyhocks are biennial plants.

bonemeal fertilizer made from ground animal bones, used to improve root growth.

bonsai the Japanese art of dwarf tree and shrub cultivation. Also, the dwarf plants themselves.

border garden a garden of flowers, herbs, shrubs, etc., grown along the perimeter of a property.

bosquet a grove of trees in a park. Also known as a bosco.

bottle garden a terrarium created in a bottle.

bower a recess shaded with leafy plants.

boxwood an evergreen shrub often trimmed to form hedges, borders, or mazes. Also known as box.

broadcast to spread or scatter seed over a wide area.

broderie plants trimmed with embroidery-like designs. Also known as ricami.

cane any major stem of a raspberry, blackberry, rose, or bamboo plant.

capsule a dry seed pod that bursts when fully mature.

chaniwa a Japanese tea garden.

clairvoyée a windowlike hole cut into a hedge.

cloche a transparent cover used to protect plants from frost or insect damage.

clone an exact genetic copy of a plant.

cold frame a large box constructed as a miniature greenhouse, with a glass cover over a soil bed where plants can be protected and grown during frost season.

cole crops all crops in the cabbage family, including broccoli, cabbage, cauliflower, collards, kale, and kohlorabi.

common name a name by which a plant is known to the public, as opposed to its botanical name.

companion planting the planting of two different plants next to each other, either because the color or textures enhance one another or because one may provide necessary shade for the other.

compost decomposing organic matter used for fertilizer.

conservatory a formal greenhouse employed for the display of plants and flowers.

cordon pruning all stems except the main one on a fruit tree, a technique employed when space is limited.

cottage garden an English garden style characterized by seemingly haphazard plantings of flowers, herbs, vegetables, and climbing vines.

cover crop any crop planted to keep weeds down or add humus to the soil between seasonal plantings.

creeper any plant that grows like a vine across the ground, such as a creeping fig or an ivy.

crocking any materials such as gravel or shells added to the bottom of plant container to aid with drainage.

cross pollination the successful transport of pollen from the flower of one plant to the flower of another, necessary in many plants for the setting of seed.

cultivate to break up topsoil to destroy or prevent weeds and to allow nutrients and water to sink into the ground more readily.

cultivar a plant created by cultivation and not found in the wild.

cutting a portion of a plant cut away to be used to propagate additional plants.

dark-dependent seeds seeds that are able to germinate only in the darkness of a soil cover.

deadhead to pinch off dead and dried-up flower heads to improve appearance or to induce new blooms.

dibble a pointed tool used to make holes in soil for planting.

dormant oil an oil containing fungicides or pesticides and applied to trees and shrubs in their dormant period, as in the late fall.

double digging turning over the soil to an extra deep level, to loosen it and make it easier for roots and nutrients to penetrate.

drip irrigation a method of watering through which a hose, often with several holes in it, is left to trickle along plants for long periods.

dwarf any variety of plant that naturally grows to a smaller size than normal.

edger any long-handled tool with a blade used for producing a perfectly trimmed edge along turf or sod.

edging plant any low plant that looks appealing aligned along an edge of a garden or walkway.

espalier a shrub or tree trained to grow in a flat, symmetrical plane up along a wall. Also, the trellis or frame used to train a plant to grow in this manner.

everblooming designating a plant that blooms all season.

exotic any nonnative or foreign plant, but especially those from another part of the world.

field-grown designating any plant that has been grown in the field as opposed to in a pot.

flat a shallow box of seedlings.

floriculture flower gardening.

forcing forcing a plant to flower prematurely by starting them indoors in the preseason.

foundation planting any plants or shrubs planted to hide the foundation of a house.

frost tender vulnerable to damage from even mild frost, as are most tropical plants.

furrow a channel made in soil for the planting of seeds or seedlings.

germination the sprouting of a seed.

graft to join the shoots or buds of two plants to create a plant with shared characteristics.

greenhouse a glass or plastic-enclosed shelter for growing plants.

green manure a cover crop such as rye grass that is grown and tilled into the soil to add nutrients.

greensand a sediment composed of sand, clay, glauconite, and multiple trace minerals, used as a natural fertilizer.

ground cover low-lying shrubbery or other plants that spread, require little maintenance, and can be used to cover unsightly areas.

habit the ultimate shape of a plant as it grows and matures.

ha-ha a sunken fence or moat to keep out animals and to provide a clear view of a garden area.

harden off to gently acclimate a plant to cold, wind, or sun by gradually increasing exposures.

hardiness the natural ability of some plants to withstand frost and extreme cold.

hardpan severely compressed soil, through which water and nutrients may not be able to penetrate.

hardscape all nonplant items in a landscape, such as benches, birdbaths, arbors, rocks, walkways, etc.

heeling in temporarily burying the roots of a plant to protect it until it is ready to be permanently planted.

heirloom plant a plant that has survived more than 50 years and may be passed down from generation to generation.

herb a plant from which is derived a natural medicine or seasoning for food.

herbicide any chemical solution used to kill plants.

hoe a long-handled tool with a flat blade, used for cultivating and other gardening tasks.

honey dew the sticky fluid secreted by aphids and left on plants.

horticulture the growing of plants.

hotbed similar to a cold frame, but with heated soil.

hot cap a plastic cap placed over vulnerable seedling to protect it from cold weather or birds.

hothouse a heated shelter for plants.

humus decomposed plant material used as fertile soil.

hybrid a new species of plant created when two different varieties of plants are crossed.

hydroponics a gardening method in which plants are grown without soil, in a nutrient-rich solution.

ikebana Japanese flower arranging.

indeterminate growing for an indefinite amount of time, as some tomato plants.

indigenous plants plants native to an area.

infertile lacking nutrients, as a poor or exhausted soil.

interplanting mixing plants that bloom at different times in order to keep the garden interesting all season long.

invasive spreading rapidly and pushing out other plants. Invasive plants can be difficult to eliminate once established.

iron chelate vital nutrient fed to plants when leaves begin to turn yellow.

Japanese garden a garden style often employing bamboo, mondo grasses, pine, and small pools of water containing koi.

knot garden originating in Tudor times, a low-lying garden composed of an intricate hedge laid out in a geometric pattern, which is interplanted with flowers and herbs.

landscape architect one who designs major components of a garden, such as drainage, grading, walkways, and rock walls, and performs general construction.

lattice an open framework used to encourage the growth of vines or other climbing plants.

layering a technique used to propagate a plant. A branch leading off the parent plant is buried in the ground, which eventually forms roots and a new plant.

leaf cutting a technique used to propagate a plant. A leaf is cut from a parent plant and placed in vermiculite or perlite to create new plants.

leggy descriptive term for tall, spindly growth with little vegetation, due to a deficiency of sunlight.

lime a soil amendment containing calcium.

loam a mixture of sand, clay, organic matter, and silt, found in the topmost layer of soil.

manure tea a mix of water with manure, used as fertilizer.

microclimate in a small area, temperatures and moisture levels that differ from those of surrounding areas, and in which a plant with specific needs may be grown.

mixed border a border garden with a blend of perennials, annuals, shrubs, and grasses.

moon garden a garden planted with night-flowering plants, such as moonflowers.

mowing strip a narrow cement, brick, or other pavement that separates a garden from the lawn, and which can easily be mowed over without damaging the garden's plants.

mulch shredded or chipped material, often organic, placed around plants to help control weeds and to prevent roots from freezing.

naturalized designating plants that have been acclimated to a region other than their native one.

nursery a gardening center that grows and tends plants, shrubs, and trees.

organic natural and previously living, not synthesized by humans.

ornamental a plant grown for the beauty of its flowers or foliage rather than as a food.

parterre as French garden laid out in a pattern.

patté d'ole three avenues branching out from a central location.

perennial a plant that lives three years or more and may reflower again and again.

pergola a trelliswork arbor on which climbing vines or roses are trained to grow.

perlite granular volcanic rock, used to aerate potting soil.

pH a measure of a soil's level of acidity and alkalinity. A level of 1 is the most acid, whereas 14 is the most alkaline.

piscina a fish pool in a garden, especially Roman.

pleached alley a sheltered walk formed by the interlacing branches of two rows of trees.

pleaching plaiting trees or shrubs together, sometimes to form a wall.

pocket garden a small niche garden or a garden planted with dwarf varieties.

propagation any one of several methods of creating new plants.

prune to trim.

raised bed a vegetable or flower garden in soil that is mounded or raised above the surrounding land, often held together by wood.

reseeders any plants or flowers that drop seeds on the ground to grow next season.

retaining wall any wall built into a hill or slope to control erosion.

revert to turn back into its original species, an occurrence of some cultivars.

ricami see BRODERIE.

rock garden a small landscaped garden featuring various small plants and rocks. Also known as a rockery.

root-bound designating a potted plant whose roots have outgrown their containment, thwarting new growth.

rosarian a rose expert or hobbyist.

rotation switching the location of plants in the garden each year to cut down on soil-borne spread of disease.

row covers any transparent cover used to trap heat and protect plants from harsh weather.

sen-tei a Japanese water garden.

scion a shoot or bud of a woody plant, used in grafting.

side-dress to place fertilizer on the soil around plants but not work it into the ground.

soaker hose a hose with hundreds of tiny holes from which water trickles gradually into a garden.

soil amendment any fertilizer or organic or inorganic matter added to soil to improve it for optimum plant growth.

spading fork a long-handled implement with long tines, used for loosening up hardened ground.

specimen plant any striking plant, often used in a landscape as a focal point.

staking tying plants, especially tall-growing ones, to wooden stakes sunken in the ground, to prevent blowdowns from strong winds.

succession planting to plant and replant on a weekly basis in order to keep a steady supply of crops or flowers later in the season.

sucker a shoot that grows out of the roots of a plant.

sunken garden a garden that is recessed below ground level, for visual interest.

sweet soil see ALKALINE SOIL.

terrace a raised portion of earth, like a step, on which plants are grown, often part of a series of such on a hill.

terra-cotta a type of fired clay commonly used for pots in gardens.

terrarium a glass or plastic box or bottle for growing small plants.

thicket tangled undergrowth consisting of various shrubs, vines, and plants.

thinning the removal of smaller seedlings between larger ones to improve growth.

tokonoma a flowered alcove in a Japanese garden. Also, topiary hedges, shrubs, or trees pruned into fantastic or animal-like shapes.

top-dress to spread fertilizer or compost along the surface of the ground.

top soil the top layer of soil, which is usually the most fertile.

transplant to uproot and move a plant from one location to another.

trellis a lattice frame for climbing plants.

trowel a small scooplike implement used for digging holes for planting.

truck garden a garden from which vegetables, herbs, and flowers are sold at a market.

vernalization the extended period of cold climate some plants, such as apple trees, must be exposed to in order to bear buds in the spring.

victory garden a home or community garden grown to bolster the food supply during World War II.

vineyard a plantation of grapes, kiwi, or other vine crops.

volunteer a plant that spreads to an adjacent property, by wind, birds, or other means.

Garden Pests and Diseases

aphid a tiny greenish, sap-sucking insect that leaves behind a sugary dewlike substance that attracts ants.

black spot a fungal disease caused by moisture, most often seen on roses.

brown rot a common fungus that infects fruit.

canker a disease found on soft or rotten stems, caused by bacteria and fungi.

cutworm any of various caterpillars that cut down and feed on the tender new shoots of cabbage, corn, and other plants.

damping off fungal decay of a young seedling, often caused by overwatering or a soil-borne disease.

dieback the death of the tips of branches and shoots, caused by pests or disease.

dormant oil an oil used to coat fruit trees and kill insects and their eggs. Also known as horticultural oil.

fungicide a chemical solution used to control fungi and the diseases it causes.

fusarium a fungal disease of herbaceous plants.

gypsy moths destructive caterpillars which in the larval stage can defoliate entire trees.

horticultural oil see DORMANT OIL.

insecticide natural or synthesized chemicals used to kill or ward off insects.

Japanese beetle extremely damaging insect, imported from Japan and now widespread in the United States. Its larvae eat the roots of grass and the adults eat holes in a massive variety of plants.

mildew damaging fungi that cover plant leaves with a downy or powdery white residue.

neem an organic insecticide that is not toxic to humans.

nematode a root-eating, microscopic roundworm.

root rot fungal disease affecting a plant's roots, caused by poor drainage.

rotenone an organic insecticide derived from the roots of tropical legumes.

scald discolored and injured plant tissue caused by overexposure to sunlight. Also known as sun scald.

verticillium a fungal disease that causes wilting and kills plants.

GEOLOGY AND LANDFORMS

A-horizon the zone of soil, rich in organic matter, immediately below the surface.

allochthonous referring to a geological object created in a location other than where it was found, as a glacial erratic.

alluvial fan deposits of alluvial material, such as rock and silt, that fan out and form an apron at a mountain's base or lower slope; the land counterpart of a river delta.

alluvium any deposits of sand, mud, or silt created by moving water.

amber tree resin that has turned to stone, the interior of which may contain preserved insects or other small, prehistoric items of interest.

anticline strata of rock bent into an arch, the reverse of a syncline.

aquifer an underground pocket of rocks, gravel, or other permeable material through which groundwater flows.

archipelago a group or scattering of related islands.

arroyo a dried-up stream channel often found in desert areas. Also known as a wadi or wash.

asthenosphere the zone between 50 and 250 kilometers below the surface of the Earth where rock is heated and pressurized sufficiently to flow; responsible for many of the Earth's vertical and horizontal movements.

astrogeology geology of celestial bodies.

Atlantic Ridge a mountain range under the mid-Atlantic Ocean extending from Iceland to Antarctica.

autochthonous referring to a geological object created in the location where it is found.

badland a desert area of eroded ridges, peaks, and mesas.

bajada a series of coalescing alluvial fans at the base of a mountain or mountains.

basin an expansive depression in the Earth, which fills with deposits of sediment.

basin and range topography any broad expanse of land characterized by fault-bounded mountains and sediment-filled valleys.

batholith a huge igneous mass with a surface area of at least 100 square kilometers and increasing in size as it extends downward, intruded into other rock and found under or within mountain ranges. Also known as a pluton.

bedding the layers in sedimentary rock.

bedding plane the surface area separating one deposit of sedimentary rock from another of different character.

bedrock any rock layer underlying soil or sediment.

B-horizon zone of soil below the A-horizon.

biostratigraphy the science of determining the ages of rock layers and how they were distributed or deposited by the study of the fossils they contain.

bolson a flat desert valley surrounded by mountains that drains into a shallow central lake.

Burgess shale world-famous, 505-million-year-old shale formation in Canada, renowned for its high-quality fossils of bizarre, prehistoric creatures.

butte a mesa that has eroded so that its width and length are less than its height. Also known as a monument.

calcareous containing calcium carbonate, formed from the shells of bivalves.

Cambrian explosion a broad, evolutionary expansion of new animal types and complexities that, according to the fossil record, appeared mysteriously 530 million years ago.

carbon 14 a radioactive isotope of carbon that has a half-life of 5,730 years. Used to date objects or events up to 50,000 years ago.

carbonate a mineral made up largely of calcium carbonate, from seashells and coral formations.

Carboniferous period a geological period from 359.2 million to 299 million years ago, named for the widespread beds of coal laid down at the time.

cast a fossilized replica of an organic object, formed when sediment fills a mold of the object.

compaction any fossil that has been flattened, either by the weight of an overlaying of rock or by a glacier.

compression a trace of fossilized organic matter, the remains of a crushed organism.

concretion a mass of rock, often egglike or spherical in shape, and formed by accumulation of successive layers of sediment around a leaf, shell, fossil, or other object that serves as a nucleus, and is usually broken open by fossil collectors in search of such artifacts. Concretions are sometimes mistaken for fossilized dinosaur eggs.

continental drift the drifting of the continents due to spreading of the seafloor.

continental shelf a sloping shelf of a continent that extends into the ocean then descends sharply.

coprolite fossilized animal feces.

core the inner portion of the Earth, beginning approximately 2,900 kilometers down.

craton the large, generally immobile center portion of a continent.

creep the gradual sliding or slipping of soil and surface material down a slope.

crust the outermost shell of the Earth, extending about 35 kilometers down.

deflation wind erosion of unconsolidated material.

delta the large, delta-shaped deposit of silt found at the mouth of rivers.

dendrite appearing on some rocks, a tiny branching line made up of iron and manganese oxides, evidence of water filtration.

deposition an accumulation of material, such as silt, seashells, minerals, or the process of accumulation.

diagenesis the changes that occur to a fossil after burial.

dike a long formation of igneous rock intruded into the fissure of another rock.

dome an upfold of rock forming the shape of an inverted cup.

drill core a tube-shaped or elongated shaft of mud, rock, sediment, or ice extracted from the Earth for laboratory study.

drumlin an elongated hill, 8 to 60 meters high and 0.5 to 1 kilometer in length, consisting of rocks and gravel deposited by a glacier.

eon the longest division of geological time, sometimes denoting two or more eras. Sometimes used to denote a span of 1 billion years.

epoch a subdivision of geological time denoting a portion of a period.

era a major division of geological time comprising one or more periods.

erosion the wearing away of a surface or geological feature by wind, rain, river flow, etc.

erratic a boulder that is out of place in its environment, having been transported over long distances by a glacier.

escarpment a cliff.

esker a winding ridge of stratified glacial deposits, stretching from a few meters to as long as 160 kilometers.

eustatic change worldwide change of sea level produced by an increase or decrease in amount of ocean water.

evaporite any salt deposit left behind when seawater evaporates.

extrusive rock rock solidified from magma that has flowed out of the earth and onto the surface.

fault a fracture in strata or, on a larger scale, the Earth's crust.

floodplain an area bordering a stream that periodically floods.

fold bend or wrinkle in rock formed when rock was in a plastic state.

fold mountain a mountain consisting of sedimentary rocks that have been folded over and elevated.

fossil fuels underground deposits of hydrocarbons, including petroleum, methane, coal, and natural gas, formed from the fossilized remains of millions of tons of prehistoric plants and animals, with phytoplanktons and zooplanktons transforming largely into petroleum and terrestrial plants and organisms transforming largely into coal.

frost action erosional process caused by the expansion of water through repeated cycles of freezing and thawing.

geocentric pertaining to the center of the Earth.

geochronology the history of the Earth as marked by geological events.

geodesy the science of the measuring of Earth's size, shape, and weight.

geomorphology the study of land forms.

geosyncline a basin in which thousands of meters of sediments have accumulated and which may ultimately become compressed into a mountain system.

Gondwanaland hypothetical Southern Hemisphere continent thought to have broken up in the Mesozoic era and now the continents of Africa, India, Australia, South America, and Antarctica.

guyot flat-topped mountain under the sea.

igneous rock rock formed from the cooling and solidification of magma.

inselberg a vestigial mountain reduced by erosion to a rocky nubbin or isolated "island," found in ancient desert areas.

intrusive rock rock that has solidified from magma after intruding into or between other rocks.

island-arc deeps deep sea trenches bordering some continents; some reach depths of 9,000 meters.

kame a steep hill of stratified glacial drift.

karst topography an area characterized by numerous sinkholes and caverns, due to limestone erosion.

Kerguelen-Gaussberg Ridge a mountain range under the Indian Ocean between India and Antarctica.

kettle a depression in a large accumulation of glacial drift caused by an ice block melting and later forming a lake.

koppie pile of boulders formed by the weathering and breakdown of inselbergs.

lava extruded from a volcano, any molten rock or molten rock that has cooled and hardened.

lithosphere the outermost layer of the Earth, comprising the crust and the upper mantle.

loess an accumulation of loose silt, deposited by wind as dust.

lowland any land at or slightly above sea level.

magma molten rock beneath the surface of the Earth.

magnetic reversal a complete shift of Earth's magnetic field, which, if occurring today, would make a compass needle point south instead of north. Such reversals have taken place several times throughout the Earth's history.

magnetostratigraphy the study of magnetized rocks to determine magnetic reversals in the Earth's past.

mantle the layer of Earth between the crust and the core.

marl forming in a water environment, a loose deposit of clay and calcium carbonate.

melange different types of rocks grouped together.

metamorphic rock rock that has changed or "metamorphosed" into other rock through heat, pressure, or chemical processes.

metamorphism the process by which a rock is altered through heat and pressure.

microfossil a tiny fossil, often requiring study through a microscope.

mid-ocean ridge a long, elevated rise in the seafloor, caused by the eruption of basalt and formation of new crust.

mineralization the process by which minerals infiltrate a dead organism and turn it into a fossil.

Mohorovicic discontinuity (Moho) the base of the Earth's crust, ranging from about 13 kilometers under the oceans to about 40 kilometers under the continents.

mold an impression of an organism, left behind to fossilize in rock.

monolith slender, eroded butte that eventually topples over.

monument a butte.

moraine a large accumulation of glacial till or drift.

oceanic trench an elongated trough on the ocean floor, caused by subduction activity.

orogeny the process by which mountains are formed.

outcrop any bedrock that has become exposed from the surrounding soil.

paleogeography the geography of a land as it was in the geologic past.

paleomagnetism Earth's magnetic field as it was in the geologic past.

Pangaea the huge, hypothetical ancient supercontinent from which all of today's continents are thought to have split off.

Panthalassa the huge, hypothetical universal ocean surrounding the supercontinent Pangaea before it divided.

peat a deposit of decomposed plant remains from a swamp or marsh.

peneplain a flat or nearly flat land surface resulting from an advanced stage of erosion.

pingo a mound or hill, sometimes more than 100 meters high, formed by expanding permafrost, found frequently in arctic regions.

plate any one of the seven major lithospheric plates, consisting of either heavy basaltic ocean crust or lighter granitic continental crust, that cover the Earth and float on the plastic upper mantle.

plate tectonics the interaction and subsequent effects of the Earth's lithospheric plates colliding and scraping against one another.

pluton any mass of igneous rock formed beneath the Earth by the hardening of magma.

regression a recession in sea level, exposing new land.

rift a long crack in the Earth's crust.

rift valley a valley formed by faulting.

salt dome a dome formed in sedimentary rock by the upward flow of a large mass of salt.

seafloor spreading the expanding of the seafloor along mid-ocean ridges, forming new crust.

seamount a mountain under the sea.

sedimentary rock rock formed by the accumulation and bedding of silt, gravel, rocks, and organic matter, easily identified by its distinctive layering or strata.

seismic prospecting a technique of determining the nature of an underground rock structure by setting off explosive charges and measuring the time the shock waves take to travel varying underground paths.

seismograph an instrument that records vibrations of the Earth, particularly during an earthquake.

seismology the study of earthquakes.

sinkhole an area of ground, usually consisting of limestone or some other soluble material, that collapses due to water erosion.

strata collective term for layers of sedimentary rock.

stratification the layering of sedimentary rock, with changes of color or texture from one bed to the next.

stratigraphy the study of rock layers, their ages, and how they were laid down or deposited.

stratum a single layer of sedimentary rock.

subduction the descending of one lithospheric plate under another.

subduction zone the area where one lithospheric plate descends beneath another, known by a high frequency of earthquakes.

syncline strata bent downward in an upside-down arch; the reverse of an anticline.

taphonomy the study of the history of a fossil, from the time the organism is first preserved through when it is uncovered by a paleontologist. Skeletons, for example, may become disarticulated because of water flow, or some fossils may become flattened due to compression by a glacier or the accumulation of many layers of sediment.

tectonic referring to the actions of the Earth's crust.

terrane a piece of the Earth's crust that tears off from one tectonic plate and becomes attached to another.

thermal plume in the upper mantle, a huge column of upwelling magma located in a fixed position and therefore known as a "hot spot." Thought to be responsible for volcanic activity.

topography collective term for the layout and all of the geological features in a given area of the Earth's surface, including hills, mountains, valleys, lowlands, etc.

tor a large rock or pile of rocks rising 6 to 9 meters (19.5–29.5 ft)—actually a mass of granite eroded to give the appearance of individual stones. Seen frequently in England.

trace fossil an incomplete or partially destroyed fossil, or any slight evidence of an organism, such as a tiny burrow or a footprint.

upland any high ground or highland, but not reaching the height of a mountainous area.

uplift the raising up of Earth's crust from tectonic forces. Also the lifted Earth itself.

weathering the gradual erosion of large rocks into smaller ones.

GEOLOGICAL TIME

(The Phanerozoic eon is measured from 544 million years ago to the present. Precambrian time is measured from 4,500 to 544 million years ago.)

m = million years ago

Era	Period	Epoch
Cenozoic	Quaternary	Holocene 11,000–present Pleistocene 1.8m–11,000
	Tertiary	Pliocene 5m–1.8m Miocene 23m–5m Oligocene 38m–23m Eocene 54m–38m Paleocene 65m–54m
Mesozoic	Cretaceous 146m–65m Jurassic 208m–146m Triassic 245m–208m	
Paleozoic	Permian 286m–245m Carboniferous 360m–286m Pennsylvanian 325m–286m Mississippian 360m–325m Devonian 410m–360m Silurian 440m–410m Ordovician 505m–440m Cambrian 544m–505m	
Proterozoic	Neoproterozoic 900m–544m Mesoproterozoic 1,600m–900m Paleoproterozoic 2,500m–1,600m	
Archean (3,800m–2,500m)		
Hadean (4,500m–3,800m)		

GLACIERS AND ICE

ablation the melting and evaporation of ice from a glacier.

arête a steep-sided, serrated mountain ridge formed by glacial erosion.

bergschrund the crevasse or group of crevasses where the head of a glacier is pulling away from a mountain wall.

bergy bit National Weather Service's term for a broken-off chunk of iceberg, bobbing 3–16 feet (1–5 m) above the surface of the water and extending 1,076–3,229 square feet (100–300 sq m) across.

black ice any thin patch of roadway ice that tends to be so clear it is nearly invisible and consequently causes numerous car accidents.

brash ice fragments of floating, broken ice, measuring less than 6.5 feet (2 m) across.

calving the breaking away of large chunks of ice from the end of a glacier; in tidewater glaciers the fallen chunks become icebergs.

cirque a bowl-like or amphitheater-like depression in the side of a mountain, formed by glacial movement.

cold glacier a glacier with no surface melting during summer months; its temperature is always below freezing. See WARM GLACIER.

crevasse a crack or fracture in a glacier.

dendrochronology the study of a tree's growth rings to determine past climatic changes and fluctuations in glacial movement and growth.

drift rocks and gravel carried by glaciers and eventually deposited. Also known as till.

drift ice any ice floating on the surface of a body of water.

drumlin an elongated hill consisting of compacted drift or till left by a glacier.

dust well a hole in the surface of a glacier, formed by a clump of dirt or dust that absorbs more sunlight and melts surrounding ice.

erratic a glacially deposited rock that differs from native rocks.

esker a long, winding ridge of till deposited by water flowing through a glacial tunnel.

fjord a glacier-carved valley inundated by the sea to form a long, narrow inlet. Also spelled fiord.

firn granular snow a year old or more at the accumulation zone or head of a glacier.

floe a large slab of sea ice sometimes measuring several miles across and usually consisting of many small ice chunks frozen together.

glacial lakes lake basins carved out by glacial activity. These include (1) rock basin lake, a depression ground out of bedrock; (2) cirque lake, a lake in the side of a mountain, also known as a tarn; (3) moraine lake, formed when glacially dumped drift dams a river or stream; (4) kettle lake, formed within a depression in the moraine itself; (5) ice-dammed lake, formed when the glacier itself dams a stream.

glacial pavement bedrock paved over by glaciers, leaving telltale scrapes, scars, gouges, or a polished appearance.

glaciation the covering and altering of the land by glacial ice.

glacier a mass of accumulated, compacted snow consolidating into ice. A glacier forms when more snow falls than melts over several successive seasons. Types of glaciers include (1) ice sheet, a large sheetlike glacier spreading out in all directions; (2) continental glacier, an ice sheet that covers a large portion or all of a continent, such as the Antarctic ice sheet; (3) valley glacier, a glacier confined to a valley; (4) cirque glacier, a glacier confined to a cirque; (5) piedmont glacier, the glacial portion that emerges from the mouth of a valley and surrounds the foot of a mountain.

glaciere a cave in a glacier.

glaciologist one who studies ice in all its forms.

glaciology the study of ice in all its forms.

glaciospeleology the study of glacier caves.

growler a small chunk of ice, measuring no more than 215 square feet (20 sq m), broken off from an iceberg.

hanging glacier a glacier that has positioned itself on a high shelf and hangs over a valley, posing a major avalanche danger.

hanging valley a secondary valley whose floor is much higher than the larger valley into which it leads; originally formed by a small, tributary glacier leading to a larger one.

horn a sharp, steeply descending peak formed by the headwalls of three or more cirques.

hummock a mound of broken ice, pushed up by pressure.

hummocked ice pieces of broken ice forced atop one another by pressure and forming a mound.

ice age any cold period in Earth's history marked by extensive glaciation and alternated with a period of warmth. The most recent ice age, extending from approximately 2 million to 10,000 years ago and consisting of at least four large-scale glacial advances, was the Pleistocene epoch.

iceblink a yellowish glare in the sky over an ice field.

icefall an avalanche of ice.

ice field any floating sheet of ice greater than 6 miles (10 km) across.

ice floe any floating sheet of ice less than 6 miles (10 km) across.

indicator a glacially transported rock that can be traced back to its original bedding ground.

kame mounds of stratified sand and gravel deposited along the edge of a glacier by glacial streams.

kettles depressions in moraines, often filling with water and creating lakes anywhere from 10 meters to 10 kilometers in diameter.

loess wind-transported silt and clay, ground fine and deposited by glaciers, and responsible for creating the rich, loamy soils and billowing topography of the Midwest.

moraine a large accumulation of glacially deposited rocks and boulders (till).

moulin a whirlpool of melted water and rocks that falls through a crevasse and carves out a shaft through a glacier to the ground. Also known as a glacier mill.

névé glacial or mountain snow that becomes ice. Also known as firn.

nunatak a hill or mountain peak surrounded by a glacier.

pack ice a large slab of sea ice consisting of chunks and floes held closely together.

pancake ice evolving from frazil or slush, rounds of ice of various sizes, resembling pancakes.

permafrost permanently frozen ground.

Pleistocene epoch a period from approximately 2 million to 10,000 years ago, marked by alternating cold and warm climates and increased glacial activity. Four major glacial advances—when ice covered as much as two-thirds of North America in depths reaching 3,000 meters—are recognized during the Pleistocene epoch. From oldest to youngest, these are known as the Nebraskan, the Kansan, the Illinoian, and the Wisconsin, collectively referred to as the Ice Age.

pressure ridge a ridge of sea ice uplifted by horizontal pressure.

regional snow line the altitude in which more snow accumulates than melts in the summer season, thus eventually forming a glacier.

rock flour rock pulverized by a glacier and carried off by running water.

sastrugi large, sharp ridges or irregularities carved into a bed of snow by wind.

serac a pinnacle of ice upraised on the surface of a glacier by the intersection of two or more crevasses.

snow bridge an arch of snow formed over a crevasse.

striations scratches and grooves left on rocks and bedrock by passing glaciers.

surge a sudden or rapid advancement of a glacier, sometimes having catastrophic consequences.

till a mixture of powdered rock, gravel, and rocks carried and deposited by a glacier.

trimline the boundary between old, larger trees untouched by glacial movement and younger, smaller trees that sprouted after ice receded.

warm glacier one that reaches melting temperature during summer.

LAKES, PONDS, AND SWAMPS

alkali lake a lake with a high content of sodium carbonate.

battery a large island of decayed vegetation and bottom material floated to the surface of a swamp by swamp gas; the island then floats, grows new vegetation, and gradually roots itself to the bottom.

bayou a marshy inlet or outlet of a lake or river.

benthos the plants and animals that inhabit the bottom of a pond, lake, or other body of water.

bitter lake a lake with a high content of sodium sulfate.

blowup the act of swamp gas blowing bottom material to the surface of a swamp.

boatman an aquatic insect that skims the surface of water.

bog a spongy wetland characterized by peat deposits, floating sedge or sphagnum mats, heath shrubs, and coniferous trees.

brackish describing a mixture of salt water and freshwater, such as found in coastal marshes.

caldera a crater lake formed by volcanic activity.

cirque a small circular basin lake found on the side of a mountain.

detritus particles of decaying plants and animals used as a source of food by many aquatic animals.

dimictic a lake whose waters overturn twice a year, due to temperature mixing, most commonly found in temperate regions.

eutrophic of a body of water, having its oxygen depleted by lush vegetation.

eutrophication the gradual filling-in of a lake by the growth of vegetation and rising sediment so that it gradually becomes a pond, then a marsh, then a swamp, and then finally dries up, the natural aging process of all lakes.

eyes small areas of open water in mat-covered bogs.

fen a marsh or bog.

floaters floating plants, such as water lilies and duckweed.

foxfire luminescence caused by the decaying of wood by certain fungi, seen in swampy areas at night.

hammocks tree islands found in swampy areas.

ice scour a relatively shallow lake formed by glaciers making a shallow depression over a level area.

kettle a natural lake formed in a depression in a glacial moraine.

lacustrine like a lake or pertaining to a lake.

lagoon the pond or body of water within a coral atoll, or any small body of water connecting with a river, lake, or sea.

limnologist one who studies lakes.

limnology the study of lakes.

littoral the shore area from the waterline to the plant line.

loch Scottish word for a lake.

marsh the shallow body of water partially filled in with vegetation, evolving from a pond.

methane marsh or swamp gas formed by decaying plants.

mire swampy ground or deep mud.

monomictic a lake whose water overturns once a year, due to temperature mixing.

moraine lake a lake formed when rocks and debris dumped by a glacier dam a river.

morass soft, wet ground, as in a marsh or bog.

muskeg a mossy bog found in northern, coniferous forest regions.

oligotrophic a body of water with a high oxygen content and largely devoid of plants and animals.

oxbow lake a lake formed when a bend or meander in a river is cut off from the main flow and isolated.

paternoster lakes a series of glacier-carved basins filled with water and resembling a string of beads.

peat decayed and partially carbonized vegetable matter found in bogs and used for fuel.

plankton tiny plants and animals that float or swim near the surface of water.

playa lake a shallow, temporary lake that forms in a desert playa or basin.

Pleistocene the epoch of glacial activity beginning 2.5 million years ago, when many of Earth's lakes were formed.

pluvial lake a lake that formed during a period of increased rainfall and decreased evaporation, most notably in nonglaciated southern regions of North America during the time of the last ice age.

quaggy yielding under foot, such as boggy ground.

quagmire marshy or boggy ground.

quaking bog a bog with a floating mat of vegetation, which trembles or "quakes" when disturbed.

seiche lake oscillations, or the tilting back and forth of lake water.

slough a slow, meandering stream that drains a swamp, or a place of deep mud or mire.

sphagnum a common bog moss.

succession the natural evolution of a body of water from a lake to a pond to a marsh and to a swamp, or the gradual filling-in of vegetation and sediment that causes a body of water ultimately to dry up.

swamp a wetland characterized by moss, shrubs, and trees such as cypress and gums; a marsh with trees.

swamp gas methane produced by decaying vegetation.

tannin the chemical released from peat or tree bark that colors water brown or tealike.

tarn a mountain lake formed in a cirque.

Wisconsin ice sheet the glacial ice sheet responsible for the formation of the U.S. Great Lakes.

METEOROLOGY

advection the horizontal movement of air, moisture, or heat.

air mass large mass of air with nearly uniform temperature and moisture.

air stagnation an air mass full of smoke, gases, and dust that has stalled over an area and cannot be cleansed due to a lack of breeze or wind.

astraphobia fear of thunder and lightning.

atmospheric pressure weight of a given volume of air. Also known as barometric pressure.

atmospherics lightning-based electrical disturbances causing radio noise and static and interfering with telecommunications. See WHISTLER.

ball lightning a mysterious and controversial electrical phenomenon, associated most often with thunderstorms; unlike lightning, it takes on the form of a sphere of various sizes, which may dart, hover, and glow for several seconds at a time.

barometer an instrument that measures atmospheric pressure and can be used to help predict storms.

barometric pressure see ATMOSPHERIC PRESSURE.

Bermuda high in the North Atlantic off North America, a migrating, subtropical area of high pressure.

blue jet similar to a sprite, a blue electrical discharge whose flash appears over a thunderstorm, 25 to 30 miles (40–48 km) above Earth.

bust meteorologist's slang for an inaccurate forecast.

Celsius scale by which temperature is measured in many areas outside of the United States. The freezing point is 0 degrees and the boiling point is 100 degrees.

condensation the change of a substance from a vapor to a liquid; the opposite of evaporation.

convection the transfer of heat by the vertical motion of air.

depression an area of low pressure.

dew point the temperature at which air becomes saturated; a further drop in temperature causes condensation followed by precipitation.

Doppler radar more accurately referred to as pulse-Doppler radar, a radar system that reads returned echoes to detect the presence, speed, and direction of precipitation, whether rain, hail, or snow.

El Niño taken from the Spanish for "the child," since it usually appears during Christmastime, it is a unusually warm flow of water from the Pacific Ocean toward South America.

eye of the storm circular area of light winds and fair weather in the center of tropical storms.

Fahrenheit scale used to measure temperature in the United States. Freezing is 32 degrees and the boiling point is 212 degrees.

fair descriptive term for clear, pleasant, and largely windless weather.

front the line of divergence between air masses of different characteristics.

fulmineous referring to thunder.

heat lightning an erroneous term. Heat lightning is normal lightning that flashes at such a great distance that its thunder cannot be heard.

heat wave very hot and humid weather that lasts for two days or more.

high a high-pressure system, usually associated with fair weather.

Indian summer any unusually warm period in the middle of autumn.

La Niña a periodic cooling of the surface waters of the Pacific off the coast of South America, which causes changes in weather patterns elsewhere in the world.

lightning a powerful electrical discharge, reaching temperatures of 54,000 degrees Fahrenheit (29,982° C) and carrying 40 kiloamperes (40,000 amperes) of electric current or more; most often released during a thunderstorm, from cloud to cloud, from cloud to air, or from cloud to ground. Lightning bolts can stretch anywhere from 1 mile to more than 100 miles in length. The near-instant superheating of the surrounding air creates a shock wave that produces thunder.

lightning rod a conductive metal rod erected over the roof of a building to attract lightning and draw it safely down into the ground.

low a region of low pressure, often associated with precipitation and windy conditions.

meteorologist one who is trained to forecast the weather.

radiosonde installed in a weather balloon, an instrument or probe that measures altitude, atmospheric pressure, temperature, humidity, and wind speed and radios the data to a ground computer. A type of radiosonde known as an ozonesonde measures ozone.

ridge an elongated area of high barometric pressure.

sheet lightning an erroneous term. Sheet lightning is actually normal lightning, but the bolt is obscured by distance and cloud cover, resulting in a broad flash that reflects for great distances.

sprite any large, reddish-orange, electrical discharge whose flash appears 25 to 60 miles (40–96 km) above a thunderstorm.

storm surge the raising of shoreline water level by storm winds; also known as storm tide or storm wave.

super cell the most powerful and long-lasting type of thunderstorm, characterized by a continuously rotating updraft that generates not only heavy rain, hail, and wind but may also spawn tornadoes and dangerous downdrafts.

temperature inversion a flipping of normal atmospheric conditions, when air that is normally cold at higher elevations is actually warm, while cold air stays at low elevations. Inversions, which can trap smog close to the ground and sometimes spawn thunderstorms, are caused by less dense warm air masses moving over dense, cool ones, but they can occur simply when the Sun goes down or when the Sun is low on the horizon, as in winter.

transient luminous event any electrical discharge, including sprites and blue jets, occurring in the upper atmosphere.

trough an elongated area of low pressure.

weather balloon a hydrogen-filled balloon that carries instruments to high altitude to measure atmospheric pressure, temperature, humidity, wind speed, and, sometimes, ozone levels. Also known as a sounding balloon.

whistler a descending whistling noise heard over the radio and caused by lightning.

MOUNTAINS

adret French term referring to the side of a mountain that receives the most sunlight and warmth, used in the Alps. See also UBAC.

aiguille a needlelike peak or pinnacle.

alpenglow a peak's rosy glow before sunrise or just after sunset.

alpenhorn a very long, wooden horn used to convey signals in the Alps or other mountainous regions.

alpine any lofty or towering mountain comparable to an alp. Also used to describe the elevation above 4,800 feet, where vegetation grows in a stunted fashion or not at all.

alpinist a mountain climber.

avalanche a dangerous fall or slide of a large mass of snow, ice, or rocks down the side of a mountain.

avalanche wind a powerful and sometimes dangerous wind generated by an avalanche.

banner cloud a stationary cloud seen frequently over the lee side of some mountains, such as the Matterhorn.

basin a U-shaped bowl created by a glacier.

butte a steep-sided mountain usually having a level top.

cairn a trail marker built of piled rocks, often used near summits.

cirque a large bowl-like or amphitheater-like hollow in the side of a mountain, carved out by snow, ice, and glacier activity.

col a saddle or low pass between two summits.

cordillera a group of parallel mountain ranges.

cornice an overhanging mass of snow or ice; it resembles an ocean wave and is known to collapse and cause avalanches.

couloir a deep. wide gully that acts as a funnel for falling snow, ice, or rocks. Also known as a coulee.

crag a steep and weathered mass of rock.

dome a type of mountain formed by the upwelling of molten rock through a crack in the Earth, causing surface mounding or bulging; when the surface crust is eventually eroded away, a dome of hardened lava remains.

escarpment a sheer cliff, a scarp.

faulted block mountain mountain formed by a massive uplifting of the Earth.

folded mountain a geological term describing a mountain formed by corrugation and compression of the Earth.

glacial erratics boulders left by glaciers that differ from native rocks, frequently seen near mountainous areas.

flank the side of a mountain.

hogback any sharp ridge or ridges with steeply sloping sides.

inselberg a vestigial mountain reduced by erosion to a rocky nubbin or isolated "island," found in ancient desert areas.

Krumholz "crooked wood"; the stunted vegetation caused by severe cold and wind at high elevations. The Krumholz zone is found wherever alpine vegetation has been twisted and dwarfed by the elements, usually above 4,800 feet.

massif a mountain that forms a mass of peaks.

matterhorn a sharp, steeply descending peak, usually formed by glacial erosion.

monadnock a massive rock that has resisted erosion better than surrounding rock and therefore remains standing as a large hill or small mountain.

mountain sickness an illness brought on by oxygen deprivation at high altitudes; the symptoms include headaches, nausea, and general weakness.

nunatak a mountain surrounded by glacial ice.

oread in Greek mythology, a mountain nymph.

orography the study of mountains.

piedmont pertaining to the foot of a mountain, as a piedmont glacier.

pinnacle the top or peak.

piton French term for a pointed peak.

plateau an elevation with a broad, flat top; mesa; tableland.

rain shadow the leeward side of a mountain, which receives far less rain than the windward side.

rarefied of or relating to the thinner air supply at high elevations.

ridgeback the lengthwise crest of any ridge.

rime ice a freezing fog found at high altitudes that settles on rocks and vegetation. Also known as verglas.

saddle the lowest point between two summits.

scree loose slopes of rock fragments and boulders.

seamount a mountain under the sea.

shoulder a humpback or false ridge.

sierra a mountain range or chain.

skirt the skirting of trees around the mountain below the alpine line.

specter of the brocken greatly enlarged shadow of a climber seen projected on a cloud or mist near a summit; named after a peak in Germany.

spur a lateral ridge projecting from a mountain.

table mountain a mesa, plateau.

talus collective term for the boulders, rocks, and gravel fragments often found at the base of cliffs and steep slopes.

tarn a mountain lake, often occupying a cirque.

tundra the barren area where little vegetation grows, above 4,800 feet.

ubac French term for the side of a mountain that is coldest because it receives the least amount of sunlight.

PRECIPITATION

acid rain rain or snow containing high levels of sulfuric or nitric acids, which are produced by fossilfuel-burning industry and internal combustion engines, and have been shown to damage vegetation, foul drinking water, and intensify erosion of buildings and other outdoor structures.

arid describing any area that is very dry and tends to lack precipitation of any kind.

blizzard any storm characterized by steady winds of at least 35 miles per hour (56 km/hr) with heavy snowfall that sharply reduces visibility and lasts for three hours or more.

condensation the change of a substance from a vapor to a liquid; the opposite of evaporation.

corn snow that has melted and refrozen to form a rough, granulated surface.

dew point temperature at which air becomes saturated; a further drop in temperature causes condensation followed by precipitation.

downdraft a column of cool air that rapidly descends to ground level, usually accompanied by precipitation.

evaporation the dispersal of moisture from surface water into the atmosphere.

firn old, compacted, and hardened snow; with further compacting it becomes glacial ice.

graupel falling pellets of snow; also known as soft hail.

humidity moisture content of the air.

hydrologic cycle the process of maintaining a constant water vapor content in the atmosphere by surface evaporation of oceans, lakes, rivers, and moist soil, and by transforming such moisture into a precipitable form. The three phases of the hydrologic cycle are evaporation, condensation, and precipitation.

hydrometeors collective term for all types of precipitation.

hyetography the study of rainfall.

hygrometer a device for measuring the amount of humidity in the air.

lake effect snow a heavy snowfall caused by cold, arctic air passing over a large expanse of warmer lake water and pulling up water vapor, freezing it, and turning it into snow, most notably occurring over the U.S. Great Lakes.

precipitation classification drizzle—fine droplets barely reaching the ground before evaporation; mist—fine droplets that usually evaporate before reaching the ground; hail—frozen droplets produced from violent convection in thunderstorms; sleet—frozen rain; rime—freezing fog.

rain gauge a device for measuring the amount of precipitation in a given time period.

saturation 100 percent humidity, the maximum amount of moisture the air can hold.

snow blindness temporary blindness caused by bright sunlight reflecting off snow.

snowblink a yellowish or whitish glow over a snowfield.

snowflake classification the seven basic types of snowflake are star, hexagonal plate, needle, column, capped column, spatial dendrite, and irregular.

thundersnow a snowstorm, often heavy, with thunder and lightning.

whiteout zero visibility caused by blizzard conditions.

RIVERS AND STREAMS

Acheron in Greek and Roman mythology, the river of woe, one of the five rivers surrounding Hades.

alluvial fan the debris consisting of silt, gravel, and rocks deposited by rivers along the foot of mountains, creating a fanlike series of ridges.

alluvium any debris eroded by or deposited by a river, such as silt, gravel, rocks, and boulders.

aquifer groundwater, or any natural underground reservoir of water.

bar a ridgelike deposit or accumulation of sand or silt in or along a river.

bed the bottom of a river.

benthos plants and animals inhabiting the bottom of a river.

bight a curve or bend in a shoreline.

billabong an Australian term for a waterway filled with water only during rainy season.

boil a water current that "boils" or upwells into a convex mound.

braided river a river divided into several intertwining branches or "braids" created by a series of built-up sandbars or banks.

branch one division of a forked river or a smaller river joining a larger one; a tributary.

brook a small stream.

cataract a waterfall.

channel the deepest part of a river.

chute a descending and steep and narrow passage of water.

creek a small, shallow stream.

delta a triangular-shaped island of deposited sediment forming downstream at a river's mouth.

detritus particles of decaying plants and animals used as a source of food by many aquatic animals.

eddy the backward-rotating current found behind rocks or other obstructions above the surface.

estuary the body of water affected by tides, where the mouth of a river meets the sea.

feeder any branch that joins into a larger watercourse.

fjord a long arm or river of ocean water running between high cliffs or banks.

floodplain any flat area that may be flooded by a river when it overflows its banks.

fluvial referring to rivers or things found in or formed by rivers.

ford a shallow portion of a river allowing people to cross on foot.

fork portion of a river that branches into two parts.

freshet an overflow of a stream due to heavy rains or melting snow.

gradient the rate of descent over a section of river, usually measured in feet per mile.

haystacks the large, standing waves that form at the bottom of rapids wherever the current is decelerating.

headwaters small brooks and streams that join to form a river.

hummock a flow of current forming a hump over a rock.

hydraulics the science of water in motion.

hydrologist one who studies the dynamics of water.

hydrophobia the fear of water.

kill a creek.

levee an embankment built along the shore of a river to protect from flooding.

meander to wind or wander aimlessly, as a river.

milldam a dam constructed across a river to raise its water level and pressure in order to turn a mill wheel.

millrace the river or channel of water used to turn a mill wheel.

moraine a huge deposit of boulders, gravel, and silt left behind by a receding glacier and responsible for damming up some rivers to form lakes.

oxbow a noose-shaped loop of water forming along the side of a river, sometimes separating from the river entirely to form a pond.

pitch a section of rapids that is steeper than surrounding sections.

pool slow-moving deep water.

race a portion of a river that is moving swiftly, especially due to a narrowing.

rapids swiftly moving white water broken by rocks.

riffles a shallow stream with small ripples caused by a bed of cobbles, rocks, and gravel.

rill a tiny stream or brook.

rip a wave or waves caused by a collision of currents in swiftly moving water.

riparian referring to a riverbank area.

riverhead a river's source.

rooster a standing wave with a crest that turns back on itself, sometimes known to swamp canoes or rafts.

runnel a tiny brook or stream.

runoff water from rain or melted snow coursing over the ground or through sewers into a waterway.

shoal a shallow area surrounded by deeper water.

sluice an artificial channel for conducting water.

souse hole a foamy, violently turbulent eddy; also known as a white eddy.

spring a water source issuing from underground.

Styx the river of hate, one of the five rivers in Greek mythology surrounding Hades.

tongue a smooth passage of black water flowing between two rocks or obstructions, often leading into a chute.

torrent a rough and swiftly flowing stream.

tributary a stream or river that "contributes" its water to a larger river or body of water.

vortex a whirlpool.

watershed the area from which a river receives its water.

whirlpool water pulled by current forces into a rotating motion that exerts a powerful draw on surrounding water or debris.

white water rapids.

ROCKS AND GEMS

acroite a colorless variety of tourmaline.

adularescent having a lustrous, bluish-white hue, as a moonstone.

adularia a variety of moonstone, characterized by a semitranslucent and whiteish-blue hue.

agate a type of porous quartz that forms several different colors.

agglomerate a pyroclastic rock consisting mostly of volcanic bombs.

alexandrite a variety of quartz that appears blue-green when viewed outside and reddish-purple under indoor or artificial light.

alluvium sand, mud, gravel, and rocks carried and deposited by rivers.

almandine a type of common garnet characterized by colors ranging from red or purplish red to orange-brown.

amber yellowish, translucent fossilized resin from coniferous trees.

American ruby a ruby in name only, actually a pyrope garnet.

amethyst a type of purple or sometimes mauve-colored quartz.

ametrine a type of quartz containing both amethyst and citrine colors.

ammolite the shell of an ammonite, an ancient sea mollusk, that has been pressurized, fossilized, and mineralized.

amygdule a cavity in igneous rock filled with secondary minerals, such as calcite or quartz.

anthracite a hard, lustrous, jet-black coal formed from prehistoric plant material.

anticline a folded mass of rock with strata sloping down on both sides from a common peak.

aquamarine a variety of beryl, blue or turquoise, the color often reminiscent of seawater. It is also found in yellows, pinks, and whites.

aquifer fractured rocks or unconsolidated sand or gravel pockets containing large amounts of groundwater.

asterism a starburst effect seen in such gemstones as garnets, sapphires, and rubies.

aventurescence a kind of sparkle seen in some gemstones, due to trace deposits of mica, hematite, or pyrite.

azurite a copper-based mineral characterized by a pale to deep blue color.

baffa diamond a fake diamond, actually made of rock crystal.

banded agate a type of agate characterized by layers of color.

basalt dark, igneous rock formed by volcanoes.

batholith a huge igneous mass—with a surface area of at least 100 square kilometers (40 square miles) and increasing in size as it extends downward—intruded into other rock and found under or within mountain ranges. Also known as a pluton.

bedrock the continuous solid rock exposed at the surface or just beneath the soil or overburden.

benitoite a rare blue gemstone found in California.

beryl a grouping of related gemstones that, in addition to red and green beryl, includes aquamarine, emerald, and morganite.

bitumen a soft coal formed from prehistoric plant material.

black opal a type of quartz that is dark and iridescent.

black pearl a dark pearl ranging in color from gray to peacock green to brown and sometimes artificially treated to enhance color, taken from a mollusk found in the Indo-Pacific Ocean. Also known as Tahitian pearl.

bloodstone a soft type of chalcedony, composed of green jasper with red iron oxide spots. Also known as heliotrope.

blue diamond a rare and valuable diamond containing trace amounts of boron, which creates a bluish hue. The Hope diamond is the most famous blue diamond.

blueschist metamorphic rock formed under extreme pressure.

blue topaz a brown or colorless topaz until heated, after which it turns blue.

Bohemian diamond a fake diamond, actually rock crystal.

Bohemian ruby a fake ruby, actually a pyrope garnet.

bort industrial grade diamonds.

boulder train a line of boulders following the historical path of a glacier.

breccia broken pieces of rock cemented or bonded together with other types of rock.

cairngorm a yellowish-brown smoky quartz, once used in the manufacture of Celtic jewelry.

calcite a crystalline form of calcium carbonate.

calcium carbonate derived from deposits of seashells, the major component of limestone and chalk.

California ruby a fake ruby, actually a pyrope garnet.

canary diamond a variety of diamond characterized by its deep yellow color.

carat unit of weight used in weighing precious gems; 1 carat equals 0.2 gram. Also the measure of the purity of gold; 24 carats equals pure, 100 percent gold; 18 carat gold is 75 percent gold and 25 percent alloy; and so forth.

carbonaceous of sedimentary rock, containing dark organic matter.

carbonado an opaque black diamond used in drill bits. Carbonados, which are mined in South America and Africa, are thought to have been deposited by an asteroid impact 3 billion years ago.

carnelian a variety of chalcedony, characterized by its translucent red or orange color, which may be banded with either color.

cat's eye otherwise known as chatoyant chrysoberyl, a yellow or greenish-yellow stone, characterized in its center by what resembles a slitlike pupil of a cat.

chalcedony colored quartz with a milky appearance.

chalk derived largely from fossil seashells, a soft, light-colored calcite.

champagne diamond a pinkish-brown diamond.

chatoyancy in a gemstone, having a cat's eye–like effect, specifically from inner bands of reflected light.

chatoyant chrysoberyl see CAT'S EYE.

chemical weathering the erosion of rocks through oxidation and hydration.

chert fine-grained quartz, once used by Native Americans for spearheads, arrowheads, and knives.

chrysoberyl a yellow-green crystal mineral.

chrysolite a transparent variety of olivine, sometimes sold as gemstones and thought by some to have magical qualities.

cinnabar the mineral mercury sulfide, characterized by color ranging from cinnamon to brick red.

cinnamon stone a brownish variety of garnet. Also called essonite.

citrine a type of quartz characterized by its yellow or orange color, sometimes mistaken for imperial topaz.

coal sedimentary rock formed by deposits of compressed plant matter.

cognac diamond a brownish-colored diamond.

conglomerate a sedimentary rock composed of a cluster of particles, gravel, and pebbles held together by clay.

corundum an extremely hard family of stones of crystallized aluminum that includes rubies and sapphires.

country rock rock into which magma has been intruded.

crystallize to turn to crystal or to form crystals.

Culinan diamond a world-record diamond, weighing 3,106 carats, found in South Africa in 1905. Also known as the Star of Africa.

Cupid's darts see RUTILATED QUARTZ.

dacite light-colored, igneous volcanic rock.

diamond a pure carbon crystal, the hardest mineral known, used in jewelry and for industrial cutting and abrading. Clear crystal diamonds are the most common, but they can also be blue, yellow, green, black, white, pink, and violet.

diatomite a sedimentary rock formed by nanoplankton.

dolomite a sedimentary rock with a high concentration of calcium-magnesium carbonate.

drift sand, gravel, and rocks deposited by a glacier.

drumlin an elongated hill of compacted rocks and gravel deposited by a glacier.

druse a layer of quartz crystals that form on another stone and especially inside a geode. Also known as drusy.

emerald a valuable green gemstone in the beryl family.

erratics rocks or boulders transported by glaciers that differ from native rocks.

esker a long, winding ridge of sand and gravel deposited by a glacial stream.

extrusive of magma, ejected out onto the Earth's surface.

fault a break or large crack in a continuous rock formation.

feldspar a common group of hard crystal minerals including calcium, sodium, potassium, and other materials.

flint a very hard form of silica, best known as a spark producer when struck against steel.

fold a bend in rock strata.

fool's gold popular name for pyrite, a bright, metallic, brassy yellow rock often mistaken for gold.

frost agate a form of agate with white, frostlike marks.

fuchsite a glassy, deep green variety of muscovite.

garnet a group of minerals, the most popular of which is pyrope. Often, a red, semiprecious crystal resembling a pomegranate seed, but garnets come in all colors except blue.

gastrolith any stone ingested by an animal to aid in digestion.

geode a globular rock with a cavity lined with minerals.

glacial pavement rock paved over by glaciers, leaving telltale scrapes, scars, and gouges, or a polished appearance.

gneiss a common metamorphic rock similar to granite.

granite a hard igneous rock composed of quartz, feldspar, and mica; a popular building material.

greenstone an alternate name for nephrite, a variety of jade.

heliotrope see BLOODSTONE.

herkimer diamonds a clear form of crystal quartz, not an actual diamond.

hornblende a green or black mineral, found in igneous rock, and one of the components of granite.

humus the dark, organic matter found in soil.

hyacinth opal a yellow or orange form of opal. Also known as girasol.

igneous rock a class of rocks formed from cooled magma or lava.

imperial jade an emerald-green form of jade.

imperial topaz a very valuable form of orange-yellow topaz.

intrusive of or relating to igneous rock or magma that forces its way into or between other rocks and solidifies before reaching the Earth's surface.

ironstone a heavy, sedimentary rock with a high iron content.

jacinth a red, translucent zircon used as a gemstone.

jade a very hard stone, composed of two different minerals, jadeite and nephrite, and highly prized for its beauty. Although it comes in different colors, the green variety is most sought after, especially for jewelry.

jasper an opaque quartz that may be red, yellow, brown, or green, with swirls and bands of colors.

karst a topography of limestone characterized by numerous sinkholes or caverns.

lapidary one who cuts and polishes gemstones.

lapilli small volcanic fragments from pebble to cobble size.

lapis lazuli a semiprecious stone characterized by its royal blue color interspersed with gold flakes of pyrite and white streaks of calcite.

limestone a sedimentary rock composed of calcium carbonate from deposits of various marine creatures.

lithification the process of rock formation.

loess deposits of windblown silt.

mabble a metamorphic rock, often white and swirled with various colors.

malachite an opaque, semiprecious stone, usually greenish because of its high copper content.

marble metamorphosed limestone.

marbled having swirls of colors, like marble.

matrix the natural rock in which a gemstone is embedded.

melanite a black garnet.

metamorphic rock rock that has been "metamorphosed" or altered by heat, steam, or pressure to form other types of rocks.

Mexican diamond not an actual diamond but rock crystal.

mica a soft, transparent mineral that forms in sheets that can be peeled or flaked off, and which can appear in various colors.

Mohs scale a scale, from 1 to 10, designating in gemstones the degree of their hardness and resistance to scratches, with diamonds being the hardest of all and rated a 10. A diamond can scratch all other gems, but it cannot itself be scratched.

moldavite a rare green and glassy gemstone formed by meteorite impacts.

moonstone a variety of feldspar, characterized by a milky, bluish luster. See ADULARESCENCE.

morganite a brittle, translucent pink gemstone, a member of the beryl family.

moss agate a green agate with dendrites of green, red, or black.

nanodiamonds also known as microdiamonds, tiny diamonds created by the impact of a meteorite on Earth.

nephrite a semiprecious variety of jade, often used to make vases and carvings.

nugget a lump of precious metal, such as gold.

obsidian a lustrous black volcanic glass found in lava flows and occasionally found in other colors.

oil shale a shale rich in organic material, suitable for energy conversion.

onyx a variety of agate, found in pure black but more often banded in black and white and a variety of other colors. Often cut into cabochons, cameos, and beads.

oolite a tiny round grain or pellet made of calcium carbonate or quartz found in limestones and dolomites.

opal an iridescent, semiprecious stone, usually having numerous inclusions that create rainbowlike reflections.

ore any earth material from which useful commodities can be extracted.

outcrop a jutting out or other natural exposure of bedrock.

overburden loose rock material lying on top of bedrock.

peacock pearl a very dark, naturally formed green pearl.

Pearl of Allah also known as the Pearl of Lao Tzu, the largest pearl ever found, weighing in at 14 pounds (6.4 kg), and actually taken from a giant clam.

pegmatite a coarse igneous rock composed of multiple elements, including feldspar, mica, and quartz, which may also be found with aquamarine, topaz, or tourmaline.

Pele's hair threadlike strands of volcanic glass.

peridot a variety of olivine, an olive-green gem found in lava flows and in meteorites, sometimes mistaken for emerald.

petrify to turn wood or any other organic material into stone by the intrusion of dissolved minerals.

petroglyph a line drawing or carving on a rock face.

petrology the study of rocks and minerals.

petrous pertaining to or resembling a rock.

placer deposit an alluvial or glacial deposit of sand and gravel that contains valuable minerals.

pumice a volcanic rock of a "frothy" appearance, often light enough to float on water.

pyroclastic containing consolidated volcanic fragments.

pyrope a form of garnet, characterized by its blood-red color, and sometimes misleadingly sold as a ruby under the names American ruby, Bohemian ruby, California ruby, Cape ruby, Montana ruby, and Rocky Mountain ruby.

quartz a crystalline mineral found in various forms and colors and includes amethyst, aventurine, citrine, opal, and others.

quinzite opal a red or pink opal.

rimrock on the edge of a plateau, the topmost layer of sheer wall.

riprap a layer of broken stones applied to an embankment of a river, lake, or ocean to help prevent erosion.

rose quartz a pink to red quartz.

rubellite a red tourmaline.

ruby a precious stone found in pink, red, purple, and brown and rated second in hardness to diamonds.

rutilated quartz a crystal containing needles of titanium dioxide, which create asterisms, and usually cut into a cabochon. Also known as Venus's hair stone and Cupid's darts.

rutile a needlelike inclusion found in some gemstones, creating asterisms or other effects.

sandstone rock made of sand grains bonded together.

sapphire a precious gem; a blue lustrous variety of corundum. Sapphires in colors other than blue are known as fancy sapphires.

scoria a porous volcanic rock.

scree gravel and small rocks that pile up at the foot of cliffs or steep slopes. Sometimes used interchangeably with talus.

sedimentary rock rock made by settled mud, silt, sand, cobbles, pebbles, and organic matter, forming layers or "strata."

shale a fine-grained, sedimentary rock formed by compaction in water.

shocked quartz quartz that has become deformed due to massive pressure, as occurs around a nuclear detonation or a meteorite impact. Scientists use shocked quartz to verify that craters around the Earth were formed by meteorite impacts and not volcanic activity.

silica silicon dioxide, a mineral widely found in sand, quartz, and agate, used in the manufacture of glass.

skarn a metamorphic rock varied in color and containing a mix of minerals, including garnet, pyroxene, magnetite, and others.

slate a fine-grained, metamorphic rock made up of quartz, muscovite, and other minerals; it is famous for its use in roofing shingles.

soapstone a soft rock composed of talc, serpentine, and magnetite and recognized by its soapy feel.

star sapphire a sapphire with inclusions of rutile needles, creating asterisms.

strata layers or beds of rock.

stratification the layering of sedimentary rock.

striation a scratch or gouge on a rock caused by a passing glacier.

stromatolite forming in shallow water, a short, pillarlike rock made from colonies of microorganisms, the oldest-known life-forms in the fossil record, appearing in rocks as old as 3.5 billion years.

talus similar to and sometimes used interchangeably with scree, an accumulation of rocks larger than fist-size, at the foot of cliffs or steep slopes.

tanzanite a rare gem, famous for producing three different colors—sapphire, violet, and burgundy—when rotated. Tanzanite is reddish-brown when taken from the ground and turns blue or purplish when heated.

till rocks and gravel deposited by a glacier. A large accumulation of till is known as a moraine.

topaz a valuable gem that comes in a variety of colors, including transparent, but the most valuable are yellow-pink and brown. Topaz must be heated and irradiated to produce its famous blue color.

tourmaline a semiprecious stone found in black, brown, violet, and pink colors. It is often found with two different colors.

treated stone any stone that has undergone irradiation, heating, or staining to improve its color.

tuff rock composed of compacted volcanic ash, usually no larger than coarse gravel.

turquoise a blue or bluish-green gem, commonly used in Native American jewelry of the Southwest.

vein a rock fracture filled with minerals.

ventifact a rock that has been shaped or polished by windblown materials.

Venus's hair stone see RUTILATED QUARTZ.

vug a cavity in a rock that sometimes may become lined with minerals, such as quartz.

watermelon tourmaline a form of tourmaline that is red on the inside and green on the outside, and also the reverse.

waxy designating any waxy luster, such as found on a moonstone or turquoise.

xenolith a rock found within a rock, usually occurring when magma flows and then hardens over an existing rock.

SEAS AND OCEANS

(*Also see* BEACHES AND SHORES)

abyssal pertaining to the depths of the oceans, the abyss.

abyssal hill a submarine hill reaching 700 meters in height, smaller than seamounts.

abyssal hills province any area of seafloor completely occupied by abyssal hills.

abyssal plain an extensive flat area of the seafloor.

abyssal zone a term originally denoting any depth of ocean beyond the reach of fishermen but now generally recognized as at least 1,000 meters and extending to about 6,000 meters, the beginning of the hadal zone. Contrast with the bathyal zone.

Antarctic Circumpolar Current the world's largest ocean current, it circles the globe and feeds cold water into the Atlantic, Pacific, and Indian Oceans.

bathometer an instrument used to measure the depth of ocean water.

bathyal zone an upper layer of ocean water, extending from 100 meters to about 1,000 meters down (the actual depth varies with local light penetration), marked by a more varied and richer fauna and higher water temperature.

bathymetry the measurement of ocean depths.

bathyscaphe a free-diving, deep-sea research vessel or miniature submarine with a manned observation compartment attached to its underside.

bathysphere a manned, spherical diving chamber lowered by cables.

Beaufort scale a scale in which wind speeds are assigned the code numbers 0 to 12, corresponding to "calm" to "hurricane." At sea, estimates of wind force are often taken from the appearance of the sea by the use of the Douglass sea and swell scale in conjunction with the Beaufort scale.

benthic realm the sea bottom and all the creatures that live on it or within it.

benthic storm a muddying of water extending for hundreds of feet in all directions, caused by powerful eddies swirling over the ocean bottom and stirring up sediments, the underwater equivalent of a sand storm.

benthos the ocean floor and the organisms living on it.

bioluminescence the glow or light emitted from several different types of sea organisms, including some fish at deep levels.

caldron a large, steep-sided, pot-shaped depression in the seafloor.

cold wall the northern boundary of the Gulf Stream, where temperature of the water drops by as much as 18°F outside the stream itself.

continental shelf the submerged shelf of a continent, at its end descending sharply to the seafloor.

Coriolis effect the deflective or curving force explaining the clockwise movements of currents in the Northern Hemisphere and the counterclockwise movements in the Southern Hemisphere.

cross seas a condition occurring when two opposing waves meet head-on and form a towering crest.

dead water a body of water, particularly common in the fjords and seas of Scandinavia, that mysteriously slows or nearly stops the forward progress of ships; thought to be caused by a thin layer of freshwater floating above a layer of denser, salty water that, when mixed, creates a train of slow-moving, submerged waves that exert a powerful drag on vessels passing over it.

deep a deep-sea plain within a large basin.

deep-scattering layer a large body of free-swimming sea organisms, such as fish or squid, that confuses sonar readings by creating a "false bottom" or false seafloor.

doldrums equatorial ocean regions characterized by flat, calm seas and little or no wind.

Douglass sea and swell scale a scale of numbers assigned to descriptive terms (0 = calm, 8 = precipitous, 9 = confused, etc.) to denote the sea's state with a second scale of numbers (0 to 99) to denote low to heavy swells.

eddy a swirling current running contrary to the main current; may be caused by two currents meeting head-on or side-long.

El Niño a colloquial Spanish term for the Christ child now applied to a warm current of ocean water that moves into the coastal waters of Peru around Christmastime; the warm waters smother an upwelling of cold water normally in place here with disastrous effects on sea life and worldwide wind and weather patterns.

Emperor Seamounts the largest chain of submarine mountains in the Pacific; links with the Hawaiian Seamounts.

eustatic change a worldwide change of sea level produced by an increase or decrease in the amount of seawater.

fathom a measurement of sea depth; 1 fathom equals 6 feet.

fathometer a sonic depth finder.

fetch the distance wind travels from one point on the sea to another and its relation to the size of waves created; the longer the fetch, the bigger the waves.

fracture zone an area of submarine fractures in the Earth's crust, marked by troughs, ridges, and mountains.

Graveyard of the Atlantic approximately 220 miles southeast of Cape Hatteras, North Carolina, a site of strong local currents and storms with a powerful undercurrent running underneath the Gulf Stream, the combined causes of thousands of shipwrecks here.

graybeards choppy, frothy waves.

Gulf Stream a warm ocean current originating in the Gulf of Mexico and flowing east around Florida, up the southeast coast of the United States, then east again to the North Atlantic Current.

guyot a flat-topped mountain under the sea.

gyre the circular path followed by oceanwide currents.

hadal zone the deepest layer of ocean water and all its fauna, starting from 6,000 meters down; usually within a trench. Also known as the ultra-abyssal zone.

hole a sinkhole or vertical chimney in the seafloor.

hydrography the study of the sea to determine its use for navigation.

ichthyology the study of fish.

internal wave a submerged or underwater wave, often invisible from the surface.

island-arc deeps deep-sea trenches bordering some continents; some reach depths of 9,000 meters.

meander a bend or bulge in an ocean current that breaks off, forms an eddy, and moves off independently of the current that spawned it.

Mid-Atlantic Ridge originally called the Dolphin Rise, after the ship that discovered it, a long chain of mountains under the mid-Atlantic stretching from Iceland to Antarctica.

nautical mile 6,080.2 feet.

neap tide the minimal or low-moving tide occurring after the first and third quarters of the Moon, when the Sun's tidal force acts at right angles to that of the Moon.

nekton collective term for all free-swimming sea creatures, such as fish, squid, or whales.

North Atlantic gyre the large, rotating current of the North Atlantic. There is also the South Atlantic gyre.

North Pacific gyre the large, rotating current of the North Pacific. There is also the South Pacific gyre.

ocean acoustic tomography the scientific technique of using sound transmitters and receivers to map such underwater properties as currents and eddies.

oceanography the study of the oceans.

Panthalassa the huge, hypothetical universal ocean surrounding the hypothetical supercontinent of Pangaea before it divided. Also known as the Tethys Sea.

pelagic region the open ocean waters, as opposed to the ocean floor.

phytoplankton the microscopic ocean plants living on or near the surface, the bottom of the sea's food chain.

plunger a wave with a convex back and a crest that falls suddenly and violently, usually found on or near shore.

province any region of the seafloor united by a common feature.

Puerto Rico Trough the deepest spot in the Atlantic and the second deepest in all the oceans, 30,246 feet or 9,219 meters.

red tide a bloom of phytoplankton that colors the water red and releases powerful toxins that kill large masses of fish and other sea life; the toxin released by some phytoplankton accumulates in mussels and clams and often proves fatal to humans who eat these shellfish.

ring a meander that has broken off from the main current.

sapropel black organic ooze or sludge, the source material for petroleum and natural gas, found in great accumulations under the ocean.

Sargasso Sea not actually a sea in itself but a section of the North Atlantic (a section the size of the continental U.S.) between the West Indies and the Azores, noted for its small, floating meadows of seaweed.

Sargasso weed the free-floating seaweed, known for its centuries-long life span, that occupies the Sargasso Sea.

sea elements the elements that make up the sea, primarily (96.5 percent) oxygen and hydrogen, followed in order of prevalence by chlorine, sodium, magnesium, sulfur calcium, potassium, bromine, carbon, strontium, boron, silicon, and others.

seafloor spreading the expanding of the seafloor along mid-ocean ridges, forming new crust.

sea high an abyssal hill.

seamount a submarine mountain over 700 meters in elevation.

seamount chain a series of seamounts.

seascarp a long, high cliff or wall, often part of a fracture zone.

seaway a sea route taken by vessels.

seiche a wave that oscillates from a few minutes to a few hours, due to either seismic or atmospheric disturbances.

shoal a shallow area, a hazard to navigation.

sill the ridge or saddle between two basins, troughs, or trenches.

slick a patch of smooth surface water surrounded by rippled water, the result of internal wave flow but often mistaken for an effect of wind action.

sounding measurement of the depth of water.

spiller a wave with a concave back and a crest that breaks gradually and continuously, usually found offshore.

spindrift sea spray.

spring tide the very high tide occurring at new and full Moon and reinforced by the gravitational pull of the Sun.

submarine bar an underwater sandbar.

submarine fan a large, offshore deposit of sediment, sometimes stretching for hundreds of miles and fanning out into the shape of a cone or apron, originating from the mouth of a large river. Also known as a submarine delta or submarine apron.

submarine spring a freshwater spring upwelling from the seafloor.

terrace a steplike section of the seafloor.

Tethys Sea one of the names for the huge, universal sea that hypothetically surrounded the supercontinent of Pangaea before it divided. Also known as Panthalassa.

thalassic pertaining to the oceans.

thalassophobia the fear of the ocean.

tidal bore a high, dangerous wave caused by a surging incoming tide upstream in a narrowing estuary or by the collision of tidal currents. Also known as an eagre.

trench a steep-sided, narrow depression in the seafloor.

trough same as a trench but gently sided.

tsunami a seismic sea wave, caused by an earthquake, frequently large and dangerous. Erroneously referred to as a tidal wave.

turbidity current an avalanche of sediment-laden water, moving as fast as 50 miles per hour down a continental slope into deeper water and stirring up silt; known to gouge out channels in the seafloor.

upwelling an upwelling of cold, deep water into upper, warmer water layers.

vent an opening on the seafloor releasing heat or volcanic debris.

zooplankton drifting sea worms, jellyfish, and crustaceans.

SOIL

acidic soil soil with a high hydrogen-ion content, sometimes referred to as sour.

agrology soil science.

alkaline soil soil with a high hydroxyl-ion content, sometimes referred to as sweet.

alluvium soil deposited by water such as a flowing river.

duff on a forest floor, leaf litter and other organic debris in various stages of decay.

edaphic pertaining to the soil.

eluvium soil and mineral particles blown and deposited by the wind.

frost heaving bumps and mounds produced at ground level due to the expansion of ice in soil.

gumbo fine, silty soil, found frequently in southern and western United States, and known for the sticky mud it produces when wet.

hummock a low area with deep, rich soil.

humus decomposing plant and animal tissue in and on the surface of the soil.

loam a mixture of soil consisting of sand, clay, silt, and organic matter in proportions conducive to healthy plant growth.

mesic of soils, moist but well drained.

mulch collective term for any material such as straw, leaves, or sawdust spread on soil to cut down water loss and weed growth.

mull an upper mineral layer mixed with organic matter.

peat partially decomposed plant material having little inorganic matter and accumulated in wet areas such as bogs.

pedology the study of soil.

permeability the quality of allowing the penetration of water or other material through the soil.

pores any spaces between solid particles in soil.

stratification individual layers or beds of soils.

TREES, FORESTS, AND JUNGLES

aerial roots tiny roots that allow jungle vines to cling to host trees.

alameda a tree-bordered walk.

arborculture cultivation of trees and shrubs.

arborculturist one who practices arborculture.

arboreal pertaining to trees, or living on or among trees.

arboretum a tree garden, usually featuring several varieties.

A-story botanist's term for the crowns or top story of the tallest trees in a jungle.

bast the soft-tissued inner bark, often used in making thread and rope.

beard the bristlelike hairs sometimes found growing out of petals or leaves.

beauty strip a narrow stand of trees left intact to hide a clearcut from view from a road or body of water.

blowdown any trees knocked down by wind.

bole the trunk, especially of a large tree.

bonsai a Japanese art form of dwarfing or miniaturizing trees or shrubs by pruning.

bosky thickly treed or shrubbed.

bower a shaded recess created by boughs or twining plants.

bromeliad any member of a family of plants that are usually found growing from cracks or crevices in the trunks or branches of jungle trees.

brush an area of low vegetation, such as shrubs and bushes.

B-story the jungle trees and plants growing below the A-story, from 30 to 110 feet up.

burl a warty protuberance found on some tree trunks.

bush rope slang for jungle vines.

buttresses the large, radiating, aboveground root systems supporting many jungle or swamp trees.

cambium the thin layer beneath a tree's bark that produces new wood cells.

canopy the uppermost story of a forest or jungle.

cauliflorous of plants that blossom from the side of a tree trunk or branch, commonly found in jungles.

chaparral a thicket of shrubby trees.

chlorosis a yellowing of leaves, a symptom of nutritional deficiency.

clearcut a practice of some lumber companies in which all or almost all of the trees in a given area are cut down, leaving a barren landscape.

cloud forest a wet, mountain forest or jungle frequently shrouded in mist.

conifer any evergreen tree or shrub.

conk the wood-eating tree fungus found projecting from the trunks of some trees.

copse a thicket of small trees or shrubs.

covert an area of thick growth offering a hiding place or shelter for animals.

crown the leaf canopy or top portion of a tree.

C-story the tree and plant growth extending from 20 to 30 feet above ground in a forest or jungle.

deadfall a jumble of fallen trees and branches.

deciduous of or relating to any type of a tree that sheds its leaves seasonally.

dendrochronology the study of a tree's growth rings to estimate dates of past events, such as forest fires and droughts.

dendrologist one who studies trees.

dendrology the study of trees.

D-story in a jungle or forest, the plants growing from 10 to 20 feet high.

duct a pit or gland, usually filled with sap or resin.

Dutch elm disease a fungus that attacks elms, blocks the flow of sap, and kills the trees.

epiphytes plants that root and grow from the cracks and crevices of a tree's trunk or branches, such as bromeliads and orchids.

E-story in a jungle or forest, the undergrowth of small herbaceous plants and trees.

gall a tumor or nub appearing on the trunk or on a branch, produced and lived in by an insect.

glade a grassy, open space in a forest.

gland a secreting pore or duct exuding resin or sap.

gnarl a twisted or knotty protuberance, as on an old branch.

grove a small stand of trees with little or no underbrush.

growth rings darkened rings within a trunk, used to define the tree's age and stages of growth.

heartwood the center of a tree trunk, containing dead wood and acting as a receptacle for waste.

knot a tough, ringed section of wood marking the past location of a branch or limb.

lateral root a root that extends horizontally from the base or taproot of a tree.

liana a great, woody jungle vine, sometimes growing as thick as a man's waist, found in most jungles.

litter rotting leaves, stems, and debris of a forest or jungle floor.

midrib the central vein or nerve of a leaf.

mor a thick, acidic humus blanket consisting of decayed fir and spruce needles found on a forest floor.

motte a grove or stand of trees on a prairie.

nerve the principal vein of a leaf.

orchard a cultivated stand of fruit or nut trees.

phloem the spongy layer of inner bark.

pitch pocket a concentration or pocket of resin in the wood of a conifer.

pollard a tree with its top cut to stimulate new root growth.

prop roots roots that curve out from a trunk above ground, giving the appearance of stilts, and commonly found in jungle areas where root systems are shallow.

rain forest a thick, tropical, mostly evergreen forest that receives at least 100 inches of rain per year.

ramose having many branches.

resin secretions, hard or liquid, from small chambers or passages within a tree.

sapling a young tree approximately 2 to 4 inches around.

sapwood the wood between the bark and the heartwood, paler and lighter than heartwood.

scrub any collection of low trees and shrubs.

second growth growth that replaces that removed by cutting or by fire.

scurf flaky bark, as a birch.

shelterbelt in a field, a strip of trees or shrubs providing shelter from the elements.

stand any close grouping or line of trees.

stoma a breathing pore of a leaf.

strangler a jungle plant (fig or banyan) starting life as a vine on the branch of a host tree, then working its way down to ground level to root; in time it grows woodier and thicker and may fully encompass the host tree, sometimes killing it.

sunscald localized injury to bark or cambium caused by high heat and sunlight.

sylva collective term for the forest trees of a region.

taiga subarctic coniferous forests consisting of small trees.

taproot the first and strongest central root of a tree, usually growing straight down.

thicket dense underbrush.

topiary trees or shrubs sculpted into fantastic shapes through pruning.

virgin forest a forest untouched by humans.

weald British term for a woodland.

windbreak a line or grouping of trees planted to act as a brake against the wind's erosive action, especially around a farm.

windfall branches and leaves knocked off by the wind.

windthrow trees knocked over by the wind.

VALLEYS

dale a broad, open valley, especially those found in England and Scotland.

dell a small, forested valley.

drowned valley a valley that has been submerged under water.

glen long, narrow, steep-sided valley, usually having a river or stream in the bottom.

rift valley land that has sunk between two faults, forming a long, relatively narrow valley.

vale a valley, usually with a river.

VOLCANOES

aa Hawaiian term for a rough, crumbly type of hardened lava.

accretionary lava ball: a semi-solidified glob of lava, from fist-size to boulder-size, on a river of lava or on the slope of a cinder cone.

active volcano a volcano that is either erupting currently or that has erupted within recorded history and will probably erupt again.

andesite a darkish volcanic rock comprised of silica, iron, and magnesium.

ash tiny particles of pulverized rock blown out of a volcano.

ashfall an accumulation of ash that has fallen out from an eruption.

basalt a dark, igneous rock produced by volcanoes.

basal wreck the truncated cone left after the eruption and collapse of a volcano.

base surge the explosive reaction of lava when it meets with water.

blister a hollow bubble or doming of a crust of lava, usually about one meter in diameter, formed by hot gas.

block any block-shaped rock ejected in an eruption.

blowhole a secondary crater or vent through which hot gas is discharged.

bomb a solidified blob of molten rock ejected from a volcano.

caldera a large crater formed by a volcanic eruption, often evolving into a lake.

cataclysm any violent upheaval, inundation, or deluge.

cinder cone a conelike mound formed by escaping volcanic gas and ash.

clastic of any ejaculate, broken or fragmented; sand is a clastic material.

composite volcano a volcano having more than one major vent. Also, any volcano with a vent and a dome.

compression waves seismic ground movement similar to the movement of a slinky toy.

conduit any natural cavity or passage through which magma flows.

continental drift the natural movement or migration of continents toward or away from one another, responsible for volcanic activity worldwide.

crater the mouth of a volcano.

curtain of fire one or more lava fountains spewing from a long fissure and resembling a curtain.

dacite a light-colored volcanic rock comprised of silica, sodium, and potassium.

debris avalanche a sudden slippage and flow of a mass of rocks, water, snow, mud, trees, or other debris down a slope.

detachment plane in an avalanche or landslide, the surface from which a mass disengages itself.

diatreme a conduit filled with fragmented rock or breccia.

dike a tabular sheet of igneous rock that intrudes into other rock.

dome a rounded or blocky mass of semi-hardened lava extruded from a vent.

dormant of volcanoes, inactive or "sleeping."

ejecta any material thrown out from an erupting volcano.

episode a volcanic event of any duration.

eruption volcanic explosion and release of superheated mass under pressure.

eruption cloud a column of ash, gas, and rock fragments rising from an eruption.

extinct volcano a volcano that is inactive and is likely to stay that way for the foreseeable future.

extrusion the emitting of magma along the surface of the earth.

fault a crack in the surface of the earth.

fissures fractures on the slope of a volcano.

flank eruption an eruption that occurs not at the top of a volcano, but from its side.

fumarole a gas or steam vent frequently found in volcanic areas.

harmonic tremor continuous seismic disturbance, thought to be related to the subterranean flow of magma.

hot spot any volcanic area having a history of tens of millions of years of activity.

hyaloclastite a deposit of fragments and granules formed by lava or magma after reacting to water.

hydrothermal reservoir a mass of porous rock containing hot water.

intrusion the entering or infiltration of magma into existing rock.

lahar a hot mudflow or ash flow down a slope.

lapilli tiny to small stone fragments ejected in an eruption.

lava molten rock after it flows out of a volcano, as opposed to magma.

lava lake a large body of molten lava in a crater, vent, or depression. Also, depending on size, a lava pond.

lava tree the hollow impression of a tree that has been engulfed and destroyed by lava.

lava tube a subterranean passage or cavern where lava once flowed.

magma underground molten rock. Magma technically becomes lava once it flows out of a volcano.

magma chamber any underground cavity holding magma.

magnitude the power, measured by numerical value, of an earthquake.

monogenetic designating a volcano that formed in a single eruption.

monticule a secondary volcanic cone of a volcano.

mudflow see LAHAR.

nuée ardente French term for a fiery cloud or superheated mass of gas and clastic material, considered to be the most devastating weapon in a volcano's arsenal. The cloud fries flesh and carbonizes wood on contact and literally sterilizes the landscape. Often hot enough to melt iron and moving as fast as 100 miles per hour, it has been described as a napalm explosion and gas attack rolled into one.

obsidian volcanic glass.

pahoehoe Hawaiian term for smooth-textured lava with the appearance of congealed molasses.

paroxysm an eruption of extreme violence and magnitude.

Pele's hair strands of spun glass, created by blow-off from fountains or cascades of lava.

Pele's tears tear-shaped drops of glass formed with Pele's hair.

phreactic explosion an explosion of steam caused when water and hot volcanic rock meet.

pillow lava pillow-shaped blobs of lava, formed underwater.

pipe a vertical magma conduit.

pit crater a crater that forms not from venting or eruption but from sinking of the ground.

plastic that which can be molded, such as lava or magma.

plate tectonics the interplay of the 10 massive fragments or plates of Earth's broken crust, forcing continents to migrate and new crust to be formed, all related to volcanic activity.

plug the solidified lava that fills the throat of a volcano. Highly resistant to erosion, the plug may remain standing as a solitary pinnacle after the outer shell of the mountain or volcano has worn away.

plug dome a mound of hardened lava that fills and caps a vent.

pluton a large igneous mass formed deep in Earth's crust.

polygenetic forming through many eruptions.

pumice a light, porous stone frequently ejected by volcanoes and known for its ability to float on water.

pyroclastic flow an avalanche of hot gas and ash.

pyrotechnics the "fireworks" caused by a volcano.

repose the period of time between eruptions.

rhyolite a light-colored volcanic rock comprised of silica, potassium, and sodium.

rift system the ocean ridges where new crust is formed and Earth's tectonic plates are drawn apart.

Ring of Fire a ring of high earthquake and volcanic activity that extends around the Pacific Ocean.

scoria a type of bomb that is filled with air cavities yet is heavier than pumice.

seafloor spreading the expansion of the seafloor along ridges, and the creation of new crust with the separation of Earth's tectonic plates.

seamount a mountain or volcano under the sea.

seismograph a device that senses and records vibrations of the Earth.

shield volcano the largest type of volcano (such as those found in Hawaii) but the least explosive due to a low silica content.

skylight an opening in the roof of a lava tube.

solfatara a fumarole that emits sulfurous gases.

spatter cone a pile of basaltic material forming a cone over a fissure or vent.

stratovolcano a volcano that emits lava and ejects rock matter.

subduction zone the ridge where two tectonic plates meet and one overrides the other.

talus a slope comprised of broken rocks.

tephra collective term for all elastic material ejected in an eruption, from sand-sized particles to chunks of rock 200 feet wide.

tilt the slope of a volcano's flank as measured against itself in the past or against another reference point.

tiltmeter a vulcanist's tool for measuring the growth rate of a bulge in the side of a volcano.

tremor continuous seismic activity due to the flow of magma.

tsunami a massive ocean wave formed by an earthquake or a volcanic eruption, or sometimes when an entire flank of a volcano collapses into the sea. A tsunami can travel from one side of an ocean to another.

tuff rock formed from volcanic activity.

tumulus a hardening sheath of cooling lava that forms over a hotter, flowing river of lava below.

vent any opening through which hot gas or molten materials escape.

volcanic pipe a large shaft of solidified magma, topped by a crater; a rich source of diamonds and other gems.

volcanic winter a drop in worldwide temperature due to volcanic activity, especially that which obscures part of the sky and the Sun's rays with volcanic ash.

volcanologist a scientist who studies volcanoes and volcanic activity. Also known as a vulcanist.

vulcanist see VOLCANOLOGIST.

Vulcanus the Roman god of fire.

WIND AND STORMS

Aeolus the Greek god of wind.

anemometer three-cupped device that rotates with the wind to measure its velocity.

backing wind a wind that gradually shifts counterclockwise through the compass; the opposite of a veering wind.

Beaufort scale a scale in which wind speeds are assigned the code numbers 0 to 12, corresponding to "calm" to "hurricane."

blustery National Weather Service's descriptive term for winds from 15 to 25 miles per hour; interchangeable with breezy and brisk.

breeze classification light—4 to 7 mph; moderate—13 to 18 mph; fresh—19 to 24 mph; strong—25 to 31 mph; gale—39 to 46 mph; strong gale—47 to 54 mph; storm wind—55 to 63 mph; violent storm wind—64 to 72 mph; hurricane—73 and up (mph = miles per hour).

breezy National Weather Service's descriptive term for winds from 15 to 25 miles (24–40 km) per hour. Also known as blustery and brisk.

brisk National Weather Service's descriptive term for winds from 15 to 25 miles (24–40 km) per hour. Also referred to as blustery and breezy.

cat's paw any slight breeze that lightly ripples the sea's surface.

chinook any warm dry wind descending the leeward slope of a mountain; known as a foehn in Europe.

chubasco a violent squall on the west coast of tropical and subtropical North America.

condensation funnel a funnel cloud comprised of condensed water droplets.

cordonazo hurricane-borne wind blowing from the south on the west coast of Mexico.

Coriolis force force resulting from the Earth's rotation, which causes and deflection.

cyclone a massive rotating storm measuring hundreds or thousands of miles across, turning counterclockwise above the equator and clockwise below, generally less violent than a hurricane.

derecho a very large and powerful windstorm spawned by a line of thunderstorms. Derechos usually stretch for 250 miles (460 km) or more and are characterized by sustained winds from at least 58 miles per hour (92 km/hr) to an excess of 100 miles per hour (160 km/hr).

doldrums steamy equatorial regions with dead-calm winds and flat seas.

dust devil a rapidly whirling column of wind that sucks up dust and resembles a miniature tornado, seen over deserts.

dust-tube tornado see LANDSPOUT.

elephant trunk tornado a long, sinuous tornado that stretches sideways across the sky and then touches down, resembling an elephant's trunk.

eolian pertaining to or caused by the wind.

etecians any winds that recur each year, or the recurring northerly summer winds over the eastern Mediterranean.

harmattan a dry, dusty wind of the west coast of Africa, blowing from the deserts.

hurricane a massive, cyclonic storm system that forms in tropical waters and, rotating clockwise in the Southern Hemisphere and counterclockwise in the Northern Hemisphere, produces torrential rain, high waves, sustained winds reaching 155 miles per hour (249 km/hr) or more, and dangerous storm surges that can flood entire cities. Hurricanes feed on heat from rising, moist air and lose their strength as they travel over land. Hurricanes spawn thunderstorms and can even produce tornadoes. Also known as a cyclone, tropical cyclone, or a typhoon.

jet stream strong winds beginning at 30,000 feet and increasing in velocity (up to 200 miles per hour or more) at 35,000 to 40,000 feet.

khamsin hot, dry southerly wind in Egypt in spring.

landspout slang for a characteristically smooth and tubular tornado, similar to a waterspout in appearance. Unlike normal land tornadoes, they form without mesocyclones and are generally smaller and weaker. Also known as a dust-tube tornado.

macroburst a powerful downdraft that is at least 2.5 miles (4 km) across, lasts from five to 20 minutes, and can cause as much destruction as an F3 tornado.

mesocyclone difficult to see with the naked eye and often only perceived on radar, an area of strong rotation, generally from 2 to 6 miles in diameter, and from which tornadoes may be spawned.

microburst a powerful downdraft less than 2.5 miles (4 km) wide that lasts less than five minutes and can create dangerous wind shear situations, a hazard to aircraft.

mistral stormy, cold northerly wind that blows down from the mountains along the Mediterranean coast.

monsoon seasonal wind that blows along the Asian coast of the Pacific from the Indian Ocean; the summer monsoon is characterized by heavy rains.

multiple vortex tornado any tornadic storm having two or more funnel or debris clouds appearing simultaneously and usually revolving around one another.

nor'easter a powerful storm that brings heavy snow and sometimes hurricane-force winds along the northeast coast of the United States and Canada.

rope a thin, tubelike tornado that is weakening and dissipating.

roping out slang for the narrowing of a funnel cloud as a tornado weakens and dissipates.

Saffir-Simpson Hurricane Wind Scale a measure of a hurricane's strength, given on a scale of 0 to 5, and used to predict the level of damage and danger to be expected as the storm passes. Category 1 has wind speeds of 74–96 miles per hour (119–153 km/hr) and a storm surge 4 to 5 feet above normal, while Category 5 has wind speeds greater than 155 miles per hour (249 km/hr), with a storm surge 18 feet (5 m) above normal.

satellite tornado any smaller, weaker tornado revolving around a larger one.

shamal a northeast wind of Mesopotamia and the Persian Gulf.

simoon scorching hot, dry wind of Asiatic and African deserts.

sirocco warm winds blowing from northern Africa to the Mediterranean area.

snow devil a waterspout that forms under a snow squall.

squall a sudden violent burst of wind, usually accompanied by rain.

stovepipe see WEDGE.

tehuantepecer powerful northerly wind of the Pacific off southern Mexico and northern Central America, occurring during the cold season.

tornado an extremely dangerous spinning column of air spawned from a thunderstorm, especially a supercell. Most tornadoes form when a layer of cold, dry air overlies a layer of warm, moist air. As the ground heats up during the day, the moist air rises, forming thunderstorms. Above and below the storms, opposing winds create wind shear, rolling and spinning the rising air, which can then rotate into a tornado. Tornados can create winds that whirl at 300 miles per hour (500 km/hr), strong enough to completely flatten entire towns.

tornado alley in the United States, a broad, flat area from west Texas to North Dakota, where dry, cold air from Canada and the Rockies sweeps down and meets with warm, moist air from the Gulf of Mexico, resulting in the creation of more tornadoes than any other location in the world, especially in the month of May.

trade wind a consistent wind of 10 to 15 miles per hour.

tropical depression a cyclonic storm forming in tropical regions and not quite achieving hurricane status, with sustained winds of less than 39 miles per hour (62 km/hr). Tropical depressions sometimes evolve into hurricanes.

veering wind a wind that gradually shifts clockwise through the compass; the opposite of a backing wind.

waterspout a tornado, which may or may not be associated with a mesocyclone, that appears over a body of water, characterized by a vortex made up of water. The most typical waterspout is unassociated with a mesocyclone and is generally weaker than most other types.

wedge a broad tornado that is wider than it is tall and may, in fact, be as wide as 1 mile. Also known as a stovepipe.

windfall timber, fruit, or any debris knocked down by the wind.

windshear the shearing force of a sudden powerful burst of wind, a noted hazard to aircraft.

wind sock cone-shaped bag hung at airports for detecting wind direction.

zephyr a west wind, or any gentle wind.

FINANCE

INTERNATIONAL MONETARY UNITS

Afghanistan afghani

Albania lek

Algeria dinar

American Samoa dollar

Andorra euro

Angola kwanza

Anguilla dollar

Antigua and Barbuda dollar

Argentina peso

Armenia dram

Aruba guilder (also florin or gulden)

Australia dollar

Austria euro

Azerbaijan manat

Bahamas dollar

Bahrain dinar

Bangladesh taka

Barbados dollar

Belarus ruble

Belgium euro

Belize dollar

Benin franc

Bermuda dollar

Bolivia boliviano

Bosnia and Herzegovina marka

Botswana pula

Brazil real

British Virgin Islands dollar

Brunei ringgit (Bruneian dollar)

Bulgaria lev

Burkina Faso franc

Burma kyat

Burundi franc

Cambodia riel

Cameroon franc

Canada dollar

Cayman Islands dollar

Central African Republic franc

Chad franc

Chile peso

China yuan (renminbi)

Colombia peso

Congo, Democratic Republic of franc

Congo, Republic of the franc

Costa Rica colon

Côte d'Ivoire franc

Croatia kuna

Cuba peso

Cyprus euro

Czech Republic koruna

Denmark krone

Djibouti franc

Dominica dollar

Dominican Republic peso

East Timor dollar

Ecuador dollar

Egypt pound

El Salvador colon

Equatorial Guinea franc

Eritrea nakfa

Estonia kroon

Ethiopia birr

European Union euro

Falkland Islands pound

Fiji dollar

Finland euro

France euro

French Guiana euro; franc

French Polynesia franc

Gabon franc

Gambia dalasi

Georgia lari

Germany euro

Ghana new cedi

Gibraltar pound

Greece euro

Greenland krone

Grenada dollar

Guadeloupe euro; franc

Guam dollar

Guatemala quetzal

Guinea franc

Guinea-Bissau franc

Guyana dollar

Haiti gourde

Honduras lempira

Hong Kong dollar

Hungary forint

Iceland krona

India rupee

Indonesia rupiah

Iran rial

Iraq dinar

Ireland euro

Israel shekel

Italy euro

Jamaica dollar

Japan yen

Jordan dinar

Kazakhstan tenge

Kenya shilling

Korea, North won

Korea, South won

Kosovo euro

Kuwait dinar

Kyrgyzstan som

Laos kip

Latvia lat

Lebanon pound

Lesotho loti; rand

Liberia dollar

Libya dinar

Liechtenstein franc

Lithuania litas

Luxembourg euro

Macau pataca

Macedonia dinar

Madagascar Malagasy ariary

Malawi kwacha

Malaysia ringgit

Maldives rufiyaa

Mali franc

Malta euro

Martinique euro

Mauritania ouguiya

Mauritius rupee

Mexico peso

Micronesia, Federated States of dollar

Moldova leu

Monaco euro

Mongolia Mongolian togrog

Montenegro euro

Montserrat dollar

Morocco dirham

Mozambique metical

Myanmar kyat

Namibia dollar, rand

Naura dollar

Nepal rupee

Netherlands euro

Netherlands Antilles guilder

New Zealand dollar

Nicaragua cordoba oro

Niger franc

Nigeria naira

Northern Cyprus Turkish lira

Norway krone

Oman rial

Pakistan rupee

Palau dollar

Palestine Israeli new shekel, Jordanian dinar

Panama balboa, dollar

Papua New Guinea kina

Paraguay guarani

Peru nuevo sol

Philippines peso

Poland zloty

Portugal euro

Puerto Rico dollar

Qatar rial

Romania leu

Russia ruble

Rwanda franc

Saint Kitts and Nevis dollar

Saint Lucia dollar

Saint Vincent and the Grenadines dollar

Samoa tala

San Marino euro

São Tomé and Príncipe dobra

Saudi Arabia riyal

Senegal franc

Serbia and Montenegro dinar; euro

Seychelles rupee

Sierra Leone leone

Singapore dollar

Slovakia euro

Slovenia euro

Solomon Islands dollar

Somalia shilling

Somaliland shilling

South Africa rand

Spain euro

Sri Lanka rupee

Sudan Sudanese pound

Suriname Surinamese dollar

Swaziland lilangeni

Sweden krona

Switzerland franc

Syria pound

Taiwan dollar

Tajikistan somoni

Tanzania shilling

Thailand baht

Togo franc

Tonga pa'anga

Trinidad and Tobago dollar

Tunisia dinar

Turkey lira

Turkmenistan manat

Tuvalu dollar

Uganda shilling

Ukraine hryvnia

United Arab Emirates dirham

United Kingdom pound

United States and its territories dollar

Uruguay peso

Uzbekistan som

Vanuatu vatu

Venezuela bolivar

Vietnam dong

Virgin Islands dollar

Yemen rial

Zambia kwacha

Zimbabwe dollar

STOCKS, BONDS, COMMODITIES, AND MARKET TERMS

acquisition the purchase of a controlling interest in one company by another.

across the board stock market activity in which prices move in the same direction.

air pocket stock any stock that plummets sharply, as an aircraft hitting an air pocket.

American Stock Exchange the stock exchange second in trading volume to the New York Stock Exchange. It is located in New York and handles mostly small to medium-size companies. Also known as Amex and the curb.

analyst a person who analyzes companies and their securities and makes buy and sell recommendations.

arbitrage earning a profit by buying a security from one market and selling it back to another market at a higher price. The practice of taking advantage of price discrepancies between two markets. Also, speculating in the stock of a company that is about to be acquired by another company.

arbitrageur one who uses arbitrage to turn a profit. Also known as an arb.

baby bond a bond with a face value of less than $1,000, for small investors.

back-end load a service fee paid by an investor when withdrawing money from an investment, such as a mutual fund.

back off of a stock that has suddenly dropped in price after rising.

bailout a large infusion of cash, loans, stocks, or bonds from an institution or government to a struggling company to rescue it from going bankrupt or out of business.

barometer stock a large stock, such as General Motors, whose market activity reflects the market as a whole. Also known as a bellwether.

bear a person who is pessimistic about the stock market and who believes prices will continue to fall. Opposite of a bull.

bear market a pessimistic market with falling prices over an extended period of time. Opposite of a bull market.

bear raid the practice of selling a large quantity of a stock to force its price down and then rebuying it at the depressed price.

bellwether a security, such as IBM stock, whose price activity indicates which direction the rest of the market will go.

belly up of a company that is going or has gone bankrupt.

bid and asked respectively, the highest price offered for a share of stock at a given time and the lowest price a seller will sell it for. The disparity between the two is known as the spread.

Big Blue nickname for IBM, International Business Machines.

Big Board the New York Stock Exchange.

Black Friday any sharp drop in a financial market. Also known as a Black Monday.

blue chip a common stock of a large corporation, such as IBM, that has had a long history of strong management and profit growth.

blue sky laws laws protecting the public from securities fraud.

boiler room a room or enterprise in which salespeople use high-pressure tactics to sell high-risk or fraudulent securities to investors over the telephone.

bond an interest-bearing certificate of debt, a form of corporate or government security; a formal IOU.

bond ratings a rating system ranging from AAA (very safe; not likely to default) to D (in default) that illustrates a bond issuer's financial health and predicts the probability of default.

bottom fisher an investor who seeks out a stock whose price has dropped to its lowest levels.

boutique a small brokerage house dealing in specialized stocks.

broad tape in brokerage firms, the enlarged, electronic Dow-Jones ticker tape that continuously displays new financial developments.

broker one who buys and sells securities on behalf of another.

bucket shop a brokerage firm that illegally gambles with its clients' holdings without the clients' awareness.

Buck Rogers a security whose price soars or rises sharply in a short period.

bull one who is optimistic about the market and who believes prices will continue an upward trend. Opposite of a bear.

bull market a prolonged period of rising stocks in the market. An optimistic market.

buying on margin buying securities on credit.

buyout the purchase of a controlling interest in a company.

cash cow a company that generates a lot of surplus cash flow.

cats and dogs speculative stocks with unproven track records; high-risk stocks.

churning the unethical frequent trading of a client's holdings in order to generate more commissions.

closely held of a corporation's controlling stock, held by only a small number of shareholders.

Comex Commodity Exchange; the New York-based exchange that trades in aluminum, copper, gold, and silver.

commodities grains, foods, metals.

common stock in a corporation, shares of ownership granting the holder a vote on important company issues as well as entitling him to dividends or a share of the profits.

contrarian an investor who follows a buying or selling strategy opposite or contrary to what most other investors are doing.

controlling interest owning 51 percent or more of a corporation's voting shares.

cornering the market buying a security or commodity in a large enough volume to control its price, an illegal practice.

correction a reversal, usually downward, of a stock's price trend.

crash a collapse of the stock market.

credit default swap a form of insurance to cover losses on securities in which a buyer makes a payment to a seller, who must pay the buyer if the financial instrument, such as a bond or loan, goes into default, which could occur in a bankruptcy.

cyclical stock a stock that rises or falls in accordance with the strength or weakness of the economy.

day order a purchase or sell order given to a broker that is good for only one day.

debt instrument a collective term for any formal IOU, such as a bond.

dividend earnings distributed to shareholders, usually paid quarterly.

dog a poorly performing stock.

dollar-cost averaging investing a set amount of money on a regular schedule, regardless of share prices or market conditions, a strategy which ultimately results in more shares purchased at lower cost, increasing long-term profits.

Dow-Jones industrial average the daily price average of 30 selected blue chip stocks, used as a market indicator or barometer.

Dun & Bradstreet a firm that obtains credit information on various companies and publishes same in reports and a ratings directory.

exchange traded fund (ETF) a basket of securities that serves as an alternative to mutual funds. ETFs are traded on the American Stock Exchange just as individual stock is; unlike mutual funds, ETFs may be purchased on margin or sold short. They must, however, be purchased through a broker.

Fannie Mae nickname for the Federal National Mortgage Association, a corporation that buys mortgages from lenders and sells them to investors.

Fed, the the Federal Reserve System and the Federal Reserve Bank.

fill or kill a purchase or sell order that will be canceled unless it is executed immediately to take advantage of brief price changes.

flag market a market in which prices are neither rising nor falling.

floor the trading floor of the New York Stock Exchange.

floor broker a person who executes buy and sell orders on the floor of an exchange.

floor trader a person who executes orders on the floor of an exchange on his or her own behalf.

foreign crowd members of the New York Stock Exchange who trade in foreign bonds.

401K an employee retirement plan, through which a portion of one's pay is put aside, matched by the employer, and saved tax-deferred until withdrawal.

fourth market institutional investors who trade securities in large volume between one another to save on broker commissions.

Freddie Mac nickname for the Federal Home Loan Mortgage Corporation (FHLMC) and the mortgage-backed securities it packages and sells.

freeriding the buying and selling of securities quickly on margin and without paying any cash, a violation of fair credit use.

friendly takeover a takeover of one company by another that is welcome and unopposed.

front-end load a sales charge paid when mutual fund shares are purchased.

fungible securities, bearer instruments, or commodities that are interchangeable in value.

futures commodities such as metals, grains, foods.

futures market a commodity exchange, such as the New York Coffee, Sugar and Cocoa Exchange or the Minneapolis Grain Exchange.

gilt-edged security any high-quality stock or bond.

Ginnie Mae nickname for the Government National Mortgage Association (GNMA) and the securities it guarantees.

going public the process of a private company offering shares to the public and subsequently becoming a publicly held company.

gold bond a bond through which interest is paid according to the price of gold.

goldbug an analyst or investor who specializes in gold.

graveyard market a bear market.

greenmail a payment made by a company takeover candidate to the potential acquiring company to prevent the takeover, a form of legal blackmail.

gun jumping trading securities on information that has not yet reached the public.

hard money strong, secure currency of an economically stable country. Also, gold.

hedge any means of protecting one's investments against losses.

hemline theory the theory that stock prices rise and fall with the hemlines of women's dresses and skirts.

homerun a highly profitable gain in a stock in a brief period of time.

hot issue a newly issued stock that proves extremely popular with investors.

hung up of a stock or bond that has dropped below its purchase price, that cannot be sold without a loss.

in-and-out trader a trader who takes advantage of sharp price movements by buying and then reselling a security in the same day.

Individual Retirement Account (IRA) a plan that allows a taxpayer to put away $2,000 of income per year tax-deferred until withdrawal at retirement.

inside information privileged information concerning a corporation that has not been made public and is therefore illegal to trade on.

insider in a corporation, one who is privy to such information as an impending takeover attempt, a future earnings report, or other development affecting stock prices. Insiders would include top executives, directors, and large shareholders.

institutional investor banks, insurance companies, mutual funds, and others who trade in large blocks of securities.

IPO initial public offering. A company's first sale of stock to the public.

IRA see INDIVIDUAL RETIREMENT ACCOUNT.

junk bond a high-risk, high-yield bond with a credit rating of BB or less, often used to finance takeovers.

Keogh plan a retirement plan in which a self-employed person can put away up to 20 percent of earnings and deduct them from his income for tax deferral.

killer bees law firms, PR firms, investment bankers, and others involved in warding off a company takeover attempt.

lamb an inexperienced or naive investor.

leg a long-lasting trend in the market. A trend on its second or third leg is a very long trend.

leveraged buyout the takeover of a company with the use of borrowed money.

leveraged stock a stock bought with credit.

liquidity the ease or speed with which an investment can be converted into cash.

load a mutual fund sales or service charge.

long of an investment posture, holding on to securities in the belief they will rise in value.

long bond a bond that takes more than 10 years to mature.

manipulation the buying and selling of large blocks of securities to give the illusion of activity and to influence other investors into buying or selling.

margin the amount of money an investor must have on deposit with a broker in order to purchase securities on credit, specifically at least 50 percent of the purchase price.

margin account an account held by a broker, which allows a client to buy securities on credit.

melon slang for a large dividend.

meltdown the stock market crash of October 1987.

money market fund a mutual fund that invests in short-term corporate and government debt.

mortgage-backed security a residential mortgage loan, purchased from banks and mortgage companies in large bundles or pools, either by a government institution or a private investment firm and converted into security based on the collective principal and interest payments to be made by borrowers.

municipal bond a bond issued by a state or local government agency to finance a large project.

municipal revenue bond a bond issued to finance a project that will eventually generate its own revenues, such as a toll bridge.

mutual fund a diversified investment fund trading in many different stocks, bonds, commodities, or money market securities.

NASDAQ National Association of Securities Dealers Automated Quotations system; it provides brokers with price quotations.

new issue a new stock or bond offering.

New York Coffee, Sugar and Cocoa Exchange a commodities exchange trading in futures contracts.

New York Cotton Exchange a commodities exchange trading in futures contracts in cotton, orange juice, and propane.

New York Curb Exchange the American Stock Exchange, or Amex.

New York Mercantile Exchange an exchange trading in oil, gasoline, palladium, platinum, and potatoes.

New York Stock Exchange originating in 1792, the oldest and largest stock exchange in the United States. Also known as the Big Board and the Exchange.

Nifty Fifty the current 50 favorite stocks of institutional investors.

noise stock market movement caused by factors other than general market sentiment.

no-load fund mutual fund shares purchased directly, without a broker, so no sales fee is charged.

nonvoting stock stock, such as preferred stock, that does not give the holder a vote in important corporate affairs.

not rated referring to a security or a company that has not yet been rated by a securities rating company, such as Dun & Bradstreet.

odd lot a purchase or rate of less than 100 shares. See ROUND LOT.

off-board not traded on the floor of the New York Stock Exchange, as OTC stocks sold over the phone.

on margin of securities, buying on credit.

open outcry in a commodity exchange, the shouting out of buy and sell offers by traders looking for buyers and sellers.

opm slang for other people's money, as used when buying securities on credit.

option a right granted to buy or sell a security at a locked-in price by a specific date.

option, call the right (bought by a fee or premium) to purchase shares of a security at a locked-in price by a specific date.

option, put the right (paid for with a premium) to sell a specific number of shares of a stock at a specific price by a specific date.

order ticket a buy or sell order form with all the information needed for a broker to make a transaction on behalf of his client.

OTC over-the-counter, referring to those securities traded not on an exchange floor but over the telephone by securities dealers.

outstanding a corporate finance term referring to stock held by shareholders.

overbought referring to a security that has risen too far in price and is due for a price decline or correction.

oversold referring to a security that has dropped sharply in price and is due for an increase.

over-the-counter see OTC.

overvalued referring to a stock whose price has been driven higher than what is justified by the company's earnings potential.

Pac Man strategy named after the video game in which characters gobble each other up, a defensive strategy of attempting to take over a company that is trying to take over your company, achieved by buying up the threatening company's common shares.

painting the tape a form of illegal manipulation in which two or more investors buy or sell securities among each other in order to influence other investors into buying or selling.

par the face value of a security.

parking temporarily placing assets in a safe, low-risk investment until market volatility passes.

penny stock a stock that generally sells for under $1 per share.

period of digestion a period of price volatility followed by price stability after the release of a new stock issue.

phantom stock plan a company incentive in which an executive's bonus is paid according to the company's stock growth.

pit where commodities are traded, as distinguished from the floor for stock trading.

plow back of a new company, to put earnings back into the business instead of paying it out in dividends.

poison pill a device or strategy of a company that is threatened with being taken over to make its stock appear unattractive to the potential acquiring company.

portfolio an investor's diversified holdings.

portfolio manager a professional who chooses investments and manages the financial portfolios of others.

preferred stock stock in which dividends are paid preferentially over that of common stock; however, it is usually nonvoting stock.

premium bond a bond that sells for a higher price than its face value.

price/earnings ratio a stock price divided by earnings per share for the previous year or projected for the coming year. Also known as the multiple, or P/E, ratio.

prospectus a circular containing information on a company's history, finances, officers, plans, and so forth, sent to potential investors in a stock offering.

publicly held of a company with shares, held by the public.

pure play Wall Street term for a company that specializes in only one business, as distinguished from a conglomerate.

quotation a bid and asked price on a security or commodity.

quotation board in a brokerage house, an electronic display of current price quotations.

radar alert the monitoring of unusual trading in a company's stock in order to detect an impending takeover attempt. Also known as shark watching.

raider one who attempts to take over a company by buying up a large portion of its stock.

rally a rise in stock prices after a flat or bear market.

rating a rating of securities and credit risk by rating services such as Standard and Poor's Corporation.

registered competitive trader a New York Stock Exchange member who trades securities on his own behalf.

resistance level the high-water mark of a security's price; it is difficult to break through due to market psychology.

return profit on an investment.

rigged market a market being rigged by manipulators.

rollover the moving of assets from one investment to another.

round lot in stock, 100 shares or a multiple of 100.

round-tip trade a security that is purchased and then resold within a short period of time.

Sallie Mae the National Student Loan Marketing Association.

S&P Standard and Poor's

scalper an investment adviser who purchases a security and then recommends it to clients in order to drive up its price and take a quick profit.

scorched earth a strategy of a company threatened with being taken over of making itself less attractive to the potential acquiring company, achieved by selling off the most desirable part of its business. Also known as shark repellent.

scripophily collecting stock and bond certificates for their "collectible" value rather than as securities, as a baseball card collector.

seat a purchased membership on an exchange.

securities stocks, bonds, notes, and similar items.

securities and commodities exchanges where securities, options, and futures contracts are bought and sold.

Securities and Exchange Commission (SEC) a federal agency that regulates and oversees investment companies, over-the-counter brokers and dealers, investment advisers, and the exchanges to protect the public from fraudulent practices.

selling short selling borrowed stocks in anticipation of a drop in price, after which the stocks may be repurchased at a lower price to make a profit.

shakeout a development in the market that scares investors into selling off their stock.

share a unit of ownership in a corporation or mutual fund.

shareholder an owner of stock in a corporation.

shark one who attempts a hostile takeover of a company; a corporate raider.

shark repellant collective term for any device or strategy used to ward off a hostile takeover attempt.

shark watcher a firm hired to monitor trading in a company's stock in order to detect an impending takeover attempt.

sideways market a flat market.

sleeper a new stock issue with great potential that is overlooked by investors.

sleeping beauty a corporation rich in assets and ripe for a takeover attempt.

soft currency currency that cannot be interchanged with another country's currency, such as the Russian ruble.

SPDRS Standard and Poor's Depository Receipts. A group of ETFs that track the Standard and Poor's index. Also known as spiders.

speculation investing in high-risk securities with the belief they will produce a higher yield.

speculator one who trades in high-risk securities.

spiders see SPDRS.

split an increase in the number of shares held by corporate shareholders with no change in equity. For example, a two-for-one split would double the number of shares owned but halve their value. A stock split is made to improve the stock's marketability.

spread the difference between a stock's bid and asked price.

stag an investor who regularly purchases then quickly resells securities within a short period of time to make a fast profit.

Standard and Poor's Corp. a company that offers several investment and ratings services.

Standard and Poor's index a measurement of the average up or down movements of 500 widely held common stocks, known as the S&P 500.

stock an equity or ownership interest in a corporation through which earnings are paid out according to the number of shares owned. Stock may also entitle the holder to a vote in important corporate affairs.

stock exchange the marketplace where stocks and bonds are traded.

stock watcher a service that monitors trading on the New York Stock Exchange to prevent unethical or fraudulent trading practices.

stop order an order to a broker to buy or sell a security when it reaches a specific price.

Street, the short for Wall Street.

street name securities held in the name of a broker instead of the name of the owner, as required when securities are purchased on margin.

strip to buy stock only for their dividends.

sweetener a bonus feature tacked on to a security to make it more attractive to investors.

swooner any security that is overly sensitive and reacts poorly to bad news in the marketplace.

tailgating a broker's practice of buying or selling for his own account the same security an influential client has just placed an order on, an unethical use of privileged trading information.

take a flyer to invest in a high-risk security; to speculate.

takeover a buying-out of the controlling interest in a corporation and, in hostile instances, the installment of new management.

target company a corporation that is threatened with a takeover.

TARP Troubled Asset Relief Program, the largest component of the government program in 2008 to address the subprime mortgage crisis by buying assets and equity from financial institutions.

ticker the electronic display of stock exchange trading activity.

toehold purchase the purchase of 5 percent of a takeover target's stock, which requires the buyer to file with the Securities and Exchange Commission if a takeover attempt is forthcoming.

tombstone the plain or unadorned advertisement in a newspaper of a new stock offering.

ton bond investor's slang for $100 million.

toxic asset any asset that cannot be sold without incurring a large loss.

trader one who buys and sells securities.

triple watching hour the massive trading that occurs when options and futures on stock indexes expire on the last trading hour of the third Friday of March, June, September, and December.

turkey a poorly performing investment.

twisting broker's unethical practice of persuading a client to make frequent trades in order to generate more commissions.

undervalued referring to a security that is selling for less than what analysts believe it is worth.

underwriter the investment banker who insures and distributes a corporation's new issue of securities.

undigested securities new stocks or bonds that have yet to be purchased due to a lack of investor interest.

unlisted security a security traded over the counter as distinguished from one traded on the floor of a stock exchange.

volatile a term commonly used to describe an unstable or rapidly fluctuating stock price or stock market.

volume the number of securities traded in a specific period.

voting stock stock that entitles the holder to a vote in important corporate affairs.

Wall Street in lower Manhattan, the financial district where the New York Stock Exchange, American Stock Exchange, and many investment-oriented firms are located. Also known as the Street.

war babies the stock and bonds of companies involved in defense contracts.

war brides war babies.

whipsawed of a security, bought just before its price drops and then resold just before its price rises.

white knight an acquirer or acquiring company that is welcomed by a takeover target.

white squire a white knight who buys less than a controlling interest in a corporation.

widow and orphan stock any very reliable and safe stock that pays high dividends.

zero-coupon bond a long-term investment bond through which interest is only paid at maturity.

FOOD AND DRINK

APPETIZERS

angels on horseback oysters wrapped in bacon.

antipasto Italian term for appetizer. The plural is antipasti.

baba ghanoush a Middle Eastern dip made from mashed eggplant, garlic, olive oil, and tahini, usually served on pita bread. Also spelled baba gannoujh.

buffalo wings spicy, fried chicken wings or chicken wing pieces, usually coated in hot sauce or barbecue sauce, reportedly originating in a bar in Buffalo, New York, in the 1960s. Traditionally, buffalo wings are served with celery sticks and a dip of blue cheese dressing.

canapé a cracker or small piece of bread spread with meat, cheese, or other topping.

caviar the salted eggs of sturgeon or salmon, eaten as a spread.

coquilles St. Jacques minced scallops served in their shells and topped with a creamy wine sauce and grated cheese.

crudités raw vegetables cut up and usually served with dip.

dim sum any of a variety of Asian appetizers that most often consist of dough casings filled with minced vegetables or meats.

dolma rice, lamb, and onion wrapped in grape or cabbage leaves and marinated with olive oil and lemon, served cold.

falafel a deep-fried patty or croquette made from ground chickpeas and seasonings. Also, a pita bread sandwich made of this.

finger food any small food or tidbit that can be picked up in one's hands and eaten.

gougère a delicate cheese puff that looks like a small dinner roll, made from Gruyère cheese, flour, butter, and eggs, and sometimes flavored with nutmeg or sprinkled with salt.

kickshaw any tidbit or delicacy.

knish a pillow of dough stuffed with potato, meat, or cheese, baked or fried.

nachos tortilla chips topped with guacamole, salsa, bean dip, or chopped onion or tomatoes, etc., and covered with melted cheese.

nosh a snack. Also, to eat a snack.

pâté a spread of pureed seasoned meat.

pâté de foie gras a spread made from fattened goose liver.

rollmop a filleted herring rolled around a pickle or onion.

rumaki a marinated chicken liver and a slice of water chestnut wrapped in bacon.

smorgasbord an assortment of appetizers and other foods, which may in themselves be eaten as a whole meal.

tapa a snack served with beer or sherry.

BEER

alcohol-free beer any beer having no more than 0.5 percent alcohol by volume.

ale a fruity brew that is made by quick fermentation at high temperatures. Ales typically have a higher alcohol content than lagers.

amber beer between pale and dark in color.

barley the grain used to make malt.

barley wine a fruity, winelike ale with a high alcohol content and a coppery color.

barrel a container for holding beer, equal to two kegs, or 31 gallons.

Belgian lace the latticework of foam that streaks down a glass after a drink of beer is taken.

Berliner Weisse a cloudy wheat beer with high carbonation and low alcohol content.

bitter popular dry British draft ale that is bronze to deep copper in color.

black and tan a blend of dark and pale beers, such as pilsner and porter.

black malt malted barley intensely roasted to provide a dark hue and a burned flavor to stouts and dark beers.

bock a very strong, malty Bavarian dark lager, traditionally drunk in early spring to mark the new season.

body the fullness of flavor and feel of a beer on the tongue

bouquet the aroma of a beer.

brewing the process of making beer.

brown ale a dark brown ale flavored with caramel malt and low in alcohol.

caramel malt a sweet, golden malt with a nutty flavor, used in dark ales.

craft beer any beer made by a small, independent brewer with traditional ingredients and methods.

cream ale a mild American ale.

doppelbock "double bock"; a very strong, dark brown beer, originating in Germany.

draft beer beer on tap from a keg.

dry beer a light brew with a higher alcohol content and little aftertaste.

eisbock a very strong bock beer, with a higher alcohol content.

fermentation the multiday process of yeast's conversion of simple sugars into alcohol and carbon dioxide.

fermenter in the brewing process, the tank used for conversion of simple sugars to alcohol.

head the foam at the top of a beer after pouring.

hops a beer spice derived from the flowers of a perennial vine.

ice beer a smooth lager made by chilling to the point of crystallization.

keg a beer container that holds 6.88 cases of beer or 15.5 gallons.

lager a smooth, crisp beer made by storing for long periods at low temperatures.

lambic a strongly acidic wheat beer originally produced in Belgium.

light beer a watery, low-calorie beer, usually pilsner. May also designate a low alcohol beer.

malt barley that has germinated and been allowed to dry.

malt liquor a strong, pale lager, originating in America.

maple brown ale a brown ale made with maple syrup as a sweetener.

mash the brewing ingredients of ground malt and water.

mashing brewing process of blending ground malt and water in a vessel.

mash tun the vessel in which the mashing process takes place.

microbrew a beer made by a small, independent brewery and distributed locally.

microbrewery a small, independent brewery that produces a high-quality, often distinctly flavored beer or line of beers, usually distributed regionally.

Oktoberfest famous beer-drinking festival that takes place in Munich, Germany, in the fall.

pilsner a dry, pale, golden-colored lager, aged in wood. Also spelled pilsener.

porter a heavy, dark brown English brew made from roasted barley.

Scotch ale a very strong, malty ale, originating in Scotland.

stout extra dark beer made with roasted malts.

weisse a very pale or white beer from Germany. Also known as weissbier.

wheat beer a beer made with malted wheat and malted barley.

BOTTLES AND GLASSES

beer mug a heavy drinking glass, often made of metal or earthenware and having a handle.

brandy snifter a glass distinguished by its medium stem and large, slightly tapering bowl, somewhat reminiscent of a balloon.

champagne glass a slender, tapering glass with a medium stem.

cocktail glass a small, stemmed glass with a triangular bowl. Also known as a martini glass.

Collins glass a tall, straight glass.

cooler a tall, narrow glass.

cordial glass a small, narrow glass with a long stem.

deep-saucer champagne glass a glass having a tall stem and broad, saucerlike cup and holding six ounces or more.

delmonico similar to a cocktail glass but having a slightly taller, narrower cup.

fifth a bottle holding one-fifth of a gallon.

goblet a large, round, handleless glass.

highball glass a large, straight glass, broader than a Collins glass and slightly narrower than an old-fashioned glass.

Irish coffee glass a large glass with a short stem and a handle.

jeroboam a wine bottle holding four-fifths of a gallon.

jigger a very small measuring glass, holding one-and-a-half ounces of fluid.

magnum a wine bottle holding two-fifths of a gallon of wine or liquor.

margarita glass a stemmed glass with a double-domed bowl.

martini glass see COCKTAIL GLASS.

old-fashioned glass a large, broad-mouthed glass.

parfait glass a tall, conical, tapering glass with a short stem and a round base.

pilsner glass a narrow, tapering beer glass with a round base.

pony a small liqueur glass.

pousse glass a tall glass with a short stem.

punch cup a small cup with a handle.

schooner a large beer mug.

seidel a large, bulging beer mug, sometimes having a hinged lid.

sherry glass a small, stemmed glass with a conical bowl.

shot glass a very small glass that holds approximately one swallow's worth, or a "shot," of liquor.

sour glass a small, stemmed glass with a conical bowl, similar to a cordial glass.

split a small bottle holding approximately six ounces. Also, a drink of half the usual amount.

stein a large, earthenware beer mug.

tankard a large mug, sometimes of pewter or silver, with a handle and a hinged lid.

tumbler a round, straight drinking glass without a base, stem, or handle.

wine glass a small glass with a long stem. Its bowl is slightly broader than that of a cordial glass. The white wine glass has a slightly narrower and taller bowl than the red wine glass.

BREADS

anadama a yeast bread made from cornmeal and molasses.

babka a Polish sweet bread flavored with rum, raisins, almonds, and orange peel.

bagel a chewy, donut-shaped roll that is boiled and then baked and traditionally spread with cream cheese.

baguette a long, slender loaf of French bread with a crispy crust.

baker's yeast the yeast used to make bread rise.

banneton a woven basket in which bread may be allowed to rise and which then conforms to the basket's shape before baking.

bannock a flat Scottish cake made from oatmeal or barley meal and usually baked on a griddle. Also, a very large scone or biscuit.

bap a floury yeast roll eaten for breakfast in Scotland.

barm brack an Irish bread flavored with raisins or currants and traditionally served with tea.

batarde a loaf of white bread that is slightly larger than a baguette.

baton a loaf of white bread slightly smaller than a baguette.

batonnet a loaf of white bread, smaller than a baguette.

bialy similar to a bagel, a chewy yeast roll topped with chopped, sautéed onions.

black bread any very dark bread, usually made from dark or whole rye flour.

bleached flour flour that is either allowed to age and lighten in color naturally or that has been doctored with a chemical bleaching agent, or both.

Boston brown bread see BROWN BREAD.

boule a round loaf of bread. Also, a rounded mass of dough.

bran the husks of any grain, such as wheat, rye, oats, etc.

breadstick a small, dry, crunchy baton of bread, usually seasoned.

brioche a rich, French roll or bread made from flour, butter, and eggs, sometimes used to encase cheese or sausage, and made into various shapes.

brown bread A dark, sweet bread made from molasses, cornmeal, and wheat or rye flour and usually steamed. Also known as Boston brown bread.

bruschetta grilled bread brushed with olive oil and garlic.

challah a loaf of rich white bread usually shaped in a twist or braid, eaten by Jewish people on the sabbath and holy days.

chapati an Indian flatbread made from whole wheat and grilled or fried.

corn bread a flat bread made of cornmeal, milk, flour, and eggs, and either baked or fried.

corn dodger a baked or fried cake of cornmeal.

corn pone a small oval loaf of corn bread, originating in the American South.

couche a linen wrap used to hold dough while it rises.

croissant a French, crescent-shaped roll resembling a puff pastry.

crostini toasted bread brushed with olive oil and served with cheese, bean puree, tomatoes, or other topping.

croutons toasted or fried bread cubes or pieces served on salad and in soups.

crumb professional baker's term used to refer to the texture and feel of a bread.

crumpet an English batter cake cooked on a griddle and often toasted.

egg wash a mix of egg and milk or water brushed over bread before baking to enrich color and create glossiness.

English muffin a flat yeast roll, usually cut in half and toasted.

ficelle a long, slender loaf of French bread, about one-half the size of a baguette.

focaccia a round, flat Italian bread flavored with olive oil, salt, and herbs.

French bread a loaf of white bread, in various shapes and sizes, with a crusty exterior and chewy interior.

hardtack wafers of unleavened bread, formerly used as rations for the military.

hot cross bun a yeast bun flavored with raisins, currants, or other dried fruits and topped with a cross of icing, traditionally eaten during Lent.

hush puppy a fried ball of cornmeal.

kaiser roll a very large, round roll, used for sandwiches.

knead to mix and shape dough with the heels of the hands.

leavener any substance, such as yeast or baking powder, used to make bread rise.

matzo thin, crisp, unleavened bread, eaten by Jews during Passover. Also spelled matzoh.

Melba toast a very thin slice of bread that is toasted.

muffin baked in a cuplike mold, a quick bread that may be made with various flours and flavored with a wide array of fruits or nuts.

nan an East Indian flat bread made from white flour. Also spelled naan.

pita originating in the Middle East, a round, flat bread, sometimes having a pocket for stuffing with a wide variety of fillings.

papadum a thin, crisp bread made from lentil flour and seasonings, originating in India.

popover a very light and airy muffin.

pumpernickel a dark bread made of a mixture or rye and wheat flour, often flavored and colored with molasses.

quick bread any bread leavened with baking soda or baking powder rather than yeast, which can be baked immediately. Muffins, biscuits, and corn bread are quick breads.

rise the expansion of any yeast dough. The yeast ferments sugars, which form carbon dioxide, thereby making the dough rise and expand.

rye bread made from rye flour or a mix of rye and wheat flour. Rye bread is often flavored with caraway seeds.

scone a biscuitlike cake, sometimes flavored with currants and usually spread with butter.

sourdough a slightly sour-tasting bread made from dough that is allowed to sit in a warm place for a time while its yeast ferments and produces a sour flavor.

spelt an ancient wheat variety occasionally utilized by specialty bakeries.

tortilla a flat round of unleavened corn flour bread, baked on a griddle.

unbleached flour flour that has no chemical additives and lightens naturally as it is allowed to age.

unleavened referring to bread with no yeast or other leavener to make it rise.

whole wheat bread made from wheat that has not been overprocessed and which has its bran or husks intact.

yeast the single cell fungi used to ferment sugars and create carbon dioxide, which makes bread rise.

yeast bread any bread whose leavening agent is yeast as opposed to baking soda or baking powder.

COCKTAILS

Alexander a drink made of gin, cream, crème de cacao, and a nutmeg garnish.

Barbary Coast a drink made of gin, rum, scotch, white crème de cacao, and light cream.

bird of paradise a drink made of tequila, white crème de cacao, amaretto, and cream.

black Russian a drink made of vodka and Kahlua.

bloody Mary a drink made of vodka, Worcestershire sauce, tomato juice, and seasonings.

bourbon slush a drink made of hot tea, lemonade concentrate, orange juice concentrate, bourbon, sugar, and water.

bull shot a drink made of vodka, beef bouillon, a dash of Tabasco sauce, a dash of Worcestershire sauce, and salt and pepper.

cocotini a drink made of coconut-flavored rum and triple sec, with the edge of the glass rimmed with shredded coconut.

cosmopolitan a drink made of vodka, triple sec, cranberry juice, and lime juice.

daiquiri a drink made of rum, lime juice, and powdered sugar.

gimlet a drink made of gin and sweetened lime juice.

gin rickey a drink made of gin, club soda, lime, and ice.

gin and tonic a drink made of gin and tonic water, garnished with a peel of lime.

Harvey wallbanger a drink made of vodka, orange juice, and Galliano.

highball a drink made of whiskey and a carbonated beverage or water.

hot toddy a drink made of bourbon, boiling water, sugar, cloves, and cinnamon.

hurricane a drink made of dark rum, light rum, lime juice, and passion fruit syrup.

Irish coffee a drink made of Irish whiskey, brown sugar, and black coffee topped with whipping cream.

kamikaze a drink made of vodka, triple sec, curaçao, and lime juice.

Long Island iced tea a drink made of gin, rum, tequila, and vodka on ice.

Manhattan a drink made of rye or Irish whiskey, vermouth, angostura bitters, and a twist of lemon.

margarita a drink made of tequila, sweet and sour mix, and orange-flavored liqueur, with the lip of the glass rimmed with salt.

martini a drink made of gin, dry vermouth, and an olive.

mint julep a drink made of bourbon, sugar, water, mint leaves, and rum.

mojito a drink made of mint syrup, light rum, lime juice, and club soda, and garnished with a lime wheel.

old fashioned a drink made of bourbon, bitters, soda, and sugar.

piña colada a drink made of rum, pineapple juice, and coconut cream.

pink lady a drink made of gin, grenadine, and cream.

Rob Roy a drink made of scotch, vermouth, and a cherry garnish.

rusty nail a drink made of scotch and Drambuie.

sangria a drink made of red wine, fruit juice, and brandy.

screwdriver a drink made of vodka and orange juice.

sea breeze a drink made of vodka, cranberry juice, and grapefruit juice garnished with a wedge of lime.

sex on the beach a drink made of peach schnapps, vodka, pineapple juice, and cranberry juice.

shark bite a drink made of rum, orange juice, sour mix, and grenadine.

Singapore sling a drink made of gin, cherry brandy, lemon, club soda, and powdered sugar.

sloe gin fizz a drink made of sloe gin, sweet and sour, soda, and a cherry garnish.

slow comfortable screw a drink made of sloe gin, Southern Comfort, and orange juice.

sombrero a drink made of Kahlua and cream.

tequila sunrise a drink made of tequila, orange juice, cranberry juice, and ice.

tidal wave a drink made of rum, vodka, brandy, bourbon, and lime.

vodka collins a drink made of vodka, lemon juice, club soda, and sugar, and garnished with a cherry.

whiskey sour a drink made of whiskey, sweet and sour, and a cherry.

white cosmo a drink made of Cointreau, vodka, white cranberry and lime juices, and a twist of orange.

COFFEE

acerbic professional taster's term for an acrid and sour flavor.

acidy professional taster's term for a sharp but pleasant flavor.

affogatto a dessert of vanilla ice cream drenched in espresso.

alpine cafe a dessert coffee made of instant coffee, brown sugar, and vanilla extract.

Americano an espresso with hot water added to make a full cup of coffee.

Arabian coffee a specialty coffee made of coffee, sugar, cinnamon, cardamon, and vanilla.

arabica the most popular variety of coffee bean, which is native to Africa but is also grown in South America. Also known as Arabian coffee.

barista an espresso bartender.

battery acid slang for a bad cup of coffee.

blackstrap slang for a bad cup of coffee.

blond and bitter slang for coffee with cream and no sugar.

blond and sweet slang for coffee with cream and sugar.

body professional taster's term for the sense of heaviness, richness, and thickness a coffee stimulates at the back of the tongue.

bon bon a cappuccino with chocolate mint liqueur topped with whipped cream, shavings of white chocolate, and a cherry.

bouquet the combined aromas in coffee.

brackish professional taster's term for salty or alkaline flavors.

bready professional taster's term for coffee that has been inadequately roasted.

breve an espresso with half-and-half or partially skimmed milk.

brew to make coffee.

briny professional taster's term for coffee that has been roasted too long.

buttery professional taster's term for coffee rich in natural oils, exuded from beans with a high fat content.

café amaretto a latte with almond syrup.

café au lait a coffee with boiled milk.

café con leche a dark roast coffee with sugar and heated milk.

café crème a large cup of espresso with an ounce of heavy cream.

café mocha a latte with chocolate.

caffe con panna a demitasse of espresso topped with whipped cream.

caffe corretto an espresso with cognac or other liqueur.

caffe freddo a chilled espresso.

caffeine a strong stimulant found in coffee.

caffe latte see LATTE.

cappuccino an espresso capped with foamed milk and sometimes sprinkled with cinnamon or powdered chocolate.

caramel a latte with caramel flavoring.

carbony professional taster's term for a burned taste, typical for a very dark roast.

cinnamon roast professional taster's term for a light roast.

crema the brown foam on the surface of a cup of espresso.

dark roast a bittersweet roast, sometimes with a hint of caramel flavor. French and espresso are dark roasts. Italian and Spanish are even darker and have a smokey, somewhat burned taste.

demitasse a small or half-size cup for serving straight espresso.

doppio a double shot of espresso.

decaf decaffeinated coffee.

decaffeinated having the caffeine removed.

earthiness professional taster's term for a flavor reminiscent of dirt.

espresso arabica bean coffee made with hot water or steam that is pressed through fine, compressed coffee and served in a small cup.

espresso con panna an espresso topped with whipped cream.

espresso machiato espresso with steamed milk or foam on top.

frappuccino a chilled or iced cappuccino.

French roast a very dark roast with a bittersweet, somewhat smoky flavor.

granita a latte with frozen milk.

Guatemalan an aromatic variety of coffee with a rich, nutty flavor.

hazelnut a variety of coffee flavored with hazelnut.

Irish cream a rich and creamy-flavored blend.

Italian a dark, bittersweet roast with a slightly smoky flavor.

java slang term for any coffee.

Joe slang term for coffee.

Kona a rich gourmet coffee grown on volcanic rock on the mountain slopes of Hualalai and Mauna Loa on the west coast of the island of Hawaii.

latte an espresso with steamed milk. Also known as caffe latte.

light roast a roast characterized by a sharp and acidic taste.

machine oil slang for a bad cup of coffee.

Mexican a light-bodied coffee grown in Mexico.

mochaccino cappuccino with chocolate.

paint remover slang for a bad cup of coffee.

paint thinner slang for a bad cup of coffee.

robusta a common bean but less flavorful than Arabica.

sour professional taster's term for unpleasantly sharp.

soy latte a latte made with soy milk.

Sumatran a heavy-bodied coffee grown in Sumatra.

supremo the highest grade of coffee.

sweet professional taster's term for coffee lacking bitterness or harshness.

Turkish coffee a coffee served with the fine grounds.

unleaded slang for coffee with no caffeine.

vanilla nut a variety blended with vanilla beans to provide a vanilla flavor.

Viennese roast a mix of medium-roasted beans with a smaller amount of dark French-roast beans.

Vienna a rich-bodied, light roast.

COOKING TERMS

(*Also see* FRENCH COOKING TERMS)

acidulated water water with a small amount of lemon juice or vinegar, used to preserve the color of sliced fruits.

al dente Italian term meaning, "to the bite," which refers to the doneness of pasta, which should be not too soft and not too hard.

alfresco eaten outside.

bain marie see WATER BATH.

baron a thin strip of a vegetable.

baste to pour, squirt, brush, or spoon melted butter or cooking juices on a food to prevent it, especially a roast, from drying out.

baton a slender, sticklike piece cut from a vegetable, roughly ¼ × ¼ × 2 inches long.

beat to stir or strike briskly with a spoon or whisk, or to blend with an electric mixer until a substance becomes fluffy.

binder an ingredient added to other ingredients to help them blend more readily.

blacken to fry and char, especially fish, in hot pepper and spices.

blanch to boil or scald a vegetable briefly, to reduce cooking time.

blend to mix thoroughly.

braise to sear meat in fat and then simmer in stock in a covered pan.

bread to cover with bread crumbs.

broil to cook with radiant heat over a food.

brown to fry until brown.

butterfly to cut a piece of meat or poultry almost all the way through down the middle and spread open.

caramelize to cook sugar until it liquefies and turns golden brown. Can refer to the cooking of natural sugars found in fruits and vegetables as well.

carbonado to score and broil meat.

charbroil to broil or grill to the point of burning or charring.

clotted cream a cream that is made thicker and richer by cooking.

coddle to cook in water very gently and slowly without boiling.

creole made with sauteed onions, green peppers, tomatoes, and seasonings.

deep-fry to submerge a food completely in fat or oil and fry it.

deglaze to add wine or stock to a pan and scrape off bits of meat or other browned matter from a cooking, and use everything in a sauce.

dehydrate to remove water or to dry to preserve.

desiccate to dry or dehydrate.

devil to add hot seasonings, such as cayenne or mustard, to a food.

dice to cut into tiny cubes.

draw to remove the internal organs, as in a game animal.

drawn butter butter that is melted, clarified, and seasoned.

dredge to coat with flour, bread crumbs, or cornmeal.

dry roast to roast without oils.

duchess pureed potato enriched with cream and molded into ornamental shapes, which are baked and then arranged around a roast or fish platter.

emulsify to bind two ingredients together by stirring, whisking, shaking, or adding a third ingredient that acts as a blending agent.

escargot butter butter flavored with lemon, parsley, and garlic.

fillet to cut out the bones of meat or fish.

five-spice powder a Chinese spice mix consisting of cinnamon, pepper, star anise, clove, and fennel.

Florentine in the style of Florence, Italy, served with spinach and a cheese sauce.

fold to use gentle cutting strokes to combine a mixture.

forcemeat any meat or fish finely chopped and seasoned and used for a stuffing.

fricassee to cut up and brown.

fritter any meat, fish, vegetable, or fruit dipped in batter and either deep fried or sautéd.

garnish to decorate a dish, as with parsley.

glaze to coat with sugar syrup, egg, etc.

gratin topped with bread crumbs and/or cheese and browned in the oven.

grecque in the Greek style, with tomatoes, peppers, and fennel.

gremolata a flavoring mixture consisting of parsley, garlic, and lemon peel, used in Hungarian goulash and other dishes.

hard-boil to cook an egg until the yolk becomes solidified.

infuse to impart flavoring from one food item into another, as a tea bag infuses flavor into water.

larding placing vegetables or strips of fat into a piece of cooking meat to keep it from drying out.

macerate to bathe or steep fruits in wine or liquor.

marinate to bathe or steep a food in a seasoned sauce or other liquid for an extended time; to tenderize and to impart flavor.

mince to chop very finely.

nap to coat lightly with sauce.

nuke slang, to cook in a microwave.

panbroil to cook in a frying pan with little or no grease.

parboil to boil briefly without fully cooking; to soften hard vegetables, such as potatoes or carrots, for cooking with softer vegetables requiring lesser cooking times.

pare to slice off the outermost layer or skin, especially of a fruit.

pickle to preserve in spiced brine or vinegar.

poach to cook, especially eggs, in water at or near the boiling point.

reduce to concentrate and thicken a liquid by boiling away water.

refresh to place hot food into cold water to halt the cooking process.

render to melt down or remove fat.

roast to cook in an oven in an uncovered pan.

salt to preserve by coating with salt.

scald to briefly submerge fruits or vegetables into boiling water to loosen their skins for easy peeling.

scallop to bake with a sauce and a topping of bread crumbs. Also, to cut in the shape of a scallop.

scallopini a thin slice of meat sautéed in wine. Also spelled scallopine.

sear to brown meat rapidly with high temperature, either in a frying pan, over a grill, or under a broiler.

seed to remove seeds from a fruit or vegetable.

season to add spices or flavorings to a food. Also, to remove warps from a cast-iron pan by heating it in an oven for an extended time. Oiling the cooking surface before the pan is placed in the oven also helps to create somewhat of a natural nonstick surface.

shred to cut into threads and strips.

shirr to bake eggs in a buttered dish, often with crumbs and cheese.

sieve to strain food or liquid through a strainer or sieve.

sift to introduce air and to strain out large clumps by shaking dry ingredients through a mesh device or sifter.

simmer to cook over low heat, just below the boiling point.

skin to remove the skin of poultry or fish.

smoke to hang or lay foods over a smoky fire for an extended period to either preserve a food or impart a smoky flavor to it. Can also be achieved with a home smoker.

soft-boil to boil an egg for a brief time so the yolk remains soft.

steam to cook in a steamer basket just above boiling water in a covered pan.

sweat to cook vegetables in fat over very low heat.

tenderize to soften and make meat easier to chew by either marinating it or by pounding it for an extended time with a mallet.

truss to tie or bind up for cooking, as a turkey's legs.

vandyke small zig zags cut into fruit or vegetable halves, which are used as a garnish.

water bath a very gentle method of cooking delicate foods and preventing them from breaking or curdling. The food is placed in a container, which is then placed in water that is gently heated. Also known as a bain marie.

whip to beat until fluffy and airy.

whisk to beat or stir with a whisk.

zest to shave off the outermost layer of skin on an orange or lemon, used for flavoring.

French Cooking Terms

accolade an arrangement of two chickens, ducks, or fish back to back on a serving platter.

affriole fresh from the garden.

aillade garlic sauce.

à la bayonnaise in the style of Bayonne—garnished with braised onions and gherkins.

à la béarnaise in the style of Béarn—a thick sauce made from eggs, butter, and mustard.

à la Beauharnais in the style of Beauharnais—garnished with artichokes in tarragon sauce.

à la bigarade in Seville-orange style—served with sour-orange sauce.

à la boulangère in the style of the baker's wife—served with fried onions and potatoes.

à la broche served on a skewer.

à la calédonienne baked in butter, parsley, and lemon juice.

à la carte ordering items separately instead of in combination.

à la châtelaine in the style of the lady of the castle—garnished with celery, artichoke hearts, baked tomatoes, and sautéed potatoes.

à la Clermont in the style of Clermont—garnished with fried onions and stuffed potatoes.

à la cordon bleu in blue ribbon style—stuffed with ham and cheddar cheese and topped with creamy mushrooms.

à la crapaudine in toad style—chicken broiled and trussed to resemble a toad.

à la créole in creole style—served with onions, peppers, and tomatoes.

à la Croissy in the style of Marquis de Croissy—with carrots and turnips.

à la diable in devil style—deviled or served spicy.

à la duchesse in duchess style—a fish served with oyster sauce; a meat served with braised lettuce and duchesse potatoes; or a soup with asparagus tips and truffles.

à la fermière in the style of the farmer's wife—a roast served with turnips, carrots, celery, and onions.

à la flamande in Flemish style—with braised cabbage, carrots, potatoes, and pork.

à la florentine in the style of Florence—garnished with spinach.

à la forestière in the style of the forester's wife—with mushrooms and potato balls browned in butter.

à la française in French style—with mixed vegetables and hollandaise sauce.

à l'africaine in African style—curried and spiced.

à la genèvoise in Geneva style—with red wine sauce.

à la Godard in the style of Godard—garnished with truffles and mushrooms.

à la grecque in Greek style—with olives, oil, and rice.

à la Hong Kong Hong Kong style—with noodles and rice.

à la hongroise Hungarian style—with paprika and sour cream.

à la julienne in Juliana style—with thin strips of vegetables.

à la king mushrooms in a creamy white sauce with red pimentos.

à l'allemande in German style—garnished with potatoes and sauerkraut.

à la Luzon in Luzon style—with pork and rice.

à la macédoine in Macedonian style—with diced fruits and vegetables.

à la Marengo in Marengo style—served with a sauce comprised of mushrooms, tomatoes, olives, olive oil, and wine.

à la meunière in the style of the miller's wife—a fish sautéed in butter, dipped in flour, and served with a butter and lemon sauce.

à la milanaise in Milan style—dipped in egg, bread crumbs, and parmesan cheese.

à la mode de Caen in the style of Caen—with leeks, vegetables, and wine, prepared with tripe.

à la moscovite in Moscow style—garnished with caviar.

à la napolitaine in Neapolitan style—a meat served with eggplant and tomatoes or spaghetti served with tomato sauce and cheese.

à l'andalouse in Andalusian style—a soup served with eggplant, red peppers, and rice.

à la neige in snowy style—served with egg whites or rice.

à la normande in the style of Normandy—in a sauce of butter and cream, with mushrooms or apples.

à la parisienne in Parisian style—garnished with small, sautéed potatoes and braised celery.

à la périgourdine in the style of Périgord—with truffles or truffle-based sauce.

à la portugaise in Portuguese style—with olive oil, garlic, onions, and tomatoes.

à la provençale in Provençale style—with mushrooms, onions, tomatoes, olive oil, and garlic.

à la reine in the queen's style—chicken with truffles and mushrooms in a puff pastry "crown."

à l'arménienne in Armenian style—with rice pilaf.

à la Rossini in the style of Rossini—with a sauce of madeira wine, mushrooms, goose liver paste, and truffles.

à la Soubise with onion puree.

à la tartare minced beef served raw with capers and a raw egg.

à l'indienne in East Indian style—with curried sauce or curried rice.

à l'italienne in Italian style—with artichoke bottoms and macaroni.

à point medium.

assaisonnement seasoning.

au beurre noir with browned butter sauce.

au blanc in white style—with a white sauce.

au bleu in blue style—cooked fish in vinegar.

au brun cooked in brown sauce.

au gras in the fat. Cooked in the broth or gravy.

au gratin with a crust of bread crumbs or grated cheese and browned slightly.

au maigre lean style, without fat.

au naturel food served uncooked, unseasoned, in its natural state.

au vin blanc made in white wine.

aux fines herbes served with finely chopped chives, onions, parsley, shallots, and sorrel.

batterie de cuisine all the necessary kitchen utensils and equipment.

beurre butter.

beurre blanc a butter sauce flavored with wine or vinegar and seasonings, used on fish, chicken, or vegetables.

beurre fondu melted butter.

beurre noir browned butter sauce seasoned with parsley and wine vinegar.

bien cuit well done.

blanc d'oeuf egg white.

boeuf épicé spiced beef.

bon appétit a salutation meaning, eat well

bouquet garni herbs tied in a cheesecloth bag and cooked with sauces, soups, stews, and other dishes to flavor them. The most common combination is thyme, parsley, and bay leaf.

buisson a mound of food.

canard à la presse pressed duck.

cannelé fluted; pastry crust or decoratively cut vegetables.

carottes à la flamande Flemish-style carrots—cooked in sugar and cream.

carte de vins wine list.

carte du jour menu of the day.

champignons au gratin baked mushrooms with a crust.

chapon a breadcrust cooked in soup.

château potatoes parboiled and braised potatoes.

chausson puff pastry.

chef de cuisine the head chef.

civet rabbit stew made with blood and red wine.

concassé a coarse chopping of a vegetable, especially tomato.

consommé clear soup; broth, bouillon.

coq au vin rouge chicken cooked in red wine.

coquille a pastry shell resembling the shell of a scallop.

Cordon Bleu Blue Ribbon, a Paris cooking school.

crème chantilly vanilla-flavored whipped cream.

crème vichyssoise leek and potato cream soup served cold.

crêpe a thin pancake.

croustade a crust dish made of bread or a pastry shell fried in deep fat.

croûte au pot crust for the pot; clear soup with floating toast pieces.

du jour of the day; today's.

duxelles sautéed mushroom hash.

entrée the main dish in the United States; appetizer in France.

épigramme a meal having two different kinds of fish or meat. It may also include the same fish or meat cooked in two different ways.

filet mignon boned steak.

flambé flaming; any food served aflame—a brandy or rum coating set on fire.

flan custard dessert.

florentine served on a bed of spinach.

fond de cuisine stocks, broths.

fromage cheese.

galette a form of thin pancake.

garbure bacon and cabbage soup.

garçon boy; waiter.

gratiné to top with cheese and/or bread crumbs and brown in the oven.

haute cuisine artful, highly skilled, or professional food preparation.

hors d'oeuvre appetizer.

julienne to cut into long, thin strips.

limande lemon sole.

macédoine a medley of fruits or vegetables in a dessert, sauce, or salad.

macédoine de fruits fruit salad.

maître d'hôtel flavored with lemon and parsley, commonly used on fish.

mirepoix a mixture of chopped onions, carrots, and celery sautéed in butter, used to flavor soups, stews, and sauces.

nappé napkined; lightly coated with icing or sauce.

nouvelle cuisine a cooking style emphasizing simpler, lighter dishes made with very fresh ingredients and presented in an artistic fashion.

oeuf egg.

oeufs à la coque soft-boiled eggs in shell.

oeufs farcis deviled eggs.

omelette aux fines herbes omelette with herbs.

omelette aux pointes d'aspèrges omelette with asparagus tips.

pain bread.

paner to coat with bread crumbs.

pâté liver or meat paste.

pâte d'amandes almond paste.

pâte d'anchois anchovy paste.

pâté de foie gras goose liver paste.

paysanne peasant style; meat or poultry braised and served with bacon and buttery vegetables.

persillade chopped parsley garnish.

petit pain a roll.

pièce de résistance set piece; the main dish or main course.

pointes d'asperges asparagus tips.

poivrade peppery sauce.

pomme de terre potato.

potage crème d'orge cream of barley soup.

potage purée à la reine puree soup in the queen's style; cream of chicken soup.

potage purée de marrons chestnut soup.

potage Rossini cream of onion soup with grated cheese.

potage velours velvet soup; a very smooth carrot and tapioca soup.

potpourri rotten pot; hodgepodge; a mixture of things.

poulette a young hen.

printanière springlike; refers to mixed vegetables cut into decorative shapes.

puree to mash or grind-up food until it is smooth.

ragoût de mouton mutton stew.

ratatouille a stew composed of eggplant, squash, tomato, onions, and olive oil.

ravigote revive; strongly seasoned white sauce.

remoulade remolded; mayonnaise seasoned with anchovy paste, capers, gherkins, herbs, and mustard.

ribaude baked appled dumpling.

ris de veau sweetbread of a calf.

rissolé to brown potatoes in deep fat.

riz au lait rice pudding.

roulade rolled up.

roux reddish brown, browned butter and flour mixture, used to thicken sauces, soups, and stews.

saignant underdone; bloody.

sauce suprême a rich white sauce made from chicken stock and cream.

sauté to cook or brown quickly in preheated fat or oil in a pan.

serviette napkin.

smitane sour cream.

sommelier wine steward.

soufflé inflated; a light and fluffy baked dish made as a dessert or as a main dish.

soupçon suspicion; a pinch or hint of an ingredient.

soupe à l'oignon onion soup.

talmouse cheesecake.

tourte a round, meat-filled pie.

vinaigrette salad dressing of olive oil, vinegar, and seasonings.

zéphir anything light and frothy.

DESSERTS

Cakes

angel food cake a light, white cake with a spongy texture, made with egg whites.

baba a small cake flavored with candied fruits and a rum glaze.

baked Alaska a sponge cake topped with ice cream, which is itself topped with meringue, that is quickly browned in the oven.

batter the mix of flour, eggs, and milk used to make cakes.

blintz a pancake filled with cottage cheese and fruit.

Boston cream pie a two-layer cake with frosting and a cream filling.

Bundt cake any cake baked in a Bundt pan.

Bundt pan a tube cake pan with fluted sides.

carrot cake a cake made with carrots, spices, eggs, sugar, and flour.

cheesecake a rich cake usually made from cream cheese, eggs, and sugar.

coffee cake a sweetened bread flavored with spices, nuts, or fruit and sometimes topped with icing or a glaze.

cupcake a small muffin-shaped cake baked in a cuplike mold and often topped with icing.

dacquoise a cake made from nut meringues and layered with whipped cream or a chocolate filling.

devil's food cake a rich cake made with chocolate or cocoa.

election cake created in the 18th century to celebrate election day, a yeast cake flavored with nuts, candied fruit, and raisins soaked in sherry.

fruitcake traditionally made at Christmas, a cake made from candied fruits, nuts, citron, and spices.

gateau a rich, layered cake with cream filling.

genoise a rich sponge cake made from eggs and butter and often filled with cream.

gingerbread cake a cake flavored with ginger and molasses.

jelly roll a layer of sponge cake that is spread with jelly and rolled into a spiral.

kuchen a German coffee cake sometimes containing nuts and raisins.

kugelhopf a yeast cake flavored with currants, raisins, or almonds, typically eaten at breakfast.

ladyfingers small, fingerlike sponge cakes.

layer cake any cake having two or more sections, one atop the other, and separated by icing or jelly filling.

madeleine a small cake baked in a shell-shaped mold.

marble cake a cake made with two different colors of batter to give the illusion of marbling.

panforte a rich cake flavored with candied fruits and nuts.

pannetone an Italian cake made of a dough loaded with candied fruit, raisins, and nuts.

petit four a small sponge cake or slice of sponge cake, usually with icing.

pound cake a cake made of about one pound of each of the main ingredients of sugar, flour, butter, and eggs.

Sally Lunn a flat, sweetened tea cake shaped like a wheel.

savarin a ring-molded cake soaked in a rum syrup.

savarin pan a ring mold used to make savarins.

strawberry shortcake a biscuit smothered with whipped cream and strawberries.

simnel cake a fruitcake.

spice cake any cake flavored with spices.

sponge cake a light cake with a spongy texture, made from flour, eggs, and sugar, and no shortening.

stollen a sweetened German bread with fruit and nuts.

tiramisu an Italian sponge cake layered with cheese and chocolate sauce and drenched in an espresso syrup.

torte originating in Austria, a rich layered cake with frosting and ground nuts.

upside-down cake a cake that is baked with fruit on the bottom but is overturned when served so the fruit serves as a topping.

wedding cake a rich, multitiered cake, topped with frosting and figurines of the bride and groom.

Cookies

almond cardamom a cookie made from flour, butter, sugar, ground cardamom, cream cheese, almond paste, eggs, and vanilla.

animal cracker a small, crisp cookie cut into the shape of an animal.

biscotti hard, dry Italian cookies flavored with almonds, hazelnuts, chocolate, or anise seed.

chocolate chip a cookie made from shortening, sugar, eggs, flour, chocolate chips, and vanilla.

date cookie a cookie made from dates, pecans, butter, sugar, eggs, and flour.

drop cookie any cookie formed by dropping dough from a spoon onto a pan, rather than rolling, shaping, or cutting them.

fortune cookie a thin, hollow cookie shell stuffed with a small slip of paper with one's "fortune" or a bit of wisdom written on it, served in Chinese restaurants.

ginger snap a crispy cookie flavored with ginger and molasses.

gingerbread cookie a cookie flavored with ginger and molasses and often cut into the shape of a man.

hermit a spicy cookie made from butter, sugar, flour, eggs, allspice, cinnamon, cloves, molasses, raisins, and walnuts.

honey drop a cookie made from butter, sugar, eggs, orange zest, honey, and mace.

jumble a thin, ring-shaped cookie topped with sugar.

macaroon a chewy cookie made from egg whites, coconut, sugar, and sometimes almonds.

molasses cookie a chewy cookie flavored with molasses.

no-bake cookie a cookie that requires no baking. An example is a cookie made from oatmeal, cocoa, and sugar.

oatmeal cookie a cookie made from rolled oats, shortening, sugar, eggs, milk, flour, and sometimes raisins, walnuts, or chocolate chips.

palmier a cookie in the shape of a palm leaf, made from sliced puff pastry and folded.

peanut butter cookie a cookie made from peanut butter, shortening, brown sugar, eggs, milk, vanilla, and flour.

pignoli cookie a flourless cookie made from almond paste, sugar, confectioner's sugar, egg whites, and pine nuts.

ratafia a macaroon flavored with a sweet liqueur made from wine, brandy, and almonds.

rugulach a cookie made from cream cheese dough stuffed with chocolate or jam, nuts, raisins, etc. Also spelled rugelach.

shortbread a buttery but crumbly Scottish cookie that is sometimes flavored with almonds, cinnamon, lemon, ginger, and cumin.

snickerdoodle a crispy cinnamon cookie, sometimes textured with oatmeal.

spice cookie a cookie made from butter, sugar, eggs, cinnamon, nutmeg, ground cloves, flour, milk, and currants.

sugar cookie a cookie made from confectioners' sugar, brown sugar, butter, vegetable oil, eggs, vanilla, flour, and sprinkled with granulated sugar.

Toll House cookie a kind of chocolate-chip cookie, reportedly originating at the Toll House Restaurant in Whitman, Massachusetts, in 1930.

tuiles paper-thin cookies flavored with almonds, vanilla, and lemon.

Other Desserts

apple pan dowdy an apple-pie-like dessert having a crust on the top but not on the bottom.

belle Hélène a dessert of pears and ice cream covered in chocolate sauce.

charlotte a baked dessert of bread slices placed in a mold and covered with fruit.

chocolate mousse a light and fluffy but rich dessert made of eggs, whipped cream, sugar, and semisweet chocolate.

brown Betty baked apple pudding with bread crumbs.

clafoutis batter-topped fruit, especially cherries, baked until puffy.

crème brûlée egg custard topped with caramel.

crêpe a thin pancake folded and loaded with a variety of sweet fillings.

crêpes suzette a crêpe rolled in an orange sauce and served with flaming brandy.

croquembouche cream puffs dipped in caramel and stacked to form a pyramid.

flan an open tart filled with pastry cream and topped with fruit. Also, a baked egg custard covered with caramel.

gelato an Italian sherbet made from whole milk, eggs, and sugar.

melba a dessert comprised of pears or peaches with vanilla ice cream and raspberry sauce.

mincemeat pie a sweet and spicy pie made of a crust covered in a filling of raisins, chopped apples, wine, and beef fat.

shoofly pie an open pie flavored with molasses and brown sugar.

truffle a candy made of chocolate and butter, shaped in a ball.

Pastries

baklava a Greek dessert made of layers of flaky pastry filled with ground nuts, sugar, cinnamon, and butter and glazed with a honey syrup.

Banbury tart a small British pastry flavored with raisins or currants.

barquette an oval pastry shell that may hold a variety of fillings.

Bavarian cream a blend of pastry cream, whipped cream, gelatin, and a variety of fruit flavorings.

beignet a square doughnut covered with powdered sugar or a glaze of flavored syrup.

bumper a large turnover.

cannoli a deep-fried Italian tube-shaped pastry filled with ricotta cheese flavored with sugar, cinnamon, vanilla, chocolate chips, or candied fruit.

chantilly a sweetened whipped cream flavored with vanilla.

cornet a cone-shaped pastry shell, which may be filled with whipped cream.

cream puff a flaky pastry shell filled with whipped cream.

cruller a doughnut in the shape of a twist rather than a ring.

Danish a flaky pastry topped with icing and packed with a fruit filling.

doughnut a deep-fried ring of sweetened dough, which may be plain or glazed with various icings or flavorings.

éclair a pastry stuffed with custard or whipped cream and topped with frosting.

frangipane a pastry cream made from eggs, butter, flour, and either finely ground almonds or macaroons.

fritter fried batter containing fruit.

jelly doughnut a pillow-shaped doughnut stuffed with jelly.

linzertorte an Austrian pastry with a dough flavored with ground nuts and cinnamon, and a filling of raspberry jam, cranberries, or apricots, and sometimes a layer of almond paste.

marzipan an almond paste used in cakes and candies and sometimes itself molded into figures or animals and eaten as a dessert.

meringue a cake or pie filling or topping made from beaten egg whites sweetened with sugar and frequently browned in the oven. Also a hardened shell made from this and filled with ice cream or fruit.

mille-feuille small, rectangular puff pastry filled with pastry cream.

napoleon a puff pastry filled with custard.

pastry cream a custard mixed with flour.

patissier a baker who specializes in cakes and pastries.

phyllo very thin sheets of dough, used in a variety of pastries and desserts.

profiterole a small cream puff.

schnecken dough rolled around a mix of cinnamon and nuts or other ingredients to create a spiral shape, and baked.

scone a biscuitlike pastry that is sometimes sweetened with currants.

strudel a baked pastry filled with cheese, cherries, and apple slices.

sweet roll a roll made of sweetened dough and flavored with seasonings, raisins, and nuts.

tart a fruit-, jam-, or jelly-filled pastry.

tartlet a small tart.

timbale a small pastry shell that can be stuffed with various minced or creamy fillings.

turnover flattened dough covered in filling and then folded into a triangular shape and baked.

DINNER DISHES

beef bourguignonne beef, mushrooms, onions, and seasonings stewed in wine.

beef stroganoff sautéed beef, onions, and mushrooms in a sour cream sauce.

beef Wellington a pastry casing stuffed with rare roast tenderloin and paté de foie gras.

boiled dinner a dish comprised of boiled potatoes, cabbage, turnip, carrots, onions, and often, ham.

Boston baked beans navy beans flavored with molasses and salt pork.

bubble and squeak a British dish consisting of fried potato, cabbage, and often, meat.

burrito a tortilla stuffed with meat, beans, or cheese.

cabbage rolls a mixture of rice and ground meat rolled in cooked cabbage leaves.

calzone a pizzalike turnover filled with meat, cheese, and sauce.

cannelloni tubular pasta in sauce.

cassoulet a bean and meat casserole.

cheese soufflé a puffy and creamy dish made from egg yolks, beaten egg whites, cheese, and a white sauce.

chicken à la king diced chicken in a creamy sauce with mushrooms, green peppers, and pimentos, served on toast or rice.

chicken cacciatore an herbed chicken with tomatoes and white wine.

chicken cordon bleu a breaded chicken stuffed with ham and cheese.

chicken divan a chicken breast with broccoli or asparagus in a cheese sauce.

chicken Kiev a breaded and deep-fried chicken breast stuffed with butter and chives and served with brown rice or kasha.

chicken Marengo a casserole or stew consisting of chicken, onions, mushrooms, tomatoes, and wine, served over toast and garnished with shrimp, crayfish, or fried eggs.

chicken Marsala chicken flavored with Marsala wine.

chicken tetrazzini a chicken casserole in a cream sauce with noodles, cheese, and mushrooms.

chili dog a hot dog smothered in chili.

chimichanga a meat-filled tortilla sometimes served with salsa, sour cream, or cheese.

chop suey stir-fried meat or fish and usually, bamboo shoots, bean sprouts, celery, water chestnuts, mushrooms, and onions flavored with soy sauce and ginger and served with rice.

chow mein a Chinese-American dish of meat, celery, bean sprouts, and fried noodles.

clams casino broiled clams on the half shell topped with a dressing.

coq au vin chicken, red wine, mushrooms, and onions.

corn dog a carnival staple of an impaled hot dog coated in cornmeal batter and fried.

cornish pasty a semicircular pie or dough casing containing bits of steak, potato, onions, and turnip, originally carried to work by English coalminers.

croquette a ball of minced meats or vegetables, breaded and deep-fried.

deviled egg a hard-boiled egg cut in half and the yolk removed, mashed, and blended with mayonnaise and seasonings, then returned to the egg white.

duck à l'orange roast duck served with an orange sauce.

egg foo young a Chinese-American dish consisting of eggs, onions, bean sprouts, and shrimp or pork.

eggroll a tubular dough stuffed with minced shrimp or chicken and vegetables and deep-fried.

eggs Benedict sliced English muffins topped with poached eggs on ham and covered with hollandaise sauce.

empanada a South American pastry stuffed with beef, cheese, or ham, and spinach and onions or other vegetables, and deep fried. There is also a dessert version with fruit filling.

enchilada a meat- or cheese-filled tortilla covered with a sauce.

escargot snails.

fajita grilled beef or chicken strips rolled into a soft tortilla with onions, green peppers, melted cheese.

fettucini flat pasta noodles, used in a variety of dishes.

fish and chips British favorite of fried fish and French fries.

fondue melted Swiss or Gruyère cheese with eggs and wine and seasonings, served with bread and vegetables. A variation is fondue bourguignonne in which diners cook strips of meat in a pot of hot oil and dip them in sauce.

fricassee cut up and stewed (or fried) chicken or meat with carrots, onions, dumplings, or noodles cooked in its own gravy.

fried rice boiled rich scrambled with eggs, scallions, pork, or shrimp.

frijoles Mexican-style beans.

frittata an Italian omelet with diced meat and vegetables and sometimes cheese.

gefilte fish seasoned balls of minced fish cooked in stock or tomato sauce.

haggis a Scottish dish comprised of the minced heart, liver, and lungs of a calf or sheep, along with beef fat, oatmeal, onions, and seasonings, boiled in the stomach of the animal.

hash fried or browned meat and potatoes.

jambalaya a Creole dish consisting of rice, tomatoes, peppers, onions, and any variety of meats, including shrimp, crab, ham, chicken, duck, game bird, oysters, or sausage.

kabob skewered meat and vegetables, especially lamb, tomatoes, green peppers, and onions, broiled or grilled. Also spelled kebab.

kedgeree an Indian and British dish consisting of smoked fish, eggs, rice, bechamel sauce, and curry.

kishke a Jewish dish made from a cow or chicken intestine stuffed with matzo meal, onions, and seasonings.

knish a Polish dish comprised of a pillow of dough stuffed with potato, meat, or cheese, either baked or fried.

lasagna an Italian dish comprised of wide strips of pasta in tomato sauce and cheese.

lobster Newburg lobster served in a sauce consisting of butter, cream, egg yolks, sherry, and seasonings over toast or rice.

lobster Thermidor lobster meat mixed with a cream and cheese sauce and mushrooms, and repacked in a half of a lobster shell and browned.

London broil a flank cut of beef, broiled.

manicotti tubes of pasta stuffed with meat or cheese and served with tomato sauce. Also, the pasta itself.

meatloaf a baked loaf of ground beef, pork, or other meat, mixed with onions, eggs, bread crumbs, and various other ingredients.

moussaka a casserole made from eggplant, ground lamb, and eggs and flavored with onions, tomatoes, and a white sauce.

ossobuco veal flavored with wine, olive oil, tomatoes, and seasonings and served with rice.

paella a Spanish dish with many variations, but generally made of chicken, shellfish, vegetables, and rice and flavored with saffron.

Peking duck a Chinese specialty of a whole duck (including the head), roasted until the skin is very crispy. It is typically served in slices served on a pancake (mu-shi) topped with hoisin and plum sauce, which is then rolled up and eaten with the hands.

pemmican a mixture of dried meat, melted fat, flour, and molasses, with variations.

poi a Hawaiian dish made from cooked tarot root mashed into a paste.

pepper steak steak strips sautéed with green or red peppers and onions. Also, steak coated with ground peppercorns and fried or broiled.

piccata thin slices of veal or chicken that are breaded and sautéed in a sauce made of white wine, butter, and lemon.

potpie a pie made from beef or chicken in a gravy with potatoes, carrots, etc.

pot roast a large, tough cut of meat, which must be braised for a long time to tenderize it.

quiche a savory custard pie, typically containing cheese, spinach, ham, and mushrooms.

ravioli pillow-shaped pasta stuffed with meat or cheese and served in sauce.

rigatoni large pasta tubes with ridges.

rissole a ball of minced meat, fish, or vegetables, sometimes breaded, and encased in pastry and fried.

Salisbury steak a patty of ground beef and egg flavored with bread crumbs, onions, and seasonings.

sashimi a Japanese dish of thin slices of raw fish, often served with soy sauce, wasabi, and pickled vegetables.

sauerbraten a pot roast marinated in vinegar seasoned with garlic, onions, peppercorns, and bay leaves and served with dumplings.

scrapple ground and boiled pig with cornmeal and seasonings.

schnitzel veal or pork cutlets breaded and deep-fried.

shepherd's pie a ground meat pie covered with mashed potato and gravy.

shrimp scampi large shrimp broiled in a garlic sauce.

spring roll a log-shaped casing of dough filled with minced meats, seafood, or vegetables, deep-fried or steamed.

steak tartare ground beef mixed with raw egg, onions, and seasonings and eaten raw.

sukiyaki a Japanese dish of thinly sliced meat and vegetables with soy sauce and sake.

surf and turf a dish in which seafood and beef are served on the same plate, usually lobster and steak.

sushi a Japanese dish comprised of vinegar-flavored rice, raw fish, cooked egg, and vegetables.

Swiss steak a thick steak pounded with flour and cooked with tomatoes and onions and seasonings.

taco a folded tortilla stuffed with meat, cheese, lettuce, tomatoes, etc.

tamale cornmeal dough stuffed with minced meat and red peppers and steamed or baked in corn husks.

tempura Japanese specialty of batter-dipped and deep-fried fish, shrimp, and vegetables.

terriyaki a Japanese specialty of meat or fish marinated in a seasoned soy sauce.

tortellini small rings or pillows of pasta stuffed with cheese, meat, or vegetables and served in sauce or broth.

LIQUEURS

abisante a licorice-flavored liqueur used as a substitute for absinthe.

abricots, crème d' a French apricot liqueur.

absinthe a green liqueur having a high alcohol content and a bitter licorice flavor, derived from wormwood and other herbs.

advokaat eggnog liqueur.

almondrado a blend of almond liqueur and tequila.

amande, crème d' liqueur made from almonds.

amaretto an almond-flavored liqueur made from the pits of apricots.

amer picon a French aperitif made from gentian, oranges, and quinine.

anise a licorice-flavored liqueur made from anise seeds. Also called anisette.

apry a liqueur made from apricot pits.

B and B a blend of brandy and Benedictine.

Benedictine a blend of brandy, sugar, and 27 different herbs, including hyssop, mint, and melissa; developed by French Benedictine monks.

cacao, crème de a blend of chocolate and vanilla beans.

café bénédictine a blend of Benedictine and coffee liqueur.

café orange a coffee and orange liqueur.

cassis, crème de liqueur derived from black currants.

cerise, crème de French cherry liqueur.

Chartreuse a spicy, French blend of brandy, plants, and more than 100 herbs.

chéri-suisse a cherry and chocolate liqueur.

cherry marnier French cherry liqueur having a slight almond flavor.

cherry rocher French cherry liqueur.

choclair American chocolate and coconut-flavored liqueur.

chococo a chocolate and coconut liqueur from the Virgin Islands.

cocoribe a coconut and rum liqueur.

coffee liqueur a coffee bean liqueur.

coffee sambuca a blend of coffee liqueur and Sambuca.

Cointreau French liqueur derived from orange peels.

cordial médoc a French blend of brandy, crême de cacao, cherries, and oranges.

Curaçao a liqueur derived from curaçao orange peels.

Drambuie a blend of scotch, heather, honey, and herbs.

fraises, crème de strawberry liqueur.

framboise French raspberry liqueur.

Galliano a liqueur flavored with anise and vanilla.

glayva a blend of scotch, anise, honey, and herbs.

Grand Marnier French blend of cognac and orange flavor.

Irish Mist blend of Irish whiskey, honey, and orange.

Kahlua a Mexican coffee liqueur flavored with vanilla.

kummel a caraway-flavored liqueur.

mandarine cognac with tangerine flavor.

maraschino cherry and almond liqueur.

menthe, crème de a liqueur flavored with mint leaves and menthol.

Midori a Japanese liqueur having a honeydew melon flavor.

noyaux, crème de almond-flavored liqueur made from the pits of apricots, cherries, peaches, and plums.

ouzo Greek anise-flavored liqueur.

parfait d'amour a liqueur flavored with several ingredients, including lemon, coriander, anisette, vanilla, orange, and flowers.

pasha a Turkish coffee liqueur.

peppermint schnapps liqueur flavored with mint.

Pernod licorice-flavored liqueur.

prunella a plum-flavored liqueur.

rock and rye a blend of rye, rock candy syrup, and fruit juice.

roiano an Italian liqueur flavored with anise and vanilla.

ron coco liqueur flavored with coconut and rum.

rose, crème de liqueur made from vanilla and spices.

Sabra an Israeli liqueur flavored with chocolate and orange.

Sambuca an Italian, licorice-flavored liqueur.

sciarada Italian liqueur flavored with lemon and orange.

sloe gin liqueur made from sloe plums.

Southern Comfort New Orleans peach-flavored whiskey.

Tia Maria Jamaican liqueur made from coffee beans and spices.

tuaca Italian brandy with citrus and milk.

Van der mint chocolate mint.

Wild Turkey bourbon flavored with spices.

Yukon Jack Canadian whiskey flavored with citrus and herbs.

SALADS

Caesar salad greens, anchovies, croutons, grated cheese, and a dressing made from olive oil, lemon juice, and garlic.

caponata eggplant, tomatoes, zucchini, celery, pine nuts, and raisins, seasoned with olive oil and vinegar.

four-bean salad kidney beans, great northern beans, chickpeas, green beans, red wine vinegar, balsamic vinegar, and olive oil. A variation of three-bean salad.

Greek salad lettuce, tomatoes, cucumbers, olives, and onions, sprinkled with feta cheese.

Mandalay salad spinach, sesame seeds, rice wine, vinegar, and sesame oil.

Mediterranean salad plum tomatoes, red onions, green beans, red potatoes, green olives, mixed greens, olive oil, vinegar, and lemon juice.

potato salad potatoes, hard-boiled eggs, celery, onions, peppers, and mayonnaise, with many variations.

Russian salad potatoes, carrots, peas, red pepper, parsley, mayonnaise, and vinegar.

salade niçoise a variable salad, often made of tuna, anchovies, potato, hard-boiled eggs, tomatoes, olives, and green beans in a vinaigrette dressing.

tabbouleh a Middle Eastern salad made from bulgur wheat, olive oil, lemon juice, and chopped tomatoes, scallions, parsley, and mint leaves. Also spelled tabouli.

three-bean salad see FOUR-BEAN SALAD.

Waldorf salad a salad made from apples, diced celery, walnuts, lemon juice, mayonnaise, and sour cream.

SAUCES AND MARINADES

alfredo a pasta sauce made of cream, butter, parmesan cheese, and sometimes garlic.

allemande a marinade made from onions, peppers, vinegar, and seasonings, used on fish and chicken.

béarnaise a creamy sauce made with egg yolks, butter, shallots, wine, vinegar, and spices, used on meat and fish.

béchamel a white sauce made with cream and thickened with a roux, used to enrich other sauces.

Bercy a white sauce made from creamed butter, fish stock, white wine, shallots, and parsley.

bordelaise a brown sauce made with meat stock, onions, red wine, flour, and seasonings, used on meat.

brown sauce any sauce made from meat stock and flour browned in butter or fat.

carbonara a pasta sauce made from eggs, parmesan cheese, and cured pork belly.

charmoula a Middle Eastern sauce made from stewed onions, honey, and vinegar and seasoned with a mixture of cinnamon, cloves, pepper, cumin, and paprika, used on meat and fish.

chasseur sauce a sauce made from mushrooms, white wine, and butter.

chutney an East Indian relish made from various fruits, sugar, spices, and vinegar or lemon juice.

cornstarch a starch made from corn, used to thicken sauces. Also known as corn flour.

coulis a puree of vegetables or fruit, used as a sauce in soups and sometimes simply to enhance other sauces.

Cumberland sauce an English sauce made from currant jelly, wine, and orange and lemon juice, used on ham and game.

duck sauce used in Chinese food, a thick sweet-and-sour sauce made from apricots, plums, sugar, and seasonings.

escabeche a marinade made from peppers, onions, vinegar and spices, used on fish or chicken.

espagnole a thickened veal stock simmered with a mix of seasonings, such as a bouquet garni, and wine.

hoisin sauce used in Chinese food, a dark and spicy sauce, similar to barbecue sauce, and made from fermented rice, soy, vinegar, sugar, and chili.

hollandaise a creamy sauce made from butter, egg yolks, and lemon juice.

hot sauce any type of spicy, mildly hot, or extremely hot sauce, with hot peppers or chilies as the main ingredient.

jus a sauce made from natural meat juices or gravy.

mayonnaise a creamy salad or sandwich dressing made from eggs, olive oil, seasonings, and lemon juice or vinegar.

miso fermented soy bean paste, used in Japanese soups and sauces.

mole any one of several thick Mexican sauces made from chilies, nuts, seeds, tomatoes, cinnamon, cumin, coriander, and chocolate, used on meat or poultry.

Mornay a rich white sauce made from egg yolks and various cheeses, used on fish and vegetables.

mount to carefully whisk and blend chunks of cold butter into a sauce.

mousseline a hollandaise sauce enriched with egg whites or whipped cream.

nantua a white sauce made from crayfish, butter, cream, and truffles.

Newburg a rich sauce made from butter, cream, egg yolks, and sherry.

nuoc-mam a Vietnamese fish sauce made from fermented fish or shrimp.

oyster sauce a sweet and salty Chinese dipping sauce flavored with oysters, cornstarch, clam juice, garlic, onion, ginger root, soy sauce, and sugar.

pesto an Italian pasta sauce made from Parmesan cheese, olive oil, garlic, basil, and ground pine nuts.

pistou a pestolike sauce made from olive oil, garlic, basil, and Parmesan cheese.

puttanesca pasta sauce made from tomatoes, anchovies, onions, black olives, capers, and chilies.

ravigote a sauce made from oil and vinegar, onions, capers, parsley, and tarragon, used on meats and fish. Also a velouté with white wine, vinegar, butter, cream, and mushrooms.

red-eye gravy a gravy made from ham and flour fried in coffee and water.

rémoulade a French sauce made from mayonnaise, mustard, pickles, capers, anchovies, and herbs, and served cold with meat or seafood. Also used as a salad dressing.

rouille a thick, creamy sauce made from hot peppers, olive oil, and garlic.

roux a mixture of flour and butter or other fat, used to thicken sauces and stews.

salsa a hot sauce made from tomatoes and chilies.

shoyu a Japanese soy sauce that is sweeter and less salty than Chinese soy sauce.

soy sauce a dark and salty Asian sauce made from fermented soy beans.

sweet-and-sour sauce an Asian sauce made from vinegar, sugar, ketchup, peanut oil, garlic, ginger, and cornstarch.

Tabasco a very hot and spicy sauce made from vinegar, red peppers, and salt.

tapenade a spread of sauce made from black olives, anchovies, capers, olive oil, and spices, used on grilled meat or fish.

tartar sauce a sauce made of mayonnaise and chopped pickles and sometimes with onions and olives, for use on fish.

tzatziki sauce a sauce made from yogurt, cucumber, garlic, olive oil, and lemon juice, used on calamari.

velouté a white sauce made from stock, cream, butter, and flour.

Welsh rabbit a cheese sauce flavored with ale, dry mustard, pepper, and Worcestershire sauce, usually served over toast, sometimes with bacon.

white sauce a roux blended with milk, cream or stock, with seasonings.

Worcestershire sauce a spicy sauce made from soy, vinegar, anchovies, tamarind, molasses, and cloves, used on meat and poultry.

SOUPS, STEWS, AND BROTHS

alphabet soup a soup in which small pieces of pasta are cut into the shape of letters of the alphabet.

billy bi a French soup made with mussels, cream, onions, and seasonings.

bird's nest soup a very expensive Chinese soup made from the nest of a small Asian bird.

bisque a thick and creamy soup of shellfish, with the shells, cream and sometimes, Cognac. This soup is also made with rabbit or fowl. Sometimes also, a creamy vegetable soup.

blanquette a veal or chicken stew with onions and mushrooms and enriched with cream.

borscht an eastern European soup of beets or cabbage, along with potatoes, beans, meat, or sausage. The most popular beet version is served cold with sour cream.

bouillabaisse a rich stew comprised of fish, lobster, or shrimp, with vegetables and a broth made from white wine, olive oil, garlic, saffron, fennel, and orange peel.

bouillon a clear broth made from cooking beef, chicken, fish, or vegetables in water.

bourride a French stew with poached fish, onions, and a broth thickened with mayonnaise and seasoned with crushed garlic.

broth a liquid flavored with meat or vegetable stock and seasonings.

brown stock brownish liquid derived from water and browned bones and meat with vegetables and seasonings.

Brunswick stew a stew of the American South, originally made from rabbit or squirrel, but today from chicken, corn, onions, tomatoes, and okra.

burgoo originally a thick stew of the American South, made from rabbit or squirrel, but today made from a combination of pork, veal, lamb, beef, or poultry, with a wide array of vegetables, which may include potatoes, onions, carrots, cabbage, corn, okra, lima beans, and others.

caldo verde a Portuguese soup of cabbage, potatoes, sausage, broth, and oil.

callaloo a West Indian stew comprised of taro leaves, crab meat, pork, okra, yams, and coconut milk.

chili con carne a Southwest or Mexican dish usually of ground beef, beans, tomatoes, and chilies or chili powder.

chowder any chunky seafood stew.

cioppino a spicy Italian stew made of fish, shellfish, tomatoes, onions, green pepper, and red wine.

civet a French stew comprised of wild game marinated in red wine and stewed with bacon and onions.

cock-a-leekie a Scottish soup of chicken, leeks, and barley.

consommé a clear broth.

court-bouillon a broth most often used to poach fish, made of water, white wine, lemon juice, onions, celery, carrots, and herbs.

daube a beef stew in a wine broth with vegetables and herbs.

egg drop soup a broth into which beaten eggs have been added.

French onion soup an onion soup topped with toast and cheese and baked in the oven.

fumet a rich broth made from boiled bones, wine, and herbs, used to flavor soups and sauces.

gazpacho a Spanish soup of pureed tomatoes, cucumbers, peppers, and onions, with oil and vinegar, served cold.

glace any highly reduced or concentrated stock used to enrich stews, soups, and sauces.

goulash a beef or veal stew made with onions and sometimes other vegetables, seasoned with paprika.

gumbo a soup of chicken, seafood, or ham, along with tomatoes and other vegetables, thickened with okra pods.

Irish stew a stew made from lamb or mutton, potatoes, onions, and other vegetables.

lobscouse formerly, a sailor's stew, made from meat, vegetables, and hardtack.

madrilène consommé made with tomatoes.

matelote a French fish stew made with egg yolks, cream, wine, pearl onions, and mushrooms.

matzo ball soup a chicken soup with dumplings made from unleavened bread meal.

menudo a spicy Mexican soup made of tripe, calf's feet, chilies, and hominy.

minestrone a thick, meatless Italian soup with pasta, barley, and beans or peas, or other vegetables.

miso soup a Japanese soup made from fermented soya beans, onions, and seaweed.

mulligan stew originally a stew made by hoboes on the road, now any stew made from bits and pieces of whatever one has on hand.

mulligatawny originating in India, a curried chicken soup with rice and coconut.

navarin a French stew made from mutton or lamb, with potatoes, turnips, and onions.

oxtail soup a soup made with a skinned ox, beef, or veal tail.

pasta e fagioli an Italian bean and pasta soup, served with sausage.

pepper pot a thick, hotly seasoned soup made from tripe, meat, vegetables, and dumplings. Also known as Philadelphia pepper pot. Also, a West Indian stew made of meat or fish and cassava juice and red pepper.

potage French soup thickened with cream or egg yolks.

pozole a Mexican soup made from pork or chicken with hominy, chilies, onions, and cilantro. Also spelled posole.

ragoût a spicy stew of meat, fish, or vegetables.

ramen a broth with wheat flour noodles, vegetables, and sometimes, meat.

ratatouille a vegetable stew of eggplant, zucchini, tomatoes, onions, peppers, garlic, and olive oil.

Scotch broth a Scottish soup made of lamb or mutton, with barley and vegetables.

shark's fin soup an Asian soup made with shark's fin, stock, and various seasonings.

slumgullion any stew made from inexpensive ingredients.

soup du jour at a restaurant, the soup of the day.

split pea soup a thick soup made from peas and ham.

stock the liquid created after cooking meat, fish, or vegetables and seasonings in water.

vichyssoise traditionally, a rich, creamy soup made from potatoes and leeks, served cold. Modern versions are sometimes made with apples, carrots, and zucchini.

waterzooi a Flemish stew made of fish or chicken and various vegetables with a sauce enriched with eggs and cream.

wonton soup a Chinese soup of clear broth and small dumplings filled with minced meat, seafood, or vegetables, flavored with scallions, celery, and soy sauce.

TEA

Assam a deep red-colored tea with a strong flavor, grown in Assam, India.

astringent professional taster's term for a distinctly dry taste or sensation.

bergamot the oil of the bergamot orange, used as flavoring in Earl Gray black tea.

black tea the most commonly drunk tea, from oxidized or fermented green tea leaves which make a reddish-colored tea.

boba see BUBBLE TEA.

body a sense of fullness or heaviness on the tongue.

brassy having a harsh, acidic flavor.

brisk having an astringent flavor or feel.

bubble tea a dessert tea originating in Taiwan. It comes in multiple colors and flavors, such as passionfruit, peach, mango, chocolate milk, black tea, and others, and contains dark balls of chewy tapioca which sink to the bottom of a cup and are sucked up with a straw. Also known as pearl tea, milk tea, and boba.

caffeine a strong stimulant found in many teas.

cambric tea a hot drink made of milk, sugar, and weak tea.

Ceylon general name for a variety of teas from Sri Lanka.

chai spiced black tea with milk and sugar.

Darjeeling a fine, highly astringent tea grown near the Himalayas of India.

Earl Gray a black tea flavored with bergamot.

flat describing teas lacking in astringency.

green tea tea made from unfermented tea leaves.

gunpowder green tea in the form of pellets.

hard descriptive term for pungent.

heavy professional taster's term for full bodied and deep colored.

herb tea any variety of tea made from leaves of plants other than the tea plant.

high tea a British custom of having a snack with tea in the late afternoon.

iced tea chilled tea.

jasmine a variety of black tea scented with jasmine.

keemun a fine black tea grown in China.

lapsang souchong Chinese black tea that is dried in bamboo baskets over pine fires, giving it a distinctly smoky flavor.

macha finely ground green tea used in Japanese tea ceremonies.

milk tea see BUBBLE TEA.

oolong lightly fermented, full-bodied black tea with a somewhat fruity aroma, from China and Taiwan.

orange pekoe a variety or grade of large whole leaf tea from India and Sri Lanka but is not orange in flavor.

pearl tea see BUBBLE TEA.

pekoe a variety of small whole-leaf black tea from India and Sri Lanka.

pungent very astringent.

raw professional taster's term for bitter.

samovar an urn with a spigot, used to make tea in Russia and elsewhere.

sassafras tea an herb tea made from the sassafras root, but no longer made because of its possible carcinogenic properties.

tea ceremony an elaborate tea-drinking ritual involving multiple preparations and utensils, practiced by the Japanese.

tisane any herb tea other than that using tea leaves.

woody professional taster's term for tea that tastes like hay.

Yunnan distinctly spicy tea harvested in southwest China.

WINES AND WINE TERMS

Asti Spumante Italian sparkling white wine.

astringency the quality of wine that makes the mouth pucker, especially found in red wines.

Bardolino a light red wine produced in northern Italy.

Barolo a rich Italian red wine from Piedmont.

Beaujolais a light and fruity French red wine from southern Burgundy.

Beerenauslese wine made from individually picked grapes rather than bunches.

blanc de blancs French term meaning, "white of whites," referring to the lightest, most delicate white wines made from all white grapes.

body flavor intensity.

Bordeaux a city in France's southwestern wine region.

Botrytis cinerea a beneficial mold that grows on late-harvest grapes that helps to produce a rich, sweet wine.

bouquet the fragrance of a wine.

brut French term referring to the driest of all champagnes.

Burgundy French region renowned for producing fine wines.

Cabernet Sauvignon a red grape used in the making of exceptional red wines, especially those of Bordeaux and California.

Catawba an American, light red grape used in white and sparkling wines.

cave French term for cellar.

Chablis a town in northern Burgundy region of France, renowned for its dry white wines.

champagne sparkling white wine.

château any vineyard property in Bordeaux.

chewy wine connoisseur's term to describe great-bodied red wines, having a strong taste and aftertaste.

Chianti a dry red wine produced in the Monti Chianti region of Italy.

claret the English term for Bordeaux red wines.

clos French term for a stone-walled vineyard.

coarse wine connoisseur's term, having a rough flavor with no finesse.

complex wine connoisseur's term, with multiple flavor overtones.

decant to pour out wine slowly into a decanter to eliminate its sediment.

demi-sec champagne term meaning half-dry.

Diamond U.S. white grape used to produce tart white wine and champagne.

Dom Perignon the 17th-century French cellarmaster known as the inventor of champagne.

dry not sweet.

finesse wine connoisseur's term, a distinct and delicate flavor.

finish a wine's aftertaste.

flabby wine connoisseur's term, having a poor quality with weak, characterless flavor.

flat wine connoisseur's term, having a dull flavor; also of a sparkling wine, having lost its effervescence.

flinty wine connoisseur's term to describe a dry white wine, having a crisp flavor.

Gallo a giant winery in California.

Gamay a red grape from which Beaujolais is made.

green young, unaged, high in acidity.

Grenache a red grape used in dessert wines and rosés.

hard having the flavor of tannin; barely aged.

Inglenook California winery known for its Cabernet Sauvignon wines.

Kabinett German term meaning the driest of wines.

Madeira a fortified Portuguese wine, similar to a sherry in flavor.

mellow wine connoisseur's term, soft with full flavor.

Moselle German river and adjacent area where delicate white wines are produced.

must the juice drawn from the grapes in the first step of wine making.

musty wine connoisseur's term, having a flavor similar to old, rotten wood, as a moldy wine cask.

Napa Valley renowned wine-producing region north of San Francisco, California.

nose boquet of a wine.

pétillant French term for a wine with slight sparkle.

Petite-Syrah a grape that produces a deep red wine.

Pinot Blanc a white grape used mostly for blending.

Pinot Chardonnay a white grape that produces French white Burgundies and California white wines.

piquant wine connoisseur's term, having a lively and not unpleasant acidic flavor.

port Portuguese blended dessert wine.

Rheingau renowned wine-producing region on the banks of the Rhine in Germany.

Rhine wine German white wine produced on the banks of the Rhine River.

rosé a fruity, pink-colored wine.

rough wine connoisseur's term, not aged long enough and having a puckerish or coarse aftertaste.

Sauternes in Bordeaux, a wine district known for its sweet white wines.

sec French term for dry.

sherry Spanish wine fortified with brandy.

short wine connoisseur's term, having a taste that is only briefly perceived.

Soave Italian dry white wine.

soft a low alcohol content.

sommelier French term for a wine waiter who has keys to and great knowledge of the wine cellar. A wine steward.

spritzer a cold drink made of wine mixed with sparkling water.

tannin a substance in wine known to produce an astringent flavor.

tart having a sharp flavor.

Tokay Hungarian white dessert wine.

Trockenbeerenauslese German term for a white wine produced from a very late harvest of grapes that has been infected with botrytis.

varietal wine any wine named after the principal grape it is made from.

vin ordinaire French term for a cheap, red wine.

vintage the year of a grape's harvest, as labeled on a bottle of wine.

vintner a wine merchant.

wine cooler a mixed cold drink of wine, fruit juice, and soda water.

woody wine connoisseur's term, having a woody taste as if it were left too long in its cask.

Zinfandel a red grape that produces a fruity red wine when young. When aged, it produces a rich, complex wine.

FURNITURE

BEDS

bunk bed two beds stacked one atop the other on a single, adjoining frame.

canopy bed a four-poster bed.

davenport multiple definitions, one of which is a sofa bed.

four-poster bed a bed having four corner posts for suspending a canopy. Also, a bed with four posts but no canopy.

futon a Japanese couch consisting of an adjustable frame and one large, folded cushion, which unfolds with the frame to form a bed.

Murphy bed a bed that folds up into a closet or special cabinet when not in use, designed for small spaces.

sleigh bed a bed resembling a sleigh, popular in the first half of the 1800s. It is characterized by a high, back-curving, scrolled headboard and footboard.

tester a canopy.

trundle bed a very low bed mounted on wheels and stored under a normal-size bed, popular from the 15th through the 19th centuries.

Tuscan bed from the Italian Renaissance period, an ornately-carved, four poster bed with a gilded headboard.

waterbed a modern, plastic bed filled with water, originating in the 1960s.

BUREAUS, CABINETS, AND CHESTS

armoire a tall cupboard, wardrobe, or closetlike cabinet with doors and shelves for clothing, but also used in modern times as an entertainment center holding a television, stereo, DVD player, etc.

apothecary chest a low chest with several small drawers, once used to store medicines, but today employed to hold numerous small items.

ark a medieval chest with a rounded cover.

art cabinet a cabinet having a glass front and various display shelves or niches and sometimes mirrored backs for showing off small ornamental items, popular in Victorian times.

bachelor's chest a chest of drawers with a hinged leaf that doubled as a writing surface when opened, popular in the 18th century.

blanket chest a small, boxlike chest for holding blankets or quilts. Sometimes called a hope chest.

bowfront any cabinet with a rounded or convex front.

breakfront a style of cabinet divided into three sections, with the middle section projecting slightly, popular in Chippendale case pieces.

buffet a cabinet having shelves and cupboards for dishes and silverware and other dining room items.

canterbury formerly a rack for holding music, now a magazine rack.

case furniture generic term for any furniture intended to hold or store something, such as a cabinet or bureau.

chest on chest a tall chest of drawers topped by a smaller chest of drawers.

chiffonier a tall and narrow chest with many drawers and often, a mirror.

coffer a medieval chest with a rounded top, made for transport.

commode a low chest with either doors or drawers, originating in the late 17th century.

dresser a chest of drawers for clothes, often having a mirror.

entertainment center an armoire-like cabinet with multiple compartments for a television, DVD player, CD player, and so on, and which may or may not have hinged doors.

étagère a freestanding, open cabinet with shelves, used to display knickknacks, curios, or other small items.

Guilford chest originating in the 17th century, a four-legged chest with a single drawer, usually painted with floral motifs.

Hadley chest originating in the late 17th century, a chest with four short legs and one or more drawers, usually paneled, carved, and stained, with floral and vine decorations.

highboy a tall chest of drawers on tall legs, often crowned with a pediment.

hope chest a small, boxlike chest, traditionally used by a young woman to accumulate and store blankets, linens, and/or clothing in anticipation of marriage.

hutch a chest or cabinet with drawers and cupboards.

lowboy a low chest or table with drawers and short legs.

pediment an arched crown on top of tall case furniture. The arch is often broken in the center and called a broken pediment.

plinth the base on which a chest with no legs sits.

pot cupboard a small cabinet originally designed to store a chamber pot, washbasin, and pitcher, from the 1700s through the 1800s.

pot table similar to the pot cupboard, a cylindrical cabinet, intended to hold a chamber pot, originating in the 1800s.

wardrobe a tall cabinet in which clothes may be hung, and underneath is usually attached a chest of drawers, now largely replaced by closets.

CHAIRS AND SOFAS

arm stump on an armchair, the vertical member that supports an armrest.

balloon chair a round-backed Hepplewhite chair, reminiscent of a balloon.

banquette a long, upholstered bench, most often used in a restaurant waiting area.

Barcelona chair a padded leather chair without arms, supported by an X-shaped frame.

barrel chair a semicircular, upholstered chair.

basket chair a wicker chair with a rounded and hooded back.

bergère a French-designed, fully upholstered armchair with a loose seat cushion and closed sides, originating in the 18th century.

Boston rocker originating in the 19th century, an American rocking chair with a spindle back and curved wooden seat, often painted or stenciled.

Brewster chair originating in the 17th century, a Jacobean-style chair constructed of turned wood and numerous spindles and sometimes having a rush seat.

butterfly chair a canvas sling chair on a metal frame.

cabriole sofa originating in the 18th century, a sofa having a rounded back that curves into its arms. It may or may not have curved cabriole legs.

camelback sofa a sofa originating in the 18th century, characterized by a large, rounded back, as that of a camel.

canapé an upholstered settee.

caning woven rattan strips used in seats and seat backs.

captain's chair a Windsor chair with a low, curving back, popular in the 19th century.

Carver chair similar to the Brewster chair but having fewer ornamental spindles. A straight-backed chair with every element constructed of turned wood except the seat, which was made of planks or rush, a Jacobean design of the 17th century.

chaise longue "long chair." An upholstered chair or sofa having a long extension for supporting the legs, as a recliner. Also spelled chaise lounge.

Chesterfield an overstuffed couch or sofa with upright, rolled arms and no exposed wood elements.

club chair modern name for a wing chair.

couch a sofa.

davenport a large, American-designed sofa, sometimes available as a sofa bed.

deck chair a folding, portable chair, used on cruise ships.

director's chair a collapsible canvas and wood chair on two X frames, made famous by movie directors and used for their portability.

divan an armless, backless, upholstered couch that can be used as a bed, originating in France in the mid 1800s.

dos-à-dos a seat or sofa in which sitters are seated back to back.

duchess a style of chaise longue of the 17th century, consisting of an upholstered chair and matching footstool or two upholstered chairs and matching footstools, each of which could be used separately or pushed together to form one long chaise longue. Also known as a duchesse brisée.

fainting couch see RECAMIER.

fauteuil an upholstered chair with open arms.

fiddleback a chair back design that resembles the outline of a violin, used in Queen Anne-style chairs.

Hitchcock chair originating in the 19th century, a chair having turned front legs, a black finish, and a stencil design on the back.

ladder back a wooden chair with back slats hung like the rungs of a ladder.

lolling chair see MARTHA WASHINGTON CHAIR.

love seat an abbreviated form of sofa, consisting of two seats instead of three or four.

Martha Washington chair a chair with an upholstered seat and a high, upholstered back, with bare arms and slender, tapering legs, originating in New England in the Federal period. Also known as a lolling chair.

placet a very low, four-legged stool, with a fabric seat, popular in the 17th century.

platform rocker a rocking chair that "rocks" on mounted springs, popular in the second half of the 1800s and into the early 1900s.

recamier a kind of sofa or chaise longue popular in the 1800s, characterized by a narrow, curving backrest that stands at an end instead of along the sofa's length, and combined with a curving footboard. Also known as a fainting couch.

recliner an upholstered chair that can be shifted, either with one's body weight or with a lever so that its back drops back in a reclining position and a footrest folds out to support the legs.

sectional a couch made up of individual components that can be arranged in different configurations.

slipper chair a low, armless, upholstered chair, used in a bedroom.

settee a wooden bench with arms, usually upholstered and capable of seating two or three people. It preceded the sofa in the 17th century.

settle a wooden bench similar to the settee, but without upholstery. It was sometimes built with a storage space underneath a hinged seat.

sofa a long, upholstered seat with upholstered back and arms, originating in the mid-1700s.

swivel chair an office chair with capability to revolve or pivot in any direction.

tablet chair a chair in which one arm has been expanded to form a writing surface, used in schools as a desk.

tête-à-tête an S-shaped seat on which two people can sit and face each other.

Windsor chair originating in 17th-century England, a very popular wooden spindle or splat chair with a saddle seat and sometimes a curving back with bentwood arms, manufactured in many variations.

wing chair an upholstered chair with a high back and winglike projections on either side, originating in the 17th century.

DECORATIVE AND CONSTRUCTION ELEMENTS

acanthus leaf wood carving inspired by the lobed, spiny leaves of the acanthus plant, most popular in the 18th century and found on cabriole legs in Queen Anne furniture and others.

acorn a carved or turned ornament resembling an acorn and used as a finial on a chair or bed post.

adaptation that which captures the essence of a style or period without necessarily having exactly the same elements.

amorini decorative carvings of boys, adorning upscale furniture of the 1600s and later.

anthemion ornamental motif resembling a spray of honeysuckle flowers, either carved or painted, popular in the 18th and 19th centuries, especially on the neoclassical anthemion-back chair.

antiquing the process of purposely making a piece of furniture look much older than it is, to give it the appearance of an antique. Various methods include scratching, gouging, staining, scrubbing with dirt, fading or roughing off layers of paint with bleach or acid baths, or exposing the wood to harsh weather or even plugging it with small nail holes to mimic wormholes. Also known as distressing. Also, a casual term for shopping for antiques.

applied ornament any carving or other ornament that must be attached separately with nails or glue. Also known as an appliqué.

apron a board, sometimes decorative, sometimes merely structural, running between and connecting the legs of a table just beneath the table's top. On chairs, the apron runs just below the seat. On a cabinet, it runs along the base. Also known as a skirt.

arabesque any highly complex decorative work consisting of twining foliage and flowers, geometrical scrolls, mythological figures, or animals that may be carved, painted, or inlaid.

arcade a carved ornamentation consisting of a line of arches. Also, a chair back with this form.

arrow spindle a decorative, turned rod or spindle carved in the shape of an arrow.

astragal small, convex beading.

auger flame a finial resembling a corkscrew or carpenter's auger; it appears on American Chippendale furniture.

backsplat a central slat of wood in a chair back.

ball and claw a fanciful footing for a chair or table, consisting of a ball within a carved foot, such as a crane's foot or a dragon's claws.

ball foot a round, turned foot. Also known as a bun foot.

baluster a column or slat supporting a rail, as in a chair back.

bamboo turning a combined technique of turning and painting to give the illusion of bamboo, popular in the 1800s.

banding contrasting inlay used as a decorative border around drawer fronts.

barley-sugar twist a carved spiral, as on a turned leg or column.

bas-relief a carving that projects only slightly from the surface it decorates.

beading any decorative edging, molding, or trim reminiscent of a flattened line of beads.

bellflower a vertical alignment of carved or painted bell-shaped flowers, a popular ornament used in Federal-style furniture.

bentwood any curved wood element, created by steaming. Bentwood is used in Windsor bow-backed chairs and bentwood rockers.

bevel a sloping edge carved into wood for a decorative effect.

bird's eye a circular coloration or marking in wood grain, reminiscent of a bird's eye, found most often in maple.

block foot on a table or chair, a square foot and straight leg.

bobbin turning a series of small globes or spheres turned into a table or chair leg, popular in the 17th and 18th centuries.

bombé on a chest or commode, having a bulge or convex shape, most often found on baroque designs. Also, the chest itself.

bonnet top an unbroken pediment form found on late 17th- and early 18th-century highboys or secretaries.

borax cheap, poorly made furniture awarded as premiums for purchasing Borax soap from the 1920s and later. The furniture was noted for its grossly overstuffed upholstery, plastic moldings, and simulated wood panels.

boss a raised, round or oval ornament or knob.

bowfront a convex front.

bracket foot on a chest of the 18th century, a foot that extends out from both intersecting sides of a corner.

broken pediment a pediment whose scrollwork on either side does not meet.

bulb turning turned wood in the shape of a bulb or swelling, used on table legs in Renaissance furniture.

bun foot see BALL FOOT.

burl decorative veneer or inlay cut from a knot or warty protrusion on a tree trunk or branch. Also, the protuberance itself.

cabachon an ornament resembling an unfaceted gem or alternately, a cashew nut.

cable decorative molding reminiscent of twined rope.

cabriole an S-shaped leg or a leg reminiscent of that of a goat, introduced in the 17th century.

cane bamboo or rattan stems. Also known as caning.

caryatid an ornamental, sculpted support in the figure of a woman, found in Directoire, Empire, and Regency styles.

castor a wheel and swivel, used as rolling footing for various pieces of furniture, originating in the 16th century.

channeling decorative grooves or furrows.

chinoiserie ornamental motifs of Asian landscapes, people, and designs, popular in the 17th and 18th centuries.

chip carving chiseled decorations, usually of geometrical design, gouged into roundels and typically found on panels in medieval chests.

cinquefoil an ornament comprised of a five-lobed leaf in a circle, found on Gothic furniture.

console a decorative bracket supporting a tabletop or a cornice.

coquillage a rococo-style ornamental motif of scallop shells.

cornice decorative molding around the top of a cabinet.

cornucopia a carved or painted ornamental motif featuring a horn filled with flowers and fruit, appearing on Renaissance, Federal, and art deco-style furniture.

cup turning turned wood in the shape of an upside-down cup or a right-side up cup with a domed lid. The design originated on the legs of some Jacobean furniture.

dentils decorative, teethlike blocks that project from a cornice. Also, dentil molding.

distressed describing a piece of furniture that is purposely dented, scratched, and worn to give it an aged or antique appearance.

distressing see ANTIQUING.

double open-twist turning wood that is turned and carved to make it appear as if it is intertwining.

dovetail a connective joint made of tapering fingers that are joined with others for a strong hold, found in drawer construction.

dowel a wooden rod or pin used to connect or hold two pieces together.

drake foot a carved footing in the shape of a duck's foot.

ebonized stained black to simulate expensive ebony woods from India and Africa.

eclectic a style that uses a blend of other styles.

egg and dart decorative molding characterized by alternating oval and arrow forms, seen on cornices.

embossing the stamping of a design on wood to simulate carving.

ergonomic design any modern design elements incorporating that which conforms to human comfort, safety, and ease of use.

escutcheon a plain or ornamental plate or shield, usually found around a keyhole or drawer pull.

fancy faces veneers that are cut and matched with other veneers to make an appealing or exotic pattern, used on cabinet facades, drawer fronts, and doors.

faux artificial, simulated.

feathered a wood grain pattern resembling feathers, as seen on mahogany and satinwood.

festoon any carved or painted ornament reminiscent of a garland, a strand of rope, or a loop of flowers or scallops.

fiberboard any cheap style of furniture made from compressed wood fibers and glue. Also, the wood itself.

figure a distinct marking or characteristic of a wood grain, such as mottles, feathers, waves, burls, crotches, and crossfire.

finial an ornamental tip on the top of a spire or cabinet.

flame finial a finial carved to resemble a ball of flame.

fluting decorative vertical channels or grooves.

foliate of an ornamental element, resembling a leaf or leaves.

French foot see SCROLL FOOT.

French scroll see SCROLL FOOT.

fretwork decorative carving in the configuration of lattice or other intersecting lines. Also known as latticework.

gallery rail a decorative rail along the border of a table or sideboard.

gouge carving decorative incising made by chisel cuts, found on gothic and Pennsylvania Dutch furniture.

graining painting technique that produces a wood grain effect.

grotesque a carved or painted insect, bird, human head, griffin, or other strange beast, used as ornament on Renaissance, baroque, and rococo furniture.

guilloche a decorative band of interwoven curves.

half column a decorative column portion, sometimes seen on highboys and secretaries.

half turning any wood turned on a lathe and then cut in half lengthwise for application as a decorative element.

haut relief a carving that projects high off the surface it decorates. Also known as high relief.

incised carved or engraved into a surface, as opposed to being raised above it.

inlay a panel or strip of inserted wood, grain, or mother of pearl, as a decoration.

intaglio any design incised or engraved into a surface.

in the white designating unfinished wood or furniture.

Japanning furniture finish made of either gesso, paint, or varnish, used to simulate lacquer, which in the 17th and 18th centuries was unavailable except in Asia and particularly in Japan.

lambrequin on a table or chair, a decoratively scalloped apron.

latticework see FRETWORK.

laurel leaves decorative motif of a band or wreath of laurel leaves, popular in neoclassical furniture of the 18th and 19th centuries.

liming lightening the color of wood by dipping it into a solution of lime, originating in the 16th century.

lozenge an ornament in the shape of a diamond.

lunette a half-moon or semicircular ornamental piece that may be carved, inlaid, or painted, sometimes in the configuration of a fan.

marquetry decorative wood inlay, often using different shades and kinds of woods.

mask a grotesque carving of a human face, used as an ornament in Renaissance, baroque, and rococo furniture.

molding any decorative trim used to dress an edge of a surface.

monopod the leg of a chair or table carved into the shape of an animal head or body, used in French Empire-style furniture.

motif design elements or ornamentation, often repeated to create a theme.

palmette a palm leaf motif, used as decoration on Renaissance and neoclassical furniture.

parquetry a geometrical pattern of contrasting woods, inlaid on a piece of furniture.

paw feet table or chair feet carved in the shape of animal feet, most popularly, a lion's.

piercing carving that cuts all the way through wood, creating open decorative work.

Prince of Wales feathers popular in the 18th century and found on Hepplewhite furniture, a decorative motif of three standing ostrich feathers tied together, the heraldic symbol of the Prince of Wales.

putto on European Renaissance and later styles, an ornament in the configuration of a winged infant or cupid.

quatrefoil a cloverlike ornament enclosed in a circle, found in Gothic and Neo-Gothic styles.

rabbet a channel cut into wood to act as a receptacle to the butt end of another piece of wood, forming a joint.

rail any horizontal bar or member supported by vertical members, as on a chair back.

rake the lean or slant of a vertical element, as the inclination of a chair back.

ram's horn arm a decorative scroll resembling a ram's horn at the end of a chair arm, found on baroque furniture.

rattan any furniture made from the bark (caning) or reeds (wicker) of the rattan palm of Asia, originating in the West in the early 1800s.

reeding carved vertical ridges, similar to fluting, on table and chair legs, especially in the late 18th century.

reel and bead turning turned wood comprised of alternating balls and ovals, found on medieval furniture.

relief any ornamental element projecting from a flat surface.

ring pull a drawer handle comprised of a ring of brass or other metal.

ring turning turned wood consisting of close-set, grooved rings.

rosette a carved, inlaid or painted ornament resembling a flower.

roundel a circular ornament often containing a decorative motif.

saber leg a chair or sofa leg reminiscent of a slightly curving sword, popular in the late 18th and 19th centuries.

scroll any decorative spiral, usually carved.

scroll foot a footing carved into the shape of a spiral or scroll, found on baroque and rococo furniture, especially at the end of cabriole legs. Also known as French foot or French scroll.

scrollwork any carved or incised spirals.

serpentine undulating or curving in form, as the front of some cabinets, popular in rococo furniture.

singerie a decorative motif featuring clothed monkeys in various human activities, including card-playing, found on rococo furniture, often with chinoiserie.

skirt see APRON.

strapwork a geometrical pattern of interlaced bands, either painted or carved, reminiscent of leather strappings, found in mannerist and Renaissance furniture.

suite any matching set of furniture.

teardrop handle a drawer pull in the shape of a teardrop, popular during the Victorian period.

trumpet turning turned wood resembling an upturned horn with a domed top.

turned referring to any wood carved, or "turned," on a lathe.

twist turning turned wood resembling rope, found on the legs of some 17th-century furniture.

varnish a special tree resin dissolved in oil, turpentine, or alcohol, rubbed on wood to create a hard, glossy surface.

vase and ball turning turned wood in the shape of small vases alternating with spheres.

veneer a thin layer of expensive or more visually appealing wood attached over a cheaper wood.

water leaf an ornamental motif resembling undulating laurel leaves, found on American Empire furniture and others of the 18th and early 19th centuries.

wicker generic term for either rattan strips or willow twigs used in making wicker furniture, originating in ancient Egypt.

STYLES

Adam a style made popular by architect Robert Adam, from 1760 to 1790, characterized by the use of light-colored woods with classical motifs and inlays but an overall reduction in ornamentation from the previously popular rococo style of the 1750s.

Adirondack a rustic or camp-style furniture, made of hickory and hickory bark, from 1898 to the 1940s.

American Empire a style derived from French Empire and British Regency from 1810 to the 1830s, characterized by the use of reeding, paw feet, and water leaf motifs.

art deco a style prominent in the 1920s and 1930s, characterized by glass and chrome elements and the use of decorative arcs, zigzags, lozenges, and other geometric patterns. Known during the period as Jazz Moderne or Art Moderne.

art nouveau "New Art." An ornate French style arising from about 1890 through 1910, characterized by frequent use of the "whiplash curve," an S-shaped line ending in one or more reverse curves. Tiffany lamps fall into the art nouveau category.

arts and crafts a style popular from 1890 to 1914, characterized by an emphasis on craftsmanship and simple forms and ornamentation. Exposed joinery is a characteristic of the style.

baroque a rich, dramatic style of furniture from the 17th to early 18th centuries, characterized by extensive ornamentation in the form of carvings, inlays, gilding, and chinoiserie.

Bauhaus a minimalist style so named after the form of German architecture inspired by Walter Gropius.

Biedermeyer a German style arising in the 1800s, and borrowing from Empire styles, noted for its plain, square, but strong forms and light woods accented with black enamel.

campaign furniture a type of furniture that can be folded or broken down for easy transport, used mainly by the military in British India from the late 18th through the 19th centuries.

Chippendale rococo style of the 18th century, most noted for its graceful lines, ball and claw feet, and cabriole legs, named after the English cabinetmaker Thomas Chippendale.

classical any style of furniture based on ancient Greek and Roman designs.

colonial any American style originating during the original settlements, from approximately 1700 to 1776. It borrowed from many previous styles, such as Jacobean and Puritan, and could be simple or ornate but was most commonly utilitarian.

colonial revival a style inspired by the original colonial styles, prominent from the 1870s through World War I and after.

contemporary any modern style.

cottage a style of inexpensive furniture of the late 19th century, characterized by decorative paintings of fruits and flowers.

Directoire a French style of furniture, popular from 1805 to 1815, noted for its simple, utilitarian design and details borrowed from ancient Greece and Rome. Mahogany was frequently used in construction, and typical ornaments included diamonds, stars, wreaths, lyres, and laurel branches. Saber-legged sofas, Grecian couches, and lyre-back chairs were characteristic pieces. The style enjoyed a renaissance in 1950s America.

early American style of the late 1600s through early 1700s, characterized by trestle tables and slat-back chairs, and simple or no ornamentation.

Elizabethan a heavily carved, massive style originating in the second half of the 1500s in England.

Empire a massive style of the early 1800s, characterized by bronze ornamentation, and decorative carvings of bees, crowns, laurel leaves, and mythological figures. The most popular drawer pull of the period was a lion head with a ring in its nose. Popular woods used in construction included mahogany and rosewood.

Federal an American style following the American Revolution, characterized by the use of veneer, inlay, and brass feet. Brass drawer pulls with bald eagle or dove designs were common as was the use of mahogany in construction. Duncan Phyfe was among the most famous Federal-style designers.

French Empire early 1800s style characterized by the heavy use of ebony, rosewood, and mahogany, with tops often made of marble and ornamentation that ranged from lions and sphinxes to torches and Roman eagles.

Georgian a style originating in the 1700s, characterized by such decorative elements as eagle heads and talons, lion heads and claws, and satyrs' masks.

Gothic a heavy medieval style known for its large trestle tables and chests banded with wrought iron.

Gothic revival a style derived from medieval times, popular in England and America in the 1800s.

Hepplewhite a late 1700s and early 1800s style named after the cabinetmaker George Hepplewhite, largely based on Adam and neoclassical styles. It is characterized by the use of serpentine and bow fronts on chests of drawers and Prince of Wales feather motifs or shield configurations on chair backs. Other ornamentation included carved eagles and stars and urns.

horn furniture chairs or settees partially or wholly made from the horns or antlers of deer, elk, buffalo, or cattle, originating in the Middle Ages, and made later in the 19th century as novelty pieces.

Jacobean English style of the early 17th century, often with dark finishes and sometimes ornamented by heavily turned legs, arabesques, and Italianate carvings. Also known as Pilgrim furniture.

Louis XIV a style originating in the early 1600s, featuring carved motifs of animals, mythological creatures, and garlands of flowers.

mannerist an eccentric furniture style originating in the 16th and 17th centuries, characterized by the use of grotesque ornamentation, including oddly postured human figures, with arabesques and strapwork, popular in northern Europe.

mission an early 20th-century style characterized by exposed joinery and simple, rectilinear forms with little ornamentation.

modular a style of furniture in which individual units can be stacked or placed in varied configurations, as in a sectional couch.

neoclassical any Greek, Roman, or Egyptian styling revivals of the late 1700s. Many furniture styles are considered neoclassical, including Adam, Louis XVI, French Empire, baroque, and others.

Phyfe, Duncan American furniture maker of the first half of the 1800s, noted as the main creator of the American Empire style. Phyfe's work was characterized by the use of figured mahogany veneers, decorative reeding and fluting on legs and posts, and paw feet made of brass. Chairs with lyre-shaped backs, and tables and sofas with gracefully out-curving feet were also characteristic. Also, the furniture or furniture style itself.

Pilgrim see JACOBEAN.

pop-art furniture an unconventional style of the 1960s through which designers thumbed their noses at convention and constructed everything from chairs shaped like baseball gloves to settees reminiscent of false teeth.

Queen Anne an 18th-century British style of furniture characterized by serpentine arms, cabriole legs, rounded frames, and walnut veneers. Wing chairs became widely popular during this time.

revival a style that incorporates a previous style, but most commonly colonial.

rococo 18th-century European style noted for its highly ornate scrollwork and other decorative elements. The use of chinoiserie, serpentine fronts, cabriole legs, and shell and flower motifs were characteristic. One extreme ornament of the style was called singerie, which was consisted of clothed monkeys involved in various human activities, such as card-playing.

rustic a very simple, utilitarian style, reminiscent of something handmade in the country.

shabby chic a popular style of the 1990s, characterized by eclectic, nonmatching furniture, sometimes purchased second-hand.

Shaker originating in the 1800s and still manufactured today, a practical, unadorned style of furniture designed by the Shakers, an American religious sect.

Sheraton style originating in the 1700s, featuring painted ornamentation, contrasting veneers, and decorative inlays.

spool furniture furniture consisting of ribbed legs, posts, and crossbars made from lengths of wood originally intended as spools for holding thread, very popular in the second half of the 1800s.

TABLES AND DESKS

Beau Brummell an elaborate, multicompartment dressing and shaving table with mirror, designed for men in the 18th century.

card table a portable, square table with legs that fold in or collapse for easy storage. Originating in the 17th century, it sometimes had dished corners for holding money.

cellarette a small wooden chest used to store wine and liquor, popular in the late 18th and early 19th centuries. A metal-lined version could be filled with ice to keep wine cool.

coffee table any low table on which coffee may be served, but usually one set in front of a couch in a living room.

console table any table attached to a wall.

credenza a sideboard or buffet. Also, a serving table with cupboard.

davenport a British-designed desk with drawers and compartments on the sides and a hinged lid that folds down to form a writing surface on the front.

drop-leaf a hinged panel that can be folded down or up to increase or decrease the length of a table. Also, the table itself.

drop-lid desk a desk having a hinged lid that pulls down and can be used as a table.

gateleg table a drop-leaf table with extra legs that can be swung out to support the leaves.

handkerchief table a table with a top in the shape of a folded, triangular handkerchief, with one triangular drop-leaf.

harvest table a long, narrow, rectangular table with drop-leaf sides, popular in the 1700s.

huntboard a small, portable table or sideboard for serving food and drink outside.

library table a large table on which multiple people may write.

loper a sliding arm used to support a leaf on a table or the fall front on a desk or cabinet.

occasional table any coffee table or end table.

Parsons table a simple, low, square or rectangular table made of plastic.

pedestal table a tea table supported by a singled column that branches into three legs at the bottom.

Pembroke table a drop-leaf table with two hinged leaves on either end, originating in the mid 18th century.

piecrust table a circular tea table with a scalloped rim, giving the appearance of a piecrust, originating in the 18th century.

quadrant a curving bracket used to support the fall front of desks from the late 18th to the early 19th centuries.

rolltop desk see TAMBOUR DESK.

sideboard usually set against a dining room wall, a table with one wide, shallow drawer and surrounded by deeper drawers or cabinets, for serving food and drinks.

spiderleg table a gateleg table from the 18th century, noted for its extremely slender legs.

tambour desk a desk with a flexible cover made of narrow wooden strips attached to cloth that can be rolled up or down to open and close the desk. Also known as a rolltop desk.

tea table any small table used to serve tea.

HUMAN BODY AND MIND

CANCER AND TUMORS

(*Also see* SURGICAL AND MEDICAL PROCEDURES AND RELATED TERMS *in* MEDICINE)

adenocarcinoma a common form of cancer originating in a gland.

Adriamycin a cancer-fighting chemical used in chemotherapy and frequently causing hair loss.

angioblastoma a cancerous tumor consisting of tissue from blood vessels.

angiogenesis inhibitor any one of several experimental drugs that cut blood flow to tumors and kill cancer cells while leaving normal cells healthy.

arrhenoblastoma an ovarian tumor known for its masculinizing effects.

astroblastoma a malignant brain tumor.

basal cell tumor a small, common skin cancer frequently found around the nose or under the eyes, usually treatable with surgery or X-rays.

benign not cancerous; not malignant.

biopsy taking a tissue sample from a tumor to help make a diagnosis.

Burkitt's lymphoma a non-Hodgkin's lymphoma usually producing a tumor in the abdomen, most often seen in teens and young adults.

carcinogen any substance that causes cancer.

carcinoma any cancer formed from the cells lining organs.

carcinoma in situ a localized cancer that has not spread and is therefore easier to treat.

carcinomatosis cancer that has spread to or invaded other parts of the body.

carcinosarcoma a malignant tumor of the lining and muscles of the uterus.

chemotherapy the treatment of cancer with drugs or chemicals.

chondrofibroma a benign tumor consisting of cartilage and fibrous tissue.

chondrosarcoma a malignant tumor composed of cartilage.

choriocarcinoma malignant cancer formed in the sexual organs.

cystadenoma a benign tumor containing cysts.

dermatofibroma a benign tumor of the skin.

eosinophilic tumor a tumor of the pituitary gland that in children sometimes causes extreme growth spurts (gigantism).

ependymoma a type of brain tumor.

feminizing tumor an ovarian tumor that in children may cause premature menstruation and precocious breast development; in older women, it may cause new breast growth and a return of vaginal bleeding.

fibroadenoma a common benign tumor made of fibrous and glandular tissue found in the breast.

fibroid tissue benign uterine tumor made of muscle and fibrous tissue.

gamma ray a type of radiation used in treating malignancies.

germinoma a tumor of the testicle.

Hodgkin's disease a malignant lymph disease that spreads to the spleen, liver, and bone marrow, most often seen in young adults.

Kaposi's sarcoma a vascular cancer characterized by the development of purple nodules on the skin, most often seen in patients with AIDS.

leukemia collective term for a family of malignant diseases of white blood cells and blood-forming marrow; some cause death within weeks, whereas others may last 20 years or more.

Leukeran an anticancer medication used in treating leukemia.

lipoma common benign tumor made of fat and found beneath the skin.

liposarcoma a malignant tumor composed of fat tissue.

lumpectomy surgical removal of a tumor or mass.

lymphoblastoma a malignant tumor of the lymph glands.

malignant deadly, potentially fatal, cancerous.

masculinizing tumor of the ovary ovarian tumor that may produce such masculine traits as a deepening voice and facial hair in women.

mastectomy the surgical removal of a breast as a treatment for cancer.

melanoblastoma malignant skin tumor arising from pigment cells.

melanoma a skin mode that has become cancerous.

metastasis the spread of cancer from one body part to another.

metastasize to spread from one part of the body to another.

monoclonal antibodies cloned antibodies used as a treatment to resist cancer growth.

myclocytic leukemia a fatal form of leukemia.

myeloma a malignant tumor of bone marrow.

myofibroma a benign tumor made of muscle and fibrous tissue.

myoma a benign tumor of muscle.

myosarcoma a malignant tumor of muscle.

neoplasm a tumor; a growth.

nephroma a kidney tumor.

oncogenic carcinogenic.

oncology the branch of medicine cornered with tumors and tumor growth.

osteogenic sarcoma a malignant bone tumor.

papilloma a benign growth of mucous membranes.

photochemotherapy cancer treatment consisting of drugs or chemicals exposed to ultraviolet radiation, which has been shown to increase effectiveness.

polyp a benign growth or tumor arising on a stalk from mucous membranes.

radioresistant of a tumor, unaffected by radiation therapy.

radiotherapy radiation therapy.

remission a reversal of a cancer in which cancer cells may be present in the body, but all signs of tumors and symptoms are gone.

resectable that can be surgically removed.

sarcoma a malignant tumor composed of bone, muscle, or fat.

SU5416 a powerful angiogenesis inhibitor.

thermography measuring the amount of heat given off by different body areas. Cancerous growths give off slightly higher heat.

Warthin's tumor a benign tumor of the parotid gland.

Wilm's tumor a malignant tumor of the kidney found in young children.

CONCEPTION, PREGNANCY, AND CHILDBIRTH

(*Also see* SEXUALITY)

abortion the spontaneous or medically induced termination of a pregnancy.

abruption placentae separation of the placenta from the uterine wall.

active phase during the first stage of labor, the phase characterized by contractions lasting about 60 seconds and occurring every two to five minutes.

afterpains postbirth pain and cramping caused by contractions of the uterus as it returns to its normal size.

alpha fetoprotein (AFP) a protein produced in the liver of a fetus and passed through the placenta into the mother's bloodstream; a high amount of AFP in the mother's blood indicates a neural tube defect.

amniocentesis the taking of a small sample of amniotic fluid in order to determine the presence of genetic or other disorders in the fetus.

amnion the innermost bag containing the fetus and amniotic fluid; one of two layers making up the amniotic sac.

amniotic fluid waters, urine, and other fluids in which the fetus floats in the uterus.

amniotomy the medically induced rupturing of the amniotic sac to speed up labor.

anencephaly a congenital defect in which only a small part of the brain develops.

antepartum before labor or before childbirth.

anterior position the head position most frequently assumed by an infant during birth, specifically head first and face down.

Apgar score a system for rating a baby's general health at birth, specifically a number score from 0 to 2 for each of five characteristics: heart rate, respiration, muscle tone, reflexes, and color.

artificial insemination the depositing of semen into the cervix through a plastic tube.

blastocyst the earliest form or stage of embryonic development.

bloody show a discharge of blood and mucus, a symptom of impending labor.

bonding the emotional attachment that grows between parents and child before and after birth.

Bradley method childbirth techniques involving the husband or partner as labor coach and the use of slow, rhythmic breathing and relaxation to control pain.

Braxton-Hicks contractions often mistaken for true labor contractions, actually mild and intermittent prelabor contractions that go away within a few hours.

breech presentation the delivering baby presenting itself feet first or buttocks first.

caul the fetal membranes that sometimes cover the head during delivery.

cephalic disproportion the condition of a woman's pelvis being too small for the baby's head to pass through.

cephalic presentation a head-first presentation.

cerclage the temporary closing of the cervix through suturing to prevent premature delivery.

cervical os the opening between the uterus and the vagina.

cervix the neck of the uterus.

cesarean section the surgical removal of a baby through the abdominal wall of the mother.

chloasma brown patches or pigmentation that appear on the skin and face of some pregnant woman, known as the "mask of pregnancy."

chorion the outermost or second of two membranes containing the fetus.

chorionic villus sampling removal and evaluation of a small portion of the placenta to determine the presence of genetic abnormalities in the fetus.

chromosomes the rod-shaped bodies in a cell on which the genes are located.

circumcision surgical removal of the foreskin of a male infant's penis.

colostrum the yellowish or whitish fluid secreted from a mother's breast during the last weeks of pregnancy and prior to the production of breast milk.

congenital existing before or at birth, usually used to describe medical conditions.

contraction the uterine muscular action that dilates the cervix during labor.

cordocentesis the taking of a blood sample from the umbilical cord to test for genetic blood disorders.

couvade the sympathetic symptoms of pregnancy developed by the father.

crib death *see* SUDDEN INFANT DEATH SYNDROME.

crowning during childbirth, the point when the full diameter of the baby's head appears from the vaginal opening.

deoxyribonucleic acid (DNA) the protein containing genetic information.

differentiation the splitting and specializing of cells to become individual body parts.

dihydrotestosterone the hormone responsible for the development of fetal genitalia.

dilation and evacuation an abortion performed by suction.

doula a Greek word for a "woman who serves." Any woman trained to provide childbirthing advice as well as physical and emotional support to a mother-to-be before, during, and after birth.

dystocia a problematic or difficult labor.

ectoderm the outermost layer of embryoblast cells that become the skin, hair, nails, and nervous system.

ectopic pregnancy the development of the fertilized egg outside the uterus, in the fallopian tubes.

edema fluid build-up in the body tissues during pregnancy, causing swelling.

embryoblast the innermost cells of a blastocyst, from which the embryo develops.

embryo transfer the transferring of a donor embryo into another woman's uterus for development.

endoderm the innermost layer of embryoblast cells that develop into the gastrointestinal tract, the liver, and the lungs.

endometritis inflammation of the lining of the uterus.

endometrium the uterine lining to which the fertilized ovum is attached.

endoscopy the employment of a lighted instrument to examine an inner body cavity.

epididymis the passage through which sperm travel from the testicles to the vas deferens.

epidural a local anesthesia administered to block pain from the lower part of the body during labor.

episiotomy during labor, an incision made from the vagina down toward the anus to create more room for the passage of the baby's head.

external cephalic version manipulation of the uterus to position the fetus head down.

fallopian tubes the tubes extending laterally from either side of the uterus, through which the egg passes each month.

fetal alcohol syndrome various mental and physical defects found in a newborn infant due to a mother's consumption of alcohol.

fetal monitor an instrument that measures fetal heart rate and uterine contractions during labor.

fetoscopy the introduction of a fetoscope (an optical device) through the mother's abdominal wall to visually examine a fetus, take skin and blood samples, or perform surgery.

fontanel one of the two soft spots in a baby's skull to allow molding through the birth canal and to allow for new brain growth in the first 18 months of life.

fraternal twins twins developed from two fertilized ova.

funic souffle sound of fetal blood rushing through umbilical vessels.

gene the part of a chromosome controlling hereditary traits.

gynecology the branch of medicine that deals with a woman's reproductive organs.

HELP syndrome hemolysis-elevated liver enzymes—low platelet count. A complication in pregnancy causing malaise, vomiting, and abdominal pain.

human chorionic gonadotrophin the placental hormone whose presence signals that a woman is pregnant.

hysteroscopy an examination of the uterus through an endoscope.

iatrogenic prematurity delivery of an infant earlier than expected due to an inaccurate estimate of gestational age given by a physician.

identical twins see MONOZYGOTIC TWINS.

implantation the attaching of the fertilized egg to the uterine wall, occurring one to nine days after fertilization.

incompetent cervix the inability of the cervix to remain closed during pregnancy, resulting in premature birth.

instillation abortion an abortion induced by an injection of saline or prostaglandin into the amniotic sac.

inversion of the uterus when the uterus is turned inside-out during birth, occurring when the umbilical cord is pulled before the placenta is detached.

in vitro fertilization a method of conception employed in women with damaged fallopian tubes, characterized by the gathering and mixing of ova and sperm, and the implantation of any fertilized eggs in the uterus.

Kegel exercises exercises to strengthen the muscles surrounding the vagina.

labor the regular and powerful contraction of the uterus during childbirth.

lactation the production and secretion of breast milk.

lactogenic hormone the pituitary hormone, prolactin, that stimulates lactation and the growth of breasts.

Lamaze method childbirth method developed by Dr. Fernand Lamaze, consisting of exercises and breathing techniques to help women pass through each stage of labor with a minimum of trauma.

lanugo the fine coat of downy hair covering the fetus from 20 weeks until birth.

latent phase the first phase of the first stage of labor, characterized by moderate contractions occurring at 5- to 15-minute intervals and lasting 30 to 60 seconds each.

Leboyer delivery a natural childbirth method in which the child is delivered in a peaceful atmosphere and with the smallest amount of pain and mental trauma possible.

Leopold's maneuvers the examination of a woman's abdomen to determine the position of the fetus.

letdown reflex the release of milk from the alveoli of the breasts to the milk ducts, a reflex caused by the hormone oxytocin.

linea nigra a dark line or streak running from the belly button to the pubic area, seen on many pregnant women.

lochia vaginal discharge of blood, mucus, and tissue after birth.

luteal phase the ovulation phase of the menstrual cycle.

mastitis an infection of breast tissue.

meconium the greenish black, odorless stools passed by the fetus soon after birth.

menarche the onset of the first menstruation.

mesoderm the central layer of the embryolast cells from which muscles, bone, blood, and connective tissue develop.

miscarriage a spontaneous abortion.

midwife a person who delivers or assists in delivering babies.

molding the process by which the infant's head changes shape or "molds" to facilitate delivery through the birth canal.

monozygotic twins twins that develop from a single ovum. Also known as identical twins.

morning sickness nausea and vomiting during pregnancy, now referred to as pregnancy sickness.

neonatal of or pertaining to an infant from birth to 28 days.

neonatologist a physician specializing in newborns.

nurse midwife a registered nurse who has graduated from a midwifery program.

obstetrics the branch of medicine that deals with pregnancy and childbirth.

ovary the gland that produces estrogen and progesterone and that contains eggs in various stages of development.

ovulation the discharge of an egg for possible fertilization by sperm.

ovum an egg or reproductive cell.

oxytocin the pituitary hormone that stimulates uterine contractions and the letdown reflex during lactation.

parturition the process of giving birth; labor.

perineum the area between the anus and the vulva.

periodic breathing common to most preterm infants, episodes of apnea or cessations of breathing.

pica the craving or eating of bizarre substances, such as starch or clay, during pregnancy.

placenta the temporary organ through which the fetus receives nutrients and exchanges oxygen and carbon dioxide from the mother.

polydactyly having an extra finger or toe.

posterior position presentation in which the head emerges face up.

postpartum after childbirth.

postpartum depression depression suffered by some mothers after childbirth, possibly related to hormone fluctuations.

premature labor any labor that begins before the 38th week of gestation.

presentation the part of the baby that emerges first from the vaginal opening; the position of the baby at birth.

preterm infant an infant with a gestational age less than 38 weeks.

progesterone the female hormone responsible for the thickening of the uterine lining before conception.

prostaglandins a group of compounds responsible for uterine contractions.

pseudocyesis the condition when a woman is convinced she is pregnant but is not; false pregnancy.

pudendal block a local anesthetic administered through injection into the vaginal area to numb the pelvic area.

puerperal psychosis severe postpartum depression requiring hospitalization.

quickening a mother's first perception of fetal movement.

recessive inheritance inheritance trait requiring genes from both parents.

sonogram an ultrasound picture of the uterus and fetus.

stillbirth birth of a dead fetus.

striae gravidarum stretch marks.

sudden infant death syndrome (SIDS) the mysterious death of an infant thought to be healthy; also known as crib death.

teratogen any substance or factor that harms the fetus.

transition the last phase of the first stage of labor, characterized by full dilation of the cervix and contractions arriving every one to three minutes and lasting 60 to 90 seconds each.

trimester any one of the three-month divisions in the nine months of pregnancy.

ultrasound high-frequency sound waves beamed into and reflected off the body to create pictures.

umbilical cord the cord connecting the placenta and the fetus.

umbilicus the navel.

vernix caseosa a white, fatty substance coating the skin of the fetus up until birth.

zygote the fertilized egg before it divides.

DIGESTIVE SYSTEM

alimentary canal collective term for the digestive parts extending from the mouth to the anus, including the mouth, the pharynx, the esophagus, the stomach, and the small and large intestines. Also known as the gastrointestinal tract.

amylase a digestive enzyme found in saliva and pancreatic juices.

anus the outlet for excrement at the end of the alimentary canal.

appendicitis inflammation of the appendix.

appendix a wormlike sac attached to the cecum of the colon and whose function is unknown.

bile a substance produced by the liver that aids digestion through emulsification of fats.

bolus a clump of chewed food ready to be swallowed.

carbohydrate sugars, starches, and cellulose.

cholesterol a waxy, fatty substance produced by the liver or ingested in the form of saturated fat.

chyme a soupy mixture of fragmented food particles and stomach chemicals resting in the stomach after a meal and waiting to be moved into the duodenum.

cirrhosis a chronic disease of the liver characterized by hardening of connective tissue and increased blockage of circulation, usually caused by chronic alcoholism.

colitis inflammation of the colon.

colon the principal portion of the large intestine.

Crohn's disease an inflammation of any part of the GI tract or alimentary canal (usually the ileum) that extends through all the layers of the intestinal wall.

diabetes sometimes called diabetes mellitus or sugar diabetes, a disease characterized by the body's inability to properly process carbohydrates (sugars and starches), resulting in an excess of sugar in the bloodstream; the main cause is the insufficient production of insulin by the pancreas, which reduces sugar in the blood.

diverticulitis inflammation of the sacs or pouches (diverticula) that have ballooned out through the walls of the colon (usually the sigmoid colon), sometimes causing fatal obstruction, infection, or hemorrhage.

duodenum approximately the first 10 inches of the small intestine.

dysphagia difficulty in swallowing.

emulsification the separation of fat in the form of tiny globules from surrounding fluid food mass.

endoscope an instrument used for examining the alimentary canal.

esophagus the food tube leading from the pharynx to the stomach.

fundus the large curvature of the stomach, bordering the esophagus.

gallbladder a small, pear-shaped sac under the liver that receives and stores bile made by the liver.

gallstones hardened masses of cholesterol forming in the gallbladder.

gastrectomy the surgical removal of part or all of the stomach.

gastrin a digestive hormone.

gastritis inflammation of the stomach.

gastroenteritis inflammation of the stomach lining.

glucose a simple sugar.

glycogen the form of sugar stored in the liver.

hematemesis vomiting of blood.

hemorrhoids enlarged veins inside or outside the anal canal.

hepatitis a viral infection of the liver causing inflammation, characterized by jaundice and fever.

hiatal hernia a disorder in which the lower end of the stomach or esophagus protrudes through the diaphragm.

hydrochloric acid a powerful stomach acid that aids in the digestion of food.

ileocecal valve the point where the small intestine meets the large intestine.

ileostomy the surgical removal of the colon.

ileum between the jejunum and large intestine, the last portion of the small intestine.

inguinal hernia a disorder in which a loop of intestine protrudes into the groin, often the result of strain from heavy lifting, coughing, or accidents.

insulin a hormone secreted by the pancreas that regulates carbohydrate metabolism by controlling blood sugar levels.

jaundice the yellowing of the skin and whites of the eyes due to the presence of bile pigments, a symptom of an abnormality in bile processing.

jejunum the part of the small intestine between the duodenum and the ileum.

large intestine the last and largest section of the alimentary canal.

lipase a pancreatic enzyme that speeds the hydrolysis of emulsified fats.

lipids fats that are insoluble in water but soluble in certain organic solvents.

liver the largest gland in the body, it aids digestion by producing bile.

lower esophageal sphincter (les) just above the stomach, the musculature that prevents gastric contents from backing up (reflux) into the esophagus.

pancreas a large gland behind the stomach that secretes insulin to help regulate blood sugar levels.

pancreatic juice an alkaline secretion of the pancreas aiding in the digestion of proteins, carbohydrates, and fats.

pancreatitis inflammation of the pancreas, usually caused by biliary tract disease or alcoholism.

parotid gland a saliva-producing gland in the back of the mouth.

pepsin a digestive enzyme secreted by the stomach.

peptic ulcer lesion in the gastric mucosal membrane, caused by the excess production of and contact with hydrochloric acid and pepsin.

peristalsis the rhythmic muscular contractions that push food through the alimentary canal.

peritoneum the membrane that lines the abdominal cavity and covers the abdominal organs.

peritonitis acute or chronic inflammation of the peritoneum.

portal vein the vein connecting the liver and the small intestine.

ptyalin a salivary enzyme that breaks down starches.

pylorus the part of the stomach connecting with the duodenum.

reflux the backing up of stomach contents into the esophagus, causing heartburn.

serotonin a common body compound found in the blood and having several functions, one of which is to inhibit gastric secretion.

small intestine between the stomach and the colon, the part of the alimentary canal that absorbs most of the nutrients from food for distribution to other organs and other parts of the body.

solar plexus a large network of nerves located behind the stomach and supplying nerves to the abdominal organs.

sphincter a muscle that opens and closes a body opening, such as the rectum.

trypsin an enzyme that helps digest proteins.

villi fingerlike projections lining the small intestine.

EARS

aero-otitis middle ear inflammation produced by changes in altitude.

anvil the middle of the three tiny bones that transmit vibrations in the middle ear. Also known as the incus.

auditory nerve the nerve that carries electrical impulses from the ear to the brain.

auricle the external portion of the ear. Also known as the pinna.

cauliflower ear deformed ear caused by repeated trauma, mainly seen in boxers.

cerumen earwax.

cochlea the spiral cavity of the inner ear containing the organ of Corti.

conductive deafness deafness caused by any defect of the external or middle ear.

Corti, organ of in the cochlea, it contains sensory cells that code sound waves into electrical signals, which are then sent to the brain.

Darwin's tubercle a point of cartilage in the upper part of the outer ear thought to be a vestige of a pointed ear by Charles Darwin.

eardrum the tympanic membrane.

equilibrium balance of the body, as maintained by the semicircular canal of the inner ear.

eustachian tube the canal leading from the back of the throat to the ear; it allows air pressure in the middle ear to equalize with air pressure outside in order to protect the eardrum from bursting.

hammer one of the three tiny bones that transmit vibrations in the middle ear. Also known as the malleus.

incus see ANVIL.

inner ear the interior portion of the ear that contains the cochlear and auditory nerve.

labyrinth the semicircular canal of the inner ear; the organ of balance.

labyrinthitis inflammation of the labyrinth, causing vertigo and dizziness.

lop ears drooping ears.

malleus see HAMMER.

middle ear on the inside of the eardrum, the portion of the ear containing the hammer, anvil, and stirrup as well as the eustachian tube.

ossicles the three bones of the middle ear.

otalgia earache.

otitis externa painful inflammation of the external ear canal and auricle caused by bacteria. Known as swimmer's ear because it is often contracted by swimming in contaminated water.

otitis media inflammation of the middle ear that sometimes causes severe, throbbing pain, usually in children.

otocleisis obstruction of the eustachian tube.

otology the study of ear diseases.

otoplasty plastic surgery on the ears, usually to repair cauliflower ears or lop ears.

otosclerosis a hereditary disorder characterized by the development of spongy bone over the stirrup, disrupting vibrations and causing progressive deafness. It is the most common form of conductive deafness.

pinna the external ear.

semicircular canal the labyrinth.

sensorineural deafness deafness caused by damage to the inner ear, to the auditory nerve or to the auditory cortex of the brain. Also known as nerve deafness.

stapes see STIRRUP.

stirrup one of the three tiny bones that transmit vibrations in the middle ear. Also known as stapes.

tinnitus ringing in the ears.

tympanic membrane the eardrum.

vertigo a sense that one is spinning or whirling around, a symptom of inner ear impairment.

EYES

aqueous humor the nutrient-rich fluid that fills the chamber between the cornea and the lens.

astigmatism distorted vision—usually affecting peripheral vision—due to abnormal curvature of the eye.

blind spot there are no photoreceptors where the optic nerve passes through the retina, thus the eye is literally blind to any images that fall there.

cataract a clouding of the lens, obscuring vision.

choroid membrane the layer of the eyeball containing blood vessels that nourish the eye.

color blindness an inability to identify color, usually red or green; it rarely affects females.

cones light-reactive nerve cells in the retina that are responsible for detecting color.

conjunctiva the mucous membrane lining the inner eyelid and the outer surface of the eyeball.

conjunctivitis inflammation of the conjunctiva.

cornea the transparent outer membrane of the eyeball.

crocodile tear syndrome shedding tears instead of salivating in anticipation of food, a rare disorder caused by the crossing of the nerves leading to and from the salivary and lacrimal glands, usually due to injury.

detached retina loss or deterioration of vision due to the retina becoming separated from the other layers of the eyeball.

diplopia seeing double.

dry eye syndrome inadequate functioning of the tear glands, producing dry eyes.

ectropion the turning-out of an eyelid so that it lies away from the eyeball.

entropion the turning-in of an eyelid, so that it scratches the eyeball.

epicanthus an extra skin fold covering the inner angle of the eye, normal in Asians and children with Down's syndrome.

esotropia a form of strabismus in which one eye is turned or crossed inward.

exophthalmos bulging of the eyeballs, caused by overactivity of the thyroid gland.

exotropia a form of strabismus in which one eye is turned or crossed outward.

floaters floating specks sometimes seen before the eyes; they're usually harmless, dead blood cells.

glaucoma increased intraocular pressure due to overproduction of aqueous humor or an obstruction of its normal flow; it causes visual defects or blindness.

grayout a blurring or temporary loss of vision in airplane pilots due to an oxygen deficiency.

helerochroma iridis the condition of having one blue eye and one brown eye, present in 2 out of every 1,000 people.

hyperopia farsightedness; the ability to see things far away but not close up.

keratitis acute or chronic inflammation of the cornea caused by an infection by herpes simplex type 1 virus.

lacrimal glands tear glands; they keep the eyes constantly moist.

lazy eye a loss or lack of vision in one eye due to misalignment of the eyes.

lens behind the iris, the transparent body that changes shape to focus on objects at various distances.

muscae volitantes the condition of seeing floating specks before the eyes.

myopia nearsightedness; the ability to see close up but not far away.

nystagmus jerking, involuntary movements of the eyes due to brain lesions or inflammation, alcohol or drug toxicity, or a congenital disorder.

ocular involving the eyes or vision.

oculomotor pertaining to movements of the eyes.

optic nerve the main nerve leading from the retina that transmits images in the form of electrical impulses to the brain.

orbit an eye socket.

photophobia extreme sensitivity to light, a symptom of an eye disease.

photopsia the condition of seeing flashes of light before the eyes, a symptom of an eye disease. Also known as scintillation.

pinkeye inflammation of the conjunctiva marked by redness of the eyeball.

pupil the dark spot surrounded by the iris; the iris makes it enlarge or shrink in response to light or strong emotion.

radial keratotomy a series of surgical incisions made in the cornea to cure nearsightedness, a procedure pioneered in the Soviet Union.

retina the innermost layer of the eyeball on which light rays are focused and converted to electrical signals to be sent to the brain.

retinitis pigmentosa a hereditary disorder characterized by progressive destruction of the retina's rods, resulting ultimately in blindness.

retinoblastoma a malignant tumor of the retina.

retinology study of the retina and its diseases and disorders.

sclera the white of the eye.

strabismus group of eye disorders including cross-eyes, walleyes, squinting, and general uncoordinated eye movement.

stye a staph infection of the eye producing a painful abscess at the margin of an eyelid.

trachoma a contagious disease affecting the conjunctiva and cornea that can result in blindness, commonly found in tropical regions.

20-20 vision normal vision at 20 feet.

vascular retinopathies a group of disorders caused by diminished blood flow to the eyes, causing visual defects.

vitreous humor the clear jelly in the large chamber behind the lens.

walleye strabismus with one or both eyes pointing outward. Also, an eye with a light-colored iris.

HAIR

achromotrichia lack of color in the hair; graying.

depilate to remove hair.

depilatory any substance that removes hair.

electrolysis removing hair with an electric needle.

hirsute hairy.

hirsutism abnormal hairiness on face and chest, especially in women. Also known as hypertrichosis.

male pattern baldness progressive balding thought to be caused by hormones.

melanocytes cells in the roots that give color to hair.

paratrichosis growth of hair in abnormal or odd places.

poliosis premature graying of the hair.

trichology the study of hair diseases.

widow's peak a V-shaped point of hair crowning the forehead.

BEARDS

à la Souvaroff a style in which the mustache joins with the sideburns, the chin left clean-shaven.

alfalfa early American slang for a beard.

anchor a short, pointy beard worn at the edge of the chin with a fringe extending up to the center of the bottom lip.

Assyrian a long beard having plaits or spiral curls.

aureole a rounded beard.

barbiche a small tuft of hair under the bottom lip. Also known as a barbula.

beaver early 20th-century slang for a beard or a man with a beard.

Belgrave a medium-length, neatly trimmed beard that may be square-cut, rounded, rounded with a point, or pointed.

burnside a mustache joined with sideburns, with the chin clean-shaven, named after General Ambrose Burnside in the 19th century.

cadiz a Spanish-style, pointed beard of medium length.

cathedral beard a long, flowing beard that broadens at the bottom like a fishtail, worn by clergy members in mid-16th to 17th century.

ducktail a neatly trimmed, long slender beard resembling the tail of a duck.

Dundreary whiskers whiskers grown long and hanging off the sides of the face while the chin is left clean-shaven.

forked a beard either combed or cut into two different branches or wisps. See SWALLOW-TAIL.

goatee a small, pointed beard, resembling that of a goat.

Imperial a long tuft of hair extending down from beneath the lower lip, named after that worn by Napoleon III in 1839.

Jewish a long, bushy, untrimmed beard, as that prescribed in the book of Leviticus in the Old Testament.

Lincolnesque a medium-length beard and sideburns worn without a mustache.

muttonchops side whiskers or sideburns trimmed to resemble mutton chops.

Old Dutch beard a short, square-cut beard with a clean-shaven upper and lower lip.

Olympian beard a very long, thick beard. Also known as a patriarchal beard.

pencil beard a thin ridge of beard extending from the bottom lip to the chin.

Raleigh a pointed beard, with the facial portion being closely trimmed, named after Sir Walter Raleigh.

Roman T a small, rectangular tuft hanging below the lower lip and accompanied with a straight or rectangular mustache to form the letter T.

Satyric tuft a chin tuft, as that worn by the Satyrs, the half-goat, half-man creatures from Greek mythology.

screw beard a short, slender beard that is twisted or twined, popular in the 17th century. Any twisted beard.

Shenandoah a spade beard.

spade a pointy or rounded beard resembling a spade.

stiletto a long, slender, pointed beard.

swallow-tail a thickly forked beard resembling the tail of a swallow.

tile a long, square-cut beard.

Trojan a thick, square-cut, curly beard of medium length.

Uncle Sam a beard as that worn by the cartoon figure Uncle Sam.

Vandyke a short, pointed beard usually worn without sideburns.

HAIRSTYLES

abstract a geometrical haircut in which one side is cut shorter than the other.

Afro kinky, puffed out hair, popular in the 1960s.

Afro puffs puffs of Afro-styled hair over each ear.

American Indian a style worn very long and straight and parted in the middle, sometimes worn in ponytails or braids.

bangs a fringe of hair worn over the forehead.

Beatle cut a bowl-like cut with sideburns, popularized by the Beatles in the early 1960s.

beehive a woman's high domelike hairstyle, reminiscent of a beehive, popular from late 1950s to mid-1960s.

bob a woman's short haircut, worn with or without bangs.

bouffant a style that is full and puffed out in an exaggerated fashion and held in place by lots of hairspray.

boyish bob a woman's very short haircut shingled in the back.

braids plaited hair worn down the back, over the shoulder or wound around the head.

bun a tight roll of hair held neatly at the crown of the head or the nape of the neck.

chignon a knot or roll of hair twisted into a circle or figure eight at the back of the head.

china doll short, straight hair having bangs in the front, a traditional Chinese cut.

classic pull-back long hair pulled back and tied with a ribbon or worn with a barrette.

Cleopatra hair worn long and straight down the sides, inspired by Cleopatra.

coif another word for a hairstyle.

corkscrew curls elongated curls resembling corkscrews, worn dangling at the sides.

cornrows hair braided into neat rows close to the head, a primarily black hairstyle.

crew cut a flattop, buzzcut.

dreadlocks see RASTAFARIAN DREADLOCKS.

ducktail a 1950s haircut in which the hair at the back of the head is combed to a point to resemble a duck's tail, worn by both sexes.

earmuffs a style parted in the middle with braids wound in circles about the ears.

elflocks matted or tangled hair.

empire cone a style in which the hair is pulled back smoothly through a conelike ornament and worn as a ponytail from the top of the head. The cone can also be wound with braids.

feather cut a woman's layered, slightly curled bob, popular in the 1960s and early 1970s.

fishbone braid a braid worn down the center of the back and resembling the spine of a fish. Also known as a French braid.

flattop crew cut.

flip a woman's style with ends forming a curl, worn with bangs.

French braid see FISHBONE BRAID.

French roll/twist a style in which the hair is pulled back and twisted into a roll or knot.

garçonne a woman's bob, worn by flappers in the 1920s.

Gibson girl a woman's puffy pompadour, popular early in the 20th century.

layered cut any style in which the hair is cut in graduated lengths around the head.

lion's tail a long piece of hair allowed to grow long down the back and tied with a cord to resemble a switch.

Mandinko the combination Mohawk, beard, mustache, and sideburns worn by Mr. T on television.

Mohawk a punk style in which all of the head is shaved except an upstanding brush 2 to 6 inches in height down the center of the head from front to back, inspired by the Mohawk Indians.

pageboy straight shoulder length or shorter hair having ends that are turned up, worn with bangs.

pigtails braids worn dangling on both sides of the head, popular with little girls.

pixie a short, layered style cut and combed to points around the face and forehead.

pompadour a woman's style in which the hair is swept up high from the forehead. Also, a man's style (popular in the 1950s) in which the hair is swept up high with no part from the forehead.

poodle cut short, curly hair, reminiscent of a poodle's coat.

porcupine a punk haircut characterized by long strands made to stiffen and stand up on the center of the head by mousse or gel.

punk any Mohawk, porcupine, dyed, shaved, sculpted, or spiked hair.

queue one long braid extending down the back.

Rastafarian dreadlocks a Jamaican style in which the head is covered with tight, dangling braids, shoulder length or longer.

Sassoon a woman's short, straight, skullcap-like cut with bangs and angled sides whose ends are turned under.

sculptured hair moussed or gelled and arranged in various designs. Also, hair having shaved-in designs, logos, and such like.

shag a long, shaggy bob with bangs.

shingle a tapering of the hair at the back of the head or neck.

spikes moussed or gelled hair formed into long spikes and often dyed.

topknot hair tied into a knot at the crown of the head.

Veronica Lake a woman's style with long hair parted to one side and partially covering one eye, popularized by actress Veronica Lake in the 1940s and revived in the 1960s.

wedge a style in which the front and sides are of equal length while the back is tapered close to the head, worn with short bangs; popularized by Olympic skater Dorothy Hamill in the 1970s.

HAIRSTYLES OF THE 18TH CENTURY

Adonis wig a flowing, white-powdered wig popularly worn by young European men from 1734 to 1775.

à la Belle Poule a woman's wig style crowned by a model of a three-masted ship.

à la Charme de la Liberté a woman's late-century style noted for its dressings of feathers, ribbons, and grasses.

à la Cybelle a woman's foot-high, towerlike style, as that worn by the goddess Cybele.

à la Grecque a man's style in which the hair is curled on each side and drawn into a horseshoelike fashion in back, popular in the 1780s.

à la Victime a French style popular in 1795; the hair was pulled up and away from the neck, as if in preparation for a decapitation by guillotine, and worn with a blood-red ribbon about the neck, inspired by the French Revolution.

à la Zodiaque a woman's high hairstyle dressed with ornaments of stars, the moon and the sun.

bag a wig of any type. Also a bag wig.

bag wig a man's wig in which the tail was enclosed in a black satin bag, from 1737 on. Also known as a purse wig. See BOURSE.

bourse the bag in which the tail of a bag wig was enclosed. Also known as a crapaud.

brigadier wig a wig having a double corkscrew tail tied with a bow at the nape of the neck, worn in the second half of the century.

cadogan wig a wig having a broad, straight tail folded back on itself and tied, popular in the 1760s. Also known as a club wig.

cauliflower wig a short, tightly curled, white bob wig worn by doctors and clergy in London.

gorgone a woman's style in which the hair was pulled high with loose, writhing curls, reminiscent of Medusa's serpent head.

lappet curl a corkscrew curl.

macaroni a huge, high, elaborate wig worn by dandies in the 1770s.

morning coiffure a woman's style in which hair at the back is pulled up and plaited, crossed at the crown, and then allowed to hang back to form a thick loop.

periwig a wig worn by men.

Piccadilly fringe a roll of hair near the forehead, worn by Englishmen in the first half of the century.

pigeon's wing periwig a man's wig having two horizontal rolls above the ears on either side of the head, from the 1750s to 1760s.

pigtail wig a man's wig with a long tail twirled and tied with a ribbon.

pincurls an artificial curl or curls pinned to the hair by a hairpin.

queue the tail of a wig.

snood a band or ribbon used to tie up a woman's hair.

spit curl a curl fashioned and secured to the forehead by spit.

washerwoman's style a woman's style in which hair is pulled up to form a bun at the top of the head; primarily English.

HAIRSTYLES OF THE 19TH CENTURY

à la concierge a woman's style in which long hair is pulled to the top of the head and pinned in a knot, popular from the late 19th to the early 20th century.

Apollo knot false hair coiled, looped, or plaited, and wired to stand up on the head, from 1826 on.

barley-sugar curl children's style composed of long drop curls.

beaver tail a broad, flat loop of hair hung over the nape of the neck, from 1865. Also known as a banging chignon.

blinkers a woman's style in which the hair was allowed to hang down the sides of the face.

caracalla cut a woman's short style having flattened, sausage-shaped curls.

chignon a knot or roll of hair worn at the back of the head by women.

curlicue a curl of a hair worn over the forehead by men.

giraffe mid-century woman's style in which hair is piled high in rolls, supported by a tall comb and dressed with flowers.

gooseberry wig a man's large, frizzled wig, worn in England.

Julian a woman's short hairstyle of the early 1800s.

Marcel wave woman's style in which waves were arranged around the head with a curling iron, popular in the 1890s.

neck coiffure a style in which the hair was pulled up in back and in front and gathered in curls on the crown of the head, popular in the 1890s.

MUSTACHES

à la Souvaroff a style in which the mustache joins with the sideburns, the chin left clean-shaven.

boxcar a rectangle with squared ends.

chevron like a chevron, broad in the center and narrowing toward ends that extend beyond the lips.

Clark Gable a neat, thin line.

handlebar short or long, usually thick, with ends turned up like bicycle handlebars.

Hindenburg a very long, thick mustache with turned-up ends.

horseshoe a long mustache that droops down over the chin.

Kaiser a mustache having turned up ends, as worn by Germany's kaiser in 1914.

mistletoe narrow mustache composed of two crescents, reminiscent of mistletoe leaves.

pencil line a very narrow mustache, sometimes divided in two at the center lip. Also, a line drawn on the upper lip.

pyramid a pyramid-shaped or triangular mustache.

regent a neat mustache resembling a rounded letter M or the twin peaks of round-top mountains.

Roman T a rectangular mustache worn with a narrow tuft hanging from below the lower lip, to form the letter T.

soupstrainer see WALRUS.

square button see TOOTHBRUSH.

toothbrush a short rectangle or square, as that worn by Charlie Chaplin and Adolf Hitler.

walrus a thick, broad mustache allowed to grow and droop over the upper and sometimes even the lower lip. Also known as a soupstrainer.

waxed a mustache in which the ends are waxed to create points or curves.

wings neatly trimmed mustache resembling bird wings.

HEART AND CIRCULATORY SYSTEM

aneurysm a ballooning-out of the wall of a vein, an artery, or the heart due to weakening of the wall by disease, injury, or congenital defect.

angina pectoris chest pain caused by insufficient blood to the heart muscle.

angiocardiography an X-ray of the blood vessels or chambers of the heart using a contrasting dye. The X-ray pictures resulting from the procedure are called angiograms.

angioplasty a procedure used to widen narrowed arteries by passing a balloon-tipped catheter into the diseased vessels and inflating the balloon.

aorta the large artery that receives blood from the heart's left ventricle and distributes it to the body.

aortic valve the heart valve between the left ventricle and aorta.

arrhythmia an abnormal rhythm of the heart.

arterioles muscular branches of arteries that when contracted slow blood flow and increase blood pressure.

arteriosclerosis a thickening and loss of elasticity of artery walls, also known as hardening of the arteries.

artery any vessel that carries blood from the heart to the body.

atherosclerosis a form of arteriosclerosis in which the linings of artery walls become thickened with deposits of fats, cholesterol, and other substances collectively known as plaque.

athletic heart syndrome an enlargement of the heart and slowing of heart rate in response to strenuous exercise; may also be accompanied by arrhythmias.

atria the two upper, holding chambers of the heart.

atrioventricular node special conducting tissue of the right atrium through which electrical impulses pass to reach the ventricles.

atrium either of the two upper chambers of the heart in which blood collects before being passed to the ventricles.

balloon angioplasty see ANGIOPLASTY.

blood clot a clotted mass of blood cells that normally stops the flow of blood at an injury site but can also form inside an artery wall narrowed by disease and cause a heart attack.

blood pressure the force exerted by the heart in pumping blood; the pressure of blood in the arteries.

blue babies infants having bluish skin, a sign of insufficient oxygen in arterial blood and indicating a heart defect.

capillaries tiny blood vessels that distribute blood between the veins and arteries.

cardiac pertaining to the heart.

cardiac arrest the cessation of the beating of the heart.

cardiology the study of heart function and heart disease.

cardiopulmonary resuscitation (CPR) the emergency procedure of chest compression and mouth-to-mouth breathing to help keep oxygenated blood flowing to the heart and brain in a cardiac arrest victim.

carotid artery either of the two major arteries in the neck that carry blood to the head.

catheterization an examination of the heart by passing of a thin tube (catheter) into a vein or artery and pushing it into the heart area.

cerebral thrombosis formation of a blood clot in an artery that supplies the brain.

cerebrovascular accident also known as stroke or apoplexy, an impeded flow of blood to the brain and its result.

cholesterol a fatty substance present in some foods and also manufactured by the liver; known to clog arteries over time.

cineangiography a motion picture taken of an opaque dye passing through blood vessels.

collateral circulation smaller "standby" arteries normally closed, but that may open to carry blood to the heart when a coronary artery becomes clogged.

congenital heart defect a heart defect present at birth.

congestive heart failure the inability of the heart to efficiently pump all the blood returned to it, causing blood to back up in the veins and fluid to accumulate in body tissues.

coronary arteries the two arteries arising from the aorta that provide blood to the heart muscle.

coronary artery disease narrowing of the coronary arteries that results in reduced blood flow to the heart muscle.

coronary bypass surgery surgery to improve blood flow to the heart muscle.

coronary occlusion an obstruction in one of the coronary arteries that slows or reduces blood flow to part of the heart muscle. Also known as coronary thrombosis.

cyanosis blueness of the skin, a sign of insufficient oxygen in the blood.

diastolic blood pressure the lowest blood pressure in the arteries, measured between beats of the heart.

digitalis a drug that strengthens the contraction of the heart muscle, helping to eliminate the accumulation of fluids in body parts related to congestive heart failure.

echocardiography a diagnostic technique using sound pulses and echoes to explore electronically the surfaces of the heart.

edema the accumulation of fluid in body tissues, caused by congestive heart failure.

electrocardiogram (ECG, EKG) a read-out of electrical impulses produced by the heart.

embolus a blood clot that forms in a blood vessel in one part of the body and then is carried to another part of the body.

endarterectomy surgical removal of plaque deposits in arteries.

fibrillation rapid, out-of-control contraction of individual heart muscle fibers, resulting in a partial or complete loss of pumping power in the chamber affected.

heart attack death of or damage to part of the heart muscle due to insufficient blood supply.

heart murmur extra "whishing" sound heard with heartbeat, caused by turbulence in bloodstream; a possible sign of disease.

hypertension high blood pressure.

ischemia decreased blood flow to an organ due to a restriction or obstruction of an artery.

ischemic heart disease coronary artery disease and coronary heart disease.

lipid a fatty substance insoluble in blood and partially responsible for clogging arteries.

mitral valve the heart valve between the left atrium and left ventricle.

myocardial infarction heart attack.

myocardial ischemia insufficient blood flow to part of the heart muscle.

myocardium the muscular wall of the heart that contracts and relaxes as it pumps blood.

nitroglycerin a drug that causes blood vessels to widen and therefore increase blood flow, used in the treatment of angina pectoris.

open heart surgery surgery performed on the opened heart while blood flow is diverted through a heart-lung machine.

pericarditis inflammation of the outer membrane surrounding the heart.

pericardium the outer membrane that surrounds the heart.

peripheral vascular disease diseased or clogged arteries and veins in the arms and legs.

plaque deposits of fat, cholesterol, and other substances in the linings of arteries.

pulmonary pertaining to the lungs.

pulmonary valve the heart valve between the right ventricle and the pulmonary artery.

rheumatic heart disease damage to the heart caused by bouts of rheumatic fever.

silent ischemia episodes of ischemia without accompanying pain.

sinoatrial node a mass of cells in the top of the right atrium that produces electrical impulses that cause the heart to contract.

sphygmomanometer an instrument used for measuring blood pressure.

stenosis the narrowing or constriction of an opening such as a blood vessel.

systolic blood pressure the highest blood pressure in the arteries, measured when the heart contracts or beats.

tachycardia excessively rapid heartbeat.

thrombolysis the breaking up of a blood clot.

thrombosis the formation or presence of a blood clot in a blood vessel or cavity of the heart.

thrombus a blood clot that forms in a blood vessel or cavity of the heart.

transient ischemic attack a strokelike attack caused by a temporarily blocked blood vessel.

varicose veins veins that have been stretched due to pooling of blood.

vascular pertaining to the blood vessels.

veins the blood vessels that carry blood from body tissues back to the heart; contrast with arteries.

ventricle either one of the two lower chambers of the heart.

ARTERIES

(Arteries carry blood away from the heart; veins carry blood back.)

Name	Area Supplied
acetabular	hip joint, top of thighbone
acromial	shoulder and upper back
alveolar	gums, teeth, and chewing muscles
angular	muscles that open and close eyelids; muscles controlling some facial expressions
aorta, abdominal	abdominal wall, diaphragm, abdominal organs, legs
aorta, arch	head, neck, arms
aorta, thoracic	chest, lungs, esophagus, diaphragm
appendicular	first portion of large intestine; appendix
auditory	inner ear
auricular	middle and outer ear, muscles of the lower skull and neck, scalp; salivary gland
axillary	pectoral muscles of chest; shoulder and upper arm muscles

basilar	cerebellum, pons (base of brain), inner ear
brachial	muscles of shoulder, arm, forearm, hand
bronchial	lungs and esophagus
buccal	gums, skin, and cheek; some chewing muscles
carotid, common	neck and head
carotid, external	front of face and neck, skull, back of scalp, dura mater
carotid, internal	forehead, front of brain, middle ear, eye, nose
celiac	esophagus and abdominal organs
cerebellar	base of brain, cerebellum
cerebral	brain
cervical	muscles of neck, shoulder, head
choroid	base of brain, optic tract
ciliary	iris and eye membrane
circumflex, femoral	muscles of the thigh and hip
circumflex, humeral	muscles of upper arm, shoulders
circumflex, iliac	muscles of lower back, lower abdominal wall, thigh
circumflex, scapular	muscles of upper back, back of upper arm, joint of shoulder
colic	group of arteries serving the colon
coronary	one of a pair serving the left or right atrium and ventricle of heart
cystic	gallbladder
dental	teeth and gums
digital	fingers or toes
dorsalis pedis	front of foot
epigastric, deep	lower abdomen
epigastric, superior	upper abdomen, diaphragm
esophageal	esophagus
facial	face, chewing muscles, tonsils, throat, lymph glands
femoral	lower abdomen, genitals, muscles and bones of thigh
frontal	forehead
gastric	lower end of esophagus, stomach
gastroduodenal	pylorus of stomach, duodenum, pancreas, bile duct
genicular	muscles of lower thigh; knee joint
gluteal	upper thigh, buttocks, prostate gland, bladder
hallucis	big toe, second toe
hemorrhoidal	rectum and anus, lower portion of descending colon
hepatic	liver, gallbladder, stomach, pancreas
ileocolic	appendix, cecum, ascending colon, last portion of small intestine
iliac, common	pelvic organs, genitals, lower abdominal wall
iliac, external	thigh and leg muscles
iliac, internal	pelvic organs, genitals, anal region
iliolumbar	greater psoas muscle, gluteal and abdominal muscles
infraorbital	eyeball muscles, tear gland, upper teeth, cheek, nasal area
innominate	right sides of neck and head, right shoulder, right arm
intercostal of aorta	chest wall, rib cage, muscles of upper back, spine
interosseus	forearm
intestinal	small intestine
labial	lips of the mouth
laryngeal	larynx
lingual	mouth and tongue
lumbar	back muscles, lumbar vertebrae, abdominal wall
malleolar	ankle area
mammary	breast, chest area
maxillary	ear, teeth, eye muscles, lacrimal gland, skin and muscles of face, tonsils, jaws
meningeal	skull, dura mater
mental	chin, lower lip
mesenteric, inferior	colon
mesenteric, superior	duodenum, small intestine, appendix

metacarpal	thumb, fingers
metatarsal	toes
musculophrenic	muscles of upper abdomen, diaphragm, lower ribs
nasal	nose, sinuses
nutrient	term for any artery serving a bone or bone marrow
obturator	bladder, pelvic muscles, hip joint
occipital	posterior neck muscles, back of ears and scalp
ophthalmic	orbit area, eye, sinuses
ovarian	ovary, fallopian tube, uterus
palatine	soft and hard palates, gums, tonsils, upper throat area
palpebral	eyelids, tear sac, eye membrane
pancreatico-duodenal	pancreas, duodenum, bile duct
penis	penis
perineal	base of penis
peroneal	back of leg, ankle joint, portion of foot
pharyngeal	throat, neck muscles, tonsil, ear, soft palate
phrenic	esophagus, spleen, diaphragm adrenal glands
plantar	bottom of foot
popliteal	thigh
profunda femoris	thigh, hip joint
pudendal	genitals, anal canal, muscles of inner thigh
pulmonary	lungs
radial	forearm and hand
renal	kidney, adrenal glands
sacral	rectum, sacrum, coccyx
scapular	shoulder, scapular, collarbone
sciatic	buttocks, hip area, anus
scrotal	scrotum
sigmoidal	sigmoid colon
spermatic	ureters of kidneys, spermatic cord, uterus
spinal	spinal cord
splenic	spleen, pancreas, portion of stomach
subclavian	muscles of neck and arms, shoulder, thoracic wall, spinal cord, brain
sublingual	sublingual gland, mucous membrane of mouth and gums
submental	skin of chin, muscles beneath chin
subscapular	shoulder joint, back of arm, back
supraorbital	orbit, eyelid, sinuses, forehead
suprascapular	neck, collarbone, shoulder blade, back
tarsal	toe muscles, portion of skin of foot
temporal	facial skin and muscles, eye and temple area, salivary gland
testicular	testicle
thoracic, lateral	front and back muscles of chest
thoracodorsal	side and back muscles of the chest
thymic	thymus gland
thyroid	neck, trachea, esophagus, larynx, thyroid gland
tibial, anterior	front of leg and ankle
tibial, posterior	back of leg and foot; knee area
tympanic	middle ear
ulnar	forearm, portion of hand
uterine	uterus, fallopian tubes
vaginal	vagina, bladder, rectum
vesical	prostate gland, bladder, ureters
volar arches	hand, fingers
zygomatico orbital	orbit

Blood

anemia a disease causing weakness and fatigue, due to a shortage of red blood cells or a deficiency of their hemoglobin content.

antibodies produced by the white blood cells, various proteins that fight and neutralize invading disease-causing organisms.

blood clot a jellylike mass of blood tissue formed by clotting factors to stop the flow of blood at the site of an injury.

blood count the number of red and white blood cells in a given volume of blood.

bloodletting the outmoded practice of intentionally bleeding a vein to let out supposed toxins.

blood pressure the pressure of the blood in the arteries.

bone marrow the soft material inside bones where most blood cells are manufactured.

coagulation the clotting of blood.

corpuscles blood cells.

cyanosis blue skin tone caused by a deficiency of oxygen in the blood.

embolus a blood clot formed in a vessel in one part of the body that travels to another part of the body.

erythrocytes red blood cells.

fibrin a factor in the blood that enmeshes blood cells and helps form a clot.

hemal pertaining to blood or blood vessels.

hematology the study of blood and its diseases.

hematoma a local swelling filled with blood.

hematopoiesis the process of blood cell manufacture in bone marrow.

hemoglobin the respiratory pigment in red blood cells.

hemophilia a disorder caused by a deficiency or absence of clotting factors in the blood, and characterized by uncontrollable bleeding, even from minor injuries.

hemorrhage copious or uncontrollable bleeding.

hemostasis the body's collective methods of controlling bleeding, including vasoconstriction and platelet clumping.

leukemia a disease of the blood and blood-manufacturing tissues, characterized by an increase in leukocytes or white blood cells and producing exhaustion and anemia.

leukocytes white blood cells.

pernicious anemia a severe form of anemia characterized by an abnormal development of red blood cells and accompanied by gastrointestinal disturbances and lesions of the spinal cord.

plasma a yellowish or straw-colored liquid made of protein and water in which blood cells float and circulate throughout the body.

plasma lipid the fat carried in blood.

platelets the blood component responsible for the clotting of blood.

red blood cells the blood cells that pick up oxygen in the lungs and distribute it throughout the body.

septicemia a blood infection.

sickle-cell anemia a hereditary disorder characterized by sickle-shaped or crescentlike blood cells that help protect against malaria but impede circulation and frequently cause premature deaths among blacks.

thrombocytes platelets.

thrombocytopenia the most common cause of bleeding disorders, characterized by a deficient number of circulating platelets.

thrombolysis the breaking up of a blood clot.

thrombus a blood clot.

white blood cells blood cells that manufacture antibodies for fighting and neutralizing disease-causing organisms.

VEINS

(Does not include veins that travel with arteries of the same name.)

Name	Area Drained
anterior jugular	front of neck
azygos	right side of chest wall
basilar	posterior base of brain
cavernous sinus	back of eye
cephalic	inner side of hand and forearm
common facial	side of face
coronary sinus	heart
coronary of stomach	stomach
diploic	skull
emissary	skull
external jugular	side of neck

great cardiac	heart ventricles
great cerebral	brain
great saphenous	inner side of leg and thigh
hemiazygos	left side of back and chest
hemorrhoidal	rectum, end of colon
hepatic	liver
inferior petrosal sinus	skull
inferior sagittal sinus	cerebrum of brain
inferior vena cava	abdomen, thighs, legs
innominate	head and neck
intercavernous sinus	one of a pair of large channels containing venous blood in the skull
internal cerebral	inner cerebrum
internal jugular	very large vein draining the brain, face, and neck
internal vertebral	spinal cord and spine
middle cardiac	back of heart
occipital sinus	cerebellum of brain near posterior base of skull
parambilical	navel area
plexus	any conglomeration of network of veins
portal	abdominal organs and intestines
posterior left ventricle	left ventricle of heart
prostatic	prostate gland
pudendal plexus	penis
pyloric	stomach
sinus	any large channel of venous blood
small saphenous	back of leg and foot
superior ophthalmic	eye area
superior petrosal sinus	brain
superior sagittal sinus	outer cerebrum
superior vena cava	head, neck, arms, chest well
transverse sinus	brain
vesical plexus	bladder, prostate gland
vorticose	eyeball

HORMONES

adrenalin also known as epinephrine, the fight-or-flight hormone released by the adrenal glands during times of stress, fear, anger, or loud noise. The release of the hormone increases heart rate and boosts the supply of oxygen and glucose throughout the brain and body.

anabolic steroid a class of steroids involved in muscle and bone growth and development.

androgen one of various masculinizing steroid hormones, most notably testosterone, dihydrotestosterone, and DHEA. Androgens help build and maintain bone and muscle and contribute to overall energy levels, skin elasticity, sex drive, and cardiovascular health.

androgen dominance a too-high ratio of androgens to estrogen or progesterone, which causes acne, greater facial and body hair, and possible premature balding.

andropause in middle-aged males, the rough equivalent to female menopause, with falling testosterone and DHEA levels causing increasing fatigue, fat production, muscle loss, and sleep disturbances.

bioidentical hormone a hormone made from plants such as soy and synthesized to mimic those produced naturally in the human body.

catecholamine a class of hormones, including epinephrine, norepinephrine, and dopamine, produced in the adrenal glands and released in stressful situations, as in a fight-or-flight situation or when blood sugar levels are low. Dopamine is also involved in generating the pleasurable feelings that come with rewarding experiences, especially involving food, sex, or drugs.

cortisol produced by the adrenal cortex, a stress hormone that, among other things, raises blood pressure and blood sugar and is involved in the deposition of fat.

DHEA dehydroepiandrosterone, an adrenal gland hormone that is converted to androgens and estrogen and is involved in maintaining stamina and energy levels as well as mental well-being.

dihydrotestosterone a more powerful form of testosterone that acts as a masculinizing force and, among other things, is implicated in male pattern baldness and prostate trouble.

endocrine system collective term for all of the body's glands that produce and secrete hormones.

endocrinology the medical field that deals with the body's glands and the hormones they secrete.

estradiol a form of estrogen that is involved in sexual behavior, breast development, and bone growth. According to the latest scientific studies, women with the highest levels of estradiol tend to have hourglass figures, are more self-confident, and are more likely to cheat on their long-term partners.

estrogen in women, produced primarily in the ovaries, and which includes estradiol, estrsone, and estriol, primarily female hormones responsible for everything from breast development to regulation of the menstrual cycle.

finger length ratio the ratio of length between the ring finger and the index finger, a proven indicator of testosterone exposure during fetal development and the consequent masculinization or feminization of some traits throughout life. Men typically have longer ring than index fingers, while the finger lengths in women are the same or the index finger is slightly longer. Longer ring finger lengths have been strongly correlated with assertiveness, aggressiveness, success in sports and the stock market, along with a higher probability of bisexuality.

follicle-stimulating hormone produced by the pituitary, a hormone involved in the development of puberty and in reproduction.

gastrin produced in the stomach, a hormone that stimulates the release of gastric acid or hydrochloric acid, to aid in the digestion of food.

ghrelin a hormone that, along with leptin, stimulates appetite. It is made in the stomach and pancreas.

gonadatrophic hormone secreted by the pituitary, a hormone that stimulates the ovaries and the testes.

human growth hormone (HGH) secreted by the pituitary gland, a hormone best known for stimulating height but is also involved in increasing muscle mass, the mineralization of bone, and the breakdown of fats.

hypothyroidism a deficiency in thyroid functioning, due most often to an imbalance with estrogen or with an iodine shortage, and characterized by an array of symptoms, including weight gain, fatigue, hair thinning, low sex drive, depression, and the feeling of being cold.

insulin hormone secreted by the pancreas, allowing the body's cells to absorb glucose and produce energy.

insulin resistance an abnormality in which tissue responds insufficiently to insulin and fails to take up glucose, from which energy is produced, resulting in a broad array of symptoms, including fatigue, brain fog, sleepiness, weight gain, and high blood sugar. Long-term problems often lead to type-2 diabetes and cardiovascular disease.

leptin produced by the fat cells, a hormone that regulates appetite, energy intake, and metabolism.

luteinizing hormone produced by the pituitary, a hormone that triggers ovulation and the production of testosterone.

orexin a hormone that stimulates food cravings and the desire to eat. It is also involved in maintaining wakefulness.

oxytocin a hormone that triggers the release of milk in the breast.

parathyroid hormone secreted by the parathyroid glands, a hormone that metabolizes calcium and phosphates throughout the body.

precocious puberty premature development of sexual characteristics, such as pubic hair, breasts, and enlarged genitals, experienced by preteens more commonly now than in years past due to hormonal abnormalities. Experts cite a wide range of possible causes, including increasing obesity rates, stress, exposure to chemicals, brain disorders, tumors, cysts, and infections.

progesterone a hormone that aids in regulating menstruation, pregnancy, and embryo development.

prolactin made by the pituitary and the breast, a hormone involved in keeping the breast full of breast milk during breast-feeding.

steroid any hormone involved in sexual, reproductive, and muscular development. They may also be central to metabolism and immune function. They include estrogen, testosterone, progesterone, and cortisol. See ANABOLIC STEROID.

thyroid hormone can refer to either thyroxine or triiodothyronine, which regulate metabolism, bone growth, protein synthesis, and the generation of body heat.

xenoestrogen any substance with estrogen-like effects, such as soy and some food additives. They are known to reduce sperm counts and increase breast cancer risk.

INFANTS AND BABIES

babble baby talk.

bassinet a baby bed.

bathinette a baby bathtub.

booties knitted shoes or boots.

carriage a stroller or baby buggy.

coddle to baby and spoil.

colic occurring from the age of two weeks to about four months, any unexplained distress, crying, or screaming from an otherwise healthy infant, possibly due to trapped gas in the abdomen.

coo to talk softly and lovingly to a baby.

cradle a rocking or swinging baby bed.

cradle cap a form of infant dermatitis, characterized by a yellowish, greasy crust on the scalp, and often appearing within the first three months. Also known as milk crust.

crow a contented, happy cry.

dandle to bounce a baby on one's knee or swing in one's arms.

diaper rash skin irritation caused by wet diaper.

incubator an environmentally controlled enclosure used to aid in the development of premature infants and to help prevent infection.

infanticide the murder of an infant.

fontanelle the soft spot on a baby's head, which slowly hardens after birth.

Moro reflex a normal startle reflex found in infants, characterized by spreading out and unspreading of the arms, along with crying, the absence of which may indicate motor or neurological damage.

octuplets eight siblings born at the same time.

pacifier a ring and a pliable nipple, which simulates the mother's nipple, that the baby sucks on to soothe itself.

papoose a Native American baby or baby carrier.

pule whining and whimpering.

quadruplets four siblings born at the same time.

quintuplets five siblings born at the same time.

septuplets seven siblings born at the same time.

sextuplets six siblings born at the same time.

squall a very loud cry.

stillborn a baby who is born dead.

teething the eruption and first appearance of an infant's teeth.

teething ring a pliable ring on which an infant chews to help relieve pain from teething.

test tube baby a baby conceived by in vitro fertilization.

toddling baby walking.

wean to gradually stop breast-feeding an infant.

wet nurse a woman hired to breast-feed the baby of a mother who is unable or does not wish to.

whimper to cry weakly.

witch's milk milk secreted from the nipples of some newborn infants, for up to three months, and believed to be caused by the influence of the mother's hormones. In folklore, it was thought to be used as food by the animal pets or familiars of witches. Also known as neonatal milk.

LUNGS AND BREATHING

alveolus a tiny air sac in which oxygen is transferred from the lungs to the blood.

apnea a temporary cessation of breathing, usually caused by too much oxygen or too little carbon dioxide in the brain.

asphyxia suffocation.

aspirate to inhale food or fluid into the lungs.

asthma a disease characterized by constriction of breathing passages and shortness of breath.

bronchiole one of the tiny tubes leading to an alveolus.

bronchitis inflammation of the bronchial tubes.

bronchodilator any medication prescribed to dilate the bronchial tubes.

bronchopneumonia inflammation of the bronchial tubes and the lungs; a common type of pneumonia.

byssinosis a lung disease caused by the inhalation of cotton particles.

carbon dioxide the waste gas expelled by the lungs in an exhale.

Cheyne-Stokes breathing in patients suffering grom congestive heart failure, breathing characterized by long periods of apnea followed by several deep breaths.

COLD chronic obstructive lung disease; a breakdown of the lungs resulting from long-term bronchitis and emphysema.

cystic fibrosis an inherited childhood disease characterized by the overproduction of mucus that obstructs the normal functioning of the lungs; accompanied by a susceptibility to infections.

devil's grip extreme and sudden pain in the chest that lasts two days or less; it is caused by inflammation of the chest cavity lining. Also known as acute pleurodynia.

diaphragm muscle that separates the abdominal and chest cavities; it is the main breathing muscle.

dyspnea shortness of breath.

emphysema a lung disease characterized by enlargement of the alveoli, causing breathing difficulties and possible damage to the heart.

farmer's lung lung condition caused by the inhalation of particles from moldy hay.

goblet cells lung cells that produce mucus.

hyperventilation excessive breathing with an intake of too much oxygen and exhalation of too much carbon dioxide, which may cause light-headedness, buzzing in the head, tingling of the lips, and a sensation of suffocation. Often brought on by anxiety, it may cause panic and fainting, but is usually relieved by breathing into a paper bag.

hypoxia inadequate oxygen in the lungs and blood.

intercostal muscles between the ribs, the muscles that aid in breathing.

larynx the upper portion of the respiratory tract; the voice box.

lobe one of five divisions that make up the lungs.

orthopnea having to sit up in bed in order to breathe adequately, a sign of abnormal heart function.

pharynx the throat.

pleura the membrane that envelops the lungs and lines the chest cavity.

pleurisy inflammation of the pleura, causing chest pain, especially when breathing deeply or coughing.

pneumonia a viral or bacterial infection of the lungs.

pulmonary pertaining to the lungs.

pulmonary edema excess fluid in the lungs.

respiratory centers portions of the brain that regulate breathing by monitoring levels of oxygen and carbon dioxide in the body.

spirometer a device that measures the amount of air inhaled.

stertorous breathing loud breathing, as in snoring.

stridor loud breathing caused by partial closure of the larynx.

trachea the windpipe leading to the lungs.

tuberculosis a communicable disease characterized by lesions in the tissues of the lungs.

wheeze raspy breathing due to mucus in the trachea or bronchial tubes.

MUSCULAR SYSTEM

abductor a muscle that pulls a body part away or out from center. Opposite of adductor.

abductor hallucis extending from the base of the big toe to the heel, the muscle that pulls the big toe away from the other toes.

abductor pollicis brevis extending from the base of the thumb to the hand, the muscle that bends the thumb and pulls it away from the fingers.

abductor pollicis longus from the base of the thumb to the forearm, the muscle that straightens the thumb.

adductor a muscle that pulls a body part in toward center. Opposite of abductor.

adductor brevis extending from the pubic bone to the femur, it adducts (moves inward), flexes, and rotates the thigh.

adductor hallucis from the foot to the base of the big toe, the muscle that flexes and pulls the big toe inward.

adductor magnus from the pubic bone to the femur, the muscle that flexes, rotates, and pulls the thigh inward.

adductor pollicis from the hand to the thumb, the muscle that pulls the thumb into a grasping position.

adductors, fifth finger and toe the small muscles on the back of the hand and foot that pull the little finger and little toe away from the other digits.

anconeus extending from the upper arm to the forearm, the muscle that straightens the elbow.

aryepiglottic the muscle that closes the entrance to the larynx.

auricularis in some people, a vestigial muscle that moves or wiggles the outer ear.

biceps brachii the strong upper arm muscle.

biceps femoris extending from the femur to the fibula, the muscle that flexes the knee and straightens the hip.

brachialis from upper arm to forearm, the muscle involved in bending the elbow.

buccinator the jaw muscles involved in retracting the angle of the mouth.

chondroglossus on the sides of the tongue, it depresses the tongue.

ciliary the eye muscle that makes the eye more convex to aid in focusing.

constrictor of pharynx constricts the throat muscles when swallowing.

coracobrachial from the shoulder blade to the upper arm, the muscle that flexes and pulls the arm inward.

corrugator forehead muscle that wrinkles the forehead and pulls the eyebrows together.

cremaster from the lower abdomen to the pubis, the muscles that elevates the testicles.

cricothyroid the group of muscles that work the vocal cords.

deltoid from the collarbone to the upper arm, the muscle that lifts, flexes, and extends the upper arm.

depressor a group of muscles that pull the corner of the mouth and bottom lip down.

depressor, nasal septum muscle that constricts the nostrils.

diaphragm between the chest and the abdomen, the muscle involved in inhalation.

dilator of nose muscle that widens the nostrils.

dilator of pupil eye muscle that widens the pupil.

epicranial the scalp muscle involved in raising the eyebrows.

erector clitoris a sexual muscle, it causes the clitoris to become erect.

erector penis a sexual muscle, it causes the penis to become erect.

erector pili on the skin, the tiny muscles that make body hair stand on end, causing goose bumps.

extensor carpi radialis from the humerus to the wrist bones, the muscle involved in straightening the wrist.

extensor carpi ulnaris from the humerus to the wrist bones, the muscle involved in straightening the wrist.

extensor digitorum, feet from the heel to the toes, the muscle that straightens the toes.

extensor digitorum, hands from the upper arm to the back of the hand, the muscle that straightens the fingers.

extensor hallucis from the fibula to the heel bone, the muscle that straightens the big toe and helps turn the ankle up.

extensor pollicis from the forearm to the thumb, the muscle that straightens the thumb and pulls it away from the fingers.

flexor carpi radialis from the humerus to the wrist, the muscle that bends the wrist.

flexor carpi ulnaris from the humerus to the wrist, the muscle that bends the wrist.

flexor digitorum, feet from heel bone to toes, the muscle involved in bending toes.

flexor digitorum, hands from forearm to fingers, the muscle involved in flexing or bending the fingers.

flexor hallucis from fibula to foot, the muscle that flexes the big toe.

flexor pollicis from forearm and wrist to thumb, the muscle that flexes the thumb.

gastrocnemius extending from the femur to the heel, the muscle that bends the ankle down.

gemellus from pelvis to thigh, the muscle that rotates the femur outward.

genioglossus from the lower jaw to the tongue, the muscle involved in sticking out and returning the tongue.

glosso palatine in the soft palate, the muscle that lifts the tongue.

gluteus maximus, medius, and minimus from the pelvis to the upper thigh, the muscles that straighten the hip and pull the leg away from the body.

gracilis from pubic bone to tibia, the muscle that pulls the leg inward or toward the other leg.

hamstring running down the back of the thigh, the three muscles that flex the knee.

hiacus from pelvis to femur, the muscle that flexes the hip joint.

iliocostal extending from the ribs to the spine, the muscle that straightens the spine and aids in sideways movement of the trunk.

infraspinatus from shoulder blade to upper arm, the muscle that rotates the arm sideways.

intercostal in the rib area, muscles that draw the ribs together and aid in breathing.

interossei in the hands and feet, muscles that pull the digits toward one another.

latissimus dorsi from the spine to the upper arm, the muscle involved in extending, rotating, and pulling the arm in toward the body.

levator ani forming a sling in the pelvic region, the muscle that supports the pelvic organs.

levator scapulae from the neck to the shoulder blade, the muscle that lifts the shoulder.

levator of upper eyelid the muscle that raises upper eyelid.

levator of upper lip the muscle that raises upper lip and dilates nostril.

lingual a muscle running the length of the tongue and involved in changing its shape.

longissimus the back muscle involved in straightening the spine.

longus capitus from the neck to the base of the skull, the muscle involved in bending the head.

lumbrical in the hands, the muscles that flex the fingers.

masseter from the cheekbone to the mandible, the muscle involved in chewing, especially in closing the mouth and clenching the teeth.

mylohyoid from the lower jaw to the neck, the muscle that elevates the floor of the mouth.

nasalis in the nose area, a muscle involved in some facial expressions.

oblique, abdominal extending from the ribs to the middle of the abdomen down to the pubic area, the muscle that flexes and rotates the vertebral column and supports the abdominal wall.

oblique, eyeball in the orbital cavity, a muscle involved in the eye's rotation.

oblique, head extending from the neck to the base of the skull, a muscle involved in rotating the head.

obturator from the pubis to the thigh, a muscle that rotates the thigh outward.

orbicularis oculi from the orbit to surrounding skin, muscles that close the eyelids.

orbicularis oris in the mouth area, the muscle involved in closing the mouth and pursing or puckering the lips.

palmaris from the forearm to the palm of the hand, a muscle that deepens the "hollow" of the palm.

pectineal extending from the pelvis to the thigh, a muscle that pulls the thigh in toward the other leg and flexes the hip.

pectoral extending from the clavicle, sternum, and ribs to the shoulder blade and upper arm, the muscle that flexes, rotates, and pulls the arm in toward the body.

peroneus from the leg to the foot, the muscle that helps flex and extend the ankle.

piriformis from the pelvis to the thigh, a muscle that aids in turning the thigh outward.

plantaris from the lower thigh to the heel, a muscle that bends the ankle down.

popliteus in the knee area, a muscle that rotates the knee inward.

pronator extending from the upper arm to the forearm, a muscle that rotates the forearm.

psoas from the lower back to the thigh, a muscle involved in bending the trunk and hip.

quadratis femoris in the pelvic and thigh area, a muscle involved in rotating the thigh.

quadratis lumborum from the last rib to the hipbone area, a muscle involved in bending the spine sideways.

rectus abdominus extending from the sternum to the pubis, the muscle that bends the spine forward.

rectus capitis extending from the neck to the skull, the muscle involved in bending the head forward and back.

rectus femoris from the upper thigh to the knee area, a muscle that straightens the knee.

rectus oculi in the orbital area, a muscle involved in rotating the eyes.

rhomboid from the neck to the shoulder blades, the muscle that draws the shoulders backward.

risorius in the mouth area, a muscle that pulls the corners of the mouth down.

sartorius from the hip to the tibia, a muscle involved in flexing the thigh and knee.

scalene from the neck to the first ribs, muscle that inclines the neck to either side.

semispinalis from the upper chest to the base of the skull, a muscle that inclines the head back.

serratus extending from the lower back, ribs, and chest, muscle that elevates ribs to aid in breathing.

soleus from the upper leg to the heel, a muscle that flexes the foot and aids in balance.

sphincter ani a muscle that closes the anus.

sphincter pupillae a muscle that contracts the pupil of the eye.

sphincter urethrae in the pubic area, a muscle that tightens the passage of the bladder.

sphincter vaginae in the pubic area, a muscle that constricts the vaginal opening.

spinalis extending from the neck, chest, and back, muscles that straighten the head and spine.

stapedius the middle ear muscle that moves the stapes.

sterno thyroid from the sternum to the Adam's apple, the muscle that draws the larynx downward.

styloglossus the muscle that lifts and retracts the tongue.

supinator extending from the upper arm to the lower arm, a muscle that rotates the forearm so that the palm of the hand faces up.

supra spinatus from the scapula to the humerus, a muscle that pulls the arm away from the body.

temporal from the temple to the mandible, a muscle that closes the mouth.

teres major from the scapula to the upper arm, a muscle that rotates the arm inward.

teres minor from the scapula to the upper arm, a muscle that rotates the arm outward.

thyroepiglottis the Adam's apple muscle that closes the larynx and trachea.

tibialis anterior from the lower leg to the foot, a muscle that flexes the foot up and in.

tibialis posterior from the back of the leg to the foot, a muscle that flexes the foot down and in.

transversus abdominus from the lower ribs across the abdomen, a muscle involved in bending the spine forward and supporting the abdominal wall.

trapezius from the top of the neck to the shoulder blade and shoulder, a muscle that raises shoulder and pulls it back

triceps brachii from the upper arm to the forearm, a muscle that straightens the elbow.

vastus from the thigh to the lower leg, a muscle that straightens the knee.

Muscle Diseases and Disorders

Aran-Duchenne disease a disease characterized by a progressive wasting away of muscles.

ataxia lack of muscle coordination.

atrophy withering of muscle when not used for long periods.

bursa a fluid-filled sac composed of connective tissue often present over bony projections, between tendons, and between movable areas or joints to ease friction.

bursitis inflammation of bursa.

contracture a shortening and immobilizing of a muscle; a permanent contraction.

epicondylitis inflammation of the forearm extensor tendons causing elbow and forearm pain and a weak grasp. Also known as tennis elbow.

muscular dystrophy a disease characterized by a progressive wasting of muscles, usually beginning in childhood.

myalgia muscle pain.

myasthenia gravis a disease characterized by a wasting of muscles, particularly those used in swallowing.

myokymia muscle twitching.

myopathy disease of muscle.

myosarcoma malignant tumor of muscle.

myositis an inflamed muscle.

tendinitis inflammation of a tendon.

NERVOUS SYSTEM

Brain

alexia the inability to understand the written word, a symptom of a brain condition.

amusia loss of the ability to play a musical instrument, due to a brain condition.

amygdala an almond-shaped part of the limbic system involved in producing and regulating emotion, especially fear and aggression, and is the center of the fight-or-flight response. Hyperactivity of the amygdala is seen in people with depression and social phobia. People with bipolar disorder have been noted to have smaller amygdala.

anomia the inability to remember names, due to a brain disorder.

anterior referring to any part toward the front.

anterior commissure a connecting fiber between the right and left hemispheres.

aphasia the inability to speak or articulate clearly, usually caused by a stroke.

apoplexy a stroke.

appestat the portion of the brain that regulates appetite.

apraxia the loss of muscle coordination, due to a brain condition.

arachnoid one of three protective membranes covering the brain and spinal cord.

asemia an inability to comprehend speech or the written word, due to a brain condition.

astroblastoma a malignant brain tumor.

autonomic nervous system the part of the brain and nervous system that, without conscious effort, controls breathing, digestion, blood flow, etc.

basal ganglia a knot of nerve cells, thought to be involved in motor function, found in the cerebrum.

beta rhythm the low-voltage electrical brain wave that predominates when someone is awake and alert.

blood-brain barrier a system that filters out harmful chemicals or substances from the blood and prevents them from entering and possibly damaging the brain.

brain stem the lowest and most primitive portion of the brain, located at the top of the spinal cord and involved in breathing.

Broca's region an egg-shaped patch in the left frontal cortex; it controls muscle coordination of the face, tongue, throat, and jaw and is also involved with the processing of music.

central nervous system a collective term for the brain and spinal cord.

cerebellum the portion of the brain in the back of the skull and beneath the cerebrum; it is responsible for muscular coordination and balance and may also be involved in the consolidation of long-term memories of frightening events.

cerebral cortex composed of gray matter, the heavily folded, topmost portion of the front of the brain, involved in attention, consciousness, thought, reasoning, language, and memory. It is the latest portion of the brain to evolve.

cerebrospinal fluid a clear fluid that cushions the brain and spinal cord to protect them from blows.

cerebrum the large portion of brain extending around the top of the skull; it is responsible for higher thought processes, such as perception, memory, and reasoning.

concussion unconsciousness and brain swelling caused by the brain striking the skull, due to a blow.

convolution one of several deep folds in the cerebrum.

corpus callosum the structure made of strands of fibers that connects the right hemisphere of the brain with the left.

cortex the outer surface and folds of the cerebrum.

cranium the top of the skull.

delta waves the high-voltage brain waves that predominate when someone is asleep.

dorsolateral prefrontal cortex a portion of the prefrontal cortex involved in reading and concentration.

dura mater the outer covering of the brain.

dysphasia difficulty in speaking or understanding speech, due to a brain condition.

electroencephalogram otherwise known as an EEG, a graphical recording of the electrical activity of the brain.

electroencephalograph the machine that records the electrical activity of the brain.

encephalitis inflammation of the brain.

encephalomeningitis infection of the brain and dura mater.

encephalon the brain.

encephalosclerosis hardening of the brain.

epilepsy a brain condition characterized by electrical disturbances that cause seizures and loss of consciousness.

forebrain the front portion of the brain, the latest to evolve, after the midbrain and the hindbrain.

frontal lobe the left and right lobes, located at the front of the cortex, in front of the forehead, the center of reasoning, judgment, and planning. Damage to this area, through blows to the head or illness, may cause frontal lobe syndrome, a mental disorder characterized by short attention span, tactless or insensitive behavior, impulsiveness, and criminal behavior.

fusiform gyrus a fold or convolution in the temporal lobe, active in face recognition.

Geschwind's territory in the parietal lobe of the cortex, a region that connects Broca's region with Wernicke's area and is thought to be involved in childhood language acquisition.

gray matter the gray or darker portions of the brain containing concentrated neuron cells and including the cerebral cortex, thalamus, basal ganglia, and the outer layer of the cerebellum. Gray matter is found in lower concentrations in people with bipolar disorder and schizophrenia, but it is unknown if it is the cause or the effect.

gyrus any one of the elevated convolutions at the surface of the cerebrum.

hemisphere the left or right division of the cerebrum.

Heschl's gyrus in the temporal lobe, a convolution involved in language and music processing.

hindbrain the oldest part of the brain, evolving before the midbrain and the forebrain, at the back of the head.

hippocampus in the limbic lobe, a seahorse-shaped area involved in the formation and storage of memory, which is known to shrink beginning in middle age, causing, most notably, deficiencies in face-name associations. The hippocampus is also involved in triggering memories in response to smells.

hydrocephalus a postbirth condition characterized by fluid buildup around the brain, causing enlargement of the skull.

hypothalamus located below the cerebrum, the part of the brain that regulates body temperature and blood pressure.

idiot savant syndrome injury to the left hemisphere of the brain before, during, or after birth, causing the right hemisphere to enlarge and overcompensate. The sufferer has below-average left-brain functioning while having superhuman right-brain functioning.

inferior temporal gyrus in the temporal lobe, a fold involved in the recognition of objects.

intraparietal sulcus in the parietal lobe, a sulcus involved with language and the spelling of words.

lateral temporal cortex part of the temporal lobe involved in rhyming words.

left caudate portion of the left hemisphere involved in the process of back-and-forth switching of language use in bilingual people.

left inferior parietal cortex portion of the inferior parietal cortex involved in remembering unfamiliar faces.

left prefrontal cortex portion of the prefrontal cortex involved in remembering unfamiliar faces.

limbic lobe in the cerebrum, a lobe along the corpus callosum that contains the hippocampus and the cingulate gyrus.

limbic system in the upper brain stem, the old or reptilian brain that regulates hunger, thirst, sex, fighting, and basic emotion.

lobe one of five sections of the cerebrum—the frontal, limbic, parietal, occipital, and temporal—roughly divided by deep folding.

medial prefrontal cortex portion of the prefrontal cortex involved in social memory.

medulla oblongata the base of the brain; it regulates respiration and circulation.

meningitis inflammation of the covering of the brain.

microencephalon an abnormally small brain.

midbrain the portion of the brain that evolved after the hindbrain but before the forebrain, at the center of the head.

neglect a bizarre brain condition in which one hemisphere of the brain is damaged, causing the sufferer to perceive only one side of his environment.

neocortex the latest part of the brain to evolve, which includes the frontal, temporal, parietal, and occipital lobes, the heavily wrinkled outer layer of gray matter surrounding the cerebrum; it is known to be involved with conscious thought, language, and sensory perception.

neuron one of millions of specialized nerve cells that carry electrochemical impulses in the brain.

nucleus accumbens a grouping of neurons in the forebrain, involved in laughter, pleasure, and the placebo effect.

occipital lobe a lobe of the cerebrum, at the back of the head, the center of visual processing and reading skills.

operculum in the inferior frontal gyrus, a portion of the brain involved in the coordination of other brain areas.

orbitofrontal cortex part of the frontal lobe that has been implicated in regulating personality, social functioning, sense of responsibility, and mood.

paragraphia confused or distorted handwriting, caused by a brain condition.

parietal lobe the topmost lobe of the cerebrum, the center of sensory processing involving touch, pressure, pain, and temperature. Parts of the parietal lobe are also involved in attention and language.

Parkinson's disease a disease characterized by a shuffling gait, muscular rigidity, and uncontrollable tremors, thought to be due to a chemical imbalance in the brain.

pituitary attached to the hypothalamus, the gland that controls most of the hormones in the body.

pons a bundle of nerve fibers forming a bridge connecting the cerebellum and the medulla oblongata with the frontal lobe and other brain areas.

posterior parietal cortex the back portion of the parietal lobe, involved with face recognition and communicating socially.

prefrontal cortex at the very front of the frontal lobes, the portion of the brain involved in planning and decision making.

primary auditory cortex in a gyrus of the upper part of the temporal lobe, the part of the brain that processes sound.

primary motor cortex in the posterior of the frontal lobe, part of the brain involved in movement.

primary visual striate cortex in the occipital lobe, a processing area for visual images.

prosopagnosia the inability to recognize faces, including those of close family members, due to a brain condition. The sufferer may recognize the faces, however, as soon as he hears them speak.

reticular formation the part of the brain stem that regulates wakefulness and attention; it is the part of the brain that is shut off by anesthesia.

right parietal lobe part of the parietal lobe involved in processing numbers.

sinistrality the right-brain dominance over the left brain that produces left-handedness.

somatosensory neocortex in the parietal lobe, the area involved in processing touch sensations, including pressure, pain, positioning, and movement.

stereoanesthesia the inability to identify objects by touch, due to a brain condition.

sulcus any cleft or groove in the cerebrum.

superior temporal gyrus in the temporal lobe, a gyrus containing the primary auditory cortex.

supplementary motor area in the frontal lobe, a processing area for the control of movement.

suprachiasmatic nucleus part of the hypothalamus that regulates the body's circadian rhythm or biological clock.

synesthesia the confusion of senses (seeing sounds, hearing sights, etc.), a mysterious brain condition.

temporal lobe a lobe of the cerebrum, above the hindbrain, an area involved in hearing and the processing of memory and the naming of things.

thalamus at the top of the brain stem, the structure known as the "great relay station" because it conveys signals between the brain stem and the rest of the brain. It is also the origination of the sensations of heat, cold, pain, and pressure.

water on the brain hydrocephalus.

Wernicke's area auditory processing area involved in processing language.

wet brain a disease of chronic alcoholism, characterized by fluid buildup and mental deterioration.

white matter brain tissue composed largely of axons insulated with myelin. Women have more white matter in their neocortexes than men do, while men have more gray matter than women do. See GRAY MATTER.

NERVES

Names	Function and Location
abducens	supplies eye muscles
accessory	supplies neck muscles, voice box, shoulders
acoustic	supplies the inner ear, deafness results when damaged. Also known as the auditory nerve
alveolar	supplies muscles of the mandible and sensation to teeth
ampullary	supplies inner ear and affects balance
auricular	sensation to the outer ear
axillary	muscles of the shoulders and surrounding skin

buccal	sensation to cheek, mucous membranes of mouth and gums. Also known as buccinator
cardiac	supplies the heart
carotid	in the neck, it serves the cranial blood vessels and glands of the head
cervical	muscle and skin of the neck, shoulders, and arms
chorda tympani	taste sensations in tongue; salivary glands
ciliary	contracts and dilates the pupil of the eye
cranial	12 pairs of nerves attached to the base of the brain; olfactory, optic, oculomotor, trochlear, trigeminal, abducens, facial, acoustic, glossopharyngeal, vagus, accessory, hypoglossal
cutaneous	sensation to all skin areas of the body
digital facial	skin sensation to fingers and toes; also, muscles of the face
femoral	muscles and skin of hip and thigh
frontal	skin of forehead and upper eyelid, frontal sinus
genitofemoral	sensation to skin of thigh, testicles, and the lips of the vagina
glossopharyngeal	supplies tongue, palate, and pharynx
gluteal	muscles of the buttocks
hemorrhoidal	muscles and skin of the rectum area
hypogastric	pelvic organs
hypoglossal	muscles of the tongue
iliohypogastric	muscles and skin of abdomen and buttocks
ilioinguinal	muscles of the abdominal wall, skin of thigh, scrotum, and labia
infraorbital	supplies upper teeth, nasal floor, facial skin beneath the eyes
interosseous	forearm muscles
labial	sensation to the lips
lacrimal	lacrimal gland and skin of upper eyelid
laryngeal	muscles of the larynx, esophagus, trachea, and tongue
lingual	floor of mouth and a portion of the tongue
lumbar	muscles and skin of the lower back and pelvic organs, sensation to the skin of lower abdomen and legs
mandibular	supplies chewing muscles; sensation to the lower teeth
maxillary	sensation to the skin of the upper face, palate, and upper teeth
median	muscles of the forearm; sensation to the wrist and hand
mental	sensation to the skin of the lower lip and chin
nasal	sensation to the skin of the nose
nasociliary	sensation to the eye and the eyelids
nasopalatine	sensation to the nasal septum and mucous membrane of the hard palate
obturator	hip and knee joints, inner side muscles of the thigh; sensation to the skin of all these regions
occipital	sensation to the scalp over the top and back of head; sensation to the back of the ear and back of the neck
oculomotor	eyeball muscles
olfactory	supplies the olfactory bulb and is responsible for the sense of smell
ophthalmic	sensation to the forehead, eyeball, and sinus area
optic	supplies the retina of the eye; vision is impossible without it
palatine	sensation to the gums, mucous membranes of hard palate, soft palate, and tonsils
palpebral	sensation to the eyelids
peroneal	supplies the knee joint; sensation to the skin of the leg, ankle, and foot
petrosal	serves parts of the palate and salivary glands
phrenic	diaphragm
plantar	toe muscles

plexus	collective term for any group or conglomeration of nerves
popliteal	muscles around the knee
pterygoid	jaw muscles and joints
pudendal	penis and clitoris; skin of the anus
radial	muscles of the upper arm and forearm; also supplies sensation to the skin of the arm and hand
recurrent laryngeal	larynx
sacral	pelvic organs, thigh muscles; also, sensation to these areas
saphenous	sensation to the skin of the inner side of the leg and foot
scapular	muscles that move the shoulder blade
sciatic	large nerve extending from the lower back down the back of the thigh; it supplies the skin and muscles of the thigh and leg
scrotal	sensation to the skin of the scrotum
splanchnic	groups of nerves serving the stomach, gallbladder, liver, pancreas, intestines, and other organs
supraclavicular	sensation to the skin of the neck, shoulders, and chest
supraorbital	sensation to the forehead and upper eyelid
thoracic	12 pairs of spinal nerves supplying skin and muscles of the back, arms, and abdominal wall
thoracic, lateral anterior	pectoral muscles of the chest
thoracodorsal	supplies latissimus dorsi muscle
tibial	skin and muscles of leg and foot
trigeminal	skin and muscles of face and jaw
trochlear	eyeball muscle
ulnar	muscles of the forearm, hand; sensation to the skin in little and ring fingers; responsible for painful "funny bone" sensation when struck
vagus	muscles of the throat, larynx, heart, lungs, abdominal organs
zygomatic	skin of cheek and temple

NOSE

anosmia inability to smell.

barosinusitis a sinus inflammation caused by a difference in atmospheric pressure inside and outside the nose.

columella the lower, front portion of the septum.

deviated septum a septum that has become crooked due to surgery, trauma, or abnormal growth; it often causes headaches or sinusitis; or it may block breathing through one nostril.

epistaxis a nosebleed.

nasal polyps benign nasal growth or tumors.

nasopharynx the nose and throat.

olfactory pertaining to the sense of smell.

olfactory bulbs extensions of the brain that relay odor signals to the brain.

olfactory epithelium in the roof of the nose, two yellow brown patches of membrane that trap odor molecules and act as smell receptors.

olfactory nerves transmit smell signals to the olfactory bulbs and to the brain.

osmology the study of the sense of smell.

parosima a distorted sense of smell, occurring in some cases of schizophrenia.

phantosmia odor hallucinations, suffered by some mentally ill patients.

philtrum the divot just below the nose and above the upper lip. Also known as the rhinarium.

postnasal drip mucus from the back of the nose that discharges down the throat.

rhinencephalon the portion of the brain concerned with smell.

rhinitis inflammation of the lining of the nose.

rhinology the study of the nose and its diseases and disorders.

rhinophyma a condition causing enlargement and redness of the nose. Also known as rummy nose, whiskey nose.

rhinoplasty plastic surgery on the nose; a nose job.

rhinorrhea runny nose.

septum the thin wall of cartilage separating the two nasal passages.

sinuses the four groups of air-filled, mucus-lined chambers in the facial bones: frontal, ethmoidal, sphenoidal, and maxillary.

sinusitis an inflammation of the sinuses, often resulting from the common cold.

vibrissae hairs in the nose.

ORGANS AND GLANDS

adenoids organs of unknown function in the back of the throat behind the nose.

adrenal glands resting above the kidneys, the glands that secrete a wide array of hormones, including adrenalin and cortisone. Also known as the suprarenal glands.

anus the end portion of the gastrointestinal tract whose muscular action eliminates feces.

apocrine glands sweat glands.

appendix near the large intestine, a vestigial organ whose function is unknown.

bladder in the lower abdomen, a storage sac for urine secreted by the kidneys.

bone marrow the soft tissue in the middle of bones that manufactures new blood cells.

brain the organ of mental and nerve processes, divided into two hemispheres and several suborgans.

A. cerebrum: outer and uppermost portion of the brain, responsible for higher brain functions, such as conscious thought.
B. cerebellum: behind and beneath the cerebrum at the back of the skull, the portion of the brain responsible for muscle reflexes, coordination, and equilibrium.
C. medulla oblongata: the lowest portion—oblong in shape—of the brain below the pons and extending to the spinal cord; it transmits nerve impulses.
D. pons: located below the cerebellum, it receives and transmits nerve impulses.

bronchial tubes extending from the trachea to the lungs, the tiny tubes that process air in and and out of the lungs.

breasts the outer chest organs that secrete milk.

cecum a pouch located where the large and small intestine join.

colon part of the large intestine extending from the cecum to the rectum, it absorbs water and pushes wastes toward the rectum.

Cowper's glands in men, two pea-shaped glands that secrete lubricant for the epithelium during sexual stimulation.

duodenal glands in the duodenum, tubular glands that secrete an alkaline substance to neutralize digestive acids.

duodenum the first portion of the small intestine, it receives bile from the liver and gallbladder and digestive juices from the pancreas.

esophagus the food tube extending from the throat to the stomach.

fallopian tubes two tubes extending laterally from either side of the uterus to the ovaries; the eggs from the ovaries pass through the fallopian tubes and are fertilized there.

gallbladder located on the underside of the liver, it stores bile manufactured by the liver.

gastric glands tubular glands of the stomach that secrete hydrochloric acid and pepsin.

greater vestibular glands on either side of the vagina, glands that secrete mucus for sexual lubrication.

heart the organ that pumps blood throughout the body.

ileum portion of the small intestine extending from the jejunum to the cecum.

intestinal glands glands in the intestine that secrete digestive hormones.

jejunum portion of the small intestine extending from the duodenum to the ileum.

kidneys two bean-shaped organs located in the lower back below the ribs; they regulate blood constituents and water balance throughout the body and discharge urine into the bladder.

lacrimal glands located in the upper portion of the orbit, glands that secrete tears.

larynx the upper part of the respiratory tract containing the vocal cords.

liver the large organ beneath the diaphragm that produces bile and metabolizes fats, carbohydrates, proteins, minerals, and vitamins.

lungs in the chest, five air-processing lobes that oxygenate and remove carbon dioxide from blood.

mammary glands the breast glands that produce milk.

ovaries an either side of the uterus, the female sex organs that produce progesterone, estrogen, and eggs.

pancreas near the duodenum, the organ that manufactures insulin and digestive juices.

parathyroid glands behind the thyroid in the neck, four small glands that produce parathyroid hormone for the regulation of calcium and phosphate metabolism.

parotid glands in front of each ear, the salivary glands.

penis the male sexual organ that conveys urine from the bladder and sperm from the testicles.

pharynx the passage for air and food; the throat.

pituitary gland important gland at the base of the skull, it secretes hormones that control metabolism and growth and the regulation of other glands.

prostate gland in men, a chestnut-shaped gland surrounding the urethra; it secretes the fluid in which sperm are transported in an ejaculation.

pylorus the outlet of the stomach that regulates the flow of food into the small intestine.

seminal vesicles located above the prostate gland in men, they store and discharge semen.

spinal cord from the base of the brain to the lower back, a cord containing nerves that send nerve impulses to and from the brain.

spleen beneath the diaphragm, an organ that destroys old blood cells.

stomach in the upper left portion of the abdomen, the organ that breaks down food through churning and acid action and then sends it on to the small intestine for digestion into the body.

testicles two small, ball-like organs in the scrotal sac that produce sperm and secrete male hormones.

thymus gland located beneath the sternum, it is thought to be useful in development up to the age of two, after which it degenerates.

thyroid gland on either side of the trachea, it manufactures thyroxin, which regulates body metabolism.

tongue the organ of taste; aids in chewing, swallowing, and speech.

tonsils the lymph glands located at the back of the mouth, which frequently become infected and swollen; their function is unknown.

trachea the windpipe leading to the lungs.

ureters the two urine-conveying tubes leading from the kidneys to the bladder.

uterus in women, the pelvic organ in which an embryo and fetus develops.

vagina the female sexual organ through which sperm is passed and through which a newborn is delivered.

PSYCHOLOGY AND PSYCHIATRY

abasia see ASTASIA.

abreaction the psychoanalytic process of reducing anxiety by reliving through speech or action the experiences that cause anxiety.

accident-prone referring to a person whose neurotic desire for attention manifests itself by an unusual number of accidents or injuries.

achiria a hysterical state in which a person feels he has lost one or both of his hands.

acting out the external expression, through behavior, of an internal conflict.

aeroneurosis airplane pilot's neurosis characterized by restless anxiety.

affect the outward presentation or expression of oneself or one's mood, as through body language, tone of voice, facial expressions, all of which can be read for signs of distress or depression.

affective disorder any psychological disorder arising from the emotions.

akathisia extreme restlessness, marked by pacing, fidgeting, foot-tapping, sometimes caused by psychotropic medications.

alethia dwelling excessively on past events.

altruism an unselfish concern for others or assistance to others without desire for reward.

ambivert a person with a combination of extroverted and introverted personality traits.

amnesia the total loss of memory of past events.

anaclisis the psychological attachment to a person who reminds one of his mother or father during childhood.

anniversary reaction anxiety or depression that may occur on the anniversary of a past loss or traumatic event.

anomie feelings of not being a part of society; alienation.

anorexia nervosa a psychiatric disorder characterized by extreme dieting to the point of emaciation.

anosognosia in stroke or brain damage victims, a lack of awareness of and indifference toward one's medical condition.

antidepressant any one of various medications, such as Prozac, used to change brain chemistry and treat clinical depression.

antisocial personality a personality characterized by impulsiveness, absence of conscience, and a complete disregard for others. Formerly known as a sociopath or psychopath.

anwesenheit the perception or feeling of someone's presence nearby, even though nobody is there, a normal symptom of the grief process.

anxiety uneasiness and apprehension, sometimes disabling.

anxiety hierarchy a list of situations given by an individual that are ranked for how much anxiety they produce, from slight to extreme.

aphagia inability to eat.

aphasia loss of speech or the ability to comprehend speech, often a symptom of brain disease.

asocial lacking interest in other people.

astasia hysterical state in which the person believes he or she has lost the ability to stand or walk. Also called abasia.

atavism the reverting to a primitive behavior or state of mind.

attachment a child's bond with a parent or caregiver.

attention deficit disorder (ADD) in some children, a disorder characterized by an inability to pay attention accompanied by impulsiveness.

aura a sense of strangeness, altered consciousness, or déjà vu that precedes or accompanies an epileptic seizure.

autism poorly understood brain disorder characterized by withdrawal from reality and absorption in inner fantasies.

aversion therapy a method of teaching someone to avoid a negative behavior, such as cigarette smoking, through unpleasant associations or punishment.

aversive conditioning changing someone's behavior by punishing them.

avoidant personality disorder a disorder in which one suffers from distorted thinking and irrationally avoids feared people, places, or things. Agoraphobia and social phobia fall into this category.

behaviorism a school of psychology that holds that valid data can come only from objective observation and experimentation.

belief-bias effect a behavior in which one's reasoning ability is skewed or corrupted by one's biases, values, attitudes, etc.

biofeedback with the help of a feedback machine, the self-regulating of heart rate, blood pressure, and brain waves to achieve desired results such as deep relaxation.

biometeorology the study or science of the effects of various weather patterns on human health or behavior.

bipolar disorder mental illness characterized by alternating periods of elation and depression. Also known as manic depression. See MANIC-DEPRESSIVE PSYCHOSIS.

blanking out losing one's train of thought, speech, or action, possibly indicating anxiety or exhaustion.

blocking a sudden dropout or interruption in the free or spontaneous flow of speech, possibly indicating a troubling or uncomfortable thought.

blunted affect a toned-down or bland presentation of one's emotional state.

body dysmorphic disorder a disorder in which the sufferer falsely believes that a particular body part is deformed or defective when it is not.

body image one's concept of one's own body, especially its attractiveness, which is highly prone to both negative and positive distortion.

borderline personality disorder a disorder characterized by persistent instability, impulsivity, and unpredictability accompanied by a chronic sense of emptiness and suicidal impulses.

bulimia an eating disorder characterized by bingeing followed by intentional vomiting.

burnout extreme disillusionment, stress, and exhaustion, most often referring to one's work experience.

Capgras syndrome the delusion that someone has been replaced by an impostor. The sufferer may also think that he himself has been replaced, a syndrome seen in paranoid schizophrenia and other brain disease.

cardioneurosis a neurotic manifestation of anxiety characterized by pain in the heart, palpitations, and a sensation of suffocation.

cataphasia frequent repetition of the same word or phrase.

catatonic stupor in which the person becomes motionless and mute.

catharsis the reduction of a negative emotion or impulse by the verbal expression or acting out of that emotion or impulse.

classical conditioning the teaching of an individual to relate one stimulus, such as a bell, to another stimulus, such as food, as in Pavlov's dogs.

classical paranoia an isolated paranoia revolving around a single subject in one's life, in which the person may otherwise be normal.

closure the final acts and thoughts involved in putting behind oneself any psychological trial or turmoil.

codependency an unhealthy relationship in which one is manipulated by the other two suffers from a serious problem such as a neurosis or substance abuse.

cognitive dissonance a clashing of thought processes that causes mental distress, as when someone who strongly believes murder is wrong kills someone. The person must maintain a positive image of himself and therefore rationalizes or justifies his actions in order to rid himself of psychological distress. See CONSONANCE.

cognitive reprogramming replacing negative thoughts with positive thinking to change a person's perception of himself or the world around him.

comorbidity the suffering of two or more disorders simultaneously.

compensation an ego defense in which a person compensates for deficiencies by striving for superiority in other areas.

compulsion any ritualistic behavior, often senseless, that a person feels must be carried out.

compulsive personality a personality characterized by tenseness, rigidity, overconscientiousness, and an obsession for trivial details.

conduct disorder often evolving from oppositional defiance disorder and appearing in early adolescence, a range of behavior problems, including verbal and physical abuse, cruelty to animals, truancy, stealing, fire setting, vandalism, and more.

confabulation a fantasy, sometimes mixed with fact, that unconsciously becomes a subject's memory of an event and may be strongly influenced by the power of suggestion, as in false child abuse claims. A false memory.

conformity the altering of one's behavior to fit in and mimic that of one's peers, a result of peer pressure.

consensual validation determining if one person's perception of reality matches with another's.

consonance a harmony between one's thoughts and actions.

conversion the unconscious process through which stress is converted into a physical, physiological, or psychological symptom.

conversion reaction a neurotic reaction in which overwhelming anxiety manifests itself in a physical way through bodily paralysis or through uncontrollable emotional outburst.

coprolalia inappropriate but involuntary utterances of socially unacceptable words and sentences, as seen in some people with Tourette's syndrome.

coprophagia the eating of feces.

coprophilia abnormal interest in feces.

Cotard's syndrome a delusion in which one believes he does not exist or that parts of his body do not exist, seen in schizophrenia.

culture shock a combination of symptoms, including stress, anxiety, depression, alienation, and homesickness, suffered for the first several months after moving to a foreign land.

cyberbullying the harassment, belittling, or threatening of someone via the Internet, e-mail, texting, blogs, social Web pages, etc.

dacnomania see MANIA.

decompensation the process of psychologic deterioration as a result of severe or long-term stress.

defense mechanism any thought or belief system employed to protect the ego from a lowering of esteem.

deindividualization the loss of social inhibitions and acting out of aggressions and impulses due to anonymity in a crowd or anonymity behind a mask or costume.

déjà vu the haunting feeling that one has experienced something or seen something before, even though there is no conscious memory of it.

delirium tremens alcohol poisoning characterized by hallucinations, trembling, and paranoia.

delusion a false belief about oneself or the world held despite evidence to the contrary.

delusional disorder a disorder characterized by frequent, irrational thoughts about being followed, poisoned, infected with a disease, lied to, or, sometimes, being the subject of someone else's infatuation. The disorder, however, does not include outlandish delusions on the level of aliens removing part of one's brain or leprechauns living under one's bed.

dementia loss of intellectual faculties with accompanying emotional disturbances due to organic brain disorder.

demonomania see MANIA.

denial an ego defense through which any harsh reality, such as the possibility of dying prematurely or that one is grossly overweight, is disbelieved or vigorously rejected.

dependent personality disorder a disorder characterized by passivity, helplessness, indecisiveness, and an overdependency on other people.

depersonalization a dissociative reaction characterized by feelings of unreality, separation, isolation, and a loss of identity.

depression feelings of sadness, ranging from a temporary case of the blues, which is easily cured through pleasurable activities, to clinical depression, which requires medical intervention.

derailment going off one's conversational track into unrelated subjects.

derealization an uncomfortable perception or feeling of unreality or strangeness.

desensitization the cure of a fear or phobia by gradual, step-by-step exposure to the source of the fear.

detachment social aloofness, due to apathy, denial, intellectualization, etc.

Diagnostic Statistical Manual a comprehensive classification system with criteria for diagnosis, used by mental health professionals. Commonly known as the DSM.

diffusion of responsibility the tendency for people in groups to fail to take action in an emergency due to the belief that "someone else" will act.

disinhibition the complete loss of normal human inhibition, allowing the freedom to act on animal or primitive impulses, sometimes caused by drug use or brain injury.

displacement a defense mechanism involving the transfer of feelings or actions from an unacceptable to an acceptable form.

dissociation a collective term for the various symptoms that occur when anxiety is handled by a splitting off of part of the personality and the breaking up of the sense of self, with symptoms ranging from a sense of unreality and loss of identity to fainting.

dissonance inconsistency between one's actions and one's attitudes.

distractability one's level of attention and ability to focus. May sometimes refer to a short attention span.

dominance in a social hierarchy, one's leadership and command over others, a behavior or standing that varies widely according to age, status, physical prowess, gender, intelligence, verbal skills, aggressiveness, testosterone levels, and the ability to network and form alliances with others.

doraphobia see phobia.

double blind an experiment in which neither the investigator nor the subjects know which group is receiving a real treatment and which a placebo.

dysfunction poor or maladjusted functioning; unhealthy behavior.

dyslexia a learning disorder in which a reader perceives letters and words backward or in the wrong order or may not see some letters or words at all.

dyspareunia genital pain experienced during intercourse, unrelated to any identifiable physical cause, seen in victims of rape and molestation.

echolalia a disorder in which the person repeats the last words heard.

echopraxia the involuntary mimicking of another's body movements and gestures.

ecopsychology the science of calming one's mind or relieving anxiety and depression through such natural outdoor activities as backpacking, gardening, or creating compost heaps.

ego in psychoanalytic theory, the personality component that involves rationality and governs the self.

egocentrism the inability to see someone else's point of view.

Electra complex an unconscious sexual desire of a daughter for her father.

electroconvulsive therapy electric shock therapy administered to the brain.

electroencephalograph (EEG) a device that measures the electrical activity of the brain.

emotional contagion the spreading of similar feelings throughout a group, as when one family member in a foul mood can cause others to act badly as a response, a phenomenon at the forefront of mob behavior.

emotional intelligence the ability to regulate and master one's emotions in order to think more clearly, to make better decisions, and to avoid trouble with others.

empty-nest syndrome the feelings of loss, depression, and anxiety experienced by a parent whose grown children have all moved out of the house.

enuresis bedwetting.

EQ short for emotional quotient, the emotional equivalent of IQ.

ethnocentricity believing your own beliefs and values are the only right ones; cultural bias.

ethnocentrism the belief that one's own culture and way of life are superior to all others.

etiology the causes of a disorder.

euphoria a feeling of great happiness.

evolutionary psychology the study of behavior as it has evolved through natural selection, as in the universal fear of snakes or inhibition around strangers or the tendency to choose physically robust or attractive mates, with many traits and personality quirks thriving because of their long-term survival value.

exhibitionism the compulsive desire to reveal one's genitals.

existentialism the philosophical belief that people have the freedom to make choices, decide the meaning of reality, and take responsibility for their existence.

expansive mood a mental state characterized by the free expression of one's thoughts and moods, without inhibition.

explosive personality a person prone to explosive outbursts.

extinction the fading and ultimate extinguishing of a behavior or thought process that maintained a phobia or other emotional dysfunction.

extroversion a personality trait characterized by an outward focus rather than an introspective one, marked by outgoing social behavior or great enjoyment in the company of others.

Eye Movement Desensitation and Reprocessing (EMDR) a therapeutic technique in which the eyes are intentionally moved rapidly back and forth while a past trauma is discussed and processed, resulting in diminished depression and anxiety.

factitious disorder a rare behavioral disorder in which one feigns illness by creating symptoms, for example by striking oneself to create bruises, or injecting fluid into a limb to simulate a tumor.

false memory see CONFABULATION.

fetishism a sexual deviation characterized by an attraction to inanimate objects, such as shoes, or to things like hands and feet, instead of to people.

fight-or-flight response a mental and physical alarm stage that releases adrenaline and other hormones into the bloodstream to prepare the body for fighting of fleeing.

file drawer effect the tendency of some research scientists to downplay, hide, or fail to publish study results that are negative or contrary to what they are looking for.

fixation the failure to complete the maturation process in a particular stage of development.

flattened affect an absence of emotional expression, particularly in one suffering from depression or mental illness.

flight of ideas accelerated speech, with rapid leaping from topic to topic, a symptom of mania.

flooding exposing a phobic person to his or her feared object or thing, in order to get the person over it.

folie à deux madness shared by two, a delusion suffered by two people simultaneously, as when a strong person in a household transmits his faulty belief onto his housemate.

folie à plusieurs madness of many, any delusion held by several people simultaneously.

formication a hallucination in which bugs are thought to be crawling all over one's body or under one's skin.

free association the psychoanalytic method of revealing the unconscious by asking a patient to say whatever word pops into his mind first in response to a stimulus word.

free-floating anxiety vague feelings of fear or anxiety without any observable cause or source.

Fregoli's syndrome a delusion in which the sufferer believes that different people are really just one person who is really good at donning disguises, named after Italian actor Leopoldo Fregoli, who was known on the stage as a quick-change artist.

Freudian slip an inadvertent utterance that reveals the speaker's true or unconscious feelings; a slip of the tongue.

frontal lobe syndrome a spectrum of symptoms or behaviors that suggest the possibility of brain damage in the frontal lobe. The most notable symptoms include a short attention span coupled with tactless, insensitive, impulsive, and sexually inappropriate behavior, along with indifference toward any negative consequences for one's actions. Sufferers of the syndrome have difficulty staying employed due to their offensive behavior and in fact often end up in jail. A high percentage of murderers have been found to have frontal lobe damage, most often caused by head trauma, brain tumor, or infections.

frustration-aggression theory a theory that holds that aggression occurs in response to frustration.

fugue state a dissociative reaction to anxiety in which a person runs away and has no memory of his actions over a period of time.

GAD see GENERALIZED ANXIETY DISORDER.

galvanic skin response changes in the electrical conductivity of skin as detected by a galvanometer; used as an emotional indicator.

gender dysphoria a distaste or revulsion for the behavioral or physical characteristics of one's own sex.

generalized anxiety disorder a disorder characterized by frequent, free-floating anxiety, which may or may not have an identifiable cause.

Gestalt therapy group therapy featuring one person in the "hot seat" to role-play, explore feelings, fantasies, dreams, and so forth.

glossolalia speaking in tongues.

grandiose delusion overblown feelings of self-worth and importance, rising to the level of delusional thinking.

grandiosity overblown feelings of self-worth, attractiveness, and power, which in extreme cases may be considered delusional.

groupthink cultlike behavior in which peer pressure forces members of a group to think or act alike, even when it may be irrational, erroneous, unproductive, or dangerous.

gustatory hallucination a hallucination involving taste.

habituation getting so accustomed to a stimulus that one may stop noticing it, as one who lives next door to a dog who barks all day.

hallucination a false perception; seeing, hearing, feeling, or smelling something that isn't there.

hallucinogen any substance or drug known to cause hallucinations.

hallucinosis symptoms of disordered perception—including auditory, visual, and tactile hallucinations—occurring in people withdrawing from severe alcohol abuse.

halo effect the overbroad perception of someone who exhibits a positive trait as being good in other ways as well.

Hamilton Rating Scale for Depression a measure of the severity of one's depression, based on a multiple-choice questionnaire.

Hawthorne effect the tendency for people to act differently when they are being observed, which can potentially skew research results.

hebephrenia a rare form of schizophrenia characterized by regressive behavior and a constant silly grin.

hedonism the theory that humans seek pleasure and avoid pain and that happiness represents the greatest good.

histrionic personality a personality characterized by dramatic attention seeking, excitability, egocentricity, and overdependency.

hyperactivity a childhood disorder characterized by excessive activity and a failure to inhibit motion or complete tasks.

hypergamy the selection of a mate or spouse with higher status than oneself, as younger women pursuing older, wealthier, more powerful males, an evolutionary survival strategy.

hypermnesia the strikingly vivid and disturbing recall of a traumatic event, causing anxiety, depression, and intrusive memories and thoughts, the opposite of amnesia.

hyperphagia pathological overeating.

hypersomnia excessive sleepiness.

hyperventilation a common reaction to anxiety, rapid breathing that reduces carbon dioxide in the blood, causing light-headedness, incoordination, palpitations, and a sensation of needing more air—generally resolved by breathing into a paper bag.

hypervigilance a state of heightened arousal and anxiety in which the sufferer sharply monitors his environment for signs of danger and often has an intense startle response, a symptom of post-traumatic stress disorder.

hypnagogic designating the mental state that occurs just before falling into sleep, known to cause hallucinations, which are considered normal.

hypnopompic designating the mental state that immediately follows the first stage of waking and which can sometimes produce hallucinations.

hypnotherapy therapy conducted with the patient under hypnosis.

hypnotic trance a dreamlike state of increased suggestibility.

hypoactive sexual desire disorder the lack of desire or sexual fantasies, with no evidence of a physical cause such as low testosterone, thought to be due to sexual trauma in childhood.

hypochondriasis an excessive anxiety over aches and pains and overall physical health.

hypomania a mild form of mania in which a person sleeps less, is unusually cheerful and active, and has grandiose or racing thoughts. It can mimic ordinary happiness but in fact may cause overconfidence and impaired judgment.

hysteria a neurotic state characterized by episodes of hallucinations, amnesia, and other mental aberrations.

id in psychoanalytic theory, the component of personality concerned with such instinctual urges as hunger, thirst, sex, and aggression.

idealization projecting overly positive attributes onto oneself or others.

implosive therapy a therapy technique in which a patient is harmlessly frightened as much as possible until anxiety is alleviated.

imprinting the learning of behavior patterns during sensitive periods of growth early in life.

impulsiveness the tendency to act without thinking.

inadequate personality a personality that is inept socially, emotionally, and intellectually.

inappropriate affect behavior, tone of voice, or facial expressions that are opposite of what would normally be expected in a particular context, as when someone laughs after someone dies or appears gloomy after a happy event.

incoherent not making sense; beyond understanding.

insight therapy a therapy technique that attempts to reveal a patient's hidden motives behind a specific behavior.

insomnia sleeplessness; trouble falling or staying asleep.

instinct an inborn, motivational drive, such as the sex drive or the drive to run from danger.

intellectualization overblown or abstract analysis used to rationalize disturbing feelings or troubles.

intermittent explosive disorder a disorder most often found between late adolescence and the late 20s, characterized by out-of-control, angry outbursts that may include physical abuse, thought to be caused by a shortage of the neurotransmitter serotonin.

introspection the examination of one's self and thought processes and feelings, resulting in heightened self-awareness.

introversion a personality trait characterized by an inward or introspective focus, marked by an enjoyment of solitary pursuits and comfort in one's own company.

James-Lange theory a theory that physiologic reactions to an outer stimulus produce the experience of emotion.

koro in Chinese culture, an irrational fear that the penis will retract into the abdomen and cause death.

Korsakoff's psychosis alcoholic psychosis characterized by distorted thinking and loss of memory.

lability an unstable state characterized by rapidly changing moods or behaviors.

lapsus linguae a slip of the tongue.

latency in psychoanalytic theory, the development period between age six and puberty, wherein little occurs in the way of psychosexual development.

latent content in Freudian theory, the underlying or hidden meaning of dreams.

logomania nonstop talking.

logorrhea excessive and irrational talking.

longitudinal study a study involving the same subjects over many years.

loosening of associations disjointed speech with a train of unrelated or disconnected ideas, a symptom of brain damage.

magical thinking a childlike perception of reality, through which wishful thinking is believed to bring about what one wants or that the universe has a preordained plan and that everyone will be taken care of, that coincidences hold meaning, or that everything happens for a reason, all notions unsupported by any scientific validation but which may bring people peace of mind.

malingerer someone who pretends to be ill.

mania elation or euphoria accompanied by irrational behavior, often alternating with deep depression, as in manic-depressive illness. Also, an obsession or crazed desire for something. Manias include the following:

alcohol	dipsomania
animals	zoomania
books	bibliomania
cats	ailuromania
children	pedomania
Christ, delusion that one is	theomania
dancing	choreomania
death	necromania
demons, devil, delusion that one is possessed by	demonomania
dogs	cynomania
eating	sitomania
fire	pyromania
flowers	anthomania
food	phagomania
genius, delusion that one is	sophomania
horses	hippomania
kill, desire to	dacnomania
money	chrematomania
nakedness	gymnomania
night	noctimania
open places, living out in	agoromania
pleasure	hedonomania
sex	aphrodisiomania, nymphomania
sleep	hypnomania
solitude	automania
stealing	kleptomania
sun	heliomania
talking	logomania
travel	hodomania
washing	ablutomania
wealth	plutomania
women	gynemania
woods	hylomania

manic excited.

manic-depressive psychosis a condition characterized by extreme mood swings, from normal to elated, or from normal to depressed, or a combination of all of the above.

manic episode a temporary condition in bipolar disorder when one may experience grandiose thoughts and euphoria and behave in inappropriate or irrational ways.

marasmus the deterioration and emaciation of an infant due to prolonged maternal separation and deprivation of affection.

martyr one who makes great sacrifices and puts on a display of suffering in order to elicit sympathy. One who is not happy unless he is miserable.

masochism the experience of pleasure from pain inflicted on oneself or inflicted on oneself by others.

mass hysteria a kind of emotional contagion in any group who perceive a threat—such as a terrorist attack—and who may react by crying, screaming, fighting, rioting, or getting sick.

medical school syndrome a common form of hypochondria in which a medical student believes he or she has the symptoms or signs of the disease he or she is studying.

meta analysis a collective study of many previous studies on a particular subject, conducted to uncover subtle trends or to average out findings toward a particular conclusion.

microexpressions fleeting or instantaneous facial expressions that appear and vanish quickly and that can be read by an observer trained to spot them.

Minnesota Multiphasic Personality Inventory a widely used test given by psychologists and psychiatrists to measure personality traits and psychopathology.

misanthropy an aversion to people.

misogyny an aversion to women.

morbid anxiety extreme, incapacitating anxiety.

moria childish excitement, foolishness, and the inability to act in a serious manner.

multiple personality a rare dissociative disorder in which the person develops or displays more than one distinct personality.

Myers-Briggs Type Indicator a personality test used to determine one's preferences, as toward introversion or extroversion, and other personality aspects, to aid in choosing appropriate educational and career pursuits.

mysophobia pathological fear of dirt, filth, and germs, with the repeated washing of hands, a form of obsessive-compulsive disorder. Also known as germaphobia.

Napoleon complex colloquial term for a form of inferiority complex once believed to be suffered by some people of short stature, so-called after French emperor Napoléon I (Bonaparte), who was perceived to be a small man when standing next to his oversized guards but who in reality was of normal height. The complex supposedly drives shorter men to seek power as compensation for their lack of physical stature, but studies have failed to show any real connection and is today considered a myth. Also known as short man syndrome.

narcissism excessive self-love, selfishness, and self-centeredness.

narco hypnosis hypnotizing a person who is under the influence of drugs.

necrophilism sexual attraction to or sexual intercourse with a corpse. Also, a death wish.

neologism a new or nonsensical word coined by a schizophrenic person to describe a complex or abstract state.

nervous tic an involuntary muscle spasm, particularly around the face, that is illustrative of inner tension.

nihilistic delusions delusions concerning annihilation of self or body organs.

nocebo a sham pill or treatment that, through the power of suggestion, may have a negative effect or actually make someone ill, the opposite of a placebo.

numbing shutting down one's emotional responses to reduce stress, a symptom of post-traumatic stress disorder.

nystagmus involuntary eye tics or spasms, with the eyeballs jerking rhythmically in one direction, a sign of a brain or balance disorder.

obsessive-compulsive disorder a mental disorder characterized by thoughts, actions, or rituals repeated again and again, such as checking 10 times to make sure the iron is unplugged before leaving the house.

Oedipus complex the sexual feelings of a child, usually male, for a parent of the opposite sex, and accompanied by feelings of hostility to the parent of the same sex.

olfactory hallucination a hallucination involving smells.

oppositional defiant disorder a disorder in children characterized by an unusual level of defiance, hostility, and spiteful behavior, with frequent lashings out at authority figures. Often evolves into conduct disorder.

organic behavior disorder a disorder caused by physical damage to the brain or nervous system.

organic psychiatry psychiatry emphasizing the physical causes of behavior disorders.

Othello syndrome a syndrome characterized by delusional jealousy and repeated accusations of infidelity, with the scantest of evidence or no evidence at all, and may include constant surveillance of one's partner and eruptions of violence, named after the Shakespearean character who murdered his wife out of the irrational belief that she was adulterous.

out-of-body experience the mysterious but false perception that one is floating outside of one's body and sometimes even observing it. Although little is known about them, out-of-body experiences have been strongly associated with psychedelic drugs, trauma, near-death experiences, and the state of mind that occurs between waking and sleeping.

overvalued idea not quite reaching the level of delusion, a strongly held or extreme belief that is not held by the rest of society.

panic disorder a disorder in which a subject coming face to face with an irrationally feared object may hyperventilate, break into a cold sweat, suffer out-of-control heartbeat, and even pass out, and consequently takes pains to avoid that object.

paradoxical psychology any counterintuitive therapy technique or approach, such as telling a person who is afraid of failure that they probably will fail. Also known as reverse psychology.

paramnesia a state of confusion between one's fantasies and dreams and reality.

paranoid ideation belief that one is being persecuted, targeted, harassed, or treated unfairly, but not quite rising to the level of a delusion.

paranoid personality disorder a disorder characterized by the irrational mistrust of others.

paranoid schizophrenia a schizophrenic disorder in which the person suffers from delusions of persecution.

paraphrenia a late-life schizophrenia with paranoid ideation.

parasomnia any odd behavior or disorder that occurs during sleep.

passive-aggressive personality a chronically discontented, petulant, fault-finding personality that reveals inner hostility by such passive actions as "forgetting" promises or by vacillating between passive dependency on others and stubborn independence.

pathological gambling an addictive behavior in which the sufferer gambles incessantly, causing financial and personal problems.

pedophilia sex act between an adult and child.

persistent sexual arousal syndrome a mysterious disorder in which women experience constant symptoms of genital stimulation and the sensation of imminent orgasms, originally thought to be psychological in origin but now associated with restless leg syndrome and overactive bladder.

personality disorder a personality dysfunction characterized by any one of various maladaptive behaviors, causing difficulty in the sufferer and sometimes in those around him.

phantosmia odor hallucinations.

phobia an irrational fear of a person, place, or thing. Phobias include the following:

animals	zoophobia
animal skin or fur, touching	doraphobia
blood	hemophobia
blushing	erythrophobia
bridges	gephyrophobia
burial alive	taphephobia
cancer	cancerphobia
cats	ailurophobia
children	pedophobia
cold	psychrophobia
confinement in enclosed space	claustrophobia
crowds	demophobia
dark	nyctophobia
dead bodies	necrophobia
death	thanatophobia, necrophobia
defecation	rhypophobia
depths	bathophobia
dirt	mysophobia
dogs	cynophobia
eating	phagophobia
failure	kakorrhaphiophobia
fire	pyrophobia
flood	antlophobia
foreigners or strangers	xenophobia
ghosts	phantasmophobia
heights	acrophobia
infinity	apeirophobia
insects	acarophobia, entomophobia
knives	aichmophobia
lice	pediculophobia
marriage	gamophobia
medicine	pharmacophobia
men	androphobia
mice	musophobia
missiles	ballistophobia
money	chrematophobia
night	nyctophobia
noise	phonophobia, acousticophobia
number 13	triskaidekaphobia
ocean	thalassophobia
old age	gerontophobia
open spaces	agoraphobia
pain	algophobia
poison	toxicophobia
precipices	cremnophobia
responsibility	hypengyophobia
ridicule	catagelophobia
robbers	harpaxophobia
sex	coitophobia, genophobia

sharp objects	aichmophobia
sin, committing	peccatiphobia
sleep	hypnophobia
snakes	ophidiophobia
snow	chionophobia
solitude	autophobia
speaking	lalophobia
spiders	arachnophobia
stars	astrophobia
strangers	xenophobia
sunlight	heliophobia
thunderstorms	astraphobia, brontophobia
touched, being	haptephobia
venereal disease	cypridophobia
women	gynophobia
work	ergophobia

physiognomy the science of determining someone's personality simply by looking at his or her face. High testosterone, for example, reveals itself by widening the face, squaring the jaw, and jutting out brow ridges. Such facial structures have been correlated with a higher propensity for aggression and other masculine behaviors.

placebo a sham pill or treatment, which, presented as real medicine, often has measurable curative effects.

positive psychology a psychological movement developed in the late 1990s in which psychologists encourage unhappy clients to focus on the positive, especially one's strengths, and to cultivate a sense of gratitude and optimism instead of relying on making drastic changes in their lives in order to find contentment.

positive reinforcement a method of changing one's unhealthy behavior through a reward system.

posthypnotic suggestion a suggestion given to a hypnotized person that is performed after coming out of the trance.

postpartum depression depression sometimes suffered by new mothers directly after the birth of a child, possibly due to hormone fluctuations.

post-traumatic stress disorder extreme symptoms of stress manifesting themselves weeks, months, or years after experiencing a traumatic event.

power of suggestion the influence of a statement made with confidence and authority by a respected or charismatic person that may change someone's perception of reality or even persuade the person to do something he or she otherwise would not do, as a hypnotist with an audience participant.

prefrontal lobotomy partial surgical removal of the frontal brain lobes from the thalamus, a procedure used to treat psychiatric conditions in the 1930s and 1940s.

pressured speech rapid, nonstop, loud speech, often carried on even when people are not listening.

primal scream therapy therapeutic method that encourages patients to vent repressed emotions and frustrations from past hurts through loud screaming and violent demonstrations.

prodromal referring to any kind of presymptom that indicates an impending seizure, disease outbreak, mental breakdown, etc.

projection an ego defense mechanism in which an awareness of one's undesirable traits or thoughts is repressed and attributed to someone else.

proxemics the study of such nonverbal expression as physical distance maintained between two or more people in a social situation and their body orientation toward one another.

pseudocyesis false pregnancy, a symptom of conversion hysteria.

pseudoseizures false seizures, characterized by staring, stiffness, jerking, and an altered state of consciousness, a dissociative trance state.

psychic blindness the loss of vision, caused by hysteria or brain lesions.

psychoanalysis the Freudian school of thought emphasizing the study of the unconscious mind and the accompanying therapy which strives to bring unconscious desires into consciousness and to resolve conflicts dating back to childhood.

psychobabble psychological terminology and jargon.

psychodrama role-playing psychotherapy in which personal conflicts and fantasies are acted out in front of a group.

psychogenic amnesia the loss of memory of portions of the past that are threatening or painful.

psychogenic pain disorder chronic or severe pain without any identifiable source.

psychopharmacology the study of the effects of drugs on behavior.

psychophysiological disorder any physical pain or illness having a psychological cause. Also known as psychosomatic disorder.

psychosomatic disorder a disorder in which physical symptoms are brought on by emotional turmoil.

psychotherapy talk therapy.

psychotropic drugs mood-altering drugs.

rationalization justification of one's actions (often negative) through self-convincing but erroneous or dishonest thought processes.

reaction formation the adoption and display of behaviors and principles that may in fact be completely opposite of what one really feels, especially when one's true feelings are socially unacceptable.

regression returning to a state of immature or primitive behavior.

reinforcement reward or punishment to either encourage a behavior or stop it.

relationship-contingent self-esteem a sense of self-worth that is overly dependent on the positive feedback from one's romantic partner, causing a cycle of neediness and obsessiveness and following even minor spats depression and anxiety.

repression the blocking out of unpleasant or anxiety-provoking thoughts.

retrograde amnesia forgetting events immediately prior to a traumatic event but remembering everything earlier.

Rorschach test a test in which a person gives his interpretation or tells what he sees in special cards marked by distinctive inkblots, a means of revealing the unconscious.

Rosenthal effect phenomenon of human behavior through which experimenters' tend to find the results they want or expect due to their own bias and unconscious manipulation of parameters, named after Robert Rosenthal.

SAD seasonal affective disorder. Feelings of depression suffered by some people during the winter months, when sunlight is greatly reduced, which has been shown to cause changes in brain chemistry.

sadism the condition of deriving sexual pleasure from inflicting pain on someone.

savant syndrome having a low IQ but being extraordinarily talented or skilled in one area, such as music, art, or numbers.

schadenfreude the secret sense of delight one may feel at another's misfortune.

schizoid personality disorder a personality disorder characterized by an extreme lack of interest in forming relationships, including sexual ones, and often marked by emotional coldness and indifference to all people, including family members.

schizophrenia a severe psychotic illness affecting the regulation of emotion, thought processes, moods, and personality, with a wide range of symptoms, from delusions to hallucinations.

schizotypal personality disorder a personality disorder characterized by extreme fear of others and a lack of close relationships but that often goes beyond ordinary shyness with aspects of magical thinking, belief in the paranormal, and various odd or eccentric behaviors. Studies show the people with this disorder tend to be more creative than normal. Van Gogh, Emily Dickinson, and Isaac Newton are thought to have had schizotypal personalities.

screen memory a false memory, manufactured to shroud a more painful and real one, as in child abuse cases.

seasonal affective disorder see SAD.

selective serotonin reuptake inhibitor a class of drugs used to treat depression and anxiety.

self-actualization living out one's full potential, especially creatively, despite difficulties or flaws in one's makeup.

self-fulfilling prophecy fulfilling one's own fear of failure—for example, by failing to even try a task, or by being so consumed with feelings of inadequacy that it becomes impossible to focus efficiently on the job at hand.

self-mutilation the cutting or burning of oneself, an expression of anxiety, rage, or self-punishment.

serotonin in the brain, a neurotransmitter that plays an important role in the modulation of mood, sleep, sexuality, and aggression and is targeted by antidepressant drugs when levels are low.

sexual aversion disorder a disorder characterized by feelings of disgust toward sex, resulting in its avoidance. If no physical cause is found, it may be a result of sexual trauma in childhood.

shell shock combat neurosis characterized by jumpiness, fear of noise, and inability to sleep or relax.

short man syndrome see NAPOLEON COMPLEX.

social desirability bias the tendency for people who are polled to give answers that are more socially acceptable than accurate, as when someone is asked how often they attend church or if they would ever steal money from a friend. Such bias often skews survey and polling results.

social facilitation the enhancement of an individual's performance due solely to the presence of other people.

sociopath one with a mental illness marked by a deficient social conscience and a tendency to commit antisocial acts, such as murder.

somatization all ego defense mechanisms causing physical pain or illness as a means of expressing psychological pain.

somatoform disorder any one of various disorders, including hypochondriasis, in which the sufferer reports various aches, pains, or other physical symptoms of which no medical or biological causes can be found. The symptoms may signal the presence of depression or other mental distress.

splitting a childlike perception that views a person who does one bad thing as all bad, and a person who does something good as all good, without being able to see a mix of traits, sometimes used by adults as a form of defense mechanism.

SSRI see SELECTIVE SEROTONIN REUPTAKE INHIBITOR.

startle response a reaction of one's nervous system to a loud noise or sudden movement, the intensity of which may indicate heightened anxiety and stress, as seen in post-traumatic stress disorder.

stereotyped movements unnecessary and repetitive body movements such as rocking, hand-wringing, head banging, clapping, skin-picking, waving, etc.

stigma that which brands one with a negative or shameful reputation, as in having a mental illness.

Stockholm syndrome ironic behavior in which a hostage or kidnap victim comes to sympathize with his captors and may even assist them.

subjective reality one's own perception of reality, which may be different from someone else's.

sublimation the modification of an instinctual impulse into a socially accepted one.

subliminal information received by the brain on an unconscious level, as in subliminal advertising.

submissiveness a behavior characterized by frequent deference, eagerness to please, and other approval-seeking actions.

suggestibility level of receptiveness to the power of suggestion; the level to which one may be persuaded or manipulated to believe or act on something.

superego in psychoanalytic theory, the personality component involving morals, ideals, and conscience.

superiority complex a personality disorder in which one acts superior but actually feels inferior.

suppression the moving of unacceptable thoughts to the unconscious.

symbiosis a mutually beneficial relationship between two or more people.

syncrony the unconscious or conscious matching or mimicking of another's gestures, body language, and speech to enhance rapport.

syndrome a collection of symptoms that point to an underlying disease or disorder.

synesthesia sensory confusion, to the point of seeing a noise as a color, evidence of a problem in the brain.

tachylogia rapid and excessive talking; manic speech.

tactile hallucination a hallucination that one is being touched or electrically shocked or that bugs are crawling under one's skin.

tend and befriend response in times of stress, the tendency in mothers to make friends and alliances, especially to help protect their children.

thought broadcasting a delusion that one's thoughts can be heard by others.

thought insertion a delusion that one's thought or thoughts have been planted in one's mind by another.

transcendental meditation a relaxation technique involving intense concentration on a specially chosen word or "mantra."

transference in psychoanalysis, the exchanging of feelings toward a significant person in one's past to one's therapist.

traumatic learning associating a frightening event with a neutral event so that the neutral event causes fear or anxiety.

trichotillomania the pulling out of one's own hair, to the point of leaving bald spots.

trigger any sound, smell, sight, or sensation that evokes a painful memory and may cause anxiety or depression.

Truman syndrome a syndrome in which the sufferer believes his life is being taped or recorded and broadcast to the nation, named after the movie *The Truman Show,* in which the main character is secretly filmed throughout his life.

type A personality a personality or temperament characterized by a high level of hostility and aggression.

type B personality a personality or temperament characterized by relaxed, easygoing behavior.

visualization using the imagination as a tool to help one "see" how a goal can or could be accomplished.

voyeurism sexual pleasure from secretly observing the naked bodies or sex acts of others.

warrior gene the monoamine oxidase A gene, which in a variant form has been implicated in a tendency toward displaying a higher level of aggression when provoked, found in about one-third of the Western population.

withdrawal the isolating of oneself, mentally and physically, from others, marked by extreme reserve and a need for solitude.

word association a method of revealing the unconscious mind by citing a series of words and asking one to cite the first word each given word elicits in the mind.

word salad incohesive or incomprehensible speech, seen in schizophrenia.

zoosadism deriving sexual pleasure from harming animals.

SEXUALITY

abstinence refraining from sex.

AC/DC slang for bisexual.

adrenogenital syndrome a genetic disorder in which a female is born with male-like genitals due to a malfunctioning adrenal gland.

adultery sexual relations with someone other than one's spouse.

afterglow a feeling of deep relaxation and fulfillment after having sex.

age of consent the age at which it becomes legal to engage in consensual sex.

ambisexual see BISEXUAL.

anal sex any sex act involving the anus.

anaphrodisiac any substance that diminishes sexual desire.

anaphrodisis lack of sexual desire.

anorgasmic incapable of achieving orgasms.

aphrodisiac any thing, substance, or activity that arouses sexual desire.

around the world slang for the kissing of another's entire body as a prelude to intercourse.

asexual having no sexual feelings.

autoeroticism sexually stimulating onself, especially by masturbation.

B&D short for bondage and discipline.

bang slang, to have sex with.

birds and the bees euphemism for sex usually used with children.

bisexual enjoying sex with both genders. Also known as ambisexual. Also, one who does this.

blow job slang for fellatio.

blue balls slang for severe sexual frustration in males caused by lack of ejaculation.

booty call the act of calling another person by phone for sex. Also, the act of soliciting it in person.

celibacy abstinence from sex.

celibate abstaining from sex.

chastity sexual abstinence.

cherry slang for the hymen.

circle jerk slang for a circle of adolescent males masturbating together.

climax an orgasm.

clit short for clitoris.

clitoris the highly sensitive female sex organ, located above the vaginal opening.

coitus sexual intercourse.

coitus interruptus a crude birth control method through which the penis is removed from the vagina before ejaculation.

condom a latex sheath pulled over the penis to prevent sperm and semen from entering vagina. Also known as a rubber.

consummation sexual intercourse on one's wedding night.

copulation sexual intercourse.

crabs slang for pubic lice, spread through sexual contact.

cuckold the husband of a female who is having or has had sex with another male.

cum slang for semen.

cunnilingus oral sex performed on a female.

cybersex sexual flirtation or sexual simulation between two people in an Internet chat room or other computer medium.

daisy chain any sex act in which three or more people participate and are joined together.

deflower to have intercourse with a virgin.

dildo a female sex device in the shape of a penis.

doggy style a sexual position in which the male thrusts into the female from behind, as dogs do.

dominance overpowering behavior used to arouse a partner sexually.

dominatrix a woman who acts in a domineering fashion in order to give sexual pleasure.

eating out slang for cunnilingus.

ejaculation the release of sperm and semen by a man upon reaching orgasm.

erectile dysfunction the inability of the male to achieve an erection. Also, impotence.

erection the enlarged, rigid state of the penis during sexual arousal.

erogenous zone any area of the body, such as the earlobes, that arouses sexual feelings when stimulated.

eros Greek word for erotic love.

erotica art or literature with sexual content.

erotophobia feelings of guilt, shame, or fear involving one's sexuality.

fellatio oral sex performed on a male.

flaccid the state of the penis in its relaxed, nonaroused state.

foreplay activities, such as kissing and caressing, that lead to intercourse.

fornication sex between two people who are not married.

French kiss a kiss in which the tongue is inserted in another's mouth. Also known as a soul kiss.

frigid outmoded term for sexually unresponsive, usually referring to women.

gang bang any sex act in which three or more people participate.

gigolo a male prostitute.

give head slang, to perform oral sex.

go down on slang, to perform oral sex.

group sex any sex act in which three or more people participate.

G-spot (Grafenberg spot) an erogenous zone or area of sexual pleasure located on the upper wall of the vagina about two inches in.

hand job slang for the stimulation of a partner's sexual organ by fingering, caressing, or pumping.

hardcore explicit pornography.

hard on slang for an erection.

hermaphrodite a person with male and female sex characteristics. Also known as intersexual.

heterosexual attracted sexually only to members of the opposite gender. Also, one who is only attracted to the opposite gender.

homosexual attracted sexually only to members of one's own gender. Also a male who has sex with another male.

hymen a thin membrane that may cover part or all of the vagina in virginal women. Contrary to popular belief, the hymen can be broken in various ways before the first sexual experience. Also known as the maidenhead.

impotence see ERECTILE DYSFUNCTION.

incubus a male demon that has sex with a female while she sleeps.

insatiable never tiring of sex.

inseminate to ejaculate inside a vagina and impregnate.

intercourse the sexual act of insertion and thrusting of the penis inside the vagina.

intersexual see HERMAPHRODITE.

jerk off slang, to masturbate.

John the customer of a prostitute.

Kama Sutra an ancient Indian text on sex, once forbidden.

Kegel exercises pelvic squeezing exercises known to improve or strengthen orgasms.

kinky referring to any unusual, adventurous, or experimental sex acts or persons who practice such.

knock boots slang, to have sex.

know biblical euphemism, to be sexually intimate or to have had sex with someone.

libido sexual desire or drive.

lie with euphemism, to have sex with.

lust a powerful feeling of desire for another.

maidenhead see HYMEN.

making out kissing, holding, and caressing. Sometimes used to refer to a sex act.

ménage à trois see THREESOME.

missionary position a standard sexual position in which the male thrusts from on top of the female, who is lying face up.

monogamy the practice of having sex with only one partner.

necking kissing and caressing; making out.

nymphet a young teenage girl who is sexually active or flirtatious.

nymphomania insatiable sexual desire in females.

nymphomaniac a female who is sexually insatiable.

one-night stand one-time sex with a stranger or someone only casually known.

oral sex any sex act performed with the mouth or lips on a sex organ.

orgasm the climax of any sex act, resulting in pleasurable convulsions and, in the male, ejaculation of semen and sperm.

outercourse a form of sex consisting only of foreplay and simulated intercourse outside of the body, recommended by sex therapists to aged couples, and especially to older men who have problems attaining an erection.

penetration entry of the penis into the vagina.

pheromones natural body scents thought to attract sexual interest in others.

polyamorous having or enjoying sex with multiple partners.

premature ejaculation ejaculation that occurs too early during sexual relations, before the female is adequately stimulated.

priapism a medical condition in which an erect penis fails to return to a flaccid state.

promiscuity frequent sex with varied partners.

quickie slang for simple sexual intercourse, usually without foreplay.

ravish to force a woman to have sex; to rape.

refractory period the postejaculation period when no new ejaculation is possible.

riding bareback slang for having sex without a condom.

rubber see CONDOM.

scopophilia pleasure derived from viewing erotic photos.

score slang, to find someone to have sex with or to have sex with someone.

seduce to entice another into having sex.

semen in an ejaculation, the fluid that contains sperm.

sex surrogate a professional counselor who may act as a sexual partner to a client in order to teach or to help alleviate various anxieties.

sex therapist a professional who counsels couples or individuals with sexual difficulties.

sexually transmitted disease (STD) any one of various infections spread through sexual contact, including AIDS, chlamidia, genital warts, gonorrhea, herpes, pubic lice, syphilis, etc.

sixty-nine position in which oral sex is mutually performed simultaneously, especially with one partner on top of the other.

sleep with euphemism, to have sex with.

softcore pornography that features nudity but little or no explicit sex.

soul kiss see FRENCH KISS.

Spanish fly a substance attained from beetle juice, which is alleged to increase sexual desire.

sperm the spermatozoon, or male seed, contained in semen that seeks out the female's egg, causing impregnation.

statutory rape having sex with someone who has not yet reached the legal age of consent.

STD see SEXUALLY TRANSMITTED DISEASE.

submission giving in to another's domineering behavior, for sexual pleasure.

succubus a female demon that has sex with a man while he sleeps.

swinging the exchange of sexual partners between couples.

taboo anything sexual that the general population feels should be forbidden.

testosterone one of the main hormones known to influence sexual desire.

threesome any sex act in which three people participate. Also known as a ménage à trois.

titillation arousal or sexual thoughts.

tumescence the engorgement and rigidity of the penis during arousal.

union euphemism for sexual intercourse.

venereal disease a sexually transmitted disease.

venery the satisfaction of one's sexual desire.

Viagra a drug that aids penile erection.

vibrator a sexual aid used to stimulate a female.

virility sexual potency.

voyeur one who gains pleasure by watching others engage in sex.

voyeurism gaining pleasure by watching others engage in sex.

wet dream while sleeping, the ejaculation of semen during a sexually charged dream.

HOMOSEXUALITY

berdache a male who dresses and acts as a female, accepted in some cultures as a third gender with magical powers.

butch lesbian behavior or dress that is very masculine. Also, a very masculine woman.

catamite a boy in a sexual relationship with a man.

drag queen a man who wears the clothing of a female.

dyke pejorative slang for a lesbian.

gay either homosexual or lesbian in sexual orientation.

glory hole a small hole through which a penis is inserted in order for two males to participate anonymously in oral sex.

homophile one who is homosexual or who supports homosexual lifestyles.

homophobia a fear or hatred of homosexuals.

in the closet secretly homosexual.

latent hidden or under the surface, as some people's homosexual tendencies.

lesbian a female who has sex with other females.

lezzie slang for a lesbian.

out to make known one's homosexuality to friends and family. Also, to come out.

outing making known one's homosexuality or that of another.

out of the closet openly homosexual.

Sapphic referring to lesbian sex.

sodomy anal or oral sex performed on a male.

Sexual Deviations

analingus oral sex involving the anus.

asphyxophilia sexual arousal from being choked or smothered.

autoerotic asphyxia/strangulation strangling or suffocating oneself for sexual pleasure.

bestiality sex with animals. Also known as zoophilia.

bondage the practice of tying one up or being tied up for sexual pleasure.

bondage and discipline the practice of tying one up and spanking or whipping for sexual pleasure.

coprophilia the derivation of sexual pleasure from feces.

crime against nature any sexually perverted act.

date rape forced, unlawful sex with an unwilling partner during a date.

deviance any unusual sexual behavior or sexual behavior considered abnormal by current cultural standards.

erotomania an extreme sexual desire or obsession. Also refers to the obsessive feelings and behavior (spying and stalking) of a deranged fan toward a celebrity and the belief that the celebrity cares for them.

exhibitionism enjoyment and sexual arousal gained from showing off one's body or sexuality, especially in public.

exhibitionist one who enjoys or is aroused by showing off their body or sexuality, especially in public.

fetish an obsessive sexual fascination with a thing, such as a pair of shoes, or a body part, such as the feet.

fetishistic transvestism sexual arousal by a man when he dresses in female attire.

flagellation whipping for sexual gratification.

flagellomania sexual enjoyment from being whipped.

flash to expose one's genitals, often inappropriately, as in a public place.

flasher one who exposes his or her genitals, often inappropriately, as in a public place.

frottage gaining sexual stimulation by rubbing up against another person, such as in a subway.

golden shower urination on a partner to either give or get sexual stimulation.

incest sex with a family member other than one's spouse.

indecent exposure nudity in public.

infantilism sexual pleasure derived from acting like a helpless baby.

kleptophilia sexual pleasure from stealing.

klismaphilia sexual arousal from receiving or giving enemas.

masochism gaining sexual pleasure by being abused, either physically or mentally.

masochist one who gains sexual pleasure from being abused, either physically or mentally, by one's partner.

molestation a sex act performed on an unwilling or helpless victim.

paraphilia any perversion or fetish.

pedophilia sexual relations with children.

peeping Tom one who spies on women, often through a bedroom window.

rape forced sex on an unwilling partner; sexual assault.

sadism gaining sexual pleasure from inflicting pain, either mental or physical, on one's partner.

sadist one who gains sexual pleasure from inflicting pain on others.

snuff film a filmed record of a victim's murder, providing a form of deviant sexual pleasure.

urolagnia sexual pleasure from the drinking of urine.

zoophilia BESTIALITY.

SKELETAL SYSTEM

astragalus the anklebone that connects with the heel bone.

atlas the first vertebra of the neck.

axis the second vertebra (below atlas) of the neck.

calcaneus heel bone.

caluarium the top of the skull.

capitate the large center wrist bone.

carpal eight small bones of the wrist: greater multangular, lesser multangular, capitate, hamate, lunate, navicular, triquetrum, pisiform.

cartilage elastic or fibrous connective tissue that sometimes transforms into bone; gristle.

clavicle the curved shoulder or collarbone above the first rib.

coccyx the vestigial tailbone.

concha a small, scroll-shaped bone of the outer side of the nasal cavity.

coxa hipbone.

cranium the skull, consisting of the occipital bone, two parietal bones, two temporal bones, a sphenoid bone, and and ethmoid bone.

cuboid a small, cubelike bone in the foot.

cuneiform the small bones of the foot.

ethmoid the T-shaped nasal bone at the front of the skull.

femur the thighbone, the longest and heaviest bone in the body.

fibula the outer leg bone extending from the knee to the ankle.

frontal the flat bones forming the front of the skull and parts of the orbit and nose.

humerus the long arm bone between the shoulder and elbow.

hyoid the U-shaped bone in front of the neck above the larynx.

ilium the upper part of the hipbone.

incus in the middle ear, the anvil.

ischium part of the hipbone.

lacrimal the smallest bone of the face.

malar cheekbone.

malleus in the middle ear, the hammer.

mandible the lower jawbone.

marrow the tissue inside certain bones that manufacture new blood cells.

maxilla the upper jawbone.

metacarpal the five slender bones of the hand.

metatarsal the five bones of the foot.

nasal the bridge of the nose.

navicular the small, boat-shaped bones of the hands and feet.

occipital the lower back of the skull.

palatine one of two bones making up the hard palate, nose, and orbit.

parietal the two bones making up the sides and roof of the skull.

patella kneecap.

pelvis the hipbones, sacrum, and coccyx collectively.

phalanges fingers and toes.

pubis the front lower part of the pelvis.

radius the long bone of the forearm, from the elbow to the wrist.

ribs 12 on each side.

sacrum the five fused vertebrae of the lower back, part of the pelvis.

scapula shoulder blade.

sesamoid the small bones embedded in some tendons, especially in the hands and feet.

skull see CRANIUM.

sphenoid the front of the base of the skull and part of the nasal and orbital cavities.

stapes in the middle ear, the stirrup.

sternum the breastbone where the ribs and collarbone are attached.

talus the astragalus.

temporal the sides of the base of the skull.

tibia the large leg bone extending from knee to ankle.

tympanic collectively, the three small bones of the middle ear, the incus, malleus, and stapes.

ulna the inner forearm bone, from the elbow to the wrist.

vertebrae the spinal column, consisting of 33 vertebrae.

vomer the bone forming the back of the nasal septum.

zygoma cheekbone.

BONE DISEASES, DISORDERS, AND BREAKS

Colles fracture the most common type of wrist fracture, involving the radius and ulna bones.

comminuted fracture a bone splintered into many pieces.

compound fracture a fracture accompanied by a flesh wound through which the bone may protrude.

countertraction used in traction to pull bones together and realign them after a break.

crepitation the sound of broken bones when they rub together. Also the cracking of joints.

fatigue fracture a fracture of the metatarsal shaft, usually caused by prolonged marching or walking. Also known as a march fracture.

Kirschner wires the wires threaded through broken bones to help pull them back together.

marble bone a disease in which bones become extremely dense. Also known as Albers-Schönberg disease.

ossification the transformation of connective tissue or cartilage into bone.

osteoarthritis a disease characterized by a wasting away of bone and cartilage.

osteochondritis inflammation of bone.

osteoclasis intentionally rebreaking a bone in order to reset it in a more accurate alignment.

osteofibrosis degeneration of bone marrow.

osteogenic sarcoma a malignant bone tumor.

osteology the study of bones.

osteoporosis a condition frequently found in elderly women in which the bones become brittle and easily broken, due to a calcium deficiency.

pathologic fracture a fracture due to a disease process rather than an injury.

Pott's fracture the most common type of lower leg fracture, involving the tibia and fibula.

scoliosis curvature of the spine.

spur a small, projecting growth of bone.

traction the pulling together and alignment of bones by a system of ropes and pulleys.

TEETH

alveolus the socket of a tooth.

bicuspid premolar teeth, between the molars and canines.

bruxism gnashing or grinding the teeth, especially during sleep.

canine teeth the sharp, pointy front teeth. Also known as cuspids.

caries cavities.

cementum the bonelike tissue covering the roots of the teeth.

cusp the pointed part of a tooth.

cuspid see CANINE TEETH.

deciduous teeth temporary teeth; first teeth, or baby teeth. Also known as milk teeth.

dedentition loss of teeth.

dentalgia toothache.

dentition the eruption of the teeth through the gums.

denture false teeth; artificial teeth.

enamel the hard, smooth substance covering the crown of a tooth.

gingivitis inflammation of gums; early form of gum disease.

gumboil an abscess found in the root of a rotting tooth.

impaction a condition in which one tooth lies nearly on its side and is wedged tightly against another tooth, usually involving wisdom teeth.

incisor teeth the eight front cutting teeth.

macrodontia abnormally large teeth.

malocclusion a condition in which the top and bottom teeth fail to meet or clench together properly, causing problems with biting and chewing.

masticate to chew.

milk teeth see DECIDUOUS TEETH.

molars the large teeth at the back of the mouth used for grinding and chewing.

odontectomy removal of teeth.

odontology dentistry.

odontoma a tumor formed from the tissue involved in tooth growth.

periodontal surrounding a tooth.

periodontal disease any disease of the tissues surrounding the teeth.

periodontitis inflammation of the gums, loss of bone tissue, and the formation of pockets around the teeth. Also known as pyorrhea.

plaque a sticky film made of mucus, food particles, and bacteria; it forms on teeth after eating.

premolars the teeth between the canines and the molars.

pyorrhea see PERIODONTITIS.

tartar a yellowish concretion on the teeth composed of calcium phosphate.

wisdom teeth the last or rearmost molars on each side; they erupt during late adolescence.

SKIN

achromasia a condition of lacking skin pigmentation, as an albino. Also known as leukoderma.

acne common skin condition, characterized by pustules and cysts, particularly on the face; caused by hormonal changes during puberty.

acrogeria premature wrinkling.

alopecia hair loss; balding.

blackhead a plugged sweat gland.

boil a painful, contagious skin swelling caused by bacteria.

carbuncle a group of interconnected boils forming a large, painful mass that discharges pus from several locations.

chloasma brown patches frequently seen on the skin of pregnant women, due to hormonal changes.

collagen skin's network of connective fibers.

contact dermatitis any skin inflammation caused by contact with an irritant, such as poison ivy.

corn a horny, thickening of the skin around the toes, usually formed by friction.

cradle cap an infant scalp condition characterized by greasy, scaly, yellow patches.

cutaneous relating to the skin.

cuticle the hardened skin around the base of fingernails and toenails.

derma skin.

dermabrasion a method of removing scars by scraping off the top layers of skin.

dermatitis inflammation of the skin.

dermatologist a skin specialist.

dermatology the study of skin.

dermis the second layer of skin, below the epidermis.

eczema an acute or chronic inflammatory skin disorder characterized by redness, thickening, crusting, and the formation of papules and vesicles.

epidermis the outermost layer of skin.

erysipelas a streptococcus skin infection characterized by sharply defined red areas and accompanied by high fever. Also known as St. Anthony's fire.

exfoliation the constant process of skin peeling or skin cell shedding.

hives an allergic skin condition characterized by the eruption of itchy welts or blotches.

impetigo a contagious skin disease seen in children and the elderly and characterized by the eruption of itchy, crusting blisters.

keratin produced by the epidermis, the tough skin substance that nails and hair are made from.

keratinization the process by which the epidermis creates new keratin for use in nails and hair.

keratosis an overgrowth and thickening of the skin.

lentigo a brownish spot on the skin, unrelated to a freckle.

leukoderma see ACHROMASIA.

lichen any skin eruption.

lichen planus a common skin disease characterized by the eruption of itchy, reddish purple spots on the skin.

lupus erythematosus an acute or chronic skin disease marked by a scaly rash and often forming a butterfly pattern over the nose and cheeks.

lupus vulgaris tuberculosis of the skin, usually affecting the face.

melanin the dark pigment produced by skin.

melanoma cancer originating from skin pigment cells; a malignant mole.

melanosis the pigmentation or darkening of the skin after prolonged exposure to sunlight.

mole a congenital growth on the skin composed of a pigmented cluster of cells.

nevus any mark or growth present on the skin since birth.

panniculus adiposus a layer of fat beneath the skin.

papule a pimple.

piebald skin patchy areas of skin lacking in pigment, a mysterious condition. Also known as vitiligo.

portwine stain a wine-colored birthmark.

pruritus itching of the skin.

psoriasis a chronic, noncontagious skin disease characterized by reddish patches covered with silvery scales.

pustule a small, pus-filled abscess.

rosacea an inflammatory skin disorder characterized by the eruption of papules and pustules and the dilation of facial capillaries.

St. Anthony's fire see ERYSIPELAS.

scabies a skin infestation of mites (commonly known as itch mites) causing the formation of itchy lesions.

scleroderma pathologic thickening and hardening of the skin, sometimes with color changes.

sebaceous cyst a cyst containing smelly, fatty material.

sebaceous gland a skin gland that produces and secretes oil (sebum) to help keep the skin moist.

strawberry birthmark birthmark resembling a strawberry, caused by dilated blood vessels.

subcutaneous the layer of fat tissue beneath the dermis. Also, a general term for beneath the skin.

tag a skin polyp or small outgrowth of skin.

vesicle a blister.

vitiligo see PIEBALD SKIN.

wheal a hive; a skin swelling.

Zeiss gland an oil-secreting skin gland.

SLEEP

advanced sleep phase syndrome a disorder in which one's sleep cycles are engaged too early in the evening, resulting in early bedtimes and subsequent early wakeups.

altitude insomnia a form of insomnia that occurs at high altitudes and is usually accompanied by headache and loss of appetite.

arousal awakening from sleep.

arousal disorder term referring to either sleepwalking or night terrors.

biological clock a physiological cell mechanism that regulates one's sleep-wake cycles.

brain waves the brain's electrical activity, which changes through the various cycles of sleep.

bruxism teeth-grinding during sleep.

chronotherapy the therapeutic use of light to change sleep-wake patterns.

circadian referring to a period of 24 hours.

circadian rhythm any 24-hour cycle within the body's regulatory system, and especially the sleep-wake cycle.

conditioned insomnia a form of insomnia in which the sufferer is so afraid of his inability to fall asleep that he cannot relax enough to drift off and thus fulfills his own fear. Also known as learned insomnia.

CPAP machine continuous positive airway pressure machine. In patients who suffer from obstructive sleep apnea, a device that blows air through a mask and into the nasal passages in order to keep the airway open during sleep, thus preventing breathing cessation and disturbed sleep.

delayed sleep phase syndrome a natural sleep cycle that has become out of sync with the sleeper's desired bedtime, causing drowsiness later than normal.

delta sleep stages 3 and 4 sleep, the deepest phase of sleep, when the brain produces mostly delta waves and its electrical activity slows dramatically.

drowsiness a strong feeling of sleepiness, marked by droopy or heavy eyelids.

electroencephalogram a measurement of the brain's electrical activity. Also called an EEG.

entrain to train one's behavior to align with the body's natural cycles, for example, to avoid going to bed until one feels drowsy.

enuresis bed-wetting.

GABA gamma-aminobutyric acid. In the brain, a neurotransmitter involved in sedation, muscle relaxation, and sleep.

homicidal sleepwalking related to sleepwalking, killing or attempting to kill someone during sleep.

hypersomnia excessive sleep.

hypnagogia that which occurs between the state of sleep and wakefulness, including hallucinations, out-of-body experiences, geometrical or other meaningless imagery behind the eyes, etc.

hypnagogic of the mental state that occurs just before one falls asleep or after one begins to wake.

hypnagogic hallucination unrelated to REM or dream sleep, a hallucination that occurs just as one is falling into or out of sleep and is considered normal.

hypnic jerk caused by a normal electrical disturbance as one falls asleep, a sudden muscle jerking in a leg, arm, or jaw, as if one has been startled.

Hypnos in Greek mythology, the personification of sleep.

hypnotics a class of drugs that facilitate sleep.

insomnia trouble falling or staying asleep.

jet lag the temporary fatigue and insomnia travelers suffer when staying in a different time zone, due to a shift in their natural sleep-wake cycle.

Klein-Levin syndrome a disorder characterized by excessive sleep, up to 20 hours at a time, and uninhibited sexual behavior.

light sleep stage 1 or stage 2 sleep, characterized by a lack of dreaming, from which sleepers may be easily awakened.

light therapy the use of very bright light to set or reset one's biological clock. It is also used to help regulate moods, especially in cases of seasonal affective disorder.

lucid dreaming any dream state in which the dreamer is aware that he is dreaming and can control part of its contents. Also known as conscious dreaming.

melatonin a sleep-regulating hormone secreted by the pineal gland.

micro-arousal a partial or brief awakening from sleep, usually not remembered by the sleeper.

micro-sleep a brief dozing, usually lasting no more than a few seconds, which may occur several times a day in people who are chronically sleep-deprived.

Morpheus in Greek mythology, the god of dreams.

narcolepsy a sleep disorder in which sufferers experience excessive daytime sleepiness and may sometimes fall uncontrollably into deep sleep at any time.

natural short sleeper one who sleeps one to three hours less than average but feels fully refreshed during the day.

nightmare a frightening or horrifying dream that occurs during REM sleep and may awaken the sleeper.

night terrors suffered by some young children, a vivid hallucination occurring during a partial awakening from deep sleep, accompanied by panic and often crying. Unlike nightmares, night terrors do not occur during dream or REM sleep and are usually not remembered.

nocturnal referring to the night or occurring at night.

nocturnal sleep-related eating disorder a disorder suffered by sleepwalkers, who get up and not only walk around during sleep but also eat and then don't remember doing so.

non–24-hour sleep-wake syndrome a disorder in which one may sleep at different times, with drowsiness coming in unpredictable fashion day by day, seen most often in blind people.

NREM non-REM sleep. Sleep without dreams or the rapid eye movement that accompanies dream sleep.

obstructive sleep apnea a cessation of breathing during sleep, caused by the closing off of part or all of the airway, triggering awakenings.

parasomnia any disorder that occurs during sleep and disturbs it.

periodic limb movement disorder also known as nocturnal myoclonus, the involuntary movement of one or more of the limbs while sleeping.

phase advance getting out of bed earlier in the morning in order to feel drowsy and fall asleep earlier in the evening.

phase delay sleeping later in the morning and consequently feeling drowsy later in the evening than normal.

Pickwickian syndrome obstructive sleep apnea that results in deficient air intake throughout the day and night, seen in obese patients. Also known as obesity-hypoventilation syndrome.

polysomnogram a physiological recording of a sleeper's breathing, brain waves, muscle movements, etc., to measure for disturbances and overall sleep quality.

rebound insomnia after cessation of sleep medications, a return or worsening of insomnia.

REM sleep a cycle of sleep that recurs throughout the night and is characterized by dreaming and by rapid eye movement under the eyelids.

REM sleep behavior disorder a disorder in which one gets out of bed, experiences hallucinations, and may physically act out a dream as it is happening, often seen as evidence of brain damage or brain tumors.

restless legs syndrome a sleep disorder characterized by involuntary jerking of the legs or a sensation of bugs crawling underneath the skin of one's legs, requiring movement of the legs for relief.

serotonin a neurotransmitter involved in moods, memory, and sleep. A shortage may cause problems with insomnia.

sexsomnia related to sleepwalking, the performing of sexual acts during sleep.

sleep apnea cessation of breathing during sleep by all causes, including obstructions in the airway and by brain abnormalities that allow the sleeper to simply stop taking breaths.

sleep architecture the cycles of sleep and their durations as they occur throughout the night and as they change over time with age, and also as graphed out on a chart.

sleep cycle any distinct stage of sleep, such as REM sleep, or light, stage 1 sleep.

sleep debt the long-term loss of sufficient sleep, resulting in daytime fatigue, loss of memory, and other deficiencies.

sleep disorder any abnormality occurring during or around sleep, including insomnia, restless legs syndrome, sleep apnea, etc.

sleep fragmentation interrupted sleep.

sleep hygiene habits and techniques used to assure a good night's sleep, such as avoiding caffeine, going to bed at the same time every night, keeping the bedroom cool and dark, etc.

sleep hyperhidrosis extreme sweating during sleep.

sleep paralysis the inability to move the body during REM sleep, to prevent the sleeper from acting out his dreams.

sleep talking talking during sleep, usually occurring during dream sleep. Also known as somniloquy.

sleep walking getting up during the deepest stages of sleep and walking around, common among children ages four to 12. Also known as somnambulism.

somnambulism see SLEEP WALKING.

somniloquy see SLEEP TALKING.

somniphobia fear of falling asleep, which can occur with an anxiety disorder or as a result of sleep apnea.

Somnus in Roman mythology, the personification of sleep.

snoring the noise made by vibrations of the soft palate when inhaling during sleep.

suprachiasmatic nucleus a part of the brain that regulates the biological clock and the sleep-wake cycle.

unihemispheric sleep seen in dolphins and some birds, a form of sleep in which only one-half of the brain slumbers while the other half remains awake.

SOCIOLOGY AND CULTURE

affirmative action a controversial government program or policy aimed at providing increased educational and employment opportunities for minorities or women through such means as hiring quotas, legal incentives, or easing of qualifying standards.

ageism prejudice and discrimination against the elderly.

alienation an individual's sense of separation or isolation from society; the absence of a sense of community.

altruism doing good for others without the desire or requirement of any kind of reward.

amalgamation the blending of the races through intermarriage and creation of mixed-blood offspring.

anarchy the absence of government, police, and other organized controls of human behavior.

anthropocentrism the belief that human beings are at the center of all meaning and creation.

anthropomorphism the attribution of human traits to animals or objects.

anti-Semitism prejudice and discrimination against Jews.

apartheid a controversial policy of racial segregation and discrimination originating in 1948 in South Africa, and largely repealed in 1991.

aristocracy a group of people deemed superior to others and, by virtue of heredity, placed in positions of power.

asceticism the philosophy or lifestyle of hard work, deprivation, and high morals as an expression of one's "goodness."

asphalt jungle the city as a place of danger, with many of the same Darwinian dynamics as found in the wild.

assimilation the process by which a minority or member of a minority becomes increasingly like those in the majority through adoption of customs, language, and attitudes.

bigotry intolerance for those of another race, religion, sexual orientation, etc.

bourgeois of the middle class or middle-class values.

caste a system of classes and subclasses in Hindu society, composed primarily of five main groups: Brahmans (priests), Kshatriyas (nobles and warriors), Vaisyas (traders and farmers), Sudras (servants), and Harijan (untouchables).

chauvinism fanatical bias toward one's own class, race, or gender; the belief that one's own group is superior to all others.

cheerful robots a term attributed to those in society who accept their place and status, no matter how lowly, without much complaint.

class a social stratum, ranked as low, middle, or high, according to wealth and education.

class consciousness awareness of one's status in society or where one fits in the socioeconomic hierarchy.

conformity molding oneself to be like others in the community in order to fit in and be accepted.

convention a social norm; a traditional way of thinking or acting.

counterculture a subculture that rejects the ways of the dominant culture.

culture shock the disequilibrium or stress that occurs when one visits or moves to a foreign country or culture with different languages, attitudes, practices, and customs.

custom a traditional practice.

desegregation the opening of schools and places of employment to all races, particularly after a period of segregation.

deviance a behavior or attitude that is out of step with the norm of a culture.

discrimination preferential treatment for one's own kind and rejection of those who are different.

double standard a social norm in which a specific behavior is acceptable in one gender or group but not in another.

establishment collective term for those with power and influence over society.

ethnic cleansing purifying a population through genocide.

ethnocentrism the belief that one's own ethnic group is superior to all others.

ethos the values and attitudes subscribed to by a particular group or culture.

eugenics the use of selective breeding as a tool to heighten national intelligence, control genetic diseases, and generally improve the human stock.

feminism the advocacy of equal rights and opportunities for both sexes.

flag-waving zealous patriotism or chauvinism.

folkways traditions and customs of a culture, usually handed down through the generations.

future shock a reference to the inability of some humans to evolve and thrive in a highly technological or rapidly advancing world. The term originates from a book, *Future Shock,* by Alvin Toffler.

gay rights the issue of civil rights for homosexuals, such as the right to marry someone of one's own sex.

gender bias prejudice against those of the opposite sex and bias toward one's own.

gentrification the displacement of lower-class citizens with those of the middle class, in a community undergoing renewal.

glass ceiling the invisible, prejudicial barrier that prevents women or minorities in some corporations from advancing to the highest levels.

global village the amalgamation of nations and cultures into a more unified whole, as facilitated by internationally shared television programs and movies, global business expansions, worldwide travel, and increased communications, as via the Internet.

grassroots movement any cultural or political movement started and maintained by the common people.

groundswell a sudden mass or outpouring of support for a cause; momentum for a popular cause that can be used to advance changes in law or behavior.

groupthink the tendency of people in groups to conform or adjust their attitudes to be in step with one another.

hate crime a crime motivated primarily by racism, sexism, or homophobia, and which sometimes comes with higher legal penalties.

Holocaust the genocide of Jews in World War II by the German Nazis.

homophobia hatred and prejudice against homosexuals.

humanism the philosophy or belief that human beings can be good and moral without influence from a religion or belief in God.

iconoclasm rejection of traditional beliefs and institutions.

ideology any set of guiding beliefs or principles, whether religious, political, or social.

indoctrination the teaching, imbuing, or brainwashing of an individual to a specific group's way of thinking.

internalization the adoption of the attitudes or beliefs of others as one's own.

isolationism a national "hands-off" policy that disregards the troubles in other nations; uninvolvement in the politics of other countries.

Jim Crow from a 19th-century minstrel routine that evolved into a pejorative epithet for blacks, a general reference to any discriminatory laws that separate blacks from whites.

jingoism zealous patriotism and contempt toward foreign countries.

Ku Klux Klan a society, known for wearing white hoods to keep the identities of members secret, that is highly prejudiced against blacks and other minorities, maintains the philosophy of white supremacy, and sometimes commits terrorist acts.

lower class the poor, uneducated, laboring class.

lunatic fringe any extremists advocating radical solutions to social problems.

male-bashing female gender bias; the practice of some females of harshly and unfairly stereotyping males.

master race a "superior" race, or the fanciful belief that such a rare exists and should therefore dominate all "inferior" races, a philosophy of Adolf Hitler and others.

matriarchy rule or government by women.

middle class those in a society who earn a moderate income and may or may not have higher educations.

misery index any measure of national and regional well-being, especially concerning employment and inflation.

moral majority a religion-and-morals-oriented segment of the United States, claiming to make up the majority of the population while working to influence the national agenda.

mores the morals, ethics, customs, and ways of a society or culture.

movement a growing organization of social or political activists working to effect change in a specific area.

multiculturalism the expression of or providing for diverse cultures in a single society, in schools, in the workplace, and in everyday life.

nationalism patriotism and devotion to one's own culture; the desire for independence from other nations.

nihilism the philosophy that morals are a human invention and do not exist in the natural world. Also, the advocacy of positive societal change through anarchy.

nonviolence a philosophy of pacifism, according to which change can be brought about by peaceful means.

outing making public the fact that someone else is gay or lesbian.

passive resistance activism that attempts to create change by nonviolent means, such as through sit-ins, boycotts, economic sanctions, or noncompliance.

patriarchy government rule by males.

politically correct acutely aware of the past injustices suffered by minorities, women, ethnic groups, the disabled, and other groups, and thus attempting to act and speak with a degree of sensitivity that is devoid of prejudice, stereotyping, or offensive notions of any kind. Sometimes taken to an extreme.

power elite those in society holding influential positions.

prejudice negative feelings toward those of another race, ethnic group, gender, sexual orientation, etc., that stem from stereotyping, broad generalizations, unfounded notions, and general ignorance.

Promise Keepers a Christian men's movement, originating in the 1990s, through which men gather and make promises to maintain sexual fidelity and work to strengthen their marriages.

provincialism small-town thinking that, through lack of worldly experience with a broad spectrum of people, is prejudicial and tends to stereotype those who are different. Also, concern for only one's own town or region.

quota system a program that requires a minimum number of minorities or women to be hired for specific positions in an institution, company, etc., to guarantee equal opportunities for all and to counter any form of discrimination.

racism prejudice and discrimination toward another race; stereotyping those of another race. Also, the belief that one's own race is superior to others.

rally a public gathering to raise support for a common cause.

religious right a broad group of religiously oriented people with conservative or Christian values and their own political agenda.

riot a turbulent or violent group demonstration or protest.

reverse discrimination discrimination against one who has long been part of a majority and thus who has never or rarely experienced such an indignity, as a white male being turned down for a job taken by a minority member to meet a quota system.

sacred cow a person, thing, institution, or belief that is considered taboo to question or criticize in any way.

scapegoating accusing a minority for a society's problems, economic or otherwise.

segregation separation of races, at schools or other institutions.

separatism the advocacy of segregation of the races.

sexism prejudice and discrimination against members of the opposite sex; gender stereotyping.

sexual harassment inappropriate and unwanted sexual advances, flirtation, humor, remarks, etc., in a school, place of employment, or other social setting.

sit-in a peaceful protest against some social wrong, characterized by the demonstrators sitting down in a group and blocking pathways, doors, etc., and refusing to move for an extended period.

social Darwinism the belief or observation that genetically and biologically superior people rise to the top of a social group and the inferior ones become relegated to the bottom.

social engineering the application of the findings of sociology studies to improve social conditions.

socialization the learning by experience of the ways of social groups and society.

stereotype a faulty characterization in which one believes what is true of one member of a group must be true of all members; an inaccurate perception based on limited experience.

taboo that which is strictly forbidden by a society. That which must not even be spoken about or mentioned.

third world of a nation, poor, developing.

tokenism the hiring of a single minority member or a small number them, largely for appearances.

tolerance acceptance of people and social groups who are different.

upper class a group of people in society who are wealthy and often highly educated.

upwardly mobile moving up in social class, due to economic or educational gains.

values the morals, ethics, and guiding principles of a society.

WASP white Anglo-Saxon Protestant.

white supremacy the prejudiced philosophy that whites are superior to other races.

women's liberation the granting of women the same rights and privileges men enjoy; the cultural freedom to choose how one will live.

yuppie young urban professional. A young person with a high-paying job and a penchant for buying all the nicer things of life.

LANGUAGE

BRITISH WORDS AND SLANG

ankle biter rug rat; toddler or baby.

anorak parka.

arctic refrigerated truck.

arse ass.

arse-load shit-load.

articulated lorry a trailer truck.

aubergine eggplant.

back garden backyard.

badger to bug; to pester.

ballocks see BOLLOCKS.

banger sausage.

barmy foolish; crazy.

barrister a lawyer of the high court.

beefburger hamburger.

berk idiot.

bird female; girlfriend.

biscuit cracker; cookie.

bit of fluff sexual partner.

bit of a knob creep; jerk.

bit of skirt babe.

black treacle molasses.

blast! damn!

bleeding idiot frigging idiot.

bloke guy; man.

bloody frigging; damned.

bloody hell! frigging hell!

blooming euphemism for bloody; frigging.

bobby slang, for a policeman.

bollocks nonsense; crap. Also spelled ballocks.

bonnet hood (of a car).

boot trunk (of a car).

braces suspenders.

bridge roll hot dog bun.

bugger-all nothing; zip.

bugger off! screw off! go away!

bum butt.

caravan camper; trailer; mobile home.

car park parking lot.

chemist pharmacist; druggist; drugstore.

chips french fries.

cinema movie theater.

collywobbles butterflies in the stomach.

cookery book cookbook.

cotton thread.

courgettes zucchini.

cow an overweight or stupid woman.

crikey! holy mackeral! holy crap!

crisps potato chips.

crossroads intersection.

cupboard closet.

dab hand a highly skilled person.

daft silly; stupid.

diversion detour.

dog's breakfast/dog's dinner a mess.

draughts checkers.

dressing gown robe.

dustbin trash can.

dustman garbage collector.

face flannel washcloth.

fag cigarette.

fairy cake cupcake.

flat apartment.

football soccer.

fortnight two weeks.

gangway aisle.

gobsmacked slang for surprised; shocked.

guv'nor chief; boss.

have it off to have sex.

headmaster principal.

Herbert a dull person.

hire to rent.

holiday vacation.

hoovering vacuuming.

ice lolly Popsicle.

in the altogether naked.

ironmonger hardware store.

Joe Bloggs Joe Blow; Joe Schmo.

jumble sale yard sale; garage sale; flea market; rummage sale.

jumper turtleneck; sweater.

knackered tired.

knackers! balls!

knickers lingerie; underpants.

knickers in a twist in a difficult or awkward situation.

knocking shop slang for a brothel.

knock someone up wake someone up.

larder pantry.

lead leash.

lift elevator.

limited (Ltd.) incorporated (Inc.).

loo bathroom; toilet.

lorry truck.

luv babe; sweetheart; darling.

mad aleck an overactive child, possibly with attention deficit disorder; smart aleck.

marks (school) grades.

mate friend.

maths math.

mileometer odometer.

mince hamburger meat; chopped beef.

ministry department.

motorway highway; freeway.

mucking about/around messing around.

mum-mummy mom-mommy.

nappy diaper.

noughts and crosses tic-tac-toe.

nutter nut; nutcase; crazy person.

petrol gasoline.

pig's breakfast a mess.

pin board bulletin board.

pissed drunk; smashed; hammered.

piss off to screw off; to fuck off.

plait braid.

plaster Band-Aid.

plasticene modeling clay.

plimsolls sneakers.

polka dots chocolate chips.

polo neck turtleneck.

post to mail.

pram baby carriage.

queue line.

quid a buck (money).

rasher slice of bacon.

ring telephone.

rubber eraser.

rubbish garbage.

scally an irresponsible miscreant, originating from scalawag.

shag slang, to have sex.

shop store.

sideboards sideburns.

silencer muffler (car).

skittles bowling pins.

sleeping policeman speed bump.

smalls underwear.

snog to make out.

sod idiot.

solicitor a lawyer of the lower court.

spanner monkey wrench.

spot on you've got it.

spots pimples; zits.

spotty Herbert a fool.

squire chief; boss.

state school public school.

sticking plaster adhesive tape.

sticky wicket a difficult, awkward situation.

stone pit (fruit).

sweets candy.

swimming costume bathing suit.

tin can.

torch flashlight.

trainers sneakers; running shoes.

trainspotter nerd; geek.

trousers pants.

tube subway.

twit idiot.

wanker idiot; jerk.

wardrobe closet.

washing powder laundry detergent.

Welsh dresser hutch.

window licker nut; nutcase.

wing fender (car).

DRUG WORDS AND SLANG

Cocaine and Crack

Angie cocaine.

apple jacks crack cocaine.

aspirin powder cocaine.

bad crack cocaine.

badrock crack cocaine.

batman cocaine.

bazooka cocaine; crack; crack mixed with tobacco in a joint; coca paste and marijuana.

beamer one who smokes crack.

beamers crack cocaine.

Belushi a mixture of cocaine and heroin.

Bernice cocaine.

Big C cocaine.

bipping snorting cocaine and heroin.

biscuit 50 rocks of crack.

blanca cocaine.

blow cocaine.

Bolivian marching powder cocaine.

bolo crack cocaine.

bone a $50 chunk of crack.

bones crack cocaine.

Cadillac cocaine.

California cornflakes cocaine.

candy cocaine; crack.

caps crack.

chocolate rock crack smoked with heroin.

cocaine an addictive stimulant derived from coca leaves.

coke cocaine.

crack highly purified cocaine in the form of pebbles, which are smoked.

crack baby a premature infant who may be malformed and suffer learning difficulties, caused by crack use in the mother.

crackhead one who regularly uses crack.

crack pipe a homemade or other pipe used to smoke crack.

crisscrossing snorting a line of cocaine with a line of heroin.

eightball a mix of crack and heroin.

freebase a highly purified or concentrated form of cocaine for smoking. Also, to prepare or use cocaine in this way.

line one dose of cocaine snorted.

moonrock crack mixed with heroin.

nose candy cocaine.

Peruvian cocaine.

primo crack mixed with heroin.

primos cigarettes mixed with cocaine and heroin.

snort to inhale cocaine through the nose.

snow cocaine.

speedball crack mixed with heroin; crack and heroin smoked in combination. Also, to mix crack and heroin and either shoot up or smoke it.

stardust cocaine.

toot cocaine.

tooter straw used to snort powdered drugs.

HEROIN AND LSD

acid LSD.

acid head one who uses LSD.

Aunt Hazel heroin.

babysit to watch over someone experiencing their first drug trip or an unpleasant drug trip.

batman heroin.

Big D LSD.

black pearl heroin.

black sunshine LSD.

black tabs LSD.

blotter LSD.

blue barrels LSD.

blue microdot LSD.

blue moons LSD.

boomers LSD.

brown bombers LSD.

brown sugar heroin.

California sunshine LSD.

caps heroin. Also, crack.

DOA heroin.

doses LSD.

Dr. Feelgood heroin.

glass heroin.

heroin derived from morphine, a white crystalline powder causing feelings of euphoria.

horse heroin.

hype a heroin addict.

LSD lysergic acid diethylamide, a psychedelic drug causing hallucinations and delusions.

methadone a synthetic narcotic with more tolerable withdrawal effects, used as an alternative to heroin to help addicts break their addiction.

moonstone the addition of a small amount of methylenedioxymethamphetamine in a bag of heroin.

mud heroin.

poppy heroin.

psychedelic causing delusions, hallucinations, or other misperceptions, from ingesting psychedelic drugs, such as LSD.

salt heroin.

scag heroin.

smack heroin.

spoon a measure of heroin, 1/16 ounce.

sugar heroin.

tabs LSD.

tripping under the influence of drugs, especially LSD or another hallucinogenic.

white nurse heroin.

witch heroin.

Z one ounce of heroin.

MARIJUANA

A-bomb a marijuana joint mixed with heroin or opium.

Acapulco Gold a variety of Mexican marijuana that is partially gold in color.

African bush marijuana.

African woodbine marijuana joint.

amp marijuana dipped in embalming fluid.

astro turf marijuana.

atom bomb blend of marijuana and heroin.

Aunt Mary marijuana.

bad seed marijuana.

bale a large block of marijuana.

bama poor-quality marijuana. Also known as bammy.

bamba marijuana.

bammer low-potency or poor-quality marijuana.

bammy see BAMA.

banano a marijuana joint laced with cocaine.

B-40 a cigar that has been filled with marijuana and dipped in malt liquor.

black gold high-quality marijuana.

blunt a cigar in which the tobacco has been removed and replaced with marijuana, sometimes mixed with cocaine.

bogard to hog a marijuana joint instead of passing it around to others. Also spelled bogart.

bomb a giant marijuana cigarette.

bong a water pipe used to smoke marijuana.

boo marijuana.

brick one kilogram of marijuana.

buda a marijuana cigarette mixed with crack.

buddha a marijuana cigarette mixed with opium.

buzzed under the influence of marijuana.

Cambodian red a variety of marijuana grown in Cambodia.

candy blunt a joint soaked in codeine.

chronic marijuana.

Colombian a variety of marijuana from Colombia.

dank marijuana.

dime bag a $10 bag of marijuana.

dojah marijuana.

doobie a marijuana joint. Also spelled doobee.

dusting adding another drug to marijuana.

fry sticks marijuana joints dipped in embalming fluid.

ganja marijuana.

grass marijuana.

hay marijuana.

hit a single inhalation from a joint.

homegrown marijuana grown in one's backyard or home.

jay a joint.

joint a hand-rolled cigarette of marijuana.

lid one ounce of marijuana.

Mary Jane marijuana.

matchbox ¼ ounce of marijuana.

Maui wowie marijuana grown in Hawaii.

nickel bag a $5 bag of marijuana.

Panama Red a variety of marijuana.

pot marijuana.

rasta marijuana.

reefer marijuana.

roach the butt end that remains after the majority of a joint has been smoked.

roach clip a small alligator or other clip used to hold a roach, for smoking.

rolling papers cigarette papers used to hand-roll joints.

shotgun the blowing of marijuana smoke from one smoker's mouth into another's.

sinsemilla a powerful variety of marijuana.

skunkweed marijuana.

speedboat marijuana laced with PCP and crack and smoked.

stoned under the influence of marijuana.

Thai sticks marijuana bundles soaked in hashish oil.

toke a single inhalation from a marijuana joint.

wackytabacky marijuana.

water pipe a pipe in which marijuana or hashish is filtered through water.

weed marijuana.

woolah blunt a mixture of marijuana and heroin in a cigarette.

Zig Zag popular marijuana rolling papers.

Other Drug Terms

addict one who is addicted to a drug.

agua methamphetamine.

ames amyl nitrite.

amp short for amphetamine. Also, marijuana dipped in embalming fluid or formaldehyde.

amped under the influence of amphetamines.

amphetamine an addictive, crystalline stimulant.

angel PCP.

angel dust PCP.

angel hair PCP.

angel mist PCP.

Arnolds steroids.

bagging inhaling chemicals from a bag; getting high from inhalants.

bang inhalants.

barbies depressants.

barrels LSD.

batmans MDMA.

battery acid LSD.

beam me up, Scotty crack and PCP.

beast heroin, LSD.

belladonna PCP.

bennie amphetamine.

bens amphetamine. Also spelled Benz.

Bermuda triangles MDMA.

Bianca methamphetamine.

bibs MDMA.

Big O opium.

bindle a small packet of powdered drugs.

bitch methamphetamine.

black beauty methamphetamine.

black birds amphetamine.

black bombers amphetamine.

black cadillacs amphetamine.

black dust PCP.

black hash opium mixed with hashish. Also known as black Russian.

blank any pill or drug having low or no potency.

blizzard methamphetamine.

blue devils methamphetamine.

blue nile MDMA.

bullet isobutyl nitrate.

bumblebees amphetamine.

burned out a state of brain damage or other impairment due to chronic drug abuse. Also, having collapsed veins due to numerous drug injections.

burnout one who is permanently apathetic or impaired due to chronic drug use.

buttons mescaline.

buzz drug-induced high.

buzz bomb nitrous oxide.

cactus mescaline.

cactus head mescaline.

candy man drug dealer.

cats in the hats MDMA.

chalk crack; amphetamine.

crank amphetamines or methamphetamines; heroin; crack.

criss cross amphetamine.

crossroads amphetamine.

crystal meth amphetamines or methamphetamines.

date rape drug gamma hydroxybutrate (GHB), a central nervous system depressant.

dead road MDMA.

E ecstasy.

ecstasy methylenedioxymethamphetamine (MDMA), favorite illegal drug used at dance parties.

Egyptians MDMA.

eightball 1/8 ounce of methamphetamine; a mix of crack and heroin.

elephant flipping under the influence of PCP and MDMA.

elephants MDMA.

eye-openers amphetamine.

fiend one who regularly uses drugs.

footballs amphetamine.

GHB see DATE RAPE DRUG.

glading using inhalants.

glass amphetamine.

go amphetamine.

greenies amphetamine.

green triangles MDMA.

gum opium.

hammerheading mixing MDMA with Viagra.

H-bomb ecstasy mixed with heroin.

horse heads amphetamine.

high under the influence of drugs; euphoric or in another state of consciousness.

hippie flip mixing mushrooms with MDMA.

huffer one who uses inhalants.

huffing using inhalants.

ice a smokable form of methamphetamine.

Jerry Garcias MDMA.

kilo a bundle of drugs weighing one kilogram.

lid poppers amphetamine.

lightning amphetamine.

liquid X see DATE RAPE DRUG.

love pill MDMA.

mainline to inject a drug.

marathons amphetamine.

MDMA methylenedioxymethamphetamine, the usual basis for ecstasy.

Medusa inhalants.

mesc mescaline.

mescaline a powerful psychedelic drug derived from the buttonlike tops of a spineless cactus of the southwest.

methamphetamine a stimulant derived from amphetamine.

moon mescaline.

moon gas inhalants.

opium derived from poppy seeds, a yellow-brown narcotic.

Oxycontin an abused painkiller.

oz inhalants.

paper a quarter gram of methamphetamine.

PCP phenylcyclohexylpiperidine, a potent psychedelic drug.

peeper one who uses MDMA.

pep pills amphetamine.

peyote mescaline.

piggybacking simultaneous injection of two illicit drugs.

pink panthers MDMA.

pixies amphetamine.

playboy bunnies MDMA.

point a needle for injecting drugs.

quaalude methaqualone, a crystalline powder used as a hypnotic and as a sedative.

quarter moon hashish.

red devils MDMA.

rig a needle for injecting drugs.

rippers amphetamine.

rolls royce MDMA.

roofers benzodrazepines. Also known as roofies.

rush inhalants.

scooby snax methamphetamine.

sextasy ecstasy mixed with Viagra.

shiznit methamphetamine.

69s club slang for MDMA.

slammer a needle for injecting drugs.

smurfs MDMA.

snap amphetamine.

snort to sniff inhalants or cocaine through the nose.

soap GHB. Also, crack.

speed methamphetamines or amphetamines.

stacking taking illicit steroids.

stars MDMA.

stash a place or container where illicit drugs are stored or hidden.

stoned intoxicated by drugs; high.

sugar heroin; cocaine; crack.

supermans MDMA.

swans MDMA.

swerve methamphetamine.

tar opium.

Tom and Jerries MDMA.

troll use of LSD with MDMA.

truck drivers amphetamine.

tweaked high on methamphetamine.

tweety birds MDMA.

uppers amphetamine.

valley girl GHB.

water methamphetamine; PCP. Also, blunts.

white cross amphetamines or methamphetamines.

wired high on methamphetamine or other drug.

GRAMMATICAL TERMS

adjective a word that describes or limits a noun or a pronoun.

adjective, descriptive a word that describes a noun or a pronoun, such as a "beautiful" woman.

adjective, limiting a word that limits a noun or a pronoun, such as "ten" apples, "five" fingers, "triple" play.

adjective, proper a descriptive adjective derived from proper noun, such as "American" music.

adverb a word or term that modifies a verb, adjective, or another adverb, for example, he ran "quickly," or his pants were "really" strange, or she walked "very" softly.

agreement in a sentence, the agreement of verbs and other components in mood, tense, or number.

antecedent a word, phrase, or clause to which a pronoun refers.

antithesis a contrast of ideas within a sentence or paragraph.

appositive a noun or noun phrase placed next to another of the same as a means of explanation, for example, Boggs, "the third baseman," caught the ball.

clause a group of words, including a subject and a predicate, constituting one unit of a compound sentence.

climax in a sentence, the placement of the most important idea last or in the last clause, for strongest impact.

conjugation the inflection of verbs.

conjunction a word that connects clauses or sentence parts, such as "and," "but," "because," "as."

contraction a shortening of a word by the removal of one or more of its letters, replaced by an apostrophe, such as "I'll" (I will), "can't" (cannot).

dangler a misplaced modifier that gives a sentence an unintended and sometimes humorous meaning, for example, "Riffling through my papers," the blue jay appeared at the window.

double negative the incorrect use of two negatives in one sentence, such as He "doesn't" know "nobody" there.

gerund the verb form ending in "-ing," when used as a noun.

infinitive a verb form without limitation of person or number.

inflection the change of a word's form to indicate case, gender, mood, tense, or voice.

interjection an exclamation, especially one that can stand alone, such as "Oh!" or "Heavens!"

modifier a word or clause that limits or qualifies the meaning of another word or words.

noun a name of a person, place, thing, quality.

noun, abstract the name of an idea, quality, or other abstraction, such as happiness, knowledge, etc.

noun, collective a name of more than one thing, such as class, club, team.

noun, concrete a name for something that can be perceived through the senses, such as shirt, sky, clouds, smoke, foot.

noun, diminutive a name of something small or young, such as duckling, kitchenette, booklet, ringlet.

noun, gender a noun that indicates sex, such as bachelor, sister, buck, doe, widow, widower.

noun, proper a name of a person of place, or institution, such as Mary, Chicago, *New York Times*.

paradigm a list or table of all the inflectional forms of a word or class of words.

plural a form of a word expressing more than one, such as apples, people, baskets.

predicate in a clause or sentence, a verb and its modifiers.

prefix a form or affix placed at the beginning of a word to alter its meaning, as "pre" in prefabricate or "re" in rerun.

preposition a word that indicates the relation of a substantive to a verb, adjective, or other substantive, such as at, by, in, to, from.

pronoun a word that serves as a substitute for a noun to prevent awkward repetition in a sentence.

sentence, complex a sentence having one principal clause and one or more subordinate clauses, for example, "We are going now because it is late."

sentence, compound a sentence having two or more independent clauses, for example, "The fire is out, and I am going home."

sentence, declarative a sentence that states, asserts, or affirms, for example, "The dog is mine."

sentence, exclamatory a sentence that expresses sharp emotion, for example, "The dog got away!"

sentence, imperative a sentence that commands, as in "Do not come any closer with that dog."

sentence, interrogative a sentence that questions, as in "Did you see the brown dog?"

singular denoting one of a thing, as distinguished from the plural form of a word.

split infinitive an infinitive in which the word "to" is separated from the verb, as in "to really think."

suffix a form or affix added to the end of a word to alter its meaning, such as "ly" in badly or "ness" in fondness.

tense the verb form denoting past, present, or future, for example, "They were, they are, they will be."

verb a word that expresses action, such as "run," "hit," "sing," "throw," "drive."

verb, auxiliary a helping verb that modifies the meaning of a principal verb; for example, in the sentence I have eaten, "have" is auxiliary.

verb, causative a verb causing an action and usually having the suffix "en," such as whiten, brighten, shorten, tighten.

verb, copula a linking verb, such as "be," "become," "seem," "get."

voice, active refers to the performing of an action by the subject in a sentence, as in "He painted the picture," as distinguished from the passive voice.

voice, passive refers to the subjects of a sentence being acted upon, as in "The picture was painted by him."

MAFIA/ORGANIZED CRIME TERMS AND SLANG

administration the ruling members of an organized crime family.

associate one who works with the Mafia but who may not be "made," or sworn in.

babbo a stupid underling.

bent car stolen car.

books, the the membership in a crime family.

bootlegging illegally copying of music, videos, etc., and selling them for profit.

borgata a crime family. Also known as a brugad.

boss in the Mafia, the head of a family. Also known as a chairman or don.

broken brought down in rank.

brugad see BORGATA.

burn to murder.

button one who has been sworn in to a crime family.

canary an informer. Also known as a rat or squealer.

can opener a safecracker.

capo the head of a crew, or group of soldiers.

capo di tutti capi boss of bosses.

capo regime see UNDERBOSS.

chairman see BOSS.

chased run out of the Mafia; banished.

Chicago overcoat a coffin.

cleaning slipping away from someone who is following on foot or in a car; giving the slip.

clip to murder.

clock to track or take note of someone's comings and goings.

comare a mistress of a Mafia member.

compare a friend.

con a confidence game or swindle.

Cosa Nostra Italian for "this thing of ours," referring to a Mafia family.

crew a group of soldiers.

don see BOSS.

empty suit a powerless wanna-be who hangs out with mob members.

enforcer one who acts as an intimidator and threatens, beats up, or even kills.

extortion the use of threats, such as that of burning down a business, to extract money from victims.

family collective term for members of the Mafia.

fence one who receives stolen goods.

finger to identify.

garbage business see WASTE MANAGEMENT BUSINESS.

gift euphemism for a bribe.

goodfella see MAFIOSO.

goombah slang for a friend or compare.

graft illegal profit.

hit to murder.

hot place a place under surveillance by the police.

hush money any money paid to someone to keep them quiet.

juice interest paid to a loanshark.

larceny stealing.

loanshark one who loans money at exorbitant interest rates.

made referring to one who has been inducted into the Mafia.

Mafia an organized society of criminals, of largely Italian or Sicilian descent.

mafioso a member of the Mafia. Also known as a goodfella or wiseguy.

mobster a member of a criminal gang; a mafioso.

MS-13 Mara Salvatrucha, a violent gang from Central America that has spread across the United States and has become notorious for home invasions, carjackings, robberies, extortion, weapons smuggling, and drug dealing. Members typically have tattoos with the number 13 or the letters MS.

off the record referring to a communication or activity conducted without the knowledge or permission of the administration.

omerta the code of silence sworn to by any member of the Mafia, upon penalty of death.

packing carrying a gun.

piece a gun.

pinched arrested.

pop to murder.

put a contract out on to arrange to have someone killed.

racketeer one who obtains money through various illegal means, such as fraud, bootlegging, or extortion.

racketeering taking part in extortion, bootlegging, or fraud.

rat see CANARY.

shake down to blackmail or frighten someone for money.

skim to take gambling profits without declaring them on one's taxes.

soldier a low-ranking member.

squealer see CANARY.

swag stolen goods.

underboss in the Mafia, one who is second in command.

waste management business euphemism for the Mafia or organized crime. Also known as the garbage business.

whack to murder.

wiseguy see MAFIOSO.

Witness Protection Program legal and physical protection offered by U.S. federal government for those who would testify in court with evidence of unlawful activities.

PRISON SLANG

agitator any prisoner who stirs up trouble, especially in provoking fights.

all day a life sentence.

bail property or money held by a court to allow a suspect to avoid jail time until a trial.

bean slot a narrow opening in a cell through which a meal tray may be passed or the prisoner may be handcuffed before leaving the cell.

bird on the line an alert that someone is eavesdropping.

bitch a homosexual or someone who is considered weak.

black market an illegal selling and buying of goods, such as bootleg alcohol, drugs, or cigarettes, by barter system by inmates.

blanket party throwing a blanket over someone and beating him. Because the victim cannot see, the person actually landing the blows may remain anonymous.

bone the dominant one in a relationship, especially a sexual one.

bong a can wrapped with several windings of toilet paper, which is lit on fire and allowed to burn slowly, used to heat water for cooking.

brig a jail on a ship.

brogan a state-issued work boot.

bullet a one-year sentence or period of time.

bunkie one who shares a bunk bed with an inmate.

capital punishment the death penalty.

cell block the section of a prison that contains the cells.

cell gangster one who talks tough while in the safety of his cell but who becomes quiet and submissive on the outside. Also known as a cell warrior.

cellie slang for a cellmate.

cellmate one who shares a prison cell with another.

chair electric chair.

checking saying something offensive to someone to see if they will dare to say anything back, a method of dominating without fighting. It may go so far as punching someone in the chin, to determine how far he or she can go with keeping a weaker inmate in check.

clique any group of prisoners who hang out together, forming a strong defense against rivals.

cliqued on when a group of prisoners who hang together beat up an individual outside the clique.

C.O. a corrections officer.

commissary a kind of in-prison store where prisoners may purchase approved goods with money placed in their account, either from doing various prison work or sent from family members.

con a convict.

conjugal visit a visit from a spouse, in a private room, for sexual purposes.

contraband any forbidden items, such as drugs or alcohol or weapons.

cooler slang for a prison.

count a check or headcount of prisoners, taking place several times a day.

death row an area of prison cells that hold those awaiting execution. May also refer to being sentenced to death, as in *on death row.*

dime slang for a 10-year sentence.

drop an item delivered or smuggled to someone in prison, often from an outdoor work detail.

dropped taken down to the floor by a corrections officer.

dungeon solitary confinement.

eyeballing staring at, as an inmate, sometimes for intimidation purposes.

fishing line any string or torn sheet used as a line to toss items down to another's cell.

fishing pole any contrivance, but especially a rolled newspaper with a paper clip on one end, used to retrieve kites or other items thrown over from another's cell.

fix up to give another inmate more food than he is due, as a favor.

funky describing an inmate who neglects to shower.

gasser one who throws blood, urine, or excrement on a prison staff member, behavior that is considered a felony in many states.

gated released from prison.

hard time a sentence served in a maximum security prison.

hole any cell used for solitary confinement or segregation purposes, but especially one that is cold, dark, and windowless.

hustle one's means for making money or bartering value, including drugs, tatooing, sexual favors, etc.

incarcerate to put in jail or prison.

infirmary a prison's medical facility.

ink tatoo

inmate a prisoner.

jail one or more holding cells for those awaiting trial or serving a sentence of less than a year.

jailhouse lawyer an inmate who has schooled himself in law and prison regulations.

kite a note passed between prisoners.

lifer one who is serving a life sentence.

man slang for any correctional officer or person in authority.

nickel slang for a five-year sentence.

parole an early trial release of a prisoner, before his jail term is up, during which he must report to a parole officer and avoid illegal activity of any kind, to prove himself worthy of living in society.

parole board state officials who meet with an inmate to decide if he should be released, before the end of his sentence.

penitentiary a correctional facility for serious criminals, particularly murderers.

P.O. parole officer.

prison any correctional facility used for incarcerating convicts for a year or more.

rabbit one who tries to escape or has a history of attempts to escape.

rat one who snitches or informs on another inmate.

recidivism committing crimes, even after serving jail time. The failure to rehabilitate oneself.

recidivist one who breaks the law again and again, even after jail time.

remand the detention of a suspect before a trial.

runner one who is attempting an escape.

shank a homemade knife made from scrap metal. Also, to stab someone with such an object.

shiv a small, homemade knife made from ordinary items, such as a sharpened toothbrush. Also, to stab someone with such an object.

spit mask a face mask fitted over a prisoner to prevent him from spitting on a prison official.

state issue any items provided by the state, such as clothing, shoes, toothbrushes, soap, etc.

super max any maximum security prison.

tats tattoos

wack sack a psychiatric ward.

ward a division or wing of a prison containing cells.

warden the head of a prison.

yard any outdoor recreation area.

yolked very muscular, as an inmate who works out every day.

URBAN STREET AND RAP SLANG

a'ight pronounced "ite," short for all right.

all that having several great qualities; excellent.

all up in my business meddling; failing to mind one's own business.

all up in my grill up in my face; confrontational.

ax to ask.

baller one who has attained a high measure of success in either making money or attracting women, or both. Also, an impressive basketball player.

'bama short for Alabama, referring to a stereotypical loser from a rural area; one who is stupid and unsophisticated and lacks style.

bang to fight or kill. Also, to have sex with someone. Also, a party, especially one with attractive girls.

banger a gang member. Also, one who enjoys hard rock or metal.

beamer a BMW car.

benjamins money, especially $100 bills, which have Benjamin Franklin's picture on them.

Benz short for Mercedes Benz.

biatch alternative pronunciation and spelling of bitch.

bling bling silver, gold, platinum, or diamond jewelry; expensive clothing, cars, etc. Also known as bling blang.

blood a member of the Bloods gang in Los Angeles, California. Also, a blood brother or member of one's own race or family.

bomb, the stunning; fantastic; the best. Someone or something that is truly impressive. Also, marijuana mixed with heroin.

bone to have sex. Also, the penis.

boo a friendly nickname, used for a boyfriend or girlfriend.

booty the rear or backside.

booty call a call to arrange to have sex.

bootylicious deliciously attractive or sexy.

boo-yah! exclamation of triumph, after winning a game or trumping someone verbally.

boy a male friend.

bounce to get up or leave.

braw derived from bro or brother, a friend; buddy; pal.

brother a friend, especially a black male.

buggin' stressing out or worrying. Also, acting strange.

burner a very large, multicolored piece of graffitto that takes up an entire wall or subway or railroad car.

bust to execute or perform skillfully.

busta someone having low status; a loser or weakling.

bust a cap to shoot a bullet. Also known as bust a slug.

bust a nut to ejaculate.

butter, like smooth; performing well or admirably.

cap bullet.

check yourself be aware of one's own behavior.

cheddar money.

chickenhead a stupid person who talks a lot. Also, a female who perform oral sex.

chill to calm down; relax.

chronic potent, homegrown marijuana.

clique on the West Coast, a group of friends one hangs out with.

cracker a white bigot.

crew the group of friends one hangs out with. Also known as a posse.

crib one's home or bedroom.

dawg see DOG.

def good; excellent.

def jam a great song; album; CD, etc.

dis to disrespect or insult.

do to have sex with someone.

dog to insult someone. Also, a term of endearment for a friend. Also, one who cheats on his girlfriend. Also known as dawg.

dope great; excellent. Also, drugs.

down with to agree or be friends with.

drive-by a gang activity in which a person is shot from a passing car.

drop to hit someone hard enough to knock the person down or unconscious.

dub a wheel rim.

feel me understand me; feel my presence.

flossin' showing off one's wealth.

fly attractive; beautiful.

foo short for fool.

forty a 40-ounce bottle of malt liquor.

fo' sheazy for sure.

fo' shizzle for real.

fo' shizzle, my nizzle for sure, my nigger.

fo' sho' for sure.

freak a woman who is sexually attractive, promiscuous, or sexually aggressive. Also, to have sexual relations.

freak dancing sexually explicit dancing.

freak train a line of dancers performing sexually suggestive moves.

freestyle ad-libbed rap lyrics.

fresh good; cool.

frontin' lying.

fugly extremely ugly.

game charm and conversational skills, especially when trying to win a female's attention and affections.

gangbang to commit crimes as part of a gang.

gangsta a gangster; gang member.

gangsta rap rap music with violent or gangster-related lyrics.

ghetto-fabulous fabulous.

grill teeth; also, one's smile.

haten' being mean and disrespectful.

hater a racist.

ho short for whore.

homeboy a male friend from one's neighborhood.

homegirl a female friend from one's neighborhood.

homey short for homeboy or homegirl.

hood neighborhood.

hoodrat an undesirable person from the hood.

ill cool; great.

it's all good it's all acceptable and fine.

jack to rob someone; to steal.

keep it real be sincere; don't be phoney.

kickin' it hanging out with a friend or friends.

krunk totally wild and exciting.

lowrider a car that rides very low to the ground, due to altered suspension. Also, one who drives this kind of car.

mack to make a pass at; to flirt. Also, to take advantage of.

my nizzle euphemism for my nigger.

off the chain exciting; excellent. Also known as off the hook.

phat rich; excellent.

player one who is promiscuous; a playboy. Also known as playa.

poser one who tries to appear as someone he or she is not.

posse see CREW.

props praise.

punk to steal or take.

represent to perform at one's best; to do one's family and friends proud.

scrub someone with low status.

shiznit euphemism for shit.

shizzle, the something exceptional or excellent; the bomb.

skank a nasty, promiscuous, or unclean female.

slammin' awesome; excellent.

smak, talkin' talking in derogatory, insulting fashion.

step off get back; leave it alone.

stoked happy and excited.

'sup? see WAZZUP?

triflin' cheating on one's boyfriend or girlfriend. Also, backstabbing.

trippin' out of one's mind; hallucinating, as if on drugs; irrational.

wack crazy.

wazzup? what's up?

VOICE AND PHONETICS

affricate a consonant produced by the tongue and hard palate, such as the "ch" sound in chicken, the "tch" sound in match, and the "dge" sound in judge.

alveolar sound a sound produced by the tip of the tongue touching the area of the alveolar ride, such as *s, t,* and *d.*

articulate to speak or pronounce clearly.

brogue an Irish accent; any strong accent.

burr a trilling of the letter *r,* as in Scottish pronunciation. To speak with a burr.

cacology improper pronunciation of words.

cadence the measured flow of one's speech; modulation.

consonant a speech sound produced by teeth, tongue, or lips, as distinguished from vowel sounds.

dental produced by the tip of the tongue near the front teeth, such as the letter *d.*

dentiloquist one who speaks with clenched teeth.

dialect the manner of speech, idiom, and pronunciation of a region, as in a southern dialect.

elocution the manner of speaking, especially public speaking.

enunciate to articulate or pronounce words clearly.

fricative a consonant produced by forcing air through a partially closed passage, such as *f, v, s, z, sh, th.*

glossolalia nonsensical, incoherent speech, especially that associated with the mentally ill.

inflection a varying of tone or pitch.

intone to chant; to speak in a singing voice, as a prayer; to speak in a monotone.

labial formed by closing or partially closing the lips, such as *b, m, w.*

labialize to round a vowel.

labiodental produced by the lips and teeth, such as the letters *f* and *v.*

labionasal produced by the lips and nose together.

labiovelar combining labial and velar sounds, as the word "quick."

lallation lulling sounds, as with a baby; baby sounds.

linguistics the science of language and speech.

mellifluous of a tone of voice, rich, smooth, or resonant.

modulation the variation of volume, tone, or pitch; a variation of inflection.

monotone a tone of voice lacking inflection or expression.

morpheme the smallest meaningful unit of language.

nasal resonating through the nasal activities, as the pronunciation of the suffix "ing" or the letter *n.*

orotund forceful and resonant.

paralinguistics all forms of communication that accompany speech, as in tone of voice, speech tempo, gestures, facial expressions.

phoneme the smallest unit of speech.

plosive designating a burst of air, as produced by pronouncing the letter *p.*

sibilant suggestive of a hissing sound, as in *s, sh, z, zh.*

sibilate to hiss.

singsong a rising and falling of voice pitch, often used when taunting another.

stentorian having a loud, powerful voice.

uvular sound a sound produced by the uvula or by the back of the tongue touching the uvula.

velar produced by the back of the tongue on the soft palate, as the letter *g* in "great." Also known as a guttural sound.

voiceless spoken without the use of the vocal cords, as the consonants *t* and *p.*

vowel a sound or letter produced by the passage of air through the larynx, as distinguished from consonants.

WORD GAMES

acrostic a poem, paragraph, or other composition in which initials or other conspicuous letters combined spell out a word or message.

alternade the creation of two words from one by assembling alternate letters, as in "calliopes": CLIPS ALOE

anagram a word or phrase created by transposing the letters in another word or phrase.

antigram same as an anagram but with an altered word or phrase that is the opposite or reverse in meaning to the original word or phrase.

beheadment the removal of an initial letter of a word to form a new word, as in blather to lather.

charade dividing a word—without changing letter placement—to form multiple words, as in "significant": sign if I can't.

charitable word a word that remains a word when any one of its letters is removed, such as "seat": eat, sat, set, sea.

curtailment removing the last letter of a word to leave another word, as in "goon" to "goo."

kangaroo word a word that contains within itself another word that is a synonym of itself, as in "evacuate" to "vacate."

letter rebus a rebus composed of letters only, as in a "B" standing for "abalone" (a B alone).

linkade joining two words with one overlapping letter to create a new word, as in "pass" and "sing" to form "passing."

lipogram a composition written entirely without the use of a particular letter, such as Ernest Wright's *Gadsby,* which does not contain the letter *e* anywhere in its text.

metallege transposing two letters in a word to create another word, as in "nuclear" to "unclear."

nonpattern word a word in which each letter is used only once.

palindrome a word spelled the same backwards as forwards, such as "redivider" or a phrase spelled the same each way, as in "A man, a plan, a canal, Panama."

pangram a phrase or sentence containing all the letters of the alphabet, constructed with as few letters as possible.

paronomasia making a pun out of a popular expression, as in "the rock-hunting nudists left no stone unturned and no stern untoned."

piano word a word in which all of its letters can be played as notes (a, b, c, d, e, f, g) on a musical instrument, such as "cabbage."

rebus a visual puzzle using pictures, symbols, letters, numbers, characters, and so on, that must be deciphered by reading it aloud, as in YYURYYUBICURYY4 me = too wise you are, too wise you be, I see you are too wise for me.

reversal a word that becomes another word when read backwards as, in "live" to "evil."

stinky pinky a noun joined with an adjective that rhymes, such as "fat cat."

Tom Swiftie the creation of a quotation followed by a punning adverb, such as "'Your eggs are on fire,' he said hotly."

transposition creating new word by rearranging the letters of another word, as in "ocean" from "canoe."

typewriter word a word that can be typed on a single row of a typewriter, such as the word "typewriter."

univocalic of a sentence in which only one vowel can be used, as in "it sits in its pit."

WORDS ABOUT WORDS

accidence area of grammar that deals with the inflection of words.

A-copy new reporting term for trite or "lazy" copy lifted directly from a public relations press release.

acronym a word formed from the initial letters of a name, such as laser (light amplification by stimulated emission of radiation) or MADD (Mothers Against Drunk Driving.)

adage a frequently quoted saying or proverb.

addendum something added or that will be added, as a supplement.

ad hominem appealing to emotion rather than logic or reason, as when assaulting an opponent's character rather than his arguments.

ad ignorantium Latin term referring to a statement made by a speaker that is true only to the degree of the listener's ignorance.

ad infinitum to infinity; going on forever, without end.

ad-lib to make an impromptu, unrehearsed, or improvised remark, speech, and so on.

ad nauseam to the degree of nausea; to a sickening or ridiculous degree.

adnomination punning.

affectation in speech or writing, an unnatural, pretentious, or show-offy style that calls attention to itself.

affix an element of a word that is attached to other elements, such as a prefix or suffix.

agglutination the formation of new words by the combining of other words or word elements, as in disfigure-ment or broncho-scope.

allegory a story or anecdote that uses metaphor to illustrate a deeper truth.

alliteration in speech or writing, a string of two or more words with the same-sounding initial consonants, as in "the silly sods sunk Sally's ship Sunday."

allonym a pen name that is the borrowed name of another, as distinguished from a pseudonym.

allusion an indirect, incidental, or casual reference that is more meaningful or significant than its presentation would imply.

alphabet soup the extravagant use of initialisms or acronyms, a common practice of the government and the military.

altiloquence any pompous speech or writing.

ambiguity a wording, remark, speech, story, or similar term having more than one meaning.

amphibology an unintentional ambiguity resulting from poor sentence construction, as in "faulty propellers will ground beef lift rescue plan."

anachronism a person, thing, word, saying, and suchlike placed in the incorrect time in history, as a character in a World War II novel who uses the words "groovy" or "floppy disk."

anacoluthon in speech or writing, an unexpected change of syntax arriving at midsentence, such as "the flowers were in—but no, they weren't in bloom, come to think of it."

analogy a similarity in comparison between two different things or concepts; making a point by illustrating the similarities between two dissimilar things.

ananym one's name spelled backwards, sometimes used as a pseudonym.

anaphora the repetition of words or phrases for effect, as in "a big, bad man with a big, bad idea for a big, bad world."

anastrophe the reversal of the normal or standard order of words in a sentence construction, for effect, as in "off his rocker he goes."

anecdote a short, interesting account of an incident, often illustrating someone's personality or some historical event.

Anglicize to alter a word or name so that it sounds English, as in Arthur Greenburger to Art Green.

annotation a critical or explanatory note accompanying a literary work.

anonym an anonymous person or an anonymous publication. Also, a concept or idea that has no word to express or describe it.

antiphrasis a form of sarcasm or irony in which the exact opposite of the normal line is used, for effect, as in saying, "Great, wonderful!" in response to your car being stolen, or "it's a tough job, but someone's got to do it," when judging a beauty contest.

antithesis the juxtaposing of sharply contrasting ideas or words, as in "a noisy kind of peace can be found in the camaraderie of war."

antonym a word opposite in meaning to another word. The opposite of a synonym.

aphorism a brief statement that succinctly illustrates a principle or truth.

apocope the omission of a letter at the end of a word, as in "thinkin'" for "thinking."

apocrypha literary works of questionable authenticity or authorship.

aporia admitting to speechlessness; at a loss for words.

apostil an annotation in the margin.

archaism in speaking or writing, a word or expression that is out of date or antiquated, as in "forsooth, fair maiden."

argot any special vocabulary or jargon used by a group or class of people.

aside on the stage, a portion of dialogue intended for the ears of the audience only; any confidential dialogue.

assonance a resemblance in sound of words, syllables, or vowels, for effect, as in "winking, blinking, thinking—the robot looked about with alarm."

asyndeton leaving out conjunctions such as "and" between clauses, for effect, as in "we went to the store, walked in quietly, ordered three pounds of ham, left."

a verbis ad verbera from words to blows.

axiom a universally recognized truth or principle.

ballyhoo hype, exaggeration.

barb a sharp-tongued remark; a caustic observation.

barbarism the use of a word that is nonstandard or not accepted by society.

belles lettres literary works appreciated for their aesthetic value rather than their educational content, such as poetry, drama.

bidialectalism the use of two dialects, one informal and one formal or proper, within a language.

bilge worthless talk.

blarney sweet-talking flattery.

blather long-winded, stupid talk.

blurb a brief statement of praise or laudatory quote on a book cover.

bon mot a witticism.

brickbat an insult or blunt criticism.

bromide a common and overused remark or observation; a platitude.

cablese an extremely brief or shorthand style of writing, as in that found in a telegram.

cacography poor handwriting. Also, incorrect spelling.

cacology poor or improper pronunciation or diction.

cant whining, pleading, or monotonous speech. Also, any moral, hypocritical language. Also, the jargon of a group or class.

catachresis the incorrect use of a word that has been confused with another word. Also, a paradoxical figure of speech, as in "Latin has always been Greek to me."

catchfools words that are sometimes confused with one another because of their similarity in sound or spelling, for example, masticate and masturbate, deprecate and depreciate. Also known as dangerous pairs.

causerie any conversational or casual piece of writing.

charientism an insult so subtly presented that it is believed by the recipient to be unintended.

chestnut a joke, story, or expression that has been around and repeated for too long.

cheval de bataille a phrase referring to a person's pet topic or favorite argument; literally, battle horse.

cheville an extraneous word added to the end of a line of poetry to make it flow evenly; literally, a rag.

circumlocution evasive or indirect language achieved by wordiness.

classicism any ancient Greek or Roman word or phrase in English.

cliché any tired, trite, unoriginal, stale, and overused expression.

clinquant a show-off style of writing.

clipped word a word that is clipped of letters or syllables or altered in some way for use in informal speech, such as "flu" for "influenza" or "fish pole" for "fishing pole."

coinage the invention of a new word or expression.

colloquial in speech or writing, characteristic of any natural conversational language; informal.

colloquialism an informal expression of everyday speech.

colloquy a formal or mannered conversation.

commoratio the pounding home of a point by repeating its principles in different words.

communiqué an official communication or announcement.

compendium a short summary.

comprobatio flattering a person in order to win him over in an argument.

connotation the implied or suggestive meaning of a word other than its literal one.

consensus gentium fallacy "common opinion of the nations." The use of the erroneous argument that something must be true because so many people believe it to be true.

constructio ad sensum the construction of sentences by sound or instinct rather than by grammatical rules.

contraction the shortening of a word through removal of one or more of its letters, sometimes indicated by an apostrophe, as in "isn't" for "is not."

conundrum a perplexing riddle or problem whose answer involves a pun.

corruption an alteration of a word or term; an improper word usage.

creole a type of language that evolves when two groups having their own languages integrate. Also known as creolized language.

dangler a misplaced modifier that gives a sentence an unintended and often humorous meaning, as in "Rifling through my papers, the elephant appeared in front of me."

dead metaphor a metaphor that has become clichéd.

decapitable sentence a poorly constructed sentence characterized by overlapping subordinate clauses. Also known as an accordion sentence.

diacritical mark a mark over a character or letter to indicate accent or pronunciation.

dialect a provincial form of a language, characterized by its own idiom, pronunciation, or grammar.

dichaeologia any form of rhetoric used to defend one's failure by blaming it on everything and everybody but oneself.

diction use and choice of words in speech and writing.

digression straying from the main topic.

dilogy any statement that has an unintentional double meaning.

dissertation a treatise; a formal and in-depth investigation or observation of a subject, often a requirement for a degree.

double entendre an ambiguous word or statement with an underlying meaning that is risqué or provocative.

double negative the incorrect use of two negatives in one sentence, as in "he doesn't know nobody there."

doublespeak wordy, evasive, or obscure language used to gloss over a subject or hoodwink listeners with circumlocution.

echoic word a word that sounds like the subject it represents, as in "tick-tock," "crackle," "pop," "swish," "gong."

elegy a poem or expression of lament, usually for the dead.

eloquence the fluent, persuasive use of language; expressiveness.

embolalia inserting useless words or utterances into speech to stall for time while collecting one's thoughts, such as "uh, you know, like, I mean, you know."

enallage improper use of tense, mood, or gender, for example, calling a herd of cows a herd of cow, or calling a woman a guy.

enunciate to pronounce words clearly and correctly.

epistolary written in the style of a letter or letters, as some novels.

epithet word or term that characterizes a person or thing. Also, an adjective or descriptive word that forms part of a name, as in Richard the Lion-Hearted.

eponym a person from whom a place or thing is named, as in Washington, Addison's disease, Phillips screwdriver.

equivocate to speak ambiguously in order to confuse or mislead.

esprit de l'escalier the witty comment or snappy reply you wish you had said to someone earlier if you had only thought of it, literally; wit from the staircase.

etymology the origin and development of words; the derivation of words.

etymon the root or earliest form of a word, as a foreign word from which an English word is derived. A word's original meaning.

euphemism a substitution of an offensive word or phrase with a more acceptable one, as in "passed on" for died.

eusystolism the substituting of initials for complete words, as a form of euphemism, as in "S.O.B." "B.S."

exemplum a short story or anecdote given to illustrate a moral.

exonym the foreign-language spelling of a native geographical name.

exposition a presentation of explanatory information, as distinguished from narrative or description.

expressionist of a style of prose characterized by the use of symbolism and surrealism.

extemporaneous performed with little or no preparation, as an impromptu speech.

extrapolate to make an inference beyond the known facts; to surmise.

eyewash flattering or misleading talk.

facetiae humorous or ribald writings, anecdotes, sayings.

faction nonfiction presented in the style of fiction.

faux pas a socially unacceptable or embarrassing remark; literally, false step.

felicity any apt choice of words.

Freudian slip a slip of the tongue that inadvertently reveals what's on the mind of the speaker.

fused metaphor the incorrect joining of two metaphors; for example, "my monkey to bear" (my cross to bear; a monkey on my back).

fustian pompous or pretentious speech or writing.

Gallicism an English word or phrase derived from French.

glib speaking easily and fluently but superficially, smugly, or insincerely.

grammatism being overly concerned about the proper use of grammar.

hack a writer more concerned with making a buck than creating fine art; one whose writing is trite.

hackneyed trite, clichéd, unoriginal, banal.

heterography inconsistent spelling usage, as in letters that are pronounced differently in different words, like the *g* in "good" and "geriatric," or the *c* in "car" and "cite."

heteronym a word having the same spelling as another but with a completely different meaning and pronunciation, as in "bass" (fish) and "bass" (drum) or "bow" (ribbon) and "bow" (boat).

heterophemy the inadvertent or incorrect use of a word that is similar in spelling or pronunciation to another word, such as "cinnamon" for synonym. Also, the use of a euphemism with a pregnant pause, as in "the president is . . . indisposed . . . if you know what I mean."

Hispanicism a Spanish word used in English, such as jalapeño, machismo.

hobbyhorse a pet topic or argument.

Hobson-Jobson the alteration of a foreign word into English, for example, "compound" from the

Malay "kampong," or "grouper" from the Portuguese "garoupa."

homograph a word identical in spelling with another word but having a different pronunciation, as in "bass" (fish) and "bass" (drum).

homonym a word spelled and pronounced the same as another word but having a different meaning, for example, "bow" (ship) and "bow" (down).

homonym slip the incorrect writing of one word for another with the same or nearly the same pronunciation, for example, "too" for "two," or "then" for "than."

homophone a word pronounced the same as another but having a different spelling and meaning, such as "peace," and "piece."

hybrid the joining of two words or word elements from two languages to form a new word.

hyperbole an exaggeration used as a figure of speech, such as "I could eat a horse," or "this hangnail is killing me."

hyperurbanism the inaccurate imitation of upper-class speech by someone with a lower-class dialect.

hypophora reasoning with oneself out loud.

ideogram a character or symbol, such as $, &, or #. Also, any character used in Chinese writing.

idiolect the unique language of an individual.

idiologism a quirk or characteristic of an individual's speech.

idiom a particular form of speech within a language, as used in a specific community or group. Also, words, phrases, and expressions that cannot be translated literally into a foreign language, such as "life's a bitch," or "join the rat race."

idioticon a dictionary of dialect.

inarticulate unexpressive; unable to speak fluently or persuasively.

innuendo a subtle implication or allusion, usually of something negative.

inversion the altering or reversal of normal word order for effect, for example, "through the grass we did run."

irony the use of words to convey the opposite of their literal meaning, especially in a sarcastic or humorous way, for example, "his wit was as sharp as a wet sponge."

Janus word a word having two meanings the exact opposite of each other, such as "inflammable," or "cleave."

jargon meaningless gibberish; the special language of a class, profession, or group.

jawbreaker a word that is difficult to pronounce.

je ne sais quoi literally, I don't know what; a certain indescribable something.

King's English normal or proper, understandable English.

laconic terse; reserved.

lallation any noise or utterance typical of a baby.

lapsus calami a slip of the pen.

lapsus linguae a slip of the tongue.

Latinism a Latin word or phrase used in English.

leading question a question designed to prompt a desired answer.

legalese legal jargon.

lethologica the inability to recall a word that is on the tip of one's tongue.

lethonomania forgetting names.

lexicography the compiling and writing of dictionaries and word books.

lexicology the study of word histories, derivations, meanings, and similar pursuits.

lexicon a dictionary, vocabulary book, foreign language word book, or similar publication.

linguistics the study of language and speech.

litotes a form of irony or understatement, achieved by the use of inverted phrasing, for example, "not bad," or "I can't disagree with that."

localism a word or expression unique to a particular community or region.

loganamnosis an obsession to remember a forgotten word.

logomasia an extreme distaste for certain words.

lost positives words whose positive forms are no longer in common use, such as "gruntled" from "disgruntled."

lyricism prose executed in a poetically descriptive style.

malapropism the incorrect use of a word that sounds similar to another word, often with humorous results, for example, "I'll sue him for defecation (defamation) of character," or "a pigment (figment) of the imagination."

malonym a metaphor, cliché, or popular expression in which an incorrect word is used, for example, "let's go hole (whole) hog on this," or "you can lead a horse to water but you can't make him think (drink)."

mealymouthed dishonest, evasive; overly euphemistic in speech.

meiosis a form of understatement or underemphasis used to achieve an ironic effect.

melioration the acquisition of a positive meaning by a word that has traditionally had a negative meaning, for example, "bad" is now sometimes used as the equivalent of "cool" or "good."

mendaciloquence artful lying.

metaphor a figure of speech characterized by an implied comparison between two things that are different, for example, "all the world's a stage," or "the evening of life," or "the company is a big ship to turn around."

metastasis in a debate, the mentioning of a subject in a casual manner, as if it were trivial.

metathesis the historical transposing of letters or syllables in a word to create a new, permanent spelling or pronunciation, such as, Old English "brid" to "bird."

metonymy a figure of speech that substitutes a word or phrase with a word or phrase that is closely associated, as in "brass" for military officers, or "the Crown" for British monarchy.

metric prose prose with a poetic rhythm.

mincing word a coyly euphemistic word used to avoid using an undainty word.

misnomer an incorrect word, name, title, belief, and so forth.

mixaprop a fusion of a mixed metaphor and a malapropism, for example, "It took more wind out of his sails than a fish without water."

mixed metaphor the incorrect fusing of two or more metaphors in a single sentence, such as "if he faces the music, it will fall on deaf ears."

neologism a newly created word or expression; an old word given a new meaning. Also, a meaningless or nonsense word coined by a mentally ill person.

nom de plume a pen name; a pseudonym.

non sequitur a remark that is not relevant to the argument at hand; an inference that does not follow from the premise; literally, it does not follow.

nosism the annoying use of "we" to denote oneself in speech or writing.

nudis verbis in naked words.

obfuscate to make unclear or obscure; to use overblown or highly technical language pretentiously.

officialese bureaucratic jargon; government obfuscation; official, formal language.

off-the-cuff spoken casually without preparation.

onomatopoeia the use of a word that sounds like what it represents, such as "chirp," "boom," "gurgle," "swish."

oxymoron a figure of speech characterized by the juxtaposition of words that seem incongruous or contradictory, as in a "cheerful pessimist," "cruel kindness," "eloquent silence."

pabulum insipid writing or ideas; mindless drivel.

padding intentional wordiness, used to lengthen a written work or speech.

palilogy repeating a word in a sentence, for effect.

pan a bad review.

pap pabulum.

paradiastole the use of euphemistic language to describe something, as in describing a brothel as a "spirited household."

paradox an apparently contradictory statement that may nevertheless be true, for example, "The man in the time travel story travelled back in time, shot his parents, and then ceased to exist."

paraphrase to restate in different words.

parataxis the use of sentences without conjunctions, especially "and" or "but."

parlance a characteristic manner of speech.

paroemiology the subject of proverbs.

paronym a word having the same derivation or root as another word, as in "beautiful" and "beauteous."

parrot to repeat mindlessly what someone else has said; to imitate without understanding, as a parrot.

pathopoeia agitating or arousing emotion through rhetoric.

pedantry showing off one's education through speech or writing.

periphrasis the overuse of words, especially indirect ones, to say something. Also, any indirect statement.

personification giving human attributes to abstractions or inanimate objects.

philology the study of historical linguistics.

philophronesis acting submissive and humble in order to mollify someone's anger.

phoneticism spelling a word differently than normal to illustrate its pronunciation, such as the Australian word "mate" spelled "mite."

platform rhetoric the form of oratory most commonly used by politicians.

platitude a trite remark; an obvious or simple observation presented as if it were brilliant.

poetic license breaking the standard rules of form, diction, style, in poetry or prose.

polysyndeton the frequent use of conjunctions, especially "and," in a sentence with multiple clauses.

pontificate to speak with pompous authority.

prosonomasia a form of pun composed of someone's name, for example, Larry Bird-beak, Katherine Lipburn.

pseudandry the use of a man's pen name by a female writer.

pseudogyny the use of a woman's pen name by a male writer.

psychobabble the jargon used by psychologists and psychiatrists, and especially by those who try to imitate them.

purple prose overblown, overwritten, flowery, or ornate prose; overly poetic prose.

red herring an irrelevant issue designed to draw attention away from the matter at hand, frequently used by politicians and mystery writers.

redundancy unnecessary repetition, as in "merge together," "erupt violently," "gather together," "free gift."

rehash stuff that has been done before; old, reworked material.

rejoinder a reply to a reply.

repartee witty or clever banter.

rhetoric the art of persuasive oratory or writing; the style, content, and structure of speech or writing.

rhetorical question a question that requires no answer; a question with an obvious answer.

satire a literary work that uses irony, wit, and humor to expose evil or folly.

satirist a person who writes satires or who uses wit and humor to expose evil or folly.

saw an old saying often repeated.

semantics the study of the development and change of word meaning throughout history.

simile a figure of speech characterized by the comparison of two unlike things, as in "he hissed like a snake," or "the cliffs rose like cathedral spires."

Socratic irony feigning ignorance in a debate in order to win a point.

soliloquy a dramatic monologue; a speech made aloud to oneself when alone.

spoonerism an inadvertent transposing of word sounds, as in "Hoobert Herver," for "Herbert Hoover," or a "White Horse souse" for a "White House source."

staccato a form of speech or writing characterized by the frequent use of short, abrupt sentences, for effect.

stemwinder a crowd-agitating speech.

stream of consciousness in speech or writing, inner dialogue, or the articulation of one's thoughts and emotions.

succinct articulated clearly and to the point with the use of as few words as possible.

suppressio veri suppressing the facts; deliberately ignoring or failing to mention information that may alter someone's decision, as in a court trial.

surrealistic descriptive and evoking images of dreams, nightmares, hallucinations, and the unconscious.

synecdoche a figure of speech in which a whole is represented by a partial description or expression, or vice versa, as in "The Sox won two of three games," instead of "The Boston Red Sox baseball team won two of three games."

synonym a word having the same or similar meaning to another word, such as "car" and "automobile." The opposite of antonym.

syntax the manner in which words, clauses, and sentences are constructed or arranged.

tacenda things that are better off left unsaid.

terse succinct, to the point.

transliteration the altering of letters or words to fit them into another language, as "snap, crackle, pop" translates to "poks, riks, raks" in Finnish.

trite unoriginal, stale, banal.

tu quoque in a debate, accusing a rival of criticizing that which he himself is guilty of.

twaddle foolish, silly talk.

verbatim word for word.

verbiage wordiness.

vernacular native language of a region. Also, trade jargon or idiom.

vogue word a currently hip-to-use word; a word in fashion.

waffle to speak vaguely or evasively.

weasel word any word used to mislead, evade, or whitewash.

whitewash to gloss over a wrong.

LAW

CONTRACT LAW

adhesion contract a contract that heavily favors one party over the other, raising suspicions that the agreements in the contract may have been coerced or involuntary on the part of the disfavored party.

bad faith willful failure to follow through on a contractual obligation.

binding obligatory.

boilerplate any universal or formal language used in a standard contract or legal document.

breach of contract the failure to carry out or follow through on a contract agreement.

consideration the giving or promise of money, goods, or services in return for something else of value, the basis for any contract; the inducement offered to enter into a contract.

covenant an agreement to carry out or perform some duty or promise, as in a deed.

covenantee the person a covenant is intended for.

covenantor the person who makes a covenant.

duress any inducement or action by a person that compels another to do something he or she wouldn't ordinarily do, such as making a threat to force someone to sign a contract.

earnest something of value, such as money, given by one party to another to bind a contract.

escalator clause a clause in a contract that provides for a higher price to be paid if certain conditions occur.

escape clause a clause allowing a person to get out of a contract and be free of liability if certain conditions do or do not occur.

in extremis most often refers to the writing of a will when death is impending, but it can also refer to any contract written under "extreme circumstances" that could possibly alter the interpretation of the contract.

meeting of the minds mutual understanding and agreement to the terms of a contract between two parties.

mitigation of damages understanding that a damaged party in a contract must not do anything that will increase the amount of damages.

notary public one authorized to administer oaths, to take depositions, and to witness and certify the signing of documents.

postnuptial agreement an agreement entered into by a husband and wife that determines how assets will be distributed in the event of death or divorce.

prenuptial agreement an agreement entered into by a couple intending to marry that determines how assets will be distributed in the event of divorce or death.

proviso a stipulation or condition.

rider an amendment or addition added to a contract.

severable contract a contract in which the agreements are considered as separate and independent so that a breach of any agreement does not void the contract as a whole.

CRIMINAL AND TORT LAW

(*Also see* CONTRACT LAW, PROBATE LAW, PROPERTY AND REAL ESTATE LAW)

ABA American Bar Association.

abscond to skip town or otherwise avoid court action through hiding or concealing oneself.

abuse of process using process for a purpose other than that intended by law.

accessory one who assists or facilitates others in a crime.

accessory after the fact one who knowingly receives or assists a person who is being sought for committing a felony.

accessory before the fact a person who plans a crime, gives advice about a crime, or commands others to commit a crime, but who does not actively commit the crime.

accomplice a partner in the commission of a crime.

accusatory instrument an accusation, an indictment, or information that forms the basis for a criminal charge.

ACLU American Civil Liberties Union.

acquiescence any behavior that implies consent, such as remaining silent and failing to raise an objection when an accusatory statement is made.

acquit to set free one who has been absolved of charges.

action the prosecuting of one party by another for a misdeed or for protection of rights or other reasons.

ad damnum the amount of damages sued for.

additur an increase of the amount of damages, awarded by the court when a jury award is deemed inadequate.

adjourn to break temporarily from a court proceeding through recess.

Admiralty court a court or tribunal having jurisdiction over actions related to the sea, such as maritime contracts or injuries at sea.

admissible evidence evidence acceptable to the court.

affidavit a written statement made by a person under oath before the court or a notary public.

affirmative action taking tangible action to eliminate the abuses of past discrimination, as through racial quotas in schools and the workplace.

against the weight of the evidence a situation through which a new trial may be ordered because a jury has, in the judge's opinion, given a verdict that is unsupported by the evidence.

age of consent age at which one may marry without parental consent. Also, the age at which a person may consent to sexual intercourse without the risk of statutory rape or sexual assault being charged to the other party.

aggrieved party the person who has been hurt or damaged in a lawsuit.

aid and abet to facilitate or assist knowingly another person in the commission of a crime.

alias otherwise or also known as.

alibi a provable accounting of a person's whereabouts at the time a crime was committed.

alienation of affections malicious acts or behavior by a third party—such as a mother, father-in-law, or outside lover—that interferes with a marriage and alienates one spouse from another.

amnesty a pardon excusing a person of a crime, such as draft evasion.

antitrust laws statutes that help to maintain free competition in the marketplace and that punish any acts by a person or corporation that unfairly restrain a competitor.

appeal to take a case to a higher court in the hope that it will deem the lower court's judgment incorrect and either reverse the judgment or order a new trial.

appellant the party who appeals a decision.

appellate court a court that reviews the rulings and judgments of a lower court.

a priori from cause to effect.

arbitration the settling of disagreements between two parties by an agreed-upon third party, most used in disputes involving labor contracts.

arbitrator the impartial, chosen person who arbitrates a dispute.

arraign to accuse of a wrongdoing or to call a person to answer a charge.

arraignment the formal charging of the defendant with an offense.

artifice a fraudulent device used to commit a crime.

assault, aggravated an assault resulting in serious bodily injury to the assaulted, or any assault judged to be particularly atrocious or depraved.

attachment the seizing of a defendant's property for the payment of a plaintiff's judgment award.

attorney-client privilege the privilege of confidential communication between client and attorney, in which information cannot be shared with any other party without consent from the client.

attorney general the chief attorney of the federal government or of each state government.

attractive nuisance the tort doctrine that requires a person who keeps any dangerous object or thing on his or her property that might attract children to protect those children from possible injury, such as by removing the door of an abandoned refrigerator or by fencing a swimming pool.

bail a form of security paid to ensure that the defendant will show up for court proceedings.

bail bond the document used in the release of a person in custody.

bailiff a court officer in charge of keeping order and guarding jurors.

bailment the process of providing bail for a defendant. Also, the delivering of goods or personal property to one in trust.

bailsman one who gives bail for another.

bait and switch an unethical practice wherein a retailer advertises a particularly good buy to attract customers and then coerces or persuades the customers into buying a much more expensive model than the one advertised.

barrister the English equivalent of a trial lawyer.

bench the court. The bench where the judge sits.

bench warrant a court order issued to have a person seized and brought into court to take part in proceedings.

Bill of Rights the first 10 amendments to the U.S. Constitution.

blue law state or local Sunday closing law.

bond a written instrument that guarantees performance of obligations—such as the payment of fees—through sureties. Also, an amount paid as bail.

bondsman a person who provides a bond for another for a free.

burden of proof the burden of substantiating claims, accusations, or allegations, a responsibility falling on the plaintiff in a court action.

bylaws any in-house rules or laws of a corporation, organization, or association.

canon church law.

capital offense an offense punishable by death.

care in a negligence case, the amount of care a custodian must give to a thing in order to avoid a charge of negligence, which, depending on circumstances, may be great care, ordinary care, reasonable care, and slight care.

caveat let him beware. An urging of caution.

caveat emptor let the buyer beware.

chief justice in a court with more than one judge, the presiding judge.

circumstantial evidence indirect, secondary, or incidental evidence from which a judge or jury might make inferences.

civil action an action filed to protect a civil right.

civil penalties fines and money damages.

class action an action filed on behalf of a group.

clean hands the doctrine holding that claimants seeking justice must not themselves have taken part in an illegal or unethical act relating to the claim.

clear and convincing of a standard of proof, beyond a preponderance of the evidence but less than beyond a reasonable doubt; more than the degree of proof required in civil cases but below that required by criminal cases.

collusion a conspiracy to commit fraud or other illegal activity.

common law law based on court decisions, customs, and usages, as opposed to law based on codified written laws.

common-law marriage a marriage not based on any formal ceremony or legal filing but on personal agreement between the two parties to become husband and wide, followed by a substantial period of cohabitation.

compounding a felony refusal of a felony victim to prosecute the felon in exchange for a bribe.

conjecture inference from incomplete evidence.

conspiracy two or more people conspiring to commit a crime.

contempt of court an act that obstructs the administration of justice or that demonstrates disrespect for the court's authority.

contumacy defiance of the court's orders or authority.

corpus delecti the facts proving a crime.

crime of passion a nonpremeditated crime committed under the influence of heat of passion or extreme sudden rage.

cross-examination the questioning of a witness by the lawyer other than the one who called the witness, concerning information previously given in the initial examination.

D.A. district attorney.

damages monetary award given to the damaged party in a court action.

damages, double an award twice the normal or standard amount given to the injured party as a form of punishment to the wrongdoer.

damages, exemplary any compensation that exceeds actual damages, awarded to punish the wrongdoer.

damnum absque injuria any loss or injury caused without any wrongdoing by a person or persons, such as by an act of nature, or any damage caused by a lawful act; any damage in which the law provides no recourse.

decriminalization the changing of a law so that what was once a criminal act is no longer so and is therefore no longer punishable by law.

defalcation failure of a trustee to pay out money when it becomes due.

default judgment a judgment made against a defendant for failure to appear in court.

defraud to commit fraud.

degree of proof the degree of evidence necessary for the awarding of damages or conviction of a suspect. The degrees of proof include "preponderance of the evidence," "clear and convincing," and "beyond a reasonable doubt."

deliberate to consider all the facts of a case after all the evidence has been given.

de minimis acts too trivial or unimportant to be dealt with in a court of law.

demonstrative evidence weapons, stolen goods, photographs, or other objects displayed in court to help clarify or add evidence to a case.

deposition a pretrial statement taken from a witness under oath.

desuetude discontinuance from use, referring to laws that have become obsolete and are no longer enforced.

dictum a dogmatic or opinionated pronouncement by the judge concerning a case.

diminished capacity a defense that pleads diminished mental capacity of the defendant, which often lessens a sentence in a criminal conviction.

disbar to rescind the license and right of an attorney to practice law due to unethical or illegal conduct.

district attorney the prosecuting attorney of a given district.

divestiture a selling off of property or assets by an offending party as ordered by the court to prevent the offender from enjoying the gains or "spoils" of his crime, usually used in the enforcement of antitrust laws.

docket the list of cases pending on a court's calendar.

double jeopardy a provision in the Fifth Amendment to the Constitution preventing a second prosecution in a criminal case; regardless of the outcome of the first trial.

embracery obstructing justice by trying to bribe or otherwise influence a juror.

entrapment a defense used in criminal law that excuses a defendant if it is proven he or she was lured into a crime by police inducement and that the crime would not have occurred if it had not been for that inducement.

estoppel a restraint to prevent one from contradicting a previous statement.

executive privilege the right of the president to refuse to disclose confidential information that may impair government functioning.

exemplar nontestimony evidence of identification such as fingerprints, blood samples, handwriting samples, and voice recordings.

exigency any emergency occurrence that excuses one for breaking the law, such as speeding to the hospital with a person having a heart attack.

expungement of records the court-ordered annulment and destruction of all records of arrest and court proceedings concerning a defendant arrested but not convicted.

extenuating circumstances circumstances that justify or partially justify an illegal act and that qualify guilt or blame.

extortion the crime of using one's position in business or government to extort or obtain illegally money or property through abuse of power.

extradition the process through which a criminal is transferred or surrendered by one nation to another or from one state to another.

facilitation the statutory offense of aiding another to carry out a crime.

fairness doctrine a requirement of broadcasters to air contrasting viewpoints on controversial issues.

famosus libellus a slanderous or libelous letter, handbill, advertisement, written accusation, or indictment.

felony any crime considered more serious than a misdemeanor, such as homicide, robbery, burglary, rape, arson, or larceny.

felony murder a murder committed in the act of another felony, such as a robbery, burglary, or rape.

fiduciary pertaining to one who holds something in trust for another.

first-degree murder any murder that is willful, deliberate, and premeditated.

foreman among a jury, the spokesman and presiding member.

forensic relating to, belonging to, or used in courts of justice.

forensic medicine a branch of medicine employed to assist in legal matters.

fratricide the murder of one's brother.

fraud willful deceit resulting in harm to another.

Freedom of Information Act the federal law requiring that documents and other materials held in federal offices must be released to the public upon request, although with a few exemptions.

fresh pursuit the right of the police to enter another jurisdiction in order to arrest a felon.

fruit of the poisonous tree doctrine the doctrine that prevents the use of evidence originating from illegal conduct on the part of an official on the grounds that such "tainted" evidence cannot be trusted.

gag order a court order restricting outside comments about a case.

garnish to attach wages or other property.

graft profiting dishonestly from public money through one's political connections.

grand jury a jury of 12 to 23 persons employed to evaluate accusations and persons charged with crimes to determine whether a trial is warranted.

gratis given without reward; free, for nothing.

gross of behavior, willful, inexcusable.

habeas corpus the common-law writ designed to prevent unjust imprisonment; law enforcement authorities must obtain a judicial determination of the legality of putting a particular person in custody.

hearing a preliminary judicial investigation of evidence to determine issues of fact.

hearsay rule a rule holding that evidence based on the statements of those other than testifying witnesses is inadmissible.

homicide the killing of one person by another.

hostile witness any biased witness whose testimony may be prejudiced against a court opponent.

hung jury an indecisive jury that cannot agree on a verdict.

ignorantia legis non excusat ignorance of the law is no excuse.

immaterial irrelevant.

immunity immunity from prosecution or exemption from a rule or penalty, sometimes granted to witnesses to get them to testify.

impaneling the jury selection process. Also, a list of those serving on a jury.

impeach to charge a public official with malfeasance while in office.

implied consent consent presumed or inferred from someone's action, inaction, or silence.

impound to place something in the custody of the police or other authority.

in articulo mortis in the moment of death.

in camera proceedings held in a judge's chambers or out of public view.

indictment a written statement formally charging one with a crime and submitted to a grand jury.

inferior court any court whose decisions may be judged by a higher court.

in invitum against the will of another.

injunction a court order that prohibits someone from carrying out a particular action.

injuria non excusat injuriam one wrong doesn't justify another wrong.

inquest a judicial inquiry. Also, a coroner's inquiry into a cause of death.

interrogation police questioning of suspects.

journalist's privilege the privilege of the media in some cases to keep sources of information confidential.

J.P. justice of the peace.

jump bail to fail to appear in court after posting bail.

jural pertaining to law and justice.

jurisprudence the science and philosophy of law.

jury of the vicinage a jury selected from the neighborhood where the crime was committed.

justice synonymous with judge.

laches a doctrine providing a defense to the defendant when the opposing party has delayed prosecution for an unusual amount of time.

larceny stealing.

leading question a query by lawyers in which the question to a witness suggests the wanted answer; allowed in court only in cross-examination.

libel malicious publication of falsehoods that defame a person.

lien a claim or hold on the property of another that secures a debt.

litigants the parties involved in a lawsuit.

litigation legal process.

loan sharking loaning money with extremely high interest rates.

majority, age of when one legally becomes adult, usually considered to be age 18.

malfeasance a wrongful act.

malice the desire to harm others; an act performed with the willful disregard for the welfare of others.

malice aforethought a thought-out design, without justification, to harm others; the state of mind that distinguishes murder from manslaughter.

malicious arrest the arrest of a person without probable cause.

malicious prosecution an action to collect damages caused by a previous prosecution without probable cause and with malice.

malum in se an act that is illegal because it is inherently evil as judged by society. See MALUM PROHIBITUM.

malum prohibitum an act that is illegal because it is prohibited by law for the welfare of the public and not necessarily evil.

mandate an order issued from a superior court to a lesser court.

manslaughter the killing of another without malice aforethought.

manslaughter, voluntary killing in the heat of passion.

manslaughter, involuntary killing someone accidentally, as through reckless driving.

material relevant, important.

material witness a witness whose testimony is absolutely vital to a case.

matricide the killing of one's mother.

mediation the settling of disputes out of court.

medical examiner coroner.

mens rea the evil intent or state of mind that accompanies a criminal act; in legal terms, the states of mind include "intentionally," "knowingly," "recklessly," and "grossly negligent."

Miranda rule the requirement to read a person his or her rights (right to remain silent, right to a lawyer's presence, etc.) during an arrest and before police interrogation.

miscarriage of justice damages to a party due to court errors during litigation, sometimes requiring a reversal of judgment.

misdemeanors any crimes considered less serious and having less severe punishment than felonies.

misfeasance performing a lawful act in a dangerous or injurious manner.

misjoinder the joining of separate counts in an indictment.

mistrial a trial that is voided and terminated before a verdict is reached, due to a hung jury, court errors, or death of a juror or an attorney.

mitigating circumstances circumstances that lessen a person's guilt in a crime.

modus operandi the manner of operation; the method used by a criminal in accomplishing a crime.

moot court a make-believe court held in law schools to argue a moot case.

moral certainty to be certain beyond a reasonable doubt, but to be less so than absolutely certain.

moral turpitude depravity, dishonesty, vileness.

motion in a court proceeding, a request for a ruling.

negative pregnant a denial that, by being noticeably qualified or modified, implies an affirmation of facts.

negligence the failure to exercise care in a degree that would be expected from a reasonable person.

negligence, criminal reckless negligence resulting in injury or death. Also known as culpable negligence.

nemo est supra legis no one is above the law.

nolle prosequi Latin for "do not pursue," referring to a motion to dismiss a case because evidence for a successful prosecution is insufficient.

non compos mentis not of sound mind.

non vult contendere he will not contest. A defendant who neither confesses guilt nor contests the charges against him, thereby acquiescing to being treated as guilty by the courts.

nuisance anything indecent, offensive, obstructive, or disturbing to the free use of one's property.

pain and suffering a type of damages that can be recovered when the opposing party's wrongdoing results in emotional or physical pain.

palimony support payments similar to alimony but given to the partner in a defunct nonmarital relationship.

pander to pimp; to serve the sexual desire of others. Also, to promote obscene literature and movies.

panderer a pimp; one who serves the sexual interests of others.

paralegal a legal assistant.

paternity suit an action filed to determine the father of an illegitimate child and to gain financial support for that child.

patricide the killing of one's father.

penal pertaining to punishments or penalties associated with breaking the law.

penal code the body of laws concerning crime and its punishment.

perjury lying while under oath, a criminal offense.

petit jury a trial jury, as opposed to a grand jury. Also known as a petty jury.

physician-patient privilege the privilege of physicians to keep all forms of communication from a patient confidential unless the patient consents otherwise.

plaintiff in a court action, the person who files suit.

plea bargaining the negotiation between the prosecutor and the accused of a mutually satisfactory disposition of a case to expedite proceedings, usually involving a guilty plea in exchange for a lesser sentence.

plead to argue, persuade, or present a case in court.

polling the jury the surveying by the judge of the jurors for their individual decisions concerning the verdict, as requested in some cases by a criminal defendant.

polygraph a lie detector.

postmortem after death. Refers to the examination of a body by a coroner to determine cause of death.

power of attorney granting someone in writing the authority to perform specific acts on his behalf.

precedent a past court case decision that is used as an authority or reference for deciding future cases.

prejudice having a bias in favor of one of the parties in a lawsuit. Also, a preconceived notion of guilt or innocence concerning a party without knowing the facts.

premeditation thinking over something beforehand, an element distinguishing murder from manslaughter.

presentment a written accusation made by a grand jury stemming from its own investigation.

presumption a supposition; a strong probability.

presumption of innocence the principle that the accused is presumed innocent until proven guilty.

priest-penitent privilege the privilege granted to a priest, rabbi, or minister to keep confidential any confessions of a church member unless the church member consents otherwise.

probable cause the required element in a legal search and seizure or in an arrest.

pro bono publico for the public welfare. Most often refers to an attorney representing a case without compensation. A pro bono case.

prosecution the carrying out of a suit in court. Also, the party filing the suit.

prosecutor the person or public official who conducts a prosecution.

prurient interest a shameful interest in sex and nudity. **public defender** a government-appointed attorney who defends those unable or unwilling to hire their own attorney.

puffing the extravagant claims made by salespeople concerning their wares, generally not acceptable as a representation of fact or as the basis for fraud.

purloin to steal.

psychotherapist-patient privilege the privilege of a psychiatrist or psychologist to keep all forms of communication from a patient confidential unless the patient consents otherwise.

quid pro quo compensation; something for something.

racketeering obtaining money through fraud or extortion or through a conspiracy to commit fraud or extortion.

raised check a check whose original amount has been altered.

real evidence any object, such as a murder weapon or photograph, that can be examined and used as evidence in court. Also known as demonstrative evidence.

reasonable doubt in a criminal trial, the doctrine describing the degree of certainty a juror must have concerning evidence in order to return a guilty verdict against the accused. He must be certain beyond a reasonable doubt.

rebuttal evidence any evidence that contradicts or counteracts other evidence.

recidivist a habitual offender.

recusal the disqualification of a judge or jury due to conflict of interest, bias, or prejudice.

rejoinder the defendant's answer in response to the plaintiff's reply or replication.

remittitur a reduction of a jury's excessive verdict, made by the judge. Opposite of additur.

replication the plaintiff's reply to the defendant's answer.

rescue doctrine a doctrine holding that a negligent person causing an injury to someone is also liable for any injury that befalls the rescuer of a victim during a rescue attempt.

respondeat superior let the superior reply. A doctrine holding that an employer is liable for damages caused by an employee in the course of his duties.

restraining order similar to an injunction but issued without a hearing.

retainer an advance payment to an attorney for services.

retreat, duty to in some jurisdictions, the duty to flee a threatening situation as opposed to defending oneself by injuring another, generally not applicable in one's own home, however.

scienter knowingly. "Guilty knowledge" of the falsity of one's statements or representations made when committing a fraud.

scintilla speculative evidence that is considered not substantial.

search warrant after reviewing evidence for probable cause, a judge's formal authority granted to the police to search a suspicious person's residence, work, or other locale for the gathering of evidence of a crime. A search warrant is unnecessary when a suspect consents to a search, or in cases of hot pursuit, when an officer follows a suspect into a hiding place, or when an officer is trying to stop a suspect from destroying evidence.

second-degree murder unpremeditated murder with malice aforethought.

service to serve notice or to deliver a pleading or other document in a lawsuit to the opposing party.

sham pleading pleading that is unsupported by the facts.

sheriff's sale the sale of a judgment debtor's property by the sheriff to satisfy an unpaid judgment, mortgage, or lien.

shield laws laws protecting the confidentiality between a news reporter and his or her source. Also includes laws protecting rape victims from questioning about past sexual experiences.

show-up similar to a police lineup, but only with one suspect facing a witness.

sidebar the part of a courtroom out of earshot of the jury and used by the judge and attorneys to discuss issues that would be improper for the jury to hear.

slander false words spoken publicly that damage the reputation of another.

standing mute refusing to plead guilty or not guilty.

statute of limitations any statute that puts a time limit on when judicial action can be taken against someone.

statutory rape engaging in sex with a minor.

stay a court-ordered postponement of an event or action.

stay of execution a court order in which a judgment is postponed for a specific amount of time.

strict liability liability for injuries or damages stemming from dangerous activities (such as the use of explosives) even if those activities are carried out lawfully and with extreme care. Liability without fault or negligence.

subornation of perjury the crime of persuading another to lie in court.

subpoena a court order to force a witness to appear at a judicial proceeding; a subpoena to testify.

subrogation one's fulfilling of an obligation on another's behalf.

suit a broad term for any court proceeding undertaken for the pursuit of justice.

suitor a litigant in a court case.

summation the closing arguments made by each party's counsel in a trial.

summons an order or notification served to a defendant to appear in court or risk a default judgment.

sunshine laws laws that require meetings held by government agencies to be open to the public.

superior court any court that reviews the decisions of lower courts.

suppression of evidence preventing the use of illegally seized evidence or any evidence that may unfairly bias a jury.

supreme court the highest appellate court in a jurisdiction or state.

Supreme Court the highest court in the United States, consisting of nine justices and having jurisdiction over all other courts.

surety one who promises to fulfill certain obligations, particularly financial ones, if his principal fails to do so; one who takes on a liability for another's debt; a bondsman.

surety bond a bond issued by a surety guaranteeing the fulfillment of another's obligations.

tacit implied.

tainted evidence evidence that cannot be relied upon because of its questionable source, based on the fruit of the poisonous tree doctrine.

taking the Fifth pleading the Fifth Amendment right not to provide evidence that will incriminate oneself.

testify to give statements while under oath in a court proceeding.

testimony statements or evidence given by a witness while under oath.

tort any wrongful act, damage, or injury associated with a breach of lawful social behavior as opposed to a breach of a contract.

tortfeasor one who commits a tort.

transcript a certified, written record of what occurred and what was said in a court proceeding.

trial, bench a trial with a judge but no jury.

unclean hands see CLEAN HANDS.

usury an excessive or illegal rate of interest on a loan.

verdict, false a verdict unsupported by the facts.

vicarious liability the liability of an employer for the actions of an employee while conducting the duties of his job. Also known as respondent superior.

vice crimes immoral indulgences such as gambling, prostitution, and pornography.

vicinage an area of neighborhood where a crime was committed or where jurors are called from.

vis major a greater force, referring to an act of God or an act of nature.

voice exemplar a tape recording of a person's voice used as identification in a court proceeding.

voir dire examination an evaluation and a qualifying of prospective jurors.

volenti non fit injuria the volunteer suffers no wrong. In tort law, any person willingly engaging in an activity cannot collect damages if that activity causes injury.

wanton grossly negligent.

warrant a court order issued to have someone arrested.

writ a court order issued to compel someone to carry out some activity or to stop them from carrying out some activity.

writ of execution the court's enforcing of a judgment by levying the judgment debtor's property.

PROBATE LAW

advancement an advance granted to a child from a living parent's will.

bequeath the giving of a gift of personal property in a will.

bequest a gift of personal property.

causa mortis the law that states that a gift given in anticipation of death is void if the giver survives.

disinherit to cancel or terminate another's inheritance.

forced heirs heirs who cannot be disinherited, such as a spouse and children.

holographic will a will written, dated, and signed by the testator himself.

in extremis most often referring to the writing of a will when death is impending, but also referring to any contract written under "extreme circumstances" that could possibly alter the interpretation of that contract.

intestate one who has died without drawing up a will.

legacy bequest.

nuncupative will a dying declaration or oral will given by an ill person incapable of drawing up a formal will.

probate a proceeding in which the elements of a will are authenticated and found legal.

probate court a court that deals with the probate of wills.

testacy leaving a valid will upon death.

testator one who makes a will.

PROPERTY AND REAL ESTATE LAW

abandonment the relinquishing of rights or property by one person to another.

appurtenant an easement, covenant, or other burden attached to a property.

burden any restriction limiting the use of one's land, such as restrictive zoning or a covenant.

chattel personal property; movable property or belongings, as distinguished from real estate.

clear title a title without encumbrances or limitations that would make legality questionable.

cloud on title any problem with a title to real estate that impairs or defeats clear title.

community property property acquired by the combined efforts of husband and wife during their marriage.

conservator a person appointed by the court to care for property owned by one deemed incapable of managing the property.

covenant a binding agreement to do or not to do something, often incidental to a deed.

covenantee the person a covenant is intended for.

covenantor the person who makes a covenant.

easement the granted right to use another person's land.

eminent domain the right of the state to take private land for public use.

encumbrance any burden, such as an easement, covenant, or lien on the title of a property.

en ventre sa mere the law of property providing that an unborn child or fetus has the same rights as one who has already been born.

postnuptial agreement an agreement entered into by a husband and wife that determines how assets will be distributed in the event of death or divorce.

prenuptial agreement an agreement entered into by a couple intending to marry that determines how assets will be distributed in the event of divorce or death.

property settlement a division of property between a divorcing husband and wife.

real property land, including any buildings thereon.

run with the land covenants and their passing of burdens or benefits on to succeeding owners of the property, even though they didn't originally contract for them.

subdivision a dividing of land into separate parcels.

tenancy-at-will an agreement between landlord and tenant that works as a kind of open-ended lease in which tenancy may be terminated at any time upon 30-day written notice by either party.

title proof of ownership or possession of property.

title search a search through public records to establish ownership of a property and any liens, encumbrances, and so on, on that property.

MAGIC AND THE OCCULT

abracadabra originally, a magic word derived from the name of the gnostic deity Abraxas. When chanted or worn around the neck in the form of letters arranged in a pyramid, it was thought to prevent illness or cure a fever.

abraun a talisman made of wood or mandrake, carved into the shape of a human and dressed; used to protect the home from evil.

absent healing a form of faith healing in which healing powers are mentally projected to a remote person who is ill.

adept one who is highly accomplished in the magical fields.

aeromancy divination by reading objects in the sky, such as clouds or comets.

agent one who is the subject or focus of a haunting, or who may unwittingly cause a haunting.

akasha a mystical fifth element.

akashic record the memory of all of human history, including thoughts and events, stored in the astral plane.

alchemist one who practices alchemy.

alchemy the ancient pseudoscience of turning base metals—by chemical and spiritual means—into gold or silver. Also, the search for an elixir for human immortality.

alectryomancy divining an answer to a question through the order in which a bird reveals letters by eating the grains set on top of them.

aleuromancy a divination technique in which messages are rolled into balls of flour and given to subjects at random, still practiced today in the form of fortune cookies.

All Hallow's Eve Halloween. In ancient times, the Celtic and Druid New Year. Also, the sabbat of Samhain, a gathering of witches held on October 31 to mark the seasonal transition.

almadel a talisman made of wax and inscribed with images, symbols, or the names of angels.

alomancy a divination technique that uses the sprinkling of salt to create patterns which can be read.

altar a table, tree stump, flat stone, or other place where Wiccan rituals are performed.

ambrosia in Greek and Roman mythology, the food and drink of the gods that imparted immortality to any human who ate it.

amniomancy a divination method that allows the practitioner to read a caul on a newborn's head.

amulet a charm worn around the neck to ward off evil.

anaphrodisiac any herb concoction that reduces or eliminates sexual desire.

anathema a sorcerer's curse, usually against another witch.

angelica in the 15th century, a medicinal herb worn around the neck, especially by children, to protect against the plague or a sorcerer's spell.

animism the belief that everything in nature has a soul or form of consciousness.

ankh of ancient Egyptian origin, a cross with a loop at the top, a symbol of life and knowledge, commonly carried by the gods and today used by modern witches in rituals.

anoint in Wiccan rituals, to purify with special oils or holy water.

anthroposomancy a divination method in which a person's face and body are read for signs or omens.

apantomancy the practice of taking as omens the crossing of paths with various birds or animals, including black cats.

apophenia the projection of mystical meanings onto coincidences or other random occurrences of everyday life, such as when a clock stops on the day a relative dies or when a cloud takes the shape of a dollar sign and prompts one to buy a lottery ticket.

apparition a ghost.

apport an object that materializes out of thin air, especially at a séance.

arcane referring to any knowledge that is secret or hidden.

arithmancy divination by numbers, a method that preceded numerology.

asagwe a Haitian voodoo dance, known as the salute to the loas.

aspergillum in Wiccan tradition, a bundle made from herbs and twigs and used to sprinkle holy water. Also known as an asperger.

asport an object that vanishes into thin air, especially at a séance.

asson a seed-filled rattle used in voodoo ceremonies.

astraglomancy divination by the throw of dice.

astral body a ghostlike double of a physical being in the midst of astral projection.

astral plane a parallel dimension through which astral bodies may operate.

astral projection the "leaving" of the physical body and traveling in spirit to wherever one desires.

astrology the pseudoscientific art of divining one's character and fate by the positioning of celestial bodies at birth.

astromancy a divination technique in which the stars are read for omens.

athame in Wicca, a black double-edged knife used in witch rituals to direct energy by drawing magic circles and diagrams but not for actual cutting.

attunement in Reiki teaching, the clearing of the body and energy channels to prime it for healing energy.

augur originally, an ancient Roman cleric who interpreted omens and signs; now, any soothsayer or prophet.

augury the study of omens to divine the future.

aura a mystical radiance believed to surround some people and objects.

aureole a halo or any circle of light around the head of a mystical person.

auspice divining the future by the actions of birds.

austromancy a divination technique in which the winds are listened to for possible omens.

autokinetic effect an error in perception in which a stationary point of light, such as the planet Venus, may appear to be moving, and especially so when bolstered by the power of suggestion, a phenomenon thought by many skeptics to explain some UFO sightings.

automatic art drawing or painting through spirit guidance or the unconscious.

automatic writing a communication technique in which a medium in a trance state allows a spirit to control his hand and write messages.

automatism collective term that encompasses the field of automatic writing, drawing, painting, and speaking.

Avalon Island of the Apples, a mythical, Celtic paradise.

balefire in Wiccan practice, a large ceremonial fire lit during Beltane, Midsummer, and Yule.

bane a negative energy.

banishing ritual a ceremony that attempts to banish evil influences by various means, including the recitation of prayers and swinging a sword to inscribe pentagrams in the air.

Beltane in Wicca, a witch's festival that takes place on the evening of April 30 and continues through May 1, it celebrates the union of the god and goddess and is also known as Walpurgis.

Bermuda Triangle also known as the Devil's Triangle, a broad expanse of ocean covering points from

Miami to Bermuda to Puerto Rico, where numerous ships and planes have vanished, allegedly due to aliens or other unexplained forces.

besom in Wiccan culture, a straw broom used by witches to sweep away negative energy and to purify a circle, especially during handfasting and Candlemas ceremonies. In the Middle Ages, a besom was traditionally placed around a hearth to protect the opening from evil spirits.

bewitchment the casting of a spell over another.

Bible code named after a book by the same name, an alleged hidden code left by God in the Bible, through specific letter sequencing, which reveals prophecies and other truths.

bibliomancy divining the future by randomly choosing a passage in a book, especially the Bible.

binding the use of magic to restrain someone from doing something.

black art sorcery or witchcraft.

black magic any form of magic used for evil purposes.

black mass in Satanism, a ceremony in which the Lord's Prayer is recited backward and, according to legend, unbaptized children are sacrificed to the devil.

bletonism a divination technique in which water currents are read for omens.

blood of the Moon in Wicca, the menstrual period, when women are thought to have their greatest power.

bokor a sorcerer who practices voodoo.

boline in Wiccan culture, a traditional white-handled knife used to harvest herbs, carve symbols, and cut wands.

Book of Shadows in Wicca, any book of spells, potions, or rituals that may be kept by an individual witch or by a coven. See GRIMOIRE.

boucan in voodoo, a ceremonial bonfire that represents the relighting of the Sun, especially at the end of the year.

bune wand old Scottish term for a witch's broomstick.

Burning Time, the historical low point, between the 1500s and 1600s, when the Catholic Church killed thousands of pagans and witches.

cabalistic having a hidden meaning.

candle magick a spellcasting technique in which colored candles are used to represent people, places, or things.

Candlemas in Wiccan tradition, a fire festival celebrating the goddess of fertility and the horned god, held on February 2.

capnomancy a divination technique in which smoke rising from a fire is read for signs or omens.

cartomancy divining the future by reading a deck of cards, such as the tarot.

cauldron a very large kettle used by witches to concoct potions or burn incense.

censer an incense holder used during purification rituals. Also known as a thurible.

ceraunoscopy divining the future by reading the patterns in lightning.

cerealogist derived from Ceres, the goddess of agriculture, one who studies and interprets mysterious crop circles.

ceromancy divining the future by reading the shapes formed by melting wax.

chakra in Kundalini yoga, any one of various energy centers located from the base of the spine to the top of the head, believed by some to have healing powers.

chaldean pre-18th-century term for an astrologer, soothsayer, or sorcerer.

chalice in Wicca, a cup made of earthly materials, such as crystal, glass, or animal horn, used in rituals and for holding sacramental wine.

channeling acting as a medium to receive communications from the spiritual or unseen world.

chanting the recitation of repetitious words or phrases to change one's state of consciousness.

chi Chinese term for the healing supernatural energy hidden in the universe and throughout nature, including in humans.

chiromancer a palm reader.

chromotherapy in modern witchcraft, the use of colored lighting to bathe and heal sick people.

cingulum in Wicca, a cord used to measure circles and for binding. It is also worn during dancing rituals and may be infused with power, which can be stored in multiple knots.

circle in Wicca, a group of people gathered for a ritualistic purpose. Also, the purified, circular space itself, traditionally 9 feet in diameter, where rituals are performed.

circle healing a Wiccan healing method in which a sick person sits in the center of a circle, surrounded by a coven, who direct healing energy toward her.

circumambulation an ancient, widespread practice of holding out the right hand toward and walking around an object or person, as a show of reverence during a ceremony; it was also practiced to cure disease, bring good luck, or purify. Also known as a holy round.

clairaudience the ability to hear things nobody else can hear, especially emanations from a spiritual or otherworldly plane.

clairvoyance the ability to perceive what cannot be seen in the physical world.

clairvoyant one with the ability to perceive what cannot be seen in the physical world.

cleansing removing negative energy, by various purifying methods and rituals.

cledonomancy the ability to predict what will be said next in a conversation.

cleromancy divining by the drawing of lots.

coco macaque in voodoo, a magical walking stick with the ability to kill enemies.

cold reading a psychic's reading of a subject's mind and background or that of his loved ones, living or dead, with no information to go by except positive responses to queries and statements made by the subject.

collective hallucination a false perception experienced by several people simultaneously through the power of suggestion.

communal reinforcement the process by which outlandish pseudosciences and faiths are promulgated by authority figures, reinforced without critical investigation by the media, and then believed by the masses, often simply because so many others believe.

confabulation sometimes mixed with facts, a fantasy or false memory that unconsciously becomes an actual account of an event or happening and which may be sincerely believed by the holder.

conjure to summon a spirit with black magic.

consecrate to purify or make sacred, often with holy water or salt.

countercharm a charm used by witches to neutralize or reverse a charm or spell employed by another.

counterspell a spell used by witches to neutralize or reverse the spell cast by another.

coven traditionally, a group of 13 witches. In Wicca, any group of witches.

covener any member of a coven.

covenstead any meeting place used by a coven.

cowen in witchcraft, one who is not a witch.

Craft, the a common term for Wicca.

crone any practicing witch who has passed menopause or the age of 50.

crop circle any of various geometric patterns created in open fields by the crushing of tall grasses or other plants, believed by some to be messages from aliens.

cryptozoology the study of hidden animals such as Bigfoot and the Loch Ness monster.

crystal any transparent mineral, such as quartz, believed to have magical powers and used in healing and other New Age practices.

crystal ball a glass ball into which fortunetellers gaze to "see" the future.

crystalomancy divining by gazing into a crystal ball or pool of water.

crystal power healing powers thought to exist in the vibrations and frequencies given off by various crystals and gems.

curse an invocation of bad luck or misfortune to befall someone.

cynanthropy the ability to turn oneself into a dog.

dactylomancy divination technique in which a dangling ring on a cord is swung like a pendulum over numbers, letters, or words.

déjà vu the haunting feeling that one has visited a place before or has experienced something at an earlier time or in a past life.

dematerialize to vanish.

demoniac one possessed by a demon.

demonic possession the invading of one's body and mind by a demon, resulting in bizarre, out-of-control behavior.

demonology the study of demons.

demonomancy divination through the calling forth of demons.

deosil in Wicca, clockwise motion, or the direction of the Sun's apparent path over Earth, symbolizing positive energy.

diabolism worship of Satan; sorcery.

Dianic in Wicca, referring to a coven who places the goddess above the horned god in importance.

direct writing any writing that appears magically, without the aid of a medium's hand.

divination foretelling the future by supernatural means.

divine fallacy skeptic's term for the belief that if something is amazing or miraculous or cannot be explained, God must have done it.

divining rod a forked stick used in dowsing to locate water.

doppelganger a spirit or ghost who haunts its living double or twin.

dowser one who searches for underground water with the use of a divining rod or other "magical" tool.

dowsing the pseudoscientific art of locating underground water by the use of a divining rod or other "magical" tool.

drawing down the Moon in Wicca tradition, a ritual held to pull down energy into a witch from the full Moon.

drawing down the Sun in Wicca tradition, a ritual held to pull down energy into a male witch from the Sun.

druid predating Christianity, a Celtic priest or religious teacher who prayed to various deities, performed human and animal sacrifices, and practiced astrology and wizardry.

ear candling an ancient practice of inserting a hollow candle into the ear to draw out not only ear wax but negative energy.

ectoplasm a white, ethereal matter that may issue from mediums during a séance or trance.

eke-name in Wicca, a witch's secret alternative name, given to herself to represent her new life in a coven and used only among other witches.

elixir any magical potion, especially one charged by a crystal.

enchantment the state of being under a spell; bewitchment.

eneagram a nine-lined drawing representing nine personality types and capable of predicting one's type.

entity a spirit or ghost

envoutement the use of voodoo dolls as representatives of real people, to transmit pain or healing to remote subjects.

esbat in Wicca, any meeting of a coven under a full Moon.

ESP extra sensory perception. A power of perception beyond what is normal; the ability to sense the thoughts of others or things that cannot be physically seen.

ethereal otherworldly; spiritual.

evil eye a flash of an angry glance, believed in folklore to cause harm.

evocation the calling forth of spirits.

exorcism the casting out of a demon from someone's body with prayers and incantations.

faith healing healing illness by prayer alone.

familiar a spirit in the form of an animal, especially a cat, owl, bird, mouse, snake, or weasel, used by a witch as a companion or helper.

fata morgana a mirage resembling castles.

fetch an apparition of a living person, an omen of that person's death.

fetish an object believed to have magical powers, such as a rabbit's foot.

flying ointment described in print as early as 1456, a poisonous blend of herbal oils, especially that of hemlock, belladonna, wolfsbane, and henbane, mixed with animal fat and rubbed on the skin to enable a witch to fly.

Forer effect the eager acceptance of a broad or vague description of one's personality traits, as constructed from astrological profiles, which could in reality apply to anyone but which are nevertheless perceived to be unique to oneself. So named after testing performed by psychologist Bertram Forer.

friggatriskaidekaphobia a superstitious fear of Friday the 13th.

geomancy divining the future by reading figures in dirt.

glossolalia see SPEAKING IN TONGUES.

gnosis knowledge of spiritual matters by intuition, especially that claimed by the Gnostics.

gnostic a member of the ancient, pre-Christian sect that believed in gnosis.

grimoire dating back to the 13th century, a witch's notebook that, in medieval times, contained information on summoning angels and demons, as well as details on potions and divination techniques. The Wiccan Book of Shadows is the modern equivalent.

handfasting a Wicca wedding.

hand of glory in medieval black magic, a charm made from the severed, mummified hand of a hanged criminal.

haruspicy divining the future by reading the entrails of animals.

haunting a recurrent visitation or appearance of a ghost or spirit before a particular person or in a particular location.

healing touch the ability to cure someone's ills simply by touching them.

heliomancy divination technique in which the Sun is studied for signs or omens.

Hell-broth in medieval witchcraft, a potion made up of various repulsive ingredients, such as animal guts, skulls, bugs, etc., made famous by the witches in *Macbeth*.

henbane in medieval witchcraft, a poisonous plant and one of the ingredients in an ointment used to enable witches to fly.

hermetic relating to Hermes Trismegistus or Thoth the Egyptian god, alchemist, and astrologer.

hex in American folklore, and especially among the Pennsylvania Dutch, an evil curse.

hex sign in American folklore, and especially among the Pennsylvania Dutch, a round symbol containing a five, six, or eight-sided star, placed or painted on doors, windows, and barns to protect against evil spirits.

high priest/priestess an accomplished witch and the leader of a coven.

hippomancy a divination technique in which the gait of horses is studied for signs or omens.

holy round see CIRCUMAMBULATION.

holy water in Wicca tradition, a liquid blessed by a Wiccan under a full Moon.

hoodoo a form of sorcery borrowing from elements of voodoo, practiced by rural American blacks in Louisiana.

horned god in pagan witchcraft and Wicca, the personification of masculine power or sexuality in the universe, unrelated to Satan.

horoscope an astrologer's exact plotting of the stars and planets at a specific time, such at a person's birth, or a chart of such. Also, a prediction of one's future based on such plotting.

hot reading dishonest technique used by mediums and psychics to gather information about a subject before a reading, by going through purses, eavesdropping, or using preperformance fact-finding interviews that are disguised as casual chats.

hydromancy divining the future by peering into water.

hydromantia a divination technique in which one stares into a pool or bucket of water and summons images of gods, spirits, or the future.

hypersensory perception above-normal powers of observation, a natural trait in some, and in others cultivated by learning to read body language, tones of voice, and other subtle social cues, sometimes mistaken for psychic abilities.

I Ching Chinese text comprised of 64 hexagrams, that can be interpreted to divine one's future. The hexagrams are chosen randomly by flipping numbered coins and adding the final total.

ichthyomancy a divination technique in which fish are observed for signs or omens.

ideomotor effect psychological term referring to body movements influenced by suggestion or by the unconscious mind, such as when a dowser's rod suddenly points downward or when a Ouija board pointer turns on its own.

imprecation a curse.

incantation the utterance of a magical spell or charm.

inedia the ability to live without food, as some who profess to be nourished by holy spirits or the universal life force. Those who claim to survive off the holy breath alone are known as breatharians and are followers of Therese Neumann of Bavaria, who lived from 1898 to 1962.

initiation in Wicca, a ceremony that formally brings another person into a coven.

intuitive one who has a powerful sense of intuition, to the point of having psychic abilities, sometimes known as a sensitive.

intuitive healer one with the ability to locate, diagnose, and cure disease with ESP and healing touch alone.

invocation an appeal to or conjuring up of a god, goddess, or spirit.

jinx that which brings bad luck.

joss stick in Chinese religious tradition, a fragrant incense burned to ward off evil.

juju the black magic used by West African witch doctors to cast out demons. Also, an amulet, charm, or fetish.

Key of Solomon any one of various versions of a famed medieval grimoire, allegedly originating with King Solomon and giving information on conjurations, invocations, and curses. It is famous for providing details on invisibility, animal sacrifices, and the summoning of demons or spirits, and even gives advice on what clothing to wear when practicing sorcery.

lampadomancy divining the future by reading fire, especially a flame in a lamp.

left-hand path the practice of sorcery or black magic.

lepanthropy the ability to change into a rabbit or hare.

levitation the act of floating in midair, by an object or a person, through supernatural means.

libanomancy divination technique in which the smoke rising from incense is read for signs or omens.

libation in witchcraft and Wicca, any water or wine used in rituals and usually poured on an altar or in a fire.

Litha in Wicca, the celebration of the summer solstice, from June 20 to 23. Originally, celebrants leapt over fires to promote fertility.

lithobolia evil spirits who rain down rocks at people or their houses.

loa in voodoo, a spirit who takes control of someone during a trance.

loco in voodoo, a spirit of healing.

lots, casting of divination technique employing thrown dice or marked bones.

Lourdes in 1858 in France, the town near a grotto by the River Gave de Pau, at which 14-year-old Bernadette Soubirous claimed to have seen the Virgin Mary some 18 times, which has since been validated by the Catholic Church as the site of no less than 67 miracles, especially healings, and is now visited by 5 million people a year, who take a drink of the water there to bring about their own healings.

love potion concocted by a witch, an aphrodisiac, sometimes intensified by the use of incantations and spells.

luck ball in hoodoo, a charm wound inside a ball of yarn and worn.

lycanthropy the ability or power to transform oneself into a werewolf.

macumba a form of voodoo of Brazilian origin.

mage an accomplished magician.

magic modern illusions created by stage performers through explainable and nonmystical techniques.

magical thinking psychological term referring to the belief that everything in the universe is interconnected and full of mysterious powers that can be tapped.

magick original spelling for the art of supernatural witchcraft, as distinguished from the magic of modern-day entertainers and sleight-of-hand artists.

magick candle in medieval witchcraft, a candle made of human fat, which glowed brighter when brought near the location of buried treasure.

maledict to curse or hex.

malediction a curse or a hex.

maleficia the misfortunes that befall those who cross a sorcerer.

malkin a cat who serves as a witch's familiar.

mambo a Haitian voodoo priestess.

mandrake a highly poisonous plant used in medieval witchcraft and, according to folklore, the most powerful of all magical ingredients. Spirits were thought to inhabit the roots, which look like little men, and it was believed that these roots could be asked questions, to which they would shake or nod their heads.

manifesting the taking on of magical powers by ordinary humans, brought about by simply using creative visualization and by willing one's wishes onto the universe.

medicine dance among Native Americans of the Plains in North America, a dance employed to summon helpful spirits.

medicine lodge among various tribes of North American Native Americans, a structure where rituals were held.

medicine man in primitive cultures, one who is thought to possess mystical powers and has the ability to summon supernatural help. Also known as a shaman or a witch doctor.

medium one who acts as a receptor or channel to receive spirits or spiritual messages.

mesmerism hypnotism or the practice of spellbinding. Also, animal magnetism.

meteoromancy divination through the observation of meteors.

metoposcopy the reading of someone's forehead to determine their character or future.

mistletoe plant widely believed by the druids to hold magical, healing properties.

mojo bag in modern witchcraft, a red flannel bag filled with herbs to ward off disease and negative energy.

mugwort in witchcraft, a healing herb also known as Saint John's plant (not to be confused with St.-John's-wort). It was believed that sleeping on a pillow full of it would enhance dreams and strengthen psychic abilities. Sachets of it were also thought to aid in astral projection and to ward off evil spirits.

mumbo jumbo in the western Sudan, a shaman who protects against evil spirits. Also, a fetish. More widespread, a magical-sounding incantation that may or may not be meaningless.

myomancy divination through analysis of the squeaks and squeals of mice and rats, practiced in ancient Egypt and Rome.

mysticism belief in the spiritual world or other dimension that cannot be perceived by the human eye.

nagalism the worshipping of serpents.

Nazca lines geometric lines and shapes created by the clearing of stones and topsoil from the Peruvian desert by the Nazca people, from 200 B.C. to A.D. 600. Because of the massive scale of the lines, they are often speculated to be the work of aliens.

necromancy divining the future by communication with the dead.

nephelomancy divining the future by studying the speed and characteristics of clouds.

nimbus the glowing aura around a deity.

numerology the study of numbers as an influence in one's life.

obeah a belief system originating among African and Caribbean blacks, characterized by the use of magic ritual.

obeah-man one who practices obeah.

occulta cult activity of medieval times, often featuring black magic and witchcraft.

occultist one who studies mysticism and the occult.

oculomancy divination through interpreting the characteristics of the eyes.

Odic force named after the god Odin, a mystical force thought to emanate from magnets and crystals.

offering in Wicca, a gift presented to the goddess or horned god.

oinomancy divination through the reading of patterns in spilled wine.

old religion, the witchcraft.

omen a sign of things to come; a portent.

oneiromancy divination of the future through the interpretation of dreams.

onomatomancy divination through the interpretation of the letters in one's name.

ooscopy divining the sex of a fetus by storing and hatching a chicken egg between a pregnant woman's breasts; the sex of the chick would determine the sex of the child. Also known as ovamancy.

ophiomancy divination through the use of serpents.

oracle a prophet or spiritual medium. Also a shrine of such a personage.

ornithomancy divining the future by reading the flight patterns of birds.

out-of-body experience the release of one's soul or spirit—said to sometimes occur during close brushes with death—when one may actually view one's abandoned physical body from a remote location. See ASTRAL PROJECTION.

palmistry the pseudoscientific art of reading palms to divine one's fate.

papyromancy a divination technique in which a piece of paper is folded or crumpled and the resulting lines and creases are read.

paranormal that which cannot be explained or is beyond human perception.

parapsychology the study of psychic or mental powers beyond scientific comprehension.

pareidolia seeing something meaningful in random or coincidental images, such as the face of Christ in a slice of toast or a ghost in a passing wisp of fog, a common form of illusion that is strengthened by the power of suggestion.

past life a life or multiple lives lived in another time, recalled with faint memories brought forth through hypnosis.

past life regression through hypnosis or other trancelike states, mental traveling to the past to visit one's former life.

pendulum a weight at the end of a cord, swung back and forth as a divination technique.

pentacle a symbol of the element of Earth, a pentagon within a circle, often worn as a pendant.

pentagram a five-pointed star and symbol of paganism.

phantasm a ghost; a phantom.

philosopher's stone a stone or substance believed in the Middle Ages to have the ability to turn base metals into gold.

philter a love potion.

poltergeist a noisy ghost who moves things around.

possession occupation by an evil spirit or demon of one's soul, mind, or body.

precognition "seeing" or "knowing" what will occur in the future.

prescience knowledge of what will occur in the future.

prophecy prediction of what will occur in the future.

prophesy to make a prediction of what will occur in the future.

prophet one who has the ability to see into the future and make predictions, as if acting as a channel for God.

psephomancy divining the future through the use of pebbles.

pseudoscience any false science based on fanciful theories or wishful thinking. Pseudoscience is distinguished from real science by its lack of peer review and controlled, unbiased testing.

psi psychic powers or extra sensory perception.

psychic having the ability to read minds or predict the future. A person with this ability.

psychic detective one who solves crimes through the use of extrasensory perception.

psychic surgery the simulation of surgery on a patient by a psychic healer, who sometimes may hold up a chicken liver or chicken heart to falsely represent a removed tumor. Psychic surgery is a thriving business in many third-world countries.

psychokinesis the ability to move objects by the power of one's mind alone. Also known as telekinesis.

psychometry a divination method through which an object is touched by a medium, thereby forming a connection to the object's owner, which may be used to solve disappearances and murders.

Ouija board a board game in which participants place their fingertips on a pointer which supposedly acts as a medium for the spiritual world and answers questions by pointing to letters that spell out words and messages.

revenant one who returns from the dead.

rhabdomancy divining the future by a divining rod.

runes magical letters or characters.

Satanic cult a group that worships Satan and carries out evil deeds or rites.

Satanism worship of Satan.

scarab an Egyptian talisman in the shape of a beetle.

scatomancy divining the future by examining animal droppings.

scry to divine the future by reading the images in reflective surfaces, such as mirrors, bowls of water, or crystal balls.

séance an assembly at which a medium calls to spirits to communicate with those in attendance.

second sight the ability to foresee the future.

seer a prophet or clairvoyant.

selective thinking ignoring or devaluing evidence that is contrary to one's beliefs in order to maintain one's dogma or illusions.

shadow ghost in a photograph, any mysterious shadow.

shamanism a Native American and Asian practice or belief through which a skilled medium communicates with the spiritual world and employs magic to heal or to divine the future.

shoehorning skeptic's term for the claiming of an accurate prediction of an event by a psychic after the event has passed. Vague or broad statements made before the event are simply made to fit the event.

shotgunning skeptic's term for a psychic's method of presenting a broad scattering of interpretations and impressions, knowing that some will inevitably be accepted as meaningful by the listener.

shrewstone old term for a crystal ball.

sigil a magical symbol, often a geometric figure or configuration, originally used to represent various demons and angels.

sixth sense another term for extrasensory perception.

skyclad in Wicca, nudity, in which some rituals may be performed.

smudge to burn incense or sage and wave it over a space or object to cleanse or rid it of negative energy.

smudgestick a bundle of incense or sage used in smudging.

solitary a witch who practices witchcraft independently and not part of a coven.

soothsaying predicting the future.

sorcerer one who practices black magic or sorcery, as a wizard.

sorceress a female who practices black magic or sorcery.

sorcery witchcraft or black magic.

sortilege divining the future by the choosing of lots.

speaking in tongues the speaking of nonsensical strings of syllables or gibberish during trancelike states by followers of some Christian denominations, especially Pentecostals, who believe they are possessed of the holy spirit. Also known as glossolalia.

specter a ghost.

spell any formula or incantation that causes someone to fall into a trance or involuntarily behave in a prescribed manner.

spellbind to cast a spell or put someone into a trance.

spiegelschrift automatic writing that appears in reverse and thus requires a mirror to read it.

spirit photographs photographs with hazy images of ghosts in the background, a result, according to skeptics, of double exposures, film processing errors, and reflections.

spirit writing messages conveyed through a medium's handwriting by spirits.

stichomancy divination through the reading of random passages in the Bible or other mystical tome.

stigmata most often seen in pious subjects, any mysterious or unexplained bleeding emanating from the same areas as the wounds suffered by Christ during his crucifixion, specifically in the hands and feet or the side of the head, allegedly due to a deep faith and sympathy with Christ.

subjective validation skeptic's term for the acceptance of a psychic's readings by a subject, due more to mental cooperation, specifically with eagerness to believe and desire for the psychic to succeed, rather than any real psychic ability.

Summerland in Wicca, a life-after-death paradise in which a subject prepares for his or her next incarnation.

Sun gazing also known as Sun yoga or solar yoga, gazing at the Sun for brief periods of time, with the belief that it will bring nourishment. Proponents sometimes claim never to have to eat because all of their nutritional needs are met by sunlight.

supernatural that which is beyond the understanding of science and the physical world, as spirits or witchcraft.

sympathetic magic any form of magic that employs components that correspond with real-life counterparts, as voodoo dolls may represent actual people and can be acted upon as such, or as a long line in the palm may be taken to mean the subject will live a long life.

synastry comparing astrological charts to determine if two people would be compatible.

synchronicity a concept created by Swiss psychiatrist Carl Jung, who in addition to believing in astrology, ESP, and telepathy, maintained that coincidences hold meaning and that when a coincidence occurs, the universe is trying to communicate something.

talisman an object or charm believed to have magical powers, such as an amulet, sometimes used as protection against evil.

tarot cards a set of 22 pictorial cards symbolizing various forces of nature along with human vices and virtues, used in fortune-telling.

telekinesis moving objects from a remote position without touching them.

telepathy communication with the mind; thought transference.

therapeutic touch a form of therapy in which a healer moves his hands over a patient to direct the flow of energy and induce healing.

third eye psychic ability; extrasensory perception; the ability to see the future.

thoughtography also known as nensha, the burning of images onto surfaces or into someone's mind by psychic abilities.

touched affected by a spirit. Also, demented.

transfiguration when a spirit medium is temporarily possessed and takes on a different appearance, possibly that of the spirit itself.

voodoo a polytheistic religion originating in Africa and mainly practiced in Haiti. Also, any of the charms, fetishes, or curses used in its practice. Also, a practitioner of spells and necromancy.

vortex a powerful eddy through time and space through which one may travel to another dimension.

Walpurgis Night April 30, the night according to medieval Christians on which a witches' sabbath was thought to take place.

warlock a male witch; a sorcerer.

water witch old term for a dowser.

wax reading divination through the interpretation of melted wax patterns left by a burning candle.

whammy a spell, hex, or jinx.

white magic magic employed for good.

Wicca a pagan religion or form of nonevil witchcraft in which female practitioners care for the Earth and our environment.

witch a female who uses black magic or sorcery.

witch ball a glass globe hung in a window to protect against evil spirits.

witchcraft the spells, formulas, incantations, etc., used by a witch.

witch hunt from approximately 1480 to 1700, irrational hunts for people who appeared to be witches, resulting in the hysterical executions of tens of thousands of innocents, sometimes by burning at the stake.

witch's ladder in Wicca, a cord tied with 13 knots, used for counting during chants or meditations.

wort old word for an herb.

wraith a ghost or vision of a living person that is said to appear just before that person dies.

xenoglossia the magical acquisition, mastery, or knowledge of a language one has never studied.

Yule in Wicca, a celebration of the winter solstice, the longest night of the year, from December 20 to 23, featuring gift exchanges and feasting. It was adopted and altered by Christians and made into Christmas.

Zenner cards a deck of 25 cards with pictures of geometric shapes, used to test for ESP.

zodiac the celestial pathway followed by the sun, moon and planets, divided into 12 astrological signs.

zombie in voodoo, a snake spirit. Also, a corpse brought back to life, or the force causing this to happen.

FENG SHUI

bagua an octagonal mirror used to reflect chi.

chi the energy force or breath of the universe. Also spelled qi.

feng shui ruler a measuring stick showing lucky measurements.

five elements fire, water, wood, earth, and metal.

geomancer a practitioner of feng shui.

luo pan a wooden compass used to determine the flow of cosmic energy, or chi.

pakua an octagonal amulet, with eight sections or trigrams.

qi see CHI.

shifu a master or teacher of feng shui. Also known as sifu.

yin and yang opposing energy forces. Yin is considered negative, and yang is positive.

MEDICINE

EQUIPMENT AND INSTRUMENTS

autoclave an apparatus that sterilizes medical instruments by steam.

biopsy needle a needle used in obtaining biopsy material.

bistoury a slender surgical knife, used most frequently to open an abscess.

bougie a slender, flexible probe made of rubber or silk and used in the diagnosis and measurement of strictures in the esophagus, the urethra, and other organs.

bronchoscope a tubular instrument inserted through the mouth and down the throat to inspect the trachea and bronchi.

caliper a forcepslike instrument used to measure thicknesses, especially body fat.

cannula a tube designed to fit into the various body channels for the withdrawing or delivering of fluids.

capnograph an instrument that monitors the amount of carbon dioxide in exhaled air.

cardiograph an instrument that records the activity of the heart.

catgut suture material made from the intestines of sheep; it is eventually absorbed by the body.

catheter a slender tube inserted into a body channel to extract or deliver fluids.

catheter, cardiac a slender tube passed through a blood vessel in an extremity to the heart to take blood samples and pressure readings.

CAT scanner computerized axial tomography; an X-ray instrument producing three-dimensional images. Also known as a CT scanner.

cautery an electrical instrument used to scar or destroy abnormal tissue.

Cavitron a motorized scalpel that cuts through delicate flesh but leaves blood vessels and ductal tissue intact; used in brain and liver surgery.

centrifuge a machine that separates substances of varying densities by subjecting them to centrifugal (whirling at high speed) force.

clamp an instrument clamped on a cut blood vessel to stop bleeding; a hemostat.

clip a metal clip used to hold tissues together.

colposcope a microscope used to directly examine the vagina and cervix.

coreometer an instrument that measures the size of the pupil of the eye.

costome an instrument used to cut through ribs.

cryoprobe an instrument that freezes malignant tissue in order to destroy it.

culdoscope a lighted instrument passed through the vagina and into the pelvic cavity to examine the organs there.

curet a spoonlike instrument used to scrape away diseased tissue and growths or to collect tissue samples.

cystoscope a long, metal tube used to inspect the inside of the bladder.

cytoanalyzer an electronic apparatus that analyzes smears thought to contain malignant cells.

cytometer a device that counts and measures blood cells.

defibrillator an apparatus that delivers an electric current to the heart to restore normal heart rhythm.

dilator an inflatable instrument used to enlarge the opening of an organ or internal cavity.

dioptometer an instrument used to measure eye refraction for the purpose of determining eye defects.

drain a tube or wick used to drain fluid from a wound, sometimes assisted by a pump.

EEG see ELECTROENCEPHALOGRAPH.

EKG electrocardiogram. A recording or readout of the heart's electrical functioning, as recorded by a cardiograph or electrocardiograph.

electroencephalograph an instrument used to record the brain's electrical waves.

electromyograph an instrument that records the electrical impulses of contracting muscles.

electron microscope an extremely powerful microscope utilizing electrons rather than visible light to produce magnified images of objects too small for an ordinary microscope to resolve.

elevator surgical hand tool used to pry up bone fragments.

endoscope collective term for a family of instruments used to examine hollow organs or body cavities, such as gastroscope, proctoscope, and cystoscope.

ergograph an instrument that measures the physical output of a muscle.

fetoscope a fetal stethoscope.

file one of a family of instruments used for cutting, smoothing, or grinding.

flowmeter a device used to measure the flow of a liquid as it is dispensed.

fluoroscope an X-ray device in which X-rays are passed through the body to strike a fluorescent screen and render a live picture of the internal organs in motion.

forceps a tongslike instrument used for grasping, clamping, and extracting tissue.

forceps, bulldog forceps used for clamping cut blood vessels.

forceps, capsule forceps used to extract the lens of the eye in cataract surgery.

forceps, hemostatic locking forceps used for clamping cut blood vessels.

forceps, mosquito tiny hemostatic forceps.

forceps, obstetrical forceps used to grasp the head of the fetus.

forceps, rongeur forceps for gouging out bone.

forceps, thumb forceps used to hold soft tissue while suturing.

gastroscope an instrument passed through the mouth and into the stomach to examine the stomach lining.

gouge a chisel-like instrument for cutting out bits of bone.

guillotine a rib cutter.

Hagedorn needle a surgical needle with cutting edge, used to sew up skin. Also, the finger-pricking needle used to draw blood.

hemocytometer a device that determines the number of red blood cells in a blood sample.

hemodialyzer an apparatus used to purify or eliminate wastes from the blood, an artificial substitute form a diseased kidney.

hemostat an instrument used to stop bleeding by clamping a cut vein or artery.

kangaroo tendon suture material derived from the tails of kangaroos.

keratome a knife used to cut into the cornea of the eye.

lancet a surgical knife used for puncturing.

laryngoscope a lighted hollow tube used for examining the larynx.

linear accelerator an X-ray machine used for delivering radiation for the treatment of malignancies.

mecometer an instrument used to measure a newborn.

micrometer an instrument used to measure microscopic objects.

microsyringe a syringe designed to measure out precise, tiny portions of fluid.

microtome a lab device for slicing thin sections of tissue for examination with a microscope.

MRI magnetic resonance imaging; a noninvasive internal imaging technique employing magnetic properties instead of X-rays.

ophthalmometer an instrument used to determine problems with vision.

ophthalmoscope an instrument used to inspect the retina or rear lining of the eye.

osteotome a surgical bone chisel.

oximeter an infrared sensor attached to the ear and finger to measure the concentration of oxygen in a patient's blood.

otoscope a lighted instrument for examining the ear.

panendoscope a cystoscope that provides a panoramic view of the interior of the bladder.

pelvimeter a caliperlike instrument for measuring the size of the pelvis or birth canal.

Penrose drain a rubber tube with a gauze center inserted into a wound to drain fluids. Also known as a cigarette drain.

plexor a rubber-headed hammer used in percussion.

Politzer's bag a device used to inflate the middle ear.

proctoscope an instrument used to examine the anus and rectum.

protractor an instrument for removing shrapnel or bullets from a deep wound.

retractor an instrument used in surgery to pull an organ or body part out of the way of work being performed.

rhinoscope an instrument for examining the nasal passages.

rongeur plierslike instrument with sharp edges for cutting bone.

scalpel a thin surgical knife.

serrefine a small clamp used for clamping blood vessels.

sigmoidoscope a lighted tube used to inspect the rectum and sigmoid portion of the large intestine.

snare an instrument fitted with a wire loop used for snaring and severing a tumor or polyp.

speculum an instrument used to enlarge a body cavity, especially for visual inspection.

spirometer a device for measuring the rate and volume of air inhaled and exhaled by the lungs.

splint a support for an injured area or broken bone.

splint, airplane a large support that holds the arm up and to the side of the body.

splint, banjo a support and traction splint made of wire and rubber and resembling a banjo, for a broken finger.

splint, T a T-shaped support for the upper back, used in cases of broken collarbones.

sponge a surgical pad used to absorb fluids.

stent a small, slotted tube inserted into a coronary artery to help hold it open and to keep blood flowing freely. It may be treated with antirejection medicine to prevent the overgrowth of tissue around it.

stethoscope a listening instrument used to amplify internal body sounds.

suture a stitching material used to sew up tissue and wounds. Surgical thread.

suture, catgut suture made from sheep intestine; it is gradually absorbed by the body.

suture, button stitches in which the ends are passed through buttons and tied off.

suture, cobbler a suture with a needle attached to each end.

swab an absorbent material wrapped around a stick or a wire for cleaning wounds or administering medication.

syringe the device used for injecting and withdrawing fluids.

tenaculum tongslike instrument used to hold a body part.

urethroscope a lighted instrument used for inspecting the urethra.

MEDICAL FIELDS AND SPECIALTIES

Phenomenon Studied	Name of Specialty
aging	geriatrics, gerontology
allergies	allergology
anesthesia	anesthesiology
bacteria	bacteriology
birth	obstetrics
blood	hematology
body function	physiology
body movement	kinesiology
bones	osteology, osteopathy
bones, muscles, and tendons	orthopedics
cells	cytology
children	pediatrics
digestive system	gastroenterology
disease, as examined by diseased tissue	pathology
disease causes	etiology
disease classification science	nosology
disease identification	diagnostics
ear, nose, and throat	otolaryngology
ears	otology
epidemic and contagious disease study	epidemiology
eyes	ophthalmology
eyes, visual acuteness testing	optometry
feet	podiatry, chiropody
female reproductive organs	gynecology
glands	adenology
gums	periodontics
hearing	audiology
heart	cardiology
hernias	herniology
hormones and the glands that secrete them	endocrinology
immune system	immunology
internal organs	internal medicine
intestine	entrology
joints	arthrology, rheumatology
kidneys	nephrology
liver	hepatology
lungs and breathing	pulmonary medicine, pulmonology
lymphatic system	lymphology
mental disorders	psychiatry
mental processing behind behavior and consciousness	psychology
mouth	stomatology, oralogy
muscles	myology, orthopedics
nervous system	neurology, neuropathology
newborns	neonatology
nose	rhinology
parasites	parasitology
plastic surgery	plastic surgery, cosmetic surgery
poison and toxins	toxicology
rectum and anus	proctology
rheumatic disease	rheumatology
serums	serology
sexually transmitted diseases	venereology
skin	dermatology
skull	craniology
spinal manipulation and correction	chiropractic
stomach	gastrology
symptoms	symptomology
teeth	dentistry
teeth straightening	orthodontics
tissue	histology
tumors	oncology

ulcers	helcology
urinary and urogenital tract (kidney, ureter, bladder, prostate, penis, urethra)	urology
veins	phlebology
viruses	virology
X-rays, radiation therapy	radiology

MEDICAL TERMINOLOGY AND TESTS

acupuncture the insertion of needles into strategic locations in the skin, as a means of relieving pain either locally or throughout the body.

angina severe chest pain caused by insufficient blood flow through the heart.

angiography an X-ray examination of the blood vessels around the heart.

antinuclear antibody test a blood test used to detect the presence of antinuclear antibodies, which signal the presence of an autoimmunity problem.

arterial blood gases a blood test that measures levels of oxygen and carbon dioxide to determine how well the lungs move oxygen into the blood and take carbon dioxide out.

arthrocentesis a procedure in which a sterile needle and syringe are used to drain fluid from a joint.

arthroscopy a diagnostic or treatment procedure that employs a tubelike viewing instrument called an arthroscope to examine the inside of a joint.

Asclepius in Greek mythology, the god of medicine, the son of Apollo.

asymptomatic without symptoms.

auscultation listening for body sounds through a stethoscope to aid in determining normal health.

autoimmunity the process of a body's own immune system working against itself, especially in causing inflammation, as in various diseases such as lupus and rheumatoid arthritis.

autopsy an examination of a corpse to determine the exact cause of death.

barium a whitish contrast medium given orally or through an enema to highlight the gastrointestinal tract under an X-ray.

b.d. in prescription writing, an abbreviation for the Latin *bis in diem,* meaning twice daily. Also written as b.i.d.

Bence Jones protein test a urine test given to detect the presence of a bone tumor.

Benedict test a test for detecting sugar in the urine.

bimanual a two-handed examination of a body area.

biopsy the removal and study of tissue to determine a diagnosis, especially of tumors.

blood count an analysis or calculation of the concentration of various components, such as white blood cells, red blood cells, and platelets, in a sample of blood. Also known as a complete blood count.

blood liver enzymes test a test employed to detect the presence of certain liver enzymes in blood, a hallmark of liver damage.

blood transfusion a transfer of blood from a donor to a patient.

bone-density scan a screening test that employs two X-ray beams to measure bone thickness and determine if osteoporosis is present.

bone graft a transplant of part of a bone from one place in the body to another.

bronchoscopy an examination of the trachea and bronchi through the insertion of a bronchoscope.

bruit a murmur heard through the stethoscope over the heart or an artery; an abnormal sound.

caduceus a serpent coiled around a staff, the official insignia of medicine.

cancer antigen 125 (CA 125) a test of a blood sample or fluid from the chest to detect the presence of CA 125, a protein found in high amounts in tumor cells.

cardiopulmonary resuscitation (CPR) a method of reviving someone whose heart and breathing have stopped, by means of compressing the chest and blowing air into the lungs via the victim's mouth.

CAT scan see COMPUTERIZED AXIAL TOMOGRAPHY.

CEA carcinoembryonic antigen; a protein molecule used as a marker in blood for the presence of a tumor somewhere in the body.

certifiable disease any disease that is contagious and therefore must be reported to the board of health.

Cheyne-Stokes breathing in patients suffering from congestive heart failure, breathing characterized by long periods of apnea (no breathing) ending with several deep breaths.

chronic of long duration, as some diseases.

colonoscopy an internal examination for polyps or tumors in the colon through means of an inserted viewing instrument.

complete blood count see BLOOD COUNT.

computerized axial tomography (CAT scan, CT scan) an X-ray scanning of a body part that, unified with a computer, produces a cross-sectional view or three-dimensional image.

contusion a bruise.

coronary angioplasty a procedure in which a balloon-tipped catheter is inserted through an artery in the groin or arm and thread to a coronary artery that has narrowed through disease; the balloon is then inflated, expanding the size of the artery.

CPR see CARDIOPULMONARY RESUSCITATION.

CT scan see COMPUTERIZED AXIAL TOMOGRAPHY.

culture laboratory-grown germs for the purpose of identification and testing.

dialysis a treatment procedure that with the aid of various technologies mimics the duties of the kidneys in filtering waste from the blood and removing excess water, employed in patients with kidney damage.

diaphanography passing a light through the breast to examine shadows, which may reveal signs of disease.

diathermy the application of heat.

diuretic an agent prescribed to increase the amount of urine passed.

DOA abbreviation for dead on arrival, a term used by ambulance paramedics, police, and emergency room staff.

dosimetry the science of determining the exact dosage of medication.

DPT child's immunization against diphtheria, pertussis, and tetanus.

echocardiography an ultrasound method of revealing the workings of the heart.

emetic an agent that stimulates vomiting.

enteral nutrition feeding through a tube passed through the nose and into the stomach.

epidemic a disease affecting a large group of people at the same time in the same community.

epidemiology the study of the occurrence and spread of a disease.

eponym the name of an illness, disorder, or medical tool as named after the person who first described it or invented it.

euthanasia the mercy killing of someone who is terminally ill.

expectorant a medicine that promotes the expulsion of mucus from the lungs.

extremis on the point of dying.

forensic medicine medical technology used to help solve crimes.

gavage feeding through a tube leading directly into the stomach through a hole created surgically in the abdominal wall.

gene therapy the substitution of abnormal genes with healthy ones as a treatment for a genetic disorder or disease.

GOMER slang term for a whining, complaining patient; an acronym for "Get out of my emergency room."

guaiac test a test for blood in the stool.

Heimlich maneuver an emergency procedure used to dislodge an object or piece of food caught in someone's throat, by means of applying sharp, sudden pressure to the abdomen below the rib cage.

hematocrit test a blood test to determine the ratio of blood cells to plasma, used to diagnose anemia.

hemoglobin a blood test to determine whether hemoglobin is too high or too low. A low level may indicate anemia, and a high level, the presence of tumors.

Hippocrates Greek physician known as the father of medicine, who lived before Christ's time and is the author of the Hippocratic oath.

Hippocratic oath an oath all physicians take promising to follow a code of ethical, professional conduct.

hydrogen breath test a test to measure the amount of hydrogen in one's breath, which can point to problems in digesting carbohydrates, such as lactose intolerance.

hyperbaric oxygenation therapy the use of high-pressure oxygen to treat carbon monoxide poisoning and burns.

hypochondriac a person excessively concerned about his health.

immunization vaccination with various antigens to active the immune system to produce antibodies as a protection against future infections.

incipient in the early stages.

informed consent a patient's legal consent to perform a treatment, procedure, or test after being informed of the risks involved.

inoculation the injection of a vaccine into the body.

intravenous within or via a vein.

intubation insertion of a tube through any part of the body for diagnostic or treatment purposes.

LASIK laser in-situ keratomileusis; a procedure to correct nearsightedness through the cutting away of corneal tissue by means of a special knife and a laser.

lavage washing out of an organ.

lesion collective term for damage to tissue, including abscesses, herpes, ulcers, tumors, and injuries.

liver blood test a blood test to measure liver enzymes to detect possible damage to the liver.

locum tenens Latin term for the temporary taking over of a practice of one doctor by another.

lower G.I. series lower gastrointestinal series; an X-ray exam using barium as a contrast medium to reveal detail in the colon. Also called a barium enema.

lumbar puncture the insertion of a needle into the spinal canal at the lower back to withdraw fluid for diagnostic purposes or to administer antibiotics or cancer drugs. Also known as a spinal tap.

magnetic resonance imaging (MRI) the use of an imaging technique employing magnetic properties instead of X-rays to reveal the interior of the body.

mammography the X-ray imaging of breast tissue.

mammogram an X-ray image of breast tissue, used to detect cancer.

Mantoux test a skin test for tuberculosis.

Mazzini test a test for syphilis.

methylene blue test an injection of dye that should appear in the urine within 30 minutes if the kidneys are functioning normally.

MRI see MAGNETIC RESONANCE IMAGING.

myringotomy an incision made in the eardrum to remove fluid and for the insertion and long-term placement of a ventilating tube, as a treatment for chronic ear infections.

nosocomial referring to the hospital, especially a disease or infection acquired while in the hospital.

nostrum a quack medicine.

occult hidden or concealed, as in blood in the stool.

organotherapy the use of hormones and tissue extracts from animals to treat human diseases.

oximetry the measurement of the concentration of oxygen in the blood, through sensors (oximeters) attached to the ear and finger.

palliative a medicine that soothes symptoms but does not cure the underlying disease.

palpation feeling with the hands the contours of a body part to help make a diagnosis.

panacea a cure-all; a universal remedy.

pandemic an epidemic that has spread across an entire state or country.

Pap test a test used to detect cancer in the cervix or uterus. Also known as Pap smear.

paracentesis drawing off fluids from a body cavity.

patch test a technique in which skin is scratched and exposed to various allergens, such as cat dander or nut protein, to test for allergic reactions. Also referred to as a scratch test.

paternity test a test to determine the father of a child by matching blood types.

pathogen any bacteria or virus capable of causing disease or infection.

percussion tapping the chest, abdomen, and back and listening for sounds in response, usually used as a method of detecting lung congestion.

per os by mouth, often abbreviated p.o.

per rectum through the rectum, often abbreviated p.r.

PET scan see POSITRON EMISSION TOMOGRAPHY.

pharmacopoeia a book listing medicinal drugs and their formulas; the U.S. Pharmacopoeia was first published in 1820.

placebo a fake medicine given in experiments and sometimes having a positive medicinal effect due to psychological phenomena.

position, Fowler's a position in which the patient is lying down with head raised about 20 inches to aid in draining pus in cases of peritonitis.

position, knee-chest a position in which the patient rests on elbows and knees with rump up for rectal exam.

position, lithotomy a position in which the patient is lying on back with knees up and legs spread, for a pelvic exam.

position, recumbent lying flat on back.

position, Sims a position in which the patient rests on the left side with the right leg bent and pulled up, for a rectal exam.

position, Trendelenburg's a position in which the patient lies with head 1 to 2 feet below knee level, to increase blood flow to the head to prevent shock. Also known as the shock position.

positron emission tomography (PET scan) an X-ray technique that captures detailed images of body tissues as injected radioactive molecules decay and produce positrons, or antiparticles of electrons.

PreVue test a highly accurate blood test used to diagnose Lyme disease.

PRK photorefractive keratectomy; a procedure to correct visual impairment by reshaping the cornea through the removal of tissue with a beam of ultraviolet light.

p.r.n. in prescription writing, a term meaning "whenever necessary."

prodromal symptoms the earliest symptoms of a disease.

prognosis the prediction of the outcome of a disease.

prognosticate to make a prediction of the course a disease will take.

prosthesis any artificial body part, such as a limb or valve.

prothrombin time test a test to determine the time it takes blood to clot.

protocol the records of a patient's case.

PSA prostate specific antigen; a blood test to detect cancer in the prostate.

quack a phony doctor.

radionucleotide test the injecting of a radioisotope into the arm to determine heart damage.

rale clicking sound made by a congested lung, as heard through a stethoscope.

reflex, Achilles ankle reflex caused by a blow to the large tendon above the heel.

reflex, Babinski the reflexive rising of the big toe and fanning of the small toes when the sole of the foot is scratched, often a sign of brain disease.

reflex, patellar the knee-jerk reflex.

relapse the return of a disease after apparent recovery.

remission a temporary or permanent halting of a disease.

resonance the sound of the lungs when they are clear and normal.

rhonchus wheezing sound heard through a stethoscope when excess mucus is present in the trachea.

Schultz-Charlton test a skin test to determine immunity to scarlet fever.

sigmoidoscopy an examination of the lower colon with a flexible tube.

Snellen test a vision test in which perfect vision is signified by the number 20/20.

socialized medicine a health care program paid for by the government through taxation.

somnoplasty a treatment for snoring in which heat is applied to remove excess tissue from the uvula and soft palate.

sonography reflection of sound waves recorded photographically to produce images of the interior of the body. Also known as ultrasound.

s.o.s. in prescription writing, a term meaning "if necessary."

spinal tap see LUMBAR PUNCTURE.

stat a hospital code word meaning "immediately."

stress test a test of the endurance and functioning of the heart, as measured during exercise.

submarine nanoparticle a developing technology consisting of a nanoparticle designed to carry and deliver drugs directly to cancer cells and eradicate faulty proteins while leaving surrounding healthy cells untouched.

sweat chloride test an analysis of perspiration to detect cystic fibrosis.

systemic affecting the entire body.

terminal fatal; near death.

thyroid blood test a test for levels of thyroid hormones to determine if the thyroid is underactive, overactive, or normal.

t.i.d. in prescription writing, an abbreviation for the Latin *tres in diem,* meaning "three times daily."

tilt-table test a test in which a patient is placed on an adjustable table that is tilted upward from a horizontal position in order to measure blood pressure deficiencies related to fainting.

TPN total parenteral nutrition; feeding of all nutrients through the veins.

traction the drawing or pulling together of broken bones in order to promote healing.

triage in disaster medicine, the sorting of patients by the seriousness and type of injury in order to provide treatment first to those who need it most.

Triage Cardiac System a machine that measures the level of critical cardiac enzymes to determine quickly if a patient has had a heart attack.

two-step test exercise to test the heart under exertion and to determine the presence of angina pectoris.

ultrasound see SONOGRAPHY.

upper endoscopy the insertion of a flexible tube down the esophagus for examination of the esophagus, stomach, and duodenum.

upper G.I. series upper gastrointestinal series; an X-ray exam employing barium as a contrast medium to reveal detail in the esophagus, stomach, and duodenum.

urea breath test a test performed to detect the presence of *Helicobacter pylori,* a bacteria that causes inflammation and ulcers in the stomach.

urinalysis an analysis of urine to detect the presence of various diseases.

ventilation transfer of air into and out of the lungs.

vital capacity test a breathing test of lung capacity, an accurate predictor or life span.

MEDICINE CHEST

acetaminophen a pain reliever and fever reducer.

Adrenalin see EPINEPHRINE.

aloe vera a plant whose leaves contain a gel that is proven to soothe and help heal burns.

amoxicillin a broad-spectrum antibiotic.

ampicillin a broad-spectrum antibiotic.

analgesic any pain reliever.

anesthetic any one of various agents used to dampen or eliminate pain sensation, some of which can also be used to bring about unconsciousness.

angiogenesis inhibitor any drug that inhibits the growth of tumors by attacking their ability to produce new blood vessels.

anodyne a pain reliever.

antacid any agent used to neutralize acid in the stomach.

antagonist a drug that interferes with or counteracts another drug.

antibiotic a widely used medicine of various forms, such as penicillin or the tetracyclines, derived from fungi or bacteria, that kills or inhibits the growth of some infectious microorganisms.

antibody a protein produced by the body's immune system to fight off foreign substances such as bacteria or viruses.

anticoagulant a substance used to inhibit blood clotting.

anticonvulsant a drug that prevents seizures or convulsions.

antidepressant any of a variety of drugs used to treat depression, such as Prozac or Zoloft.

antidote any agent administered to neutralize poison.

antiemetic a drug that prevents vomiting.

antigen any foreign substance, such as bacteria, viruses, or toxins, that triggers a response from the immune systems, which produces antibodies as a defense.

antihistamine drug that blocks the body's release of histamine, used to control allergic reactions.

antipruritic an itch reliever.

antipyretic a fever reducer.

antiseptic inhibiting the growth of germs.

antispasmodic drug that controls or prevents muscle spasms.

antitussive a cough suppressant.

antivenin an antidote to animal poison, such as from a snakebite.

aphrodisiac fantasy agent that heightens sex drive.

aspirin common pain reliever and fever reducer that is also used to prevent heart attacks or reduce the severity of a heart attack in progress.

astringent an agent that constricts tissue and slows the flow of blood.

AZT azidothymidine, a drug used to combat the symptoms of AIDS.

bactericide any agent that kills bacteria.

bacteriostat any agent that inhibits the growth of bacteria.

barbiturate a drug that depresses the central nervous system and induces sedation or sleep.

benzocaine a topical or local anesthetic.

beta-blocker drug that inhibits the excitability of the heart to help treat angina, hypertension, and arrhythmia.

bicarbonate of soda baking soda, used as an antacid.

booster shot a second vaccination administered several months or years after an original one to prevent immunity levels from dropping.

botox botulinum toxin; derived from a deadly poison, a substance most commonly injected into the forehead to relax contracted muscles and consequently reduce wrinkles. It is also used to combat headache and back pain and to help control involuntary muscle spasms.

broad-spectrum capable of fighting a wide array of microorganisms.

bronchodilator any drug, often in the form of an inhalant, that relaxes bronchial smooth muscle and opens airways during an asthma attack or allergic reaction.

camphor a substance used in liniments and in treatments for flatulence.

capsicum red pepper, used as a topical analgesic and an expectorant.

castor oil a laxative.

cathartic a laxative.

catholicon a panacea, or cure-all.

chloroform formerly used as an anesthetic, now in treatments for flatulence and as a liniment.

codeine a painkiller and cough suppressant derived from morphine.

cortisone a steroid hormone used in various diseases, such as Addison's disease.

cortisone injection an injection of cortisone to treat inflammation, especially in joints.

cytotoxin a drug that inhibits cell division and is effective in slowing or stopping the growth of cancer cells.

decongestant any agent used to relieve nasal congestion.

depressant any drug that depresses the central nervous system and produces a sedative effect.

diazepam popular tranquilizer and muscle relaxant, known more widely by its trade name, Valium.

digitalis derived from foxglove, a heart stimulant used to treat heart failure.

disinfectant any cleaning agent used to destroy bacteria or other microorganisms.

diuretic any drug that increases the output of urine, used to reduce edema.

DPT a vaccination against diphtheria, whooping cough, and tetanus, commonly administered during childhood.

dressing a bandage or other protective wrapping, applied with or without medication to a wound.

echinacea extract of the purple coneflower, used to boost immunity and help lessen the severity of colds.

elixir a mixture containing alcohol or glycerine, used to mask the taste of a bitter or foul-tasting medicine.

emetic any agent used to induce vomiting.

ephedrine a bronchodilator used in the treatment of asthma and allergies.

epinephrine a naturally occurring hormone released by the adrenal glands during stress to increase heart rate and blood pressure; its synthesized version (Adrenalin) is used as a heart stimulant and bronchodilator and is commonly carried by those with severe allergies to prevent anaphylaxis.

erythromycin an antibiotic used to fight staph and strep infections.

expectorant a cough medicine.

general anesthetic a surgical anesthetic that renders a patient unconscious.

germicide any agent that kills microorganisms.

ginkgo an extract from the leaves of the gingko tree, noted for improving mental performance by increasing blood flow to the brain.

ginseng a natural plant product to boost energy levels.

hypnotic any sedative or sleep-inducer.

ibuprofen a pain reliever and anti-inflammatory agent.

immunosuppressant any drug that suppresses the immune system, used to prevent the body rejecting transplanted tissues and organs.

insulin a pancreatic hormone that regulates blood sugar levels, the manufactured version of which is used in the treatment of diabetes mellitus.

interferon a natural cell protein that helps to prevent a virus from replicating.

iodine an antiseptic used to dress wounds.

ipecac a plant extract given in the form of syrup to induce vomiting.

kava a natural root extract believed to relieve tension.

laxative any substance used to purge the bowels.

L-dopa drug used in the treatment of Parkinson's disease.

lidocaine a local anesthetic that is also used to stop heart arrhythmia.

liniment any rubbing compound used to soothe aching muscles and relieve stiffness.

lymphocyte a white blood cell involved in the body's natural immune system.

local anesthetic any topical substance used to numb or stop sensation in a specific area.

methadone a narcotic used as a substitute for morphine or heroin to help those dependent on these drugs to cure their addictions.

MMR a vaccine used to prevent measles, mumps, and rubella, administered during childhood.

morphine a powerful painkiller and sedative extracted from opium.

narcotic a painkilling and sedating drug, such as morphine, that is usually addictive.

natural killer cell a natural cell or lymphocyte in the body that defends against viruses and tumors.

neomycin a broad-spectrum antibiotic, commonly used on the skin and in the eyes.

nitroglycerin a vasodilator used in episodes of severe angina to open blood vessels and help restore blood flow to the heart.

OD an overdose; to overdose.

opiate any one of various drugs derived from opium, such as morphine and codeine.

opium an extract of the poppy flower, a powerful and addictive narcotic used for painkilling and sedation.

OTC over-the-counter; available without a doctor's prescription.

overdose an excessive dose of medicine, causing ill effects or even death.

palliative any medicine that relieves symptoms but does not cure the underlying illness.

panacea a mythical cure-all.

patent medicine any trademarked medication that can be purchased without a doctor's prescription.

penicillin a broad-spectrum antibiotic.

pharmaceutical any drug or medication available at a pharmacy.

pharmacology the study and science of drugs and their effects on the body.

pharmacopoeia a book containing information on drugs and their ingredients, their preparation, their proper dosages, etc.

pharmacy a drugstore.

phenobarbital a barbiturate with a sedative effect, used to treat anxiety and insomnia.

physic a laxative.

placebo a sham pill or treatment that, presented as real medicine, often has measurable, curative effects, used in double-blind medical studies to test the efficacy of authentic medications.

polio vaccine either the Sabin (live virus) or the Salk (dead virus) vaccine, to prevent polio.

poultice a folk remedy composed of a warm, moist dressing made from meal, bread, clay, or other substance and applied to soothe an aching or inflamed body part.

prednisone a synthetic steroid used in the treatment of allergies and rheumatic diseases.

prescription a doctor's written order to a pharmacy for a medication.

procaine a local anesthetic known more widely by its trade name, Novocain.

prophylactic any agent that prevents disease, such as a vaccine. Also, a condom.

psychedelic more often known as an hallucinogenic, any substance that causes altered states of consciousness and may cause hallucinations.

psychoactive any drug that affects the mind, thinking processes, mood, etc.

purgative a laxative.

quinine drug used in the treatment of malaria.

Sabin vaccine see POLIO VACCINE.

St.-John's-wort the yellow-flowered *Hypericum* plant, an extract of which has been shown to relieve mild to moderate depression.

Salk vaccine see POLIO VACCINE.

sedative any drug used to relieve anxiety or induce sleep.

sodium barbital a sedative.

soporific any drug that induces sleep.

steroid any of various hormones, including cortisone, progesterone, the male hormone androgen, and the female hormone estrogen, synthetic versions of which are used in hormone replacement therapy and in muscle building.

stimulant any substance that excites the central nervous system and increases alertness, such as caffeine.

streptokinase a bacteria-produced enzyme used to break up artery-clogging blood clots, especially in cases of myocardial infraction and pulmonary embolism.

streptomycin a broad-spectrum antibiotic, especially used in the treatment of tuberculosis.

sulfa drug any one of various drugs derived from sulfanilamide, used to treat a broad range of infections, such as those involved in conjunctivitis, bronchitis, leprosy, malaria, dysentery, gastroenteritis, and urinary infections, by preventing the growth of bacteria. Also known as a sulfonamide.

sulfonamide see SULFA DRUG.

synergist any medicine that produces a more powerful effect when combined with another medicine.

tetracycline any one of various bacteria-derived antibiotics used to treat a wide range of bacterial infections, including syphilis.

tolerance the decline of a drug's effectiveness in a patient over time, causing the need for higher dosages.

topical applied to a localized area outside the body, such as the skin.

tranquilizer any drug used to relieve anxiety and induce sleep.

troche a lozenge.

vaccine any inoculation administered to prevent a disease.

valerian a plant-derived sedative.

vasoconstrictor any drug that narrows the blood vessels, used to maintain or raise blood pressure during shock or surgery.

vasodilator any drug that widens the blood vessels, causing an increase in blood flow, used to improve circulation and to treat angina.

vermicide any drug used to destroy worms in the intestines.

vitamin any one of various substances, derived from plant and animal products, essential for the body's health and functioning.

warfarin an anticoagulant used to help prevent embolism.

withdrawal unpleasant side effects, which may include sweating, vomiting, shaking, strong cravings, etc., experienced when a patient stops taking certain drugs.

SURGICAL AND MEDICAL PROCEDURES AND RELATED TERMS

ACL surgery surgical reconstruction or repair of the anterior cruciate ligament of the knee, using a graft from the patient's own body.

adenectomy removal of a gland.

adenoidectomy removal of the adenoids.

adenotonsillectomy removal of the tonsils and adenoids.

adrenalectomy removal of the adrenal glands.

anesthesia, caudal injection of an anesthetic agent into the lower spinal canal.

anesthesia, endotracheal an anesthetic agent administered through a tube placed into the mouth or nose and down into the trachea or windpipe for inhalation.

anesthesia, epidural injection of an anesthetic agent just outside the spinal canal.

anesthesia, general the administration of a full-body anesthesia involving loss of consciousness.

anesthesia, intravenous injection of an anesthetic agent into a vein.

anesthesia, local an anesthetic agent used in a limited or confined area of the body.

anesthesia, spinal an anesthetic agent injected directly into the spinal fluid of the spinal canal.

anesthesia, topical a local anesthetic applied to a body surface.

appendectomy removal of the appendix.

approach surgical term referring to the method used and route taken to reach a particular organ.

arthroscopy examining the inside of a joint with a lighted instrument.

biopsy removal of tissue samples for the purpose of diagnosis, especially of tumors.

breast augmentation the implantation of saline-filled silicone bags under the breast and chest muscle to create fuller breasts.

Brunschwig's operation removal of all of the pelvic organs in order to stop a massive spread of cancer.

bypass a blood vessel graft supplied to an area with inadequate blood supply due to clogging of an artery. Also, an operation to shunt intestinal contents from one section of an intestine to another.

canthoplasty plastic surgery on the upper eyelid.

catheterization the passing of a slender tube into a body channel to extract or deliver fluids.

catheterization, cardiac passing a tube through a blood vessel in an extremity and threading it to the vessels of the heart for taking blood samples and pressure readings.

cauterization the burning away of abnormal tissue by electric current, heat, or caustic material.

celiotomy any surgery that opens up the abdomen.

cephalotrypesis cutting a hole through the skull to diagnose or treat a brain disease.

chemonucleolysis injecting a herniated disk with an enzyme in order to dissolve it.

chemotherapy the employment of chemicals to treat infections and tumors.

cholecystectomy removal of the gallbladder.

cholecystogastronomy surgically joining the gallbladder to the stomach.

choledocholithotomy removal of stones from the common bile duct leading from the gallbladder.

circumcision the surgical removal of the foreskin of the penis on a male infant.

clone a genetically identical descendant created asexually through somatic cell nuclear transfer.

closed-chest massage an emergency method of restarting a heart that has stopped beating, specifically by pressing down rhythmically on the breastbone with the palm of the hand 80 times per minute.

closure the suturing of a wound; closing a wound.

colectomy removal of all or part of the large intestine.

colostomy a procedure to bring the large intestine to the abdominal wall, where an opening is made.

craniotomy a skull surgery that exposes the brain.

cryogenics the science of using cold as a medical treatment.

cryosurgery surgery employing extreme cold to destroy diseased tissue.

cryothalectomy the application of extreme cold to the thalamus of the brain; it destroys the area responsible for producing the palsy of Parkinson's disease.

curettage the scraping of tissue to obtain samples or to remove diseased tissue and growths.

cystectomy the removal of a cyst.

denervate to purposely cut a nerve in a body area in order to relieve pain.

divinyl ether an inhaled anesthetic agent.

electrocoagulation the coagulation of tissue through the use of an electric current.

embolectomy surgical removal of a blood clot in an artery to restore normal circulation.

encephalography an X-ray technique revealing parts of the brain.

endoscopic retrograde lithotripsy the passing of an instrument through the bladder and into the ureter to remove stones.

endoscopic shock wave lithotripsy disintegrating and eliminating kidney stones by the use of shock waves instead of surgery.

enhanced external counterpulsation (EECP) a noninvasive medical therapy used to eliminate or reduce angina. The procedure employs a device that delivers pulses of pressure to the legs that are timed with the patient's heartbeats. Over a course of 35 or more treatments, the technique lowers the pressure that the heart must pump against and increases the rate of return of blood to the heart, reducing pain from angina.

enterectomy removal of part of the intestine.

esophagectomy removal of the esophagus.

esophagoscopy the passing of an instrument down the throat to inspect the esophagus.

ether an inhaled anesthetic agent.

ethyl chloride a local anesthetic agent that freezes any tissue it comes in contact with.

ethylene an anesthetic gas.

eviscerate to open the abdomen and pull out the intestines.

excision the surgical removal of a tissue or organ.

face-lift plastic surgery to remove wrinkles.

flap a section (graft) of flesh that includes subcutaneous fat, muscles, nerves, arteries, and veins transplanted to another part of the body by microsurgery.

fluoroscopy a technique of producing live X-ray images of the internal organs in motion on a fluorescent screen.

fundal plication a procedure to correct a hiatus hernia by wrapping the upper end of the stomach around the intruding portion of the esophagus.

gamma knife radiosurgery a surgery that employs an irradiation machine to concentrate gamma rays on brain and other tumors to destroy them. The method is used when tumors are difficult or otherwise impossible to remove surgically.

gastrectomy removal of part or all of the stomach.

gastric lavage prior to surgery, the washing out of all stomach contents.

gastrostomy the surgical creation of an opening into the stomach through the abdominal wall, when feeding through the mouth is not possible.

gingivectomy the surgical removal of part of the gums.

glossectomy removal of the tongue.

graft the transplanting of tissue from one part of the body to another. Also, the tissue so transplanted.

graft, auto a graft taken from the patient's own body.

graft, fascial a graft consisting of fibrous tissue.

graft, full thickness a graft containing all layers of the skin.

graft, split thickness a graft consisting of only part of the layers of the skin.

hemostasis the stopping of bleeding, achieved in surgery by clamping and tying off blood vessels.

hernioplasty surgical repair of a hernia.

heterograft a graft taken from an animal for use on a human.

homograft a graft taken from the body of another person.

hypodermic beneath the skin, as a hypodermic injection.

hysterectomy removal of the uterus.

incise to cut surgically.

incision a surgical cut.

intubation the passage of a tube into a body channel.

keratectomy removal of the cornea of the eye.

Kraske's operation removal of the rectum, coccyx, and part of the sacrum.

laparoscopy a minimally invasive surgical technique in which a small incision is made in the abdomen through which instruments may be inserted to perform a wide array of tasks, from examination of tissue to organ removal.

laryngectomy removal of the larynx (voice box).

lidocaine a local anesthetic agent.

lipectomy the removal of excess body fat.

liposuction a plastic surgery process in which excess fat is sucked from the body as a means of weight loss.

lobectomy removal of one of the five lobes of the lungs.

lobotomy removal of the front portion of the brain as a treatment for severe mental illness.

lumpectomy the removal of a tumor or mass.

mammoplasty plastic surgery to improve the appearance of the breasts.

mastectomy removal of a breast.

mastoplasty plastic surgery to reduce the size of the breasts.

McBurney's incision an angular incision in the lower right abdomen, for removal of the appendix.

myectomy removal of part or all of a muscle.

myringotomy an incision into the eardrum to remove pus.

nephrectomy removal of a kidney.

neurosurgery surgery of the brain, spinal cord, or nerves.

nitrous oxide the anesthetic gas better known as laughing gas.

Ober operations in cases of paralysis, the transplanting of muscles and tendons.

odontectomy removal of the teeth.

oophorectomy removal of an ovary.

oral surgery surgery of the mouth or gums.

osteoclasis the deliberate rebreaking of a bone to more accurately set its alignment.

otoplasty plastic surgery to correct such ear deformities as flop ears and cauliflower ears.

palatoplasty repair of a cleft palate.

pancreatectomy removal of the pancreas.

pentothal an intravenous anesthetic agent.

percutaneous transluminal coronary angioplasty X-ray imaging of the coronary arteries with the aid of catheterization and a contrast medium or dye.

perfusion the injection and permeation of a fluid into a body part.

perineoplasty after childbirth, the repair of torn tissue between the vagina and the rectum.

phantom limb pain after an amputation, sensation or perceived pain from the limb that was severed, a poorly understood psychological phenomenon.

phlebectomy the removal of a vein.

pneumonectomy removal of a lung.

postoperative after surgery.

procaine a local anesthetic agent.

prolapsed referring to an organ that has fallen out of its normal position.

prostatectomy removal of the prostate gland.

purse-string operation the closing of the cervix with a purse-string suture in order to prevent premature childbirth or miscarriage.

radial keratotomy surgery originating in the Soviet Union and involving several incisions made in the cornea of the eye to cure nearsightedness.

radio frequency face-lift a nonsurgical face-lift that uses high-powered radio waves to diminish wrinkles and sags by contracting and tightening the skin.

radiosurgery use of radiation in surgical treatment.

rejection reaction the body's attack on foreign substances, including organs or tissues donated from another person, which can often be counteracted by special drugs.

rhinoplasty plastic surgery to improve the appearance of the nose.

rhytidectomy plastic surgery to remove skin wrinkles.

salpingectomy removal of a fallopian tube.

salpingoplasty opening a closed passage in a fallopian tube to cure sterility.

septectomy surgery to correct a deviated septum in the nose.

shunt a bypass.

sigmoidectomy removal of the sigmoid portion of the large intestine.

somatic cell nuclear transfer the method of creating a cloned embryo by inserting the nucleus of a cell into a hollowed-out egg and treating it with chemicals to initiate embryonic cell division. The clone contains the cell donor's genes and a small amount of DNA from the egg.

splenectomy removal of a spleen.

staphylorrhaphy repair of a cleft palate.

sternal puncture taking by needle a marrow sample from the breastbone to test for blood disease.

sternotomy cutting the sternum apart in order to gain access to the heart.

suture to stitch or sew up a wound. Also, the thread used for this purpose.

suture, button suturing technique in which the ends of the thread are passed through buttons and tied off.

suture, catgut suture material made from sheep intestine; it is gradually absorbed by the body.

suture, cobbler a suture with a needle attached to each end.

suture, continuous a suture having only two ties, at the beginning and end of a wound.

suture, interrupted a suture having several ties and separate strands.

suture, inverting a suture that turns in tissue on all sides of a wound.

suture, purse-string a continuous, inverting suture forming a circle.

tamponade stopping blood flow by inserting a cotton sponge in a wound.

tapping the removal of body fluids with a needle.

temporal-cortical bypass an artery bypass applied to the surface of the brain to help restore blood flow.

therapeutic cloning the cloning of human embryos from which may be harvested stem cells. The stem cells can be cultured into cell colonies for use in the creation of various tissues for transplants.

thoracoscopy an examination of the chest cavity by a special instrument.

thyroidectomy removal of the thyroid gland.

tissue engineering the creation of living tissue in the laboratory. Skin and organ cells can be grown by various means, but full organ growth is still in the experimental stage. On the experimental front, liver and kidney cells are grown and "assembled" with microscopic tubes made of a biocompatible polymer that serves a circulatory system.

tissue typing the matching of compatible tissue or organs in transplant operations to help prevent rejection reaction.

trachelectomy removal of the cervix and the neck of the uterus.

tracheotomy an emergency incision into the trachea to open up the airways and relieve suffocation.

transfusion the infusing of donor blood into a patient's vein.

trans-sex surgery removal or altering of the sexual organs as an aid in changing one's sex from male to female, or vice versa.

trepanning boring a hole through the skull.

tubal ligation surgically closing the fallopian tube to prevent pregnancy.

ureteroscopic ultrasonic lithotripsy disintegration of stones in the ureter by means of sound waves.

vaginoplasty repair of a torn vagina after childbirth.

vasectomy sterilization technique involving the cutting of the vas deferens, the tube through which sperm is transported.

Wertheim operation removal of the uterus, fallopian tubes, ovaries, and surrounding tissue to cure extensive cancer.

MILITARY

AIR FORCE AND AIRCRAFT

(includes naval aircraft)

A-4 see SKYHAWK.

A-6 see INTRUDER.

A-7 see CORSAIR II.

A-10 see THUNDERBOLT II.

AC-130 see HERCULES.

aeromedical evacuation the transport of patients to and between hospital facilities by air.

aeromedical evacuation coordinating officer an officer in charge of aeromedical evacuations.

aeromedical staging unit a medical unit operating at an air base or airstrip.

aeronautical chart a map showing features of the Earth to aid in air navigation.

afterburning in the exhaust jet of a turbojet engine, the process of fuel injection and combustion.

afterflight inspection the inspection for defects in an aircraft after a flight; may also include the replenishment of fuel and the securing of the aircraft.

AH-1J see SEA COBRA.

airborne alert a state of aircraft readiness in which aircraft are already in the air and prepared for combat.

airborne assault weapon a full-tracked gun providing antitank capability for airborne troops.

airborne battlefield command and control center an aircraft equipped with communications, data link, and display equipment, employed as an airborne command post or as an intelligence relay facility.

air combat fighter an F-16; a single engine, supersonic, turbofan tactical fighter/bomber capable of employing either nuclear or nonnuclear weapons.

air controller one assigned to the control of aircraft by radar, radio, or other means.

air corridor a restricted air route intended for friendly aircraft only.

aircraft arresting barrier a barrier device used to stop the forward motion of an aircraft in an emergency landing or aborted takeoff.

aircraft arresting cable spanning the landing surface or flight deck, a cable used to catch an aircraft's arresting system to stop its forward motion.

aircraft arresting hook a hook device on the bottom of an aircraft to engage arresting gear, especially on the flight deck of an aircraft carrier.

aircraft arresting system a series of components used to catch aircraft and stop their forward progress during landings or aborted takeoffs.

aircraft dispersal area an area on a military installation where aircraft are dispersed or spread apart when parked, with the intention of avoiding large-scale destruction in the event of an enemy air raid.

aircraft marshaller one who directs aircraft on the ground by the use of batons.

aircraft marshalling area the area where aircraft line up before takeoff or where aircraft assemble after landing.

aircraft scrambling from a ground alert, the immediate takeoff of aircraft.

BLU-82 a 15,000-pound bomb. Also, more popularly known as a daisy cutter.

bunker buster the GBU-28 Penetrator, a bomb designed to penetrate earth and concrete in order to destroy buried bunkers.

C-17 Globemaster III a large, jet-powered cargo plane.

Corsair II an A-7; a single-seat, single-turbofan engine, all-weather light attack aircraft designed to operate from aircraft carriers, armed with cannon and capable of carrying a wide assortment of nuclear and nonnuclear missiles.

crash locator beacon an automatic beacon device to aid forces in locating a crashed aircraft.

critical altitude the maximum altitude an aircraft can fly and still function properly.

cruising level the altitude maintained throughout most of a flight.

curve of pursuit the curved path described by a fighter plane making an attack on a moving target while holding the proper aiming allowance.

DADCAP dawn and dusk combat air patrol.

daisy cutter see BLU-82.

dart a training target towed by a jet and fired upon by a practicing fighter aircraft.

day air defense fighter a fighter aircraft capable of engaging in combat only in daylight and in clear weather.

DC-130 see HERCULES.

Delta Dagger a single-engine turbojet all-weather interceptor with supersonic speed and armed with Falcon missiles. Also known as an F-102A.

Delta Dart a supersonic, single-engine turbojet all-weather interceptor armed with Falcon missiles with nonnuclear warheads and Genie rockets with nuclear warheads. Also known as an F-106.

destroy, beam in air intercept, a code meaning "the interceptor will be vectored to a standard beam attack for interception and destruction of the target."

destroy, cutoff in air intercept, a code meaning "intercept and destroy. Command vectors will produce a cutoff attack."

destroy, frontal in air intercept, a command meaning "the interceptor will be vectored to a standard frontal attack for interception and destruction of the target."

destroy, stern in air intercept, a command meaning "the interceptor will be vectored to a standard stern attack for interception and destruction of the target."

diplomatic authorization authority for a flight over or a landing on foreign soil obtained through diplomatic channels.

dispenser on fighter aircraft, a container used to carry and release submunitions.

ditching a controlled crash-landing in the water.

drone an unmanned, remote-controlled aircraft used primarily for reconnaissance.

droop stop a device that helps prevent helicopter rotor blades from drooping excessively after the engine has been shut off.

dropmaster the person in charge of the preparation, inspection, loading, lashing, and ejecting of materials for an airdrop.

drop message a message dropped by air to a ground unit.

duck in air intercept, a code meaning "trouble headed your way."

dumb bomb any unguided bomb.

dummy run a practice bombing run.

E-1B see TRACER.

E-2 see HAWKEYE.

EA-6A see INTRUDER.

EA-6B see PROWLER.

Eagle a twin-engine supersonic, turbofan, all-weather tactical fighter employing a variety of weapons and capable of long-range missions through in-flight refueling. Also known as an F-15.

ejection the emergency escape from an in-flight aircraft by means of an independently propelled seat or capsule.

ejection, sequenced a system that ejects crew members one at a time in an emergency situation, to avoid midair collisions.

elevator in air intercept, a code meaning "take altitude indicated."

emergency scramble in air intercept, a code meaning "carrier addressed immediately launch all available fighter aircraft as combat air patrol."

endurance the time an aircraft can continue flying without refueling.

engage to fire upon an enemy aircraft.

escort an aircraft assigned to protect other aircraft.

extraction parachute an auxiliary parachute used to release, extract, and deploy cargo from aircraft in flight.

F-4 see PHANTOM II.

F-5A/B see FREEDOM FIGHTER.

F-14 see TOMCAT.

F-15 see EAGLE.

F-16 see AIR COMBAT FIGHTER.

F-35 Lightning II a joint strike fighter jet.

F-100 see SUPER SABRE.

F-101 see VOODOO.

F-102A see DELTA DAGGER.

F-104 see STARFIGHTER.

F-105 see THUNDERCHIEF.

F-106 see DELTA DART.

F-111 a twin-engine, supersonic turbofan, all-weather tactical fighter armed with nuclear or non-nuclear weapons and capable of taking off from or landing on short runways.

F-117A see STEALTH FIGHTER.

F/A-22 Raptor the most advanced tactical jet fighter in the United States air arsenal, noted for its ability to carry air-to-air missiles internally in order to maintain its stealthiness.

faded in air intercept, a code meaning "contact has disappeared from reporting station's scope, and any position information given is estimated."

faker a friendly aircraft simulating a hostile aircraft in training exercises.

famished in air intercept, a code meaning "have you any instructions for me?"

feet dry in air intercept, a code meaning "I am over land."

feet wet in air intercept, a code meaning "I am over water."

ferret an aircraft especially equipped to detect and analyze electromagnetic radiation.

firebee a remote-controlled, subsonic drone acting as a target to test and evaluate weapon systems employing surface-to-air or air-to-air missiles. Also known as BQM-34.

firepower umbrella the range or distance a naval unit's weaponry can reach, within which is hazardous for enemy aircraft to fly.

flare to change the flight path of an aircraft to decrease the rate of descent for landing.

flight deck in some aircraft, an elevated cockpit.

foam path a path of fire extinguisher foam laid on a runway to help prevent an explosion or fire in an emergency or crash landing.

fox away in air intercept, a code meaning "missile has fired or been released from aircraft."

freddie a controlling unit.

Freedom Fighter a twin-engine supersonic turbojet, multipurpose tactical fighter/bomber. Also known as F-5A/B.

free drop the dropping of equipment or supplies from an aircraft without the use of parachutes.

free lance in air intercept, a code meaning "self-control of aircraft is being employed."

Galaxy a large cargo transport aircraft powered by four turbofan engines. Also known as C-5A.

gate in air intercept, a code meaning "fly at maximum possible speed."

glide bomb a bomb fitted with airfoils to provide extra lift.

glide mode a flight control system that automatically positions an aircraft to the center of a glide slope course.

go around mode a flight control system that automatically terminates an approach and initiates a climb mode when needed.

grand slam all enemy aircraft sighted are shot down.

H-2 see SEA SPRITE.

H-3 see SEA KING.

H-46 see SEA KNIGHT.

harassing harassing attacks by air, designed to aid ground units in battle.

Harrier a single-engine, turbojet light attack aircraft designed to take off vertically or from short runways. Also known as an AV-8.

Hawk a mobile, surface-to-air missile system that provides nonnuclear, low-to-medium altitude air defense coverage for ground forces. Also known as MIM-23.

Hawkeye a twin turboprop, multicrew airborne early warning and interceptor control aircraft designed to operate from aircraft carriers. It carries a long-range radar and integrated computer system for the detection and tracking of airborne targets. Also known as E-2.

HC-130 see HERCULES.

heading the direction an aircraft is headed expressed in degrees clockwise from north.

heads up in air intercept, a code meaning "enemy got through."

helicopter lane an air corridor reserved for helicopters during operations.

helipad a reserved area used specifically by helicopters when parking, taking off, or landing.

heliport airport facility specifically designed to service helicopters.

Hercules a troop and cargo transport equipped with four turboprop engines.

hypersonic speeds equal to or exceeding five times the speed of sound.

imagery sortie a single reconnaissance flight to obtain photographic and other visual information.

instrument flight a flight controlled by reference to instruments only.

interceptor an aircraft used to identify, intercept, and engage enemy targets.

in the dark a code meaning "not visible on my scope."

Intruder a twin-engine, turbojet, two-place, long-range, all-weather, aircraft carrier-based, low-altitude attack aircraft armed with an assortment of weapons, including Sidewinder, Bullpup, napalm, or all standard navy rockets. Also known as an A-6.

Iroquois a light, single-rotor helicopter used for cargo and personnel transport and sometimes armed with machine guns or light rockets.

Jet Star a small, fast transport aircraft powered by four turboprop engines. Also known as a C-140.

judy a code meaning "I have contact and am taking over the intercept."

jumpmaster the person who manages or supervises a team of parachutists.

jump speed the airspeed at which parachutists can safely jump from an aircraft.

KA-6 see INTRUDER.

KC-97L see STRATOFREIGHTER.

KC-135 see STRATOTANKER.

landing roll the rollout or deceleration of an aircraft from touchdown to taxi speed.

laydown bombing a low-altitude bombing run in which delay fuses or delay devices are used to allow the aircraft time to escape the effects of its own bombs.

liner a code meaning "fly at speed giving maximum cruising range."

LOCAP low combat air patrol.

loft bombing a low-altitude bombing run in which the aircraft drops its bombs as it begins to pull up or climb.

machmeter an instrument displaying the Mach number of the aircraft.

mach no a code meaning "I have reached maximum speed and am not closing my target."

mach yes a code meaning "I have reached maximum speed and am closing my target."

mark a term used to designate the exact time of a weapon's release, usually preceded by the word "standby."

mark mark command from ground controller for an aircraft to release its bombs.

Mayday distress call.

merged a code meaning "tracks have come together."

midnight a code meaning "changeover from close to broadcast control."

MIM-23 see HAWK.

MIM-72 see CHAPARRAL.

MOAB massive ordnance air-blast bomb; a 21,500-pound bomb dropped from an aircraft, sometimes used for intimidation purposes alone. Also known as the mother of all bombs.

music in air intercept, a term meaning electronic jamming.

napalm powdered aluminum soap or similar compound used to gelatinize oil or gasoline for use in napalm bombs.

NATO airspace the airspace above any NATO nation and its territorial waters.

near miss a near collision with another aircraft in flight.

negative term meaning "no" in air communications.

night cap night combat air patrol.

no fly zone an area designated off-limits to aircraft, usually by military order.

no joy a code meaning "I have been unsuccessful," or "I have no information."

notice to airmen a notice containing information on any change in any airport facility, service, procedure, or hazard. Also called NOTAM.

offset bombing any bombing procedure that uses a reference or aiming point other than the actual target.

oranges, sour a code meaning "weather is unsuitable for aircraft mission."

oranges, sweet a code meaning "weather is suitable for aircraft mission.

orbiting a word meaning circling, or circling and searching.

ordnance collective term for pyrotechnic weapons, including bombs, guns and ammunition, flares, smoke, and napalm.

Orion a four-engine, turboprop, all-weather, long-range, land-based antisubmarine aircraft capable of carrying an assortment of search radar, nuclear depth charges, and homing torpedoes. Also known as a P-3.

OV-10 see BRONCO.

overshoot a landing that is aborted.

P-3 see ORION.

pan a code meaning the calling station has a very urgent message to transmit concerning the safety of a ship, aircraft, or other vehicle or of some person on board or within sight.

pancake a code meaning "land," or "I wish to land."

pathfinder aircraft an aircraft with a specially trained crew carrying drop zone/landing zone marking teams, target markers, or navigational aids and that precedes the main force to the drop zone or landing zone or target.

pattern bombing the uniform distribution of bombs over a particular area.

payload the cargo and passengers on a flight.

Phantom II a twin-engine, supersonic, multipurpose, all-weather jet fighter/bomber capable of operating from land or from aircraft carriers and armed with either nuclear or nonnuclear weapons. Also known as an F-4.

photoflash bomb a bomb designed to produce a brief and intense illumination for medium-altitude night photography.

pogo a code meaning "switch to communications channel number preceding 'pogo.' If unable to establish communications, switch to channel number following 'pogo.'"

point of no return the point at which an aircraft is incapable of returning to base due to a low fuel supply.

popeye a code meaning "in clouds or area of reduced visibility."

pounce a code meaning "I am in position to engage target."

precision bombing bombing directed at a specific target.

Provider an assault, twin-engine transport that can operate from short, unprepared landing strips to transport troops and equipment. Also known as a C-123.

Prowler a twin turbojet engine, quadruple crew, all-weather, electronic countermeasures aircraft designed to operate from aircraft carriers. Also known as an EA-6B.

prudent limit of endurance the time during which an aircraft can remain airborne and still retain a given safety margin of fuel.

punch a code meaning "you should very soon be obtaining a contact on the aircraft that is being intercepted."

purple a code meaning "the unit indicated is suspected of carrying nuclear weapons."

RA-5 see VIGILANTE.

radar picket radar picket combat air patrol.

radio beacon a radio transmitter that emits a distinctive signal used for the determination of bearings, courses, locations, and so on.

radio fix the location of an aircraft by determining the direction of radio signals coming to the aircraft from two or more sending stations, the locations of which are known.

reconnaissance a mission undertaken to obtain, by visual observation or other detection methods, information about the activities and resources of an enemy; or to secure data concerning the meteorological, hydrographic, or geographic characteristics of a particular area.

reconnaissance by fire disclosing an enemy's position by firing or shooting at its general vicinity and waiting for the flashes of return fire.

reconnaissance in force a mission designed to discover or test an enemy's strength.

RF-4 see PHANTOM II.

roll the rotation of an aircraft in flight.

S-2 see TRACKER.

S-3 see VIKING.

salvo the release or firing of all ordnance of a specific type simultaneously.

saunter a code meaning "fly at best endurance."

scan a code meaning "search sector indicated and report any contacts."

scram a code meaning "am about to open fire. Friendly units keep clear of indicated contact, bogey, of area."

scramble an order directing takeoff of aircraft as quickly as possible.

Sea Cobra a single-rotor, dual crew, light attack helicopter armed with a variety of machine guns, rockets, grenade launchers, and antitank missiles. Also known as an AH-1J.

Sea King a single rotor, medium-lift helicopter utilized for air/sea rescue and personnel and cargo transport in support of aircraft carrier operations. Some may be equipped for antisubmarine operations. Also known as an H-3.

Sea Knight a twin-rotor, medium-lift helicopter utilized for personnel and cargo transport. Also known as an H-46.

Sea Sprite a single-rotor light lift helicopter utilized for air/sea rescue, personnel and cargo transport, and antisubmarine operations from naval vessels. Also known as an H-2.

Sea Stallion a single-rotor heavy-lift helicopter utilized for personnel and cargo transport. Also known as a CH-53A.

sick a code meaning "equipment indicated is operating at reduced efficiency."

side-looking airborne radar an airborne radar, viewing at right angles to the axis of the vehicle, which produces a presentation of terrain or moving targets.

skip bombing a method of aerial bombing in which a bomb is released from such a low altitude that it slides or glances along the surface of the water or ground and strikes the target at or above water level or ground level.

skip it a code meaning "cease attack"; "do not attack."

Skyhawk a single-engine, turbojet attack aircraft designed to operate from aircraft carriers, and capable of delivering nuclear or nonnuclear weapons, providing troop support, or conducting reconnaissance missions. It can act as a tanker and can itself be air refueled. Also known as an A-4.

Skytote a small unmanned airplane that takes off like a helicopter and can deliver supplies to troops in otherwise inaccessible locations, such as cliffs or rough terrain. It may also be used for surveillance.

snake mode a control made in which the pursuing aircraft flies a programmed weaving flight path to allow time to accomplish identification functions.

snow a narrow band of jamming signals swept back and forth over a wide band of frequencies; sweep jamming.

sortie an operational flight by one aircraft.

spitting in air antisubmarine operations, a code meaning "I am about to lay, or am laying, sonobuoys. I may be out of radio contact for a few minutes."

splashed in air intercept, a code meaning "enemy aircraft shot down."

spoofer a code meaning "a contact employing electronic or tactical deception measures."

Starfighter a supersonic, single-engine, turbojet fighter capable of employing nuclear or nonnuclear weapons. Also known as an F-104.

Starlifter a large cargo transport powered by four turbofan engines, capable of intercontinental range with heavy payloads and airdrops. Also known as a C-141.

state chicken a code meaning "I am at a fuel state requiring recovery, tanker service, or diversion to an airfield."

state lamb a code meaning "I do not have enough fuel for an intercept plus reserve required for carrier recovery."

state tiger a code meaning "I have enough fuel to complete my mission as assigned."

static line a line attached to a parachute pack and to a strop in an aircraft so that when the load is dropped the parachute is automatically deployed.

Stealth Bomber a bomber, otherwise known as the B-2, specially designed in the shape of a flat, flying wing in order to render it invisible to enemy radar.

Stealth Fighter a combat fighter/bomber with stealth (radar-eluding) design. Also known as F-117A.

stern attack an attack by an interceptor that terminates with a heading crossing angle of 45° or less.

stick a number of paratroopers who jump from a door of an aircraft during one run over a drop zone.

stick commander jumpmaster.

strafing the delivery of automatic weapons fire by aircraft on ground targets.

strangle a code meaning "switch off equipment indicated."

strangle parrot a code meaning "switch off Identification Friend or Foe equipment."

Stratofortress an all-weather, intercontinental, strategic heavy bomber powered by eight turbojet engines; capable of delivering nuclear and nonnuclear bombs, air-to-surface missiles, and decoys. Also known as a B-52.

Stratofreighter a strategic aerial tanker/freighter powered by four reciprocating engines; it is equipped to refuel bombers and fighters in flight. Also known as a KC-97L.

Stratotanker a multipurpose aerial tanker/transport powered by four turbojet engines; it is equipped for high-speed, high-altitude refueling of bombers and fighters. Also known as a KC-135.

stream take off aircraft taking off in a column formation.

subsonic less than the speed of sound.

Super Sabre a supersonic, single-engine, turbojet, tactical fighter/bomber. Also known as an F-100.

supersonic greater than the speed of sound.

tally ho a code meaning "target visually sighted."

Thunderbolt II a twin-engine, subsonic, turbofan, tactical fighter/bomber capable of taking off or landing on short fields and of delivering an assortment of weapons; has an internally mounted 30mm cannon and can be refueled in flight. Also known as an A-10.

Thunderchief a supersonic, single-engine, turbojet-powered tactical fighter capable of delivering nuclear weapons as well as nonnuclear bombs and rockets; equipped with a sidewinder weapons and can be refueled in flight. Also known as an F-105.

tied on a code meaning "the aircraft indicated is in formation with me."

Tomcat a twin turbofan, dual crew, supersonic, all-weather, long-range interceptor designed to operate from aircraft carriers. Also known as an F-14.

toss bombing similar to loft bombing but performed at any altitude.

Tracer a twin-reciprocating engine, airborne radar platform designed to operate from aircraft carriers. Its mission is the detection and interception control of airborne targets. Also known as an E-1B.

Tracker a twin-reciprocating engine, antisubmarine aircraft capable of operating from carriers, and designed primarily for the detection, location, and destruction of submarines. Also known as an S-2.

tracking a code meaning "by my evaluation, target is steering true course indicated."

train bombs dropped in short intervals or sequence.

turbojet a jet engine whose air is supplied by a turbine-driven compressor, the turbine activated by exhaust gases.

vector a code meaning "alter heading to magnetic heading indicated."

Vigilante a twin turbojet engine, dualcrew, supersonic all-weather reconnaissance aircraft designed to operate from aircraft carriers. It carries a wide assortment of photographic and electronic surveillance systems. Also known as an RA-5.

Viking a twin turbofan engine, multicrew antisubmarine aircraft capable of operating off aircraft carriers. Also known as an S-3.

Voodoo a supersonic, twin-engine turbojet air interceptor with twin cockpits. Also known as an F-101.

Walleye a guided air-to-surface glide bomb; it incorporates a contrast-tracking television system for guidance.

Wild Weasel an aircraft specially modified to identify, locate, and destroy ground-based enemy air defense systems.

wingman an aviator subordinate to, and in support of, the designated section leader; also, the aircraft flown in this role.

zippers target dawn and dusk combat air patrol.

ARMY, GROUND FORCES, AND GENERAL MILITARY TERMS

(*Also see* ROBOTICS *in* ELECTRONICS)

Abrams the U.S. forces premier battle tank, having either a 105mm or 120mm gun and a top speed of 40 miles per hour with a four man crew. Also known as the M-1.

all available a request or command for all available fire to be aimed at the same target.

anticrop operation the employment of anticrop agents to destroy an enemy's source of food.

antimateriel agent a chemical or natural substance used to deteriorate or damage enemy equipment.

antipersonnel mine a mine designed to cause casualties to personnel.

antitank mine a mine designed to immobilize or destroy a tank.

armored earthmover a heavy, full-tracked bulldozer used to clear obstructions and fill antitank ditches, used by the engineering unit. Also known as the M-9.

armored personnel carrier a lightly armored, highly mobile, full-tracked vehicle, amphibious and air-droppable, used for transporting personnel.

armored-vehicle-launched bridge a 60-foot folding bridge mounted in place of a turret on an M-60 or M-1 tank; used to span antitank ditches.

army corps a tactical unit larger than a division and smaller than a field army; usually two or more divisions together with auxiliary arms and services.

army group the largest formation of land forces, normally consisting of two or more armies or army corps.

assault echelon a unit scheduled for an initial assault on an area.

back tell the transfer of information from a higher to a lower echelon of command.

ballistics the science of missiles or other vehicles acted upon by propellants, wind, gravity, temperature, or other forces.

banana clip a curved or crescent-shaped ammunition clip holding 30 rounds.

barrage a prearranged barrier of fire designed to protect friendly troops and installations by impeding enemy movements across defensive lines. Also, a protective screen of balloons that are moored to the ground and kept at given heights to hinder operations by enemy aircraft.

basic encyclopedia a compilation of identified installations and physical areas of potential significance as objectives for attack.

basilage the marking of a route by a system of dim beacon lights enabling vehicles to be driven at normal speeds under blackout conditions.

battery left a method of fire in which weapons are discharged from the left one after the other, usually at five-second intervals.

battery right same as battery left, but starting from the right.

billet shelter for troops. Also, to quarter troops.

biological agent a microorganism that causes disease in humans, plants, or animals or causes the deterioration of materiel.

blister agent a chemical agent that injures the eyes and lungs, and burns or blisters the skin. Also called vesicant agent.

blood agent a chemical compound, including the cyanide group, that affects bodily functions by preventing the normal transfer of oxygen from the blood to body tissues. Also called cyanogen agent.

blood chit a small cloth chart depicting an American flag and a statement in several languages to the effect that anyone assisting the bearer to safety will be rewarded.

blue forces forces used in a friendly role during NATO exercises.

booby trap an explosive or other injuring device deliberately placed to cause casualties when an apparently harmless object is disturbed or a normally safe act is performed.

boot slang for a soldier fresh out of boot camp.

bound a single movement, usually from cover to cover, made by troops under enemy fire.

Bradley infantry fighting vehicle having twin missile launchers to use against enemy tanks and one 22mm cannon firing armor-piercing slugs. Also known as the M-2 and M-3.

breaching securing passage through a minefield.

bridgehead an area of ground held or to be gained on the enemy's side of an obstacle.

briefing the giving of instructions or information.

brigade a unit smaller than a division to which are attached groups and/or battalions and smaller units.

cache a hidden supply of food, medicine, water, and communication equipment, for use in evasion tactics.

call for fire a request for fire on a specific target.

camouflage any material used to hide equipment and installations within an environment.

camouflage detection photography infrared photography designed to detect camouflage and what is hidden beneath it.

camouflet the resulting cavity in a deep underground burst when there is no rupture of the surface.

canalize to restrict operations to a narrow zone by use of obstacles or by fire or bombing.

cargo carrier highly mobile, unarmored, full-tracked cargo and logistic carrier capable of traversing inland waterways.

catalytic attack an attack designed to bring about war between two powers through the disguised machinations of a third power.

Chaparral a short-range, low-altitude, surface-to-air, army air defense artillery system.

chemical mine a mine containing a chemical agent designed to kill, injure, or incapacitate personnel.

cinderella liberty liberty that ends at midnight.

civilian internee a civilian who is interned during armed conflict for security reasons.

civilian internee camp an installation established for the internment of civilians.

click slang for kilometer.

cluster bomb a large bomb that releases mini bombs or mines that spread over a large area.

combat engineer see SAPPER.

combat engineer vehicle, full-tracked 165mm gun an armored, tracked vehicle that provides engineer support to other combat elements; equipped with a heavy-duty boom and winch, dozer blade, 165mm demolition gun, and a machine gun.

contact mine a mine detonated by physical contact.

continuous illumination fire a type of fire in which illuminating projectiles are fired at specified time intervals to provide lighting over a specified area or target.

counterguerrilla warfare operations conducted against guerrillas.

countermining tactics and techniques used to detect, avoid, and/or neutralize enemy mines.

culture any feature of terrain that has been constructed by humans, including roads, buildings, canals, and all names and legends on a map.

danger close in artillery support, information in a call for fire to indicate that friendly forces are within 600 meters of the target.

D-day the unnamed day on which a particular operation is to commence.

debriefing instructions not to give away or discuss classified information. Also the interviewing of one returning from a mission in order to gather intelligence data on other vital information.

decontamination station a facility equipped to clean personnel of chemical, biological, or radioactive contaminants.

decoy any phony object, installation, or person intended to deceive the enemy.

DEFCON defense readiness conditions; a system of progressive alert postures for use between the joint chiefs of staff and the commanders of the armed services.

defilade to shield from enemy fire or observation by using natural or artificial obstacles.

defoliant operation the use of defoliating agents on trees, shrubs, and any foliage to make a clearing for military operations.

demilitarized zone a defined area where military installations or military forces are prohibited.

demolition belt an area sown with explosive charges, mines, and other obstacles to deny use of the land to enemy operations and as a protection to friendly troops.

demolition tool kit the tools, materials, and accessories of a nonexplosive nature necessary for preparing demolition charges.

deployment the extension or widening of the front of a military unit to battle formation. Also, the relocation of forces to desired areas of operations.

detachment a part of a unit separated from its main organization for duty elsewhere.

division a tactical unit larger than a regiment or brigade but smaller than a corps.

Dragon a portable antitank weapon consisting of a small missile and launcher.

dump a temporary storage area, usually out in the open, for bombs, ammunition, equipment, and suchlike.

Duster a self-propelled, twin 40mm antiaircraft weapon for use against low-flying aircraft. Also known as M-42.

echelon any subdivision of a tactical unit.

enfilade sweeping gunfire across the length of a line of troops.

envelopment surrounding the enemy.

Excalibur a 155mm artillery shell with its own guidance system to increase accuracy.

FCS Future Combat Systems. A developing system of weapons, including robots and combat vehicles, that can communicate with each other over a wireless network.

flamethrower a weapon that shoots incendiary gas. Nicknamed zippo.

flash blindness temporary or permanent loss of vision caused by intense flash from an explosion.

flash suppressor a device attached to the muzzle of a weapon to diminish its flash upon firing.

Fritz nickname for the Kevlar helmet worn by the army and marines. The helmets resemble those worn by the Germans in World War II.

glad bag derogatory slang for a body bag.

grunt slang for an infantryman.

guerrilla a member of an independent raiding band.

gun carriage a mobile or fixed support for a gun.

howitzer a high-trajectory cannon with a barrel longer than a mortar.

hum-vee modern equivalent of the jeep.

IED improvised explosive devices; homemade, remote-control bombs built by enemy guerrilla fighters, commonly employed by Iraqi resistance.

igloo space in an earth-sheltered structure, an area designed for the storage of ammunition and explosives.

klick kilometer.

KP kitchen police; mess hall duty.

laser rangefinder a device that uses a laser to determine the distance to an object.

litter a basket or frame utilized for the transport of the injured.

logistics the science of carrying out the movement and maintenance of troops.

mark a call for fire on a specific location to indicate targets.

materiel all items, including ships, tanks, aircraft, weapons, repair parts, and equipment, but excluding real property (installations, utilities, etc.) necessary to equip, maintain, and support military activities.

mess dining facility.

military currency currency prepared by a power and declared by its military commander to be legal tender for use by civilian and military personnel in the areas occupied by its forces.

mopping up finishing off the last remnants of enemy resistance in an area.

mortar a muzzle-loading, high-trajectory cannon with a shorter range than a howitzer.

muzzle brake a device attached to the muzzle of a weapon that utilizes escaping gas to reduce recoil.

napalm powdered aluminum soap or similar compound used to gelatinize oil or gasoline for use in napalm bombs or flame throwers. Also, the gelatin substance itself.

NATO North Atlantic Treaty Organization, an international military and peacekeeping alliance composed of 19 Western nations, including the United States and Canada, originally formed in 1949 for mutual protection against Soviet aggression.

nerve agent a potentially lethal chemical agent that interferes with the transmission of nerve impulses.

orange forces those forces used in an enemy role during NATO exercises.

ordnance explosives, chemicals, pyrotechnics, guns, ammunition, flares, napalm.

parlimentaire an agent or person sent behind enemy lines to communicate or negotiate openly with the enemy commander.

phonetic alphabet a list of standard words used to identify letters in a message transmitted by radio. The authorized words, in order: Alpha, Bravo, Charlie, Delta, Echo, Foxtrot, Golf, Hotel, India, Juliet, Kilo, Lima, Mike, November, Oscar, Papa, Quebec, Romeo, Sierra, Tango, Uniform, Victor, Whiskey, X-ray, Yankee, and Zulu.

pillbox a small, low fortification that houses machine guns, antitank weapons, and other weapons. It is usually constructed of sandbags or concrete.

pressure mine a mine that responds to pressure.

pull rank to use one's rank to force someone to do something.

purple forces those forces used to oppose both blue and orange forces in NATO exercises.

PX post exchange; a military store.

radar fire gunfire aimed at a target that is tracked by radar.

ratline an organized effort for moving personnel and/or materiel by clandestine means across a denied area or border.

recoilless rifle a weapon capable of being fired from either a ground mount or from a vehicle and capable of destroying tanks.

reconnaissance patrol a patrol used to gain tactical information concerning the enemy.

retrograde movement military doublespeak term for retreat.

rules of engagement directives issued by military authority, that specify the circumstances and limitations under which forces shall engage in combat with the enemy.

sabotage deliberately damaging or destroying an object or facility to interfere with or obstruct the national defense of a country.

safing applying mechanisms, catches, and so on, and similar means to make weapons and ammunition safe to handle.

salvo the simultaneous firing of several weapons aimed at the same target.

sapper an engineer who is responsible for clearing minefields and roadside bombs and who also lays mines and repairs or builds bridges, roads, and airfields. Also known as a combat engineer.

scopehead slang for radarman.

sheaf planned lines of fire that produce a desired pattern of bursts with rounds fired by two or more weapons.

sheet explosive plastic explosive in sheet form.

shelling report any report of enemy shelling containing information on caliber, direction, time, density, and area shelled.

sortie a sudden attack made from a defensive position. Also known as a sally.

sos chipped beef on toast; favored military meal.

splash in artillery support, the word transmitted to an observer or spotter five seconds before the estimated time of the impact of a salvo or round.

spoiling attack a tactical maneuvere employed to seriously impair a hostile attack while the enemy is in the process of forming or assembling for an attack.

spotting observing and reporting deviations of artillery fire to aid in homing in on a target.

strafing the firing of aircraft weapons upon ground units.

submunition any munition that is designed to separate from its parent munition to explode independently.

surprise dosage attack a chemical attack carried out too quickly for defending troops to mask or protect themselves.

thermal imagery infrared imagery useful in revealing camouflage and all object and personnel hidden behind camouflage.

tone down a form of camouflage in which surfaces of objects are made to blend in with their surroundings.

tracer bullets treated to create a glowing trajectory.

trench burial a quick burial method employed when casualties are heavy.

triage the evaluation and classification of casualties to determine the order and type of medical attention needed.

vesicant agent see BLISTER AGENT.

Vulcan an army air defense artillery gun that provides low-altitude air defenses; it is a six-barreled, 20mm rotary-fired weapon.

zulu time Greenwich Mean Time.

ELECTRONIC WARFARE

(radar, electronic deception, etc.)

balloon reflector a balloon-supported confusion reflector producing false echoes.

barrage simultaneous electronic jamming over a wide area of frequency spectrum.

burn-through range the distance at which a specific radar can discern targets through the external interference being received.

chaff radar confusion reflectors, which consist of thin, narrow metallic strips of various lengths and frequency responses, used to reflect echoes for confusion purposes.

clutter permanent echoes, clouds, or other atmospheric echo on radar scope.

crystal ball radar scope.

doppler radar a radar system that differentiates between fixed and moving targets by detecting the apparent change in frequency.

electromagnetic intrusion the intentional insertion of electromagnetic energy into transmission paths in any manner, with the objective of deceiving operators.

electronic imitative deception the introduction into the enemy electronic systems of radiations imitating the enemy's own emissions.

electronic jamming the deliberate radiation, reradiation, or reflection of electromagnetic energy for the purpose of disrupting enemy use of electronic devices and systems.

electronic manipulative deception the alteration of friendly electromagnetic emission characteristics, patterns, or procedures to eliminate revealing, or convey misleading, indicators that may be used by hostile forces.

gadget radar equipment. May be followed by a color to indicate state of jamming. The color code used is green—clear of jamming; amber—sector partially jammed; red—sector completely jammed.

gull a floating radar reflector used to simulate a surface target at sea for deceptive purposes.

masking the use of additional transmitters to hide a particular electromagnetic radiation as to location of source and/or purpose of the radiation.

meaconing a system of receiving radio beacon signals and rebroadcasting them on the same frequency to confuse navigation.

music in air intercept, electronic jamming.

radar beacon a receiver-transmitter that sends out a code signal when triggered by the proper type of pulse, enabling determination of range and bearing information by the interrogating station or aircraft.

radar camouflage the use of radar absorbent or reflecting materials to change the radar echoing properties of a surface of an object.

radar fire gunfire aimed at a target that is tracked by radar.

radar netting the linking of several radars to a single center to provide integrated target information.

radar picket any ship, aircraft, or vehicle stationed at a distance from the force protected for the purpose of increasing the radar detection range.

radar tracking station a radar facility that tracks moving targets.

radiation intelligence intelligence derived from the electromagnetic emissions of enemy equipment.

radio deception sending false dispatches, using deceptive headings, employing enemy call signs, and so on, over the radio to deceive the enemy.

radio silence a condition in which all or certain radio equipment capable of radiation is kept inoperative.

SIGINT signals intelligence. Personnel and equipment employed in gathering and processing signals intelligence.

INTELLIGENCE, ESPIONAGE, DECEPTION, AND PSYCHOLOGICAL WARFARE

accommodation address a secure address from which an agent may communicate with his superiors. The accommodation may be perfectly innocent but may also only appear that way to the public.

acoustical surveillance employment of electronic devices, including sound-recording, receiving, or transmitting equipment, for the collection of information.

acoustic intelligence intelligence derived from the collection and processing of sound.

agent one who is employed by an intelligence agency to gather intelligence. In the CIA, an agent is directed by a case officer.

agent authentication providing an agent with personal documents, accoutrements, and equipment that have the appearance of authenticity.

agent-in-play an agent who is actively gathering intelligence while under the direction of enemy intelligence services.

agent net an organization for secret purposes that operates under the direction of a principal agent.

ambush the surprise capture of an agent by enemy intelligence.

base a small CIA post.

biographical intelligence intelligence collection concerning foreign personalities.

black referring to illegal concealment.

black, living living under illegal concealment.

black border crossing getting across a border by the use of illegal concealment.

black list a counterintelligence list of enemy collaborators, sympathizers, intelligence suspects, and others.

black ops top-secret operations.

black propaganda propaganda that purports to emanate from a source other than the true one.

blow to expose, usually unintentionally, the secret cover of a person, installation, or operation.

bridge agent in the CIA, a messenger who takes a message from a case officer to an agent in the field.

brush pass a surreptitious handoff of a note, message, photograph, computer disk or other sensitive material between a case officer and an agent.

bug a concealed microphone or listening device.

bugged of a room or object, secretly equipped with a microphone or a listening device.

burn to deliberately expose the secret cover of a person, installation, or operation.

burn notice an official statement of one intelligence agency to other agencies that an individual or group is unreliable.

case officer in the CIA, one who recruits and supervises agents.

cell a small group of individuals who work together for secret or subversive purposes.

Central Intelligence Agency (CIA) agency of the United States, established in 1947, that gathers international intelligence and conducts counterintelligence programs.

chokepoint any narrow passage, such as a bridge, where agents can easily monitor the comings and goings of a subject.

CIA see CENTRAL INTELLIGENCE AGENCY.

CID the Clandestine Imaging Division; a branch of the CIA in charge of photographic and video surveillance, and other intelligence gathering.

cipher a secret code or code system. Also, a message written in code or the key to its deciphering.

Citadel, the a secret U.S. government department that gathers and processes signal intelligence from foreign nations.

civil censorship censorship of civilian communications, such as messages, printed matter, and films in territories occupied or controlled by armed forces.

clandestine in secret.

Clandestine Service the CIA branch that carries out secret operations.

classified information information kept secret to protect national interests or national security.

cold war a state of international tension in which political, economic, technological, sociological, psychological, and paramilitary measures short of overt armed conflict are employed to achieve national objectives.

collection the gathering of intelligence.

communication deception use of devices, operations, and techniques to confuse the communications link or navigational system of the enemy.

compartmenting the sharing of sensitive information only among others who absolutely must know, a security method used by various intelligence groups. Vertical compartmenting is the strict limiting of information up or down a chain of command. Lateral compartmenting is the strict limiting of information among peers.

compromised referring to a breach of security or secrecy.

concealment device any device such as a miniature recorder or camera inside a pen, used to gather and transport information.

confusion agent an agent dispatched to confound the intelligence or counterintelligence of another nation rather than to collect information.

counterdeception efforts to negate, neutralize, or diminish the effects of a foreign deception operation.

counterespionage the detecting, neutralizing, exploitation, and prevention of espionage activities by another country.

counterintelligence any misinformation used to deceive the enemy.

countersabotage action designed to detect and counteract sabotage.

countersubversion action designed to detect and counteract subversion.

courier a messenger or espionage agent carrying secret documents.

cover any type of facade employed to protect one's identity or purpose; a disguise, a phoney job or name, or a made-up excuse for being at a particular sensitive location.

cover stop a stop made by an agent, such as into a store, to give the impression to anyone following, that his trip is innocent.

covert operation any secret or undercover operation.

critical intelligence any information of extreme importance, such as indications of the imminent outbreak of hostilities.

cryptanalysis the converting of encrypted messages into plain text without having knowledge of the encryption key.

cryptology the science of hidden, disguised, or encrypted communications.

cryptonym a code name.

cultivation a deliberate and calculated association with a person for the purpose of recruitment, obtaining information, and so forth.

dangle operation a ruse in which one who appears to be a rich resource of intelligence, but who is in reality a double agent, is made obviously available for plunder by enemy intelligence.

dead drop any secret location used as a place to drop off information or packages for someone else to pick up at a later time.

dead telephone a technique of communicating a message by means of a telephone signal without the need of speech. It may be as simple as letting the phone ring 13 times and then hanging up.

declassify to cancel the security classification of an item of classified matter.

decrypt to convert encrypted text into plain text by deciphering and decoding.

diplomatic cover the guise of a diplomatic official who is actually a case officer for the CIA and may use diplomatic immunity to avoid prosecution by a foreign nation.

disinformation inaccurate information broadcast about troop strength, secret maneuvers, or other military plans to deceive the enemy.

double agent an agent who has infiltrated enemy intelligence and works for them as a "quasi" spy while gathering information for the other side.

dual agent an agent who works for two or more agencies, collecting information for both.

elicitation acquisition of information from a person or group in manner that does not disclose the intent of the interview or conversation.

ELINT CIA abbreviation for electronic intelligence.

encipher to convert plain text into unintelligible form by means of a cipher system.

encrypt to convert plain text into unintelligible form by means of cryptosystem.

escape line a planned route to allow personnel engaged in clandestine activity to depart from a site when the possibility of apprehension exists.

espionage actions directed toward the gathering of information through clandestine operations.

evasion and escape intelligence processed information prepared to assist personnel to escape if captured by the enemy or to evade capture if lost in enemy territory.

evasion and escape net the organization within enemy-held areas that operates to receive and move military personnel to friendly control.

exfiltration operation an operation designed to rescue or help a defector or CIA operative get safely away from a critical situation, or out of a hostile country entirely.

eye, the among a group of agents, one who maintains visual surveillance on a subject.

Federal Bureau of Investigation (FBI) the United States agency that investigates and protects against terrorist attacks, foreign intelligence, organized crime, white-collar crimes, and other crimes, and often assists local police forces.

foreign instrumentation signals intelligence (FISINT) intelligence information derived from electromagnetic emissions from enemy hardware, machinery, weapons, and other sources.

FSB the Federal Security Service for the Russian Federation, a successor of the KGB.

gray propaganda propaganda from an unidentified source.

GRU the military intelligence agency for Russia.

handler in the CIA, a case officer in charge of a particular active agent.

hard target country any nation which the CIA perceives to be difficult to infiltrate and gather intelligence from.

HUMINT CIA abbreviation for any form of human intelligence.

imagery intelligence intelligence gathered from the use of photography, infrared sensors, lasers, electro-optics, and radar sensors.

IMINT CIA abbreviation for imagery intelligence, particularly satellite photos.

infiltration the placing of an agent within enemy territory.

infiltration, black crossing a border through illegal concealment.

infiltration, gray crossing a border with the use of false documentation.

infiltration, white legal crossing of a border.

intelligence any form of information, whether in the form of text, photos, videos, intercepted electronics communications or other media concerning another nation's political or military operations.

KGB the intelligence-gathering agency of the Soviet Union, formed in 1954.

legend the false identity used by a CIA case officer. The identity is frequently that of an actual, but deceased person.

microdot a photo reduced to the size of a pinhead.

mole a spy; a double agent who has worked undetected among the enemy for a significant length of time.

overt operation the collection of intelligence openly, without concealment.

padding extraneous text added to a message for the purpose of concealing its beginning, ending, or length.

penetration the recruitment of agents within, or the infiltration of agents or monitoring devices into, an enemy organization.

perception management see PSYCHOLOGICAL OPERATIONS.

political intelligence intelligence concerning foreign and domestic policies of governments.

psychological consolidation activities planned psychological activities in peace and war directed at a civilian population in order to achieve desired behavior that supports military objectives.

psychological media all forms of communication media.

psychological operations (PSYOP) planned operations designed to influence the emotions and reasoning of a foreign audience. Also known as perception management.

psychological warfare the planned use of propaganda and other psychological tools to influence the opinions, emotions, attitudes, and behavior of hostile foreign groups.

PSYOP see PSYCHOLOGICAL OPERATIONS.

quisling a traitor.

radar intelligence intelligence derived from data collected by radar.

radiation intelligence intelligence derived from the emissions of electromagnetic energy from foreign devices, equipments, and systems but excluding those generated from nuclear weapons.

radio deception deceiving the enemy through the sending of false dispatches, deceptive headings, and enemy call signals over the radio.

receptivity the vulnerability of a target audience to psychological operations.

safe house a secret and secure house or apartment where spies may meet.

SIGINT signals intelligence; intelligence gathered by intercepting telephone, radio, or other communications.

signal site any location used to signal information to another, through the use of a chalk mark, strip of tape, etc.

station any major CIA base of operations.

subversion action designed to undermine the military, economic, psychological, or political strength of a regime or its morale.

surveillance the secret watching or monitoring of a person or location to gather intelligence.

takedown the dismantling of a network of foreign agents.

target intelligence intelligence gathered concerning a potential target for destruction.

tradecraft all the techniques used by the CIA to gather information, avoid detection, etc.

white propaganda propaganda disseminated and acknowledged by the sponsor.

MILITARY INSIGNIA AND RANKS

(commissioned officers)

ARMY, AIR FORCE, AND MARINES

general of the army, air force five silver stars, one 2-inch stripe, four ½-inch stripes.

general four silver stars, one 2-inch stripe, three ½-inch stripes.

lieutenant general three silver stars, one 2-inch stripe, two ½-inch stripes.

major general two silver stars, one 2-inch stripe, one ½-inch strip.

brigadier general one silver star, one 2-inch stripe.

colonel silver eagle, four ½-inch stripes.

lieutenant colonel silver oak leaf, three ½-inch stripes.

major gold oak leaf, two ½-inch stripes.

captain two silver bars, two ½-inch stripes.

first lieutenant one silver bar, one ½-inch stripe, one ¼-inch stripe.

second lieutenant one gold bar, one ½-inch stripe.

chief warrant officer (W-4) silver bar with four enamel bands, one ½-inch stripe.

chief warrant officer (W-3) silver bar with three enamel bands, one ½-inch stripe.

chief warrant officer (W-2) silver bar with two enamel bands, one ½-inch stripe.

chief warrant officer (W-1) silver bar with one enamel band.

NAVY AND COAST GUARD

fleet admiral five silver stars, one 2-inch stripe, four ½-inch stripes.

admiral four silver stars, one 2-inch stripe, three ½-inch stripes.

vice admiral three silver stars, one 2-inch stripe, two ½-inch stripes.

rear admiral (upper half) two silver stars, one 2-inch stripe, one ½-inch stripe.

rear admiral (lower half) one silver star, one 2-inch stripe.

captain silver eagle, four ½-inch stripes.

commander silver oak leaf, three ½-inch stripes.

lieutenant commander gold oak leaf, two ½-inch stripes, one ¼-inch stripe.

lieutenant two silver bars, two ½-inch stripes.

lieutenant (jg) one silver bar, one ½-inch stripe, one ¼-inch stripe.

ensign one gold bar, one ½-inch stripe.

chief warrant officer (W-4) silver bar with three enamel bands, one ½-inch stripe.

chief warrant officer (W-3) silver bar with two enamel bands, one ½-inch stripe.

chief warrant officer (W-2) gold bar with three enamel bands, one ½-inch stripe.

MISSILES, NUCLEAR WEAPONS, AND ROCKETS

absolute dud a nuclear weapon that fails to explode.

active material material, such as plutonium and certain isotopes of uranium, that is capable of supporting a fission chain reaction.

acute radiation dose total ionizing radiation dose received at one time and over a period so short that it is fatal.

afterwinds wind currents set up in the vicinity of a nuclear explosion directed toward the burst center, resulting from the updraft accompanying the rise of the fireball.

air-breathing missile a missile with an engine requiring the intake of air for combustion of its fuel, as in a ramjet or turbojet.

airburst an explosion in the air, above ground.

air-to-air guided missile an air-launched guided missile for use against air targets.

ballistic missile any missile that does not rely on aerodynamic surfaces to provide lift and consequently follows a ballistic trajectory when thrust is terminated.

ballistic missile early warning system an electronic system for providing detection and early warning of attack by enemy intercontinental ballistic missiles.

base surge a cloud that rolls out from the bottom of the column produced by a subsurface burst of a nuclear weapon.

beam rider a missile guided by an electronic beam.

blast wave diffraction the passage around and envelopment of a structure by a nuclear blast wave.

booster an auxiliary or initial propulsion system that travels with a missile and that may or may not separate from the parent craft when its impulse has been delivered.

camouflet the underground cavity created by a subterranean nuclear detonation.

captive firing a firing test of short duration, conducted with the missile propulsion system operating while secured to a test stand.

chronic radiation dose a dose of ionizing radiation received either continuously or intermittently over a prolonged period of time, that may or may not cause radiation sickness and death, depending on the dose rate.

cloud top height the maximum altitude to which a nuclear mushroom cloud rises.

command destruct signal a signal used to operate intentionally the destruction signal in a missile.

condensation cloud a mist or fog of water droplets that temporarily surrounds the fireball following a nuclear detonation in a relatively humid atmosphere.

contamination the deposit and/or absorption of radioactive material on and by structures, areas, personnel, or objects.

controlled effects nuclear weapons nuclear weapons designed to achieve variation of the intensity of specific effects other than normal blast effect.

critical altitude the altitude beyond which an air-breathing guided missile ceases to perform adequately.

critical mass the minimum amount of fissionable material capable of supporting a chain reaction.

cruise missile guided missile, the major portion of whose flight path to its target is conducted at approximately constant velocity.

decay, radioactive the decrease in the radiation intensity of any radioactive material over time.

destruct system a system that, when operated by external command, destroys the missile.

dirty bomb an early or less-advanced form of the atom bomb, which has an inefficient blast effect but produces large amounts of radiation or nuclear fallout.

Doomsday Clock introduced in 1947, a symbolic clock—showing the world on its face—maintained by the Bulletin of the Atomic Scientists and regularly reset to show how close the earth is to nuclear apocalypse, or "midnight."

dosimetry the measurement of radiation doses by dosimeters.

dwarf dud a nuclear weapon that, when launched at a target, fails to provide the expected blast yield or destruction.

electromagnetic pulse the electromagnetic radiation from a nuclear explosion caused by Compton-recoil electrons and photoelectrons from photons scattered in the materials of the nuclear device. The resulting electric and magnetic fields may couple with electrical systems to produce damaging current and voltage surges.

fallout the precipitation to Earth of radioactive particles from a nuclear cloud; also applied to the particles themselves.

fallout safe height of burst the height of burst at or above which no military significant fallout will be produced as a result of a nuclear weapon detonation.

fireball the luminous sphere of hot gases that forms a few millionths of a second after detonation of a nuclear weapon and immediately starts expanding and cooling.

fire storm stationary mass fire within a city that generates strong, inrushing wind from all sides; the winds keep the fires from spreading while adding fresh oxygen to increase their intensity; a side effect of a nuclear blast.

fission the splitting of the nucleus of a heavy element into two nuclei of lighter elements, with the release of substantial amounts of energy.

fission products a general term for the complex mixture of substances produced as a result of nuclear fission.

flare dud a nuclear weapon that detonates with expected yield but at an altitude much higher than intended so that its effects on a target are lessened.

free rocket a rocket not subject to guidance or control in flight.

ground zero the point on the surface of the Earth at, or vertically below or above, the center of a planned or actual nuclear detonation.

guided missile a missile whose flight path is controlled by external or internal mechanisms.

hard missile base a launching base that is protected against a nuclear explosion.

initial radiation the radiation, essentially neutrons and gamma rays, resulting from a nuclear burst and emitted from the fireball within one minute after burst.

intercontinental ballistic missile a ballistic missile with a range from 3,000 to 8,000 miles.

kiloton weapon a nuclear weapon, the yield of which is measured in terms of thousands of tons of trinitrotoluene (TNT) explosive equivalents, producing yields from 1 to 999 kilotons.

launcher a structural device designed to support and hold a missile in position for firing.

megaton weapon a nuclear weapon, the yield of which is measured in terms of millions of tons of trinitrotoluene (TNT) explosive equivalents.

NORAD North American Air Defense; the protective radar system network monitoring the airspace over the United States and Canada.

nuclear column a hollow cylinder of water and spray thrown up from an underwater burst of a nuclear weapon, through which the hot, high-pressure gases formed in the explosion are vented to the atmosphere.

nuclear exoatmospheric burst the explosion of a nuclear weapon above the atmosphere, from above 120 kilometers.

operation exposure guide the maximum amount of nuclear radiation a commander of a unit considers safe to be absorbed during an operation.

radiation sickness an illness, resulting from excess exposure to ionizing radiation. The earliest symptoms include nausea, vomiting, and diarrhea, followed by loss of hair, hemorrhage, inflammation of the mouth and throat, and general fatigue.

rainfall, nuclear the water that falls from base surge clouds after an underwater burst of a nuclear weapon. This rain is radioactive.

rainout radioactive material brought down from the atmosphere by precipitation.

rem roentgen equivalent mammal; 1 rem is the quantity of ionizing radiation of any type that, when absorbed by humans or other mammals, produces a physiologic effect equivalent to that produced by the absorption of 1 roentgen of X-ray or gamma radiation.

roentgen a unit of exposure dose of gamma or X-ray radiation. In field dosimetry, one roentgen is equal to 1 rad.

Safeguard a ballistic missile defense system.

salted weapon a nuclear weapon that has, in addition to its normal components, certain elements that capture neutrons at the time of the explosion and produce radioactive products over and above the usual radioactive weapons debris.

sea skimmer a missile designed to fly at less than 50 feet above the surface of the sea.

short-range ballistic missile a ballistic missile with a range of 600 nautical miles.

soft missile base a launching base not protected against a nuclear explosion.

spray dome the mound of water spray thrown up into the air from the shock wave of an underwater detonation of a nuclear weapon.

stellar guidance a system that refers to certain preselected celestial bodies to guide a missile.

tolerance dose the amount of radiation that may be absorbed by a person over a period of time with negligible health effects.

TOW missile a wire-guided missile.

two-man rule a system designed to prohibit access by an individual to nuclear weapons and related components by requiring the presence at all times of at least two authorized persons, each capable of detecting incorrect or unauthorized procedures with respect to the task to be performed.

warhead that part of a missile or rocket that contains the nuclear or thermonuclear system, high-explosive system, or chemical or biological agents intended to inflict damage.

zero point the center of a burst of a nuclear weapon at the instant of detonation.

TYPES OF MISSILES AND ROCKETS

ADM-20 see QUAIL.

AGM-28A see HOUND DOG.

AGM-45 see SHRIKE.

AGM-53 see CONDOR.

AGM-65 see MAVERICK.

AGM-69 see SHORT-RANGE ATTACK MISSILE.

AGM-78 see STANDARD ARM.

AGM-84A see HARPOON.

AGM-142 see HAVE NAP.

AIM-4 see FALCON.

AIM-7 see SPARROW.

AIM-9 see SIDEWINDER.

AIM-54A see PHOENIX.

AIR-2 see GENIE.

Condor an air-to-surface guided missile that provides standoff launch capability for attack aircraft. Also known as AGM-53.

cruise missile highly accurate, computer-guided missile having a land range of up to 1,552 miles. See TOMAHAWK.

Falcon an air-to-air guided missile; optional nuclear warhead. Also known as AIM-4.

Genie an air-to-air, unguided rocket equipped with a nuclear warhead. Also known as an AIR-2.

HARM high-speed antiradiation missile; it homes in on radar signals from surface-to-air missile sites and destroys them.

Harpoon an all-weather, antiship cruise missile capable of being employed from ships, submarines, and aircraft. It is turbojet-powered and employs a low-level cruise trajectory. Also known as AGM-84A.

Have Nap a camera-guided missile. Also known as the AGM-142.

Hawk a mobile, surface-to-air missile system that provides nonnuclear, low-to-medium altitude air defense coverage for ground forces. Also known as MIM-23.

Hellfire an air-to-surface antitank missile.

Hound Dog a turbojet-propelled, air-to-surface missile designed to be carried externally on the B-52; it is equipped with a nuclear warhead. Also known as AGM-28A.

Lance a mobile, storable, liquid propellant, surface-to-surface guided missile, with nuclear and nonnuclear capability. Also known as XMGM-52.

LGM-25C see TITAN II.

LGM-30 see MINUTEMAN.

LGM-118A see MX.

Mace a missile guided by a self-contained radar guidance system or by an inertial guidance system and characterized by its long-range, low-level attack capability. Also known as MGM-13.

Maverick an air-to-surface missile with launch and leave capability. It is designed for use against stationary or moving small, hard targets such as tanks, armored vehicles, and field fortications. Also known as AGM-65.

MGM-13 see MACE.

MGM-29A see SERGEANT.

MGM-31A see PERSHING.

MGM-51 see SHILLELAGH.

MIM-23 see HAWK.

Minuteman a three-stage, solid-propellant, ballistic missile guided to its target by an all-inertial guidance and control system. It is equipped with a nuclear warhead and is designed for deployment in underground silos. Also known as LGM-30.

MIRV multiple independently targetable reentry; a missile having two or more warheads aimed at different targets.

MX an intercontinental ballistic missile (ICBM) with multiple warheads. Also known as LGM-118A.

Patriot a land-mobile surface-to-air antimissile used to protect small areas, such as an airfield.

Pershing a mobile surface-to-surface inertially guided missile of a solid-propellant type; it has a nuclear warhead capability. Also known as MGM-31A.

Phoenix a long-range air-to-air missile with electronic guidance and homing. Also known as AIM-54A.

Polaris an underwater, or surface-launched, surface-to-surface, solid-propellant ballistic missile with inertial guidance and nuclear warhead. Also known as UGM-27.

Poseidon a two-stage, solid-propellant ballistic missile capable of being launched from a specially configured submarine operating in either its surface or submerged mode. The missile is equipped with nuclear warheads and a maneuverable bus that has the capability to carry up to 14 weapons that can be directed at 14 separate targets. Also known as UGM-73A.

Quail an air-launched decoy missile carried internally in the B-52 and used to deceive enemy radar, interceptor aircraft, and air defense missiles. Also known as ADM-20.

RGM-66D see STANDARD SSM.

RIM-2 see TERRIER.

RIM-8 see TALOS.

RIM-24 see TARTAR.

RIM-66 see STANDARD MISSILE.

Sam-D an army air defense artillery, surface-to-air missile system.

Sergeant a mobile, inertially guided, solid-propellant, surface-to-surface missile with nuclear warhead capability, designed for short-range targets up to 75 miles. Also known as MGM-29A.

Shillelagh a missile system mounted on the main battle tank and attack reconnaissance vehicle for employment against enemy armor, troops, and field fortications. Also known as MGM-51.

short-range attack missile an air-to-surface missile, armed with a nuclear warhead, launched from the B-52 and the FB-111 aircraft. Also known as AGM-69.

Shrike an air-launched antiradiation missile designed to home on and destroy radar emitters. Also known as AGM-45.

Sidewinders a solid-propellant, air-to-air missile with nonnuclear warhead and infrared, heat-seeking homer. Also known as AIM-9.

Sparrow an air-to-air solid-propellant missile with nonnuclear warhead and electronic-controlled homing. Also known as AIM-7.

Spartan a nuclear surface-to-air guided missile formerly deployed as part of the Safeguard ballistic missile defense weapon system. It is designed to intercept strategic ballistic reentry vehicle above Earth's atmosphere.

Sprint a high-acceleration, nuclear surface-to-air guided missile designed to intercept strategic ballistic reentry vehicles above Earth's atmosphere.

Standard Arm an air-launched antiradiation missile designed to home on and destroy radar emitters. Also known as AGM-78.

Standard Missile A shipboard, surface-to-surface and surface-to-air missile with solid-propellant rocket engine. Also known as RIM-66.

Standard SSM a surface-to-surface antiradiation missile equipped with a conventional warhead. Also known as RGM-66D.

Stinger a lightweight, portable, shoulder-fired, air defense artillery missile weapon.

Subroc submarine rocket; submerged, submarine-launched, surface-to-surface rocket with nuclear depth charge or homing torpedo payload, primarily antisubmarine. Also known as UUM-44A.

Talos a shipborne, surface-to-air missile with solid-propellant rocket and ramjet engine. It is equipped with nuclear or nonnuclear warhead, and command, beam-rider homing guidance. Also known as RIM-8.

Tartar a shipborne, surface-to-air missile with solid-propellant rocket engine and nonnuclear warhead. Also known as RIM-24.

Terrier a surface-to-air missile with solid-fuel rocket motor. It is equipped with radar beam rider or homing guidance and nuclear or nonnuclear warhead. Also known as RIM-2.

Titan II a liquid-propellant, two-stage, rocket-powered intercontinental ballistic missile guided to its target by an all-inertial guidance and control system. The missile is equipped with a nuclear warhead and designed for deployment in underground silos. Also known as LGM-25C.

Tomahawk an air-, land-, ship-, or submarine-launched cruise missile with conventional or nuclear capability.

Trident II a three-stage, solid-propellant ballistic missile capable of being launched from a Trident submarine. It is equipped with advanced guidance, nuclear warheads, and a maneuverable bus that can deploy warheads to multiple targets; its range is over 4,000 miles. Also known as UGM-96A.

UGM-27 see POLARIS.

UGM-73A see POSEIDON.

UGM-96A see TRIDENT.

US Roland a short-range, low altitude, all-weather, army air defense artillery surface-to-air missile system.

UUM-44A see SUBROC.

XMGM-52 see LANCE.

NAVY AND MARINES

(*Also see* SHIPS AND BOATS *in* TRANSPORTATION)

acoustic mine a mine that responds to the sound of a passing ship.

acoustic minehunting the use of sonar to detect mines.

Aegis an integrated shipboard weapon system combining computers, radars, and missiles to provide a defense umbrella for surface shipping.

afloat support logistic support providing fuel, ammunition, and supplies outside the confines of a harbor.

air boss on a carrier, one who supervises the flight deck.

airdale slang for a naval aviator.

air wing aboard an aircraft carrier, the officers and crew members assigned to aircraft.

amphibious assault ship a naval ship designed to embark, deploy, and land elements of a landing force in an assault by helicopters, landing craft, and amphibious vehicles.

amphibious reconnaissance a reconnaissance mission to survey a shore area, usually in secret.

angled deck on an aircraft carrier, a landing deck that is slightly offset by 10 degrees to port to make it easier for a bolter to take off again after an aborted landing.

antenna mine a mine fitted with an antenna that, when touched by a ship, explodes the mine.

antirecovery device any device in a mine designed to prevent an enemy from discovering how its exploding mechanism works.

antisubmarine barrier any line of devices or mobile units arranged to detect or deny passage to or destroy hostile submarines.

antisubmarine carrier group a group of ships consisting of one or more antisubmarine carriers and a number of escort vessels whose primary mission is to detect and destroy submarines.

antisubmarine minefield a minefield laid specifically against submarines.

antisubmarine rocket a surface ship-launched, rocket-propelled, nuclear depth charge or homing torpedo.

antisubmarine screen an arrangement of ships that protects or screens another ship or group of ships against submarine attack.

antisubmarine torpedo a submarine-launched, long-range, high-speed, wakeless torpedo capable of carrying a nuclear warhead for use in antisubmarine and antisurface ship operations.

antisweep device any device in the mooring of a mine or in the circuits of a mine to make sweeping of the mine more difficult.

antisweeper mine a mine with a mechanism designed specifically to damage mine countermeasure vehicles.

antiwatching device a device fitted in a moored mine that causes it to sink should it show on the surface, so as to prevent the position of the mine from being disclosed.

armed sweep a sweep fitted with cutters or other devices to increase its ability to cut mine moorings.

arresting gear any device, such as a chain, used to catch a landing aircraft and help bring it to a stop. Also, overrun gear.

attack aircraft carrier a large ship designed to operate aircraft, engage in attacks on targets afloat or on shore, and engage in sustained operations in support of other forces.

attack cargo ship a transport ship carrying combat cargo.

balls to the wall slang term for full speed.

bandit a hostile aircraft.

battery all guns, torpedo, tubes, searchlights, or missile launchers of the same size or caliber or used for the same purpose on one ship.

battery left a method of fire in which weapons are discharged from the left, one after the other, at five-second intervals.

battery right a method of fire in which weapons are discharged from the right, one after the other, at five-second intervals.

beachhead hostile shore position captured by amphibious units.

beachmaster unit a naval unit supporting the amphibious landing of one division.

beach minefield a shallow-water minefield blocking the way to a shoreline or beach.

bingo code word for running out of fuel.

blue shirt on an aircraft carrier, an aviation boatswain's mate, who wears a blue shirt and who is responsible for positioning and securing aircraft to the deck.

blue water any deep water.

boatswain a warrant officer or petty officer in charge of the deck crew and riggings.

bogey an unidentified aircraft.

bolter on an aircraft carrier, an aircraft that misses a landing by failing to hook the arresting wire and must go around for another try.

boot slang for a rookie, fresh out of boot camp.

bosun's whistle a metal whistle blown to call attention to a special announcement.

bottom a mine that remains on the seabed.

bottom sweep a wire or chain sweep close to the bottom.

bounce to practice landing on an aircraft carrier.

bouquet mine a mine in which a number of buoyant mine cases are attached to the same sinker so that when the mooring of one mine case is cut, another mine rises from the sinker to its set depth.

brass slang for officers.

bravo zulu code term for well done.

bulldog code word for a cruise missile.

call for fire a call for gunfire support.

cat short for catapult.

catapult on the deck of an aircraft carrier, the device that helps launch aircraft into the air.

cinderella liberty liberty in which one must return to ship by midnight.

clearance diving the use of divers to locate, identify, and dispose of mines.

clock code position the position of a target in relation to a ship with dead-ahead position being 12 o'clock.

Close-In Weapon System an onboard, short range missile defense system consisting of a radar tracker and a Gatling gun, two versions of which are the Vulcan Phalanx and the Goalkeeper.

CO commanding officer.

coffeepot slang for a nuclear reactor.

cold shot on an aircraft carrier, an inadequate catapult shot, due to compromised power, often resulting in a crash of an aircraft.

concentrated fire the fire of the batteries of two or more ships directed against a single target.

conn control of the ship's course. Also, in a submarine, the conning tower or control room.

convoy a number of ships escorted by other ships or aircraft in passage together.

cooky slang for a ship's cook.

creeping mine a buoyant mine held below the surface by a chain, which is free to creep along the seabed under the influence of current.

crossdeck pendant across the deck of an aircraft carrier, the cable that catches the hook of an aircraft to arrest landing.

customer ship the ship that receives replenishment supplies from another ship.

cutter a device fitted to a sweep wire to cut or part the moorings of mines.

dan to mark a position or a sea area with dan buoys.

dan buoy a temporary marker buoy used during minesweeping operations to indicate boundaries of swept paths.

dan runner a ship running a line of dan buoys.

datum the last known position of a submarine after contact has been lost.

debarkation the unloading of troops and cargo from a ship.

deck ape slang for a deck crew member who does manual labor. Also known as a knuckledragger.

decoy ship a ship camouflaged with its armament and fighting equipment hidden.

deep minefield an antisubmarine minefield set deep enough so that surface ships can cross it safely.

destroyer a high-speed warship armed with 3-inch and 5-inch dual-purpose guns and various antisubmarine weapons.

ditty bag a drawstring bag used to hold toiletries and other small items.

dock landing ship a naval ship designed to transport and launch amphibious craft.

drifting mine a mine free to move under the influence of waves, wind, or current.

dummy minefield a minefield containing no live mines.

endurance the amount of time a ship can continue to operate without refueling.

ensign the lowest-ranking naval officer.

flattop an aircraft carrier.

flemish to coil a rope neatly on deck.

flight deck the runway on an aircraft carrier.

floating mine a mine visible on the surface of the sea.

flooder a mine that floods after a preset time and sinks to the bottom.

flotilla an administrative or tactical organization consisting of two or more squadrons of destroyers or smaller types together with flagships and tenders.

foul deck on an aircraft carrier, a deck that is currently unsafe to land on.

fresnel lens on an aircraft carrier, a system of lights used to provide glide slope visuals for approaching aircraft. Also known as the lens. A glowing yellow image projected by the lens, known as the ball, moves up and down and aligns with a row of green lights to illustrate a perfect glide slope. The ball turns red when an aircraft is too low and in danger of crashing. Also found at naval air stations.

frigate a warship designed to operate independently or with strike, antisubmarine warfare, or amphibious forces against submarine, air, and surface threats; its armament includes 3-inch and 5-inch guns and advanced antisubmarine weapons.

fubar short for fucked up beyond all recognition.

general quarters a condition of readiness when naval action is imminent; all battle stations are fully manned and alert and ammunition is ready for instant loading.

guided missile cruiser a warship designed to operate with strike and amphibious forces and armed with 3-inch and 5-inch guns, advanced area-defense anti-air-warfare missile system, and antisubmarine weapons.

guided missile destroyer a destroyer equipped with Terrier/Tartar-guided missiles, naval gun battery, long-range sonar, and antisubmarine weapons.

guided missile frigate a frigate equipped with Tartar or SM-i missile launchers and 70mm gun battery.

guinea pig a ship used to determine if an area is free of influence mines.

gunny slang for a marine gunnery sergeant.

hashmarks stripes on the sleeve that mark years of service.

head on a ship or boat, a toilet.

heaving deck on an aircraft carrier, an unstable deck, caused by wind and waves.

heavy-lift ship a ship with a lift capacity of 100 tons.

homing mine a mine fitted with a propulsion system that homes on a target.

hot rack a bed that must be shared among crew members for lack of space.

hydrofoil patrol craft a fast surface patrol craft.

hydrographic chart a nautical chart showing depths of water, nature of bottom, contours of bottom, and related information.

jarhead slang for a marine.

knuckledragger see DECK APE.

lap a section or strip of area assigned to a single minesweeper.

LCS littoral combat ship. A small warship that is designed to operate near shorelines.

leatherneck a marine.

lens, the see FRESNEL LENS.

lifer one who makes the navy or marines a lifelong career.

Mayday a distress call.

minesweeping the technique of searching for and clearing mines from an area.

net sweep a two-ship sweep using a netlike device designed to collect or scoop up seabed or drifting mines.

obstructor a device laid with the goal of obstructing mechanical minesweeping equipment.

ocean station ship a ship providing a number of services, including search and rescue, meteorological information, navigational aid, and communications facilities.

offshore patrol a patrol operating in coastal waters.

oiler a tanker equipped to replenish other ships at sea.

ordnance collective term for bombs, guns, ammunition, and other pyrotechnic devices.

otter in naval mine warfare, a device that, when towed, displaces itself sideways to a predetermined distance.

Phalanx a close-in weapons system providing automatic, autonomous terminal defense against antiship cruise missiles. The system includes self-contained search and track radars, weapons control, and 20mm M-61 guns.

ping jockey slang for a sonar operator, after the sound signal made by sonar.

polliwog slang for a sailor who has yet to cross the equator.

q-message a classified message relating to navigational dangers, navigational aids, mined areas, and searched or swept channels.

Q-ship a decoy ship.

rack a bed.

rack time sleep time.

redshirt on an aircraft carrier, an aviation crew member who loads bombs and ammunition and who wears a red shirt. Also, a member of a carrier crash team.

rising mine a mine having positive buoyancy that is released from a sinker by a ship influence or by a timing device.

romper a ship that has moved more than 10 miles ahead of its convoy and is unable to rejoin it.

rotorhead slang for a helicopter pilot or crew member.

salvo in naval gunfire support, a method of fire in which a number of weapons are fired simultaneously upon the same target.

shadower a maritime unit observing and maintaining contact with an object overtly or covertly.

sheaf in naval gunfire, planned lines of fire that produce a desired pattern of bursts with rounds fired by two or more weapons.

shellback slang for a sailor who has crossed the equator.

ship influence in naval mine warfare, the magnetic, acoustic, and pressure effects of a ship, or a minesweep simulating a ship, that is detectable by a mine.

ship's company the crew members and officers dedicated to the running of a ship, as opposed to those in the air wing, assigned to aircraft.

snipes slang for onboard engineers, machinists, boiler technicians, and mechanics, who work primarily below decks.

sonar a sonic device used primarily for the detection and location of underwater objects.

sonobuoy a sonar device used to detect submerged submarines and to relay its information by radio.

Spec Ops special operations.

spotter an observer who reports the results of naval gunfire and who may also direct fire on designated targets.

spotting observing and communicating the accuracy or inaccuracy of naval gunfire in order to make necessary adjustments.

squadron an organization of two or more divisions of ships.

squid slang for any sailor.

stateroom an officer's living quarters.

sterilizer a built-in device that renders a mine inoperative after a certain amount of time.

TACAN Tactical Air Navigation, a radio navigation aid.

tin can slang for a destroyer.

Top Gun the Navy Fighter Weapons School at Fallon Naval Air Station in Nevada, where pilots learn fighter tactics.

torpedo defense net a net employed to close an inner harbor to torpedoes fired from seaward or to protect an individual ship at anchor or under way.

tractor group a group of landing ships in an amphibious operation that carries the amphibious vehicles of the landing force.

twidget slang for an electronics or computer technician.

vampire code for an antiship cruise missile.

very deep draught ship a ship with a laden draught of 45 feet or more.

weather deck any deck exposed to the elements.

SUBMARINES

anechoic covering any covering material used to absorb sonar pulses to help prevent detection by an enemy vessel.

awash a partially submerged state in which only the conning tower can be seen above the surface.

ballast seawater flooded into wraparound or other tanks to allow a submarine to submerge or descend.

ballast tanks wraparound tanks or other tanks used to hold water or compressed air.

bathyscaphe a free-floating bathysphere with ballast and depth controls.

bathysphere a spherical diving bell having windows for observation.

blow the tanks to empty the ballast tanks by filling them with compressed air.

boomer a ballistic missile submarine.

bridge the conning tower, specifically where the periscope is located.

cavitation the noise produced by bubbles formed by propellor action, a crucial factor in detecting submerged submarines.

chicken of the sea slang for a ballistic missile submarine whose main objective is to stay hidden from the enemy.

clear datum to leave an area where a submarine has been detected or has given its position away.

conning tower the tower or superstructure, now called the sail, that contains the bridge and the periscope.

control room the room containing the control panels for diving, planning, steering, and other movements.

crush depth the deepest depth a submarine can go before being crushed by pressure.

datum the point where a submarine has been detected or has given its location away.

depth charge a bomb dropped from a ship to explode at a certain depth or on contact with the submarine.

draft the depth of water required for a submarine to float.

fairwater more common term for the conning tower.

fish slang for a torpedo.

fleet ballistic missile submarine a nuclear-powered submarine designed to deliver ballistic missile attacks from submerged or surface positions.

hangar a missile tube.

helm the control area where the submarine is steered.

helmsman one who steers the vessel.

hydrophone a submersible microphone used to detect sounds from ships or submarines.

hydroplanes horizontal rudders or fins located fore and aft that swivel to deflect water flow around the hull to lift or drop the nose, used to ascend or descend. Also known as planes.

lifeguard submarine a submarine used in rescue operations in enemy territory.

mess the crew meal room.

periscope the viewing apparatus that is raised surreptitiously above the surface of the ocean to observe enemy craft or terrain.

ping the sound made by an active sonar system.

ping jockey slang for a sonar operator, after the sound a sonar system makes.

planesman crew member who operates the hydroplanes.

powerplant a diesel-electric or nuclear-drive motor.

reactor a nuclear reactor in nuclear submarines.

rudder the adjustable plane used to steer the submarine.

sail a conning tower. Also known as a fin.

sail plane a fin located on either side of the conning tower.

screws the propellors.

scrubber a system that clears carbon dioxide out of the air.

snorkel air-intake and exhaust pipes in diesel-electric submarines. Also known as a snort.

snorkeling moving just below the surface with the snorkel raised above the surface for taking in and expelling air.

sonar acronym for sound navigation ranging, a system that transmits and receives reflected sound waves to detect submarines and submerged objects.

sonobuoy a sonar device used to detect submerged submarines, which, when activated, relays information by radio.

SOSUS sound surveillance system; a system of listening hydrophones on the seabed linked to stations on shore.

submarine havens specified sea areas for submarines in noncombat operations. Also known as submarine sanctuaries.

Subroc a submerged, submarine-launched, surface-to-surface rocket with nuclear depth charge or homing torpedo, primarily intended for use against other submarines.

torpedo an underwater missile ejected from a tube in the submarine by compressed air; it is propelled to its target by two propellers powered by an electric motor.

torpedo defense net a net employed to close an inner harbor to torpedoes fired from seaward or to protect a ship at anchor or underway.

Trident a nuclear-powered submarine armed with long-range Trident ballistic missiles.

U-boat submarine, especially a German one.

wolfpack a group of submarines working together in a line to destroy enemy vessels.

WORLD WAR II SLANG

NOTE: Some terms in this section are pejorative

Army

ack-ack machine gun or antiaircraft gun.

archies antiaircraft guns.

armored cow canned milk.

army banjo shovel.

Aussies soldiers from Australia.

AWOL absent without leave. Also, a wolf on the loose, or after women or liquor.

baby food cereal.

barker a large artillery gun.

battery acid coffee.

beans nickname for a commissary officer.

bear grease general-issue soap.

big boot general.

blackout coffee.

blackstrap coffee.

blanket drill sleep.

blitz a bombing.

blow it out of your bag shut up.

B-19 a fat woman.

bobtail a dishonorable discharge.

bog pocket a cheapskate.

brass hat a staff officer.

brig jail Also known as the clink, stockade, hoosegow.

brown bombers army laxatives.

bucking trying to get a promotion.

bucking for a section 8 trying to get discharged through any means possible.

bulldog military police.

bunky a buddy, friend, or pal.

Butch nickname for a commanding officer.

cackle jelly eggs.

camel corps infantry.

camp happy a little touched in the head.

canteen an army retail store.

cat beer milk.

cat stabber a bayonet.

CB confined to barracks.

cheese toaster bayonet.

chest hardware medals.

chicken a very young recruit.

chili bowl a military haircut.

civvies civilian clothes.

Clara all-clear air raid signal.

corn Willie tinned corn beef.

corpuscle corporal.

cowboy a tank driver.

cream on a shingle creamed beef on toast.

croot recruit, rookie, bozo, bucko.

crow chicken.

crowbar hotel any jail.

crumb hunt kitchen inspection.

daisy may a denim fatigue hat.

devil's piano a machine gun.

ditty bag bag for keeping valuables in.

dog fat butter.

dog house the guardhouse.

dog tag the metal identification tag worn around the neck.

drive it in the hangar shut up.

duds shells that fail to explode.

elephant trap a large hole dug for refuse.

faint wagon ambulance.

fisheyes tapioca with raisins.

fly one wing low to be drunk.

foxhole a pit dug to protect oneself against enemy fire.

frogskin a dollar bill.

fuzzie-wuzzies winter trousers.

garrison shoes any dress shoes.

general's car a wheelbarrow.

Gertrude a soldier working in an office.

GI general issue.

GI Jesus the chaplain.

goldfish canned salmon.

goof burner one who smokes marijuana.

goofy discharge a discharge given for mental illness.

grandma low gear in a jeep or other vehicle.

grubber lowest ranking.

hay sauerkraut.

hi Jackson a friendly greeting.

hip flask a .45-caliber pistol.

hitch an enlistment.

housewife a sewing kit.

Irish grapes potatoes.

jack money.

Jerries Germans; German planes.

John L's long Johns.

jumping Jesus a chaplain in a paratrooper unit.

Kendall did it an oft-repeated buckpassing line.

kennel rations hash or meat loaf.

KP duty assisting the cook in food preparation, serving, and cleanup; kitchen police.

krauts Germans.

lacy of a soldier, effeminate.

laid out for inspection unconscious.

leatherneck a marine.

light chassis a woman with a great figure.

Li'l Abners army shoes. Also known as groundhogs.

low on amps and voltage out of ideas.

machine oil pancake syrup.

Mae West a life jacket worn like a vest.

maneuvers putting the make on a woman.

Matilda one's blanket roll.

meat wagon ambulance.

mess gear knives, forks, spoons.

nappy nickname for the barber.

noncom noncommissioned officer.

on the beam, are you are you OK?

padre chaplain.

paint remover coffee.

pantywaist a sissy.

pea shooter rifle.

pill rollers medical corps.

pineapple hand grenade.

pipped shot, as in "he got pipped."

pocket lettuce dollar bills. Also known as happy cabbage.

police up to pick up, clean up.

popeye spinach.

popsicle motorcycle.

post exchange merchandise store; the PX.

prang an avoidable airplane crash.

propeller wash B.S.

ptomaine domain the mess hall.

pull rank to remind another of one's higher rank, as a coercive tactic.

PX post exchange.

Q company a recruit receiving company.

quiff a girl.

rabbit food lettuce, celery, carrots.

Rachel high gear in a jeep or other vehicle.

red nose shrapnel.

rudily doo not worth a damn.

sand and specks salt and pepper.

sawbones an army doctor.

shimmy pudding Jell-O. Also known as shivering Liz.

skirt patrol looking for women.

slingshot pistol.

snafu situation normal all fouled up.

snap snap hurry up, on the double.

squirrel cage the psychoanalyst's office.

stocks and bonds toilet paper.

swampseed rice.

tarheel soldier from the U.S. South.

three seventy three square meals and 70¢, a day's wages.

tin titty canned milk.

tommy Thompson submachine gun.

Waldorf, the mess hall.

Australian Soldiers

billy a can for boiling tea in.

bloke a man.

bloody very "damned," for example, "bloody good," "bloody stupid."

bonzer excellent.

boshter great.

bosker fine.

bush the back country. American equivalent of the "boonies."

chivvy back talk.

cliner a woman.

cobber a buddy.

cow bad.

deener a shilling.

dingbats Italians.

dinkie cute.

dinkum the real thing; genuine; real.

Jerries Germans.

knocked up tuckered out; tired; bushed.

larrikin drunk.

Matilda a bundle of personal articles.

nips the Japanese.

Pommies Englishmen.

punting betting.

Sheila a nice-looking woman.

shikkered drunk.

shivoo a party.

squatter a farmer.

station a farm or ranch.

stone a measurement of weight.

stonkered shell-shocked.

tucker food.

zack sixpence.

Marines

belly robber the cook.

boogies Japanese airmen.

boondockers field shoes.

boot a new recruit.

boot camp recruit training camp.

brig rat prisoner.

butcher a medical officer.

canned Willie canned beef.

cattle boat a troop transport boat.

cub one who has not yet crossed the Arctic Circle.

deck ape one who swabs the deck.

ding how OK, derived from the Chinese.

ditty box a small box for personal articles.

dogface soldier.

dragon back one who has crossed the 180th meridian.

FiFi anyone's girlfriend.

flatfoot marine's nickname for a sailor.

48 a two-day leave.

frog sticker a bayonet.

gooks natives.

go to hell cap a garrison cap.

gunny a gunnery sergeant.

iron kelly steel helmet. Also known as a tin derby.

Jackson a marine's call to another soldier, "Hey, Jackson."

jamoke coffee.

joe coffee.

Maggie's drawers a red flag waved to indicate a complete miss of the target on a shooting range.

old issue an old marine.

padre chaplain. Also, Holy Joe.

pearl diver a marine assigned to kitchen duty, especially washing dishes.

pollywog a marine who has not yet crossed the equator.

punk bread.

ring tails gunner's nickname for the Japanese.

run aground to get into trouble.

scuttlebutt gossip.

shack mammy a native woman of the South Pacific.

sick bay a hospital dispensary.

sinkers doughnuts. Two for a nickel at the time.

slopchute a beer parlor.

swabby nickname for a sailor.

sweetheart one's rifle.

twist a dizzy to roll a cigarette.

Navy

admiral's watch a good night's sleep.

airedale a naval aviation recruit.

alligator an amphibious tank.

arctic boat refrigerator boat carrying meat. Also known as the beef boat.

armory the gun maintenance shop.

ashcan a submarine depth charge.

AWOL absent without leave.

baffle painting ship camouflage painting.

battlewagon a battleship.

belay stop that or shutup.

bells denotes the time of day. 1 A.M. = 2 bells, 2 A.M. = 4 bells, 3 A.M. = 6 bells, 4 A.M. = 8 bells, 5 A.M. = 2 bells, 6 A.M. = 4 bells, 7 A.M. = 6 bells, 8 A.M. = 8 bells, 9 A.M. = 2 bells, 10 A.M. = 4 bells, 11 A.M. = 6 bells, noon = 8 bells. Same cycle repeated for P.M. hours.

bilge water B.S.

bird boat an aircraft carrier.

blow a storm at sea.

boot a newly enlisted sailor.

boot camp a six-week naval training camp on shore.

brass the gold stripes on an officer's sleeve.

brig an onboard jail.

brightwork any metal finishings that need polishing.

brownnose one who kisses an officer's feet; an officer's favorite.

buzzard any eagle insignia.

calk off to sleep.

canary a beautiful woman.

canteen onboard retail store.

captain of the head one ordered to clean the toilets.

Chicago piano an antiaircraft gun.

cigar box fleet boats carrying landing craft, tanks, and infantry for a shore attack.

coiled up his ropes died.

collision mats waffles.

commissary bullets beans.

crow an ugly woman.

cut of his jib a sailor's appearance or behavior.

EPD extra police duty; cleaning and polishing.

fish a torpedo.

flashing his hash throwing up from seasickness.

flying coffin a PBY navy patrol bomber.

foo foo perfume.

forecastle lawyer one who claims to know all navy regulations.

four-oh 4-0; perfect; OK.

four-striper captain.

French leave to leave a ship without permission.

funnels smokestacks.

furlough any liberty lasting over 72 hours.

galley ship kitchen.

gangway to get out of the way.

gig captain's private boat.

gilligen hitch an imaginary knot in a rope.

give it the deep six to throw it overboard.

gob sailor.

gone native of a sailor, overly friendly with natives on shore.

gooks natives of the South Seas.

goos goos Filipinos.

hammock what a sailor sleeps in.

heave out and lash up morning greeting to get out of bed and roll up one's hammock.

honey barge the garbage barge.

houligan navy sailor's nickname for the Coast Guard.

katzenjammers the shakes after a night of heavy drinking ashore.

liberty shore leave of 48 hours or less.

limey a British sailor.

mail buoy an imaginary mail box on a buoy; new recruits were told in all seriousness to leave their mail on this buoy for the mailman to pick up.

mast, called to the called in for a reprimanding by the captain.

mess meals; the meal room.

mokers the blues.

mosquito boat a light, quick boat equipped with small guns.

muck up to clean up.

mud hook anchor.

old man the captain.

one striper an ensign.

ordinary seaman a seaman second class.

peacoat a waist-length, blue wool coat.

pigboats submarines.

pipe him aboard to welcome a high-ranking officer or dignitary aboard by blowing the boatswain's whistle.

plotting room a room where maneuvers were planned over maps and instruments.

pollywog a sailor yet to cross the equator.

scrambled eggs the gold insignia on an officer's cap.

seagull a loose woman who follows the fleet around from port to port.

sea legs accustomed physically and mentally to life at sea.

send a fish to fire a torpedo.

shellback an experienced sailor; one who has crossed the equator.

shivering Liz Jell-O.

sick bay onboard hospital.

skibbies the Japanese.

slop chute a garbage chute leading to the ocean.

slushy nickname for the cook.

smukes dollars.

sparks a wireless operator.

step off the plank to get married.

straight as a deck seam trustworthy.

submarine ears hard of hearing.

swab a large mop.

three sheets in the wind drunk.

three striper a commander.

two and a half striper a lieutenant commander.

two striper a lieutenant.

watch a four-hour watch duty.

watch cap a black, knitted stocking cap.

wicky wicky hurry up; chop chop; on the double.

NURSES

Annie nickname for a nurse anesthetist.

arthritis of the cerebellum, have to be stupid.

bedpan alley the hospital.

blues the two-tone blue uniforms worn during the war.

brown kitties bronchitis.

dock the hospital.

doctorine a woman doctor.

follow-up man mortician.

gubbins dirty dressings.

idiotorium hospital for the mentally ill.

inkie an incubator baby.

misery hall an emergency room.

scrub nurse a nurse who follows sterile procedures in order to handle operating room instruments.

sick bay ship hospital.

stiffy a paralyzed person.

stink kitchen a chemical laboratory.

temperature, don't run a don't get excited.

WACs

arsenal wear general issue lingerie.

barracks bags bags under the eyes from working a night shift.

blow boy bugler.

boll weevils heavy brown cotton stockings.

book rack bunk bed.

burp class a defense class on gas warfare.

canteen cowboy soldier who hangs out at the canteen to flirt with the women.

cool good.

cut off a scene to leave.

dry ammunition cosmetics.

gigs demerits.

GI Jane an OK person.

gravy good-looking, as in "he's gravy."

gruesome twosome regulation shoes.

hair warden the camp hair stylist.

jeep jockeys women auto mechanics in Motor Transport.

jubilee reveille.

monkey suits general issue coveralls.

night maneuvers fooling around with a man.

put a nickel in it hurry up.

scoff to eat.

screwy as a toad a nut case.

square from Delaware a hick girl from a small town.

WAC Women's Army Corps.

WAC shack the barracks. Also known as the Wackery.

wolfing looking for men.

MUSIC

KEYBOARD INSTRUMENTS

baby grand a small grand piano, usually no more than 5 feet in length.

bandoneon the Argentine equivalent of an accordion, characterized by notes that are produced by buttons instead of a keyboard.

calliope any organ played or activated by steam.

celesta a small, keyboardlike instrument in which keys depress hammers that strike tuned steel bars, creating a haunting bell-like sound; invented in 1886 and used in T chaikovsky's "Dance of the Sugar Plum Fairy."

clavichord a stringed keyboard set in a rectangular box and producing soft sounds, popular from the 16th to the 18th centuries.

concert grand the largest size of piano, usually about 9 feet in length.

concertina a simple accordion with buttons in place of a keyboard.

damper any device that mutes or stops the sound vibrations of an instrument, as in the small pieces of felt-covered wood used in a piano.

damper pedal on a piano, the right-hand pedal that raises all dampers, allowing all of the strings to vibrate freely.

harpsichord a pianolike instrument having strings that are plucked instead of being struck by hammers; popular from the 16th to the 18th centuries and still in use.

hydraulos a type of pipe organ invented by the Greeks, notable for its regulation of air pressure by the displacement of water in special chambers.

key any of the individual levers on a keyboard.

manual a keyboard played by the hands as opposed to one played by the feet, as an organ pedalboard.

pedal any one of the two or three foot pedals controlling volume and tone on a piano.

pedal organ the section of organ pipes, often of low pitch, operated by an organ's pedal board.

piano keyboard in which keys activate hammers that strike tuned strings.

player piano a mechanical piano that plays tunes automatically by means of air pressure and special perforated music roles.

soundboard the resonant board over which strings are strung in a piano or harpsichord.

spinet a small harpsichord, popular from the 16th to the 18th centuries.

stop in organs, a lever or knob that stops air to a particular set of pipes; the set of pipes so affected is also called a stop.

synthesizer a modern keyboard instrument capable of producing or reproducing hundreds of different sounds through electronic means.

virginal a small, rectangular harpsichord popular from the 15th to the 17th centuries.

wind chest the air chamber in some organs.

MUSIC DIRECTIVES
(tempos, volume, etc.)

accelerando accelerating gradually.

adagietto a slow tempo, slightly faster than adagio.

adagio a slow tempo, faster than largo, slower than andante, specifically from 98 to 125 quarter notes per minute.

adagissimo extremely slow tempo.

ad libitum ad-libbing tempo, rhythm, accents, notes, and so on.

affettuoso with tenderness.

affrettando in a rushed manner.

agilmente lightly and nimbly.

agitato in an agitated, restless manner.

allargando slowing down and increasing in volume.

allegramante brightly.

allegretto a fast tempo; faster than andante but slower than allegro.

allegro a fast and lively tempo.

allentando slowing down.

altra volta encore.

ancora repeat.

andante a moderate tempo between adagio and allegro.

ängstlich a German directive to perform in a fearful, tense manner.

animato spirited.

appassionato with passion.

attaca attack. A direction to begin the next movement quickly without a break.

Aufschwung German term for "soaring," "lofty."

ballo in dance tempo.

bocca chiusa to be hummed.

bouche fermée to be hummed.

bravura a directive to sing or play confidently a passage requiring a high degree of skill.

brusco in a brusque manner.

burlesco in a comical manner.

calando lowering, softening.

calcando gradually quickening.

calmando in a quiet and calm manner.

cedez French directive to slow down.

commodo a relaxed, leisurely manner.

crescendo with increasing volume.

da capo a directive to repeat from the beginning until you reach the word "fine" (end). Often written as D.C.

decrescendo decreasing in volume; growing softer.

delicato delicately.

delirio deliriously, in a frenzied manner.

diminuendo decrescendo.

dolce softly and sweetly.

dolente slowly and with sorrow.

doppio movimento double the previous speed.

dramatico dramatically.

eilend German directive to perform in a hurried manner.

élargissant French directive to slow down and broaden the music.

elegante with grace and refinement.

encore French directive to repeat.

facile fluently.

fastoso in a dignified manner.

festoso in a joyful, festive manner.

feurig German directive to perform in a fiery manner.

fiero boldly.

forte loudly.

fortissimo very loudly.

frettoloso in a rushed manner.

funerale mournfully.

furioso wildly and furiously.

geheimnisvoll German directive to play in a mysterious manner.

Generalpause German term for a "general rest," usually referring to a silence lasting one or more measures and involving all musicians.

grave slowly and solemnly.

heftig German directive to perform lightly and cheerfully.

indeciso tentatively or indecisively.

innig German directive to play with deep sincerity.

inquieto in an agitated manner.

lamentoso mournfully.

larghetto a slow tempo between largo and andante, specifically from 69 to 98 quarter notes per minute.

largo a very slow tempo, specifically from 42 to 69 quarter notes per minute.

legato smooth-flowing with no pauses, opposite of staccato.

lestissimo very quickly.

malinconico in a melancholy manner.

mancando progressively softer.

marcato with sharp accents.

mezza voce to sing at half the singer's normal volume.

mezzo forte with moderate loudness.

mezzo piano with moderate softness.

militare, alla with a military air.

ossia refers to an alternative and often easier way of performing a particular passage.

parlato "spoken."

pathétique with deep feeling.

pianissimo very softly.

prestissimo the fastest tempo possible.

presto a very fast tempo, from 182 to 208 quarter notes per minute.

ravvivando continuously speeding up the music.

ritardando gradually slowing the tempo.

ritenuto slowing the tempo at once.

schleppend German directive to perform in a dragging manner.

sciolto nimbly and lightly.

seconda volta Italian term referring to a second ending or a second time played.

slancio, con with dash.

sospirando in a plaintive manner.

sotto voce softly.

spiritoso with high spirit.

staccato with quick, light, broken or detached notes.

strisciando a very smooth legato.

tacet Latin directive to remain silent throughout a passage.

teneramente with tenderness.

tonante very loudly.

tranquillo in a tranquil manner.

tre, a Italian directive for three instruments to play the same music at the same time.

vide directive alerting a musician that a particular passage may be omitted if desired.

vigoroso with vigor.

vivo lively.

volti subito turn the page quickly so the music will continue flowing without a break.

zoppa, alla in a syncopated rhythm.

Directives to Individual Instruments

bois a direction to play with the wood of a bow as opposed to the hair.

chiuso to "close" an instrument by inserting a hand into its bell to muffle or change its pitch.

coperto "covered," referring to a cloth to be placed over a drum to muffle or mute its sound.

deux, à French directive for two instruments to play the same music at the same time.

Frosch, am German directive to play with the part of the bow closest to the hand.

gauche French directive to play a note or passage with the left hand.

gedämpft German directive to mute or muffle a tone.

jeté French directive for a violinist to let the bow bounce several times on the strings. Also known as ricochet.

licenza, con alcuna Italian directive allowing a musician some creative license in performing a particular passage.

martelé French directive for a violinist to bow with brief, short strokes, producing a staccato effect.

martellato Italian directive for a piano player to strike the piano keys very hard, as a hammer.

m.d. mano destra or "right hand." A directive to play a piece or passage with the right hand.

m.s. mano sinistra or "left hand." A directive to play a piece or passage with the left hand.

muta Italian directive for wind instrument players to switch instruments or for timpanists to change the tuning of a drum.

ondeggiando Italian directive to a violinist to "rock" the bow back and forth over the strings to produce a tremolo or undulating effect.

pavillons en l'air French directive to a horn player to play with his horn or bell pointing up to project sound further and more powerfully.

piqué French directive to a violinist to bow in an intermittently detached or bouncing manner to produce a slurring, staccato effect.

pizzicato in music for violin or cello, a directive to pluck the strings with the fingers or thumb instead of or in addition to bowing.

punta play with the point of the bow.

sautillé French directive to a violinist to bounce the upper portion of the bow off the strings.

scordatura Italian directive to change the tuning of a stringed instrument in order to perform a particular composition.

sinistra play with the left hand.

sopra in keyboard music, a directive to cross one hand over the other to play a particular passage.

sordino, con Italian directive to a player of a stringed or wind instrument to use a mute.

sotto in keyboard music, a directive to cross one hand under the other to play a particular passage.

spiccato Italian directive to a violin or cello player to play in staccato style with the portion of the bow between the frog and the midpoint.

talon, au French directive to a violinist or cellist to play with the frog end of the bow.

MUSIC TERMS

accent emphasis on a particular note or chord.

accent, apogic a tone held for a longer time than others.

accent, dynamic a tone played louder than others.

accent, tonic a tone higher in pitch than others.

acciaccato playing the notes of a chord not quite simultaneously, but in quick succession from bottom to top.

accidentals collective term for the signs that raise or lower a pitch or that cancel these; includes sharp, double sharp, flat, double flat, and natural.

acoustics the science of sound properties.

air a simple melody.

aleatory music musical compositions with elements left to chance or the whims of the individual musician.

alto the second or third highest voice class of instruments—alto clarinet, alto sax, and so on.

answer repeating an original theme in a lower or higher register.

answer, call and the repeating or nearly repeating of a theme played by one instrument by another instrument, creating a kind of echo effect.

answer, real an answer played exactly the same as the original theme, with the exception of being in a higher or lower key.

answer, tonal an answer in which the distances between the notes are played differently than in the original theme.

anthem a hymn or composition set to words from the Bible.

anticipation the playing of a single note before a chord that harmonizes with that chord.

aquarelle a delicate composition.

arabesque the musical counterpart to arabesque architecture, an ornate or florid melody section.

arpeggio a chord in which the notes are played individually in quick succession instead of simultaneously.

arrangement the arrangement of a composition for another medium than that for which it was intended. Also known as a transcription.

ASCAP American Society of Composers, Authors and Publishers.

aubade French term for early morning music as opposed to a serenade or evening music.

augmentation the lengthening of the time values of notes in a composition, for example, from quarter notes to half notes or from half notes to whole notes. Opposite of diminution.

bagatelle French term for any short composition, usually for piano.

bar a measure; a bar line. Also, a guitar chord made by one finger laid straight across all six strings and pressed down.

bar line the vertical line in a musical staff that separates two measures.

baroque a term borrowed from baroque architecture to describe the musical developments between 1600 and 1750, characterized by growing complexity and the popular use of contrasts.

bass the lowest voice in a family of instruments.

baton the stick used by the conductor to direct a symphony orchestra's timing, phrasing, volume, and so forth.

battle music any musical composition in which battle sounds are re-created.

bebop jazz style, frequently with a fast tempo, originating in the 1940s and characterized by scat singing, complex rhythms, and off-time beats. Also known as bop.

berceuse French term for lullaby, usually involving an instrumental composition.

bitonality playing two keys simultaneously.

blues originally a form of jazz song, characterized by depressing themes, a slow tempo, and having flatted thirds and sevenths.

BMI Broadcast Music Inc., an American performing rights society.

boogie woogie jazz piano style popular in the 1930s and 1940s, characterized by the left hand playing a repeating bass pattern while the right plays a melody.

bowing the employment of a bow over the strings of a violin, cello, or other stringed instrument.

break in jazz, an improvised solo.

brevis a double whole note, the longest note in use.

bridge passage a short musical passage that helps one body of a composition flow smoothly into another body.

broken chord a chord in which notes are played not simultaneously but in quick succession; an arpeggio.

buffa comic, as in comic opera.

cadence rhythmic flow, beat. Also, a progression of chords or notes leading to the close of a composition.

cadence, deceptive a cadence that ends on a note or chord other than what the listener expects or anticipates. Also known as an interrupted cadence.

cadence, imperfect a cadence that gives the impression that more music is to follow and is therefore used in the middle of a composition.

cadence, masculine a cadence that ends on a strong beat as opposed to one that ends on a weak beat, as a feminine cadence.

cadenza a virtuoso solo performance near the end of a composition.

calypso music originating in the West Indies and especially in Trinidad, characterized by high syncopation and repetition, and improvised lyrics of a humorous or topical nature.

cantata a vocal or instrumental composition of several movements that include arias, duets, and choruses; a type of opera.

chamber music music in which each part is played by a single instrument as opposed to several instruments in an orchestra; music performed by a trio, quartet, quintet, or other group.

chamber orchestra a small orchestra of 40 players or less.

chord any simultaneous playing or sounding of three or more notes.

chord, chromatic a chord played along with one or more notes that are out of key.

clef the symbol at the beginning of a musical staff indicating the pitch of the notes.

coda the final or closing passage of a movement.

colpo the stroke of a bow.

composition a piece of music.

concertmaster the first violinist and assistant conductor.

concerto a composition for the orchestra and one or more soloists, usually performed in three movements.

concert pitch the pitch to which orchestral instruments are tuned, specifically the A above middle C to a frequency of 440 cycles per sound.

conservatory a school of music instruction.

consonance in-tune, harmony; pleasant-sounding. The opposite of dissonance.

consort a small instrumental ensemble.

counterpoint the combining of two or more different melodies to create a richer tapestry of sound. Similar to polyphony or the use of multiple voice parts.

cross rhythm the playing of two different rhythms at the same time.

decibel one unit in the measurement of sound volume.

demisemiquaver a thirty-second (1⁄32) note.

diminution shortening the time values of notes, such as whole notes to half notes, half notes to quarter notes. Opposite of augmentation.

discord a harsh or unpleasant-sounding chord, dissonance.

dissonance harsh; unpleasant-sounding; disharmony.

Dixieland New Orleans jazz combining elements of ragtime and blues, originating in the early 20th century.

dotted note a note with a dot over it is to be played lightly and quickly, or staccato. A dot after a note has half of its time value added to it. That is, a dotted quarter (¼) note equals ¼ note plus ⅛ note, and so on. A double dot after a note adds three-fourths the time value to that note, so a double-dotted ¼ note equals ¼ note plus ⅛ note, plus 1⁄16 note.

double-handed a musician who can play two different instruments well.

downbeat the first beat in a measure, named for the starting downswing of a conductor's baton.

duet a performance by two musicians.

duple meter two beats per measure.

dynamics the graduations of sound volume, from soft to loud.

ear, playing by playing music without notation, either by memory or by improvising.

ear training the teaching of pitch and rhythm recognition.

echo a softly repeated musical passage.

eighth note a note having a time value equal to ⅛ of a whole note.

eighth rest a rest or silence lasting as long as an eighth note.

elegy a sad song, vocal or instrumental, lamenting the death of someone or something.

embouchure the placement, shaping, and actions of the mouth, lips, and tongue in achieving proper pitch, tone, and effects in a wind instrument. Also, the mouthpiece of a wind instrument. See TONGUING.

enharmonics notes, intervals, or chords that sound the same but differ by name. For example, C sharp is the equivalent of D flat, D sharp the equivalent of E flat.

ensemble a small performing group of musicians.

étude French term for "study," referring to an instrumental composition designed to test and improve a player's skills, or any difficult piece containing arpeggios, trills, scales, and such like.

expression marks collective term for musical directives, including tempo, volume, technique, phrasing, and mood, often expressed in Italian.

fanfare a short piece for trumpets to announce the arrival of royalty or to begin some festivities.

fantasia any musical composition that relies more on the whims of the composer than on any standard form; music of an improvisational or fanciful quality. Also, a short mood piece.

finale the final movement in a composition.

fine Italian word for "end."

flamenco Spanish music with vocals, guitar, and percussive accompaniment by castanets and fingernail tapping on the belly of the guitar.

flat the pitch of a note subtracted by half a tone; an accidental that lowers the pitch by this amount. Also, of a note, played slightly below the correct pitch.

florid music that is highly ornamented.

frog the part of the violin bow that tightens the horsehair.

fughetta a short fugue.

fugue a polyphonic composition in which themes are sung sequentially by two or more performers and in imitation of the previous performer; a complex form of a round or canon.

fugue, double a fugue having two themes or subjects.

fugue, triple a fugue having three themes or subjects.

glissando sounding up or down the scale of an instrument very rapidly, as drawing one finger up or down the entire length of a piano keyboard or a fingerboard of a guitar, or moving the slide of a trombone to its full extension and back; the sound this produces.

gospel music with themes that center on Christ and salvation, often performed with a choir, originating in African-American churches.

grand opera any lavish or artistic opera production.

half note a note having a time value equal to ½ of a whole note.

half rest a rest or silence lasting the same length of time as a half note.

hemidemisemiquaver a sixty-fourth ($^1/_{64}$) note.

hootenanny a performance by folk singers, usually with sing-alongs from the audience.

hymn any religious song praising God.

imitation the echoing or repetition of one singer's part by another.

improvisation music that is spontaneously generated, made up, faked, and so on.

incidental music music providing background atmosphere in a play or movie. Also, any music played between the acts of a play.

interlude a short passage within a composition, usually an instrumental section between vocals. Also, any incidental music played between acts of a play.

intermezzo originally, a musical playlet, often comic, inserted between acts of a play from the 16th to the 18th centuries. Today, a short piece of music performed to illustrate the passing of time in a play or opera. Also, an interlude.

interval the distance between the pitches of two notes, measured in tones and half-tones. Also, two notes played in unison.

intonation the production of pitch by an instrument. Good intonation is the production of accurate pitch.

jam any informal or unprepared performance by a pop, rock, jazz, or folk group. A jam session.

key signature following the clef on a musical staff, the sharp or flat symbols that indicate which key the music is in.

lament a composition of mourning.

ledger short extension lines appearing above or below the five standard staff lines, used to underscore very high or very low notes.

libretto the text of an opera.

lullaby any gentle song intended to put a baby to sleep.

lyrics the words of a song.

maestoso any stately musical passage or movement.

maestro master, as in master musician.

mariachi a Mexican ensemble consisting of at least one of each of the following: guitar, violin, harp, and bass guitar.

measure the section of music contained between two bar lines; same as a bar.

medley a performance of portions of favorite tunes played one after the other.

melisma one syllable of a lyric carried or sung through several notes.

melismatic pertaining to melisma.

melody a group of notes, catchy or at least memorable in some way, making up part or all of a song. Most songs usually have more than one melody.

meter refers to how many beats per measure are in a particular composition.

minstrel a musician or entertainer of the Middle Ages.

minuet music in moderate triple meter, intended for the dance of the same name.

M.M. Maelzel's metronome, used to sound the precise tempo at which a passage or composition is to be played.

modulation the changing of keys within a single composition.

motif the briefest sequence of notes that can be defined as a melody, such as the opening four notes of Beethoven's Fifth Symphony.

movement a major section within a composition, often having its own key signature, and often set apart from following movements by a brief pause.

musicology the study of music.

mute any muffling device used on an instrument to lower its volume or alter its tone.

natural any note not raised or lowered by a sharp or a flat.

nocturne French term pertaining to the night, specifically music that conjures up images of the night and romance in the night. Also, a piano melody played with the right hand accompanied by soft broken chords played by the left.

noel a Christmas carol.

notation the writing down of music.

octave all eight notes of a minor or major scale. Also, the interval between the bottom and top notes of the scale.

octet eight; having eight voices or eight instruments; a composition for eight musicians, and similar groupings.

ode a lyrical poem sometimes set to music.

opera buffa comic opera.

operetta an opera of a lighter or more humorous nature.

opus work; the word is usually followed by a number to designate the order in which a particular work was produced by a composer; for example, opus 27 would designate a composer's 27th work, although not all compositions are so numbered.

oratorio religious text set to music and involving soloists, chorus, and orchestra, usually performed without scenery, costumes, or special effects.

orchestra, symphony an orchestra capable of playing symphonies, usually having at least 90 musicians.

orchestration the writing and dividing of parts of a composition to be played by the individual instruments of an orchestra.

ornaments any notes added to a composition to put extra pizzazz into a piece; embellishments; flourishes.

overblow to blow so hard into a woodwind that it raises its normal pitch one octave higher (slightly higher for clarinets), a technique used in playing many musical compositions.

overture a composition of instrumental music preceding or introducing an opera, oratorio, or play.

paraphrase a theme, melody, or passage in a composition that is repeated in a different way.

passion a musical composition set to the Passion, the gospel account of the week's events leading up to the crucifixion of Christ.

pasticcio any composition created by several composers, or a montage of the works of several composers as assembled by an arranger.

pastoral any music that conjures up images of life in the country.

pedal tone the lowest pitch attainable on a wind instrument.

philharmonic amalgamation of two Greek words, "love-harmony." Another name for an orchestra or musical society.

pitch any note in the range between the lowest and the highest notes.

pitch pipe a small wind instrument used to demonstrate proper pitch.

polyrhythmic having more than one rhythm played at the same time.

portamento similar to a glissando but with smaller note intervals, thus limiting its execution to the violin, trombone, and voice, in which no separation of notes of half notes (as by frets) exist.

program music music that tells a story or depicts a mood or emotion.

quarter note a note with a time value equal to ¼ of a whole note.

quarter rest a rest or silence equal to the time value of a quarter note.

quartet an ensemble of four musicians or a composition written for four musicians.

quintet an ensemble of five musicians or a composition written for five musicians.

ragtime a highly syncopated piano music performed with a quick tempo, popular in the United States early in the 20th century.

R&B abbreviation of rhythm and blues.

rap music originated by black performers in the United States in the 1980s, characterized by a strong beat and recitative singing style.

refrain a section or verse of a musical composition that is repeated at regular intervals and especially at the end of each stanza.

reggae black Jamaican music characterized by off-time beats and simple, repetitive lyrics.

reprise a repetition of or return to an original theme of a composition.

rest a pause or silence.

retrograde refers to a melody that is reversed so that the first note becomes the last, and vice versa.

rhapsody a free form or improvised composition depicting a mood or emotion.

rhythm and blues black American music originating after World War II, combining elements of jazz and blues and characterized by loud volume, a driving beat, and usually depressing lyrics; the forerunner of rock and roll.

riff any short melodic phrase played on an instrument, but particularly on jazz or rock guitar.

rock and roll term coined in 1951 by disc jockey Alan Freed to describe a new type of music evolving from rhythm and blues and characterized by heavy drum beats, loud, jangly guitars, and youthful lyrics.

score the music written for a movie or play; any musical composition for orchestra.

secondo in a piano duet, the lower of two parts.

semiquaver British equivalent of a sixteenth (1/16) note.

septet an ensemble of seven musicians or a composition written for seven musicians.

serenade an instrumental composition similar to a sonata. Also, a love song sung under the loved one's window.

sextet an ensemble of six musicians or a composition written for six musicians.

sharp an accidental that raises the pitch of a note by one-half. Also, of a note, played slightly above the correct pitch.

sight-reading performing music on sight without previous practice.

signature the key and meter signs at the beginning of a composition.

sixteenth note a note equal in time value to $\frac{1}{16}$ of a whole note.

sixteenth rest a rest or pause equal in time value to a sixteenth note.

sol-fa syllables the syllables do, re, mi, fa, sol, la, ti.

sonata an instrumental composition in three to four movements with each differing in key, mood, and tempo.

sonatina a sonata with shorter or fewer movements.

soul style of 1960s music derivative of blues and gospel and often characterized by lyrics with black themes.

spiritual a type of religious song with complex rhythms, developed by black Americans in the 1800s.

staff the set of horizontal lines upon which notes are written and designated a pitch.

stanza in sings with a poetic text, a verse or set of verses. Also, the introductory passage of a song, followed by the chorus.

steel band an ensemble of musicians playing steel drums.

stereophonic recorded with two or more microphones with the intention of playing it back through two or more speakers.

suite an instrumental composition consisting of several movements usually involving dance music, and each in the same key; a popular form from 1600 to 1750.

symphonic poem program music, or music that depicts a scene or story or emotion, usually performed in one extended movement.

symphony a long orchestral composition in four movements, similar to a sonata but performed by the entire orchestra.

syncopation changing time signatures suddenly, accenting the weak beat instead of the strong; off-time rhythms and beats, used widely in jazz, blues, ragtime, and jazz-rock fusion.

time signature at the opening of a composition, a sign consisting of two numbers, one over the other, the top designating beats per measure, the bottom the time value of the note receiving the beat.

toccata a highly elaborate and difficult keyboard composition featuring arpeggios, scales, ornaments, and other techniques.

tonguing the placement and action of the tongue to produce different pitches and effects in a wind instrument.

tonguing, flutter silently pronouncing the letter *r* repeatedly to produce a tremolo effect in the flute.

transcription see ARRANGEMENT.

transpose to change the key of a composition in writing and in performance.

treble a high-pitched instrument.

tremolo a shaking or trembling effect produced by quick changes in volume, as in flutter tonguing on the flute.

trill a commonly used musical ornament produced by very quick alternation of a note with another note one-half or one full tone above it.

troubadour a poet-musician of the 12th to 13th century.

vamp to improvise an accompaniment when another musician is playing a solo, especially in a jazz composition.

vaudeville comic songs of the early 18th century French opera. Also, in the 20th-century United States, a variety show.

virtuoso an exceptionally skilled musician.

whole note note with the longest time value.

whole rest a rest or pause with a time value equal to one whole note.

PERCUSSION INSTRUMENTS

bass drum the largest, deepest-sounding drum. On a drum set, the floor drum that is kicked by a pedal.

bell lyre a portable glockenspiel.

bongos small Cuban drums played with the fingers, thumbs, and heels of the hands.

campanella a small bell.

carillon a set of tuned bells or chimes originating in the 13th century, usually hung in a church tower and played either automatically or by means of a keyboard and pedals.

castanets small, wooden clappers clicked together rhythmically in the hands, used in Spanish dances.

Chinese crash cymbal a crash cymbal with its edge turned up, providing a distinctive crashing sound when struck.

Chinese wood block a 7- to 8-inch block of slotted wood, making a distinctive "tock" sound when struck by a drumstick, popular with jazz drummers. Also known as a clog box.

choke cymbals two cymbals fixed face-to-face on a pedal and rod device and clapped together or struck with drumsticks to keep time or to add flourishes to the beat. More popularly known as a high-hat.

claves wooden stick approximately 8 to 10 inches long and clacked together to add percussion accompaniment in Latin music.

cowbell an actual cowbell with the clapper removed, used in percussive accompaniment.

crescent a Turkish instrument consisting of an inverted crescent hung with small bells.

cymbal, crash a cymbal designed to be struck powerfully to produce a loud crash.

cymbal, finger a pair of tiny, 2-inch cymbals placed on finger and thumb and rung together, of ancient origin but still in use in Greece and Turkey.

cymbal, ride a pop music cymbal that is played lightly to help keep the rhythm or beat.

cymbal, sizzle a type of crash cymbal embedded with loose rivets that produce a "sizzling" sound when struck.

glockenspiel a xylophonelike instrument having two rows of tuned steel bars arranged like the keyboard of a piano. A portable lyre-shaped version used in marching bands is known as a bell lyre.

gong a large bronze cymbal suspended by a cord and struck with a mallet.

grelots sleigh bells.

guiro a hollow gourd cut with a row of deep lines that are scraped with a metal prong to produce a rasping sound, used as percussive accompaniment in Cuba, Puerto Rico, and other Caribbean countries.

jingling Johnnie a crescent.

kettle drum see TIMPANI.

maraca a dried gourd filled with seeds and used as a rattle in Latin American music.

marimba a xylophonelike instrument of Central America. It is distinguished from the xylophone by a row or rows of wooden bars with resonant gourds or tubes projecting underneath.

mridanga a two-headed Indian drum shaped like a barrel and played primarily with the fingertips.

pedal on a timpani, the foot pedal that changes the tension and pitch of a drumhead. Also, the foot or "kick" pedal of a bass drum.

roto toms modern, single-headed tom-toms whose pitch can be altered simply by rotating their heads slightly, used primarily in rock bands.

snare drum a somewhat flat drum fixed with a series of metallic strands or snares and used to carry the main beat in most modern music.

steel drum a Caribbean drum originally made from an oil drum, characterized by a multidented head, with each dent producing a different pitch; noted for its pleasing, tinkling sound, and popularly used in calypso music.

tablas a pair of Indian drums, one made from a log, the other made of metal.

tampon a double-headed drumstick shaken back and forth by the wrist to produce a roll on a bass drum.

tam-tam a gong.

timpani a large, kettle-shaped drum tuned to a specific pitch that can be changed instantly by means of a foot pedal. Also known as a kettle drum.

tom-toms small, supplemental drums used primarily for fills, rolls, and flourishes; usually mounted on the bass drum.

triangle a steel rod bent into the shape of a triangle and "clanged" by a metal stick.

tubular bells chimes.

vibraphone an instrument similar to the xylophone and marimba, having two rows of tuned metal bars with resonators fitted with lids that open and close to provide a continuous vibrato effect; a popular jazz instrument.

xylophone an instrument similar to a marimba, characterized by two rows of wooden bars of graduating length and struck by hammers to produce a "rattling skeleton" sound.

STRINGED INSTRUMENTS

aeolian harp named for the Greek god of winds, a stringed boxlike instrument placed in a window and played automatically by the wind, known since biblical times and popular from the 16th to the 19th centuries.

archlute a large lute with a double neck.

autoharp a type of zither in which strings are plucked or strummed while chords are produced by depressing keys.

balalaika a triangular shaped guitar with a long neck and three strings, used for accompanying folk songs in Russia and Eastern Europe.

bandurria a flat-backed, 12-string guitar used in Spain and Latin America.

banjolin a short-necked banjo with four strings.

baryton an 18th-century guitarlike instrument consisting of six melody strings played with a bow and from 16 to 40 "resonant" strings that could be plucked in accompaniment or simply left to vibrate in sympathy with the melody strings.

bass guitar low-toned guitar having four strings to play the bass line of a melody.

belly the upper body surface of a stringed instrument over which the strings are stretched.

bissex an 18th-century guitar having six strings that were plucked or strummed and another six strings that vibrated in sympathy.

biwa a Japanese, short-necked lute with four strings.

bouzouki a pear-shaped stringed instrument used in Greece as an accompaniment in folk songs.

bow a pliable stick strung with horsehair and used on stringed instruments (violin, viola, etc.) to create sound.

bridge a piece of wood or metal where the strings are attached on the belly of a guitar, lute, or similar instrument.

capo a device clamped over the strings of a fret to shorten the length of vibrations and to facilitate the playing of certain keys. Also known as a capotasto.

cello a bass violin having four strings and stood on the floor when played.

chitarrone a large lute (up to 6½ feet) having between 11 and 16 strings, used for accompanying baroque music in the 16th and 17th centuries.

chyn a seven-stringed zither of ancient China, still in use.

cittern a flat-backed, pear-shaped guitar having four to 12 pairs of strings that were plucked or strummed by a quill plectrum, popular in England in the 16th and 17th centuries.

clarsach a small Celtic harp, still in use in Scotland.

colascione a European, long-necked lute having 24 movable frets, originating in the 16th century.

course in lutes and guitars, two or more strings that are tuned the same and played at the same time to provide greater volume when needed.

crwth an ancient Welsh lyre played with a bow. Also known as a crowd, crouth, or cruit.

double bass the largest and deepest-sounding member of the violin family.

dulcimer an instrument consisting of a shallow box over which 10 or more courses of strings are stretched and struck with small hammers.

dulcimer, Appalachian a three-stringed member of the zither family, plucked or strummed while it rests on one's lap.

esraj an Indian instrument with four melodic strings and 10 to 15 sympathetic understrings, played with a bow.

fingerboard the fretted or unfretted portion of the neck of a stringed instrument; where the chords are made.

frets the wood or metal strips on the fingerboard of a guitar, lute, or similar instrument, that act as guides for locating proper pitch.

frog the part of a violin bow that tightens the horsehair.

gittern an early form of guitar having four pairs of strings, originating in the Middle Ages.

gusle a long-necked, one-stringed instrument having a shape like a pear or a heart and played with a bow by Yugoslavian folk singers.

hardanger fiddle a violinlike instrument of Norway having four regular strings and four to five understrings that vibrate in sympathy, used in folk music.

Hawaiian guitar a lap-held guitar with metal strings that are stopped with a steel bar that is held or slid along with the left hand while the strings are strummed or plucked with the right hand, notable for its nasal, vibrato effects.

hurdy-gurdy an ancient stringed instrument played with a rosined wheel turned by a crank instead of by a bow, still used in European folk music today.

Irish harp a small harp having 30 to 50 brass strings that are plucked with the fingernails as opposed to using the fingertips, as a standard harp.

kantele a flat soundboard or psaltery having as many as 25 strings that are plucked or strummed while held in the lap.

kithara a widely used, lyre-shaped, harplike instrument of the ancient Greeks.

koto the Japanese national instrument, specifically a 13-stringed (strings made of waxed silk) soundboard 6 feet in length and resting on the floor.

lira da braccio an early version of the violin, about 28 inches long and having seven strings; invented in Italy in the 15th century.

lute a guitarlike instrument having a pear-shaped body, a broad, flat neck, a bent-back pegbox, and several pairs or courses of strings, widely used throughout the 16th century.

lyra an ancient Greek stringed instrument with a bowlike body made of tortoiseshell. The name was later applied to the rebec and the hurdy-gurdy.

lyre collective term for a large family of harplike instruments including the lyra, kithara, crwth, and rebec.

mandolin a small member of the lute family, having a pear-shaped body and four pairs of strings; used today in folk and country music.

peg any one of the wood or plastic pins turned to adjust the tension and pitch of a string; a tuning peg.

pick a plectrum; any device used for plucking or strumming.

plectrum a pick.

ponticello the bridge of a violin or other stringed instrument.

rebec a medieval instrument shaped like a pear and having two or three strings and played by a bow.

sarangi Indian stringed instrument carved from a single block of wood, played by bowing in an upright position.

sarod an Indian, short-necked lute with a twangy sound similar to a banjo.

samisen a long-necked, fretless lute having three strings that are struck rather than plucked; widely used in Japan.

sitar an East Indian, long-necked lute having 16 to 20 movable frets with five to seven regular or melody strings and 11 to 13 sympathetic strings underneath; made of a single block of wood or gourd.

sound hole any of the holes cut into the belly of a stringed instrument.

sound post in many stringed instruments, the wooden dowel connecting the belly with the back; it helps to carry vibrations.

sympathetic strings in older stringed instruments, a series of strings that are not plucked, strummed, or bowed but are simply left to vibrate when other strings are played.

tambura a long-necked lute of India, characterized by strings that are always played open and capable of producing only four, dronelike sounds.

tanbur a popular long-necked lute played in the Near East and southeastern Europe.

theorbo a bass lute, popular from 1600 to 1800.

ukulele a small, four-stringed guitar of Portuguese and Hawaiian origin, used in folk songs.

vihuela a popular Spanish lute of the 16th century.

vina an Indian zither similar to a sitar.

viola a lower-pitched and slightly larger version of the violin, known for its solemn, husky tones.

zither a folk instrument consisting of a flat, wooden soundbox over which as many as 42 strings are stretched.

VOCALS AND SONG

absolute pitch the ability to remember, identify, and sing tones accurately without the aid of hearing another tone. Also known as perfect pitch.

a cappella singing without instrumental accompaniment.

alto high; a low-register voice of a female (contralto) or a high-register or falsetto voice of a male. A register below soprano.

answer, call and the repeating or nearly repeating of a theme sung by two or more singers in succession.

antiphonal sung by two singers or two groups in a choir alternately.

aria a long, elaborate solo vocal piece with instrumental accompaniment, associated with operas, cantatas, and oratorios.

ariette a short aria.

ballad a simple, narrative song, usually of a sentimental or romantic nature.

barcarolle a type of song sung by Venetian gondoliers.

baritone midrange of a male voice, about halfway between tenor and bass.

bass the lowest male voice.

basso buffo a bass singing voice, most fitting of comic opera.

basso cantante a bass singing voice characterized as light and sweet.

basso profundo a bass singing voice characterized as especially deep and powerful.

canon a musical composition featuring echoing voice parts that overlap, for example, "row, row, row your boat."

canon, double a musical composition with two simultaneous canons or a total of four voices singing the same lines at slightly different times.

canon, free a canon in which the imitation or echoing portion is sung in a slightly different way than the original.

canon, mixed a canon accompanied by independent voice parts and melodies.

canon, retrograde a canon with the imitation/echo portion sung backward from the original.

canticle a chant or hymn other than a psalm with words taken directly from the Bible.

cantillation free-rhythm chanting, as in Jewish liturgies.

cantor in Jewish worship, the chief singer of the liturgy. Also, the leader of a choir.

carol to sing joyfully; a Christmas song, usually with several parts.

castrato a male singer who underwent castration before puberty in order to remain an alto or soprano in the Italian opera of the 17th and 18th centuries.

chant a monophonic, nonrhythmic, unaccompanied form of singing.

chest voice the lowest register of the human voice, said to emanate from the chest. See HEAD VOICE.

choral of, relating to, or sung by a chorus or choir.

choral symphony a symphony with choral music.

compass the complete range of a voice, from the lowest to the highest note that can possibly be attained.

contralto the lowest range of a female voice; the range between soprano and tenor.

croon to sing softly.

diction the clear and proper enunciation of song lyrics.

falsetto a method of attaining an unnaturally high pitch in a male voice, a technique notably used by such pop vocal groups as the Bee Gees and the Four Seasons.

glee club a chorus consisting of males and/or females or both that perform glees and other types of songs.

glees brief, unaccompanied songs for men's chorus, usually having three to four voice parts, popular in the 1800s.

head voice the high-pitched voicing that causes the sensation of vibrations in the singer's head.

homophony a composition with one central voice part, as opposed to polyphony or several voice parts.

lyric a light, sweet voice.

madrigal a vocal composition having two or more movements and five or six voice parts.

mezza voce Italian music notation directing the singer to sing at half his or her normal volume.

mezzo soprano a female voice with a range halfway between alto and soprano.

parlante Italian music notation directing a singer to approximate the sound of speech.

pathétique French music notation directing the singer to express deep feeling.

patter song a type of comedic opera song sung very quickly and in a speechlike style.

plainsong chanting.

polyphonic having several voice parts.

prima donna in opera, the lead female singer.

primo uomo in opera, the lead male singer.

recitative a style of operatic singing similar to speech and with few changes in pitch.

round a simple form of a canon; a song with two or more voice parts that echo, imitate, or overlap one another, such as "Three Blind Mice" or "Row, Row, Row Your Boat."

scat style of jazz singing characterized by nonsensical syllables and other vocalizations other than lyrics.

serenade a love song, especially one sung under a lover's window at night.

shanty a work song sung by sailors to keep time in jobs involving teams. "Blow the Man Down" is a typical shanty.

solfeggio a vocal exercise employing the sol-fa syllables (do, re, mi, fa, sol, la, ti).

soprano the highest range of a female voice; the highest range of a young boy.

syllabic characterized by one note sung for each syllable of the lyrics.

tenor the highest range of a male voice.

WIND INSTRUMENTS

alpenhorn a long (sometimes as long as 12 feet) wooden horn used in the Alps to convey signals, call cattle, or play simple melodies.

aulos a shrill wind instrument of ancient Greece, characterized by several finger holes and a double reed; played two at a time, one in each hand by a single performer.

Bach trumpet a high-pitched trumpet originating in Bach's day and used in many of his compositions.

bagpipe Scottish instrument producing a haunting, droning sound through the use of several pipes and a windbag pumped with the arm.

bamboo pipe a simple recorderlike instrument made of bamboo.

barrel organ an instrument consisting of a wooden barrel with fixed pins or projections that automatically force air into organ pipes with each rotation, usually capable of playing only one tune.

basset horn a type of alto clarinet invented in the 18th century, characterized by a long, slender body and an up-curving metal bell, used frequently in the operas of Wolfgang Amadeus Mozart and Richard Strauss.

bassoon a very long (8½ feet doubled over) member of the oboe family producing sounds that are sometimes exceptionally comedic or sad.

block flute a recorder or flageolet.

bombardon a type of bass tuba.

bore the conical or cylindrical tube of a wind instrument.

cor de chasse a brass hunting horn originating in the 17th century.

cornet a small brass instrument similar to a trumpet and used in military bands.

crook a curved piece of tubing connecting to the reed with the body of a woodwind; it makes the instrument easier to hold.

crumhorn a J-shaped woodwind of the 16th and 17th centuries.

double reed a mouthpiece consisting of two pieces of cane bound together and between which air is blown; used in the oboe, English horn, bassoon, and others.

drone on a bagpipe, any one of the pipes producing a continuous unchanging pitch.

English flute a recorder.

English horn an alto oboe.

euphonium a brass tenor tuba rarely used in orchestras but frequently seen in brass and military bands.

fife a small flute with six finger holes and having a lower pitch than a piccolo; usually used in military bands.

fipple flute another name for a recorder or flageolet; any flute blown from one end, as a whistle.

flugelhorn a brass instrument similar to a cornet but having a wider bore.

French horn a coiled brass instrument with a flaring bell 11 to 14 inches in diameter, used in orchestras and noted for its mellow sound.

harmonium a keyboardlike instrument that sounds like a pipe organ but is designed to work as a giant harmonica, specifically with air blown through reeds by pedal-operated bellows, popular in the 1800s.

heckelphone a woodwind similar to an oboe but having a larger bore and a more powerful tone, developed in 1904.

helicon a large bass tuba that coils around the musician's body to facilitate carrying it in a marching band.

key any one of the small finger levers that open and close over hard-to-reach holes.

key bugle a bugle having keys to produce a wider range of notes, largely replaced by the valved cornet in 1850. Also known as the Kent bugle.

mellophone an instrument similar to the French horn but easier to play; primarily used in marching bands.

musette a French bagpipe popular in the 17th and 18th centuries.

oboe a double-reeded woodwind shaped like a clarinet and widely used in many orchestral compositions.

oboe, baritone a large oboe with a pitch an octave below its standard counterpart.

ocarina a small, potato-shaped instrument having 10 holes and producing a whistlelike sound.

oliphant a horn made from an elephant tusk.

panpipes an instrument consisting of four to 12 small pipes of graduating length banded together and blown into to produce different notes; known as a syrinx by the ancient Greeks. Also known as the pan flute.

piccolo a small flute having a pitch one octave higher than a flute.

saxhorn a brass instrument similar to a flugelhorn but having a funnel-shaped mouthpiece, used in marching bands.

shakuhachi a Japanese flute, blown like a recorder and made of bamboo.

shofar an ancient instrument made of a ram's horn, used for more than 3,000 years to signal the New Year in Jewish religious services.

sousaphone a large bass tuba or helicon.

uilleann pipes Irish bagpipes.

valve any one of the valves or pistons on a brass instrument (except trombone) engaged to produce a different pitch.

woodwinds collective term for all the wind instruments that were originally made from wood, but now including the saxophone, flute, piccolo, oboe, English horn, bassoon, clarinet, and basset horn.

OCCUPATIONS

FARMING

acre a square of land measuring approximately 209 feet (61 m) per side.

auger a spinning, spiral shaft that is used to convey grain in and out of storage bins.

baler a machine that compresses and ties hay or straw into rectangles or round bales to facilitate storage.

barn raising the erection of a new barn with the help of neighbors, family, and friends, a popular event in rural America.

bin any storage unit, often concrete or corrugated metal, for grain.

biochemicals environmentally friendly chemicals derived from natural sources, including enzymes, hormones, and pheromones, for use as insect repellants or to prevent insect mating and growth.

biosolids either animal manure or sewage from sewage treatment plants, spread on fields to fertilize crops.

bocage farmland divided into fields by hedges and small trees, especially in France.

broadcast to spread seeds in a uniform manner.

bunker silo a horizontal silo built above or below ground.

bushel common unit of volume for the measurement of dry grains or produce, which may vary in weight according to the crop. A bushel of wheat, for example, weighs 60 pounds (28 kg), and a bushel of corn weighs 56 pounds (25 kg).

byre a cow barn.

cash crops any crops intended to be sold for money, as distinguished from crops grown to feed livestock or to be consumed by the farmer's family.

cereal grains the grains typically used in the manufacture of cereals, specifically barley, oats, rice, and wheat.

cock a cone-shaped pile of hay or straw. Also known as a haycock.

combine a large harvesting machine that cuts, threshes, cleans, and bags grain.

commodity any agricultural goods.

compaction compression of soil by tractors or other large farm machinery.

compost decomposing organic matter used as fertilizer.

contour farming plowing and planting that follows the contours of uneven terrain to help prevent water runoff and soil erosion.

corncrib a storage building having slatted sides for the drying of corn.

cover crop a fast-growing crop sown to prevent erosion of the soil.

cow path a walled or fenced pathway leading from the barn and past crops to pasture for cows.

croft a small subsistence farm—usually comprising no more than 5 acres—in Scotland. The term is sometimes applied to small farms in other countries as well.

crop dusting applying pesticides on crops by airplane, helicopter, or other means.

cultivate to develop soil with plowing and fertilizer in order to grow crops.

cultivator an implement that breaks up the soil and uproots weeds around crops.

custom harvester any company with equipment and transport vehicles hired by a farmer to harvest and deliver crops.

disk to cut up the soil with rotating disks.

disk harrow a harrowing implement employing metal disks to break up the soil.

domesticate to tame, raise, and breed animals, usually for profit.

draft animal any animal, such as a large horse or ox, bred or used for pulling.

drill an apparatus pulled behind a tractor that cuts a groove in soil, drops seeds, and then covers the soil.

dry farming collective term for the methods used to raise crops where there is little rainfall and no irrigation. The crops chosen are those well-adapted to near-drought conditions; moisture-stealing weeds are carefully culled, and a mulch is placed over the soil to keep moisture from evaporating too quickly in the sun.

elevator a conveyor system that carries hay bales to the upper story of a barn.

erosion the running or blowing off of soil, especially topsoil, caused by wind, rain, overgrazing by livestock, or too frequent cultivation.

extension agency from an agricultural university, a research and educational branch set up to serve local farmers.

fallow barren; to leave a field unseeded after plowing.

federal crop insurance insurance provided to farmers from the U.S. government to protect against unforeseen hardship, such as storm damage, early frosts, plant diseases, pests, etc.

feed a mix of grains and nutrients fed to livestock.

feed grains corn, milo, and soybeans.

feed lot an enclosed area where cattle are fed a high grade of feed to fatten them for market.

fertilizer any nutrient added to the soil to enrich it for growing crops.

flail a threshing or husk-loosening tool composed of two or more sticks attached by a chain that is swung at grain, largely outmoded due to modern harvesting methods.

flail chopper a machine used to cut and load standing forage crops.

fodder livestock feed, such as cornstalks, hay, and straw.

forage harvester a machine that cuts up forage such as corn.

4-H an agricultural organization through which children and teens learn various aspects of farming.

frost hollow a low area or hollow that tends to draw cold air from higher elevations and thus produces more killing frosts—avoided by farmers.

furrow the long channel or rut cut into soil by a plow.

grain elevator a large storage facility for grain, usually made up of multiple bins, silos, or tanks.

grange a local organization of farmers that serves as a social outlet and center for support.

green manure crop a crop, such as legumes, that restores nitrogen to the soil.

harrow an implement having either spikes or disks for leveling, breaking up clods, and refining plowed soil.

harvest to pick crops by hand, or to gather them through use of a farm machine, such as a combine.

harvester any reaping machine.

hay any grasses cut and prepared for livestock feed. As a verb, to cut and prepare grasses for fodder.

haycock see COCK.

hayfork a pitchfork.

hayloft an upper story of a barn, where hay is stored.

headland the unplowed perimeter of a field, where the tractor and equipment can be driven and maneuvered without damaging crops.

herbicide any chemical used to kill weeds.

humus nutrient-rich part of soil that contains naturally composted plant matter or manure.

husbandry the business of farming.

hydroponic a method of growing through which plants are fed nutrients without the use of soil.

insecticide any chemical used to kill insects.

ley farming sowing an arable plot with grass to be used as pasture for several years.

livestock any farm animals, such as cows, sheep, pigs, chickens, or others, usually raised for profit.

manure waste matter from farm animals, often spread on soil to enrich it.

manure spreader a machine used to spread fertilizer uniformly.

moldboard plow the classic, wedge-shaped plow, used by farmers for centuries.

monoculture the raising of the same crop in the same fields year after year.

mower a machine that cuts or mows hay.

organic farming natural farming that uses no chemicals, artificial fertilizers, insecticides, etc.

pastoral farming the breeding and raising of cattle, sheep, horses, goats, reindeer, or other grass-eating animals.

pasture grass fields for grazing livestock.

pesticide any chemical used to kill insects.

planter a seeding machine that meters out and distributes seeds at uniform depths and intervals.

plow to turn over the soil to prepare it for planting, often done by a tractor. Also the tractor itself.

plowshare the cutting edge of a moldboard plow.

rake a tined or toothed implement pulled by a tractor to gather loose hay or to windrow hay for baling.

rotation of crops changing the type of crops grown in a field each year or every few years to help control weeds, pests, and diseases and to help maintain the fertility of the soil.

scythe an old-fashioned implement composed of a long, curving blade held by a bent handle, used for mowing and reaping.

sickle a small version of a scythe with a straight, one-handed handle.

silage chopped feed that may be composed of any numbers of crops, including grasses, corn, clover, or sorghum, and fermented in storage for use in winter.

silo a cylindrical storage building for fodder.

spreader any machine used to spread manure, lime, or other material in a uniform fashion.

straw the stems of plants, such as wheat, used for animal bedding.

subsistence farming crops and animals raised not to be sold but to be consumed by the farmer's family.

terracing plowing a shelf into a slope to slow water runoff.

thresh to separate grains or seeds from straw by beating the stems and husks.

thresher a machine that threshes.

tiller an implement having rotary tillers or blades for breaking up or plowing soil.

timothy the most commonly grown hay grass on U.S. farms.

truck farming intense farming of vegetable crops and their quick shipment to market by trucks.

waterway any human-made, canal-like trough for catching and directing runoff away from cultivated areas.

weed any unwanted plant that competes with crops for nutrients and water.

windrow a long pile of hay left to dry in a field before being baled or bundled.

FIREFIGHTING

air tanker a large airplane equipped with a tank for dropping water or chemicals on a forest fire.

borate a saltlike substance used to put out fires.

borate bomber a large airplane equipped with a tank for dropping borate on a fire.

bucket brigade nickname for rural firefighting team comprising people in a line handling down buckets of water.

conflagration a huge, out-of-control fire that extends over a large area or through several buildings.

coop the communication center where calls are received in a fire station.

fire break a strip of land burned or plowed to stop the spread of an oncoming fire.

fire door a heavy door designed to hold back fire for at least 30 minutes.

fire wall a fireproof wall.

fog pattern a broad cloud of water sprayed continuously over an area to keep firemen cool while they work.

gooseneck crane a hinged crane equipped with water nozzles, used for fighting fires high up. Also known as a snorkel.

mars light the red, flashing beacon atop a fire truck.

outrigger a support leg that extends out the side of a ladder truck to help stabilize it.

pack pump a water tank worn on the back, used to carry water to brush fires.

resuscitator apparatus that forces air into the lungs of people suffering from smoke inhalation.

snorkel see GOOSENECK CRANE.

superpumper a huge pump used to draw water from a river, lake, or other body of water.

tillerman one who steers the rear portion of a long ladder truck.

turnout coat a firefighter's waterproof, fireproof coat.

turntable the platform and hydraulic motor that raises a ladder and turns it on a ladder truck.

water cannon a cannon capable of shooting water up to 500 feet. Also known as a deluge gun.

FUNERAL SERVICES

algor mortis the cooling of the body after death.

arrangement room in a funeral home, a room where the family meets with the funeral director to make burial arrangements.

aspiration the removal of abdominal fluid or gases from the deceased.

bereaved those mourning the deceased.

burial case see CASKET.

burial certificate a legal permit authorizing burial.

burial vault a container that holds a casket after burial to help prevent the collapse of a grave.

casket a long boxlike container made of wood, metal, or plastic in which the deceased is placed for burial. Also known as a coffin or burial case.

casket coach see HEARSE.

casket veil a transparent veil draped over the casket to prevent flies from landing on the deceased.

catafalque a draped framework on which a casket rests during a funeral service and while the deceased awaits burial.

coffin see CASKET.

columbarium a vault with multiple niches for holding urns containing cremains.

coroner a medical officer who investigates and determines cause of death, especially if anything other than natural causes are suspected.

cortege a funeral procession.

cosmetology the art of applying cosmetics to the deceased to make him or her appear lifelike.

cremains the ashes and remains of the deceased after cremation.

cremation the burning of a corpse to reduce it to bone fragments, which are then pulverized.

crematory a furnace for burning dead bodies. Also, the building that houses such a furnace.

crypt a vault used to hold remains.

death certificate a legal document signed by an attending physician registering the cause of death.

death notice a small notice on the obituary page of a newspaper announcing a death and scheduled funeral services.

deceased dead. Also, one who has died.

disinter to dig up or remove the remains of the dead from its burial or holding place.

disposition the final resting place for the body or remains of the deceased.

door badge a spray of flowers hung from the bereaved's doorway to announce a death in the family.

embalm to disinfect and temporarily preserve the deceased by injecting the veins and arteries with preserving and antiseptic fluids.

embalmer one who works to disinfect and temporarily preserve the body of the deceased through the use of chemicals.

entombment placement of the deceased in a mausoleum.

exhume to dig up the remains of the deceased from the burial site.

family car the limousine the immediate family members of the deceased ride in during a procession to the cemetery.

family room in a funeral home, a room where family members may retire to grieve in private.

flower car a car that transports floral arrangements to the cemetery.

final rites a graveside funeral service.

first call the first meeting between a funeral director and the family of the deceased, usually at the home of the deceased.

funeral coach see HEARSE.

funeral director one who runs a funeral home and arranges for the care and burial of the deceased and who may act as a counselor to the bereaved. Also known as a mortician or undertaker.

funeral home an establishment that embalms and otherwise cares for the remains of the deceased and arranges for burial. Also known as a mortuary.

funeral spray cut flowers or a floral arrangement sent to the home of the deceased or to the funeral home.

grave the hole in the ground into which a coffin containing the deceased or an urn containing the cremains of the deceased is placed.

grave liner a container into which a casket is placed to protect it from the collapse of a grave.

hearse a vehicle that carries a corpse to its gravesite. Also known as a casket coach or funeral coach.

honorary pallbearer one who acts as part of an honor guard for the deceased but who does not carry the casket.

hospice an organization made up of volunteers and nurses who care for the dying in their home.

inquest an inquiry by a jury into the cause of death.

in state of the deceased, presented for viewing by the bereaved.

inter to bury a body in a grave.

interment the burying of a body in a grave.

inurnment the playing of the deceased's ashes into an urn after cremation.

medical examiner a physician who performs autopsies on those who die by suicide, criminal action, or other violent means.

morgue a facility where unknown dead bodies are stored until they can be identified by relatives and then examined for cause of death.

mortician see FUNERAL DIRECTOR.

mortuary see FUNERAL HOME.

mortuary science the art and science of embalming and preparing a body for burial.

niche a small space in a wall for holding cremains in an urn.

obituary a death notice appearing in a newspaper.

pallbearers friends or family of the deceased who carry the casket during a funeral service or as needed.

preparation room in a funeral home, a room used to ready a body for burial.

preparation table a table on which a body rests while it is being embalmed and otherwise prepared for burial.

procession a slow-moving line of vehicles, including a hearse, proceeding from the funeral service to the cemetery.

purge a putrefied discharge of intestinal material from an orifice of the deceased due to inadequate embalming.

register a sign-in book in which visitors to the funeral home register their names during a service.

reposing room the room in which a body lies in state in its casket until the funeral.

restorative art dermatological repair of damaged features of the deceased.

rigor mortis the stiffening of the muscles after death.

slumber room in a funeral home, a room in which the deceased may lie in a bed before being placed in a casket.

trade embalmer an independent embalmer who may work for several different funeral homes.

undertaker see FUNERAL DIRECTOR.

urn a container in which cremains are held.

vigil among Roman Catholics, a service held the night before the funeral.

visitation in a funeral home, a scheduled time when friends and family may pay their respect to the deceased.

wake a viewing of the deceased before burial, sometimes lasting all night long.

POLICE AND DETECTIVES

(*Also see* LAW)

accelerant police lab term for gasoline, kerosene, turpentine, or diesel fuel, any of which may be used in an arson fire.

A.C.U. anticrime unit.

A.D.A. assistant district attorney.

adipocere the waxy, soapy substance made up of fatty acids and insoluble salts that forms on a corpse, especially in a moist environment. Also known as grave wax.

A.K.A. also known as; alias.

alias any false name used by a criminal.

A.P.B. all points bulletin, issued to help locate a fleeing suspect.

at large of a criminal, yet to be apprehended.

automatism a crime performed unconsciously, as when sleepwalking. Defendants in rare cases have been found innocent by using such a defense.

bag 'em slang, to place a corpse into a body bag.

ballistics the study of firearms and bullets, used to identify weapons employed in a crime, the locations of the criminals when they fired them, etc.

banker a dealer or other street person who holds cash paid out for drugs.

baton a police officer's small club, carried on his or her person for defensive purposes. Also known as a nightstick or billy club.

beat the territory or neighborhood in which a police officer makes his or her patrol.

billy club see BATON.

black powder method a method of revealing latent fingerprints. Glassware cleaner and black powder are used to enhance prints on adhesive tape.

blank lineup a police lineup in which an actual suspect in a crime is not included, a test used to determine the veracity or credibility of a witness.

bloodstain pattern analysis the study of the shapes, locations, and patterns of bloodstains to determine a victim's location; whether he or she was lying, seated, or standing when attacked; how much the victim struggled, and so on.

blotter at a police station, the computer register or database (formerly a book) in which arrests are recorded.

blowfly also known as a bluebottle or greenbottle, a metallic-colored fly characterized by its ability to quickly zero in on a decaying corpse, on which it lays eggs. Because the eggs develop into larvae in a predictable time span, their presence can be used to help determine time of death, often to within a day or two, or less.

bobby British colloquialism for a police officer.

book to record an arrest and register the person arrested.

book, the the rules and regulations of police procedure and law.

boost to shoplift.

bounty a reward offered for the successful capture of a criminal.

bounty hunter one who hunts and captures wanted criminals for posted rewards.

bucket the city jail.

bulletproof vest a vest made from Kevlar, a bulletproof mesh, often worn under a police uniform.

bunco-forgery a division in a police department that handles consumer fraud, bribery cases, computer database crimes, fraudulently printed checks, counterfeit money, forged airline tickets, theft of bank checks and check writing equipment, credit card fraud, forged prescriptions, pickpocketing, and similar crimes. The responsibilities of such a division may vary somewhat from department to department.

bust slang, to arrest.

bystander effect a psychological phenomenon in which the more bystanders there are to witness a crime the less likely anyone will step in to help the victim.

canary slang for an informer.

C of D chief of detectives.

C of O chief of operations.

chop shop a facility yard or garage where stolen cars are stripped of their parts by thieves.

citizen's arrest an arrest made by one who is not a police officer, a legal act by any U.S. citizen.

cognitive dissonance a form of psychological denial in which a criminal's attitudes and moral beliefs are inconsistent with his actions.

collar slang for an arrest. Also, to arrest.

commissioner the city official who oversees a police chief and police department.

composite drawing a drawing made by a police artist from details given by more than one witness.

computer forensics the analysis of a suspect's computer and its stored data to uncover a wide range of criminal behavior, from child pornography to computer hacking to terrorism.

coroner an elected public officer who is a pathologist and who determines the cause of death in cases in which foul play is suspected.

corpus delecti all of the evidence and facts surrounding a homicide.

corrosive fingerprint technique a new forensic technique used to reveal fingerprints on bomb fragments, bullet casings, or guns, even after the prints have been thoroughly washed or wiped off. The suspect fragment or item is coated in a special conductive powder, similar to photocopier powder, and electrically charged. The powder, attracted to the natural corrosion caused by the oils in fingerprints, forms around the corrosion, revealing print details.

crack to solve a case.

crackdown a tightening of police enforcement against a particular crime.

crime lab a laboratory that may work either within or independently of a police department to investigate and process toxics, explosives, narcotics, inflammables, unknown specimens, fingerprints, blood samples, urine, semen, saliva, hairs and fibers, DNA typing, tire impressions, footprints, firearms identification, document analysis, and so forth.

crime scene staging the altering of a crime scene by a criminal, in order to mislead investigators. A premeditated murder, for example, may be staged to look like a simple robbery gone wrong.

criminalist a crime lab specialist or technician.

criminology the study of all facets of crime.

C.S.U. crime scene unit.

dactylography the study of fingerprints as a means of criminal identification.

D.B. dead body.

defensive wounds wounds that appear on the hands, fingers, and arms of assault or murder victims who tried to fight off their assailants.

depersonalization a form of denial in which a murderer objectifies a victim in a variety of ways, including covering the victim's face or disfiguring it beyond recognition in order to remain detached.

detective a police officer who investigates crimes.

detention the holding of a criminal by the police.

division see PRECINCT.

disorganized referring to criminal behavior that is largely unplanned, sloppy, and impulsive and leaves lots of evidence behind.

DNA database an archive of DNA profiles from serious criminals, used to provide matches when DNA evidence is left behind at crime scenes.

DNA fingerprinting the identification of a criminal by examination of DNA in blood, hair, semen, etc., left behind at the scene of a crime.

DOA dead on arrival.

dragnet a coordinated, all-out search for a criminal.

entrapment the luring of someone into an illegal act, disallowed by law.

facial identification system (FIS) computerized system for matching facial features and identifying criminals.

false arrest an arrest of a person for reasons that are legally unsupportable.

false confession a coerced confession given by an exhausted suspect, who is in fact innocent of any crime. Police, using old-style interrogation techniques, may intentionally or unintentionally intimidate, manipulate, or brainwash suspects who are young, mentally retarded, mentally ill, or elderly into admitting guilt when no guilt exists. Such techniques are increasingly being abolished.

Federal Bureau of Investigation (FBI) a division of the United States Department of Justice, a national agency assigned to investigate such crimes as bank robberies, espionage, kidnapping, sabotage, government fraud, and civil rights violations, originating in 1908.

finger to accuse a person of a crime based on evidence.

FIS see FACIAL IDENTIFICATION SYSTEM.

forensic anthropology the analysis of bones to determine a homicide victim's age, gender, and any traumas or diseases suffered. May also be used to identify remains through DNA analysis.

forensic artist an artist who sketches a picture of a suspect by eyewitness accounts, often aided by computer programs.

forensic chemistry a crime lab specialty involving the analysis and identification of fibers, hairs, particles, paints, dyes, chemicals, etc.

forensic entomology the study of insects, especially their attraction to corpses and when they tend to lay eggs on them. Time of death can sometimes be determined by the presence of insects and their eggs alone.

forensic geology the study and analysis of stones and soils, sometimes used to narrow down or pinpoint where a criminal has walked or driven by residue left on shoes or tires.

forensic medicine the science involved in uncovering the medical facts concerning a criminal law case.

forensic pathology medical specialty used to determine the cause and time of death.

forensic sculptor a crime lab artist who sculpts a three-dimensional likeness of a victim or suspect.

forensic serology the study and analysis of body fluids, used to identify victims or suspects through blood typing, semen, DNA, etc.

frisk to pat down a suspect in search of weapons or contraband.

fugitive section a division within a large department that investigates and captures fugitives.

garden room slang for the morgue.

gas-chromatography mass spectrometer a crime lab machine used to identify substances, especially illicit drugs, with a high degree of accuracy.

geographical profiling forming a pattern of locations where serial crimes are being committed, which may provide a clue to the perpetrator's home neighborhood.

headspace the area directly above burned debris in the aftermath of an arson fire. In a set fire, accelerant evaporates and forms hydrocarbons, which are deposited above the fire. Lab analysis via "headspace gas chromatography" can identify the presence of these hydrocarbons, although sometimes "sniffer" dogs may be used.

heat slang for the police.

heist a robbery.

hit man a contracted killer.

holding pen a cell where the newly arrested wait to be booked.

homicide division the division within a department that investigates and processes murders.

hostile attributional bias a common psychological malfunction in which faulty perception of hostile intent impels a criminal to assault or attack someone.

hot slang for stolen.

hydrocarbons residue formed during the evaporation of accelerants in a fire, used as evidence in arson cases.

I.A.D. Internal Affairs Division; a division that investigates complaints against police or other department personnel.

ingratiation a technique in which an interrogator flatters and befriends a suspect in order to get the suspect to drop his or her guard.

Integrated Ballistics Identification System an archive of bullet and shell evidence from crime scenes across the United States. Computers are employed to look for matches.

inventive witness a witness who makes up or embellishes details in order to be involved in a case and feel important.

informer one who provides police with information concerning a crime.

john a prostitute's male customer.

jumper a bail jumper.

K-9 division trained police dogs, used in sniffing out drugs, in tracking and attacking fleeing suspects, or in locating corpses.

latent fingerprints fingerprints formed by perspiration or oils, which cannot be seen by the human eye but can be revealed by a variety of techniques.

lead a clue.

leading question a question posed by interrogators in a manipulative or misleading way in order to elicit the desired response from witnesses or suspects. The answer given to such a question is often inadmissible in court.

lie detector see POLYGRAPH.

lineup a group of men or women arranged in a line, from which a witness must identify a suspect in a crime.

liquid-chromatography mass spectrometer a variation of the gas-chromatography mass spectrometer, used for similar purposes.

lividity discoloration of a body caused by the pooling of blood after death; it can be used to help determine the time of death.

Luminol a chemical used to detect blood, even when diluted 10,000 times.

manhunt a coordinated search for a fugitive.

mark a victim of a crime; a dupe.

marshal a U.S. federal officer in charge of processing court orders.

maximization an interrogation technique in which a detective tries to convince a suspect that the police have much more evidence in a case than they really do in order to elicit a confession.

medical examiner (M.E.) one who is not an elected official, as a coroner is, but rather is hired by a county or city to perform the same duties.

microexpressions very brief and partial facial expressions that occur after being shown or told something with emotional content and which occur too quickly to fully conceal. Such expressions are readily detected by a skilled interrogator.

minimization an interrogation technique in which a detective plays down the seriousness of a crime or casts blame on others or circumstances, in order to relax a suspect and get him or her to confess.

Miranda rule law that requires an arresting officer to read an arrestee his or her constitutional rights, including the right to an attorney and the right to remain silent.

M.O. modus operandi; a criminal's method of operating.

most wanted list the FBI's roster of extremely dangerous criminals at large.

moulage a cast impression of a footprint or shoe print.

MP military police.

nab informal, to catch or arrest.

narc slang for a narcotics officer.

narcotics division a division that handles crimes dealing with narcotics.

nightstick see BATON.

odontology the study of the characteristics of teeth, sometimes used to identify remains.

on the take receiving stolen or illegal goods or money.

organized referring to criminal behavior that is carefully planned, with evidence meticulously hidden.

Organized Crime Intelligence Division a division that investigates and gathers information on members of organized crime.

orthotolidine solution chemicals used to detect the presence of blood in a stain.

ouchteriony test a crime lab test used to determine if a bloodstain is human or animal.

paddy wagon a vanlike vehicle designed to hold and transport several arrestees simultaneously, as during a riot.

palynology the study and identification of pollens. Pollens left on clothing can sometimes be used to narrow down or even pinpoint where a suspect has been in the recent past because some plants may only grow in a limited or specific territory.

pepper spray defensive tool used by an officer in subduing a noncompliant suspect in a crime; the highly irritating ingredients held in a can are sprayed directly at the face of the suspect, causing temporary breathing difficulties and blindness.

petechial hemorrhage any one of tiny, pinlike hemorrhages that form below the skin, especially under the eyelid, in a strangulation or asphyxiation case.

piece a gun.

pit maneuver a technique of stopping a fleeing criminal by steering a cruiser into the tail end of the getaway car and spinning it around.

plainclothes officer a police officer or detective who works in street clothes to help hide his or her identity.

polygraph an apparatus having sensors that are attached to a criminal suspect to measure blood pressure and respiration during interrogation. Also known as a lie detector.

precinct a station house or the area of a city that a station house serves. Also known as a division.

private detective a detective unaffiliated with a police department who is hired by an individual to investigate a crime, carry out surveillance, find a missing person, etc.

private eye a private detective.

probable cause the belief, based on evidence, that someone has committed a crime, necessary for issuance of search or arrest warrants by the court.

profiling the controversial practice of pulling a motorist over in his or her car on the basis of age or race, as opposed to any wrongdoing or suspicious activity.

psychological profile a report developed by a psychologist detailing a criminal's likely psychological makeup, based on profiles from criminal behavior in past crimes.

psychopathic personality an impulsive personality largely or entirely lacking in conscience or sense of remorse.

rape kit a kit used by investigators to collect semen or other biological material from a rape victim.

rap sheet a criminal's record of arrests and convictions.

reverse paternity DNA a test used to identify a person's blood by analyzing the DNA of the individual's parents.

rifling the spiraling grooves inside a gun barrel that leave distinctive markings on bullets when fired. Every gun barrel has its own distinctive pattern that, when imprinted on bullets, can be used as identification and evidence.

R.K.C. resident known criminal.

scanning electron microscope in a police lab, a high-tech microscope used to search for particles present in gunshot residue.

Scotland Yard the headquarters of the Criminal Investigation Department of the London Metropolitan Police.

search warrant a court order allowing a police officer to search a suspect's residence for evidence of illegal activity.

selective recall a suspect's suspiciously sharp memory of where he was and what he was doing when questioned by an interrogator about a crime. Suspects often supply too many precise details when providing alibis concerning the day and location a crime took place. Such memory is doubly suspicious when the suspect cannot produce similar details about the day before or after a crime took place.

shadow to tail or follow a suspect.

signature a particular way a serial offender performs an illegal act, or a telling detail left behind at a crime scene that identifies a criminal.

sniffer dog a dog trained to sniff out illicit drugs, bombs, or accelerants used in an arson fire.

speed trap an area along a road where a police officer hides in order to catch speeders.

spike strip a mat composed of long, sharp spikes, laid down in the middle of a road to pierce the tires of a motorist fleeing from the police.

stakeout waiting and observing surreptitiously at a location for a crime to occur.

stun gun a small electric gun that fires a wired, dart-like projectile and incapacitates a fleeing or struggling suspect by jolting the person with up to 50,000 volts of electricity, causing complete loss of muscle control. Also known as a Taser.

super glue fuming a technique used to reveal latent fingerprints. Super glue is heated to boiling, creating a gas that coats everything around it. A component of the glue adheres to the amino acids, fatty acids, and proteins in the oil secretions from fingertip ridges and turns them white. Also known as cyanoacrylate fuming. Developed by the Japanese in 1978.

surveillance observation or spying on a criminal suspect by the police or a detective.

SWAT Special Weapons and Tactics; an elite police force with paramilitary training.

sweep a large-scale crackdown on a particular crime in a specified area, resulting in numerous arrests.

swoop a massive and simultaneous convergence of police or police cruisers at a particular site to make an arrest of a group of suspects, such as drug dealers.

tactical officer an officer who works in plain clothes to make drug and vice arrests.

Taser see STUN GUN.

tear gas a gas that causes severe eye irritation and temporary blindness, used by law enforcement to control unruly or rioting crowds.

third degree a method of police interrogation largely outmoded by the 1930s but practiced in some precincts as late as the 1950s; it was characterized by officers aggressively and exhaustively grilling a suspect under bright lights, and sometimes included beatings, in order to force a confession.

.38-caliber a service revolver, the sidearm of choice among plainclothes detectives, due to its smaller size and relative ease of concealment compared with the .357 Magnum.

.357 Magnum the sidearm of choice for many police officers on patrol; it is larger and more powerful than the .38 preferred by plainclothes detectives.

time of death medical examiners and coroners determine time of death of murder victims through various means: by body core temperature (which in the brain or liver drops an average of 1½ degrees per hour), by the extent of body stiffening (rigor mortis), by the pooling (lividity) of the body's blood, by the clouding of the corneas, by the drying of tissues, and by the presence or absence of purge fluid, which leaks out of the intestines after a certain amount of time.

tin slang for a police officer's badge.

TOD time of death.

trace analysis division in a police lab, an expert or team of experts who examines and identifies hairs, fibers, paints, papers, and other crime scene evidence.

trolling vice term for sending a plainclothes officer to an area frequented by prostitutes in order to make arrests for solicitations.

vice division a division that processes cases involving gambling, prostitution, and pornography.

vigilante one who takes the law into his or her own hands.

voiceprint an electronically generated, graphic reproduction of a person's voice, used for identification purposes.

warrant a writ authorized by a judge to have an individual arrested.

watch a police shift.

watch commander a lieutenant or captain who supervises police officers during a shift.

whip an officer in charge.

wired carrying a concealed recording device.

X-ray diffraction machine in a police lab, a machine used to identify explosive materials.

zapped slang for shot.

POLITICS AND ECONOMICS

act a bill after it passes the House of Representatives or the Senate or both.

activist one who works for a cause.

advance man a publicity person who schedules speeches, conferences, and so on, for a candidate or an incumbent.

adventurism risky or reckless government action, either domestically or in foreign affairs.

advise and consent the power of the Senate to advise the president and consent to proposed appointments or treaties.

amendment a proposal to revise, or an actual revision of, a bill, motion, or act.

apolitical lacking interest in politics, or the tendency to refuse to participate in politics out of apathy or disgust.

armchair strategist one who criticizes or remarks on political events from a comfortable position and particularly with the advantage of hindsight.

back channel the secret or informal circuit of communication used by the CIA and other government agencies.

backer one who supports a political candidate financially.

balance of power the theory that peace is maintained only when nations share equal power.

ballyhoo sensational or exaggerated promotion of a candidate or issue.

bandwagon a popular issue jumped on by politicians in order to be seen as part of the majority.

bargaining chip a negotiating concession.

barnstorm to tour rural areas to make campaign speeches.

bellwether a trendsetter.

bigger bang for the buck in military terms, a weapon or military system that delivers the most for the money.

big stick the deterrent of a large and powerful defense.

bill a proposed law.

bipartisan pertaining to both political parties; relating to the working together of two political parties, despite differences, to achieve a common goal.

black hats political opponents; the bad guys.

bleeding heart liberals extreme liberals—in the view of extreme conservatives. "Bleeding hearts" are suckers for sob stories and are quick to pledge tax money to cure a variety of social ills.

bloc a group of representatives with a common interest.

blue-ribbon panel a committee chosen for their expertise to look into a particular matter.

boll weevils nickname for southern conservative Democrats.

boom and bust an economy that follows cycles of prosperity and depression.

boondoggle any government project in which taxes are wasted through poor planning, incompetence, and inefficiency.

brain trust a group of well-informed advisers.

bread-and-butter issue any political issue that affects the voters' pocketbooks.

brinksmanship risk-taking politics often involving threats, and particularly the threat of military or nuclear intervention, with the goal of trying to make an opponent concede.

brouhaha an uproar, as over a controversy.

buck-passing passing the burden of responsibility to someone else.

bully pulpit a prominent high position that allows a politician to moralize and pontificate.

bureaucracy government administration composed of bureaus headed by nonelected officials. Also, any government office that, through convoluted channels and overly strict adherence to rules, impedes or slows down action.

business cycle the normal up and down cycling of the economy, from expansion and boom to contraction and recession, usually occurring roughly every three to five years and characterized by rising unemployment during downturns and rising inflation during expansions.

cabinet the heads of executive departments who serve as advisers to the president.

cant the vernacular used by a politician; pet words and phrases used by politicians.

canvass to gauge support for a candidate before the vote.

card-carrying denoting a member or supporter of a cause or organization, such as a card-carrying member of the ACLU.

caucus a meeting to select candidates and plan a campaign.

centrist one who tends to favor policies that fall between the left-leaning ideals of the Democratic Party and the right-leaning Republican Party, or one who takes a middle position on any issue.

chamber the House of Representatives or the Senate.

civil disobedience resisting the law to promote a cause.

cloture in the Senate, the process by which debate time is limited to one hour per senator.

coattail the winning of a congressional seat by party association with a popular presidential candidate.

cold war nonmilitary hostilities between two nations.

communist economy an economy based on the sharing of goods and services and overseen and managed by a government.

congress any assembly of government representatives, but especially Congress, the national legislative body of the United States, comprising the Senate and the House of Representatives.

Congressional Record the printed daily account of the debates and votes of the House and Senate, published by the Government Printing Office.

congressman/congresswoman a member of the U.S. House of Representatives.

conservative one who is generally opposed to change; a supporter of the status quo.

constituency collective term for the citizens of a legislative district. In the case of a senator, a state.

constituent a citizen of a particular legislative district.

consul an official appointed to a foreign city to represent its commercial interests.

consulate the office of a consul.

coup d'état the sudden takeover or overthrow of government.

cronyism favoritism toward friends, resulting in sometimes questionable political appointments and reciprocal backscratching.

cult of personality the blind following of a charismatic leader, such as a dictator, in which an aura of power is maintained through propaganda and pervasive indoctrination via various media outlets.

dark horse a candidate whose chances of winning an election are slight to none.

deep-six to throw out or get rid of something, often with the hope that it will never be found or discovered.

deflation a nationwide dropping of prices for goods and services.

delegate a person chosen to represent a constituency at a convention.

delegation a group of representative from an organization or area.

demagogue a politician who appeals to the greed, fears, and prejudices of the voters; a spellbinding orator who panders to voter selfishness.

Democratic Party evolving from the principles of Thomas Jefferson and further refined by Andrew Jackson and Martin Van Buren, the left-leaning or liberal-oriented one of the two major political parties of the United States, symbolized by the mascot of a donkey, and most often characterized by members who tend to favor labor unions, abortion rights, gay rights, gun control, affirmative action, regular upward adjustments of the minimum wage, extensive social services including welfare, and strong environmental policies with business-limiting regulations.

depression a period of extreme economic downturn, marked by plunging manufacturing, employment, and sales of goods, along with rising bankruptcies and tighter credit, and noted for being more severe and protracted than a recession.

despot a tyrant or dictator.

détente the thawing or opening up of relations between two nations previously hostile toward one another.

diplomacy the maintaining of positive relations or negotiations between nations.

diplomat a government official who maintains relationships and carries out negotiations with a foreign nation. Also responsible for protecting the rights of American citizens in a foreign country.

diplomatic corps collective term for all of the diplomatic officials assigned to one nation.

diplomatic immunity rights protecting diplomats from prosecution for crimes in other countries.

dissident one who strongly disagrees with those in power or who reports and protests government abuses of power.

divide and rule any method of gaining power by keeping one's enemies divided and therefore less of a threat.

domestic affairs political affairs within a nation's own borders.

dove a pacifist who philosophically rejects war as a solution to problems.

dyed-in-the-wool referring to a die-hard partisan through and through.

elder statesman an older, experienced, and highly respected politician.

electoral college collective term for persons elected from each state to cast electoral votes for the president and vice president.

electorate persons eligible to vote.

embargo a trade ban, often enacted to protest the action of another country.

embassy the residence or office of an ambassador in the capital of another nation.

engrossed bill official copy of a bill after it has been passed.

executive order a presidential order.

executive privilege the right of the president to withhold information from Congress.

executive session a meeting closed to the public.

extremist one whose views are seen as extreme or radical.

fact-finding trip a trip or junket overseas to gather information on a foreign issue.

faction a dissenting group within a larger group.

fed any high-ranking employee of the U.S. government.

fence-mending tending to one's local constituency, for example, reestablishing ties with local politicians or media.

fence, on the straddling either side of an issue; being unwilling or unable to decide one way or another.

figurehead one who appears to be in power but in reality is not.

filibuster a long-winded speech or debate made by a senator in a minority as a last-ditch attempt to alter the opinion of the majority or to delay a vote. Also made to draw public attention to an issue.

fiscal conservative one who advocates placing strong limits on government spending and taxes.

fiscal year the 12-month period for the use of federal funds, beginning October 1.

floor where debating and voting takes place in a legislative chamber.

football, political any issue exploited by a politician for partisan gain.

franking privilege the free use of postal services by senators and representatives.

free market economy an economy that is driven and maintained by the forces of supply and demand and private enterprise rather than the dictates of government.

gag rule a rule that limits the time for debate in a legislative body.

gerrymander the adjusting of representative districts to conform to a voting pattern or favor one party over another.

good soldier a politician willing to put aside his own interests for those of his party.

GOP Grand Old Party; the Republican Party.

graft profiting by political corruption.

grandstanding delivering a speech or making comments specifically designed to elicit cheers and applause from an audience.

grassroots of or having to do with the common people and basic, fundamental issues.

green party a formal political group or affiliation interested in advancing the care and conservation of the environment and also often advocates nonviolence, civil rights, and social justice.

green politics any politics advocating for the protection or conservation of the environment.

groundswell popular support for an issue or a politician.

hack a loyal worker for a political party.

hardball, play to adopt a tough, no-nonsense political stance, with the liberal use of blunt language, threats, and consequences.

hatchetman a politician's associate who makes vicious attacks against the opposite party.

hat in the ring, to throw one's to announce one's candidacy.

hawk one who readily advocates war as a means of solving problems.

henchman a member of a politician's staff; a right-hand man; used pejoratively.

Hill, the Capitol Hill; the legislative branch of the federal government.

hopper the box where proposed bills are placed in a legislative chamber.

impeach to formally charge a politician with wrongdoing while in office.

imperialism expanding a nation's authority by acquiring new territories, exploiting another land's resources, and so on.

incumbent a politician already in office who is running for reelection against a challenger.

independent a nonpartisan politician. Also, a person who votes for a candidate and not for a candidate's party affiliation.

inflation the rising of prices, due to various economic forces.

initiative the proposal of a new statute, amendment, ordinance, etc., by the gathering of signatures of registered voters on a petition by ordinary citizens, to put the issue in front of a legislative body for consideration or to force a popular vote. Also known as a citizen's initiative.

interest group any group, such as the National Rifle Association, that lobbies members of Congress to represent its interests.

intransigent unable to be persuaded; entrenched in one's beliefs; uncompromising.

Iron Curtain term coined by Winston Churchill in 1946 to illustrate the political divide between democratic Western Europe and communist Soviet Union and Eastern Europe.

isolationism the foreign policy of minding one's own business or remaining neutral in international disputes.

joint chiefs of staff the four highest-ranking U.S. military officers: the chiefs of staff of the army, navy, and air force, plus an appointed chairman; they advise the secretary of defense on the nation's military matters.

joint committee a committee of members from both legislative bodies.

joint session a meeting of members of both legislative bodies.

junket a trip taken by a politician at taxpayer expense, ostensibly for research into foreign affairs but often suspected of being more of a free vacation.

kangaroo ticket a ticket in which the candidate for vice president is more popular than the candidate for president.

keynote speech the main address designed to rouse emotions or loyalty at a convention.

kitchen cabinet influential close friends and minor officials who advise the president informally.

knee-jerk liberal a liberal intellectual who thinks only superficially about issues.

laissez-faire the policy of little or no government intervention into economic issues, with the belief that the private sector will take care of itself.

lame duck a politician whose term is nearly over and whose power is subsequently diminished, especially after being freshly defeated by a challenger in an election.

landslide a huge election victory.

leading economic indicators a set of 10 statistics used to predict if the economy will expand or contract in the next year. These include manufacturer's new orders, delivery of new merchandise to vendors, new orders for equipment, new building permits, money supply, manufacturer's average work week, initial jobless claims, the rise or fall of the S&P 500, the spread between long and short interest rates, and consumer confidence.

left wing the part of a political organization advocating reform or overthrow of the established order.

legislation laws passed by a legislative body.

liberal one who advocates government action to protect individual liberties and rights; one who is broadminded.

liberalism a political orientation evolving from the philosophies of Thomas Jefferson and others and characterized by strong support for individual rights and freedoms and the belief that church and state should be kept separate. Liberals tend to favor government social programs, better access to education, stringent environmental protections, and the adoption of universal health care.

litmus test issue an issue that tests a politician's ideology, whether liberal or conservative or something in between.

lobby the attempt to influence an elected official into voting a certain way on important legislation. Also, an organization that does the influencing.

lobbyist one who tries to influence a politician's decision on an upcoming vote.

logrolling voting for a colleague's issue so he will return the favor and vote for yours; backscratching among politicians.

Machiavellian alluding to politics based on cunning and deceit rather than on morals, so-called after Niccolò Machiavelli, a Renaissance political theorist who believed humans were evil by nature and thus best governed as such.

majority leader the head of the majority party in the House or Senate.

managed news government news released to the press to serve its own interests.

mandate a demand by the people to an elected official to carry out some action or to take a certain course of action, such as getting tough on environmental issues.

McCarthyism any kind of investigative probe that compromises one's rights and invades one's privacy unjustly.

minority leader the head of the minority party in the House or Senate.

moderate one who takes a middle-of-the-road position on an issue.

mollycoddle to pamper or spoil constituents at taxpayer expense, for example, to vote for every welfare program that is proposed.

mossback one strongly opposed to progress and change.

mouthpiece a politician's spokesperson.

muckraker a journalist who works to expose government corruption and incompetence.

mudslinging the trading of insults and unsubstantiated charges between politicians; a smear campaign.

mugwump one who frequently votes the opposite of his party's wishes.

nonpartisan neutral; not favoring any one party; irrelevant to party ideology.

old guard nickname for conservative Republicans.

oligarchy a government run by a few individuals, such as one run by one family.

ombudsman a government official who investigates citizen complaints against the government and tries to counteract its bureaucracy.

Oval Office the office of the president.

pacifist a peace lover.

pairing an agreement between two politicians not to appear at an upcoming vote since their votes would cancel each other out.

palace guard the president's closest circle of advisers and friends; used pejoratively.

paper tiger a nation that flaunts a degree of power it does not have. Also, any danger that has been exaggerated or blown out of proportion.

partisan of a particular party's principles and beliefs; favoring or supporting any one party.

party a large political group with specific beliefs, goals, and guiding principles, such as the Republican Party or the Democratic Party.

party line the ideology, policies, and philosophy of a political organization.

pecking order a hierarchy; the chain of command from top to bottom.

Pentagonese abstruse military jargon.

perks the fringe benefits and special privileges accrued to politicians and people in power.

platform a set of promises and goals to accomplish adopted by a candidate for office.

playing politics working more for the good of one's party than for the public interest.

play in Peoria the question "How will it play in Peoria?" refers to the reaction and acceptance of an issue or idea from America's heartland.

plum, political an appointed office or position with good pay for little or no work.

point of order in a legislative meeting, an objection that a rule of order is not being followed correctly.

politico a politician or one who is active in politics.

pork barrel the federal or state treasury from which a share of funds are taken by politicians for local projects.

presidential succession the political officials who move up in power in case something befalls the president in office. Specifically, the line of power is passed from the president to the vice president, followed by the speaker of the House, the president pro tempore of the Senate, the secretary of state, and the secretary of the treasury.

president of the Senate the vice president serves as the president of the Senate, but rarely presides. See PRESIDENT PRO TEMPORE.

president pro tempore a senator chosen to take the place of the vice president as president of the Senate.

pressure group any organization that seeks to influence politicians through a variety of means.

primary an election of candidates for an upcoming general election.

progressive tax a tax based on a citizen's ability to pay. See REGRESSIVE TAX.

protectionist one who advocates protecting American jobs and products by charging steep tariffs on competing imports.

psephology the study of elections and voting patterns.

pump priming using federal money to provide momentum for a sagging economy.

pundit a columnist or broadcaster educated in politics and serving as an analyst or observer.

puppet a politician controlled or manipulated by others.

puppet government a nation controlled by the government of another nation.

purge to eliminate, either through violent or nonviolent means, opposition in a party or government.

quorum the minimum number of members of a legislative body who must be in attendance before official business can be conducted.

radical one who strongly advocates change in government.

radicalism the belief in, advocacy for, or acting out of any extreme or revolutionary ideals.

reactionary one who favors returning to the politics and policies of the past.

Reaganomics economic policies promoted by former president Ronald Reagan. They included a reduction of government spending and taxes, reduced regulations for business, and a limiting of inflation by the control of the money supply.

recession a period of prolonged economic downturn, usually lasting from one to two years and marked by falling manufacturing, employment, and sales of goods. Recessions are handled in different ways by politicians, often with tax cuts by Republicans and increased government spending to stimulate employment by the Democrats. Not as severe or prolonged as a depression.

red herring an issue used to distract the public from a more important issue, such as inflation.

referendum a submission to the public of an act, amendment, or statute for a vote.

regressive tax a tax that affects the poor more than the rich.

Republican Party created in 1854, with Abraham Lincoln serving as the first Republican president, the right-leaning major political party of the United States, symbolized by the elephant mascot and most often characterized as pro-business, with ideas such as a loosening of regulations that limit the free market, private charity programs to replace government services, and the shrinking of government with the goal of lower taxes. Republicans also tend to oppose abortion, minimum wages, affirmative action, gay marriage, and any additional gun controls. Also known as the GOP, or Grand Old Party.

rhetoric persuasive debate, argument, speech, or B.S., widely used by politicians.

right wing the part of a political organization opposed to progress and favoring a return to the politics of the past.

roll call vote a vote in which the name of each member of a legislative body is called out and answered with either a "yea" or a "nay."

rubber chicken circuit election campaign touring and speaking at public luncheons and dinners in which the menu offerings are the least important part of the program.

rubber-stamp to give routine approval to a bill or measure.

sacred cow any institution or subject that is considered taboo to criticize or tear down, such as Social Security.

sanctions punitive measures such as restrictions on trade, taken to alter another nation's behavior.

secretary of state the chief foreign policy adviser to the president.

Security Council the U.N. council responsible for maintaining peace and preventing war.

sedition the inciting of a rebellion against the government.

senator a member of the U.S. Senate.

separation of powers in a democracy, a system of checks and balances in which power is divided into branches. In the United States, power is split between the executive branch, the legislative branch, and the judiciary.

sergeant at arms the legislative officer who controls access and maintains order in a legislative chamber.

shoo-in a candidate who is a sure winner in an election.

shuttle diplomacy the shuttling back and forth between capital cities of a diplomat involved in negotiations.

sleeper legislation that has more than the expected effect after being passed. Also, an amendment tacked onto a bill to soften or alter its meaning.

smear campaign an election campaign in which politicians slander one another.

sobriquets affectionate nicknames given to politicians, such as the Father of Our Country, Rough Rider, the Chief.

sovereignty a nation's authority over its own affairs; self-government; independence.

Speaker of the House the Speaker of the House of Representatives, second in the line of succession after the vice president.

spin control the manipulation of the public's perception of a controversy or scandal, through omitting, twisting, or softening of facts.

spin doctor a politician's representative who manipulates the public's perception of a controversy or scandal by omitting, twisting, or softening facts; one who puts something negative in a positive light.

splinter group a dissenting group that splits off from a larger organization.

split ticket a ballot voting for candidates of more than one party.

stagflation a period of economic stagnation with high inflation and unemployment.

statesman a skillful politician who is perceived as exceptionally wise, diplomatic, and above partisan politics.

steering committee an organizing group of legislators who facilitate the passage of bills.

stemwinder a crowd-rousing speaker or speech.

stimulus package a very large spending package legislated by Congress to help revive a flagging economy, by creating work, funding various infrastructure projects, and sometimes also cutting taxes.

straw man a weak opponent or weak argument set up intentionally to be easily vanquished.

straw vote a sample or informal vote or poll taken before an election. Also known as a straw poll.

stump to make speeches in an election campaign.

suffrage the right to vote.

sunset clause a provision in a regulation that expires after a set amount of time and must be voted on to maintain it after the termination date.

supply side economics an economic engine through which growth is spurred by boosting profit motive and by cutting income and capital gains taxes, for the wealthy and big businesses.

swing vote the population of people who vote for a candidate and not necessarily for the candidate's party affiliation.

swing voter one who has the power to decide an election one way or the other.

table a bill to kill a bill or to remove it from consideration.

teller vote a House vote characterized by members passing by tellers who count them as either "for" or "against."

totalitarian authoritarian, highly controlling of the people.

trickle-down economics an economic strategy in which taxes are cut for businesses and the wealthy, thereby, in theory, providing heightened profit incentive, which in turn results in expansion of new business and the creation of more jobs for the middle and lower classes.

trickle-down theory the economic theory that giving aid to corporations, for example, in the form of tax breaks or other benefits, results in a trickling down of benefits for employees and other citizens, ultimately resulting in stimulating the economy.

two-party system a political system having only two major parties, as in the United States.

unilateralism the use of military force without the assistance of other nations.

USA PATRIOT Act acronym for Uniting and Strengthening America by Providing Appropriate Tools Required to Intercept and Obstruct Terrorism, a bill signed into law in 2001 in response to the 9/11 terrorist attacks to broaden the powers of law enforcement to conduct surveillance and searches, to tap phone lines, to inspect e-mails and financial records, and to detain foreign suspects on U.S. soil.

veto a president's objection to a bill in which the bill is returned unsigned to a legislature.

voice vote a vote in which all in favor say "yea" and all opposed say "no" or "nay."

vox populi Latin term for "voice of the people," a belief that the people as a whole have the ability to make the best political decisions.

waffle to hedge; to be wishy-washy and uncommitted to an opinion; to use weasel words.

Ways and Means Committee the tax-writing and other revenue-raising committee of the House of Representatives that oversees Social Security, Medicare, and unemployment benefits. All new tax bills must pass through this committee.

weasel words ambiguous or unclear language used by politicians.

welfare state a government that provides an economic safety net (welfare) to its citizens.

whip the assistant to the leader of a party in the House or Senate.

witch-hunt a hysterical investigation with rampant finger-pointing and blame-casting.

write-in on a ballot, the writing in of a candidate's name by a voter.

Government Forms, Systems, and Philosophies

anarchy the complete absence of a governing force.

aristocracy a governing body composed of people born of upper-class parentage, with power handed down from generation to generation.

autarchy absolute power or sovereignty; a country under such rule.

autocracy a government or nation ruled by one powerful person, as a dictator.

autonomy independence from outside influence or rule.

Bill of Rights the first 10 amendments to the U.S. Constitution, which guarantee, among other rights, the freedom of religious worship, of the press, and of assembly, and the rights to petition the government and to keep and bear arms.

capitalism an economic system based on free enterprise, in which property, companies, shops, etc., are privately owned and products and services are produced for profit.

collective any operation or governing system controlled by all the workers involved.

collectivism ownership and control of an operation or governing system by the people involved in it.

colonialism the governing or control of a dependency by a governing nation.

common law collective term for all the customary laws and principles handed down in society through the generations.

commonwealth a state or nation governed by its people.

communism a single-party ruling system in which the government restricts private property and controls the economic production and distribution of goods and services, which are equally shared among the people.

conservatism a political philosophy or platform characterized by a belief in traditional policies and values.

constitution a collection of written laws and principles used as a guide for government.

Constitution, U.S. the fundamental guiding laws and principles, including the Bill of Rights, or the document on which these are recorded, of the United States.

constitutional government any government employing the guiding principles of a constitution.

democracy a government run for and by the people through the power of their votes.

despotism a government in which one person has absolute power.

dictator one with absolute power; a despot.

dynasty rule handed down to family members from generation to generation.

egalitarianism a philosophy or system of equal rights for everyone.

fascism a form of government headed by a dictator, and often characterized by racist attitudes, an aggressive use of military and police forces, and a strong suppression of any socialist or democratic opposition.

federalism a system of government in which power is shared between a nation and its states.

feudalism a European system in effect from the ninth to the 15th century in which property owned by a lord was tended by vassals, who were required to pay dues and to serve in the military.

kingdom a territory ruled by a king.

liberalism a political belief system characterized by openness to change and progress and the granting of government aid to those deemed underprivileged or in need.

libertarian one who advocates free thought and action.

matriarchy a governing body ruled by one or more females.

meritocracy any group of leaders selected to office for their high IQs, achievements, or special abilities.

monarchy a government headed by a leader who inherits the position and remains in power for life, such as a king or an empress.

municipal referring to a local political unit, such as a city.

nationalism devotion to one's own nation and its independence from others.

Nazism totalitarian system or ideology of Adolf Hitler's National Socialist German Workers Party, characterized by expansionist goals, zealous nationalism, and notions of racial supremacy.

oligarchy government by a small group of people, such as a family.

Parliament the national legislature, composed of the House of Commons and the House of Lords, and an elected prime minister, of Great Britain.

patriarchy a governing body ruled by one or more males.

plutocracy a government composed of wealthy individuals.

police state a state in which the government represses citizens and any political opposition through a secret national police force.

principality any territory ruled by a prince.

puppet government a false government installed and controlled by another.

regency in a monarchy, one who is appointed to lead in place of another who is disabled or deemed too young for the position. Also the period during which the substitute rules.

republic any nation headed by a president and representatives elected to office by citizens.

socialism a social system based on collectivism.

sovereignty self-rule and independence.

technocracy a governing body headed by technical experts.

theocracy a governing body headed by religious leaders.

totalitarianism a system of absolute control by a single group, party, or dictator.

tyranny an oppressive system in which one person is given absolute power.

welfare state a system in which the state takes responsibility for citizen education, employment, health care, and retirement needs.

International Relations

accord agreement or harmony between two nations.

alien one from another country; a nonnative or noncitizen.

alliance a joining of forces between two or more nations for economic or military reasons.

ally a friendly nation associated with another for a common cause.

ambassador the highest-ranking diplomatic official of a nation.

annex to acquire and incorporate a territory into a state.

asylum government's formal protection from extradition granted to a refugee.

attaché a diplomatic official or staff member of an ambassador.

axis of evil term coined by former president George W. Bush, in describing Iran, Iraq, and North Korea, in 2002.

balkanize to divide a territory into small political units, especially ones that may become antagonistic or hostile toward one another, so-named after the formation of the Balkan states (Yugoslavia, Albania, etc.) after World War I.

banana republic any small, Latin American country having a shaky political foundation and a limited economy, often based on a single crop controlled by foreign interests.

bilateralism agreement of two nations to work together for the common good.

bloc a group of legislators or nations working together for a common cause.

blowback CIA term for any revenge action inflicted on a civilian population of a government that secretly attacked a terrorist group or rogue nation.

Bush Doctrine a state philosophy held by former president George W. Bush that countries that sponsor or harbor terrorists should be dealt with on a par with the terrorists themselves.

cartel an alliance of international politicians or corporate officials formed in order to control production, pricing, etc., in order to monopolize or at least dominate a business, such as oil.

chancellery the office, building, or the staff of an embassy or consulate.

chancellor the head secretary of an embassy. In some European countries, the prime minister.

chargé d'affaires a diplomatic officer filling in for an ambassador or carrying out a low-level task.

cold war a nonphysical war in which hostilities and political tensions are greatly heightened between two or more nations; originally named after the strained relations and economic competition between the United States and the Soviet Union following World War II.

consul a diplomatic official assigned to take up foreign residence and who acts as a representative for citizens and businesses from his own country.

consulate the residence or office of a consul.

consul general highest-ranking consul in charge of all other consuls in a foreign nation.

convention an agreement between nations.

covenant a legal agreement.

delegate one appointed to act as a representative.

détente a relaxation of hostilities and tensions between nations; a period of warming relations.

diplomacy the art of international relations, encompassing skills for defusing tensions, forging alliances, and negotiating compromises.

diplomat government's representative in a foreign nation, particularly one who is highly skilled in defusing tensions, forging alliances, and negotiating compromises.

diplomatic corps the diplomatic staff residing in a foreign country.

diplomatic immunity government-sanctioned exemption from taxation and legal prosecution granted to a diplomat residing in a foreign nation.

domino theory the theory that if a form of objectionable government, such as communism, is left unchecked, it will eventually spread to neighboring states.

Egyptian Islamic Jihad a terrorist group now allied with al-Qaeda that works to overthrow the Egyptian government and replace it with an Islamic state.

embargo the government-ordered prohibition of trade with another nation, concerning either a single commodity or many.

embassy the office building and personnel of an ambassador.

emigrant one who leaves his native land to take up residence in a foreign country.

émigré one who has abandoned his own country and taken up residence in another, particularly for political reasons.

emissary a representative or agent on a mission.

entente an agreement between nations stipulating mutual cooperation and action.

envoy a diplomatic representative, sometimes acting as a messenger, sent on a specific mission.

exile the voluntary or forced emigration of a citizen due to political differences. Also, the period of time spent out of one's country for this.

expatriation the removal of oneself from one's homeland, due to political differences.

extradition the surrender and delivery of a foreign criminal to the authorities in his homeland.

foreign policy a government's philosophy and program for dealing politically with another nation.

free trade trade between nations that is unrestricted by tariffs, quotas, etc.

GATT General Agreement on Tariffs and Trade; an international agreement to facilitate international trade.

General Assembly governing body of the United Nations, made up of all the representatives from member nations.

Geneva Conventions international treaties signed from 1864 to 1949, in Geneva, Switzerland, requiring combatants in war to treat civilians and prisoners of war humanely.

glasnost Soviet movement of the 1980s to open itself to greater political criticism and heightened influence from the West.

Hamas literally, Islamic Resistance Movement, a Palestinian militant organization whose goal has been to establish an Islamic state in Palestine and has been involved in suicide bombings and rocket attacks to that end.

Hezbollah a Shiite Muslim political group with a militant wing that the United States defines as terrorist. Active in Lebanon, it is a major provider of social services.

immigrant one who takes up residence in another nation, leaving behind his homeland.

immigration the entry of foreigners who have left their homeland to take up residence in another country.

imperialism the practice of government expansion into other territories or countries, by force or through economic or political domination.

insurgents terrorist forces who travel from their home countries or bases to fight in a war in another country, to further their cause.

International Court of Justice the world court of the United Nations that judiciates international disputes.

International Monetary Fund a specialized agency of the United Nations that promotes international trade and currency stabilization.

Iron Curtain metaphor for the political and ideological divide between the Soviet Union and the West from 1945 to 1990.

isolationism a philosophy or practice of noninteraction with other nations, either politically or economically.

jihad an Islamic term with varied meanings, including "struggle," but also, broadly, holy war.

League of Nations an international peacekeeping organization formed after World War I; it dissolved in 1946, following World War II.

legate an emissary of the pope.

minister a diplomatic representative ranking second to an ambassador.

Monroe Doctrine U.S. militarily enforced policy of closing off the unsettled portions of North and South America in 1823 to any colonization attempts by Europe.

most favored nation a country granted normal status by the United States, thereby allowing the same advantageous trade rights and privileges in trading with the U.S. as granted to other preferred countries. Also, most-favored-nation, as an adjective; of or relating to this status.

NAFTA North American Free Trade Agreement; agreement signed in 1994 to relax trade restrictions and eliminate tariffs between the United States, Canada, and Mexico.

NATO North Atlantic Treaty Organization; a military alliance formed in 1949 with the United States and several European nations to provide mutual protection against outside aggression, particularly from the Soviet Union, now having 19 member nations working together in peacekeeping and defense missions.

naturalization the process or certification of becoming a legal citizen of a foreign country.

nonaligned nation any nation that is not an ally of any superpower nation.

OPEC Organization of Petroleum Exporting Countries; an alliance of oil-producing nations that works to set production limits, prices, etc., of petroleum.

plenipotentiary any diplomat who may rank below ambassador but may be, nevertheless, vested with complete authority.

protocol diplomatic rules of etiquette, ceremony, and procedure.

al-Qaeda a worldwide ring of militant Islamic organizations working together to undermine Western influence in the Middle East, best known for its attack of the United States on September 11, 2001, when jet aircraft were hijacked and rammed into the twin towers of the World Trade Center in New York City and the Pentagon outside Washington, D.C.

refugee one fleeing from his homeland to another country, due to economic or political strife, or war.

rogue nation any country that sponsors terrorism and has weapons of mass destruction.

saber rattling the subtle threatening of one nation toward another nation through a show of force or demonstration of power.

sanction a penalty levied on a nation that has violated international law.

secretary-general an executive officer of the United Nations.

secretary of state the head of U.S. foreign affairs.

Security Council peacekeeping council of the United Nations, with members who are frequently rotated.

shuttle diplomacy diplomacy conducted by an official traveling back and forth between nations.

sovereignty self-government; independence from the rule of another nation.

State Department the U.S. office of foreign affairs.

statesman a politician with broad, international appeal and respect who is called on to handle delicate foreign affairs.

state terrorism any terrorist acts conducted or sponsored by a government.

suicide bomber one who straps bombs to himself or herself and blows up a group of people or a building, such as a government facility, to further a militant cause.

summit an international conference of the highest-ranking government officials.

superpower any nation with exceptional political, economic, and military clout.

Taliban a radical Islamic group that ruled Afghanistan from 1996 to 2001 and, after removal by military forces, continued to disrupt the new Afghan government and additionally worked to take over a portion of Pakistan, specifically the Swat Valley, in 2009. The group is most notorious for implementing a severe form of sharia, law that forbids women from being educated and, among other proscriptions, bans television, movies, dancing, kite flying, and beard trimming.

tariff a government-imposed tax on an imported good.

territorial waters waters falling within a state's jurisdiction, specifically within 3 miles, or 4.8 kilometers, from shore.

third world the poor or developing nations of Asia, Africa, and Central and South America.

trade balance an equal or near-equal ratio between nations of imports to exports.

treaty a legal agreement between two nations, usually concerning the maintenance of peace and trade.

United Nations an international organization formed after World War II to seek peaceful solutions to conflicts and to facilitate trade, cultural, and humanitarian exchanges between nations.

Warsaw Pact also known as the Warsaw Treaty Organization, an alliance formed by Albania, Bulgaria, Czechoslovakia, East Germany, Hungary, Poland, Romania, and the Soviet Union in 1955 for mutual protection against NATO and democratic expansion, dissolved in 1991.

PUBLISHING AND JOURNALISM

Afghanistanism journalist's term for the avoiding of local controversy by focusing news coverage on distant lands.

allege one of the most frequently used hedge words of journalists who wish to avoid being sued for libel. See LINDLEY RULE.

angle a story's point of view or perspective.

AP Associated Press.

blacksmith an uninspired but industrious reporter who simply pounds out stories day after day.

blue-pencil to edit; to make corrections in a manuscript.

bogus fillers or stock features to be replaced by hard news in a later edition of a daily newspaper.

boil down to condense a story.

bootjacking the hawking of newspapers on the street. **break** where a newspaper story stops on one page to be continued on another page.

bright a brief, light human-interest story.

bulldog the early edition of a daily newspaper, usually printed the night before.

bullpup the first edition of a Sunday newspaper, a portion of which may be printed well before Sunday.

bury a story to place a story on an inner page of a newspaper.

byline the reporter's name, which appears above the beginning of a story.

canned copy press releases, publicity releases, features from syndicates—any prewritten material. Also known as A-copy or handouts.

circulation the average number of copies of a newspaper or magazine sold in a given period.

city editor the newspaper editor who covers city news; he or she works in the city room.

clean highly polished and needing little or no editing.

cold dope statistics.

colored story a biased or slanted piece of reporting.

comma chaser slang for a copy editor.

copy any written or illustrated material to be printed.

copyboy/copygirl one who runs errands; a gofer in a newsroom.

copy editor the editor who checks for style, grammar, and other errors, and makes corrections in manuscripts for the printer.

correspondent a reporter who sends in news stories from remote locations.

crusade a journalist's dedicated effort to expose some wrongdoing, such as government corruption.

cub a new, inexperienced reporter.

date file a file of important anniversaries, holidays, and upcoming events to be covered.

dateline at the beginning of a newspaper story, the line indicating the story's point of origin. Formerly, the dateline included the date.

deadline the day or time a story must be submitted for publication.

dirty heavily edited and marked.

editorial a personal opinion column. Also, all written copy other than advertising.

editorializing a reporter's insertion of a personal viewpoint in a story.

fair comment the legal right of a reporter to report the facts of a story as he or she understands them to be as long as the facts are presented fairly and without malice.

feature a large article or story, usually of human interest and not necessarily newsworthy.

filler short, stock items, used to fill space in a newspaper or magazine.

five W's the five questions that must be answered in every news story—who? what? where? when? and why?

Fleet Street the London press.

fluff a trite story or article.

freelance writer a nonstaff reporter who submits assigned or unassigned (unsolicited) stories to a newspaper or magazine.

gonzo journalism journalism style given a free rein; wild, outrageous reporting from a personal viewpoint, as that of Hunter Thompson.

hack any writer or reporter more concerned with making a buck than creating fine writing.

handout a press release.

hedge word any word used by a journalist as protection from a libel suit, as in, "alleged," "reportedly," "reputed."

investigative journalism reporting in which several interviews are conducted along with exhaustive research.

John Garfield still dead story any rehashing of old news.

keyhole journalism unethical journalism that ignores people's right to privacy; gossip news.

kill to cancel a story.

leader a newspaper's lead story.

leg man a reporter who travels to the scene of news and phones in a story to the rewrite editor.

libel any published, false accusation; an untrue, defamatory statement.

Lindley rule a rule to be followed when using nonattributable material, such as sensitive material, by which vague phrases such as "according to official sources" are used. Also known as deep background.

managed news a government-controlled release of news. A government news release in its own interest.

morgue the reference files or reference room of a newspaper.

mouthpiece a publicist or public relations officer; a press secretary.

muckraker a journalist who exposes corruption.

op-ed a newspaper page usually located opposite the editorial page and devoted to opinion columns.

over the transom of unsolicited copy, received through the mail from freelance writers.

peg the main point or thrust of a story.

photojournalism telling a story with photographs.

press agent a publicity agent.

press gallery a reserved area in a government or other building for use by the press.

press kit publicity material, such as information and photos, handed out or mailed to reporters and newspapers on behalf of a corporation, organization, or movie star.

press pass a card confirming affiliation with a newspaper or magazine and used to gain free admission to a specific event.

press release a handout of a suggested article provided by corporations, universities, other institutions, and press agents to gain publicity.

privileged communication the legal right of journalists to keep the names of their sources confidential. See SHIELD LAW.

puff a trite publicity piece.

put to bed to make the final preparations for printing.

rag nickname for a newspaper with a poor reputation.

railroad to hurry a story from writing to composing with no editing in between.

retraction a correction noting inaccurate reporting in a previous edition.

rewrite editor an editor who rewrites stories called in over the phone or who rewords press releases.

sacred cow a person or institution favored by members of the press and that they hesitate to criticize or investigate for a story.

scoop to learn of a story and publish it before the competition. Also, the story itself.

shield law the law that protects reporters from revealing their sources.

silly season a slow news period characterized by trivial news or no news.

skinny inside information.

slant the perspective or point of view of a story.

slush unsolicited manuscripts from freelancers.

spike to kill a story. Also a story held for later use.

spot news current news.

squib a short news item.

staffer a staff reporter, as distinguished from a freelance reporter.

state editor the editor at a large newspaper in charge of state news.

stringer a part-time freelancer who sends in stories from remote locations.

tabloid a half-sized newspaper characterized by sensational stories and photographs.

think piece an editorial or analysis of the news.

UPI United Press International.

vignette a very brief news item.

wire editor the editor in charge of news received from the Associated Press and other wire services.

wire service a news service, for example the Associated Press or United Press International.

yellow journalism journalism that is irresponsible, sensational, and exploitive.

Book Publishing

academic press a small press or university press specializing in scholarly books.

acknowledgments the author's thanks to interview subjects, research assistants, family members or colleagues, and others who aided in the writing and production of the book.

acquisitions editor at a publishing house, an editor in charge of purchasing manuscripts for publishing into books.

adaptation a novel converted to a screenplay, or vice versa.

addendum new or additional material added to a book after its initial publication.

advance an amount of money paid by a publisher to an author up front (in advance of publication), usually based on a minimum projection of sales.

anthology a book of short stories or other selected writings by one or more authors.

appendix supplementary information printed at the back of a book, usually before the index.

auction the bidding for the purchase of a valuable author's book by several publishers.

audio book a book recorded on tape, sometimes as read aloud by the author.

authorized biography a biography written with the permission and cooperation of the subject, as distinguished from an unauthorized biography.

autobiography a biography written by oneself.

backlist a term referring to a publisher's books that have been in print for a significant amount of time yet continue to sell well, such as classics or reference books.

belles lettres literary works appreciated for their aesthetic value rather than their educational content, such as poetry or drama.

bibliography a list of books to read for additional information, printed at the back of a book before the index.

biography a person's life story, written by another.

blockbuster a hugely successful book.

blue pencil a reference to an editor's corrections on a manuscript page, originally performed in blue pencil.

blurb a glowing review or testimonial from a noted person on a book's jacket.

bodice ripper a form of romance novel in which the courtship gets rough.

book producer a company or individual who provides a range of services for publishers, from hiring writers and artists for specific jobs, to performing various design and editing tasks, to arranging printing. Also known as a book packager.

brand-name author an author who writes consistently successful and popular books.

breakout book a novel of exceptional size, scope, or content, written by an experienced author with previously unspectacular sales but that a publisher believes in and promotes heavily in order to make the author a household name.

chapbook a small booklet or paperback containing poems or ballads.

coffee-table book a large, illustrated book, purchased primarily for its pictures.

colophon a publisher's logo, usually printed on the spine of a book.

commercial fiction popular fiction that can be counted on to generate large sales.

copyediting the final editing and correcting of stylistic and grammatical errors in a manuscript.

copyright the legal right of ownership of a piece of written material, such as a book.

cyberpunk a subcategory of science fiction featuring high technology and violent themes.

dedication author's tribute to a loved one or other important person at the beginning of a book.

desktop publishing publishing carried out in a home office, with ordinary word-processing equipment.

Edgar an award presented by the Mystery Writers of America for best mystery novel of the year.

e-book an electronic book, sold over the Internet or in a bookstore, for reading in an electronic device.

epic a larger-than-life story of a legendary hero.

epilogue a closing note sometimes used to tie up loose ends, illuminate a point, or hint at the future, following the main body of a book.

escalator a bonus paid by a publisher to an author when a book attains specified goals, such as 100,000 sales or appearance on the New York Times bestseller list.

flap copy description, blurbs, author's capsule biography, or other copy found on a book's flaps.

flyleaf a blank page at the front or back of a book.

footnote a supplementary note printed in small type at the foot of a page.

foreword an introductory piece preceding the main body of a book.

formula novel a novel that features a proven plotline, such as boy meets girl, boy loses girl, boy wins girls back, to elicit reader interest.

frontispiece an illustration preceding the title page of a book.

frontlist a publisher's newest releases.

genre kind, type, or category of book—western, science fiction, romance, and so on.

ghostwriter a writer who writes a book for someone else, who may or may not give credit to the real author.

glossary a list of definitions of words encountered in a book.

Golden Spur an award presented by the Western Writers of America for best western novel of the year.

gothic horror a horror novel that takes place in an old mansion or castle.

gothic romance a romance novel that centers on a naive girl or woman victimized by an evil man and courted by a heroic man, all taking place in or around an old mansion or castle.

hack a writer who churns out books quickly and is concerned more with making a buck than producing fine art.

hardcover a book printed with a hardback cover as opposed to a paper one.

hard SF hard science fiction; a science fiction novel emphasizing technology.

historical romance a romance novel featuring a story that takes places in the past.

imprint a division with its own distinctive line of books, that may be only one of many different imprints of a publishing company.

index a directory located at the back of a book of terms, names, etc., arranged alphabetically with page numbers, for quick location in the text.

instant book a book published quickly in order to take advantage of some timely event. Also known as a quickie.

interactive fiction a novel, usually for children, that offers several plot alternatives for the reader to choose.

International Standard Book Number (ISBN) an internationally recognized identification number printed on the back of a book. The ISBN includes an item number and a code identifying the country of origin and publisher.

literary agent one who represents authors in the sale of rights to their books.

literary book an avant-garde, experimental, or highly styled novel that usually has limited sales; a noncommercial book featuring a high degree of writing skill.

literati those with great knowledge concerning literature.

magnum opus an author's masterpiece.

managed text a textbook whose writing is supervised by a professor.

manuscript a book in typewritten form, as submitted by an author to a publisher.

mass-market paperback a rack-size, commercial paperback sold in magazine outlets as well as bookstores.

midlist books expected to have only moderate sales appeal.

monograph a small, scholarly book on a single subject.

Nebula an award presented by the Science Fiction Writers of America for best science fiction novel or story of the year.

New Age collective term for a category of books that includes metaphysical, spiritual, holistic, astrology, mysticism, and faith healing interests.

Nobel Prize in literature prestigious annual award composed of a gold medal and a large cash prize given to the author of an outstanding body of work, as originally endowed by Alfred Nobel.

novelization the writing of a novel based on a movie or TV script.

novella a short novel, from 7,000 to 15,000 words. Also known as a novelette.

omnibus a collection of works by a single author or on the same theme.

option the right retained by a publisher to publish an author's next book.

O.S.S. obligatory sex scene, as found in many commercial novels.

out of print referring to a book that is no longer published or sold.

overrun a surplus of printed books. A printing of books that exceeds the demand.

over the transom of an unsolicited manuscript, sent to a publisher by a freelance writer or a freelance writer's agent.

pen name a fictitious name used by an author who wishes to remain anonymous. A pseudonym; nom de plume.

piracy the illegal use or republishing of another's copyrighted material without permission.

plagiarism using the writing of another author and trying to pass it off as one's own.

point of view the perspective a story is written from, as from a single lead character, or several characters, or from the author.

police procedural a mystery or crime drama featuring methods of police investigation.

preface an introductory text preceding the main body of a book.

prequel a novel that details a preceding storyline to a novel previously published.

proofreader a freelance or staff reader who checks manuscripts or typeset pages for errors.

proposal an author's presentation of a new book idea to a publisher, usually composed of three sample chapters, and other sales material.

pseudonym a pen name.

public domain material that has no copyright protection and can be freely reprinted without permission.

publicist on the staff of a publisher, one who publicizes a newly released book to various media outlets.

Pulitzer Prize prestigious annual award granted to the authors of outstanding works of American fiction, drama, poetry, biography, autobiography, history, nonfiction, and journalism, originating with an endowment made by Joseph Pulitzer to Columbia University in 1917.

pulp fiction poor-quality novels that were once printed on cheap, pulp paper.

purple prose flowery or overly ornate writing; the excessive use of adjectives and adverbs, a weakness of inexperienced writers.

remainder an overstocked book sold at a low price.

reprint a hardcover book republished in a paperback format.

revision a rewrite of a manuscript, or previously published book, to add or delete information, correct copy, etc.

roman à clef a novel depicting actual events and real people given fictional names.

roman-fleuve a very long novel, sometimes published in several volumes, that follows multiple generations of a family or group.

royalties a percentage of a book's profit paid to the author by the publisher after a certain number of books have been sold and the author's advance has earned out.

saga a long novel following multiple generations of a family or group.

self-publishing the publishing of a book by an individual as opposed to a publishing company.

sequel a novel published as a follow-up to an earlier novel. **serial** a long story published in separate installments.

serial rights rights purchased by a magazine or newspaper to publish excerpts from a book.

SF science fiction.

sidebar a block of text set off from the main text to highlight a peripheral subject or interesting tidbit.

signature the folded and printed sheets ready for binding.

slush pile stacks of unsolicited manuscripts that pile up at publishing houses.

small press a small publisher that issues a select number of books each year, usually with limited distribution and negligible payment for the authors.

space opera a science fiction adventure similar to Star Wars.

Stoker Award award given by the Horror Writers of America for best horror novel.

stream of consciousness an author's presentation of the thoughts and feelings of a character or characters.

subplot a secondary storyline to a more important plot or storyline.

subsidiary rights individual book rights sold for foreign and translation sales, motion picture and television sales, serialization sales, electronic and audio editions, etc.

subtext in a story, the meaning between the lines.

sword and sorcery a fantasy novel featuring a mythical past with warriors, witches, warlocks, elves, magic, and suchlike.

synopsis a brief description of a novel.

thriller any mainstream novel filled with high danger and adventure and white-knuckle suspense.

tie-in a novelization of a motion picture or television show.

tour de force a masterful work by an author.

trade book a commercial hardcover book intended for a general audience, as distinguished from a college textbook.

trade paperback same as a trade book, but in paperback format.

trilogy a story published in three volumes.

trim size the dimensions of a book.

unabridged containing the complete information or text; not condensed.

unauthorized biography a biography written without the cooperation of the subject.

vanity press a publisher who publishes books that are paid for by their authors.

verisimilitude realism or the appearance of realism in fiction; a skillful quality of truth in description, characterization, etc.

voice an author's own distinctive writing style, characterized by choice of vocabulary, tone, point of view, richness or starkness in description, etc.

whodunit popular colloquialism for a mystery.

writer's block psychological problem in which an author is unable to write, due to loss of confidence in one's abilities, lack of inspiration, general procrastination, etc.

YA abbreviation for young adult books.

Book Sizes

atlas folio a book that measures 25 by 50 inches.

double elephant folio any book that measures 50 inches tall or taller.

duo decimo any book that measures 5 by 7¼ inches.

elephant folio any book that measures 23 by 25 inches.

folio any book that measures 12 by 19 inches.

imperial octavo any book that measures 8¼ by 11½ inches.

medium octavo any book that measures 6 by 9¼ inches.

octodecimo any book that measures 4 by 6½ inches.

quadragesimo-octavo any book that measures 2½ by 4 inches.

royal octavo any book that measures 6½ by 10 inches.

sexodecimo any book that measures 4 by 7½ inches.

super octavo any book that measures 7 by 11 inches.

Book Terms

back matter see END MATTER.

biblia abiblia worthless books or literature.

bibliobibuli people who read too much and who have little or no other interests.

biblioclasm the burning or destruction of books.

biblioclast one who burns or destroys books.

bibliogony the production of books.

biblioklept one who steals books.

bibliomancy divination by books.

bibliomania a passion for collecting books.

bibliopegy bookbinding as an art.

bibliophagist a devourer of books.

bibliophile one who loves books.

bibliophobia a fear of books.

bibliopoesy the making of books.

bibliopole a bookseller.

bibliotaph one who hides or hoards books.

bibliotheca library.

boards on a hardcover book, the front and back covers.

body matter the central or main text.

dust cover also known as a dust jacket, a protective covering, usually made of glossy paper.

end matter the glossary, the bibliography, and the index. Also known as back matter.

end sheet one sheet making up both the flyleaf and the pastedown.

flyleaf the blank page at the front or back of a book.

fore edge the edge of the pages, opposite the spine, sometimes gilded for fancy books.

front matter coming before the main text, the copyright page, title page, acknowledgments, copyright, dedication, table of contents, foreword, preface, and introduction.

headband a cloth band that protects the spine.

hinge where the covers bend upon opening.

incunabula books printed before A.D. 1500.

joint the groove where the boards are joined and bend upon opening.

tail the bottom of a book.

wrapper the cover on a paperback book.

Footnote Abbreviations

abr. abridged.

anon. anonymous.

app. appendix.

ca. (circa) approximately.

cf. (confer) compare.

col. column.

ed. editor.

e.g. for example.

esp. especially.

et al. and others.

etc. (et cetera) and so forth.

et seq. and the following.

f. and the following page.

ff. and the following pages.

fl. flourished.

ibid. in the same place.

id. the same.

i.e. that is.

inf. below.

loc. cit. in the place cited.

ms. manuscript.

mss. manuscripts.

N.B. take special note of.

n.d. no date.

n.s. new series.

op. cit. in the work cited.

o.s. old series.

p. page.

par. paragraph.

pass. throughout.

pl. plate.

pp. pages.

pt. part.

pub. published, publisher.

q.v. which see.

r. reigned.

repr. reprinted.

ser. series.

sup. above.

suppl. supplement.

s.v. under the word.

trans. translation.

v. see.

vide. see.

viz. namely.

Headline Types

blank a second line of a headline, usually in smaller type.

banner a large headline extending all the way across the top of the front page. Also known as a streamer.

barker similar to a kicker but set in larger type than the headline beneath it.

bikini head a headline illuminating a portion of a story.

binder line an inner-page headline stretching over two or more related stories.

bumping heads abutting headlines.

circus makeup a headline using different kinds or sizes of type to draw attention.

crossline the middle line of a three-section headline.

cutline a caption under a picture.

deadhead a vague, abstract, or lackluster headline. Also known as a flathead or a wooden head.

drophead a headline set underneath a banner, and which refers to the same story.

jump head a shortened or abbreviated headline indicating the continuation of a story from a previous page.

kicker a small-type, teaser line set above the headline. Also known as an eyebrow, highline, teaser.

overline a headline set above a picture.

ribbon a one-line headline set in smaller type than a banner but with a width greater than one column.

rocket head a displayed or bold-type quotation set in the middle of a story.

scarehead any alarmist or sensational headline.

screamer a very large banner headline set in bold print.

second coming type the largest and boldest headline type, reserved for stories on a par with the second coming of Christ. Also known as studhorse type.

skyline head a banner headline set above the masthead, at the very top of the front page. Also known as an over-the-roof head.

stock head a standby headline used when another line or story is killed.

subhead a small headline placed within a story.

tombstones two headlines with similar construction that are set beside one another.

PERFORMING ARTS AND BROADCASTING

DANCE

alegrías Spanish gypsy dance performed by a lone female, with moves reminiscent of those made by a bullfighter.

bamba a Mexican dance in which a sash is thrown on the floor and is tied together by the feet of a dancing couple.

bambuca the national ballroom dance of Colombia.

barn dance any dance social held in a barn or town hall, with various forms of square dancing.

beguine a variation of the rumba, originating in Cuba and Martinique.

belly dance a Middle Eastern dance performed by a solo female, characterized by stomach undulations.

big apple a swing dance with a caller, originating in South Carolina in the 1930s.

black bottom a solo or couples dance succeeding the Charleston in the 1920s, and characterized by a combination of shuffling, stomping, and swaying knees.

bolero a lively Spanish dance in 3?4 time performed with castanets and punctuated with sharp turns and sudden stops.

boogie-woogie an African-American, hip-swaying jazz dance.

booty dancing see FREAK DANCING.

bossa nova a lively, sambalike Brazilian dance for couples.

Boston jive a variation of the lindy hop with kicks.

break dance American dance originating in the 1980s, characterized by spins and acrobatic moves performed solo—often in a prostrate position—on the floor.

bump 1970s American disco dance characterized by dancers bumping hips.

bunny hop congalike dance of the 1950s featuring three hops instead of a kick.

cancan originating in Paris in 1890, a dance performed by women and characterized by high kicking and skirt lifting.

cha-cha a variation of the mambo, characterized by a triplet beat, a quickstep, and a shuffle.

Charleston a lively American dance of the 1920s, made famous by many vaudeville acts.

chipaneca Mexican dance in ¾ time in which the dancers ask the audience to clap hands with them.

choreographer one who designs a series of dance steps and moves, especially for a show.

choreography a planned progression of steps and movements, as designed by a choreographer for a show.

clogging dance of the Blue Ridge Mountains, featuring double time stomping and tap steps in wooden-soled shoes.

conga an African-Cuban dance in 2?4 time, popularized in the 1930s, and characterized by a long chain of dancers performing three successive steps, followed by a kick.

contredanse a French square dance originating in about 1600.

cossack a Russian dance featuring squatting dancers with arms folded.

cotton-eyed Joe a country and western dance in which dancers move around the room and stomp, shuffle, and kick.

fandango a progressively accelerating Spanish dance performed with castanets and snapping fingers, and further characterized by the couples freezing temporarily when the music pauses and then resuming.

faruca a Spanish gypsy dance characterized by double turns, falls, and heel work.

flamenco Spanish gypsy dance characterized by foot stomping and hand-clapping.

fox-trot a couples ballroom dance performed in 2/4 or 4/4 time.

freak dancing slang for any sexually explicit dancing. Also known as booty dancing.

freak train slang for a train of dancers dancing in a sexually explicit manner.

freestyle any invented form of dance, sometimes combining elements from many other dances, as in rock and roll dancing.

galop a lively Hungarian dance featuring glissanding and galloping steps, popular in the 19th century.

hornpipe a lively sailor's dance performed with the music of a hornpipe.

hula a Polynesian dance featuring undulating hips and gestures of the hands and arms to tell a story.

hustle a popular American disco dance of the 1970s.

jacking rapidly rippling the torso back and forth, especially to match the beat of the music, as part of any disco dance.

jitterbug a lively swing dance, a variation of the lindy hop.

jive a fast swing dance combining elements of the lindy hop and jitterbug, noted for its triple step performed on the toes.

juba American slave dance of the 1800s, characterized by hand-clapping and slapping of the knee and thighs.

lambada passionate and sensuous Brazilian couples dance with close body contact, and combining elements of various other Brazilian dances.

limbo West Indies dance in which dancer tries to bend as far back as possible while shuffling under a progressively lowered pole.

lindy hop named after Charles Lindbergh's first crossing of the Atlantic in an airplane, a popular swing dance characterized by its high-flying, acrobatic moves.

locking robotic-like movements through which a dancer freezes or locks and collapses into successive poses and moves.

mambo a Caribbean dance in 4/4 time, resembling the rumba.

minuet a slow and stately dance originating in 17th-century France, featuring groups of dancers performing courtly gestures.

Mexican hat dance a Mexican folk dance featuring a male's dance around a sombrero.

moonwalk a glissanding backwards walk giving the impression of floating on air, made popular by Michael Jackson in the 1980s.

moshing counterculture dance form in which dancers aggressively slam into each other, in a dance area called a "mosh" pit, originating in the 1980s. Also known as slamdancing.

paso doble a Spanish march in which a male dancer moves as a bullfighter and employs his female partner as a "cape."

polka lively Bohemian dance for couples characterized by a hop followed by three short steps.

quadrille a French square dance performed by four couples.

quickstep a quick fox-trot popular in Europe.

rave an all-night dance party.

reel a lively, Scottish folk dance.

rumba a Cuban dance that evolved by mimicking the movements performed in farm labor, such as shoeing a mare, but is now perceived as sexual.

running man modern American dance step reminiscent of someone running in place, originating in the 1990s.

samba a Brazilian dance performed in 4/4 time.

shimmy a shaking of the whole body, originally an African-American dance of the 1880s, now incorporated as an element of freestyle dancing.

swing see JITTERBUG, JIVE, LINDY HOP.

tango Latin American dance performed in 2/4 or 4/4 time, characterized by dips and long, glissading steps.

tarantella a lively and whirling Italian folk dance performed in 6/8 time.

twist a hip-wiggling rock and roll dance originating with Chubby Checker in the 1960s.

two-step a country and western dance with lots of twirls, originating in the 1800s.

vogue posing like a photo model while incorporating other dance forms, such as modern jazz, gymnastics, and yoga, so named after the song and video by Madonna.

BALLET

arabesque a position in which the dancer balances on one leg, the other leg extended backward with straight knee while the arms hold one of various poses.

assemblé a jump in which the dancer thrusts one leg up and then springs off of the other.

attitude grecque an arm position with one arm curving overhead one way and the other arm curving downward toward the legs in the opposite direction.

attitude à terre a leg position in which one foot is pointed sharply to the side while the other leg is bent at the knee and slanted in back with its foot bend over and toes scraping the floor.

baisse lowering the heel or heels to the floor after standing en pointe.

ballerina a female ballet dancer.

ballerina, prima a ballet's leading female dancer.

ballonné a leap beginning and ending with one foot touching the opposite leg at the knee (grand ballonné) or at the ankle (petit ballonné).

barre the bar at hip level that runs along the walls of a ballet dancer's practice room.

barre work classroom practice of balance and movements while the hand rests lightly on the barre.

basque, grand pas de a movement in which the dancer thrusts the front leg forward and springs so that the supporting leg rises as the first leg descends.

battlements, grand throwing one leg up high with knee straight and foot pointed while the body is kept as still as possible.

battlements, tendus sliding out one leg along the floor until the foot is fully pointed and then returning to the starting position.

beat to strike or slap calves together.

bourrée, pas de gliding across the floor on the toes with quick, mincing steps.

cabriole a movement in which the dancer, with one leg raised, springs from the supporting leg and executes a single, double, or triple beat.

cambre bending from the waist in any direction.

chassé sliding the foot out in any direction while keeping the heel flush on the floor.

chat, pas de a movement in which the dancer brings one foot up to the opposite knee or ankle and leaps sideways.

cheval, pas de scraping the ground like a horse with one foot while hopping on the other foot.

choreographer one who creates dances and steps.

choreography the steps and movements of a ballet.

ciseaux, pas de leaping and splitting the legs wide apart to the side or from front to back. Also known as the grand écart.

collé jumping steps in which the legs and feet are held tightly together in the air.

coryphée the rank below a principal dancer and above those in the corps de ballet.

coupée to put down one foot while lifting the other.

course, pas de a succession of running steps.

danseur a male ballet dancer.

danseur, premier the leading male ballet dancer.

défilé, le grand on closing night of a ballet, an onstage parade of all the members of the ballet company.

deux, pas de any dance performed with two people.

divertissement a ballet that shows off the talents of its dancers but does not tell a story.

enlèvement the act of lifting another dancer into the air, who then strikes a pose.

en pointe on the tip of the toe.

entrechat a jump straight up performed with beats and rapid changes of leg position.

fermé a position in which the feet are closed together in opposite directions.

gargouillade a jump in which the legs are brought underneath the dancer, with the feet describing small circles in midair.

glissade sliding or gliding by the soles of the feet. Also known as glisse.

jeté a leap from one foot to the other.

leotard the form-fitting elastic garment worn in dance practice. Also known as tights.

limbering exercises performed to loosen up the body.

mime stylized gestures used to illustrate a passage in a story.

pas step or dance.

pas couru running steps.

pas marché a stylized walk, with the legs swung wider apart than is natural.

piqué stepping sharply onto one toe while keeping the leg straight. Also known as jeté sur la pointe.

pirouette whirling on the toes of one foot.

pistolet throwing the left leg up, then springing with the right and performing a beat followed by a change in leg position, a second beat, and a final leg change before landing with the left leg in the air.

plié a bending of the knee or knees.

pointe a dancer is en pointe when she is standing on the tips of the toes. Also describes the specially blocked shoes used for performing en pointe.

pose placing an extended foot on the ground.

promenade pivoting on the heel.

révoltade a leap in which the dancer appears to jump over his own raised leg.

rolling standing with body weight centered on either the inside or outside of the feet.

rosin a substance used to prevent slipping on the dance floor.

sauté a jump in which the takeoff and landing are in the same position.

sickle foot when the natural line of the leg is curved inward. Also known as serpette.

sissonne a jump made with a landing on one foot with the raised foot touching the supporting leg at the knee or ankle.

soubresaut a jump in which the legs are clung together without a change in position.

soutenu to be performed slowly.

spotting when turning or spinning, leaving the head frozen in the same position until the last possible moment. A spin in which the head follows far behind the body's rotation.

taquete small, quick steps on tiptoes.

temps de pointe steps performed en pointe.

tiroirs, faire les when two lines of dancers cross and recross on the stage while performing the same steps or movements.

toe shoes ballet shoes.

tour en l'air springing straight up and executing a single, double, or triple turn in midair.

tutu the traditional ballet skirt.

variation solo.

JAZZ DANCING

allegro brisk movements.

arabesque balancing on one leg with the other leg raised high to the rear and the arms upraised.

attitude a balancing on one leg with the other leg extended and upraised to the front.

back bend a standing position with the back arched and the arms upraised toward the ceiling.

barre warmup exercises performed in a studio at a horizontal bar.

barrel leap turn a leaping turn made with arms extended.

barrel turn a turn on one foot with arms extended.

battement a leg kick from the hip forward or back.

body roll a roll or flex of the body from the knees and progressing to the thighs, pelvis, torso, and head.

catch step two steps in any direction timed to one and a half counts of the music.

chaine quick turn made in two steps.

chest lift from a supine position, the chest is lifted forward to an upright position.

compass turn a turn on one foot with the other leg extended and making a full circle.

contraction a drawing together of the body.

corkscrew turn an ascending or descending turn starting and ending with the legs crossed.

coupé a brisk exchange of foot position.

dégagé lifting and pointing a fully arched foot.

demi-plié bending halfway at the knees.

en croix describing the shape of a cross.

en dedans circling into the body.

en dehors circling away from the body.

fouetté a sharp movement from one direction to another.

frog position a seated position with the legs pulled up, bent at the knees, and the feet touching each other.

glissade a sliding step.

grand plié bending fully at the knees with heels raised off the floor.

hitch kick a scissors kick performed with toes pointed.

hop leaping off and landing on the same foot.

inverted long jazz arm the arms extended out to the sides with palms facing up.

isolation isolating and moving one body part in contrast to the rest of the body.

jazz hand palm out, hand facing forward with fingers extended.

jazz sissonne a leap starting and ending with the feet placed together.

jazz split a slide and split to the floor ending with one leg fully extended and the other bent at the knee.

knee hinge kneeling and arching or "hinging" the torso backward.

knee slide sliding across the floor on one's knees.

knee turn a turn performed on both knees.

leap turn a two-step turn and jeté.

outside turn a turn on one foot.

pas de bourrée a three-step series in any direction.

passé moving the leg or foot from front to back.

pelvis roll a circling motion of the pelvis.

pirouette a spinning turn performed on one foot.

plié bending at the knees.

plié-relevé position a position in which the knees are flexed and the heels are raised off the floor while the arms are outstretched to the sides.

port de bras the placement or movement of the arms.

promenade a pivot on the ball of the foot.

renversé bending while making a turn.

rond de jambe performing a circling movement with the leg.

sauté any jumping or leaping movement.

seat spin spinning on the seat of one's pants.

side jazz walk a sideways walk with the knees in the demi-plié position.

spiral turn a winding turn.

stag leap a leap during which the front foot is lifted to the knee of the back leg.

sundari Oriental head motions.

swastika a seated position in which one leg is flexed forward and the other flexed back, a configuration resembling a swastika.

tabletop a position in which the torso is bent over and laid out flat parallel to the floor to resemble a tabletop.

tombé letting the body fall forward, back, or to the side onto a leg in the plié position.

tour to turn the body.

triple three steps taken with two counts of the music.

Square Dancing

Alamo style a circle of dancers join hands, with every other dancer facing outward.

all around your left-hand lady a move in which the corners dance around each other right shoulder to right shoulder.

allemande a forearm grasp and a swing through made by the corner dancers.

arky couple either two men or two women.

arm swing grasping another's forearm and swinging around.

around one a designated couple turn their backs to one another and both move behind the nearest person.

bend the line breaking up a line of dancers by having the end dancers move forward and the center dancers move back.

break to release hands.

California twirl a move in which a couple raise joined hands to form an arch, which the lady passes under. Also known as frontier whirl.

call a singing direction for the next dance movement, made by the caller.

caller the person who sings or chants out dance directions.

cast off in a line of couples, the center dancers separate and move forward while the end couples join hands and move back.

centers any dancers inside the square or inside any other formation.

cloverleaf couples in a double line break off from the corners, turn back around, and describe a cloverleaf pattern while trailing couples follow.

courtesy turn a couple joins left hands and wheel counterclockwise.

crisscross one couple divides another couple, who then close and cross trails to exchange places.

curlicue while holding an arch, the gent walks around the lady, who then backs under the arch, so they end up facing opposite directions while still holding hands.

dive through two couples form an arch, which another couple passes under.

Dixie chain with couples in a single file line, the ladies pull through from right to left hands, followed by the gents, ending in a single file.

dosi around facing dancers move forward and pass around each other back to back.

do-si-do to do-si around.

fold one dancer steps forward and turns to face his or her partner.

frontier whirl see CALIFORNIA TWIRL.

gents traditionally, how male dancers are addressed.

grand chain four ladies move in a right-hand star to opposite gents, who courtesy turn them.

grand right and left weaving in and out around other dancers in a circle, the ladies pulling by in one direction while the gents pull by in the other until partners meet.

hash calls freestyle calls—none of which necessarily rhyme—made spontaneously by the caller. Also known as patter.

hinge the couple turn to face each other, step forward, and join right hands.

hoedown a square dance; also, music traditionally played at a square dance.

honor a call to bow to your partner.

Indian style single file.

look her in the eye a call to face your partner.

make an arch a call for two dancers to join and raise hands overhead to create an arch.

ocean wave four dancers facing in alternate directions form a line and join hands palm to palm at shoulder height; each dancer then takes a step forward and a step back for an undulating effect.

pack saddle star a star in which four dancers form a hub by grabbing each other's wrists.

pass through facing couples pass through one another and end up back to back.

patter see HASH CALLS.

peel off each dancer in a couple separates and turns back while the trailing couple squeezes between them, separates, and turns back to end up in a line facing the opposite direction.

pigeon wing clasping hands with the elbows pointed up.

promenade with hands crossed, right to right, left to left, with gents' palms facing up, couples follow each other in a circle counterclockwise.

promenade wrong way a promenade danced clockwise.

pull-by two people lightly clasp hands and swing each other through a line or formation.

rock it taking a short step forward and tapping the other foot then stepping back and tapping the other foot. Also known as balance.

sashay (chassé) a couple standing side by side move out of line and sidestep past one another.

set a square.

singing calls predetermined calls that are sung to the music, as distinguished from hash calls.

skirt work the ladies flaring their skirts to the sides.

spread it wide a call to change a hold around the waist to an outstretched handclasp position.

square the square formed by four couples.

square your sets a call to dancers to come onto the floor and form squares.

star dancers touch hands at shoulder height to form a hub, which they circle around. In singles, to grasp hands at shoulder height and rotate around one another.

swing walking around your partner while holding the waist and hands.

trade a side-by-side couple turn to face each other, then walk around each other, and end up side-by-side facing the opposite direction.

trailing following the dancer or dancers in front of you.

wrong way any movement in the opposite direction of normal.

Tap Dancing

bells a click of the heels while in midair.

brush a sweep of one foot forward, diagonally, or backward while lightly brushing the floor.

buck a move consisting of a stomp of the right foot followed by a hop left on the left foot, a slap down on the right, a slap down on the left, a step right, and then a repeat of the entire move starting on the left foot.

buffalo a leap and a landing on the right while raising the left foot and shuffling it forward and back, followed by a leap and landing on the left foot and a return to the starting position.

chug sliding forward on the ball of the right foot while simultaneously dropping the heel sharply.

coffee grinder in a squatting position with the hands touching the floor, one extended leg describes the action of a coffee grinder by rotating around in a complete circle.

cossack a difficult Russian folk dance with the body in a squatting position and the arms folded at chest level while the legs kick out alternately.

cramp roll a step forward of one foot while raising the heel, followed by a step forward of the other foot with raised heel, then a drop of both heels in quick succession.

dig a step in which the arms are held aloft gracefully to the sides while each foot crosses the other alternately and taps the floor once.

doll hop a step followed by a hop with one leg, followed by another step and a hop with the other leg.

falling off the log a mixture of shuffles and cross steps that produce the illusion of the dancer losing his balance and falling off a log.

flap a brush with the right foot followed by a step on the right foot, producing two sounds.

heel drops moving the right foot forward with the toe pointed up and heel touching the floor, then moving the foot back and repeating with the left foot while arms are placed one over the other at chest level.

heel plate an optional plate placed on the heel of a shoe for tapping.

hop a hop and landing on the same foot.

nerve taps tapping the floor in quick succession with the toe of one foot, frequently used in practice to develop speed and flexibility.

riff a toe tap and a forward slide of the foot while scuffing the heel.

scuff scuffing or scraping the floor with the heel.

shuffle a brush of one foot forward and then back, producing two sounds.

shuffle leap a shuffle followed by a leap and landing on the same foot, producing three sounds.

soft shoe any slow, soft dance with light tapping and a variety of intricate steps, originally performed with sand on the floor.

stamp a tap made by the entire foot, instead of just the ball.

step a simple raising and lowering of one foot, with the weight of the body shifted to that foot.

step-clap a step followed by a hand clap, then repeated with the other foot.

time step any of various combinations of shuffles, flaps, and steps.

toe heel tapping with the ball then the heel of one foot, producing two sounds.

toe point tap a tap with the tip of the toes.

FILM

adaptation a screenplay adapted from a novel, biography, or other source.

aleatory technique a film technique in which scenes are not specifically planned and are left to chance.

arc light a powerful set light.

art director the designer in charge of sets, costumes, or both.

artifact a visual defect in a film.

auteur French term for a movie director who "authors" a film by exercising personal artistic vision.

backlighting lighting that originates behind the subject for a silhouetting effect.

back lot a large plot of land owned by a studio for constructing outside sets.

barn doors the louvers or blinders that are adjusted on large set lights to increase or decrease illumination.

best boy on a set, the assistant to the chief electrician.

billing the position and status given to an actor's name in publicity and in a movie's credits. The actor given top billing is usually listed first and often in the largest letters. Equal billing is shared between two or more actors. Diagonal billing is when top actors are listed side by side, with equal height of lettering, but because the name positioned on the left is considered to have higher status, the names are transposed in different promotional materials.

biopic a movie based on an actual person's life; a biographical movie.

bit player an actor with a small part or role.

black comedy a comedy in which the humor springs from such dark subjects as death, political incorrectness, prejudice, etc.

blacklisting in 1950s America, Senator Joseph McCarthy's formal discrimination against filmmakers who were thought to be communists.

blockbuster in the past, any motion picture that takes in more than $100 million in ticket sales, but increasingly, due to higher ticket prices and inflation, a motion picture earning $150 million or more. The term originated with the British military during World War II, after the massive, city-block-levelling bombs they dropped on German cities.

blocking setting up and rehearsing a scene, including determining where the actors should stand or move, where the cameras should shoot from, and so on.

blooper a muffed line spoken by an actor or a scene that goes awry, cut from a movie but sometimes archived for use on blooper shows.

boffo industry slang for box office hit.

boom a long, mobile arm used to suspend a microphone above the action and out of view of the camera.

bootleg an illegally copied and distributed movie, often of poor quality. Also, the underground industry that illegally copies and sells movies.

B picture any second-rate, low-budget movie.

breakdown script a list of actors, props, and equipment needed for a scheduled day of shooting.

cameo role a role in which only a brief appearance is made by a major actor.

camp exaggerated homosexuality or other wild behavior, such as actors appearing in drag, used for comedic effect.

card a type of credit optical in which names and titles fade in and out in the same position.

cast all of the actors appearing in a movie.

casting the department headed by a casting director, in charge of auditioning and hiring actors.

casting couch reference to the most notorious location for a trade of sexual favors for a role in a motion picture, allegedly common in the old days of movie making, but less so today.

casting director the person in charge of auditioning and hiring actors.

cell one of thousands of individual drawings on celluloid sheets used in creating animation or cartoons.

changeover cue a dot in the corner of a film's frames to cue the projectionist to start the next reel.

character actor an actor who is natural at playing a certain personality type, such as a crotchety old man or a sex siren, and who in fact may be called to play the same type again and again in other movies. Such actors may be unconvincing in any other role.

Cinemascope a film process invented by 20th Century Fox in which anamorphic lenses are used to squeeze film scenes onto 35mm film so that they can be unsqueezed and expanded by a theater projector to create an image more than twice as wide as it is high.

cinematographer a motion picture photographer. Also known as the director of photography.

cinematography motion picture photography.

cinematology the study of films.

cinema verité a realistic or documentary style of filming, sometimes with a handheld camera, under as natural conditions as possible and with little or no input from the director.

cinephile a person who loves movies.

cinerama a wide-screen process that employed three synchronized cameras and is now outmoded.

clapper a handheld chalkboard with data describing the next shot; the sound of a clapstick on its top signals the start of the next scene. Also known as a slate.

color cards cards showing a scale of colors, used as a guide to correct colors when filming.

colorization the computerized process of transforming black-and-white film into color.

commissary a movie studio's cafeteria.

continuity consistency in the images presented in a movie from scene to scene. For example, an actor may be shown with unkempt hair in one shot and then perfectly combed hair in the next shot, or a prop visible on a table in one scene may mysteriously vanish in a following shot because someone on the set inadvertently removed it, thereby breaking continuity. It is the script supervisor's job to monitor continuity from shot to shot and keep careful notes concerning every detail, including lighting, environmental conditions, positions of the actors, prop locations, etc., and have a "continuity report" available at all times.

costume supervisor one who is in charge of the creation, sizing, and authenticity of costumes.

coverage a brief, written review of a script submitted to a producer or studio.

cover set an alternative set used when outdoor shooting is spoiled by rain.

cover shot see MASTER SHOT.

craft service a company or caterer responsible for providing snack tables for the cast and crew.

crane shot an aerial shot taken from a crane or suspended mechanical arm.

crawl the rolling credits at the end of a movie.

credits at the beginning and end of a film, the list of all the people in the production crew, including the actors.

crosslighting lighting that originates from the sides.

cut to to switch from one scene to another.

dailies prints from a day's shooting, viewed by the director and others to determine if any shots need to be filmed again. Also known as rushes.

dialogue coach a person who teaches actors how to speak a foreign language or with an accent.

director the person who directs the action of the actors, sets scenes, coordinates other technicians, and so on.

director's cut a version of a movie as the director prefers it with complete artistic control and little or no studio input.

director of photography see CINEMATOGRAPHER.

direct to video a movie sold only on VHS tape or DVD and not previously released in theaters.

docudrama a movie based on a real event.

dresser one who assists the actors with their costumes.

dub to record dialogue, foreign dialogue, or sound effects in a studio after the film has been shot.

editing the cutting, splicing, and final arrangement of scenes in a film.

editor one who cuts, splices, and determines the final arrangement or length of scenes in a film.

effects track the soundtrack containing sound effects, to be mixed with other soundtracks.

epic a heroic movie with a story line that frequently spans many months or years.

executive producer a producer who handles only the business and legal matters on the making of a film.

extra a person hired to play a nonspeaking part in the background of a scene, frequently as a member of a crowd.

film noir French term meaning, literally, "black film," used to describe some American movies made in the 1940s that were notable for their low-key or dark lighting effects.

final cut the edited, finished film.

flashback a scene that departs from the present and shows an event from the past.

flood short for a floodlight.

focus puller a member of the camera crew who adjusts the camera's focus during filming.

foley to reproduce the sound of a body movement, such as footsteps or rustling clothes, in a recording studio for dubbing onto film.

foley stage a large room with several different types of floor (brick, wood, tile, etc.) used to dub in the sound of footsteps in a film.

foley studio a recording studio in which the picture and soundtrack are played while sound effects are added to match the action of the actors, for example, clothes rustling or footsteps.

gaffer a set electrician and light specialist.

giraffe an adjustable boom microphone.

grip a set assistant or stagehand; one in charge of props.

handheld a handheld camera, used for natural, documentary like effect.

Hays Office the office of former Postmaster General Will Hays, who was appointed by the Motion Picture Producers and Distributors to develop a general code to guide producers on how much sex, violence, or offensive language could be allowed in films. Notoriously strict, the Hays Production Code was introduced in 1934 and remained in effect until 1967, when it was abolished.

high concept descriptive term for a highly commercial plot, script, or idea for a movie. A high-concept movie usually has top actors, bigger-than-life action, a clever premise appealing to the largest body of potential movie-goers, and a vast potential for profit.

hit the mark during a shot, a cue from the director to move to a designated spot on the set.

honeywagon a trailer or truck used as a dressing room while shooting a film on location.

horse opera a western.

hot set a movie set on which a scene is currently being shot.

independent a movie shot and produced by a filmmaker unaffiliated with a major studio.

indie an independent film.

in the can slang, referring to a movie that is shot but not ready for distribution.

kenworthy a special crane, sometimes computer programmed, used to film miniature sets.

klieg light a floodlight.

leader the black strip of film showing countdown numbers at the beginning of the film.

letterbox a format in which a widescreen motion picture can be presented on video with a top and bottom band of the television screen blocked out.

lip-synch to match recorded speech with the actors' lip movements on film.

location manager a person who is in charge of arranging for shooting in a given location and securing any necessary permissions from property owners and authorities.

location scout one who searches out appropriate locations for shooting.

lock it down, speed, action "Lock it down" is announced by the assistant director to quiet everyone on the set for shooting. The director of photography or camera operator then announces "speed," so the director will know when the camera is operating at the correct speed. "Action" is then called by the director to commence performance of a scene.

looping lip-synching on short loops of film.

Macguffin a term coined by director Alfred Hitchcock, referring to a plot element which at first appears meaningless to the audience but which becomes important later on.

married print the soundtrack and film combined into one unit.

master shot a long shot that takes in an entire scene. Also known as a cover shot.

method actor an actor who practices a form of naturalistic acting first popularized in the 1930s.

Mickey Mousing combining whimsical music or musical effects with the actions of the actors, a technique frequently used in cartoons and sometimes in comedic movies.

mix to combine different soundtrack elements, such as dialogue, music, and sound effects.

mogul the head of a movie studio.

Moviola an editing machine.

MOW movie of the week; a made-for-television movie.

nickelodeon an early form of American movie theater, with admission costing a nickel.

novelization a novel adapted from a movie.

on location of filming, in an actual setting, such as an airport, rather than in a studio mockup or set.

optrack an optical soundtrack on a married print; it is composed of a photo image of sound modulations on the side of the film.

outtake a portion of film deleted by the editor.

overlap sound dialogue or sound that continues as the scene fades out. Also, dialogue or sound that begins before the scene fades in.

Panavision wide-screen process that supplanted Cinemascope.

Pan-Cake a makeup used on actors to darken skin.

pickup a motion picture produced and shot by one studio and purchased by another.

pitch a verbal presentation of a story or movie idea from writers to producers.

postproduction any additional elements that must be performed or added after the principal film has been shot, most notably editing and special visual effects.

postsynchronization the recording of the soundtrack after the film has been shot.

practical set a studio set, such as a bedroom mockup, with parts that actually work, such as doors, windows, and so on. Also, any on-location set.

premiere the first public showing of a movie.

prequel a movie featuring a story line that precedes in time the related story line of another movie already produced and shown.

print the physical movie or film itself, or a reel of a movie.

producer the person who secures financing, purchases the script, hires artists and technicians, and oversees a film's production.

production assistant an all-around assistant who performs a wide variety of odd jobs on a set.

production manager a budget supervisor in charge of purchase orders and the hiring of crew.

product placement an appearance of a commercial product, such as a name-brand soda or beer, in a motion picture as a passive paid advertisement and prearranged by the producer and advertiser.

prompter a person who helps the actors with their lines.

prop any object used in a film, for example, a chair, table, inkwell, gun, or elephant.

property a film story.

prosthetic appliance a fashioned piece of latex or gelatin attached to an actor's face or body, as when playing an alien.

rough cut the first cutting and splicing of a film by the editor, in which scenes are placed in the correct general order according to the script.

rushes see DAILIES.

scenic artist a set artist who paints, textures, plasters, letters, creates signs, and more.

score the music composed for a film.

screening the showing of a movie on a screen or in a theater.

screenplay a film story, with dialogue and descriptions of action in the script.

screen test an audition of an actor in front of a camera.

screenwriter a script writer.

script supervisor the person in charge of film continuity, for example, making sure details in one shot (such as which side the actor's hair is parted on or whether a jacket is zipped or unzipped) match those in another shot, even though filmed days or weeks apart. Formerly known as the script girl.

Sensurround a gimmicky movie sound system in which stereo speakers are placed in front, in back, and sometimes on the sides of a theater.

set the location where a film is being shot.

shooting script a script having directions for camera angles, shots, and so on, as well as dialogue.

slate see CLAPPER.

sound effects all sounds, other than music or dialogue, added to film after shooting.

sound stage a building in which sets are built and dismantled for filming.

soundtrack the optical or magnetic track on the side of a film; it contains the music, dialogue, and sound effects.

spaghetti western a European western, usually made in Italy or Spain, popular in the 1960s.

spec script a movie script written on speculation, as opposed to an assignment, with the hope of landing a sale to a producer or studio.

splice to join two pieces of film.

spotting session a meeting in which the director, composer, and editor decide where the music will play in the film.

stand-in a person who takes the place of an actor on a set while a shot is being set up.

Steadicam a special, handheld, waist-supported camera that provides smooth, shake-free shots on a par with dolly shots.

still a photo or enlarged frame from a film, used for publicity.

stock footage existing film borrowed or purchased from a film library and used in a new film.

storyboard a series of captioned drawings showing planned camera shots.

streamer a long line drawn on a film to cue an actor that a scene to be dubbed with dialogue is coming up. Also used to cue conductors for accurate placement of music.

sword and sandal slang for biblically based movie epic, named after the costumes and props used.

sword and sorcery slang for a fantasy epic.

take a recording of scene. The director may order several takes of the same scene to make sure everything works as planned.

test screen to screen a movie in front of a test audience to measure reaction. If reaction is poor, parts of the movie may be reshot before nationwide release.

track the rails on which the camera rides in a tracking shot.

treatment a detailed description or outline of a film idea, as given by the author.

turnaround a process in which a script that has been purchased and has gone through preproduction fails to get made and is made available for sale to other studios.

typecasting the casting of a character type to fit a specific character role.

walla a sound effect of a murmuring crowd.

wild shooting shooting a film without simultaneous recording of the sound.

wild sound sound recorded apart from the actual filming.

wild walls on a set, temporary walls that can be assembled and disassembled quickly.

wrangler an animal handler. Also, a handler of all kinds of nonanimal items. The person responsible usually has a certain amount of expertise with the item.

wrap the end of shooting for the day.

Special Effects and Camera Techniques

animatronics electronically or radio-controlled puppets of animals, humans, monsters, etc.

back projection the projection of a still or moving background through a translucent screen behind the actors, now largely outmoded by front projection and other techniques. Also known as rear projection.

blue screen a process employing a blue screen and color filters to produce matte shots. Also known as a traveling matte. In television, it is performed electronically at the touch of a button and is known as chroma-key.

CGI computer-generated imagery.

chroma-key see BLUE SCREEN.

claymation an animation technique employing clay or plasticine models and stop-action photography.

composite the digital or photographic combination of two or more images on a piece of film.

crab dolly see DOLLY.

crosscutting showing alternating scenes in quick succession to illustrate parallel action.

cutaway a quick switch to a scene of action taking place at the same time as the previous scene, or on a related subject.

day-for-night photography filming night scenes in daylight by using dark filters over the camera lenses.

detail shot an extreme closeup.

dissolve an optical effect in which one scene gradually fades out and melds into another scene.

dolly a rolling platform on which a camera is mounted to gain mobility. Also known as a crab dolly.

dolly shot a shot taken from a rolling dolly.

Dutch angle a canted camera angle that produces a tilted image on the movie screen.

dynamation the process of combining live action with stop-action photography, using split-screen techniques originating with special effects artist Ray Harryhausen in 1958.

establishing shot a shot that establishes the location of the upcoming scene.

extreme long shot a panoramic shot taken from a great distance.

fade-in an optical effect in which a dark background slowly brightens to reveal the next scene.

fade-out an optical effect in which the picture slowly darkens to black.

filter a gelatin, glass, or plastic plate placed over a camera lens to produce various light or color effects.

fisheye lens an extreme wide-angle lens that distorts images and makes the horizon appear distinctly curved.

flag a device positioned in front of a light to create shadow.

flash cutting editing a section of film into brief scenes that quickly succeed each other.

flash frame a scene consisting of few frames, or even one frame, that passes so quickly the audience barely perceives it.

flick pan see SWISH PAN.

freeze frame the repetition of a single frame of a movie to give the illusion that the action has frozen.

ghosting a special-effects technique that makes an actor or prop appear as a ghostly image, achieved through superimposition or reflective shots. Also, a dubbing technique in which a professional singer's voice is dubbed over or with that of an actor's to give the illusion that the actor can sing.

glass shot an effect in which the camera films a shot through scenery painted on glass, with the action occurring behind the glass.

gobo a wooden screen placed in front of a light to dim it or to cast a shadow.

green screen the same as blue screen, but green in color and often producing better results.

high-hat shot a shot taken from near floor or ground level looking up.

highlighting using a thin beam of light to illuminate a part of the actor's face.

jump cut a scene that jumps abruptly into another scene; the joining of two discontinuous shots.

mask a shield placed over a camera lens to give the illusion of peering through binoculars or a keyhole.

Massive a computer program that gives virtual life and random reactions to digitally created characters.

matte artist an artist who creates backgrounds for matte shots.

matte shot a special effect in which part of one scene is masked and combined with another to produce a realistic depiction of something that is normally too difficult or too expensive to shoot, for example, an astronaut filmed in a studio and melded into an image or photograph of space to produce an illusion of an astronaut floating in space.

mocap see MOTION CAPTURE.

morph to alter, or "metamorphose," the shape or appearance of an actor or object on screen through computer-generated special-effects techniques.

morphing a computer-generated special-effects technique in which actors or objects on screen can be altered in shape or appearance.

motion capture a special effects technique in which a live actor wears a body suit rigged with sensors that digitally record, or "capture," his or her movements. Animators add the captured movements to computer-generated images of the actor to convey realism in a digital landscape. The technique can even be used on animals, such as horses, to film dangerous scenes. Also known as mocap.

optical printer an apparatus that combines a projector and a camera with facing lenses, for creating composite shots.

overcrank to run the camera at a greater speed than normal to produce slow-motion images.

pan to film from side to side.

pixilation stop-action photography effect in which an inanimate object is moved between each frame or a small number of frames so that on film the object appears to move on its own, as if by magic.

point-of-view shot a shot as seen from a character's perspective.

pullback a shot in which the camera is pulled back to reveal a larger portion of the scene.

pushover an optical effect similar to a wipe, in which a new scene appears to push the preceding scene off the screen.

rack focus a change of focus from a subject in the background to a subject in the foreground, or vice versa, without moving the camera.

reaction shot a shot that shows a character's reaction to the action around her or him.

rear projection see BACK PROJECTION.

Rembrandt lighting backlighting method modeled after the techniques of the famous Dutch painter, in which a soft light is projected from behind a character for a subtle halolike effect, popularly used in the movies of the 1930s and 1940s.

reverse-angle shot a shot of an opposite view, as when switching from one character to another during alternating dialogue.

ripple dissolve an optical effect in which a wavering image serves as a transition to either a flashback, a flash-forward, or a dream sequence.

rotoscoping an animation method in which live action in a film is traced over.

scrim a plate placed in front of a light to produce shadow.

soft-focus slightly out-of-focus, as achieved by placing Vaseline or a special filter over the camera lens; used to soften lines in romantic shots.

split screen an optical effect showing two different scenes on one frame.

squib a tiny explosive charge used to simulate gunshots.

stop-action photography a special-effects technique in which objects are filmed one frame at a time, allowing the object to be moved between frames. The resulting moving image is known as pixilation.

substitution shot a shot in which the action is stopped midscene and the actors freeze in place. A substitution is made, either for an object or by a dummy representing one of the actors. The shot may be used, for example, when one of the characters is about to have his head cut off or some other unpleasantry.

superimposition a special effect in which one scene is superimposed over another, most notably used in creating scenes with ghosts. Also known as a super.

swish pan a rapid, blurring pan of a scene that serves as a transition into the next scene. Also known as a flick pan, whip pan, or zip pan.

synthespian a digitized actor with computer-generated enhancements.

time-lapse photography a method of compressing real time into a much shorter span of time in film by shooting frames at timed intervals.

tracking shot a moving camera shot on a dolly, on rails, or on foot.

traveling matte see BLUE SCREEN.

trucking shot a rail or dolly shot.

two-shot a shot of two characters simultaneously, as distinguished from a shot cutting back and forth between actors during dialogue.

undercrank to run the camera at a slower speed than normal to produce fast-motion images.

washout a fade to white.

whip pan see SWISH PAN.

wipe an optical effect in which one scene moves from left to right, or vice versa, to knock out another scene and therefore serve as a transitional device.

zip pan see SWISH PAN.

zoom a shot that, by means of automatic focus, zooms in close to a distant subject.

RADIO

AM amplitude modulation; a radio signal that travels along the surface and curvature of the Earth and thus has a much larger broadcast area than FM.

audio news release a taped news or publicity piece sent to radio stations by publicists for broadcast.

band a range of radio frequencies.

beeper slang for an interview recorded over the telephone, formerly requiring a series of beeps to indicate to listeners that the interview was not being broadcast live.

booking board a posted calendar listing future programs and interview guests.

B-rate the cheapest commercial rates, for airing late at night or on Sunday morning.

breakers the new recordings receiving the heaviest air time.

Broadcast Music, Inc. (BMI) a nonprofit organization of music publishers and composers who collect royalties of up to 12¢ each time a performer or member's recording is played over a radio station.

call letters the identification letters of a radio station, usually beginning with the letter W if located east of the Mississippi and K if located west of the Mississippi. Canadian call letters begin with C; Mexican call letters begin with X.

class I station a 50,000-watt AM station having FCC protection of frequency for up to 750 miles. Also known as a clear channel station.

class III station a 5,000-watt station operating on an unprotected, regional channel.

clear channel station a maximum-power AM station having frequency-protected range of up to 750 miles. Also known as a class I station.

cool out to lower the volume of background music at the end of a commercial.

cough button a switch used by an announcer or DJ to turn off the microphone during a cough or sneeze.

cue burn damage to the beginning of a record, due to heavy cueing.

cue up to set a record, tape, or CD in cue position for immediate play.

DAB digital audio broadcasting.

dead air silence during a radio broadcast, a taboo.

delay time a seven-second delay between a talk show's broadcast and transmission, within which any obscenities from callers may be deleted.

digital radio a new transmission system, properly called digital audio broadcasting, that is projected to replace AM and FM by 2015. Digital broadcasting delivers clear and crisp audio without hiss, interference, flutter, distortion, or fading but requires a digital receiver. With digital radio, music and speech are converted to electronic ones and zeros, or bits, and stored, played, and transmitted. Also known as high-definition radio.

disk record.

disk jockey one who plays records, tapes, and CDs over the radio.

DJ disk jockey.

DJ copy a record with only one side recorded on.

drive time important broadcast hours in the morning and late afternoon, when people listen in their cars on their way to and from work.

explosive a loud, explosionlike noise produced by speaking too close to the microphone.

feed broadcasts sent from a national network to local stations, or vice versa.

field strength the power of a station's broadcasting signal.

FM frequency modulation; straight-line radio signals that cannot be received beyond the horizon and therefore have a much smaller range than AM signals; however, FM signals provide high-fidelity reception with little or no static.

FM flutter hisses, pops, and phasing effects caused by reflections of radio signals off tall buildings and mountains.

ground wave a radio signal that travels along the Earth's surface, as distinguished from one that goes into space as it meets the curvature of the Earth.

high-definition radio see DIGITAL RADIO.

high frequency a frequency between 3 and 30 megahertz.

indie slang for an independently owned radio station.

low frequency a frequency between 30 and 300 kilocycles per second.

network a group of affiliated radio stations and their headquarters.

outcue the last four or five words in a song, interview, or newscast, that serve as a cue to the engineer or disk jockey to begin another record, commercial, or program.

performance royalties fees paid by radio stations for the rights to play the songs of music publishers and composers.

picket fencing the fading in and out of an FM station at the fringe of its broadcast range.

playlist a schedule of the day's recordings to be played on the air.

PSA public service announcement.

rolloff the faint edges of a radio signal, when a station hasn't been tuned in properly.

rumble low-frequency vibration.

satellite radio a pay radio service that delivers a wide array of clear-signal music, news, or talk programs.

shock jock a radio program host who is obnoxious, obscene, irreverent, and controversial.

shock radio talk radio featuring loud, rude, or obnoxious hosts who insult their guests and listeners.

simulcast the simultaneous broadcast of a program on television and radio.

sound bite a brief note from a newsworthy person, aired as part of a newscast.

standby guest an emergency stand-in guest used in case a scheduled guest fails to appear.

tape delay a system used on call-in programs, in which a phone call is taped and delayed before airing, to eliminate obscenities.

trailer a brief, promotional piece on an upcoming program, usually played at the end of another program.

translator a station that does not have its own programming but rebroadcasts that of other stations.

upcutting the unethical cutting of part of a network program in order to create more space for local commercials.

urban contemporary radiospeak for inner-city black music.

voice-over a narrator's voice heard over the background music of a commercial.

STAGE AND THEATER

aboard slang for on stage.

above at or toward the back of the stage; upstage.

ace a 1,000-watt spotlight.

act one segment of a play.

actor-proof of a powerfully written play, impervious to poor acting performances.

Actors' Equity Association the 30,000-member actors' union; they are issued Equity cards and are paid according to Equity scale.

apple box a 14″ × 24″ platform used to elevate a performer on stage.

apron the portion of a stage in front of the arch.

arc follow spot a powerful spotlight used to follow a performer.

arena theater theater in which the stage is surrounded by seats.

argentine a shiny sheet of metal that simulates a window on a piece of scenery.

artist's assistant one who assists and escorts a performer from the dressing room to the stage, especially in an opera.

ashcan a 1,000-watt floodlight.

audience dress a rehearsal before an audience, before the show's actual opening.

audit stub the ticket portion retained by the theater for accounting purposes.

a vista of a scene change, made while the curtain is still up.

baby spot a small spotlight, usually 750 watts.

backdrop a painted curtain serving as background scenery.

backing light lighting originating from behind a set or scenery.

backstage the nonperformance area in the wings.

bad laugh laughter from the audience at an inappropriate moment.

balcony a second or third upper floor. A first upper floor is a mezzanine or dress circle. A fourth floor is frequently called a gallery.

balcony box an area reserved for spotlights.

balcony lights lights operated from a balcony box.

balcony operator the person who operates the balcony lights.

band call a musicians' rehearsal.

band shell an outdoor bandstand having a concave back wall and roof.

barn doors adjustable louvers in front of a spotlight to control the intensity of its beam. Also known as blinders, flippers, or shutters.

bastard amber a pink amber gel commonly used to color stagelights.

batten a strip of wood or metal from which scenery or lights are hung.

beam projector a spotlight used to project a sharply defined or narrow beam, to simulate a moonbeam or sunbeam.

bedroom farce a comedy centering on antics in the bedroom.

below at or toward the front of the stage; downstage.

billboard pass a free ticket given to a local retailer in exchange for displaying theater advertising.

black comedy a comedy based on macabre or morbid subjects.

blackout a complete darkening of stage lights to indicate a passage of time or the end of a scene.

blackout switch a switch that controls all of the stage lights.

blind seat a seat with an obstructed view.

block to indicate performer positioning and movements by marking the stage with chalk or tape.

boffo a box office hit.

bomb crater a depression or pit in a stage floor.

bon-bon a 2,000-watt spotlight directed on the face of a performer.

dakota a line of dialogue that leads into or cues a song.

dark house a nonperformance night at the theater.

dead pack scenery to be removed from the stage, as distinguished from live pack, or scenery to be placed on stage.

dim the house to turn out the houselights over the audience.

dinner theater a theater that combines a meal with a show.

dog a small town or noncritical location where the bugs are worked out of a show, as in "to try a show out on the dog."

door list a list of people admitted free to a show. Also known as the house list.

double cast casting two performers for the same role, in case one gets sick. See UNDERSTUDY.

downstage the front of the stage, toward the audience. Also at or toward the front of the stage.

dramatis personae a list of characters in a play.

drapery setting scenery composed of painted curtains or backdrops.

dress a stage to furnish a stage with scenery, furniture, props, and so on.

dresser a wardrobe assistant; an assistant to the wardrobe chief.

dress extra an extra who provides his own costume and is consequently paid on a higher scale.

dress-room list a posted list of dressing rooms assigned to performers.

drop any stage curtain that can be raised or lowered.

farce a wacky comedy based on wild or unlikely or ludicrous situations.

first-night list a list of reviewers, sponsors, and other VIPs invited to attend an opening night, as distinguished from the second-night list.

five minutes to curtain the traditional warning call to all performers five minutes before the show. Also, "five minutes, please."

flashpot receptacle that holds flash powder that is ignited to produce smoke, fire, or explosive effects.

flat an upright piece of painted scenery.

flood a floodlight or broad-beamed light.

fly a floor, platform, or loft over the stage, for lights and other equipment. Also, to suspend scenery from above the stage floor.

fly crew the crew who operate the overhead lights and other equipment on the fly.

fly gallery a sidewall platform where scenery lines are sometimes secured.

fly plot a diagram of lighting placement in the fly; a rigging plan.

footlights a row of lights along the foot of the stage, sometimes recessed in a trough, sometimes not.

front of the house the box office, lobby, and business offices at the front of a theater.

full-dress a full dress rehearsal.

gel a colored plastic (formerly made from gelatin) filter placed in front of a light to produce a colored beam.

go to table to rehearse lines while sitting around a table with other performers.

grave a hole in the stage.

green room a performers' waiting room near the stage.

ground row a piece of background scenery that simulates a landscape, skyline, horizon, or other location.

head spot a spotlight directed on a performer's head.

high comedy comedy having witty, intelligent dialogue, as distinguished from low comedy.

hit the boards slang for to go on stage.

horseshoe staging seating that forms a horseshoe configuration around the stage.

hot of a microphone, live.

houselights the lights that illuminate the audience.

icebreaker an opening number in a musical.

intermission bell a bell, chime, or buzzer rung to alert the audience that intermission is nearly over.

keg light a 500-watt spotlight shaped like a beer keg.

kill to turn off the lights or to remove scenery from the stage.

klieg light a large, powerful, wide-angle spotlight.

lap dissolve the fading out of one light and brightening of another, for effect.

legitimate theater serious plays and musicals, as distinguished from burlesque and vaudeville.

light rehearsal a practice run of light changes and lighting cues.

light tower a tower, often of scaffolding, on which lights are hung.

live pack scenery to be placed on the stage, as distinguished from dead pack, or scenery to be taken off or that has already been used and put away.

live stage a stage with scenery.

loge a theater box in the front section of a mezzanine or balcony.

low comedy slapstick or physical comedy, as distinguished from high comedy.

lyric theater a theater specializing in producing musicals.

makeup call the time a performer must report to the makeup department.

marquee at the front of a theater, the projecting, rooflike structure advertising the upcoming show and its top performers.

matinee an afternoon show.

melodrama a play in which the emotions are acted out in an exaggerated fashion.

noises off sound effects made from off-stage.

Obie annual award given to those involved with off-Broadway productions.

off Broadway low-budget or experimental productions performed in theaters other than those in the Broadway and Times Square area of New York.

oleo a painted curtain used as background for a brief scene while the set is changed from behind.

open full to start the show with the entire cast on stage.

opening night the first formal performance before an audience and critics.

opry house slang for an old theater.

orchestra pit the space below the stage where the musicians play.

overture a musical lead-in to a musical production number.

page a curtain to pull a curtain together so that the two halves meet at midstage.

pan to slowly sweep a spotlight from left to right, or vice versa.

Pan-Cake performers' heavy makeup.

papering the house giving away numerous free tickets in order to fill the theater.

parapet a low wall along a balcony.

parquet a theater's main floor, also known as the orchestra.

pass door a door providing access to backstage from the auditorium.

passion play a play centering on the suffering of Christ.

peanut gallery slang for a top balcony or gallery, where lower-class patrons ate peanuts.

perch an offstage platform on which a spotlight is sometimes placed.

pigeon a platform or riser, smaller than an apple box, used to elevate a performer.

pin spot a spotlight having a very narrow beam.

pit the orchestra pit.

play to the balcony to direct one's performance to the cheaper seats in the balcony, from which the lower classes are quicker to applaud. Also, to play to the gallery.

pool hall lighting dim, overhead lighting, used for effect in some scenes.

positions! the last call for performers to take their positions before the curtain rises.

practicals stage props that actually function, as distinguished from replicas.

practical set a set having real walls and props that work, as distinguished from facades and replicas.

production number any extravagant act or musical number involving many or all members of the chorus, dance troupe, or other performers.

program a brochure describing the show and its performers, given or sold to audience members.

prologue an introduction to a play.

prompt box a hoodline projection or alcove in the center of the stage in which a prompter is positioned out of view of the audience.

prompt corner location where the prompter positions himself, usually downstage right.

prompter one who assists actors in remembering lines while the show is in progress. He keeps track of the dialogue by means of a prompt book.

prop any object, from a cigarette lighter to a sofa, used in a show.

property personnel the stage crew responsible for props.

proscenium the front of the stage, from the front curtain to the orchestra; the apron.

quick study a performer particularly adept at learning his role and accompanying lines.

raisonneur in a play, a character who observes the action, comments on it, and serves as a narrator to the audience.

rake the slant or inclination of a stage. A raked stage slopes down from back to front.

revue a musical composed of sketches and songs.

royal box boxed seating near the stage, reserved for royalty or other VIPs.

rumble pot a receptacle in which boiling water and dry ice is mixed to create fog effects.

score the music written for a show.

set designer one who designs and creates a set.

set dressings set furnishings, decor.

snake a special cable that combines several cables, used with stage lighting.

soliloquy talking to the audience or to oneself on stage.

spot a spotlight.

SRO standing room only; a packed house.

stagehand a helper who assembles, dismantles, and moves scenery; operates the curtain; and performs other tasks.

stagestruck having the sudden desire to become a stage performer, usually occurring while watching a stage show.

strike to take down a set.

theater party a performance given for charity, with the beneficiaries often making up part of the audience.

thrust stage a stage that extends out into the middle of an audience.

tormentor a curtain or piece of scenery that conceals the wings of a stage or backstage.

tragedy a play or drama that ends sadly or in tragedy.

trapdoor a door in the stage floor through which performers may enter or exit.

understudy a performer who rehearses the role of another in case a stand-in is needed.

upstage the portion of the stage furthest from the audience. Also, at or toward the back of the stage.

wagon stage a mobile set on wheels, used to facilitate the changing of sets.

walk-through a rough rehearsal.

wardrobe mistress one responsible for costumes.

white light district a theatrical district. Also known as a white way.

TELEVISION

ABC American Broadcasting Company.

affidavit of performance a notarized list of commercials and public service announcements and their air dates and times, provided to the sponsors.

affiliate a local station, frequently independently owned, that contracts to air the programs of a particular national network.

announcer booth in a studio, a small booth where off-camera voice-overs or announcements are made.

Arbitron the TV ratings company that measures the size of a TV viewing audience by means of an electronic meter placed on TV sets.

arc a curving movement left to right (arc right/left) of a TV pedestal camera, as ordered by the director.

art director a supervisor of the art department.

assemble edit the simultaneous recording of audio, video, cue, and control tracks on a tape.

associate director in the control room, an assistant to the director, whose commands are the ones heard by the camera operators.

atmospheric effects specialist a special-effects person who simulates fog, rain, thunder, lightning, smoke, and so on.

audio operator the audio technician responsible for a program's sound quality.

back lot studio property where outdoor scenes are occasionally shot.

backtiming a method of ending a live program exactly on time by providing a rehearsed final segment that can be made shorter or longer at will. Also, in news programs, the time when the last segment must be aired to match the time deadline.

balop a large slide of art work, used as a background scene.

bat blacks to fade out or to fade to black.

bear trap slang for an alligator-type clamp used to attach lights in a studio. Also known as a gaffer grip.

big head a closeup of a performer's head.

billboard the credits at the opening and closing of a program. Also, an announcement made on behalf of the sponsor, such as "This program brought to you by . . ."

bird a satellite used for TV transmission.

bird, lose the to lose the transmission of a TV signal through a satellite.

birding slang for television transmission via satellite.

black level TV control signals that are blocked out of the picture.

blackout the prohibition of local sports coverage due to contract agreements, intended to draw the maximum audience to the local stadium.

block to provide indications or markings of camera or performer placement and their movement during rehearsal.

blunting airing a program of similar content to that of a competing station at the same time.

boom a long, movable arm, crane, or pole used to hold a microphone.

bump to cancel a guest on a talk show.

bumper a transitional device between program segments, such as a fade-out, or an announcement such as, "We'll return after these messages."

cable puller a studio assistant responsible for power, sound, and picture cables who follows camera movements and pulls cables out of the way to prevent entanglement.

call sheet a schedule sheet showing the dates and times a cast and crew must appear for a production.

camera cue a red warning light indicating when a camera is actually shooting. Also known as a cue light or tally light.

camera mixing mixing shots in succession from two or more studio cameras.

camera rehearsal a full dress rehearsal in which camera placement and movements are planned or blocked.

camera riser a platform that elevates a camera.

canned prerecorded, such as canned laughter.

cast to hire a performer for an acting part. Also, the collective term for all of the performers in a show.

casting director the director who casts the performers for a show.

casting file a file of performer biographies.

cattle call an open audition, usually mobbed by acting hopefuls, for a bit or minor part in a program.

catwalk a narrow walkway or scaffolding above the studio, from which lights can be hung and accessed.

CBS Columbia Broadcasting System.

cc closed-captioned for the hearing-impaired; the superimposing of captions over a TV program, seen only by those viewers with special decoders.

chain break during a program break, a brief spot for station identification. Also, a local commercial up to 20 seconds long.

cherry picker a mobile crane holding a boom and camera for moving, outdoor shots; it has three seats, for the director, the camera operator, and the camera assistant.

cinemobile a large vehicle containing dressing rooms and store rooms, used when taping on location.

circle-in a transitional optical effect in which the picture forms a circle and diminishes, while a new scene enlarges from a small circle. Also known as iris-in.

circle wipe an optical effect in which a scene begins as a dot on the screen and enlarges to wipe out the previous scene.

clean entrance a direction to a performer to enter a scene from off-camera, as distinguished from the camera following the performer into the action.

closed set a set or studio closed to the public.

color bar a vertical strip of graduating colors for color testing of TV transmission. The colors are white, yellow, cyan, green, magenta, red, blue, and black. Also known as a colorburst.

come in a director's command to move the camera in closer on the subject.

control room the technical room where the director and engineers control the audio and video.

cover shot a wide shot revealing location at the start of a scene.

crab shot a shot in which the camera moves left or right on its dolly or truck.

crane a cherry picker.

crane grip the crane or cherry picker operator.

crawl the moving credits at the end of a TV show. Also, any text seen moving across the bottom of the TV screen, as a weather or news bulletin.

credits the acknowledgments of cast and crew at the start or end of a program.

creeper a small camera dolly.

cue card a large card with a performer's lines printed on it. Also known as a flip card or an idiot card.

cue light an ON THE AIR warning light; also a red camera light to indicate shooting.

cue line a line spoken by one actor that serves as a cue to another actor.

cue sheet a schedule of cues and timings.

cyclorama a curved backdrop or wall used on a stage or studio to give the illusion of sky.

day for night filming a night scene in broad daylight by the use of special dark filters.

dead roll starting a program at its normal time but not broadcasting it until a late sporting or other event is over, at which time the program is "joined already in progress."

deaf aid a small earpiece used by reporters, anchors, and others.

decryption the decoding and unscrambling of pay cable TV signals.

defocusing dissolve an optical transition effect in which one camera goes slowly out of focus while another camera shoots a different scene that slowly comes into focus.

delayed broadcast the common practice in the Pacific time zone of airing a TV show later than it originally was transmitted.

delay time the seven seconds of delay time between broadcast and transmission in which obscenities may be removed on a live call-in talk show.

detail set a set used for closeups, having many props and details. Also known as an insert set.

detail shot an extreme closeup.

diagonal dissolve an optical effect in which two corners of a scene merge on screen.

Digital Video Effects an electronic special-effects system.

discovery shot a shot that zooms in on something the viewer had previously overlooked or failed to perceive.

dissolve an optical effect, such as fade-in, fade-out, or fade-to-black, serving as a transition to the next scene.

dolly grip one who pushes a camera dolly.

dolly-in a director's command to move the camera closer to the subject.

doll-out a director's command to move the camera away from the subject.

dolly shot a moving camera shot made on a dolly. Also known as a truck shot or tracking shot.

dolly tracks rails on which a camera and dolly ride during outdoor shots where the ground is uneven.

dress extra an extra who provides his own costume and is thus paid more.

dressing room a room used for dressing and makeup.

dress plot a list of actors' costumes and the order in which they will be worn throughout a program.

dry block a rehearsal without cameras.

dub to record in sound effects, music, dialogue, or foreign dialogue onto a sound track.

ducker a device that automatically lowers volume of background music to allow a voice-over to be heard.

dupe a copy of a taped TV program.

ear prompter a small audio ear plug through which an actor can listen to other actors' lines and play off them.

editor the person in charge of cutting and splicing videotape to put scenes in their proper sequence.

electronic character generator a typewriter-like device that produces on-screen lettering and characters for sports scores, weather reports, stock updates, and other reports.

electronic matte the combining electronically of images from two different cameras.

electronic still store an electronic storage unit holding photographic slides and titles.

elephant doors the large doors entering onto a TV studio.

embargo the prohibitions against the media's releasing certain news until a particular date or time.

encryption the process of scrambling TV signals to protect pay TV networks from theft of service.

endcue the last four or five words spoken by a performer, newscaster, or anchor, for example, used as a cue for the control room engineer and director to cue the music and credits. Also known as outcue.

ESU engineering setup. The projection of an image over the shoulder of a news anchor during a news story.

explosion wipe an optical effect in which an upcoming scene appears to expand from the center of the screen.

explosive a loud, sharp sound produced by speech made too close to a microphone, the bane of audio engineers.

extra an actor in a small nonspeaking role.

eye bounce the technique of looking down and sideways while on TV. Looking down without a sideways glance gives a shifty-eyed or fearful appearance.

facade a fake building having only a front wall and nothing behind it, often used on western programs.

fade an optical effect in which the picture fades in or out.

favor an instruction to the cameraman to focus in on a subject.

feed broadcasts transmitted from a network to local stations or vice versa.

field strength the strength of a local station's broadcast signals.

filter mike a microphone used to simulate the sound of someone's voice over the telephone.

first assistant cameraman one who adjusts a camera's focus to a performer's movements away or toward the camera. Also known as a focus puller.

fishbowl in a studio, an observation booth for sponsors and others involved with the program.

fishpole a long microphone boom.

flashcaster a device used to superimpose news, weather, and other bulletins onto a crawl at the bottom of the TV screen.

flash-pan a superfast pan shot that blurs the picture and serves as a transition to the next scene.

flip wipe an optical effect in which a scene appears to turn over, as a page, to reveal a new scene.

floodlight a broad, bright studio light.

foley a sound effect dubbed in, such as footsteps, clothes rustling, or glasses clinking.

foley artist one who performs sound effects in a recording studio.

foley stage where foley effects are performed.

footage a length of video tape.

freeze frame a optical effect in which tape is frozen at the end of a program to provide a still picture over which credits are run.

futures editor a TV news editor who is responsible for getting coverage of upcoming news events.

gaffer a chief electrician on a set or in a studio.

green room a waiting room for guests who are scheduled to appear on a talk show.

grip a stage or studio hand; a general set assistant.

half shot a camera shot halfway between a long shot and a closeup.

hammers set or stage assistants to the grip, not to be confused with set carpenters.

hammocking scheduling a poor program between two highly rated programs to increase the poor program's ratings.

handbasher an 800-watt, handheld set light.

hiatus time off between a program's shooting schedule, especially during summer reruns.

high-definition television (HDTV) a new generation of televisions having a higher resolution or sharper image.

honeywagon a trailer with dressing rooms and other facilities, for shooting a program on location.

hot microphone a live microphone.

intercutting taking several shots of the same scene from various angles and splicing them together for a more effective viewpoint.

interstitial programming the airing of short programs between long programs to break up the monotony.

iris-in see CIRCLE-IN.

jump a cue to step on another performer's lines; to react too early to a cue.

key to light a set. Also, to superimpose text onto the screen.

key light any main source of light on a set.

klieg light a powerful, wide-angle light used on sets.

lap dissolve an optical transitional effect in which one scene is gradually replaced by another.

late fringe TV ratings term for viewers who watch from 11 P.M. to sign-off.

laugh track prerecorded laughter dubbed over a comedy show at appropriate moments.

lavaliere a microphone worn around the neck, as a necklace.

lead-in an introductory announcement leading in to a program.

legend titles or other text keyed onto the screen.

letterbox format the showing of a movie on TV with its original theater aspect ratio (width to height of picture), in which horizontal bands appear on the top and bottom of the TV screen.

live mike a microphone that is on.

live on tape referring to a program recorded as it actually happened or was performed, but not actually live when transmitted or broadcast.

location a real setting (e.g., an airport) as distinguished from a studio set, where a portion of a program is shot.

location manager a production assistant who plans and arranges for shooting on location.

location scout a production assistant who finds and reserves locations for shooting.

makeup call the time at which a performer must report to the makeup department.

master of ceremonies the host of a TV program; the MC or emcee.

match dissolve an optical transitional effect in which a scene fades and is replaced by a similar or nearly identical scene, but at a later time.

maxi-brute a powerful arc spotlight containing nine 1,000-watt lights in three rows. Also known as a nine-light.

minicam a portable TV camera used when taping on-location news.

network collective term for a group of affiliated TV stations that air the same programs.

O/C script directive for "on camera."

one-key one 1,000-watt floodlight. A 1,500-watt light equals one-and-a-half key.

open-ended of a national program or commercial, having a portion in which a local announcer can add local information.

opening billboard an opening preview or the opening credits of a program. Also, an announcement of sponsors, such as "brought to you by . . ."

opticals optical effects; examples are dissolves, fades, superimpositions, and wipes.

outcue the last four words in an interview, dialogue, or newscast, used as a cue to the engineers and director to roll music and run the credits. Also, known as endcue.

outtakes unused portions of a program tape, edited out due to flubbed lines or other mistakes.

pan a bad review of a program. Also, a direction to the cameraman to sweep slowly across a scene for a panoramic effect.

pan and scan the method by which a motion picture's widescreen aspect ratio is changed to make it suitable for TV broadcast. See also LETTERBOX FORMAT.

Pan-Cake the heavy makeup used by performers.

paper cut a written schedule or list of cuts and splices keyed to time cues made before the actual editing takes place.

PAR light a commonly used spotlight having a parabolic aluminized reflector.

people meter an electronic system for tracking TV viewers to establish ratings, adopted by A. C. Nielsen in 1987 to replace the diary system.

Pepper's ghost a simple special-effects method of producing a ghost image. A camera shoots through an angled mirror to create a reflection of the subject; invented by scientist John Henry Pepper.

performance royalties payments made by a broadcaster to a songwriter or publisher for the right to play their music.

pod a group of commercials.

poop sheet a trivia information sheet on athletes, used by sports announcers between plays in a game.

preempt to broadcast a special in place of a regularly scheduled program.

preview monitor a monitor from which the director chooses the picture to be used by various cameras.

prime time the time period having the largest viewership, from 8 P.M. to 11 P.M.

producer one in charge of financing and staffing a show. In addition to the business end of a program, a producer may also oversee some creative aspects of a show.

prompter a device that enables an actor or announcer to read off a script while looking into the camera. See PROMPTER SCRIPT, TELEPROMPTER.

prompter script a script transmitted to a monitor on top of or beside a camera, or superimposed on the camera lens itself for reading but not seen by the TV audience.

quad split an optical effect in which four different scenes appear on the screen at the same time.

residual a royalty or payment made to a performer for use of their taped performance beyond the original contract.

ripple dissolve a dissolve or fade in which the scene ripples or wavers into the next scene, as in a dream sequence or flashback.

rostrum camera a camera designed to shoot artwork on a table, for animation.

rotoscope a prism and lamphouse device used on a special-effects camera to produce traveling mattes.

rug slang for background music in a commercial.

scale minimum standard fee for a performer or model.

scoop the most frequently used light in TV, specifically a 1,000-watt floodlamp having a shovel-like reflector. Also known as a basher.

set the location of a TV production; the scenery, furnishings, props, lighting, and equipment of a TV program.

set and light director's order to get the set and lighting ready for shooting.

shaky-cam slang for a handheld camera.

shooting log a notebook with details of a day's shooting and the camera equipment used. Also known as a camera log.

shooting schedule the schedule of when each shot in a movie or TV show will be made, usually out-of-sequence to the storyline but later edited in order.

shot box on a TV camera, a control panel for zoom and other focus changes.

signature montage a sequence of brief, identifying scenes used as an introduction to a program.

simulation a reenactment of an event, used frequently in news programs.

simulcast a program broadcast simultaneously on radio and TV, as a concert or presidential speech.

sister station a TV station affiliated with the same network as another station.

sitcom situation comedy.

snake a special studio cable that combines several cables.

sound bite a quick clip of a quote made by a politician or other newsworthy person, aired on a newscast.

sound dissolve the fading out of sounds in one scene followed by the fading in of sounds from an upcoming scene, a transitional device.

spider a junction box for several electrical outlets, used in studios.

spider dolly a camera mount comprising projecting legs on wheels.

splice to join two pieces of film or tape together.

splicing charge a fee sometimes charged for splicing a commercial into a program.

split screen an optical effect in which two or more scenes are shown on the screen at the same time.

squib a gunpowder charge held in a gelatin capsule, detonated from a distance to simulate gunfire.

squibbed bag a squib placed in a blood bag (imitation blood) and detonated on or under clothing to simulate gunshot wounds.

stable a group of performers under contract with a single agent or network.

standby guest on a talk show, an "extra" guest used as a stand-in in case another guest doesn't show up.

standing set a permanent or semipermanent set used repeatedly, as on a soap opera.

still store an electronic memory unit that stores graphics and photos for use in news programs.

storyboard a sequence of cartoons and sketches that illustrate a proposed commercial. Also used in movies to plan how scenes will be shot.

strike to tear down a set.

sweeps TV ratings periods in November, February, May, and July, noted for the airing of sensational programming in order to attract a large audience.

syndicate a service that distributes a TV program to subscribing stations.

syndication the distribution of a program to subscribing stations.

systems cue an audio, visual, or spoken signal for local station identification.

tabloid TV a pseudo news program featuring sensational stories.

take a 42 an order to take a 42-minute meal break, as prescribed for crew members by union rules.

talent coordinator on talk shows, one who auditions, interviews, and schedules guests.

tally light a red light illuminated on a camera when shooting.

tape to record a program on videotape.

teaser a brief preview or promo of an upcoming show to attract viewers.

technical director the assistant director who oversees the technical aspects of a studio and studio control room.

teleplay a play written or adapted for TV.

TelePrompTer tradename for a brand of prompter, now used generically. See PROMPTER.

tight two-shot director's order to cameraman for a head shot of two people.

tongue left/right a command to extend a cranemounted camera out horizontally to follow the action.

topic box a window or visual on the screen above a newscaster's shoulder to identify the topic.

trades, the the trade publications of show business, such as *Variety,* and *Hollywood Reporter.*

trailer a brief, promotional piece of a coming attraction.

transportation captain the head of a studio's transportation and moving department.

truck shot a moving dolly shot. Also, to move the camera sideways.

tulip crane a crane on which a camera platform can be mounted for aboveground shots.

12-14 unit a mobile, remote news truck capable of transmitting at 12 gigahertz and receiving at 14 gigahertz.

two-shot a closeup of two people.

upcutting the unethical practice of cutting off part of a network program in order to insert more local commercials.

V-chip a computer chip in a television set that has the ability to "read" the ratings of television shows and, when programmed, can automatically block the viewing of certain programs by children.

veejay video disk jockey.

video operator the control room engineer who operates the camera control units and monitors and is responsible for the overall picture quality.

videotape magnetic tape on which sound and pictures can be recorded.

voice-over a narrator or announcer's voice heard over a commercial or program.

white coat rule an FCC rule that prohibits actors from wearing white lab coats while pitching a medical product unless it is clearly stated that the actor is not a physician or related professional.

wild shot a camera shot taken without accompanying sound.

wild sound real or natural sounds that are recorded, as distinguished from studio sound effects.

wild track a sound track recorded independently of the visual track.

wild wall a set wall that can be dismantled quickly, usually for the insertion of a TV camera.

wind machine a large fan used to simulate wind.

wipe any optical effect that cleans or wipes off the image on the screen.

RELIGIONS

ANCIENT RELIGIONS

ANCIENT EGYPTIAN WORSHIP

Amun the king of the gods.

Anubis the jackal-headed god of the dead and guardian of tombs and cemeteries.

Aten the sun, worshiped exclusively for a time by order of Pharaoh Akhenaten.

Geb earth god.

Hathor cow-headed goddess of the sky and, later, goddess of love, dance, and the underworld.

Horus hawk-headed god of the sky and light.

Isis queen of gods; goddess of motherhood and fertility.

Khnum ram-headed god of the upper Nile and the creator of humankind.

Maat goddess of justice.

Nepthys goddess of the dead.

Nut goddess of heavens.

Osiris the supreme god of Egypt and the judge of the dead.

Ra (Re) the sun god; the king of the gods and father of humans; portrayed as a lion, cat, or falcon.

Sebek god of water.

Seth evil god of darkness and storms, often portrayed with the head and a pig.

Thoth originally, the moon god, but later associated with wisdom and magic; portrayed with the head of an ibis.

GREEK AND ROMAN MYTHOLOGY

(The Romans adopted many of the Greek deities; those that are exclusively Roman are noted as such.)

Acheron the underworld river of woe.

Achilles the Greek warrior who slew Hector and who was himself killed by a wound to his vulnerable heel by Paris.

Adonis the beautiful youth loved by Aphrodite.

Aecus a judge of the dead in Hades; son of Zeus.

Aeetes keeper of the Golden Fleece.

Aegeus he drowned himself after thinking his son had been killed; Aegean Sea named after him.

Aeolus keeper of winds.

aether the pure upper air breathed by the Olympians.

Ajax the Greek warrior who killed himself because the armor of Achilles was given to Odysseus.

Amazons the women warriors who lived near the Black Sea and who supported Troy against the Greeks.

Amphitrite the wife of Poseidon.

Andromeda the daughter of Cepheus and Casiopeia; she was rescued from a sea monster by her husband Perseus.

Anteros the god who avenged unrequited love.

Aphrodite (Venus) goddess of love and beauty; the daughter of Zeus; and mother of Eros.

Apollo the god of the sun, prophecy, music, medicine, and poetry.

Arachne the woman who challenged Athena to a weaving contest; she was changed to a spider.

Ares (Mars) god of war; son of Zeus and Hera.

Argo the ship Jason sailed on his quest for the Golden Fleece.

Argus the hundred-eyed monster slain by Hermes; his eyes were said to have been placed in the peacock's tail.

Arion the musician saved from drowning by a dolphin.

Artemis (Diana) goddess of the moon, hunting, and chastity.

Asclepius the god of medicine; the son of Apollo.

Astraea the goddess of justice; daughter of Zeus and Themis.

Athena (Minerva) goddess of wisdom and the arts.

Atlas he was condemned to support the world on his shoulders for warring against Zeus.

Bacchus god of wine; son of Zeus and Semele.

Bellona Roman goddess of war.

Briareus the monster with a hundred hands; son of Uranus.

Calliope the goddess of epic poetry.

Calypso a sea nymph who delayed Odysseus on her island for seven years.

Cassandra the prophetess who was never believed; daughter of Priam.

centaur a half-man, half-horse.

Cepheus the king of Ethiopia; father of Andromeda.

Cerberus the three-headed dog guarding the entrance to Hades.

Charon the ferryman who carried the souls of the dead over the River Styx to Hades; son of Erebus.

Charybdis the personification of a whirlpool off the Sicilian coast opposite a cave.

Chimera a fire-breathing monster with the head of a lion, body of a goat, and tail of a serpent.

Chiron the centaur who taught Achilles and Hercules.

Chronos the personification of time.

Circe the sorceress who transformed the men of Odysseus into swine.

Clio the goddess of history.

Cronus (Saturn) the god of harvest; ruler of the universe until overthrown by his son Zeus; son of Uranus and Gaea.

Cupid see EROS.

Cyclops a one-eyed giant. See POLYPHEMUS.

Daedalus the builder of the Labyrinth; father of Icarus.

Danae princess of Argos.

Daphne a nymph who was changed to a laurel tree.

Demeter (Ceres) goddess of agriculture.

Diana see ARTEMIS.

Diomedes the prince of Argos and a hero at Troy.

Dione Titan goddess; mother of Aphrodite.

Dionysus (Bacchus) god of wine; son of Zeus.

dryads wood nymphs.

Echo a nymph whose unrequited love for Narcissus made her fade away so that only her voice remained.

Eos (Aurora) goddess of dawn.

Erato goddess of lyric and love poetry.

Erebus the dark region that must be passed before reaching Hades; spirit of darkness.

Eros (Amor, Cupid) god of love; son of Aphrodite.

Eurystheus king of Argos who imposed the 12 labors on Hercules.

Euterpe goddess of music.

Flora Roman goddess of flowers.

Fortuna the Roman goddess of fortune.

Furies the avenging spirits.

Gaea the goddess of earth, mother of Titans. Also known as Gaia.

Ganymede the cupbearer of the gods.

Golden Fleece the fleece of the golden ram, quested for by Jason.

Gorgons the three female monsters who had snakes growing out of their heads; gazing upon them turned the beholder to stone. See MEDUSA.

Graeae the Gorgons' three sentinels; they shared one eye between them.

Hades the abode of the dead.

hamadryads tree nymphs.

Harpies women with the bodies of birds.

Hecate goddess of sorcery.

Helen fairest woman in the world; her kidnapping caused Trojan War; daughter of Zeus and Leda.

Helios (Sol) god of the sun.

Hephaestus (Vulcan) god of fire; son of Zeus and Hera.

Hera (Juno) queen of heaven; wife of Zeus.

Hercules strongman and hero; performed the 12 labors (killing Nemean lion, killing Lernaean Hydra, capturing Erymanthian boar, capturing Cretan bull, etc.) to win immortality.

Hermes (Mercury) the god of physicians and thieves; messenger of the gods; conducted dead to Hades.

Hippolyta the queen of the Amazons.

Hyacinthus the beautiful youth Apollo loved but accidentally killed; Apollo made a hyacinth grow from his blood.

Hydra the nine-headed monster slain by Hercules.

Hymen the god of marriage.

Hyperion the father of Helios.

Hypnos (Somnus) the god of sleep.

Icarus fell into the sea and drowned after wax wings melted when he flew too close to the sun; son of Daedalus.

Iris goddess of rainbow.

Janus the Roman god of gates and doorways, depicted with two opposite faces.

Jason the leader of the Argonauts in the quest for the Golden Fleece.

Juno see HERA.

Jupiter see ZEUS.

Lucina the Roman goddess of childbirth.

Mars see Ares.

Medea the princess sorceress who helped Jason obtain the Golden Fleece.

Medusa the Gorgon whose head was cut off by Perseus.

Melpomene the goddess of tragedy.

Midas the king of Phrygia; all he touched turned to gold.

Minos the king of Crete; after death he became a judge of the dead in Hades; son of Zeus and Europa.

Minotaur the half-man, half-bull kept in the Labyrinth in Crete; slain by Theseus.

Mnemosyne the goddess of memory.

Momus the god of blame and ridicule.

Morpheus the god of sleep and dreams.

Muses the nine goddesses of arts and sciences: Calliope, Clio, Erato, Euterpe, Melpomene, Polymnia, Terpsichore, Thalia, Urani. The daughters of Mnemosyne and Zeus.

naiads the nymphs who preside over brooks, springs, and fountains.

Narcissus the beautiful youth who fell in love with and pined away for his own reflection in a pool, and was transformed into a flower.

Nemesis the goddess of retribution and revenge.

Neptune see POSEIDON.

Nereids the sea nymphs who attended Poseidon.

Nike goddess of victory.

nymph any female spirit of nature.

Nyx goddess of the night.

Oceanus a Titan and god of the sea circling the earth.

Odysseus (Ulysses) king of Ithaca and leader of the Greeks in the Trojan War.

Oedipus king of Thebes; was abandoned at birth; grew up to unwittingly kill his father and marry his mother.

oreads mountain nymphs.

Orion a great hunter made into a constellation.

Pales Roman goddess of shepherds and herdsmen.

Pan god of woods and fields.

Pandora the woman who opened the box and unwittingly released all the ills of humankind.

Paris he slew Achilles; son of Priam.

Pegasus the winged horse that left Medusa's body after her death.

Pelops his father cooked and served him to the gods.

Penates the gods of Roman households.

Persephone (Proserpine) queen of the underworld; wife of Pluto.

Perseus he killed Medusa and rescued Andromeda from a sea monster; son of Zeus and Danae.

Pleiades the seven daughters of Atlas; they were changed into a constellation.

Pluto god of Hades; brother of Zeus.

Plutus god of wealth.

Polyphemus the Cyclops who ate six of Odysseus's men.

Pomona Roman goddess of fruits.

Poseidon (Neptune) god of the sea; brother of Zeus.

Priam king of Troy.

Priapus god of procreation and the guardian of gardens; the personification of an erect phallus.

Procrustes a giant who stretched or shortened victims to make them fit one of his iron beds; slain by Theseus.

Prometheus the Titan who stole fire from heaven and gave it to humans; punished by being chained to a rock, where vultures ate from his liver each day.

Proteus a sea god who could change his shape.

Pygmalion king of Cyprus; carved statue of maiden who was brought to life by Aphrodite.

Python the serpent slain by Apollo.

Remus brother of Romulus; was slain by Romulus.

rivers of the underworld Acheron (woe), Cocytus (wailing), Lethe (forgetfulness), Phlegethon (fire), Styx (souls carried across it by Charon).

Romulus son of Mars; raised by a wolf after being abandoned as an infant; he killed his brother Remus; founded Rome in 753 B.C.

Saturn see CRONUS.

satyrs woodland goatlike gods or demons.

Scylla a rock opposite Charybdis, personified as a sea monster who devoured sailors.

Selene goddess of the moon.

Silvanus Roman god of woods and fields.

Sinis the giant who used pines to catapult victims against the side of a mountain; slain by Theseus.

Sirens the deities who entranced sailors to their deaths by their songs.

Sisyphus king of Corinth; condemned to relentlessly roll a heavy stone to the peak of a hill, where it always fell back down again.

Sol see HELIOS.

Sphinx a winged monster having the head of a woman and the body of a lion; killed those who could not answer her riddle; killed herself when Oedipus answered it correctly.

Styx the river on which Charon ferried souls to Hades.

Tantalus the king who, condemned to Hades, underwent the torture of standing in water that always receded when he tried to drink it.

Tartarus the underworld below Hades.

Tellus Roman goddess of earth.

Terminus Roman god of boundaries and landmarks.

Terpsichore goddess of choral dance and song.

Terra Roman goddess of earth.

Thanatos the personification of death.

Theseus son of Aegeus; slew Minotaur, Procrustes, and Sinis.

Titans the original gods before the Olympians.

Triton son of Poseidon.

Uranus personification of the sky; father of the Cyclopes and Titans.

Venus see APHRODITE.

Zeus (Jupiter) the ruler and father of all the Olympian gods; son of Cronus and Rhea.

MONSTERS AND FABULOUS CREATURES

(*Also see* GREEK AND ROMAN MYTHOLOGY)

Abaia in Melanesian mythology, a great eel who caused floods whenever a fellow fish in his lake was caught.

Aitvaras Lithuanian flying dragon hatched from the egg of a cock, considered a good household spirit.

Alan Philippine half-human, half-bird who lived in gold houses in forests and hung upside-down from trees.

Alicha in Siberian mythology, a beast who lived in the sky and swallowed the sun and moon periodically.

Amarok a giant wolf in the mythology of Eskimos.

Ammut an ancient Egyptian creature, part hippo and part lion with the jaws of a crocodile; it ate the hearts of sinners.

Anubis jackal-headed Egyptian god and judge of the dead.

Apop in Egyptian mythology, a sea serpent hiding in darkness.

argopelter a beast of American lore; it lived in the trunks of trees and threw pieces of wood at innocent passersby.

Argus in Greek mythology, a hundred-eyed monster; its eyes were ultimately used to decorate the peacock's tail.

bagwyn heraldic beast with the tail of a horse and the horns of a goat.

baku in Japanese mythology, a tapirlike creature that feeds on the bad dreams of humans.

banshee in Irish and Scottish legend, a spirit having one nostril, a large front tooth, long, streaming hair, webbed feet, and red eyes from continuous weeping and wailing. According to legend, she washes the clothes of a man destined to die and, if caught washing by a mortal, must disclose the name of the man and grant three wishes.

baobhan sith a Scottish evil spirit appearing as a beautiful girl in a green dress, which hides her deerlike hooves. She and others seduce young men and suck their blood.

basilisk a 6-inch-long desert serpent described by Pliny and others. A glance from this creature caused death, as did its poisonous breath. It could itself be killed by a weasel, by a cock crowing, or by seeing its own reflection in a mirror.

behemoth in the Apocrypha, a large beast sometimes identified as a hippo. Now taken to mean any large beast.

bergfolk Scandinavian fairies and brownies and the like; the evil outcasts of heaven who live in banks, mounds, and mosses; they could make themselves invisible or change their shape, and were frequently accused of stealing corn and ale.

boggart a mischievous, brownielike spirit that haunts the north of England.

brollachan a creature or spirit without form, responsible for mysterious occurrences.

brownie a small, shaggy, humanlike creature with shabby clothing. In England and Scotland, brownies took bread and milk in exchange for household labor; some had the magic ability to settle swarming bees.

bugaboo a small, evil creature that comes down chimneys and snatches naughty children; a favorite of baby-sitters.

bunyip an Australian man-killer who lived in deep pools and streams.

Caecus in Roman mythology, a cave-dwelling, fire-breathing half-beast, half-man who killed humans and aligned their heads in its lair. The son of Vulcan, slain by Hercules.

calygreyhound heraldic, antelopelike beast having the forelegs and claws of an eagle and the rear legs and feet of an ox.

Centaur in Greek mythology, a creature with a human front and the body and hind legs of a horse; known for its benevolence and wisdom.

Cerberus the three-headed dog with serpent manes that guarded the gates of Hades; kidnapped by Hercules.

cetus a sea monster with the head of a greyhound and the body of a dolphin.

ch'i-lin a Chinese unicorn.

chimera Homeric beast having a front like a lion, a middle like a goat, and a rear like a serpent; sometimes depicted with the three heads of these beasts.

cuero a giant octopus of South America having clawed tentacles and ears covered with eyes.

Cyclops a cave-dwelling, one-eyed giant described in the *Odyssey.*

devil fish heraldic compound beast of the devil with a fishlike body.

devil's dandy dogs fiery-eyed, fire-breathing dogs of Cornish legend who followed Satan over the moors on stormy nights.

dobie a brownie guardian of hidden treasure.

dragon a creature taking many forms, sometimes winged, sometimes fire-breathing; usually known for guarding a huge hoard of treasure.

dragon tygre a heraldic compound beast.

dragon wolf a heraldic compound beast.

drake from Celtic and Germanic folklore, a dragonlike ogre that hunts and travels on horseback; it lives in a place and eats humans.

dwarf in Scandinavian mythology, a little man with a large head and a long beard, born from the earth or from mold. It lives in a hollow hill or mound, and sunlight will turn it to stone. Dwarves are usually talented metalsmiths.

elf a little, humanlike creature dwelling underground; noted for its love of music, dancing, mischief, and practical jokes.

enfield heraldic beast having the head of a fox, the body of a lion, the hindquarters of a wolf, and the talons of an eagle.

Erymanthian boar a giant boar driven into a snowdrift and trapped there by Hercules.

fachan an evil Irish spirit known for killing and mutilating travelers; it had one eye in its forehead and one hand protruding from its chest, and it was covered with feathers.

falcon-fish heraldic compound of a fish and a falcon with a hound's ears.

falin Scottish mountain demon.

faun in Greek legend, part goat, part man, similar to a nymph.

fire-drake a cave-dwelling, fire-breathing dragon who hoarded treasures of the dead.

fuath a Scottish water spirit with webbed feet and yellow hair.

Gabriel Ratchet a ghost hound heard yelping in the sky in the midst of severe storms, believed to be a portent of death.

Ganesha in Hindu culture, a creature having a human body and an elephant head.

gargouille a dragon who made waterspouts in the Seine; the inspiration for gargoyles.

gargoyle a fantastic medieval sculpture having a wide-open mouth for spouting rain- or wastewater near the roofs of buildings.

Geryon a three-headed, three-bodied man joined at the waist, shot by Hercules.

ghul an evil spirit encountered by travelers in the Arabian desert.

gigelorum a microscopic beast of Scottish folklore; it made its nest in a mite's ear.

Girtablili in the Babylonian epic of creation, a half-man, half-scorpion.

glastig in Scottish folklore, a half-woman, half-goat who wore green and was kind to the old and feeble but who liked to misdirect travelers.

gremlins rabbitlike creatures who sabotaged airplanes and pulled pranks in World War II. Were believed to live in holes around airfields.

griffin in Indian and Arabian folklore, part lion and part eagle.

grylio a medieval, salamanderlike creature said to poison apples in apple trees.

gryphon a griffin.

Harpies vulturelike birds having the head and breasts of women, from Greek legend.

hidebehind a mysterious creature known to hide behind trees and sneak up on lumberjacks in North America; they were never seen, however.

hippocampus a half-horse, half-fish with a serpent's tail; it pulled Poseidon's chariot.

hodag a horned, human-eating beast with a spiked back, said to live in the swamps of Wisconsin.

hoop snake a snake said to hold its tail in its mouth and roll about like a wheel, from American lore.

hydra a beast with seven to nine heads, one of which is immortal. If any of the heads were cut off the blood would cause a new head to grow back. Hercules killed this beast by burning the heads and burying the immortal head under a rock.

jinshin uwo the giant fish on which Japan was thought to float; the lashing of its tail was the explanation for earthquakes.

kraken a sea creature said to be a mile and a half in length in sailor lore of the 1600s and later, and probably based on the giant squid.

leprechaun an Irish fairy less than 2 feet in height, believed to haunt wine cellars and to guard huge hoards of treasure.

Leviathan the great fish of Hebrew myth.

lindorm a snakelike, heraldic dragon.

Loch Ness monster the elusive lake monster of Scotland.

Medusa the snake-headed Gorgon who turned people to stone.

minocane a heraldic beast, half-child, half-spaniel.

Minotaur a bull-headed man kept in a labyrinth and slain by Theseus.

monoceros a howling beast something like a cross between a rhino and a unicorn.

orc according to Pliny, "an enormous mass of flesh armed with teeth," based on the killer whale.

Orthos two-headed guard dog, brother to Cerberus.

padfoot a devil dog who haunted the area of Leeds, England.

Pan the Greek god of the woods and fields; a humanlike creature having the belly and legs of a goat.

Peist the Irish dragon whom St. Patrick imprisoned.

phoenix in Egyptian mythology, a brilliantly colored bird who lives more than 500 years, then consumes itself in fire and rises anew from the ashes.

puk a small, household dragon who brings treasure to its master.

roc in Arabian legend, the giant, eaglelike bird who carried off young elephants and ate them.

rumptifusel a large, vicious beast who slept wrapped around a tree and was often mistaken for a fur coat by passing lumberjacks.

safat a dragon-headed creature that flew so high in the sky it vanished from sight.

salamander a cold-bodied lizard thought by the Greeks to live in fires.

satyr fish a winged, heraldic beast with the head of a satyr and the body of a fish.

satyrs manlike creatures with legs, hindquarters, and horns of a goat; they were the attendants of Bacchus and Pan.

serra a flying sea monster with a lion's head and a fish's tail.

side Irish fairy who lived in barrows.

stringes Greek vampire who sucked the blood of sleeping victims and brought nightmares.

thunderbirds from Native American folklore, giant birds whose flapping wings were thought to be the cause of thunder.

tritons dolphin-tailed beasts with humanlike faces, the conch-blowing attendants of Neptune.

troll in Scandinavian folklore, a large, evil fairy or elf who could charm men and who was scared away by church bells. Trolls who roamed at night were turned to stone if caught in daylight. Standing stones are thought to be the petrified bodies of trolls.

were-jaguar South American version of a werewolf.

werewolf a wolf disguised as a human.

wodewoses mute, club-wielding ogres with shaggy green hair who kidnapped women and ate children in medieval times.

wyvern heraldic flying serpent with a barbed tail and legs like an eagle's.

MODERN RELIGIONS

BUDDHISM

ahimsa the doctrine of nonviolence and the unwillingness to harm any living creature, including animals for food.

Amida Buddha the Buddha of "immeasurable light."

bhakti the love and devotion a follower feels for someone more spiritually advanced.

bodhi the Buddhist term for enlightenment, the spiritual awakening all Buddhists strive for.

bodhisattva in Mahayana Buddhism, a being or person devoted to attaining enlightenment for all living things.

bodhi-tree the fig tree under which Siddhartha Gautama attained enlightenment while meditating.

Dalai Lama the spiritual leader of Tibetan Buddhism. Every new Dalai Lama is believed to be a reincarnation of the former Dalai Lama.

dharma the path to enlightenment, specifically living a life of generosity, love, and wisdom.

dukkha the Buddhist belief that everything eventually leads to suffering.

enlightenment spiritual awakening; the state of being a Buddha; supreme bliss, perfect wisdom and compassion, and profound insight into the meaning of life. Also known as nirvana or the transcendental.

five precepts a set of rules for moral behavior; in general, don't lie, steal, kill, drink or use drugs, or misconduct oneself sexually.

Four Noble Truths life lessons taught by Buddha: (1) everything leads to suffering; (2) suffering is caused by desire or greed; (3) eliminating desire and greed eliminates suffering; (4) the pathways of enlightenment are open to anyone who lives morally and meditates.

Gautama, Siddhartha the founder of Buddhism, known as the Buddha.

lama a Vajrayana Buddhist from Tibet who is spiritually learned and developed.

lotus position a seated position in which the legs are folded tightly together, used in meditation.

mantra "instrument of thought"; a word or phrase representing spiritual meaning, recited repeatedly during meditation.

nirvana enlightenment.

prayer wheel a Tibetan Buddhist apparatus consisting of a wheel on which papers inscribed with mantras are attached; the wheel is rotated to release the efficacy of the mantras.

rosary a circle of beads sometimes used when reciting mantras.

satori the sudden achievement of enlightenment.

stupa a Buddhist shrine in the shape of a mound or dome, usually containing a sacred object or marking a sacred place.

Wesak a festival celebrating the enlightenment of Buddha or his birth and death, held in May on the day of the full moon.

zazan meditation in the lotus position.

Zen the Chinese and Japanese school of Buddhism focusing on the attainment of enlightenment through meditation.

CHRISTIANITY

abbess the female superior of an abbey; the female version of an abbot.

abbey a monastery or convent.

abbot the male superior of an abbey or monastery.

ablutions the washing of the hands before or after certain religious ceremonies, such as before Catholic Mass.

abomination anything repugnant to God.

absolution the forgiveness of sins.

acolyte one who assists a priest or minister at the altar, for example by lighting or extinguishing candles or handling the offerings.

Acts of the Apostles the New Testament book describing Christian history.

Advent the birth of Christ; the Second Coming of Christ. Also, the four weeks preceding Christmas.

Adventists, Second a denomination that believes that the Second Coming will soon arrive and prophesies the date.

Adventists, Seventh-Day a denomination that believes that the Second Coming will soon arrive but does not prophesy a date.

agape in the early Christian Church, a love feast or communal meal of thanksgiving held with the Eucharist.

agnostic one who neither believes nor disbelieves in God due to a lack of evidence or proof.

Agnus Dei the Lamb of God; an icon representing this.

agrapha Greek for "things that are not written," referring to any words of Jesus not included in the Bible's four Gospels but found in other sources.

All Saints' Day observed on November 1, a day commemorating martyrs and saints.

All Souls' Day observed on November 2, a day of prayer commemorating those Christians believed to be in purgatory.

almsgiving giving gifts or money to the poor, a religious practice around the world.

amen Hebrew for "to trust," denoting faithfulness.

anathema one who is damned; a ban or excommunication.

Angelus a Roman Catholic prayer recited at 6 A.M., noon, and 6 P.M. to commemorate the Annunciation. Also the bell used to announce this prayer.

Annunciation the angel Gabriel's announcement to the Virgin Mary that she would conceive a son.

anoint to apply oil to the body to initiate one into divine service.

Antichrist "he who is against Christ." The great antagonist or "man of lawlessness" posing as a religious leader who will be defeated and banished with Christ's Second Coming. Also known as "the beast."

Apocalypse the last book of the New Testament; a revelation of the world to come.

Apocrypha collections of proverbs, sermons, and texts excluded from the Hebrew Bible because they were thought not to be inspired by God. Roman Catholic Bibles include all but two of these texts in the Old Testament. Protestants however, consider them uncanonical.

apostasy the abandonment of one's religious faith.

apostate one who gives up his faith.

Apostle one of the 12 witnesses chosen by Christ to preach the Gospel.

Apostles' Creed the oldest statement of Christian faith, sometimes ascribed to the 12 Apostles, beginning, "I believe in God the Father Almighty, maker of heaven and earth. . . ."

archangel a chief or high angel, including Michael, Gabriel, and Raphael.

archbishop the highest-ranking bishop; he oversees an archdiocese.

archdeacon a priest who oversees a territory and assists a bishop.

archdiocese in the Roman Catholic Church, a diocese under the jurisdiction of an archbishop.

Ark of the Covenant the ornate, acacia wood chest containing the Ten Commandments, carried by Hebrews into battle, and responsible for bringing down the walls of Jericho. Sometimes referred to as the footstool of God.

Armageddon "mountain of Megiddo." The location of the final battle between the forces of the Lord Jesus Christ and the Antichrist, as prophesied by the Bible in Revelation 19:16.

Ascension Christ's ascent to heaven on a cloud, commemorated on the 40th day after Easter Sunday, known as Holy Thursday.

Ash Wednesday the first day of Lent, the 40-day period of fasting and repentance preceding Easter. The name is derived from the ash of burned palm branches (from Palm Sunday) dabbed in the configuration of a cross on members of the congregation by a priest.

Assumption in Roman Catholic and Eastern Orthodox Churches, a feast on August 15 to commemorate the taking into heaven of the Virgin Mary.

atheism the disbelief in the existence of God.

atonement the making of amends for sins.

avarice greed, one of the seven cardinal or "deadly" sins.

baptism a ceremony through which a young child or an adult becomes a member of the church. In Baptist churches, adults are fully immersed in water. In the Eastern Church and Roman Catholic Church, young children are sprinkled with or immersed in water three times and sometimes anointed with oil.

Baptist Church the Christian Protestant church that baptizes adults but not infants.

beatification the step prior to canonization, in which the pope declares a deceased person to be blessed and therefore worthy to be prayed to for help or guidance.

beatific vision seeing God directly.

Beelzebub in the New Testament, the "prince of demons"; synonymous with Satan.

Benedictines nuns or monks who conduct their lives by the Rule of St. Benedict—with emphasis on stability, study, work, worship, and obedience to the abbot.

benediction the act of blessing at the end of a service. In the Roman Catholic Church, the Benediction of the Blessed Sacrament.

benefice any property held by a church.

bishop a high-ranking minister in the Roman Catholic, Anglican, and Orthodox Churches, and others who oversees a diocese.

blaspheme to speak evil against God; to curse the name of the Lord.

breviary a books of hymns, prayers, and instructions for reciting daily services in the Roman Catholic Church.

canon ecclesiastical laws, codes, or authoritative writings of a religion. Also, the books of the Bible officially accepted by the Christian Church.

canonical hours the prayers that, according to canonical law, should be recited at specific times of the day. Also, the hours when these prayers are said.

canonize in the Roman Catholic Church, to declare a deceased person a saint after beatification.

canticle a song or chant with words taken from biblical text; a nonmetrical hymn.

cardinal an official elected by the pope to advise and assist him in governing the church. Cardinals rank just below the pope in the Catholic hierarchy; they are responsible for electing a new pope when one dies.

catechism a short book that, in question-and-answer format, instructs candidates for confirmation in Christian doctrine.

celebrant the presiding priest or minister at the consecration of the bread and wine at Holy Communion or Mass.

celibacy the practice of abstaining from sexual intercourse, a requirement of the Catholic priesthood; the vow of celibacy.

chaplain a rabbi, priest, or minister serving a hospital, prison, school, or military base.

charge a parish.

Charismatics Christians who believe they are blessed with the gift of tongues, healing, or prophecy.

cherubim the second order of angels, below archangels.

chrism in the Roman Catholic and the Orthodox Church, the holy oil used in confirmation rituals.

christening the ceremony of baptizing and giving a name to an infant.

collect a short prayer before the reading of the epistle in the Mass of the Roman Catholic Church.

College of Cardinals the body of cardinals in the Roman Catholic Church.

communion fellowship. See EUCHARIST.

conclave a secret meeting of cardinals to elect a new pope. Also, the location of this meeting.

concupiscence theological term for the desire for the forbidden, especially sex; lust.

confession the admission of sins to a priest in the Roman Catholic Church.

confessor a male saint who did not die a martyr's death, such as most monks, bishops, priests, religious laypersons.

confirmation a service admitting a baptized infant or adolescent into the Christian Church.

consecrate to bless or make sacred. To change bread and wine into the body and blood of Christ in the Roman Catholic Church.

consistory a meeting of cardinals to conduct business or to appoint bishops.

contrition repentance for having sinned.

convocation an assembly of clergy members to discuss church affairs.

Coptic Church the Christian churches of Egypt and Ethiopia.

corrupt text any Bible passages that have been modified.

covenant a testament or agreement between church members to defend and support the faith.

Dead Sea Scrolls several parchment scrolls dated from about the 1st century and discovered in caves near the Dead Sea in 1947. The scrolls include hymns, laws, teachings, and the oldest texts of the Old Testament of the Bible.

dean in the Roman Catholic Church, a priest who oversees several parishes. Also, the superior of a cathedral.

defrock to remove the authority from a minister due to unethical behavior.

denomination any branch or sect of the Christian Church.

diocese a district supervised by a bishop. Also known as an eparchy in the Eastern Orthodox Church.

dispensation in the Roman Catholic Church, a bending of the rules in cases of hardship, for example, allowing someone to ignore the fast on Good Friday for health reasons.

district superintendent in the Methodist Church, a supervisor of ministers in a district.

divine office in the Roman Catholic Church, the public prayers, psalms, hymns, and readings.

divinity the essence of God and all divine things.

Eastern Orthodox Church the churches of Eastern Europe, Russia, and the eastern Mediterranean. Also known as the Orthodox Church.

ecclesiastic a priest or minister; a clergyman.

ecumenical pertaining to the unity of the Christian Church around the world.

Epiphany a festival held on January 6 in the Catholic, Orthodox, and Protestant Churches to commemorate the visit of the wise men at Christ's birth.

Episcopal Church the Anglican Church in the United States, Canada, and Scotland. Unlike other Protestant churches, Episcopal churches are governed by bishops.

epistle one of the letters written by the Apostles in the New Testament and recited as part of a service.

Eucharist the main sacrament commemorating the Last Supper. The bread and the wine, as the body and blood of Christ, are eaten and drunk by worshipers. Also known as Communion, Holy Communion, and Mass.

evangelism spreading the word of Christ throughout the world through missions.

evangelist one who spreads the word of Christ.

evensong an Anglican evening service similar to Catholic vespers.

ex cathedra "from the chair"; referring to a pronouncement made by the authority of one's office.

excommunication the cutting off from or exclusion from the Catholic Church membership or from religious rites, especially that of receiving Holy Communion, due to certain transgressions against the church.

faith healing the healing of a sick person through prayer and faith in God rather than through medical intervention.

Franciscans the order of Anglican and Roman Catholic friars, founded by St. Francis of Assisi.

friar similar to a monk, but not bound to a single community. A Franciscan, Dominican, or Carmelite.

fundamentalism the 20th-century Protestant movement that holds that the Bible is infallible and should be taken as the literal truth, despite scientific or historical evidence to the contrary.

genuflect to get down on one knee in worship.

glossolalia speaking in tongues, a gift of the Holy Spirit. An unknown language spoken to communicate visions or prophecies, especially in the Pentecostal Church.

Good Friday the day on which Christ's Crucifixion is commemorated.

Gospels the four accounts of the life and death of Christ by Matthew, Mark, Luke, and John.

hagiarchy a country governed by holy men. Also, a hierarchy of saints.

hands, laying on of healing someone by channeling God's power through touch.

Hebrew Bible the Old Testament.

heresy anything against traditional religious doctrine or dogma.

heretic one who dissents from his religion's doctrine or dogma.

Holy Communion the service of the Eucharist.

Holy Innocents Day a festival held on December 28 commemorating the murder of Bethlehem's male children under two, as ordered by King Herod.

Holy Land Israel or Palestine.

holy orders the rite of ordination to the priesthood.

Holy Week the last week of Lent.

host the round wafers of unleavened bread used in Holy Communion.

Immaculate Conception in the Roman Catholic Church, the doctrine that holds that the Virgin Mary was free from original sin since her conception.

infidel a member of another religion, in regard to Christianity or Islam. Also, one with no religious beliefs.

intercession the Roman Catholic or Orthodox Christian's prayer to a saint requesting that they pray directly to God on their behalf. Prayers made through saints or angels are believed to be more effective.

Isa Arabic for Jesus.

Jesuit a member of the Society of Jesus, a Roman Catholic order.

King James Bible the translation of the Bible into English ordered by King James I; it was first published in 1611.

kiss of peace a greeting kiss in the Roman Catholic Mass, the Orthodox Eucharist, and the Lutheran Communion.

laity the nonclergy members of a congregation.

lauds the hour of morning worship in Catholic divine office.

lectionary a book containing lessons from the Bible to be read at services.

Lent the 40-day period, beginning with Ash Wednesday, before Easter Sunday.

litany a prayer of supplications recited by a clergy alternating with replies from the congregation, either sung or spoken.

liturgy the rite of the Eucharist. Also, public worship or any religious ritual. Also, the Book of Common Prayer.

Lutheran Church the Protestant Church that follows the teachings of Martin Luther.

Madonna the Virgin Mary. Also, any depiction, such as a painting, of the Virgin Mary.

martyr one killed for his religious beliefs.

Mass the Roman Catholic term for the Eucharist or Holy Communion.

Maundy Thursday the day of the Last Supper and the day Jesus washed the feet of his disciples.

mendicants friars who take a vow of poverty and live entirely from alms.

Mennonites the Protestant denomination that baptizes adults, stresses nonresistance, and rejects war and violence.

missal in the Roman Catholic Church, a book containing a year of instructions, readings, and prayers for the Mass.

monotheism the belief in only one God.

nones the service that takes place at 3 P.M. at Roman Catholic and Eastern Orthodox churches.

original sin the first sin—that of Adam and Eve eating of the tree of knowledge of good and evil.

Palm Sunday the Sunday before Easter; it commemorates Christ riding into Jerusalem on a donkey, when palms were spread in welcome before him.

papacy the supreme office of the pope.

papal authority the leadership of the pope in governing the Roman Catholic Church.

parish a local Catholic or Anglican community within a specific territorial district.

paschal candle in Roman Catholic and several Anglican churches, a tall candle lit the night before Easter and kept burning near the altar until the feast of the Ascension or Pentecost Sunday. Also known as the Easter Candle.

Passion the suffering of Christ from the Last Supper to his Crucifixion, on our behalf, as recounted from Gospels as a part of Holy Week services.

pastor "shepherd." A minister in the Lutheran, Baptist, and Pentecostal Churches.

patriarch the highest-ranking bishop in the Eastern Orthodox Church.

patron saint in the Roman Catholic Church, a saint who has been designated as a special guardian or protector of a nation, community, profession, group, individual, and so forth. Also, any saint for whom an individual is named at baptism.

penance a sacrament comprising contrition, confession, the imposition of a good work, or the saying of prayers and absolution.

penitent one who has sinned and wishes to repent. Also, a person who confesses his or her wrongdoings to a priest at confession.

Pentecost a festival held on the seventh Sunday after Easter to commemorate the descent of the Holy Spirit after Christ's Ascension. Also known as Whitsunday or Whit Sunday.

Pentecostal Church a multidenominational group of churches stressing the need for believers to receive the Baptism of the Holy Spirit. Most noted for congregation members who spontaneously "speak in tongues" during a service and who claim to have the gift of healing or prophecy.

plainsong a method of chanting psalms or hymns.

polytheism a belief in more than one god.

pontiff the pope.

pope the head of the Roman Catholic Church and the bishop of Rome.

Presbyterian Church the Christian Protestant denomination with a doctrine based on the teachings of Calvin. Noted for its lack of elaborate rituals and plain churches.

presbytery a minister's house, often located beside a church.

primate in an Anglican district or group of dioceses, the highest-ranking bishop. Also, the highest-ranking bishop in a country.

proselyte one who converts from one faith to another.

psalter a book of psalms from the Old Testament.

rector in the Anglican Church, a clergyman in charge of a parish.

rectory the house of a Catholic priest or an Episcopal minister.

requiem a Roman Catholic funeral mass set to music to aid the deceased through purgatory to heaven.

resurrection the restoration of the life of Jesus by God after Christ's Crucifixion. Also, the rising of souls from the bodies of the dead.

rosary a circle of beads used as an aid to prayer. Also, a prayer to God directed through the Virgin Mary.

sacrament any one of several rites performed in the Christian Church to receive God's grace. In the Roman Catholic Church, these include baptism, confirmation, the Eucharist, matrimony, orders, penance, and extreme unction. In the Protestant Church, only baptism and the Eucharist are considered sacraments.

Sanctus a hymn sung before the prayer of consecration at a Eucharist service.

sanctus bell a bell rung at Roman Catholic Mass to draw attention to the consecration of the bread and wine.

see the center of a bishop's diocese.

seminary a religious training institution for priests and ministers.

seven virtues in Roman Catholic theology, prudence, justice, fortitude, temperance, faith, hope, and charity.

shunning an Amish and Mennonite practice of refusing to socialize with excommunicated members in any way.

synod an ecclesiastical council.

theophany a manifestation of God, as through fire or thunder.

tithe one-tenth; to donate one-tenth of one's income to the church, practiced by some Christians according to Mosaic law.

Transfiguration a festival held on August 6 to commemorate Christ's appearance before the Apostles. Known as the Feast of Tabor in the Eastern Orthodox Church.

Trappist a strict order of monks, known for their fasting and extended periods of silence.

Trinity the Holy Trinity; the Father, the Son, and the Holy Ghost.

Unification Church founded by Korean Sun Myung Moon in 1954, the church having a doctrine based on a conglomeration of Christian and Taoist ideas.

Unitarian Church the church noted for its philosophy that all faiths lead to the same truth and for its readings from the sacred texts of various religions, including Christianity, at services.

Vatican the palace home of the pope in Vatican City.

vestments ecclesiastical garments.

vicar in England, a priest who oversees a parish.

vicar of Christ the pope, as representative of Christ on earth.

Hinduism

Agni the god of fire.

ahimsa the doctrine of nonviolence held by many Hindu sects, epitomized by the Hindu leader Mahatma Gandhi.

arti the sacred flame, offered in a lamp to the gods during services.

ashram a communal house where followers or students of a guru live.

avatar the incarnation of a god. Nine avatars are believed to have descended from heaven, including Rama and Krishna, to reestablish law and worship. One remains to come (Kalki), who will destroy the world.

avidya spiritual ignorance, a cause of much suffering.

Bhagavad Gita "the Song of the Lord," a highly influential book of 700 verses featuring the spiritual guidance given Prince Arjuna by his charioteer, Krishna (an incarnation of God), on the battlefield.

Bhagavan "Blessed One" or "Lord," referring to holy men or the god Vishnu.

bhakti knowing God through love and devotion.

Brahma the god of creation and the source of wisdom. Brahma is usually portrayed as having four heads and often seated on a lotus or flying on a swan. He is not widely worshipped by Hindus.

Brahman the Universal Spirit in everyone and everything.

Brahmin the highly revered priestly caste of Hinduism. Brahmins carry out sacrifices and other ceremonies.

chakras places in the body other than the brain where consciousness resides, according to Hindu yoga; the genitals, the navel, behind the lower breastbone, the throat, and between the eyebrows.

chela the student of a guru.

chit Hindu word for consciousness.

Deva "shining being," a god.

dharma caste duties and obligations.

Durga the greatly venerated wife of the god Shiva.

Durga Puja a main festival honoring the goddess Durga.

Ganesha the four-armed, elephant-headed god and son of Shiva, widely worshiped as a "remover of obstacles"; a symbol of luck and prosperity, especially in western India.

guru a spiritual teacher.

Hanuman the Hindu monkey god.

Indra god of rain, thunder, and war.

Janmashtami a festival celebrating the birth of Krishna.

Kalki the last avatar or incarnation of Vishnu; he is due to come in the future and destroy the world to make way for the creation of a new world.

Kamadeva god of love and desire.

karma the central Hindu belief that what goes around comes around; that is, one's fate in life is determined largely by one's behavior earlier in life or in a previous life and that bad karma can be reduced or eliminated by performing good works and living a moral life.

Krishna the widely popular black god and avatar of Vishnu. Many Hindus use Krishna as the name of God.

Kshatriya the warrior caste; the caste second only to the Brahmins.

lingam an erect phallus, the symbol of the god Shiva.

lotus position the yoga position in which the legs are folded tightly together, used in meditation.

mantra a word or phrase repeated continuously in meditation to clear the mind of all intrusive thoughts.

moksha "liberation"; the release from the bondage of endless reincarnation and karma, the highest goal of Hindus; it is achieved by living a good life and creating good karma.

naman three vertical lines worn on the forehead of Vaishnavia, in Vaishnavism.

niyama purifying oneself through discipline, according to Hindu yoga.

om Sanskrit for "yes" or "so be it," a sacred word uttered before prayers.

puja worship; it is performed three times per day by Orthodox Hindus.

Rama the seventh avatar; an incarnation of Vishnu.

Sacred Thread Ceremony Hindu boy's initiation rite of second birth and passage to maturity.

sadhu an ascetic holy man.

sannyasin one who abandons all material things except for a pot, a loincloth (dhoti), and alms in an attempt, along with meditation, to achieve moksha; an ascetic.

Shaivism worship of the God Shiva.

Shiva the god of life, death, and rebirth, symbolized by an erect phallus.

Sudra the lowest caste of the Hindu caste system, specifically servants and peasants.

Sikhism largely Indian religion, originally guided by gurus, but now authorized by the Sikh scriptures known as the Adi Granth. Sikhs believe in a formless God who is beyond human comprehension. Karma and reincarnation are accepted beliefs.

Trimurti the three forces of God; Brahma, the creative force; Vishnu, the preserving force; and Shiva, the destructive force.

untouchables formerly, those peasants outside the caste system; physical contact with them would "pollute" a caste member and so they were avoided. Such discrimination still exists in rural areas. Also known as the Scheduled Caste or panchamas.

Vaishnavism worship of the god Vishnu, thought by some to be the Supreme Being.

Vaisya the third Hindu caste, ranking below Brahmins and Kshatriyas. Specifically, merchants and businessmen.

vedas Hindu scriptures.

Vishnu the god who preserves life, thought to be the Supreme Being by some followers.

Yama god of the underworld.

yoga a school of Hindu philosophy that combines mental and physical disciplines, noted for its meditation and system of exercises used to achieve spiritual well-being.

yogi one who practices yoga.

Islam

adhan the call to prayers at dawn, midday, midafternoon, sunset, and after dark.

Allah Supreme God; the same God as that pronounced by Moses and Jesus.

al-Rahim one of Islam's 99 Beautiful Names of God, meaning "the compassionate."

al-Rahman one of Islam's 99 Beautiful Names of God, meaning "the merciful."

ayatollah an authority and interpreter of Muslim law.

azan the call to prayer from the minaret of a mosque.

Bismalah a call for Allah's blessing.

Black Stone in the courtyard of the great mosque at Mecca, a sacred stone kissed and touched by pilgrims.

Dome of the Rock in Jerusalem, a domed shrine over the rock from which Muhammad is said to have ascended to heaven.

Fatiha the first chapter of the Koran, used as a prayer on many occasions.

five pillars of Islam the five requirements of the Islamic religion: repeating the creed, praying five times per day, giving alms, fasting, and making at least one pilgrimage to Mecca in one's lifetime.

hajj the pilgrimage to Mecca to visit several sacred sites, including the Black Stone.

halal a term similar to kosher in Judaism, meaning food has been judged fit to eat by Islamic dietary law; for example, an animal about to be slaughtered must be facing the direction of Mecca, and its blood must be completely drained before butchering.

imam the leader of prayer in a mosque.

infidel one who belongs to any faith other than Islam.

Jahannam Islamic term for hell.

jihad spreading the faith and fighting against the enemies of Islam. Also, a holy war.

Kaaba the stone sanctuary in Mecca that contains the Black Stone.

Koran the sacred text that contains the revelations of Allah as made to Muhammad. Also spelled Qur'an.

Lailat-ul-Bara'h the Night of Forgiveness, a Muslim festival devoted to forgiveness.

Lailat-ul-Qadar the Night of Power, a Muslim festival celebrating the giving of the Koran to Muhammad.

Mecca in Saudi Arabia, the most sacred city of Islam, where Muhammad, the prophet of God, was born.

minaret the mosque tower from which the faithful are called to prayer.

Moslem see MUSLIM.

mosque a building for Muslim worship.

muezzin the one who calls the faithful to prayer from the minaret of a mosque.

Muhammad the prophet of God or Allah; he received revelations from God and is the founder of Islam.

mullah a Muslim scholar who interprets Islamic law.

Muslim an adherent of the Islamic religion. Also spelled Moslem.

prayer mat a mat or carpet laid to face Mecca and kneeled on to conduct prayers. Also known as seggadeh.

purdah a term referring to the Koran teaching that women must keep their bodies covered and let only their faces and hands show in public to protect their virtue.

Qur'an see KORAN.

Ramadan a month of daily fasting between sunrise and sunset accompanied by religious study. It is the ninth month of the lunar calendar.

Salam Alaikum "Peace be upon you," a common Muslim greeting.

Salat the prayers that must be recited five times per day to satisfy one of the five pillars of Islam.

Shiites Muslims belonging to the minority Shia sect.

shirk the most severe Muslim sin—putting anything on a par with Allah.

Siyam the Muslim requirement to fast during Ramadan.

Sunnis members of the largest Islamic religious group who adhere only to the teachings of Muhammad.

zakat the giving of alms, one of the five pillars of Islam.

JUDAISM

Adonai the name of the Lord, pronounced this way whenever the letters YHWH occur in the Torah.

amidah "standing"; the prayer recited at all Jewish services.

anti-Semitism discrimination against Jews.

Bar Mitzvah the initiation rite of a 13-year-old boy, who reads aloud from the Torah and becomes accepted as an adult and as a member of the religious community.

Bas Mitzvah the equivalent of a Bar Mitzvah for 13-year-girls. Also known as Bat Mitzvah.

cantor the chief singer or prayer leader in a synagogue.

Chanukah see HANUKKAH.

dietary laws in Orthodox Judaism, traditional laws pertaining to the consumption and preparation of foods; for example, pork, shellfish, and birds of prey cannot be eaten. Foods fit to be eaten are called kosher.

Elohim Hebrew name of God used in the Torah.

Ezrat Nashim the women's section of a synagogue.

Gehenna Greek name for hell; in Hebrew, Hinnom.

Gentile anyone not a Jew.

Halakah the body of laws in the Torah and the Talmud.

Hanukkah a festival commemorating the victory of the Maccabees over the Syrians in 165 B.C. and the rededication of the Temple of Jerusalem. The festival is noted for its ritual of Jewish families lighting a candle every night for eight nights and placing each candle into a menorah (candelabra). Also known as the Festival of Lights. Also spelled Chanukah.

Hasidim strict Orthodox Jews, known for their black, widebrim hats, long black coats, and earlocks. Also spelled Chasidim.

Hebrew Bible the Old Testament of the Christian Bible; it contains the five books of the Law known collectively as the Torah.

Jehovah name of God.

Jew a believer in Judaism or a person descended from the Hebrew people. By Jewish law, must be a child of a Jewish mother.

kaddish a prayer recited when mourning the loss of a relative to help reaffirm faith.

kaftan the long, black coat worn by Hasidic Jews.

kashrut the code stating which foods are kosher.

kosher of food, fit to eat and unrestricted under Jewish dietary law.

matzoh the unleavened bread eaten for eight days by Jewish families over Passover to commemorate the exodus of the Israelites from slavery in Egypt.

menorah a seven- or nine-branched candelabra.

Messiah the representative of God who will come to earth at the end of the age to established the Kingdom of God on earth.

mezuzah a scroll with passages from the Hebrew Bible, kept in a box on every doorpost of a Jewish home.

Mishnah Jewish oral law, passed down through the ages.

mitzvah a commandment or duty; a good deed or charitable act.

mohel a Jew who performs circumcisions.

ner tamid in a synagogue, the everburning oil lamp in front of the ark.

Orthodox Judaism traditional Judaism, known for its strict adherence to the Law, or Torah; for example, no Orthodox Jew shall marry a gentile, no nonkosher foods shall be eaten under any circumstance.

Passover the eight-day festival commemorating the flight of the Jews from slavery in Egypt and their exodus to the Promised Land. Also known as Pesach or the Feast of Unleavened Bread.

rabbi a Jewish minister.

Rosh Hashanah the Jewish New Year, celebrated in late September or early October.

Sabbath Saturday, the seventh day of the week; a day of rest to honor God.

seder the Passover meal commemorating the Israelites' escape from Egypt. Features of the meal include unleavened bread, four glasses of wine each, a bone of lamb, and green vegetables.

sheitel a wig worn by Orthodox Jewish women in accordance to the rabbinical rule that holds that a woman must keep her hair covered in the presence of any man other than her husband.

Shema a prayer said in the morning and in the evening in Jewish homes. It begins, "Hear O Israel, the Lord Our God, the Lord is one. . . ."

siddur a Jewish prayer book.

synagogue a Jewish house of worship.

tallith a prayer shawl worn by Jewish men during morning prayers.

Talmud a collection of rabbinical writings forming, along with the Torah, the basis of authority for Judaism. It includes scriptural interpretations, dietary rules, advice for daily living, and sermons, among other writings.

tefillin two small leather boxes containing scrolls from the Torah and strapped to the forehead and left arm of Jewish men during weekday morning services.

Torah the Hebrew Bible; the five books of the Old Testament attributed to Moses.

Weeks, Feast of a summer festival commemorating the receiving of the Ten Commandments by Moses.

Western Wall the Wailing Wall. A vestige of the foundation of the Temple of Jerusalem, where Jews go to pray.

Yahweh the name for God; it is always written as YHWH and never spoken aloud because of its sacredness. See ADONAI, JEHOVAH.

yarmulke the skullcap worn by Jewish men.

Yom Kippur the holiest of all Jewish holidays, devoted to prayer, confession of sins, repentance, and fasting. Also known as the Day of Atonement.

SCIENCE

ANTHROPOLOGY AND ARCHAEOLOGY

aborigine a native inhabitant.

abrading stone any stone used to smooth or sharpen wood, bone, or other stone.

absolute dating any method that uses specific physical or chemical measurements, such as carbon-14 dating, or historical associations, such as historical documents or dates on coins, to determine age within a limited time frame.

alidade a sighted rule used for drawing lines of sight and measuring angles, a surveyor's tool.

amino acid dating a dating method that determines age by measuring changes in amino acid structure, which occur at a known rate in bone and other organic material, and can be used with artifacts up to 100,000 years old.

amphora a large, round ceramic container, used for centuries to store oil, wine, grain, etc., and often found in ancient shipwrecks.

anthropoid any ape such as the gorilla, chimpanzee, gibbon, or orangutan characterized by its resemblance to humans; resembling a human or ape.

archaeologist an anthropologist who specializes in archaeology.

archaic *Homo sapiens* the first modern human subspecies, living 250,000 years ago, and characterized by broad, somewhat Neanderthal-like faces.

Archaic period in North American prehistory, the years between 10,000 B.C. and 3000 B.C.

archeomagnetic dating a method of dating burned rock or clay, as from a hearth or kiln, by using Earth's magnetic field. Superheating aligns iron particles within the rock or clay to the magnetic North Pole, which changes location over time.

Ardipithecus ramidus African, prehuman ancestors who may have walked upright at least part of the time. Their oldest remains date from 4.4 million years ago.

articulated referring to bones that are still joined rather than separated or scattered.

artifact any object made or employed by humans, especially one of interest to archeologists.

assemblage any grouping of artifacts, particularly from the same site.

atlatl a bone or wood implement with a hand grip and a hook in which the end of a spear was inserted, used to hurl a spear with greater velocity.

Australopithecus anamensis African, prehuman ancestors whose shin bone remains are thicker than the shin bones of a chimpanzee, evidence of upright walking. They lived from 3.9 to 4.2 million years ago.

Australopithecus afarensis prehuman ancestors living in East Africa from 3 to 4 million years ago; the most famous fossils are those of "Lucy," who stood only 3 1/2 feet tall.

Australopithecus africanus African, prehuman ancestors living from 2 to 3 million years ago, and characterized by slightly larger braincases than *A. afarensis.*

Australopithecus boisei prehuman ancestors living in another part of Africa at the same time as *A. robustus,* with slightly larger builds, from 1.5 to 2.6 million years ago.

Australopithecus robustus prehuman ancestors, characterized by their huge teeth and heavy jaws requiring supporting skull crests, living in Africa from 1.5 to 2.6 million years ago.

barrow a human-made mound, especially one found over a grave; a tumulus.

bipedal walking on or having the ability to walk on two feet.

bison jump any site on top of or at the foot of a cliff, especially in the Americans Plains, where there is evidence that humans tricked bison into leaping to their deaths for easy slaughter.

bowsing thumping the ground with a mallet or other heavy tool to listen for differences in ground resonance, used to locate buried chambers.

B.P. abbreviation for before present, before the present day.

Bronze Age the period beginning from around 5000 to roughly 500 B.C., depending on region, when metals (bronze and copper) were first used to construct tools and weapons.

burial mound a mound of soil under which people were buried.

butchering station a location within a site that contains evidence, such as a large number of bones, of the regular butchering of animals.

cairn a human-constructed pile of rocks, sometimes found over a burial site.

carbon-14 dating a dating method that measures the amount of radioactive decay in an artifact's carbon-14 content and can be used to date organic objects as old as 75,000 years.

catalog a recording of artifacts and where they were found at a site; also spelled catalogue.

Caucasoid a widespread human race, making up approximately 55% of the world's population, and characterized by light skin; they evolved in the north and especially in Europe.

cave art cave paintings left by Cro-Magnon people in France and elsewhere, from around 30,000 years ago and later.

ceramic referring to pottery.

chert a rock similar to flint but found in variable colors and chipped off to form projectile points.

chronology a time line of historical events in the order in which they happened.

cist a stone coffin, from the Neolithic period.

clovis point a fluted, leaf-shaped stone projectile point, used by Native Americans to kill large prey.

codex a handwritten manuscript, especially a Christian or Mesoamerican one.

convergent evolution the principle that those from different lineages can develop similar characteristics as a response to environmental similarities.

Copper Age the beginning period of the Bronze Age, when copper and bronze were used in the manufacture of tools and weapons.

coprolite fossilized feces.

core a sampling, often cylindrical, of a segment of soil, ice, tree wood, etc., analysed to find clues about climate, volcanic activity, forest fires, plant growth, and the like.

Cro-Magnon man a highly intelligent and advanced human ancestor with exceptional artistic and tool-making abilities, living from 10,000 to 40,000 years ago, and characterized by a broader face than that of a fully modern human.

cross-dating dating an archaeological site by using the established date and evidence of similarities from another site.

cuneiform pictographic writing, developed and used by the Sumerians around 3500 B.C.

curate to look after archaeological artifacts, as in a museum.

curator one who looks after an archaeological collection, as in a museum or a repository.

Darwinism from naturalist Charles Darwin, the theory of evolution or survival of the fittest.

debitage the waste products, particularly chips, left over from the making of stone tools.

dendrochronology the technique of determining age by counting the growth rings on long-lived trees.

dental pick a tool with a tiny point, used to scrape off very small debris, bits of soil, etc.

dig an archaeological excavation.

dolmen a neolithic monument composed of a large flat stone laid across two or more standing stones.

effigy mound a mound of soil constructed into the shape of an animal or bird.

evolution the natural process that allows strong, thriving individuals, well adapted to their environment, to pass their genetic heritage on to healthy offspring, while struggling individuals tend to die off; the survival of the fittest.

faunal dating a method that uses specific or known evolutionary changes in an animal to help determine the age of a site where that animal's bones are found.

feature that which cannot be removed from an archaeological excavation, such as a fire pit or post molds.

fieldwork work and research that takes place outside, usually at a dig, rather than in an office or laboratory.

flake a thin, flat chip of stone removed during the making of a stone tool or weapon, sometimes used as a hide scraper.

flexed burial a burial in which the body is found in a fetal position.

flint a black, hard quartz that gives off sparks when struck with steel.

flotation a screening technique in which soil is placed in a drum of water, with lighter materials—usually seeds, carbonized plant remains, and small bone fragments—floating to the top.

fluorine dating a dating method that determines approximate age by measuring how much fluorine a bone has absorbed from groundwater, a known rate.

fossil beach a former beach raised far above sea or lake level.

genealogy a history of ancestral descent; a record or charting of lineage.

grid the dividing of an excavation into precise squares, used to accurately place and record where artifacts are found.

ground penetrating radar the method of sending radar pulses through the soil, with bounced-back signals indicating the presence of hidden structures or features.

hammerstone any strong or very hard stone used to work or chip bone or other stone.

hand ax a stone cutting tool from the Paleolithic period.

hide scraper a stone or bone implement used to scrape away hide from flesh.

hieroglyphics pictographic writing used by the ancient Egyptians.

hominid a human or any two-legged, prehuman ancestor.

hominoid belonging to the family of apes and humans; resembling a human being.

Homo erectus prehuman ancestors who employed fire and lived from 27,000 to 1.8 million years ago, with remains found in Africa, China, and Europe. Known as "Upright man," its inner ear structure, where the body's sense of balance is centered, appears more humanlike than that of any hominid that came before.

Homo ergaster prehuman ancestors who lived in Africa's Rift Valley 1.4 to 2 million years ago and may have been the first, along with *H. habilis,* to migrate to Asia.

Homo habilis prehuman ancestor commonly referred to as "handy man" because they constructed stone tools. They are thought to have migrated to Asia, and lived from 1.5 to 2 million years ago.

Homo heidelbergensis prehuman ancestors characterized by large faces, massive brow ridges, and very low foreheads. They lived from 200,000 to 500,000 years ago; their remains have been found in Africa, China, and Europe.

Homo rudolfensis prehuman ancestors who were among the first to develop simple stone tools and lived in the Rift Valley of Africa from 1.9 to 2.5 million years ago.

Homo sapiens neanderthalensis "Neanderthal man"; living from 30,000 to 137,000 years ago, a tool-building, humanlike ancestor characterized by a strong, stocky body and a brain that was actually slightly larger although less intelligent than that of a modern human; they are thought by some to have blended into the modern human lineage through mating.

Homo sapiens sapiens "Double wise man," fully modern humans.

housepit a depression in the ground, created when a dwelling collapses and decays.

index fossil the remains of a creature that existed for a relatively short amount of time and thus can be used to roughly date artifacts by the strata it is found in.

in situ in its original location or position.

Iron Age the period beginning from roughly 1600 B.C., when iron was first used in manufacturing tools and weapons.

Java man the first specimen remains of *Homo erectus,* found in Java in 1891.

kitchen midden a refuse heap, especially of kitchen scraps, studied by archaeologists to determine what a primitive group ate.

knapping the chipping off of flakes from a stone to create a tool or weapon.

level a layer of excavation, sometimes naturally divided from other layers by strata.

lithic made of stone. Also referring to any artifact or tool made of stone.

locus an association of features within a site.

looting the stealing of artifacts from an archaeological site.

luminescence dating a measurement of the amount of light energy stored in the crystals of calcite, feldspar, and quartz. The energy, which is stored at a known rate, is released after heating, and ages can be established from a few hundred to several hundred thousand years.

magnetic dating any method that uses magnetic minerals and their positioning in relation to Earth's magnetic field to establish approximate ages of artifacts.

mano a grinding stone, often made from a cobble. Elaborate versions may have a handle or be shaped like a rolling pin. Used with a metate.

megafauna large Ice Age animals, such as mammoths and mastodons.

Mesolithic period the middle Stone Age period, from 10,000 B.C. to roughly 8000 B.C., noted for the human development of the microlith and boats.

metate a flat or basinlike stone slab used for grinding.

microlith a small flint tool set in bone or wood, used for cutting and scraping, from the Mesolithic period.

midden a deposit of trash artifacts, such as food scraps, shells, bones, charcoal, ash, etc.

milling station also known as a milling stone, a stone slab or basin having a depression or mortarlike cup, used for milling or grinding grain.

missing link any one of the hypothetical or supposed human ancestors that would provide a model of an exact intermediary between ape and human and thus "prove" human evolution, now an outmoded notion.

Mongoloid a widespread human race making up approximately 33% of the world's population, characterized by yellowish skin, straight black hair, and epicanthic folds around the eyes; they evolved in and largely inhabit Asia.

monolith a large single-stone monument.

Negroid one of the three main human races, making up approximately 8 percent of the world's population, and characterized by dark skin, curly hair and a broad nose; they evolved in Africa.

Neolithic period the late Stone Age period extending from 8000 B.C. to the advent of the Bronze Age, noted for the development of human settlements, advancing farming techniques, textile weaving, and the domestication of animals.

nitrogen dating a method of determining age by measuring the loss of nitrogen in bone, which occurs at a known rate.

obsidian a volcanically formed glass that primitive people used to make very sharp blades and cutting tools.

Paleoindians the earliest known people living in the Americas.

Paleolithic period the early Stone Age period, from 2 million years ago to roughly 10,000 B.C., noted for its hunter-gatherer human ancestors and their increasing sophistication in the construction of stone tools.

paleopathology the study of diseases of the past, and the evidence of injuries and illnesses as found on skeletons.

palynologist one who studies pollens and spores. Preserved specimens can provide a picture of what the local plant ecology might have been like at a given time.

petroglyph a carving, inscription, or work of art on a stone.

pictograph a picture painted on a rock.

Piltdown man prehuman fossils found in Piltdown, England, in 1908, thought to be up to a million years old and touted as the great "missing link," but later proved to be part of a hoax.

pipe stem dating a dating method that helps determine the age of American colonial sites by measuring clay pipe stem diameters, which were typically reduced in size from 1620 to 1800.

point see PROJECTILE POINT.

post mold a circular discoloration of ground, left from the rotting of a post.

potassium-argon dating a method of determining the age of a lava flow by measuring the rate at which its potassium-40 content decays into argon.

pot hunting the looting of archaeological sites, often by thieves wanting to sell in the antiquities market.

potsherd a piece of broken pottery; an archaeological artifact.

primitive ancient, prehistoric; crude and unsophisticated.

projectile point any stone point attached to either a spear or an arrow.

proton magnetometer a device composed of a sensor and a recording device that is moved over the surface of a site in a grid pattern to locate magnetic anomalies underground, the source of which could be anything from an iron object to pottery kilns, hearths, or tombs.

provenance the source or documented history of ownership of an artifact, used in archaeology to establish authenticity and therefore value. Also synonymous with provenience, although provenience is sometimes defined as the exact location where an artifact is found.

radiocarbon dating see CARBON-14 DATING.

radiometric dating any dating method employing the measurement of radioactive decay, such as with carbon 14 or potassium argon, to determine age.

red ochre iron oxide, used as a pigment by Native Americans.

relative dating a very broad dating method in which artifacts may be compared to other similar artifacts elsewhere and given an earlier, later, or contemporary designation.

remote sensing any one of a number of techniques, including ground-penetrating radar, electroresistance surveying, and magnetic resonance, used to uncover the location of buried artifacts.

screen a wooden frame and mesh used to sift out tiny bits of artifact from soil.

shard a broken piece of glass or ceramic.

site any location of archaeological interest, where remains of human activity can be found.

site steward one who protects a site from vandals and thieves.

stele a large, upright stone monument bearing an inscription or design.

Stone Age the period from roughly 2 million years ago to roughly 6000 B.C., and divided into three sub-ages, the Paleolithic, the Mesolithic, and the Neolithic. The age is named for the advancement of the construction of stone tools.

Stonehenge an arrangement of upright stone slabs in Salisbury Plain, England, constructed during the Neolithic period.

strata natural layers of sediment.

stratigraphic column created over centuries, a column or block of layered soil deposits, with the most recent material usually located at the top and the oldest on the bottom. However, in some geological circumstances, such as earthquake or volcanic activity, a column may be upended, with the oldest materials on top.

stratigraphy the layering and sequencing of soil deposits over centuries.

Sumerians advanced human culture of Mesopotamia credited with the invention of writing after 4000 B.C.

survey the close examination of ground in order to find clues of past human occupation or activity.

transit a surveyor's tool used in the field to measure angles and help make accurate topographic maps.

tree ring dating see DENDROCHRONOLOGY.

trilithon a prehistoric monument composed of a large, horizontal slab resting on two standing or upright slabs.

troglodyte any prehistoric, prehuman or human cave dweller.

tumulus a prehistoric grave mound; a barrow.

vestige an outmoded physical remnant of an ancient physical characteristic or organ on a modern human, such as an appendix or canine teeth.

Woodland the period of North American prehistory from 3000 to 1300 B.C., a time that marks the beginning of the appearance of pottery.

ASTRONOMY

Drake equation formulated by Dr. Frank Drake in 1960 in preparation for the meeting in Green Bank, West Virginia, that established the search for extraterrestrial intelligence (SETI) as a scientific discipline. It suggested that a large number of extraterrestrial civilizations would form, but that technological civilizations tend to destroy themselves quickly.

Epsilon Eridani harboring a star by the same name, the closest solar system to our own, approximately 62 trillion miles out, and thought to contain a similar system of planets and asteroid belts. It was the fictional location of the planet Vulcan, home to *Star Trek*'s Spock.

Fermi paradox named after Enrico Fermi, who marveled over the high probability of extraterrestrial civilizations across the galaxy yet puzzled over the complete lack of radio signals from them.

Formalhaut-B orbiting the star Formalhaut, the first planet outside our solar system captured visibly in a photograph, in 2008. Although larger than Jupiter, it is 1 billion times fainter than the star it orbits.

giant molecular cloud in interstellar space, a massive cloud of mostly hydrogen molecules, sometimes containing enough material to create millions of suns.

Great Silence, the astronomers' term for the complete lack of radio signals received from other intelligent beings across the galaxy, a puzzle considering how many habitable planets there are likely to be.

heliosheath a region outside the termination shock, where the solar wind slows, thickens, and mixes with interstellar gases.

protoplanet a planet in the process of formation.

protoplanetary debris revolving around a star, a giant ring or cloud of dust and debris from which planets eventually form.

protostar a very dense area of a molecular cloud, where a star is in the process of forming.

termination shock a region outside the solar system where outer space begins and the solar wind drops below supersonic speeds, the furthest distance spacecraft from Earth have traveled.

CHEMISTRY

absolute zero the lowest temperature theoretically possible, –273.15°C or –459.67°F, in which no heat or motion can exist.

absorption the taking in or soaking up of a gas or liquid, by a liquid or a solid.

accelerator a catalyst that starts or speeds up a chemical reaction without itself being changed.

acid a corrosive compound having a pH less than 7.0 and a hydrogen ion activity greater than water.

activator any substance having the ability to increase the action of a catalyst.

additive a substance combined with another to alter its form, consistency, properties, etc.

adsorption the attachment of a layer of gas, liquid, or solid onto the surface of another substance without being absorbed.

alkali an ionic salt of an alkali metal or alkaline earth metal element.

alloy a metal containing two or more elements.

amphoteric capable of reacting as either an acid or a base.

anion a negatively charged atom or atom grouping.

anticatalyst a substance that stops or slows a chemical reaction, especially by weakening the action of a catalyst.

atmosphere a measure of air pressure, specifically 1 atmosphere is equal to that experienced at sea level.

atom the smallest component of an element.

atomic mass the total number of protons and neutrons in an atom's nucleus.

atomic number the total number of protons in an element.

atomic symbol on the periodic table, the symbol that corresponds to each element.

atomize to transform a liquid into a fine spray, mist, or aerosol. Also, to nebulize.

Avogadro's number the number of atoms or molecules in one mole or 6.02×10^{23}. Also known as Avogadro constant. See MOLE.

base the opposite of an acid, a chemical compound with a pH above 7.0; an alkali. Ammonia is a base.

biodegradation the breaking down and transformation of organic substances, usually through the release of enzymes by microorganisms.

buffer solution a solution added to a mixture to maintain pH at a constant level, used in fermentation and other processes.

catalysis through the use of a catalyst, the speeding up of a chemical reaction.

catalyst any substance used to start or speed up a chemical reaction.

cation an atom or atom grouping with a positive charge.

chain reaction a series of chemical reactions, with each change setting up the necessary products for the next.

charcoal a porous substance made from wood, bone, or coconut, used to absorb gases and liquids.

chelation the removal of metal ions from a solution, used in medicine to treat lead or mercury poisoning.

chemist one who studies and works with chemicals to create useful compounds and mixtures, to determine the chemical makeup of materials, or to perform medical testing and research.

chemoluminescence a glow or giving off of light, produced by a chemical reaction.

chromatography originally named for the process of separating pigments, now encompassing the separation of any mixture, specifically by passing it through another material, with some components naturally sticking to the material better than others.

cleavage the breaking up of chemical bonds into smaller molecules.

closed chain in a molecule, a string of atoms that forms a loop or ring.

colloid a mixture that appears homogeneous but contains components that have incompletely dissolved. Aerosols, foams, and emulsions are all colloids.

compound any mixture of two or more elements.

concentration an increase in density or strength, achieved by removing water, impurities, or other substances. Also, the volume of a substance within a mixture of others.

condensation the changing of a gas into a liquid.

conductor any material that allows an electrical current to pass through it.

decompensation reaction the breaking down of large molecules into smaller ones.

deposition the process through which a gas turns into a solid without forming into a liquid first.

dilution the thinning of a concentrated liquid by adding another liquid or a solvent.

distill to separate components in a mixture by heating them.

electrochemistry a branch of chemistry involving the study of chemical reactions with voltage applied, or the creation of voltage throughout chemical reactions themselves.

electrolysis forcing an electrical current through a cell to produce an electrochemical reaction.

electrolyte any compound that when dissolved in water can conduct electricity.

element any pure substance that cannot be broken down into any other component elements.

emulsion any blend of two liquids that cannot be mixed, such as oil and water, and will eventually separate.

equilibrium in a chemical substance, a state of stability, when no further reactions or changes can take place.

exothermic referring to any reaction that creates heat.

extraction the separation of compounds in a mixture by the addition of a solvent and then subjecting it to shaking.

formula the constituent elements in a molecular compound, written out as a set of symbols and numbers.

half-life the amount of time it takes to break down half of a chemical component or to convert it into another product.

heterogeneous referring to a mixture with two or more separate components that are unevenly mixed.

homogeneous referring to any mixture that has been thoroughly blended and has a uniform composition.

imbibition the absorbing of a liquid by a solid.

immiscible incapable of being mixed or blended, as oil and water.

inert tending to be chemically nonreactive or inactive.

inhibitor any chemical or chemical compound used to slow or stop a reaction.

insulator any material through which electricity is unable to flow.

intermediate any chemical that is temporarily created by a chain reaction and then consumed by that reaction.

kinetics the study of chemical reaction rates.

mass spectrometry the process in which an ionized sample is passed through electric and magnetic fields to determine molecular formulas in a substance.

molarity the number of moles in a dissolved solution, a measure of concentration.

molar mass the weight of one mole of a given compound.

mole a unit of mass equaling 602 billion trillion atoms or molecules, or 6.02×10^{23}. Also known as Avogadro's number.

molecule a group of bound atoms.

monomer a small or simple molecule that may bond with other monomers to form a polymer. Amino acids are monomers that bond with others to form proteins.

orbital the space around the nucleus of an atom where electrons can be found.

osmosis the passing or diffusion of molecules of liquid solvent through a semipermeable membrane, from an area of high concentration to an area of lower concentration.

parts per million a measure of a very small amount of a substance within a much larger volume of another substance, for example one drop of food coloring to a million drops of water.

periodic table a table listing the elements with their symbols, arranged by order of their atomic numbers and structure.

pH a measure of how acidic or alkaline a substance is.

phase the physical state of matter, either a gas, liquid, or solid.

poisoned of a chemical reaction, slowed, stopped, or corrupted by an inhibitor.

polymer a large molecule made up of a chain of monomers. Plastic is a polymer.

precipitate a particle or particles of matter that becomes separated from a solution.

product the substance that is created after all chemical reactions have ceased.

reactant see REAGENT.

reagent any compound, mixture, or substance, other than a solvent or catalyst, added to another substance to test for chemical reaction in order to expose the presence or absence of a specific chemical. Also known as a reactant.

rectify to refine or purify by distillation.

reversible reaction a chemical reaction that can produce a product that may be reverted back to its original constituents.

solute that which gets dissolved when immersed in a solvent.

solution a homogeneous mixture.

solvent any substance, usually liquid, with the ability to dissolve other substances.

sorption absorption of a gas by a solid.

stoichiometry the study of the relationships of the volumes of substances and reactants in a chemical reaction, used to calculate how much of various chemicals will be needed to make a final product.

sublimation the process through which a solid turns into a gas without first turning into a liquid, the best example being dry ice.

suspension any solution in which particles have not dissolved.

synthesize to combine two or more elements in order to create a new substance.

titration an analysis to determine the concentration or volume of a reactant.

valency the power within an element to combine with others, measured by its ability to combine or displace atoms. A variant of valence.

volatile any unstable substance that can change rapidly from a solid to a vapor. Also, unstable, as an adjective.

zymergy the chemistry involved in the fermentation process, as in the making of beer or wine.

COMETS

aphelion the point of a comet's orbit farthest from the Sun.

coma the cloud of diffuse gas and fine particles that surrounds and obscures a comet's nucleus.

dust tail a relatively short, curving tail with a high silica content that, reflected by sunlight, gives off a yellowish hue. Also known as a type-II comet.

elliptical orbit an orbit that traces the path of an ellipse.

exotic ice small components of comet ice made from methane, ammonia, carbon dioxide, or another nonwater source.

fireballs fiery meteors that crash to Earth and are frequently mistaken for comets.

flourescence the radiating of blue fluorescent light from electrically charged monoxide molecules in a comet's coma.

gegenschein "counterglow"; the faint, eerie glow seen in the sky exactly opposite from where the Sun has set, caused by reflected light from a huge ring of cometal debris enveloping the Sun. Same as the zodiacal light but seen in the opposite side of the sky.

hyperbolic comet a distant comet that follows a hyperbolic orbit.

ion tail a long, straight tail colored blue by electrically charged molecules absorbing blue light from the Sun and reradiating it to Earth. Also known as a type-I comet.

long-period comet a comet that takes centuries to complete its orbit.

nucleus the ball of dirty ice at the center of a comet.

Oort cloud a vast, unseen repository of more than 1 trillion comets surrounding the Sun at a distance of 50,000 astronomical units.

perihelion the nearest point to the Sun in a comet's orbit.

perturbation a disturbance in the orbit of a comet by the gravity force from a nearby planet or other large body.

rocket effect the melting and vaporizing of comet ice, forming jets of gas and a rocketing effect that disturbs the orbital path of the comet.

short-period comet a comet that completes its orbit every few years.

type-I comet see ION TAIL.

type-II comet see DUST TAIL.

zodiacal light same as gegenschein but seen in the opposite side of the sky, above where the Sun has set.

CONSTELLATIONS

CONSTELLATIONS OF THE NORTHERN HEMISPHERE

Latin Name	English Equivalent
Andromeda	Andromeda
Aquila	Eagle
Auriga	Charioteer
Boötes	Herdsman
Camelopardalis	Giraffe
Canes Venactici	Hunting Dogs
Cassiopeia	Cassiopeia
Cepheus	Cepheus
Coma Berenices	Berenice's Hair
Corona Borealis	Northern Crown
Cygnus	Swan
Delphinus	Dolphin
Draco	Dragon
Equuleus	Foal
Hercules	Hercules
Hydra	Sea Serpent or Monster
Lacerta	Lizard
Leo Minor	Little Lion
Lynx	Lynx
Lyra	Lyre
Ophiuchus	Serpent Bearer
Pegasus	Pegasus
Perseus	Perseus
Sagitta	Arrow
Serpens	Serpent
Triangulum	Triangle
Ursa Major	Great Bear (Big Dipper)
Ursa Minor	Little Bear (Little Dipper)
Vulpecula	Fox

CONSTELLATIONS OF THE SOUTHERN HEMISPHERE

Latin Name	English Equivalent
Antlia	Air Pump
Apus	Bird of Paradise
Ara	Altar
Caelum	Sculptor's Tool
Canis Major	Greater Dog
Canis Minor	Lesser Dog
Carina	Keel
Centaurus	Centaur
Cetus	Whale
Chameleon	Chameleon
Circinus	Compasses
Columba	Dove
Corona Australis	Southern Crown
Corvus	Crow
Crater	Cup
Crux	Southern Cross
Dorado	Swordfish
Eridanus	River
Fornax	Furnace
Grus	Crane
Horologium	Clock
Hydrus	Water Snake
Indus	Indian
Lepus	Hare
Lupus	Wolf
Mensa	Table
Microscopium	Microscope
Monoceros	Unicorn
Musca	Southern Fly
Norma	Square
Octans	Octant
Orion	Orion (the Hunter)
Pavo	Peacock
Phoenix	Phoenix
Pictor	Painter
Piscis Austrinus	Southern Fish
Puppis	Poop (deck of *Argo*)
Pyxis	Mariner's Compass
Reticulum	Net
Sculptor	Sculptor

Scutum	Shield
Sextans	Sextant
Telescopium	Telescope
Triangulum Australe	Southern Triangle
Toucan	Toucan
Vela	Sail
Volans	Flying Fish

CONSTELLATIONS OF THE ZODIAC

Latin Name	English Equivalent
Aquarius	Water Bearer
Aries	Ram
Cancer	Crab
Capricornus	Goat
Gemini	Twins
Leo	Lion
Libra	Scales
Pisces	Fishes
Sagittarius	Archer
Scorpius	Scorpion
Taurus	Bull
Virgo	Virgin

ELEMENTS

actinium, aluminum, americium, antimony, argon, arsenic, astatine, barium, berkelium, beryllium, bismuth, bohrium, boron, bromine, cadmium, calcium, californium, carbon, cerium, cesium, chlorine, chromium, cobalt, copper, curium, darmstadtium, dubnium, dysprosium, einsteinium, erbium, europium, fermium, fluorine, francium, gadolinium, gallium, germanium, gold, hafnium, hassium, helium, holmium, hydrogen, indium, iodine, iridium, iron, krypton, lanthanum, lawrencium, lead, lithium, lutetium, magnesium, manganese, meitnerium, mendelevium, mercury, molybdenum, neodymium, neon, neptunium, nickel, niobium, nitrogen, nobelium, osmium, oxygen, palladium, phosphorous, platinum, plutonium, polonium, potassium, praseodymium, promethium, protactinium, radium, radon, rhenium, rhodium, roentgenium, rubidium, ruthenium, rutherfordium, samarium, scandium, selenium, silicon, silver, sodium, strontium, sulfur, tantalum, technetium, tellurium, terbium, thallium, thorium, thulium, tin, titanium, tungsten, ununbium, ununhexium, ununpentium, ununquadrium, ununtrexium, uranium, vanadium, xenon, ytterbium, yttrium, zinc, zirconium.

EVOLUTION

allopatric a mode of speciation, through which one group of a population breaks away from another, becomes geographically isolated, and changes gradually over time due to differences in environmental pressures.

biased gene conversion unrelated to natural selection, a process that speeds up the rate of evolution in certain genes, through both positive and negative mutations, which may spread rapidly throughout a population.

catastrophism theory of evolutionary change brought about by a worldwide catastrophe, such as a collision with an asteroid and resulting climate change.

cladistics the classification of species according to evolutionary lineage. Also known as phylogenetics.

cladogram a diagram showing the branching off of life-forms as they evolved into different forms. Also called a family tree or tree of life.

classification in modern biology, a hierarchical arrangement of life-forms in related groupings, specifically by species, genus, family, order, class, phylum, and kingdom.

coevolution the ongoing adaptation of two or more animals in the same geographical range, through which changes in one lead to changes in the other, as predator and prey.

common ancestor the forebear from which two different species branched off and evolved their own traits.

convergence the independent development of the same useful trait in two or more different species, as wings are convergent in birds and bats.

creationism a religious explanation for all of Earth's diversity, through which an all-powerful god created all life-forms in their present state, a belief system derived from the Bible and discredited by mainstream science.

Darwinism Charles Darwin's scientific theory that life continuously evolves and species change over time due to environmental pressures and natural selection.

exaptation a new use for a body characteristic or component that originally evolved for a different purpose.

extinction the dying off of an entire species.

eugenics a term coined in 1883 by Francis Galton designating a scheme to manipulate evolution by allowing only strong, intelligent people to breed, thus creating a super race of humans, an idea that fell out of favor after World War II.

evolution, theory of a widely misinterpreted term. Not a hypothesis, as popularly believed, but an explanation of evolution, based on observed, proven, and verified facts, that remains open to adjustments and additional information.

fitness overall health, strength, and ability to mate and successfully raise offspring, a major component in evolution.

genetic drift changes in a gene pool, due merely to chance rather than forces in the environment.

gradualism a theory of gradual change over time, in contrast with catastrophism.

heredity the inheritance of genes and traits from one's parents and grandparents.

hopeful monster slang term for a mutant or mutated animal that, through major structural change, has the potential to spawn a new type or variation of a species. Major mutations, though, are more often harmful than beneficial.

intelligent design a religious explanation for life and all its complexity, through which an all-powerful god designed and created all, discredited by mainstream science because it cannot be tested or proven.

macromutation a large-scale mutation, resulting in significant change in an animal. Most macromutations are of no benefit and usually cause more harm than good.

micromutation a small or microscopic mutation, many of which are needed to bring about significant change in an animal.

missing link an outmoded term for a transitional animal or fossil, a developmental form between two distinctly different species.

mutation a mistake or change in genetic material, due to various forces, that along with other mutations may result in a change in an animal's traits. Mutations are often detrimental, but they are occasionally beneficial enough to be passed on successfully to generations of offspring.

mutualism the development and adaptations of two species that evolve side by side and benefit from each other, as flowers and bees.

natural selection the natural law governing all life, through which organisms best adapted to their environments survive and pass on their successful traits to their offspring, while poorly adapted forms eventually die out.

phyletic gradualism in contrast to punctuated equilibrium, the theory that evolution proceeds gradually over time, without big jumps or rapid changes.

phylogenetic tree see CLADOGRAM.

phylogeny the study of the relationships between species, as in a family tree.

punctuated equilibrium a theory that maintains that evolution does not always follow a slow or gradual path, and that change can come quickly in bursts, for example, as a result of catastrophic environmental changes, as when a comet or asteroid strikes the Earth and radically alters the climate, or when a species lives in relative isolation and changes to fit its own microenvironment.

Scopes monkey trial the famous 1925 trial of the teacher John Scopes, who was convicted of illegally teaching evolution to his students and was fined $100, the long-term effect of which was to prevent evolution from being covered in school textbooks until the 1960s.

selective pressures any environmental stresses, such as change of climate, drop in food sources, increased predation, or others, that force a life-form to either change environments or develop new traits, as through evolution.

speciation the change of one species and branching off into another, usually due to differences in surroundings.

taxonomy the biological classification of life-forms.

trait a characteristic.

vestigial referring to a body part or trait that has diminished in size, function, or importance over the years, such as canine teeth in humans.

young earth creationism religious explanation of creation, based on the Bible, from which it is believed the Earth is only a few thousand years old, a notion discredited by mainstream science.

MOON

albedo the percentage of light received from the Sun that is reflected off the Moon's surface (approximately 7 percent). (The Earth reflects about 40 percent of received sunlight.)

Apennines a 600-mile-long mountain range with summits rising to 15,000 feet (one mountain, Mt. Huygens, rises to nearly 20,000 feet) located in the Moon's northeast quadrant.

apogee point of the Moon's orbit farthest from the Earth.

blue moon the rare occurrence of a full moon appearing twice in one month.

Clavius a large, walled plain 145 miles across in the Moon's southeast quadrant; from its depressed interior, walls rise 17,000 feet.

Copernicus one of the most famous of the Moon's craters, 56 miles in diameter.

crater an impact hole or depression caused by a meteor.

craterlet a small crater.

cusp a horn of the crescent moon.

domes mound structures resembling pingoes on Earth.

gibbous of a Moon phase, between half and full.

harvest moon the full moon that rises early in the evening nearest the time of the autumnal equinox, September 23, providing illumination for the fall harvest.

hunter's moon the first full moon following the harvest moon, providing illumination for hunters.

Luna in Roman mythology, the goddess of the Moon.

lunacy a form of insanity once thought to be caused or influenced by the Moon.

lunar eclipse darkening of the Moon caused by the Earth coming between it and the Sun.

lunar month the period between successive new moons: 29 days, 12 hours, 44 minutes.

mare a large dark plain on the Moon, in ancient times thought to be a sea. Its plural form is "maria."

Mare Imbrium the "sea of showers"; a circular plain, or mare, 700 miles in diameter in the northeast quadrant of the Moon.

Mare Tranquillitatis the "sea of tranquillity"; the sight of Moon landings, in the northwest quadrant.

new moon in a position between the Sun and Earth, the first phase of the Moon, with its unlit side facing Earth; at sunset, it may appear as a very narrow crescent.

nimbus moon the Moon with an apparent halo or nimbus, caused by the refraction of light by ice crystals in high, thin cirrus or cirrostratus clouds of Earth.

occultation the passing of the Moon in front of another celestial body, thus obscuring it.

Oceanus Procellarum the "ocean of storms," largest of all lunar marias, with an area of 2 million square miles.

perigee the point of the Moon's orbit nearest to Earth.

phases the dark side of the Moon facing Earth is called the new moon (more accurately defined as a "black" moon because it is invisible from Earth). The first sliver of moon is called the crescent. The thickened crescent is the first quarter. Between the half and full moon is the gibbous, followed by full and a reversal of phases.

ray an impact line or crack radiating out from some craters.

rille a narrow trench.

selenian pertaining to the Moon.

selenography the study of the Moon's surface.

selenology the study of the Moon.

terminator the line separating the daylight side from the night side.

Tycho the famous rayed crater, 54 miles in diameter in the southeast quadrant.

wane shrinking phase of the Moon.

wax growing phase of the Moon.

PARTICLES AND PARTICLE PHYSICS

accelerator a machine that uses electric or magnetic fields to accelerate a beam of charged particles to a very high level of speed and energy.

alpha particle a positively charged particle made up of two protons and two neutrons.

amu atomic mass unit.

annihilation the collision and disappearance of a particle and an antiparticle, and the subsequent formation or appearance of a different particle and antiparticle.

antiparticle see ANTIMATTER.

antimatter antiparticles (antifermions) with the opposite properties of particles. If a particle has a positive charge, the antiparticle will have a negative charge. The reverse is also true. The muon, for example, has a negative charge and the antimuon has a positive one.

antiquark the antiparticle of a quark.

atom the smallest particle of any element or matter. It consists of a nucleus containing protons and neutrons, and electrons that move around the nucleus.

atomic mass the weight or mass of an atom as expressed in unified atomic mass units, with one unit equal to $\frac{1}{12}$ of the mass of a carbon-12 atom.

atomic mass unit unit of atomic weight, with one unit equal to $\frac{1}{12}$ of the mass of a carbon-12 atom.

atomic number the number of protons in a nucleus. Atoms of the same element have the same atomic number.

atomic theory the theory that everything is made up of atoms and subatomic particles and that physical phenomenon can be explained by their interactions.

atomic weight the weight of one atom of a given element, expressed in atomic mass units.

atom smasher an accelerator.

baryon a hadron composed of three quarks and subject to strong interactions.

beta particle a high-energy electron or positron ejected by a radioactive nucleus.

B-meson an extremely short-lived meson.

boson any of a class of subatomic particles, including mesons, weakons, classons, and photons, that do not obey the Pauli exclusion principle. All particles are either bosons or fermions.

carbon dating a technique for determining the ages of substances or objects that contain carbon by measuring how much carbon 14 remains in them.

carbon 14 a radioactive isotope of carbon, having a half-life of 5,730 years, and subsequently used to determine the age of carbon-containing fossils, archaeological artifacts, and so forth.

CERN Center for European Nuclear Research; an international accelerator facility near Geneva, Switzerland.

chain reaction a series of self-sustaining nuclear reactions.

charm a characteristic in particles that predicts the lack of reaction between certain particles and that accounts for the long life of the J particle.

classon either a photon or a graviton, which have neither mass nor charge.

cold fusion hypothetical method of creating unlimited energy by fusing atoms in a test tube with much lower temperatures and pressures than traditionally believed to be possible.

collider an accelerator that creates two beams of charged particles that collide head on, used for research and experimental purposes.

color the distinguishing characteristic of quarks that determines their behavior in the strong interaction.

cosmic rays particles of energy radiating from space.

critical mass the minimum amount of fissionable material needed to cause a nuclear explosion.

curie a unit of radioactivity equal to the quantity of a radioactive isotope that decays at 37,000,000,000 disintegrations per second.

cyclotron a circular accelerator in which particles in a magnetic field are propelled by alternating high-frequency voltage, to study interactions.

dalton an atomic mass unit.

decay a process in which a particle gradually disappears and is replaced with a different particle or particles.

deuterium an isotope of hydrogen.

deuteron the nucleus of deuterium, used in accelerator collisions of particles for research purposes.

$E = mc^2$ Albert Einstein's formula, energy equals mass multiplied by the velocity of light squared, which can be used to explain the loss of mass in a nuclear reaction and its ultimate conversion to energy.

electron a subatomic particle or lepton with a negative charge. A cloud of electrons surround an atomic nucleus.

dose a quantity of radiation absorbed by a body.

dosimeter a device containing photographic film, which darkens the more it is exposed to radiation. It is worn and monitored by people who work around radiation sources. Also known as a film badge.

electromagnetic force one of the four fundamental forces of nature, the interaction between particles caused by their electric and magnetic fields. Also known as electromagnetic interaction.

electron a negatively charged particle that moves around the nucleus of an atom.

electroweak force the combined effects of the electromagnetic and weak forces.

elementary particle any indivisible subatomic particle in a nucleus, such as a lepton, quark, weakon, or classon.

exclusion principle the law of physics that states that no two identical particles can have the same set of quantum numbers or occupy the same quantum state. More formally known as the Pauli exclusion principle.

fast neutron a neutron that can produce fission.

Fermilab the Fermi National Accelerator Laboratory in Batavia, Illinois.

fermion a subatomic particle with peculiar angular momentum or spin and which cannot exist in the same state simultaneously as any other fermion. Electrons, protons, neutrons, quarks, and leptons are all fermions.

film badge see DOSIMETER.

fissile fissionable. The isotopes uranium 235 and plutonium 239 are highly fissile.

fission a nuclear reaction through which an atom is split, releasing massive energy.

flavor designating any one of the types of quarks or leptons. in quarks, the flavors are up, down, charm, strange, top, and bottom. In leptons, the flavors are electron, muon, tau, electron neutrino, muon neutrino, and tau neutrino.

fundamental interaction any one of the four fundamental forces of nature—electromagnetic, weak, strong, and gravitational.

fusion a nuclear reaction through which two atoms combine to form another element, releasing massive energy. It is the primary energy of stars.

gamma ray electromagnetic radiation with a high penetration power, produced by nuclear reactions.

Geiger counter an instrument used to detect and measure the presence of ionizing particles.

gluon a massless subatomic particle that binds quarks through strong force to form hadrons, such as protons and neutrons.

grand unified theory the theory that strong, weak, gravitational, and electromagnetic forces are variations of the same force.

graviton a theoretical subatomic particle or string without mass or charge, a possible unit of gravity.

gravity one of the four fundamental forces of nature, the attractive force or pull created by any mass.

hadron a subatomic particle composed of quarks and antiquarks that interacts strongly with other particles.

heavy water in nuclear reactors, water with a high content of deuterium atoms.

half-life the time it takes half of the atoms in a radioactive substance to disintegrate or decay into another element.

isobars atoms having the same atomic weight but different atomic numbers.

isomers atoms having the same number of neutrons and protons but having different energy states.

isotones atoms with the same number of neutrons but different atomic numbers.

isotopes atoms with the same atomic number but different number of neutrons.

kaon an unstable meson produced in a high-energy particle collision. It contains a strange quark and an anti-up and anti-down quark or an anti-strange quark and an up or down quark.

k meson a kaon.

lamda particle an electrically neutral baryon.

lepton a subatomic particle involved in weak interactions with other particles. Electrons, muons, and neutrinos are leptons.

mass number the total number of neutrons and protons in a nucleus.

mass spectroscope a device that uses magnetic fields and electric fields to measure the mass of charged particles.

meltdown the overheating and melting of the core of a nuclear reactor, due to accidental loss of coolant.

meson an unstable particle composed of a quark and an antiquark that is subject to the strong force.

molecule two or more atoms bound together to form the smallest particle of any one element.

muon a subatomic particle created from a decayed, charged pion. It has a negative charge and itself decays into an electron.

neutrino a lepton with very little mass and no charge and that interacts only weakly. It exists in three flavors: the electron neutrino, the muon neutrino, and the tau neutrino.

neutrons electrically neutral particles, making up part of an atom's nucleus, along with protons.

nuclear physics the study of the atom's nucleus and its components.

nuclear force see STRONG FORCE.

nuclear reactor a device in which atoms undergo fission and heat energy is created.

nucleon any particle in the nucleus of an atom; a proton or neutron.

nucleus the core of an atom, composed of protons and neutrons. Its plural form is nuclei.

nuclide any of a class of atoms having the same number of protons, neutrons, and energy content.

orbitals orbiting paths where one or two electrons will almost always be found around a nucleus.

particle a subatomic object with both mass and a charge.

Pauli exclusion principle see EXCLUSION PRINCIPLE.

photon a massless subatomic particle, the quantum unit of electromagnetic radiation or light.

pi meson a pion.

pion part of the binding force of an atomic nucleus, any one of three types of mesons with a positive, negative, or neutral charge.

positron the antiparticle of the electron.

proton a positively charged particle, making up part of an atom's nucleus.

quantum mechanics the physical laws and dynamics concerning particles, their electric charges, momentum, etc.

quantum theory a theory that states that energy is made up of pulsing quanta and that the amount of energy carried by photons is proportional to the frequency of the emitted electromagnetic radiation.

quark a fundamental particle and building block of protons, neutrons, and other elementary particles. There are six variations, or flavors, known as up, down, strange, charmed, bottom, and top.

rad a unit of radiation that is absorbed.

radiation any one of various emissions of energy, including gamma rays, X-rays, neutrons, alpha particles, beta particles, etc.

radiation sickness a potentially fatal illness with such symptoms as nausea, bleeding, hair loss, diarrhea, and a compromised immune system, caused by overexposure to radiation.

radioactivity emissions of particles or electromagnetic rays.

radioelement any radioactive element.

radioisotope any radioactive substance, whether natural or humanmade.

radiotherapy the use of radiation to treat disease, particularly cancer.

rem a unit used to measure the deleterious effects of ionizing radiation on living tissue, the equivalent of one roentgen of X-rays or gamma rays.

roentgen a unit of exposure of ionizing radiation, as that from X-rays.

Rutheford-Bohr atom originating in 1911 by Ernest Rutheford and Niels Bohr, the erroneous theory of electrons circling in a regular orbit around a nucleus, as planets around the Sun.

scintillation a flash of light emitted by a phosphor when it absorbs a photon or ionizing particle.

slow neutron also known as a thermal neutron, a slow-moving neutron capable of fission.

spin a particle's rotation in a consistent direction about an axis.

stable referring to a particle that does not decay or disintegrate into another element.

string as proposed in string theory, a vibrating, one-dimensional stringlike particle with length but no thickness, postulated as the basic unit of all matter. Strings interact by splitting and joining.

string theory any one of several theories that states that the basic unit of matter or reality in the universe is not the point of a particle but a vibrating, one-dimensional stringlike particle that splits and joins with other strings. The basic string theory requires that spacetime have 26 dimensions, while an advanced theory, the superstring theory, requires 10 such dimensions. String theory provides a unifying structure to explain the behavior of natural forces and elementary particles; however, the theory cannot be proven. (The term *string theory* increasingly refers to superstring theory.)

strong force one of the four fundamental forces of nature, a force that binds quarks, antiquarks, and gluons and makes hadrons. Also known as nuclear force or strong interaction.

strontium 90 a dangerous radioactive isotope, found in fallout following a nuclear explosion.

subatomic referring to the interior of an atom or that which is smaller than an atom.

supercollider a giant, high-speed particle accelerator.

superstring theory see STRING THEORY.

tau the heaviest lepton.

thermonuclear reaction an occurrence of fusion created by extremely high temperatures. One of a chain of such reactions that occur continuously on the Sun and stars.

tracer a radioisotope with a short half-life placed inside a substance that is injected into the body and tracked. High levels of the radioisotope in an organ may indicate cancer.

weak force one of the four fundamental forces of nature, it is involved in the interchange of energy, mass, and charge within the nuclei between leptons and quarks and their antiparticles. The weak force is responsible for the change of one particle into another. Also known as weak interaction.

weakon any one of three large particles, the neutral Z particle, or the positive and negative W particles, involved in the weak force.

WIMP weakly interactive massive particle; a hypothetical subatomic particle with a large mass that interacts weakly through gravity, a possible form of dark matter in the universe.

SPACE

accelerating universe the expansion of the universe, with galaxies receding into the far reaches of space at greater and greater speeds. This is the most widely accepted model of the universe.

accretion disk a massive, rotating disk of gas and dust surrounding a newborn star or a black hole.

active galactic nucleus an extremely bright and energized region at the center of some galaxies, thought to be a giant accretion disk surrounding a black hole.

albedo the amount of light reflected off a celestial object.

aphelion a planet or comet's point of orbit farthest from the Sun.

asterism a group of stars not belonging to any of the 88 recognized constellations.

asteroid a very large rocky mass, ranging in size from a half mile to 600 miles across, that travels through space. Also known as a minor planet.

asteroid belt a ring of asteroids orbiting the Sun between Mars and Jupiter.

astral of or pertaining to the stars.

astrobiology the science concerning life or the potential for life on other planets.

astrology a pseudoscience that claims to be able to predict one's destiny according to the position of celestial bodies when one was born; widely discredited by science.

astronomical unit mean distance of the Earth from the Sun—92,900,000 miles—used to express the distances of other celestial bodies.

astronomy the study and observation of the universe.

astrophysics the science concerning the physical properties of the universe, such as light, chemical makeup, gravitational forces, etc.

aurora the colored bands or streamers of light that appear across the night sky when charged particles from the Sun interact with Earth's magnetic field. In the Northern Hemisphere, the aurora is known as the northern lights, or aurora borealis. In the Southern Hemisphere, it is the southern lights, or aurora australis.

big bang the prevailing theoretical model of the creation of the universe, in which it is postulated that an infinitely hot dot of matter smaller than an electron exploded 13.7 billion years ago and rapidly expanded to form all of the gases, matter, stars, and galaxies in existence today.

binary a double star, each revolving around the other.

black hole a star that has exploded and collapsed to infinity, leaving behind a gravity force so powerful that nothing can escape it, including light.

blueshift the decrease in wavelength of light emitted by a celestial object that is moving toward an observer.

bolide a bright meteor or fireball.

brane theory a theoretical model in which the universe is postulated to be a three-dimensional membrane residing in a four-dimensional space that cannot be perceived and is accessible only to gravity.

brown dwarf a mysterious celestial object composed of gas that is smaller than a star but larger than a Jupiter-size planet and that radiates small amounts of energy.

catena a chain of craters.

cephid variable a yellow supergiant star that expands and shrinks every three to 50 days.

closed universe a theoretical model of the universe in the shape of a sphere that closes in on itself.

comet a celestial body composed of ice and rock.

conjunction orbital position of an inferior planet when it is directly between the Earth and the Sun or when it is at the exact opposite side of the Sun from the Earth. Also the orbital position of a superior planet when it is on the opposite side of the Sun from Earth.

conservation of energy and mass law of physics that holds that the amount of energy and mass in the universe remains unchanged.

constellation a group of stars, named for an object, animal, or mythical figure.

cosmic microwave background microwave and other radiation remaining from the big bang; it is present in every part of the sky.

cosmic ray a stream of ionizing radiation from space, largely of protons, alpha particles, and other atomic nuclei.

cosmic year the time it takes the Sun to travel around the center of the galaxy, roughly 225 million years.

cosmogony the study of the creation of the universe.

cosmological principle the principle that states that matter is evenly distributed throughout space.

cosmology the study of the form, content, and evolution of the universe.

culmination the point when a celestial object reaches its greatest possible altitude above Earth's horizon.

curvature of space according to Albert Einstein's theory of gravitation, massive objects in space, such as stars, cause space to curve and light to bend.

cyclic model any one of a number of hypothetical models of creation in which the universe expands and then contracts and either collides with an unseen, parallel universe, ultimately forming a new universe, or which re-creates the big bang and expands anew in an endless cycle.

dark matter composing a large portion of the universe, matter that cannot be seen but can be perceived through its gravitational effects.

declination the position of a star as located through the combination of two coordinates, east-west (right ascension) and north-south of the celestial equator.

Doppler effect the change in wave frequency, with light or sound, as a source moves toward or away from an observer. An example is the sound of a train whistle as it approaches, passes directly in front of, and recedes from an observer. The pitch sounds as if it is lowered as the train passes and shrinks into the distance. The Doppler effect allows scientists to determine, among other things, if stars are moving away or toward us. It can also be used to determine the velocity of an object detected by radar.

eclipse the obscuring of one celestial body by another, most notably when the Moon passes in front of the Sun.

ephemeris a chart or table providing the future positions of celestial bodies.

event horizon the outer perimeter of a black hole, at which the force of gravity is so powerful that matter would have to exceed the speed of light in order to escape.

evolved star an older star that has converted most or all of its store of hydrogen into helium.

extrasolar planet any planet lying outside of our solar system, of which scores have been discovered.

flare star a star whose brightness can increase by as much as two to 100 times in a matter of minutes, then return to normal.

galaxy a large grouping of stars, sometimes consisting of billions of stars. Also known as an island universe.

galaxy cluster a grouping of galaxies held in close association by the strength of their collective gravity. A super cluster may hold as many as tens of thousands of galaxies across 100 million light-years of space.

geocentric relating to the Earth as a center; relative to the Earth.

geosynchronous orbit an orbit in which a satellite or other object keeps pace with the Earth's rotation. Also known as a geostationary orbit.

globular cluster a spherelike cluster of old stars, sometimes numbering in the hundreds of thousands.

gravitational clustering the natural tendency for a large mass, such as a galaxy, to attract other masses, including stars and galaxies, and to grow ever larger over time.

gravitational lens a massive object in space, such as a galaxy, that distorts, bends, or magnifies the light from objects behind it.

gravitational wave as predicted by Albert Einstein's general theory of relativity, a hypothetical wave, oscillation, or disturbance originating in a black hole or other source and thought to travel unimpeded across space.

Great Red Spot a massive perpetual storm on the surface of Jupiter.

Hubble constant the ratio of a galaxy's velocity in traveling away from the Earth divided by its distance from the Earth.

Hubble's law a law that states that due to the expanding universe, the velocity of a galaxy moving away from Earth is directly proportional to its distance from Earth.

hydrogen the Sun's primary gas and the most common element throughout space.

inferior planets the planets Venus and Mercury, whose orbits are closer to the Sun than Earth's.

interferometer the combination of two or more optical telescopes to produce sharper focus. Also, two or more radio telescopes combined to magnify radio signals.

interstellar dust dust particles between the stars.

interstellar space the vast regions of empty space between the stars.

inverse square law a law of physics that holds that gravity decreases with the square of the distance between two masses. Doubling the distance between two masses, for example, would reduce gravity by three-quarters. The same law applies to the magnitude or brightness of stars. Doubling a star's distance reduces brightness by three-quarters.

irregular galaxy a galaxy without an organized form, such as a spiral or globe.

island universe see GALAXY.

Kuiper belt a disk-shaped swarm of 200 million comets and comet fragments located from just beyond the orbit of Neptune and extending past Pluto.

light-year an astronomical unit of measurement, specifically the distance light travels in a year, approximately 5,880,000,000,000 miles.

Local Group, the a cluster of more than 30 galaxies, including Andromeda, the Milky Way, and the Magellanic Clouds.

Magellanic Clouds two irregular galaxies that can be seen with the naked eye in the southern sky.

magnetosphere the magnetic field that surrounds a planet.

magnetotail the outer portion of a planet's magnetosphere, which is pushed away from the Sun by the solar wind. It is so named because it forms a cometlike tail that extends away from a planet's night side.

magnitude a scale for measuring the apparent brightness of celestial bodies, the brightest being negative, zero, or first magnitude, the dimmest visible to the naked eye being sixth magnitude.

meridian the great circle passing through the sky's zenith and touching the north and south horizons.

meteor a rock or metal fragment entering Earth's atmosphere and burning up. Popularly known as a shooting star.

meteorite a meteor that is not completely burned away by the atmosphere and strikes the Earth.

meteoroid any one of the small rocks that travel throughout space and are officially designated as meteors when they enter Earth's atmosphere and flare across the sky.

meteor shower a raining down of a mass of meteors to Earth, caused when Earth passes through a cloud of debris from an old comet. Many meteor showers occur annually because the Earth passes through the same debris clouds on the same day or week each year.

Milky Way the galaxy of 100 billion stars within which the Earth and Sun are located. The faintly luminous band or river of stars that crosses the night sky in summer, which most people call the Milky Way, is actually only one arm of the galaxy, which is a spiral. The constellation of Sagittarius serves as a beacon for the galaxy's center.

minor planet see ASTEROID.

northern lights see AURORA.

nova an erupting star that temporarily brightens.

occultation the obscuring of a small or distant celestial body by a larger or closer body, such as the Moon passing in front of a star or planet.

old referring to a moon or planetary surface with numerous craters, an indication of great age.

Oort Cloud a vast belt thought to contain a trillion or more comets, located in the outermost reaches of the solar system, from one light-year out from the Sun to approximately halfway to the nearest star, Proxima Centauri.

open universe a theoretical model in which the universe never ends but expands infinitely in every direction.

opposition orbital position of a superior planet when it is on the opposite side of the Earth from the Sun.

orbit the path followed through space by a celestial body.

parallel universe a hypothetical, unseen universe that is postulated to exist in another dimension and that may have played a role in the creation of our own universe.

parsec astronomical unit of measurement equaling 3.26 light-years.

patera a shallow crater.

perigee point in the orbit of the Moon closest to Earth.

perihelion point of a body's orbit nearest the Sun.

planetesimal any one of the millions of small orbiting bodies that may have come together to form the planets.

proper motion the motion of the stars not related to the Earth's rotation.

protogalaxy a "baby" galaxy in its earliest stages of formation.

Proxima Centauri the nearest star to the Sun, located 4.22 light-years away; it requires a telescope to be seen.

pulsar a neutron star that emits X-rays or other types of radiation.

quasars quasi-stellar radio sources, the oldest and most remote visible objects in the universe, and among the most mysterious. They are believed to be active galactic nuclei powered by supermassive black holes. Also known as quasi-stellar objects.

radiant point where meteor showers appear to originate in the sky.

radio astronomy the study of radio frequency radiation from space through radio telescopes.

radio telescope a giant, dish-shaped telescope that gathers faint radio signals from space.

red giant a cool, red star many times larger than our sun.

redshift the shift of an emitted light's spectrum to a lower frequency, specifically toward the red end, when the light's source—a galaxy or other celestial body—moves away from an observer. The farther away an object is, generally, the larger the redshift exhibited. Astronomers use the light spectrum emitted by a celestial body to determine if it is moving away or toward us.

relativity, general theory of Albert Einstein's theory that matter causes space to curve. First published in 1916, this theory expands on his theory of special relativity, developed in 1905. In the general theory, Einstein postulated that large masses attract smaller masses, not because of some invisible force waves but because large masses "warp" space, just as a heavy ball placed in the middle of a rubber sheet warps the space around it and will cause other balls to roll toward it.

relativity, theory of special Albert Einstein's widely accepted and largely proven theory describing the laws of particles moving at close to the speed of light, which are different from those governing particles moving at slower speeds. Although the speed of light is always the same, no matter if an observer is in motion or standing still, Einstein postulated that moving clocks tick more slowly than stationary ones because time is literally slowed down. This effect is especially pronounced when approaching speeds near that of light.

retrograde an orbit of a satellite that is or appears opposite that of the Earth's rotation. Also, an orbit of a celestial object that is opposite of Earth's orbit around the Sun.

satellite an object or moon in orbit around a planet.

scintillation the apparent "twinkling" of the stars, which is caused by refraction of light passing through Earth's atmosphere, especially close to the horizon.

SETI Search for Extraterrestrial Intelligence; a scientific program dedicated to finding intelligent life in outer space through the gathering and study of radio waves.

Seyfert galaxy a type of spiral galaxy with an intensely bright nucleus and thought to contain a black hole.

shooting star a meteor.

sidereal as measured with respect to the stars.

singularity the center of a black hole, where matter is believed to be immensely compacted and dense and the force of gravity infinitely powerful.

solar wind a stream of gas continually blown out from the Sun at hundreds of kilometers per second.

solstice position of the Sun when farthest north (summer solstice) or farthest south (winter solstice) in the sky.

southern lights see AURORA.

spacetime the four-dimensional continuum composed of the three dimensions of space with time, through which an event can be precisely plotted.

spectroscope an instrument astronomers use to separate light into its component colors, creating a spectrum that can be analyzed to determine what elements a celestial body is made of.

spiral galaxy a galaxy in the configuration of a spiral or pinwheel, with the oldest stars clustered in a sphere in the center and the youngest stars forming the outer arms.

star a fiery sphere of gas; a sun.

starburst galaxy a galaxy in which new stars are rapidly forming.

superior planets the planets Mars, Jupiter, Saturn, Uranus, Neptune, and Pluto, whose orbits are farther from the Sun than the Earth's.

supermassive black hole a black hole that resides at the center of a galaxy and may contain the mass of millions of consumed stars.

sunspot cooler area visible as a dark spot in the surface of the Sun.

supernova an exploding star that increases its brightness thousands of times, dimming only after a period of months.

supernova remnant a nebula surrounding the site of an earlier supernova explosion.

symbiotic stars two stars so close together they exchange gases and mass.

terminator the line that delineates the dark side of a planet or moon from the lighted side.

transit method a method of discovering new planets by observing if a star dims temporarily, which sometimes means a planet or another star has passed in front of it.

uranography the mapping of the stars.

uranometry the scientific measurement of the distances, brightness, and positions of celestial bodies.

variable star a star with a varying magnitude or brightness.

white dwarf a tiny star comparable in volume to the Earth but with a mass equal to the Sun's and a density a million times that of water.

young referring to a moon or planetary surface that has a small number of craters, an indication of the planet's age.

zenith the point in the sky directly overhead.

zodiac the 12 constellations aligned along the ecliptic through which the Sun, Moon, and most of the planets travel.

zodiacal light a hazy band of light consisting of dust illuminated by the Sun and sometimes seen from Earth.

SUN

acronical occurring at sunset

bright spots X-ray and ultraviolet flashes on the Sun's surface closely associated with intense magnetic fields.

chromosphere the reddish solar atmosphere between the photosphere and the corona.

corona the tenuous outer atmosphere of the Sun extending into space for millions of miles but generally only visible during an eclipse.

coronal holes holes in the Sun's Corona created by openings in the Sun's magnetic fields through which are emitted high-speed solar wind particles; largely responsible for the magnetic storms on Earth.

coronal mass ejection a massive bubble of gas that periodically explodes from the Sun and discharges a wave of charged particles into space and toward Earth, disrupting satellite functioning and occasionally blacking out entire cities. Also known as a solar storm.

facula a bright spot on the surface of the Sun, especially near its perimeter.

filament a finger of cool gas suspended above the photosphere that may appear slightly darker against the brilliance of the Sun's surface.

flare an eruption on the Sun, causing a brightening and a jet of radiation and particles to be ejected into space, sometimes toward Earth. Flares occur most often near sunspots.

gegenschein a faint reflection of the Sun that may form on dust particles and appears in the evening sky opposite where the Sun has set.

granulation a reticular pattern of small bright areas or cells on the surface of the Sun.

helio referring to the Sun.

heliocentric relating to the Sun as a center; relative to the Sun.

heliolatry worship of the Sun.

Helios in Greek mythology, the sun god who drove his chariot across the sky from east to west each day.

heliosphere an area encompassing the area of the Sun and solar system out beyond Pluto, where the solar magnetic field can be found.

heliotaxis the movement of an organism in response to sunlight.

heliotherapy sunlight therapy.

heliotrope any plant that bends or turns to follow the daily path of the Sun.

mock sun a false image of the Sun, often watery in appearance, formed by the refraction or bending of light by hexagonal crystals of ice in the air. Also known as a sun dog.

neutrino produced by thermonuclear fusion in the Sun's core, a massless particle that has the bizarre ability to pass through physical objects such as the Earth.

penumbra the outer, lighter-colored border of a sunspot.

photosphere the visible surface of the Sun.

plage a bright spot or granulation appearing in the chromosphere.

plasma an electrically-charged, gaslike substance emitted by the Sun.

prominence a cool jet, stream, or arch of gas that rises from the chromosphere and into the corona, visible during an eclipse.

proton-proton chain the nuclear process by which energy is produced and hydrogen is converted into helium in the core of stars, including the Sun.

Ra Egyptian sun god.

sigmoid an S-shaped formation of plasma on the surface of the Sun that presages a coronal mass ejection.

Sol the Latin name for the Sun.

solar constant the total radiant energy put out by the Sun on a continuing basis, specifically 1,369 watts per square meter as measured above Earth's atmosphere.

solar cycle the 11-year cycle of sunspot and solar flare activity, known to cause, at its peak, increased magnetic storm effects on Earth. Also known as sunspot cycle.

solar eclipse the obscuring of the Sun caused by the Moon passing in front of it.

solar flare a huge tongue of gases and particles extending suddenly from a catastrophic explosion on the Sun's surface to millions of miles out into space.

solar nebula the massive cloud of gas and dust that collapsed and contracted to form the Sun approximately 5 billion years ago.

solar oscillation a pulsation of the Sun.

solar storm see CORONAL MASS EJECTION.

solar wind particles and gases spewed from the Sun at speeds exceeding 1 million miles per hour.

spicule a thin jet of bright gas emitted from the sun.

sun dog see mock sun.

sunspot a dark spot on the Sun's surface having a lower temperature than its surrounding area and strongly associated with intense magnetic fields.

sunspot cycle see SOLAR CYCLE.

umbra the dark, central region of a sunspot.

variable star a star with varying luminosity; the Sun is variable but to only a slight degree.

SPORTS

ARCHERY

American round a competitive round in which each contestant shoots 30 arrows at 60 yards, 30 at 50 yards, and 30 at 40 yards.

animal round a competitive round in which each contestants shoots at lifelike animal targets from 10 to 60 yards.

archer's paralysis a psychological problem in which the archer "chokes" under pressure, loses his aim, or becomes incapable of releasing when aligned on target.

arm guard an inner forearm covering made of leather or plastic; it protects the bow arm from the bow string.

barebow shooting without a sighting aid on a bow.

battle clouts a competition in which 36 broadhead arrows are shot 200 yards to a large target.

belly the side of the bow closest to the bow string.

blunt an arrow with a flat tip, used to stun small game.

bow the pliable wood and fiberglass apparatus that holds the bowstring.

bow hand when shooting, the hand that holds the bow.

bowsight a sight or aiming aid on the top half of the bow.

bowstring the synthetic or waxed linen string that is pulled back and released to protect an arrow.

bow weight a bow's draw weight.

broadhead a hunting arrow having a broad head or two or more blades.

bullseye the center of a target.

clout a 48-foot target with a 1½-foot center, used for long-distance shooting and scored the same as a standard-size target.

clout shooting shooting at a clout from 120 to 180 yards away.

crest a row of colored stripes around an arrow's shaft below the fletching; they are used as an identification aid.

crossbow a bow held sideways and fired by a trigger mechanism from a special stock. Its short arrows are known as bolts.

draw to pull the bowstring back.

drawing hand the string hand.

draw weight the force required to pull a bow back one arrow length.

drift deviation of an arrow's flight due to wind.

feather any of the three stabilizing feathers on the shaft. See FLETCHING.

field archery competition featuring various targets located outside in fields or woods to simulate hunting conditions.

fingerstalls thimblelike, protective covers worn on the string fingers.

fletching the feathers attached to an arrow shaft to stabilize its flight. Also known as flights.

flight shooting nontarget, distance shooting competition.

foot bow a bow held with the feet while the string is drawn back with both hands, used in distance shooting competition.

green an outdoor shooting range.

king's round a crossbow competition in which contestants shoot six bolts each at a target 40 yards away.

longbow a straight, medieval-style bow.

loose to release the bowstring to project an arrow.

Mediterranean draw pulling the drawstring with three fingertips of the string hand.

Mongolian draw pulling the drawstring with the thumb and index finger.

nock the groove in the limb of the arrow for inserting the bowstring. To insert the bowstring into this groove.

petticoat the nonscoring, outer fringe of a target.

popinjay shooting a competition in which archers shoot blunt arrows at artificial birds.

quiver a case for holding arrows.

string dampener a rubber fitting that deadens the twang of the bowstring upon release, used when hunting.

wand a long, narrow target, usually 6 feet by 2 inches.

wand shooting a competition in which 36 arrows are shot at a wand from 60 to 100 yards.

AUTO RACING

aerofoil a wedge or wing mounted above the front or tail of a car to produce better adhesion to the road.

apron the low edge of a racetrack, used to get on and off the track.

banking the sloping of a racetrack, especially around curves.

blown said of a motor when a major part (such as a piston seizing from overheating) breaks and produces smoke.

broadslide making a turn while sliding sideways.

bump drafting a controversial practice of slamming into the rear end of a car in front of a racer in order to maintain momentum.

catch tanks special tanks fitted on a race car to help prevent fluids from leaking on and fouling the track.

chicane a tight ess or curve.

chute the fast straightaway section of track in front of the grandstand.

crew chief the supervisor of the pit crew.

dogging driving bumper to bumper with the car ahead in an attempt to pressure a mistake.

drafting the technique of driving directly behind another car to create a vacuum that allows both cars to go faster and to conserve fuel. Also known as slipstreaming.

drag a straightaway race over a short distance, usually a quarter mile.

drift a four-wheeled, sideways slide.

ess an S-shaped turn.

factory team a racing team sponsored by the manufacturer of the race car.

flags a blue flag held still warns of a competitor on one's tail. When waved it warns of a competitor about to pass. A yellow flag indicates an obstruction or hazard ahead. When waved it indicates extreme danger ahead. A green flag means "go, the track is clear." A black flag held up with a board with the number of an offending car is an instruction for that car to pull over at the pits at once, due to some hazard such as leaking oil. A red flag means stop. A white flag indicates that one is entering the final lap. It may also be used to indicate a caution—for example, an ambulance or service vehicle is on the track ahead. A checkered flag indicates the end of the race.

flying start a running start, as distinguished from a standing start.

formula one car a single-seat race car with a 1500cc turbocharged rear engine producing more than 900 horsepower.

formula two car a single-seat race car with a 2000cc, fuel-injected, nonturbocharged rear engine producing 325 horsepower, discontinued in 1984.

formula three car a single-seat race car with a nonturbocharged 1600cc, fuel-injected rear engine producing 165 horsepower.

funny car a drag racing car having an engine mounted in the middle and the driver's seat located far in the back.

Grand Prix an international race for formula cars.

grid positions the starting positions of a line of cars, with the fastest qualifiers usually up front.

groove the quickest or most efficient pathway along a racetrack.

hairpin a very sharp, direction-reversing turn.

hang out the laundry in a drag race, to release the parachute at the end of the race.

heel and toe working the accelerator and brake with the toe and heel of the right foot while working the clutch with the left foot.

Indy car a single-seat race car with a 2650cc rear engine producing 750 horsepower; may be turbo or nonturbo.

infield the area within an oval track.

lap to overtake a competitor who then falls one track length behind.

lap of honor a slow lap taken around the track by the winner.

marbles dirt, gravel, and rubber shavings from skidding tires that collect on certain parts of a track and can make drivers lose control.

marshal one of several track officials responsible for lining up the racers, inspecting work in the pits, and similar duties.

NASCAR National Association for Stock Car Auto Racing.

nerf bar a side or front bumper that prevents a competitor's car from striking one's wheels.

NHRA National Hot Rod Association, the sanctioning body for drag racing.

pace car the noncompeting lead car that sets the pace through one or two laps before the race begins.

paddock where the cars are kept and prepared for a racing event.

pit board a message board used by a pit crew to communicate with a driver.

pit crew the staff of mechanics who service a race car during a pit stop.

pits areas along the track where a team of mechanics repair and service each car during stops in a race.

pit stall the location of the pit crew and service supplies, where a pit stop takes place.

pit stop a stop in the pits during a race to have a car serviced, refueled, or repaired.

pole position the front inside position granted the driver with the best qualifying time. The most coveted starting position.

production car a stock car.

rail a dragster with the engine mounted in front of the rear wheels.

rally a long-distance race.

restrictor plate a metal plate mounted at an engine's intake to limit power, a safety feature required for many racers.

retaining wall the outside wall that prevents cars from accidentally running off the track or crashing into the grandstand.

reverse start a start in which the fastest qualifying cars are lined up last.

roll bar a hollow steel tube that prevents the roof of a car from collapsing on top of a driver in the event of a rollover.

roll cage a network of roll bars for increased protection of the driver during a crash and rollover.

shoes racing tires.

short track a track that is less than a mile long.

shutdown to defeat a competitor in a drag race.

shutdown strip the end of the racing strip where dragsters slow down and stop.

slicks smooth, treadless tires.

slingshot a passing method in which the trailing car pulls out of the draft of the leader, which produces a vacuum that pulls the lead car back.

slipstream the vacuum created behind a fast-moving car.

spoiler an aerodynamic device for improving handling of the car at high speed.

sponsor any large company that pays a race team to advertise a product on their car or uniforms.

sprint car a single-seat race car having a wheelbase of at least 84 inches and a front engine producing 575 horsepower.

stage to align a drag racer at the starting line.

stock car a standard sedan modified for racing. Also known as a production car.

superspeedway a racetrack that is one to two miles long, or longer.

T-bone to crash into another car broadside or to run straight on into a retaining wall.

tire tether Kevlar straps that prevent tires from flying off and injuring someone during a crash.

tri-oval a racetrack in the configuration of an oval with a hump, or fifth turn.

weight jacking adjusting the weight of a car to give more traction to one side or the other.

BASEBALL

AAA the principal minor league from which the major league draws players.

abbreviations box score and scorecard abbreviations include some of the following:

A	assist
AB	at bat
AL	active list, American League
B	bunt
BA	batting average
BB	base on balls/walks
BK	balk
CG	complete game
CS	caught stealing
DH	designated hitter, doubleheader
DL	disabled list
DP	double play
E	error
ER	earned run
ERA	earned run average
F	foul out
FC	fielder's choice
FO	force out
FP	fielding percentage
G	game
GS	games started
H hit	
HB	hit batter
HR	home run
IP	innings pitched
IW	intentional walk
K	strikeout
KC	strikeout, called
KS	strikeout, swinging
LOB	left on base
LP	losing pitcher
OF	outfield
PB	passed ball
PO	put out
R	run
RBI	runs batted in
S	sacrifice
SB	stolen base
SF	sacrifice fly
SHO	shutout
SO	strikeout
SS	shortstop
T	total time of game
2B	double
3B	triple
TP	triple play
WP	wild pitch, winning pitcher

aboard on base; as in "two men aboard."

ace a team's best pitcher.

air it out to hit a ball deep into the outfield or over the wall for a home run.

alive a pitch that appears to rise or move on its own accord.

alleys the open areas between the center fielder and the left fielder and the center fielder and the right fielder.

Annie Oakley a free pass to a game.

apple old slang term for the baseball.

around the horn describing a double play in which the ball is fielded by the third baseman, thrown to the second baseman for one out, and then thrown to the first baseman for the second out.

artillery a team's best batters.

Astroturf brand name of a type of artificial grass.

back-door slide intentionally sliding wide of the bag to avoid being tagged out and then quickly grabbing the bat with the hand.

backstop the screen behind home plate that protects the spectators from being hit by foul balls.

bad-ball hitter a batter who tends to swing indiscriminately at pitches outside the strike zone and who either strikes out a lot or produces a lot of fly balls.

bad hop a hit or thrown ball that takes an unexpected hop, making it difficult to field.

bag commonly used term for either first, second, or third base.

balk an illegal motion made by a pitcher with the intention of deceiving a base runner into starting a run for the next base.

balloon a slow-pitched ball that, to the batter, appears big and easy to hit.

baptism the roughing up of a smooth, new baseball with special mud, performed by the umpire prior to a game.

barrel the heavy, top, or hitting portion of a bat.

base on balls a walk. A batter's pass to first base after the pitcher pitches four balls out of the strike zone, at which the batter doesn't swing.

bases loaded runners on every base.

basket catch catching a fly ball at belt level with cupped hand and glove, a risky technique.

batfest an inning or game with an unusually high number of hits.

batter's box either one of the 6-foot by 4-foot rectangles a player must stand in while at bat.

battery collective term for the pitcher and catcher.

batting average a percentage determined by dividing the number of hits a player has by the number of times he has been up to bat. 1.000, would be perfect. More realistically, however, .300 is excellent and .400 or above is extraordinary and rarely achieved.

bazooka a powerful throwing arm.

bean to hit a batter in the head with a pitched ball.

beanball a ball intentionally pitched at the batter's head to intimidate or to move him back away from the plate.

beanball war retaliatory pitches at a batter's head by both teams.

behind in the count referring to a batter, having more strikes than balls; referring to a pitcher, having more balls than strikes.

bellywhopper a head-first, diving slide into a base.

benchwarmer a player who rarely plays and can usually be seen sitting on the bench.

big guns artillery.

bleachers the cheap seats or benches located around the outfield.

bloop to hit a short fly ball that lands between the infielders and outfielders for a hit. Also known as a Texas Leaguer.

blooper a short fly ball that lands between the infielders and outfielders for a hit.

blow it by to pitch a ball so fast that the batter can't possibly hit it.

blow smoke to throw fastballs; also throw smoke.

bobble commonly used term for a hit ball that is mishandled or dropped.

box score in newspaper sports sections, a statistical rundown of a game.

box seats the best and most expensive seats in a ballpark, located around first base, third base, and home plate.

boys of summer originally a name for the Brooklyn Dodgers of the 1950s but now connoting all baseball players.

bread-and-butter pitch a pitcher's most effective pitch.

breaking said of a curveball as it "breaks" high, low, fast, or slow.

breaking ball any pitch that alters its trajectory by rising, dipping, or curving.

break the wrists the determining factor in whether a batter has taken a full swing at the ball, missed, and produced a strike; to swing the arms and turn the wrists far enough to be considered a strike.

break-up slide an intentional sliding collision with a defensive player to break up a double or triple play.

brushback pitch a ball pitched deliberately close to the batter's body in order to move him back away from the plate. This is a method of regaining some of the strike zone the batter had crowded out.

bug on the rug a ball bouncing elusively on artificial turf.

bullpen located beyond the outfield, one of two practice or warmup areas for relief pitchers.

bullpen ace a team's most effective relief pitcher.

bunt a lightly hit ball that rolls only a few feet from home plate, used as a sacrifice hit to advance a base runner. If executed well, it can also serve as a hit to get the batter to first.

bush slang for unprofessional or unsportsmanlike play, named after lesser minor leagues such as A or AA, otherwise known as the bush leagues.

bush league the A or AA minor leagues or lower leagues.

buzzer a ball pitched so fast that it literally "buzzes."

cannon a powerful throwing arm.

caught leaning of a base runner who has taken too much of a lead from the base, picked off for an out.

caught looking of a batter, called out on strikes.

cellar commonly used term for last place.

chalk the white powder used to mark lines and boxes in the playing field. Lime is also used.

change-up a ball thrown to resemble a fastball but that actually moves slowly, used to throw off a batter's timing. Also, any slow ball thrown after a number of successive fastballs, to damage a batter's timing.

check swing a half swing; a partial swing not counted as a strike because the wrists weren't broken.

cheese slang for a fastball. Also known as cheddar.

choke to perform badly in a critical situation. Also, to choke in the clutch.

choke up on the bat to place the hands high up on the handle of the bat to achieve greater control of the swing.

chop a quick, downward swing that usually results in a grounder.

chopper a hit ball that strikes the ground then bounces high.

circus catch a spectacular or acrobatic catch.

clean the bases to get a hit that drives all men on base safely home.

cleanup position in a batting lineup, the fourth batter, who is usually the best batter. The fourth batting position is the one most likely to produce runs.

closer the closing relieving pitcher; the pitcher intended to end the game.

clothesline a line drive to the outfield.

clubhouse collective term for a team's locker room, showers, lounge, and manager's office.

clutch a critical situation.

clutch hitter a player who can be counted on for producing a hit in clutches. A player who doesn't choke.

coaches' boxes the 5-foot by 20-foot rectangles where the coaches stand, to the right of first base and to the left of third base.

corked bat a bat whose barrel has been illegally hollowed out and filled with cork or rubber to facilitate hitting the ball further.

curveball a ball pitched with a high degree of spin, causing it to drop or curve suddenly as it nears the plate.

cut ball a ball that has been deeply scratched or nicked, giving it unusual dynamics when pitched.

daisy clipper/daisy cutter a sharply hit ground ball that skims over the grass.

deer slang term for a fast base runner.

designated hitter a 10th player designated to hit in place of the pitcher, but only in the American

League. In the National League, the pitchers hit for themselves.

doctor to alter illegally a baseball with nicks, scratches, abrasions, or moisture or to alter illegally a baseball bat by filling it with cork or rubber.

donut the heavy, doughnutlike weight slipped over a bat to aid a batter in warming up.

doping taking illegal substances, such as steroids, to boost performance.

double play two outs produced by fielders during one play.

down the alley a fastball pitched through the middle of the strike zone.

downtown a home run's destination, particularly an out-of-the-park home run.

draft the drawing of players from high schools, colleges, minor leagues, and free agents.

drag bunt a slow-rolling bunt hit down the first-base line.

dribbler a slow-moving ground ball.

dugout the enclosed bench area of either team.

earned run average the average number of runs a pitcher gives up per nine innings, a statistic of his overall performance.

emery ball a baseball that has been illegally scuffed by an emery board or other abrasive object.

English the spin imparted on some pitched balls.

error a fielding misplay that allows the offensive team to advance to a base.

fan to strike out or to strike someone out.

farm system the network of minor leagues from which the major leagues draw players.

fastball a very fast pitched ball with a straight trajectory.

finesse pitcher a pitcher who utilizes a variety of clever pitches rather than speed to strike out batters.

fingering the proper placement of the fingers on the ball (especially in relation to the seams) to execute such pitches as curveballs, knuckleballs, and sliders.

fireballer a pitcher particularly adept at throwing fastballs.

$5 ride in a Yellow Cab slang phrase for a home run, especially one hit out of the ball park.

flat-footed slang term for caught off-guard or unprepared.

forkball a downward-breaking pitch thrown with the index finger and middle finger spread far apart.

foul ball a ball hit out of play.

four-bagger slang for a home run.

free agent a professional player who is not under contract and is free to negotiate with any team.

fungo bazooka an apparatus that automatically shoots balls into the air for fielding practice.

goat nickname for a player who makes a game-losing mistake.

goat's beard the small, protective flap hanging down from the chin of a catcher's or umpire's mask.

go down looking to strike out on a called third strike.

go down swinging to strike out by swinging the bat and missing.

go downtown to hit a home run.

go signal a signal given from a coach to a player to steal a base, to continue advancing around the bases, or to swing at the next pitch. Also known as the green light.

grand slam a home run hit with the bases loaded.

greaseball a baseball illegally altered with Vaseline, hair tonic, lard, or other substance to change its dynamics when pitched.

ground rule double an automatic two-base hit awarded whenever a hit ball lands in fair territory and then bounces out of play into the stands.

gun a powerful throwing arm.

gun down to throw out a base runner.

hesitation pitch a pitch in which the pitcher pauses momentarily after his windup in order to throw off the batter's timing.

home whites the home team's traditional uniforms.

horsehide slang for the baseball.

hot corner said of third base because balls are hit sharply there.

hot stove league whimsical name for any group of men who discuss, debate, and gossip about baseball during the off-season.

hummer slang for a fastball.

infield fly rule an automatic out called by an umpire when an infield pop fly is hit with two or more men on base and less than two outs. The automatic out prevents a fielder from intentionally dropping the ball in order to set up an unfair, double-play force situation.

inning one of nine rounds of play in which each team comes to bat once and is allowed three outs.

intentional walk deliberately throwing four balls outside the strike zone to intentionally walk a feared batter in order to pitch to a less talented batter. Intentional walks are also given in order to set up force plays.

knuckleball a ball held against the knuckles or fingernails and pitched without spin to make it more readily affected by wind and air currents.

laugher a game dominated by a team to a ludicrous degree.

loft one to hit a high fly ball.

lollipop slang for a slow or very easy pitch to hit.

lumber slang for the bat or bats.

minors the minor leagues.

moon shot slang for a long home run.

mustard velocity. A good fastball has a lot of mustard on it.

MVP abbreviation for most valuable player.

no-hitter a game in which a pitcher does not give up a hit to the opposing side.

no pepper the stenciled signs found in many ball parks prohibiting pepper games—the infield batting and fielding drill involving several players and frequently damaging the playing field.

nubber a weak infield hit.

off-speed pitch any pitch slower than a fastball; a slow pitch.

on deck batter the next player scheduled to bat after the batter at the plate.

opposite field hitter a batter who frequently hits a ball into the field opposite from the side he bats from, indicative of a late swing.

palm ball a ball held between the thumb and palm and thrown off-speed [with a pushing motion].

pennant title of a league championship.

pennant race race for the championship.

perfect game a game in which a pitcher gives up zero hits to the opposing team.

pinch hit to bat in place of another player.

pinch hitter a replacement batter, usually a better hitter than the one he replaces.

pinch runner a replacement runner, one who runs considerably faster than the man he replaces.

pine tar pine resin substance used on the batter's hands to improve grip on the bat.

pine tar ball a baseball illegally doctored with pine tar.

pitch around a batter to frustrate a batter by pitching the ball outside, inside, low, high, and generally out of comfortable swinging range, a method of giving an intentional walk but with a chance of a strikeout.

pitcher's duel a pitcher-dominated game in which no or few hits are made by either team.

pitchout in a potential base-stealing situation, a pitch purposefully thrown high and outside to put the catcher in perfect position for throwing out a base stealer.

place hitter a hitter adept at hitting the ball in any direction he desires.

pop-up a high fly ball hit over the infield; a pop fly.

pull the ball to swing at the ball early so that it is hit to the same side of the field batted from.

quail a pop fly that drops in safely for a hit. Also known as a dying quail.

RBI runs batted in.

relief pitcher a pitcher who replaces the starting pitcher or another relief pitcher.

ride the bench/pine to sit out play until called in to substitute for another player.

rifle a powerful throwing arm.

rip one to hit the ball hard.

road grays traditionally, the uniforms used when a team is playing an away or road game.

rookie a first-season or first-year player.

rope a line drive.

roster the list of active players on a team.

Rotisserie League Baseball a game of imagination and statistics in which enthusiasts draft players and monitor their statistics throughout the season to determine the best team overall.

rounders one of the old British games that baseball is descended from.

rubber the 6-inch by 24-inch rubber plate set on top of the pitcher's mound that must be toed or touched during an actual pitch.

rubbing mud the commercial mud (Lena Blackburne Rubbing Mud) used to rub the gloss off of new baseballs.

sacrifice any hit that gets the batter out but advances a teammate to the next base or home.

scout a person who scouts schools and minor leagues for up-and-coming players.

scouting report a written evaluation of an up-and-coming player in school or in a minor league.

screwball a pitch that curves inside instead of outside. Also known as a reverse curve.

scuffed ball an illegally doctored ball.

seventh-inning stretch the old custom of stadium fans standing and stretching their legs in the seventh inning.

shag flies to practice catching fly balls.

shake off a sign a pitcher's shake of the head in refusing to deliver a pitch suggested by the catcher's signals.

shoestring catch a catch of a fly ball at shoe level.

shortstop the infield player's position between second and third base.

shotgun slang for a powerful throwing arm.

shutout a game in which the losing team fails to score any runs.

sidearm a type of pitch delivered in a manner between underhanded and overhanded.

sign one of several types of secret signals conveyed by catchers and coaches to players on the field or up at bat.

sign stealing deciphering an opposing team's signals and using them to advantage.

sinker a pitch thrown with a roll of the wrist, causing the ball to dip or sink suddenly at the plate.

sinking fastball a fastball that acts like a sinker.

6-4-3 a double play started by the shortstop (6), who throws the ball to the second baseman (4), who completes the play by throwing to the first baseman (3).

600 home run club an exclusive hitter's club with only three members, Hank Aaron, Babe Ruth, and Willie Mays.

six o'clock hitter a term describing a player who bats well in practice but performs poorly in a game.

slider a lightly spinning curveball that breaks suddenly but with less curve than a standard curveball.

slump a period in which a player or team plays poorly.

smoker a fastball.

smoking of major velocity, as in a smoking fastball.

southpaw a left-handed player, but usually referring to a pitcher.

speed gun an electronic apparatus used to measure the speed of pitched balls.

spitball a ball illegally altered with spit or moisture in order to change its pitching dynamics.

split-fingered fastball a fastball pitched like a forkball and that sinks suddenly.

squibber a weakly hit ball that passes or drops in for a base hit.

standup double/triple a hit that allows a batter enough time to reach second or third base without having to slide.

steal to advance safely to the next base by a surprise run.

stopper a team's best starting or relief pitcher.

switch hitter a player adept at hitting either left-handed or right-handed.

Texas Leaguer a weakly hit ball that manages to get over the infielders' heads for a base hit.

3-6-3 a double play begun by the first baseman (3), who throws the ball to the shortstop (6), who throws back to the first baseman.

throw smoke to throw a fastball. Also known as to blow smoke.

triple play getting three outs in one play, a rarity.

unearned run a run scored but not charged to a pitcher's earned run average due to circumstances beyond his control, such as an error.

Vaseline ball a ball illegally doctored with Vaseline.

warning track the dirt track skirting the length of the outfield wall or fence; it acts as a warning to help prevent players from accidentally colliding with the wall when attempting to field a ball.

whiff to strikeout.

BASKETBALL

air ball a ball so poorly shot it misses hitting either the backboard or the rim.

alley-oop a shot in which the ball is caught in midair and slam-dunked before the player's feet touch the floor.

assist a pass by one player to another that results in a score.

backboard the board or fiberglass structure that holds the hoop and net, today referred to as the "glass."

backcourt the defense's forecourt, a definition that changes with possession of the ball.

backcourt foul a foul committed by an offensive player while in his backcourt.

backcourt violation a violation levied on a team that fails to move the ball out of its backcourt within 10 seconds after gaining possession, resulting in loss of possession.

back door play when an offensive player under the basket darts behind a defender to receive a pass.

bank shot a shot caromed off the backboard and into the basket.

baselines the short boundary lines at the ends of the court behind the baskets.

blocking foul a defensive player moving illegally into the path of an offensive player.

body fake using body language to fake a defender into moving in the opposite direction to the way you wish to go with the ball.

bomb a shot taken from long range.

box out maneuvering in front of a defender to gain the best position for a rebound.

brick a poor shot, usually an air ball.

bucket a scored basket.

center circle the circle at midcourt used for the center jump at the start of a game.

charging a personal foul violation given to an offensive player who runs into a defender who has established position (is standing still when hit).

cold of a player having missed several shots in a short period of time.

crashing the boards slang for aggressive rebounding.

D popular term for "defense."

double dribble a violation in which a player with the ball starts a dribble, stops and holds the ball, then starts a dribble again and moves his feet.

double team two defensive players guarding one offensive player.

downtown long-range shot.

draw a foul a player deliberately positioning himself to be fouled in order to be awarded a free throw.

dribble to stand, walk, or run while bouncing the ball on the floor.

driving the lane driving quickly through the free-throw lane for a closeup shot.

dunk a shot made by jumping high in the air and throwing the ball through the hoop from above. Also known as a slam dunk, stuff, or a jam. Also to make a dunk.

fallaway a shot taken while falling or fading back away from a defender to get a clear path to the basket.

fast break getting downcourt at a dead run to score a basket before defenders can get back to cover.

feed passing the ball to a player in shooting position.

field goal percentage ratio of shots taken to shots scored.

forced shot a shot taken in a rush, when in poor position or when off balance.

forwards the two players who usually cover the corner areas on either side of the basket.

foul out to commit more fouls than are allowed and be forced to leave the game.

free throw a free shot taken at the free-throw line, awarded to a player who has been fouled.

free-throw lane 19-foot by 16-foot painted lane running from the free-throw line to the end line. Also known as the three-second area.

free-throw line the line where a fouled player takes a free shot, 15 feet in front of the basket.

free-throw percentage ratio of free throws taken by a player to free throws made or scored.

frontcourt the area closest to the basket of the offensive team.

frontcourt players the two forwards and center.

full-court press close and aggressive guarding by the defense all over the court from the time the ball is inbounded.

goaltending the act of a defensive player blocking a shot near the basket as the ball in flight is descending, a violation in which a basket is automatically scored to the offensive team.

guards the positions played by smaller players skilled in ballhandling and dribbling; they generally cover the perimeter of the offensive and defensive zones.

hacking hitting an opponent's arm with the hand, a foul violation.

Hail Mary a shot that requires a prayer and the guidance of God to go in the basket. Making this shot is known as "throwing up a prayer."

hang time the time a player making a jump shot "hangs" in the air, related to leaping ability.

hook shot a one-handed, over-the-head arc shot. Also called skyhook.

hot hand a player on a hot shooting streak.

intentional foul a foul committed intentionally in order to stop the game clock, usually in the closing seconds of a game.

jump ball at the start of a game or when two opposing players wrestle over the ball, a procedure that determines possession: tossing the ball up and having the opposing players jump for it and tap it to a teammate.

jump shot a shot taken while jumping.

layup the closest and easiest shot, made by a player who has moved under the rim.

offensive foul a foul committed by a member of the team with the ball.

one-and-one in amateur ball, a bonus shot given if the first free throw goes in. In the NBA, the second shot is always taken.

outlet pass a long, downcourt pass.

palming turning the ball over in the palm while dribbling, a violation giving possession to the other team.

penalty situation a situation in which free throws will be awarded to a fouled player because a team has used up its allowable fouls for the quarter.

penetration penetrating through defenders to the basket.

percentage shot a shot, usually at close range, that has a high probability of going in.

personal foul illegal physical contact, including hacking, charging, holding, and fighting.

pick a screen created when an offensive player stands still and intentionally blocks the path of a defender so a teammate can get open for a pass or a shot.

pick and roll moving off a pick and running toward the basket for a pass, a method of eluding a defender.

pivot pivoting on one foot to avoid a traveling violation.

point guard a guard who directs the offense.

post the pivot position: the high post is near the foul line; the low post is near the basket.

power forward a forward particularly adept at rebounding and defense.

pullup driving toward the basket, stopping suddenly, and taking a jump shot.

pump fake faking a shot to the basket (double-pump fake: pumping the arms twice in faking a shot).

rebound getting possession of the ball off the backboard.

reverse dunk dunking the ball from a backwards position.

run and gun a quick-moving, quick-shooting game strategy.

scoop shot an underhand shot taken while running close to the basket.

screen when a player with the ball "hides" behind a teammate and takes an uncontested shot.

shot clock the clock that displays the time left for the offensive team to take a shot, 24 seconds with each new possession.

sixth man the first substitute player off the bench.

slam dunk see DUNK.

stutter step a swiftly switching foot movement used to fake an opponent.

swish a perfect shot that enters the net without touching the rim.

team foul a foul charged to a team's allowance (four per period in the NBA).

10-second rule the offensive team must bring the ball up over the midcourt line within 10 seconds or lose possession.

3-second violation when an offensive player stays within the free-throw lane for more than three consecutive seconds.

trap to double-team a player with the ball in an attempt to make a steal.

traveling taking more than two steps without dribbling the ball. Also known as a walking.

24-second rule requires a team to shoot within 24 seconds after gaining possession of the ball.

walking see TRAVELING.

zone defense defenders guarding an area or zone instead of man-to-man.

BODYBUILDING

abs short for the abdominal muscles.

anabolic steroids a controversial synthetic hormonal compound known to help increase muscle mass.

barbell a lifting component composed of a long handle and weighted disks on either end, for two-handed exercises.

bench press a lift of a barbell or weighted pulley mechanism up over the chest while lying on one's back on a bench.

blast to repeatedly work a muscle to failure and beyond. Also, to fry, thrash, or torch.

bulking intentionally gaining fat and muscle mass to increase body size.

burn the painful sensation produced by a muscle as it is subjected to a build-up of lactic acid from an extreme or prolonged work load.

cheat to use momentum or incorrect technique to facilitate lifting of a heavy weight.

circuit training moving quickly from one exercise to another, with little rest, in order to increase intensity and gain an aerobic benefit.

creatine a natural acid that provides energy to the muscles during contraction, used as a supplement by some bodybuilders.

crunch a situp.

cut see DEFINITION.

deadlift a straight lift of a barbell off the floor, an extremely effective, all-around muscle-building exercise.

definition sharply defined muscle mass with an apparent absence of body fat. Bodybuilders often refer to someone with sharp muscle definition as being ripped, shredded, sliced, or cut.

dumbbell a lifting component composed of a small handle with weighted disks on either side, used for one-handed exercises.

flat of a physique, inadequately trained. See FULL.

fly an exercise usually performed with dumbbells while lying on one's back on a bench. The dumbbells are lifted simultaneously in an arc until positioned over the chest.

flush the flooding of blood into muscle tissue, occurring naturally from heavy lifting.

freak popular slang term for someone who appears inhumanly muscular, with massive, billowing muscle tissue.

free weights any weights, such as a barbell or dumbbell, that can be used on their own, and are not part of an exercise machine.

full of a physique, fully billowing with eye-popping muscular definition. The opposite of flat.

glutes short for the gluteus maximus, the muscles of the buttocks.

guns slang for the biceps or the biceps and triceps together.

hardbody any well-toned physique.

isolation concentrating the use of a single muscle to make a lift or press.

isometric exercise a form of exercise pitting one set of muscles against another.

juice slang for anabolic steroids.

lats short for the latissimus dorsi muscles of the back.

military press a seated lift of weights from chest level to an overhead position.

pecs short for pectoral muscles.

pull-up an exercise performed while hanging by the hands on a bar. The exerciser lifts his body until his chin is over the bar, then returns to the original position. Also known as a chin-up.

pumped of muscles, having the billowing and engorged appearance naturally taken on as they are flushed with blood and metabolites from a heavy workout.

push-up an exercise performed in a prone position, with hands and toes supporting the body on the floor, while the arms lift the body until elbows are straight or nearly so.

pyramiding the method of building bigger muscles by increasing the weight lifted but reducing the number of repetitions.

quads short for the quadricep muscles.

rep short for repetition; one lift or press.

set a number of repetitions.

shredded see DEFINITION.

situp an exercise in which one lies on his back and slowly raises his upper body off the floor to a certain point.

sliced see DEFINITION.

six-pack slang for a sharply defined abdominal wall, separated by six distinct sections, known collectively as the rectus abdominus muscle. Also called a washboard stomach.

spotter one who stands by another as a dangerous lift is performed, to aid in preventing a slip that could cause injury. A spotter may also assist in completing particularly difficult lifts.

stack any group of training-enhancing supplements taken as part of a complete bodybuilding program.

thrash see BLAST.

toning the slight growth of muscle and simultaneous reduction of body fat that comes from exercise, giving the appearance of a more sharply defined musculature overall.

vascular referring to the visible engorged veins on a physique with sharp definition.

weight machine any machine composed of various resistance training components, such as lifts, presses, etc., usually worked by a pulley system.

washboard stomach see SIX-PACK.

wheels slang for the big leg muscles, such as the quadripeds.

BOWLING

address position the starting stance before the approach and delivery.

anchor the best bowler on a team; he or she usually bowls last.

apple the ball.

approach the runway or prerelease area, 15 feet in front of the foul line.

arrows guide marks near the foul line used for aiming the release of a ball.

baby split a 2-7 or 3-10 split.

backswing the movement of the arm behind the back prior to release.

backup a ball that curves in the opposite direction of a hook, specifically right for right-handers and left for left-handers.

balk to cross the foul line without releasing the ball.

ball return track the channel in which balls are rolled back to the rack.

barmaid a pin hidden from sight behind another pin. Also known as one in the dark or a sleeper.

bed the surface of the lane from the foul line to the pit.

bedposts the 7-10 split. Also known as goalposts, fenceposts, and mule ears.

belly the widest portion of a pin.

bellying releasing a ball far to the right to compensate for a lane that hooks too strongly.

big ears a split leaving the 4, 6, 7, and 10. Also known as the big four, and double pinochle.

blank a bowling ball without holes.

blind score a predetermined score given to a team to cover an absent member.

blocking an illegally manufactured oil buildup in the middle of a lane that helps guide balls to the strike zone.

blow a rack to bowl a strike that leaves no deadwood.

boccie an Italian bowling game.

body English the contortionistic body language used by bowlers after a release in a vain attempt to "control" the ball.

bonus in tenpins, the extra points added to a score for making a spare or a strike.

bowling on the green lawn bowling.

bridge the space between holes in a bowling ball.

Brooklyn hitting the opposite pocket from the release hand, specifically the 1-2 pocket for right-handers and the 1-3 pocket for lefties. Also known as a crossover, or Jersey.

bucket a 2, 4, 5, 8 spare for right-handers or a 3, 5, 6, 9 spare for lefties. Also known as a basket or bread basket.

bury to deliver the ball into a pocket, usually for a strike.

candlepins cylindrical wooden pins 15¾ inches high. Also, the bowling game using these pins and small balls without holes, as distinguished from tenpins.

cheesecake a lane that tend to produce higher scores than others. Also known as pie alley.

cherry to chop off the front pin so that it fails to knock down any neighboring pins. Also known as to pick a cherry or to leave a cherry.

chop same as cherry.

Christmas tree a 3-7-10 split for right-handers or a 2-7-10 split for lefties.

Cincinnati an 8-10 split. Also known as a Cincy.

clean game a game without misses or splits.

conditioner lane oil.

convert to make a spare.

count the pinfall from the first ball of a frame following the frame in which a spare or strike has been made. The bonus points.

crank to impart a ball with rotation to make it hook.

creeper a slow-rolling ball.

curve a wide hook.

deadwood pins that have been knocked down and remain on the pin deck.

deck the portion of the lane the pins rest on; the pin deck.

deuce a score of 200.

dodo an illegally weighted ball.

double two strikes in a row.

double pinochle a 4-6-7-10 split; big ears.

double wood two pins left standing, one behind the other.

dress the lane to oil a lane in preparation for a game.

duckpin a pin similar to a tenpin but shorter and squatter, used in the game of duckpins.

dump to release a ball with the fingers and thumb simultaneously in order to prevent it from hooking or curving.

Dutch 200 a game of 200 made with alternating spares and strikes.

English spin on the ball.

fast lane a lane in which the hooking action of balls is diminished.

fenceposts see BEDPOSTS.

field goal a shot that goes between split pins and misses everything.

fill the pinfall of one ball counted after a spare; the bonus.

fill the woodbox to throw a strike with the last ball of the game.

finger to snap the fingers upward when releasing to impart lift or spin on a ball.

foul to step on or over the foul line during delivery, an infraction resulting in the forfeiture of any pins knocked down.

foul line the line marking the end of the approach and beginning of the lane.

four horsemen a 1-2-4-7 or 1-3-6-10 leave.

frame one-tenth of a game; one inning or period of play in a game.

full hit a ball that hits the headpin too high and misses or barely touches the 2 or 3 pin behind.

full roller a spinning ball that hooks sharply into a pocket.

goalposts see BEDPOSTS.

grandma's teeth a 7-8-10 or 7-9-10 split.

graveyard a lane that tends to yield low scores.

Greek church a 4-6-7-8-10 or 4-6-7-9-10 split.

grinder a delivery with a powerful hook or curve.

groove a worn track or rut in a lane caused by the impact of balls over an extended period of time.

gutter the channel on either side of a lane that catches poorly thrown balls.

gutter ball a ball that rolls into the gutter.

gutter shot a delivery down along a gutter that hooks or veers out as it reaches the pins.

half Worcester a 3-9 or 2-8 split.

handicap points added to the score of a player or team to make competition even.

hang a pin to miss knocking down a strike by one pin.

headpin the front or number 1 pin. May be called the kingpin in some usage.

high board a high or raised board in a lane that alters a ball's trajectory.

high hit a ball that hits the headpin straight-on.

high-low-jack a 1-7-10 split.

holding lane a lane that diminishes a ball's hooking action. Also known as a fast lane or stiff alley.

hole a strike pocket.

hook a ball thrown with rotation that veers into a strike pocket.

inning a frame.

Jersey see BROOKLYN.

kegler a bowler.

kegling another name for bowling.

kickbacks the side boards running parallel to the pit.

kingpin the central pin; the number 5 pin. In some usage the headpin may be called the kingpin.

lane the 60-foot alley between the foul line and the pit.

laying out the ball delivering the ball smoothly onto the lane without bounces.

leave the pins left standing after delivering the first ball in a frame.

lift snapping the fingers up when releasing to impart rotation on the ball.

line a 10-frame game.

loft a poor delivery in which the ball flies up out of the hand and bounces harshly onto the lane.

mark a spare or a strike.

mixer a well-thrown ball that produces a violent tumbling action among the pins. Also known as a sweeper.

mother-in-law the 7 pin.

move in to start the approach in a center position.

move out to start the approach from a corner position.

mule ears the 7-10 split; bedposts.

nosedive a ball that hits the headpin straight-on.

one in the dark see BARMAID.

open frame a frame without a spare or a strike.

PBA Professional Bowlers Association.

picket fence a 1-2-4-7 or 1-3-6-10 leave.

pie alley see CHEESECAKE.

pin deck see deck.

pinfall the pins that are knocked down by a ball, or all the pins knocked over in a single frame.

pinsetter the apparatus that sets the pins and resets the pins on the deck.

pit the sunken area below the end of a lane, where balls and knocked-down pins are collected.

pocket the area most likely to yield a strike when hit with the balls; for right-handers, this is between the 1 and 3 pins; for lefties, the 1 and 2; the strike pocket.

power player a player who relies more on powerful deliveries to knock down pins than on finesse.

pumpkin a weakly thrown ball with little or no hooking action.

rack a setup of 10 pins.

railroad a split.

read the lane to roll practice balls in order to determine a lane's quirks or imperfections.

ringing 8 the 8 pin left standing alone.

rob the cradle to knock down only one pin in a baby split.

roundhouse a wide curving trajectory.

running lane a lane in which hooks can easily be made into the pocket. Also known as a slow lane.

scratch a player's score without any handicap added in. Also, a nonhandicap game.

setup a rack.

short pin a pin that is knocked down but that fails to knock down any of its neighbors.

skittles a British bowling game in which a wooden ball or disk is used to knock down nine pins.

sleeper any pin hidden behind another pin; a barmaid.

slow lane see RUNNING LANE.

sour apple the 5-7 split.

spare 10 pins knocked down with two balls in a single frame.

split any combination of pins left standing with a gap or gaps between them.

spread eagle a split leaving the 2, 3, 4, 6, 7, and 10 pins.

strike 10 pins knocked down on the first ball rolled. To make a strike is known as to carry a rack.

strike out to roll three strikes in a row in the last frame of a game.

strike pocket pocket.

string one game; 10 frames.

sweep bar the bar apparatus that collects fallen pins from the deck.

sweeper see MIXER.

tenpins the modern game of bowling, characterized by its large balls with drilled holes and its wide-bottomed pins, as distinguished from candlepins.

300 game a game with 12 consecutive strikes for a score of 300.

wood the pins.

Woolworth a split leaving the 5-10.

Worcester a split leaving everything but the 1 and 5.

BOXING

apron the perimeter of the ring floor extending outside the ropes.

arm puncher a boxer who does not put the weight of his body behind his punches.

babyweight the weight division below lightweight.

bagged fight a fixed fight.

bantamweight the weight division with a 118-pound limit.

below the belt received below the belt; it is an illegal punch that results in loss of points.

bob and weave to move the head and upper body up and down and back and forth to elude punches.

bolo punch an exaggerated form of the uppercut, having a swing that begins below the hop.

bout a match.

breadbasket slang for the abdomen.

break to pull away from a clinch.

butt to butt the opponent with the top of the head; a foul if intentional.

canvas the floor of the ring.

cauliflower ear a swollen, deformed ear resembling cauliflower, caused by repeated blows.

clinch to hold or embrace the opponent either from exhaustion or to avoid being hit.

cold cock to knock someone out with one punch.

combination a quick succession of varied punches.

cornerman the assistant or trainer who comes into the ring at the end of a round to advise his fighter. See CUT MAN.

crazy bag a small, leather punching bag strung with elastic cords from floor to ceiling, used to develop timing. Also known as double-end bag.

cross a punch thrown across the opponent's punch.

cruiserweight weight division with a 190-pound limit; found in the WBC only

cut man a cornerman responsible for stopping the flow of blood from a fighter's cuts.

dance to use footwork to elude an opponent.

decision a win awarded on the basis of points, as distinguished from a knockout.

double up to throw two punches in quick succession.

draw a bout that ends in a tie.

drop one's guard to momentarily drop one's guard hand, leaving the jaw open and vulnerable to a punch.

featherweight weight division with a 126-pound limit.

feint to fake a move in order to deceive the opponent.

fistic concerning boxing.

flyweight weight division with a 112-pound limit.

footwork moving the feet to elude an opponent's punches.

foul an illegal punch, for example, one behind the head or below the belt.

glass jaw a boxer who is easily knocked unconscious.

go the distance to complete all rounds of a bout without being knocked out.

gouge to stick one's thumb into the eye of the opponent.

granite chin a boxer who is not easily knocked out.

guard the hand that guards the facial area.

handler trainer.

haymaker a powerful punch.

heavy bag a large, heavy punching bag suspended from the ceiling and used to develop strength.

heavyweight the weight division over 175 pounds.

heel to strike an opponent with the heel of the hand, a foul.

hook a circular punch thrown from the side.

jab a quick, straight punch.

kidney punch an illegal punch to the lower back or kidneys.

knockdown a blow that knocks a fighter to the canvas; he must get up within 10 seconds or lose the bout.

knockout the point in a match when a fighter is knocked unconscious or fails to get up from a knockdown within 10 seconds, thus losing the bout. Also known as a KO.

lead the jabbing hand.

light heavyweight weight division with a 175-pound limit.

lightweight weight division with a 135-pound limit.

low blow a blow below the belt.

mandatory eight count a rule in which a knocked-down boxer must wait at least 8 seconds before resuming the fight, a safety factor.

middleweight weight division with a 160-pound limit.

mix it up to exchange punches.

mouse a black eye.

neutral corner either of the two corners not used by the fighters and their cornermen; where a fighter must stand for the count after knocking down an opponent.

one-two punch a short left jab followed by a right cross.

on one's bicycle performing footwork.

over and under a head punch followed by a body punch.

overhand punch a punch that starts high and swings down on the opponent's head or upper body.

peanut bag a very small speed bag, used to develop reflexes and timing.

prizefighter a professional boxer.

pugilism the sport of boxing.

pugilist a boxer.

pull a punch to punch with only a portion of one's strength; to hold back.

punch-drunk dazed; mentally deficient or slow in speech due to blows to the head over an extended period.

put away to knock an opponent out.

rabbit punch an illegal blow to the back of the neck.

referee the official who oversees a match.

roadwork boxer's training term for long-distance running to build stamina.

roll with the punch to move one's head back with the thrust of a punch to lessen impact.

round in a professional bout, one three-minute period.

roundhouse a broad or wide, sweeping hook.

shadow box to spar with an imaginary opponent.

shake the cobwebs to shake off a daze after being punched in the head.

slugfest an exchange of blows without regard to defense.

south of the border below the belt.

spar to practice boxing with a sparring partner.

sparring partner one who serves as a practice opponent.

speed bag a pear-shaped punching bag hung at eye-level that bounces back rapidly with each punch, used to develop speed.

split decision a decision in which one official has a scoring disagreement with the other two officials.

square circle another name for the boxing ring.

standing eight count a count of eight given by the referee to a stunned boxer who has fallen but is able to stand.

stick to jab.

sucker punch a surprise punch.

Sunday punch one's best punch.

take out to knock out an opponent.

tale of the tape the weight and measurements of the two boxes before the bout, and how they match up.

technical draw a bout that ends in a draw due to an accidental injury.

technical knockout the awarding of a win to a fighter when his opponent is injured, or unable or too stunned to resume fighting. Also known as a TKO.

telegraph a punch to communicate unwittingly by body language to an opponent what the next punch will be.

throw in the towel to concede defeat by literally throwing in a towel from the fighter's corner.

thumb to gouge.

TKO see TECHNICAL KNOCKOUT.

under and over a punch to the body followed by a punch to the head.

uppercut a punch starting low and hooking straight up with bent elbow to the opponent's head.

WBA World Boxing Association.

WBC World Boxing Council.

weigh-in the inspection of weight before a bout to assure each opponent falls within the divisional weight limit.

welterweight weight division with a 147-pound limit.

BULLFIGHTING

banderilla a 24-inch-long, barbed dart stuck into the bull's neck or shoulder. Several banderillas are usually driven in to these areas to weaken the bull's neck muscles and therefore make it impossible for it to lift its head.

burladero a wooden shelter located near a wall that a matador can run into and hide behind to escape a charging bull.

capework the technique of drawing the bull close by waving the cape.

cuadrilla a team that assists the bullfighter in the ring.

gore to pierce with the horn of the bull.

matador the bullfighter.

muleta the red cloth waved to entice the bull into charging.

pass a passing of the bull past the matador's cape, or muleta.

pic a picador's lance.

picador one of the cuadrilla on horseback who prods the bull in the neck with a lance.

veronica a pass in which the matador stands still and waves the bull by him with the cape.

CANOEING

(*Also see* RIVERS AND STREAMS *in* ENVIRONMENT)

amidships in or toward the middle of a canoe.

aft toward the back of the canoe.

astern behind the canoe.

bailer a scoop used for bailing water.

beam width of a canoe at its widest point.

blade the paddle end of an oar.

bow front of the canoe.

bowman the paddler or passenger occupying the front.

bow stroke the basic paddle stroke made by the bowman to propel the canoe forward with no effort to steer.

broadside either side of a canoe.

Canadian stroke stroke originated by the Canadian Indians in which the sternman passes the paddle blade through the water at a slight angle and finishes with a quick outward stroke, used to avoid fatigue on long excursions.

draw the depth of water displaced by a canoe when floating, also known as the draft.

duffle the apparel and equipment of a canoeist.

freeboard the distance from the waterline to the gunwales.

grip top end of a paddle.

gunwales pronounced "gunnels"; the upper edges of the sides of a canoe.

haystacks standing waves that form at the bottom of rapids wherever the current is decelerating.

hummock a flow of current that forms a "hump" over a rock.

jam stroke a stroke that brakes the forward motion of a canoe by plunging the blade straight down into the water and holding it.

J stroke a steering stroke with a finishing twist made by the sternman.

keel narrow strip running along the underside of a canoe to prevent sideslipping in wind or current; a wider version is known as a shoe or river keel.

lining an alternative to portaging, where a rope is attached to bow and stern to guide the canoe around hazards and obstructions from the safety of shore.

painter a line used to tie or tow a canoe.

pillow a rounded rock partially or fully concealed beneath black water.

port the left side of a canoe facing forward.

portaging carrying a canoe over land between two bodies of water.

ribs skeletal bracketing running between gunwales.

riffles small ripples in shallow stream caused by numerous submerged rocks or cobbles.

rips river waves larger than riffles but smaller than rapids.

rooster a river wave with a crest that turns back on itself, sometimes swamping canoes. Also known as a curler.

souse hole violent foamy turbulence where water plunges over boulders, sucks air along with it, and creates dangerous and unpredictable hydraulic properties. Also known as a white eddy.

sponsons air chambers built into the gunwales running the length of a canoe.

starboard the right side of a canoe facing forward.

sternman the paddler at the rear of the canoe.

stern rudder stroke placing the paddle astern or alongside of a canoe and using it as a rudder, known as the lazy man's way to steer.

tongue a smooth passage of black water between two rocks.

yaw to deviate from course or sway, caused by wind or current.

yoke a frame fitting anchored at the gunwales allowing a canoe to be shouldered while carried upside down.

CURLING

besom the broom used for sweeping the ice clean.

bitter a stone just touching the outer ring of the house.

bonspiel a curling tournament.

broom a besom.

build a house to align the stones in an advantageous position so that they protect each other.

button the first circle out from the center of the house.

chap and lie the delivery of a stone that knocks out an opponent's stone and takes its place.

close a port to fill a gap between two stones.

curling stone a polished, circular stone about 12 inches in diameter, weighing 42 to 44 pounds, and having a removable handle on top.

heavy ice rough ice that slows the momentum of a thrown stone.

hog a stone that fails to clear the far hog line.

hog line the line 7 yards in front of the tee past which a stone must come to rest or be removed from play.

house a 12-foot circular area at each end of a rink, where the stones are delivered.

pebble to sprinkle hot water on the ice to create bumps and increase friction for better control of the stones.

rink the 138-foot by 14-foot playing area having a series of concentric rings (houses) at each end where the stones are delivered.

rock a curling stone.

shot rock the stone lying nearest the center of the house.

skip the captain of a curling team.

sooping sweeping of the ice to clear it of any debris.

sweeping sooping.

take-out knocking an opponent's stone out of play.

tee the circular area inside the house.

wick to carom off another stone.

DIVING

armstand dive any dive begun with the diver standing on his or her hands at the edge of the diving board.

backflip a backward somersault.

back header a backwards dive in which the head hits the water first.

back jackknife a board-facing dive in the jackknife position.

backward dive a dive in which the diver faces the board, leaps off, turns backward, and hits the water feet first. Also, a dive in which the diver faces away from the board and enters the water headfirst.

backward somersault a dive started facing the board, followed by a backward somersault.

degree of difficulty in competition, the degree of difficulty of a dive and its factoring in the final score.

diving well the deep end of a pool.

full gainer a reverse dive with a somersault.

half gainer a backflip ending headfirst and facing the board.

jackknife a dive in which the body describes the positioning of a closing and opening jackknife, with the body doubled over and hands touching the ankles followed by an extension straight into the water.

springboard a diving board.

swan dive a dive in which the head is tilted back and the arms extended out to the sides.

tuck a diving position in which the legs are tucked or folded up into the chest.

twist any twisting dive.

FENCING

à droit against the right.

à gauche against the left.

aids the three balancing fingers of the weapon hand.

appel a beat or stamp of the foot used to fake an opponent into action.

balestra a short, forward jump followed by a lunge.

beat a sharp blow to the opponent's blade.

bind to take an opponent's blade from a high line diagonally to a low line, or vice versa.

bout one match or fight.

breaking ground backing up a step; retreating.

break time an intentional pause taken between movements to throw off an opponent's timing.

cadence the rhythm in which movements are made.

ceding a parry a yielding parry characterized by a return to the guard position, used as a defense against a taking of the blade.

change of engagement engaging the opponent's blade in a new line.

circular parry a circular blade movement used to pick up an opponent's blade and move it. Also known as a counter parry.

compound attack an offensive action composed of one or more feints.

corps-à-corps body contact between fencers.

coulé a graze made down the opponent's blade.

coup double a double hit.

coupé "cut-over;" passing over the opponent's blade.

covered position a defensive position taken to protect from a direct line or thrust of attack.

croisé taking of an opponent's blade by using the forte to force the blade down.

cut to hit with the side of a saber blade to score.

dérobement evading the opponent's attempt to take the blade.

development an arm extension and lunge.

disengage to pass the blade under an opponent's blade.

electric fencing fencing in which points are registered by an electric apparatus.

engagement when opposing blades are in contact with one another.

épée a short dueling weapon similar to a foil but with a fluted blade and a larger guard. Also, the style of fencing used with an épée.

feint a fake attack or movement made to deceive an opponent.

fencing jacket a lined, protective jacket worn by fencers.

flèche a running attack with arm extended.

foible the outer portion and tip of a fencing weapon, as distinguished from the forte.

foil a fencing sword with a thin blade and cup guard.

forte the inner portion of a blade, nearest the grip, as distinguished from the foible.

froissement a deflecting attack made on an opponent's blade.

gauntlet a protective glove with flaring cuff.

guard the protective cup or disk near the grip of a fencing weapon.

high lines target areas located above the weapon hand.

hit to hit the opponent with the point (or with an edge of a saber) to score.

in quartata a step taken to the side to avoid being hit with the opponent's blade.

invitation opening up a vulnerable area to encourage an opponent to make an attack.

judge the director who, with the assistance of the other judges, makes rulings on hits and nonhits.

jury the president (director) and judges that officiate a fencing bout.

lunge a thrusting attack forward.

making ground advancing.

measure the distance from which a fencer can make a hit with a full lunge; the measure varies with the fencer's body size.

molinello a saber cut made with a full swing of the forearm instead of a less powerful wrist cut.

on guard a stance of balance and readiness, characterized by the feet set apart at right angles, the hips faced three-fourths to the front, both knees bent, and both arms raised in a defensive position.

orthopedic grip a sword grip providing greater control than the standard handle or "French" grip.

parry to deflect the opponent's attacking sword.

passata sotto ducking under an attacking sword while simultaneously thrusting one's blade at the opponent.

piste the area in which a bout is held.

prise de fer a taking of the blade.

pronation the hand position with the knuckles facing up.

reassemblement taking a half step back and standing erect.

redoublement a renewal of attack while lunging.

reprise a renewal of attack following an on guard position.

riposte offensive moves taken by a fencer who has successfully parried.

saber a dueling sword similar to a foil but having a wraparound guard and a wider, flatter blade that scores points with the point and with the cutting blade itself. The style of fencing used with sabers.

sabreur a fencer who uses a saber.

stop hit countering offensive action with offensive action; attacking an attack.

straight thrust a straight thrust of the weapon into a target area.

supination hand position with the palm upward.

taking the blade taking possession of an opponent's blade; the engagement, bind, croisé, and envelopment.

touché touched.

trompement deceiving the opponent's parry or defense.

underplastron a protective undergarment worn over the upper sword arm and chest.

FISHING

anadromous fish that spawn in freshwater but spend most of their adult lives in the sea.

angling sport fishing, with a pole, line, and hook.

attractant scents added to lures to help attract fish.

bag limit the legal number of fish one can take from a body of water.

bait any organic matter used to attract fish, but especially worms, insects, bait fish, crayfish, shrimp, and squid.

barb at the end of a fishhook, a second point or spur that helps prevent the fish from wriggling free.

bass boat a boat with a shallow draft, specifically designed for bass fishing.

bird's nest a mass entanglement of one's line, usually around the reel.

bobber attached to the fishing line at the surface, a plastic float or ball that bobs up and down as a fish strikes the bait.

bottom feeder any fish that stays near or on the bottom of a body of water, such as a flounder, catfish, or carp.

bottom fishing letting one's lure or bait drop all the way to the bottom or keeping it just above, to attract bottom feeders.

bumping intentionally hitting a log or rock with a lure during a cast, known to attract the attention of some fish.

buzz bait a lure with blades that agitate or buzz the surface of the water as it is pulled in.

buzzing pulling in a spinnerbait or buzz bait quickly across the top of the water to cause splashing and therefore simulate a wounded fish.

cane pole a simple fishing pole made of bamboo with no reel.

casting reel a reel with a revolving spool.

catch and release a practice in sport fishing to catch a fish and then throw it back alive.

chum live, dead, ground-up, or bloodied bait or various scents added to the water to attract fish.

commercial fisherman one who fishes for money or for a living.

crank bait a wood or plastic lure that when still floats on the surface of the water, but when pulled in dives under and appears to swim like a baitfish.

creel a basket or carrier for fish.

deadfall a tree that has fallen into the water and provides shelter for fish.

deadsticking a passive fishing technique in which the bait is left to lie still in the water for long periods.

deep-runner a crank bait designed to run at depths of 10 feet or more.

depthfinder a sonar device used to locate underwater features and schools of fish. Also known as a fishfinder.

doughball bait made from bread or dough, used in carp fishing.

drag in a reel, a device that controls the amount of hold on a line, allowing a strong fish to pull out some line, to help prevent line breakage.

dry fly in dry fly fishing, a fly that floats on the surface of the water.

eyelet one of the rings on a pole through which the line passes.

fighting chair at the back of a boat, a chair fitted with a harness and belt, in which a fisherman straps himself for security and leverage while pulling in extremely large fish, such as marlin.

flat a shallow stretch of water where fish tend to spawn.

flipping carefully swinging a line and letting a lure drop delicately into a fish-sensitive area, such as underneath a vegetation mat or between bushes.

flutterbait a lure that when dropped into the water, flutters down to the bottom like a dying baitfish.

fly specifically an aquatic fly of interest to trout fishermen, specifically caddis flies, mayflies, and stoneflies.

fly reel used in fly fishing, a reel designed to hold heavy line.

fly fishing a method of fishing with imitation flies at the end of a heavy, buoyant line.

forage fish small fish who produce in large numbers and serve as prey for predator fish.

fry baby or very young fish.

gaff a heavy metal hook used to haul in large fish.

game fish any sport fish or fish eagerly sought after by fishermen and usually subject to strict catch limits.

grub a plastic lure resembling a short worm.

hackle in fly fishing, small chicken feathers used in tying flies.

hatchery a kind of fish farm where fish are raised for later stocking ponds, lakes, and rivers.

hawg slang for any very large bass.

hip boots rubber boots that go all the way up the legs, used for wading.

jig a lure that may be in the shape of a frog, grub, insect, or fish, or which may have eye-catching hairs or feathers.

jig and pig a jig and a pork rind.

jigging moving a lure up and down in the water to attract fish.

leader an extrastrong line attached to the end of the fishing line and to the lure, for added resistance against a fish's cutting teeth.

livebox any container designed to keep either bait or fish alive.

lunker any very large bass.

lure any artificial bait used to attract and catch fish.

mat a vegetation canopy covering the surface of the water, a hideout for bass.

mealworm a small beetle larva, used to catch crappies and sunfish.

nest any area in which fish lay their eggs.

nightcrawler a large worm used for bait for a variety of fish.

nongame fish any fish not considered a sport fish and usually less regulated than a game fish.

outrigger a setup of polls that allows trolling with multiple lines, and without tangling.

poaching illegal fishing.

redd a trout or salmon nest, often just a depression in gravel, where eggs are deposited.

reel on a fishing pole, a spooling mechanism that holds the line.

rise rippling water at the surface, evidence of a fish rising to the bait.

roe fish eggs.

school any group of fish swimming together.

sinker a small, heavy weight attached to the end of a line to make it sink with the bait.

skipping a casting technique in which a lure is skimmed over the surface of the water, to make it skip like a flat rock.

slot limit a size range of fish that can be kept, as regulated by law on a particular body of water.

smolt freshwater preadult stage of an anadromous fish.

smoltification the physical changes that occur in anadromous fish to allow them to thrive in salt water.

snap a small, metal pin that can be easily latched and unlatched for the quick attachment or release of hooks, sinkers, lures, etc.

spawning the issuing of eggs into the water by a female fish and fertilization by the males.

spincaster a push-button, closed reel with a small frontal opening through which the line passes and is prevented from tangling.

spinning reel a reel on which line is cast from a stationary spool.

spook to scare off fish by making noise or casting moving shadows over the water.

spoon resembling a spoon, a lure that wobbles in the water to attract fish.

stock to load a body of water with fish from a hatchery.

strike a taking or biting of the bait by a fish.

swivel a small, twin-ringed, swiveling device that attaches between a lure or leader and line, to prevent tangling of the line.

tackle box a multi-compartment box for holding lures, hooks, swivels, sinkers, etc.

test referring to the strength of a fishing line.

tower on a large sport-fishing boat, a tower that can be climbed to look out for tuna or other schools of sport fish.

treble a three-point hook, used on many lures.

trolling running a long length of line behind a slow-moving boat, in order to cover more than one area where fish may be.

trolling motor a very small, electric motor used to quietly propel a boat around areas of fish.

trotline a line with several hooks run across a stream.

weedless spoon a spoon with a guard for fishing in weedy waters.

weir a fence constructed to trap fish.

winter kill a die-off of fish in small bodies of water, due to oxygen depletion.

FOOTBALL

air it out to throw a long pass.

armchair quarterback a know-it-all fan who criticizes play from the stands or while watching a game on TV.

arm tackle to tackle solely with the arm or arms.

audible a play called verbally at the line of scrimmage, often to change a planned play made in a huddle.

back one who plays in the backfield, either offensively or defensively.

backfield the backs.

backfield in motion illegal motion of one or more players in the backfield prior to the snap.

back judge the downfield judge who watches for clips, pass interference, and out-of-bounds plays.

backpedal to run backward, as a quarterback.

Big Ben see HAIL MARY.

birdcage the protective face bars on a helmet.

blind side the side unseen by the quarterback when in position to pass and the side from which most quarterback tackles, called a blind-side tackle, occurs.

blitz a surprise rush by more than the usual number of defenders toward the quarterback.

body block to throw oneself sidelong into an opponent to block his path.

bomb a very long pass.

bootleg a play in which the quarterback fakes a handoff, then runs in the opposite direction with the ball hidden behind his hip.

box-and-chain crew the sideline crew responsible for marking the line of scrimmage with the down box and 10-yard measuring chain. Also known as the chain gang.

break a tackle to break free from a tackle and continue running.

broken play a play that goes awry, usually due to miscommunication. Also known as a busted play.

bullet a powerfully thrown line-drive pass.

butt block to illegally tackle or block an opponent by driving or butting one's helmet into his body.

carry to run with the ball.

center in the offensive line, the center player who snaps the ball to the quarterback to start play.

chain gang see BOX-AND-CHAIN CREW.

chicken-fight a series of standing blocks made in quick succession against an opponent to keep him away from the quarterback.

chuck to intentionally bump the receiver as he begins his run from the line of scrimmage.

circle pattern a circular pattern run by a receiver to elude a defender.

circus catch any acrobatic or spectacular catch.

cleats football shoes with projections for traction on the soles. Also, the projections themselves.

clipping illegally hitting an opponent without the ball from behind, a foul resulting in a 15-yard penalty.

clothesline to tackle by swinging an arm stiffly into an opponent's head or neck, a foul resulting in a 15-yard penalty.

color commentator a radio or TV sports announcer who analyzes the plays and discusses and criticizes strategy.

comeback a play in which the receiver runs a straight pattern, then turns abruptly back toward the quarterback for a pass.

completion a completed forward pass.

conversion to kick the ball through the goalposts for one extra point after a touchdown.

corner short for cornerback.

cornerback one of two defensive backs positioned at the outside end positions to cover sweep runners and wide receivers for passes.

corner blitz a blitz on the quarterback by one or both cornerbacks.

cross pattern a pass pattern in which two wide receivers run downfield along opposite sidelines, then turn and cross paths.

cut to change direction abruptly.

decline a penalty the option of an offended team to refuse a penalty award when it is not advantageous.

defensive back a cornerback, safety, or other player positioned behind the linebackers who defends against passes and running plays.

defensive end one of two defensive players positioned on the end of the line of scrimmage who rushes the quarterback or defends against sweep plays.

defensive tackle one of two players positioned next to, and inside of, a defensive end on the line of scrimmage.

defensive unit players who specialize in defense.

delay of game an infraction resulting in a 5-yard penalty.

dime defense a defense using six backs.

doping taking illegal substances, such as steroids, to boost performance.

double reverse a play in which a back hands the ball off to a teammate running in the opposite direction, who in turn hands off to another teammate running in the original direction.

down the point when play is stopped or the ball is declared dead. Also, one of four chances to advance the ball 10 yards with each possession.

draw play a play in which the quarterback backpedals as if to pass and thereby draws a rush by the defense, but instead hands off to a back who runs through the gap left open by the rushing defenders.

drive a series of play advancing a team downfield.

duck a slow-floating pass that is easy to intercept. Also known as a dying quail.

eat the ball of a quarterback, to let himself be tackled in a play than risk being intercepted by defenders who are covering the receivers closely.

eligible receivers the six players on the offensive team that are eligible to receive a forward pass, specifically the backs and the two ends.

encroachment having a part of one's body over the line of scrimmage just prior to the snap, an infraction resulting in a 5-yard penalty.

end run a play in which the ballcarrier runs around one end of the line.

ends the two players positioned at either end of the line of scrimmage.

end zone the goal zone at either end of the field.

extra point after a touchdown, one extra point added for successfully kicking the ball through the goalposts.

face mask a bird cage. Also, an infraction in which an opponent is grabbed or tackled by the face mask, a 5- to 15-yard penalty.

fair catch a signal to the officials that the ball receiver wishes to catch the ball without being tackled and is therefore marking the ball down without advancing it.

field goal three points scored by kicking the ball through the goalposts.

first and 10 first down and 10 yards to go to reach another first down.

flag a diagonal pass pattern in which the receiver runs downfield and cuts diagonally toward a corner of the end zone. Also, the flag thrown by an official to signal an infraction.

flak jacket a padded, rib-protecting jacket worn like a vest.

flanker flare a short flip pass to a back still in the backfield and moving toward the sideline.

flea-flicker a lateral or a handoff followed by a surprise pass. Also, a pass followed by a lateral.

fly pattern a pass pattern in which the intended receiver runs at top speed straight downfield.

formation the alignment of the defense or offense at the line of scrimmage.

free safety a defensive back positioned well behind the line of scrimmage, who is responsible for covering midfield for running plays or passes but who is "free" to assist other defenders in covering receivers.

front line the players aligned along the line of scrimmage.

fullback an offensive back who plays behind the quarterback and blocks or carries the ball on handoffs. A powerful but relatively slow-moving running back.

fumble to drop the ball.

gang tackle to tackle the ballcarrier with more than one tackler.

goal line the line marking the beginning of the end zone, over which the ball must be carried or passed to a teammate for a touchdown.

goalposts the U-shaped upright standing on either endzone through which goals are kicked.

gridiron a football field.

ground the ball to intentionally throw the ball to the ground or out of bounds to avoid being tackled for a loss of yardage behind the line of scrimmage, an infraction resulting in a 10-yard penalty and a loss of a down.

guards the two offensive linemen who flank the center and block.

Hail Mary a long pass, usually into the end zone, that requires "divine intervention" to be completed. Also known as Big Ben. To make a Hail Mary is known as "throwing up a prayer."

halfback the offensive player positioned in the backfield who acts as a receiver or ballcarrier, more commonly known as a running back.

hang time the elapsed time a kicked or thrown ball is suspended in the air.

hike a command to snap the ball to begin play.

hitch a pass pattern in which the receiver runs downfield, then cuts abruptly to the outside for a pass.

hitch and go a pass pattern in which a receiver fakes a hitch, then continues straight downfield for a pass.

huddle the huddling together or meeting of players in which plays are planned between downs.

I formation an offensive formation in which the tailback, halfback, and fullback form a line behind the quarterback.

illegal motion illegal motion of a player set on the line of scrimmage just prior to the snap.

incompletion a pass not caught.

ineligible receiver a player not permitted to catch a forward pass.

interception a passed ball intended for an offensive receiver but caught by the defense, resulting in an automatic exchange of possession.

kicking team a team's members who specialize in executing punts, field goals, and extra points.

late hit tackling or running into an opponent after the ball has been whistled dead, an infraction resulting in a 15-yard penalty.

lateral a pass thrown underhanded or overhanded in a backwards or sideways direction.

leg whip to intentionally use one's legs after falling to trip up an opponent.

linebackers the defensive players positioned just behind the line who back up the defensive linemen.

line judge the official who keeps time and watches for encroachment, offsides, and illegal motion at the line of scrimmage.

lineman a player positioned on the line of scrimmage.

line of scrimmage the imaginary line that marks where the ball is down and separates the defensive line from the offensive line.

man-for-man a defensive strategy in which each receiver is guarded by only one man.

middle linebacker the linebacker positioned behind the middle of the defensive line.

Monday morning quarterback a fan who criticizes his team's play by using 20/20 hindsight the day after the game.

naked reverse a play in which a team's blockers all move in one direction to draw the defense while the ballcarrier moves in the opposite direction.

nickel back a back that replaces a linebacker in the nickel defense.

nickel defense a defense that uses five backs, the extra back replacing a linebacker.

nose guard a defensive lineman positioned in the center of the line. Also known as a middle guard or nose tackle.

nutcracker a practice drill in which a team's ballcarriers are subjected to tackles by one or more players.

offside being positioned beyond or over the line of scrimmage prior to the snap.

onside kick a low, tumbling, easily fumbled kick made by a team behind in the score in the last moments of a game in the hope of regaining possession of the ball.

on the numbers a well-placed pass reaching the receiver at chest height, or "on the numbers."

outlet man a backup receiver used when the primary receiver is closely guarded or when the quarterback is under pressure to get rid of the ball.

overtime an extra period at the end of a game to determine the winner when the score is tied.

pass rush a rush by the defense to tackle the passer.

personal foul hitting, kicking, clipping, tripping, face-masking, or other unnecessary roughness, a 15-yard penalty.

pick off to intercept a pass.

pigskin nickname for the football.

pitchout a pass toward the sidelines and behind the line of scrimmage.

placekick a kick made from a tee or a teammate's hold on the ground.

play-action pass a play in which a handoff is faked to the running back, who pretends to hold the ball in his arms while the quarterback passes.

playbook a book containing a team's strategies and diagrammed plays.

pocket behind the line of scrimmage, a pocket formed by blockers which the quarterback steps into to evade the pass rush.

point spread in betting, the number of points by which one team is estimated to beat another team in a game.

pop a strong tackle or block.

post pattern a pass pattern in which the receiver runs downfield along the sideline, then makes a cut toward the goalposts.

prayer a pass requiring "divine intervention" to be completed; a Hail Mary.

primary receiver the planned receiver in a play, as distinguished from a backup or outlet man.

pump to pump or cock the throwing arm once or twice to fake a pass to deceive the defense.

punt a kickoff in which the ball is dropped in the air and booted before it hits the ground, executed when possession must be relinquished on fourth down.

punt return catching a punted ball and advancing as far downfield as possible before being tackled.

QB quarterback.

quarterback the player who calls signals, takes the snap from the center, and either runs, hands off, or passes the ball.

quarterback draw a play in which the quarterback drops back as if to pass, then runs straight ahead through a gap left by the defense.

quarterback sneak a play in which the quarterback takes the snap and immediately runs forward with the ball through the defense for short yardage.

quick count an unusually quick count that signals the ball to be snapped much earlier than the defense would normally expect, used to throw off the defense's timing.

quick out a pass pattern in which a receiver crosses the line of scrimmage, then cuts abruptly to the outside for a quick, short pass.

quick release a quarterback's ability to release the ball quickly when throwing.

receiver any offensive player eligible to receive a pass, specifically the backs and two ends (wide receivers).

red dog a blitz by the linebackers.

referee the leading official in charge of a game; he conducts the coin toss at the start of a game, explains fouls, administers penalties, and keeps track of the down, among other things.

reverse a play in which the ballcarrier running in one direction hands off to a teammate running in the opposite direction.

rollout left or right lateral movement made by the quarterback after receiving the snap.

roughing the passer charging into or tackling the passer after the ball has been thrown, a 15-yard penalty.

running back the more commonly used name for a halfback or a fullback.

rush to advance the ball downfield by a running play rather than a passing play.

sack to tackle the quarterback.

safety a score of two points awarded to the defensive team when a ballcarrier on offense is downed on or behind his own team's goal line. Also, a defensive back.

scrambler a quarterback adept at scrambling.

scrambling the eluding of tacklers by the quarterback behind the line of scrimmage.

screen pass a pass to the side of the line of scrimmage.

scrimmage a practice game.

secondary the defensive backfield made up of the cornerbacks and safeties. Also, the area where these players are positioned.

shank to kick the ball off the ankle or side of the foot instead of the instep.

shiver to thrust the forearms up sharply to deflect an opponent's block.

shoestring catch a catch made at shoe level.

shotgun offense a spread-out formation in which the quarterback stands several yards behind the center to receive the snap in order to set up a pass play.

signals the quarterback's code used at the line of scrimmage to call the snap.

slant a diagonal pass pattern.

sled a padded steel frame on skids, used in blocking practice.

slot in the offensive line, the space between a tackle and an end.

slot formation a formation in which a running back is positioned in the slot between the tackle and the split end.

snap the center's passing of the ball between the legs to the quarterback to start play at the line of scrimmage.

spike after scoring a touchdown, the ritual of slamming the ball to the ground.

spiral the smooth, nontumbling spin of a well-thrown ball. Also, to throw a spiral.

split end a pass receiver positioned far to the outside of the line of scrimmage. More commonly known as a wide receiver.

split the uprights to kick the ball through the goalposts for a field goal or extra point.

squib kick a low, tumbling kick difficult to field without fumbling.

straight-arm to hold one's arm out stiffly to block a potential tackler.

strip the ball to knock or poke the ball out of the ballcarrier's hands and cause a fumble.

strong safety the safety lined up opposite the strong side of an offensive line.

strong side the side on which the tight end is positioned.

stutter step a faked step in one direction; a short, deceiving step or momentary change in running rhythm to throw off the timing of a pursuer.

submarine to duck below a lineman's block.

sudden death overtime.

sweep to run to one side behind a wave of blockers.

tackle to knock or pull the ballcarrier down to the ground to stop play.

tackling dummy a stuffed bag used in tackling practice.

tailback in an I formation, the back positioned farthest behind the quarterback.

TD a touchdown.

T formation a formation in which the backs assume the configuration of a T, with the fullback positioned far behind the quarterback and between the two halfbacks.

thread the needle to throw a perfectly placed pass between two or more defenders into the hands of a receiver.

throw for a loss to tackle a passer behind the line of scrimmage for a loss of yardage.

tight end an offensive lineman positioned at the end of the line of scrimmage near the tackle.

touchback an occurrence in which the ball is kicked into the opposite team's end zone and downed; it automatically brings the ball out to the receiving team's 20-yard line.

touchdown a goal or score of six points, made by successfully running or passing the ball into the opponent's end zone.

turnover a loss of possession of the ball due to a fumble or an interception.

umpire an official positioned behind the defensive line who assists the referee and is also responsible for inspecting players' equipment before a game.

unnecessary roughness kicking, hitting or butting, or tackling an opponent after the play is dead, all 15-yard penalties.

uprights the goalposts.

weak side the side of the line without the tight end.

wide receiver a pass receiver positioned on the end of the line. Also known as an end, split end, or flanker.

wishbone a formation, similar to the T, in which the halfbacks are positioned on either side and slightly behind the fullback.

zebra any of the officials, so nicknamed for their black-and-white striped shirts.

zone coverage a strategy in which each defender plays a zone instead of a man, as distinguished from man-to-man coverage.

FRISBEE

arcuate vanes the slightly raised diagonal ribs on a Frisbee.

Bernoulli principle the principle of physics by which air flowing over the top of a Frisbee's curved areas is slowed, producing lift.

cheek the inside face of the rim or lip.

crown see CUPOLA.

cupola the raised center area. Also known as the crown, cabin, or dome.

dancing skips see SKIP FLIGHT.

drop a sudden loss of waft.

flight plate the top portion of the disk from rim to rim.

Frisbee finger separation of the fingernail from the nail bed, caused by an errant catch.

hyperspin a shot imparted with extra torque; it produces a hovering flight with little or no warp.

Hyzer angle the left or right angle or deviation from which the disk is thrown, producing a turning flight.

lift the lift from a wind current that propels a disk from a waft to a higher flight plane.

lip the rim.

Mung angle the upward pitch angle of the disk when released. Also known as the attack angle.

navel the indentation in the center of the cupola.

skip flight a disk thrown with negative Mung that bounces off the ground and rises.

tailskating a poor throw, having an extreme Mung angle, which produces a sharply ascending and sharply descending flight with no waft.

thermals rising warm air, used by a veteran disk thrower to create lift.

waft floating cleanly without disturbance.

wane the gradual loss of waft; it evolves into wasting.

warp the sideways turning in the opposite direction of spin, occurring at the end of a disk's flight.

wasting the descent and loss of power in a disk's last stage of flight.

wax the stabilizing period after release, when the Mung angle levels out.

well synonymous with climb.

whelm the release of the disk. Also known as the hatch.

yawing spinning.

GOLF

ace a hole made in one stroke.

addressing the ball preparing for a stroke by setting the body in the proper stance and lining the club up with the ball.

albatross scoring three strokes under par for a particular hole. Also known as a double eagle.

approach a stroke to the putting green or pin, usually a medium-length shot.

apron the grass surrounding the putting area; also known as the fringe.

away furthest from the hole; the golfer with the "away" ball shoots first.

back door the back of the hole. A ball "drops in the back door" when it precariously encircles the hole then miraculously drops in from the rear.

back side in an 18-hole course, the second nine holes. Also called the back nine.

backspin a reverse spin put on the ball to stop it from rolling too far on the putting green.

backswing the swing motion from the ground to the back of the head.

baffy a No. 5 wood (club) with a face angle similar to a No. 3 or No. 4 iron.

bail out to sink an extra-long putt to keep from losing a hole.

banana ball an extreme slice sending the ball curving in an arc in the shape of a banana.

barranca a deep ravine.

beach any sand trap on a course.

bend one to hook or slice a ball.

birdie scoring one stroke under par for a particular hole.

bisque a handicap stroke that may be used on any hole on the course.

bite club action of putting backspin on a ball.

blade a type of putter.

bladesman name used to describe a superior putter.

blast to launch huge cascades of sand when playing a ball out of a sand trap. Also known as to explode.

blind hole a putting green that cannot be seen by a player who is about to approach.

bogey scoring one stroke over par at a particular hole.

bold a stroke that is too strong.

borrow sloping a ball to compensate for a slight rise or curve in the putting green.

brassie No. 2 wood, used when long-distance strokes are needed (originally named for its brass sole plate).

bunker a depression in bare ground, usually covered with sand; a sand hazard.

bunt a short shot.

bye the unplayed holes left after a match has been won.

caddie the person who carries the player's clubs and assists during a match.

can to make a putt and get the ball in the hole.

cap the top part of a club shaft.

carry the distance between where the ball is struck and where it makes its first bounce on the ground.

casting a poor swing technique in which the hands are used too much to control the start of the downswing. Also known as hitting from the top.

casual water a temporary pool or puddle of water or a bank of snow not considered part of a course's official hazards; a player is allowed to remove his ball from casual wear without penalty. Also known as a casual lie.

chipping iron an iron used for making chip shots.

chip shot a short, low shot, frequently with overspin, taken near the putting green.

choke to move the grip further down on the handle of a club. Also to psychologically collapse under pressure and blow an easy shot.

chop to hack the ball with a club to give it extra spin.

chump an opponent who poses little or no competition.

cleek No. 4 wood with a face angle similar to a No. 1 or No. 2 iron.

closed stance a stance in which the left foot is placed over the line of flight with the right foot back.

clubbing a player advising another player which club to use on a particular shot.

club head the portion of the club that strikes the ball.

clubhouse collective term for lockers, restaurant, bar, and meeting rooms.

clubhouse lawyer a person who knows even the most obscure golf rules and who generally makes a pain of himself by advising everyone.

collar the edge of a sand hazard.

course rating a scale defining the playing difficulty of a particular course in comparison to other courses, expressed in strokes and fractions of a stroke.

cup hole.

cut shot a high, soft shot that stops rolling almost immediately after hitting the green.

dead imparted with so much backspin that a ball stops without rolling after hitting the green.

deuce a hole made in two strokes.

dimples the indentations on a golf ball.

divot a slice of turf hacked out by a club during a stroke.

dogleg a curve in the fairway to the right or left.

dormie a situation in which the opponent must win every remaining hole to tie a match.

double bogey scoring 2 over par at a particular hole.

double eagle a score of 3 under par. Also known as an albatross.

down the number of strokes a player is behind his opponent.

draw an intentional hook shot.

drive to hit the ball from a tee.

driver No. 1 wood, used for the maximum distance shot.

dub a poor shot; a missed shot.

duck hook a severe hook hit low to the ground, sometimes causing people on the sidelines to "duck."

duffer a poor golfer. Also known as a hacker.

dunk to hit a ball into a water hazard.

eagle scoring two strokes under par at a hole.

explode see BLAST.

face the hitting surface of a club's head.

fade a ball that "fades" to its left or right at the end of its flight.

fairway the manicured terrain between the tee and the putting green.

fan to swing the club and miss the ball completely. Also known as to whiff.

fat shot a shot in which the club has partially struck the ground before hitting the ball, resulting in a high, low, or weak flight.

feather hitting a long, high shot that curves slightly from left to right and then settles with little roll.

flagstick the flagpole placed in a hole to show its location from a distance.

flash trap a small sand bunker, usually shallow.

flier a ball without spin that travels farther than expected.

floater a ball that is hit high and appears to float lightly across the sky.

fore the word shouted to warn players downfield of the impending flight of a ball.

forecaddie a person whose primary responsibility is to mark the position of a player's ball on the course.

fringe see APRON.

frog hair the short grass around the edge of the green.

front side on an 18-hole course, the first nine holes.

gimme a short putt easily made.

go to school to learn the lay of a green by watching the roll of a putt from another player.

grain the direction in which the grass on a putting green lies after being cut.

grasscutter a low, line-drive shot that skims the grass.

green the whole golf course. (The putting greens are where the holes are located and are frequently referred to as the "green" as well.)

greens fee the fee paid to play on a golf course.

gross a player's score before a handicap is subtracted.

hacker a poor golfer.

halfswing a swing in which the club is brought only halfway back.

halve to make a hole in the same number of strokes as the other player(s).

handicap a stroke or strokes given to a player of lesser ability than his opponent to help even out a match.

handicap player a player who usually plays above par and is thus given a handicap.

hanging lie a ball that comes to rest on a downhill slope.

hazard a bunker or water trap.

heel to hit the ball from the top of the club head near the shaft, resulting in the ball taking off at right angles to the line of play.

hole-in-one a hole made in one stroke. Also known as an ace.

hook a ball that curves to the left.

iron any club with a metal head.

lateral hazard a water hazard running alongside or parallel to the line of play.

lie the place where the ball comes to rest after a shot.

links originally a name for a seaside golf course but now describing any course.

lip the rim of the hole.

loft the height a ball reaches in the air. Also the angle a club face is set at in order to give a ball more lift or "loft."

marshal a person who keeps spectators in line and orderly in a golf tournament.

mashie No. 5 iron.

mashie iron No. 4 iron.

mashie niblick No. 7 iron.

match a golf game played by holes rather than a course. The player winning the most holes wins the match.

midiron No. 2 iron.

mid mashie No. 3 iron.

Mulligan a second shot allowed off the first tee in nonprofessional or casual games.

neck the socket where the shaft of a club joins the head.

net a player's score after his handicap has been subtracted.

open a tournament open for both amateurs and professionals.

open stance a stance in which the left foot is placed in back of the ball's flight path, allowing a player to face in the direction he wishes to hit.

out of bounds the ground outside the course.

overclubbing using a bigger club than is necessary for a particular shot so that the ball travels further than desired.

par the theoretical number of strokes considered necessary to get the ball in the hole; hitting below par, or with fewer strokes, is superior; hitting above par, or with more strokes, is considered inferior.

penalty stroke a stroke added to a player's score for breaking a rule.

pin the flagstick.

pitch a short, lofting shot to the putting green, often with backspin.

pitch and run same type of shot as a pitch but without the high arc or backspin, allowing the ball to roll after it hits the putting green.

pitching niblick No. 8 iron.

pitching wedge an iron used for making pitch shots.

playing through the point in playing a hole when one group of players catches up to another group and is allowed to pass ahead.

plugged lie a ball that has been buried in the sand of a bunker. Also known as a fried egg.

pot bunker a small, deep bunker.

pull a ball hit straight but nonetheless to the left of target.

punch a low shot "punched" into the wind with a short, slamming swing.

push opposite of a pull.

putt to stroke the ball lightly, as on a putting green.

putter No. 10 iron.

putting green the short-cropped area around the hole.

quail high a long, low shot.

rabbit a ball that bounces erratically after landing.

referee the person who sees to it that all rules are followed.

rough any areas of relatively long grass on a course.

run the distance a ball rolls after striking the ground.

sand trap a sand hazard; bunker.

sand wedge an iron designed for shots out of sand traps.

scoop a poor swing technique in which the club head dips.

scoring lines the indented lines on the faces of irons.

scratch to play at par.

scruff cutting the turf with a club head.

scuffing hitting the ground behind the ball with a club head.

short game collective term for pitching, chipping, and putting.

skulling hitting a chip or pitch shot too far.

sky hitting the ball too low with the club head, sending it "skyward" in a flight resembling a pop fly in baseball.

skywriting a poor swing technique in which the club head makes a looping motion at the top of the backswing.

slice a shot that curves to the right of target.

slider a low shot that bounces erratically.

snake a very long putt.

snipe a severely hooked ball that dives quickly.

sole the bottom of a club head.

spade mashie No. 6 iron.

spoon No. 3 wood.

spray an extremely poor shot hit far off line.

sudden death when a match is tied at the end of the allotted number of holes, the continuation of play until one opponent wins a hole.

sweet spot the center of the face of a club.

tee a wooden or plastic plug on which the ball is balanced for driving. Also, the area of the first shot of each hole.

thread a shot through a narrow opening between two obstacles.

toe the outer part of the club head.

toe job a ball hit too much from the club toe.

top hitting the ball above center, causing it to roll or hop.

turn starting the second nine holes.

underclubbing using a club designed for shorter distances when longer distance is needed.

unplayable lie a ball in a position where it cannot be played.

up the number of holes a player is ahead of his opponent.

waggle flexing the wrists and slightly swinging the club back and forth before hitting the ball.

wedge a club with a heavy flange on the bottom.

whiff to miss the ball completely.

wood a club with a wooden head.

yips shaking that causes a player to miss a short putt.

GYMNASTICS

aerial cartwheel a leaping, midair cartwheel, as performed on the balance beam.

afterflight in a pommel horse or other routine, the finishing fight leading to a landing.

back lever on the rings, a position in which the legs are extended out so that the body describes an L-shape.

back Moore on a pommel horse, making circling movements with hands on one pommel or behind the back.

balance beam a 16½-foot-long by 4-inch-wide raised, padded beam, adjustable to various heights.

barani a half-twisting front somersault.

beat the bar on the uneven bars, to strike the lower bar with the abdomen or hips with a whipping motion.

compulsory in a competition, a required exercise or routine.

crash mat the foam safety mat that serves as a cushion for landings or falls.

cross grip on the horizontal bar, a grip in which one hand is crossed over the other; it is used to turn the performer during a swing.

croupe the rear portion of a pommel horse. When facing the horse from the side, the croupe is always on the left.

Deltchev on the uneven bars, a cross-gripped downswing followed by a half turn and a front somersault.

Diamadov on the parallel bars, a full twisting forward swing to a one-armed handstand.

dismount the finishing exercise and flight of a routine.

double flyaway a horizontal bar dismount consisting of a giant downswing followed by a release on the upswing and the execution of two somersaults before landing.

elgrip an unusual grip, similar to the hand position used with a swimmer's backstroke.

English position a handstand position in which the hands are held closely together.

flip flop on the balance beam, a backward flip that stops at a handstand and follows through to a standing position. Also, any somersault.

full-in short for "full in to back somersault out"; more specifically, a backward somersault followed by a second backward somersault with a full twist.

full-out short for "back somersault in to full out"; more specifically, a somersault followed by a second somersault with a full twist.

giant swing on the bar or on the rings, an exercise in which the entire body is swung end over end by the hands.

half in–half out a somersault with a half twist followed by another somersault with a half twist.

handspring a jump through a handstand in tumbling or over the vault horse.

handspring vault running up to a horse and flipping over it by upending oneself with a moving handstand.

hanging event an exercise on the horizontal bar or rings.

Hecht dismount on the horizontal bar, a high-swinging dismount.

horizontal bar the raised gymnastics bar; it stands about 8½ feet high.

horse short for pommel horse.

hurdle to leap or hop over.

iron cross on the rings, a position in which the arms are extended out sideways to describe the shape of a cross. Also known as the cross.

layout a straight-out body posture maintained during certain exercises.

limber similar to a walkover but with the legs kept together.

lunge a starting position for some tumbling exercises, characterized by the arms held outstretched overhead and one leg extended with bent knee forward.

mount the starting exercise of a routine.

neck as viewed from the side, the right position of a pommel horse.

Olympic order the event order in professional competition. In men's competition, the order is floor exercise, pommel horse, still rings, long horse vault, parallel bars, and horizontal bar. In women's, the vault, uneven bars, balance beam, and floor exercise.

one-arm giant a giant swing performed with a one-handed grip.

overgrip the most natural hand grip, with the palms of the hands facing away from the gymnast.

parallel bars two 11-foot rails set parallel to each other about 5 feet, 9 inches from the floor.

pike a position in which the body is bent forward at the hips.

planche a position in which the gymnast balances his body parallel to the floor or apparatus.

pommel horse an upholstered, four-legged support having wooden handles (pommels) on the top.

press a very slow, graceful movement to a handstand.

puck position a cross between a tuck and a pike.

rings the still rings. Once known as the flying rings.

routine a series of exercises.

run a series of tumbles.

Russian Moore performing pivots around both pommels of a pommel horse.

saddle on a pommel horse, the area between the pommels; the middle of the horse.

scissors swinging the body and scissoring the legs back and forth across the pommel horse.

spotting the act of assisting or standing by to catch a gymnast in the event of a fall.

spotting belt a training belt suspended by ropes and worn by a gymnast when learning a new exercise to help prevent injuries.

step-out a landing position in which one leg follows the other instead of hitting at the same time.

still rings the rings, flying rings.

streulli on the parallel bars, a backward roll on the upper arms, followed by an extension to a handstand.

stuck landing a perfect or still landing, as if being "stuck" to the floor.

stutz on the parallel bars, swinging from a handstand downward and forward to upward.

symmetry alignment of body parts during an exercise.

tinsica a walkover executed with one hand placed in front of the other.

tuck a somersaulting position in which the legs are folded tightly into the chest and held by the arms.

uneven bars two raised horizontal bars placed one beneath and out from the other.

vault a leap or a leaping somersault over a vault horse.

vault horse same as a pommel horse but without the pommels. It is vaulted over lengthwise.

walkover wheeling around from feet to hands and back.

whip-up while straddling the balance beam, swinging the legs up and backward.

HOCKEY

assist a pass to a teammate that results in a goal.

attacking zone the offensive zone; the area of the goal being shot at.

backcheck checking an opponent in the defensive zone.

backhand a pass made with the back of the stick blade.

backline the defensemen.

banana blade a stick blade with a special curve built in to help control the puck.

bench minor a two-minute penalty assessed to a team whose coach, manager, trainer, or player not currently on the ice commits an infraction, usually unsportsmanlike conduct.

blade the bottom or shooting portion of a stick.

blocking glove the large, protective glove worn by the goaltender to deflect pucks. Also known as a blocker.

blue lines the two wide blue lines that divide the rink into the attacking zone, the defensive zone, and the neutral zone. They are used to determine offside and pass violations.

board check to push or bodycheck an opponent into the wall or fence surrounding the rink.

boarding illegal or excessively violent board checking, resulting in a penalty.

boards the fence or wall that surrounds the rink.

bodycheck to bump an opponent with the upper body in order to gain access to the puck.

breakaway to break away from defenders and move quickly toward the goal with the puck.

butt-ending illegally poking an opponent with the butt of the stick.

catching glove the glove used by the goalie to catch the puck in midair, worn on the opposite hand to the blocking glove.

center the central player on the forward line who takes part in most faceoffs and is frequently the player who takes the puck in for a shot on goal; the position played between the two wings.

center ice the neutral zone between the blue lines at the center of the rink.

change on the fly to send in a substitute player while the puck is still in play.

charge run into an opponent from behind, an illegal play.

charging a foul called on a player who deliberately runs into an opponent from behind.

check see BODYCHECK, HOOK CHECK, POKE CHECK.

chippy of a player, team, period of play, or game, excessively rough.

clear to move the puck into a position of safety away from one's own goal or out of the defensive zone entirely.

crease the 8-foot by 4-foot marked rectangle in front of the goal.

cross-check to bump an opponent with the stick help up high across the body, an illegal play.

cut down the angle to move out from the goal to meet an oncoming opponent with the puck to reduce his visual angle to the goal.

defensemen the two players who help the goalie defend the goal.

deke to fake a move and deceive an opponent.

drop pass a pass in which a moving player stops the puck and leaves it in place for a player from behind while continuing to move on.

faceoff a method of restarting play by lining up two opposing players against each other and dropping the puck between them in a designated faceoff circle.

faceoff circle one of five 15-foot circles in which faceoffs are executed at the ends and middle of the rink.

flip pass a pass in which the puck is lifted up off the ice and flicked over an opponent's skate or stick.

forecheck to check an opponent in his defensive zone.

forwards the center and the left and right wings; the forward line.

freeze the goalie to fake a goalie with a deceptive move or shot.

give-and-go to pass the puck to a teammate, then skate quickly past a defender to receive a return pass.

goalie the goaltender; the player positioned directly in front of the goal.

goal judge one of two officials who make rulings on goals.

goal light on either side of a rink, the red light turned on behind the goal when a goal is scored.

goals against average the statistic indicating the average number of goals a goalie allows per game.

goaltender a goalie.

hat trick three goals scored in a single game by the same player. See PURE HAT TRICK.

high stick to strike an opponent with a stick held above the shoulders, an illegal play.

hip check a body check with the hip.

hook check an attempt to steal the puck from an opponent from behind or from the side with the stick blade.

hooking illegally catching and holding an opponent with the crook of the stick.

icing illegally shooting the puck from behind the center red line and across the goal line of the opponent where it is first touched by an opponent, excluding the goalie.

kick save stopping a shot on goal by sticking a foot out to block it.

kill a penalty to avoid being scored against when shorthanded a player due to a penalty.

left wing the largely offensive position played on the left side of the rink.

linesmen two officials who make icing and offside calls, conduct faceoffs, and otherwise control the game.

major penalty a 5-minute penalty, levied on a player for unnecessarily rough play or for fighting.

man advantage the advantage of a full team playing against a shorthanded team.

minor penalty a two-minute penalty levied on a player for minor infractions.

mucking scrambling and battling for the puck in the corners. Also known as digging.

neutral zone the center area of the rink, between the two blue lines.

NHL National Hockey League.

offside a violation in which a player is present in the attacking zone as the puck crosses the blue line. Receiving an illegal pass in this position.

penalty removing a player from the game for a specified amount of time for committing an infraction or foul.

penalty box where penalized players must sit out their penalty time.

penalty killing percentage statistic that indicates the times a team has avoided being scored against when playing shorthanded.

penalty minutes a statistic of total penalty time served by a player or team in a game, series, or season.

penalty shot a free shot on goal defended only by the goalie.

period one of three 20-minute time periods in a game.

poke check poking the puck away from an opponent with the blade of the stick.

policeman an intimidating player with a reputation for quick retribution against any rough play from the opposing side.

power play any man-advantage situation.

power play goal a goal scored on a power play.

puck a 3-inch rubber disk.

pull the goalie in a catch-up situation in the final moments of a game, to remove the goalie and substitute him with an offensive player to strategically increase the odds of scoring a game-tying goal.

pure hat trick a score of three consecutive goals by the same player with no points scored by others in between.

rag the puck to handle the puck for a lengthy period of time.

red light the red goal light.

red line the wide center line that divides the rink in half.

referee the official who enforces rules of the game.

referee's crease the marked semicircle in front of the penalty timekeeper.

roughing excessively roughing up an opponent, an infraction.

rush to move the puck into the attacking zone toward the goal.

save to prevent a goal.

screen to position oneself between the goalie and a teammate preparing to shoot on goal to block the goalie's view.

shadow to guard an opponent closely.

shorthanded short one or more team members.

slapshot a hard, driving shot made with a high backswing of the stick.

slashing illegally slashing an opponent with the stick.

slot the area extending 10 yards out from the goal, from which most goals are scored.

smother the puck to fall on and cover the puck with one's body in order to stop play.

snap pass a quick pass made with little stick movement.

spearing illegally stabbing or poking an opponent with the stick blade.

split the defense to break through two or more defenders into the attacking zone.

stick check stealing the puck away from an opponent with the stick.

take a penalty to commit an infraction intentionally in order to stop play.

take the body to give or receive a body check.

trailer a teammate who skates behind the puckhandler for a possible drop pass.

wing one of two players who play on the right and left sides of the rink.

Zamboni the vehicle used to resurface or freshen the ice between periods.

HUNTING

area drive a hunting method in which one or more hunters drive or scare out game from woods while another hunter waits in ambush along game trail.

bag to shoot and capture a game animal.

bag limit the maximum number of game animals that may be taken legally by one hunter in a hunting season or period.

baiting a method of attracting game by spreading food along game trails, illegal in many areas.

blind a camouflaged or hidden shelter from which a hunter waits to ambush game. A duck blind.

blood to expose a hunting dog to the scent or blood of its prey.

buck fever a psychological problem in which the hunter chokes up under pressure and is unable to aim or shoot at a sighted deer.

buckshot lead shot in large sizes for shooting deer and other big game.

cast the ranging about by a dog in search of game or in search of the game's scent.

deadset a dog's stance when game is located.

decoy a fake duck used to attract other ducks to a hunting area.

deer rifle commonly, a .30-.30, .30-.06, or .308.

gun dog a hunting dog trained to flush out and retrieve small game. A pointer, setter, or retriever.

spoor collective term for the droppings, tracks, shed hair, or other signs of game on a trail.

spread the width of a set of deer antlers.

stool a bunch of decoys grouped together.

MOUNTAINEERING

(*Also see* MOUNTAINS *in* ENVIRONMENT)

arrest to slow and stop the fall of a climber by gripping and squeezing the belaying rope.

avalanche cord a long, brightly colored length of cord allowed to trail behind a climber in an avalanche zone; the rope facilitates the location of a climber if buried under an avalanche.

belay any object, such as a rock, a climber uses to tie himself to for security. Also, holding or securing a rope for a fellow climber. Also, playing out a rope to a climber ahead.

bergschrund a crevasse located where a glacier has broken away from a mountain.

bivouac to make a temporary, makeshift shelter on a mountainside. Also, the shelter itself.

brake bar a short bar that attaches to a carabiner to slow or stop a rope during rappeling.

buttress a projection, usually flanked by a gully on either side, on a mountainside.

carabiner a ring having a spring catch, used to connect ropes to pitons.

chimney a narrow, vertical passageway through which a climber may pass.

chockstone a stone wedged in a crack and used as a handhold.

cliff hanger a hook attached to any small projection or crack and hung with a foot stirrup.

cornice a wavelike overhang of ice and snow, notorious for starting avalanches.

couloir a ravine or gorge up the side of a mountain; it provides an easy ascent route, but it is dangerous because it serves as a channel for falling rocks.

crampon toothed, metal boot attachments to increase traction on ice.

crevasse a crack or fissure in a glacier.

descendeur a waist line device for gripping rope and slowing descent when rappeling.

etrier a short rope ladder.

exposure the state of being dangerously exposed on a precipitous cliff or steep flank with open space below the climber's feet.

freeclimbing climbing without the aid of pitons and bolts or any kind of mechanical assistance.

glacis a rock slope up to 30 degrees.

glissade to slide down a slope by the soles of one's feet.

ice ax a spiked, adzelike tool used for cutting steps in ice or used as a belay anchor.

ice hammer a tool with one end having a hammer and the other a long spike.

ice screw a threaded spike screwed into the ice.

mantel to climb up onto a shelf or ledge by holding onto its edge and swinging one leg up and over, as in climbing out of a pool.

mountain sickness sickness encountered at above 10,000 feet where air is thin; symptoms include headaches and nausea, which disappear during the descent.

pendulum traversing a steep face by swinging sideways on a rope; a horizontal rappel.

piton a metal spike, wedge, or peg driven into rock or ice to secure a climber.

rappel to descend a cliff face by the use of ropes.

serac a high wall or tower of ice, hazardous to climb.

slab to move diagonally up a steep slope to make climbing easier.

stance a rest spot on a cliff climb.

summit pack a small backpack for carrying climbing gear and clothing.

switchback to zigzag to counter steep slopes. Also, a trail that zigzags to facilitate climbing.

traverse to move sideways across a slope or cliff.

RACQUETBALL

ace a serve that scores a point without a return from the opponent.

around-the-wall ball a ball played off high on the sidewall that then strikes the front wall, the opposite sidewall, then the floor.

avoidable hinder interference from an opponent that could have been avoided; a violation resulting in a side-out or a point to the player interfered with.

back court court area between the back wall and the short line.

backhand same as a backhand in tennis, with the racquet hand sweeping forward from the opposite side of the body.

backhand corner the court area on each player's backhand side.

backspin rotation or bottom spin imparted on a ball by angling the sweep of the racket.

back wall shot a ball played after it bounces off the rear wall.

block one player getting in front of the other after a shot.

ceiling ball a ball shot into the ceiling and rebounding off the front wall, then bouncing high off the floor toward the back wall, a common defensive shot.

ceiling serve any serve that strikes the ceiling before or after contact with the front wall.

crotch any of the junctures where floor and walls meet or where ceiling and walls meet.

crotch shot a shot played into any juncture between floor and wall or ceiling and wall.

cutthroat a game in which three players compete against each other.

dead ball any ball no longer in play, due to interference or being shot out of the court. Also, any old ball that has lost its bounce.

donut a score of zero.

doubles a game in which two teams, of two players each, compete against one another.

down-the-line pass a shot hit straight along a sidewall that returns straight and close to that sidewall, making it difficult to return.

drive serve a low drive into the front wall that rebounds low and fast into the rear court.

English spin imparted on the ball.

face the hitting surface of a racquet.

fault an illegal serve.

fly ball a ball played directly off a wall without a first bounce on the floor.

forehand a stroke in which the ball is hit on the same side as the racquet hand.

forehand corner the court area where each player hits forehand shots.

front court the part of the court near the front wall.

gun hand the hand that is used to grip the racquet.

half-volley hitting a ball on the short hop or the instant it bounces up from the floor.

hypotenuse shot a low shot played from a rear corner to the opposite front corner.

inning one round of play, in which both players have served.

isolation strategy in doubles play, playing the majority of shots to the weaker or less skilled of the two opponents.

kill shot an extremely low shot off the front wall, which barely bounces and is difficult for an opponent to retrieve.

lob a soft, high-arching serve that drops into one of the rear corners.

long an illegal serve that bounces off the front wall and flies all the way to the back wall without touching the floor.

mercy ball a dangerous situation in which a player attempting to hit a ball might accidentally strike the opponent by swinging the racquet, so consequently he or she chooses not to and lets the ball go by. In most cases the play is taken over.

offhand the hand that does not grip the racquet.

pinch shot a kill shot played into a sidewall first.

portsider a left-handed player; southpaw.

rally the continuous return of the ball by each player until an error is made.

reverse corner kill a kill shot hit crosscourt into the far front corner.

rollout the ball rolling out from the wall after a kill shot.

service box the serving area, marked by the service line and the short line.

short line the line marking the rear of the service box halfway between the front wall and the back wall.

side-out loss of service due to a missed shot or penalty.

straddleball any shot that passes between the legs of a player.

sweet spot the area of the racquet face providing the most power and control, usually the center.

technical one point subtracted from a player's score due to unsportsmanlike behavior, such as swearing or stalling.

tension the degree of tightness in the stringing of a racquet.

thong the loop tethered to the butt of a racquet, used as a safety device to keep the racquet from flying out of the hand during play.

volley to strike the ball off a wall before it bounces on the floor.

wallpaper ball a shot that returns as closely as possible along a sidewall without touching it.

z-ball a shot that bounces high off the front wall corner into a sidewall, across to the opposite sidewall, then onto the floor, tracing a Z pattern.

RODEO

bareback riding the riding of a wild, bucking horse for eight seconds while hanging on with only one hand.

bronc short for bronco, an unbroken or improperly broken horse.

bulldog to wrestle a steer to the ground by grasping its horns and twisting its head down.

bull riding riding a bucking bull for eight seconds while holding on with one hand.

calf roping roping a calf from horseback, then wrestling the calf to the ground and tying three of its legs.

chute a narrow stall in which a wild horse or bull is held for mounting and release into the arena.

clown a clown who runs into the arena to distract a bull after a rider has been thrown.

hazer an assistant, noncompeting rider who guides a steer in a straight line to make it easier for a contestant to leap onto the steer and wrestle it down.

pickup man a horseman who rides beside a contestant on a bucking bronc to prevent the rider from being kicked or trampled if he falls off.

saddle bronc riding a competition in which each contestant must ride a saddled, bucking horse for 10 seconds while holding on with one hand and continuously spurring the animal.

steer roping same as calf roping but with a full-grown steer.

steer wrestling an event in which each contestant must wrestle a steer to the ground by grabbing onto its head or horns. Also known as bulldogging.

team roping an event in which two contestants working together try to rope a steer around the neck and two hind legs and immobilize the animal as quickly as possible.

SCUBA AND SKIN DIVING

anoxia oxygen depletion from holding one's breath too long when skin diving; it sometimes results in an underwater blackout.

bends, the a dangerous body reaction in which gas bubbles lodge in joints and tissues, causing crippling pain; it occurs when breathing compressed air at below 33 feet and failing to decompress on the return ascent. Also known as decompression sickness.

buddy breathing the sharing of air from one tank by two divers by passing the mouthpiece back and forth.

buddy line a line tied between two divers to keep them together, especially at night or in murky water.

buddy system a safety system in which each diver is responsible for the well-bring of a fellow diver while in the water.

buoyancy compensator an inflatable vest used in addition to a weight belt to help control buoyancy.

decompress to make a slow ascent or to stop at certain depths for specific times to allow gas bubbles accumulated in tissues to be eliminated by the body to avoid contracting the bends.

decompression the lessening of water pressure on a diver as he ascends.

decompression sickness see BENDS, THE.

decompression tables U.S. Navy tables indicating how much decompression time is required for various depths and dives.

depth gauge a wrist gauge that measures water pressure or depth.

diver down flag a red flag with a white diagonal bar; it is flown from a boat or floated on the surface of the water to warn boaters of divers nearby.

dolphin kick fishlike motion in which the legs are kicked or flapped up and down in tandem.

nitrogen narcosis the dangerous narcotic effect suffered by a diver breathing compressed air at below 100 feet. Also known as rapture of the deep.

rapture of the deep see NITROGEN NARCOSIS.

regulator the breathing apparatus that regulates the flow of air from the air tanks.

scuba an acronym for self-contained underwater breathing apparatus.

snorkel a J-shaped tube with a mouthpiece on one end and an air hole extending above the surface on the other end.

spear gun an underwater trigger gun that shoots small spears for stalking fish.

stride entry the most common method of entering the water from boatside, specifically by taking a giant stride feet first into the water. Also known as the giant stride entry.

weight belt a belt having attached weights to cancel the body's natural buoyancy underwater.

wet suit a thick, skintight, neoprene rubber suit that draws in water, which is heated by the body and helps protect against the cold.

SKATEBOARDING

bank see RAMP.

boardslide see RAILSLIDE.

caballerial a 360-degree rotation in midair while riding fakie.

carve to skate in a long, curving arc.

cruise to travel or coast along steadily without performing tricks.

deck the platform of a skateboard.

fakie, ride to ride backward.

goofy-foot a stance with the right foot planted forward on the board.

grind to slide intentionally on the skateboard's axles over a curb or railing.

half-pipe a U-shaped ramp.

jam to skateboard with others in a group.

kickflip kicking or flipping the skateboard into the air with one's toe.

longboard a long skateboard used for cruising as opposed to performing tricks.

mongo-foot the propelling of the board along with the front foot instead of the back.

ollie a jumping trick performed by kicking the tail of the board.

one-eighty (180) a half rotation performed in midair.

nollie a jumping trick performed by kicking the nose of the board.

nose the front of a skateboard.

railslide sliding along a rail or ledge. Also known as a boardslide.

ramp a wood or concrete rise on which to gain speed or perform tricks. Also known as a bank.

skatepark a skateboarding area built up with ramps.

slam to fall off the board and get hurt.

tail the back end of a skateboard.

three-sixty (360) a full rotation performed in midair.

trucks the front and rear axles of a skateboard.

SKATING

arabian a flying spin in which the body is stretched out parallel to the ice.

axel a jump of 1½ revolutions.

axel, double a jump of 2½ revolutions.

axel, inside an axel in which the takeoff and landing are executed on the same foot.

axel, triple a jump of 3½ revolutions.

Bielmann spin a spin in which one leg is held outstretched high overhead.

camel a spin executed in an arabesque position.

Choctaw a forward to backward turn.

crossfoot spin a spin in which one foot is crossed over the other.

deathdrop an arabian with a landing into a back sit spin.

death spiral a pairs move in which the man holds the woman by the arms and pulls her in a circle with her back arched and her head near the ice.

figures the figure eight and its variations; the figures executed in a patch session.

flying camel a flying spin ending in a back camel.

flying sit spin a flying spin that ends with a sitting spin.

free dancing skate-dancing to music.

freestyle jumps, spins, and footwork executed to the sound of music. Also known as free skating.

Grafstrom spiral an arabesque executed with bent knees.

hydrant lift a pairs move in which the man lifts the woman over his head with her legs split.

Lutz a one-revolution jump.

overhead lift a pairs move in which the woman is held high over the man's head with her back arched.

pair sit spin a sit spin in which the skating couple embrace.

patch in competition, a "patch" of ice designated to each skater to lay out figures on. A patch session.

pivot a spin with one toe pointed into the ice.

Russian split a jump split in which the skater touches his or her toes.

Salchow a one-revolution jump started off a back inside edge and ended on a back inside edge on the opposite foot.

serpentine a figure comprising three circles; a three-lobe figure.

spin a rapid rotation on one spot on the ice.

split a jump in which the legs are split or spread wide apart.

spread eagle a gliding position with one skate facing forward and one skate facing backwards.

stag a split jump executed with the leading leg bent at the knee.

stroking gliding and propelling oneself over the ice.

Zamboni the vehicle or machine that resurfaces the ice on a rink.

SKIING

avalement "swallowing" a mogul, or absorbing the shock of skiing over a bump by retracting the knees and feet.

back moebius a jump in which the skier does a backward somersault in a straightout body position while performing a 360° twist of the body.

backscratcher an acrobatic jump in which the tips of the skis point straight down while the tails touch or "scratch" the skier's back.

ballet a kind of dance on skis performed with a series of graceful freestyle maneuvers.

biathlon a competition combining skiing and rifle marksmanship.

christie a parallel turn made by leaning into the turning direction.

compression turn a turn used on bumpy terrain in which the skier absorbs the bump by retracting or relaxing his legs, then twisting them at the crest to perform a turn.

corn old, coarse, granulated snow.

cornice an overhanging shelf of ice and snow, hazardous to skiers, and known to collapse and cause an avalanche.

crust snow with a hardened surface.

daffy an acrobatic jump in which the skis are scissored in midair.

edging cutting the edges of the skis into the snow to aid in maneuvering; also, walking sideways up a slope.

fall line the direction of a slope's descent.

freestyle avant-garde, acrobatic, or ballet-style skiing.

gelendesprung any ski jump made in a crouching position.

gondola a covered ski lift.

helicopter an acrobatic jump in which the skier spins around 360° in the air, as a helicopter blade.

herringbone a skier's method of walking uphill in which steps are taken at diagonal or wide angles.

kick turn a stationary turn in which one ski is lifted high in the air and swung around to the desired direction.

killer kick an acrobatic maneuver in which the skier "sits" on the back of one ski and kicks the other high in the air, followed by a quick, slicing turn.

langlauf cross-country running on skis.

mogul a bump, hump, or rise of snow.

mogul field a slope with numerous humps.

mule kick an acrobatic jump performed with the skier's knees bent out sideways at a 90° angle.

Nordic skiing cross-country skiing.

peacock's tail an acrobatic maneuver in which the skier makes a complete turn on the uprighted tips of the skis.

powder deep, soft snow.

rambling cross-country walking on skis, a slower and more relaxed form than langlauf.

ramp a slope linking different levels of a mountain.

reverse crossover same as a stepover, only with one ski crossed over the other from behind instead of the front.

royal christie a classical ballet skiing maneuver in which one ski is lifted far behind the skier and brought forward gracefully to make a turn.

royal spin a complete turn with one ski held in the air and turned in pirouette fashion.

schuss to ski straight down a steep slope without turns or traverses.

sideslipping slipping sideways while making a turn.

sidestepping walking sideways up a hill with skis on.

sitzmark the form left in the snow by a skier who has fallen backward.

skijoring skiing while being towed by a horse or vehicle.

slalom a race over a winding course marked with posted flags.

snow cannon a cannonlike device that shoots a spray of water into cold air, forming ice and snow, used by ski resorts.

snowplow bringing the tips of skis together in a V shape or snowplow formation to slow descent or brake. Also known as a wedge.

somersault a backward or forward somersault in the tucked or untucked position.

spatula the front or curved-up end of a ski.

star turn a stationary turn made by raising and putting down the skis alternatively, creating a radius or "star" in the snow.

stepover a ballet maneuver in which one ski is stepped over the other, followed by a royal christie.

swallowing absorbing the impact of a mogul by relaxing or retracting the legs and feet.

undulation a swell or wave in the snow.

traversing a diagonal run across a slope.

washboard a series of small, bumpy waves in the snow.

wedelns a series of very fast and slight changes in direction made by flexing the body joints.

SKYDIVING

automatic opener a device calibrated to deploy automatically a parachute at 1,000 to 1,200 feet, used with student jumpers.

auxiliary chute a reserve parachute.

bag deployment the fabric container enclosing the parachute canopy.

batwings rigid or semirigid surfaces attached to the arms and body to facilitate gliding and slow descent, used illegally.

breakaway the jettisoning of the main parachute to deploy the reserve chute; the cutting of suspension lines to release the canopy.

cloth extensions sections of fabric sewn into the armpits and crotch area to facilitate gliding and to slow descent; not the same as batwings.

crabbing directing the descending parachute sideways to the wind.

delta position a freefall position in which the arms are held back at the sides with the head held low, to increase the rate of descent.

deployment the release and unfurling of the parachute from its pack.

deployment device a sleeve or bag that contains the canopy, slows its opening and reduces shock.

docking joining hands (or other body parts) with another diver in midair.

drop altitude the altitude at which a skydiver jumps.

drop zone a specified area where a skydiver plans to land.

exit point the point in the air, often over a landmark on the ground, where a jumper exits the plane.

freefall the portion of the jump in which the parachute is not yet deployed. Also, any jump in which the chute is deployed at the skydiver's discretion, as distinguished from a static line jump.

frog position a freefall position in which the jumper assumes a spread-eagle posture with arms upraised.

glide horizontal movement through the sky.

groundhog any nonjumping spectator on the ground.

hank to pull or yank on a steering line.

harness the webbing and strapping that cradles the jumper and connects with the suspension lines.

holding directing the canopy against the wind to slow ground speed.

hop 'n' pop pulling the ripcord immediately after exiting from the plane.

inversion a deployment malfunction in which the canopy becomes turned completely or partially inside out.

jumpmaster an experienced jumper and jump leader; one who oversees the jumps of students.

line-over a deployment malfunction in which one or more lines get caught up over the top of the canopy. Also known as a Mae West.

opening point the point in the air at which the jumper should pull the ripcord in order to land within the specific jump zone.

opening shock the shock or pull felt by the jumper when the chute opens.

oscillation the swinging back and forth of a jumper under a descending canopy, usually occurring during turns.

pack collective term for the parachute assembly, including the container, canopy, connector links, risers, suspension lines, and reserve chute.

pack tray the container part that holds the lines when stowed.

paraboots special shock-absorbent boots worn by jumpers.

pilot chute a small parachute used to help deploy the main parachute.

PLF parachute landing fall; a method of landing in which impact is distributed across several points of the body instead of to the feet and ankles alone.

poised exit an exit made from an airplane wing or strut.

relative work working with others in midair to create formations or to conduct stunts.

reserve the auxiliary chute.

running directing the parachute to fly with the wind to increase ground speed.

smoke flares used to make the jumper easier to spot from spectators on the ground.

spotting choosing the airplane course and a ground landmark over which to jump in order to land at a desired location.

stall the loss of lift.

static line a line attached from the aircraft to the parachute; it automatically deploys the parachute as soon as the jumper exits the plane.

steering lines short lines connected to the suspension lines, used to steer the canopy. Also known as toggle lines.

streamer a deployment malfunction in which part of the canopy clings together and fails to unfurl.

suspension lines the cords connected to the harness from the canopy.

terminal velocity the fastest speed a body can reach while dropping through the air, approximately 120 miles per hour, reached about 12 seconds after exiting an airplane, depending on body position.

toggle lines see STEERING LINES.

tracking assuming the best body position for horizontal movement.

wind drift indicator a weighted strip of crepe paper, usually about 20 feet long, dropped out of an airplane to determine the amount of drift a jumper can expect during descent.

SNOWBOARDING

air a reference to being or getting airborne, often called catching air.

alley-oop a 180° rotation.

backside where the heels are planted on a snowboard.

bail to crash or fall.

boarder cross competition a race in which competitors run a gated course composed of various jumps and turns.

bone to ride with one or both legs straightened.

bonk to strike a rock or log.

boosting getting up in the air off a jump.

caballerial a rotation of 360°.

carve to make a turn.

catching air boosting.

chatter board vibrations produced at high speeds and through turns, reducing control.

corduroy a surface of finely ridged snow, like corduroy pants, created by the grooming of a snowcat.

crater to crash, especially when one leaves a hole in the snow afterward.

crippler air a stunt composed of a 90° rotation, followed by a flip, and another 90° rotation.

cruise an easy, straightforward run without tricks or stunts.

dampening a method of reducing chatter or vibrations by laminating rubber into the board.

double-handed grab a stunt in which the snowboard is grabbed with both hands while in midair.

dragon a machine used to groom half-pipes.

duckfoot a stance in which the toes are pointed outward.

effective edge running the length of the board, the metal edge that comes in contact with the snow.

fakie, ride to ride backward, with the foot that is normally planted in back in the front.

540 air a 540° rotation in which the boarder ends up riding backwards or fakie.

flail to ride wildly out of control, especially with windmilling arms.

flying squirrel air bending at the knees and grabbing the back of the board with both hands while in midair.

freeriding riding freely downhill without halfpipe stunts or jumps.

freestyle riding halfpipes, and performing stunts and jumps, as opposed to freeriding.

goofy goofy-footed.

goofy-footed riding a board with the right foot in the front position, as opposed to regular-footed.

half-pipe a U-shaped ramp of snow.

handplant a planting of one or two hands in the snow to facilitate a rotation stunt.

hucker one who hurls him- or herself wildly over jumps and crash-lands.

invert any stunt in which the rider's head is temporarily below the snowboard, as a simple flip.

inverted aerial a stunt in which a boarder turns upside down in midair.

inverted 720 an inverted aerial with a 720° rotational flip.

Japan air a stunt in which the front of the board is grabbed and pulled up to the level of the head.

jib to ride a snowboard on a surface other than snow.

kink a bump, notch, or uneven patch of snow in a halfpipe, causing difficulty.

leash a line attaching from the front foot to the board, used to prevent the board from running down the mountain on its own.

lip the top edge of a halfpipe wall.

McEgg an inverted stunt in which the rider plants the front hand on a halfpipe wall and rotates 540°, landing in a forward-riding position.

McTwist an inverted aerial with a 540° rotational flip.

900 air a 900° midair rotation, landing in the forward-riding position.

nose the front tip of the board.

ollie a flat-ground leap or springing off the ground by the strength of one's legs, particularly from the back of the board, and without the aid of a mound of snow.

180 air a 180° midair rotation ending riding fakie.

pipe dragon a machine used to shape and cut halfpipes.

quarterpipe a halfpipe with only one wall.

railing making very hard and fast turns.

regular-footed with left foot planted in the forward position, as opposed to goofy-footed.

revert to rotate from riding fakie to forward or vice versa.

rolling down the windows descriptive term for the wild arm-swinging a boarder uses to regain balance.

skate to propel oneself on flat areas.

snowcat a specialized vehicle that can plow or groom snow either with its treading or with various attachments.

stance the positioning of the feet on the board.

stick to make a jump landing with balanced form.

tail the rear of the snowboard.

tail wheelie riding on the tail with the board's nose in the air.

360 air a 360° rotation in midair.

traverse to slide across the face of a hill as opposed to straight down it.

tuck a crouching position that helps cut wind resistance and increase speed.

wall either wall of a half-pipe.

SOCCER

back a fullback; a player who plays defense in the backfield.

back heel to kick the ball backward with the heel of the foot.

back pass to pass the ball to a player behind.

banana pass to kick the ball off-center to impart it with spin, which produces a curving or "banana" trajectory. Also known as a banana kick, bending the ball, or curling the ball.

bending the ball see BANANA PASS.

bicycle kick a volley in which the player upends himself and kicks the ball with his legs scissoring overhead. Also known as a hitch kick, overhead volley, reverse kick, and scissors kick.

block tackle to block the ball with one's foot or body to prevent an opponent from stealing it.

blue card in indoor soccer, a blue card held up by the referee to indicate that a player is being cited with a time penalty.

board in an indoor soccer match, to push an opponent into the fence or wall surrounding the field, an illegal play.

book to issue a yellow or other card to a player for a foul or for unsportsmanlike behavior.

boots commonly used name for soccer shoes.

box the penalty area or penalty box.

bully a mad scramble for a loose ball by both sides in front of a goal.

card to issue or show a yellow or other card.

catenaccio Italian term for "big chain," a largely defensive mode of play characterized by close, man-to-man coverage and one free man or sweeper who stand guard behind three or four fullbacks.

caution to issue a caution to a player; to card or book. A second offense may result in ejection from the game. See RED CARD.

center back the central defender, usually placed in front of a goal.

center circle at the center of the field, the circle from which kickoffs are taken at the start of each half.

center forward the position played closest to the opponent's goal; the offensive position also known as the central striker.

center halfback a midfield player who plays both offensive and defensive roles.

change on the fly in indoor soccer, to take out a player and send in a substitute while the ball is still in play.

charge to rush the shoulders of an opposing player to push him away from the ball, a legal tactic.

charge, illegal deliberate body contact that is violent or dangerous or in an area other than the shoulders, an infraction resulting in a free kick awarded to the offended team.

chest trap to stop a ball in flight with the chest.

chip to kick a high, lofting shot over the head of a defender. Also known as a lob pass.

clear to kick or throw the ball (by the goalie only) out of the goal area.

collecting the act of catching and gaining control of a passed ball with the feet.

convert a corner to score with an awarded corner kick.

convert a penalty to score with a penalty kick.

corner at each corner of the field, a small, quarter circle from which corner kicks are made.

corner kick a direct free kick from a corner taken by the offense after the ball has been propelled out of bounds past the goal line by the defense.

crease in indoor soccer, the 16-foot by 5-foot rectangular area in front of a goal.

cross pass a pass from one side of the field to the other.

curling the ball see BANANA PASS.

cut down the angle the goalie's defensive tactic of running out to meet an opponent with the ball to cut down the opponent's visible shooting area to the goal.

defender a fullback or halfback.

direct free kick a direct free kick awarded to a team that has been seriously fouled by the opposing team.

dribble to propel the ball forward with light taps of the feet.

drop ball in a nonpenalty stoppage, a method of restarting play in which the referee drops the ball between two opposing players.

dropkick to drop the ball and kick it as it bounces, a kick made by the goalie.

drop pass stopping the ball while on the move and then leaving it or passing it backward to a player moving up from behind.

face off two opposing players facing each other during a drop ball.

feinting faking a move to elude an opponent.

flick to crisply pass or jab the ball with the outside of the foot. Also, to bounce the ball off the head for a pass or an attempted goal.

football another name for soccer. Also, the soccer ball.

forward a front line offensive player, responsible for moving the ball close to an opponent's goal and taking shots.

fullback a defender in the last line of defense in front of a goal.

ghost to face into the background or play casually in the hope of being left undefended at a later, more critical time.

give-and-go to pass to a player, break away from a defender, and then receive a quick return pass.

goalie the goalkeeper.

goalkeeper the player who guards the goal to prevent shots from entering the net and scoring. The goalie.

goal line the boundary line at either end of the field.

goals against average the statistic indicating the average number of goals a goalie allows per game.

hack to kick an opponent, a foul.

hacker a dirty player who frequently commits fouls against opponents.

halfback one of several midfield players involved in offense and defense.

half-volley kick kicking the ball the instant it bounces up from the ground.

handballing illegally touching the ball with the hands.

hat trick three goals scored by the same player in a single game.

heading propelling the ball with the head.

head trap stopping an in-flight ball with the head.

heavy pitch a slow playing field, such as one that is wet or has long grass.

heel pass kicking a pass with the back of the foot.

hitch kick see BICYCLE KICK.

indoor soccer soccer played on a smaller field with fewer players (six per team instead of the standard 11) and slightly different rules.

inside left, inside right the inside forwards on the left or right sides of the field.

jockeying maneuvering or shepherding an opponent with the ball into a more tightly defended area.

juggling keeping the ball in the air by bouncing it continuously on the knees, feet, or head.

kill the ball to stop or trap a moving ball.

linesman one of two officials who assist the referee in making calls.

linkman a midfielder or halfback.

lob a high, arcing pass or shot.

major penalty a penalty in which the offending team must play short a player for five minutes.

marking guarding an opponent.

midfielders the offensive and defensive positions in the middle of the field.

MISL Major Indoor Soccer League.

NASL North American Soccer League.

nutmeg to kick the ball between a defender's legs and continue on down the field.

offside being in an illegal position on the opponent's side of the field, specifically between the goal line and the ball, the instant the ball is played with less than two opponents nearer the goal.

offside trap a strategic play to lure an opponent into an offside position in order to gain possession of the ball.

off the ball away from the ball.

outside left, outside right the forwards on the outside right or outside left of the field. Also known as wings or wingers.

penalty arc outside each penalty area in front of the goal, a half radius from which penalty kicks are made.

penalty area in front of and around the goal, the 44-yard by 18-yard marked rectangular area from within which a goalie may handle the ball. A foul committed in this area results in a penalty kick being awarded to the offended team.

penalty kick a direct free kick taken from the penalty arc or penalty spot.

pitch the traditional name for a soccer field.

placekick to kick a ball that has been set motionless on the ground.

policeman a center back; the central backfield defender.

power play in indoor soccer, the man advantage of one team when the other team has temporarily lost a player due to a time penalty.

power play goal in indoor soccer, a goal scored while the defending team is short one man.

pull the goalkeeper a last-ditch effort to score a goal in the closing minutes of a game by replacing the goalie with a field player, which leaves the net open and vulnerable but provides one extra potential scorer.

punt a goalie's long kick away from his goal.

push pass a short pass made with the inside of the foot.

red card a red card held up by the referee when a player is ejected from a game.

referee the official who oversees a game and who is assisted by two linesmen.

scissors kick see BICYCLE KICK.

screen while dribbling, to keep the body between the ball and a defender. Also known as shielding.

shadow to guard an opponent closely.

show the ball while dribbling, to make the ball appear easy to steal in order to lure a defender closer to or away from a certain position.

slide tackle an attempt to kick or steal the ball away from a dribbler by sliding into the ball feet first.

sole trap trapping a moving ball against the sole of the foot and the ground.

striker the center forward; a forward.

sweeper a player who represents the last line of defense before a goalkeeper; he plays in front of or behind the back line.

tackle to use the feet to dislodge or steal the ball away from an opponent.

tackle through the ball to run into an opponent while attempting to tackle the ball; it often results in the assessment of a foul.

targetman the central striker, who receives air balls to shoot on goal or to pass to players close to the goal.

thigh trap to trap or stop a moving ball with the thigh.

throw-in the method in which a ball is returned to play after going out of bounds.

touch the out-of-bounds area along the sidelines.

touchlines the sidelines.

trap to stop a ball in motion with the feet, knees, thighs, chest, or head. Also known as to kill the ball.

volley kicking a ball in midair, before a bounce.

wings players positioned on the outside or flanks of a line. Also known as wingers.

yellow card a yellow card held up by the referee to show that a player has been cautioned for an infraction.

SQUASH

ace a shot so well placed that the opposing player cannot even make contact with it with his racquet.

alley shot a shot close to the side walls. Also known as a rail shot.

back wall shot bouncing the ball off the back wall powerfully enough so that it reaches the front wall without touching the floor.

boast bouncing the ball off a sidewall powerfully enough so that it reaches the front wall without touching the floor.

boast nick a boast shot aimed in such a way as to strike the front wall and junction of the floor and sidewall in quick succession so that the ball rolls out and is impossible for the opposing player to hit back.

corner shot a ball played into the sidewall close to the front wall and striking the front just above the tell-tale, from which it drops short to the floor making for a difficult return.

crosscourt shot a shot that crosses the court and sometimes forces the opposing player to use his backhand.

die of the ball; to fail to bounce, and therefore declared dead.

doubles squash played by four players.

drive a slamming shot taken after the ball bounces.

drop nick a soft shot in which the ball hits the junction of the floor and sidewall and rolls out, making it impossible to return.

drop shot a low, soft shot that bounces only slightly, making it difficult to return.

fault an incorrect serve.

foot fault when the server's foot is in an illegal position when serving.

gallery the bleachers or seated area for spectators.

get getting to and returning a difficult shot.

half-volley a ball played after one bounce.

length a play that results in the ball dying before it reaches the back wall.

let the replaying of a point.

let point a point awarded to a player who has been deliberately interfered with by an opponent during play.

lob a high shot against the front wall.

nick any ball that strikes the juncture of floor and wall and rolls out for an impossible return.

Philadelphia boast a reverse boast.

putaway an irretrievable shot.

rally when two opponents return several shots back and forth before a point is finally scored.

service box the quarter circle in the corner of a service court in which a player must have at least one foot while serving.

tell-tale the line just above the floor on the front court, below which a shot is illegal.

volley a ball played in the air.

SURFING

aerial a trick in which the board is pulled up by the rails to become airborne.

air referring to getting some air or getting airborne with one's board.

angling riding across a wave instead of directly toward shore.

axe a serious wipeout.

backhand surfing with one's back facing the wave.

bail out to leap off the surfboard just before wiping out.

barney a new surfer or one with poor skills.

barrel inside the hollow of a breaking wave. Also known as a tube.

blown out referring to waves that have been turned into unridable chop by the wind.

body surfing floating on or riding a wave without a board.

bomb an extremely large wave.

boogie board a small foam board that a rider kneels or lies on to surf waves.

choppy broken wave conditions that make it difficult or impossible to surf.

cutback a very sharp turn back toward the breaking part of a wave.

face the part of a wave that is ridden by surfers.

forehand surfing while facing the wave. Also known as front side.

goofy-footed riding with the right leg forward, most commonly used by left-handed surfers.

hang five to curl the toes of one foot over the nose of the board.

hang ten to curl the toes of both feet over the nose of the board.

jacking the sudden rise or steepening of a swell as it passes from deep water to shallow.

jake a beginner who causes problems for other surfers.

kick out to leave a wave by riding up over the top of it.

kiteboarding surfing on a small board while being towed by a kite. Also known as kite surfing.

leash a board tether attached to the surfer's ankle.

mushy any weak, low waves.

natural-footed a stance in which the left leg is forward, typical for a right-handed surfer.

nose the front of a surfboard.

nose ride riding on the front of a board.

overhead referring to waves taller than the surfer, with double overhead being twice the surfer's height, and triple overhead being three times the height.

over the falls one of the worst types of wipeout, when a surfer crashes down with the lip of a breaking wave and is driven into the seafloor.

pearl a wipeout caused by the front of the board dipping into the water, a hazard of riding on a steep wave.

pocket the steepest part of a wave, just in front of the breaking portion.

rail the sides of a board.

rip current a strong, reverse current that pulls.

roundhouse cutback a sharp, 180° turn back toward the broken part of a wave.

set a group of waves.

shortie a wetsuit with short arms and legs.

shoulder the edge of a breaking wave.

soup the whitewater portion of any breaking or broken wave.

switchfoot changing one's normal stance to the opposite stance.

tail the rear of a surfboard.

360 three-sixty; a trick in which the board is whipped around 360° on a breaking wave.

tube the inside of a breaking wave; the barrel. Also, as a verb, to ride inside a wave.

wet suit a neoprene outfit worn to keep surfers warm in cold conditions.

TENNIS

ace a perfectly placed serve that an opponent is unable to return.

ad in short for advantage in.

ad out short for advantage out.

advantage in in the server's advantage; the point won by the server after deuce.

advantage out the receiver's advantage; the point won by the receiver after deuce.

alley along either side of the court, the long, additional area used only in doubles play.

approach shot a shot that allows a player to move toward the net.

attack the net to move quickly toward the net for a volley or a kill shot.

Australian grip a grip halfway between the eastern and the continental.

backcourt the rear portion of the court, between the baseline and the service line.

backhand a stroke taken from the left side of a right-handed player's body (opposite for a lefty).

backspin reverse spin on a ball.

baseline the line marking the ends of the court.

baseline judge one of two linesmen who watch the baseline and call balls out of play.

blitz to bombard an opponent with a quick succession of fast, hard shots.

block volley to return a ball without swinging the racket; letting the ball bounce passively off the face of the racket.

break to win a game against the server.

break point the point that will win a game against the server.

butt the end of a racket handle.

cannonball a fast, hard serve.

carry literally to carry or hold the ball in play on one's racket, a penalty situation resulting in the loss of the point.

centerline the line dividing the service boxes.

changeover the switching of courts by the opposing players after every odd game in a set.

chip a soft, backspinning shot that dips and barely clears the net. Also known as a dink.

chop a shot made by a chopping swing of the racket, which imparts the ball with heavy spin.

clay court a court surface made of clay.

closed face the face of the racket when it is tilted down toward the ground or down toward an incoming ball, as distinguished from an open face.

continental grip a popular grip that can be used for either forehand or backhand shots, characterized by the palm facing down and the index finger and thumb forming a V around the left side of the handle.

crosscourt shot a ball hit diagonally across the court.

cross slice a short, slicing motion of an open racket; it gives the ball backspin and sidespin simultaneously. Also known as a cut stroke.

Davis Cup an annual international teams tournament.

dead slang for out of play.

default to forfeit a game, set, or match by failing to complete it.

defensive lob a very high, deep lob, executed to give a defensive player time to get into better position for the opponent's next shot.

deuce when players reach a tie score of 40 to 40. To win, one player must score two points in a row.

die of a ball, to fail to bounce, such as when imparted with underspin.

dink see CHIP.

double fault the failure to deliver a legal or inbounds serve within two tries.

double hit to hit the ball twice in the same play, an infraction resulting in the loss of the point.

doubles a game with four players, two to a side.

down-the-line shot a shot hit straight down the sideline.

down-the-T shot a shot hit straight down the middle of the court, along the center service line.

drag volley a volley hit with an open racket, imparting some backspin.

drive a hard groundstroke.

drop shot a soft shot that barely clears the net and is therefore difficult for an opponent in the backcourt to reach.

eastern grip popular forehand grip in which the player "shakes hands" with the racket handle in a natural hand position. Also known as the shake hands grip.

error a failed return.

face the stringed, hitting surface of the racket.

fast court a court in which the ball tends to skid or bounce quickly, as on wood or grass.

fault failure to deliver a legal or in-bounds serve.

15 the first scoring unit or point.

flat a serve or shot executed with little or no spin.

follow-through the finishing portion of a swing.

foot fault stepping on or over the baseline while making a serve; two consecutive faults result in the loss of the point.

forecourt the area between the net and the service line.

forehand a shot executed on the right side of the body by a right-handed player (opposite for a lefty).

gallery the spectators' seating area.

gallery play a showoff shot made to stir up a reaction from the spectators.

game point a point that wins a game if made by the player who is ahead.

game set a game-winning point in a set-winning game.

Grand Prix a yearlong, worldwide tournament circuit played by professionals, who earn points and prize money for a year-end championship.

grand slam winning the Australian, U.S., French, and Wimbledon singles championship in the same year.

grass court a court made of grass and known for its fast surface.

groundstroke a stroke made after an incoming ball has bounced, as distinguished from a volley.

gut a racket's string material, made from animal intestines.

half-volley to strike the ball immediately after a bounce.

jam to stroke the ball directly at an opponent's body in order to force an off-balance return.

jump smash a powerful, overhead shot made while jumping in the air.

kick the speed, height, and direction of a ball that has bounced up from the ground.

kill a hard, fast shot that eludes the opponent.

let a serve that nicks the top of the net and must be replayed.

linesman any one of the line judges who makes calls on whether a ball hits in or out of court.

lob a high, arcing shot.

love a score of zero.

match winning the best of three or more sets.

mixed doubles doubles in which each team has one male and one female.

moon ball a very high lob.

net judge a judge who sits on one side of the net and calls any lets on a serve.

open a tournament open to professionals and amateurs.

open face the face of the racket when it is titled back away from an incoming ball, as distinguished from a closed face.

overhead a stroke hit with the arm over the head, as a serve.

passing shot a shot that passes by an opponent who is close to the net.

poach in a doubles game, to move intentionally into a partner's territory to attempt a surprise kill shot.

point the first point is 15, the second is 30, the third is 40, and the fourth is game. Four points wins a game.

point penalty a subtraction of one point for unsportsmanlike conduct.

power player a player who uses powerful serves and drives to win a game, as distinguished from a touch player.

punch volley a volley made by partially swinging or punching the racket.

put away to execute a kill shot.

rally a long exchange of shots between opponents before someone finally fails to make a return.

serve and volley to serve then quickly rush the net for a return volley.

service a serve.

service box slang for service court.

service break winning a game against the server.

service court either of the 13½-foot by 21-foot rectangular boxes on both sides of the court in which the ball must land when served.

service line the line marking the boundaries of the service boxes.

set a scoring unit, specifically the first six games won by one player by a margin of two.

set point a point that will win a set if the leading player scores.

sidespin a sideways spin imparted on the ball by a sideways slice of the racket.

singles court the court area measuring 78 feet by 27 feet.

slam a smash.

slice hitting under and across a ball to impart it with underspin and sidespin.

slow court a court surface that produces high, rebounding balls, as in clay.

smash a powerful, overhead stroke.

sphairstike the original name for tennis, as coined by its inventor.

spin ball rotation producing a curved flight path and an unpredictable bounce.

spin it in to serve a ball with spin.

stop volley a soft volley that barely drops over the net, used when the opponent is in the backcourt.

straight sets consecutive wins.

sudden death a tie-breaker game.

sweet spot the middle of the racket face; the optimum hitting surface.

tennis elbow painful condition characterized by inflammation of the tendons around the elbow, caused by twisting and general overuse of elbow in tennis.

throat the neck of the racket handle, just below the head.

topspin forward rotation imparted on a ball by brushing the racket face up and over the ball.

touch player a finesse or control player, as distinguished from a power player.

umpire the official seated in a high chair at one end of the net; he keeps the score and makes rulings.

underspin backward rotation imparted on a ball by brushing the racket face down and under the ball.

volley to hit the ball in the air, before it bounces on the ground.

Wimbledon the tennis championships held in Wimbledon, England.

THOROUGHBRED RACING

(*Also see* HORSES *in* ANIMALS AND INSECTS)

acey deucey a riding style to facilitate balance during turns in which the right stirrup is shorter than the left.

across the board betting on one horse for win, place, and show.

aged a horse seven years of age or older.

airing an exercise run. Also, a race in which the horse runs only at exercise speed.

also-ran a horse that did not finish in the money.

alter to castrate.

ankle boot a protective leather or rubber bootie for the fetlock.

ankle cutter a horse that strikes and cuts a fetlock with the opposite hoof while running.

apprentice a student jockey.

armchair ride a victory won without having to prod the horse.

baby a two-year-old.

baby race a 2- to 4-furlong race for two-year-olds.

back to slow down.

backstretch the straightaway at the far side of the track.

bangtail a bobbed or shortened tail.

barrel the torso of a horse.

barrier the starting gate.

bear in to move toward the inside rail.

bear out to move to the outside of the track, especially during a turn.

bend a turn in the track.

bit the mouth bar to which the reins are secured.

blanket finish a very close finish.

blind switch the position of being blocked by other horses in front and the decision to either drop back and go around them or wait for an opening.

blinkers the eye pieces that partially block a horse's vision, used to keep concentration focused on the track to the front.

blowout a brief workout to warm up a horse before a race.

boat race a fixed race.

bobble to stumble.

bolt to run off in a panic, as when some horses see the starting gate.

boot to kick the horse to make it run faster.

Boots and Saddles the bugle call accompanying the horses entering the track for post parade.

bottom the horse assigned to the outside post position.

break in the air to leap upward instead of out at the starting bell.

break maiden to win the first race of one's career, pertaining to either jockey or horse.

brittle feet hooves that chip easily.

bucked shins inflamed shins, due to stress.

bull ring a small track.

buzzer an illegal, battery-powered, vibrating device used to scare a horse into running faster.

calculator the clerk who calculates pari-mutuel odds.

cannon the foreleg between the ankle and the knee.

canter a slow gallop.

card a racing program.

carry the target to run last from start to finish.

chalk horse the favorite to bet on.

chalk player one who bets on favorites.

choppy abnormally short strides, due to lameness.

chute an extension of a stretch to provide a long, straight run from starting gate to first turn.

claiming race a race in which a horse is subject to purchase.

clerk of the scales the official who weighs riders and tack before and after a race.

clocker one who times workout runs, used as information for betting.

clothes horse blanket.

clubhouse turn a bend or turn in the track closest to the clubhouse. In races that begin on the homestretch, the first turn.

colors riders' colorful, identifying costumes.

croup the uppermost hindquarters of a horse.

cuppy of a track, broken into clods and hoofprints.

daily double winning a bet by correctly picking both winners of two races.

dark referring to a track's nonracing day or night.

dark horse an underrated horse; a sleeper.

dead heat when at least two horses vie for the finish line nose-to-nose.

dead weight weights added to a saddle to raise the overall weight of rider and tack.

deep of a track, freshly harrowed.

derby race for three-year-olds.

disqualify officially to drop back a horse's finishing position due to interference or illegal weight.

dope sheet horseracing information sheet.

drench to give medicinal liquid to a horse.

dwell to break slowly at the gate.

eighth a furlong.

eighth pole a colored post marking ⅛ mile, or 1 furlong, from the finish line.

exacta picking the winner and place horses.

fade to tire and fall behind at the homestretch or before.

farrier a horseshoer.

fast track a dry, hard track.

fetlock the ankle of a horse.

field collective term for all the entrants in a race.

film patrol the crew that films the race to monitor for interference or other fouls.

five-eighths pole a post marking 5 furlongs from the finish line.

flash a change of odds shown on the tote board.

flatten out position of an exhausted horse, specifically with its head hung low and even with its body.

footing a track's surface condition.

freelance a jockey who works independently and is not contracted by any one stable.

freshener time allotted for rest to restore a horse's energy.

frog the fleshy cushion on the sole of the hoof.

furlong ⅛ of a mile.

futurity a race in which horses are entered before they are born.

gad a jockey's whip.

gallop a horse's fastest gait, in which all four feet are intermittently off the ground at the same time.

gelding a castrated male horse.

gentleman jockey an amateur jockey.

graduate to break maiden.

groom the stable assistant who grooms the horse and escorts it to the paddock for a race.

grunter an out-of-condition horse.

gumbo a heavy mud track.

half-mile pole the pole located 4 furlongs from the finish line.

hand a measure of equine height, specifically 4 inches.

handicap the assigning of weights to equalize competition. Also, to study the records of horses' past performances to help in choosing a future winner.

hand ride to teach a horse to take longer or faster strides by pulling on its head at the beginning of each stride.

hat trick a jockey's winning of three races on a single program.

hayburner a horse that costs more money to maintain than it is worth.

head of the stretch the last portion of the final turn.

heat a race.

herd to turn a horse to block another from gaining a superior position.

homestretch the straightaway in front of the stands.

hop to drug a horse illegally.

hot-walker a stable assistant who walls a horse to cool it off after a race.

impost the weight a horse must carry in a handicap race.

infield the area inside of the track, where the tote board is located.

inquiry an official investigation of a race to determine if it was run fairly.

irons stirrups.

jockey the rider. Also, to jockey for position during a race.

juvenile a two-year-old.

kiss the eighth pole to finish way behind.

lead pony the horse and rider that lead thoroughbreds to the post.

leather a whip.

length 8 to 9 feet.

maiden a jockey or horse that hasn't won a race yet.

mile pole a colored post marking 1 mile to the finish line.

monkey crouch a riding style characterized by a low crouch over the horse's withers.

muck out to clean out a horse's stall.

mudder a horse that runs especially well on muddy tracks.

nightcap the final race on a card.

objection a jockey's complaint of a foul.

odds board the tote board.

odds on odds of less than even money.

off the board to finish out of the money.

off-track betting betting conducted away from the track.

outrider the mounted escort who leads horses to the post.

overland making wide turns.

paddock a saddling enclosure or stall. Also, a pasture.

pari-mutuel a betting system in which the winners collect all the money bet by the losers, minus house percentage.

pasteboard track a fast track that is thin and hard.

pinched back getting pocketed and pushed back behind a group of horses.

pocket being surrounded by other horse.

pony any nonracing, working horse on a track, such as a lead pony.

pool the total amount bet.

post the starting gate.

pull to hold a horse back intentionally to prevent it from winning.

punter one who plays the horses.

quarter pole the colored post 2 furlongs from the finish line.

quinella betting in which the bettor tries to pick the first two finishers.

racing secretary the track handicapper and official who assigns weights in handicap races.

rack up to run into or interfere with several horses at once.

rate to hold back a horse early in a race to help conserve its energy for the home-stretch.

roar loud coughlike breathing of a horse.

runner a messenger between the people in the clubhouse boxes and the mutuel window.

run wide to run too far out from the inside rail and waste ground.

saliva test a drug test performed on winning horses.

save ground to hug the inside rail, the most efficient means of saving ground and running the track faster.

scenic route a wide run covering too much ground; an inefficient run.

scratch the withdrawal of an entrant from a race.

scratch sheet a racing tip sheet featuring graded handicaps, scratches, and so on.

seat the rider's posture on a horse.

sex allowance a weight concession granted to female horses running against males.

shed row row of barns near the backstretch.

shoe board a sign listing the types of shoes worn by the entrants.

short an out-of-shape horse that fades in a stretch.

shut off to cut in front of another racer and block him out.

silks see COLORS.

sixteenth pole the pole marking half a furlong from the finish line.

skin to roll the surface of a track to make it harder and faster.

sleeper an underrated horse.

sophomore a three-year-old horse.

spit out the bit said of an exhausted horse who refuses to go any further.

sprint any short race, about 7 furlongs or less.

stake the commission paid to the winning jockey or trainer.

stall gate a starting gate having individual compartments for each horse.

stewards the three officials of racing law who judge races.

stiff to hold back a horse intentionally to prevent it from winning.

string collective term for the horses owned by one stable.

tack collective term for the saddle and other equipment placed on the horse.

three-eighths pole the colored pole marking 3 furlongs from the finishing line.

three-quarters pole the colored pole marking 6 furlongs from the finish line.

tout a trainer, groom, stable boy, jockey, or other person connected to the sport who provides "inside information" on a horse or race for a fee.

trackmaster person in charge of maintaining the track.

Triple Crown winning the Kentucky Derby, the Preakness Stakes, and the Belmont Stakes.

urine test a drug test for horses.

valet one who cares for a jockey's clothing and carries his tack.

walking ring an oval walking area near the paddock where the horses are walked for the purpose of observation by the betting public. Also known as the parade ring.

walkover a race in which every horse is scratched but one, who can win simply by walking in.

washy of a horse, sweaty.

weigh-in the weighing of jockeys with tack after a race is over.

weigh-out the weighing of jockeys with track before a race begins.

whoop-de-doo an aggressive riding style in which the horse is frequently whipped and is allowed to run as fast as possible without restraint.

TRACK AND FIELD

anchor one who runs the last leg of a relay race. Also, the last leg of the race itself.

baton in a relay race, the tube passed from one runner to another.

bell lap the last lap of a multi-lap race, marked by the ringing of a bell.

bonk to become exhausted to the point when only slow running is possible. Also, known as hitting the wall.

bounding in the triple jump, the series of leaps made.

break-line the point on a track where runners may change lanes.

carbo load to consume a high carbohydrate diet for three days leading up to a long race, to maximize glycogen or energy stores.

changeover in a relay race, the handing over of a baton from one runner to another.

cross-country a running race ranging over open terrain, grass, or through woodlands, rather than over a formal track.

decathlon a two-day competition of 10 different events, often determining bragging rights for greatest all-around athlete. The events are the 100 meters, long jump, shot put, high jump, 400 meters, 110 meter hurdles, discus, pole vault, javelin, and the 1,500 meters.

discus a disk or plate thrown for distance in the discus competition. Also the competition itself.

doping the illegal practice of using performance-enhancing drugs, such as steroids.

exchange zone in a relay race, the limited area in which the baton must be passed to the next runner.

false start an early takeoff by one or more runners at the start of a race, requiring a second start.

fartlek a Swedish term for a workout that incorporates a mix of fast and slow running.

fast twitch muscle fiber muscle fiber used to produce explosive speed but which tends to have little endurance.

field event any nonrunning event, such as throwing or jumping.

five K a 5,000-meter, or 3.1 mile, race.

400 meters one lap around the track.

hammer throw a ball attached to a wire, which is thrown as far as possible by competitors.

heat any individual race within a round of races.

heptathlon a competition of seven track and field events, specifically javelin, hurdles, high jump, long jump, shot put, sprint, and 800 meter race.

high jump an event in which competitors try to leap over a high bar, unaided by poles.

hit the wall see BONK.

hurdle one of several waist-high, fencelike barriers that must be leapt over in a hurdles race.

intervals a practice workout in which a course is run at high speed with slow jogs in between.

javelin a spearlike projectile thrown in the javelin competition.

kick at the end of a race, an all-out sprint.

lap one circuit around the track or other course.

leg one portion of a relay race.

long distance designating any race of 5,000 meters or more.

marathon a very long running race of 26.2 miles, or 42.2 kilometers.

meet a competition between two or more teams.

mile, the four times around the track.

pole vault a competition in which competitors run at high speed and vault over a high bar, by the use of a long pole.

runner's high a feeling of happiness or euphoria after a long race, caused by the release of feel-good brain opiates or endorphins.

shot put a competition in which competitors throw a heavy metal ball as far as possible.

slow twitch muscle fiber muscle fiber involved in endurance running but not producing explosive speed.

spikes shoes fitted with spikes for extra traction.

split the time taken at a designated portion of a race, usually at a mile marker, to provide information to the runner about his speed.

sprint a full-out run at top speed over a short course.

staggered start a starting line-up in which runners are staged at varying points behind each other, to compensate for running around a curve, where the outside runner would otherwise have a disadvantage.

starting blocks the blocks on which a runner braces his feet at the start of a race.

tail wind an advantageous wind that helps propel a runner from behind.

takeoff board a 4-foot-long board from which long jumpers and triple jumpers must take off and leap.

ten K a 10,000 meter, or 6.2 mile, race.

throwing circle the circle within which a competitor must throw a discus, shot put, or hammer.

triple jump a competition in which an athlete must perform a hop, step, and a jump in succession to achieve the greatest distance.

ultra marathon any race more than 26.2 miles.

VO2max the maximum amount of oxygen that can be used by the body; aerobic capacity.

walk a speed walking race in which competitors must keep one foot on the ground at all times, and the forward leg must be kept straight, to prevent a running gait.

wind-aided helped by a tailwind.

VOLLEYBALL

antennas the vertical rods at either edge of the net; a ball striking the antenna on either side is deemed out of bounds.

attack block an aggressive attempt to stop the ball before it passes over the net.

back set a set made by a setter overhead and back to a spiker.

block a defensive move by one or more players to block passage of the ball over or near the net.

bump pass another name for a forearm pass, a ball played underhand off the pressed-together forearms.

candy cane a hard, sizzling jump serve that hooks.

contacted ball a ball that touches or is touched by a part of a player's clothing.

crosscourt serve a serve made to the opponents' right-hand sideline.

dig an underhand save close to the floor, used to retrieve or play off a spike; a spiked ball that is saved and passed.

digging saving and passing a powerfully spiked ball.

digging lips slang term for digging someone's best spike or shot repeatedly.

dink a deceptive variation of the spike in which the ball is not smashed with the hand but flicked over blockers by the fingertips.

dive diving to retrieve a ball before it touches the floor and scores.

double block two defenders rising up at the same time to block a spike or other shot.

English spin on the ball.

facial a ball that is spiked into someone's face. Also known as getting mudpacked.

fault a violation of the rules.

floater a ball struck in such a manner as to avoid giving it spin; the result is a ball that when struck may float left or right, rise or drop, or follow an erratic trajectory.

forearm pass a bump pass.

foul a violation of the rules.

line serve a serve made down the opponent's left sideline.

lollipop slang term for a soft serve easily returned by the opposition.

mudpacked, getting see FACIAL.

netting touching the net while the ball is in play; the offending team loses possession of the ball or loses a point.

off-speed spike a spike struck deceptively soft to throw the blockers' timing off.

overhand pass the standard pass executed with both hands held at head height or above.

seam the open space between two serve receivers, or any vulnerable area between players.

service area where the ball is served, specifically both right rear corners of the court at end lines and extending 6 feet back.

serving rotation the rotation of servers on each new possession of the ball, the players moving clockwise into their new positions.

set an overhand pass that places the ball into good position for a teammate to spike over the net.

setter the player whose primary function it is to set the ball to the spiker.

side out the transfer of the serve to the defensive team after the offensive team fails to score a point.

sizzling the pits spiking the ball directly into a blocker's armpits.

spike a ball that is struck powerfully into the opponent's court.

spiker the player who executes the spike.

thrown ball any ball that is judged to be thrown instead of struck, a foul violation.

WINDSURFING

abeam at right angles to the board.

aft toward the stern.

apparent wind the wind felt by the windsurfer, not the true wind one would feel if standing still.

backing wind a wind that is changing direction in a counterclockwise manner.

beam reach a wind blowing from abeam at 90° to the board's course.

bearing away sailing away from the wind.

beating sailing a zigzagging course to windward close-hauled.

bow the front or nose of the board.

break the point where a wave breaks.

camber the degree of curve or fullness in a sail.

carve to cut a turn at high speed.

cavitation when the small fin or fins at the back of the board fail to grip the water, causing the stern to slip and slide sideways.

cleat a hook or fitting on which line is secured.

clew the outside corner of a sail; it attaches to the end of the wishbone.

clew-first to sail with the outside corner of the sail pointed into the wind, used in freestyle and as a means of changing course.

close-hauled sailing as close to the wind as possible.

close reach the wind blowing slightly forward of abeam.

cross seas waves or current that strikes the board from abeam.

daggerboard the large, removable center fin that prevents the board from sliding sideways. See STORM DAGGERBOARD.

donkey kick a method of kicking the back of the board down to facilitate launching or jumping off a wave.

dry suit a neoprene suit to protect the wearer from cold water and hypothermia.

duck tack to duck under the rig, as opposed to walking around it, when tacking.

eye of the wind the exact direction from which a wind is blowing.

fin a skeg or daggerboard.

following seas waves or current moving toward the board from behind.

foot the bottom of the sail.

freestyle the performance of stunts on the board. In noncompetition, also known as hotdogging.

freshening wind a wind growing in strength.

fresh wind a wind of 17 to 21 knots.

gybing see JIBING.

harden to bring the said closer to the body.

head the top of the sail.

head sea current or waves that strike the board head on or from the front.

hull the board itself, minus the rig.

hypothermia dangerous loss of body heat, due to extended exposure to cold water or air.

jibing turning from one tack to another so that the stern passes through the eye of the wind. Also spelled gybing.

leech the edge of the sail between the clew and the head.

leeward the side farthest from the wind. Opposite of windward.

leeway sideways movement of the board to leeward.

luff the edge of the sail from the head to the tack.

luff up to change course and sail closer to the wind.

marginal sail a sail used in hard winds.

mast same as a mast in a sailboat.

mast foot the portion of the mast that attaches inside the mast foot well.

offshore wind a wind blowing from the land to the water.

onshore wind a wind blowing from the water to the land.

outhaul the line that pulls the clew out to the end of the wishbone.

pintail a board having a tapered tail for better control in strong winds.

plane to skim lightly across the surface of the water.

port when looking forward, the left side of the board.

pumping pumping the rig back and fort to produce added wind in the sail.

purling surfing the bow straight into a wave and going head over heels.

rail the side of the board.

railing sailing with the board slightly inclined on its side.

regatta a meeting of windsurfers who compete in events or races.

rig all of the rigging above the universal joint; collective term for the mast, sail, and wishbone.

roundboard a board having a rounded belly, faster but less stable than a regular board.

running sailing with the wind coming from directly behind.

scoop curvature at the nose of the board.

skeg a small fin at the stern of the board to prevent the tail from sliding.

slalom to jibe and tack.

starboard when looking forward, the right side of the board.

stern the back of the board.

storm daggerboard a short daggerboard.

tack the corner of the sail by the universal joint.

tacking a method of changing course in which the nose of the board passes through the eye of the wind.

trim to let the sail in or out as wind conditions change.

universal joint at the mast foot, the apparatus that allows the rig to be inclined and to be swung 360°.

uphaul the line used to pull the rig up out of the water.

veering wind a wind that is changing direction in a clockwise manner.

wetted area the portion of board touched by water, producing drag.

windward the side of the board nearest the wind.

wishbone the booms.

WRESTLING

advantage position the on-top position.

amplitude a throw with exceptional height. Exceptional height on a throw scores extra points in some styles of wrestling.

ankle ride manipulating an opponent in a disadvantaged position by lifting his ankle.

arm throw locking the opponent's arm and executing a throw by rotating the body.

back-arching a throwing method in which the wrestler grasps his opponent and literally bends over backward, causing the opponent to flip over and be pinned.

bear hug a body lock made with the arms around the torso.

body lock a bear hug.

breakdown flattening an opponent on the mat on his belly or side.

chicken wing wrapping an arm around an opponent's arm and pinning it behind his back.

counter wrestling reacting to an opponent's offensive moves instead of initiating such moves.

crossface a headhold across the jaw to the opponent's far shoulder.

disadvantage position the bottom position.

dump to pull an opponent's leg out from under him in order to flip him onto his back.

escape to get out of a bottom position into a neutral position.

fall see PIN.

far side cradle a pinning technique in which the opponent's head and knee are held together.

fireman's cradle hooking an arm under an opponent's crotch and flipping him over.

freestyle the style of wrestling used in the Olympics and other international competition.

Greco-Roman wrestling an international and Olympic style of wrestling that limits the use of the legs and feet.

half nelson a pinning hold in which an arm is thrust under the opponent's arm and locked over his neck or head.

hammerlock a hold in which the opponent's arm is pinned up and behind his back.

headlock a hold in which an arm is wrapped around the opponent's head.

key to react to an opponent's reactions and adjust an attack accordingly.

lookaway a method of raising and turning the head to counter a half nelson.

nearfall a vulnerable position in which the shoulders are exposed to the mat but are not touching.

pin to hold both of an opponent's shoulder blades to the mat for a set amount of time to win the bout. Also known as a fall.

pommeling battling with the arms and hands to gain upper body position.

reversal when a wrestler in the bottom position breaks out and gains control of the man on top.

riding manipulating an opponent from the top position.

roll an attempt at an escape and reversal by rolling out from under an opponent.

scrimmage to practice wrestling maneuvers.

setups false movements or changes of stance that trick an opponent into a vulnerable position.

sitout escaping from a disadvantaged position by sitting up abruptly.

slam an excessively powerful throw to the mat, resulting in a penalty.

snapdown a takedown in which the opponent's head is snapped back into the mat.

snatch attacking the opponent's leg at the knee. Also known as a high single.

souplesse a body throw made with the back-arch.

standup escaping an opponent's hold by standing up abruptly.

takedown throwing an opponent down on the mat from a neutral position.

turk lifting one leg of an opponent, then tripping the other leg out from under him for a takedown to the mat.

YOGA

Ananda a gentle style of yoga noted for its thoughtful affirmations.

asanas literally, "comfortable position"; the various body positions or poses of yoga.

ashram a retreat or school where yoga and spirituality are taught or practiced.

ashtanga yoga a style or discipline of yoga that incorporates breath control with stretches and postures that work together to realign the spine, detoxify the body, and build strength and stamina. Also known as power yoga.

bandha a body lock.

chakras one of seven energy centers thought to be spinning like wheels along the spine. If any of these is under- or overenergized, disease is thought to occur in the body.

cobra a yoga position in which one lies on the floor and curls the upper body up and back.

dhyana the quieting of the mind through meditation and reflection.

downward dog starting from an upward dog position, the raising of the hips and pressing of the heels into the floor, reminiscent of a dog stretching.

fish a yoga position in which one lies on the back while arching the chest.

guru a spiritual teacher.

half-lotus a position in which one is seated on the floor with legs folded in and ankles crossed. An easier position to attain than a regular lotus.

Hatha yoga a form of yoga that uses difficult but low-impact stretches and postures performed with controlled breathing to induce a sense of calm.

kundalini as held by yoga philosophy, the spiritual energy hidden in all beings.

Kundalini yoga a form of yoga that employs breath techniques to heat the body and stimulate the energy center at the base of the spine.

lion a body position in which one sits on the heels with hands resting on the knees while simultaneously widening the eyes and fully extending the tongue from the mouth.

locust a yoga position in which one lies on the stomach and raises one or both legs up in the air.

lotus a position in which one is seated on the floor with legs crossed and both feet resting souls-up on opposite thighs.

mantra a hymn or excerpt of text taken from any one of the four sacred Hindu books known as the Veda and chanted as part of a prayer or meditation.

mudra a hand gesture that directs one's life current.

nadi a channel of energy thought to carry the life force throughout the body.

om a popular meditation sound chanted over and over again to help free the mind of distracting or troubling thoughts. The sound represents all that is, all that was, and that will ever be. Also spelled aum.

plough a body position in which one lies on the back and raises the straightened legs slowly up and back over one's head.

power yoga see ASHTANGA YOGA.

prana life energy; life force.

pranayama breath control or conscious breathing.

samadhi the path to enlightenment. A trancelike state of oneness or deep meditative focus.

samskara an emotion from past experience thought to be recorded within the cells and nervous system of the body.

Sanskrit ancient Indic language from which many yoga terms are derived.

sattwic the ideal yogic diet, consisting of pure, fresh, organic or healthful foods.

Shakti feminine energy or expression, thought to reside at the base of the spine.

Shiva male energy or expression, thought to reside at the crown of the head.

sirshasana a headstand thought to increase brain power.

suryanamaskara a "salute to the sun." In ashtanga yoga, a focusing of one's concentration and breath while performing an opening series of stretches and warm-ups to increase flexibility for deeper postures to follow.

Tantra yoga a sensual form of yoga, most noted for its use of a sacred sexual union.

tapas the warming of the body through stretches and postures to burn off toxins or release them through perspiration.

upward dog from a prone position, a posture in which the body is supported by the hands, thighs, and backs of the feet on the floor, while the torso is arched upward and the head pointed toward the ceiling, reminiscent of a dog stretching.

vinyasa the combination of breath and movement.

yogashala a yoga house; a special place where yoga is practiced.

yogi one who practices yoga.

yogini a female practitioner of yoga.

TOOLS

APPARATUS

ampule a small glass vial, most often used to hold pharmaceutical hypodermic solutions. Also known as an ampoule.

autoclave a pressurized appliance used to sterilize items by raising internal temperatures to above the boiling point.

barometer an instrument for measuring atmospheric pressure.

beaker a cylindrical glass vessel with a wide mouth.

bell jar a bell-shaped vessel, open at the bottom, for containing gases and other tasks.

Buchner funnel a funnel in which a filter paper is inserted and used in filtering substances by suction.

Bunsen burner an apparatus that produces a gas flame, used to heat substances.

burette a cylindrical, test tube–like vessel, with volume measurements along its side and a stopcock at its bottom, for precisely dispensing liquids.

calorimeter a device for measuring the heat released during chemical reactions.

centrifuge a device that rotates substances in order to separate their individual constituents, particularly lighter ones from denser ones.

cold finger a finger-shaped apparatus used to produce a cold surface.

condenser a large glass tube containing another tube through which hot liquids and gases pass to distill.

crucible a cup or bowl-shaped vessel, usually porcelain or metal, used to hold chemical mixtures heated to very high temperatures.

desiccator a heavy glass bowl or pot with a tight-fitting lid and sometimes a stopper for drawing out air, used with a desiccant to prevent moisture from contaminating a substance.

Erlenmeyer flask a flask with a conical base.

evaporating dish a flat, open dish used to facilitate the evaporation of liquids.

flask a vessel that comes in various shapes and sizes but is generally wide-bodied with a narrowing neck.

fleaker a flat-bottomed vessel with a narrow neck and flared rim, for holding liquids.

funnel a laboratory vessel with a very broad mouth and a narrow neck, used to ease the pouring of liquid between containers without spilling.

glove box a sealed, largely transparent box with two holes for inserting one's hands into attached gloves, through which one may perform tasks without breaking the airtight seal, for working in a vacuum or to protect oneself from hazardous chemicals.

graduated cylinder a glass or polypropylene vessel with volume measurements on the side.

hydrometer a cylindrical device used to measure the density of a liquid.

litmus test a test of pH of a substance, performed with dyed filter paper or a solution of litmus in water. Blue litmus turns red when exposed to acid and red litmus turns blue when exposed to an alkaline substance. A neutral substance turns litmus paper purple.

mortar a hardened bowl in which substances are crushed, usually with a pestle.

pestle an implement used to crush substances in a mortar.

petri dish a shallow dish used to culture cells.

pipette similar to a dropper, a cylindrical vessel that uses a vacuum component for drawing up or dispensing precise amounts of fluids.

pycnometer a stoppered flask with a capillary tube for siphoning out air bubbles, used for determining fluid densities.

retort a glass vessel with a long, bent-over neck and a bubblelike container, for heating and distilling liquids.

still an apparatus in which liquids are distilled, that is, heated, boiled, and cooled to condense the vapors. Most notably used to concentrate alcohol content.

Syracuse watch glass a shallow, flat-bottomed dish.

test tube a glass tube, open at the top, that holds liquids, especially during heating. Also known as a culture tube.

thermometer a meter or device used to measure temperature.

vacuum chamber any enclosed space, such as in a glovebox, in which air may be removed by a vacuum pump.

Woulff bottle a two or three-necked bottle used for absorbing gases.

CUTTING TOOLS AND KNIVES

glass cutter a toothbrush-shaped metal tool with a notched head and a small cutting wheel, used for scoring and cutting glass.

hawk's bill snips tin snips used for cutting tight circles.

linoleum cutter a short, wood-handled knife with a hooked blade, used for cutting vinyl and linoleum flooring.

oilstone a stone made of aluminum oxide or silicon carbide, used to sharpen blades. Also known as a whetstone, benchstone, sharpening stone, or hone stone.

precision knife a pencil-like metal knife with a small, triangular blade, used for cutting paper and other light materials. Also known as an Xacto knife.

razor knife a wooden or plastic handle with a slot for holding a razor blade.

tin snips heavy, metal shears used for cutting thin metals. Types of tin snips include aviation, duckbill, hawk's bill, and universal.

utility knife a hollow, metal handle with a retractable blade, used for cutting soft material, such as drywall or roofing products.

HAMMERS AND NAIL PULLERS

ball peen hammer a standard hammer with a rounded back surface instead of claws. Also known as a machinist's hammer.

brad driver a small, spring-loaded, screwdriverlike tool used to drive brads (tiny nails).

cat's paw a crowbarlike steel bar with a slotted tip for pulling up nails.

claw hammer the standard hammer with nail-pulling claws. Also known as a carpenter's hammer.

deadblow hammer a mallet with a head filled with shot to prevent rebounding.

engineer's hammer a very small sledgehammer.

mallet a wood-handled hammer having a cylindrical or square head made of wood, rubber, or plastic; it is used primarily to pound chisels and to manipulate metal.

maul a sledgehammer.

nail gun a gunlike apparatus that automatically drives nails without hammering.

nail set a thick, nail-like shaft with a pointed tip, pounded with a hammer to countersink nails.

rip hammer a hammer having straight claws, used in flooring work.

sledgehammer a hammer with a long or short handle and a very heavy, oblong head for driving chisels, wedges, and spikes, and for demolition.

tack hammer a hammer with a square, narrow head that has been magnetized to hold tiny tacks and nails for driving.

tack puller a screwdriverlike tool with a clawed tip for prying out tacks.

PLIERS

end nippers metal pliers with wide, beveled jaws, used for pulling out or cutting off nails.

fence pliers multiuse pliers with jaws to pull wire, a hammerlike end for driving staples into posts, and a hook or claw for pulling staples out, used to erect wire fences.

lineman's pliers square-jawed pliers for cutting and manipulating wire. Also known as electrician's pliers or wiring pliers.

locking pliers pliers that can be locked or clamped onto an object; the adjustable jaws are widened or closed by turning a screw in the wrench's handle. Also known as Vise-Grips.

long-nose pliers needle-nose pliers used to hold and manipulate wire, especially in tight spaces.

slip-joint pliers a metal pliers with jaws that are adjusted for size by means of a pivoting joint in its neck.

tongue-and-groove pliers long, straight-handled pliers with jaws that are adjusted by a pivot and a series of grooves.

wire cutters pliers with curved handles and jaws for cutting wire.

SAWS

azebiki a short, thin Japanese saw with a double-edged blade, for starting cuts in the middle of a panel or board.

backsaw a handsaw with a spined, rectangular blade with fine teeth, used for making precise cuts, especially when used with a miter box. Also known as a miter box saw.

band saw a large, stationary power saw with a blade in the configuration of a loop that continuously rotates through a table guide; used for making curving for elaborate cuts.

bayonet saw see RECIPROCATING SAW.

buck saw a large, bow-shaped handsaw with large teeth, used for cutting logs or branches.

circular saw a popular, high-speed power saw with a circular blade, used primarily for making straight cuts.

compass saw a small, fine-toothed hand saw with a curved handle and a long, thin blade (sometimes pointed), used for cutting holes and curves. Also known as a keyhole saw.

coping saw a small hand saw with a very short and narrow blade held in a U-shaped metal frame, used for making fine, precise, or decorative cuts. Also known as a fret saw or a scroll saw.

crosscut saw the most commonly used handsaw; it has a wood or plastic handle with a long, tapering toothed blade and is used for sawing wood across the grain.

dovetail saw a small backsaw with a small hand grip.

dozuki a thin, hatchetlike saw with very fine, sharp teeth, for cabinet work and for cutting joints such as dovetails.

hacksaw a hand saw with a fine-toothed blade, used for cutting metal or plastic.

hole saw a drill bit having a small cuplike saw blade, for making perfect holes.

jig saw see SABER SAW.

keyhole saw see COMPASS SAW.

miter box a boxlike cutting guide having 45° and 90° cutting slots, for making perfect angle cuts.

pocket saw a flexible wire that has been coated with fine particles of tungsten carbide; it can be carried in a pocket, is used for rough cutting, and is popular with campers.

radial arm saw a circular saw mounted permanently in a stationary table; it is used for a variety of cuts and can be angled 90°.

reciprocating saw an elongated, upright power saw used for cutting in tight spaces or for cutting through walls and nails at the same time, as in renovation work. Also known as a bayonet saw.

rip saw same as a crosscut saw but having teeth designed for cutting wood with or along the grain, such as down the length of a board.

ryoba a Japanese saw resembling a meat-cutter's knife; its blade has teeth on both sides—one side for crosscutting and one side for ripping.

saber saw a portable power saw with a short, thin blade that bobs up and down, used for making elaborate cuts. Also known as a jigsaw.

table saw a stationary table in which a circular saw protrudes from a slot; wood is fed into the saw, unlike a radial arm saw.

veneer saw a small saw for cutting veneer or for making shallow cuts.

SCREWDRIVERS

offset screwdriver an S-shaped screwdriver that is turned as a crank, used for getting at screws in tight spaces. Also known as a cranked screwdriver.

Phillips head screwdriver a common screwdriver with a cross or crisscross head, for use with Phillips head screws.

return spiral ratchet screwdriver a ratcheting screwdriver with a blade turned by pushing down on the handle.

screw-gripper screwdriver a screwdriver with a split blade for holding screws in place, for one-hand use.

spiral ratchet screwdriver a screwdriver with a ball-like handle and a ratcheting mechanism.

stubby a short screwdriver for use in tight spaces.

WEIGHTS AND MEASURES

astronomical unit (AU) the average distance of the Sun from the Earth, about 93,000,000 miles, a commonly used measurement of distance in astronomy.

bale a large bundle, such as cotton, weighing approximately 500 pounds.

board foot 144 cubic inches—12 inches by 12 inches by 1 inch.

bolt 40 yards, a measurement for fabric.

Btu British thermal unit; the amount of heat needed to raise the temperature of 1 pound of water 1° Fahrenheit.

carat 200 milligrams, for weighing precious stones.

chain 66 feet; 80 chains in a mile; a measurement used in surveying. Also known as Gunter's chain.

cubit an ancient unit of measurement, derived from the length of the forearm to the tip of the middle finger, approximately 17 to 22 inches.

decibel a unit of loudness, specifically the softest amount of change the human ear can detect.

freight ton as a measurement for mass cargo, the equivalent of 40 cubic feet of freight.

great gross 12 gross, or 1,728.

gross 12 dozen, or 144.

hand derived from the width of the hand, specifically 4 inches, as used to measure the height of horses.

hertz a unit of frequency equal to 1 cycle per second.

hogshead two liquid barrels; 14,653 cubic inches.

horsepower a unit of power equal to 745.7 watts; the power necessary to lift 33,000 pounds for a distance of 1 foot in one minute.

karat a measurement denoting the purity of gold, for example, 12 karat gold is 50 percent gold and 50 percent alloy; 24 karat gold is 100 percent pure gold.

knot a unit of speed equal to 1 nautical mile per hour, or about 1.15 statute miles per hour.

league a unit of distance equal to 3 miles.

light-year an astronomical unit of measurement, specifically the distance light travels in a year's time, about 5,880,000,000,000 miles.

link a surveyor's unit of measurement equal to 0.01 chain, or 7.92 inches.

magnum a 2-liter bottle.

nautical mile 6,076 feet, or 1,852 meters.

parsec an astronomical unit of measurement equal to 3.26 light-years, or 19.2 trillion miles.

pi the ratio of the circumference of a circle to its diameter, approximately 3.14159265.

pipe a unit for measuring liquids, the equivalent of 2 hogsheads.

ream a unit for measuring paper, the equivalent of 500 sheets.

roentgen a unit of radiation exposure produced by X-rays.

score a group of 20 units or items.

sounding a measured depth of water.

sound, speed of approximately 1,088 feet per second when measured at 32° Fahrenheit at sea level; the speed varies according to altitude and temperature.

span a measuring unit derived from an outstretched hand, the equivalent of 9 inches, or 22.86 centimeters.

square 100 square feet; used in construction.

stone in Great Britain, the equivalent of 14 pounds avoirdupois.

therm 100,000 Btus.

township a unit of measurement used in surveying, specifically the equivalent of 36 square miles.

tun 252 gallons, as used for measuring wine or other liquids.

WRENCHES

adjustable wrench a common steel wrench with adjustable jaws for loosening or tightening nuts and bolts. Also known as a Crescent wrench.

Allen wrench an L-shaped, hexagonal rod, used for turning hexagonal screws or bolts. Also known as a hex key.

box wrench a steel wrench with a toothed ring on each end, for loosening or tightening nuts and bolts.

chain wrench a wrench with a chain on one end, used when a powerful torque is needed, as for pipes or pipe fittings.

combination wrench a steel wrench with standard open jaws on one end and a box wrench (toothed ring) on the other.

Crescent wrench brand name for an adjustable wrench.

crow's foot wrench a standard, open-jawed wrench with a special hole in its neck in which a socket wrench can be inserted for driving; commonly used in hard-to-reach areas.

deep-throat socket wrench a hollow, steel tube with hexagonal openings on either end, for turning nuts and valves. Also known as a plumber's wrench.

faucet spanner a flat, metal bar having various openings on its ends and down its length, used in several plumbing applications.

monkey wrench a large, heavy adjustable wrench used in plumbing.

nut driver a screwdriverlike wrench with a hex opening at the end of its shaft for turning hex nuts and bolts in tight places.

nut splitter a P-shaped tool used to cut away nuts that are frozen or irretractable.

pipe wrench a large, heavy adjustable wrench with toothed jaws, used by plumbers for turning pipes and pipe fittings.

socket wrench a steel wrench with a head containing a ratcheting mechanism and a square plug on which variably sized sockets are attached, for turning nuts and bolts in limited space.

spanner a British word for a wrench. Also, a plumbing wrench with special notches for loosening faucet nuts.

spud wrench a metal wrench with large open jaws on either end, used to turn oversized nuts, such as those used in plumbing fixtures.

strap wrench a wrench with a fabric strap on one end, used for turning pipes without making scratches.

TRANSPORTATION

AUTOMOBILES

accelerator the gas pedal, attached to the throttle in the carburetor or fuel-injection system.

additive a fluid added to gas or oil to improve performance.

afterburner an exhaust manifold that burns off carbon monoxide and fuel in the exhaust system to produce extra power.

airbag a bag located in a steering wheel, dashboard, or side door that automatically inflates to protect passengers from injury in an accident.

air cleaner above the carburetor, the round receptacle that holds the air filter.

air filter located in the air cleaner, the round filter that removes dirt and dust from the air before it enters the carburetor.

airfoil a winglike structure that captures air and helps to press the automobile into the road to improve traction and cornering. Also known as a spoiler.

alignment the proper positioning of the front wheels for optimum handling and minimum tire wear.

all-wheel drive a drive system that, unlike four-wheel drive, engages all four wheels at all times, with a center differential that allows each wheel to rotate at different speeds, improving on-road traction. Also known as full-time four-wheel drive.

alternator a generator device that produces alternating current for powering the electrical equipment while the engine is running.

antifreeze a solution that lowers the freezing point and raises the boiling point of water in the cooling system. Also known as coolant.

antiknock agents any substance added to gasoline to raise its octane number and prevent it from knocking, pinging, or detonating.

antilock brakes brakes designed to prevent locking of the wheels during heavy braking.

antiroll bar see SWAYBAR.

automatic transmission a transmission in which gear ratios are changed automatically, thus eliminating the need for a stick shift and clutch.

axle the shaft to which the wheels are attached.

backfire an explosion of the air-fuel mixture in the intake or exhaust system.

badge engineering auto manufacturer's term for a car model sold under a variety of names under which only the trim and name badges differ.

ball joint a ball-and-socket joint providing flexibility to the steering linkage and suspension system.

battery the electrochemical component used to store and produce electricity.

bearings any ball or roller-type bearings that absorb friction between two moving parts.

beater slang for any near-wreck of a car that is nevertheless still in drivable condition.

bleed to remove air from a brake system, fuel-injection system, or cooling system to aid the smooth flow of fluid.

blown of an engine, ruined, usually from a seized piston.

blue books a variety of books that list the current prices paid for used cars.

body putty a pliable material used to fill in or smooth dents. Also known as bondo.

bore the diameter of the cylinder hole.

brake drum mounted on each wheel, a metal drum whose insides are pressed against by the brake shoes to slow or stop a car.

brake fade temporary loss of a brake's gripping power due to the generation of high temperatures from overuse.

brake lines the tubes and hoses through which brake fluid flows from the master cylinder to the brakes.

brake lining attached to each brake shoe, the heat-resistant asbestos lining that presses against the brake drum to slow or stop a car.

brake shoes the arc-shaped pieces of metal that, lined with heat-resistant asbestos, are pressed against the brake drums to slow or stop a car.

Breathalyzer a device that detects and measures the presence of alcohol in one's breath, used by police to stop drunk drivers.

bushing a protective liner or sleeve that serves as a barrier against noise and friction.

butterfly valve a small, pivoting metal plate or disk that regulates the flow of air into the carburetor.

cam in the camshaft, a lobed disk that activates the opening and closing of valves.

camber wheel alignment term for the outward or inward tilt of the top of a wheel that improves handling and lessens tire wear.

camshaft the shaft with lobed cams that operate the valves.

carburetor the device that vaporizes fuel, mixes it with air in appropriate proportions, and then delivers the mixture to the intake manifold.

carburetor barrel the part of the carburetor in which air flows and is mixed with fuel.

caster wheel alignment term referring to the wheel positioning that provides the greatest steering stability.

catalytic converter a mufflerlike afterburner in the tailpipe that burns away unburned or harmful gases.

charging system the system that generates and stores electricity, comprising the fan belt, the alternator (or generator), and the battery.

chassis the frame that supports the body and motor of a car. In some usage, a collective term for all the parts of a car except the body and fenders.

cherry automotive slang for a used car that has been kept in perfect condition.

choke a plate or valve that chokes off the amount of air entering the carburetor to help produce a richer air-fuel mixture for cold starting.

clear coat a nonpigmented, protective coating of paint that improves a base paint's durability and gloss; used on most modern cars.

clutch a coupling that engages and disengages the engine from the transmission to facilitate the changing of gears.

clutch disk at the end of the driveshaft, a spinning plate that is forced against the flywheel when the clutch is engaged.

clutch pedal in a manual transmission, the pedal to the left of the brake that disengages the clutch when pressed.

coil in the ignition system, a transformer that amplifies the voltage from the battery and relays it to the distributor and the spark plugs.

coil springs the large, shock-absorbing springs near the front and sometimes the back wheels.

combustion chamber the space between the piston and the cylinder head, where the fuel-air mixture is compressed and ignited.

compact any small car.

connecting rod the rod that connects the piston to the crankshaft. (Breaking a connecting rod is known as throwing a rod.)

convertible any car with a retractable roof.

coolant an ethyl glycol solution; antifreeze.

cooling system the system that prevents the engine from overheating by cooling and circulating a mixture of coolant and water through water jackets in the engine block. The cooling system comprises the fan, radiator, thermostat, water jackets, and water pump.

coupe a two-door, two-passenger car.

crankcase the lower portion of the engine that surrounds the crankshaft above the oil pan.

cranking engaging the starter and turning over the engine.

crankshaft the main rotating shaft in the engine, with cranks attached to the connecting rods to convert up-and-down motion into circular motion. The crankshaft transmits power from the pistons to the driveshaft.

crankshaft pulley at the front of the crankshaft, a wheel that drives the fan belts and alternator.

creeper the rolling board a mechanic moves around on while lying underneath a car.

cruise control a device that automatically maintains a car's speed at a preset level and is disengaged by the brake.

curtain side airbags airbags that are mounted above side windows in the front and back and inflate in a side impact, protecting passengers from flying glass and from head injuries.

cylinder in the engine block, the hollow pipe in which the piston is housed and moves up and down.

cylinder head above the engine block, the part of the engine that encloses the cylinders and contains the combustion chambers and, in most cases, the valves.

dead axle an axle that does not deliver power to a wheel.

detonation see KNOCKING.

diesel engine an engine without a carburetor that burns diesel oil rather than gasoline.

dieseling a condition (unrelated to diesel engines) in which the engine continues to sputter after the ignition has been turned off. Also known as afterrunning.

differential located between the rear wheels, an arrangement of gears that drives the rear axle and allows each of the wheels to turn at different speeds when cornering.

dipstick a metal stick used to check fluid levels in a fluid reservoir.

disc brake a brake system consisting of two pads that squeeze opposite sides of a rotating disc to slow a car or bring it to a stop.

disk brakes brakes of padded calipers that grab a disk on the wheel to slow or stop the car.

distributor the device that distributes a proportional amount of electricity to each spark plug, in sequence.

distributor cap an insulated cap with a central terminal for the coil wire and a series of outer terminals for the spark plug wires, with voltage delivered to each by the rotor.

double clutching releasing and depressing the clutch while in neutral to facilitate coupling of the fly-wheel and the clutch disk, used mostly in truck-driving.

double-overhead-cam engine an engine having two camshafts in each cylinder head to activate the valves.

downshift to shift to a lower gear to help slow the car and help prevent brake wear.

driveshaft the spinning shaft that transmits power from the transmission to the differential.

drive train collective term for the clutch, transmission, driveshaft, differential, and rear axle.

dual carbs having two carburetors on one engine.

DUI driving under the influence of alcohol.

DWI driving while intoxicated.

dynamometer a device used to measure engine power.

ECU electronic control unit.

electrical system the system that generates, stores, and distributes current to start the car and to power electrical equipment, comprising the alternator, battery, regulator, wiring, ignition distributor, and ignition coil.

electrolyte the battery's mixture of sulfuric acid and water.

engine block the main framework or block containing the cylinders and other engine parts. Also known as the cylinder block.

engine flywheel in manual transmissions, a spinning metal plate at the end of the crankshaft that engages and disengages with the clutch disk.

ethanol an alternative fuel, often made from corn, that can be used to either supplement or replace gasoline.

exhaust manifold a device that, through several passages, receives exhaust gases from the combustion chambers.

exhaust system the system through which exhaust flows, from the exhaust manifold to the catalytic converter to the muffler and out the tailpipe.

fan between the radiator and the engine, a spinning fan that draws cooling air through the radiator.

fan belt the rubber belt that connects the fan with the alternator.

fastback a car with an aerodynamically slanting roof.

firewall the protective, insulated wall dividing the engine compartment from the passenger interior.

Flexcar trade name of a company that, through membership, makes cars available for sharing with others in designated spots throughout major cities in the United States.

flex fuel vehicle any vehicle designed to run on either gasoline or ethanol or a mixture of the two.

float bowl in the carburetor, the reservoir that holds a small quantity of gasoline to be vaporized.

fog lamps specialized lights that cast a low, broad beam and reduce reflected light, increasing visibility in fog, mist, and haze.

four-barrel a four-barreled carburetor, with the third and fourth barrels operating only at high speed or when accelerating, as in a large V-8 engine.

four by four (4×4) a vehicle equipped with four-wheel drive.

four-stroke cycle the four—down, up, down, up—piston strokes that complete the intake, compression, power, and exhaust cycle.

four-wheel drive a drive system that sends power to all four wheels instead of two but must be turned on by the driver, unlike all-wheel drive.

four-wheel independent suspension system a system in which the wheels are supported separately with no axles to connect them, which improves handling and helps to minimize road shock.

four-wheel steering a system through which the rear wheels may be used to steer along with the front.

4WD four-wheel drive.

fuel-air mixture the "mist" of gasoline and air that is compressed and ignited in the cylinders.

fuel filter a fuel line device that removes dirt and other contaminants from gasoline flowing through it.

fuel injection a system that replaces the carburetor by using an electronic sensing device to deliver a proportional amount of fuel to the combustion chambers according to engine speed and power needs.

fuel injector nozzles in fuel-injection systems, the nozzles that inject fuel into the combustion chambers. Also known as fuel injector valves.

fuel lines the hoses through which gasoline flows from the gas tank to the carburetor.

fuel pump the pump that draws gasoline from the gas tank into the fuel lines and on to the carburetor or fuel-injection nozzles.

fuel system collective term for the fuel tank, fuel lines, fuel pump, fuel filter, and the carburetor or the fuel injection system.

full-time four-wheel drive see ALL-WHEEL DRIVE.

gasket a rubber, cork, paper, or metal plate seated between two parts to seal out fluids and help prevent premature wear.

gasohol an alternative fuel made of a mix of gasoline and ethanol.

generator a device that generates electricity from mechanical energy.

GPS global positioning system; a satellite and onboard system that provides exact location of one's automobile, allowing pinpoint computerized directions to any destination.

halogen headlights gas-filled headlights that are brighter and last longer than standard incandescent lights.

head gasket the seal seated between the cylinder head and the engine block.

heads-up display a projection of instrument data onto the lower windshield on the driver's side, helping to keep the driver's eyes on the road.

hemi short for hemispherical combustion chambers, located in the cylinder heads and noted for their ability to generate extra power.

HIDS high-intensity discharge headlights; controversial headlights that use electricity to ionize xenon gas and create a blue-white glow that is brighter than that produced by halogen headlights. Opposing-side drivers sometimes complain that oncoming HIDS are blinding.

horsepower the energy required to lift 550 pounds 1 foot in one second. The pulling power of the engine.

hot-wire a method of starting a car's ignition without a key.

hybrid an innovative automobile powered by both gasoline and electricity.

hydroplaning also known as aquaplaning, the gliding or sliding of a vehicle over a thin layer of water as the tires lose traction or contact with the road.

idiot lights slang for the dashboard signals that light up to warn of impending oil depletion, overheating, or other malfunctions.

idle engine speed when in neutral or when the car is not moving.

idle speed screw at the outside bottom of a carburetor, a screw that can be turned to adjust idle speed.

ignition interlock a device that pairs a Breathalyzer with an ignition lock to prevent drunk drivers from starting a car.

ignition system collective term for the coil, battery, distributor, and spark plugs.

independent suspension a suspension system that allows two wheels connected by an axle to move up and down separately in response to road shock.

intake manifold a set of pipes through which the fuel-air mix flows from the carburetor to the cylinders.

internal combustion engine an engine in which fuel is burned internally rather than in an outside source, as in a steam engine.

jack any device used to jack a car up off the ground to facilitate mechanical repair. Types of jacks include hydraulic, scissors, and tripod.

knocking a metal knocking sound (resembling marbles rattling in a can) in the engine caused by a loose bearing, faulty timing, or low-octane gas. Also known as pinging or predetonation.

leaf springs rear wheel springs comprising metal plates of graduated lengths one atop the other, which flex to absorb road shock.

lowrider a car modified to ride extremely close to the ground.

lube grease pastelike oil used to lubricate a number of moving parts, especially in the steering linkage and suspension system.

lubrication system the system that lubricates moving parts in the engine, comprising the oil, oil pan, oil pump, oil filter, and oil gauge.

lug nuts the large nuts that lock the wheel onto a car.

MacPherson strut a combination spring and shock absorber, for superior shock dampening.

manual transmission a transmission requiring a stick shift and clutch to change gears.

master brake cylinder the cylinder that holds brake fluid and compresses it through the brake lines to the brakes when the brake pedal is engaged.

misfiring a malfunction in which the fuel-air mixture in one or more cylinders fails to combust.

muffler a device in the exhaust system that muffles the noise of escaping exhaust.

octane rating the rating that reflects a gasoline's antiknock properties; the highest octanes produce the least amount of engine knock or ping.

odometer the dashboard mileage meter.

oil filter a filter that removes dirt and other contaminants from oil as it circulates through the lubrication system.

oil pan the pan that stores oil, located below the crankcase.

oil pump a crankcase pump that draws oil from the oil pan through the lubrication system.

Onstar an automotive service with an on-call staff, an onboard global positioning system receiver, an embedded mobile phone, and an engine interface. The service provides directions to lost drivers, unlocks doors by remote control, monitors engine performance, notifies drivers of mechanical problems, contacts emergency personnel when an airbag is deployed, and tracks stolen vehicles. The remote staff may be contacted with the push of a button.

overdrive a special gear, such as fifth gear in a five-speed transmission, that allows the drive wheels to turn faster than the engine, to facilitate coasting and fuel saving at high speed.

overhead cam a camshaft situated above the cylinder head instead of below the cylinders, to remove the need for valve-activating push rods.

oversteer a problem of rear-wheel drive cars in which inadequate road adhesion by the tires causes a partial or full spinout during a turn.

passing gear in an automatic transmission, a low gear that is automatically engaged to provide a short burst of speed when the accelerator is sharply depressed.

pinging see KNOCKING.

piston the cylindrical plug that moves up and down inside the cylinder to compress the fuel-air mixture and to force the connecting rods to rotate the crankshaft.

piston rings the metal rings installed in grooves in the pistons to prevent fuel-air leaks into the crankcase.

points the current-regulating, metal terminals in the distributor.

power brakes a brake system that employs hydraulic or vacuum pressure to assist in braking.

power steering a steering system that employs hydraulics to facilitate steering.

power train the drive train.

pressure cap the radiator cap.

push rods the rods that extend between the camshaft lifters and the rocker arms and are pushed up by the cam lobes.

rack-and-pinion steering a steering system in which a pinion on the end of the steering shaft meshes with a notched bar or rack, noted in sports cars for its quick response.

radiator at the front of the engine, the squarish receptacle that cools fluid passing through it by means of numerous air ducts.

rear obstacle warning system a system of sensors on a rear bumper that detects obstacles while moving in reverse and flashes or sounds an alarm to the driver.

remote car starter a transmitter, usually placed on a keychain, which can start a car or unlock doors from up to 500 feet away, most often used to prewarm the interior of a car on a cold day or precool it with the air conditioner on a hot day.

resonator a small, secondary muffler that further reduces exhaust noise on some car models.

rings piston rings.

roadster an open, two-seater car with a retractable top.

rocker arms arms that rock or pivot on shafts as the camshaft rotates, opening and closing the valves.

rotor located on top of the distributor shaft, the device that conducts current in sequence to the spark plug terminals.

rpm revolutions per minute.

running rich a condition in which too much gas and too little air is consumed by the engine, resulting in sooty or black exhaust.

SAE abbreviation used with oil gradings, meaning Society of Automotive Engineers.

sedan a two- or four-door car, seating four to seven passengers.

shift-on-the-fly referring to the ability of a vehicle to shift into four-wheel drive without having to stop and lock the front hubs first.

shimmy a distinct vibration or side-to-side shaking of the front wheels, caused by a bent rim, a shifted tire belt, a loose suspension part, or a loose steering linkage part.

shock absorber a device placed at each wheel to help limit bounce and compression when driving over bumps or when stopping quickly.

slant engine an engine in which the cylinder block is slanted from the vertical.

sludge an engine-fouling conglomeration of oxidized oil, gas, and water that reduces lubricating efficiency.

spark plug a plug that screws into the cylinder head and delivers a spark to the combustion chamber to ignite the fuel-air mixture.

spoiler see AIRFOIL.

springs any springlike devices, such as coil springs, leaf springs, or torsion bars, that absorb road shock.

stabilizer bar a shaft between the lower suspension arms that reduces swaying or lurching of the car on sharp turns or curves.

starter the small electric motor that turns the crankshaft to start the engine.

steering linkage the interconnections between the front wheels and the steering wheel.

stroke the distance of one stroke of a piston from the top to the bottom of a cylinder, or vice versa.

strut a shock absorber and mounting plate.

subcompact a very small, two-door, two-passenger car.

supercharger a device that pressurizes the air-fuel mixture to increase engine power.

suspension system collective term for the springs, shock absorbers, steering linkage, stabilizers, and torsion bars.

swaybar part of the suspension system, a stabilizing bar or rod mounted between wheels to reduce body lean when turning. Also known as an antiroll bar.

synchromesh a system that matches engine and gear speed to prevent grinding of the gears when shifting.

tachometer the rpm or engine speed gauge on the dashboard.

tailpipe the last portion of the exhaust system.

telematics generic term for remote services, such as Onstar, that work via GPS systems, mobile phone, and remote sensors.

toe in to align the front wheel so that they point inward slightly, for better handling at high speeds.

torque the turning or rotational force produced by an engine at the crankshaft.

torsion bar a bar that produces spring by twisting, especially over an uneven road.

transaxle on front-wheel drive or rear-engine cars, a unit that combines the functions of the transmission, differential, and clutch at the drive axle to eliminate the need for a driveshaft.

transmission the gear box that, through various gear ratios, transmits power from the engine to the drive axle.

transverse engine an engine mounted between the drive wheels, as in frontwheel drive cars.

tune-up a maintenance procedure in which parts of the ignition system are adjusted or replaced. A typical tune-up may include an adjustment of the idle speed, the fuel-air mixture and the timing, the gapping and replacement of spark plugs and points, and the replacement of the rotor and condenser.

turbocharger a supercharger powered by hot exhaust gases.

undercoating a rustproofing material applied underneath a car.

understeer a specific type of tire slippage common to front-wheel drive vehicles. In slick conditions, the vehicle continues on a straight path even after turning the steering wheel.

valves the engine devices that open and close to allow or stop the flow of fuel and air or exhaust gases.

V-8 an eight-cylinder engine, with the cylinders mounted in two rows forming an angle or V.

venturi in the carburetor, the narrowed passageway that creates a vacuum to draw fuel from the float bowl.

water jackets the engine channels through which coolant flows to cool the engine.

water pump the device that pumps coolant and water through the cooling system.

wheelbase the distance down the center from front axle to rear axle.

Zev zero emission vehicle, an electric or alternate-powered car producing no polluting exhaust.

Zipcar trade name of a company that, through membership, makes cars available for sharing at designated locations throughout the United States.

AVIATION

aerodynamics the branch of physics concerning the laws of motion of air under the influence of gravity or other forces.

aileron any one of the hinged movable surfaces or flaps on the trailing edge of a wing, used for executing banks or rolls.

airfoil any surface, such as a wing or an aileron, providing lift or aerodynamic control.

air speed indicator the instrument displaying air speed.

altimeter an instrument consisting of an aneroid barometer, used to determine altitude.

altitude the distance or height above land or water.

amphibian a plane equipped to take off or land on either water or land.

angle of attack the set of an airfoil as it meets the air, determining the amount of lift or other aerodynamic control.

approach approaching an airport for landing.

artificial horizon a gyrostabilized instrument displaying the airplane's pitching and rolling.

autopilot a gyroscopically controlled device that automatically keeps an aircraft steady or is programmed for various maneuvers, such as climbing to a desired altitude.

aviator a pilot.

aviatrix a female pilot.

backwash the powerful air current driven behind an aircraft by its propellers; also known as prop wash or the slipstream.

bank to turn right or left by rolling or tilting an airplane laterally in flight.

barnstorming an exhibition of stunt flying.

bearing the horizontal direction of an aircraft in flight.

belly landing an emergency landing on the bottom of the fuselage, with the landing gear retracted.

biplane a plane with two sets of wings.

black box the flight data recorder, actually colored orange and situated in the tail, impervious to crashes due to its reinforced construction.

bogie a four-, six-, or eight-wheeled truck on a main landing leg.

bogy slang for an unidentified flying object.

cabane the framework and struts that support the wings at the fuselage.

cabin the cockpit.

camber the curve of a wing from its leading edge to its trailing edge.

CAT abbreviation for clear air turbulence.

ceiling the maximum altitude to which an aircraft can climb under specific weather conditions.

chandelle a high-performance 180° climbing turn, usually only performed at air shows or in combat.

clean slang term for an in-flight plane, having all landing gears, flaps, or other extendable devices retracted.

clearance permission from air traffic control to proceed.

cockpit the cabin or compartment accommodating the pilot, the copilot, the controls, and the instruments.

cockpit voice recorder a cabin recorder used to record dialogue of the flight crew and radio transmissions, used for safety and crash review purposes.

cowling the removable covering protecting the top and sides of an airplane motor.

critical speed the lowest possible speed of an aircraft in which control can be maintained.

crosswind a wind striking a plane broadside, creating a hazard for landing.

dead reckoning plotting a position by using calculations combining speed, course, time, and wind.

deadstick an emergency descent and landing with the engines shut down.

delta wing a triangular-shaped wing.

dihedral angle the angle attained when the main wings are inclined up from the center of the fuselage so that the tips are higher than the remaining portion of the wings, for lateral stability.

dive a steep descent.

drag the resistance the surrounding air exerts on a moving airplane.

drone an unmanned, radio-controlled airplane, often used for military reconnaissance missions.

Dutch roll a sudden roll and yaw caused by a wind gust.

elevator a hinged horizontal surface on the tail assembly, controlling the up-and-down direction of an airplane.

ELT emergency locator transmitter. An aircraft radio transmitter automatically activated on crash impact with the ground or water, used to aid in location by rescuers.

ETA estimated time of arrival.

FAA Federal Aviation Administration, the government agency that oversees aviation in the United States.

fin the fixed vertical stabilizer at the tail helping to control roll and yaw.

flameout loss of combustion in a gas-turbine engine, resulting in a complete loss of power.

flap any one of the movable surfaces on a wing used for producing either lift or drag.

flight data recorder see BLACK BOX.

flight path an air course or route.

fly-by-wire of pilot controls, activated by electronics or fiber optics rather than mechanical connections.

fuselage the long body portion to which the wings, tail, and landing gear are attached.

glide a slow descent without engine power.

glidepath the descending path a plane follows when approaching for landing.

glider a motorless airplane towed aloft and used for recreational soaring.

global positioning system (GPS) a satellite-based navigational system, used by commercial carriers and the military.

GPWS ground proximity warning system. An onboard radar system that sounds an alarm when an aircraft is too close to the ground.

hangar an aircraft shelter and workshop.

holding pattern a circling pattern made by aircraft awaiting landing clearance at an airport.

hydraulics the fluid-based controls used to maneuver flaps, brakes, landing gear, and other apparatus.

hypersonic greater than five times the speed of sound.

hypoxia a medical condition caused by lack of oxygen at or above 12,500 feet, marked by a sense of euphoria, increasing disorientation, and, eventually, unconsciousness.

Icarus in Greek mythology, the son of Daedalus, who flew so high on artificial wings that the sun melted the wax fastenings and he fell into the sea and drowned.

icing the formation of ice on any part of an aircraft, but especially the airfoils.

ILS instrument landing system; a landing system comprising marker beacons, high-intensity runway lights, and two radio beams that provide vertical and horizontal guidance to pilots.

inertial navigation system a self-contained airborne system that continuously computes and displays navigational data, replacing the need for a navigator on many flights.

jet engine an engine that mixes oxygen and fuel, converting them into a powerful jet of heated gas, which is expelled under high pressure.

jet stream a river of high-speed winds, usually circulating from west to east at high altitudes, used to aid jet flights when traveling in the same direction.

knot 1 nautical mile per hour, the standard measurement of speed in aviation, equal to 1.1515 miles per hour.

lazy eights alternating 180° climbing and descending S-turns, usually executed for show.

lift the aerodynamic forces that lift an aircraft.

longeron a long spar running from the bow of the fuselage to the stern.

loran long range navigation; a system in which the position of an aircraft is plotted by comparing the time intervals between radio signals from a network of ground stations.

Mach the ratio between the speed of an aircraft and the speed of sound. For example, an aircraft flying at Mach 2 would be traveling at two times the speed of sound.

marshaller a taxiway crew member who uses bats or batons to direct aircraft ground traffic.

marshalling ground crew signaling with batons to direct aircraft ground traffic.

Mayday the international distress call.

microwave landing system a radio landing aid guiding aircraft to a runway from several directions by a microwave beam.

payload cargo, baggage, and passengers.

pitching the nose of an airplane forced up or down by wind.

port light the red light situated on the left side of aircraft, an identification and anticollision aid. See STARBOARD LIGHT.

pressurize in an aircraft compartment, to create an air pressure higher than the low atmospheric pressure found at high altitudes.

prop wash the powerful air current driven behind an aircraft by its propellers; also known as the slipstream.

red-eye an overnight or late-night flight.

rib one of the fore-and-aft supporting members in a wing.

roll to roll left or right; also an acrobatic maneuver in which the craft is rotated completely around while maintaining course.

roll-out the distance an aircraft requires to come to a safe stop after touchdown.

rudder the hinged surface on the tail that is used to turn the airplane left or right.

slipstream the airstream behind the propeller.

sonic boom the explosion heard when an aircraft breaks the speed of sound.

sortie an aircraft sent out on a single military mission.

spin an out-of-control, rotating descent, evolving from a stall.

spinner the spinning, cone-shaped covering over the propeller hub.

spiral a tight, descending turn or series of turns.

spoiler one of the special flaps raised on the wings to "spoil" lift by disrupting airflow, used to slow an aircraft or greatly increase the rate of descent.

stabilizer a fixed horizontal surface on the tail to which the elevator is attached, providing longitudinal stability.

stack when landings are delayed, two or more aircraft circling one above the other at 1,000-foot intervals awaiting approach clearance.

stall the loss of lift when airspeed is too slow, resulting in the nose pitching down and the plane fluttering like a falling leaf.

standing waves the currents of air created by a strong wind blowing over a mountain, hazardous to aircraft.

starboard light the green light situated on the right side of aircraft, an identification and anticollision aid.

strobes the bright, white flashing lights situated on the wingtips as an anticollision aid.

supersonic faster than the speed of sound.

TACAN tactical air navigation system; an electronic navigational aid used principally by the military.

taxi to maneuver an airplane on the ground.

TCAS traffic alert and collision avoidance system; an onboard, radar-based collision alerting system.

thermal a rising column of warm air, adding lift to light aircraft.

thrust the force of the engines that propel the craft forward.

three-point landing a perfect landing.

torque the left-turning twisting motion of an aircraft caused by the right-turning propeller, compensated by special rigging automatically, but corrected only manually in some aircraft above cruise speed.

turboprop a turbojet engine connected with a propeller.

turbulence disturbed air.

VTOL vertical takeoff and landing aircraft; any aircraft, such as a helicopter, with the capability of lifting straight up into the air.

wind shear a rapid change of wind direction or speed affecting airflow over the wings, extremely hazardous to aircraft low to the ground.

AIRCRAFT

BALLOONS

aeronaut balloon pilot or passenger.

aerostation the art of operating a lighter-than-air craft.

altimeter device that measures the altitude of an aircraft by sensing differences in air pressure.

anemometer device that measures wind speed.

apex the top of a balloon.

apex rope rope attached to the top of the balloon used during inflation to control the balloons movement; also known as a crown line.

appendix sleeve at the bottom of a balloon where the balloon is filled and through which expanding gas escapes.

attitude the balloon's position relative to the horizon.

ballast disposable weight, usually in the form of sandbags, used to maintain altitude or to slow a descent.

balloonmeister authority responsible for the safe operation of ground-based balloon activities.

basket the basket that carries the aeronauts, controls, and fuel; also known as a gondola.

blast-off high-speed liftoff used in windy conditions.

blast valve high-pressure fuel valve.

blimp an airship.

burner unit that burns propane gas to heat the envelope of the balloon.

ceiling distance between the ground and cloud cover.

chase crew crew members who assist in the launch and chase the balloon in flight to aid in its landing.

deflation port panel of the upper envelope that detaches to allow hot air to escape to aid in deflation.

dirigible a powered balloon with directional controls.

envelope interior balloon fabric that contains the hot air.

equator area of the balloon's greatest girth.

gondola see BASKET.

gore length of balloon fabric tapering at the end to form sections when sewn to other gores.

helium nonflammable lighter-than-air gas.

hydrogen flammable lighter-than-air gas.

mouth the opening at the base of a balloon.

pyrometer instrument that displays the temperature of the hot air near the top of the balloon.

redline temperature the hottest temperature a balloon fabric can withstand without damage.

rip line a line that is pulled to open the deflation port.

sink rate of descent.

sparker device for igniting the burner's pilot light.

telltale heat-sensitive material near the top of a balloon providing a warning of dangerously high temperatures.

tether anchor line.

thermal rising column of warm air.

variometer device that measures vertical airspeed or the rate of climb or descent.

Blimps

ballast bags 50-pound bags hung from a ring encircling the car to help maintain proper weight when loads are light.

ballonets fitted within the large gas bag, two smaller bags that are filled with air to add weight or emptied of air to subtract weight.

bite the volume of air propeller moves, according to the propeller's pitch and speed.

blimp a nonrigid dirigible.

car attached to the underside of the gas bag, the gondola that carries the pilot, passengers, controls, fuel tanks, and other equipment.

Dacron the rubberized fabric a blimp's gas bag is made from.

dirigible any steerable, lighter-than-air craft.

gas bag the large, helium-filled bag that provides lift.

gondola the car.

hangar a large building where a blimp is inspected and maintained.

helium the lighter-than-air gas that fills the gas bag.

mast a large post to which the nose of a blimp is attached when parked or moored on the ground. The mooring mast.

nose lines lines leading from the nose, used by ground crew to stabilize the blimp during takeoffs and landings.

riggers ground crew work on a blimp's fabric and ropes.

rigid a dirigible having a fabric cover stretched over a rigid framework that is filled with individual gas cells.

trim to balance the blimp in flight by adjusting the amount of air in the ballonets.

wind sock the conelike sock erected on a landing field to indicate wind direction.

zeppelin a large, cigar-shaped dirigible having a rigid body.

Helicopters

autorotation an unpowered descent in which the rotor blades are rotated by air currents alone.

clutch the control used to engage and disengage the rotors from the engine to allow autorotation.

coaxial rotor system a dual-rotor system mounted one atop the other and rotating in opposing directions.

collective pitch lever the pilot's left-hand control, used to change the pitch of the main rotor blades.

compound helicopter a cross between an airplane and a helicopter, having rotary and fixed-wing components.

cyclic pitch stick the pilot control that changes the pitch of the blades individually, affecting the speed and direction of flight.

flight deck the cockpit.

heliport a helicopter landing pad or landing facility.

lateral rotors dual rotors aligned to the left and right of the body.

rotor brake the control that engages and disengages the main rotor system.

skid the landing feet or rails, as distinguished from wheels.

stall loss of lift.

tail rotor a rotor mounted on the tail to counteract the torque produced by the main rotor.

tandem rotor system a dual-rotor system aligned fore and aft.

Airports

approach lights the platformed lights—some raised as high as 200 feet—leading to a runway. See SEQUENCE FLASHERS.

apron the main loading area.

barrette closely spaced approach lights that from the sky appear as a solid bar of light.

blast fences fixed barriers or walls protecting passengers and equipment from jet-engine wake.

cab the glassed-in enclosure atop the control tower.

centerline approach system the runway approach system used as the national standard, characterized by flashing blue lights paired with white centerline bars leading to white crossbars at 1,000 feet, red crossbars at 200 feet, and a green bar at the threshold of the runway.

centerline lights 200-watt, white lights embedded into the runway.

clearway the clear area past the end of the airport, over which aircraft make their ascent.

control tower the airport nerve center manned by controllers who oversee taxiing, takeoffs, and landings, recognized by its tower and glass-enclosed cab.

flight service center the facility that provides pilots with information on weather, local conditions, winds, routes, and other conditions.

hangar an aircraft storage and maintenance building.

holding bay a large waiting area just off the runway where, in peak hours, pilots must wait in line for takeoff.

holding point a marked threshold along the side of a runway where the second aircraft in line stops and waits for the aircraft in front of it to take off.

marshallers airport personnel who direct taxiing aircraft into or out of parking positions by signals made with batons or paddles.

microwave landing system a system that guides aircraft to the runway by a microwave beam that scans a large area of sky.

rollout lanes high-speed turn-off lanes serving the runway.

safeway pneutronic parking system a system of pressure pads embedded in the aircraft parking and docking area that sense the position of aircraft and direct the pilot left or right.

sequence flashers white strobe lights that blink in sequence to help guide pilots toward the centerline of the runway. One component of the approach lights.

snow lights raised lights marking the edges of the runway when others are buried beneath snow.

taxiway the strip an aircraft drives on leading on or off the runway.

touchdown zone lights the white lights marking the touchdown zone of the runway.

visual approach slope indicators adjacent either side of the touchdown zone, a system of lamps projecting aligned, red and white beams indicating a pilot's angle of approach.

wind sock a bright, conical sock indicating wind speed and direction.

CARRIAGES AND COACHES OF THE 19TH CENTURY

barouche a four-wheeled vehicle having facing seats to accommodate six people, popular with families. The barouche's collapsible top quickly converted it into an open vehicle, which made it the popular choice as a parade carriage for presidents and other dignitaries.

brougham an English-designed, boxlike carriage enclosing two to four passengers, pulled by one horse.

buggy see TOP BUGGY.

cabriolet a one-horse, two-wheeled carriage having two seats and a collapsible top.

chaise a one-horse, two-wheeled open carriage with folding hood. Also called a shay.

coachman the driver of a coach or carriage.

Concord the most popular stagecoach of the period, built in Concord, New Hampshire. It could carry up to nine people inside and as many as a dozen outside, hanging off and around the roof.

conestoga a dory-shaped wagon having a hooped canvas roof, used for long-distance traveling and pulled by a team of six horses.

covered wagon a smaller, lighter version of a conestoga.

curricle an English, two-wheeled open carriage, pulled by two horses.

dormeuse a French traveling carriage.

draft horse a large, strong horse capable of pulling a carriage. Also called a dray.

dray horse a draft horse.

drummer's wagon a merchandise wagon used by salesmen (drummers) serving storekeepers. They were noted for their painted scenes and gilt scrolls decorating the sides.

freight wagon a huge wagon having 6-foot wheels with 1-inch-thick iron tires, noted for making permanent ruts in roads all over the country.

gee driver's traditional command to horses to turn right. See HAW.

gig a one-horse, two-wheeled, American-designed open carriage.

governess cart an open cart for pulling children, for fun.

grocer's wagon a large, open-top wagon.

gurney a rear-entry cab that seated four passengers, popularly used in New York.

hack a one-horse cab. Also, a driving horse.

hansom a one-horse cab or cabriolet, noted for having its driver's seat located high in the back of the vehicle instead of at the front.

haw a driver's traditional command to horses to turn left. See GEE.

landau A German-designed, four-wheeled, closed carriage having two passenger seats and a roof made in two sections, the rear of which could be folded down.

omnibus a horse-pulled bus.

phaeton a two-horse carriage having a collapsible top, the vehicle of choice among physicians and women.

prairie schooner same as a conestoga but having a flat, boxy body rather than a boatlike one.

road coach an English-designed traveling carriage similar to a stage coach.

rockaway a multipassenger carriage with a roof extending over the driver to protect him from the elements. The rockaway was noted for its front window through which the driver and passengers could converse.

shay see CHAISE.

Studebaker an open farm wagon pulled by two horses.

surrey a family vehicle having two long seats facing forward and, frequently, a fringed canopy top.

top buggy a one-horse buggy accommodating one or two people, used for errands and short excursions.

Victoria an elegant wagon resembling a giant slipper on wheels. It had plush upholstery and a collapsible top and was used by the upper class.

SAILING

(*Also see* SHIPS AND BOATS)

abeam at right angles to the vessel.

ADF automatic direction finder, a radio direction finder.

aft near or at the stern.

aground hung up on the bottom or on shore.

ahull when a vessel is hove-to with all of its sails lowered.

alee on the side of the boat opposite to the wind direction.

all standing all sails flying.

aloft overhead.

anchorage a safe place to lay anchor, preferably protected from wind and current.

anchors aweigh a directive to raise the anchor.

anchor light a white light illuminated on the forestay at night.

anemometer a device for measuring wind speed.

antifoulant a chemical agent, such as copper, used in boat paint to retard the growth of algae and barnacles on the bottom of the boat.

aport to the port or left side of the vessel.

apparent wind the wind strength and direction as perceived on a moving vessel; not the actual wind.

ashore on shore.

aspect ratio the ratio of sail height to sail length, for example, a tall, narrow sail is said to have a high aspect ratio.

astern toward or at the stern.

athwartship abeam.

autopilot a device used in tandem with a compass on a boat's steering apparatus to automatically maintain a constant course.

auxiliary an engine used on a sailboat when the wind fails.

back a sail to fill a sail with wind from an opposing direction in order to slow the vessel.

backing wind a wind direction that is changing in a counterclockwise fashion.

backstay a wire rigged to control the amount of bend in a mast.

ballast any heavy objects or substance, such as sand, stones, water, laid in the bottom of a vessel to help stabilize it, especially in heavy seas.

barber hauler an adjustment for a jib sheet to change the sheeting angle.

bare poles said of a vessel sailing with all sails furled, when the wind is powerful enough to move the boat without sails.

barnacles marine animals that attach themselves to a boat's bottom.

barometer an instrument that measures atmospheric pressure.

batten a strip of wood, plastic, or metal fitted into a sail's pockets to help maintain the sail's correct shape.

beach to sail a vessel onto the shore.

beam the width of a vessel at its widest point.

bear away to alter course away from the wind. Also known as to bear off or fall off.

bearing position or direction in relation to something else.

beat to sail to windward close-hauled while tacking; to make a series of tacks on an upwind course.

Beaufort wind scale a wind and sea classification scale, from 0 (flat calm) to 12 (hurricane winds with waves reaching 14 meters).

becalmed unable to move due to wind failure.

belay to wrap or secure a line around a cleat or belaying pin.

belaying pin a wood or metal pin around which line is secured.

bend a sail to attach a sail to the boom and mast.

berth a docking space. Also, a sleeping compartment.

bilge the area beneath the cabin floor, where water (bilge water) tends to collect.

binnacle an encased compass mounted on a pedestal.

bitt a short post on a deck or dock, used for belaying mooring lines.

bitter end the last link of an anchor chain as it is let out. Also, the end of any line.

blanket the loss of wind when one boat positions itself directly upwind of a downwind boat.

block a pulley.

blooper an L-shaped sail.

board to get on or walk on a boat.

boat hook a pole used to aid in mooring or for securing another boat.

boom the spar on which the bottom or food of a sail is secured.

boom vang a tackle attached to the boom to keep it from rising.

bosun's chair a seat in which a crew member is hoisted to conduct work aloft.

bow the front of a vessel.

bowline a mooring line at the bow. Also known as a painter.

bowsprit a spar projecting beyond the bow, for attaching a headsail.

break ground to break an anchor free from the sea bottom.

breakwater a barrier to protect a harbor from heavy seas.

brightwork collective term for all metal fittings and varnished woodwork.

broach to lose control of the boat, which swings about sideways.

bulkhead a partition.

bulwarks the raised sides of a vessel, above the upper deck.

buoy a flotation device, sometimes having bells and lights, for marking banks, channels, and hazards.

burgee a yacht club pennant.

cabin living space below deck.

camber the curvature of a sail.

cast off to release mooring lines and set sail.

catamaran a twin-hulled sailboat.

centerboard the large center fin or plate, used in place of a keel; it helps prevent rolling. See DAGGERBOARD, KEEL.

chock a deck fitting through which lines are passed.

cleat a one- or two-prolonged fixture around which line is belayed.

clew the lower aft corner of a fore-and-aft sail.

clinometer an instrument that measures a vessel's sideway inclination or heel.

close-hauled as close to the oncoming wind direction as possible without luffing.

clove hitch a temporary mooring knot that comes united with sideways tension.

cockpit where the steering wheel or the tiller is located.

come about to alter a boat's course from one tack to another.

companionway a stairway or ladder descending to the cabin.

cordage commonly used term for any thick line or rope.

course heading; direction.

crabbing moving sideways through the water; making leeway.

cradle the framed support upon which a vessel rests on shore.

cringle a ring through which rope is threaded in a sail. Also known as a grommet.

daggerboard a small, daggerlike centerboard, commonly found on small boats.

dead ahead directly ahead.

dead reckoning navigating by deduction through knowledge of current position, speed, and heading.

deep-six to throw something overboard.

doldrums equatorial region of the ocean, notorious for its dead calms, the bane of sailors.

downhaul the tackle used to increase tension on the luff of a sail.

draft the portion of a vessel that is submerged. Also known as the draw.

drifter a headsail used in faint winds.

drogue a conelike sea anchor.

earing a short line used to secure a reefed sail to the boom.

ensign a national flag.

fall off see BEAR OFF.

fender any kind of cushioning hung over the hull of a boat to protect it from contact with a dock or another boat.

fend off to push off with the feet, hands, or a boat hook to avoid contact with another boat or a dock.

fetch to sail close-hauled without the need to tack.

fittings hardware and fixtures on a vessel.

fix an exact position, as deduced by navigational skills.

flemish to coil a line flat on a deck in order to dry it uniformly.

following sea current that is traveling in the same direction as the vessel.

foot the bottom edge of a sail.

fore near or at the bow.

fore and aft from the bow to the stern.

foredeck the deck portion forward of the mast.

foresail a triangular sail attached forward of the mast and pronounced "for's'l."

forestay rigging extending from the top of the mast to the bow to keep the mast from moving backwards.

foul to entangle.

founder the sinking of a boat as it fills with water.

freeboard the portion of the hull that is not under water.

furl to roll up a sail on its boom or spar.

galley a kitchen.

gangplank a bridge walk set as a ramp between a vessel and the dock, to facilitate boarding.

Genoa a large headsail or jib.

ghosting sailing in a calm when the wind is apparently absent.

gimbals fixtures that allow objects, such as a lamp, a barometer, or a compass, to swivel and remain level in rough seas.

gunkholing sailing in shallow waters.

gunwale the uppermost edge of the hull's sides, pronounced gunnel.

guy a line or wire.

halyard any line used to hoist a sail.

hand one of the crew.

hard alee to come about.

harden up to sail closer to the wind.

hatch a doorway in a deck.

hawser a heavy line used for mooring or towing.

head the top edge of a sail. Also, a toilet.

heading the direction the boat is sailing in.

headsail any sail set forward of the mast, such as a drifter, jib, or Genoa.

head sea current that is running in the opposite direction of the vessel.

heave crew's pulling together.

heave to stop forward motion by backing the headsail.

heaving line the mooring line with weighted end, tossed to someone on a dock.

heel the lean or angle of a vessel when sailing.

helm the steering wheel or the tiller.

helmsman the person who steers.

hike to lean far out over the side of a boat to help counter extreme heeling.

hiking straps footstraps used to help secure crew members when hiking.

hoist to raise a sail.

hold a storage area below deck.

hove down extreme heeling.

in irons stopped while turning against the wind.

jib a triangular headsail.

jib boom extending beyond the bowsprit, a spar to take an extra headsail.

jibe to tack while sailing downwind.

jury-rig to construct a makeshift part to replace a damaged part, a required skill of sailors.

kedge a means of freeing a boat that has run aground on a sandbar, specifically by throwing an anchor in front of the boat and then pulling the boat free. Also, the small anchor used for this purpose.

keel the fixed fore-and-aft member or backbone of a vessel's bottom.

kite a spinnaker.

labor to roll and pitch in heavy seas.

landfall the first sighting of land.

lanyard any short piece of line used to secure a loose object, such as a pail or a tool, or for fastening riggings.

lash to secure a loose object with line.

launch a small boat used to carry people from land to a moored vessel, or vice versa.

lay up to store a boat during winter.

lazarette a small storage compartment in the stern.

leading edge the front portion of a sail.

lee to leeward; on the side of the boat protected from the wind.

leech the unattached edge of a triangular sail.

leeward the direction the wind is blowing, pronounced loo'ard.

leeway sideways motion of a boat, pushed by the wind or current.

line rope.

list leaning of a vessel caused not by wind or current but by unbalanced weight on board.

log an instrument fixed to a vessel's keel for measuring speed. Also, a journal of daily courses, distances sailed, weather conditions, and similar entries.

luff the leading edge of a sail.

luff up to sail into the wind, causing the leech of the sail to flap.

mainsail the main or largest sail on a boat, pronounced "mains'l."

make fast to secure a line.

Marconi-rigged a triangular sail rigged fore and aft. Also known as Bermuda-rigged.

mast the large, vertical spar to which sails are attached.

masthead the top of the mast.

masthead fly at the masthead, a weathervane or wind indicator.

midships in or near the middle of the ship. Also known as amidships.

mizzenmast the aftmost mast on a yawl or a ketch.

moor to tie up a boat.

mooring an anchorage, often marked with a buoy and pennant.

outhaul the line used to increase tension on the foot of the mainsail.

painter see BOWLINE.

passage a voyage from one place to another.

pay off to turn the bow away from the wind.

pay out to let out line.

piloting navigating.

pinch to sail too close to the wind.

pitch the rockinghorse-like, fore-and-aft motion of a vessel moving over waves.

pitchpole the complete somersaulting of a vessel in very heavy seas.

planing skimming across the water.

plot to draw out a course and bearings.

port the left side of a vessel when one is looking forward; opposite of starboard.

porthole a window.

port tack a tack in which the wind is blowing over a vessel's port side.

pram a small dinghy, used as a tender.

pulpit the safety rail at the bow and the stern.

quarters the living and sleeping space below deck.

raise a light to spot a light on shore.

rake the angle of a ship's mast in relation to the deck.

ratlines rope steps made of small lines tied across the shrouds; the crew can climb aloft on them.

reach to sail with the wind abeam.

ready about a directive to stand by to ready for coming about.

reef to reduce the mainsail and secure its unused part, usually in preparation for storm winds.

reeve to pass a line through a hole.

regatta sailing races.

ride to lie at anchor; to ride out a storm while at anchor.

rigging collective term for the lines and wires used to uphold the mast and manipulate the sails.

roll the side-to-side motion of a vessel in heavy seas.

rudder the movable plate at the bottom or rear of a hull, used to steer the boat.

run to sail with the wind directly behind the vessel; sailing with the wind.

running lights the lights that must be illuminated on a vessel at night.

scud to run before the wind in a gale.

sea anchor a floating anchor that helps stabilize a boat during a storm.

scuppers drains or openings along the gunwales to allow the flow of rough seas over the deck.

set to hoist sails.

sheets lines attached to the sails for trimming.

shrouds wires that stabilize the mast and keep it from bending.

slack tide a brief period of no current movement at the turning of the tide.

slip a berth at a dock.

spanker a fore-and-aft rigged sail on the aftermast of some vessels.

spar a mast, boom, bowsprit.

spill the wind to take the wind out of a sail by moving it out of position.

spinnaker a large, three-cornered sail added to increase downwind speed.

square-rigged having four-sided sails set abeam or athwartships.

starboard the right side of the boat when facing forward, opposite of port.

starboard tack a tack in which the wind blows from starboard to port.

staysail a triangular sail set behind the headsail.

steerage way reaching a high enough speed to steer the vessel.

stem the tide to make headway against the current.

stern the rear of the boat.

storm sails small, strong sails used for their ease of control in stormy weather.

strike to lower a sail.

surfing picking up speed by intentionally riding on top of a wave.

swamp to flood with water.

tabernacle the deck housing for the bottom of the mast.

tack the lower front corner of a sail. Also, the side of the boat opposite the side the sails are on. See TACKING.

tacking switching tacks by turning the bow into the wind.

tail to pull or haul in a line.

take in to lower a sail.

telltales short strings of yarn attached to the shrouds as indications of wind direction.

tender a small boat, such as a dinghy, used to go to and from shore or to other vessels.

tight cover to position one's vessel in a race so that the competitor's vessel loses airflow into his sails.

tiller a steering stick attached to the rudder.

topside on deck.

transom the aftmost board at the stern.

trim the angle of a sail in relation to the wind direction. Also, to adjust a sail's angle.

trimaran a trihulled vessel.

trysail a small, triangular sail used in stormy weather in place of a mainsail.

turn turtle to capsize completely; to go belly up.

under the lee a position protected by the wind, for example, behind a land barrier or downwind of another vessel.

veering wind a wind that is changing direction in a clockwise fashion.

wake the foamy, turbulent water left behind a vessel.

weather the windward side of a vessel.

weigh anchor to raise the anchor.

winch a reel-like apparatus for winding line.

windage the area of sail actually collecting wind.

windward the side of the boat that is taking the wind directly.

yard a spar on which a square sail is hung.

yaw a drifting turn, caused by heavy seas.

Crew of a Large 18th- or 19th-Century Sailing Vessel

able seaman a senior deck hand responsible for rigging, manning guns, and occasionally taking the helm.

boatswain warrant officer responsible for supervising crew and the ship's maintenance. He would beat the crew to get them to work harder; he also served as an executioner. Also spelled bosun or bos'n.

boatswain's mate a petty officer who assisted the boatswain.

cabin boy one who waited on and served as a "gofer" for officers.

call boy one who carried the pipes and whistles of the boatswain and sometimes relayed whistled commands to other parts of the ship.

carpenter ship's carpenter; a petty officer responsible for the upkeep of all woodwork on board.

cockswain the helmsman of a ship's auxiliary boat; the head of this boat's crew.

conder a lookout who gives directions to the helmsman; one who cons or directs a ship from a lookout position.

deck hand in the merchant navy, a rank below chief officer and boatswain.

deck officer in the merchant navy, an officer who keeps watch on the bridge.

efficient deck hand a deck hand over the age of 18 who has passed a competency test and who has served for at least one year.

first mate chief officer ranking just below master on a merchant navy vessel.

foretopman a seaman whose station is the fore topmast.

helmsman the seaman who steers the vessel. Also known as the quartermaster, wheelman, or steerman.

lady of the gunroom Royal Navy slang for seaman responsible for the gunner's stores.

lamp trimmer a seaman responsible for maintaining all oil lamps on a vessel.

lee helmsman the assistant to the helmsman who stands at the lee side of the wheel.

master the commander of a merchant navy vessel. Short for master mariner.

master at arms officer in charge of maintaining law and order on board.

mate first rank below the master. The mate is responsible for organization and navigation. Same as first mate.

midshipman the lowest-ranking commissioned officer.

ordinary seaman seaman who has not yet qualified for able seaman status.

petty officer a noncommissioned naval officer.

quartermaster in the merchant navy, the helmsman. In the Royal Navy, a supervisor of the helmsman.

sailmaker a crew member who constructs and repairs sails and other items made of canvas.

steward crew member in charge of catering, provisioning, and maintaining the living quarters.

storekeeper crew member in charge of stores and their issuance to crew.

supercargo short for superintendent of cargo; the owner or representative of the owner of a ship's cargo who travels on board a merchant vessel.

warrant officer in the Royal Navy, a senior ranking, noncommissioned officer.

yeoman in the Royal Navy, an assistant to the navigator. Also, an assistant to a storekeeper.

Sailing Terms of the 18th and 19th Centuries

badge an ornamental window or likeness of a window decorated with marine figures near the stern of a sailing vessel.

barbarising swabbing a deck with sand and cleanser.

belay it much-used saying for "stop it" or "shut up."

bilboes iron bars on the deck to which prisoners were shackled on some warships.

blood money money paid to innkeepers or a boarding house for finding men to fill vacancies on a ship's crew.

bluff bowed a vessel having a broad bow that pushes through the water instead of slicing through it.

broken backed a worn-out or structurally weakened vessel with a dropping bow and stern.

caboose a chimney housing in the cook's galley on a merchant ship. Also, the galley itself.

close quarters wooden barriers on a deck, behind which crew could fight off and shoot at enemy boarders.

coach on a large man-of-war, a stern compartment used as captain's quarters.

cobbing disciplinary action practiced by the British navy, specifically tying a man down on deck and spanking him with a board.

cockpit in a man-of-war, an emergency medical compartment under the lower gundeck.

cod's head and mackerel tail slang describing a vessel having a bluff bow and a narrow or tapering stern.

company the crew of a ship.

cuddy a cabin in the fore of a vessel.

cut of his jib sailor slang for the way a person characteristically looks or behaves.

dead door a wooden shutter sealing a window.

dog watch deck watch from 4 P.M. to 8 P.M.

ducking disciplinary action in which a man was dunked repeatedly in the sea while being hung from a yardarm, a practice abandoned at the end of the 17th century.

graveyard watch deck watch from midnight to 4 A.M.

grog rum diluted with water, a ration of the Royal Navy.

hardtack slang for ship's biscuits.

keel hauling disciplinary action in which a man was pulled underneath the keel of a ship by ropes from one side to another, a practice abandoned in the 19th century.

lady's hole a small storage compartment.

lazarette a quarantine room for persons with contagious diseases. Also used as a holding room for troublemakers or as a storeroom.

magazine on a man-of-war, a storeroom for gunpowder and other explosives.

marry the gunner's daughter to be flogged on a Royal Navy vessel.

mess deck a deck on which the crew took its meals; also, a mess room.

monkey poop a low poop deck.

mustering calling a crew together for a drill or inspection.

piping the side sounding the boatswain's whistle as a salute to an arriving or departing officer of high rank.

portage seaman's wages for one voyage.

powder room compartment where gunpowder was kept in bulk on a man-of-war.

ram bow on a man-of-war, a bow equipped with an iron or bronze projection used for ramming enemy vessels.

reefer a pea jacket worn by midshipmen.

roundhouse a deckhouse aft of the main mast.

sailroom a compartment where sails were stored.

saloon on a merchant ship, the officers' mess. Also, a main passenger accommodation.

salt horse salt beef, a staple of seamen.

scrollhead ornamental scroll work at the stem of a ship instead of a figurehead.

scuppers channels cut through the sides of a ship to drain off deck water.

scuttle any small hatchway, usually fitted with a lid.

shanghai to kidnap a sailor from one vessel to enlist him to duty on another vessel, a practice in American ports in the 19th century.

shanty song sung by crew to keep work in unison, especially when heaving ropes.

sick bay a medical compartment for persons with injuries or illnesses.

slop room compartment for storing extra clothes for crew.

slops extra clothes kept on board for new sailors too poor to have their own changes of clothes.

steerage accommodations forward of the main cabin.

tabernacle the three-sided square casing in which a mast is stepped and clamped.

ward-robe a fortified room where valuables taken from enemy vessels were stored.

whaleback slang for a vessel whose deck has a steep arching from middle to sides to drain off water.

SHIPS AND BOATS

(*Also see* SUBMARINES *in* MILITARY: NAVY AND MARINES)

abeam at right angles to the keel.

aft at, near, or toward the rear of the ship.

air port porthole, for light and ventilation.

aloft in the upper rigging above decks.

amidships at or near the middle of a ship.

anchor, bower the main or largest anchor on a ship, carried in the bow.

anchor, kedge small anchor used for kedging or warping, freeing a vessel from shoals.

anchor, sea conical cloth bag dragged behind a vessel to reduce drift; also known as a drogue.

anchor, stream anchor about one-third the weight of a bower, used when mooring in narrow channels or in a harbor to prevent the vessel's stern from swinging.

argosy large merchant ship, or any fleet of merchant ships.

astern in the rear of a vessel.

auxiliaries collective term for the various motors, winches, pumps, and similar equipment on a vessel.

ballast any portable or fixed weight carried to make a vessel more stable or seaworthy. Types of ballast include sand, concrete, lead, scrap, pig iron, and seawater.

ballast tanks water tanks that are filled or emptied to aid in a vessel's stability; also used in subs for submerging.

batten strip of wood or steel used in securing tarpaulins.

beam the extreme width of a vessel.

berth bed, bunk, or sleeping compartment. Also, any place where a ship is moored.

bilges the rounded portions of a ship's bottom or shell.

bilge pump pump that removes water from the bilges.

binnacle a stand that houses a compass for easy viewing.

block a pulley or system of pulleys.

boiler steam generator.

booby hatch access hatch on the weather deck with a hood and sliding cover to keep water out.

bollard iron or wooden fixture on a vessel or dock to which mooring lines are attached.

boss the curved or swollen portion of the ship's underwater hull around the propellor shaft.

bosun boatswain—petty officer in charge of rigging, sail maintenance, anchors, and deck operations.

bosun's chair a seat for hoisting a person aloft for repairs.

bow front of a ship. Also known as a prow.

bowsprit spar that projects over the bow, used to hold the lower ends of head sails, or used for observation.

bridge an observation platform, often forming the top of a bridge house or pilot house, giving a clear view of the weather deck.

bulkhead any one of the partition walls that divide the interior of a ship into compartments or rooms.

cabin the living quarters for officers and passengers.

cabin boy one who waits on the passengers and officers of a ship.

cabin class ship accommodations above tourist class but below first class.

capstan drum- or barrel-shaped apparatus operated by hand or by motor for hauling in heavy anchor chains.

cargo hatch the large opening in the deck to permit loading of cargo below.

cargo net net used to haul cargo aboard.

cargo port an opening with a watertight door in the side of a ship to allow the loading and unloading of cargo.

chafing gear rubber hoses, sheaths, and other materials used to protect ropes from wearing where they rub on sharp edges.

chart house small room adjacent to the bridge for charts and navigating instruments.

cleats piece of wood or metal having two projecting arms or horns on which to belay ropes.

clinometer instrument that indicates the angle of roll or pitch of a vessel.

companionway a hatchway in a deck with a set of steps or ladders leading from one deck to another.

cordage collective term for all the ropes on a vessel.

cradle wooden frame where boats are stowed on shore.

cross tree athwartship pieces fitted over the trees on a mast.

crow's nest lookout perch attached to or near the head of a mast.

cuddy a small cabin.

davit small crane on a ship's side for hoisting boats or supplies.

deadlight a porthole lid or cover.

deep waterline the depth of a vessel in the water when carrying the maximum amount of allowable weight or cargo.

derrick a type of crane used for hoisting and swinging heavy weights.

door, airtight a door constructed to prevent the passage of air.

door, watertight a door constructed to prevent the passage of water.

draft the depth of a vessel below the waterline. Also spelled draught.

draft marks numbers on a vessel's bow or stern indicating the draft or depth of the vessel below the waterline.

dry dock a hollow floating structure designed to submerge in order to float a vessel into it, and then to lift the vessel out of the water for repairs or construction.

fantail the overhanging stern section on some vessels.

fathom nautical unit of measurement, in the United States 6 feet, or 1.829 meters.

fender protective plate, bundles of rope, old tires, or other material running along the side of a ship to prevent scratches and dents from rubbing against other vessels or piers.

fetch the distance from a wind's point of origin over the sea to a vessel, affecting the height of waves. Also, to swing around or veer.

fin a projecting keel.

flotilla fleet of small vessels.

flotsam and jetsam debris, goods, or cargo cast or washed from an imperiled or wrecked ship.

flukes the hooks or holding claws of an anchor.

fore the front of a ship or bow area.

fore and aft lengthwise of a ship.

forecastle structure on the upper deck of a ship toward the fore; the crew quarters on a merchant ship.

foul the sea growth or foreign matter covering the underwater portion of a ship's shell.

founder to sink after filling with water.

galley kitchen.

gangplank board or platform used for boarding passengers or cargo.

gangway an opening in a ship's side for the passage of freight or passengers.

grapnel similar to a small anchor, a device used for recovering small items dropped overboard or to hook onto lines from a distance.

graybeards choppy, frothy waves.

gunwale the upper edge of a side of a vessel.

guys wires, ropes, or chains used to support booms, davits, and suchlike.

halyards light lines used in hoisting signals or flags; also, the ropes used in hoisting gaffs, sails, or yards.

hatchway accessway or opening in a deck.

hawse hole through which the anchor chain is hoisted or released; any hole through which a chain or cable is passed.

hawser rope or cable used in mooring or towing.

head toilet.

heave to to stop the forward motion of a vessel and lie dead in the water.

heel the leaning of a vessel to one side, caused by wind, waves, or shifting cargo.

helm the steering apparatus, including the tiller, the rudder, and the wheel.

hog scrub broom used for scraping a ship's bottom underwater.

hold space below deck for cargo.

jack ladder ladder with wooden steps and side ropes.

jury temporary structures, such as makeshift masts or rudders, used in an emergency. Also known as jury-rigging.

keel the main structural member running fore and aft along the bottom of a vessel, also known as the backbone.

keelson a beam running above the keel of a vessel.

knot unit of speed, 1 nautical mile (6,080 feet) an hour.

lanyard rope having one free end and one attached to any object for the purpose of remote control; also, any rope used for fastening riggings.

lee the side of a vessel sheltered from the wind, or leeward; opposite of the windward side.

list deviation of a vessel from an upright position, caused by waves, wind, bilging, or shifting cargo.

magazine storage compartment for the stowage of ammunition.

mast upright pole on the center line of a ship's deck, used for carrying sails or for supporting rigging, cargo, and boat-handling gear.

messroom compartment where crew members eat their meals. An officer's meal compartment is sometimes called a wardroom messroom.

mooring the operation of anchoring a vessel or securing it to a mooring buoy, wharf, or dock.

mooring lines chains, ropes, or cables used to tie a ship to a wharf or dock.

nautical mile 6,080 feet.

panting the pulsations of the bow and stern bottoms as the vessel rises and plunges in rough seas.

pea jacket short, heavy woolen seaman's coat.

pelorus navigational instrument similar to a compass, used in taking bearings. Also known as a dumb compass.

pilot house navigational center near the front of a vessel, providing an unobstructed view in all directions except directly aft.

pitching rising and falling of a vessel's bow as it rides other waves.

pitchpoling the flipping over of a vessel in rough seas, from front to back.

plunger wave with a distinctly convex back with a crest that fails suddenly and violently, usually found near shore. See SPILLER.

poop the structure or raised deck at the aft of a vessel.

port the left side of a vessel when looking from aft forward.

pudding fender material constructed of ropes, canvas, leather, or old tires to prevent chafing or denting from piers or other vessels.

regatta a boat race or series of boat races.

rigging collective term for all ropes, chains, or cables used to support masts, yards, booms, and similar equipment.

roll motion of a vessel from side to side in rough seas.

rudder flat slab of metal or wood used in steering a vessel.

scuppers deck drains or gutters for carrying off rain- or seawater.

scuttlebutt drinking fountain.

shellback veteran sailor or old salt.

shroud set of ropes stretched from the masthead to a vessel's side, used for support or to ascend the mast.

sick bay medical service area.

sounding measurement of the depth of water.

spar pole serving as a mast, boom, gaff, yard, bowsprit, and suchlike.

spiller wave with a concave back and a crest that breaks gradually and continuously, usually found away from shore.

starboard the right side of a vessel when looking forward.

stateroom a private room for passengers or officers.

stem the front of a bow.

stern the aft or rear of a vessel.

superstructure any structure built above the uppermost complete deck, such as a pilothouse or bridge.

tack any change of course or veering of a vessel to one side in order to take advantage of a side wind.

tiller an arm attached to the rudder for operation of the rudder.

turn turtle to capsize.

wake wash or churning water left behind a ship's passage.

weather deck uppermost continuous deck exposed to the weather.

windlass a drumlike apparatus used for hoisting heavy anchor chains and hawsers.

yard a spar attached at its middle to a mast and running athwartship as a support for a square sail, halyard, lights, and other equipment.

yardarm outer end of a yard.

SPACEFLIGHT

SATELLITES AND SPACE PROBES

Apollo a NASA program comprising a series of manned lunar missions, beginning in the 1960s, and ending in the 1970s.

Ares 1 a NASA rocket currently in development to take the next generation of astronauts into space.

astronaut Latin term for "sailor of the stars." A space traveler.

attitude a satellite's orientation in orbit, for example, pointed toward Earth or the Sun.

burn the firing of a spacecraft's thrusters.

Canopus a bright star used as a reference point in a space probe's navigation.

Cassini a two-story high space probe launched in 1997 to explore Saturn and its moons.

Chandra a boxcar-sized, X-ray observatory launched in 1999 to study X-ray sources at the centers of galaxies.

Corot a French probe set for launch early in the 21st century to search for planets around distant stars.

cosmonaut Russian term for an astronaut.

cruise a probe's travel time between planets.

decay the gradual loss of a satellite's orbital altitude due to Earth's gravity.

Deep Space 1 a spacecraft launched in 1998 to test spacecraft technologies.

Deep Space 2 twin probes launched in 1999 to analyze Martian subsurface soil, but which ultimately failed.

downlink to send radio signals from a spacecraft to Earth.

DSN Deep Space Network, the Jet Propulsion Laboratory's spacecraft tracking facility.

ERV earth return vehicle; any part or component of a probe that returns to Earth.

ESA European Space Agency.

escape velocity speed required to propel a spacecraft beyond Earth's gravitational forces.

explosive bolts explosive bolts detonated to separate experimental packages or other subsystems while in orbit.

Galileo a space probe launched in 1989 to collect data on Jupiter and its moons.

Gemini NASA program featuring the first manned extravehicular activity in orbit, and the first manned docking of two spacecraft, 1965–1966.

Genesis a spacecraft launched in 2001 to collect solar wind particles.

geosynchronous orbit an orbit synchronized with the turning of Earth so that the satellite stays above the same area of Earth at all times.

Giotto a space probe launched to collect data on Halley's Comet in 1986.

gravity assist the use of a planet's gravity to deflect or slingshot a space probe deeper into space.

heavy space plane an experimental shuttle craft capable of "flying" into orbit by using ejector ramjet engines combined with rocket engines.

HESSI High Energy Solar Spectroscopic Imager; a probe to be launched early in the 21st century to study solar flares.

horizon sensor on a satellite, an onboard sensor that perceives Earth's horizon as an aid to maintain proper attitude.

Hubble Space Telescope a large, orbiting observatory, launched in 1990 from the space shuttle.

hydrazine space probe's onboard fuel used for attitude-adjusting rockets.

hydrogen peroxide a fuel sometimes used to power a satellite's maneuvering rockets.

International Space Station an orbiting space station composed of 100 separate elements, which will stretch more than 100 meters long when completed and built cooperatively by 16 nations. The first two component modules, the *Unity* and *Zarya,* were linked by shuttle astronauts in 1998. Construction was slowed and in question after the loss of the space shuttle *Columbia* in 2003.

ion engine an experimental engine employing solar panels to accelerate charged atoms of xenon to create propulsion in space probes.

JPL Jet Propulsion Laboratory; the scientific facility and body of scientists in Pasadena, California, that oversees and maintains a space probe's mission.

Kepler launched in 2009, a spacecraft that trails Earth's orbit and searches a group of 100,000 stars in our galaxy for evidence of Earthlike or habitable planets.

lander any vessel designed to land on a planet or moon.

launch corridor a flight path.

launch window a span of time within which a satellite or probe must be launched in order to meet economic, trajectory, or orbital location requirements.

lightcraft an experimental spacecraft powered by high-intensity laser light or microwave energy beamed from the ground to the bottom of the vessel to concentrate heat and create thrust.

Lunar Prospector a space probe launched in 1998 to survey and collect data from the moon.

Magellan a probe launched in 1989 to map by radar the surface of Venus and to take measurements of the planet's gravity.

Mariner any one of various planetary probes, launched from 1962 to 1973.

Mars Direct Plan an inexpensive, speculative plan for sending humans to mars sometime around 2020.

Mars Express an orbiter and lander mission to Mars conducted by the European Space Agency. The mission failed when its landing craft, *Beagle,* attempted to touch down on Mars on December 25, 2003; it did not return radio signals and was presumed "lost."

Mars Global Surveyor a space probe launched in 1996 to map the planet Mars.

Mars Odyssey an orbiter that reached Mars in October of 2001 and circled the planet to collect data on radiation and surface minerals. It also served as a communications relay for the rovers *Opportunity* and *Spirit.*

Mars Pathfinder a planetary probe that landed on Mars in 1997 and radioed back photographs of a rock-strewn Martian desert.

Mars Surveyor a planetary probe launched in 1998 and 1999 in two parts to explore the south pole of Mars.

Mercury a NASA program featuring the first manned, suborbital and orbital missions, from 1961 to 1963.

microprobe a small probe launched from a larger, main probe.

Mir a Russian orbital space station, launched in 1986 and retired in 2001 when it reentered Earth's atmosphere.

modules independent subsystems on a satellite or probe.

NASA National Aeronautics and Space Administration.

NEAR Near Earth Asteroid Rendezvous; a space probe launched in 1996 to collect data on Eros, a 40-kilometer-long asteroid in the solar system's main asteroid belt.

Opportunity* and *Spirit two planetary rovers that landed on opposite sides of Mars in January 2004 and gathered data on climate and geology and searched for evidence of past life forms.

orbit a path followed by a spacecraft or satellite around a planet or moon, and held in place by gravitational forces.

Orion shaped like the Apollo spacecraft but three times larger, a space capsule designed to carry four astronauts to the *International Space Station* in 2015 and to the Moon by 2020. In an expandable form, it may carry as many as six astronauts to Mars.

Pathfinder Rover an all-terrain vehicle launched from the Mars Pathfinder to explore the surface of Mars.

payload collective term for cargo, gear, and passengers taken into space by a spacecraft.

photovoltaics see SOLAR CELLS.

Pioneer any one of various lunar or planetary probes launched from 1958 to 1978.

pod any detachable component of a space vessel.

propellant any fuel providing a vessel's thrust.

reentry a satellite's reentry into Earth's atmosphere from orbit.

retro rocket an engine producing reverse thrust to slow a vessel.

rover any all-terrain vehicle launched from a lander to survey a planet's surface.

Salyut any one of seven Russian orbital space stations, launched from 1971 to 1986.

scramjet a speculative engine designed to capture massive amounts of air to burn with liquid hydrogen or other fuel, to be used to "fly" future spacecraft into orbit like jets.

scrub to cancel a launch or mission.

Skylab a U.S. orbital space station launched in 1973, and employed for scientific research; it eventually deorbited.

solar cells photovoltaic cells aligned on paddles extending out from a satellite or probe to absorb and utilize solar energy to power onboard systems.

solar probe scheduled for launch in 2007, a probe that will fly very close to the Sun to collect data on its corona and take high-resolution photographs of its surface.

Soyuz a Russian space program highlighted by the first orbital transfer of crew from one craft to another, from 1967 to 1981.

space tether connected between two space vessels, a several-miles-long line employed to "throw" one of the craft into higher orbit, by use of momentum or of electricity generated by Earth's magnetic field.

Spirit see *OPPORTUNITY* AND *SPIRIT*.

Sputnik 1 the first artificial satellite launched into space, by the Soviets in October 1957.

Stardust a space probe launched in 1999 to collect the dust from a passing comet and bring it back to Earth.

station keeping maintaining a satellite's orbital altitude by firing onboard rockets.

subsystems any onboard instruments or modules.

telemetry the science of taking measurements from a distant point.

tracking station a ground station that tracks satellites.

trajectory flight path of a space probe.

uplink to send radio signals from Earth to a spacecraft.

Venera any one of several Russian probes studying the planet Venus.

Viking either one of two U.S. spacecraft that landed on Mars in 1976, analyzed its soil, and radioed back photographs of its terrain.

Vostok Russian space program highlighted by the first manned spaceflight and the first woman in space, 1961–1963.

Voyager either of two probes of the outer solar system, noted for radioing back spectacular photographs of Jupiter, Saturn, Uranus, and Neptune, from 1979 through the 1980s.

X-33, X-34 experimental shuttle vessels under development.

SPACE SHUTTLE

abort to stop a mission in progress, usually due to some malfunction.

airlock a chamber between a pressurized and an unpressurized compartment, or between a pressurized compartment and space.

attitude the orientation or position of the shuttle relative to the Earth's horizon or other reference point.

automatic landing mode a computer-controlled guidance system capable of landing a craft without human assistance.

avionics the electronics systems monitoring the control of the flight.

barbecue mode rolling the shuttle slowly along its axis to diffuse external heat.

bearing the angular or horizontal direction of a shuttle or other spacecraft after launch.

beta cloth a flameproof spacesuit material made of glass fibers.

blackout a loss of radio signal.

booster see SOLID ROCKET BOOSTERS.

bulkhead any wall of a compartment.

Canopus a bright star used in space navigation to help orient a vessel.

capture the capturing of a satellite or other payload by the remote manipulator arm.

cargo bay the unpressurized midsection of the shuttle's fuselage; it has hinged doors that open wide to space.

crawlerway the reinforced roadway over which space vehicles are transported from an assembly building to the launchpad.

crew egress the crew exitway.

crew ingress the crew entryway.

deck any of three decks on the shuttle: the flight deck, the mid-deck, and the lower deck.

delta wing a triangular wing configuration, as found on the shuttle.

deorbit burn the firing of a retro rocket to slow the craft's orbit for either changing orbit or preparing for reentry into Earth's atmosphere.

deployment the deployment of a payload, such as a satellite, into space.

dock to join two vessels together in space.

downlink a radio broadcast from the shuttle to Earth.

emergency exit system an escape mechanism composed of seven "slidewires" and passenger baskets, which can be ridden to the ground from orbiter up until 30 seconds before launch.

entry the reentry of the shuttle into Earth's atmosphere.

EVA extravehicular activity; activities carried out by crew outside a pressurized compartment, where spacesuits are needed.

flame trench the concrete pit located under a launchpad; it directs rocket flame away from the spacecraft.

flare to pitch the spacecraft nose up to reduce speed for landing.

flying brick the nickname for the shuttle.

g the force of gravity; 1 g equals the gravity of Earth; 5 g's equal five times the gravity of Earth, and so on.

geosynchronous orbit an orbit that stays in sync with the earth's rotation, 22,300 miles above the equator.

gimbal an apparatus having ball joints to allow movement in several directions, as a rocket nozzle.

glide slope the landing approach.

Goddard Space Flight Center the center in Greenbelt, Maryland, that operates and maintains the space flight tracking and data network.

hypergolic propellants propellants such as nitrogen tetroxide and monomethylhydrazine that ignite on contact with one another.

hypersonic exceeding five times the speed of sound; above Mach 5.

Kennedy Space Center the launching base for the shuttle, located in Cape Canaveral Florida.

LOX acronym for liquid oxygen.

Lyndon Johnson Space Center located near Houston, Texas, the center that designs, develops, and tests spacecraft, selects and trains astronauts, and plans missions.

Mach a term denoting the speed of sound; for example, Mach 2 is twice the speed of sound, Mach 3 is three times the speed of sound.

microgravity the near-zero gravity experienced while in orbit above Earth.

micrometeoroids tiny meteor particles the size of sand grains, known to erode the exterior of the shuttle on impact.

mission specialist a specialist or expert on the shuttle's payload or scientific mission.

mission station a station on the aft flight deck, where payload operations are carried out.

orbiter the shuttle.

payload changeout room a launchpad room where payload is loaded into the shuttle cargo bay.

pilot the second in command of a flight after the commander.

pitch up-and-down rotational movement of the nose.

remote manipulator system in the cargo bay, a large mechanical arm used to retrieve or deploy satellites.

retro rocket a rocket that fires in the opposite direction of the shuttle's flight, to slow momentum.

roll an inflight rolling motion of the shuttle along its axis.

rudder a movable surface on the tail to control yaw. Also known as the speed brake.

solid rocket boosters the two solid-propellant rockets that lift the shuttle up to an altitude of 25 miles and then are jettisoned.

spacelab a modular laboratory in the orbiter, used by mission specialists to conduct experiments.

speed brake a split and spread rudder that increases drag and slows the shuttle during the landing phase.

telemetry shuttle flight mission data transmitted to Earth.

umbilical an electrical and life support cable attached to an astronaut when working outside the shuttle while in orbit.

uplink radio transmission from Earth to the shuttle.

Vernier engine an engine providing slight thrust for small changes in shuttle position.

vertical stabilizer the tail.

window a period of time within which a mission must be launched or concluded.

yaw left-right rotation of the nose.

Shuttle Acronyms

ADI attitude direction indicator.

A/G air-to-ground.

AMI alpha-Mach indicator.

APU auxiliary power unit.

CSS control stick steering.

DCM displays and controls module.

EMU extravehicular mobility unit.

EVA extravehicular activity.

HSI horizontal situation indicator.

IUS inertial upper stage.

IVA intravehicular activity.

LCC launch control center.

LOS loss of signal.

MCC Mission Control Center.

MCC-H Mission Control Center, Houston.

MET mission elapsed time.

MLP mobile launcher platform.

MMU manned maneuvering unit.

OMS orbital maneuvering system.

OPF orbiter processing facility.

PAM payload assist module.

PLSS portable life support system.

RCS reaction control system.

RMS remote manipulator system.

SCAPE self-contained atmospheric pressure ensemble.

SOMS shuttle orbiter medical system.

SRB solid rocket booster.

SSME space shuttle main engine.

SSUS spinning solid upper stage.

tacan tactical air navigation.

TDRS tracking and data relay satellite.

TPS thermal protection system.

WCS waste collection system.

TRAINS AND RAILROADS

bank grade.

berth bed in a sleeping car.

bogies the wheeled trucks on which railroad cars ride.

boxcar the enclosed, boxlike freight car.

brakeman conductor's assistant who maintains and inspects the brakes.

bumper a small top barrier at the end of a track.

cab the driving compartment.

caboose a car with sleeping and eating facilities for the crew; it is pulled at the end of the train.

coach a car for carrying passengers.

coaling road a coal track.

coupler the clamping device that allows each car to lock onto another car.

crossbuck the X-like railroad crossing warning sign.

crow the peep of a steam whistle.

dead-end bay a substation.

dining car a car in which meals are served.

downtrain from the home terminal.

driver the engineman.

engineer one who operates the engine.

engine road a track leading to the engine house.

flatcar a riding platform without roof or walls, for hauling large objects.

gauge the width between the two rails of a track.

gondola an open, shallow freight car.

grade the slope or inclination of a track.

grade crossing an intersection of a road and a rail crossing.

highball a railroad signal to go full-speed ahead.

hopper car a freight car having large funnels or hoppers for carrying and dispensing grains.

linear induction motor the electric motor that powers a maglev train.

livestock car a boxcar having open slats for the transport of livestock.

locomotive the electric or diesel-powered engine that pulls the cars.

locomotive shed an engine terminal.

maglev train an unwheeled train that, levitated on a magnetic field, is free from friction and can travel at great speeds.

marshalling classifying and sorting cars in a yard.

marshal yard a freight yard.

monorail a single-railed track.

piggyback car a flatcar designed to haul the trailers of tractor-trailer trucks.

platform a landing for passengers beside the tracks at a station.

platform car a flatcar.

Pullman trademark name for a parlor or sleeping car, designed by George Pullman.

redcap a porter in a railway station.

refrigerator car a refrigerated car for hauling perishables.

regulator the throttle.

rolling stock collective term for all of a railroad's wheeled vehicles.

roundhouse a facility, often with a turntable, for repairing and switching locomotives.

semaphore a signaling apparatus employing lights or pivoting arms.

shed master an engine house foreman.

shunting switching tracks.

signal box a signal tower or station.

signal gantry a raised frame spanning one or more tracks and on which are mounted signal lights.

sleeper a railroad tie. Also, a sleeping compartment or car.

switch the apparatus that is adjusted to shunt a train onto another track.

tank car a cylindrical car designed to haul fuels and other fluids.

turntable a rail platform that rotates to turn a locomotive in the opposite direction.

wagon slang for a freight car.

wagon-lit a sleeping car.

yard a receiving and holding yard for trains and cars.

EAPONS

CLUBS AND HAMMERS

chigiriki a heavy ball suspended on a 4- to 6-foot chain, which is attached to a long shaft and swung about to strike or entangle an enemy; of Japanese origin.

horseman's hammer a combination hammer and pick mounted on a shaft, used by horsemen to knock out or kill an enemy.

kusarigama a Japanese pick hammer with a long chain and weighted ball at the end.

mace a club with a weighty or spiked end.

morning star a spiked ball on a chain suspended from a shaft.

truncheon a heavy club.

war-flail one or more heavy weights attached to a short chain or chains on a shaft.

DAGGERS

anlace a dual-edged, medieval dagger.

baselard a dagger having a crosspiece as a guard for the hand at the pommel.

bodkin a medieval dagger or stiletto.

bowie knife U.S. fighting and hunting knife having dual edge at the tip.

dudgeon dagger having a handle made out of wood of the same name. Also, the hilt of any dagger.

fullers grooves in a dagger blade.

grip the handle.

hilt the handle.

jambiya classic Arabian dagger with dual-edged, curved blade.

khanjar Indian and Persian dagger having a jade or ivory, pistol-like grip and a forward- or backward-curving handle.

knuckle-guard a bar or shield at the hilt to protect the fingers.

kris classic Malay dagger with a wavy blade.

misericord in medieval times, a narrow dagger used to deliver death quickly to an already wounded knight.

pommel the knob at the butt end of some daggers, sometimes highly ornamented.

pugio an ancient Roman military dagger having a very broad blade and a narrow grip.

quillon dagger a dagger having quillons.

quillons two side projections at the guard or hilt.

rondel a medieval dagger having a disklike pommel and guard and a narrow blade, used from 1320 to 1550.

skean Irish and Scottish dual-edged dagger.

stiletto dagger having a very narrow blade for stabbing or thrusting only.

swordbreaker a dagger having a deeply notched blade for catching and breaking the blade of a sword.

GUNS AND BULLETS

assault rifle any automatic rifle intended to be used for an assault or attack on humans.

automatic any gun that fires continuously while the trigger is pressed.

barrel the metal tube through which bullets are projected after firing.

baton rounds shotgun projectiles that stun but do not kill; used in riot situations.

bayonet a knife mounted on the barrel of a rifle for use in hand-to-hand combat.

bead a small projection on the muzzle of a gun, used for sighting.

birdshot small shotgun pellets used in bird hunting; may also be used to control a crowd in riot situations.

bluing the colored finish on the metal parts of a gun.

bolt a sliding rod that pushes a cartridge into the firing chamber.

bolt-action a gun having a manually operated bolt.

bore the inside portion and diameter of the barrel, extending from the breech to the muzzle. Also known as the gauge.

box magazine a rectangular or square magazine.

brass catcher a firearm attachment that catches spent cartridges ejected from an automatic or semiautomatic rifle.

breech the rear portion of a gun, behind the bore.

buck and ball a cartridge having a round ball and three buckshot.

buckshot large shotgun pellets used for large game.

bullet, cannelured an elongated, grooved bullet.

bullet, elongated a long bullet, as distinguished from a round one.

bullet, flat-point a bullet having a flat nose.

bullet, hollow-point a bullet having a hollow nose; it produces a wider area of damage on impact.

bullet, metal-case a bullet in which a metal jacket covers the nose.

bullet, soft-point a bullet having a lead tip; it produces a wider area of damage on impact.

bullet, wad-cutter a cylindrical, flat-topped bullet noted for making clean holes, used for target practice.

bullpup a firearm in which a magazine is inserted in the buttstock, behind the trigger mechanism.

butt the bottom of the grip on a pistol; the portion of a rifle placed against the shoulder when firing. Also known as the buttstock.

caliber the diameter of the barrel hole.

carbine a rifle having a barrel less than 22 inches in length.

cartridge the container holding the explosive charge.

centerfire cartridge a cartridge having its primer in the center of its base.

chamber the rear portion of the barrel; it receives the shell or cartridge.

choke a device that alters a shotgun muzzle to achieve a desired shot pattern.

clip a receptable used to hold several cartridges that are loaded simultaneously.

cock a hammer.

cylinder a revolving cylinder containing several cartridge chambers.

derringer a single-shot, pocket-sized pistol having a short barrel, the ultimate firearm for concealment.

double-action of a revolver capable of firing successive shots simply by pulling the trigger without having to first cock the hammer.

drift deviation laterally of a bullet's trajectory.

drum a round, spring-loaded magazine.

duckbill choke a muzzle attachment on a combat rifle used to spread shot in a wide line to hit more than one advancing target.

ejector a device that ejects a cartridge case.

firing pin the projection on the firing mechanism that strikes the primer or cap to detonate the powder charge.

flash hider a muzzle attachment used to conceal the flash of firing, especially at night.

fléchette a finned projectile used in a combat shotgun to produce greater wound penetration.

gauge the interior diameter of a shotgun barrel. Also known as the bore.

grip the handle on a pistol.

hair trigger a sensitive trigger requiring only a light pull to release it.

hammer the cock or lock portion that strikes the primer of a cartridge to fire it.

jacket a covering on a bullet.

kick the recoil after firing.

lock the mechanism that detonates a charge. Also, to engage the safety.

machine pistol a compact, automatic, or semiautomatic firearm.

magazine in a repeating firearm, the receptacle or clip that holds and advances the ammunition to the chamber.

muzzle the mount or front of the barrel, from which the bullets emerge.

muzzle brake a rifle attachment that reduces recoil by diverting internal gases.

muzzle velocity the speed of a bullet as it emerges from the muzzle.

pistol carbine a pistol having a removable shoulder stock to allow it to be fired as a rifle.

recoil the kick of a gun after firing.

revolver any pistol with a rotating, chambered cylinder allowing firing in quick succession.

rimfire cartridge a cartridge with its primer rimming the base, as distinguished from a centerfire cartridge.

riot gun a short shotgun that fires nonlethal projectiles in riot control situations.

safety a lock or mechanism that is set to prevent the unintentional firing of a gun.

shotgun a gun that fires a number of small pellets instead of a single bullet with each shot.

sight any bead or device aligned with the eye to facilitate aiming.

silencer see SUPPRESSOR.

single-action referring to a firearm that must be manually cocked before each shot.

stock the wooden part of a rifle that rests against the shoulder when firing.

submachine gun a light, handheld machine gun that fires standard pistol rounds.

suppressor a noise-suppressing, baffled tube attaching to the muzzle of a gun. Also known as a silencer.

tracer bullet a bullet that leaves a glowing trail, allowing its trajectory to be seen at night; used in the military.

trigger pull the pressure necessary to pull and release a trigger; descriptive terms include hair trigger, creeping pull, dragging pull, still pull, hard pull, smooth pull, and fine pull.

TYPES OF GUNS

antique guns blunderbuss, breechloader, Colt six-shooter, dueling pistols, flintlock, gatling gun, musket, muzzle loader.

automatic and semiautomatic handguns Beretta Pistola Automatica 9mm, Beretta Pistola Automatica Brevetto 7.65mm, Charter .38, Colt Police .45, Lugar 7.65, 9mm Parabellum, Mauser C96, Remington, Singer, .357 Magnum (several makers), Walther .38.

machine guns Barrett, British Lancaster, British Sterling, Calico 100, AK 47, Colt AR-15, Harrison and Richards, Plainfield, Ruger Mini 14, Sten, Thompson, Universal, Uzi.

revolvers Browning, Colt, Ruger Bearcat .22, Ruger GP 100-.357, Mauser Dan Wesson .44 Magnum, Dan Wesson .22 Magnum, Dan Wesson .41 Magnum, Smith and Wesson .44 Magnum, Smith and Wesson .25, Smith and Wesson Police 86.

rifles, carbines, shotguns Browning, Calico, Enfield, Harrison and Richards, Martin, Mauser, Plainfield, Remington, Ruger, Shiloh, Winchester.

POLE ARMS

(halberds, lances, pikes, etc.)

bardiche a Russian poleax used from the 16th to the 18th centuries.

bill a large curving or hooking blade (with the cutting edge on the inside, as a scythe) attached to a long pole.

catchpole a long pole with spring arms, used to catch a man by an arm or leg and pull him off his horse during battle. Also known as a mancatcher. See SLEEVE TANGLER.

glaive a long, broad knifelike blade attached to a long pole.

halberd a weapon head consisting of an ax blade, a sharp spike or point, and a beak, attached to a long pole; used in the 15th and 16th centuries.

half-moon a broad, two-pronged blade in the shape of a crescent moon, a Spanish weapon.

hammer a weapon head consisting of a sharp hammer head on a long shaft, for piercing armor or knocking an enemy out through armor.

lance a sharp metal head on a long shaft, used by soldiers on horseback.

mancatcher see CATCHPOLE.

military fork a two-pronged fork mounted on a long shaft.

partisan a weapon head consisting of a broad spear tip with a crescent base attached to a long shaft.

pike 16-foot shaft with sharp point, used to defend musketeers against attacking cavalry in the 17th century.

poleax a broad ax blade mounted on a long shaft.

quarterstaff a simple wooden staff.

ranseur a weapon head consisting of one long point and two shorter points or blades projecting from its base. Also known as a corsèque or spetum.

sleeve tangler a Japanese, multitoothed pole used to catch or snag apparel in order to pull an enemy off a horse.

spontoon a short pike.

thrusting spear a long-shafted spear with a broad, sharp point meant for stabbing instead of slashing.

trident a three-pronged fork on a long shaft.

SWORDS

baldric a tooled-leather belt worn across the chest to support a sword.

broadsword any sword with a broad blade.

claymore a large, dual-edged broadsword used by the Scottish Highlanders.

cutlass a relatively short sword with a curved blade, used by 18th-century sailors and pirates.

ensiform shaped like a sword.

épée a fencing sword having a cupped handle and a blade with no edge but a blunt point.

Excalibur King Arthur's famous sword.

falchion a short sword with a broad, curving blade.

false edge of a single-edged sword, a tip sharpened on both sides.

foil a thin-bladed fencing sword with a flat guard.

gladiate shaped like a sword.

hand-and-a-half an intermediate or smaller sword than a two-handed sword.

hanger any short sword hung from the side of the body and used as a backup for a larger sword. Also known as a sidearm.

hilt a sword handle.

knuckle-bow a knuckle guard at the hilt.

one-hand sword a very short sword.

pommel the knob at the end of the hilt, sometimes weighted to help balance the sword.

quillons small side projections at the hilt.

rapier a long, slender, dual-edged sword with a cupped hilt, used in the 16th and 17th centuries. An 18th-century version had no cutting edge but a sharp point for thrusting.

saber a heavy sword with a slightly curved blade, used by the cavalry. Also, a two-edged sword used in fencing.

scabbard a sword sheath.

scimitar an Oriental sword with a curved blade.

shamshir classic Persian and Indian saber with a curved blade.

sidearm see HANGER.

smallsword a small sword used as a fashionable costume item in the 17th and 18th centuries.

spear point a symmetrical blade with a sharp point.

two-hand sword a very large sword requiring two hands to swing.

TORTURE AND PUNISHMENT

Amnesty International an international organization that works to protect human rights and to eliminate executions and torture.

bastinado beating the soles of the feet with a stick or a cudgel.

boot one of various iron or wooden fittings placed over the foot or leg, which was then hammered through with wedges to apply pressure, sometimes to the breaking point.

breaking wheel originating in ancient Greece and used throughout the Middle Ages, a large, wooden, spoked wagon wheel, on which a victim was tied and then beaten with cudgels, clubs, or hammers. The resulting broken limbs would then sometimes be braided around the spokes, for display purposes.

burning at the stake in the Middle Ages, a method of execution in which heretics and witches were tied to a stake and burned alive, abolished in the late 18th century.

crucifixion originating in the sixth century B.C., a form of torture in which a victim was tied or nailed to a cross and left to hang. The victim sometimes had to carry the cross on his back to his place of execution and, once there, might also be impaled or have his legs broken. The most famous crucifixion victim was Jesus Christ.

cruel and unusual punishment general term for any form of torture, banned by the English Bill of Rights in 1689, and formally banned in the Eighth Amendment to the U.S. Constitution in 1787.

drawn and quartered one of the most severe forms of torture, originating in England for the crime of high treason. The punishment called first for a brief hanging, through which the victim was nearly killed but not quite. Partially revived by water, the victim would then be dragged onto a table, where his genitalia was removed, his abdomen cut open, and his intestines pulled out by a roller and then burned before his eyes. A decapitation followed and the remaining body was then hacked into four pieces, all of which were put on public display. After 1814, the punishment was changed, with the victim hanged until dead, after which he was sliced up. All forms of the punishment were abolished in 1870.

dungeon as part of a castle, an underground prison, where prisoners were isolated for great lengths of time.

forcipation pinching one's flesh with forceps or pincers.

heretic's fork a pitchforklike device, with double prongs and a strap that was placed around the neck. On one end, the prongs would be set under one's throat, and on the other into one's sternum, causing great pain. Used during the Spanish Inquisition.

impale to drive a sharp stake into someone.

iron maiden originating in the late 18th century, a tall iron case or cabinet in which a victim was placed and stabbed with knives or nails through strategically placed holes.

keelhauling a form of punishment used on sailors in the Dutch navy and the British Royal Navy, from the 1500s until 1853, through which a sailor tied to a rope was pulled under the hull of a ship and cut up by barnacles as he passed. If pulled too slowly, the victim would drown.

mock execution a form of psychological terror in which a blindfolded victim is told that he is about to be executed, with every step in the process carried out, including gunfire at close range, but with no actual physical harm done, used to coerce a prisoner into a confession.

picana similar to a cattle prod, an electrically charged wand that is hooked to a car battery or a transformer, through which power is adjusted to apply electric shocks to prisoners.

pitchcapping a form of torture in which a paper cap filled with hot tar or pitch is forcibly placed on a victim's shaved head and then later torn off, pulling up shreds of skin and flesh in the process. Used by British soldiers on Irish rebels in 18th-century Ireland.

Procrustes in Greek myth, the son of Poseidon. He was notorious for his iron bed, on which he cut off the legs of victims who were too tall for it. Conversely, he stretched on the rack those who were too short.

rack a wooden frame fitted with a roller at one or both ends, to which hands and feet were attached. By means of an incremental turn of a handle, the limbs were stretched to the point of breaking.

run the gauntlet made famous by the Roman military, a form of punishment in which a disgraced soldier would be made to run through two rows of men, who would strike him as he passed.

scavenger's daughter used in the Tower of London, a metal rack through which head, hands, and legs were strapped, and the victim made to bend and compress oneself so forcefully that blood would ooze from the nose and ears. Also known as the iron shackle or the stork.

scold's bridle an iron muzzlelike apparatus fit around the head, with a mouthpiece that stuck the tongue with sharp spikes if the wearer stirred or spoke, used as punishment for mouthy or troublesome women, including workhouse inmates in England and Scotland in the 1600s. Also known as the Branks.

scourge a multithonged whip or flail.

shunning in some Christian sects, the act of ignoring and avoiding someone who has sinned or acted out in some way against the church.

star chamber in the English court of law and operating out of the palace of Westminster from the 15th century to 1641, a secret court that tried cases without juries, witnesses, or the possibility of appeal, and which punished those found guilty with whippings, cutting off of ears, imprisonment, and the pillory. As an adjective, any secret, arbitrary, or strict institution of law that disregards human rights.

strappado used during the Middle Ages, a form of torture in which victims' hands were tied behind their backs and then pulled up into the air by another rope, which dislocated the arms. Also known as a reverse hanging.

tarring and feathering in Europe and in the American colonies in the 1700s, a form of mob punishment in which one was stripped to the waist and covered in tar and then plastered with or rolled in chicken feathers and made to ride in a cart through town as a form of humiliation.

Third Geneva Convention created in 1949, an international treaty agreement that spells out how prisoners of war are to be cared for during their captivity and that prohibits all forms of torture.

thumbscrew used during the Middle Ages, a vice placed over a victim's finger, thumb, or toe, and slowly crushed.

tocks similar to a pillory, a contrivance of boards that lock in a sitting victim's feet, hands, or head, or sometimes all of these. Used to publicly humiliate military deserters or minor offenders from the Middle Ages through colonial America.

torture chamber any room used for torture, where various torture devices may be set up, used from as early as Roman times and widespread during the Middle Ages, with the most notorious being used during the Spanish Inquisition.

Tower of London a fortress and prison in central London, famous for holding a torture chamber, which included such devices as the rack and the scavenger's daughter.

waterboarding originating during the Spanish Inquisition or earlier and used by the United States on suspected al-Qaeda suspects after the 9/11 attacks, a form of torture in which a victim is put on his back, with his hands and feet tied and his head inclined, while water is then poured over the mouth and nose to simulate drowning.

water ingestion a form of torture in which a victim has water forced down his throat, sometimes to the point of death, used against American soldiers by the Japanese in World War II.

whipping boy as part of the English court in the 1600s and 1700s, any boy who served as a substitute to a young prince when punishment for the prince's misbehavior was called for. The substitute, usually a close companion, would be whipped or beaten either for the prince's poor school performance or for acting out. The practice arose because a prince could not be physically punished by anyone other than the king, who was often away or too busy to attend to disciplinary matters.

WORDS AND EXPRESSIONS YOU SHOULD KNOW

Following are "big" words and phrases that turn up again and again in magazines such as *Time* and *Newsweek* and in the speeches of the world's most articulate speakers. These are words and terms every literate person should know, to sharpen both comprehension and communication skills.

abdicate *vb.* (AB duh KAYT) to give up one's position, office, or power. *The outraged citizens forced the king to abdicate the throne.*

aberration *n.* (AB uh RAY shun) a deviation from the norm. *The hot weather we've had this January is an aberration.*

abhor *vb.* (ab HOR) to loathe or detest. *I abhor people who are habitually late.*

abject *adj.* (AB jekt) the absolute worst or most extreme. *The migrants slept in their car and were living in abject poverty.*

abominable *adj.* (uh BOM un uh bul) horrible; awful. *That the homeless were forced out of the shelter this winter was abominable.*

abridge *vb.* (uh BRIJ) to shorten or reduce. *My editor asked me to abridge my book, as I've gone well over the contracted word length.*

absolve *vb.* (ub ZOLV) to free from blame; to exonerate. *The attorney was certain the new evidence would absolve his client.*

abstain *vb.* (ub STAYN) to refrain from doing something; to hold back. *I am finally going to abstain from pipe-smoking forever.*

abstinence *n.* (AB stuh nens) the act or condition of going or living without something. *When it comes to alcohol, I plan to practice abstinence.*

abstract *adj.* (AB strakt) nonrepresentational; not easily identified or defined. *We had a difficult time trying to understand Aunt Mary's abstract art.*

abstruse *adj.* (ab STROOS) incomprehensible or understood by only a few. *Einstein's theories are quite abstruse.*

acclimate *vb.* (AK luh mayt) to adapt or accustom oneself. *It takes time to acclimate oneself to the cold of the Arctic.*

accolades *n.* (AK uh LAYDZ) honor or recognition for something well done. *The movie is winning accolades from critics.*

accomplice *n.* (uh KOM plis) one who accompanies or helps another commit a crime. The thief's accomplice was also found guilty but given a lesser sentence.

accord *n.* (uh KORD) agreement; harmony. *The two nations suspended hostilities and reached accord.*

according to Hoyle according to the book or to the highest authority, so-named after card game expert Edmond Hoyle. *We've constructed everything according to Hoyle, so we should be successful.*

accost *vb.* (uh KOST) to approach or greet, especially in an aggressive manner. *Be prepared for every salesman in the store to accost you.*

Achilles' heel *n.* (uh KILL eez HEEL) a metaphor for a serious weakness, from the myth of Achilles, who was invulnerable everywhere except on his heel. *The lack of research and development turned out to be the company's Achilles' heel, as it ultimately had to bow to the competition.*

acid test *n.* any test of value or genuineness, so-named after the jeweler's nitric acid test to determine the authenticity of gold. *The acid test of a good politician is her following through on campaign promises.*

acquiesce *vb.* (AK wee ESS) to yield; to give in. *The opponents of the bill were in the majority, so we decided to acquiesce without a fight.*

acquit *vb.* (uh KWIT) to free or clear one from legal charges. *The jury voted to acquit the defendant.*

acrid *adj.* (AK rid) sharp or bitter in flavor or odor. *The toddler spit out the acrid-tasting vinegar.*

activism *n.* (AK tiv iz um) involvement in a cause; work for political or social change. *His activism in the environmental movement has raised awareness of air pollution.*

acumen *n.* (AK yuh mun) sharp or intelligent judgment. *She had exceptional business acumen and would soon rise to the corporation's top echelon.*

adage *n.* (AD ij) a saying or proverb; a universal truth. *"Honesty is the best policy" is a popular adage.*

adamant *adj.* (AD uh munt) unyielding; refusing to give in. *My brother refused to give me another slice of pizza; no matter how much I begged, he remained adamant.*

adept *adj.* (uh DEPT) highly capable; skilled. *With all forms of carpentry, she was impressively adept.*

adherent *n.* (ad HEER unt) a supporter, of a cause or a person. She was an adherent of the Democratic Party.

ad hoc *adj.* (AD hok) assembled for a specific purpose. *They formed an ad hoc committee to look into the matter.*

ad infinitum *adv.* (ad in fi NITE um) infinitely; on and on forever. *Alarmists are concerned that the human population will continue to grow ad infinitum.*

adjudicate *vb.* (uh JOO di kayt) to judge and settle a legal case. *It requires great patience and intelligence to adjudicate a dispute fairly.*

ad lib *vb.* (AD LIB) to improvise or perform without preparation. *Caught off guard, the congresswoman was forced to ad lib a speech.*

admonish *vb.* (Ad MON ish) to criticize or warn in order to correct errant behavior. *The boys were admonished for playing on the train tracks.*

ad nauseam *adv.* (AD NAWZ ee um) to a sickening degree. *He listed all his awards and accomplishments ad nauseam.*

adroit *adj.* (uh DROYT) highly skilled with one's hands; also mentally agile. *He was particularly adroit at playing scales on the piano.*

adulterate *vb.* (uh DULT uh RAYT) to pollute or make impure. *The protesters warned that the discharge from the planned paper mill would adulterate the nearby river.*

adversary *n.* (AD vur ser ee) opponent; enemy. *The champion boxer pummeled his adversary and won the match by a knockout.*

adverse *adj.* (ad VURS) unfavorable or antagonistic. *The show is cancelled due to adverse weather conditions.*

adversity *n.* (ad VUR sit ee) hardship or highly trying conditions. *In losing several players to injuries, our team has suffered great adversity.*

advocate *n.* (AD vuh kut) 1. a supporter of a cause or person. *He is an advocate of racial equality. —vb.* 2. to support a cause. (AD vuh kayt) *Our congressman, unfortunately, tends to advocate higher taxes.*

aesthetic *adj.* (es THET ik) concerning that which is beautiful or pleasing to the eye. *The artist had an exceptional aesthetic sense, as his work always drew admiration.*

affectation *n.* (AF ek TAY shun) a phony put-on; an act or pretense; a behavior that is unnatural. *Her English accent was an obvious affectation, as she had spent her entire life in New York.*

affidavit *n.* (AF uh DAY vit) a written statement made under oath. *We were required by law to provide an affidavit, which was witnessed by an official of the court.*

affinity *n.* (uh FIN i tee) an attraction or positive feeling toward someone or something, often due to some kinship or sense of similarity. *It's natural to experience an affinity toward one's cousins.*

affluent *adj.* (AFF loo unt) wealthy; rich. *We drove through the affluent side of town and marveled at the beautiful mansions.*

affront *n.* (uh FRUNT) an insult; an offensive remark or action. *Refusing to attend the wedding would be an affront to the bride and groom.*

agenda *n.* (uh JEN duh) a list of things to be done. *I have an extremely busy agenda today.*

agile *adj.* (AJ ul) nimble, alert, and quick. *A World leader must have an especially agile mind.*

agnostic *n.* (ag NOS tik) one who believes that the existence of God cannot be known or proven. *An agnostic doesn't completely eliminate the possibility of a God, as an atheist does; rather, he requires more evidence for believing either way.*

alarmist *n.* (uh LARM ist) one who panics, often unnecessarily, and overreacts to every threat. *It is easy to convince an alarmist that the world will end.*

albatross (around one's neck) a metaphor used to symbolize a burden of guilt or disgrace, derived from the albatross that was shot and hung around the neck of the Mariner in "The Rime of the Ancient Mariner." *The president's scandalous love affairs will remain forever as an albatross around his neck.*

alchemy *n.* (AL kem ee) any apparent magical process, as that of turning base metal into gold, or concocting a formula into a medical cure-all. *Although some people would like to believe in magic, alchemy is clearly a pseudo-science and has no place in the world of modern technology.*

alienate *vb.* (AYL ee un ayt) to estrange; to cause to be emotionally distant. *It's easy to alienate people—just insult them.*

allege *vb.* (uh LEJ) to accuse or assert without proof. We allege that Ralph stole the last doughnut; however, we don't have sufficient proof to convict him.

allusion *n.* (uh LOO zshun) an indirect reference. *By saying that someone has "an albatross around his neck," you're making an allusion to "The Rime of the Ancient Mariner," the original source of the albatross metaphor.*

aloof *adj.* (uh LOOF) distant; remote; withdrawn. *Shawn was unusually aloof and barely said three words to us all night.*

alter ego *n.* another side of one's personality. (Also, a close companion.) *Sociopaths may be quite charming; many of us would be hard-pressed at first to discern their cold-blooded alter egos.*

altruism *n.* (AL troo iz um) unselfish concern for others; assistance to others without desire for gain. *He practiced altruism often by making anonymous donations.*

ambiguous *adj.* (am BIG yoo us) that which can be understood in more than one way and is therefore unclear. *The politician's statements were so ambiguous, we couldn't tell if she wanted to raise taxes or lower them.*

ambivalent *adj.* (am BIV uh lent) having mixed feelings. *We often feel ambivalent about city taxes; on one hand, we want better schools and services, yet on the other, we don't want to have to pay for them.*

amenable *adj.* (uh MEEN uh bul) receptive to; agreeable and willing. *I would be amenable to paying higher taxes, as long as that extra money isn't wasted.*

amiable *adj.* (AYM ee uh bul) friendly and agreeable. *At the party, everyone was in an amiable mood.*

amicable *adj.* (AM i kuh bul) friendly, with goodwill. *The two parties came to an amicable agreement and shook hands.*

amnesty *n.* (AM nest ee) an official pardon. *The political prisoners were given amnesty and released.*

amorphous *adj.* (uh MOR fus) shapeless; undefined. *An amorphous cloud drifted over our heads.*

anachronism *n.* (uh NAK ruh niz um) someone or something that does not fit into its time period; a historical inaccuracy. *A helicopter flown in Victorian times would be a glaring anachronism.*

anarchy *n.* (AN ark ee) the complete absence of law and order; chaos. *A world without government would be a world filled with anarchy.*

androgynous *adj.* (an DROJ uh nus) having characteristics of both sexes. *We couldn't tell if the androgynous rock star was a man or a woman.*

angst *n.* (ANGST) anxious unhappiness. *I'm anticipating my 50th birthday with great angst.*

animated *adj.* (AN uh MAYT id) lively and uninhibited. *It is difficult to become animated with someone until you first break the ice with small talk.*

animosity *n.* (AN uh MOS uh tee) hatred; ill will. *The divorcing couple had too much animosity to solve their differences.*

annotate *vb.* (AN uh tayt) to add notes. *The editor asked the author to annotate his book to make it easier for students to understand.*

annul *vb.* (uh NUL) to nullify or cancel. *The city council voted to annul several outmoded laws.*

anomalous *adj.* (uh NOM uh lus) out of the norm; unusual. *Santa Claus arriving on the fourth of July instead of Christmas would be quite anomalous.*

anomaly *n.* (uh NOM uh lee) an abnormality; a deviation from the norm. *A blizzard in Florida would be considered an anomaly.*

antecedent *n.* (AN ti SEED unt) that which came before. *The antecedent of the compact disk was the eight-track tape.*

antediluvian *adj.* (an ti duh LOO ve un) coming before the biblical flood and therefore very old or antiquated. *The politician's philosophy of "might makes right" was absolutely antediluvian.*

antipathy *n.* (an TIP uh thee) a strong dislike. *Many people feel a certain antipathy toward telephone solicitors.*

antiquated *adj.* (ANT i kwat id) old-fashioned; outmoded or out of date. *The crank style telephone was considered antiquated decades ago.*

anti-Semitism *n.* (AN ti SEM i tiz um) hatred or prejudice toward Jew or Judaism. *Adolf Hitler was history's strongest proponent of anti-Semitism.*

antithesis *n.* (an TITH uh sis) opposite. *The antithesis of love is hate.*

apartheid *n.* (uh PART hite) originally, the policy of racial segregation in South Africa; now, any form of segregation. *A cultural apartheid is dividing inner-city blacks from suburban whites.*

apathy *n.* (AP uh thee) complete lack of interest; indifference. *If we are to defeat political corruption, we must first conquer voter apathy.*

aplomb *n.* (uh PLOM) great poise and confidence. *She hosted the gala with exceptional aplomb.*

apocalypse *n.* (uh POK uh lips) mass destruction or devastation, as a holocaust. *Some seers predict that an apocalypse will occur in the 21st century.*

apocryphal *adj.* (uh POK ruh ful) questionable or strongly suspected to be inauthentic or erroneous. *The celebrity's so-called lost diary turned out to be apocryphal.*

appease *vb.* (uh PEEZ) to pacify or calm. *We bought a doughnut in order to appease the screaming toddler.*

apprehensive *adj.* (AP ri HEN siv) filled with anxiety, especially about the future. *I'm apprehensive about that speech I have to give tomorrow.*

apropos *adv.* (AP ruh POH) appropriate or fitting; timely. *With Arbor Day right around the corner, his speech on tree conservation was apropos.*

arbiter *n.* (ARB i tur) a mediator, negotiator, or judge. *The warring parties needed an outside arbiter to help them settle their differences.*

arbitrary *adj.* (ARB i trair ee) random; by chance or whim. *All of the apple pies were equally delicious, so the judge's decision to award a blue ribbon to Mrs. Feeney was completely arbitrary.*

arbitrate *vb.* (ARB i trayt) to mediate, negotiate, or act as judge. *A disinterested third party was brought in to arbitrate the dispute.*

arcane *adj.* (ar KAYN) mysterious or unknowable to all but a few. *The famous astrophysicist's theories were rather arcane.*

archaic *adj.* (ar KAY ik) outdated, ancient; antiquated. *Hangings and beheadings are an archaic form of criminal punishment.*

ardent *adj.* (AR dent) passionate; fervent. *In the late 1990s, many children became ardent collectors of Beanie Baby toys.*

arduous *adj.* (AR joo us) extremely difficult or laborious. *Shoveling a driveway clean after a blizzard is an arduous task.*

aristocratic *adj.* (uh ris tuh KRAT ik) of nobility or the ruling class. *Many who claim to have lived past lives also claim to have aristocratic bloodlines.*

armchair general *n.* one who strategizes or criticizes the actions of others from the safety of an armchair and without any real-world experience. *The football fan who constantly gripes about his team's plays is a classic armchair general.*

arraign *vb.* (uh RAYN) to formally accuse or charge one of a crime in a court of law. *We plan to arraign the suspect on Friday morning.*

articulate *adj.* (ar TIK yuh lut) highly expressive; verbally proficient. *Lawyers win and lose cases by their verbal skills and thus must always be articulate.*

artifice *n.* (ART uh fis) craftiness; cleverness. *The swindler separated the money from his victims with great artifice.*

aspiration *n.* (AS pur AY shun) a goal or strong desire to achieve something; an ambition. *The young girl had an aspiration to be a great basketball player, and so she practiced every day.*

assiduous *adj.* (uh SID yoo us) diligent; hard-working. *She has assiduous study habits.*

assimilate *vb.* (uh SIM uh layt) to integrate; to make adjustments and fit in. *It took me over a year to fully assimilate to Italian life.*

astute *adj.* (uh STOOT) sharp or shrewd. *When it comes to making a profit on Wall Street, my uncle is particularly astute.*

asymmetrical *adj.* (AY sim ET rik ul) of contrasting or unmatching shape or size. *The building was asymmetrical, with a dome on one side and a boxlike structure on the other.*

atheism *n.* (AY thee iz um) disbelief in God; nontheism. *Atheism is the belief that God is nothing more than an invention of the human imagination.*

atone *vb.* (uh TOHN) to make amends for a sin or a wrongdoing. *The judge made the petty thief atone for his sins by forcing him to perform five hundred hours of community service.*

atrocity *n.* (uh TROSS i tee) an outrageous or monstrous act or behavior. *Countless atrocities will occur in times of war.*

au courant *adj.* (oh koo RAHN) up to date and informed. *The model's fashion decisions were always sharp and au courant.*

audacious *adj.* (aw DAY shus) bold, especially in a way that lacks restraint and may be considered reckless. *The terrorists hatched an audacious plan to blow up the White House.*

auspicious *adj.* (aw SPISH us) favorable; propitious; denoting positive circumstances. *The first warm day of May is an auspicious time to plant a vegetable garden.*

austere *adj.* (aw STEER) severe or somber, in appearance or behavior. Also, plain and unadorned. *The prison's interior was deliberately austere.*

autonomous *adj.* (aw TON uh mus) self-directed; independent. *The island's government required no outside intervention and was completely autonomous.*

avant-garde *n.* (ah vahnt GARD) those involved in developing or using new techniques, technologies, etc., in the arts or other fields. *Those entrepreneurs who started a business over the Internet were once part of an elite avant-garde; now they're in the mainstream.*

avarice *n.* (AV ur iss) an extreme desire for wealth; greed. *His avarice made him risk all of his income at the crap tables, where he quickly lost a small fortune.*

aversion *n.* (uh VUR shun) a strong dislike. *I have an aversion to fried pig's knuckles.*

ax to grind a metaphor for a self-serving motive, especially one that may not be readily apparent to others. *He voted for the amendment not out of the goodness of his heart, as he professed, but because he had an ax to grind and would secretly benefit from the change.*

babe in the woods an innocent or naive person; a helpless person. *When I arrived in New York, I was a babe in the woods.*

backlash *n.* (BAK lash) a reprisal; a consequence from some action. *The congressman's failure to serve the needs of his constituency will result in voter backlash.*

badger *vb.* (BAJ ur) to harass, hound, or nag. *The lawyer was warned not to badger the witness.*

banal *adj.* (buh NAL) dull, especially due to overuse or overfamiliarity. *The editor rejected the author's work because it was trite and banal.*

bane *n.* (BAYN) ruin; cause of destruction. *Pollution is the bane of healthy fish stocks.*

baptism of fire a metaphor for an extremely difficult initiation. *The city experienced a major earthquake; for the new mayor, it was a baptism of fire.*

bargaining chip *n.* a thing of value that can be traded for something of equal value. *In future negotiations, the president will use free trade as a bargaining chip.*

bastion *n.* (BAS chun) a stronghold or place of great fortification. *Around the world, America is considered a great bastion of freedom.*

beachhead *n.* (BEECH hed) a metaphor for the establishment of a base of operations, especially at the shoreline of enemy territory. *The company has established a beachhead in France and has plans to expand its sales base throughout Europe.*

bear by the tail a metaphor for a very trying or harrowing predicament; the "tail grabber" either suffers great turmoil (being dragged through the underbrush), or risks being bitten or consumed (by the bear) if he lets go. *With his vote to outlaw dancing on school grounds, the principal has grabbed the proverbial bear by the tail.*

beard the lion to confront something or someone with great daring. *By taking our complaints directly to the mayor, we would beard the lion in his own den.*

bearish *adj.* (BAIR ish) pessimistic, particularly concerning the stock market. *The market on Wall Street turned bearish today as the Dow Industrial Average dropped nearly 100 points.*

beat a dead horse to argue or debate a point that has already been discussed or settled. *After refusing for the fourth time to give me a raise, my boss told me not to ask any more; I was beating a dead horse.*

beguile *vb.* (bi GUYL) to deceive, trick, or mislead. *The swindler will easily beguile you with his charm.*

behemoth *n.* (bi HEE muth) anything gigantic. *The company started as a mom and pop store but is now a franchising behemoth.*

beleaguer *vb.* (bi LEE gur) to harass or plague. *the IRS tends to beleaguer only those who attempt to cheat on their tax returns.*

bellicose *adj.* (BEL i KOHS) pugnacious, quarrelsome. *The diplomats were worried about the dictator's bellicose manner.*

belligerent *adj.* (buh LIJ ur unt) aggressive; looking for a fight. *The dictator's belligerent manner offended everyone.*

bells and whistles extras, accessories, options, or luxury items. *We bought a new computer with all the latest bells and whistles.*

bellwether *n.* (BEL WETH ur) any person or thing in a position of leadership, sometimes used as an indicator of where the followers will be headed. *Among computer companies, IBM has a long history as a bellwether.*

benchmark *n.* (BENCH mark) any standard by which others are measured. *The auto maker's newest model will serve as a technological benchmark for the competition.*

Benedict Arnold *n.* any traitorous person; coined after the American Revolution general. *Roger pulled a Benedict Arnold and went to work for the competition.*

benevolent *adj.* (bug NEV uh lent) disposed to doing good; charitable; kindly. *He was a benevolent man who gave more than half of his fortune away.*

benign *adj.* (bi NIYN) of a harmless nature. *It was a relief to learn that my tumor was benign.*

between the devil and the deep blue sea in a very difficult position; being forced to choose one of two equally unpleasant situations; similar to "between a rock and a hard place." *I'm between the devil and the deep blue sea; if I take the job in San Diego, I'll have to move, but if I don't take the job, I'll be out of work.*

bigot *adj.* (BIG ut) one who is intolerant of those of a different race, religion, political party, or sexual orientation. *Archie Bunker was a classic bigot; he looked down his nose at everyone who wasn't a white, heterosexual male.*

bigotry *n.* (BIG uh tree) intolerance for those of a different race, religion, political affiliation, or sexual orientation. *His discrimination against his homosexual neighbors was pure bigotry.*

bilk *vb.* (BILK) to swindle or cheat. *John was arrested for trying to bilk the insurance company out of a large settlement.*

black market *n.* an illegal or underground market. *The imported goods were purchased illegally through the black market.*

blasé *adj.* (blah ZAY) nonchalant, cool, unfazed. *The director was surprisingly blasé about winning an Academy Award.*

blasphemy *n.* (BLAS fuh mee) any irreverence toward God or religion. *During the Inquisition, any act of blasphemy could get you a date with the torture chamber.*

blatant *adj.* (BLAYT unt) loud or offensive. *The fan was ejected from the stands for his blatant cursing of the opposing team.*

bleeding heart *n.* one who is easily moved by sob stories, sympathizes excessively, and feels obliged to offer assistance, even when it may be counterproductive to do so. *If you believe wholeheartedly in every social welfare program ever invented, you are a bleeding heart.*

blithe *adj.* (BLITHE) lighthearted and unconcerned. *It is difficult to darken the blithe spirit of children on the last day of school.*

bombastic *adj.* (bom BAS tik) of speech or writing, pompous. *The student's speech was full of big words and sentiments but was highly bombastic.*

bon vivant *n.* (BON vee VAHN) one who savors fine food and drink and has developed refined tastes. *She was a bon vivant who loved to sample foreign dishes and fine wines.*

bourgeois *adj.* (boor ZHWAW) of the conventional middle class. *His drive to keep up financially with his neighbors was thoroughly bourgeois.*

boycott *vb.* (BOY kot) to deliberately stop purchasing something, as a means of protest. *The environmental group planned to boycott the products of all of the companies who polluted the air.*

brazen *adj.* (BRAY zun) bold in a rude way; impudent. *Everyone was shocked at the brazen remarks the protesters made to the president.*

brevity *n.* (BREV i tee) conciseness; the quality of being brief and to the point. *We only have thirty minutes to make our pitch, so brevity is paramount.*

broach *vb.* (BROACH) to open a topic for discussion. *At the meeting, we must broach the issue of higher taxes with delicacy.*

brouhaha *n.* (BROO haha) an uproar. *The finding of corruption caused a brouhaha in the Senate.*

brusque *adj.* (BRUSK) blunt, curt, or rough in manner. *The sales clerk was tired and had had a bad day, so she was understandably brusque with us.*

bureaucracy *n.* (byoo ROK ruh see) any government administration, particularly that which is inefficient. *To satisfy government bureaucracy, we had to sign seventeen different forms.*

burgeon *vb.* (BUR jun) to grow and proliferate. *With interest rates kept low, the economy tends to burgeon.*

cache *n.* (KASH) a stockpile or hiding place for the storage of food or other items. *We built a food cache up on stilts so the bears couldn't reach it.*

cacophonous *adj.* (kuh KOF uh nus) jarring or unpleasant sounding. *The rock band always made a cacophonous racket whenever they tuned their instruments.*

cagey *adj.* (KAY jee) very careful and shrewd and difficult to fool. *A fox is too cagey to be easily caught in a trap.*

cajole *vb.* (kuh JOHL) to persuade through flattery or repeated lighthearted requests. *A great salesman knows how to cajole his customers into making a purchase.*

calibrate *vb.* (KAL i brayt) to adjust for accuracy. *The butcher was required by law to calibrate his scales.*

callous *adj.* (KAL us) hard and unfeeling. *The soldier's rough treatment of the prisoner was particularly callous.*

callow *adj.* (KAL oh) immature; juvenile. *The teenager was quick to judge others but was too callow to see his own faults.*

camaraderie *n.* (kahm RAH duh ree) friendly rapport. *After winning the game, the team shared a great camaraderie.*

candor *n.* (KAN dur) complete honesty; frankness. *In all candor, I think your haircut looks goofy.*

can of worms, open a to bring up a difficult or complex problem. Similar to "open a Pandora's box." *Dress codes? Let's not open that can of worms tonight.*

capitalism *n.* (KAP i tuh liz um) an economic system allowing private citizens to pursue their own enterprises for private gain; the free enterprise system. *America's strength is due not only to its diversity but to its system of capitalism.*

capitulate *vb.* (kuh PICH yoo layt) to give in or acquiesce; to agree to terms. *It was a long battle, but the opposing party was finally persuaded to capitulate.*

capricious *adj.* (kuh PRISH us) unpredictable; by whim. *Maine has some of the most capricious weather in the country.*

carcinogenic *adj.* (kar sin uh JEN ik) cancer-causing. *Many of the compounds in cigarette smoke have been found to be carcinogenic.*

caricature *n.* (KAIR uh ku chur) a drawing or depiction of someone or something with humorously exaggerated features. *Cartoonists love to draw caricatures of famous politicians.*

carnage *n.* (KAR nij) a massacre or bloody slaughter. *The carnage of World War II was horrific.*

carnal *adj.* (KAR nul) pleasurable in a physical and especially sexual way as opposed to a spiritual way. *He was secretly attracted to his neighbor but was careful to keep his carnal desires to himself.*

carnivorous *adj.* (kar NIV uh rus) flesh-eating. *Lions and tigers are carnivorous animals.*

carte blanche *n.* (KART BLAHNSH) a granting of power or privilege to do as one pleases, as giving one a blank check. *As for spending money on research and development, the head of the laboratory was given carte blanche.*

cartel *n.* (kar TEL) a group of businesses that pool their power to control production and prices of products. *The oil cartel withheld a percentage of surplus oil until the price per barrel increased.*

Cassandra *n.* (kuh SAN druh) from the mythological character of the same name, one who predicts disaster and doom but is disregarded. *I don't want to be accused of being a Cassandra, but I think the stock market is overdue for a big crash.*

castles in the air/castles in Spain fanciful daydreams or goals too impractical to be realized. *"John," my boss said, "your idea is too impractical to work. You're building castles in the air again."*

catalyst *n.* (KAT uh list) an agent, thing, or person that gets something started, makes something happen, or facilitates or expedites these processes. *John Muir was a catalyst for the national conservation movement.*

catbird seat, in the sitting high and mighty; a position of power. *With its economy humming along, America is enjoying at least a temporary perch in the catbird seat.*

catch-22 *n.* an unwinnable situation; named after the novel of the same title. *I couldn't get the job without experience, but I can't get experience without the job; it's a classic catch-22.*

catharsis *n.* (kuh THAR sis) a cleansing of the soul; a release of great inner turmoil. *Camping in the desert for a week relieved my stress and brought about a great catharsis.*

caucus *n.* (KAW kus) a meeting or assembly, especially one formed to choose candidates or discuss a specific political issue. *We held a caucus to register our votes for political candidates.*

cause célèbre *n.* (KAWZ say LEB ruh) a widely discussed issue or controversy. *The news networks are always on the lookout to uncover the next cause célèbre.*

caustic *adj.* (KAWS tik) cutting, burning, and corrosive, as acid. *The fumes are caustic, so be sure to wear protective clothing. His caustic remarks hurt my feelings.*

cautionary tale *n.* an incident, event, or story that serves as an illustration or a warning of a hazard. *The Great Depression serves as a cautionary tale to all stock market investors.*

cavalier *adj.* (kav uh LEER) arrogantly indifferent or nonchalant. *His attitude toward the discipline of his spoiled children was cavalier; he just didn't seem to give a damn.*

caveat *n.* (KA vee aht) a warning or caution. *The police officer issued a firm caveat: either move along or be arrested for loitering.*

caveat emptor (KA vee aht EM tur) Latin term for "let the buyer beware." *When shopping over the Internet, caveat emptor.*

celibate *adj.* (SELL uh but) not sexually active; sexually abstinent. *With all of the sexually transmitted dis-*

eases out there, some think it's a good idea to remain celibate until marriage.

cerebral *adj.* (suh REE brul) pertaining to the intellect or the brain. *Some people have a more cerebral focus than an athletic one.*

c'est la vie (say lah VEE) French term for "that's life" or "such is life." *Today I struck out three times, then on the way home from the game I got a flat tire on my bike! Oh well, c'est la vie.*

chagrin *n.* (shuh GRIN) a feeling of embarrassment, shame, or annoyed unease. *I suffered only mild chagrin at noticing that my shirt was on inside-out.*

chameleon *n.* (kuh MEE lyun) one who changes or has the ability to change quickly, so-named after the color-changing lizard. *Mary is such a chameleon; I never know from one day to the next which fashion trend she is going to follow.*

champion *n.* (CHAMP ee un) a proponent, advocate or backer of some cause or person. *Martin Luther King was a champion of equal rights.*

charisma *n.* (kuh RIZ muh) an aura of great power and charm. *Great political leaders and movie stars usually share a common trait: charisma.*

charlatan *n.* (SHAR luh tun) one who professes to have great knowledge or credentials but does not; a quack; an imposter. *The charlatan tried to pass himself off as a physician, but we knew his university degrees were fraudulent.*

chaste *adj.* (CHAYST) pure, upright, moral. Also, virginal. *Nuns living in the convent were expected to be chaste.*

chastise *vb.* (CHAS tiyz) to punish one either physically or with harsh criticism. *The young boy was chastized for swearing in church.*

chauvinism *n.* (SHO vin izum) blind devotion to one's own kind and contempt for those of a different sex, race, religion, etc. *After seven years of excluding men from her company, she was accused of chauvinism.*

chicanery *n.* (shi KAY nuh ree) deception; trickery. *After my wallet disappeared, I began to suspect some form of chicanery.*

chimera *n.* (kye MIR uh) a mythological or imaginary monster made up of unmatching parts, as a goat, lion, and serpent. *By merging the three companies, they created something of a chimera.*

chronic *adj.* (KRON ik) long-term or recurrent. *I've had a chronic cough for nearly six months.*

chutzpah *n.* (HOOTS puh) nerve; guts; boldness. *You need great chutzpah to publicly challenge the president.*

circuitous *adj.* (sur KYOO i tus) roundabout; indirect. *We took a circuitous and therefore much longer path to the pond.*

circumspect *adj.* (SUR kum SPEKT) cautious; prudent. *It's always a good idea to remain circumspect around porcupines.*

circumstantial *adj.* (sur kum STAN shul) incidental or insignificant. *To convict most criminals, you must gather more than circumstantial evidence.*

circumvent *vb.* (SUR kum vent) to get around, avoid, skirt; to bypass. *We penciled in a route that would circumvent the alligator-filled swamp.*

clairvoyant *adj.* (klair VOY unt) having a sixth sense or psychic powers. *The woman claimed to be clairvoyant; that is, she could read our minds and would prove it if we paid her ten dollars.*

clandestine *adj.* (klan DES tin) in secret of undercover, as an illicit enterprise or act of espionage. *The unlucky children accidentally stumbled upon a clandestine assembly of witches.*

claptrap *n.* (KLAP TRAP) pretentious or grandstanding speech or writing intended to get applause or attention. *The politician played to the crowd by spewing his vacuous claptrap.*

clemency *n.* (KLEM un see) an act or gesture of mercy for forgiveness. *In a show of clemency, the pope embraced the thief and then sat him down for a long talk.*

clique *n.* (KLIK) a group of like-minded individuals who exclude those who are different. *High school society is composed of numerous cliques, from jocks to intellectuals to nerds.*

cloistered *adj.* (KLOYS turd) secluded or sequestered from others. *Monks live a cloistered lifestyle.*

coalesce *vb.* (koh uh LESS) to fuse, commingle, or merge to form one body. *Shake the constituent* *ingredients of a salad dressing and they will quickly coalesce.*

coalition *n.* (KOH uh ISH un) an alliance; a union. *The environmentalists formed a coalition to fight industrial pollution.*

coerce *vb.* (koh URS) to force by intimidation, threats, etc. *The older boys tried to coerce the young ones into breaking windows.*

cogent *adj.* (KOH junt) convincing *He gave a very cogent argument.*

coherent *adj.* (ko HEER unt) clear, intelligible; lucid. *The drunk was barely coherent.*

collusion *n.* (kuh LOO zhun) a conspiracy. *The criminals worked in collusion to rob the midtown bank.*

comme ci, comme ça (KUM SEE KUM SAH) French term for "so-so," or "not one way or the other." *When I asked my wife how she felt about the president following the scandal, she said, "Eh, comme ci, comme ça."*

commiserate *vb.* (kuh MIZ uh RAYT) to feel sorry for or sympathize with another. *During funerals, the bereaved commiserate together.*

compel *vb.* (kum PEL) to force; to move one to action. *The threat of a speeding ticket compels most people to follow the speed limit.*

complacent *adj.* (kum PLAY sunt) smug and self-satisfied; unworried. *Teams who enter into the championship with a complacent attitude will likely lose.*

complicity *adj.* (kum PLIS i tee) participation in a wrongful act. *The accomplice was sentenced for his complicity in the robbery and will spend five years in jail.*

compulsion *n.* (kum PUL shun) a strong force or drive. *The kleptomaniac suffers from a compulsion to shoplift.*

compulsory *adj.* (kum PUL suh ree) mandatory; required. *Taking an algebra course is compulsory.*

compunction *n.* (kum PUNK shun) the mental discomfort caused by conscience. *The sociopath kicked his cat but felt little compunction for it.*

conceit *n.* (kun SEET) overblown and unjustified self-esteem; egotism; arrogance. *He was so full of conceit, he automatically assumed he was the most intelligent man in the room.*

conciliatory *adj.* (kin SIL ee uh tor ee) friendly and placatory; willing to make amends or give in to achieve peace. *When paced with possible criminal charges, the brawlers quickly turned conciliatory.*

concise *adj.* (kun SISE) brief and to the point. *When writing a letter of complaint, it pays to be concise.*

concur *vb.* (kun KUR) to agree or arrive at an agreement. *The tax cuts proposed by the Republicans made so much sense that the Democrats were forced to concur.*

condescend *vb.* (KON di SEND) to talk down to someone or speak with someone judged as an "inferior" in a superior manner. *I respect my professor, but sometimes when I disagree with her, she condescends, and I can't stand that.*

condone *vb.* (kun DOHN) to forgive or overlook a wrongdoing. *We must never condone the taking of hostages, no matter what the rationale may be.*

conducive *adj.* (kun DOO siv) that which facilitates, leads to, or helps to bring about. *Good nutrition is conducive to optimum health.*

congenial *adj.* (kun JEEN yul) friendly, especially when others are compatible and have similar interests and tastes. *We all had much in common, which made for a very congenial atmosphere at the dinner table.*

congenital *adj.* (kun JEN i tull) that which exists before or from birth. *Sadly, the toddler was found to have a congenital heart defect.*

conjecture *n.* (kun JEK chur) speculation based on inference; guesswork. *That aliens exist on other planets is merely conjecture; nobody knows for sure.*

connive *vb.* (kuh NIVE) to collude or plot. *They were born thieves who could be counted on while in prison to connive and conspire.*

connoisseur *n.* (KON uh SUR) an authority or expert. *Our local wine connoisseur uses more than forty different words and terms to describe the taste of wines.*

consecrate *vb.* (KON suh KRAYT) to make sacred or holy or set apart as such. *The priest is scheduled to consecrate the shrine this afternoon.*

consensus *n.* (kun SEN sus) an agreement by all. *The assembly finally reached a consensus and voted to pass the resolution.*

conservative *adj.* (kun SURV uh tiv) traditional in values. *My father believed in a conservative brand of politics because he disliked progress or change of any kind.*

conspicuous *adj.* (kun SPIK yoo us) glaringly obvious; that which stands out. *Wearing a Lone Ranger mask to the supermarket will make you rather conspicuous.*

conspiracy *n.* (kun SPEER uh see) a secret group effort to commit a wrongdoing. *After the assassination, the FBI worked to uncover those involved in the conspiracy.*

consummate *adj.* (kon SUM it) accomplished; perfect. *It was no wonder all her albums sold millions of copies; she was the consummate vocalist.*

contentious *adj.* (kun TEN shus) argumentative; quarrelsome. *The contentious couple would likely solve their differences by going their separate ways.*

contingent *adj.* (kun TIN junt) subject to. We'll go to the beach, contingent upon how hot it gets.

contrite *adj.* (kun TRITE) apologetic; sorry. *It is easy to forgive someone when they're contrite.*

contrived *adj.* (kun TRIVED) overly planned, resulting in a forced or unnatural effect. *His play was replete with unbelievable coincidences; it was simply too contrived to be believed.*

conundrum *n.* (kuh NUN drum) a puzzle; a baffling problem. *Protecting the environment while keeping factories humming has long been a political conundrum.*

convivial *adj.* (kun VIV ee ul) social and fond of the party life. *The convivial party-goers performed the conga around the guest of honor.*

copious *adj.* (KOH pee us) plentiful; abounding. *The old dowser claimed to have found a copious water supply.*

cornerstone *n.* (KORN ur stohn) a vital or most vital element. *The right to vote is a cornerstone of every democracy.*

corroborate *vb.* (kuh ROB uh RAYT) to substantiate; to offer supportive information. *When putting forth a new scientific theory, it pays to have others corroborate your findings.*

coup *n.* (KOO) a brilliant move or action. *The chess champion lost suddenly with a coup by the challenger.*

coup d'état *n.* (koo day TAH) an overthrow of a ruler or government, especially by a small group. *The dictator was forced to abdicate his position after a decisive coup d'état by his opposition.*

covenant *n.* (KUV uh nunt) a contractual or binding agreement. *The community enforced a covenant restricting fences over six feet in height.*

covert *adj.* (koh VURT) secret; undercover. *The spy carried out a covert operation.*

coy *adj.* (KOY) shy or flirtatiously shy; demure. *Her coy gazes attracted the attention of the boys.*

crass *adj.* (KRASS) crude and indelicate. *We were offended by her crass remarks.*

credence *n.* (KREE dens) belief that something is true. *I don't give psychics much credence; if they could really predict the future they'd all be millionaires.*

crème de la crème (KREM duh luh KREM) French term for the "cream of the cream," or the best of the best. *All the desserts were delicious, but the chocolate cake was the crème de la crème.*

crescendo *n.* (kruh SHEN doh) an increase in intensity and accompanying climax. *The orchestra played a near-deafening crescendo.*

critical mass *n.* a metaphor used to illustrate a crisis point; the state of any problem that has grown unchecked and threatens to explode. The metaphor originates from the minimum amount of fissionable material needed to cause a nuclear explosion. *Don't wait for environmental problems to reach critical mass; do something about them now.*

cross the Rubicon to take some critical action that will result in great consequences, from which there is no turning back. Originating from the crossing of the Rubicon by Julius Caesar and his troops in 49 B.C. *By permanently giving up its electronics division, the company has crossed the Rubicon into uncharted terrain.*

cryptic *adj.* (KRIP tik) mysterious; secret; concealed. *The spies sent cryptic messages to each other.*

curry favor to win one over through flattery. *Politicians curry favor with voters by telling them how wonderful they and their home towns are.*

cursory *adj.* (KUR suh ree) performed superficially and without much attention to detail. *The clerk made a cursory inspection of her nails and then promptly started chewing on them.*

curt *adj.* (KURT) brief or abrupt to the point of being considered impolite. *The clerk was so curt and unfriendly that we decided to take our business elsewhere.*

cut the Gordian knot to solve a convoluted problem quickly. Originating from the legendary knot tied by King Gordius as a challenge to would-be conquerors of Asia Minor in 400 B.C. and cut by Alexander the Great. *The mayor cut the Gordian knot of cleaning up air pollution by simply restricting the number of cars on the roads.*

cutting edge *n.* the forefront; the vanguard. *The company is on the cutting edge of computer innovation.*

cynical *adj.* (SIN ik ul) prone to questioning the true motives of others; distrustful and skeptical. *The ex-convict claimed to have a purely altruistic reason for raising money for charity, but his parole officer was cynical.*

dark horse *n.* one who is little-known and not expected to win but may take people by surprise; an underdog. *The candidate is a dark horse, hardly known outside of his home state and is not expected to win many votes.*

dauntless *adj.* (DAWNT less) bold and unafraid. *In times of war, the dauntless and aggressive general would be difficult to stop.*

debacle *n.* (di BAH kul) a terrible failure, disaster or collapse. *Expecting a debacle on Wall Street, Mary cashed in all of her stocks and invested the money in bonds.*

debilitate *vb.* (di BIL i TAYT) to cripple or handicap. *Some sports injuries debilitate more than others, but broken bones tend to take the longest to heal.*

debonair *adj.* (deb uh NARE) graciously friendly and smooth; suave. *A lifetime of social polishing had made the prince particularly debonair.*

decadent *adj.* (DEK uh dunt) designating unrestrained indulgence leading to deterioration or decay. *Her decadent lifestyle will eventually prove her undoing.*

decorum *n.* (di KOR um) proper manners and conduct, as expected during a formal occasion. *A certain decorum is expected at funerals, so please restrain your children.*

defame *vb.* (di FAYM) to undermine the reputation of another through slander or libel. *If this newspaper defames me one more time, I will sue for libel.*

deference *n.* (DEF ur uns) the yielding of one to another, out of respect or obligation; submission. *In deference to the company, I stated only positive things about the CEO.*

definitive *adj.* (di FIN uh tiv) authoritative, conclusive. *The famous English professor wrote the definitive guide to good grammar.*

deft *adj.* (DEFT) highly skilled. *The nurse reassured me that the surgeon was particularly deft in removing tonsils.*

defunct *adj.* (di FUNGT) no longer operating or existing; out of business. *The shoe repair business that once operated on Main Street is now, sadly, defunct.*

déjà vu *n.* (day zhah VOO) the haunting feeling that one has seen or experienced the same thing before. *The conviction that I had visited the old house before was only déjà vu; in fact, I'd never been to the place in my life.*

deleterious *adj.* (del uh TEER ee us) harmful; damaging. *Overwatering may have a deleterious effect on your houseplants.*

delude *vb.* (du LOOD) to deceive; to fool. *I like to delude myself into thinking that I'm in perfect shape, when I know I'm really twenty pounds overweight.*

delusion *n.* (di LOO szhun) a false belief. *Thinking he was the greatest human who ever lived, my boss was suffering from delusions of grandeur.*

demagogue *n.* (DEM uh GAWG) a politician who panders to the whims and emotions of the voters in order to win them over. *He was a demagogue who told the voters only what they wanted to hear, not what they needed to hear.*

democracy *n.* (de MOK ru see) a government by and for the people. *In a democracy, the people get to vote on who will lead them.*

democratic *adj.* (dem uh KRAT ik) by and for the people *The democratic way to choose a leader is to vote.*

demoralize *vb.* (di MOR uh lize) to strip of confidence; to dishearten. *The loss of their star player served to demoralize the team.*

demure *adj.* (di MYOOR) shy or quiet; also, affecting shyness. *I was attracted to the demure girl who stood in the corner by herself.*

deplorable *adj.* (di PLOR uh bul) terrible; grievous. *After the party, our house was in deplorable condition.*

depose *vb.* (di POZ) to remove from power. *The citizens called for the authorities to depose the prince.*

deride *vb.* (di RIDE) to ridicule. *The wiseguys liked to stand at the edge of the dance floor and deride everyone's dance style.*

de rigueur *adj.* (de ree GUHR) necessary to fulfill the rules of etiquette or fashion. *Thankfully, nose rings are no longer considered de rigueur.*

derision *n.* (duh RI szhun) hostile ridicule. *His bid to raise taxes in order to purchase an ice-skating rink was met with derision.*

derivative *adj.* (duh RIV uh tiv) taken or borrowed from something else. *His play was highly derivative and borrowed liberally from Woody Allen.*

dernier cri *n.* (DAIR nee ay CREE) the latest thing; hip. *The dernier cri of fashion is now little, boxlike hats.*

derogatory *adj.* (di ROG uh TOHR ee) disparaging; insulting. Any more derogatory remarks about my cooking and you'll be making your own dinner.

desecrate *vb.* (DES uh krayt) to disrespect that which is sacred or holy; to profane. *The thugs planned to desecrate the holy shrine by spraypainting it with grafitti.*

despondent *adj.* (di SPON dunt) filled with sadness and despair. *After the home team lost the game, we gave the despondent players a pat on the back for a good try.*

despot *n.* (DES put) a dictator; an autocrat. *The despot rules with an iron fist.*

destitute *adj.* (DES ti TOOT) extremely impoverished. *The destitute couple begged for dimes on the street corner.*

détente *n.* (day TAHNT) a relief or easing of tensions or hostilities between nations. *We were greatly heartened by the promise of détente between the two warring leaders.*

deterrent *n.* (de TUR unt) that which hinders, blocks, or stops. *If you're worried about burglars, a tall, barbed wire fence is a good deterrent.*

detrimental *adj.* (det ri MENT ul) damaging. *Smoking is detrimental to your health.*

devil's advocate *n.* one who represents an opposing side simply for the sake of argument or as an exercise. *I don't really believe that everyone should own a gun, but in debate class I like to play the devil's advocate.*

diabolical *adj.* (di yuh BOL uh kul) of the devil; fiendish. *Beware of diabolical powers unleashed on Halloween.*

diatribe *n.* (DYE uh tribe) a critical denunciation. *My editor wrote a long-winded diatribe criticizing not only my article but also my viewpoint.*

dichotomy *n.* (di KOT uh mee) a division comprising two opposing viewpoints. *There is a broad dichotomy of opinion between the sexes.*

didactic *adj.* (dye DAK tik) educational, particularly concerning morals. *The Sunday school teacher put on a didactic skit about stealing.*

dilapidated *adj.* (di LAP i dayt ud) run-down; falling apart. *The next stiff wind would probably knock down the old, dilapidated building.*

dilettante *adj.* (DIL i TAHNT) one who dabbles in the arts or has an amateurish knowledge of a field. *I love poetry, but when it comes to writing it, I'm strictly a dilettante.*

diligent *adj.* (DIL uh junt) hard-working and persevering. *She was a diligent worker who would not quit until the job was done right.*

diplomacy *n.* (di PLOH muh see) the act and skill of cultivating and maintaining good relationships with others; tact, in international or personal relations. *The* *highest form of diplomacy must be employed to prevent international hostilities from exploding into war.*

disaffected *adj.* (dis uh FEK tid) full of resentment; alienated. *Disaffected, the laid-off workers staged a demonstration against the company.*

disarming *adj.* (dis ARM ing) hostility-reducing, often through charm. *The beauty pageant winner's smile was disarming and tended to dampen any hostility felt toward her by the losers.*

discerning *adj.* (di SUR ning) highly perceptive; sharp in judgment. *The judge cast a discerning eye over the defendants.*

disclaimer *n.* (dis KLAYM ur) a statement that releases one from legal liability. *Manufacturers of dangerous products must issue public disclaimers in order to protect themselves from lawsuits.*

disconcerted *adj.* (DIS kun SURT ed) disturbed; upset. *Dogs are often disconcerted by the sounds of an approaching thunderstorm.*

discord *n.* (DIS kord) conflict and disagreement. *There was a great discord among the panelists as the debate began.*

discreet *adj.* (dis KREET) unobtrusive, tactful, and low-key. *If you must burp at the dinner table, please be discreet.*

disdain *n.* (dis DAYN) contempt. *I feel nothing but disdain toward those who abuse animals.*

disillusioned *adj.* (DIS i LOO szhund) disturbed by a previously unseen reality. *With so much dishonesty and scandal, it is easy to become disillusioned with politics.*

disparage *vb.* (dis PAIR ij) to criticize and put down. *If you plan to disparage someone in print, be careful not to slander or libel.*

disparity *n.* (dis PAIR uh tee) a state of inequality. *There is too often a disparity between what one says and what one does.*

disseminate *vb.* (di SEM uh nayt) to distribute or broadcast. *We will disseminate the information as soon as it comes off the press.*

dissension *n.* (di SEN shun) disagreement. *There is often great dissension between Democrats and Republicans.*

dissertation *n.* (DI sur TAY shun) a lengthy and involved academic report or treatise, based on original research; a thesis. *Writing a dissertation is a requirement of one seeking a doctorate.*

dissident *n.* (DIS uh dent) one who disagrees. *The dictator threatened to throw all dissidents in prison.*

dissipate *vb.* (DIS uh PAYT) to thin or peter out; to exhaust. *The snow is finally beginning to dissipate.*

dissuade *vb.* (dis WAYD) to talk out of; to discourage. *Unless you're in top physical condition, I would try to dissuade you from climbing Mount Everest.*

divest *vb.* (di VEST) to strip or remove; to sell off one's investment. *With Wall Street turning decidedly bearish, it might be a good time to divest oneself of stocks.*

docile *adj.* (DOS ul) gentle; tame and easy to handle or train. *Thankfully, my horse was docile and never bucked.*

dogged *adj.* (DOG id) tenacious and persistent; stubborn. *To finish a marathon, you must be absolutely dogged.*

dogma *n.* (DOG muh) a strong belief, principle, moral, or set of morals. *The zealous are often blind to their own causes and dogmas.*

dogmatic *adj.* (dog MAT ik) clinging tenaciously to one's own beliefs and refusing to consider other viewpoints. *It's never wise to be dogmatic; always question your own beliefs and those of others.*

dormant *adj.* (DOOR munt) not active; in a state of sleep. *The dormant volcano hadn't erupted for more than two hundred years.*

double-blind test *n.* a medical test in which neither the administrators nor the test subjects know who is receiving placebos (sham treatments) and who is receiving real medicine, the object of which is to measure efficacy without influence of bias. *The university conducted a double-blind test on eighty-three subjects and discovered, to their horror, that placebos worked just as well as their experimental medicine.*

double entendre *n.* (DUB ul on TON druh) an ambiguous statement that can be understood in either a perfectly innocent way or in a naughty way. *The comedian was restricted from swearing and telling* *blatantly offensive jokes, so he used a lot of subtle double entendres to get laughs.*

double standard *n.* (dub ul STAN derd) a social standard that is followed unequally between sexes, races, groups, etc. *It's quite acceptable for a woman to wear a man's suit at work, but not for a man to wear a dress—a double standard.*

dour *adj.* (DOWR) gloomy, stern; sullen. *My boss is a dour man who rarely smiles.*

draconian *adj.* (dray KOHN ee un) extremely harsh. Originating from Draco, an Athenian lawmaker who, around 620 B.C., implemented laws in Greece that too frequently punished criminals and wrongdoers by death. *The despot has implemented a draconian set of punishments for anyone who commits treason.*

droll *adj.* (DROHL) oddly comical. *The comic's droll delivery of a New England accent had audience members snickering.*

dubious *adj.* (DOO be us) questionable; doubtful. *The items we purchased through the mail were of dubious quality.*

duplicity *adj.* (doo PLISS i tee) behavior that is two-faced or deceptive. *Over time his duplicity became obvious because he too frequently said one thing but did another.*

dyed-in-the-wool *adj.* (DYED in the WULL) to the very core; through and through. *I am a dyed-in-the-wool-conservationist.*

dynamic *adj.* (dye NAM ik) active; highly spirited and powerful. *We're looking for a dynamic personality for our managerial position.*

earnest *adj.* (UR nist) serious and genuine. *We made an earnest attempt to clean the basement.*

echelon *n.* (ESH uh lon) one level of a multilevel organization. *We took our complaints to the company's highest echelon, the office of the CEO.*

eclectic *adj.* (i KLEK tik) from diverse sources. *His collection of CDs was highly eclectic and included everything from pop to New Age.*

effeminate *adj.* (i FEM uh nit) feminine or unmanly. *Effeminate boys may be picked on unfairly.*

efficacy *n.* (EF uh kuh see) effectiveness. *The efficacy and safety of the new drug left much to be desired.*

effusive *adj.* (i FYOO siv) pouring out great emotion; gushing. *It's nice to be complimented, but Aunt Mary's effusive hugging and screaming over my little clay sculpture was a bit much.*

egalitarian *adj.* (i GAL uh TAIR ee un) practicing or believing in equality for everyone. *It's always wise to elect someone who has a strongly egalitarian philosophy.*

egocentric *adj.* (ee go SEN trik) seeing oneself at the center of everything; selfish. *He was so egocentric he actually believed the football players in the huddle were talking about him.*

egregious *adj.* (i GREE jus) extremely conspicuous or outrageous. *I'm sick of your egregious lies.*

elicit *vb.* (i LIS it) to bring out. *The comedian's clever pantomime was designed to elicit applause, and it did.*

eloquent *adj.* (EL uh KWUNT) articulate; persuasive through speech. *She was an eloquent speaker who could outrage or tickle with a single sentence.*

emaciated *adj.* (i MAY shee ay tid) extremely lean, as from starvation. *It had been an extremely difficult winter, and most of the deer were badly emaciated.*

emancipate *vb.* (i MAN suh payt) to free. *Lincoln's desire was to emancipate the nation's slaves.*

emasculate *vb.* (i MASS kyuh layt) to weaken; to strip one of power. *She liked to emasculate men by publicly humiliating them.*

embargo *n.* (em BAR go) a government prohibition on a specific imported good or goods. *As a punishment against inequitable trade practices, the president called for an embargo on all Japanese radios.*

embellish *vb.* (em BELL ish) to exaggerate or embroider. *It was difficult to distinguish fact from fiction because Uncle Joe tended to embellish his fishing stories.*

embezzle *adj.* (em BEZ ul) to steal, especially when in a trusted position. *The accountant tried to embezzle money from the charity but failed.*

embroider *vb.* (em BROY dur) to exaggerate; to embellish. *Uncle Joe liked to embroider his fish stories, and he could be counted on to add completely fictitious details.*

eminent *adj.* (EM i nunt) distinguished, important, high-ranking. *Mary Smith, an eminent authority on economics, is predicting a worldwide recession.*

empathy *n.* (EM puh thee) understanding of another's feelings, especially through having similar experiences or circumstances. *I've had many pets through the years, so I have great empathy for anyone who has lost one.*

emphatic *adj.* (em FAT ik) with great emphasis. *Her directive was emphatic: no more spitball fights during working hours.*

empirical *adj.* (em PEER i kul) based on real-world experience or observation, not theory. *A mountain of empirical evidence supports the existence of evolution.*

empower *vb.* (em POW ur) to grant or invest with power. *Empower people with a good education and they will accomplish great things.*

emulate *vb.* (EM yoo layt) to copy or model oneself after. *If you're going to play basketball, you'd do well to emulate the stars of the NBA.*

enamored *adj.* (i NAM urd) in love; charmed. *I'm enamored of the farm country of Pennsylvania.*

encroach *vb.* (en KROHCH) to trespass or intrude. *The sea continues to encroach on the beach, eroding more and more of the dunes with each passing year.*

endemic *adj.* (en DEM ik) restricted to a particular area; indigenous. *Lyme disease is not widespread throughout the country; rather it is endemic, especially to New England.*

engender *vb.* (en JEN dur) to create or cause. *We are active in the environmental movement in order to engender change.*

enigma *n.* (en IG muh) a mystery or riddle. *Astronomers can't yet explain everything in the universe; much of it remains an enigma.*

enlighten *vb.* (en LITE un) to educate or inform. *We took our students to the observatory to enlighten them about the universe.*

ennui *n.* (An WEE) listless boredom. *We were couped up in our log cabin all winter and suffered from terrible ennui.*

entrepreneur *n.* (on truh pruh NUR) one who starts and runs an enterprise, business, etc. *She was an aggressive entrepreneur; as soon as she closed the boutique she opened a restaurant.*

entropy *n.* (EN truh pee) a state of ongoing deterioration in a system. *The entropy found in some third world societies is difficult to turn around.*

enunciate *vb.* (e NUN see ayt) to pronounce clearly. *When giving a speech, be sure to enunciate each word clearly.*

envoy *n.* (ON voy) a representative. *A special envoy was sent to the state house to relay a diplomatic message.*

ephemeral *adj.* (i FEM ur al) fleeting; of short duration. *The appearance of a comet in our night sky was ephemeral.*

epic *adj.* (EH pik) on a grand scale; mythical, legendary; heroic; extraordinary. *Last February we were blasted by a blizzard of epic proportions.*

epiphany *n.* (i PIH fuh nee) a great revelatory experience or insight; an illumination of a truth. *The astronaut experienced a great epiphany as he orbited the Earth; next to the vastness of the universe, he suddenly realized how small his problems really were.*

epitome *n.* (i PIT uh me) the perfect example or representation. *Many thought that Jimi Hendrix was the epitome of cool.*

equanimity *n.* (EE kwuh NIM i tee) composure. *Even as his house burned down in front of him, my neighbor maintained his equanimity.*

equilibrium *n.* (EE kwuh LIB ree um) balance, composure, and stability. *Long-term power outages tend to test my family's equilibrium.*

equitable *adj.* (EK wi tuh bul) fair. *The judge divided the prizes among the contestants in an equitable manner.*

equivocate *vb.* (i KWIV uh kayt) to speak ambiguously or evasively. *When asked whether they will or will not raise taxes, politicians often equivocate.*

ergonomics *n.* (ur go NOM iks) the science of design that seeks to serve human form and facilitate functioning and productivity, especially in a work environment. *The ergonomics of the plant was considered state-of-the-art; everything was designed with worker safety, comfort, and productivity in mind.*

erroneous *adj.* (i RO nee us) incorrect; wrong. *The politician insisted that the accusations against him were totally erroneous.*

erudite *adj.* (ER yoo dite) highly educated; learned. *The professor was erudite and difficult to debate.*

eschew *vb.* (es CHOO) shun; forego; avoid. *I tend to eschew any sort of rich, fatty food.*

esoteric *adj.* (ES uh TER ik) designed for a small group; difficult for ordinary people to understand. *Only a handful of scientists truly understood the physicist's esoteric theories about the universe.*

esprit de corps *n.* (es SPREE de COHR) in a group, a common bond that unifies and facilitates friendliness and cooperation. *All of the runners in the charity marathon babbled together excitedly; the esprit de corps even spilled over to the spectators.*

estranged *adj.* (e STRAYNJD) alienated. *After the fight, the couple became increasingly estranged.*

ethereal *adj.* (i THIR ee ul) heavenly or otherworldly. Also, celestial. *The mysterious woman had an ethereal quality, almost like an angel.*

eugenics *n.* (yoo JEN iks) a highly controversial philosophy or science that claims the human population can and should be strengthened by prohibiting weaker members from procreating. *Eugenics theoretically can strengthen genetic stock, but it may do so at the price of human rights.*

euphemism *n.* (YOO fum iz um) a polite word or phrase used in place of an offensive one. *"Darn" has long been used as a euphemism for "damn."*

euphoria *n.* (yoo FOR ee uh) elation; great happiness and joy. *As the home team scored the winning touchdown, the crowd reacted with shrieks of euphoria.*

euthanasia *n.* (yoo than AY szhuh) mercy killing. *Some believe in euthanasia for people with terminal illnesses and agonizing pain.*

exacerbate *vb.* (ek ZAS ur bayt) to make worse; to aggravate. *Insulting your opponent during an argument will only exacerbate the matter.*

exacting *adj.* (eg ZAK ting) rigorous and painstaking; difficult, meticulous. *Filing an accurate tax return is an exacting task.*

exalt *vb.* (eg ZAWLT) to honor or glorify. *Our society tends to exalt athletes and ignore engineers.*

exasperate *vb.* (eg ZAS puh RAYT) to madden, infuriate, or frustrate profoundly. *If you're planning to have children, be forewarned; they will exasperate you at every turn.*

exemplary *adj.* (eg ZEM pluh ree) that which is of such quality as to be made an example of or imitated by others. *Her needlepoint is exemplary.*

exemplify *vb.* (eg ZEM pluh fye) to serve as a great example or model. *Michael Jordan will always exemplify the superstar athlete.*

exhaustive *adj.* (ex ZAWS tiv) thorough, complete. *We made an exhaustive search through our computer files but came up empty.*

exonerate *vb.* (eg ZAWN ur rayt) to prove innocent. *The attorney announced confidently that the new evidence would exonerate his client.*

exorbitant *adj.* (eg ZORB uh tunt) excessive, unreasonable. *A required twenty-five-percent tip for the wait staff is exorbitant, and I refuse to pay it.*

expedient *adj.* (ek SPEE dee unt) immediately useful. *If your toilet is overflowing, it would be expedient to use a plunger.*

expedite *vb.* (EK spi DITE) to speed things along or help to speed things along. *My real estate agent said he would expedite matters by delivering the document himself.*

explicit *adj.* (eks PLIS it) clearly and unambiguously expressed. *The movie was restricted to minors because of its explicit sex and violence.*

exploit *vb.* (ek SPLOYT) to make use of or take advantage of. *I want an agent who will exploit every opportunity to the fullest.*

expound *vb.* (eks POUND) to explain in detail. *The astronomer liked to visit schools and expound on the universe to students.*

extol *vb.* (eks TOHL) to praise; to laud. *The coach liked to extol the virtues of his team, even when they had a losing season.*

extortion *n.* (ex TOR shun) the forcing of one to pay money by means of intimidation, blackmail, or other illegal means. *The gang member was convicted* *of extortion after threatening to burn down the home of anyone who refused to give him money.*

extraneous *adj.* (ek STRAY nee us) unnecessary; superfluous. *The key to powerful writing is to cut all extraneous words.*

extrapolate *vb.* (ek STRAP uh layt) to make assumptions or draw conclusions from what is known. *With the universe populated with millions of worlds, scientists extrapolate that aliens not only may exist but may be common.*

extrovert *adj.* (EKS truh vurt) one who is sociable and outgoing. *An introvert often prefers her own company, but an extrovert more often seeks out company.*

exultant *adj.* (eg ZULT unt) jubilant. *The employees were absolutely exultant over their raises.*

facade *n.* (fuh SAHD) a front or mask; that which covers up something. *He acted perfectly happy when he was told he wouldn't get a bonus, but I think that was only a facade.*

facetious *adj.* (fah SEE shus) tongue-in-cheek; in a joking manner. *She thought I was serious when I said I was going to run for president, but I was just being facetious.*

facilitate *vb.* (fuh SIL uh tayt) to make easier; to simplify. *The facilitate mailing, please include your zip code.*

faction *n.* (FAK shun) a group with a common bond that has split off from a larger group. *A right-wing faction claimed responsibility for the bombing.*

fait accompli *n.* (FAY tuh kom PLEE) an irrevocable or irreversible act or deed. *Japan's bombing of Pearl Harbor was the fait accompli that pulled America into World War II.*

fallacious *adj.* (fuh LAY shus) false; erroneous. *You have no facts or statistics to back up your statements, so I suspect your argument is completely fallacious.*

fallacy *n.* (FAL uh see) a popularly held belief that isn't true. *That the Sun orbits the Earth instead of the other way around is a popular fallacy.*

fallible *adj.* (FAL uh bul) capable of making errors; imperfect. *Human beings are not computers; we are fallible.*

fanatical *adj.* (fuh NAT uh kul) devoted and passionate; zealous; extreme. *My best friend is fanatical about basketball and watches at least six college games every weekend.*

farcical *adj.* (FARS i kul) absurd; ludicrous. *Our attempts to put on a serious show turned farcical as the PA system broke and a spotlight came crashing down on the stage.*

fastidious *adj.* (fah STID ee us) meticulous; needing and arranging things just so. *He was a fastidious man who never seemed to have a single hair out of place.*

faux pas *n.* (foh PAH) a social blunder. *Forgetting the names of people you have just been introduced to is a common faux pas.*

fawn *vb.* (FAWN) to try desperately to please someone by flattery and servile behavior. *We watch in disgust as the underlings all fawn over the president.*

feign *vb.* (FAYN) to fake or invent. *Students and employees alike tend to feign illness most often on Mondays.*

felonious *adj.* (fel OHN ee us) criminal; evil. *His intentions of withdrawing money from the bank were purely felonious.*

fervent *adj.* (FUR vunt) passionate; heated. *She had a fervent desire to play in a professional soccer league.*

fickle *adj.* (FIK ul) changing or likely to change often; capricious. *Some teenagers are fickle and may have a crush on somebody new every month.*

fidelity *n.* (fi DEL uh tee) loyalty; faithfulness. *If your husband stayed out last night until 4 A.M., I would have to question his fidelity.*

figurative *adj.* (FIG yur uh tiv) not literal; metaphorical. *He claimed he would "die" if he didn't get an ice cream cone, but his statement was figurative; people can survive indefinitely without ice cream.*

figurehead *n.* (FIG yur HED) one who appears to be in charge and have the power but in fact does not. *Some presidents are just figureheads; it's their spouses who may have the real power.*

finagle *vb.* (fin AY gul) to manipulate, maneuver, and pull strings to get something. *My agent tried to finagle a deal in which I would play the lead in a new movie with the Muppets.*

finesse *n.* (fin ESS) delicate skill. *Some pitchers throw only fastballs, but others throw lots of different curves, relying more on finesse to strike batters out.*

finite *adj.* (FIY NITE) limited. *The earth contains only a finite amount of oil, and thus someday we'll be forced to develop an alternate energy source.*

fission *n.* (FISH un) the splitting of the atom; a nuclear reaction. *Fission is what makes an atomic bomb explode.*

fixation *n.* (fix AY shun) a neurotic preoccupation or obsession. Some men have a fixation with blonds, while others go gaga over brunets.

flagrant *adj.* (FLAY grunt) glaring and outrageous. *The star player was ejected from the game after committing another flagrant foul.*

flamboyant *adj.* (flam BOY unt) ostentatious; loud; showy. *The flamboyant hostess caught everyone's attention the moment she entered a room.*

fledgling *n.* (FLEJ ling) a beginner; a neophyte. *She fell off her skates seventeen times, but she was, after all, just a fledgling.*

flippant *adj.* (FLIP unt) disrespectful, irreverent. *Any more flippant remarks from you and I'll ask you to leave.*

flux *n.* (FLUKS) flow; constant flow or change. *To keep production in flux, the assembly line must never be allowed to shut down.*

foible *n.* (FOY bul) a minor weakness or fault. *Nobody is perfect; we all have our foibles.*

forlorn *adj.* (for LORN) hopelessly miserable. *After losing her job, she was forlorn for several weeks.*

formidable *adj.* (FORM id uh bul) difficult to face, overcome, or measure up to; highly challenging. *The champion's formidable opponent has won all of the matches he has boxed in.*

forte *n.* (FOR tay) specialty; area of expertise. *Everyone praises my roses and tomatoes, but that's no surprise; gardening is my forte.*

fortitude *n.* (FOR tih tood) strength and courage, especially during a great challenge or difficulty. *You need great fortitude to run a marathon.*

fortuitous *adj.* (for TOO it us) occurring by chance or luck. *Having an off-duty policeman just happen by as I was being mugged was fortuitous.*

fraudulent *adj.* (FROD yoo lent) deceptive; dishonest; illegal. *Most of the swindler's wealth came through fraudulent means.*

frugal *adj.* (FROO gul) thrifty; economical. *The couple was so frugal, they were able to buy their first home with cash.*

fruition *n.* (froo ISH un) completion and fulfillment, as the bearing of fruit. I brought my dreams to fruition the day I opened my own business.

furtive *adj.* (FUR tiv) secretive and sneaky. *In a singles bar, men and women make numerous furtive glances at one another.*

futile *adj.* (FYOOT ul) useless; in vain; producing no result. *Our attempt at becoming rock stars was futile; we didn't even know how to play our instruments.*

galvanize *vb.* (GAL vuh niyz) to stimulate, spur, or jolt into action. *That at least one polluted river in the city could actually be set on fire helped to galvanize the drive for cleaner water.*

gauche *adj.* (GOHSH) tactless; unrefined socially. *Whispering dirty jokes to the queen would probably be considered gauche.*

gauntlet, run the any multidirectional punishment, criticism, or ordeal. Originating from an archaic form of punishment in which a soldier would run between two lines of men being struck with clubs, ropes, etc. *Facing censure, the president will have to run the gauntlet against some formidable detractors.*

gauntlet, throw down the historically, to challenge another to a fight. Today, to challenge another to a debate or contest. *The two politicians will throw down the gauntlet and debate the issues next Tuesday before live TV.*

genie out of the bottle a metaphor alluding to the reality that once an important action has been taken, it may be extremely difficult to reverse it, as in putting the genie back in the bottle from which it sprung. *Scientists let the nuclear genie out of the bottle decades ago; ever since, many activists have worked tirelessly to try and put it back in.*

genocide *n.* (JEN uh SIYD) the extermination or partial extermination of an ethnic group. *The Nazis committed genocide against the Jews in World War II.*

genre *n.* (ZHON ruh) a category or kind, as in an art form. *Stephen King has long specialized in the horror genre.*

genteel *adj.* (jen TEEL) refined; polite. *The finishing school prided itself on churning out genteel students.*

germane *adj.* (jur MAYN) relevant; pertinent. *When we're discussing politics, I would appreciate it if you wouldn't bring up unrelated issues; try to keep your comments germane.*

glasnost *n.* (GLASS nohst) a Russian policy advocating freedom of expression and increased openness concerning social problems. *The spirit of glasnost is alive and well in Russia, where citizens now feel free to criticize their government.*

glib *adj.* (GLIB) without much thought, as an offhand or superficial comment or piece of advice. *The critic's glib remarks only served to illustrate how little he cared or knew about our art.*

grandiloquent *adj.* (gran DIL uh kwent) using big words to make an impression; bombastic. *The politician's grandiloquent speech backfired; instead of impressing us with his knowledge, he impressed us with his pomposity.*

grassroots *adj.* (GRAS ROOTS) of the common people or citizenry. *The neighborhood's housewives began a grassroots campaign to stamp out local corruption.*

gratuitous *adj.* (gruh TOO i tus) unnecessary or uncalled for. *Many movies today are filled with gratuitous violence.*

gregarious *adj.* (gri GAIR ee us) friendly and outgoing. *Most people in sales are gregarious by nature.*

grist for the mill useful material to work with. *The latest scandal should provide plenty of grist for the pundits' mill.*

grovel *vb.* (GROV ul) to fawn; to cringe and kiss up to someone. *The dutiful peasant is always expected to grovel at the king's feet.*

guile *n.* (GILE) slyness and deceit. *The swindler used sheer guile to separate victims from their money.*

gilding the lily dressing up something that is already beautiful and cannot be improved. *To people who like things natural, trimming a Christmas tree is only gilding the lily.*

gullible *adj.* (GULL uh bul) naive; prone to believing anything. *Young children are quite gullible and easy to fool.*

hackneyed *adj.* (HAK need) overfamiliar and unoriginal and therefore dull or ineffective. *Replete with clichés, the student's writing was hopelessly hackneyed.*

haggard *adj.* (HAG urd) gaunt or wild-eyed from exhaustion. *By the time they reached the summit, the climbers were out of breath and haggard.*

hallmark *n.* (HALL mark) an identifying characteristic. *One of the hallmarks of a poor economy is high unemployment.*

harbinger *n.* (HAR binj ur) a sign of things to come. *Frequent spring rain is a harbinger of May flowers.*

harrowing *adj.* (HAIR oh wing) frightening. *The rollercoaster is the most harrowing ride at the amusement park.*

haughty *adj.* (HAWT ee) arrogant and disdainful of others. *The snob gave us a haughty look and departed.*

hedonist *n.* (HEE dun ist) a self-indulgent pleasure seeker. *During weekdays, I'm a hard worker, but on weekends I tend to become something of a hedonist.*

heinous *adj.* (HAY nus) extremely wicked or evil. *Mass murder is a heinous crime.*

heterogeneous *adj.* (HET ur o GEE nee us) composed of differing elements; incongruous. *America is famous for its richly heterogeneous society.*

hiatus *n.* (hye AY tus) a break or rest from work. *I've worked without a vacation all year, so next week I'm going to take a three-week hiatus.*

hierarchy *n.* (HYE uh RAHR kee) an order of rank; a tier system of command. *In the corporate hierarchy, I was a common peon.*

highbrow *n.* (HYE brow) an intellectual; a scholar. *Don't let highbrows intimidate you; everyone has gaps in their education.*

histrionic *adj.* (his tree ON ik) theatrical or overly dramatic. *My teenage daughter claimed with all sincerity that she would die if she wasn't allowed to go to the party, but she is often histrionic.*

Hobson's choice *n.* a choice that is in reality no choice at all because it offers no alternative. *I was offered a Hobson's choice: either I would stop protesting about poor working conditions or I would be fired.*

hoist with one's own petard a Shakespearean metaphor for getting hurt with one's own offenses or weapons. The metaphor refers to a bomb (petard) blowing up in one's face. *The company polluted the river surreptitiously at night, but then were hoist with their own petard as fishermen downstream sued for the massive fish kills they caused.*

holier-than-thou *adj.* (HO lee er than THOW) self-righteous; taking a superior, moralizing stance. *Whenever anyone cops that annoying, holier-than-thou attitude, I remind them that only those who are without sin can rightfully cast stones.*

holistic *adj.* (ho LIS tik) consisting of a whole or integrated approach, as opposed to that comprising individual components. *Holistic medicine looks at the mind and the body in order to more fully understand the disease process.*

Holy Grail *n.* a metaphor for any fervently sought after object, goal, etc., so-named after the cup supposedly used by Jesus at the Last Supper, the subject of numerous medieval quests. *The Holy Grail of auto manufacturers is a car that will produce zero emissions and travel one hundred miles on a single gallon of gas.*

homage *n.* (AW mij) that which is shown or given in order to honor someone. *We paid homage to our city's philanthropists by giving them a dinner and awards.*

homogeneous *adj.* (ho mo JEE nee us) made of similar elements. *Some nations are composed of only one ethnic group and are therefore described as homogenous.*

hubris *n.* (HYOO bris) arrogant pride. *Ralph presumed that the vote for most eligible bachelor would go to him; such hubris was rather nauseating.*

humility *n.* (hyoo MIL i tee) modesty; the absence of pride or arrogance. *Joan never expected to win, and she accepted the award with great embarrassment and humility.*

hyperbole *n.* (hi PUR bul ee) exaggeration, as a figure of speech. *"I'm so hungry I could eat a horse" is a statement illustrating the use of hyperbole.*

hypochondriac *n.* (hi poh KON dree ak) one who chronically imagines himself to be sick when in reality he is not; one overly concerned with his health. *My friend is the worst hypochondriac I've ever known; he is sure that he is suffering from cancer, beriberi, and Lyme disease, all at the same time.*

hypothetical *adj.* (hi puh THET uh kul) suppositional; unproven; assumed; theoretical. *The professor asked us to imagine a hypothetical situation in which humans could travel faster than the speed of light.*

iconoclast *n.* (iye KON uh KLAST) one who disrespects and attacks society's revered beliefs, institutions, public figures, etc. *The famous atheist earned her reputation as an iconoclast when she forced prayer to be removed from schools.*

idyllic *adj.* (iye DIL ik) peaceful, rustic, pastoral. *We passed an idyllic rural scene of sheep grazing along rolling green hills.*

ignominy *n.* (IG num MIN ee) dishonor; shame. *For acting up in class, Jed had to suffer the ignominy of being sent to the principal's office.*

imbroglio *n.* (im BROHL yo) a confusing or entangled situation. *The two parties were involved in a heated imbroglio that soon boiled over into a fistfight.*

immutable *adj.* (im MYOOT uh bul) unchangeable. *The Constitution guarantees that our rights as U.S. citizens are immutable.*

impartial *adj.* (im PAR shul) unbiased; fair. *You can't be an impartial judge if one of the beauty contestants is your niece.*

impeccable *adj.* (im PEK uh bul) perfect; flawless. *We could easily see how John had been appointed as ambassador; he had impeccable manners.*

impermeable *adj.* (im PERM ee uh bul) impenetrable. *It was unfortunate we had to camp out in a downpour but fortunate that our tent was impermeable.*

impetuous *adj.* (im PECH oo us) acting in a careless or thoughtless manner. *The impetuous youth threw the rock through the window and immediately regretted it.*

impinge *vb.* (im PINJ) to encroach upon or hit up against. *If you play your stereo loud all night you impinge on the rights of others to get a good night's sleep.*

implausible *adj.* (im PLAWS uh bul) not possible or probable; unbelievable. *The boy's explanation of the spilled milk—that a ghost had knocked it over—was implausible.*

implicit *adj.* (im PLIS it) implied or suggested but not expressed directly. *Implicit in the contract was the issue of timeliness, although no deadline was expressly given.*

imposing *adj.* (im POH zing) having a powerful or grand presence. *Tourists like to gawk at the imposing skyscrapers all around New York.*

impotent *adj.* (IM puh tent) ineffectual. *The new pitcher's attempts at striking out batters were completely impotent; the opposing team hit one home run after another.*

impregnable *adj.* (im PREG nuh bul) secure or impossible to break through. *The castle's walls were ten feet thick and were thought to be impregnable.*

impressionable *adj.* (im PRESH un uh bul) easily influenced or brainwashed; suggestible. *Young children are highly impressionable, which is why they must be taught a strong sense of right and wrong from early on.*

impudent *adj.* (IM pyoo dunt) disrespectful in a bold way. *Any more impudent behavior will result in suspension from school.*

impugn *vb.* (im PYOON) to criticize or attack, especially that which is questionable. *Political opponents often try to impugn each other's records.*

impunity *n.* (im PYOON uh tee) complete freedom from punishment. *As the police lost control of the crowd, the rioters proceeded to break windows and loot shops with impunity.*

inane *adj.* (in AYN) empty and pointless. *If I have to sit through one more inane comedy show I'm going to scream.*

inanimate *adj.* (in AN uh mut) lifeless; inert. *Dr. Frankenstein's challenge was to animate an inanimate body.*

inaugurate *vb.* (in AW gyuh RAYT) to induct, initiate, or start. *We will inaugurate the president with the swearing-in tomorrow at noon.*

incessant *adj.* (in SESS unt) endless; nonstop. *The infant's incessant crying kept me awake for most of the night.*

incisive *adj.* (in SYE siv) sharp and penetrating. *The muckraker's incisive report got right to the heart of the scandal.*

incongruous *adj.* (in KON groo us) incompatible; of unmatching components. *Installing a pair of skis on a bicycle would appear rather incongruous.*

inconspicuous *adj.* (in kun SPIK yoo us) blending in and attracting little if any attention. *Shoplifters try to be as inconspicuous as possible.*

incorrigible *adj.* (in KAWR i juh bul) incapable of reform or improvement. *Incorrigible youths may as adults end up behind bars.*

incredulous *adj.* (in KREJ uh lus) unbelieving, skeptical. *As I recounted my trip aboard the flying saucer, the police officer appeared incredulous.*

indelible *adj.* (in DEL uh bul) leaving a lasting or permanent impression. *Tragedies always leave indelible memories.*

indict *vb.* (in DITE) to charge with a crime. *Although my neighbor has been indicted, the case has not yet been proven against him.*

indictment *n.* (in DITE munt) a formal charge of a crime. *The grand jury handed down an indictment against the gang members.*

indifferent *adj.* (in DIF ur unt) apathetic; uncaring. *Nature is indifferent to the suffering of animals.*

indigenous *adj.* (in DIJ uh nus) native. *The coon cat is indigenous to Maine.*

indigent *adj.* (IN duh junt) poor. *The indigent vagrant stopped people on the street to beg for money.*

indignant *adj.* (in DIG nunt) angry and resentful, due especially to an injustice. *The taxpayers are indignant; they will not pay a penny more in taxes.*

indoctrinate *vb.* (in DOK tri nayt) to teach one's beliefs to another; to brainwash. *The cult found it easy to indoctrinate and manipulate young people.*

indolent *adj.* (IN duh lunt) lazy. *If you choose to be indolent and refuse to help around here, you won't be getting any supper.*

ineffectual *adj.* (in uh FEK choo ul) ineffective; impotent; useless. *We tried to dam the flooding waters, but all our efforts were ineffectual.*

inept *adj.* (in EPT) incompetent; bumbling. *We knew the carpenter was inept when we saw his freshly built staircase collapse.*

inert *adj.* (In URT) inactive; motionless. *After stuffing themselves with turkey and pie, many of the guests became inert on the couch.*

inexorable *adj.* (in EK sur uh bul) unchangeable; relentless. *The process of evolution is inexorable and will forever mold the universe.*

infamous *adj.* (IN fuh mus) famous for something bad; notorious; having a negative reputation. *The infamous cat burglar was finally captured by police today.*

infer *vb.* (in FUR) to deduce from established facts. *With millions of planets in the universe, it would probably be safe to infer that life exists at least on a few of them.*

infinitesimal *adj.* (in fin i TES uh mul) immeasurably tiny; microscopic. *In some sensitive individuals, it takes only an infinitesimal amount of pet dander or pollen to trigger an allergic reaction.*

ingratiate *adj.* (in GRAY she ayt) to try to win one's approval or favor. *Little girls may try to ingratiate themselves with mothers who have recently baked cookies.*

inherent *adj.* (in HAIR unt) innate; native; inborn. *Michael Jordan had a tireless work ethic and practiced for long hours, but he was also blessed with an inherent athletic ability.*

innate *adj.* (in AYT) inborn; natural; native. *All mothers have an innate drive to protect their young.*

innuendo *n.* (in yoo EN doh) an indirect remark that implies something negative. *He didn't dare insult his mother-in-law directly, but he would often imply that she was officious and meddlesome through innuendo.*

inquest *n.* (IN quest) a legal investigation, such as that conducted by a coroner in an attempt to determine a cause of death under suspicious circumstances. *An inquest revealed evidence pointing to foul play.*

insidious *adj.* (in SID ee us) quietly and unobtrusively causing great damage. *Diabetes is an insidious disease; it may cause great damage long before the victim even knows he has it.*

insipid *adj.* (in SIP id) bland; dull; flavorless. *Some critics charge that television programs are growing increasingly insipid.*

insolvent *adj.* (in SOL vent) unable to pay off one's debts; bankrupt. *The company owes too many creditors money and is on the verge of becoming insolvent.*

instigate *vb.* (IN stig ayt) to incite or start. *Police say five gang members attempted to instigate a riot.*

insular *adj.* (IN sul ur) isolated or detached; narrow in opinion due to a lack of worldly experience. *The insular opinions of the remote regions of the state are in stark contrast to the more liberal views of the southern, metropolitan areas.*

insurrection *n.* (in sur EK shun) rebellion against established authorities. *The peasants banded together in a mass insurrection.*

intangible *adj.* (in TAN juh bul) imperceptible; impalpable. *The soul is intangible, yet philosophers have long pondered its existence.*

integral *adj.* (IN ti grel) essential; basic. *Math should be an integral component of anyone's curriculum.*

integrity *n.* (in TEG ruh tee) moral and ethical character. *The boy who returned my lost wallet had great integrity.*

intractable *adj.* (in TRAK tuh bul) unmanageable and stubborn. *The impish lad had to be removed from class for his intractable behavior.*

intransigent *adj.* (in TRANS uh junt) uncompromising. *It is impossible to negotiate a difficult situation with someone who is intransigent.*

intrepid *adj.* (in TREP id) bold; fearless. *Parasailing requires an exceptionally intrepid temperament.*

intrinsic *adj.* (in TRIN sik) inherent; natural. *It's unwise to challenge the intrinsic nature of bears to protect their young.*

introspective *adj.* (in truh spek tiv) contemplative and observant of one's own thoughts, feelings, and inner world. *He had an introspective bent that compelled him to examine and carefully edit all thoughts before he spoke them aloud.*

inundate *vb.* (IN un dayt) to flood or engulf. *The day following every Thanksgiving, orders for Christmas cards would inundate the greeting card company.*

irascible *adj.* (i RAS uh bul) easy to anger. *Killer bees have earned a reputation of being frighteningly irascible.*

ironic *adj.* (i RON ik) having an opposite meaning to what is said. *She said that politicians should always aspire to the highest form of sleaze, but I suspect she was being ironic.*

irrelevant *adj.* (i REL uh vunt) impertinent; unrelated; beside the point. *We're arguing about farm subsidies here, sir, and your comments about Beanie Babies are really quite irrelevant.*

irreverent *adj.* (i REV ur unt) disrespectful. *The comedians of today love to gore sacred cows and are often lauded for being so irreverent.*

irrevocable *adj.* (i REV uh kuh bul) irreversible; irretrievable. *Once this new constitution is signed, there will be no turning back; its laws will be irrevocable.*

itinerary *n.* (i TIN ur air ee) travel plan, route, or schedule. *A fall foliage tour of New Hampshire and Maine is on our itinerary next week.*

jaded *adj.* (JAY ded) tired out or bored from overindulgence. *Washington is nice, but after touring seven museums in one day, I've become jaded.*

jaundiced *adj.* (JON disd) prejudiced, hostile, and envious. *The bigot regarded the minorities dominating his city's baseball team with a jaundiced eye.*

je ne sais quoi (je ne say KWA) French term for "I know not what"; "a certain something." *People with charisma have that certain je ne sais quoi that attracts others like a magnet.*

judicious *adj.* (joo DISH us) prudent, fair, and sound in judgment. *By splitting the profits evenly three ways, we made the most judicious choice possible.*

juggernaut *n.* (JUG ur not) a powerful force or institution, sometimes followed blindly by devotees. *The company had become a juggernaut, wiping out competing mom and pop shops all over the country.*

juxtapose *vb.* (juks tuh POHZ) to place side by side. *Juxtapose the pieces of a puzzle to expedite assembly.*

Kafkaesque *adj.* (KAHF kuh ESK) nightmarish or otherworldly, as the writings of Franz Kafka. *His drug-induced hallucinations took on a Kafkaesque quality.*

kinetic *adj.* (kin ET ik) in motion; active; energetic. *The kinetic properties of electricity are difficult to comprehend.*

kismet *n.* (KIZ met) destiny; fate. *My wife thinks it was kismet that brought us together, but I say it was just dumb luck.*

kudos *n.* (KOO dohs) acclaim; praise. *She is winning kudos for her gourmet cooking.*

lackadaisical *adj.* (lak uh DAYZ uh kul) listless; careless; indifferent; unspirited. *The children's efforts to rake the yard were lackadaisical at best; even after three hours of work, the lawn remained covered in leaves.*

lackluster *adj.* (LACK lus tur) dull; bland; colorless. *The home team has been rather lackluster lately; as a result, they've lost four games in a row.*

laconic *adj.* (luh KON ik) terse; using few words. *The laconic gentleman rarely answered us with more than a grunt.*

laissez-faire *n.* (LESS ay FEHR) any noninterfering or "hands-off" policy; allowance to act as one pleases without control or regulation. *The government's laissez-faire economic policy allows for natural cycles of growth and recession.*

lampoon *vb.* (lam POON) to ridicule, satirize, or parody. *Every week, the comedy show would lampoon the president and his behind-the-scenes antics.*

languid *adj.* (LAN gwid) weak; lacking in energy. *On hot days, the workers tend to grow languid.*

languish *vb.* (LAN gwish) to grow weak, listless, or neglected. *The company is letting its typewriter business languish in favor of its word processor division.*

lascivious *adj.* (lah SIV ee us) expressing lust; lewd. *She eyed the cake hungrily and gave a lascivious moan of desire.*

latent *adj.* (LAY tunt) hidden beneath the surface. *Parents always wonder what latent abilities reside within their children.*

latitude *n.* (LAT uh tood) unrestricted freedom to act as one wishes. *The voters gave the mayor the latitude to rein in city polluters with stiff fines.*

laud *vb.* (LAWD) to acclaim or praise. *The teacher loved to laud the accomplishments of her star pupil.*

lavish *adj.* (LAV ish) generous, bountiful; rich. *The Thanksgiving table was covered with a lavish array of dishes.*

left-handed compliment *n.* a compliment that is intended or can be perceived as an insult. *My instructor told me I could write for preschoolers, which I took as a left-handed compliment.*

left-wing *adj.* (LEFT WING) liberal; leftist; radical. *"We don't need any left-wing factions telling us what we can and cannot cut down in the forest," a spokesman for the paper company was quoted as saying.*

legacy *n.* (LEG uh see) something passed down to following generations. *Michael Jordan's legacy of championship basketball will be difficult to match.*

lethargic *adj.* (leth ARJ ik) listless, sluggish. *The children were as lethargic as sloths until I promised to take them out for ice cream.*

levity *n.* (LEV i tee) light or humorous behavior, particularly at an inappropriate time. *If I may inject some levity into this funeral, I will now tap-dance with the deceased.*

libel *n.* (LI bul) published statements that are both untrue and malicious or damaging. *To prevent being sued for libel, newspapers must check and double-check facts and sources.*

liberal *adj.* (LIB ur ul) tolerant and open-minded. *His philosophy was liberal; he believed nobody should have the right to discriminate against a person for their race, gender, or sexual orientation.*

Lilliputian *adj.* (lil uh PYOO shun) tiny; miniature, as the people of Lilliput in Jonathan Swift's *Gulliver's Travels*. *I watched my children as they gleefully built a Lilliputian village out of Popsicle sticks.*

lip service *n.* talk of doing something but failing to follow through and actually do it. *Our local politicians paid lip service to the environmental movement; their words were empty promises, however, as nothing was ever done.*

literati *n.* (lit uh RAH tee) literary intellectuals as a group. *The local literati were lambasting the famous author's new book.*

litigate *vb.* (LIT uh gayt) to sue in court. *If your children continue to break our windows, we'll be forced to litigate.*

litigious *adj.* (li TIJ us) highly contentious and prone to threatening with and filing lawsuits. *In our litigious society, you can climb a ladder when you're drunk, fall off and break a leg, and then sue the ladder company for damages.*

lobby *vb.* (LOB ee) to try and persuade those in legislative power to vote in a certain way. *Lawnmower manufacturers will lobby Congress to prevent passage of a bill that would require small engines to run with fifty percent fewer emissions.*

logistics *n.* (luh JIS tiks) management, including procurement of supplies, distribution, transport, and maintenance, of any large-scale operation. *The logistics involved in sending troops overseas is nightmarish.*

loose cannon *n.* one who is out of control or unpredictable, either verbally or physically. *The ace pitcher was characterized as something of a loose cannon; he often shot his mouth off with the press and threatened management whenever they benched him.*

loquacious *adj.* (loh KWAY shus) talkative. *Radio talk-show hosts must be loquacious and quick-thinking.*

lucid *adj.* (LOO sid) clear; clear-headed. *I'm not quite as lucid when I've had a couple of drinks as when I'm sober.*

lucrative *adj.* (LOO kruh tiv) profitable. *The personal computer business continues to be highly lucrative.*

ludicrous *adj.* (LOO di krus) laughable. *The organization's continued attempts to prove the earth is flat are ludicrous.*

lukewarm *adj.* (LUHK WARM) unenthusiastic; tepid. *A few people in the audience applauded, but the overall response to the play was lukewarm at best.*

lurid *adj.* (LUR id) horrifying and gruesome; sensational or shocking. *The tabloid television program featured lurid accidents involving automobiles, airplanes, and trains.*

macabre *adj.* (muh KAHB ruh) ghastly, as scenes of death. *The horror writer was a master at depicting the macabre.*

Machiavellian *adj.* (mak ee uh VEL ee un) deceitful and crafty, so-named after Niccolò Machiavelli of the 16th century, who believed that in politics, morality should take a back seat to wiliness. *The senator's backdoor, Machiavellian politics may have accomplished what he wanted, but his reputation is now permanently tarnished.*

machination *n.* (mak uh NAY shun) a scheme or design, especially of a sneaky nature. *His covert machinations won him several converts as well as a formal nomination.*

magnanimous *adj.* (mag NAN uh mus) noble, unselfish, and quick to forgive. *My boss is unusually magnanimous and rarely says anything when I'm late for work.*

magnate *n.* (MAG nayt) a very successful and powerful businessperson. *The oil magnate arrived in town this morning to discuss the drilling of a new well in the Atlantic Ocean.*

magnum opus *n.* (MAG num OH pus) a masterpiece. *Every weekend I work on my magnum opus in progress, but it won't be ready for at least ten years.*

malaise *n.* (muh LAYZ) a physical or mental fatigue and uneasiness, especially stemming from an illness. *I went to the doctor about a general malaise I was experiencing, and he said it was probably the start of the flu.*

malevolent *adj.* (muh LEV uh lent) malicious. *The malevolent dictator needed little excuse to punish those who disagreed with him.*

malice *n.* (MAL iss) a desire to hurt others; maliciousness. *The defendant had apparently harbored great malice toward his victim.*

malignant *adj.* (mal IG nunt) deadly; harmful. *Unfortunately, the tumor was found to be malignant.*

malingerer *n.* (mah LIN gur ur) one who tries to get out of work or responsibility, especially by feigning illness. *One of my employees calls in sick almost every Monday; he is a chronic malingerer and probably should be fired.*

malleable *adj.* (MAL ee uh bul) pliable, moldable; impressionable. *Young minds are particularly malleable, so parents must use great care in teaching morals.*

mandate *n.* (MAN dayt) a strong desire by the people as manifested by an overwhelming vote. *The governor received a clear mandate from the voters to buy more land for conservation.*

manifest *vb.* (MAN uh FEST) to show or make evident. *At the séance, the spirit would manifest itself in the shape of a chained prisoner.*

manifesto *n.* (man uh FEST oh) any publicly declared political doctrine, set of beliefs, or intentions. *In the organization's manifesto was a promise to strive for world peace.*

masochist *n.* (MAS uh kist) one who takes pleasure, especially sexual, in being physically or verbally abused. *A sadist takes pleasure from inflicting pain on others, but the masochist takes pleasure from receiving it.*

maternal *adj.* (muh TURN ul) motherly. *Maternal instincts compelled the doe to protect its fawn at any cost.*

matriarch *n.* (MAY tree ark) a mother or a ruler who is a woman. *The matriarch of the family was regarded as the highest domestic authority; after all, she ruled over nine children and twenty-seven grandchildren.*

maudlin *adj.* (MAWD lin) tearfully sentimental; sentimental to a laughable or unrealistic degree. *The movie tried too hard to tug at viewers' heartstrings; unfortunately, most of the writer's attempts at pathos were merely maudlin.*

maxim *n.* (MAK sim) a basic truth stated in a simple sentence. *"All is fair in love and war" is a popular maxim.*

mea culpa *n.* (MAY uh KUL puh) my fault; I am guilty. A Latin expression admitting one's guilt. *The cat was locked out all night again? Mea culpa! I accidentally broke the pet door last night and forgot to let Morris in.*

mediate *vb.* (MEE dee ayt) to act as an intermediate and help two parties come to an agreement or settlement. *The children should not be employed to mediate between feuding husbands and wives.*

melodramatic *adj.* (mel oh druh MAT ik) overly dramatic; theatrical. *My teenager is often melodramatic; last night she announced in horrified tones that she would die if she couldn't go to the concert.*

menial *adj.* (MEE nee ul) servile; that of a servant. *She held a menial position cleaning the houses of the wealthy.*

mentor *n.* (MEN tor) a teacher, instructor, or guru. *A personal mentor can help expedite your apprenticeship as a writer considerably.*

mercenary *adj.* (MERS uh nair ee) motivated purely by money, as a hired soldier. *He didn't care who won or lost the war; his motivation as a sharpshooter was solely mercenary.*

metamorphosis *n.* (met uh MORF uh sis) a dramatic transformation. *The caterpillar undergoes an incredible metamorphosis to become a butterfly.*

metaphor *n.* (MET uh for) a figure of speech not to be taken literally, but to illustrate a point. *"The star basketball player is on fire" is a metaphor for a basketball player who is shooting extremely well.*

metaphysical *adj.* (met uh FIZ ih kul) supernatural; not of the physical world. *Astrologers take a metaphysical view of the universe, while astronomers take a physical one.*

microcosm *n.* (MI kroh KOZ um) a miniature world or reality. *The suburban sprawl in my neighborhood is just a microcosm of what is happening around the world.*

milieu *n.* (mil YOO) setting; environment. *The street corner was not the opera singer's normal performance milieu.*

militant *adj.* (MIL uh tunt) aggressive and antagonistic. *The militant environmentalists were arrested for inciting a brawl with lumberjacks.*

minutiae *n.* (mi NOO shee ee) trivial or insignificant detail. *Biographies describe a celebrity's life, right down to the finest minutiae.*

misanthrope *n.* (MIS un throhp) one who hates people. *The misanthrope shuns community and prefers to live secluded from others.*

mitigate *vb.* (MIT uh gayt) to lessen or soften the effect of something. *We tried to mitigate flood damage by sandbagging the periphery of our property.*

mollify *vb.* (MOLL uh fye) to soothe or appease. *Giving raises will temporarily mollify complaining employees.*

momentous *adj.* (moh MEN tus) important; consequential; pivotal. *The bombing of Pearl Harbor by the Japanese in World War II was momentous.*

monolithic *adj.* (mon oh LITH ik) huge and permanent, as a monolith. *The government has taken on monolithic proportions and will be impossible to dismantle.*

moot *adj.* (MOOT) subject to debate; unsettled. *Whether men or women make better managers is a moot question.*

moral soapbox *n.* a reference to a figurative or literal platform one stands on to look down at others and moralize or preach. *She got up on her moral soapbox and proceeded to point fingers at everyone in our department who had sinned against the company.*

moratorium *n.* (mor uh TOR ee um) a suspension or delay. *The city council has ordered a moratorium on all new building permits until an environmental impact study can be made.*

morbid *adj.* (MOR bid) unhealthy, from either a physical or mental standpoint. *The pyromaniac has a morbid desire to set fires.*

moribund *adj.* (MOR uh bund) dying; becoming obsolete. *Smokestack industries in America are increasingly moribund.*

motif *n.* (moh TEEF) a repeated theme or pattern. *The wallpaper featured a motif of birds, flowers, and bees.*

muckraking *n.* (MUK rayk ing) investigative journalism that focuses on corruption or unethical behavior. *The newspaper was famous for its crack muck-raking staff.*

myopic *adj.* (mi OP ik) short-sighted. *Failure to develop solar power now is indicative of this administration's myopic energy program.*

myriad *n.* (MEER ee ud) a great number; also, an infinity. *The restaurant had a myriad of menu choices.*

naïveté *n.* (ni EEV uh TAY) innocence and inexperience; lack of sophistication and knowledge. *When visiting a big city, take care to prevent street swindlers from taking advantage of your naiveté.*

narcissistic *adj.* (nar si SIS tik) vain and self-absorbed. *She stood in front of the mirror for more than an hour with a narcissistic need to preen.*

nebulous *adj.* (NEB you lus) cloudy, unclear. *The future of America's energy sources is nebulous; nobody knows if we'll be using mostly solar or nuclear power in the next century.*

nefarious *adj.* (ni FAIR ee us) evil. *The nefarious pirates threw their captain overboard and sailed away laughing.*

neophyte *n.* (NEE uh fite) an amateur or beginner. *We were told to be patient with neophytes because they hadn't acquired many skills yet.*

nepotism *n.* (NEP uh tiz um) favoritism toward relatives, in work, politics, etc. *Nepotism was widely practiced in the family business, as relatives were always hired over strangers.*

nihilism *n.* (NYE uh liz um) the belief that morals are a human invention and do not exist in the real world. Also, the advocacy of positive change through anarchy. *If you don't believe in religion or gods or morals you may be an advocate of nihilism.*

nirvana *n.* (nur VAHN uh) a state of spiritual enlightenment or bliss. *The achieve nirvana, Mary meditated faithfully for two hours every day.*

nocturnal *adj.* (nok TURN ul) active at the night. *Skunks are, for the most part, nocturnal animals, at least when human beings are around.*

nonchalant *adj.* (non shuh LAUNT) cool and indifferent. *You'd never guess he had just won an Academy Award by his nonchalant attitude.*

nostalgia *n.* (nuh STAL juh) a longing for the past; sentimental feelings toward the past. Also, homesickness. *Whenever I think of my boyhood, my heart aches with nostalgia.*

notorious *adj.* (no TOR ee us) infamous; known for something bad. *I wouldn't buy that car if I were you; it's notorious for breaking down in cold weather.*

novice *n.* (NOV is) a beginner; a neophyte. *Snowboarding isn't easy; if you're a novice, we suggest you try one of our bunny trails.*

noxious *adj.* (NOK shus) harmful. *The noxious fumes spewing from the bus made us gag.*

nuance *n.* (NOO ahns) a subtle distinction, difference, or variation. *This gemstone has a particular nuance that makes it less valuable than the others.*

nullify *vb.* (NULL uh fye) to cancel out; to make null and void. *Although it's difficult to nullify a judge's ruling, we can appeal to a higher court.*

obfuscate *vb.* (OB fuh skayt) to make confusing or impossible to comprehend. *Critics contend that politicians sometimes obfuscate the issue of tax hikes in order to prevent an uproar.*

objective *adj.* (ob JEK tiv) uninvolved and unbiased. *It's impossible to be objective when reviewing your own writing; you need a disinterested second party to give you feedback.*

oblivion *n.* (uh BLIV ee un) the state of being utterly forgotten or lost. *Save for a few classics, many of the popular novels of the 19th century have faded into oblivion.*

obnoxious *adj.* (ub NOK shus) offensive, unpleasant, revolting. *Everyone was glaring at the street thugs for their obnoxious behavior.*

obsequious *adj.* (ub SEE kwee us) overly compliant and servile. *I need an assistant who will do as I ask, but that doesn't mean I require you to be obsequious.*

officious *adj.* (uh FISH us) meddlesome or offering suggestions or directions when none are wanted. *Many backseat drivers are as officious outside of a car as they are in one.*

olive branch *n.* a peace offering. *After arguing with my spouse all day, I offered her an olive branch by asking her out to dinner.*

ominous *adj.* (OM un us) foreboding; indicative of impending disaster. *When sailing in the middle of the ocean, dark clouds on the horizon are particularly ominous.*

omnipotent *adj.* (om NIP uh tent) all-powerful. *Many people believe that God is omnipotent; that is, God can do anything.*

onerous *adj.* (OH nur us) burdensome; laborious. *Shoveling out a driveway after a blizzard is an onerous task.*

opaque *adj.* (oh PAYK) impossible to see through; impenetrable by light. *It was impossible to spy on the people inside, because the windows were opaque.*

opportunist *n.* (op ur TOON ist) one who aggressively pursues and exploits any kind of opportunity, regardless of ethical considerations. *The ambulance chaser has given lawyers the reputation of being opportunists.*

oppression *n.* (uh PRESH un) the unjust keeping down of an individual or population. *The dictator ruled his citizenry with an iron fist; his oppression of the masses kept any opposition forces down.*

optimism *n.* (OP tuh miz um) the belief or outlook that things will turn out well; a positive attitude. *In order to invest in the stock market, you should have a strong degree of optimism.*

opulence *n.* (OP yuh lens) wealth and luxury. *The people of Beverly Hills live in great opulence.*

orthodox *adj.* (ORTH uh DOKS) following approved or traditional standards. *Our children worship God in an orthodox way; every Sunday they attend church, and every night they say their prayers.*

ostensible *adj.* (uh STEN suh bul) referring to an outward appearance which may be misleading. *His ostensible reason for judging the beauty contest was philanthropic, but I suspect his real reason was to flirt with the contestants.*

ostentatious *adj.* (aws ten TAY shus) showy, ornate, loud. *The peacock is by far the most ostentatious bird in the world.*

ostracize *vb.* (AWS truh size) to exclude; to banish. *The cult would ostracize anyone who failed to follow their rules.*

pacifist *n.* (PASS uh fist) a peace lover. *A pacifist refuses to use violence to get his way; instead, he uses his wits and passive resistance.*

palpable *adj.* (PAL puh bul) capable of being touched or perceived. *The medium claimed that the ghosts attending her séance would be fully palpable.*

panacea *n.* (pan uh SEE uh) a cure-all. *Scientists have searched for a panacea for cancer for more than fifty years, to no avail.*

panache *n.* (puh NASH) a dashing style. *The model had great charisma and panache and attracted admiring stares wherever he went.*

Pandora's box *n.* in mythology, the box containing human ills opened by the curious Pandora. In modern usage, anything opened or employed that may have the potential to cause human ills. *Some experts warn that African jungles may contain a Pandora's box of deadly viruses just waiting to be sprung loose.*

paper tiger *n.* a person or nation that may look dangerous and powerful but in reality is not. *Third world tyrants like to bare their teeth to the rest of the world, but they're only paper tigers.*

paradigm *n.* (PAIR uh dime) a model serving as a base for instruction. *The Wall Street guru's investment strategy serves as an excellent paradigm for wealth building.*

paradox *n.* (PAIR uh doks) a statement or observation that contradicts itself but is nevertheless true. *Her wealth was a paradox; the more money she made, the less she enjoyed it.*

paragon *n.* (PAIR uh gon) a model of excellence. *Some consider Mother Teresa a paragon of virtue.*

paranoia *n.* (pair uh NOY uh) the belief or delusion that one is being persecuted; acute and irrational distrust of others. *Your paranoia has reached an extreme when you're certain the football players in a huddle are plotting to get you.*

paraphrase *vb.* (PAIR uh frase) to restate something not verbatim but in an approximate or roughly accurate form; to summarize. *I don't remember Kennedy's famous speech word for word, so I'll have to paraphrase.*

parochial *adj.* (puh ROHK ee ul) narrow in experience, scope, or outlook; provincial. *He had a* *parochial view of people and therefore mistrusted those of other races, ethnic groups, and sexual orientation.*

parody *n.* (PAIR uh dee) a humorous or ridiculing imitation of a show, book, song, etc. *The comedy troupe performed an irreverent parody of religious programming.*

partisan *adj.* (PART uh sun) following the tenets or beliefs of one's political party; biased. *Republicans and Democrats are expected to vote in a completely partisan manner, although one or two rogues may cross party lines.*

pass the buck to cast blame or responsibility onto someone other than yourself. *When it comes to accepting responsibility for the nation's economic woes, Republicans can be expected to pass the buck to the Democrats and vice versa.*

pastoral *adj.* (PAS tuh rul) designating the peacefulness and simplicity of rural life; idyllic. *Longing for the pastoral life, Jane bought some land and a flock of sheep and became a shepherd.*

pathos *n.* (PAY thos) that which produces feelings of pity or poignancy; also, these feelings themselves. *The movie was so steeped in pathos, most of the theatergoers left in tears.*

patriarch *n.* (PAY treek ark) a male head or leader of a group. *The tribal patriarch warned us not to cross into his territory again.*

patronize *vb.* (PAY truh nize) to talk down to; to condescend or treat as one's inferior. *Whenever I disagree with my professor, she puts on a superior expression and patronizes me.*

paucity *n.* (PAW is tee) a lack; dearth. *A paucity of money to pay bills will motivate most people to find work.*

peccadillo *n.* (PEK uh DIL oh) a minor fault or offense. *You can't criticize politicians for every little thing they've done wrong in their lives; we've all got our peccadilloes.*

pecuniary *adj.* (pe KYOO nee air ee) of money; financial. *The workers' concerns are purely pecuniary; they think they deserve higher pay.*

pedantic *adj.* (puh DANT ik) nitpicking with factual matters; overprecise or scholarly to an extreme, showy, or unnecessary manner. *Know-it-alls are frequently pedantic, much to everyone's annoyance.*

pedestrian *adj.* (puh DES tree un) unimaginative or so ordinary as to be dull. *You might have gotten the grammar right, but your story and characters are thoroughly pedestrian.*

pejorative *adj.* (pi JOR uh tiv) belittling; negative. *Any more pejorative remarks like that to your sister and you'll go to bed early.*

penchant *n.* (PEN chunt) a strong fondness for something. *I have a penchant for chocolate swirl ice cream.*

penitent *adj.* (PEN i tunt) full of regret; sorry. *The child was quite penitent after he was caught stealing cookies.*

pensive *adj.* (PEN siv) deep in thought, particularly about sad things. *My mother appeared so pensive, I was tempted to ask her what was so troubling.*

perennial *adj.* (puh REN ee ul) continuous, perpetual, or returning again and again. *The movie version of the Wizard of Oz is a perennial favorite.*

perfunctory *adj.* (pur FUNK tuh ree) performed superficially or routinely. *The border guard made a perfunctory inspection of our car and then let us go through.*

peripheral *adj.* (pur IF ur ul) along the side or neighboring. *Computers often require several peripheral components.*

perjury *n.* (PURJ ur ee) lying under oath. *Committing perjury in a court of law is illegal.*

permeate *vb.* (PERM ee ayt) to penetrate, as a thick and strong odor. *Seconds after he entered the room, his strong cologne would permeate the room and make people gag.*

pernicious *adj.* (purn ISH us) harmful; deadly. *The liberal sale of firearms in this city is highly pernicious.*

perquisite *n.* (PUR kwi zit) a fringe benefit or special privilege that stems from working at a particular job. *One of the perquisites of my job is a company car, which I'm allowed to drive at any time.*

personable *adj.* (PUR sun uh bul) friendly; sociable. *Salespeople must have personable dispositions.*

pertinent *adj.* (PUR tuh nunt) relevant. *We're talking about the weather, not football; please keep your remarks pertinent to the subject.*

perturb *vb.* (pur TURB) to annoy or trouble. *You perturb me with your constant requests for money.*

peruse *vb.* (puh ROOZ) to look over or study carefully. *Please peruse the contract at your leisure before signing.*

pervade *vb.* (pur VAYD) to spread, penetrate, permeate. *The odor of skunk pervades our neighborhood on trash night.*

pervasive *adj.* (pur VAY siv) spreading throughout. *If not countered regularly by rational thought, racism will become pervasive.*

perversion *n.* (pur VUR zshun) a sexual deviation. *Some would call Hank's foot fetish a perversion, but others would just think it was silly.*

petty *adj.* (PET ee) unimportant or trivial. *I've got enough to worry about without you burdening me with petty demands.*

petulant *adj.* (PECH uh lunt) moody and irritable. *Don't even think about asking your father for money when he is in such a petulant mood.*

philanthropy *n.* (fil AN thruh pee) humanitarianism; good deeds and charity. *She will always be remembered for her generous philanthropy.*

pièce de résistance *n.* (PEE es de ray zee STONSE) the crowning piece in a work, meal, etc. *After our appetizer and salad, we were brought the pièce de résistance, a feast of Main lobster and clams.*

pious *adj.* (PI us) very religious; having a holier-than-thou attitude. *I don't appreciate your pious attitude; what I choose to believe and how I choose to worship is my business.*

piquant *adj.* (pee KAHNT) sharp to the taste. *I like my salsa to be so piquant that my tongue feels about to burst into flame.*

placate *vb.* (PLAY kayt) to pacify or soothe; to appease. *In order to placate the screaming toddler, we gave him a cookie.*

placid *adj.* (PLAS id) peaceful, tranquil. *We told the pet store owner that any dog we bought would have to have a placid temperament, especially around children.*

plaintive *adj.* (PLAYN tiv) expressing sadness. *All the plaintive calls Bambi made in the forest would not bring back his mother.*

platitude *n.* (PLAT i tood) a clichéd remark given as if it is original or profound. *The politician obviously hadn't studied our problems in depth because the best he could do was to spew glib platitudes.*

platonic *adj.* (pluh TON ik) loving but not sexual. *I have a friend who is of the opposite sex, but our relationship is not physical—it's strictly platonic.*

plausible *adj.* (PLAWZ uh bul) believable, possible. *Joe's excuse of losing his homework to aliens wasn't plausible.*

plead the Fifth in a legal or figurative sense, to plead the Fifth Amendment of the United States Constitution, through which one refuses to testify (in court) in order to avoid incriminating oneself. *Did I steal the last piece of Aunt Mary's cake? I plead the Fifth.*

plethora *n.* (PLETH ur uh) an overabundance. *This country produces a plethora of nonrecyclable trash.*

poignant *adj.* (POYN yunt) touching; moving. *The movie's poignant story tugged at my heartstrings.*

polarize *vb.* (POH luh RIZE) to take opposite sides. *The controversial issue has only served to polarize the candidates, with each taking an opposing viewpoint.*

pontificate *vb.* (pon TIF uh kayt) to preach or lecture, particularly about one's own dogma. *The industrialist continued to pontificate on the necessity of continued economic growth, but the environmentalists in the audience were buying none of it.*

portent *n.* (POR tent) a sign of things to come. *Black clouds on the horizon are a portent of an imminent storm.*

postulate *vb.* (POS chuh layt) to assume without proof. *Although we have no concrete evidence, it's easy to postulate that life exists on other planets.*

pragmatic *adj.* (prag MAT ik) practical; real-world, as opposed to theoretical, *We'll make this company competitive again through pragmatic means, not through wishful thinking and daydreams.*

precedence *n.* (PRES uh duns) priority. *In a tornado, safety must take precedence over comfort; stay down in your basement until the storm has passed.*

precedent *n.* (PRES uh dunt) an example from the past (as in a case of law) used as a guideline for a similar occurrence, case, or development in the present. *Last week's verdict did not set any precedents; two similar legal cases in 1937 and in 1950 had identical outcomes.*

precipitate *vb.* (pri SIP i TAYT) to cause to happen, especially sooner than expected. *Alcohol won't soothe tensions in a domestic dispute; in many instances it can precipitate violence.*

preclude *vb.* (pree KLOOD) to prevent or render impossible. *Locking firearms in a cabinet should preclude most young children from the possibility of an accidental shooting.*

precocious *adj.* (pri KOH shus) unusually mature or advanced for one's age. *The precocious tike was speaking three languages at the age of four.*

precursor *n.* (pree KUR sur) that which comes before; a forerunner. *The Internet is the precursor of a truly global village.*

preeminent *adj.* (pree EM i nunt) dominant and unsurpassed. *In all categories of safety, the car we chose to buy is preeminent.*

preempt *vb.* (pree EMPT) to displace or take the place of another. *Unfortunately, the president's speech is going to preempt my favorite television show.*

premonition *n.* (prem uh NISH un) a foreboding, hunch, or forewarning. *I once had a horrible premonition that my local bridge was going to collapse, but it never did.*

prerequisite *adj.* (pree REK wuh zit) required; necessary. *Yes, I'm afraid geometry and algebra are indeed prerequisite.*

prerogative *n.* (pri ROG uh tiv) a right or privilege. *I can wear my hair any way that I want to; it's my prerogative.*

presumptuous *adj.* (pri ZUMP choo us) bold in assuming and taking too much for granted. *Frank, as usual, swaggered up to collect first prize even before the winner's name was announced; he's so presumptuous, we all want to vomit.*

pretense *n.* (PREE tens) a false front, put-on, or affection. *Under the pretense of "having a job to do," the female reporter marched boldly into the men's locker room and confronted the naked players.*

pretentious *adj.* (pri TEN shus) affected, fake; putting up a grand but false image of oneself. *Joe often behaves like an intellectual, but most people realize he is being pretentious when he misuses big words.*

prima donna *n.* (PREE muh DON uh) an egotistical, moody, whining brat. (Also, the lead female vocalist in an opera.) *We were warned not to cast one particular actress in the production because she had a reputation as a prima donna.*

primordial *adj.* (pri MOR dee ul) primitive; prehistoric. *Capturing and protecting territory is a primordial urge.*

pristine *adj.* (pris TEEN) unpolluted; untouched; pure. *The mountain lakeshore was off-limits to development and was therefore pristine.*

prodigious *adj.* (pruh DIJ us) huge, powerful; impressive. *Flying around the world in a hot-air balloon is a prodigious undertaking.*

prodigy *n.* (PROD i jee) a child with extraordinary talent or intelligence. *The five-year-old guitar prodigy played Jimi Hendrix licks with astonishing proficiency.*

profane *adj.* (pro FAYN) disrespectful and irreverent, especially regarding religious matters. *Your scoffing remarks about my religion are profane, but I'll always defend your right to free speech.*

proficient *adj.* (pro FISH unt) competent, skillful. *Sally has become a proficient gardener; her tomato plants often grow more than six feet high.*

profligate *adj.* (PROF luh git) extremely wasteful; extravagant. *The winner of the lottery was so profligate, he managed to spend all of his winnings in a single year.*

profound *adj.* (pro FOUND) of great depth or import. *Her theory that more than one god existed in the universe was profound.*

profuse *adj.* (pro FYOOS) pouring out with great volume. *The only way to stop profuse bleeding is to bandage and apply pressure.*

profusion *n.* (pro FYOO zshun) a great pouring forth; a great amount. *When we entered the swamp we were met with a profusion of mosquitoes.*

proletariat *n.* (PROH li TAIR ee ut) the working class; industrial laborers collectively. *The proletariat protested their minimum wages while the company's executives earned millions.*

proliferate *vb.* (pro LIF uh RAYT) to multiply quickly. *With America's aggressive entrepreneurs, a new successful franchise can always be expected to proliferate.*

prolific *adj.* (pro LIF ik) very productive. *She was a prolific author, producing more than three novels per year.*

promiscuous *adj.* (proh MIS kyoo us) sexually indiscriminate. *He readily admitted to being promiscuous; he'd had, he said, romances with more than fifty women.*

propensity *n.* (pro PEN sit ee) a natural inclination. *Like her mother, she had a propensity to coddle her children.*

propitious *adj.* (pruh PISH us) opportune; favorable. *May is always a propitious time of year to plant a vegetable garden.*

proponent *n.* (pruh POH nunt) a supporter, advocate, or backer. *I'm a proponent of strong environmental conservation.*

propriety *n.* (pruh PRY uh tee) proper behavior and decorum. *In church, you are expected to conduct yourself with a certain propriety.*

prosaic *adj.* (proh ZAY ik) dull; ordinary. *This story is nothing out of the ordinary; it's as prosaic as all of the other amateur entries.*

proscribe *vb.* (proh SKRIBE) to prohibit or outlaw. *The city council will meet tomorrow to draw up plans to proscribe public drunkenness in the parks.*

proselytize *vb.* (PROS uh li tize) to convert someone to one's own religion, political party, belief system, etc. *Members of the religious cult visit my house once a year in an attempt to proselytize, but I usually don't answer the door.*

protocol *n.* (PROH tuh col) a code of conduct. *When visiting the president, remember we must follow protocol exactly.*

protract *vb.* (proh TRACT) to prolong or stretch out. *The arctic cold front coming down from Canada is expected to protract winter by at least another week.*

prototype *n.* (PROH toh tipe) an original model; a forerunner or mockup. *The prototype of our solar-powered car seats only one, but the revamped model will seat two.*

provincial *adj.* (pruh VIN shul) having a narrow outlook, from lack of worldly experience, as someone living in a small town. *His provincial attitude precludes him from understanding or appreciating homosexuals.*

provocative *adj.* (pro VAWk uh tiv) provoking or stimulating. *The ad recruiting new marines was so provocative that three young men from our town immediately signed up for duty.*

prudent *adj.* (PROO dunt) wise and judicious; intelligently cautious. *Before going out on the ice, it is always prudent to measure its thickness first.*

psychotic *adj.* (is KOT ik) insane; crazy. *Believing wholeheartedly that moon monsters are after you is probably psychotic.*

pundit *n.* (PUN dit) an authority or expert serving as a critic. *The political pundits had much to criticize with the president's sexual escapades.*

pungent *adj.* (PUN jent) having a sharp odor or taste. *These spices are too pungent for my taste.*

purge *adj.* (PURJ) to eliminate, excrete, or cleanse. *To repair your computer, we must purge it of viruses.*

quack *n.* (KWACK) one who practices a profession, especially medicine, yet is unschooled and incompetent. *The quack's magical medicine turned out to be made of sugar.*

qualify *vb.* (KWAL uh fye) to modify. *Bill reported that the company would not be making any more widgets, but I need to qualify that statement; we'll make them if we get sufficient orders for them.*

quandary *n.* (KWON duh ree) a predicament. *We're in something of a quandary here; you say companies require experience to get this job, but how do we get experience if they won't hire us?*

quantum leap *n.* (KWON tum LEEP) a radical change or altering of direction. *The popularizing of* *the personal computer has produced a quantum leap toward a global information network.*

quell *vb.* (KWELL) to subdue or suppress. *In an attempt to quell inner-city violence, the mayor is advocating stricter gun control.*

que será será Spanish for "whatever will be will be." *If you've taken every safety precaution possible, there is no longer any purpose in worrying; que será será.*

quixotic *adj.* (kwik SOT ik) impractically romantic or idealistic, from the fictional character of Don Quixote. *Her dreams of spending her honeymoon on a tiny sailboat in the middle of the Pacific were quixotic; neither she nor her fiancé knew how to sail.*

radical *adj.* (RAD i cul) extreme; fanatical. *His idea to shut down all businesses that pollute was radical.*

rakish *adj.* (RAY kish) dashing, jaunty. *The women turned their heads in unison as the rakish gentleman entered the room.*

rambunctious *adj.* (ram BUNK shus) unruly; raucous and noisy. *Any rambunctious children will be removed from the museum.*

ramification *n.* (ram uh fuh KAY shun) a consequence or effect. *The loss of the nuclear plant would have several ramifications, not the least of which was significantly higher energy bills.*

rampant *adj.* (RAMP unt) growing or spreading out of control. *Population growth in many third world countries has become rampant.*

rancor *n.* (RANG kur) deep-seated hatred. *The rancor between the two parties may prevent them from agreeing on anything worthwhile.*

rapacious *adj.* (ruh PAY shus) predatory; plundering. *The rapacious pirates stole every last item of value from the government vessel.*

ratify *vb.* (RAT uh fye) to pass or officially approve. *The bill was ratified by an overwhelming vote.*

rationalize *vb.* (RASH uh nuh lize) to convince oneself through self-serving arguments that one's actions are defensible or positive when they are not; to justify one's actions. *The looter rationalized stealing the television because, after all, the shop door was unlocked and everybody but him already owned a TV.*

rebuke *vb.* (ri BYOOK) to reprimand and criticize. *The children were rebuked sharply for riding their bicycles in busy traffic.*

rebuttal *n.* (re BUT ul) a counterargument; a refutation or retort. *The defense made some strong points but we had a powerful rebuttal prepared.*

recant *vb.* (re KANT) to retract or take back something previously stated. *I'd like to recant my criticism against all cats; actually, what I meant was, I don't like some cats.*

reconcile *vb.* (REK un sile) to resolve differences or make up. *After their fight, the boys were asked to offer apologies and reconcile.*

red herring *n.* any issue or object employed to distract from a larger, more important one. *The president's vociferous focus on the booming economy was obviously a red herring to distract reporters from his past unethical behavior.*

redress *n.* (REE dress) compensation for or correction of a wrong. *The company's lawsuit seeks redress for the reporter's slanderous report.*

redundant *adj.* (ri DUN dunt) repetitive, wordy; more than what is called for. *When making a speech, you may make a point in various ways, but try to avoid being redundant.*

refute *vb.* (ri FYOOT) to argue or prove that something is wrong. *We plan to refute the newspaper's poorly researched report with facts and figures of our own.*

regale *vb.* (ri GAYL) to entertain. *The comedian regaled us with one hilarious story after another.*

regress *vb.* (ree GRESS) to retreat to an earlier stage; to progress backwards. *Don't let a teenager regress to her childhood by crying for a snack; that's embarrassing.*

reiterate *vb.* (ree IT uh RAYT) to repeat or go over what has already been said. *I will reiterate these directions only once, so I strongly urge you to take notes.*

relegate *vb.* (REL uh GAYT) to assign or consign. *As the youngest of ten children, I was always relegated to carry out the most meaningless chores in the house.*

relentless *adj.* (ri LENT less) unremitting, incessant. *The relentless rain caused the river to flow over its banks and inundate the town square.*

relinquish *vb.* (ree LIN kwish) to give up or renounce. *Even after losing to the challenger, the vanquished fighter refused to relinquish his championship belt.*

remiss *adj.* (ri MISS) negligent in one's duties. *I would be seriously remiss if I forgot to take the trash out for three weeks in a row.*

renaissance *n.* (REN i SAHNS) a revival or resurgence. *The city is undergoing something of a renaissance, with several new office buildings and a new park planned.*

renege *vb.* (ri NIG) to go back on one's word or promise. *Don't renege on written agreements unless you want to be sued for breach of contract.*

renounce *vb.* (ri NOWNCE) to give up or reject. *When Sally learned of the fraud involved, she quickly decided to renounce her belief in psychics.*

repartee *n.* (REP ar TEE) clever verbal exchanges or witty remarks. *The comedian engaged himself in some stinging repartee with his hecklers.*

repercussion *n.* (ree pur KUSH un) a consequence or effect of some action. *Repercussions from the oil embargo will include higher prices at the gas pumps.*

replete *adj.* (ri PLEET) full; rich or plentiful. *The pantry was replete with beans and rice—enough staples, in fact, to last a year.*

reprehensible *adj.* (rep ri HENS uh bul) richly deserving of criticism. *The graffiti artist's defacing of the town church was reprehensible.*

reprisal *n.* (ri PRIZE ul) retaliation; a counterattack. *You can't expect to throw eggs at someone without some kind of reprisal.*

reproach *n.* (ri PROACH) criticism and blame. *The evidence proves that my client had nothing to do with the burglary; he is above reproach.*

reprove *vb.* (ri PROOV) to give one's disapproval. *The city council vociferously reproves all violations of the noise ordinance.*

repudiate *vb.* (ri PYOO dee AYT) to reject as false. *I will loudly repudiate any allegations of unethical behavior on my part.*

rescind *vb.* (ri SIND) to repeal or abolish. *The city council thought a curfew for teens was a good idea, but public pressure will force them to rescind the experiment as of tomorrow.*

resigned *adj.* (ri ZYEND) accepting of one's fate; reconciled to reality. *I'm never going to play major league baseball, but I was resigned to that fact a long time ago.*

resilient *adj.* (ri ZIL yunt) having the ability to cope or recover quickly. *John has gone out of business, but I would never count him out; he's incredibly resilient.*

resolute *adj.* (REZ uh LOOT) determined. *I am absolutely resolute in my goal to give up smoking.*

resonate *adj.* (REZ uh NAYT) to reverberate or echo. *She gave soul-stirring speeches that deeply resonated with her constituents.*

respite *n.* (RES pit) a break or rest. *A mother of ten children needs a regular respite or she'll have a nervous breakdown.*

reticent *adj.* (RET i sunt) reserved, quiet. *Joe is so reticent with his feelings, it's hard to know what he is thinking.*

reverberate *vb.* (ree VUR bur ayt) to echo, resonate, or produce an aftereffect. *Every toll of the bell would reverberate all the way across town.*

revere *vb.* (ri VEER) to highly honor or respect. *Young athletes will always revere the superstars of sports.*

reverie *n.* (REV uh ree) fantasizing; daydreaming. *I was in the midst of pleasant reverie when a loud noise jarred me back to reality.*

rhapsodize *vb.* (RAP suh dize) to speak about with great passion; to gush. *My sons like to rhapsodize about all the latest rap groups, who are, apparently, something approaching gods.*

rhetoric *n.* (RET uh rik) words and their artful employment in speech or writing. Also, artful speech that in reality says nothing meaningful. *The crowd demanded more than rhetoric from the senator; they demanded action.*

rife *adj.* (RIFE) abounding, widespread. *The topic of evolution is rife with misunderstanding by those who are unschooled in natural science.*

rudimentary *adj.* (rood uh MENT uh ree) basic; fundamental. *Our introduction to biology was strictly rudimentary; we'll study it in more depth next year.*

ruminate *vb.* (ROOM uh nayt) to contemplate; to think about. *I like to ruminate on questions for a while before answering them.*

rustic *adj.* (RUS tik) of rural life or simplicity. *They lived in a rustic log cabin far on the outskirts of town.*

saccharine *adj.* (SAK uh rin) sickeningly sweet. *The movie's ending was so saccharine, we nearly all vomited into our popcorn containers.*

sacred cow *n.* any institution, belief, object, etc., that is considered taboo to criticize or question. *It takes great courage to gore sacred cows, as any atheist will readily tell you.*

sacrilege *n.* (SAK ruh lij) a violation of that which is considered holy or sacred. By defacing the Christian cross and knocking over the gravestones, the vandals committed a sacrilege.

sacrosanct *adj.* (SAK ruh SANKT) sacred. *The symbol of the Christian cross is considered sacrosanct.*

sadistic *adj.* (suh DIS tik) gaining pleasure by inflicting pain on another. *The torturer enjoyed great sadistic pleasure by stretching his victims on the rack.*

salient *adj.* (SAYL yunt) prominent; outstanding. *The professor tends to be verbose, so I take notes only on his most salient points.*

sanction *n.* (SANK shun) permission; formal authorization. *We have received the official sanction of the National Basketball Association to hold this game for charity.*

sanctimonious *adj.* (SANK tuh MOHN ee us) pretending to be holy or righteous. *Our preacher is rather sanctimonious when it comes to gambling; he admonishes us to stay away from it, but then he goes and sponsors bingo games for charity every Saturday.*

sangfroid *n.* (sahn FWAH) composure, especially in unnerving situations. *Even when asked to deliver an impromptu speech before five hundred people, Sally maintained her sangfroid and appeared completely unruffled.*

sanguine *adj.* (SAN gwin) cheerful and optimistic. Also ruddy in complexion. *For a woman who had suffered great personal adversity, she was remarkably sanguine.*

sardonic *adj.* (sar DON ik) bitterly mocking or sarcastic. *Any more sardonic remarks like that and you'll be asked to leave the room.*

satirical *adj.* (suh TEER uh kul) lampooning; ridiculing. *John's satirical play made a laughingstock out of the president of the United States.*

savoir faire *n.* (SAV war FAIR) great social expertise and ability. *To qualify as an international diplomat, you must first and foremost have great savoir faire.*

scapegoat *n.* (SKAYP GOHT) one who is given the blame for the actions of others. *In truth, nearly everyone on the team had a hand in losing the game, but the shortstop was made the scapegoat for making an error in the ninth inning.*

schism *n.* (SIZ um) a separation in a group, especially due to a disagreement. *A schism has formed in the church over homosexual rights.*

scintillating *adj.* (SIN til ayt ing) sparkling; twinkling. *The diamonds were absolutely scintillating under the jeweler's light.*

scrupulous *adj.* (SKROOP yuh lus) having morals and ethics; principled. *When it came to filing his taxes, he accounted for every penny and was absolutely scrupulous in his deductions.*

scrutinize *vb.* (SKROO tuh nize) to look over closely. *The teacher will scrutinize your papers for neatness and grammar, so be careful.*

secede *vb.* (si SEED) to withdraw or break away from a group. *The northern portion of our state would like to secede from the southern portion, due to vast philosophical differences.*

secular *adj.* (SEK yuh lur) unrelated to religion or spiritual matters. *Not every church takes the secular viewpoint that humans evolved from apes; some still hold to the story of Adam and Eve.*

sedentary *adj.* (SED un tair ee) unmoving; inactive. *Couch potatoes with sedentary lifestyles can expect to gain weight very quickly.*

semantics *n.* (suh MAN tiks) that which deals with words and their meanings. *Whether the problem is black and white or falls into a gray area isn't important; let's argue about solutions, not semantics.*

seminal *adj.* (SEM uh nul) originating; the first. *The launching of Sputnik was the seminal event in ushering in the satellite age.*

sequester *vb.* (suh KWES tur) to isolate, set apart, or separate from others. *We will need to sequester the sick passengers until we know what kind of virus they have.*

serendipity *n.* (SER un DIP uh tee) good fortune; a lucky accident. *I met my wife through pure serendipity; she was walking her dog and I was walking mine, and our leashes tangled.*

servile *adj.* (SUR vile) submissive or subservient, like a servant. *The slave's servile, eager-to-please demeanor won him little respect and lots more work.*

shirk *vb.* (SHURK) to neglect or ignore a responsibility. *Don't shirk your duties or you'll never get a raise.*

shrewd *adj.* (SHROOD) clever and wily; savvy. *You need to be a shrewd investor to make a profit in a bear market.*

singular *adj.* (SING gyuh lur) unique; one of a kind. *The scientists assured us that the tsunami striking our shore was a singular event and wouldn't likely ever happen again.*

slander *n.* (SLAN dur) false and damaging statements made about someone publicly. *The challenger accused the incumbent governor of corruption, but we suspected it was nothing more than slander.*

smear campaign *n.* damaging statements and accusations made to destroy, someone's reputation; mudslinging. *The two candidates mounted reciprocal smear campaigns; by the time the elections were over, both of their reputations had been thoroughly tarnished.*

sojourn *n.* (SO jurn) a visit or stay somewhere for a brief time. *I'm planning a three-month sojourn in southern California to write my novel.*

solace *n.* (SOL is) comfort or relief from difficulty. *Although we lost the game, I took solace in the fact that we would have another chance to advance in the semifinal round.*

solemn *adj.* (SOL um) serious, dignified, and somber. *The funeral was solemn.*

solicitous *adj.* (suh LIS uh tis) showing one's concern through attentiveness. *Good mothers are always solicitous toward their children when they get hurt.*

solvent *adj.* (SOL vunt) financially sound and able to pay one's bills and expenses. *The company was doing well and would remain solvent for at least another three years.*

sophistry *n.* (SOF is tree) clever argument that sounds plausible but is, in reality, full of holes; artful reasoning that misleads or deceives. *Great lawyers don't always need facts or overwhelming evidence to win cases; sometimes a bit of sophistry is all that's called for.*

sophomoric *adj.* (sof MOR ik) juvenile; immature; foolish. *Any more sophomoric pranks like that and we'll be forced to suspend you from school.*

sovereign *adj.* (SOV run) independent from the rule of others. *The island declared itself a sovereign nation and rejected any further administration from the mainland.*

spearhead *vb.* (SPEER HED) to head up or start an organization, movement, etc. *John Muir is often credited with spearheading the environmental movement.*

specious *adj.* (SPEE shus) appearing to be true but in fact being fallacious. *Your argument probably sounds quite credible to the jury, Mr. Jones, but my expert witness will, in fact, prove that it is specious.*

spite *n.* (SPYTE) hard feelings; vengeance. *The teacher flunked Jake for the year; out of spite, he egged her car.*

splitting hairs being nitpicky and too exacting. *If we're going to sit around splitting hairs all day, we'll never get this contract signed; let's just agree on a fifty-fifty deal and work out the trivial details as we go.*

spry *adj.* (SPRY) lively and active. *She was astonishingly spry for someone who would turn ninety-six next month.*

spurious *adj.* (SPYOOR ee us) false, counterfeit; not authentic. *The police officer's radio report of a flying saucer turned out to be spurious.*

squalid *adj.* (SKWALL id) filthy and run-down. *They lived in a squalid, cockroach-infested tenement building in the center of town.*

squander *vb.* (SKWAN dur) to waste. *Let's be irresponsible and squander all our money on impulse purchases and luxuries.*

stagnation *n.* (stat NAY shun) an absence of life or activity. *To bring this company out of stagnation, we must put more money into research and development.*

staid *adj.* (STAYD) serious and restrained; sober. *It's hard to get my boss to laugh at anything; he's just too staid.*

stalemate *n.* (STAYL mayt) deadlock or draw. *Management and union cut off their negotiations after reaching a stalemate.*

stalwart *adj.* (STALL wurt) strong and resolute. *I am and always will be a stalwart supporter of equal rights.*

status quo *n.* (STAT us KWO) the present state of affairs. *The president has no interest in changing his policies; he's happy with the status quo.*

staunch *adj.* (STAWNCH) strong and loyal. *Sally is a staunch supporter of gay rights.*

steadfast *adj.* (STED fast) constant and resolute; steady; loyal. *Don't let anyone talk you out of our plans; remain steadfast at all costs.*

stereotype *n.* (STAIR ee uh type) a broad and skewed characterization that ignores individuality. *The assessment that "men are pigs" is an unfair stereotype; in reality, only a certain percentage of men qualify as such.*

stigma *n.* (STIG muh) that which brands one with a negative reputation; that which causes shame. *The stigma of his criminal record stayed with the murderer long after he had been released from prison.*

stigmatize *vb.* (STIG muh tyze) to brand one with a negative or shameful characterization. *Society will continue to stigmatize criminals long after they've been released from prison.*

stipulate *vb.* (STIP yuh layt) to specify formally, especially in a contract. *Be sure to stipulate exactly what you require in the contract.*

stoic *adj.* (STOH ik) indifferent or apparently indifferent to pain, grief, pleasure, etc. *My brother once stepped on a nail, but he was surprisingly stoic about it and never even winced.*

strident *adj.* (STRI dunt) shrill and harsh. *The rock musician's guitar solo was blistering and strident.*

stringent *adj.* (STRIN junt) strict; rigorous. *This school maintains stringent rules prohibiting swearing and verbal abuse.*

stymie *vb.* (STYE mee) to impede; to put up obstacles. *Environmental regulations may stymie production at some companies, but the long-term benefits are worth the trade-off.*

suave *adj.* (SWAHV) gracious, diplomatic; smooth in social settings. *We need someone who is exceptionally suave to host this year's award ceremonies.*

subjective *adj.* (sub JEK tiv) as seen or experienced through one individual; personal; not objective. *My opinion of my own writing is subjective and is therefore unreliable.*

subjugate *vb.* (SUB juh GAYT) to dominate, control, or make subservient. *The dictator hatched a scheme that would allow him to subjugate millions of uneducated citizens.*

sublime *adj.* (sub LYME) grand, exalted; majestic. *I thought Carl Sagan's views of the universe were absolutely sublime.*

subliminal *adj.* (sub LIM in ul) that which may be sensed unconsciously but not consciously. *The company often employed subliminal advertising and would often imbed hundreds of barely perceptible dollar signs throughout its art work.*

subordinate *adj.* (suh BORD in et) secondary; under or lesser than another. *In a court setting, the bailiff is in an obviously subordinate position to that of the judge.*

subpoena *n.* (suh PEE nuh) a written order to appear in court. *The witness to the bank robbery will receive a subpoena today to appear in court.*

subservient *adj.* (sub SERV ee unt) submissive and servile. *My younger brother was subservient toward me until he was five years old, at which time he loudly asserted his independence.*

substantiate *vb.* (sub STAN shee ayt) to provide evidence or testimony to prove something true. *Thousands of scientists have substantiated Darwin's theory of evolution with studies and findings of their own.*

subterfuge *n.* (SUB tur fyooj) trickery or deception used to cover up one's true actions. *Swindlers employ clever subterfuge to separate their victims from their money.*

subversive *adj.* (sub VUR siv) working toward the overthrow of a government. *The protester was questioned by the police for distributing subversive literature to the public.*

succinct *adj.* (suk SINKT) concise and to the point. *As we have only two hours to make the award presentations, please keep your speeches succinct.*

superficial *adj.* (soo pur FISH ul) on the surface only; lacking depth. *To judge someone by their appearance alone is terribly superficial.*

superfluous *adj.* (suh PUR floo us) extraneous; unnecessary. *The editor used her blue pencil to scratch out all of the manuscript's superfluous words and sentences.*

surreal *adj.* (sur RE ul) having a dreamlike or nightmarish quality. *The abstract painter's otherworldly images were hauntingly surreal.*

surrogate *adj.* (SUR uh GIT) a substitute. *A nanny serves as a surrogate parent when mother and father go off to work.*

svelte *adj.* (SVELT) slender; lithe. *Don't even think about becoming a model unless you have a svelte figure.*

Svengali *n.* (sven GAHL ee) one who has the uncanny ability to brainwash or persuade others to do his bidding, often for evil purposes. Originating from the musician-hypnotist in the George du Maurier novel *Trilby. The cult leader was a Svengali who convinced thousands of followers that the world would end unless they donated everything they owned to him.*

swan song *n.* a final appearance, performance, or work. Originating from the myth of a song sung only once in a lifetime, by a swan as it dies. This book will be the famed novelist's swan song, as he has officially announced his retirement.

sycophant *n.* (SYKE uh fant) one who constantly flatters and is servile toward another in order to gain praise or acceptance. *The boss likes hard-working employees, but he has no respect for sycophants.*

symbiotic *adj.* (sim bee OT ik) mutually beneficial. *Bees and flowers have had a symbiotic relationship for millions of years.*

symmetry *n.* (SIM uh tree) correspondence or harmony in form; the quality of being uniform. *The artist was obsessed with balance and would arrange his pieces for hours to achieve symmetry.*

synonymous *adj.* (si NON uh mus) much the same as or similar to. *Dog is synonymous with canine; cat is synonymous with feline.*

synthesis *n.* (SIN thuh sis) the mixture or combination of components to make a whole. *Fusion is the synthesis of jazz and rock music forms.*

tacit *adj.* (TASS it) implied but not specifically expressed. *While it isn't written in our contract, we have a tacit agreement that the work will be performed in a timely manner.*

taciturn *adj.* (TASS i turn) untalkative; reserved by nature. *She was unusually taciturn and would rarely speak unless spoken to.*

tactful *adj.* (TAKT ful) diplomatic and discreet; sensitive. *It's not always easy to find a tactful way to tell someone that their fly is unzipped.*

tangible *adj.* (TANJ uh bul) capable of being touched and perceived. *We have no tangible evidence that aliens exist.*

tantamount *adj.* (TANT uh mount) equivalent; the same. *Letting children ride in the car without seatbelts is tantamount to letting them ride in a boat without life jackets.*

tawdry *adj.* (TAW dree) cheap, gaudy, and showy. *I'm afraid Aunt Mary has rather poor taste in fashion; her clothes are usually quite tawdry.*

temerity *n.* (tuh MER i tee) reckless courage or boldness. *Anyone who has the temerity to try and climb Mt. Everest without intense physical training is gambling against death.*

temperate *adj.* (TEM pur ut) moderate; mild. Thankfully, we live in a temperate climate, where it never gets too hot or too cold.

tenacious *adj.* (ten AY shus) stubbornly persistent. *The tenacious athlete thinks nothing of standing out in the rain shooting baskets for hours.*

tenet *n.* (TEN ut) a belief or principle. *It's difficult to agree wholeheartedly with all of the tenets of my church.*

tentative *adj.* (TEN tuh tiv) unsure, indefinite. *Our plans for vacation are still tentative; we could change our minds at any time.*

tenuous *adj.* (TEN yoo us) weak and insubstantial. *Their agreement to cooperate with one another is tenuous; the slightest hostility from either side could end everything.*

terse *adj.* (TURS) brief, concise. *A one-word answer is about as terse as you can get.*

testament *n.* (TEST uh ment) that which testifies to the truth or validity of something. *His fingerprints provided mute testament to his presence at the crime's location.*

tirade *n.* (TYE rayd) a long, angry speech; a diatribe. *I don't have to sit here and listen to this tirade anymore; I'm walking out.*

titillate *vb.* (TIT ul ate) to arouse or excite, especially in an erotic way. *Movie makers have long employed scantily clad actors and actresses to titillate viewers.*

torrid *adj.* (TOR id) scorching hot. *After reading her romance novels, Nancy would always fantasize about having a torrid love affair.*

totalitarian *adj.* (toh tal i TAIR ee un) authoritarian; tyrannical. *Their totalitarian form of government regulated everything, including what the people should wear for clothing.*

touchstone *n.* (TUCH stohn) a measure or test of worth or genuineness. *The health of the fish population was used as a touchstone for the effectiveness of the state's environmental regulations.*

tour de force *n.* (toor de FORS) an exceptional work, feat, or achievement. *The novelist's latest work is being called a tour de force by critics.*

transcend *vb.* (tran SEND) to surpass or exceed. *The existence of God transcends logic, but then, so does life.*

transcendental *adj.* (tran sen DENT ul) supernatural; spiritual; beyond the worldly or physical. For many, deep meditation can be a transcendental experience.

transgression *n.* (trans GRESH un) a sin; a violation of the law. *For the transgression of stealing the police officer's doughnuts, the transient was ordered by the court to perform forty hours of community service.*

transient *adj.* (TRAN shunt) transitory; passing quickly. *A comet is a rare and transient event.*

traumatic *adj.* (truh MAT ik) psychologically wounding; shocking; deeply disturbing. *Being involved in a serious car accident is traumatic.*

travesty *n.* (TRAV es tee) a farce; a poor imitation. *Our court case was ineptly handled by the judge; it was a travesty of justice.*

trepidation *n.* (trep uh DAY shun) fear; anxiety. *We approached the sleeping bear's den with trepidation.*

trite *adj.* (TRYTE) unoriginal; stale; hackneyed. *Most new writers describe scenes with words and phrases they've encountered in print before, and thus their writing is ineffective and trite.*

tryst *n.* (TRIST) a secret rendezvous made by lovers. *The two employees arranged a tryst every Saturday at midnight.*

tumultuous *adj.* (tuh MULT choo us) wild and uproarious. *The stock market suffered another tumultuous day of trading, as stock prices plummeted to new lows.*

tutelage *n.* (TOOT ul ij) instruction; teaching. *Perhaps nearly anyone could learn to write a novel under the tutelage of Stephen King.*

tyranny *n.* (TEER un ee) dictatorship; oppression. *Under the evil king's tyranny, peasants were forced to work the fields from sunup until sundown with little pay.*

ubiquitous *adj.* (yoo BIK wit us) omnipresent; seemingly everywhere. *The ubiquitous Japanese beetles are the bane of gardeners.*

ulterior *adj.* (ul TEER ee er) undisclosed; hidden. *My uncle had an ulterior motive for wanting to trim our hedges; he wanted to get a gander at the nude sunbathers next door.*

ultimatum *n.* (ul tuh MAY tum) final warning, demand, or offer. *Franky was given an ultimatum; either he would stop throwing food or he would have to leave the table.*

unassuming *adj.* (un uh SOOM ing) modest; unpretentious. *Mary was so unassuming, she truly could not believe that her painting had been awarded first prize.*

uncanny *adj.* (un CAN ee) weird and mysterious; something of or resembling the supernatural. *Her knack for guessing our ages and weights was absolutely uncanny.*

undermine *vb.* (UN dur myne) to cause damage, weaken, or sabotage. *It's OK to protest, but use care not to break the law or your efforts may actually backfire and undermine our efforts to pass new legislation.*

unequivocal *adj.* (un uh KWIV uh kul) unambiguous; clear. *The governor was unequivocal; he would lower taxes by the end of the year.*

unflappable *adj.* (un FLAP uh bul) calm and difficult to upset. *Advocates of controversial issues may face a firestorm of protest; therefore they must be absolutely unflappable.*

unmitigated *adj.* (un MIT uh gay tid) not diminished or diluted in any way; out-and-out. *If you have the unmitigated gall to come in here and ask for a raise, then I have no choice but to say yes.*

unorthodox *adj.* (un ORTH uh doks) unconventional; nonstandard. *Their form of worship is unorthodox and vociferously protested by the head of the church.*

unscrupulous *adj.* (un SKROOP yuh lus) unprincipled. *The unscrupulous used car dealer could spot a sucker a mile away.*

upbraid *vb.* (up BRAYD) to scold. *The drill sergeant took great pleasure in upbraiding new recruits for the most trivial of infractions.*

urbane *adj.* (ur BAYN) suave; refined; smooth. *The movie star was not only glamorous but urbane; she shook hands and chatted graciously with everyone she met.*

usurp *vb.* (yoo SURP) to overthrow and take over a position of power. *The terrorists attempted to usurp the prime minister's office.*

utilitarian *adj.* (yoo til uh TAIR ee un) useful or practical. *I prefer cars that are more utilitarian than showy.*

utopia *n.* (yoo TOH pee uh) an ideal world; a perfect society. *It's easy to imagine a utopia; it's quite another to build one that works.*

vacillate *vb.* (VAS uh layt) to go back and forth or be indecisive. *I can never make up my mind about what ice cream to eat; I tend to vacillate forever between vanilla and chocolate.*

vanguard *n.* (VAN gard) the leading or front members of a movement, institution, army, etc. *Our local university is at the vanguard of medical research.*

vehement *adj.* (VEE uh munt) fervent; passionate. *He made a vehement protest to the police officer, but he was given a speeding ticket anyway.*

vendetta *n.* (ven DET uh) a feud fueled by a cycle of vengeance. *The Mafia members had their own version of population control through personal vendettas.*

veneer *n.* (ven EER) a topmost layer; a facade; a cover-up. *Under his polished veneer stood a man with innumerable self-doubts.*

venerable *adj.* (VEN ur uh bul) esteemed due to age or character. *The venerable judge Jacob Jones will preside over tomorrow's murder trial.*

venturesome *adj.* (VENT chur sum) courageous and adventurous; enterprising. *Don't try to stop Sally from attempting to climb Mt. Everest; she's always had venturesome blood.*

veracity *n.* (vur ASS uh tee) truthfulness and accuracy. *The officer doubted the veracity of the drunk's statements about seeing a pink elephant.*

verbatim *adj.* (vur BAYT um) word for word; exactly as spoken or written. *I will not quote from his speech verbatim.*

vernacular *n.* (vuh NAK yuh lur) everyday or informal language. *Her vernacular was rich in regional slang.*

viable *adj.* (VYE uh bul) workable; doable; capable of surviving. *Your invention is not only viable but also has a ready market; let's patent it immediately.*

vicarious *adj.* (vi KAIR ee us) experienced indirectly or imagined through the experiences of others. *I never rode the roller coaster myself, but I get a vicarious thrill hearing others describe its twists and turns.*

vicissitudes *n.* (vi SIS i TOODS) the ups and downs and changes experienced in life. *Don't be caught off guard by the vicissitudes of life; learn to expect them and be prepared.*

Victorian *adj.* (vic TOR ee un) of the period of Queen Victoria's reign in the second half of the 19th century, characterized by its prudishness and puritanical viewpoints. Also, an ornate style or architecture from this time. *Mary is so prim and proper, she is positively Victorian.*

vigilance *n.* (VIJ uh lens) attentiveness and watchfulness. *To catch a deer munching in your garden requires great vigilance.*

vilify *vb.* (VIL i FYE) to defame and put down harshly. *This newspaper will not vilify any politician without sound reasons.*

vindicate *vb.* (VIN di kayt) to clear or absolve one of guilt or blame. *This new evidence should vindicate my client.*

vindictive *adj.* (vin DIK tiv) seeking revenge. *Just because you lost the race doesn't mean you should throw eggs at the winner's house; that's being childishly vindictive.*

visceral *adj.* (VISS uh rul) intuitive, instinctive; from one's gut. *The predator's drive to hunt is purely visceral.*

vitriolic *adj.* (vi tree OL ik) bitter and sarcastic. *I know Joe lost the race, but if he continues to be so vitriolic I'm going to have to leave.*

vivacious *adj.* (vi VAY shus) lively. *Her vivacious personality lit up the room every time she entered.*

vociferous *adj.* (voh SIF ur us) loud, noisy. *The workers made a vociferous complaint about too much overtime work.*

vogue *n.* (VOHG) in vogue; in fashion. *Nose rings aren't likely to stay in vogue long, or are they?*

volatile *adj.* (VOL uh tul) unstable; likely to explode. *I would not advise investing in the stock market when it is this volatile.*

volition *n.* (voh LISH un) conscious choice. *I'm signing up for the army of my own volition; nobody is forcing me.*

voracious *adj.* (vo RAY shus) extremely hungry or insatiable. *He cut into his steak with voracious abandon.*

waffle *vb.* (WAWF ul) to equivocate or speak ambiguously. *We don't want another governor who is going to waffle on the issues; we need someone who will make a firm decision and stick to it.*

wanton *adj.* (WON tun) wild, unrestrained; reckless. *The boys were punished for the wanton destruction of their bedrooms.*

wary *adj.* (WAIR ee) cautious; leery. It's hard not to feel wary when walking through a graveyard at midnight.

WASP *n.* (WASP) white Anglo-Saxon Protestant. *The north side of town is populated almost exclusively by WASPs.*

Waterloo *n.* (WOT ur loo) defeat. A metaphor coined after Napoleon's defeat in Waterloo, Belgium, in 1815. *Our team has beaten all challengers, but the game against our crosstown rivals next week may prove to be our Waterloo.*

whimsical *adj.* (WIM suh kul) fanciful; out of the ordinary. *His wood carvings of elves and trolls were whimsical.*

wily *adj.* (WYE lee) sly, cunning; crafty. *The wily coyote is not easily fooled.*

windfall *n.* (WIND fall) a godsend; a boon; an unexpected stroke of good fortune. *My tax refund last year came as a surprising windfall.*

wistful *adj.* (WIST ful) full of sad longing; pensive. *Whenever she was reminded of her youth, she became wistful and nostalgic.*

zeal *n.* (ZEEL) passion; great or extreme enthusiasm. *Blinded by her zeal to lose weight, Sally consumed nothing but water and crackers for three days straight.*

zealous *adj.* (ZEL us) passionate; fanatical; intense. *He was a zealous believer in ESP and scoffed at the notion that it was only pseudoscience.*

zenith *n.* (ZEE nith) the highest point; pinnacle. *At its zenith, the company was manufacturing more baby buggy bumpers than any other competitor.*

Index

B

C

D

E

G

H

I

J

K

L

M

N

P

Q

R

T

U